# THE CAMBRIDGE CRITICAL GUIDE TO LATIN LITERATURE

*The Cambridge Critical Guide to Latin Literature* offers a critical overview of work on Latin literature. Where are we? How did we get here? Where to next? Fifteen commissioned chapters, along with an extensive introduction and Mary Beard's postscript, approach these questions from a range of angles. They aim not to codify the field, but to give snapshots of the discipline from different perspectives, and to offer provocations for future development. The *Critical Guide* aims to stimulate reflection on how we engage with Latin literature. Texts, tools and territories are the three areas of focus. The *Guide* situates the study of classical Latin literature within its global context from late antiquity to Neo-Latin, moving away from an exclusive focus on the pre-200 CE corpus. It recalibrates links with adjoining disciplines (history, philosophy, material culture, linguistics, political thought, Greek), and takes a fresh look at key tools (editing, reception, intertextuality, theory).

ROY GIBSON is Professor of Classics at Durham University and has published widely on Latin poetry and prose from Cicero to late antiquity, particularly Ovid, Pliny the Younger and Sidonius Apollinaris. He is Co-Director of the Ancient Letter Collections project, which researches Graeco-Roman letter collections from Isocrates to Augustine.

CHRISTOPHER WHITTON is Professor of Latin Literature at the University of Cambridge. His publications include a commentary on Pliny *Epistles* 2 (Cambridge, 2013), *The Arts of Imitation in Latin Prose* (Cambridge, 2019) and *Roman Literature under Nerva, Trajan and Hadrian: Literary Interactions, AD 96–138* (co-edited with Alice König, Cambridge, 2018).

# THE CAMBRIDGE CRITICAL GUIDE TO LATIN LITERATURE

EDITED BY

ROY GIBSON
*University of Durham*

CHRISTOPHER WHITTON
*University of Cambridge*

Shaftesbury Road, Cambridge CB2 8EA, United Kingdom

One Liberty Plaza, 20th Floor, New York, NY 10006, USA

477 Williamstown Road, Port Melbourne, VIC 3207, Australia

314–321, 3rd Floor, Plot 3, Splendor Forum, Jasola District Centre,
New Delhi – 110025, India

103 Penang Road, #05–06/07, Visioncrest Commercial, Singapore 238467

Cambridge University Press is part of Cambridge University Press & Assessment,
a department of the University of Cambridge.

We share the University's mission to contribute to society through the pursuit of
education, learning and research at the highest international levels of excellence.

www.cambridge.org
Information on this title: www.cambridge.org/9781108421089

DOI: 10.1017/9781108363303

© Cambridge University Press & Assessment 2024

This publication is in copyright. Subject to statutory exception and to the provisions
of relevant collective licensing agreements, no reproduction of any part may take
place without the written permission of Cambridge University Press & Assessment.

First published 2024

*A catalogue record for this publication is available from the British Library.*

*Library of Congress Cataloging-in-Publication Data*
NAMES: Gibson, Roy K., editor. | Whitton, Christopher, 1979– editor.
TITLE: The Cambridge critical guide to Latin literature / edited by Roy Gibson, Christopher Whitton.
DESCRIPTION: Cambridge ; New York, NY : Cambridge University Press, 2023. | Includes bibliographical references and index.
IDENTIFIERS: LCCN 2023005305 | ISBN 9781108421089 (hardback)
SUBJECTS: LCSH: Latin literature – History and criticism.
CLASSIFICATION: LCC PA6003 .C36 2023 | DDC 870.9–dc23/eng/20230422
LC record available at https://lccn.loc.gov/2023005305

ISBN 978-1-108-42108-9 Hardback

Cambridge University Press & Assessment has no responsibility for the persistence
or accuracy of URLs for external or third-party internet websites referred to in this
publication and does not guarantee that any content on such websites is, or will remain,
accurate or appropriate.

*for John Henderson*

# Contents

| | |
|---|---|
| List of Figures and Tables | page ix |
| List of Contributors | xiii |
| Preface | xv |
| List of Abbreviations | xvi |

1. Introduction: Texts, Tools, Territories    1
   *Roy Gibson and Christopher Whitton*

2. Canons    43
   *Irene Peirano Garrison*

3. Periodisations    97
   *Gavin Kelly*

4. Author and Identity    158
   *Alison Sharrock*

5. Intertextuality    208
   *Donncha O'Rourke and Aaron Pelttari*

6. Mediaeval Latin    272
   *Justin Stover*

7. Neo-Latin    334
   *Yasmin Haskell*

8. Reception    395
   *James Uden*

9. National Traditions    447
   *Therese Fuhrer*

10. Editing    516
    *Samuel J. Huskey and Robert A. Kaster*

| | |
|---|---|
| 11. Latin Literature and Linguistics<br>*James Clackson* | 563 |
| 12. Latin Literature and Material Culture<br>*Michael Squire and Jaś Elsner* | 613 |
| 13. Philosophy<br>*Katharina Volk* | 700 |
| 14. Political Thought<br>*Michèle Lowrie* | 753 |
| 15. Latin Literature and Roman History<br>*Myles Lavan* | 817 |
| 16. Latin Literature and Greek<br>*Simon Goldhill* | 847 |
| Envoi<br>*Mary Beard* | 907 |
| *Index Locorum* | 917 |
| *General Index* | 921 |

# *Figures and Tables*

| | | |
|---|---|---|
| 3.1 | Latin Loebs, Latin Oxford Classical Texts and the Oxford Latin syllabus: chronological coverage. | *page* 116 |
| 3.2 | Selected hexameter poets from Ennius to Petrarch: word divisions in the last two feet. | 128 |
| 10.1 | Gettysburg Address: hypothetical stemma. | 527 |
| 10.2 | Manuscripts of Suetonius' *De uita Caesarum*. Stemma. | 530 |
| 10.3 | Manuscripts of Suetonius' *De uita Caesarum*. Working stemma. | 531 |
| 11.1 | Semantic map of *Venus*. | 593 |
| 12.1 | Typographic presentation of a poem by Publilius Optatianus Porfyrius (*Carm.* 26) – as published in P. Welser (1595), *Publilii Optatiani Porphyrii panegyricus dictus Constantino Augusto*, Augsburg, p. 5. Photograph by Michael Squire. | 620 |
| 12.2 | Manuscript presentation of the same poem, with *Carm.* 13 above, in Codex Palatinus Latinus 1713 (fol. 10v.; Biblioteca Apostolica, Vatican), ninth century. © Biblioteca Apostolica Vaticana (Vaticano). | 621 |
| 12.3 | Manuscript presentation of the same poem in Codex Bernensis 148 (fascicule 58, fol. 2v.; Bern, Burgerbibliothek), sixteenth century. Note the scribal error and incorrect correction in line 8. Photograph by Johannes Wienand. | 622 |
| 12.4 | Manuscript presentation of the same poem in Codex Augustaneus 9 Guelferbytanus (fol. 2v.; Wolfenbüttel, Herzog August Bibliothek), sixteenth century. © Herzog August Bibliothek, Wolfenbüttel. | 623 |
| 12.5 | Typographic presentation of an 'altar' epigram attributed to Besantinus (*Anth. Pal.* 15.25). Typesetting by Christine Luz (reproduced by kind permission). | 628 |

| | | |
|---|---|---|
| 12.6 | Latin graffito in the image of a snake, from Pompeii IV.5 (*CIL* IV 1595). | 629 |
| 12.7 | Early Hadrianic funerary altar of T. Statilius Aper (displayed in the Musei Capitolini, Rome). Photo: Reproduced by kind permission of the Institut für Klassische Archäologie und Museum Klassischer Abgüsse, Ludwig-Maximilians-Universität, Munich. | 630 |
| 12.8 | Presentation of a poem by Publilius Optatianus Porfyrius (*Carm.* 19) – in Codex Augustaneus 9 Guelferbytanus (fol. 4r.; Wolfenbüttel, Herzog August Bibliothek), sixteenth century. © Herzog August Bibliothek, Wolfenbüttel. | 634 |
| 12.9 | 'Palindrome square' inscription from Ostia, second century CE. Drawing by Michael Squire. | 637 |
| 12.10 | Selection of ten name-graffiti in the shape of ships, from early Imperial Rome and Pompeii. Reproduced by kind permission of Jane Heath. | 638 |
| 12.11 | Presentation of a poem by Publilius Optatianus Porfyrius (*Carm.* 3) – in Codex Palatinus Latinus 1713 (fol. 9r.; Biblioteca Apostolica, Vatican), ninth century. © Biblioteca Apostolica Vaticana (Vaticano). | 639 |
| 12.12 | Garima Gospels ms I (AG I, foll. 11r. and 12r. in current binding), opening of the first and second canon tables in the form of aedicules. Photograph by Michael Gervers, published by kind permission of Judith McKenzie. | 641 |
| 12.13 | The Vatican Terence (BAV, MS Vat. lat. 3868) fol. 2r., ninth-century copy (c. 825) of an Italian original of the fifth century. Photograph: Reproduced by kind permission of the Institut für Klassische Archäologie und Museum Klassischer Abgüsse, Ludwig-Maximilians-Universität, Munich. | 643 |
| 12.14 | The Augustine Gospels (Cambridge, Corpus Christi College, Parker Library, ms 286) fol. 125r., sixth-century codex, probably made in Italy. Reproduced by kind permission of the Institut für Klassische Archäologie und Museum Klassischer Abgüsse, Ludwig-Maximilians-Universität, Munich. | 644 |
| 12.15 | The Roman Virgil (BAV, MS Vat. lat. 3867) fol. 6r., late fifth or sixth century, probably made in Italy. Photo: Reproduced by kind permission of the Institut für Klassische Archäologie und Museum Klassischer Abgüsse, Ludwig-Maximilians-Universität, Munich. | 645 |

*List of Figures and Tables*   xi

12.16  The Roman Virgil (BAV, MS Vat. lat. 3867) fol. 45r.,  646
late fifth or sixth century, probably made in Italy. Photo:
Reproduced by kind permission of the Institut für
Klassische Archäologie und Museum Klassischer Abgüsse,
Ludwig-Maximilians-Universität, Munich.

12.17  Codex Arcerianus (Herzog August Bibliothek at  647
Wolfenbüttel, Cod. Guelf. 36.23A) fol. 67v., fifth or
sixth century, perhaps Italian. © Herzog August Bibliothek,
Wolfenbüttel.

12.18  The Vatican Virgil (BAV, MS Vat. lat. 3225) fol. 71r.,  650
perhaps early fifth century, from Rome. Photo: Reproduced
by kind permission of the Institut für Klassische Archäologie
und Museum Klassischer Abgüsse, Ludwig-Maximilians-
Universität, Munich.

12.19  Wall-painting from the Casa di Sirico (Pompeii VII.1.25),  657
first century CE. Reproduced by kind permission of the
Institut für Klassische Archäologie und Museum für Abgüsse
Klassischer Bildwerke, Ludwig-Maximilians-Universität,
Munich.

12.20  Obverse of *Tabula Iliaca* 4 N (= Rome, Musei Capitolini,  658
Sala delle Colombe, inv. 83a). Photograph by Michael
Squire, by kind permission of the Direzione, Musei
Capitolini, Rome.

12.21  Plaster cast of the same tablet (*Tabula Iliaca* 4 N), as  659
housed in the Archäologisches Institut und Sammlung der
Gipsabgüsse, Göttingen (inv. A1695). Photograph by Stefan
Eckardt, reproduced by kind permission.

12.22  Diagram showing the arrangement of scenes in the two  666
lateral friezes of 'oecus h' in the Casa di Octavius Quartio
(Pompeii II.2.2). Diagram by Michael Squire.

12.23  Reconstruction drawing of the east wall of the same *oecus*,  667
showing the Heracles frieze above, and the smaller Iliadic
frieze below. Photograph reproduced by kind permission
of the Archiv, Institut für Klassische Archäologie und
Museum für Abgüsse Klassischer Bildwerke, Ludwig-
Maximilians-Universität, Munich.

12.24  Fragmentary obverse side of the *Tabula Iliaca Capitolina*  670
('Capitoline Iliac tablet'/*Tabula Iliaca* 1 A: Rome, Musei
Capitolini, Sala delle Colombe, inv. 316), late first
century BCE or early first century CE. Photograph by
Michael Squire, reproduced by kind permission of the
Direzione, Musei Capitolini, Rome.

| | | |
|---|---|---|
| 12.25 | Reconstruction of the same tablet in complete state, showing the arrangement of epic cyclical scenes. Reconstruction by Michael Squire. | 671 |
| 12.26 | Europa mosaic from the Roman villa at Lullingstone in Kent, fourth century CE. Photograph reproduced by kind permission of the Archiv, Institut für Klassische Archäologie und Museum für Abgüsse Klassischer Bildwerke, Ludwig-Maximilians-Universität, Munich. | 674 |
| 12.27 | Marble funerary altar from Rome, Museo Chiaramonti, Vatican. Photograph reproduced by kind permission of the Archiv, Institut für Klassische Archäologie und Museum für Abgüsse Klassischer Bildwerke, Ludwig-Maximilians-Universität, Munich. | 680 |
| 14.1 | 'Tellus relief', Ara Pacis. With credit to Craig Jack Photographic/Alamy Stock Photo. | 762 |
| 14.2 | 'Acanthus frieze', Ara Pacis: detail. Photo: Ralph Liebermann. | 762 |

# *Contributors*

MARY BEARD is Professor of Classics emerita at the University of Cambridge, and Honorary Fellow of Newnham College.

JAMES CLACKSON is Professor of Comparative Philology at the University of Cambridge, and Fellow of Jesus College.

JAŚ ELSNER is Senior Research Fellow, Corpus Christi College, Oxford.

THERESE FUHRER is Professor of Latin at the Ludwig-Maximilians-Universität, Munich.

ROY GIBSON is Professor of Classics at the University of Durham.

SIMON GOLDHILL is Professor in Greek Literature and Culture at the University of Cambridge, and Fellow of King's College.

YASMIN HASKELL holds the UNESCO Chair in Inter-Cultural and Inter-Religious Relations at Monash University.

SAMUEL J. HUSKEY is Professor of Classics and Letters at the University of Oklahoma.

ROBERT A. KASTER is Kennedy Foundation Professor of Latin Language and Literature emeritus at Princeton University.

GAVIN KELLY is Professor of Latin Literature and Roman History at the University of Edinburgh.

MYLES LAVAN is Professor of Ancient History at the University of St Andrews.

MICHÈLE LOWRIE is the Andrew W. Mellon Distinguished Service Professor of Classics and the College at the University of Chicago.

DONNCHA O'ROURKE is Senior Lecturer in Classics at the University of Edinburgh.

IRENE PEIRANO GARRISON is Pope Professor of the Latin Language and Literature at Harvard University.

AARON PELTTARI is Senior Lecturer in Classics at the University of Edinburgh.

ALISON SHARROCK is Hulme Professor of Latin at the University of Manchester.

MICHAEL SQUIRE is Laurence Professor of Classical Archaeology at the University of Cambridge, and Fellow of Trinity College.

JUSTIN STOVER is Senior Lecturer in Classics at the University of Edinburgh.

JAMES UDEN is Professor of Classical Studies at Boston University.

KATHARINA VOLK is Professor of Classics at Columbia University.

CHRISTOPHER WHITTON is Professor of Latin Literature at the University of Cambridge, and Fellow of Emmanuel College.

# *Preface*

Putting this volume together has been an enjoyable task and a smoother process than is often the case: six years from commissioning to publication counts (it's nice to think) as a respectable enough maturation, even without a pandemic; and growing pains were minimal at most. Hence sincere gratitude to Michael Sharp and the Syndics of CUP for the invitation to edit it, to the seven anonymous readers who commented on our prospectus, and to the nineteen scholars who agreed to join us in the project. If, as we hope, you find the chapters that follow stimulating and varied, that is thanks to the intellectual energy and verve with which those contributors approached their Herculean task, writing substantial chapters whose themes and questions we suggested, but whose contents and execution they determined. First drafts were shared around the table at a workshop held in Cambridge in June 2018; we thank the participants both for making it a very congenial and invigorating occasion, and for the spirit of collaboration in which they produced and shared further drafts and responded to suggestions. Most contributors submitted their chapters in final form in late 2019; it has not been possible for them to provide systematic bibliographic updates since that date.

We gratefully acknowledge the funding from the Faculty of Classics and Emmanuel College in Cambridge, the University of Manchester and Cambridge University Press that made the workshop possible. For help with copyediting, we thank Phoebe Garrett, Laura Losito and Juliet Wilberforce.

The image on the cover is Francesco Vezzoli's remarkable *Nike Metafisica*, in an installation on the site of ancient Brixia (part of a major 2019 exhibition at the Fondazione Brescia Musei, *Palcoscenici archeologici: Interventi curatoriali di Francesco Vezzoli*). We are very grateful to Stefano Karadjov and Francesca Morandini of the Fondazione Brescia Musei, as well as to Francesco Vezzoli himself, for permission to use the image, and for kindly waiving reproduction fees.

This volume is dedicated to an exemplary scholar who does and has done so much to help us all become better readers.

# *Abbreviations*

| | |
|---|---|
| *ANRW* | *Aufstieg und Niedergang der römischen Welt*, Berlin 1972–. |
| *ASD* | *Erasmus. Opera omnia*, Amsterdam 1969–. |
| BT | Bibliotheca Teubneriana. Leipzig/Stuttgart/Berlin 1849–. |
| *CCSL* | *Corpus Christianorum series Latina*, Turnhout 1954–. |
| *CHCL* | P. E. Easterling, B. Knox, E. J. Kenney and W. V. Clausen, eds., *Cambridge History of Classical Literature*, 2 vols., Cambridge 1982–5. |
| *CIL* | *Corpus inscriptionum Latinarum*, Berlin 1862–. |
| *CLA* | *Codices Latini antiquiores*, Oxford/Osnabrück/Toronto 1934–92. |
| *CLE* | F. Bücheler and E. Lommatzsch, *Carmina Latina epigraphica*, 2nd edn, Leipzig 1930. |
| *CSEL* | *Corpus scriptorum ecclesiasticorum Latinorum*, Vienna/Berlin 1866–. |
| *CTC* | *Catalogus translationum et commentariorum*, Washington, DC 1960–. |
| *CWE* | J. K. McConica, ed., *The Collected Works of Erasmus*, Toronto 1978–. |
| *DLL* | The Digital Latin Library (http://digitallatin.org). |
| *DNP* | H. Cancik and H. Schneider, eds., *Brill's New Pauly* (online at https://referenceworks.brillonline.com). |
| DOML | Dumbarton Oaks Medieval Library, Cambridge, MA, 2010– (online at https://referenceworks.http://domedieval.org). |
| *GL* | H. Keil, *Grammatici Latini*, 8 vols., Leipzig 1855–80. |
| *HLL* | R. Herzog and P. L. Schmidt, eds., *Handbuch der lateinischen Literatur der Antike*, Munich 1989–. |

| | |
|---|---|
| *IG* | *Inscriptiones Graecae*, Berlin 1873–. |
| *IGUR* | *Inscriptiones Graecae urbis Romae*, Rome 1968–. |
| *ILS* | H. Dessau, ed., *Inscriptiones Latinae selectae*, 3 vols., Berlin 1892–1916. |
| LCL | Loeb Classical Library, Cambridge, MA 1912– (online at loebclassics.com). |
| LDLT | Library of Digital Latin Texts (published online by the DLL). |
| *LIMC* | *Lexicon iconographicum mythologiae classicae*, Zurich 1981–99 and 2009. |
| L&S | C. T. Lewis and C. Short, *A Latin Dictionary. Founded on Andrews' Edition of Freud's Latin Dictionary*, Oxford 1879. |
| LSJ | H. G. Liddell, R. Scott and H. S. Jones, *A Greek–English Lexicon*, 9th edn with revised supplement, Oxford 1996. |
| *MGH* | *Monumenta Germaniae historica*, Berlin 1826– (online at www.brepols.net). |
| *OCD*[5] | T. Whitmarsh, ed., *The Oxford Classical Dictionary: A New Digital Initiative* (oxfordre.com/classics). |
| OCT | Oxford Classical Texts. |
| ODNB | *Oxford Dictionary of National Biography*. |
| OLD | P. G. W. Glare, ed., *The Oxford Latin Dictionary*, Oxford 1968–82. With 2nd edn, 2012. |
| *PHerc.* | *Papyri Herculanenses*. See M. Gigante, *Catalogo dei papiri ercolanesi*, Naples 1979, and M. Capasso, *Manuale di papirologia ercolanese*, Lecce 1991. |
| PHI | Packard Humanities Institute database of classical Latin texts. |
| *PPM* | G. Pugliese Caratelli, ed., *Pompei: pitture e mosaici*, Rome 1990–2003. |
| RE | A. Pauly, G. Wissowa and W. Kroll, eds., *Real-Encyclopädie der klassischen Altertumswissenschaft*, Stuttgart 1893–1980. |
| *RHT* | *Revue d'histoire des textes*. |
| *RIB* | R. G. Collingwood and R. P. Wright, eds., *Roman Inscriptions of Britain*, Oxford 1965–. |
| *Tab. Vind.* | A. K. Bowman and J. D. Thomas, *The Vindolanda Writing-Tablets (Tabulae Vindolandenses II)*, London 1994. |

| | |
|---|---|
| TLG | M. C. Pantelia, ed., *Thesaurus linguae Graecae* digital library (online at http://stephanus.tlg.uci.edu). |
| TLL | *Thesaurus linguae Latinae*, Munich 1900– (online at https://tll.degruyter.com). |
| VSD | *Vita Suetonii Donatiana* (= Suetonius/Aelius Donatus, *Vita Vergilii*). |

CHAPTER I

## *Introduction*
### *Texts, Tools, Territories*

*Roy Gibson and Christopher Whitton*

The book before you aims to offer a critical overview of work on Latin literature. Where are we? How did we get here? Where to next? Fifteen commissioned chapters, along with our introduction and Mary Beard's postscript, approach these questions from (we hope) a refreshing range of familiar and less familiar angles. They aim not to codify the field, but to give snapshots of the discipline from different perspectives, and to offer suggestions and provocations for its future development. Most broadly, we hope to stimulate reflection on how we – whoever 'we' may be – engage with Latin literature: what texts do we read? How do we read them? And why?

We'll spare you potted summaries of the chapters. Instead, we divide our introduction into four parts. The first situates this *Guide* in the field, and surveys topics and approaches adumbrated in it (and some that are not). Then we elaborate on two specific thrusts. One of them, signalled most obviously by the inclusion of chapters on mediaeval Latin and Neo-Latin, is a call to decentre work on Latin literature from the 'classical' corpus. The other, related to that, is to contemplate ways in which literary scholarship can enrich and be enriched by work in adjoining disciplines: history, linguistics, material culture, philosophy. Finally, we offer 'distant reading' as a complement to the close reading that defines the field. Along the way, we draw out some of the threads of the chapters to come, and sample some of the conversations running across them.

---

\* Thanks are owed to Catherine Conybeare, Jaś Elsner, Joe Farrell, Adam Gitner, Sander Goldberg, Peter Heslin, Gavin Kelly, Myles Lavan, Carlos Noreña, Ioannis Ziogas and especially Reviel Netz for their comments on drafts of this chapter, and to Walter Scheidel for supplying a transcript of Scheidel 2020. None should be presumed to agree with the positions outlined here. This introduction focuses mainly on issues within Anglophone Classics and concentrates on Anglophone publications; we are only too aware of a large number of publications in other languages omitted here.

## A *Critical Guide*: Texts, Tools, Theories

The provenance and heft of this *Guide* might invite comparison with the Latin volume of the *Cambridge History of Classical Literature* edited by E. J. (Ted) Kenney and Wendell Clausen in 1982. In part that is apt, and not just because Cambridge University Press commissioned this book as a successor, in some sense, to that one. There too contributors pooled expertise to survey the field of Latin literature in the light of recent work, free of the obligation to cover basic information and instructed to be 'critical' (p. xiii). There are some signal differences too. Most obviously, ours is not a history,[1] nor a reference book in the traditional sense:[2] no potted biographies or bibliographies for ancient authors, no arrangement by chronology or genre, no aspiration to 'full' coverage, whatever that might mean – though we do invite you to join us in venturing beyond (even) late antique Latin, if you don't already. Hence too the shift of emphasis away from introducing and explicating primary texts, and towards reflection on modes of scholarship. Scholarly approaches have changed quite a bit since the Latin *CHCL* was commissioned in 1971;[3] it won't surprise you that 'authors' (in the biographical mode) and their 'intentions' rarely feature here except to be problematised,[4] nor perhaps that the rod of judgement wielded so often there – entertainingly but not always inspiringly[5] – is rejected in favour of a more democratic search for the merits, not the failings, of our texts.[6] The profession has evolved too, in a way reflected here: no gender parity yet, still less racial diversity, but seven of the seventeen contributions are authored by women; and each chapter in its way holds up a mirror to what we do, including Therese Fuhrer's survey

---

[1] For which we might also direct you to Conte 1994, the volumes of the *Handbuch der lateinischen Literatur der Antike* (overseen by Herzog and Schmidt) and the *Oxford History of Classical Literature* (ed. Dee Clayman and Joseph Farrell) currently in preparation. On the tradition of such histories, see Peirano Garrison (pp. 79–80) and Kelly (p. 110).

[2] A genre rapidly giving way to online resources such as Oxford Bibliographies Online and The New Pauly.

[3] The fitful evolution of the *CHCL* is related (and some stringent criticisms are levelled) by Woodman 1982.

[4] See Sharrock in Ch. 4.

[5] According to F. R. D. Goodyear, for instance, Velleius 'merits scant esteem' (p. 641), Curtius Rufus was an 'accomplished dilettante' (p. 642) and Suetonius 'possesses no original mind' (p. 663); not even Tacitus escapes a rap ('*Annals* 1–6 show a sad lack of judgment and historical perspective', p. 650). The acid isn't special to Goodyear: 'limitations disqualify Persius from greatness' (Niall Rudd, p. 510); we should keep neglecting Valerius Flaccus and Silius (D. W. T. C. Vessey, p. 558); most late antique poetry up to Ausonius forms a 'discouraging catalogue of poetasters and minor versifiers' (Robert Browning, p. 698). It's no accident, of course, that post-Augustan writers bear the brunt of it.

[6] Some might call that bland, of course; cf. Barchiesi 2001b, reviewing Taplin 2000: 'The drift of the entire survey is that there are no bad texts anymore ... '

of Latin literature studies past and present around the globe.[7] We address a broad audience: scholars and students of Latin literature first and foremost, of course; but we hope that the chapters on linguistics, material culture, philosophy, political thought, history and Greek will both serve as bridges for Latinists into these related fields, and encourage traffic in the opposite direction too. Finally, this *Guide* has been a substantively collaborative venture, encouraged in particular by a two-day workshop in June 2018, where first drafts were discussed around a table; cross-references are just the most visible consequence of those formative exchanges.

Nearer in time, and in some ways in manner, is the Blackwell *Companion to Latin Literature* edited by Stephen Harrison in 2005. That is a hybrid of literary history and 'general reference book' (p. 1), combining surveys of the field with thematic essays on such topics as 'the passions', 'sex and gender' and 'slavery and class'.[8] Perhaps its most striking feature is the cut-off point of 200 CE, reflecting a canon of convenience enshrined in the *Oxford Latin Dictionary* and in many programmes of study, but also perpetuating it. The present volume, by contrast, subjects such conventions to concerted scrutiny – one reason that it opens with Irene Peirano Garrison's chapter on canons and Gavin Kelly on periodisation (and we will have more to say about the *OLD* in a moment). And our topic is not so much Latin literature 'itself' (texts, history, genres, themes) as on how we read it: a critical guide in the maximal sense. Perhaps the nearest comparandum, or so we would like to think, is the series *Roman Literature and its Contexts* edited by Denis Feeney and Stephen Hinds;[9] like those books, the essays here are above all ideas-driven, not an encyclopaedic gathering of data; like their authors, our contributors have been encouraged to be opinionated, to adopt and address different methodologies, and to speak in whatever voice they see fit. The avowed subjectivity is programmatic, as we try to critique or at least reflect on the ideological underlay of what we do, as well as doing it.

The volume is therefore by definition partial. We have aimed for a suitable spread, and you will encounter Latin authors from Livius Andronicus in the third century BCE to Giovanni Pascoli at the turn of

---

[7] The fact that Fuhrer is the only contributor not in post in the English-speaking world is, we assure you, accident. Two others (Irene Peirano Garrison and Katharina Volk) are among the many continental European Latinists who have crossed the Atlantic. Thanks to Yasmin Haskell, our cast-list is not entirely confined to Europe and the USA.

[8] Including three chapters by contributors to the present volume. The edited collection of Taplin 2000 is a hybrid of a different kind, offering 'a new perspective' on Latin literature through eight (excellent) interpretative essays, running from 'the beginnings' to 'the end of the classical era'.

[9] For a provocative critique of that series, see Gunderson 2020: 208–14, in 'a comi-tragic retelling' of its evolution.

the twentieth CE, but, to repeat, we do not aspire to complete or even coverage; to take an extreme case, Erasmus Darwin's *The Loves of Plants* (1789) has ended up with several pages,[10] Pliny the Elder's *Natural History* none.[11] It's true, the 'classical Latin' of the first centuries BCE and CE is a centre of gravity; James Clackson, for instance, makes Catullus a *fil rouge* for his chapter on linguistics, and the *Aeneid* gets sustained treatment by Donncha O'Rourke and Aaron Pelttari on intertextuality, Michael Squire and Jaś Elsner on ecphrasis and Michèle Lowrie on political thought.[12] Such emphases reflect in part inherited canons, in part the expertise of many of our contributors (and of most Latinists in university posts). But this centre of gravity is also deliberately destabilised, both internally, by Peirano Garrison's opening reflections on marginality (pp. 52–9), and chronologically, by the three chapters that focus on post-antique material (mediaeval Latin, Neo-Latin and reception) and by the routine inclusion of late antique material in others.

In the same spirit, let us clarify that the 'Latin literature' of our title is a term of convenience, and intended inclusively. Latin is only one of two or more languages spoken by most of its authors, whether ancient or modern; from a cultural–historical point of view, 'Roman literature' might therefore be a better term for ancient texts – though not for much post-antique Latin.[13] (Of course that is only the tip of an iceberg about language, identity and above all the Graeco-Latin 'cultural hybridity' central to Simon Goldhill's chapter and recurrent elsewhere.)[14] And 'literature' is simply a practical choice: *Critical Guide to Latin* might suggest a book on linguistics; *Critical Guide to Latin Studies* seemed obscure. It is not, therefore, restrictive: if for many people 'literature' once meant high poetry above all,[15] tastes tend now to the catholic,

---

[10] Uden (pp. 433–9), exemplifying the role of classical reception in modern scientific thought.
[11] That is no reflection of the lively state of the scholarship, any more than the absence of Seneca's *Natural Questions* is. On *QNat.* see notably Williams 2012 and the translation of Hine 2010; on *HN* Beagon 1992 and 2005, Carey 2003 and Murphy 2004 remain important (see also Bispham, Rowe and Matthews 2007; Gibson and Morello 2011); Doody 2010 and Fane-Saunders 2016 are significant studies of its reception.
[12] O'Rourke and Pelttari (pp. 211–22); Squire and Elsner (pp. 658–65); Lowrie (pp. 795–804). See also *inter alios* Uden (pp. 422–7) on poetic receptions of Eclogue 2 by Anna Letitia Barbauld in the eighteenth century, and Fuhrer (pp. 499–501) on the 'Harvard' and 'European' schools in the twentieth.
[13] Cf. Peirano Garrison (pp. 80–2). Even before then, the marker 'Roman' has its own problems, of course (Lavan 2020).
[14] E.g. O'Rourke and Pelttari on translations of Greek (pp. 222–9), Clackson on Greek and Latin metre (pp. 578–82) and Volk on the Romanising of Greek philosophy (pp. 705–17). As Goldhill (p. 870) puts it, 'we cannot rely on a polarised opposition of Greece and Rome as discrete cultural entities'. We might compare the rolling process of exchange between Latin and the vernacular in mediaeval Latin and Neo-Latin (Stover, p. 290 and *passim*; Haskell, pp. 359–63), as we might compare Greek/Latin bilingual poems (Squire and Elsner, p. 635; Goldhill, pp. 890–1) with mediaeval and Renaissance macaronic texts (Stover, pp. 310–11, 314–15; Haskell, pp. 345–7).
[15] Peirano Garrison (p. 82).

*1 Introduction: Texts, Tools, Territories* 5

and our own tenor is to encourage open-mindedness. Sander Goldberg offers a working definition: 'texts marked with a certain social status, whose "literary" quality denotes not simply an inherent aesthetic value but a value accorded them and the work they do by the society that receives them'.[16] That invites a whole series of questions about canon formation, elitism and more, but is also usefully open, allowing the case to be made that 'technical' writings, for instance, should be called literature[17] – or, more to the point, that they merit *reading* with the sorts of tools and approaches typically brought to bear on it. From another perspective, the term 'literary texts' is commonly used to denote texts which have come to us through the manuscript tradition, as distinguished from those written on stone, bronze, plaster, papyrus or wood.[18] But, as Myles Lavan argues, these latter types may respond very productively to 'literary' analysis (as shown by work on the *Res gestae*, that great exception to the rule); at the same time, literary scholars stand to gain a great deal from incorporating such material into their reading of 'literary' texts – to enrich our sense of cultural context, for instance, and to profit from opportunities to look beyond the literary elite.[19] Mediaeval Latin offers a salutary perspective, as Justin Stover remarks, and the same is true of Neo-Latin: compared with their vast corpora, no definition, however generous, could be said to make ancient Latin literature an unmanageably large field.[20]

As with texts, so the topics treated here are necessarily selective. The opening two chapters on canons and periodisation interrogate two crucial ways in which texts are sorted and shifted; a third, genre, is also addressed by them, and elsewhere.[21] Alongside the chapters on philosophy and political

---

[16] Goldberg 2005: 18. Feeney 2016: 153–5 points to the situatedness of 'literature' as a modern term.
[17] As it now is, increasingly: see Formisano 2017 and e.g. Fögen 2009; König and Whitmarsh 2007; Doody and Taub 2009; Formisano and van der Eijk 2017; König 2020. Sharrock (p. 176) compares Vitruvius and Horace as a case in point.
[18] Lavan (p. 825). So too Clackson (p. 571), though he would exclude grammarians and commentators.
[19] Lavan puts that suggestion into practice with a letter from the *Vindolanda Tablets*, and makes an analogous case for texts preserved by jurists (see also Lavan 2018). In similar vein, see Lowrie (pp. 759–60) on the *Res gestae* and other inscriptions (as well as art), Clackson (pp. 568–9, 579) on the hexameters of one Iasucthan, written at Bu Njem in 222 CE, Squire and Elsner (pp. 629–32) on the altar of T. Statilius Aper, and several chapters in König, Uden and Langlands 2020. Pompeian graffiti is another case in point (Clackson, pp. 613–14; Squire and Elsner, p. 614 n. 6); so is the opportunity afforded by epigraphy to expand our canon of female Latin poets (Stevenson 2005: 49–58). On reading 'beyond the elites' see Squire and Elsner (pp. 677–82); cf. Clackson (pp. 583–4) on 'vulgar Latin' and its problems.
[20] Stover, pp. 274–5.
[21] Peirano Garrison (pp. 59–67); Kelly (pp. 142–3); Stover (pp. 280–92); Haskell (pp. 363–8). Volk on philosophy (Ch. 13) and Lowrie on political thought (Ch. 14) productively cut across genres, challenging in the process the poetry/prose divide. Stimulating reflections on the aesthetic and heuristic stakes of genre include Fowler 1979, Hinds 2000, Barchiesi 2001a, Farrell 2003 and

thought we could have set one on rhetoric,[22] and another on religion;[23] education, science and law also merit attention[24] — but choices had to be made. We have preferred to spread discussion of gender, too, across the volume, while highlighting here its continued pressing importance, whether in drawing attention to female writers[25] and calling out chauvinism ancient and modern,[26] or interrogating cultural constructions of gender[27] at a time of rising challenges to binaries and an explosion of interest in trans-ness.[28] So too with the increasing attention to other suppressed voices (the enslaved, subalterns, alien cultures)[29] and, conjoined with that, the often uncomfortable role of Classics in modern experiences of race.[30]

The tools of the Latinist's trade, too, are explored in several ways. Among those tools textual editions remain a *sine qua non*;[31] Sam Huskey and Bob Kaster (Chapter 10) introduce the principles of stemmatics, consider their limitations in the face of a text such as Servius' commentary on Virgil, and explore the opportunities and challenges of editing in a digital age with reference to the Library of Digital Latin Texts under construction at the University of

---

Hutchinson 2013; for some different approaches to generic interaction see Harrison 2007 and Papanghelis, Harrison and Frangoulidis 2013.

[22] See especially Lowrie (pp. 769–78) and Lavan (pp. 830–3); also Lavan (pp. 863–8) on rhetoric in historiography. The topic extends to the whole of Latin literature, pagan and Christian (e.g. Stover, pp. 299–300, on the homily). The current burst of creativity in this area includes Gunderson 2003, Peirano Garrison 2019 and Dinter, Guérin and Martinho 2020.

[23] See e.g. Kelly (pp. 141–3) and Fuhrer (pp. 455–6, 467, 480); also Clackson (pp. 564–74 and 586–94) on Venus, and Squire and Elsner (pp. 618–32 and 677–82) on pagan altars, actual and literary.

[24] See Peirano Garrison (pp. 59–67) on ancient educational canons. On legal literature see pp. 31–2 in this chapter, Peirano Garrison (p. 82), Lowrie (p. 778) and Lavan (p. 828).

[25] Including in this volume O'Rourke and Pelttari (pp. 240–6) on Proba, Sharrock (pp. 193–8) on Sulpicia and 'gynocriticism', Haskell (pp. 339–40) on neo-Latin poets and Uden (pp. 410–27) on Mary Wollstonecraft, Phillis Wheatley and Anna Letitia Barbauld.

[26] Sharrock (pp. 166–8) on violence in Ovid and (pp. 198–200) on feminist 'resistance'; Lowrie (pp. 793–4) on the female body in political narratives of rape and foundation; Uden (as prev. n.) on modern exclusions of women. See too Zuckerberg 2018 on the continuing appropriation of classical texts by 'antifeminists'.

[27] Lavan (p. 821) on the work of Keith and Corbeill; Goldhill (pp. 852–4) on the gender politics of Greekness.

[28] Just finding its way into print: see e.g. Traub, Badir and McCracken 2019, Starks-Estes 2020 and Surtees and Dyer 2020, this last launching a series from Edinburgh University Press, 'Intersectionality in classical antiquity'.

[29] Sharrock (pp. 167–8) and Lavan (pp. 821, 833–6) on slavery; Fuhrer (p. 480) on the Black presence in Roman Britain. Lavan (p. 821) and Goldhill (pp. 847–50) on post-colonial approaches to provincials and religious others; Haskell (pp. 374–5) on colonial encounters in Neo-Latin.

[30] Peirano Garrison (pp. 48–9); Uden (esp. pp. 419–22, 426, 430–1); see also n. 58.

[31] Progress continues to be made with classical texts, thanks to *inter alia* the opportunities of computer analysis (see p. 523 n. 21 on the 'New Stemmatics'), the relative ease and inexpense of travel around Europe and beyond, and the ongoing digitisation of manuscripts in many collections (spurred on by the pandemic). Mediaeval and neo-Latin texts are a different matter, with huge swathes of material still unedited (Stover, pp. 277–8; Haskell, pp. 375–9).

Oklahoma.[32] Further key resources – commentaries,[33] dictionaries and grammars,[34] translations[35] – are thematised across the volume, as are other 'technical' matters, style and metre among them;[36] Clackson (Chapter 11) considers more broadly what linguists can do for literary scholars. A technical matter of a different sort concerns ancient technologies of reading and their literary and sociocultural dimensions,[37] highlighted here in several contributions.[38] Modern technologies, in particular digital humanities, are another repeated port of call; we draw attention here to the range and uses of open-access corpora,[39] not least in intertextual studies, where text-comparison software is now a routine tool (though no panacea)[40] and big data computation offers new analytical approaches,[41] as well as in editing and stylistic studies;[42] and some broader advantages and disadvantages of scholarship in the age of the internet.[43]

[32] On digital editing see also Fuhrer (pp. 501–2). See too Peirano Garrison (pp. 57–9) on editing and the canon, Sharrock (pp. 182–3) on editing and the author, and Fuhrer (pp. 483–93) on different traditions of editing Lucretius, Horace, Propertius and Seneca. On transmission – the scribes and scholars who constitute a large part of classical reception – Reynolds and Wilson 2013 (orig. 1968) remains the go-to guide. The authoritative survey of Reynolds 1983 is due to be updated in Justin Stover's forthcoming *Oxford Guide to the Transmission of the Latin Classics*.

[33] Near to both our hearts, but much discussed in recent years: Most 1999; Gibson and Kraus 2002; Kraus and Stray 2016; Gibson 2021. See Fuhrer (pp. 493–6) on past and future developments, Haskell (pp. 337 and 377) on the practical and institutional challenges of commenting on neo-Latin texts, and Clackson (pp. 564–7) for a Catullan case study in evolution and tralaticiousness. On ancient commentary see especially Huskey and Kaster (Ch. 10) on Servius; also Peirano Garrison (pp. 74–7) on Macrobius and scriptural commentary.

[34] See Clackson (pp. 567, 590–4) on dictionaries and again (pp. 576, 594–98) on grammars; Stover (p. 273) on dictionaries of mediaeval Latin.

[35] Fuhrer (p. 501). Translations are ever more important as a point of access (or aid) for readers, but also a fundamental form of interpretation in themselves.

[36] On metre see Kelly (pp. 126–36) and Clackson (pp. 578–82). Stover (pp. 292–318) offers a *Stilgeschichte* of mediaeval Latin.

[37] On ancient books see Kenney 1982 and e.g. Blanck 1992 and Winsbury 2009, not to forget Birt 1882. Parker 2009 and Johnson 2010 are important sociological approaches; see also O'Rourke and Pelttari (pp. 251–5) on orality and reading communities. On the literary stakes of the poetic book, see e.g. Van Sickle 1980a and 1980b and Hutchinson 2008.

[38] Kelly (pp. 143–8) and O'Rourke and Pelttari (pp. 251–6) on the materiality of the bookroll and the codex; Squire and Elsner (pp. 632–52) on the page as aesthetic and literary space in Optatian, the Gospels and the Vatican Virgil.

[39] O'Rourke and Pelttari (pp. 257–9), Haskell (pp. 378–9) and Clackson (pp. 601–3).

[40] No tool is useful without a good workman, and there is more to life than lexis (cf. Lowrie's observation that many concepts in political thought 'operate within larger semantic fields even without being mentioned', p. 790).

[41] See O'Rourke and Pelttari (p. 259) with abundant references, and e.g. Coffee 2019 (with the other essays in Berti 2019), Bernstein 2020, Coffee and Gawley 2020, Heslin 2020 and Hinds 2020. Predictions of the future date rapidly, of course, as a glance back at (for instance) McCarty 2002 shows; this footnote, too, is fated to go stale particularly fast.

[42] Editing: Huskey and Kaster (Ch. 10). Style: e.g. Stover and Kestemont 2016; Dexter, Katz, Tripuraneni et al. 2017; Chaudhuri, Dasgupta, Dexter and Iyer 2018; Keeline and Kirby 2019.

[43] Bagnall and Heath 2018 is a valuable guide to digital resources for Latinists. In some respects the internet represents a leap backwards; problems include the proliferation of typo-ridden Latin texts

What of 'theory'? For many, the pragmatic truce that broke out after the wars of the late twentieth century – that 'easygoing pluralism' excoriated by Charles Martindale[44] – seems to hold; and our failure to poke some hornets' nests may disappoint some. That said, theory is of course omnipresent. It is thematised most explicitly by Alison Sharrock on authorship and identity,[45] O'Rourke and Pelttari on intertextuality (a subset of the discipline that continues to stimulate interest and scepticism in equal measure),[46] James Uden's survey – and revitalisation – of reception theory,[47] Lowrie's kaleidoscope of critical approaches to the end of the *Aeneid* (pp. 795–804), and Goldhill's exploration of Greek–Latin interactions in postcolonial terms (Chapter 16), but different theoretical approaches are displayed and interrogated throughout.[48] The centre of gravity is firmly cultural–historical, embraced explicitly by Kelly on periodisation (p. 119–20) and Lavan in his call for a more nuanced historicism

and a widespread return to antiquated – because not copyrighted – editions, translations and reference works, including the Victorian dictionary 'Lewis and Short' (which does, however, have some advantages; see n. 76). Conversely, the digitisation of much early modern scholarship has made important commentaries and other publications available outside the rare books rooms of libraries. So much for 'input'; output is also rapidly changing, given the opportunities for disseminating research – and pursuing polemic – in virtual print, on social media (Fuhrer, pp. 502–3) and in online seminars.

[44] '… an easygoing pluralism, involving co-existence of activities if not much active intellectual interchange, is favored within the academy – what Terry Eagleton, product of a more ideological age, used to call in his lectures "clueless eclecticism"' (Martindale 2002: 142). Cf. Sharrock (p. 185) on 'the impression that we might be living in a "post-theoretical" age (as if that were possible)'.

[45] In whose chapter you will find (e.g.) Barthes, Foucault and Derrida (pp. 184–93). See also Haskell (pp. 368–73) on 'authenticity' in Neo-Latin, Huskey and Kaster (p. 516) on authorship from a text-critical point of view, Clackson (p. 570) on linguists and intentionality; Lowrie (p. 792) advocates a move away from authors to larger conceptual histories. Several contributors unproblematically invoke metapoetics (notably O'Rourke and Pelttari, pp. 229–40, on 'self-reflexive intertextuality'), reflecting their status as a given (at least in some measure) for most or all readers of ancient literature.

[46] Also Stover (pp. 282–5) on mediaeval *imitatio*, Haskell (pp. 359–61 and 368–73) on neo-Latin intertextuality and the authentic voice; Squire and Elsner (p. 626) on Optatian (and p. 675 on '"inter-textual-pictorial" play'); Lavan (p. 841) on 'real life' intertextuality (also O'Rourke and Pelttari, pp. 254–5); Goldhill (p. 863) on the challenges of 'proof' in translingual intertextuality. Clackson (pp. 568–70) and Lavan (p. 840) remind us of the scepticism with which work on intertextuality continues to be met in many quarters, and Lowrie (p. 792) advocates for a change of approach in terms of political thought: 'To access Roman political thought as more than a collection of statements or even textual symptoms will require a concerted shift in focus from author to culture, intention to convention, reference to system.'

[47] With survey on pp. 398–406. Uden highlights resistance, exclusion and Global Classics as ways forward, using three case studies from the eighteenth century. See also Fuhrer (p. 482) on reception and reader-reception in their German/US institutional contexts. Stover's and Haskell's chapters inevitably double as studies in reception of ancient Latin, while also inviting classicists to move beyond what Philip Hardie (2018) has called 'an hour-glass model of intertextuality' (comparing a given post-antique text with an ancient one without considering what lies in between).

[48] Including, it may still need emphasising, when it comes to textual editing: as Huskey and Kaster (pp. 516–17) point out, every edition is a theory.

when addressing questions of politics and power in Roman texts;[49] so too Katharina Volk, with her manifesto for a culturally grounded reading of Roman philosophy,[50] and Uden's vindication of reception as cultural studies in the strong sense.

Where will the 'high theory' of the coming years be? Prophecy is a fools' game, but we note with Sharrock (p. 200) the still fresh shoots of ecocriticism,[51] the stirrings of posthumanism,[52] and the rich promise of the cognitive turn.[53] Queer theory continues to evolve,[54] and Global Classics is another important impulse,[55] not least in its continuing call to disciplinary self-awareness. In that spirit, we offer as one last critical tool a running self-reflexivity about the state of the discipline and its practitioners: contributors reflect explicitly on their own careers,[56] as well as on the continued imbalance in gender[57] and race,[58] the more or less explicit marginalising of areas such as post-antique and reception studies[59] and the effect on research of changing patterns of teaching and of funding structures.[60] Navel-gazing is easily mocked; but explicit reflection on individual presumptions and disciplinary norms is surely a prerequisite for truly critical engagement.

[49] As he puts it (p. 825), 'Being a good historicist requires being a good historian – and that is a non-trivial condition.'
[50] Ch. 13; so too Lavan (pp. 823–4) on Stoicism, Stover (p. 284) on mediaeval allegory, and Lowrie in her chapter on political thought.
[51] Whether in the soft sense (readings which attend to natural or human-natural relations) or a hard one (politically evaluating texts in terms of ecological ideals). Virgil's *Eclogues* has naturally been a prime target (Saunders 2008; Apostol 2015); Schliephake 2017 includes ecocritical approaches to Virgil, Columella, Lucan and Statius. Here, as often, Classics sails in the wake of English departments (e.g. Bate 1991, Glotfelty 1996, Rigby 2015), though soft ecocriticism (e.g. on landscape) of course has a long tradition.
[52] Bianchi, Brill and Holmes 2019, Chesi and Spiegel 2020.
[53] O'Rouke and Pelttari (pp. 259–60), Clackson (pp. 589–90), with Squire and Elsner (p. 652 n. 82) on the 'sensory turn'. On 'cognitive classics' see Meineck, Short and Devereaux 2019 (heavily weighted to Greek); also e.g. Riggsby 2019, a study of ancient information technologies with a strong cognitive thrust (and abundant pay-off for 'literary' readers), and Gazzarri 2020, taking a cognitive approach to Senecan metaphor.
[54] Not least into intersectionality and trans studies (see n. 28).
[55] Both as theoretical approach (see Uden, esp. pp. 428–33, and e.g. Umurhan 2018) – and as a call to decentre the tradition (cf. Seo 2019). For the important work of Andrew Laird in centring focus on Latin America, see (e.g.) Laird and Miller 2018.
[56] Sharrock (p. 184), Haskell (pp. 334–6), Uden (p. 396).
[57] See Huskey and Kaster (p. 540) and Fuhrer (p. 492) on the paucity of female textual critics in particular, and Uden (pp. 417–20) for a longer view on the education of women in Latin.
[58] Fuhrer (p. 475).
[59] See Haskell on Neo-Latin. Uden (esp. pp. 395–7 and 439–40) confronts and collapses value-inflected distinctions between philology and reception studies.
[60] Peirano Garrison (pp. 43–52) for a long view on teaching canons in the USA; Stover (p. 279) on funding work in mediaeval Latin; Haskell (pp. 355, 373–9) on the teaching and funding of Neo-Latin; Fuhrer (pp. 450–83 *passim*) on the pedagogical landscape.

## Territories (1): 'Classical' and Later Latins

One of the purposes of this volume is to highlight tools and methodologies that can be used to interrogate canonical texts in fresh or challenging ways. Another is to highlight less familiar texts. Why do we relegate so much of our corpus to the categories of 'marginal' and 'minor'? For most practising Latinists the largest single area of neglect is the literature of late antiquity and beyond: the Middle Ages, the Renaissance and – when Latin goes global – the modern and early modern eras.[61] Walter Scheidel has argued that Roman historians can only grasp what is specific to the Roman Empire if they pay equal attention to 'what happened later on in the same geographical space'.[62] Similarly, specialists in classical Latin – whom we take to be a large part of our readership – can benefit from asking what becomes of literature later on, in the same linguistic space.[63] As Joseph Farrell puts it, Latin can be appreciated 'as richer and more appealing for the diversity that it gained through time and space in the contrasting voices of many speakers':[64] there is clear advantage in shifting from an image of classical Latin as a cluster of texts ensconced within a *pomerium* to the thought that we lie only at the *beginning* of Latin literature. (The image of the *pomerium* also encapsulates the limited spatial distribution of the Latin literature of the late republic and early Empire, which is heavily concentrated within the metropolis; the north African Apuleius and Tertullian point the way to the greater geographical diversity of the future.) The accumulated expertise of those who work on the vast range of texts from late antiquity to neo-Latin and modern vernacular receptions of Latin texts has much to offer the rest of us in both teaching and research – not least a sense of our place within the world history of Latin.[65]

That is one reason why more than half the contributors to this volume are scholars who work primarily on material outside classical Latin literature. But

---

[61] See Haskell (pp. 347–8 and 356–7) on global Neo-Latin and Fuhrer (pp. 477–80) on Latin literature studies beyond Europe and the Anglophone world; Stover (pp. 278–80) and Fuhrer (*passim*) on national boundaries; on politics of global reception see again Uden (pp. 428–33) and Blanshard et al. 2020: 188–9.

[62] Scheidel 2019: 22.

[63] Where Scheidel 2019 contends that the disappearance of Rome was a precondition for future economic and social progress (a view that needs to be read against Netz 2020: 800–5 on the success of antiquity as cultural catalyst), the present volume rejects the old narrative of Latin's post-classical decline. For the trope of decline in Latin from a golden age, see Farrell 2001: 84–112.

[64] Farrell 2001: 123; cf. the agenda set out ibid. xii–xiii.

[65] For the continuing influence of early-modern commentators in the field (alongside the resources offered by modern critics), see O'Rourke and Pelttari (pp. 216–17) on Juan Luis de la Cerda; conversely for the rich patrimony offered by forgotten classical philologists of the early modern period, see (e.g.) Santini and Stok 2008.

*1 Introduction: Texts, Tools, Territories*

how is 'classical Latin' defined, and how useful or valid is such a definition? How big is the extant classical corpus, how does it relate to the corpus as perceived in antiquity, and how big is it by comparison with later eras? And how well is modern scholarship distributed across surviving Latin texts?

### *Defining Classical Latin*

'Classical Latin' is a term as various as it is exclusive. To take just chronology, it may be used to describe the Latin of all antiquity (excluding mediaeval and beyond), just the Latin of the republic and early principate (excluding later antiquity), or most narrowly the 'model' prose and verse of a few select authors (excluding, then, almost everything).[66] We use it here in the second sense, as a counterpole to 'late antique', objectionable in perpetuating a polarity which this volume sets out to challenge, but adopted as a term of convenience.[67] One powerful demarcation of classical Latin in that sense is enshrined in the *Oxford Latin Dictionary*. Issued serially from 1968 to 1982, with a second edition in 2012, the *OLD* is the flagship lexicon in the English-speaking world, and exerts due influence.[68] According to a decision taken early on, it covers texts up to around 200 CE, adding some from later,[69] but excluding even second-century Christians:[70] so for instance Ulpian (born c. 170) is in, but Tertullian (born 155) stays out.[71] It was a practical decision – to add Augustine alone would have doubled the material,[72] and the project took over half a century as it is – and not one that reflected scholarly

---

[66] The models being Cicero (or even just his oratory and dialogues) and Caesar in prose, Virgil, Horace and Ovid above all in verse. This is the norm in older grammars such as Kühner and Stegmann 1912, and remains influential, not just in education systems where prose and verse composition is privileged: commentators on imperial texts, for instance, are often prone to measure their author's usage against a 'classical' norm.

[67] Kelly (p. 107) prefers a different use, and reflects on the term 'classical'; cf. Hall and Stead 2019: 21–44 on the origins and development of 'Classics'. Zetzel 2018: 81–3 (on Fronto and Gellius) considers some differing ideas of the classical within antiquity itself.

[68] On its long gestation and vicissitudes, see Henderson 2010 and Stray 2012. The 'second edition' is essentially an aesthetic makeover, and not obviously an improvement (Whitton 2012).

[69] As late as Isidore in the sixth century and Paulus' epitome of Festus in the eighth. Others include Donatus' Terence commentary, Fulgentius Afer, Macrobius, Nonius, Priscian, Servius and the texts of *CIL*: i.e. largely paraliterary texts useful to classicists.

[70] Glare 1986: vi (= 2012: ix). The original plan had been to stop at the death of Suetonius (Henderson 2010: 147–9).

[71] Admission was granted, though, to Augustine's *City of God*.

[72] Augustine's five million words, on the estimate of Dolbeau 1998: 134–5, equal the total of all surviving Latin literature up to the first century CE. There was also a desire not to step on the toes of a dictionary of 'later Latin' under preparation for the Society for the Promotion of Christian Knowledge, which in fact never appeared; there is, however, a *Glossary of Later Latin to 600 AD* (1949) by Alexander Souter, one of the first editors of the *OLD*. See Henderson 2010: 148, 152–3; Stray 2012.

consensus: 'an irreparable blunder', said Robin Nisbet;[73] 'a terminal limit devoid of linguistic or literary validity', declared Frank Goodyear.[74] But it had significant intellectual consequences: despite many advances,[75] the *OLD* has failed to supersede its flawed Victorian predecessor 'Lewis and Short' in an important point of content (as well as in actual use),[76] and it reinforces a widespread tendency to see Latin after Apuleius as exotic. (Those educated in different systems, including a Germanic tradition centred on the *Thesaurus linguae Latinae*, whose coverage runs into the sixth century, often conceptualise the field rather differently.)[77]

The exclusion of Christian texts continued a trend that had been in train since Wolf's *Prolegomena to Homer* (1795) and perhaps earlier, as Classics extricated itself from 'philology's shadow', theology.[78] If they were parting ways in the nineteenth century, the two disciplines remained closely enmeshed in methodological terms, thanks to a mutually reinforcing investment in textual criticism and authenticity, as well as a commitment to close – very close – reading of ancient authors.[79] By the early twentieth century, the fissure was deeper. New subjects had arrived to take the place of theology as methodological allies, and the shared concerns of the

---

[73] In the *Oxford Magazine*, 14.2.1969 (as quoted by Henderson 2010: 174 n. 47), following publication of the first fascicle. Nisbet anticipated a boom in late antique Latin which the dictionary would do little to foster; whether his prediction can be called right fifty years on depends on where one is standing. Ausonius, Prudentius, Ammianus Marcellinus and Claudian have all attracted very large bibliographies, alongside the enduring colossi of Augustine and Jerome. From another point of view, it is the Latin authors of the post-Virgilian age who have been signal beneficiaries, despite the discouragements of the *CHCL* (see p. 2).

[74] Goodyear 1992: 281 (orig. 1983). Other reviewers were more temperate, but not all mild: Kenney 1970; Luck 1984.

[75] Clackson, pp. 586–9 (faulting, however, the lack of attention to diachrony in semantics).

[76] Lewis and Short 1879, including inconsistent coverage up to c. 600. Freely available on the Perseus website and cheap to download as an app, it is unlikely to be superseded as the 'big dictionary' of choice for many readers so long as the *OLD* either exists only in print (priced at over £300) or sits behind an expensive paywall.

[77] Coverage is more or less comprehensive up to the second century, but often more selective thereafter. The *Thesaurus* is one of several large research projects in German-speaking lands, also including the *Mittellateinisches Wörterbuch* and Bibliotheca Teubneriana Latina; on these and others see Fuhrer (pp. 455–6), who also notes the greater institutional support for late antique studies in parts of continental Europe. On the broad cultural context for such initiatives, see Blanshard et al. 2020: 114–15.

[78] Conybeare and Goldhill 2020, esp. ch. 1. In the terms of Blanshard et al. 2020: 82–99, the separation of Classics from theology is a matter of 'repeatedly asserted differentiation' rather than 'genetic difference'. The silent erection of barriers is nothing new in the broader history of the field: early imperial Greeks, as Simon Goldhill shows (pp. 863–7), understood how to perform their ignorance of Latin.

[79] Goldhill 2020: 33–49; cf. Peirano Garrison 2020 on Lachmann's editions of both Lucretius and the New Testament.

*1 Introduction: Texts, Tools, Territories*

Victorian age appeared antiquated.[80] As in many divorces, the former partners began to define themselves *against* one another, in an act of disavowal whose unacknowledged force shapes the discipline as we know it today.[81]

And yet classical Latin is in an important sense the brainchild of Christianity – one of which Quintilian might have approved, for all the Christian insistence on a gulf separating the heavenly concerns of Jerusalem from the affairs of Athens.[82] After the reign of Hadrian, Latin literature famously begins to fall quiet until the resurgence beginning with Diocletian in the late third century. It is hardly a uniform decline: not to mention Fronto, Gellius and Apuleius, jurisprudence flourishes and a Christian tradition gets underway, especially in north Africa. A century of political, military and economic turmoil from the late 160s onwards might be one explanation. Greek suffers a gradual decline in production over the course of the third century (at least by comparison with the peak years of the later second century); but authors of the stature of Athenaeus, Herodian, Philostratus and Plotinus flourish in the late second and early third centuries.[83] The reasons for the perhaps unequal fortunes between the two languages are unclear.[84] But as Latin literature made its return in the late third and (particularly) fourth centuries, the Christian population of the empire rocketed, from perhaps 5–10% in 300 CE to a position of clear dominance by 400.[85] This was the era in which (classical) Latin as the language of literature was gradually standardised to some degree: the pronounced stylistic experiments attempted in the age between Tacitus

---

[80] See Goldhill 2020: 57–62, esp. p. 62 'intergenerational, family conflict, the trauma of the First World War, the growth of the discipline of anthropology, and the importance of world politics after the world war . . . all worked to effect the divorce between classical philology and theology'.
[81] See Goldhill 2020: 54–7; but it might be said, given the centrality of the Greek New Testament to earlier close relations, that the effects of the divorce have been stronger on the Hellenic side than on the Latin. Classics is not uniquely guilty in this regard; see Vinzent 2019: 46–7 on institutional divides between scholars of patristics and scholars of the New Testament.
[82] See Peirano Garrison (pp. 67–77) and Kelly (pp. 140–3) on the complexity of Christian ideological responses to 'classical' Latin, and on the Christian preservation of pagan works, including a vast amount of fragmentary texts. For the use of 'Athens' by the Latin-speaking Tertullian, see Goldhill (p. 884).
[83] Netz 2020: 691–727. For the possibility of a rupture in Latin literature in the years 254–84 CE, see Farrell 2001: 9–10; cf. Kelly (p. 113) on the absence of elite genres from surviving third-century texts.
[84] Leonhardt 2013: 80–6 suggests that the growing cultural capital of Greek, evident already in the time of Trajan and Hadrian, was a factor: Greek rhetoricians and philosophers who lived in Italy did not usually write in Latin, and Roman practitioners displayed an increasing willingness to compose in Greek. However, the association of *paideia* with Greek was more likely to have been a constant across all eras.
[85] Trombley 2006.

and Apuleius in the second century seem to became rarer in the new era.[86] Such standardisation was in part due to the gradual diffusion of an accepted canon of (classical) works taught at school for emulation: Cicero and Virgil, of course; also Terence, Sallust, Horace and Livy.[87] Like most canons, it had stylistic diversity within it; in any case, as Clackson remarks (p. 584), classical Latin had never been an unchanging monolith.[88] Augustine could move seamlessly, all the same, from teaching Latin rhetoric at the schools of Carthage to those of Rome and Milan, despite consciousness of his north African ('Punic') accent.[89] It is one of the great paradoxes, then, of the *OLD* and the field it serves that the very authors and texts who colluded in creating a canon of classical Latin are so often excluded from view.

*Sizing up the Corpus*

We will return in a moment to those flimsy yet consequential barriers between classical and later Latins. First, we address some questions about scale in the classical corpus: how much literature survives, and how much was there? Surprisingly little effort seems to have been put into answering the second question; but inspiration can be found in Reviel Netz's *Scale, Space and Canon in Ancient Literary Culture* (2020), a provocative and challenging essay on the extent of Greek literature in antiquity.[90] Netz's approach cannot be mapped directly onto Latin, given the quantitative and qualitative differences between the surviving Greek and Roman corpora. But we summarise it here to gesture at the bigger picture of the ancient literary Mediterranean, and to illustrate the methodology and potential rewards of a quantitative approach.

---

[86] Stylistic experimentation lived on in the work of e.g. Ammianus, Aurelius Victor and (later) Sidonius.

[87] Leonhardt 2013: 87–8. Very broadly, the classicism of late antiquity eventually gave way to the more mannered style of the late fifth and early sixth centuries, before a temporary resurgence of the *sermo humilis* of the Vulgate; see Stover's chapter (Ch. 6). On the mediaeval educational canon (which overlaps to some degree with the late antique, besides the addition of the Vulgate and Christian Latin classics), see again Stover: like the late antique canon, the mediaeval canon allowed for significant stylistic diversity.

[88] As the Romans themselves knew. Repeated attempts to 'reform' Latin and return to classical 'stability' (Farrell 2001: 5–6, 15–17) should be read against this relative diversity in practice.

[89] Augustine, *De ord.* 2.45.

[90] Keith Hopkins once estimated the number of 'fluent and skilled literates' among early Christian communities across the whole Mediterranean at 42. This (Douglas Adams-esque) number is not of course to be taken literally, but stands as 'a symbol for a small number of unknown size' (Hopkins 2018a: 463–4). In other words, rough orders of magnitude are the order of the day.

*1 Introduction: Texts, Tools, Territories*

On Netz's projection, by the end of the second century CE around 30,000 people had written literature in Greek,[91] of whom around 10,000 had works still circulating; the latter number fell to perhaps 500 to 1,000 by the ninth century.[92] Today around 200 authors are transmitted either in whole works or in whole parts of works (i.e. one or more constituent books still whole).[93] In other words, surviving Greek authors represent perhaps 2% of the total circulating in 200 CE and well below 1% of the authors active to that date.[94]

Those proportions rise if we include fragmentary authors.[95] But to reach even a 10% survival rate from before 200 CE, we would need works or fragments of 3,000 authors.[96] The canon of the *Thesaurus linguae Graecae* runs to around 4,000 – but across a much longer span (to the fall of Byzantium); and late antique Christians are on the whole more likely to be preserved than their earlier pagan counterparts, for a simple practical reason: a text written in 400 BCE had to survive much longer before being copied onto parchment than one written in 400 CE.[97] Even including fragmentary authors, then, perhaps no more than 5% have survived in any extent. As for the quantity of surviving text, this is often assumed to be less than 1%.[98] Suppose, though, that most of our 30,000 putative writers were neither eminent nor prolific, failing to spur the sorts of efforts put into preserving the likes of Aristotle, Plutarch and Galen: that might raise the estimate to perhaps 2%.[99]

---

[91] Projecting attestations for *c*. 5,000 Greek authors in the period before 200 CE, Netz suggests that the ratio for attested authors in proportion to all pre-200 authors (attested and unattested) probably lies somewhere between 1:5 (or just below) and 1:9. In consequence, there were perhaps anywhere between 22,500 and 45,000 Greek authors active in the period before late antiquity (Netz 2020: 527–624).

[92] Netz 2020: 550–1, 557–9. Most were probably technical and philosophical writers rather than strictly belletristic; but we have already mentioned the problem of defining 'literature'.

[93] Ibid. 551.

[94] More than that, Netz (ibid. 546, 557–8) argues for a survival rate of only 15% for a putative 20,000 pre-imperial authors into the imperial period itself.

[95] See the quantitative analysis performed on the *TLG* by Berti et al. 2009: 'for the period between the 8th century B.C. and the 3rd century A.D. included, 59% of the authors is preserved only in fragments, 12% is known both from entirely preserved works and fragmentary ones, while 29% is represented by surviving works'.

[96] I.e. 60% of the probable 5,000 authors *attested* in total for the period before 200 CE (see n. 91).

[97] Or papyrus (see Kelly, p. 145).

[98] In 1494 Pietro Bembo, concerned about the disappearance of ancient Greek literature in his own time, and perhaps after some acquaintance with the *Suda*, estimated that only 1% of ancient Greek literature was still in existence; see his *Oratio pro litteris Graecis* with Wilson 2003. A similar claim has been staked in modern times (Blum 1991: 8, 13 n. 4), and is often repeated anecdotally. The true rate of survival in bulk is perhaps less than 1%, i.e. somewhere between survival rates for papyrus and stone (see next n.), even allowing for the recopying that texts regularly enjoyed and inscriptions did not.

[99] As suggested to us by Reviel Netz. For estimates of the (low) survival rate of ancient texts preserved via other media, including inscriptions, papyri and military diplomata, see Duncan-Jones 1982: 360–2; Eck 2002: 93–5; Netz 2020: 528–36. Using the genre of narrative fiction in medieval Europe

Can Netz's approach be replicated for Latin? His estimates come from probabilistic arguments based on attestations in ancient sources. Despite a high attrition rate, the surviving Greek corpus is not small, and we have plenty of attestation-rich works, including the post-classical *Suda*. Latin is perhaps as well endowed with similar texts, proportionally.[100] But there is perhaps ten times as much Greek literature down to the fifth century CE extant as there is Latin,[101] with presumably a significant multiplicative effect on attestations of lost authors. In consequence, we probably have less information about texts we know of but do not possess, and an even shakier basis for estimating what else there was. Above all, we lack the Egyptian papyri that, for Greek literature, grant direct access to antiquity and preserve many texts not otherwise selected for re-copying onto parchment. There is, then, a fundamental quantitative *and* qualitative difference between the surviving Latin and Greek corpora and what they are equipped to tell us about losses.[102]

Still, Netz provides the impetus for a quantitative approach to the Latin corpus. But we start at the other end with extant (rather than attested) authors. The *OLD* cites over 700 different whole or fragmentary works from about 370 authors, including grammarians and those embedded in the *Digest*;[103] of these, around 65 have works wholly or substantially extant. There are also around 35 unattributed works fully extant (some perhaps written by authors with attributed works extant; but to be generous to the corpus, let us assume the overlap is relatively small), and 270 or so authors of whom only fragments survive. These numbers are rough and ready (leaving aside, for instance, the *XII Tables* and similar compilations), but they offer a basic starting-point.[104]

---

(c. 600–1450 CE), Kestemont, Karsdorp et al. 2020 estimate survival rates for the total number of works on a range from 38.6% (England) to 79% (Germany) and 81% (Ireland), and the percentage of surviving documents that carried these works on a range from 4.9% (England) to 19.2% (Ireland).

[100] Where Greek features citation-rich sources such as Plutarch, Athenaeus and Photius, as well as the *Suda*, Latin offers e.g. Cicero's *Brutus*, Quintilian, Gellius, Jerome's *De uiris illustribus*, Festus and Nonius.

[101] This ratio for Greek literature down to Nonnus in the fifth century is quoted in the 1925 preface of LSJ (1996: v), and attributed to Diels 1905: 692, who wrote at a time of great rediscoveries of Egyptian papyri.

[102] Cf. Kelly (pp. 148–9) on the difficulties of applying the methods of Netz 2020 to Latin literature.

[103] For this exercise we have excluded the handful of non-juristic works from after 200 CE.

[104] Figures for authors, of course, are independent of estimates of quantity: the corpora of Cicero and Livy are massive, that of Gallus minute.

*1 Introduction: Texts, Tools, Territories*

It is safe to assume that the *OLD* does not draw on every pagan author from before 200 to survive. What percentage does it include?[105] For the period up to 140 CE, Peter White counts just over 120 poets 'of whose verse any portion is extant in a manuscript tradition';[106] 95% of them are listed among the *OLD*'s sources. If we guess that prose is less privileged, we might suppose – at least as a sighting shot – that the *OLD* cites around 80% of authors whose work substantially survives, and around 50–60% of authors who survive as fragments.[107] If so, we can project a surviving Latin classical (and pagan) corpus with 100 to 125 authors surviving in whole or whole parts and 270 to 450/540 authors in fragments. Assume an overall survival rate, as for Greek, of 5%, and we might (very) provisionally project something between 7,400 and 11,500/13,300 Latin authors before 200 CE.[108] Then again, the average Latin text was much younger by the time it was first copied onto parchment, suggesting a better survival rate; our projections should be dropped a little if so.[109] The corpus of Classical Latin as understood by the *OLD* then consists, on any reasonable estimate, of perhaps not very much more than 100 authors surviving whole or in whole parts.[110] The overall survival rate, assessed by bulk, looks – as might be expected – low.[111]

---

[105] In the preface to the first volume of *La Littérature latine inconnue* (1952), H. Bardon cited some estimates made in 1903 by one A. F. Wert (in fact A. F. West 1902): 772 Latin authors known by name, 144 with one or more works transmitted, 352 surviving as fragments quoted in other works, and 276 attested but not extant. It appears that West based his estimates on M. Schanz's 1875–87 revision of W. S. Teuffel's *Geschichte der römischen Literatur*; the figures include Latin authors down to 500 CE, 'excluding all Christian Latin and all Greek books written by Romans'. West added that of the 144 survivors, 64 had lost the majority of their books, 43 retained the greater part of their writings, and 37 possessed all or very nearly all of their works.
[106] White 1993: 211–22.
[107] The estimates are deliberately conservative, to leave room for an unknown number of fragmentary jurists and grammarians not cited. A glance at the contents list for Cornell's *Fragments of the Roman Historians* (2013) suggests that only around 50% of the authors appear in the *OLD*; collections of fragments in other prose genres perhaps register an even lower strike rate.
[108] Here as elsewhere, it is orders of magnitude that matter; the precise figures are eminently open to revision. A further question is raised: who counts as an 'author'? One definition might be: someone whose work was read and circulated beyond the (extended) family of the writer. Pliny's *Epistles* offer numerous examples of versifiers whose work would presumably have remained a family affair (e.g. the *lyrica doctissima* of Vestricius Spurinna at *Ep.* 3.1.7), were it not for Pliny's unique interest.
[109] Whether Latin produced proportionately more belletristic authors than Greek remains a subject for speculation.
[110] Classical Greek, it appears, has only twice that particular number of surviving authors; but they and their fragmentary fellow authors produced on average much more text per head.
[111] Fragmentary authors survive largely as quotations in later texts, and do not have the advantage enjoyed by Greek of extensive supplementation through papyrus finds. (Even the currently available Herculaneum papyri are mostly Greek.)

## On 'Representativeness'

It is conventional to lament the loss of large swathes of Ennius or Livy and the near or total disappearance of others such as Gallus: like Greek, and unlike many other disciplines in the humanities, scholarship on classical Latin 'has a constitutive relationship to loss'.[112] Lamentation may be misplaced in two rather different senses. In ethical terms, the neglect, indifference or cultural hostility suffered by Latin literature over the centuries might be viewed in the context of the 'epistemicide' (cultural, environmental, religious) that the Romans themselves so enthusiastically inflicted on their imperial subjects.[113] In simpler terms of scale, what survives in fact appears to be, to a perhaps surprising extent, representative of works circulating in antiquity: we have many of the authors who were most widely read.

In a famous passage of his *Education of the Orator*, written in the early 90s CE, Quintilian sets out which Greek and Latin authors a budding orator should read (*Inst.* 10.1.38–131). Towards sixty writers make the cut in Latin, including poets, historians and philosophers as well as orators. Of course, the list is not straightforwardly representative of what actually was being read in his day: Quintilian is not much interested in literature before Cicero, excludes authors alive at his time of writing, and omits several genres altogether (no biography, epistolography, fables, novels or pastoral; no *Apocolocyntosis* and no *Natural History*, to mention a couple): he is prescribing a canon, and specifically a paedagogical one (for the aspiring orator), as much preserving one. Still, in other ways his tastes look catholic, including poets whose manner and content were far from smooth or risk-free (Lucretius, Catullus, Lucan).[114] Of his nearly sixty authors, we possess over a third either whole or in whole parts, and substantial fragments of many of the rest. The spread is uneven across genres: only one of Quintilian's fourteen orators (Cicero – who of course supplies a very great deal of our extant prose), but wholes or whole parts of two-fifths of the poets and historians, and one-third of the philosophers. Still, this is a striking outcome: although perhaps only 5% (or slightly more) of classical

---

[112] Blanshard et al. 2020: 129.    [113] On Roman epistemicide, see Padilla Peralta 2020.
[114] On Roman canons (including Quintilian's), see Peirano Garrison's chapter (Ch. 2). The letters of Pliny the Younger reveal a set of tastes more thoroughly biased towards his own time and personal acquaintances (Gibson 2014): of the Latin writers he admires, we possess whole or in whole parts 45% of the poets, 36% of the historians, 12% of the orators, and none of the handful of philosophers (ibid. 206).

*1 Introduction: Texts, Tools, Territories*

Latin authors may have survived in any form at all, we seem to have a disproportionately good sample of mainstream literature as it appeared towards the end of the first century CE.[115]

Otherwise put, it appears that the classical canon that Christians would later make their own in the fourth century and beyond was already forming in the first. That suggests considerable stability in tastes, and commensurate fortune in transmission – allowing for the addition of Petronius and others who found more favour with Christian copyists than with Quintilian (whose focus on education overrides all other considerations).[116] But how 'traditional' is our own canon in research and teaching? In other words, how many of the 100 or so classical authors whose works survive wholly or substantially attract regular attention?

Answers to that question must be subjective. What counts as regular? One dedicated article each year? A monograph a decade? The expanding girth (or, nowadays, database) of *L'Année philologique* tells its own story about the increasing volume of classical research, but not about its distribution. The teaching canon remains small. The 'Cambridge Greek and Latin Classics' (better known as the 'Green and Yellows') is certainly the largest and perhaps the most widely used commentary series in the world; yet despite a pronounced expansion in range since its inception in the 1970s, it features only around twenty Latin authors.[117] Just one of those is late antique; five others, or at least their floruits, postdate Quintilian (Tacitus, Pliny, Juvenal, Suetonius and Apuleius), and two were alive when he was writing, disqualifying them from mention (Martial and Statius).[118] The remaining twelve 'Green and Yellow' authors all feature in Quintilian's list: sign of a remarkably static canon. Of course, curricula are not tied inexorably to that series; even so, probably no more than thirty

---

[115] This accords in some respects with conclusions reached by Netz 2020: 13–14 that, for Greek literature before 200 CE, prestige and popularity largely coincided: good reputation ensured wide circulation; cf. Netz 2020: 624: 'We have truly lost much of the detailed contents. We have also lost even the trace of some passing fads. What we do know, truly well, is the broad contours of the constants.' However, reading Quintilian cannot of course tell us how many Petroniuses (et al.) he omits. For the criticism that Netz takes insufficient account of the fundamental effects of Byzantine tastes on the surviving Greek canon, see the review by Elsner 2021: why did the hugely popular Menander fail to survive in manuscript form?
[116] Likewise for the wide range of styles other than strict Ciceronianism adapted by neo-Latin authors, albeit with episodes of moral panic over perceived decline in the purity of Latin: see Haskell's chapter (Ch. 7); also Stover's on anti-classical Latin styles in the Middle Ages (Ch. 6).
[117] Gibson 2021.
[118] The late-antique author is Augustine (Clark 1995, White 2019). Clark's book and Kenney 1990 (Apuleius' *Cupid & Psyche*) were the two Latin volumes in a short-lived parallel series (the 'Imperial Library') clothed in purple and mauve. See also Kelly (pp. 115–17) on similar results for coverage provided by other series of texts.

writers of classical Latin are taught with any regularity, at least in the Anglosphere.[119]

Not many more receive systematic attention in research. If we expand that to irregular or incipient research and to figures whose stock has been rising, but who remain on the edges of many scholars' horizons – prose writers such as Valerius Maximus, Velleius Paterculus, Pomponius Mela and Florus, for instance; the poets Germanicus, Grattius and Phaedrus; the pseudepigrapha pinned to Virgil, Tibullus and Ovid – we might reach a total somewhere in the sixties. The number of authors considered 'mainstream' has undoubtedly expanded in recent decades, with the rehabilitation of such previously derided figures as Valerius Flaccus, Silius Italicus and Pliny the Younger.[120] Yet there remains ample room for expansion: an already small canon is more constricted than need be.[121] And, as this volume is designed in part to demonstrate, we have the tools that we need to undertake the research. More fundamentally, as Peirano Garrison argues in her chapter on canons (Chapter 2), we need to interrogate the link between the perceived authority of the critic and the market value of a text; to recognise that a discourse of the 'minor' might be a textual strategy deliberately co-opted by an author; and to embrace marginality 'as a way of doing business'.[122]

*Looking to Late Antiquity*

This is not a call to abandon Quintilian's authors. Other constituencies within and beyond academia expect and even rely on us to curate the

---

[119] Haskell (pp. 374–5) offers suggestions for the incorporation of neo-Latin texts into classical teaching programmes.
[120] See Peirano Garrison (pp. 52–3).
[121] In his inaugural lecture of 1956, C. O. Brink entered a special plea for the study of the 'margins' of classical literature, in fear that through concentration alone on the avowed 'classics', scholars would lose sight of the broader literary canvas of a period and soon begin seriously to distort its dimensions. A case in point was the *Appendix Vergiliana*, whose poems allowed a glimpse of 'an Alexandrian continuity, culminating in Ovid and scarcely interrupted by the great Augustans', whose 'classicism' was arguably quite unrepresentative of the tastes of the day (Brink 1957: 15–19, with quotation from p. 17; Brink's successor as Kennedy Professor at Cambridge returned to the issue in his inaugural lecture: Kenney 1975: 16–17). Underworked Latin authors and texts would dominate the early decades of the Cambridge Classical Texts and Commentaries ('Orange') series established by Brink (see Gibson 2016), and still do: alongside Tacitus (Woodman 2017 and 2018), the most recent Latin authors treated are Decimus Laberius (Panayotakis 2012), Gargilius Martialis (Zainaldin 2020) and – opening the door for the first time to Christian Latin – Venantius Fortunatus (Kay 2020).
[122] On canons, margins and the question of aesthetic quality, see also Formisano 2018; Franklinos and Fulkerson 2020: 1–9.

'classic' texts, and the boom in reception studies has perhaps had the unintended consequence of focusing attention on a relatively small number of canonical works whose reception has 'gone global'.[123] We can in any case now generate more data for interpretation, frame our tasks with more precision, and ask new and challenging questions of our canonical texts. There are also limits to how far we can go in our embrace of the classical margins – albeit limits that we are far from reaching. The long arc of the late twentieth- and early twenty-first-century demand for re-evaluation of previously neglected authors was a necessary reaction to an earlier era which seemed to give little serious attention to poets other than Virgil or Horace (Quintilian was hardly so narrow). After all, why should there be a monotonous function from how 'central' an author is to how often they should be studied? But many would consider it a stretch to insist that Cornelius Nepos' *Eminent Foreign Generals* should be studied as intensively as Tacitus' *Annals*.[124] Another (and complementary) route lies across the disciplinary and institutional boundaries erected between classical philology and theology – and giving serious attention to the Latin (and mainly Christian) texts of what is called 'late antiquity'.[125]

Many (classical) Latinists will have their own prejudices to overcome. 'The field of Classics', as Peirano Garrison observes, can easily pose as a 'protector of the secular in opposition and response to the culturally hegemonic reach of monotheistic religions ... in a kind of scholarly post-enlightenment version of the separation of State and Church'.[126]

---

[123] Both issues are sensitively discussed by Formisano 2018; cf. Güthenke and Holmes 2018: 59–61 on Charles Martindale's response to the 'politics of globalization' espoused by Page DuBois in *Out of Athens* (2010).

[124] For the persistence of 'value' in the field and the need to take responsibility for 'likes' and 'dislikes', see Blanshard et al. 2020: 15–18. This is as close as we come to the sorts of value judgements encapsulated in *CHCL* (n. 5).

[125] On the term 'late antique' see Peirano Garrison (p. 47); Kelly (p. 115) issues a complementary call to expand our gaze. Two significant resources for late antique Latin literature are the forthcoming *Cambridge History of Later Latin Literature* and *Cambridge Dictionary of Later Latin Literature*, both being edited by Gavin Kelly and Aaron Pelttari; see also the *Oxford Dictionary of Late Antiquity*, edited by Oliver Nicholson in 2018. A new series of short monographs, *Cultures of Latin*, edited by Catherine Conybeare for CUP, is devoted to continuities from classical to late antique Latin and beyond.

[126] Peirano Garrison 2020: 88. She aptly quotes Shuger 1994: 3 'the sacred is ... drained, is emptied out, in order to provide modern culture with sufficient symbolic and symbolic capital to start up its own economy'; cf. Farrell 2001: 78–83 on ideologically driven neglect of Christian Latin. Also relevant is a perceived difference between the balancing of competing opinions characteristic of Roman law or ancient Judaism versus the dogmatism and hierarchy of early Christianity (traced by Hopkins 2018a: 469–75 to the rarity of literate readers within small Christian cells). For a vigorous response to such thinking (in the guise of reflections on Dodds' 1965 work *Pagan and Christian in an Age of Anxiety*), see Morgan 2019.

(Certainly the rich vein of 'republican' thinking in Roman texts analysed in Lowrie's chapter has been an important inspiration to early modern and modern theorists of the avowedly secular state.[127]) The *OLD* instantiates a version of this polarity between church and state.[128]

Yet such binary thinking is false at an elementary level in the study of literature: the language that Cicero attempted to standardise in the first century before Christ (or 'before the common era', in the dating system imposed in this volume) was largely unchanged in the essentials of morphology and syntax nearly half a millennium later. Change was already underway, of course, as Stover reminds us in his chapter, with the emergence of Christian *sermo humilis* and, in the late fifth and early sixth centuries, a non-classical 'mannered' style. And, as Peirano Garrison shows (pp. 72–3), Christian education eventually recognised a distinction between secular and ecclesiastical texts. Nevertheless, continuity in language and persistence of cultural processes demand that we think across the disciplinary gulf between classical and late antiquity. Goldhill (pp. 891–6) situates Jerome's translation of the Greek New Testament within a long tradition of Roman encounters with the literature and culture of the Greek-speaking Empire – albeit, in this case, one that eventually led to the imposition of rigid barriers between east and west. The intertextual practices of classical writers, as O'Rourke and Pelttari argue (pp. 240–51), similarly benefit from being considered as part of a continuum with the poetic centos of late antiquity and the typological reading of Jewish scriptures by Christian authors. And, Volk suggests (pp. 736–7 and 740), both Apuleius and his north African compatriot Tertullian need to be seen as operating in the same tradition of the Roman sophist.

Of course, just because we can read the Latin texts of Christian late antiquity does not mean that we are necessarily equipped to understand them.[129] Yet if we hive off to departments of history, religion or theology the responsibility for understanding the culture of this era, then we will not be able to understand fully even the intellectual milieu that produced the

---

[127] Cf. Marx's claim that the French Revolution was enacted 'in Roman costume' (Blanshard et al. 2020: 21, 38–9).

[128] If Latin students face charges of neglect of religious texts largely of late antiquity, classical Greek students face charges of neglect of the Hellenistic era (Septuagint) and early imperial age (the New Testament); see Goldhill 2020: 57.

[129] It is worth asking how far we are restricted by the effects of training within a narrowly confined canon (i.e. effects that can be eliminated by opening the canon), and how far by the human capacity to master the necessary information one needs to understand both a Catullus and a Cassiodorus.

late antique grammarians, critics and commentators such as Servius and Macrobius – considered here by Huskey and Kaster (pp. 537–40) and O'Rourke and Pelttari (pp. 250–3) – who remain fundamental to comprehension of earlier texts.[130] So too with visual commentary: in the words of Squire and Elsner (p. 652), illuminated manuscripts such as the Vatican Virgil demand respect as 'a series of responses to ... works closer to their original resonance and reception than our own reactions'. More fundamentally, as Kelly argues, 'The continuity of ... patterns of thought [across classical and late antiquity] is why periodisation matters and ... how it does intellectual harm, by narrowing our horizons and by encouraging a fundamentally unhistorical understanding of literature' (p. 119). There is also the incongruity of ignoring something so essentially Roman as late antique Christianity. It is difficult to decide, as Keith Hopkins put it, whether the transformation that followed Constantine's great decision 'should be called the triumph of the Christian church or the triumph of the Roman state'.[131]

The riches of the late antique corpus are extensive; how extensive is harder to say. Not even the *Thesaurus linguae Latinae* keeps count of all its *auctores* and *fontes*.[132] But the general impression that significantly more Latin authors from late antiquity are extant than there are from before it gets empirical confirmation from handbooks such as Part 6 of the *Handbuch der lateinischen Literatur der Antike*, dedicated to 'the age of Theodosius' (374–430).[133] Covering just fifty-five years, its two volumes treat well over 200 authors and pseudonymous or anonymous texts or collections of texts[134] – more than double the number that survive from the four centuries to 200 CE.[135] Much of this work can be said to fall outside the

---

[130] See Peirano Garrison (pp. 74–7).
[131] Hopkins 1999: 84. As for Rome's legacy, Walter Scheidel argues in *Escape from Rome* (2019) that 'the Greco-Roman legacy is far less important in the making of later European successes than is usually assumed – with the possible exception of Christianity, which rather perversely tends to be marginalised by proper classicists and many ancient historians' (Scheidel 2020). But for the dangers of assuming wholesale rupture from a 'classical' past, see Blanshard et al. 2020: 26–30.
[132] For a rough sense, the *TLL* lists over 120 authors whose name begins with A, four times the number in the *OLD*. As for works, the 2018 digital index for the *TLL* (https://thesaurus.badw.de/tll-digital/index/a.html) contains just under 5,000 rows cataloguing – in theory – either a single work or author. If we assume that around half of these rows represent cross-references or are superfluous in some way, we might (very) provisionally end up with 2,000–3,000 separate works from before 600 CE. The *Clavis patrum Latinorum* (Dekkers and Gaar 1995) attempts to list all Christian Latin texts from Tertullian to Bede.
[133] Berger, Fontaine and Schmidt 2020.
[134] A handful of lost works is included in these volumes, e.g. the histories of Nicomachus Flavianus.
[135] Parts 4 and 5 covered 117–284 and 284–374 in one volume each, suggesting that the explosion in literary activity was specifically at the end of the fourth century and start of the fifth.

realms of high literary culture; but it is hard not to be impressed by such an extraordinary outpouring of intellectual energy, and by its hardiness in survival (helped of course by the shift in this period from papyrus roll to codex, a seismic change which also brought with it a marked increase in the visualisation and illustration of the written corpus);[136] similarly with the astonishing quantities of prose produced by the likes of Augustine and Jerome. If 'definitions of the classical', as Peirano Garrison puts it (pp. 44–5), 'have been traditionally invested in claims of the universal superiority of the Graeco-Roman tradition and therefore implicitly of western culture', then a willingness to go beyond the boundaries of the classical is a necessary first step towards dismantling these attitudes.

Using bulk rather than author count, Jürgen Leonhardt estimated that Christian texts comprise around 80% of all Latin texts to survive antiquity, including inscriptions. But even the combined bulk of pagan and Christian texts is as nothing compared with the quantity of post-antique Latin. Antique texts as a whole are outnumbered by 10,000 to 1 (constituting, then, '0.01 percent of the total output');[137] classical Latin texts, therefore, by 50,000 to 1.[138] To be sure, these dizzying figures pay no attention to quality of text, and they include plenty of material (legal dissertations, for instance) which few would call literature. But Leonhardt does have a point: there is a lot of Latin out there. And much of it, particularly that of late antiquity, the high Middle Ages, the Renaissance and early modernity, is written in a form (at least) comprehensible to those trained in classical Latin.[139] Here is an ocean of material compared with the pond of classical Latin texts.[140]

One of the functions of this volume is to point the way towards this world of Latin beyond the second century CE, to decentre classical Latin, and to provide some first points of orientation. Attitudes to the Latin

---

[136] See Squire and Elsner (pp. 632–52).
[137] Leonhardt 2013: 2. Neo-Latin has lived on well past the eighteenth century: see Haskell (pp. 352–3).
[138] Ibid. 2–3 (he does not reveal the basis of his calculations). On the difficulties of estimating extant, published and lost mediaeval Latin, see Stover (pp. 272–3).
[139] Important caveats remain. Viewed as a whole, mediaeval Latin exhibits 'bewildering linguistic variety', including mannerism that borders on incomprehensibility to the classically trained; see Stover's chapter (Ch. 6), with Haskell (pp. 341–3) on some humanist responses. Scholars of Neo-Latin typically look 'sideways' to other Renaissance or early modern texts rather than 'backwards' to classical models (Haskell, p. 341); the reverse is true of classical reception scholars.
[140] This raises an important question: does the quantitative difference between classical and post-classical texts entail different interpretative parameters, so that the quantity of texts available makes a qualitative difference to the type of criticism that is either possible or appropriate? See below (pp. 33–4) on 'close' and 'distant' reading.

*1 Introduction: Texts, Tools, Territories* 25

canon in all periods *are* becoming more expansive.[141] Yet the encounters of classical Latinists with later texts (and their scholarship) are often a product of serendipity or toe-dipping.[142] We aim to provide broader vistas of landscapes ahead – without, we hope, being gripped by the 'Columbus complex', with its delusions of easy access to lands long settled by others with superior environmental knowledge and skills.[143] Since an ideal of competence in all periods of Latin is clearly impossible, we might instead aim for the 'nodal' Classics advocated by Constanze Güthenke and Brooke Holmes as a solution to the tensions between expansion (hyperinclusion) and limitation (hypercanonicity) in the discipline: 'rather than imagine the individual as encompassing a body of material, either within a field of vision or by means of her own self as the frame by which the fragments are restored to wholeness, we could imagine her as situated within a potential web of connections'. The task is to bring constituent parts of the web into contact.[144]

If the absence here of dedicated chapters on late antiquity and Christianity appears paradoxical in that light, it is positively motivated: rather than roping those areas off (as the discipline so often does), we have aimed at organic incorporation. Individual chapters routinely bring together texts which are 'classical' and 'late', pagan and Christian; and the relationships between and across them are repeatedly put under scrutiny. Peirano Garrison challenges the inherited distinction between Christian and pagan canons (pp. 67–77), and Kelly interrogates the boundaries between the classical, the late antique and the mediaeval (pp. 97–120). Stover adumbrates the vast terrain of extant (and largely unpublished) mediaeval Latin literature. 'Heterogeneous, and the product of accidental formation' (p. 275), the mediaeval canon cannot realistically be defined by the usual touchstones of period, place or literary analysis. Instead, Stover models different ways of approaching the field, with a particular emphasis on diachronic 'microhistories' of genre (particularly epic and bucolic) and synchronic histories of style, including the non-classical 'mannered' style affected by many elite literary productions. Yasmin Haskell investigates the benefits of more explicit disciplinary

---

[141] This is particularly evident in the digital edition of the *Oxford Classical Dictionary* (*OCD*[5]), which includes significantly expanded coverage of late antiquity.
[142] See Haskell's chapter (Ch. 7).
[143] The term is from Haskell 2001: 48–9 ('... we run that risk ... when we turn our classical telescopes on so many enticing New Worlds, worlds which our mere mastery of the Latin language seems to reveal to us').
[144] Güthenke and Holmes 2018, cited by Uden (p. 432).

dialogue between classical, Renaissance and early modern varieties of Latin by considering Neo-Latin as a modern discipline and historical discourse, before using old, new and hybrid genres alongside the undervalued element of 'emotion' as paths into the neo-Latin domain and its varied canons. The global reach of the Latin language well beyond Europe and North America and its continuing life as a literary medium emerge clearly from this chapter. Fuhrer demonstrates that the study of Latin can sometimes signify rather distinctive things in other intellectual cultures where disciplinary boundaries are positioned differently. In particular, varying levels of institutional investment and support for late antique or Neo-Latin studies can be detected in Europe, north America and elsewhere.[145] And Uden looks at the decentring effects of the global reception of classical texts, urging that we lessen the risk of insularity in reception studies by subjecting ourselves to refereeing processes from those beyond the field.[146]

Uden issues an invigorating call 'to transform the centre and periphery of Classics itself, reconceptualising work on Latin literature in later periods as part of the core of the discipline' (p. 432). We hope this volume may contribute in some small way to that endeavour.

## Territories (2): Disciplinary Neighbours

A second principal drive of this volume is to look afresh at relations between Latin and its fellow sub-disciplines within Classics. Specialists in Latin and Greek literature (and most are one or the other) and in ancient archaeology, art, history, linguistics, philosophy may find themselves grouped together in various institutional combinations, particularly in larger departments of Classics and Ancient History in the Anglosphere. This is proudly cited as proof that ours is the original interdisciplinary 'subject'. But how much do we have in common? What are the (largely undiscussed) problems standing in the way of more successful communication? What can we learn from one another?

To start with linguistics, a 'literary' Latinist trying to use a book such as Pinkster's *Oxford Latin Syntax* or Adams' ground-breaking trilogy on Latin bilingualism, regionalism and social variation might well come away

---

[145] Fuhrer, *passim*. Stover and Haskell also consider how national boundaries can artificially limit corpora. Formisano 2018 addresses clashes in ideas of canon and literary 'importance' between the continental European and US educational systems. On 'Classics' as a discipline, with its national differences, see Blanshard et al. 2020: 65–81.
[146] See also Peirano Garrison (pp. 43–52) on the work performed by 'reception' on the canon.

puzzled or discouraged.¹⁴⁷ Literary allusion is not admitted as part of grammatical explanation, but poorly evidenced Italic languages are freely cited; it is assumed that (reconstructed) spoken Latin is the primary point of reference as well as focus of research; single explanations are preferred to multiple competing interpretations; and Proto-Indo-European appears to be the object of baffling cultic veneration. (PIE linguists perhaps share an unacknowledged disciplinary border with theology: the existence of the invisible subject of study is ultimately a matter of faith; God is in the gaps.) For linguists, as Clackson puts it (p. 575), 'individual utterances or texts are of themselves only revealing insofar as they can give information about the language system that produced them'. The goal is to make a general statement about Latin as a language, not to explicate the apparent quirks of individual authors: literary Latinists attempting the journey from general description to particular explanation will encounter linguists travelling in the opposite direction. Yet, as Clackson argues, a better understanding of such differences will allow the two constituencies to make better use of each other's work: to take one of his examples, work on the historical semantics of *Venus/uenus* can help literary readers of Catullus as well as linguists.

If linguists and Latinists at least share a language as object of study, that has been less true of Latinists and ancient philosophers. Despite the fact that Hellenistic philosophy is preserved largely through Latin accounts of it, Roman philosophy scarcely existed as a subject for most of the twentieth century. As Volk suggests (p. 701), such devaluation has much to do with the institutional history of philosophy as a university subject, where 'what is relevant is the originality and, as it were, quality of a given argument, the way it stands up to scrutiny and improves on earlier approaches' – leaving Roman philosophy 'derivative and second rate' by comparison to Greek. (Not a view shared by all, of course.)¹⁴⁸ If we are to understand Roman philosophy, a paradigm shift is required: much philosophy in Latin was written by non-philosophers who wanted to understand how to apply the teachings of philosophy to their own lives; they wanted to make it work, not to elaborate technical innovations. The tense cultural imbrication of Rome with Greece, and assumptions (by Hellenists) of the cultural superiority of Greek over Latin – both considered by Goldhill in his chapter – provide the larger context for these struggles for recognition.¹⁴⁹

---

[147] Pinkster 2015; Adams 2003, 2007, 2013.
[148] Volk, p. 702 n. 4; also e.g. Gildenhard 2007, Baraz 2012 and Schofield 2021 on Cicero's conceptual creativity in the *philosophica*, and Gildenhard 2010 on his oratory.
[149] See also Fuhrer (pp. 453–4 and 464–5) on the perceived greater cultural prestige of Greek in the modern world compared with Latin (and reactions against this in Italy), Farrell 2001: 28–51 on the

Institutional relationships between Classics and Archaeology have not always been good, at least in the Anglosphere.[150] Many archaeologists speak of 'text-hindered' approaches or look with disdain on a field that does not annually produce vast new sets of data. To classicists, archaeological reports can seem hopelessly fragmented, their authors 'more interested in doing another dig and writing up last year's finds than in making sense of the last generation's advances'.[151] Although literary scholars often share departments with researchers who identify primarily as art historians or archaeologists, there is all too little cross-fertilisation with work on material culture, as Squire and Elsner (pp. 614–17) point out – a state of affairs that allows, for instance, the illustrated manuscripts of late antiquity mentioned earlier to fall down the cracks between Latin literature and Roman art history. More fundamentally, they argue, there is too little appreciation of the fact that ecphrasis is not exclusively a literary phenomenon, or that epic texts and representations of epic action in paintings or friezes share a common cultural framework. In sum, 'if Latin texts can help in reconstructing theories and practices of Roman seeing, so too can material objects help us to understand the conceptual framework that Roman authors and readers brought to the composition and reception of Latin literature' (p. 672).

Latin literature and Roman history, at least in the English-speaking world, are not so much guilty of ignoring one another as in serious danger of reaching a crisis after previously close relations. Viewed from the outside, the coming of that crisis may not be immediately apparent.[152] Fuhrer (p. 460), writing from the perspective of a career spent in Germanophone Classics, draws a contrast between an older German tradition of antiquarian, lexicographical and philological scholarship in Latin and an Anglophone tradition that often has stronger links with cultural history: witness the *Journal of Roman Studies*, whose pages are equally at home with a study of the army and the spread of Roman citizenship as they

---

trope of Latin's linguistic poverty, and Blanshard et al. 2020: 117–25 on the differences between 'not knowing Greek' and 'not knowing Latin'.

[150] The classic verbalisation by Redfield 1991 of antipathies between anthropology and Classics stood duty for the largely unwritten history of inter-departmental tension between archaeology and Classics until the appearance of the essays collected by Sauer 2004 on the boundaries between Graeco-Roman archaeology and ancient history; see especially Laurence 2004, and cf. Porter 2003 and Blanshard et al. 2020: 128–43 more broadly on Classics, archaeology and materiality.

[151] Hopkins 2018b: 199 n. 79 also encapsulates attitudes designed to annoy archaeologists: the latter dig up stuff for the former to analyse 'properly'.

[152] It has been long in the making; cf. Netz 2020: 26–7 on the professionalisation in the 1960s of the humanities as a whole and its different effects on sub-branches of papyrology: 'the study of documents *professionalized outwards*, while the study of literary texts *professionalized inwards*'.

are with digital analysis of Latin prose rhythm or the question of how Romans conceptualised future time.[153] Such mingling reflects to some extent the institutional structures in the Anglosphere, where experts in (for instance) literature and history more commonly cohabit than in the German-speaking world, where Latin literature and Roman history rarely share a building, never mind a library.

From the outside looking in, a relative lack of philological depth in Anglophone Latin studies – in part stemming from a lack of exposure to historical linguistics during the training of Latinists – may be compensated by a broader cultural-historical range.[154] Yet not every scholar trained in the German tradition sees advantage in the Anglosphere's stabling of subdisciplines. In his 2020 address to the American Association of Ancient Historians, Walter Scheidel called for a decoupling of Graeco-Roman history from literature. His goal was not to reinstate the continental European system, where, he argued, a narrowness of focus has isolated classical historians from History as a broader discipline. Rather, he proposed re-imagining ancient Mediterranean studies as global and comparative history: scholars might aim for expertise in 'state formation in literate state-level pre-industrial societies' rather than 'in the history of the Later Roman Empire with a side line in Augustine and Mediaeval Latin'.[155] There are clear but unacknowledged dangers in this venture. As the 'Postclassicisms Collective' observes, 'interdisciplinarity risks repeating many of the same tropes of disciplinary behavior, but on a larger scale'.[156] In any case, the ground continues to move unbidden beneath our feet. Economic, social and then cultural history dominated the agendas of the most forward-thinking ancient historians of the 1960s to the 1990s, and global history captured the biggest headlines in the first two decades of the new millennium; but new currents of thinking continue to be generated. Maintaining a global perspective remains important: the Graeco-Roman world is only one among many ancient pasts available for study, even within the ambit of the Mediterranean.[157] But, as history at the same

---

[153] Articles on these three subjects appeared in *JRS* 109 (2019).
[154] As Fuhrer suggests (p. 460); on exposure to linguistics, see Clackson (pp. 603–5). That range is illustrated also by the series *Roman Literature and its Contexts*, mentioned earlier.
[155] Scheidel 2020. [156] Blanshard et al. 2020: 79.
[157] On the 'discernable trend back to the big' in ancient history, see Shaw 2008. Blanshard et al. 2020: 182–200, esp. 193–7 advocate for 'deep immersive reading' of Graeco-Roman texts alongside 'horizontal, comparative reading' of texts from other ancient world cultures; they also comment (ibid. 87–8, 195–6) on the institutional exclusion of other ancient Mediterranean languages from Classics. For reservations about imposing the term 'classical' on other ancient pasts, see Formisano 2018: 13–14; Blanshard et al. 2020: 12–14.

time returns to a bottom-up approach and re-examines relationships with 'sources' – in part through recognition that the Roman Empire is too vast and diverse to bear many more generalisations – this is a good time for Latinists to re-examine their ties with Roman historians.

Lavan warns that the relationship between literary and historical studies is under threat: 'I think Latinists ought to be worried by the degree of disinterest [*sc.* in their work by historians], which sometimes borders on alienation' (p. 817). The historiographical turn is a case in point: transformational work has been done on the rhetoricity and literary texture of ancient historians, with important consequences for historians as well as for literary readers; but such work risks not so much being provocative, as evading 'complex questions about the relationship between historiography and history' (p. 841). So too on broader historical questions: where literary Latinists, working primarily on texts produced by or for the senatorial elite, are often fixed on political history, and (when it comes to the literature of the principate) obsessed with responses to monarchy, historians are more likely to be interested in wider social history, and in an elite perspective that goes beyond anxieties *vis-à-vis* the emperor. Latinists can perhaps find more common ground with their historian colleagues, Lavan suggests, by taking an interest in the *longue durée* of social formation (rather than particular imperial dynasties) or in the kinds of non-literary texts where skills of close reading remain in demand (inscriptions, the juristic corpora, documentary letters).

### *The Limits of Literature*

That brings us back to the question of which texts we read, and which we do not. Why study epigrams transmitted on parchment, but ignore the vast corpus of epigram inscribed on stone?[158] Perhaps the greatest challenge, however, is to re-examine our focus on texts produced by or for the Roman political elite. Finding other sorts of texts to read is clearly one direction for the future. Equally, as Lowrie shows in her chapter, we can radically change the questions we ask of elite canonical texts, and in the process move into closer contact with disciplines beyond the world of Classics. If we focus on political thought, rather than on political and dynastic history, a whole body of Latin texts can be re-evaluated for their contribution to political

---

[158] See Clackson (pp. 568–9) on inscriptional verse. On epigraphy as sub-discipline, see Blanshard et al. 2020: 69–77, including reflection on epigraphy's lack of a 'canon', but arbitrary separation from papyrology.

theory. Roman works of the classical era, unlike their Greek counterparts, are usually deemed short on abstract political theory. Yet they are rich in 'commentary... on the actual and ideal organisation of human life and the obstacles to success' (p. 756). It is important to 'probe *how* the Romans thought about politics in their own language in addition to *what* their ideas were', in poetry as well as in prose.[159] Practices of thinking, rhetoric, works addressed to emperors, reflections on the constitution, (contested) exemplarity, histories of conceptual terms, metaphor – all these become resources for understanding Roman political thought.

Political thought is not confined, of course, to canonical texts. Roman law is rich in resources for this area of study, but offers a particularly resonant example of a set of texts marginalised in the Anglosphere, at least. This corpus straddles key boundaries we have mentioned, between classical and later Latin, pagan and Christian, Latin west and Greek east. Jurists flourished in the third century CE, just as belletristic literature faltered. Roman law was one of the reasons that a Greek under Rome might want to learn Latin (so Libanius claimed),[160] and it was Justinian, ruling in Constantinople, who initiated the single most influential codification of Roman law in his *Corpus iuris ciuilis*.[161] From the eleventh century onwards, Roman law began to inform legal education and administration across Europe, giving rise to an enormous body of interpretative literature.[162] Yet the prestige of the Roman jurists is low in the Anglosphere, the degree to which Roman literature and thought are permeated by law underappreciated.[163]

One partial explanation for this relative neglect is that civil codes in the English-speaking world, unlike those of continental Europe and elsewhere,

---

[159] The embeddedness of Roman political thought shares obvious parallels with the embeddedness of philosophy in much Latin poetry (see Ch. 13 by Volk).

[160] Libanius, *Orat.* 1.234, 255; 49.27: see Nesselrath 2014: 253. On Latin in the eastern Empire see also Kelly (pp. 139–40).

[161] However, the Greek materials used to teach the corpus soon effectively superseded the Latin text; see Corcoran 2017: 101–16. Frier 2016 provides an annotated text and translation of the *Codex* of Justinian (one part of the *Corpus iuris ciuilis*).

[162] Stein 1999 gives a brief overview.

[163] As Fergus Millar suggested, 'no one will deny that... an interest [in the jurists] is rare to the point of eccentricity' (Millar 1986: 272). For recent work in a variety of national traditions (with reference to further work in those traditions), see e.g. Ziogas 2021 on Ovid and Roman law and Ziogas and Bexley 2022 on Roman law and Latin literature; Gebhardt 2009 on law and Augustan poetry; and Mantovani 2018 on the jurists as literature. For accessible introductions to Roman law and its contexts, see Riggsby 2010; du Plessis, Ando and Tuori 2016. As ever, the narrative is not straightforward or unilinear: to take a parochial example, Roman law was one of six 'caucuses' into which the Cambridge Classics Faculty was divided until the 1980s (a place later taken by the 'interdisciplinary' caucus).

largely derive from sources other than Rome. The resulting disparity in interest in Roman law carries shades of opposition between church and state and between Protestant and Catholic.[164] (The concomitant neglect of Roman law and patristic Latin perhaps renders reception of the ancient world in the Anglosphere distinctly eccentric in a global context.) The inclusion of imperial edicts in Justinian's codification gave prominence to ecclesiastical policy and religious orthodoxy,[165] and his own *Novella* 131, added in 545 CE, gave the status of law to the rulings of the great church councils of Nicaea, Constantinople, Ephesus and Chalcedon, so initiating the canon law of the church. To make things almost too neat, in 529 CE – the year which saw publication of his first edition of imperial edicts – Justinian is said to have closed down Plato's Academy in Athens. True or not,[166] the symbolic power of the story is self-evident: Justinian, codifier of Roman law and steadfast proponent of religious orthodoxy, ended a millennium-long tradition of free enquiry. Yet in terms of recognised intellectual stature, Roman law is a counterpart to the Greek philosophical corpus, and one which has doubtless had greater influence on how lives have been actually lived. Much work remains to be done here, not least in promoting conversation between specialists in Roman law, with their own set of abstract concepts, historians who mine it for data or try to reconstruct socio-economic contexts, and literary scholars studying how law shaped the thinking of other texts too[167] – if not (and why not?) reading the jurists themselves.

## Critical Reading

Roman law is cited by Lavan too as one genre where the close reading skills of Latinists might establish common ground with Roman historians. He remarks, though, that in the course of his journey away from Latin literature he has found himself 'producing fewer close readings of particular texts and more often trying to generalise about Latin language and discourse' (p. 819). This disciplinary divergence raises questions about the privileged status of 'close reading' among Latinists. The habit has been part of the genetic code of the sub-discipline since antiquity: Terence, Cicero, Virgil, Horace, Ovid, Persius, Lucan, Statius, Juvenal and others attracted

---

[164] For various senses in which 'Protestant *vs* Catholic' structures the study of Latin (and Classics), see Farrell 2001: 101–5 and 125–6; Morgan 2019: 184–5; Blanshard et al. 2020: 88–90.
[165] Corcoran 2017: 97, 100–1.   [166] Cameron 2016.
[167] See e.g. the essays collected by du Plessis 2013, especially Howley 2013 on Gellius and the law, and the work of Jill Harries (1998, 2006, 2007).

from the outset a variety of intensive reading practices, including marginal and interlinear annotations, *quaestiones* and treatises, mythological companions, single-author and *variorum* commentaries, and essayistic exposition.[168] Christian authorities likewise developed a rich tradition of linear and lemmatic commentary on biblical texts, often deriving from sermons in which oral exposition was offered of a text read aloud to a Christian congregation.[169]

This symbiosis between classical and Christian reading practices has endured into the modern era: lemmatic commentaries are characteristic of and fundamental to Graeco-Roman literature, as they are in biblical studies.[170] Literary monographs likewise tend to privilege intense work with selected key passages. Close reading is something Latin literary work is good at, and revels in; and it plays an avowedly central role in the chapters to follow. Reading across texts is also hardwired into the discipline, traditionally in the currency of 'parallels'; more recently in the contested dimensions of allusion, reference and intertextuality.[171] But what of 'distant reading'?[172] This might take us to a different set of authors from the 'minor' writers identified by Peirano Garrison, many of whom (particularly the pseudonymous poets) offer intense rewards, intertextual and other, to close readers. Keith Hopkins notoriously derided an inductive approach to history whereby credit went 'to the ancient historian who makes the best pattern out of the largest number of pieces and cites the most obscure sources relevantly':[173] he advocated rather for a deductive approach, insisting that historians first create a broader framework within which to contextualise the piecemeal ancient data.[174] Something of this method can be seen in Netz's *Scale, Space and Canon*, which attempts a survey of all Greek literature up to 200 CE in order to contextualise what we have, and to understand long-term shifts in literary culture, such as the collapse of the early imperial model of patron and author and a change in late antiquity towards the model of the teacher and his circle.

---

[168] For an overview of Roman philology and scholarship, see Zetzel 2018: esp. pp. 159–200, 253–77 on commentary and exegesis (also Zetzel 1975, 2005). On mythological companions, see Cameron 2004.
[169] See e.g. Cain 2010: 16–41 on Jerome as biblical commentator.
[170] Houlden 1990. On classical commentaries see n. 33 and pp. 19–20. [171] See n. 46.
[172] 'Distant reading' as a concept is generally traced back to Moretti 2000.
[173] Hopkins 1978: 182.
[174] E.g. the model lifetables of the United Nations offered a structure within which to analyse ages of death recorded on Roman tombstones; a hypothetical graph of steady-line growth for early Christianity allowed the testing of claims about the nature of the sect: see Kelly 2018: 3–6.

Smaller data sets than the whole of Greek or Latin literature can also be read from a distance. To take an example close to the interests of both editors of this volume, around fifty Graeco-Roman 'literary' letter collections survive in manuscript form from the period up to the sack of Rome in 410. They run to many thousands of individual letters: the correspondence of Cicero, Libanius, Augustine and Isidore of Pelusium alone consists of nearly 5,000 pieces.[175] Much of this vast corpus responds well to close reading of the sort normally practised on poetry, including readings with an explicitly intertextual focus. But perhaps as much is resistant: letters of recommendation, consolation and friendly solicitation or regard, for instance, tend to work with a relatively small number of repeated tropes. The 'Ancient Letter Collections' project run by Roy Gibson, Andrew Morrison and Antonia Sarri aims for 'distant' reading of all fifty collections by collecting data on selected aspects of each one (numbers of senders and addressees; number and range of length of letters; the arrangement of the letters in manuscripts; what else is transmitted with each collection). Andrew Riggsby suggests other ways in which we might read epistolographical corpora from a distance, by focusing for instance on discourse structure, topic modelling and sentiment analysis.[176] Biography, declamation, sermons, dialogues, commentaries and works of exegesis, martyr narratives and medical and technical texts might benefit from similar approaches. The greatest riches for distant reading are offered by digital humanities and the vast amounts of data that computer-led approaches can harvest for interpretation.[177] The greatest obstacle remains the incomplete digitisation of Latin texts in machine-readable form, particularly for later antiquity and the early mediaeval period, and the fact that databases are frequently locked behind paywalls.

There is ample place, then, for both 'close' and 'distant' reading – critical readings both – in a field which is far from exhaustion, but also ripe for expansion. If we have focused here on just some of the ways in which that expansion might be pursued – distant reading, conversations across sub-disciplinary fences, and more dialogue between classical and later Latins – we hope that this introduction has offered a suitable taste of the *Guide* that awaits.

---

[175] Cicero (*c.* 946 letters); Libanius (*c.* 1544); Augustine (*c.* 308); Isidore of Pelusium (*c.* 2000).
[176] Riggsby 2022.
[177] See pp. 6–7; also Underwood 2019 on the possibilities for new understandings through digital humanities of periodisation and shifts in theme, gender and genre in modern literary history.

# References

Adams, J. N. (2003) *Bilingualism and the Latin Language*, Cambridge.
  (2007) *The Regional Diversification of Latin, 200 BC – AD 600*, Cambridge.
  (2013) *Social Variation and the Latin Language*, Cambridge.
Apostol, R. (2015) '*Urbanus es, Corydon*: ecocritiquing town and country in Eclogue 2', *Vergilius* 61: 3–28.
Bagnall, R. and S. Heath (2018) 'Roman studies and digital resources', *JRS* 108: 171–89.
Baraz, Y. (2012) *A Written Republic: Cicero's Philosophical Politics*, Princeton.
Barchiesi, A. (2001a) 'The crossing', in S. J. Harrison, ed., *Texts, Ideas, and the Classics: Literary Theory and Classical Scholarship* (Oxford), 142–63.
  (2001b) Review of Taplin 2000, *BMCRev* 2001.12.01.
Bardon, H. (1952) *La littérature latine inconnue. Tome I*, Paris.
Bate, J. (1991) *Romantic Ecology: Wordsworth and the Environmental Tradition*, London.
Beagon, M. (1992) *Roman Nature: the Thought of Pliny the Elder*, Oxford.
  (2005) *The Elder Pliny on the Human Animal: Natural History Book 7*, Oxford.
Berger, J.-D., J. Fontaine and P. L. Schmidt, eds. (2020) *Handbuch der lateinischen Literatur der Antike. Sechster Band: Die Literatur im Zeitalter des Theodosius (374–430 n. Chr.)*, 2 vols., Munich.
Bernstein, N. (2020) 'Quantitative and qualitative perspectives on the use of poetic tradition in Silius Italicus' *Punica*', in Coffee et al. 2020, 373–88.
Berti, M. (2019) *Digital Classical Philology: Ancient Greek and Latin in the Digital Revolution*, Berlin.
Berti, M., et al. (2009) 'Collecting fragmentary authors in a digital library', in *Proceedings of the 9th ACM/IEEE-CS Joint Conference on Digital Libraries* (Austin, TX), 259–62.
Bianchi, E., S. Brill and B. Holmes, eds. (2019) *Antiquities Beyond Humanism*, Oxford.
Birt, T. (1882) *Das antike Buchwesen in seinem Verhältniss zur Litteratur*, Berlin.
Bispham, E., G. Rowe and E. Matthews, eds. (2007) *Vita vigilia est: Essays in Honour of Barbara Levick*, London.
Blanck, H. (1992) *Das Buch in der Antike*, Munich.
Blanshard, A., S. Goldhill, C. Güthenke et al. (2020) *Postclassicisms: the Postclassicisms Collective*, Chicago.
Blum, R. (1991) *Kallimachos: the Alexandrian Library and the Origins of Bibliography*, Madison, WI.
Brink, C. O. (1957) *Latin Studies and the Humanities: an Inaugural Lecture*, Cambridge.
Cain, A. (2010) *St Jerome: Commentary on Galatians*, Washington, DC.
Cameron, A. (2004) *Greek Mythography in the Roman World*, Oxford.
  (2016) 'The last days of the academy in Athens', in A. Cameron, *Wandering Poets and Other Essays on Late Greek Literature and Philosophy* (Oxford), 205–46.
Carey, S. (2003) *Pliny's Catalogue of Culture: Art and Empire in the Natural History*, Oxford.

Chaudhuri, P., T. Dasgupta, J. P. Dexter and K. Iyer (2018) 'A small set of stylometric features differentiates Latin prose and verse', *Digital Scholarship in the Humanities* 34: 716–29.
Chesi, G. M. and F. Spiegel, eds. (2020) *Classical Literature and Posthumanism*, London.
Clark, G. (1995) *Augustine. Confessions Books I–IV*, Cambridge.
Coffee, N. (2019) 'Intertextuality as viral phrases: roses and lilies', in Berti 2019, 177–200.
Coffee, N. and J. Gawley (2020) 'How rare are the words that make up intertexts? A study in Latin and Greek epic poetry', in Coffee et al. 2020, 409–20.
Coffee, N., C. Forstall, L. Galli Milić and D. Nelis, eds. (2020) *Intertextuality in Flavian Epic Poetry: Contemporary Approaches*, Berlin.
Conte, G. B. (1994) *Latin Literature: A History* (trans. J. B. Solodow, rev. D. P. Fowler and G. W. Most), Baltimore.
Conybeare, C. and S. Goldhill, eds. (2020) *Classical Philology and Theology: Entanglement, Disavowal and the Godlike Scholar*, Cambridge.
Corcoran, S. (2017) 'Roman law and the two languages in Justinian's empire', *BICS* 60: 95–116.
Cornell, T. J., ed. (2013) *The Fragments of the Roman Historians*, Oxford.
Dekkers, E. and E. Gaar (1995) *Clavis patrum Latinorum*, 3rd edn, Turnhout.
Dexter, J. P., K. Katz, N. Tripuraneni et al. (2017) 'Quantitative criticism of literary relationships', *Proceedings of the National Academy of Sciences of the United States of America* 114 (16): E3195–E3204.
Diels, H (1905) 'Der lateinische, griechische und deutsche Thesaurus', *Neue Jahrbücher für das klassische Altertum* 15: 689–96.
Dinter, M. T., C. Guérin and M. Martinho, eds. (2020) *Reading Roman Declamation: Seneca the Elder*, Oxford.
Dolbeau, F. (1998) 'Découvertes récentes d'oeuvres latines inconnues', *SEJG* 38: 101–42.
Doody, A. (2010) *Pliny's Encyclopedia: The Reception of the Natural History*, Cambridge.
Doody, A. and L. Taub, eds. (2009) *Authorial Voices in Greco-Roman Technical Writing*, Trier.
DuBois, P. (2010) *Out of Athens: The New Ancient Greeks*, Cambridge, MA.
Duncan-Jones, R. (1982) *The Economy of the Roman Empire: Quantitative Studies*, 2nd edn, Cambridge.
du Plessis, P. J., ed. (2013) *New Frontiers: Law and Society in the Roman World*, Edinburgh.
du Plessis, P. J., C. Ando and K. Tuori, eds. (2016) *The Oxford Handbook of Roman Law and Society*, Oxford.
Eck, W. (2002) 'L'empereur romain chef de l'armée. Le témoignage des diplômes militaires', *Cahiers Glotz* 13: 93–112.
Elsner, J. (2021) Review of Netz 2020, *BMCRev* 2021.06.40.
Fane-Saunders, P. (2016) *Pliny the Elder and the Emergence of Renaissance Architecture*, Cambridge.

Farrell, J. (2001) *Latin Language and Latin Culture from Ancient to Modern Times*, Cambridge.
  (2003) 'Classical genre in theory and practice', *New Literary History* 34: 383–408.
Feeney, D. (2016) *Beyond Greek: The Beginnings of Latin Literature*, Cambridge.
Fögen, T. (2009) *Wissen, Kommunikation und Selbstdarstellung: Zur Struktur und Charakteristik römischer Fachtexte der frühen Kaiserzeit*, Munich.
Formisano, M. (2017) 'Introduction: the poetics of knowledge', in Formisano and van der Eijk 2017, 12–26.
  (2018) 'Marginality and the classics: exemplary extraneousness', in Formisano and Kraus 2018, 1–28.
Formisano, M. and C. S. Kraus, eds. (2018) *Marginality, Canonicity, Passion*, Oxford.
Formisano, M. and P. van der Eijk, eds. (2017) *Knowledge, Text, and Practice in Ancient Technical Writing*, Cambridge.
Fowler, A. (1979) 'Genre and the literary canon', *New Literary History* 11: 97–119.
Franklinos, T. E. and L. Fulkerson (2020) 'Authoring, reading and exploring an *Appendix*', in T. E. Franklinos and L. Fulkerson, eds., *Constructing Authors and Readers in the Appendices Vergiliana, Tibulliana, and Ovidiana* (Oxford), 1–23.
Frier, B.W. (2016) *The Codex of Justinian. A New Annotated Translation, with Parallel Latin and Greek Text*, 3 vols., Cambridge.
Gazzarri, T. (2020) *The Stylus and the Scalpel: Theory and Practice of Metaphors in Seneca's Prose*, Berlin.
Gebhardt, U. C. J. (2009) *Sermo iuris: Rechtssprache und Recht in der augusteischen Dichtung*, Leiden.
Gibson, R. K. (2014) 'Suetonius and the *uiri illustres* of Pliny the Younger', in T. J. Power and R. K. Gibson, eds., *Suetonius the Biographer: Studies in Roman Lives* (Oxford), 199–230.
  (2016) 'Fifty shades of orange: Cambridge Classical Texts and Commentaries', in Kraus and Stray 2016, 346–75.
  (2021) 'Fifty years of Green and Yellow: the Cambridge Greek and Latin Classics series 1970–2020', in S. Harrison and C. Pelling, eds., *Classical Scholarship and its History from the Renaissance to the Present: Essays in Honour of Chris Stray* (Berlin), 175–217.
Gibson, R. K. and C. S. Kraus, eds. (2002) *The Classical Commentary: Histories, Practices, Theory*, Leiden.
Gibson, R. K. and R. Morello, eds. (2011) *Pliny the Elder: Themes and Contexts*, Leiden.
Gildenhard, I. (2007) *Paideia Romana: Cicero's Tusculan Disputations*, Cambridge.
  (2010) *Creative Eloquence: The Construction of Reality in Cicero's Speeches*, Oxford.
Glare, P. G. W., ed. (1982) *The Oxford Latin Dictionary*, Oxford.
  (2012) *The Oxford Latin Dictionary*, 2nd edn, Oxford.

Glotfelty, C. (1996) 'Introduction: literary studies in an age of environmental crisis', in C. Glotfelty and H. Fromm, eds., *The Ecocriticism Reader: Landmarks in Literary Ecology* (Athens, GA), xv–xxxvii.
Goldberg, S. (2005) *Constructing Literature in the Roman Republic*, Cambridge.
Goldhill, S. (2020) 'The union and divorce of classical philology and theology', in Conybeare and Goldhill 2020, 33–62.
Goodyear, F. R. D. (1992) Review of *OLD*, in F. R. D. Goodyear (ed. K. Coleman et al.), *Collected Papers in Latin Literature* (London), 281–7. First published in *Proceedings of the African Classical Associations* 17 (1983), 123–46.
Gunderson, E. (2003) *Declamation, Paternity and Roman Identity: Authority and the Rhetorical Self*, Cambridge.
  (2020) 'Theology's shadow', in Conybeare and Goldhill 2020, 199–224.
Güthenke, C. and B. Holmes (2018) 'Hyperinclusivity, hypercanonicity and the future of the field', in Formisano and Kraus 2018, 57–73.
Hall, E. and H. Stead (2019) *A People's History of Classics: Class and Greco-Roman Antiquity in Britain and Ireland*, London.
Hardie, P. (2018) 'A tale of two loves: the greatest hits of post-medieval writing in the Latin language', *TLS* 19.1.2018.
Harries, J. (1998) *Law and Empire in Late Antiquity*, Cambridge.
  (2006) *Cicero and the Jurists: From Citizens' Law to the Lawful State*, London.
  (2007) *Law and Crime in the Roman World*, Cambridge.
Harrison, S. J. (2007) *Generic Enrichment in Vergil and Horace*, Oxford.
Haskell, Y. (2001) 'The Columbus paradigm – or complex? – in neo-Latin studies', *SO* 76: 47–51.
Henderson, J. (2010) 'A1–ZYTHIUM: DOMIMINA NUSTIO ILLUMEA, or out with the *OLD* (1931–82)', in C. Stray, ed., *Classical Dictionaries: Past, Present, Future* (London), 139–76.
Herzog, R. and P. L. Schmidt (2002–) *Handbuch der lateinischen Literatur der Antike*, Munich.
Heslin, P. (2020) 'Lemmatizing Latin and quantifying the *Achilleid*', in Coffee et al. 2020, 389–408.
Hinds, S. (2000) 'Essential epic: genre and gender from Macer to Statius', in M. Depew and D. Obbink, eds., *Matrices of Genre: Authors, Canons, and Society* (Cambridge, MA), 221–44.
  (2020) 'Pre- and post-digital poetics of "transliteralism": some Greco-Roman epic incipits', in Coffee et al. 2020, 421–46.
Hine, H. M. (2010) *Lucius Annaeus Seneca: Natural Questions*, Chicago.
Hopkins, K. (1978) 'Rules of evidence', *JRS* 68: 178–86.
  (1999) *A World Full of Gods: The Strange Triumph of Christianity*, London.
  (2018a) 'Christian number and its implications', in Hopkins 2018c, 432–80. First published in *JBCS* 6 (1998), 185–226.
  (2018b) 'Economic growth and towns in classical antiquity', in Hopkins 2018c, 160–206. First published in P. Abrams and E. A. Wrigley, eds. (1978) *Towns and Societies: Essays in Economic History and Historical Sociology* (Cambridge), 35–77.

(2018c) *Sociological Studies in Roman History* (ed. C. Kelly ), Cambridge.
Houlden, J. L. (1990) 'Commentary (New Testament)', in R. J. Coggins and J. L. Houlden, eds., *A Dictionary of Biblical Interpretation* (London and Philadelphia), 129–32.
Howley, J. (2013) 'Why read the jurists? Aulus Gellius on reading across disciplines', in du Plessis 2013, 9–30.
Hutchinson, G. O. (2008) *Talking Books: Readings in Hellenistic and Roman Books of Poetry*, Oxford.
  (2013) 'Genre and super-genre', in Papanghelis, Harrison and Frangoulidis 2013, 19–34.
Johnson, W. A. (2010) *Readers and Reading Culture in the High Roman Empire*, Oxford.
Kay, N. M. (2020) *Venantius Fortunatus: Vita Sancti Martini. Prologue and Books 1–11*, Cambridge.
Keeline, T. and T. Kirby (2019) '*Auceps syllabarum*: a digital analysis of Latin prose rhythm', *JRS* 109: 161–204.
Kelly, C. (2018) 'Introduction – Keith Hopkins: sighting shots', in Hopkins 2018c, 1–54.
Kenney, E. J. (1970) '*Dimidium qui coepit habet*', *CR* 20: 91–4.
  (1975) *New Frameworks for Old: The Place of Classical Literature in the Cambridge Classical Course. An Inaugural Lecture*, Cambridge.
  (1982) 'Books and readers in the Roman world', in Kenney and Clausen 1982, 3–32.
  (1990) *Apuleius. Cupid & Psyche*, Cambridge.
Kenney, E. J. and W. Clausen, eds. (1982) *The Cambridge History of Classical Literature, ii: Latin Literature*, Cambridge.
Kestemont, M., F. Karsdorp et al. (2022) 'Forgotten books: the application of unseen species models to the survival of culture', *Science* 375: 765–69.
König, A. (2020) 'Tactical interactions: dialogues between Greece and Rome in the military manuals of Aelian and Arrian', in König, Uden and Langlands 2020, 134–56.
König, A., J. Uden and R. Langlands, eds. (2020) *Literary Interactions in the Roman Empire, 96–235: Cross-Cultural Interactions*, Cambridge.
König, J. and T. Whitmarsh, eds. (2007) *Ordering Knowledge in the Roman Empire*, Cambridge.
Kraus, C. S. and C. Stray, eds. (2016) *Classical Commentaries: Explorations in a Scholarly Genre*, Oxford.
Kühner, R. and C. Stegmann (1912) *Ausführliche Grammatik der lateinischen Sprache. Zweiter Teil: Satzlehre*, 2nd edn, 2 vols., Hannover.
Laird, A. and N. Miller, eds. (2018) *Antiquities and Classical Traditions in Latin America*, Hoboken.
Laurence, R. (2004) 'The uneasy dialogue between ancient history and archaeology', in Sauer 2004, 99–113.
Lavan, M. (2018) 'Pliny *Epistles* 10 and imperial correspondence: the Empire of letters', in A. König and C. Whitton, eds., *Roman Literature under Nerva,*

*Trajan and Hadrian: Literary Interactions*, AD *96–138* (Cambridge), 280–301.
  (2020) 'Beyond Romans and others: identities in the long second century', in König, Uden and Langlands 2020, 37–57.
Leonhardt, J. (2013) *Latin: Story of a World Language* (trans. K. Kronenberg), Cambridge, MA.
Lewis, C. T. and C. Short (1879) *A Latin Dictionary. Founded on Andrews' Edition of Freud's Latin Dictionary*, Oxford.
Luck, G. (1984) Review of *OLD*, *AJPh* 105: 91–113.
Mantovani, D. (2018) *Les juristes écrivains de la Rome antique: les oeuvres des juristes comme littérature*, Paris.
Martindale, C. (2002) 'Classics, theory, and thought', *Arion* 10: 141–55.
McCarty, W. (2002) 'A network with a thousand entrances: commentary in an electronic age?', in Gibson and Kraus 2002, 359–402.
Meineck, P., W. M. Short and J. Devereaux, eds. (2019) *The Routledge Handbook of Classics and Cognitive Theory*, London.
Millar, F. (1986) 'A new approach to the Roman jurists', *JRS* 76: 272–80.
Moretti, F. (2000) 'Conjectures on world literature', *New Left Review* 1: 54–68.
Morgan, T. (2019) 'Pagans and Christians: fifty years of anxiety', in C. Stray, C. Pelling and S. Harrison, eds., *Rediscovering E. R. Dodds: Scholarship, Education and the Paranormal* (Oxford), 182–97.
Most, G. W., ed. (1999) *Commentaries – Kommentare*, Göttingen.
Murphy, T. (2004) *Pliny the Elder's Natural History: The Empire in the Encyclopedia*, Oxford.
Nesselrath, H.-G. (2014) 'Emperors and empire in Libanius', in L. van Hoof, ed., *Libanius: a Critical Introduction* (Cambridge), 187–219.
Netz, R. (2020) *Scale, Space and Canon in Ancient Literary Culture*, Cambridge.
Nicholson, O. (2018) *The Oxford Dictionary of Late Antiquity*, Oxford.
Padilla Peralta, D. (2020) 'Epistemicide: the Roman case', *Classica* 33: 151–86.
Panayotakis, C. (2012) *Decimus Laberius. The Fragments*, Cambridge.
Papanghelis, T. D., S. J. Harrison and S. Frangoulidis, eds. (2013) *Generic Interfaces in Latin Literature: Encounters, Interactions and Transformations*, Berlin.
Parker, H. N. (2009) 'Books and reading Latin poetry', in W. R. Johnson and H. N. Parker, eds., *Ancient Literacies: The Culture of Reading in Greece and Rome* (New York), 186–229.
Peirano Garrison, I. (2019) *Persuasion, Rhetoric and Roman Poetry*, Cambridge.
  (2020) 'Source, original and authenticity between philology and theology', in Conybeare and Goldhill 2020, 86–109.
Pinkster, H. (2015) *Oxford Latin Syntax. Volume 1: The Simple Clause*, Oxford.
Porter, J. (2003) 'The materiality of classical studies', *Parallax* 9: 64–74.
Redfield, J. (1991) 'Classics and anthropology', *Arion* 1: 5–23.
Reynolds, L. D., ed. (1983) *Texts and Transmission: A Survey of the Latin Classics*, Oxford.

Reynolds, L. D. and N. G. Wilson (2013) *Scribes and Scholars: A Guide to the Transmission of Greek and Latin Literature*, 4th edn, Oxford.
Rigby, K. (2015) 'Ecocriticism', in J. Wolfreys, ed., *Introducing Ecocriticism in the 21st Century*, 2nd edn (Edinburgh), 122–54.
Riggsby, A. M. (2010) *Roman Law and the Legal World of the Romans*, Cambridge.
  (2019) *Mosaics of Knowledge: Representing Information in the Roman World*, Oxford.
  (2022) 'What do (Cicero's) letters count as evidence for?', in R. Gibson and R. Morello, eds., *The Epistolary Cicero: Further Readings in the Letters*, Dublin (= *Hermathena* 202–3), 265–84.
Santini, C. and Stok, F. (2008) *Esegesi dimenticate di autori classici*, Pisa.
Sauer, E., ed. (2004) *Archaeology and Ancient History: Breaking Down the Boundaries*, London.
Saunders, T. (2008) *Bucolic Ecology: Virgil's Eclogues and the Environmental Literary Tradition*, London.
Scheidel, W. (2019) *Escape from Rome: The Failure of Empire and the Road to Prosperity*, Princeton.
  (2020) 'The ancient historian on the tightrope', recorded lecture, http://web.stanford.edu/~scheidel/Scheidel%20AAH%202020%20Keynote%20Lecture.mp4
Schliephake, C., ed. (2017) *Ecocriticism, Ecology, and the Cultures of Antiquity*, Lanham, MD.
Schofield, M. (2021) *Cicero: Political Philosophy*, Oxford.
Seo, J. M. (2019) 'Classics for all: future antiquity from a global perspective', *AJPh* 140: 399–715.
Shaw, B. (2008) 'After Rome', *New Left Review* 51: 89–114.
Shuger, D. (1994) *The Renaissance Bible: Scholarship, Sacrifice, and Subjectivity*, Berkeley.
Starks-Estes, L. S. (2020) *Ovid and Adaptation in Early Modern English Theatre*, Edinburgh.
Stein, P. (1999) *Roman Law in European History*, Cambridge.
Stevenson, J. (2005) *Women Latin Poets: Language, Gender, and Authority from Antiquity to the Eighteenth Century*, Oxford.
Stover, J. and M. Kestemont (2016) 'The authorship of the *Historia Augusta*: two new computational studies', *BICS* 59: 140–57.
Stray, C. (2012) 'The *Oxford Latin Dictionary*: a historical introduction', in Glare 2012, viii–xvii.
Surtees, A. and J. Dyer, eds. (2020) *Exploring Gender Diversity in the Ancient World*, Edinburgh.
Taplin, O., ed. (2000) *Literature in the Greek and Roman Worlds: A New Perspective*, Oxford.
Traub, V., P. Badir and P. McCracken, eds. (2019) *Ovidian Transversions: 'Iphis and Ianthe', 1300–1650*, Edinburgh.
Trombley, F. (2006) 'Overview: the geographical spread of Christianity', in M. M. Mitchell and F. M. Young, eds., *The Cambridge History of Christianity. 1: Origins to Constantine* (Cambridge), 302–13.

Umurhan, O. (2018) *Juvenal's Global Awareness: Circulation, Connectivity, and Empire*, London.
Underwood, T. (2019) *Distant Horizons: Digital Evidence and Literary Change*, Chicago.
Van Sickle, J. (1980a) 'The book roll and some conventions of the poetic book', *Arethusa* 13: 5–42.
  (1980b) 'Reading Virgil's Eclogue book', *ANRW* II.31.1: 576–603.
Vinzent, M. (2019) *Writing the Early History of Christianity: from Reception to Retrospection*, Cambridge.
West, A. F. (1902) 'The lost parts of Latin literature', *TAPhA* 33: xxi–xxvi.
White, P. (1993) *Promised Verse: Poets in the Society of Augustan Rome*, Cambridge, MA.
  (2019) *Augustine. Confessions Books* V–IX, Cambridge.
Whitton, C. (2012) Review of *OLD* (2nd edn), *TLS* 20.7.2012.
Williams, G. D. (2012) *The Cosmic Viewpoint: A Study of Seneca's Natural Questions*, Oxford.
Wilson, N. G. (2003) *Pietro Bembo: Oratio pro litteris Graecis*, Messina.
Winsbury, R. (2009) *The Roman Book: Books, Publishing and Performance in Classical Rome*, London.
Woodman, A. J. (1982) Review of Kenney and Clausen 1982, *LCM* 7: 102–8.
  (2017) *The Annals of Tacitus. Books 5 and 6*, Cambridge.
  (2018) *The Annals of Tacitus. Book 4*, Cambridge.
Zainaldin, J. (2020) *Gargilius Martialis. The Agricultural Fragments*, Cambridge.
Zetzel, J. E. G. (1975) 'On the history of Latin scholia', *HSPh* 79: 335–54.
  (2005) *Marginal Scholarship and Textual Deviance: The Commentum Cornuti and the Early Scholia on Persius. BICS* Supplement 84, London.
  (2018) *Critics, Compilers and Commentators: An Introduction to Roman Philology 200 BCE–800 CE*, Oxford.
Ziogas, I. (2021) *Law and Love in Ovid: Courting Justice in the Augustan Age*, Oxford.
Ziogas, I. and E. Bexley, eds. (2022) *Roman Law and Latin Literature*, London.
Zuckerberg, D. (2018) *Not All Dead White Men: Classics and Misogyny in the Digital Age*, Cambridge, MA.

CHAPTER 2

# *Canons*

*Irene Peirano Garrison*

## The Canonised Classics

On the surface, canons appear to be an almost inescapable function of institutionalised knowledge – a hierarchy of authors, texts and methodologies that structure both our curricula and the profession in decisions on appointments and promotions, conferences and grants. As John Guillory writes: 'the canonicity of works is ... another name for their institutional mode of reception and reproduction'.[1] Canons, so the argument goes, are *practical* tools for creating and maintaining learning communities and for negotiating belonging to groups (academic, social, professional, etc.). While acknowledging the need to change the boundaries of the canon to include under-represented texts or readers, proponents of the pragmatic approach to canonical formations emphasise what they see as the sheer *inevitability* of the canon. As the argument goes, a canon, however negotiated, is indispensable for teaching and research: how else but through the negotiations of canonical formations in syllabi, reading lists, conferences and funding bodies is one to carry out the paedagogical and professional missions with which we are entrusted as scholars and teachers?

It is important to emphasise from the start that this pragmatic argument betrays defensiveness. Whether explicitly or not, such pragmatic arguments are often made in response to critiques from marginalised groups: students and scholars who are critiquing the exclusion of racial, ethnic and religious minorities from academia and are seeking to create canons, reading lists and institutions that are representative of the diversity of society. The rhetorical context in which these 'canons of practicality' are often evoked should give pause for thought even to the most committed of pragmatists.[2] What critics of the canon object to is not just the content of canonical formations – canons that are all too often too male, too white

---

[1] Guillory 2013: 269.  [2] I thank the editors for suggesting the phrase 'canons of practicality'.

and too western-centric – but also the ways in which the supposed aesthetic superiority of Homer, Virgil, etc., which is repeatedly invoked to justify the inclusion of these works into the canon and the exclusion of others, erases the process through which canonical texts have been used to defend and rationalise violence against racial, religious and other minorities and against women.[3] Such a history of reception, canon critics argue, is one that should be represented in paedagogy, and may even warrant exclusion from the canon or at the very least a redefinition of a given text's role within it. Thus canon critics do not simply want to redesign the canon out of a self-promoting agenda as charged by opponents, who often implicitly present themselves as promoters of the practical or objective defenders of great literature. Rather, they are inviting much-needed reflection on the mechanisms underpinning canonical formations, beginning with the nexus of aesthetics, ideology and power through which the canon carries out its 'practical' mission.[4]

An analysis of the canon must thus begin by reckoning with the work that canons have traditionally performed in literary studies and the role that Graeco-Roman antiquity has played in the formation of the broader discourse of canon. Even the most ardent proponents of the canons of practicality might concede that it would be reductive to see the relationship of canon and the classics of Graeco-Roman antiquity merely as the result of the mechanics of academia.[5] For one, there is practically an *equation* between classical antiquity and the canon: by its very name, Classics has traditionally legitimised itself as a field through its access to objects that claim to have intrinsic trans-historical value. Friedrich August Wolf's *Prolegomena to Homer* is hailed as the beginning of the disciplinary field of Classics to the exclusion of, for example, Christian texts, Greek Judaism and the languages of imperial peripheries.[6] If Classics is in effect coextensive with Homer, the author who most embodies the canon, it is inevitable that it should be considered a 'highly canonised' field.[7]

More to the point, as we have seen above, definitions of the classical have been traditionally invested in claims of the universal superiority of the

---

[3] Bond 2018.
[4] See Morrison 1989 on the study of African American literature as examination of 'the unspeakable things unspoken' of the American canon. On the tensions inherent in the project of creating a black canon see Gates Jr 1992: 17–42.
[5] On efforts to disentangle the idea of canonical masterpieces (works that can but need not be 'ancient') from that of the classic (a work belonging to the Graeco-Roman past) see Kermode 1983 and the introduction in Damrosch 2006: 15; Mukherjee 2013: 30–1. Still, given how definitions of the canon are deeply rooted in Graeco-Roman antiquity (see in this chapter), this distinction seems at best artificial.
[6] See Grafton, Most and Zetzel 1985: 35.    [7] Porter 2002; Formisano 2018: 5–6.

Graeco-Roman tradition and therefore implicitly of western culture. In the words of Hans-Georg Gadamer, the classical is 'a kind of timeless present that is contemporaneous with every other present' (Gadamer 2004: 299). Here Classics is deeply complicit in the formation of Euro-centrism, western-centrism and other elitist ideologies, which use the Graeco-Roman past as the underpinning for claims of trans-cultural and trans-historical superiority. It has been repeatedly observed that the notion of the classic is inextricably connected to that of empire, as for example in T. S. Eliot's terse formulation from a lecture delivered to the Virgil Society at the height of World War II in October 1944: the *Aeneid* is the classic *par excellence* because 'Aeneas is the symbol of Rome; and, as Aeneas is to Rome, so is ancient Rome to Europe. Thus Virgil acquires the centrality of the unique classic; he is at the centre of European civilization, in a position which no other poet can share or usurp' (Eliot 1974: 28–9).

The co-extensiveness of the classical with timeless trans-cultural values can take several forms: a 'quasi-Darwinian' claim that the value of the classics is tied to and evidenced by their continual survival. In this reading, 'the canon is . . . a gauge of vitality' (Bloom 1995: 39), 'the classic . . . defines itself by surviving' (Coetzee 2011: 20) or, to put it differently, it is democratically defined by the 'pleasure' it gives to successive reading communities.[8] Exceptionalist claims can also be found lurking in arguments about the value of the classical for understanding European culture or for placing western civilisations in dialogue with non-western ones.[9] The pitfalls of these paradigms are not hard to spot. On the one hand, there is a danger of constructing the canon as a *universal* mode and thus imposing culturally alien categories on non-western traditions.[10] On the other, as Emily Apter has reminded us, the methodology behind 'global literature' conjures practices of 'collectivism' and 'curatorial salvage' and other markedly colonial modes through which literature is cast as 'property', worth collecting, preserving and assessing in its 'value'.[11] Apter puts her finger on the ways in which the classical can play a role in institutional forms of knowledge that are deeply entwined with western notions of

---

[8] For the role of pleasure in the canon see Kermode 2006: 15–31. In Kermode's reading, the changes to the canon – the fall and ascent of individual authors and texts – affirm the democratic character of canonical formations.

[9] See DuBois 2010: 18 for an example of an egalitarian approach that frames Graeco-Roman antiquity as one among many civilisations: 'I see no compelling reason that our students should privilege the Greeks and Romans above all others. We should accept that the ancient Greek and Roman civilizations are part of *global* history, that they have had great influence on the development of western civilization and on its sometimes imperial ambitions elsewhere.'

[10] Trivedi 2007.   [11] Apter 2013: 326–9. On the question of collecting see also Appiah 2009.

personhood and a neoliberal emphasis on the transference of goods and market value. Finally, critics have attacked from different disciplinary angles the very narrative of a cohesive western canon as inherently fallacious and blind to the porousness of east–west categories.[12] We could recall Amitav Ghosh's attack on the myth of a cogent European Novel in the essay on his grandfather's library, which is in itself a deep critique of the discourse of the canon. Ghosh denounces the Novel as a genre both deeply rooted in a local and parochial European identity and yet intrinsically dependent from the start on imperial dislocation for its existence.[13]

Other critics such as Pierre Bourdieu and Barbara Herrnstein Smith have focused our attention on the pervasiveness of the language of value in literary analysis and the meaning of this productive intersection of economics and literature, investigating the kind of 'cultural capital' that the canon represents and how it functions in a system of exchanges within academia.[14] Central to this approach to the canon as an institutional mechanism is the critique of the contingent nature of literary judgements: the value of the text is not a property residing in the object of study but rather a positive effect arising from readers' engagement with it. In turn, those engagements are pre-shaped and pre-determined by the institutional context in which they take place.

> All value is radically contingent, being neither a fixed attribute, an inherent quality, or an objective property of things but, rather, an effect of multiple, continuously changing, and continuously interacting variables or, to put this another way, the product of the dynamics of a system, specifically an *economic* system. (Smith 1988: 30)

For whom, with whom and where we are judging and reading becomes key to understanding the very functioning of the canon as a tool for hegemonic control.[15] Indeed, work by Ankhi Mukherjee on the role of the canon in post-colonial writing has unearthed the ways in which 'the question and concept of the classic is . . . always that of the outsider'.[16] Commenting on

---

[12] Guillory 2013: 33 calls western culture the 'umbrella term under which all these different texts take shelter from the labor of critique, the labor of reading'; and see also Kermode 1983: 22–8; for a critique of the continuity between Greece, Rome and Europe see Amin 2011 esp. 165–88.
[13] Ghosh 1998: 18: 'when we read *Middlemarch* or *Madame Bovary* we have not the faintest inkling that the lives depicted in them are made possible by global empires . . . '. See also Said 1993: 80–97.
[14] See Smith 1988; Spivak 1987: 212–42; Bourdieu 1993.
[15] Keith 2000: 8–35 on the role of epic in Roman education as a tool for maintaining the male-dominated social hierarchy.
[16] Mukherjee 2013: 49.

the essays by the same title – 'What is a Classic?' – by T. S. Eliot and J. M. Coetzee, respectively written in war-torn London in 1944 and delivered in 1991, a year after the end of the Apartheid regime, Mukherjee delves deep into the ways in which both writers use the classics to explore and tackle their own peripheral status in relation to Europe (in the case of Eliot, as an American living in the UK) and the global literary stage (in the case of South-African Coetzee). Recent work on constructions of the classical in Graeco-Roman antiquity has placed a similar emphasis, for example, on the ways in which visions of the Greek classical past are shaped by the geographical and temporal liminality of imperial Greek writers of the Second Sophistic and also on how this ancient construction of Hellenism in writers such as Plutarch and Aelius Aristides has been privileged in the service of a romanticised and anachronistic attachment to a pure version of Hellenism in nineteenth-century scholarship.[17] A comparable critique of the scholarly investment in the construction of the classical past has come from the field of late antiquity.[18] Here in putting forward a vision of late antiquity as a period of extreme dynamism and vitality, even while retaining a label that explicitly relegates the period to a liminal space relative to classical antiquity, scholars have pointed to the heuristic value of the Gibbonian construct of decline and fall not for late antiquity but rather for Enlightenment history.[19]

It takes not only imagination and risk-taking to question the inevitability of the canon as an enshrined institutional and professional practice but also an intimate knowledge of the history of higher education, a high bar to clear for most classicists, including this author. The classics, including Homer and Virgil and other Graeco-Roman texts, have been the bedrock of the modern liberal arts curriculum from its earliest inception. One of the most significant documents in the history of American Higher Education, the Yale Report of 1828, contains one of the first arguments for a liberal education, as opposed to a professional one, defined as 'such a course of discipline in the arts and sciences, as is best calculated, at the same time, both to strengthen and enlarge the faculties of the mind, and to familiarise it with the leading principles of the great objects of human investigation and knowledge' (p. 30).[20] The best course of study is one which brings into exercise all the important mental faculties and is therefore both

---

[17] Porter 2006; Swain 2010; Whitmarsh 2013: 3 'the Second Sophistic has been – and remains in much current scholarship – a modern fantasy projected back on to the ancient world, an *objet petit a*, an impossible idealization of a pure, untainted aristocratic Greek tradition'.
[18] Brown 1993; Formisano 2007 and Formisano 2014.    [19] Momigliano 1980; Pocock 1977.
[20] On this document and its impact see Herbst 2004 and Adler 2020.

propaedeutic to further specialised study in the professional school and conducive to engaged participation in society by all members to whom such education might be accessible. It is important to note, however, that the case for this liberal arts curriculum inclusive of science, mathematics and what we may now term 'Humanities' is advanced in the context of the question as to whether Greek and Latin should be retained as part of the college instruction or instead eliminated because irrelevant to most professions. In some ways, though 200 years old, the report is strikingly applicable. The slippage between practicality and desirability is already at work in this early document: according to the authors since 'the literature of every country in Europe is founded more or less on classical literature ... if scholars are prepared to act in the literary world as it in fact exists, classical literature, *from considerations purely practical* [emphasis added], should form an important part of their early discipline' (p. 34). The authors make a limited claim as to the value of Greek and Latin for those going into law, medicine and theology. While Greek is especially valuable to access scripture in its 'original simplicity and purity', Latin is framed as essential for those studying modern European languages. Yet on closer inspection, the practicality of the liberal arts canon is but one part of a larger and more serious claim about the ability of the Greek and Roman writers to 'form the taste, and to discipline the mind, both in thought and diction, to the relish of what is elevated, chaste, and simple' (p. 35).

The political nature of this discourse, both in its original context and in its subsequent instantiations, cannot be understated:[21] for as scholars have demonstrated, this rhetoric went hand in hand with an appropriation of the classical past to justify modern structures of colonialism and slavery.[22] To give one contemporary example, John Calhoun, the American slavery advocate, statesman, vice-president of the United States and Yale graduate, is rumoured to have asserted that philological competence in Greek was an indicator of humanity, and one in which black people were incapable of partaking.[23] For sure these constructs were contested already in the nineteenth century:[24] African American scholars, educators and intellectuals not only actively combated these appropriations by using classical texts to challenge racist ideologies but also co-opted Graeco-Roman civilisation in the development of their nascent programme for African American culture.[25] Nevertheless, even as the authors of the Yale Report

---

[21] Rankine 2020. [22] Barnard 2017; Richard 1994. [23] Ronnick 2005: 44, 342–3.
[24] See responses in Crummell 1897; Cooper 1898: 260–1. [25] Hairston 2013.

wrestle with subtlety with transatlantic differences in the teaching of Greek and Latin at University, there is no question that the goal for which this curriculum is designed is the formation of a white male who claims European heritage as his own.

Thus, though the reconfiguration and supplementation of the curriculum in today's Anglo-American classrooms may on some level satisfy the present demand for greater inclusivity, it is important to acknowledge that the place of classical works in the liberal arts canon rests on a mixed legacy. To give one other example, in the US, debates about opening up the canon have clustered around the redefinition of the curricula for 'Great Books' courses in the context of liberal arts education in places such as Reed College, Columbia, Chicago and Yale. Demands for Great Books programmes, such as Columbia's Core Curriculum as well as similar programmes at Chicago, Berkeley, University of Virginia and later at Yale, arose in the aftermath of World War I in an effort to strengthen democracy and to avoid the mistakes that led to near annihilation in the first world conflict.[26] Originally developed as war issues training and accompanied soon by an Honours course on Great Books taught by John Erskine, 'An introduction to contemporary civilization' was designed to teach students among other things 'how to produce cheap goods without sacrificing human nature; how to achieve political and legal forms that are at once flexible and stable; how to eliminate human and material waste of any kind; how to preserve national integrity and still enjoy the benefits of international organization'.[27]

On the one hand, the founders of these programmes, men like John Erskine at Columbia, Charles W. Eliot at Harvard and Mortimer Adler at Chicago, were driven by the idea of democratising both access to the classics and their interpretation – the innovation of Great Books programmes resting as much on their curricula as on the Socratic method employed in the classroom.[28] This attempt to 'democratise' the classics was partly felt to be an answer to the development of electives in university curricula and the increased 'professionalisation' of higher education.[29] It is in response to these changes in higher education that a common curriculum, based on a set of texts once considered the bastions of social elites, was developed to educate this student body made increasingly of middle-class men from first- or second-generation European immigrant families. Here the classical past, specifically inflected as Greek, provides a *trait d'union* in

---

[26] The Great Books idea in turn has its root in late nineteenth-century Victorian culture: Lacy 2008.
[27] Coss 1919: 344.   [28] See Chaddock 2002.   [29] Bell 2011: 12–15.

the melting pot of the nascent American democracy. As Erskine writes in his essay 'The moral obligation to be intelligent':

> Our land assimilates all races; with every ship in the harbor our old English ways of thought must crowd a little closer to make room for a new tradition ... the social conditions from which these new citizens have escaped have taught them the power of the mind. They differ from each other, but against the Anglo-Saxon they are confederated in a Greek love of knowledge, in a Greek assurance that sin and misery are the fruit of ignorance, and that to know is to achieve virtue. (Erskine 1921: 22–3)

On the other hand, the emphasis on the classics' role in catalysing social and ethnic assimilation of recent immigrants and inculcating a new democratic moral order is not just built on a skewed and idealised image of the classical past but, as James Turner has argued, also can be seen to mask a Christian, and specifically Protestant, agenda by endowing the teaching of literature with 'the promise of moral formation once shouldered by Protestantism'.[30] Still, perusing Erskine's manifesto on reading Great Books one is struck by the vibrant modernity of many of his claims: in carving a space for the non-scholar to read Great Books, Erskine argues that the historical method of reading the classics does not deserve the credit it gets:

> [M]any a conscientious student has completed an elaborate study of language in the hope that in the end he would know something about literature, only to find that he knew a great deal about language. The approach to literature is always through life, and if a book no longer reflects our life, it will cease to be generally read, no matter what its importance for antiquarian purposes. (Erskine 1935: 16)

This call to examine Virgil as a book for the present has its roots in a radically modern concept of reading as a dynamic process, through which change is exerted on the past:

> [W]henever we read a book we love, we change it, to some extent. We read into it our own interpretations, and the meanings which the words have taken on in our own time. (Erskine 1935: 21)

At least two competing models of canonicity are seemingly at work. In one, the Graeco-Roman past is presented as embodying timeless values accessible through historical study. As in the case of the Yale Report of 1828, the classical canon thus conceived is a *practical* tool through which to read the

---

[30] Turner 2000: 270 and see his discussion *passim*.

present and shape the future. The other, represented in John Erkine's Great Books school, approaches the classics and the canon to which they belong more consciously as a *displacement* of the self, 'a magic surface, in which [the audience] can see themselves more clearly than elsewhere' (Erskine 1935: 23). The canon is here envisaged as a currency, a tool to make out who we are in the present moment, as opposed to a vehicle for the transmission of quantum values. It is and should be changeable not just in scope but also in definition, with works being swapped in and out as well as being radically redefined through reading. In many ways, however, both of these versions of the classical canon activate, self-consciously or not, a deep sense of intimacy with the classical past, whether through the promise of repetition or through the distorting effect of the mirror.

Thus the creation of a liberal arts canon, spanning the Graeco-Roman classics and European literature and thought all the way to the nineteenth century, implies a politically charged claim of continuity between the present and the classical past. Such a claim is deeply connected with nineteenth-century discourses of nationalism in all their sinister ramifications (e.g. anti-Semitism, Euro-centrism, Orientalism).[31] To give just one example of this complex legacy, American Great Books activists, including John Erskine himself, were deeply influenced by the programme for liberal education founded on the classics developed by Matthew Arnold, the Victorian poet and critic.[32] Arnold argued that culture was not one based on 'a smattering of Greek and Latin' or 'scientific passion' but rather that it was to be defined as 'the study of perfection':

> But there is of culture another view, in which not solely the scientific passion, the sheer desire to see things as they are, natural and proper in an intelligent being, appears as the ground of it. There is a view in which all the love of our neighbour, the impulses towards action, help, and beneficence, the desire for stopping human error, clearing human confusion, and diminishing the sum of human misery, the noble aspiration to leave the world better and happier than we found it, – motives eminently such as are called social, – come in as part of the grounds of culture, and the main and pre-eminent part. (Arnold 1869: 7)

In 'The function of criticism at the present time', an essay published in 1865 after Arnold delivered his famous lectures 'On translating Homer', the critic asks 'There is so much inviting us! What are we to take? What will

---

[31] See Winterer 2002: 136–7 in reference to nineteenth-century America; see also Stephens and Vasunia 2010 for discussion of Classics and the rise of nationalism.
[32] Lacy 2008: 403–17. See Erskine's reference to Arnold's agenda in Erskine 1921: 19.

nourish us in growth towards perfection?'[33] The answer lies in selecting 'the best that is known and thought *in the world*' [emphasis added].[34] While Arnold invites every critic to possess 'one great literature, at least, besides his own' (p. 82), his model of great literature is in practice centred on the revival of a cogent European culture founded on distinct national identities but sharing a common heritage in antiquity:

> But after all, the criticism I am really concerned with, – the criticism which alone can much help us for the future, the criticism which, throughout Europe, is at present day meant . . ., – is a criticism which regards Europe as being, for intellectual and spiritual purposes, one great confederation . . . and whose members have, for their proper outfit, a knowledge of Greek, Roman and eastern antiquity, and of one another. (Arnold 1895: 39)

Moreover, as Miriam Leonard has shown, Arnold's socially liberal programme of education through 'great literature' is in itself highly fraught: Arnold's famous call, also advanced in his 1869 *Culture and Anarchy*, to strike a balance between Hebraism and Hellenism, which Arnold viewed as the two idealised cultural forces animating world history, is both a corrective to contemporary discourses of philhellenism by French Semitics scholar Ernest Renan, among others, and an extension of it, being in no way exempt from the odious anti-Semitic rhetoric which animates it.[35]

In highlighting the complex and at times deeply troubled history of the instructional contexts in which the study of Greek and Roman Great Books is embedded the point should not be to seek out alternative 'bias-free' textual canons but rather to emphasise the political nature of these paedagogical projects and the claims to greatness therein advanced.[36] Furthermore, as we construct a history of the Latin canon, we must reckon with the role of the Graeco-Roman past in the construction of modern nostalgic canonical formations. Canons may well be practical tools but they are ideological nonetheless.

### 'Opening Up the Latin Canon'

> . . . it is a truism that a full undoing of the canon-apocrypha opposition, like the undoing of any opposition, is impossible . . . When we feminist Marxists are ourselves moved by a desire for alternative canon-formations, we work with varieties of and variations upon the old standards. (Spivak 1987: 213)

---

[33] Arnold and Pater 1895: 84.   [34] Ibid. 78.   [35] Leonard 2012: 105–38.
[36] See further North 2017.

When canonicity and the canon are framed as the 'price of doing business', the focus shifts instead to the process of negotiating and 'opening' up the canon to the under-represented or marginal. When we consider the canon first and foremost as a function of institutional practice – a hierarchical list of authors, texts and methodologies deemed for one reason or another worthier of being taught, studied and preserved – there is no question that in the past three decades, the core of Latin literature has significantly widened with a boom in areas such as post-Virgilian epic, technical literature and miscellaneous collections (e.g. Columella, Pliny the Elder, Vitruvius, Frontinus, Valerius Maximus, Aulus Gellius), pseud-epigrapha (e.g. *Appendix Vergiliana*) and late antique literature to name a few. New theoretical models and emerging methodologies have aided this expansion: some of the recent shifts that have fuelled – and in turn have been fuelled by – the expansion of the canonical core of Latin texts include, for example, the erosion of traditional boundaries between literature and history and between text and material culture, and the booming field of reception studies which has significantly expanded the historical and geographical scope of the classical scholar. The rise of a mass market for translations and textbooks, stimulated by the need to teach Greek and Latin texts in courses taught in translation to a broader set of undergraduate audiences, has further shaped the curriculum to allow for the inclusion of corpora, such as papyri, graffiti and inscriptions, previously difficult to access.[37] The extent to which the digital age will affect the curricular canon is still in question: on the one hand, the internet has made more material more easily available through searchable databases and yet the price of digital subscriptions and the practicalities of the classroom may in the end push more readers towards older translations out of copyright and therefore freely available on the web.[38] In turn, the older the material, the more likely it is to be alienating in its deployment of racist and sexist vocabulary and in its blatant misappropriation of the classical past.[39]

Most recent discussions of the canon have focused on drawing and re-drawing the boundaries of Latin and Greek literature to include the writings and perspectives of under-represented or marginalised social,

---

[37] Kennedy 2001; Hardwick 2000 and for earlier efforts to 'open up' the classics through translation see Sheets 2005 with reference to the Loeb project. For the ways in which non-literary and non-canonical corpora have been made available through translation see, for example, Lefkowitz and Fant 2016; Kennedy, Roy and Goldman 2013.
[38] Hall 2008b.
[39] Haley 2009. This is not to say, however, that current teaching tools are immune from this problem: see, for example, McCoskey 2019 with reference to the treatment of slavery in nineteenth-century Latin textbooks in contrast to current trends.

racial and gender groups, a re-kindling of the canon wars of the 1980s and 1990s.[40] It is important to consider both the politics of this 'opening up' of the canon and how such a gesture plays out with respect to the specific field of Roman literary studies and more generally of Classics. In this section, we will explore the obvious paradox at play whenever we critique the canon by calling for a change in its internal composition without calling into question its validity as a construct. As Spivak notes in the quote which opens the section, these 'alternative canon-formations' are nothing but 'variations upon an old standard'. If, as John Guillory writes, 'the point is not to make judgment disappear but to reform the conditions of its practice', what are the limits of this logic of 'substitutability' not just for the study of the marginal but also for the discipline?[41]

Work that seeks to recover the experiences of marginalised groups and the gender and race ideologies promoted by Graeco-Roman texts has laid important ground for framing traditionally peripheral constituencies as part and parcel of dominant texts and ideologies.[42] This body of research has emphasised that Graeco-Roman antiquity is in many ways in a relationship of deep alterity from modern democratic ideals of inclusivity, fairness and democracy and such an acknowledgement is surely a salutary corrective to the traditional view of Greece and Rome as the cradle of all that is good about western culture. Furthermore, the emphasis on the linguistic, racial, religious and cultural plurality of the ancient world not only provides a richer and more faithful picture of Graeco-Roman antiquity but defuses the selective appropriation of Rome and Athens as founding sites of white European culture.[43] Still, there are obvious limits to this approach to 'opening up' the canon in the field of antiquity, in which women, slaves and other minorities had restricted access to literacy. Despite the exciting volume of new work on categories and voices traditionally neglected or altogether excluded from scholarly discourse, as scholars of antiquity we must be careful to guard against what David Damrosch has called the 'insistent presentism' of postmodernity, resisting the ways in which the impetus to 'modernise' the canon excludes periods and genres in which the voices that seek representation are less present or less clearly visible.[44]

Relatedly, the incorporation of post-classical reception in the classical curriculum is another major engine of democratisation of the canon.[45]

---

[40] On the canon wars see Graff 1992.   [41] Guillory 2013: 340.
[42] Recent overviews in Liveley 2006; Milnor 2008: 16–46; Zajko 2008; Richlin 2014: 1–35; Joshel and Murnaghan 2005.
[43] DuBois 2010; Seo 2019.   [44] Damrosch 2006: 17.   [45] Rankine 2019.

Through the study of classical reception in its global dimension across time and space, the relevance of the Graeco-Roman world to different and mutually connected cultural traditions is explored in all its complexity. This emphasis on the plurality of voices that have a stake in the classical tradition is intellectually enriching as well as reparative at a time when issues of access, relevance and racism are increasingly being raised in the field.[46] While this expanded and more open-ended vision of the classical canon has met with resistance in some quarters with a growing sense of discomfort both at what is being perceived as a 'de-skilling' and loss of disciplinary competence and at the erosion of the exemplarity of the classical, other work has focused on nimble, capacious and pragmatic paradigms for constructing canons that accommodate antiquity and its reception.[47]

These expanded, revised, opened or upended canons raise fundamental questions about the mechanics of artistic *representation* and the role of communities in hermeneutical dynamics. First, the notion that, for example, a male-authored text is bound to transmit a male-centred worldview rigidly restricts the meaning of texts to the intentions of their author, obscuring the ways in which communities do not 'find' or 'stumble upon' meaning but actively *construct* it in the process of reception. Moreover, if recent work on identity has taught us anything, it is that identities are far from monolithic self-evident entities: they are rather intersectional (Crenshaw), performed (Butler) or even 'idealised imaginings' (Pratt).[48] When Stanley Fish poignantly asks whether there is 'a text in this class', we would be well advised to consider this as a question not just about the unity and comprehensibility of literary texts but also about the possibility of arriving at a definition of stable and homogenous identities based on 'shared values' of any one community.[49]

Thus the idea of opening up the canon raises critical questions about the construction of identity, community and readership. When texts are viewed not as static conveyers of meaning but instead as objects that come into being *only* in the process of interpretation, the question of whose identity, history and values are represented by or through the object will necessarily involve a complex consideration of the identities not just of makers, creators and authors but also of contemporary readers and

---

[46] Including two special issues of the *American Journal of Philology* (Greenwood 2022), where readers will find a more updated bibliography than I was able to include here after the final submission of the manuscript in 2019.
[47] Greenwood 2016; Güthenke and Holmes 2018; Martindale 2013.
[48] See the critique of communities in Guillory 2013: 276–9.   [49] Fish 1982.

audiences, as they collaborate to shape its culturally and historically situated interpretation. In this perspective, the diversifying of the canon has to be understood as a *dialogic* project involving both the identities of readers, students and scholars and the subject matter of their study.[50] Opening up the canon is a dynamic and self-reinforcing process and one which involves both readers that embody difference (social, racial, gender, etc.) accessing and studying an expanded and evolving canon and texts (peripheral, post-classical, marginal, etc.) that embody difference being 'read into' the canon by an increasingly diverse readership. As Lorna Hardwick shrewdly points out with reference to the question of whether Classics has undergone a 'democratic turn', participation is a key measure of democratisation in ensuring that Classics is not an exclusive practice and one historically co-opted to justify conservative, reactionary or hateful programmes.[51] Yet, as Hardwick argues, access is measured not just quantitatively but also *qualitatively* as the process of 're-vision' (Rich 1972), identifying paths not taken and thus revealing 'hitherto unrecognised possibilities' (Wolf 1988: 270–1) that are activated whenever the subjectivity of new readers comes into play with the work's crevices and inconsistencies.[52] Opening up the canon begins by taking seriously the inherent fragmentation of texts and by acting out our desire to cure the loss through a reading that is transformative for both the subject and the object.[53]

If approached from this angle, the process of opening up the canon involves a deep methodological shift rather than a process of substitution, an upending of priorities or, worse still, a widening that feels unmanageable. But how does this methodological shift affect approaches to specific texts and genres, especially as they pertain to Latin literature? First, the strong traction of the concept of canonicity within the field of Classics determines not just a hierarchy of texts and methodologies worthier of being taught and researched but also informs the very approach to so-called marginal texts. As a scholar of 'minor' Roman poetry, in my own research on Latin pseudepigrapha, I have had to overcome an intellectual impasse. Scholarship on Roman fakes has generally consisted of studies of individual texts aimed at proving or disproving the conventional attribution and

---

[50] Jauss' notion of 'dialogical understanding' in Jauss 1985: 9–17; and Greenwood 2010: 37 on the 'dialogism' of Caribbean receptions of the classics.
[51] Hardwick 2013. See also Hall 2008a and Dozier 2018; Krebs 2012.
[52] Rich 1972: 18 defines re-vision as 'the act of looking back, of seeing with fresh eyes, of entering an old text from a new critical direction'. Different models of readership can pave the way for a re-imagining of encounters with Graeco-Roman antiquity. See, for example, Casali 2004; Felson 2016; Hauser 2018.
[53] Najman 2017: 529 for a model of reading as 'reciprocal transformation of text and self'.

## 2 Canons

dating: are any or all the poems of the *Catalepton* by Virgil? Is the *Laus Pisonis* Neronian or Flavian? And is the writer the young Lucan? Is the writer of the *Consolatio ad Liviam* also the author of the *Elegiae in Maecenatem*? Scholarly engagement with these texts traditionally stops at whatever provisional answer one has reached on these endless and endlessly unanswerable questions, and little or no thought is given to the dynamics that gave rise to these texts.[54] The anonymity of these works is one of the factors that have positively discouraged any form of literary analysis, tied as this has traditionally been to the process of constructing and reconstructing authorial identity.[55] Yet, no less influential a factor in discouraging any interest in the cultural roots of anonymous and spurious works is the self-proclaimed role of the philologist as a defender of the canon. Here the canon cultivates a 'policing mentality' in which a select group of works considered valuable has to be kept free from unwanted impostors, while little or no interest is given to the literary dynamics of the works rejected as spurious. One is reminded of Antony Grafton's compelling image of antiquity as a train 'in which Greeks and Latins, spurious and genuine authorities sit side by side until they reach a stop marked "Renaissance". Then grim-faced humanists climb aboard, check tickets, and expel fakes in hordes through doors and windows alike.'[56] Filling the cultural vacuum which Roman pseudepigrapha has been made to inhabit means stepping out of the train-conductor role and treating these texts not as crime scenes but as creative responses to the literary past. Studying spurious Roman poetry as a literary tradition – not as an inextricable bundle of problems of authorial identities and dating – implies a fundamental repositioning of one's scholarly stance towards marginal texts but also canonical authors, a willingness to drop the role of policeman of the canon and assume instead the mask of cultural observer.

Secondly, it is important to take stock not just of how approaches to the canon shape our approach to the margins, but of how the project of the canon is shaped by a given approach to the margins. The canonical locus of study for non-canonical texts has typically been the textual edition and the commentary and to this day pseudepigrapha and other 'minor' texts are mostly studied in the context of these most traditional philological genres.[57] It is worth asking *why* this should be so and to what extent the scholarly medium, if at all, is shaping the message. From Scaliger's edition

---

[54] Peirano 2012a: 242 on the tendency to proclaim guilt without exploring motive. For a critical exploration of these issues as they interlace with gender, see Skoie 2002; Gurd 2005.
[55] Peirano 2012b.   [56] Grafton 1990: 102.   [57] Hunter 2002.

of the *Appendix Vergiliana* (1572), to Baehrens' *Poetae Latini minores* (1879–86), to Riese's (1869–70) and Shackleton Bailey's (1982) *Anthologia Latina*, to Housman's and Goold's editions of Manilius, engagement with minor Roman poetry has been surprisingly central in the tradition of textual criticism with genealogies of critics displaying their prowess and belonging to a scholarly tradition through successive and layered engagement with the inert bodies of marginal texts.[58] As Lowell Edmunds argues, 'minor literature', which these texts are seen to embody, is understood squarely in aesthetic terms.[59] Housman expressed this paradox lapidarily in a paper on the text of the *Culex*: 'Just as it is hard to tell, in Statius or Valerius Flaccus, whether this or that absurd expression is due to miscopying or to the divine afflatus of the bard, so in the *Culex* and *Ciris* and *Aetna* it is for ever to be borne in mind that they are the work of poetasters. Many a time it is impossible to say for certain where the badness of the author ends and the badness of the scribe begins' (Housman 1902: 339). Here the textual work of the critic, often framed in clinical terms as a rescue operation or restorative surgery, constitutes an affirmation and sublimation of the method of philology, as the 'aesthetic pleasure that comes from the sheer technical work'.[60]

It is also true, however, that the very method of traditional philology, which is being affirmed as the message, derives its prestige from the authority and value of the canon. The basic principle, common to both ancient and modern criticism, according to which the critic is able to judge on issues of authenticity because of his command of an author's style (*diuinatio*), rests on the loving identification with the author.[61] The critic's most important weapon is his acquaintance with each writer's most salient characteristics and his ability to use his judgement and knowledge to spot the intruder. Modern authenticity criticism has made the stylistic variable arguably more 'quantifiable' by closely studying metrics and diction and compiling lists of features which are characteristic of a given author, and distinguishing between the early and late phases of their production. Yet, to ask whether a textual variant is authentic is to judge whether it reflects what are assumed to be the standards and style of the author, that is in

---

[58] Bowersock 2011 reviews the 'scholarly line' of Manilian criticism stretching from Bentley, Scaliger and Goold, noting that 'the praise that Shackleton Bailey lavished on Goold's Loeb edition of Manilius was a kind of secular blessing from a high priest of textual criticism'.
[59] Edmunds 2010.
[60] Bowersock 2011. Edmunds 2010: 61–2 cites Shackleton Bailey's definition of the textual critic as 'a physician' who 'does not go too anxiously into the merit of what he heals; he gives his aid where it is most needed and most effectual'.
[61] For the ways in which secondary literature disrupts these categories see Sluiter 2000.

effect to think *like* the author. Some conclusions follow: the authority of the critic is intimately dependent on the value of the reconstructed text. Unsurprisingly, minor texts pose challenges precisely in that they threaten to disrupt the critic's desire to be one with the author. On the one hand, the minor text is an inert body, a kind of dummy on which the critic practises their surgical skill; on the other, as an inferior text, it must be resisted by the critic as an object of desire and identification.

However, there is one further corollary that we may be less eager to grapple with: namely that the project of the canon ultimately needs the presence of a non-canonical margin to justify itself. Taking a metaphor from the history of the book, we might think of the rejected readings in the apparatus at the bottom of a page as the paratext of philology. In Gérard Genette's formulation, paratexts such as titles, dedications, prefaces, etc. represent the outer edge of the text and, though physically liminal, hermeneutically they are in fact central to helping configure and thus deliver the text.[62] This paradox of textual criticism has been well studied by critics of philology such as Jerome McGann and David Greetham. As the latter writes, in relation to the role of the apparatus, 'the authentication of the "primary" text above is wholly dependent on the description and evaluation of the "rejected" readings below. The editors must successfully demonstrate the inadequacies of the lower text in order to convince the reader that the upper text is authentic.'[63] In other words, the presence of the text above is guaranteed by, and therefore draws its authority from, the demonstrated inferiority of the lower text. The more inadequate the lower text, the higher the authority of the upper text. We can extend this metaphor beyond the sphere of textual criticism if we see this rhetoric of inadequacy and inferiority as fundamental to the self-definition of the canon. We may choose to preserve the status quo by seeking the admission of marginal texts into the canon (thereby implicitly marginalising other texts). Or we may choose to disrupt, if not the canon as a list, at least its claim to primacy and alterity versus the margin.

## The Antiquity of the Canon

However much we may reposition ourselves in relation to both new and traditional canon formations, we must at some point grapple with the fact that the canon and the hierarchy of texts and genres on which it is built are to some extent inventions of Graeco-Roman antiquity. What does it mean

---

[62] Genette 1997.    [63] Greetham 1991: 22.

to work with canon formations in the study of Latin literature given how the Romans themselves set out to construct a national literature as a translation of the canon of another?[64] To what degree is the critical discourse of the Latin canon rooted in the very sense of belatedness and marginality built into the Roman literary tradition? To what extent does it feed upon and complement the classicism of the Second Sophistic under which the turn to the Greek classical past functioned both as a site of cultural resistance by the Greeks and as a tool of imperial control by the Roman elites?[65] And to what extent does it depart from it?

There is a unique and intimate connection between Roman literature, which starts with a translation of a Greek 'classic', Livius Andronicus' *Odyssia*, and the canon.[66] This structuring of a Latin vernacular literature as a translation and continuation of Greek literature is predicated upon the existence of a more or less fixed canon of great works. In Denis Feeney's words, 'a strongly classicizing and canonizing urge is evident from the beginning of the translation project'.[67] According to the standard narrative, the Romans of the second century BCE inherited such a 'canonising urge' from their near contemporaries, the Hellenistic scholars and poets, who were the first to systematise the study of the Greek literary past. This narrative of translation and adaptation should be revised to account for the ways in which the Hellenistic systematising of the Greek literary past was interpreted through and made to map onto Roman modes of political and social ordering.[68] Thus the Roman sources that discuss the work of Hellenistic grammarians can be read not just as storehouses of information about the third and second century BCE but also about contemporary concerns with the appropriation of Greek heritage and the globalising aspirations of the Romans. In this way, the construction of the Greek classical past can be seen as an invention of the Romans as much as of Hellenistic Greeks, and one which created an enduring legacy in modern accounts of the literary canon.

The effort to frame Roman literature as a translation of the Greek canon is evident from the earliest beginning. Ennius was supposedly referred to as

---

[64] Feeney 2016; Goldberg 2011.   [65] Connolly 2007; Porter 2005; Woolf 1994.
[66] For a critique of this paradigm see Barchiesi 2002: 'one could argue that Latin studies have been focusing on translation and transference, not on appropriation and reuse, because the discipline was trying to (re)establish itself (through many an inferiority complex) as the missing link between German Hellenophilia and European national identities'.
[67] Feeney 2016: 119.
[68] This is akin to what Joy Connolly has called the 'payoff' of Hellenism to the Romans: Connolly 2007: 31: 'Universal, globally appealing Hellenism mapped itself as the intellectual and ideological system for universal and globalizing (if not globally appealing) Roman empire.'

the *alter Homerus* already by Lucilius.[69] The early Roman dramatists focused not on contemporary theatre but on the fifth-century 'classics'.[70] Cicero expresses this 'canonising urge' in a well-known passage of the *Academica* in which he is attempting to sell the project of writing philosophy in Latin:

> Quid enim causae est cur poetas Latinos Graecis litteris eruditi legant, philosophos non legant? An quia delectat Ennius Pacuuius Accius multi alii, qui non uerba sed uim Graecorum expresserunt poetarum – quanto magis philosophi delectabunt, si ut illi Aeschylum Sophoclem Euripidem sic hi Platonem imitentur Aristotelem Theophrastum. (Cic. *Acad.* 1.3)
>
> For what is the reason why those knowledgeable of Greek letters read Latin poets and do not read Latin philosophers? Is it because Ennius entertains them, Pacuvius, Accius and many others, who have reproduced not the words but the meaning of the Greek poets? How much more will philosophers please them, if in the same way as those imitated Aeschylus, Sophocles and Euripides, they should imitate Plato, Aristotle and Theophrastus?

Ennius, Pacuvius and Accius correspond to the tragic Greek triad of Aeschylus, Sophocles and Euripides, as already proto-canonised in Aristophanes' *Frogs*. In turn, Plato, Aristotle and Theophrastus are presented as the philosophical canon.[71]

The creation of a vernacular literature seems to have been accompanied by philological work that attempted to frame the developing body of texts as a match to and replica of the existing Greek classics.[72] Gellius, for example, transmits a fragment in iambic senarii from the *De poetis* of Volcacius Sedigitus, probably composed around 100 BCE.

> multos incertos certare hanc rem uidimus,
> palmam poetae comico cui deferant.
> eum meo iudicio errorem dissoluam tibi,
> ut, contra si quis sentiat, nihil sentiat.
> Caecilio palmam Statio do comico.
> Plautus secundus facile exuperat ceteros.
> dein Naeuius, qui feruet, pretio in tertiost.
> si erit, quod quarto detur, dabitur Licinio.
> post insequi Licinium facio Atilium.
> in sexto consequetur hos Terentius,

---

[69] Lucil. 1189 Morel; Varro, *Sat. Men.* 398; Hor. *Epist.* 2.1.50.
[70] Nervegna 2007; Gildenhard 2010; Manuwald 2011: 20–2.
[71] Cf. Cic. *De or.* 3.26 where other triads drawn from art history are brought to bear.
[72] Horsfall 1993.

Turpilius septimum, Trabea octauum optinet,
nono loco esse facile facio Luscium.
antiquitatis causa decimum addo Ennium. (Gell. 15.24)

We see that many are undecided on the decision as to which comic poet they would award the palm of victory. By my judgment I shall resolve this wavering, so that if anyone thinks differently from me, they have no sense at all. To Caecilius Statius, I give the palm of victory as a comic. Plautus easily surpasses the rest in second place; then Naevius comes third with his passion. If there is a fourth place, it will belong to Licinius. I make Atilius follow next after Licinius. Let Terentius follow after these, sixth in rank. Turpilius holds seventh place, Trabea eighth. Ninth place I easily make Luscius occupy, Ennius I add as tenth on account of his antiquity.[73]

As Citroni notes, Caecilius, Plautus and Naevius constitute the initial triad, while the other six are added as an unwilling appendix (v. 12 *Si erit quod quarto detur*) to form a canon of nine.[74] Ennius is amusingly presented as a tenth extra. Volcacius compares the critical process to an athletic competition: critics are fighting (v. 1 *certare*) and uncertain to whom they should award victory (v. 2 *palmam deferant*). This is not just yet another application of the ubiquitous metaphor of criticism as a form of contest. Rather, the competition with the conferral of the palm of victory is here emphatically seen as belonging to the Greek world, as Livy reminds us when discussing the introduction of the *palma* at the *Ludi Romani*.[75] Varro's own comic list was structured in triads depending on different areas of expertise with Caecilius being the best in plots, Terence in character and Plautus in dialogue (*Sat. Men.* 399 *In quibus partibus in argumentis Caecilius poscit palmam, | in ethesin Terentius, in sermonibus Plautus*).[76] This canonising practice was later to be mocked by Horace in the *Epistle to Augustus* (Hor. *Epist.* 2.1.51 *ut critici dicunt*): as the critics say, Horace writes, Ennius is the Latin Homer, Afranius the Roman Menander, Plautus the Roman Epicharmus, while Caecilius is superior in seriousness (*grauitas*) and Terence in art (*ars*).[77] Horace ironically mocks the rigidity of these expert judgements, while at the same time criticising the in-built bias against more recent writers. Paradoxically, however, Augustan literature

---

[73] Courtney 1993: 94–6.   [74] Citroni 2005.
[75] Livy 10.47.3 *Eodem anno coronati primum ob res bello bene gestas ludos Romanos spectarunt palmaeque tum primum translato e Graeco more uictoribus datae.* Cf. Hor. *Carm.* 1.1.5–6 *palmaque nobilis | terrarum dominos euehit ad deos* with Nisbet and Hubbard 1970: 6 ad loc.
[76] Cf. Varro fr. 40 Funaioli 1907 Ἥθη ... *nullis aliis seruare conuenit, quam Titinio Terentio Attae*; πάθη *uero Trabea Atilius Caecilius facile mouerunt*; Vell. Pat. 1.17.1.
[77] And see *Epist.* 2.2.99–100 *Discedo Alcaeus puncto illius; ille meo quis? | Quis nisi Callimachus?*

can be read as an attempt not to do away with the archaic canon enshrined by Varro but to 'reboot' it, revamping with it the 'canonising urge' with which Roman literature had begun. When Horace at the end of *Carm.* 1.1 asks Maecenas to include him among the lyric poets (*Quodsi me lyricis uatibus inseres*), we are told that 'Horace's *inseres* represents the Greek ἐγκρίνειν, to "include in the canon" (οἱ ἐγκριθέντες, the *classici*)'.[78] Here the Romans are seen to transfer pre-existing Greek cultural media that predated the advent of Rome – be they a list of canonical works, scholarly or poetic genres or institutional contexts for the preservation of poetry and learning. It is typically argued that this list of the nine lyric poets was an early example of canonical formation, created by the Alexandrian grammarians to identify the foremost writers in each genre.[79] Yet, while an anonymous epigram from the *Palatine Anthology* seems to treat the canon of nine as closed (9.184 'beginning and end limit of all lyric'), another one plays with the conceit that Sappho is not the ninth lyric poet but instead the tenth muse (9.571).[80] Neither is datable for sure to the Hellenistic period.[81] The first attestation of the canon of ten Attic orators is in the second-century treatise *On Literary Styles* by Hermogenes (2.401, 403) and forms the basis for pseudo-Plutarch *Lives of the Ten Orators*.[82] Most scholars agree that this list of orators (not works), just as the list of top tragic and comic writers, remained relatively fluid well into the late Republic when Cicero seems unaware of it (see, for example, *Brut.* 285–91).[83]

It is hard to date these Hellenistic lists, let alone ascertain their function and specifically whether they functioned as 'proto-canons':[84] were

---

[78] Nisbet and Hubbard 1970: 15 ad loc. Ἐγκρίνειν is attested in late texts: for example Phot. *Bibl.* 61 20b25 'Aeschines, the son of Lysanias, called Socraticus, is reckoned by Phrynichus and others one of the greatest orators (εἰς τοὺς ἀρίστους ἐγκρίνει), and his speeches as models of Attic style, only second to those of its best representatives.' However, Emily Greenwood points out to me that it is used of the approved stories allowed in the ideal city at Plato, *Resp.* 377b–c 'We must oversee then, as it seems, the storymakers, and what they do well we must admit (ἐγκριτέον), and what they do not do well, we must reject. And we will convince nurses and mothers to tell their children the stories listed as acceptable (ἐγκριθέντας).' The verb ἐκκρίνειν is used of exclusion from the list of Seven Sages by Diodorus Siculus in the first century BCE 9 fr. 7.1: 'He was included among the Seven Sages after they excluded from the list (ἐκκρίναντες) Periander of Corinth because he had turned into a harsh tyrant.'
[79] Pfeiffer 1968: 206–7; Citroni 2005; Easterling 2012.    [80] See Barbantani 1993: 5–97.
[81] See Page 1981: 341 on anonymous 36a, b.
[82] Quintilian, however, speaks of ten orators being the product of one age in *Inst.* 10.1.74 *Sequitur oratorum ingens manus, ut cum decem simul Athenis aetas una tulerit.* And cf. Vell. Pat. 1.16.
[83] Worthington 1994: 259 attributes the rise of the canon to the Atticist movement and Caecilius of Calacte, the author of a treatise on the subject according to the *Suda*.
[84] For an argument for the invention of the Greek canon predating the Hellenistic age see Netz 2020.

Callimachus' *Pinakes* ('Tables') a catalogue of books available in the library or a list of best in the 'pragmatic sense of ... most useful or most famous authors in the different genres' (Easterling 2012: 286)?[85] If the latter, it is unclear to what extent the Alexandrian *enkrithentes* are singled out as the best for the purpose of imitation, as their later counterparts discussed in Quintilian are, or simply as the most accomplished. The Latin word *index*, which translates *Pinax*, is used both of a catalogue of books from the library (Quint. *Inst.* 10.1.57 *Nec sane quisquam est tam procul a cognitione eorum remotus ut non indicem certe ex bibliotheca sumptum transferre in libros suos possit*) as well as a list of top surviving writers in a given genre or plays by a given author (Cic. *Hort.* fr. 48 *indicem tragicorum*; Sen. *Ep.* 39.2 *indicem philosophorum*; Gell. 3.3.1 the *indices* of Plautine plays by Volcacius Sedigitus). Either way, their circulation in written editions and commentaries of surviving Greek classical authors built towards and solidified their eventual canonical status.[86]

Above all, it is worth noting the extent to which this picture of the Greek canon as a pre-ordered hierarchical field is filtered through the Roman imperial imagination. To start with, not only is the list a quintessentially Roman cultural medium;[87] Romans were also fond of displaying such lists of victories of comic or tragic poets in their homes as suggested by disparate findings of Athenian victory lists in Roman contexts.[88] Regardless of when the lists of best writers such as those attributed to Volcacius Sedigitus and Varro were ultimately created, it is important to note the extent to which the account of the scholarly work of the Alexandrians is thoroughly mediated by *Roman* sources. Indeed, besides Horace, Quintilian is the most important source for the existence of these lists. According to the Roman rhetor:

> Quo quidem ita seuere sunt usi ueteres grammatici ut non uersus modo censoria quadam uirgula notare et libros qui falso uiderentur inscripti tamquam subditos summouere familia permiserint sibi, sed auctores alios in ordinem redegerint, alios omnino exemerint numero. (*Inst.* 1.4.3)
>
> The old *grammatici* indeed were so severe in their judgments that they not only allowed themselves to mark lines with a sign of disapproval and remove

---

[85] Radermacher 1919; Witty 1958; Blum 1991: 150–1, 182–3.
[86] Most 1990: 55–6 on the creation of scholarly editions and commentaries in Alexandria and the influence they indirectly exerted on later processes of canonisation.
[87] Gildenhard 2003; Riggsby 2019.
[88] For example the fragments from the library of Tauromenion from the second century BCE, on which see Battistoni 2006; *IGUR* 216, 215 and 218, pertaining to victories in the 440s BCE on which see Olson and Millis 2012.

from the family as if they were supposititious children any books which seemed wrongly attributed, but also listed some authors in a recognised canon, and excluded others altogether. (trans. Russell 2001)

Later in the reading list, Quintilian claims that 'Apollonius does not appear in the grammarians' list, because Aristarchus and Aristophanes, who evaluated the poets, included none of their own contemporaries' (*Apollonius in ordinem a grammaticis datum non uenit, quia Aristarchus atque Aristophanes, poetarum iudices, neminem sui temporis in numerum redegerunt, Inst.* 10.1.54). It is worth stressing that these accounts of Alexandrian practice are deeply imbued with a typically Roman sensitivity to structure and social order.[89] When, in the second century CE, Aulus Gellius (19.8.15) recalls Fronto's way of calling the old cohort of orators or poets the *classici*, that is, men of the first class, he was creating a new coinage which was destined to have a long history, while all the same capitalising on a metaphorical interplay between literature and politics. As Farrell has remarked in relation to the patterning of poets' careers onto the *cursus honorum* of Roman politicians, Hellenistic genre theory entered into a deeply productive dialogue with the political and social structures of the Roman upper class.[90] Similarly, the Romans can be seen to have easily translated Hellenistic concerns with intellectual ordering into political hierarchies. It is no coincidence that in Quintilian's description of the role of the Alexandrian grammarians the marking of inauthentic passages should be characterised as *censoria uirgula notare* (*Inst.* 1.4.3 'marking lines with a sign of disapproval'). This phrase is meant to bring to mind the *nota* of the censors, the mark that was put in the *census* next to the name of disgraced people to exclude them from the list of citizens qualified to vote and stand for office.[91] Donald Russell, whose translation I gave, renders the Latin *ordo* as 'canon' but the inclusion and exclusion of books from the list can be seen to mobilise the meaning of *ordo* as social class.[92] In Quintilian's formulation, books are included or excluded from lists as citizens are included or excluded from classes (senatorial, equestrian, etc.) by grammarians who operate as Roman censors. Far from functioning as an inert metaphor, this intersection of the political and the canonical in the Roman literary imagination makes the canon an engine which both shapes and is shaped by Roman imperial ideology.

---

[89] On the relation between empire and intellectual order see König and Whitmarsh 2007; Moatti 2015.
[90] Farrell 2002. [91] Sen. *Controv.* 2.1.*praef.*24–5.
[92] See Livy 26.35.3; Val. Max. 2.2.1 *ignarus nondum a censoribus in ordinem senatorium allectum, quo uno modo etiam iis, qui iam honores gesserant, aditus in curiam dabatur.*

Another way in which the concept of the canon was already operative in Roman literature is in the clearly defined *hierarchy* of genres, adapted from the Greeks, according to which epic was seen as superior to all other genres.[93] Consequently, several genres defined themselves as 'minor', 'secondary' or even para-literary. Epigram, for example, is at the bottom of the hierarchy.[94] Prose is ranked lower than poetry with some exceptions.[95] It is useful then to explore genre, canonicity and epigonality as mutually reinforcing cultural mechanisms within a carefully structured pecking order. Just as Martial's defence of the low status of his epigrams (e.g. 1.*praef.* 7 *iocorum nostrorum simplicitate*; 11.20.10 *Romana simplicitate*) is well understood as a rhetorical strategy, not as a truthful characterisation of his style, so the epigonality of minor poets is being more and more understood as a self-conscious artistic effect.[96] The anonymous author of the *Laus Pisonis*, addressing his would-be-patron, exclaims:

> Felix et longa iuuenis dignissime vita
> eximiumque tuae gentis decus, accipe nostri
> certus et hoc ueri complectere pignus amoris.
> Quod si digna tua minus est mea pagina laude,
> at uoluisse sat est: animum, non carmina iacto.
> Tu modo laetus ades: forsan meliora canemus
> et uiris dabit ipse fauor, dabit ipsa feracem
> spes animum.                                                      (*Laus Pis.* 211–18)

Lucky young man, most worthy of a long life, distinguished glory of your people, confidently accept and embrace this token of my true affection. But if my page is less than worthy of your praise, my will is enough: my disposition is my boast, not my poetry. Only I ask that you lend your blissful presence: perhaps we will sing better and your very favour will give me strength, the very hope will make my soul productive.

We can choose to take these statements at face value and let the author's apologetic stance exercise its gravitational pull and claim, as one commentator does, that 'the poet *was* only eighteen and whoever he was evidently had his way to make'.[97] Or we can read these statements as part of a 'generic pose': either as a strategic rhetorical move designed to ingratiate

---

[93] Farrell 2003.
[94] Mart. 12.94.9 *Quid minus esse potest? Epigrammata fingere coepi*; Tac. *Dial.* 10.4 *Ego uero omnem eloquentiam omnisque eius partis sacras et uenerabilis puto, nec solum cothurnum uestrum aut heroici carminis sonum, sed lyricorum quoque iucunditatem et elegorum lasciuias et iamborum amaritudinem [et] epigrammatum lusus et quamcumque aliam speciem eloquentia habeat, anteponendam ceteris aliarum artium studiis credo* with Edmunds 2010: 37–8.
[95] Hutchinson 2009; Whitmarsh 2013: 186–208.   [96] Fowler 1995; Roman 2001.
[97] Kenney 2006: 121.

the addressee or as a result of a conscious artistic persona not dissimilar from the 'bumbling incompetence' that Zetzel has seen as the hallmark of Horace's poetic persona in the *Satires*.[98] Lowell Edmunds' invitation to isolate minor Roman texts not on the basis of aesthetic criteria but of shared literary effects such as parody and realism is very helpful. Could the minor and the marginal be approached as *textual* stratagems comparable to Roland Barthes' 'reality effect'?[99] Conversely, following Mario Telò in his study of Aristophanic comedy, we may also choose to analyse the discourse of the canon in Graeco-Roman poets with a critical eye, not always assuming that it is ultimately dependent on an idealised list (e.g. a Hellenistic grammatical list). As Telò argues in relation to Aristophanes' *Peace*, the canon of comedy is 'an imagined, self-constructed ideal ... deceptively offered as generic orthodoxy' to undercut his rivals' claims to poetic success.[100]

Latin literature offers a prime site from which to analyse the functioning of canons: for one thing, the Romans themselves saw their own literary corpus as a translation of the Greek canon. Though they inherited, translated and adapted the terminology of Hellenistic scholarship, they also uniquely shaped its intellectual tools: the modern discourse of the canon is not only rooted in the canonising project of Roman authors but also deeply connected from its inception with the ideological and political project of imperial conquest of the Romans.

## The Boundaries of the Latin Canon

According to Cicero, Latin literature 'began' in 240 BCE, when Livius Andronicus staged the first play at Rome (Cic. *Brut.* 71–3), but when and where does it end? The answer to this question involves analysing the complex relationship between the Early Church Fathers and classical antiquity against the rise of the discourse of secularism in modern academia and its impact on disciplinary fault lines. Accordingly, this section will problematise the structural distinction between classical and Christian Latin canon and emphasise instead the crucial role played by Christian sources, typically excluded from the study of Latin literature, in the shaping of the disciplinary tools, texts and reading practices of the average Latinist.

Since the birth of *Altertumswissenschaft* ('the science of antiquity') in the late eighteenth and early nineteenth century, the study of classical

[98] Zetzel 1980. [99] Barthes 1989: 141–6. [100] Telò 2016: 6.

antiquity has defined itself in opposition to the study of coeval and co-extensive civilisations, chief above all the Egyptian and the Jewish.[101] While up to the middle of the nineteenth century, scholars moved with freedom between Graeco-Roman antiquity, early Christianity, New Testament and Hebrew Bible, these are today distinct disciplinary entities with their own autonomous canons.

These disciplinary distinctions inform current narratives of the rise of the canon. It has often been observed that while the word 'canon' is derived from the Greek *kanōn*, its modern usage with reference to a selective list of authors is a post-classical coinage based on a late Christian development, not unlike the ways in which the word 'classic' is, in Mario Citroni's formulation, a 'learned reuse, in the humanistic context, of a specific metaphorical expression used by an ancient author'.[102] In classical Greek, *kanōn* refers to a 'rule' or 'standard', and hence the term is used of authors who are presented as models for imitation. For example, we know from Pliny the Elder, Plutarch and Galen that the Greek sculptor Polykleitos assigned the name *kanōn* to a statue of perfect proportions and to a treatise on the subject of the ideal bodily ratio.[103] In Dionysius of Halicarnassus, Lysias is said to be 'the standard and model of excellence in this genre [i.e. narration]'[104] while Thucydides is a 'model historian and the standard of excellence in deliberative oratory'.[105] Just as a canonical writer in the modern sense of the word is perceived to be superior, a *kanōn* is a model of recognisable value. Yet, in so far as they are held up above the rest, the *kanones* are models for the practical purposes of imitation. It is in the context of which works should be read and imitated by would-be-orators that the practice of listing model authors first begins to emerge.[106] The pragmatic context of emulation creates what at first seems to be a critical difference between the ancient and the modern construct of a list of authors. Whereas, as we have seen, the canon in the modern sense of a group of preferred works hints at the trans-historical superiority of the

---

[101] Marchand and Grafton 1997.
[102] Citroni 2005: 209. The ancient text referenced by Citroni is Gellius 19.8.15, discussed p. 65. Pfeiffer 1968: 207 mentions David Ruhnken's 1768 *Historia critica oratorum Graecorum* as the first example of the use of the word canon to mean a selective list; see also Oppel 1937; Nicolai 1992: 251–65; Metzger 1997: 289–93; Rutherford 1999: 3; Hägg 2010.
[103] See Plin. *HN* 34.19.55 *Fecit et quem canona artifices uocant liniamenta artis ex eo petentes ueluti a lege quadam, solusque hominum artem ipsa fecisse artis opere iudicatur*; Stewart 1978.
[104] Dion. Hal. *Lys.* 18.4 ὅρον τε καὶ κανόνα τῆς ἰδέας ταύτης αὐτὸν ἀποφαίνομαι.
[105] Dion. Hal. *Thuc.* 2.22 οἱ κανόνα τῆς ἱστορικῆς πραγματείας ἐκεῖνον ὑποτίθενται τὸν ἄνδρα καὶ τῆς περὶ τοὺς πολιτικοὺς λόγους δεινότητος ὅρον.
[106] See Rutherford 1999. Proto-examples of 'canons' include Dion. Hal. *De imit.* 2, Hermog. *Id.* 2, Quint. *Inst.* 10.1.

selected works of literature, the ancient list is designed to point out the virtues of each model for the purpose of imitation in the context of the training of orators (Quint. *Inst.* 10.1.45 *Sed nunc genera ipsa lectionum, quae praecipue conuenire intendentibus ut oratores fiant existimem, persequor*). Such models are not, however, to be viewed a-critically; rather, the student is invited to improve upon the model, careful to reproduce its virtues but not its faults.[107] In addition to accommodating a certain amount of fluctuation, these lists of proto-*kanones* are not list of works but of writers.

The word *kanōn* begins to be used of a closed list of texts by the early Christians in discussions of the authenticity of specific books. Thus in the early fourth century CE, Eusebius of Caesarea writes of Origen that 'in his first book on Matthew's Gospel, maintaining the Canon of the Church (τὸν ἐκκλησιαστικὸν φυλάττων κανόνα), he testifies that he knows only four Gospels [Matthew, Mark, Luke, John], writing as follows … ' (Euseb. *Hist. eccl.* 6.25.3).[108] In Eusebius, although there is continuity in the deployment of *kanōn* to isolate texts deemed to be endowed with specific virtues, the emphasis has clearly shifted from stylistic and ethical emulation to the process of sanctioning and listing works deemed morally and theologically superior. This meaning is well defined by the fourth century when Augustine and Jerome use *canonicus, -a, -um* of books belonging to a sanctioned body of work, in other words a canon. Augustine explains the origin of the canon thus understood as the Word of God in *The City of God*:

> Hic prius per prophetas, deinde per se ipsum, postea per apostolos, quantum satis esse iudicauit, locutus etiam scripturam condidit, quae canonica nominatur, eminentissimae auctoritatis, cui fidem habemus de his rebus, quas ignorare non expedit nec per nos ipsos nosse idonei sumus. (August. *De civ. D.* 11.3)

> God having spoken first through the prophets, then through himself and finally through the apostles as much as he saw fit, founded scripture of the highest authority which is called 'canonical' through which we believe in these matters which it is not fit to ignore and which we are incapable of knowing by ourselves.[109]

---

[107] Russell 1979.
[108] Metzger 1997: 18.3, in which *The Shepherd* of Hermas is described as not being part of the canon (μὴ ὂν ἐκ τοῦ κανόνος), as the first known instance of this use. Contra Pfeiffer 1968: 207 n. 4.
[109] For Augustine's delineation of the content of the Christian canon see *De doctrina christiana* 2.8.13 which gives the list of the canon (*totus canon scripturarum*).

It is standard to draw a fault line between this Christian usage of the canon as a body of authoritative works and classical lists of *kanones* as well as the later post-humanistic repurposing of the term canon to secular writings.[110] However, it is important to note that these seemingly different canonical formations stand on a well-identifiable continuum: albeit rooted in a different kind of claim about the intrinsic superiority of the work, the modern usage of the word canon retains an emphasis on emulative practices through its appeal to the place of the canonical texts in the ethical formation of readers.[111] Conversely, because of the close connection between style and character (*qualis homo talis oratio*: Cic. *Tusc.* 5.47.9; Sen. *Ep.* 114), the classical *kanones* have an unspoken potential to be used as ethical models from the very beginning.[112] Thus despite the fact that it is often claimed that Christianity has superimposed its own canon-forming gaze onto antiquity, aesthetics and ethics are deeply interwoven in formations of canons from the very beginning.

This complex entanglement of church and text raises a related point about the disciplinary divide at the heart of this narrative. To glance back at the history of what we now call 'classical scholarship', Isaac Casaubon, the renowned sixteenth-century scholar, became famous for disproving the authenticity of the *Corpus hermeticum*, which on the basis of linguistic borrowings from the Septuagint, Plato and the New Testament, he proved to be not the product of its purported date of composition but of the first centuries of the common era.[113] To jump to the nineteenth century, the rise of textual criticism is deeply connected to parallel developments in the study of 'sacred' texts: indeed Karl Lachmann, from whom, rightly or wrongly, the stemmatic method takes its name, edited both the New Testament and 'classical' texts such as Lucretius, as did Richard Bentley before him.[114]

How far back should we trace this disciplinary divide between classical and Christian Latin? The split between pagan and Judaeo-Christian literatures is arguably already encapsulated in Jerome's often-cited dream, where God appears to him and accuses him of being 'a Ciceronian, not a Christian' (*Ciceronianus es, non Christianus*, Jer. *Ep.* 22.30).[115] Echoing Tertullian's memorable question – 'what does Athens have to do with Jerusalem?' (*quid ergo Athenis et Hierosolymis?*, *De praescr.*

---

[110] Kennedy 2001; Citroni 2005.
[111] This point appears under a different guise in recent defences of the values of the humanities, for example, in Allen 2016: 43–9 and Nussbaum 2016. And see p. 50 on the Protestant roots of the secular Great Books courses.
[112] Möller 2004.  [113] Grafton and Weinberg 2011.  [114] Timpanaro 2005.  [115] See Mohr 2007.

*haeret.* 7.1) – Jerome prefaces his narrative of his own renunciation of classics by positing a radical split between classical literature (Horace, Virgil and Cicero) and Christian writings:

> Quid facit cum psalterio Horatius? Cum euangeliis Maro? Cum apostolo Cicero? Nonne scandalizatur frater si te uiderit in idolio recumbentem? Et licet 'omnia munda mundis et nihil reiciendum sit, quod cum gratiarum actione percipitur', tamen simul bibere non debemus calicem Christi et calicem daemoniorum. (Jer. *Ep.* 22.29)

> What has Horace to do with the Psalter, Virgil with the Gospels and Cicero with Paul? Surely a brother is tempted to evil if he sees you reclining at a table in an idol's temple? Although 'unto the pure all things are pure and nothing is to be rejected if it is received with an act of gratitude', still we ought not to drink from the vessel of Christ and the vessel of the devils at the same time.

Of course this uncompromising stance in Jerome's letter, written in 384, is not only belied by his literary practice, in which quotations of and allusions to classical literature abound, but also by later pronouncements. For example his letter 77, written in 398, in response to criticism from the orator Magnus who had accused Jerome of defiling the purity of the church with the filth of the pagans by his frequent quotations of secular literature (*Ep.* 77.2 *cur in opusculis nostris saecularium litterarum interdum ponamus exempla, et candorem Ecclesiae, Ethnicorum sordibus polluamus*), Jerome compares secular wisdom (*sapientia saecularis*) to the beautiful captive woman of *Deuteronomy* 21.35 for whom the law prescribes a ritual of cleansing and mourning before she becomes the wife of her captor. Jerome's desire for the captive secular wisdom is justifiable in that it proliferates the faith and does so by cutting or shaving off whatever pleasure, error and idolatry is hiding in the classical texts.[116]

Almost at the same time, Augustine lays out his programme for Christian learning in *De doctrina Christiana*, written in 396 to address the issue of the teaching of Christianity. In this important manifesto, Augustine operates under a strict dichotomy between 'Roman' and sacred authors: the latter are called canonical authors (*canonici auctores*) and encompass both sacred texts and church fathers. Much of the aim of book 4, devoted to the issue of Christian eloquence, is to show that facility

---

[116] See also *Ep.* 21.13 where the husks being consumed by the prodigal son of Luke 15:11–32 is interpreted allegorically as the consumption of the 'songs of the poets, secular wisdom and the pomp of the words of the rhetors'.

in speech can be acquired by reading and studying the Christian canon (*ecclesiasticae litterae*):

> Nec desunt ecclesiasticae litterae, etiam praeter canonem in auctoritatis arce salubriter collocatum, quas legendo homo capax, etsi id non agat sed tantummodo rebus quae ibi dicuntur intentus sit, etiam eloquio quo dicuntur, dum in his uersatur, imbuitur, accedente uel maxime exercitatione siue scribendi siue dictandi, postremo etiam dicendi, quae secundum pietatis ac fidei regulam sentit. (August. *De doctrina Christiana* 4.9)
>
> There is no shortage of Christian literature, even outside the canon which has been raised to its position of authority for our benefit; and by reading this an able person, even one not seeking to become eloquent but just concentrating on the matters being discussed, can become steeped in their eloquence, especially if this is combined with the practice of writing or dictating, and eventually speaking, what is felt to be in conformity with the rule of holiness and faith. (trans. Green 1995)

While making a case for the stylistic value of Christian literature, Augustine happily quotes and follows Cicero's theory of the three styles and his admonition that the orator be made to master all styles. After giving numerous positive examples of the different styles from both scripture and church fathers, Augustine concludes by calling for an acknowledgement of the eloquence of 'our canonical authors and teachers'.[117] This radical distinction between secular and ecclesiastical was codified in the sixth century in Cassiodorus' *Institutiones diuinarum et saecularium litterarum*, a treatise on Christian education in two books, the first on scripture and the works of Christian fathers and the second one on the secular liberal arts. Originally designed for use in the Vivarium, a monastic community he founded in his own family estate in Calabria, the book, variously excerpted and copied, was to be foundational in the Middle Ages.[118]

The church fathers' radical and self-conscious split between secular antiquity and Christian writing anticipates the disciplinary divide between Classics and theology but only to an extent. The modern secularisation of education and the loss of biblical knowledge have catalysed a contraction of the canon of Latin works taught and researched in Classics departments to works of the pagan era which, though more distant in time, are paradoxically more 'legible' to the modern secular reader, in so far as they are not

---

[117] 4.60 *canonicos nostros auctores doctoresque*. That said, Augustine's relationship with the classics is no less rich and complex than Jerome's: see Shanzer 2012 and MacCormack 1998.
[118] See the *Dialogus super auctores sacros et prophanos* of the twelfth-century monk Conrad of Hirsau for a mediaeval version of this genre in which sacred and profane authors are studied side by side.

imbued in a religious ideology that many do not consider relevant. To the extent that late antique literature has a place in the classicist canon, it tends to be approached in relation to its translation and adaptation of pagan antiquity. Despite its importance, this work privileges Christian learned poets like Prudentius, Ausonius and Claudian, while Patristics scholars focus on the study of the contemporary writings by the Early Church Fathers.[119] To some extent, this disciplinary divide inscribes a modern distinction between secular and religious onto antiquity, by relegating the study of the supposedly secular pursuit of 'literature' to the late antique scholars trained in the classical tradition, while reserving the early Christian theology for the theologians.[120] There are obvious pitfalls to this *modus operandi*: on the one hand, for some time now, scholars have focused our attention on the pivotal role played by secular fields such as, for example, grammar, in the development of Christian textuality.[121] In turn, as we shall see in a moment, this work is a reminder that the creation of the classical past is unthinkable outside of the mediation of 'Christian' sources. In short, in approaching late antiquity we should be wary of modes of interpretation which, in Debora Shuger's words from her study of the Renaissance bible, frame religion as a 'separable "layer" atop the surface of [secular] culture'; rather it is best to approach all forms of knowledge in this period as the result of complex syntheses of religious and secular discourses.[122]

Moreover, the modern marginalisation of the late antique Latin corpus affects not just Christian texts that do not fit the definition of secular literature but also contemporary works written by pagan authors or by authors whose religious stance is difficult to ascertain, as for example is the case for Martianus Capella and Macrobius. Such a dichotomy either inhibits the study of tralaticious corpora (e.g. commentaries) or else generates scholarship aimed at disentangling historical kernels rather than situating the work as a whole.[123] An interesting and complex example of this phenomenon is the *Anthologia Latina*, a compilation of Latin poems (elegies, epigrams, inscriptions, centos and other genres) assembled starting in the Renaissance with Scaliger on the basis of early mediaeval anthologies – principally the *Codex Salmasianus* (Paris lat. 10318,

---

[119] See Elsner 2004 for a discussion of the problems involved in the parallel split between 'pagan' and Christian art in late antiquity.
[120] See Pelttari 2014 for a revisionary approach to Christianity and classical antiquity in late antique poetry.
[121] Chin 2008.    [122] Shuger 1994: 193.
[123] See the helpful remarks in relation to the early scholia to Persius in Zetzel 2005.

eighth–ninth century) and the *Codex Thuaneus* (Paris lat. 8071, ninth century).[124] The collection in the *Codex Salmasianus*, which furnishes the bulk of the modern *Anthologia Latina* edited by Riese and others, originated in Vandal North Africa of the sixth century but it contains earlier material, as, for example, three epigrams attributed to the younger Seneca. The *Salmasianus* and the *Thuaneus* preserve three epigrams under the name of Seneca (*Anth. Lat.* 224, 228, 229 Shackleton Bailey), two of which are also found without any ascription in the *Codex Vossianus*, where they are followed by another sixty-nine poems. No name is attached to these epigrams, but on account of the similarity in style and content, editors have created a collection of (pseudo-)Senecan exile poetry.[125] Yet the *Codex Salmasianus* can also be approached in its own right as a witness to Virgil's reception in the scholastic environment of late antique Vandal Carthage in which earlier specimens of Virgilian pastiches such as the *Medea* of Hosidius Geta (end of the second/early third century CE) or the *Pervigilium Veneris* (of disputed date) co-exist with more recent ones.[126]

It may therefore be argued that the disciplinary divide between Classics and theology leaves much to be desired in terms of our ability to comprehend both the intellectual milieu from which the literary works of late antiquity – be their authors pagan or Christian – originated, and by extension the very corpus of texts which we comfortably group under the umbrella of the 'classical tradition'. To give one example, the *Saturnalia* of Macrobius is now thought of as the product, not of the late fourth century, as previously assumed, but of the early fifth – Cameron identified the author of this work with Macrobius Ambrosius Theodosius, praetorian prefect in 431 CE.[127] In Cameron's dating of the *Saturnalia* to 431, after the establishment of Christianity as the religion of the empire and twenty or so years after the sack of Rome in 410, it is almost impossible to maintain that Macrobius was *not* a Christian. Yet, in so far as the work makes no mention of Christianity and is set some fifty years prior to its date of composition during the Saturnalian feast of 382 or 383, on the eve of Gratian's abolishment of pagan cults in 382, it has been standard to approach the dialogue as a source for Virgilian scholarship of the earlier first and second century. Whose hermeneutics does the discussion of Virgilian

---

[124] Tarrant 1983.    [125] Holzberg 2004.
[126] Tandoi 1984: 199–201 and Kay 2013: 7–13. On Hosidius' *Medea* see Rondholz 2012; for the *Pervigilium Veneris* see Barton 2018. An analogous case study is represented by the *Epigrammata Bobiensia*, a collection compiled in the end of the fourth and early fifth century CE but which some believe include earlier materials, as for example poems by the Augustan Domitius Marsus (39, 40 = Courtney 1993: #8, 9) and the *Fabella Sulpiciae* (37), supposedly written by the Domitianic Sulpicia mentioned by Martial (10.38). On the anthology in Latin literature see Vardi 2000.
[127] Cameron 2011: 231–72.

poetry, which occupies books 3 to 6, reflect? That of the pagan elites of the characters in the dialogue, such as Quintus Aurelius Symmachus, one of the dialogue's main characters, a successful orator, statesman and leader of the unsuccessful protest against Gratian's removal of the Altar of Victory? Or that of the early imperial sources? Or of Macrobius' own Christian readers? Take, for example, Macrobius' much contested approach to Virgil as a sacred shrine, in which Praetextatus lays the ground for the exegetical discussion of the poet that follows:[128]

> Sed nos, quos crassa Minerua dedecet, non patiamur abstrusa esse adyta sacri poematis, sed archanorum sensuum investigato aditu doctorum cultu celebranda praebeamus reclusa penetralia. (Macrob. *Sat.* 1.24.13)
>
> But we, for whom a crass Minerva is unseemly, should not allow the inner places of this sacred poem to be concealed, but having examined the approaches to its hidden meanings, let us throw open its inmost shrine to be filled by the worship of the learned.

The image of commentary here deployed is spatial: interpretation is compared to an entrance into the inner space of a sanctuary (*adyta*) and hermeneutics to opening up a sacred shrine. It may be that in Cameron's words we should resist the notion that Macrobius 'saw Vergil as a sacred text, from which he planned to extract arcane religious truths'.[129] One could easily trace this language earlier on, to, for example, Tacitus' portrayal of the inner shrines of *eloquentia*.[130] A similar question arises about Virgil's divine status. The earlier attestation of the title *diuinus* for Virgil is in *Catalepton* 15, a book of pseudo-Virgilian *iuuenilia* generally dated to the first century CE. In presenting the preceding collection, the poem acts like a *sphragis* of sorts, stating that 'these too are the first beginnings of that divine poet' (*Catal.* 15.3 *illius haec quoque sunt diuini elementa poetae*). Yet when this title is repurposed in the Servian commentaries, how are we to interpret the statement that 'the divine poet always touches on the truth, even when he is engaged in some other matter' (*unde apparet diuinum poetam aliud agentem uerum semper attingere*, Serv. Dan. 3.349)? Is the commentary's approach to Virgil as 'all full of knowledge' (*totus quidem Vergilius scientia plenus est*, Serv. *ad Aen.* 6 praef.) harkening back to classical antiquity or forward to Christian allegoresis?[131] Servius, whose

---

[128] Pelttari 2014: 32–43.  [129] Cameron 2011: 589.
[130] For Macrob. *Sat.* 1.24.13 compare for example Tac. *Dial.* 12.2 *sed secedit animus in loca pura atque innocentia fruiturque sedibus sacris. haec eloquentiae primordia, haec penetralia.*
[131] The problem is compounded by the fact that the notice about the divinity of Virgil is found not in Servius, but in DS or Servius auctus ('expanded Servius'), the name traditionally given to the

commentary on Virgil probably predates the sack of Rome of 410, and who is also a character in Macrobius' *Saturnalia*, makes liberal use of allegory, a tool developed in classical antiquity but also associated with religious exegesis, both Christian and Jewish.[132] Yet it is surely confining to read 'sacred' as reflecting exclusively a supposedly hidden Christian religious agenda.[133] Rather, the question to ask is how Macrobius' or Servius' repurposing of the earlier language of the sacrality of poetry might resonate with his readership, Christian and otherwise – how in effect the religious experience of reading communities both leverages earlier representation of Virgilian and Homeric omniscience and reshapes them.

Finally, the chief disciplinary tools we use in our fields and those without which the classical tradition is materially unthinkable – the commentary, the textual edition and translation – were developed in the context of the exegesis of scripture, which was in itself read in dialogue with classical texts.[134] Many of our Graeco-Roman sources are known exclusively or almost exclusively through indirect tradition and transmitted in much later sources which have their own ethics of quotation.[135] The Latin canon presents distinctive challenges in this respect: whereas papyri, mostly from Egypt, have yielded a vast quantity of fragments from Greek literature, the vast majority of fragments of Latin literature survive as quotations.[136] Thus late antique grammatical and exegetical sources played a pivotal role in the transmission of republican literature.[137] In other cases, the mediation of Christian writers was instrumental in the survival and inseparable from the transmission of a given work: in the case of Cicero's *Topica*, for example, the text survives largely accompanied by a commentary on the text by Boethius written around 500 CE. The Boethian commentary rivalled in popularity the Ciceronian original, the

---

seventh- or eighth-century compilation of the Servian commentary. This version has long been thought to incorporate materials from an earlier commentary, probably by Servius' teacher Aelius Donatus. See Stok 2012.

[132] On Servius and allegory see Jones 1961. For a later Christian allegorical reading of the *Aeneid* see, for example, Fulgentius' development of allegorical readings of Virgil in the *Expositio Vergilianae continentiae* dated to the fifth century. Here the poet Virgil himself explains to Fulgentius that 'in each book of the poem, he introduced material of an allegorical nature, so as to display the entire course of human life in the twelve individual books' (*Exp. Verg.* 86–7).

[133] See the subtle arguments developed in relation to Macrobius in Conybeare 2020.

[134] Lössl and Watt 2011; Niehoff 2012.   [135] See, for example, O'Donnell 1980.

[136] Notable exceptions are the Gallus papyrus from Qasr Ibrim and fragment of the *Carmen de bello Actiaco* from Herculaneum (*PHerc.* 817).

[137] For example Nonius Marcellus, *De compendiosa doctrina*, to whom we owe the preservation of most of the fragments of republican literature, the commentaries on Horace by Acro and Porphyrio and those on Virgil by Aelius Donatus and Servius.

tradition of which it contaminated throughout the Middle Ages.[138] In a sense, therefore, the distinctions between scriptural and profane, classical and late, though in principle correct, threaten to foreclose a deeper conversation about the shaping of texts in the context of tradition, reading and interpretation.

### The Latin Canon: a Brief History

The canon of Latin literature is far from a straightforward entity. As we are about to see, its two constitutive elements – Latin and literature – are both subject to negotiation. On the most straightforward interpretation, a Latin canon would include only texts written in the Latin language. Yet, 'Latin' is a highly problematic term and susceptible to a variety of readings, depending upon which highly different canonical formations might be construed or imagined. The traditional and most conservative version of the canon of Latin literature begins with Livius Andronicus, Naevius and Ennius and ends with Tacitus and Juvenal and the authors of the 'High Empire', namely Apuleius, Aulus Gellius, Fronto and the *poetae nouelli* of the Antonine Age.[139] This structure is already present in Friedrich Leo's pioneering *Geschichte der römischen Literatur*, published in Berlin in 1913, and by many considered the founding text of Roman literary studies.[140] Although Leo died after the publication of the first instalment ('Die archaische Literatur') and the project was never completed, one can get a glimpse of its ambition from the treatment of Latin literature in Wilamowitz-Moellendorff's *Die griechische und lateinische Literatur und Sprache*, published in Hinneberg's *Kultur der Gegenwart*, a massive multi-volume history of world culture which came out between 1905 and 1926. There 'Die lateinische Literatur und Sprache' ('Latin literature and language') is divided into three sections: one, written by Franz Skutsch, on the history of the Latin language; one, authored by Leo, on Latin literature of antiquity; and one, written by Eduard Norden, on Latin literature in the transition from antiquity to the Middle Ages. Norden's treatment of the transitional period, which partially overlaps with Leo's, examines

---

[138] Reinhardt 2003: 73–96.
[139] Such is the chronological scope of, for example, Harrison 2005: 2 'the beginning of Christian literature about AD 200 with Tertullian and Minucius Felix is a major watershed... as a result the volume reflects the range of Latin literature commonly taught in universities'. Fantham 1996 has the same chronological limits with a deeper interest in literary culture as opposed to high literary genres in verse. The *Oxford Latin Dictionary* controversially made 200 CE its cut-off point, though with exceptions: Goodyear 1983.
[140] Gianotti 2003; Barchiesi 2002.

the development of literature from the mid-fourth century, the time of *ecclesia triumphans*, to the reconstitution of the Roman empire under Charlemagne but is careful to acknowledge that this history is partial and does not address church history (p. 484). Leo's treatment of Latin literature is chronologically arranged in three main periods: republican, Augustan and imperial, though the first section is almost equal in length to the sum of the last two. The rationale for this choice is made explicit in the beginning of the section on imperial literature: after Augustus, the Romans did not produce any literature of equal value; among the post-Augustan poets, there are some great names, also some with considerable talent but no great poets ('sind große Namen, auch beträchtliche Talente, aber keine großen Dichter', p. 454). While this history of Latin literature follows the seemingly self-evident contours of chronology, Leo's emphasis on Rome as the spiritual link ('das geistige Band der alten und neuen Weltkultur', Leo 1913: 1) between the old (Greece) and the new (Christian Europe) tailors a specific approach to Latin canon, one that privileges acts of transference and adaptations (hence Leo's intense focus on the earlier phases of Roman literature). The decadence of Roman literature is explained as the by-product of the rise of rhetoric and the metamorphosis of poetry into rhetorical art ('rhetorische Kunst'). Seneca, Juvenal, Martial and Tacitus are the highlights of this age, while Lucan and Statius are among the considerably talented but their work is dismissed within a few words. In regards to Statius, the *Thebaid* is praised as lacking 'neither power nor impetus' (p. 459) but neither the *Siluae* nor the *Achilleid* find any mention. The literature of the later empire includes the archaising movement of the Hadrianic era which with its backward-looking glance is said to have led to the collapse of Roman literature and the rise of the provinces and the lower classes, with Africa being singled out as the cradle of the novel (Apuleius) and of the first translations of the Bible (Tertullian, Augustine, etc.). There is a brief mention of Christian poetry and the section on antiquity ends paradigmatically with a treatment of Boethius' *De consolatione philosophiae*, a prison dialogue replete with classical learning and written as its author, born shortly after the deposition of the last Roman emperor, awaited execution by the Ostrogothic king Theoderic. Later to become one of the most popular works of the Middle Ages, in Leo's survey of Latin literature the *De consolatione philosophiae* comes to epitomise the end as well as the enduring legacy of Roman antiquity.

## 2  Canons

In order to understand Leo's selective focus and chronological limiting of Roman literature to the fall of the Roman empire, it is helpful to glance at earlier stages in the development of the study of antiquity. Leo's approach to the question of the originality of Latin letters was in many ways a response to German philhellenism which, starting with Winckelmann in the late eighteenth century, had elevated the Greeks and disparaged the Romans as mere imitators. And yet philhellenism in its complex relation to nationalism is in many ways responsible for the birth of Latin literary history. For it was Friedrich August Wolf, the father of *Altertumswissenschaft*, who authored the first history of Roman literature in parallel with the founding of the *seminarium philologicum* in Halle in 1787.[141] Wolf's 'History of Roman literature' is arranged in two parts. The first is a survey of known authors arranged under the names of rulers and emperors. The second is a history of the genres of Roman literature: poetry (dramatic, epic and lyric) and prose (historiography, eloquence, erudition), which surveys relevant authors in chronological order.[142] This dazzling work, which still repays reading, begins with a theoretical discussion of literary history defined as 'the coherent narrative of the fortunes of the scientific and learned enlightenment of a people' ('eine zusammenhängende Erzählung von den Schicksalen der wissenschaftlichen und gelehrten Aufklärung einer Nation', Wolf 1834: 3). This literary history is not a collection of facts but a narrative with a story to tell about the rise and fall of a nation. The canon therein constructed is thus subservient both to this narrative as a whole and to the operative concept of people: hence, for Wolf the chronological limit of Roman literary history is the deposition of Romulus Augustulus in 476 (p. 94), though some of the authors mentioned in the second part are later (e.g. Isidore and Beda). Authors writing between the demise of Latin knowledge in the sixth and its renaissance in the fifteenth century are listed in a separate appendix. Secondly, a clear connection is made between political and literary decline: the period that goes from Hadrian to the sack of Rome witnesses at once the crumbling of state institutions and the demise of literature.[143]

In order to appreciate the ideological thrust of Wolf's narrative, it is useful to compare it to that of his model (see p. 8), the *Bibliotheca Latina* of the seventeenth-century polymath Johann Fabricius published in

---

[141] Wolf 1787, more easily found as Wolf 1834.
[142] This tension between biography and genres is already at work in antiquity: besides Callimachus' *Pinakes* discussed p. 64, see Accius, *Didascalica* fr. 13 Morel; Varro and Suetonius, *De poetis*.
[143] Wolf 1834: 94 'So wie der römische Staat kränkelte, so geht es auch mit der Litteratur, Vortrag und Sprache.'

Hamburg in 1697, the most comprehensive bibliographical work of its generation which lists all known authors of the classical period as well as editions and translations, and gives a critical discussion of each work. This original edition of the *Bibliotheca* begins with Plautus and Cato the Elder, includes late antique writers like Macrobius, Claudian and Symmachus, and ends with Boethius and his younger contemporary and successor Cassiodorus. An appendix follows containing a list of fragmentary poets (beginning with Ennius), a list of Christian poets and one of ecclesiastical writers – his principal stated aim being that of providing an overview in chronological order of the totality of Latin authors, the ancient ones but not the ecclesiastics (*latinos autores veteres non ecclesiasticos, quorum scripta aetatem tulerunt, recenserem universos ordine chronologico*, Fabricius 1697: 3). The rationale given is primarily pragmatic rather than ideological – there are many editions of ecclesiastic writers available to those who are interested in this area of study such as for example Cardinal Bellarmino, *De scriptoribus ecclesiasticis* (1613).[144]

Even if we chronologically restrict the focus of study, the canon of Roman literature includes on most definitions at least some works not written in Latin: the earliest Roman historians, the annalists Fabius Pictor and Cincius Alimentus in the second century BCE, wrote in Greek. Historians of Rome also contend with the fact that Roman history written by provincial Roman elite continues to be written in Greek: to name just two notable examples, in the early second century CE, Plutarch of Chaeronea, a Roman citizen, wrote in Greek the *Parallel Lives*, a comparison of Greek and Roman history, as did Cassius Dio, a Roman senator from Bithynia who wrote a work of Roman history in Greek in the early third century CE.[145] The slippage here is due to the fact that 'Roman' denotes a political identity, shared by speakers and writers of several languages including, but not limited to, Greek and Latin (see Goldhill, Chapter 16 in this volume).[146] Latin, however, need not imply Roman: in fact, Ennius, a speaker of Greek, Latin and Oscan, only received Roman

---

[144] Fabricius 1697: 53–4: *ecclesiasticos scriptores huic bibliothecae inserere non est nostri instituti. Versantur in minibus omnium quae in illo genere utiliter literis consignantur*. Indeed, Fabricius published a separate *Bibliotheca ecclesiastica*, which begins from Jerome, in 1718. The most famous and widely circulated edition of Fabricius' *Bibliotheca Latina* was published by Johann August Ernesti (Lipsiae, 1773–4). This three-volume work reconfigured Fabricius' work to exclude the whole of *Latinitas Christiana* to a separate volume (hence the work lacks the appendix on Christian poets and excludes Boethius and other Christian writers originally included in the first edition).
[145] On Plutarch's Roman identity see Preston 2001.
[146] Josephus, who received Roman citizenship from Vespasian, wrote both in Greek and in Aramaic: Cotton and Eck 2005.

citizenship through Marcus Fulvius Nobilior in 184 BCE; Terence, whose cognomen was *Afer* ('the African'), was allegedly born in Carthage (Suet. *Vita Ter.* 1), enslaved and brought to Rome to the home of the senator Terentius Lucanus in the 160s BCE. Thus one might question to what extent other literature written in Greek from later periods might or should also have a place in a history of Roman literature: a notable case study in this category might be the epigrams written by Greek poets for Roman patrons, like Antipater of Thessalonica's poems for and about Lucius Calpurnius Piso, which would have been collected in the *Garland of Philip*, an anthology of first-century-BCE epigrams compiled some time before the death of Nero and now transmitted in the *Greek Anthology*, and other writings in Greek by literati belonging to the same circle (e.g. the works of Philodemus, the remains of which were found in a villa in Herculaneum which supposedly belonged to Lucius Calpurnius Piso's father, the consul of 58 BCE, and Parthenius of Nicaea, whose *Erotika pathemata* is dedicated to Cornelius Gallus and may have been influential with the neoterics and elegists).[147] Other influential works in the study of Roman literature and history, such as the *Res gestae*, exist in multiple parallel versions (Greek and Latin) recovered from the edges of the empire (Ancyra, Antioch and Apollonia).

As scholars become more interested in and aware of the hybridity of literary traditions in the imperial period, this sub-canon of Greek/Roman/Latin works is bound to increase in size and challenge long-standing assumptions about literary interactions in the period.[148] To push the issue further, if one were to renounce, or at least resist, the notion of 'Greek' and 'Roman' as self-contained concepts, one might construct far different canons, ones based, for example, on genres or provincial and local identities. Hence studies of the novel have already created hybrid canons, consisting of works in Latin such as Petronius' *Satyricon* or Apuleius' *Metamorphoses*, which presents itself as derived from a Greek original (1.1 *fabulam Graecanicam*), in Greek (Chariton, Achilles Tatius, Longus and Heliodorus) as well as texts that appear in multiple redactions (e.g. the *Alexander Romance*, which survives in Greek and Latin, as well as Syriac and Arabic) or Latin texts that purport to be translations of Greek originals (e.g. *Ephemeris belli Troiani* of Dictys of Crete or the *Historia Apollonii*

---

[147] Whitmarsh 2013: 137–50 and Gow and Page 1968.
[148] See the arguments about whether the later Greek epic writers such as Quintus of Smyrna or Nonnus of Panopolis knew and read Virgil or Ovid, or whether Pliny and Tacitus knew Plutarch: König, Langlands and Uden 2020 on the second century CE.

*regis*).¹⁴⁹ Local identity, whether that is understood to refer to authors or readers, might also be deployed as an organising principle to generate alternative canonical formations.¹⁵⁰ Scholars have long remarked upon the Spanish school of the Senecas, Lucan, Martial and Quintilian or that of North Africa exemplified by Apuleius, Fronto and the Christian apologetics of the second to third centuries like Tertullian, Cyprian and Minucius Felix, as well as Claudian and most notably Augustine¹⁵¹ – though less obvious might be the ways in which the local affiliations of authors might interplay with displaced audiences of provincial readers in the various peripheries of the empire.¹⁵²

Moreover, one's definition of 'literature' inevitably yields a different picture of the canon. The canon of eighteenth- and nineteenth-century literary history is structurally centred on the high genres of poetry, the apex of which marks the high period of Roman literature. By contrast a history of Latin literature centred on a canon of Latin legal writings would begin with the law of the Twelve Tables and the fragmentary remains of its early commentators, such as Sextus Aelius in the second century BCE, and extend all the way through the high classical period of Roman law in the second century CE with the works of Salvius Iulianus, commissioned in 131 CE by the emperor Hadrian to edit the Praetor's edict, Ulpian, Gaius, the author of the *Institutiones*, and Sextus Pomponius, stretching all the way into the sixth century and culminating with the *Corpus iuris ciuilis*, a magnificent compilatory work of known Roman law commissioned by the emperor Justinian in 527 CE and a source for many earlier legal sources. Conversely, a canon of Latin grammatical writings would yield a different picture altogether, beginning as Zetzel's guide does, in the second century BCE with exegetical work on Ennius and Plautus by Lampadio, Aelius Stilo, Volcacius Sedigitus and others, moving to Varro in the mid-first century BCE and to the archaist movement, and culminating with the 'classical era of Roman philology' – the centuries between the fourth and the sixth bookended by the commentaries and grammatical works of Marius Victorinus, Aelius Donatus and Servius (end of fourth–early fifth century CE) to Priscian, Boethius, Cassiodorus in the sixth century and

---

[149] That is not to say that these texts, which, with the exception of the *Satyricon*, are set for the most part not in Rome but in exotic peripheries (Egypt, Ethiopia, Babylonia, etc.), cannot tell a story about imperial Roman culture: see Connors 2008.
[150] Barchiesi 2005.
[151] Whether one can create a case for a coherent 'Latin Africanism', the appreciation of the African context may extend to analysis of non-Latin literary background, reception and audience: see the essays in Lee, Finkelpearl and Graverini 2014.
[152] Woolf 2003 with discussion of Martial 12.1; Citroni 1995.

Isidore in the early seventh century, whose massive *Etymologiae* is both a compendium of earlier pagan grammatical work and often considered a watershed between late antique and mediaeval grammar.[153] As social and cultural history become accepted components of literary study, not only the boundaries of the canon are likely to shift but also the narratives of its development. As we have just observed in the cases of the legal and grammatical corpora, historical moments considered to mark peaks and declines in the narrative of the high literary canon – the classicism of the age of Augustus, the silver age of the Neronian and Flavian age, etc. – do not appear to constitute significant shifts in these other canonical formations. Additionally, one must also guard against the tendency to construct chronological narratives of literary development loosely based on the succession of genres. Thus few would agree today with the view of post-Ovidian literature as the 'age of rhetoric' or with late antiquity as the 'age of technical knowledge', labels that prioritise poetry and some genres of prose (historiography, Ciceronian oratory, etc.), while all the while eliding from view both the long history of rhetoric in Rome beginning in the second century BCE and the development of poetic genres in late antiquity (to name just two phenomena).[154]

It is important to note that while the ancient hierarchy of genres certainly informs the discourse of canon, it is not coincidental with it. Thus authors whose works occupy a low place in the hierarchy of genres have at times occupied an important place in the canon. Statius and Lucan were immensely popular in the Middle Ages with hundreds of surviving copies but were marginal at best throughout the twentieth century, a fact memorably acknowledged by Statius' Oxford editor when he stated that 'there is such an abundance of manuscripts of the *Thebaid* that one rightly suspects that Statius had more copyists during the Middle Ages than readers in our time'.[155] The hazards of survival are sometimes responsible for changes to the canon: Catullus was lost in the Middle Ages and only came to light around 1300 in Verona. Lucretius was largely unknown until Poggio Bracciolini's discovery of a manuscript in 1417 during the Council

---

[153] See the remarks in Zetzel 2018: 201 and Copeland and Sluiter 2009: 62–71.
[154] Kenney and Clausen 1982: 1 but also Curtius 1953: 145–66.
[155] Garrod 1906: v. For a comparable shift in fortunes compare, for example, Martial's popularity during Humanism (Sullivan 2005: 262–300). Within the corpus of even the most canonical author, different works may at times be less canonical than others: see Kennedy 2002 on the circulation and reception of Cicero's letters (*Ad familiares*) and rhetorical works (*De oratore*) in relation to his speeches.

of Constance, from which point it arguably shaped not just the Renaissance's reception of antiquity but the very concept of modernity. A re-dating of an author can also engineer a turn in the fortune of their text: rediscovered by Petrarch in 1360, the *Eclogues* of Calpurnius Siculus were considered contemporary to the poems of Nemesianus, whose work is transmitted in the same manuscript and who was then identified with the third-century-CE author of the *Cynegetica*. Since 1854, when Moritz Haupt redated the Calpurnian eclogues to the Neronian period, Calpurnius has frequently appeared in literary surveys of the Neronian age, despite the challenges mounted to Haupt's arguments by Champlin and others.[156] In turn, while in contemporary discourse, the canon refers to the list of works studied and perhaps researched in schools and universities, at a time when Latin was widely spoken and read, the school canon was not necessarily coincidental with that comprised of works privately read, let alone translated.[157] Some texts barely known to specialists today were immensely popular and have complex manuscript traditions that defy neat divisions between antiquity and the Middle Ages: these include epitomators of the Roman historians such as Justinus, the epitomator of Pompeius Trogus, 'a household name' through the Middle Ages, and Eutropius, whose *Breviarium* was reworked by Paulus Diaconus in the eighth century and by Landolfus Sagax in the tenth.[158] In this class also belong the *Distichs of Cato*, a moralising work from late antiquity attributed to Cato the Elder, which was a wildly popular school text and translated already into Old English as early as the twelfth century. Finally, one must not forget that literature is in itself a relatively recent invention. To give just one example, in Oxford from its establishment in 1800 to 1972, the course of study known as Literae Humaniores – the ancestor of today's Classics degrees – was largely dominated by history and philosophy with Latin and Greek being tested through prose composition and unprepared translation.[159] If anecdotes are at all effective at conveying the lived reality of the canon, when glancing at nineteenth-century autobiographies one is struck by the frequent mentions of history and antiquarianism at the expense of what we may today identify as canonical authors. Henry Fynes Clinton, a member of Parliament and a classical scholar who studied in Oxford between 1799 and 1806, left a rich autobiography. In it he writes that when he was in school, he read 'Virgil,

---

[156] See Henderson 2013; Karakasis 2016. Against the Neronian dating see Champlin 1978 and Horsfall 1997.
[157] Hall 2008b.   [158] Reynolds 1983a: 197.   [159] Stray 2018: 31–52.

except the Georgics; almost the whole of Horace, the Gallic War of Caesar; Sallust, and the Catilinarian orations of Cicero'.[160] By the time he left Oxford, 'except the orations, read at Southwell [school], I had not studied any parts of the works of Cicero. I was ignorant of Quintilian, and Tacitus, and Pliny. I had twice perused Livy with attention.'[161]

## Conclusion

Moving between a focus on the *physical* limits of the canon across time and a review of the canon's impact as a critical mechanism, we have discussed the ways in which the very discourse of the canon has traditionally influenced scholarly approaches in the field of Latin literature and Classics broadly understood. Emphasis has been placed on the ways in which the canonised nature of the classics determines not just a hierarchy of texts and methodologies worthier of being taught and researched but also informs the very approach to non-canonical or 'para-canonical' texts. The canon in other words is not just about *what* we study, it is also about *how* we study it. Interrogating the canon of Latin texts implies a fundamental repositioning of one's scholarly stance not just towards non-canonical texts but also towards canonical authors, whose primacy should be scrutinised.

No one will dispute that the Latin canon, both in its internal structure and as a mechanism for organising knowledge, has come under intense scrutiny. But what kind of philology can we imagine outside of the discourse of the canon? And how, if at all, will the study and theoretical framing of so-called 'marginal texts' change the discipline?[162] It is critical that we modify not only our academic cores and scholarly foci to include a wider complement of texts, ancient and post-classical, but also that we change the frame of reference within which marginal texts are typically considered. This shift will involve in the first instance an awareness that the marginal status of such texts cannot be elided from any story we tell about them. We cannot apprehend marginal texts in spite of themselves and outside of the rhetoric both ancient and modern that has constituted them and at times relegated them to the periphery. Protestations of poetic incompetence, inferiority and epigonality are a trope in 'minor' texts but one that we would be well advised to resist. Statius' famous wish expressed at the end of the *Thebaid* that his poem 'not challenge (*ne tempta*) the divine *Aeneid* but rather follow it from a distance (*longe sequere*) and ever worship its footsteps' (*Theb.* 12.816–17) embodies both the canonical hold

---

[160] Clinton 1854: 5.   [161] Clinton 1854: 22.   [162] Questions raised in Formisano 2018.

of the Virgilian epic and the self-proclaimed inferiority of his successors.[163] Yet, as Philip Hardie notes, it also 'sanctifies' the canon into which the poet seeks admission in the near future: 'even if Statius advises his poem for the present to follow at a distance, the future holds *honores* that might well be those of a god'.[164] Moreover, scholars of post-Virgilian epic have pointed to the ways in which the self-conscious epigonality of texts and authors functions alternatively as a cover for critiques of their predecessor (Ganiban 2007) or as a productive mechanism for exploring a new balance between periphery and centre in the changed political environment of the Flavian era (Augoustakis 2010).

We may choose to study this discourse of canon and margin diachronically and effectively historicise the canon, not simply tracking items that have dropped in and out of it, but above all examining its changing function in history, its connection to forms of institutionalised knowledge (the Hellenistic library, the German university, etc.) and how canonical formations develop side by side with other social and intellectual structures. Or perhaps marginal texts will lead to a renewal of the discipline if we can frame marginality not as a list of physical objects (minor texts) or as a physical 'no go space' that needs to be rescued into the centre but as a *modus operandi*. In proposing marginality as a 'way of doing business', I have been inspired by the possibility of looking at the margin (or marginalisation) as a process rather than as object. One of the most acute contemporary readers of the western margin, the subaltern and the other, feminist and cultural critic Gayatri Spivak, once wrote that instead of pointing the accusing finger at the centre, we would do better to use ourselves 'as a shuttle between the centre (inside) and the margin (outside) and thus narrate a displacement' (Spivak 1987: 146). A new ethics of the periphery, as one might call it, would leverage the liminality of non-canonical texts to interrogate the ideological pressures that shape practices of reading in and out of the canon and to engage with and document processes that led to the marginalisation or exclusion of different texts at different moments by different readers. It is this ability to conceive of bold 'narratives of displacement' between canon and margin rather than reproduce new descriptions of the margins according to old narrative patterns that will ultimately open up a new way to imagine the literary space of antiquity.

---

[163] Cf. Silius' worshipping of the tombs of Virgil and Cicero as narrated in Plin. *Ep.* 3.7.
[164] Hardie 1993: 111.

## References

Adler, E. (2020) *The Battle of the Classics: How a Nineteenth-Century Debate Can Save the Humanities Today*, New York and Oxford.
Allen, D. (2016) *Education and Equality*, Chicago.
Amin, S. (2011) *Eurocentrism: Modernity, Religion, and Democracy*, New York.
Appiah, K. A. (2009) 'Whose culture is it?', in J. Cuomo, ed., *Whose Culture: The Promise of Museums and the Debate over Antiquities* (Princeton), 71–86.
Apter, E. S. (2013) *Against World Literature: On the Politics of Untranslatability*, London.
Arnold, M. (1869) *Culture and Anarchy: An Essay in Political and Social Criticism*, London.
　(1895) 'The function of criticism at the present time', in Arnold and Pater 1895, 3–86.
Arnold, M. and W. Pater (1895) *The Function of Criticism at the Present Time and An Essay on Style*, New York and London.
Augoustakis, A. (2010) *Motherhood and the Other: Fashioning Female Power in Flavian Epic*, Oxford.
Barbantani, S. (1993) 'I poeti lirici del canone alessandrino nell'epigrammatistica', *Aevum(ant)* 6: 5–97.
Barnard, H. L. (2017) *Empire of Ruin: Black Classicism and American Imperial Culture*, Oxford.
Barchiesi, A. (2002) Review of *Von Göttern und Menschen erzählen. Formkonstanzen und Funktionswandel vormoderner Epik. Potsdamer Altertumswissenschaftliche Beiträge* (ed. P. Barceló, P. Riemer, J. Rüpke, and J. Scheid), *BMCRev* 2002.06.26.
　(2005) 'Centre and periphery', in Harrison 2005, 394–405.
Barthes, R. (1989) *The Rustle of Language*, Berkeley.
Barton, W. M. (2018) *The Pervigilium Veneris: A New Critical Text, Translation and Commentary*, London and New York.
Battistoni, F. (2006) 'The ancient *pinakes* from Tauromenion: some new readings', *ZPE* 157: 169–80.
Bell, D. (2011) *The Reforming of General Education: The Columbia Experience in its National Setting*, New Brunswick and London.
Bloom, H. (1995) *The Western Canon: The Books and School of the Ages*, Orlando.
Blum, R. (1991) *Kallimachos: The Alexandrian Library and the Origins of Bibliography*, Madison, WI.
Bond, S. (2018) 'What is "the West"? Addressing the controversy over HUM110 at Reed College', *Society for Classical Study Blog*, https://classicalstudies.org/scs-blog/sarah-bond/blog-what-west-addressing-controversy-over-hum110-reed-college, accessed 6 June 2019.
Bourdieu, P. (1993) *The Field of Cultural Production: Essays on Art and Literature*, Cambridge.
Bowersock, G. W. (2011) 'The tremendous, ferocious Bentley', in *The New York Review of Books* 24.11.2011.
Brown, P. (1993) *The Making of Late Antiquity*, Cambridge, MA.
Cameron, A. (2011) *The Last Pagans of Rome*, New York.

Casali, S. (2004) 'Nisus and Euryalus: exploiting the contradictions in Virgil's *Doloneia*', *HSPh* 102: 319–54.
Chaddock, K. R. (2002) 'A canon of democratic intent: reinterpreting the roots of the Great Books movement', *The History of Higher Education Annual* 22: 5–32.
Champlin, E. (1978) 'The life and times of Calpurnius Siculus', *JRS* 68: 95–110.
Chin, C. (2008) *Grammar and Christianity in the Late Roman World*, Philadelphia.
Citroni, M. (1995) *Poesia e lettori in Roma antica*, Rome.
  (2005) 'The concept of the classical and the canons of model authors in Roman literature', in Porter 2006, 204–36.
Clinton, H. (1854) *Literary Remains of Henry Fynes Clinton Consisting of an Autobiography and a Literary Journal and Brief Essays on Theological Subjects*, London.
Coetzee, J. M. (2011) 'What is a classic?', *Current Writing: Text and Reception in Southern Africa* 5: 7–24.
Connolly, J. (2007) 'Being Greek/being Roman: Hellenism and assimilation in the Roman empire', *Millennium: Jahrbuch zu Kultur und Geschichte des ersten Jahrtausends n. Chr./Yearbook on the Culture and History of the First Millennium* C.E. 4: 21–42.
Connors, C. (2008) 'Politics and spectacle', in T. Whitmarsh, ed., *The Cambridge Companion to the Greek and Roman Novel* (Cambridge), 162–84.
Conybeare, C. (2020) 'Virgil, creator of the world', in C. Conybeare and S. Goldhill, eds., *Classical Philology and Theology: Entanglement, Disavowal and the God-Like Scholar* (Cambridge), 180–98.
Cooper, A. J. (1898) *A Voice from the South*, Xenia, OH.
Copeland, R. and I. Sluiter (2009) *Medieval Grammar and Rhetoric: Language Arts and Literary Theory, AD 300–1475*, Oxford.
Coss, J. (1919) 'The new freshman course at Columbia College', *Columbia University Quarterly* 21: 248. Reprinted in L. Menand, P. Reitter and C. Wellmon, eds., *The Rise of the Research University: A Source-Book* (Chicago, 2017), 343–5.
Cotton, H. and W. Eck (2005) 'Josephus' Roman audience: Josephus and the Roman elites', in J. Edmondson, S. Mason and J. Rives, eds., *Flavius Josephus and Flavian Rome* (Oxford), 37–52.
Courtney, E. (1993) *The Fragmentary Latin Poets*, Oxford.
Crummell, A. (1897) 'The attitude of the American mind toward the negro intellect', *American Negro Academy* 3: 8–19. Reprinted in J. R. Oldfield, ed., *Civilization and Black Progress: Selected Writings of Alexander Crummell on the South* (Charlottesville, VA, 1995), 204–13.
Curtius, E. R. (1953) *European Literature and the Latin Middle Ages*, New York.
Damrosch, D. (2006) *What Is World Literature?*, Princeton.
Dozier, C. (2018) 'Pharos', http://pages.vassar.edu/pharos/.
DuBois, P. (2010) *Out of Athens: The New Ancient Greeks*, Cambridge, MA.
Easterling, P. E. (2012) 'Canon', *Oxford Classical Dictionary*, Oxford, 275–6.
Edmunds, L. (2010) 'Toward a minor Roman poetry', *Poetica* 42: 29–80.

Eliot, T. S. (1974) *What Is a Classic? An Address Delivered before the Virgil Society on the 16th of October, 1944*, New York.
Elsner, J. (2004) 'Late antique art: the problem of the concept and the cumulative aesthetic', in S. Swain and M. Edwards, eds., *Approaching Late Antiquity: The Transformation from Early to Late Empire* (Cambridge), 271–309.
Erskine, J. (1921) *The Moral Obligation to Be Intelligent and Other Essays*, New York.
    (1935) *The Delight of Great Books*, Indianapolis.
Fabricius, Io. Alb. (1697) *Bibliotheca Latina sive notitia auctorum veterum latinorum quorumcumque scripta ad nos pervenerunt*, Hamburg.
    (1718) *Bibliotheca ecclesiastica*, Hamburg.
Fantham, E. (1996) *Roman Literary Culture: From Cicero to Apuleius*, Baltimore.
Farrell, J. (2002) 'Greek lives and Roman careers in the classical vita tradition', in P. Cheney and F. A. de Armas, eds., *European Literary Careers: The Author from Antiquity to the Renaissance* (Toronto), 24–45.
    (2003) 'Classical genre in theory and practice', *New Literary History* 34: 383–408.
Feeney, D. (2016) *Beyond Greek: The Beginnings of Latin Literature*, Cambridge, MA.
Felson, N. (2016) 'Appropriating ancient Greek myths: strategies and caveats', *Studies in Gender and Sexuality* 17: 126–31.
Fish, S. (1982) *Is There a Text in This Class? The Authority of Interpretive Communities*, Cambridge, MA.
Formisano, M. (2007) 'Towards an aesthetic paradigm of late antiquity', *AntTard* 15: 277–84.
    (2014) 'Reading décadence: reception and the subaltern late antiquity', in M. Formisano and T. Fuhrer, eds., *Décadence: 'Decline and Fall' or 'Other Antiquity'?* (Heidelberg), 7–18.
    (2018) 'Marginality and the Classics: explaining extraneousness', in Formisano and Kraus 2018, 1–28.
Formisano, M. and C. Kraus, eds. (2018) *Marginality, Canonicity, Passion*, Oxford.
Fowler, D. (1995) 'Martial and the book', *Ramus* 24: 31–58.
Funaioli, H. (1907) *Grammaticae Romanae fragmenta* vol. 1, Leipzig.
Gadamer, H. (2004) *Truth and Method*, New York.
Ganiban, R. (2007) *Statius and Virgil: The Thebaid and the Reinterpretation of the Aeneid*, Cambridge.
Garrod, H. (1906) *P. Papini Stati Thebais et Achilleis*, Oxford.
Gates, H. L., Jr (1992) *Loose Canons: Notes on the Culture Wars*, Oxford.
Genette, G. (1997) *Paratexts: Thresholds of Interpretation (Literature, Culture, Theory)*, Cambridge.
Ghosh, A. (1998) 'The march of the novel through history: the testimony of my grandfather's bookcase', *The Kenyon Review* 20: 13–24.
Gianotti, G. F. (2003) 'La storiografia letteraria: il paradigma della letteratura latina', in L. Casarsa, L. Cristante and M. Fernandelli, eds., *Culture europee e tradizione latina* (Trieste), 65–87.
Gibson, B. (2005) 'The High Empire: AD 69–200', in Harrison 2005, 69–79.

Gildenhard, I. (2003) 'The "annalist" before the annalists: Ennius and his *Annales*', in U. Eigler, ed., *Formen römischer Geschichtsschreibung von den Anfängen bis Livius: Gattungen, Autoren, Kontexte* (Darmstadt), 93–114.
  (2010) 'Buskins & SPQR: Roman receptions of Greek tragedy', in M. Revermann, ed., *Beyond the Fifth Century: Interactions with Greek Tragedy from the Fourth Century BCE to the Middle Ages* (Berlin), 153–86.
Goldberg, S. (2011) *Constructing Literature in the Roman Republic*, Cambridge.
Goldhill, S., ed. (2001) *Being Greek under Rome: Cultural Identity, the Second Sophistic and the Development of Empire*, Cambridge.
Goodyear, F. (1983) Review of *Oxford Latin Dictionary*, ed. P. G. Glare, Oxford 1968–82, *PACA* 17: 124–36. Reprinted in K. M. Coleman, J. Diggle, J. B. Hall and H. D. Jocelyn, eds., *F.R.D. Goodyear: Papers on Latin Literature* (London, 1992), 281–7.
Gow, A. and D. Page (1968) *The Greek Anthology: Garland of Philip and Some Contemporary Epigrams*, Cambridge.
Graff, G. (1992) *Beyond the Culture Wars: How Teaching the Conflicts Can Revitalize American Education*, New York.
Grafton, A. (1990) *Forgers and Critics: Creativity and Duplicity in Western Scholarship*, Princeton.
Grafton, A., G. Most and J. Zetzel (1985) *Wolf, F. A. Prolegomena to Homer, 1795. Translated with Introduction and Notes*, Princeton.
Grafton, A. and J. Weinberg (2011) *I Have Always Loved the Holy Tongue: Isaac Casaubon, the Jews, and a Forgotten Chapter in Renaissance Scholarship*, Cambridge, MA.
Green, R. (1995) *Augustine: De doctrina Christiana*, Oxford.
Greenwood, E., (2010) *Afro-Greeks: Dialogues between Anglophone Caribbean Literature and Classics in the Twentieth Century*, Oxford.
  (2016) 'Reception studies: the cultural mobility of classics', *Daedalus* 145: 41–9.
Greenwood, E., ed. (2022) *Diversifying Classical Philology*, 2 vols., Baltimore, MD (= *AJPh* 143.2 and 143.4).
Greetham, D. (1991) '[Textual] criticism and deconstruction', *Studies in Bibliography* 44: 1–30.
Guillory, J. (2013) *Cultural Capital: The Problem of Literary Canon Formation*, Chicago.
Gurd, S. (2005) *Iphigenias at Aulis: Textual Multiplicity, Radical Philology*, Ithaca, NY.
Güthenke, C. and B. Holmes (2018) 'Hyperinclusivity, hypercanonicity, and the future of the field', in Formisano and Kraus 2018, 57–73.
Hägg, T. (2010) 'Canon formation in Greek literary culture', in E. Thomassen, ed., *Canon and Canonicity: The Formation and Use of Scripture* (Copenhagen), 109–28.
Hairston, E. A. (2013) *The Ebony Column: Classics, Civilization and the African American Reclamation of the West*, Knoxville, TN.
Haley, S. (2009) 'Be not afraid of the dark: critical race theory and classical studies', in L. Nasrallah and E. Schüssler Fiorenza, eds., *Prejudice and*

*Christian Beginnings: Investigating Race, Gender and Ethnicity in Early Christian Studies* (Minneapolis), 27–50.
Hall, E. (2008a) 'Putting the class into classical reception', in Hardwick and Stray 2008, 386–97.
  (2008b) 'Navigating the realms of gold: translation as access route to the Classics', in A. Lianeri and V. Zajko, eds., *Translation and the Classics: Identity as Change in the History of Culture* (Oxford), 315–40.
Hardie, P. (1993) *The Epic Successors of Virgil: A Study in the Dynamics of Traditions*, Cambridge.
Hardwick, L. (2000) *Translating Words, Translating Cultures*, London.
  (2013) 'Against the democratic turn: counter-texts, counter-context, counter-arguments', in L. Hardwick and S. J. Harrison, eds., *Classics in the Modern World: A Democratic Turn?* (Oxford), 15–32.
Hardwick, L. and C. Stray, eds. (2008) *A Companion to Classical Reception*, Malden.
Harrison, S., ed. (2005) *A Companion to Latin Literature*, Malden.
Hauser, E. (2018) '"There is another story": writing after the *Odyssey* in Margaret Atwood's *The Penelopiad*', *Classical Receptions Journal* 10: 109–26.
Henderson, J. (2013) 'The *Carmina Einsidlensia* and Calpurnius Siculus' *Eclogues*', in E. Buckley and M. Dinter, eds., *A Companion to the Neronian Age* (Oxford), 170–87.
Herbst, J. (2004) 'The Yale report of 1828', *IJCT* 11: 213–31.
Holzberg, N. (2004) 'Impersonating the banished philosopher Pseudo-Seneca's *Liber Epigrammaton*', *HSPh* 102: 423–44.
Horsfall, N. (1993) 'Empty shelves on the Palatine', *G&R* 40: 58–67.
  (1997) 'Criteria for the dating of Calpurnius Siculus', *RFIC* 125: 166–97.
Housman, A. E. (1902) 'Remarks on the *Culex*', *CR* 16: 339–46. Reprinted in *The Classical Papers of A. E. Housman* vol. 2 (Cambridge, 2004), 563–76.
Hunter, R. (2002) 'The sense of an author: Theocritus and [Theocritus]', in C. Kraus and R. Gibson, eds., *The Classical Commentary: Histories, Practice, Theory* (Leiden and New York), 89–108.
Hutchinson, G. O. (2009) 'Read the instructions: didactic poetry and didactic prose', *CQ* 59: 196–211.
Jauss, K. (1985) 'The identity of the poetic text in the changing horizon of understanding', in M. Valdes and O. Miller, eds., *The Identity of the Literary Text* (Toronto), 146–74.
Jones, J. (1961) 'Allegorical interpretation in Servius', *CJ* 56: 217–26.
Joshel, S. and S. Murnaghan, eds. (2005) *Women and Slaves in Greco-Roman Culture: Differential Equations*, London and New York.
Karakasis, E. (2016) *T. Calpurnius Siculus: A Pastoral Poet in Neronian Rome*, Boston.
Kay, N. M. (2013) *Epigrams from the Anthologia Latina: Text, Translation and Commentary*, London.
Keith, A. M. (2000) *Engendering Rome: Women in Latin Epic*, Cambridge.

Kennedy, G. A. (2001) 'The origin and concept of the canon and its application to the Greek and Latin classics', in J. Gorak, ed., *Canon vs. Culture: Reflections on the Current Debate* (New York and London), 105–16.
  (2002) 'Cicero's oratorical and rhetorical legacy', in J. M. May, ed., *Brill's Companion to Cicero: Oratory and Rhetoric* (Boston), 481–501.
Kennedy, R. F., C. S. Roy and M. L. Goldman (2013) *Race and Ethnicity in the Classical World: An Anthology of Primary Sources in Translation*, Indianapolis.
Kenney, E. J. (2006) Review of S. Di Brazzano (ed.), *Laus Pisonis. Introduzione, edizione critica, traduzione e commento*, *CR* 56: 119–21.
Kenney, E. J. and W. V. Clausen (1982) *The Cambridge History of Classical Literature. Vol. 2, Latin Literature*, Cambridge.
Kermode, F. (1983) *The Classic: Literary Images of Permanence and Change*, Cambridge, MA.
  (2006) *Pleasure and Change: The Aesthetics of Canon*, Oxford.
König, A., R. Langlands and J. Uden (2020) *Literature and Culture in the Roman Empire, 96–235: Cross-Cultural Interactions*, Cambridge.
König, J. and T. Whitmarsh, eds. (2007) *Ordering Knowledge in the Roman Empire*, Cambridge.
Krebs, C. (2012) *A Most Dangerous Book: Tacitus's Germania from the Roman Empire to the Third Reich*, New York.
Lacy, T. (2008) 'Dreams of a democratic culture: revising the origins of the Great Books idea, 1869–1921', *The Journal of the Gilded Age and Progressive Era* 7: 397–441.
Lee, B. T., E. Finkelpearl and L. Graverini, eds. (2014) *Apuleius and Africa*, New York.
Lefkowitz, M. and M. Fant, eds. (2016) *Women's Life in Ancient Greece and Rome: A Source Book in Translation*, Baltimore.
Leo, F. (1913) *Geschichte der römischen Literatur*, Berlin.
Leonard, M. (2012) *Socrates and the Jews: Hellenism and Hebraism from Moses Mendelssohn to Sigmund Freud*, Chicago.
Lively, G. (2006) 'Surfing the third wave? Postfeminism and the hermeneutics of reception', in C. Martindale and R. Thomas, eds., *Classics and the Uses of Reception* (Malden), 55–66.
Lössl, J. and J. Watt (2011) *Interpreting the Bible and Aristotle in Late Antiquity: The Alexandrian Commentary Tradition between Rome and Baghdad*, Farnham.
MacCormack, S. (1998) *The Shadows of Poetry: Vergil in the Mind of Augustine*, Berkeley.
Manuwald, G. (2011) *Roman Republican Theatre*, Cambridge.
Marchand, S. and A. Grafton (1997) 'Martin Bernal and his critics', *Arion* 5: 1–35.
Martindale, C. (2013) 'Reception – a new humanism? Receptivity, pedagogy, the transhistorical', *Classical Receptions Journal* 5: 169–83.
McCoskey, D. (2019) 'The subjects of slavery in 19th-century American Latin schoolbooks', *CJ* 115: 88–113.
Metzger, B. M. (1997) *The Canon of the New Testament: Its Origin, Development, and Significance*, Oxford.

Milnor, A. (2008) *Gender, Domesticity, and the Age of Augustus: Inventing Private Life*, Oxford.
Moatti, C. (2015) *The Birth of Critical Thinking in Republican Rome*, Cambridge.
Mohr, A. (2007) 'Jerome, Virgil, and the captive maiden: the attitude of Jerome to classical literature', in D. Scourfield, ed., *Texts and Culture in Late Antiquity: Inheritance, Authority, and Change* (Swansea), 299–322.
Möller, M. (2004) *Talis oratio – qualis vita: Zu Theorie und Praxis mimetischer Verfahren in der griechisch-römischen Literaturkritik*, Heidelberg.
Momigliano, A. (1980) 'Declines and falls', *The American Scholar* 49: 37–50.
Morrison, T. (1989) 'Unspeakable things unspoken: the Afro-American presence in American Literature', *Michigan Quarterly Review* 28.1: 1–34.
Most, G. (1990) 'Canon fathers: literacy, mortality, power', *Arion* 1: 35–60.
Mukherjee, A. (2013) *What Is a Classic? Postcolonial Rewriting and Invention of the Canon*, Stanford.
Najman, H. (2017) 'Ethical reading: the transformation of the text and the self', *JThS* 68: 507–29.
Nervegna, S. (2007) 'Staging scenes or plays? Theatrical revivals of "old" Greek drama in antiquity', *ZPE* 162: 14–42.
Netz, R. (2020) *Scale, Space and Canon in Ancient Literary Culture*, Cambridge.
Nicolai, R. (1992) *La storiografia nell'educazione antica*, Pisa.
Niehoff, M., ed. (2012) *Homer and the Bible in the Eyes of Ancient Interpreters*, Boston.
Nisbet, R. G. M. and M. Hubbard (1970) *A Commentary on Horace: Odes, Book 1*, Oxford.
North, J. (2017) *Literary Criticism: A Concise Political History*, Cambridge.
Nussbaum, M. (2016) *Not for Profit: Why Democracy Needs the Humanities*, Princeton.
O'Donnell, J. (1980) 'Augustine's classical readings', *RecAug* 15: 144–75.
Olson, D. and B. Millis (2012) *Inscriptional Records for the Dramatic Festivals in Athens: IG II2 2318–2325 and Related Texts*, Boston.
Oppel, H. (1937) *Kanon: Zur Bedeutungsgeschichte des Wortes und seiner lateinischen Entsprechungen*, Leipzig.
Page, D. L. (1981) *Further Greek Epigrams*, Cambridge.
Peirano, I. (2012a) *The Rhetoric of the Roman Fake: Latin Pseudepigrapha in Context*, Cambridge.
  (2012b) 'Authenticity as an aesthetic value: ancient and modern reflections', in I. Sluiter and R. Rosen, eds., *Aesthetic Value in Classical Antiquity* (Leiden), 215–42.
Pelttari, A. (2014) *The Space that Remains: Reading Latin Poetry in Late Antiquity*, Ithaca, NY.
Pfeiffer, R. (1968) *History of Classical Scholarship: From the Beginning to the End of the Hellenistic Age*, Oxford.
Pocock, J. (1977) 'Gibbon's decline and fall and the world view of the late Enlightenment', *Eighteenth-Century Studies* 10: 287–303.

Porter, J. (2002) 'Homer: the very idea', *Arion* 10: 57–86.
    (2005) 'What is "classical" about classical antiquity? Eight propositions', *Arion* 13: 27–62.
Porter, J., ed. (2006) *Classical Pasts: The Classical Traditions of Greece and Rome*, Princeton.
Preston, R. (2001) 'Roman questions, Greek answers: Plutarch and the construction of identity', in Goldhill 2001, 86–119.
Radermacher, L. (1919) 'Kanon', *RE* 10.2.
Rankine, P. D. (2019) 'The classics, race, and community-engaged or public scholarship', *AJPh* 140: 345–59.
    (2020) 'Classics for all? Liberal education and the matter of Black Lives', in I. Moyer, A. Lecznar and H. Morse, eds., *Classicisms in the Black Atlantic* (Oxford), 265–89.
Reinhardt, T. (2003) *Cicero's Topica*, Oxford.
Reynolds, L. D. (1983a) 'Eutropius' and 'Justinus' in Reynolds 1983b, 159–62 and 197–9.
Reynolds, L. D., ed. (1983b) *Texts and Transmission: A Survey of Latin Classics*, Oxford.
Rich, A. (1972) 'When we dead awaken: writing as re-vision', *College English* 34: 18–30.
Richard, C. J. (1994) *The Founders and the Classics: Greece, Rome and the American Enlightenment*, Cambridge, MA.
Richlin, A. (2014) *Arguments with Silence: Writing the History of Roman Women*, Ann Arbor.
Riggsby, A. (2019) *Mosaics of Knowledge: Representing Information in the Roman World*, Oxford.
Roman, L. (2001) 'The representation of literary materiality in Martial's *Epigrams*', *JRS* 91: 113–45.
Rondholz, A. (2012) *The Versatile Needle: Hosidius Geta's Cento Medea and Its Tradition*, Berlin.
Ronnick, M. V., ed. (2005) *The Autobiography of William Sanders Scarborough: An American Journey from Slavery to Scholarship*, Detroit.
Russell, D. A. (1979) 'De imitatione', in T. Woodman and D. A. West, eds., *Creative Imitation and Latin Literature* (Cambridge), 1–16.
    (2001) *Quintilian: The Orator's Education*, 5 vols., Cambridge, MA.
Rutherford, I. (1999) *Canons of Style in the Antonine Age: Idea-Theory and Its Literary Context*, Oxford.
Said, E. (1993) *Culture and Imperialism*, New York.
Seo, M. (2019) 'Classics for all: future antiquity from a global perspective', *AJPh* 140: 699–715.
Shanzer, D. (2012) 'Augustine and the Latin classics', in M. Vessey, ed., *A Companion to Augustine* (Malden), 161–74.
Sheets, K. B. (2005) 'Antiquity bound: the Loeb Classical Library as middlebrow culture in the early twentieth century', *The Journal of the Gilded Age and Progressive Era* 4: 149–71.
Shuger, D. K. (1994) *The Renaissance Bible: Scholarship, Sacrifice, and Subjectivity*, Berkeley.

Skoie, M. (2002) *Reading Sulpicia: Commentaries 1475–1990*, Oxford.
Sluiter, I. (2000) 'The dialectics of genre: some aspects of secondary literature and genre in antiquity', in M. Depew and D. Obbink, eds., *Matrices of Genre: Authors, Canons and Society* (Cambridge, MA), 183–204.
Smith, B. H. (1988) *Contingencies of Value: Alternative Perspectives for Critical Theory*, Cambridge.
Spivak, G. (1987) *In Other Worlds: Essays in Cultural Politics*, Chichester.
Stephens, S. A. and P. Vasunia (2010) *Classics and National Cultures*, Oxford.
Stewart, A. (1978) 'The canon of Polykleitos: a question of evidence', *JHS* 98: 122–31.
Stok, F. (2012) 'Commenting on Virgil, from Aelius Donatus to Servius', *Dead Sea Discoveries* 19: 464–84.
Stray, C. (2018) *Classics in Britain: Scholarship, Education, and Publishing 1800–2000*, Oxford.
Sullivan, J. P. (2005) *Martial: The Unexpected Classic*, Cambridge.
Swain, S. (2010) *Hellenism and Empire: Language, Classicism, and Power in the Greek World, AD 50–250*, Oxford.
Tandoi, V. (1984) 'Antologia Latina', in *Enciclopedia Virgiliana* 1, 198–205.
Tarrant, R. (1983) 'Anthologia Latina', in Reynolds 1983b, 7–13.
Telò, M. (2016) *Aristophanes and the Cloak of Comedy: Affect, Aesthetics, and the Canon*, Chicago.
Timpanaro, S. (2005) *The Genesis of Lachmann's Method*, Chicago.
Trivedi, H. (2007) 'Western classics, Indian classics: postcolonial contestations', in L. Hardwick and C. Gillespie, eds., *Classics in Post-Colonial Worlds* (Oxford), 286–304.
Turner, J. (2000) *Philology: The Forgotten Origins of the Modern Humanities*, Princeton.
Vardi, A. (2000) 'An anthology of early Latin epigrams? A ghost reconsidered', *CQ* 50: 147–58.
Whitmarsh, T. (2013) *Beyond the Second Sophistic: Adventures in Greek Postclassicism*, Berkeley.
Wilamowitz-Moellendorff, U., ed. (1905) *Die griechische und lateinische Literatur und Sprache*, Berlin.
Winterer, C. (2002) *The Culture of Classicism: Ancient Greece and Rome in American Intellectual Life, 1780–1910*, Baltimore.
Witty, F. J. (1958) 'The Pínakes of Callimachus', *The Library Quarterly: Information, Community, Policy* 28: 132–6.
Wolf, C. (1988) *Cassandra: A Novel and Four Essays*, New York.
Wolf, F. A. (1787) *Geschichte der römischen Litteratur nebst biographischen und litterarischen Nachrichten von den lateinischen Schriftstellern, ihren Werken und Ausgaben*, Halle.
   (1834) *Vorlesung über die geschichte der römischen literatur* (ed. J. D. Gürtler), Leipzig.
Woolf, G. (1994) 'Becoming Roman, staying Greek: culture, identity and the civilizing process in the Roman east', *The Cambridge Classical Journal* 40: 116–43.

(2003) 'The city of letters', in C. Edwards and G. Woolf, eds., *Rome the Cosmopolis* (Cambridge), 203–21.

Worthington, I. (1994) 'The canon of the ten Attic orators', in I. Worthington, ed., *Persuasion: Greek Rhetoric in Action* (Routledge), 244–63.

Yale University (1828) *Reports on the Course of Instruction in Yale College by a Committee of the Corporation and the Academical Faculty*, New Haven.

Zajko, V. (2008) 'What difference was made? Feminist models of reception', in Hardwick and Stray 2008, 195–206.

Zetzel, J. (1980) 'Horace's *Liber sermonum*: the structure of ambiguity', *Arethusa* 13: 59–77. Reprinted in K. Freudenburg, ed., *Horace: Satires and Epistles* (Oxford, 2009), 17–42.

(2005) *Marginal Scholarship and Textual Deviance: The Commentum Cornuti and Early Scholia on Persius*, London.

(2018) *Critics, Compilers and Commentators: An Introduction to Roman Philology, 200 BCE–800 CE*, Oxford.

CHAPTER 3

# *Periodisations*

Gavin Kelly

## 1 Three Vignettes

Since the history of Latin is so long, and attempts to categorise it go back almost as long, let us begin with three snapshots of past attitudes to the periodisation of Latin literature. I came across the first when looking for the origins of the idea that Latin literature of the Roman Republic and early Empire can be divided into a Golden Age and a Silver Age. This unabashedly evaluative terminology, not seemingly ancient, is still in use, particularly in the abbreviated form 'Silver Latin'. The *Oxford English Dictionary* took me to a first recorded usage of 'Golden Age' in Dryden's preface to his *Fables* (1700),[1] and of 'Silver Age' in the preface to the *Thesaurus linguae Latinae compendiarius* of 1736 (p. xxx), a two-way Latin–English dictionary by Robert Ainsworth (1660–1743) – and this preface provides my first vignette.[2]

Ainsworth in fact provides a categorisation of four ages, which he claims to take from predecessors. There was a Golden Age from the second Punic War to the death of Augustus in 14 CE; a Silver Age from the death of Augustus to the death of Trajan in 117; a Brazen Age down to 410, the year of Alaric's sack of Rome; and an Iron Age thereafter, 'after which the purity of the Latin tongue was very much neglected'. His brief list in English (pp. xxx–xxxi) is followed by a more detailed catalogue in Latin (pp. xxxii–xxxviii) of the authors belonging to each of the ages. Ainsworth makes the important qualification that some authors write in a better or worse style than might be presumed for their age – with the overall assumption, of course, that gold is better than silver and so on. Ancient criticisms of early authors (Ennius, Caecilius) are cited, with the reflection that subsequent

---

[*] The editors set me a daunting task, and I am grateful for their trust, patience and advice. I also thank colleagues who have kindly commented on drafts (Fabio Guidetti, Aaron Pelttari, Justin Stover, Joop van Waarden, George Woudhuysen) or answered queries (Michael Höckelmann, Danuta Shanzer, Foteini Spingou, Yannis Stouraitis).
[1] 'With Ovid ended the Golden Age of the Latin tongue.'
[2] I cite Ainsworth from the first edition of 1736; pagination differs by a few pages in later editions.

Romans 'took great pains in polishing their native language' (p. xxx).³ Moreover, 'Vitruvius, who writ even in the Augustan age, sinketh in some places below the diction of his contemporaries ... the style of Valerius Maximus, the writers of the *Historiae Augustae* (*sic*), Ammianus Marcellinus, and Apuleius, is much worse than some others who lived in their times' (p. xxxi). Those praised as surpassing the style of their times include Ulpian, Lactantius, Sulpicius Severus and Claudian. Finally, 'under Theodoric the Goth, Boethius, a man of consular dignity, wrote in so pure a Roman style, that if we were ignorant of the age he lived in we should take him for a contemporary of Cicero'. These judgements are hardly profound, but that they are broadly representative for their period is suggested by Edward Gibbon's similar, politically-inflected judgement of Boethius half a century later: 'the last of the Romans whom Cato or Tully could have acknowledged for their countryman'.⁴

A few preliminary observations may be made about Ainsworth's periodisations. Firstly, the metaphor comparing Roman literature to fine and less fine metals, though inspired by ancient literature in the form of Hesiod's myth of the ages and its Latin reception and adaptation in authors like Virgil and Horace, is ultimately early modern.⁵ Secondly, the Latin literature to which the periodisation is applied comes exclusively from Rome, the Roman empire and its immediate successor states, that is, from what we call antiquity: the last author included is Cassiodorus Senator in the sixth century CE.⁶ Mediaeval and early modern Latin is simply not mentioned. Still more strikingly, only secular authors are listed and Christians are only considered if they are laymen (Ausonius, Prudentius, Boethius) or at least not solely theological in their concerns (Sidonius, Cassiodorus): no Tertullian, Ambrose, Augustine or Jerome. Thirdly, the ultimate aim of the arrangement is to establish a hierarchy of styles that should be imitated in Latin composition, with the 'Golden Age' (and specifically Cicero and his contemporaries) at the top. After all, the express purpose of Ainsworth's

---

[3] A more recent definition of the 'Golden Age', that of the *Encyclopaedia Britannica*, lets it run from *c.* 70 BCE to 18 CE. On 'archaic Latin', see section 3.

[4] Gibbon 1776–88: IV.xxxix 550; on Gibbon's adherence to conventional views on stylistic decline see Kelly 2018. Gibbon owned Ainsworth's dictionary in the 1746 edition (Keynes 1940: 47).

[5] Hesiod *Works and Days* 109–201; cf. also Ovid, *Met.* 1.89–150; Virgil, *Ecl.* 4.8–9 and *Aen.* 6.792–3. The application of the ages to literature can be traced back to at least the sixteenth century (Farrell 2001: 90–2 cites Julius Caesar Scaliger's *Poetices libri septem* 1561: 295 for awareness of this metaphor and that of the ages of a human being, discussed in what follows). In the Middle Ages, there was a practice of designating authors as golden, silver, tin and lead – but such distinctions bore no relationship to period (Hexter 2005: 14).

[6] Other early modern dictionaries often have the same limitation, some referring in their titles to the *lingua Romana* rather than *Latina*.

dictionary is to help students to develop a pure writing style. The improvements over his predecessors of which he boasts earlier in his introduction – the avoidance of dubious locutions in the English–Latin section, the inclusion in the Latin wordlist of missing words attested in good authors, exclusion of words that are not good Latin, correction of misattributions of bad words to good authors – are all directed towards that end; so too, it seems, is the avoidance of patristic works.[7] Fourthly, Ainsworth at the start remarks that, had the metallic metaphor been not traditional, his preference would in fact have been for a biological metaphor: 'the origin, growth, flourishing state, and decay of the Latin tongue may, in my opinion, be most properly represented by the different ages of man, as infancy, youth, manhood, and old age' (p. xxx). These four categories do not map directly on to his four metallic ages: Cicero and Virgil are clearly the youth or manhood of Latin rather than its infancy; Ainsworth's characterisation of the earliest Latin literature, which sits uneasily in the Golden Age, would fit better into such a schema. The biological metaphor, applied in ancient historiography to the Roman people and their political systems,[8] is also found in more developed form in the literary history of Ainsworth's contemporary Johann Funck.[9] Still more blatantly than the metallic imagery, it implies decline, and that the end of antiquity can be seen as a kind of death.

Let us turn to a second snapshot: a letter (*Ep.* 9.9) sent in the mid-1390s to the Cardinal of Padua, Bartolomeo Uliari or Oliari, by the learned Chancellor of Florence, Coluccio Salutati (1331–1406).[10] Uliari had suggested to Salutati that he make a collection of his letters to ensure his undying fame and to serve as a model for future writers (p. 79.2–6), and Salutati used his reply to unleash a splendid display of humanist learning.

---

[7] See again Ainsworth 1736: xxxi: 'In after-times the beauty of the Latin tongue declined very much, and many base words were introduced into the language, especially by the ecclesiastic and physical [i.e. medical] writers, the use of which ought to be carefully avoided by all persons studious of writing in a good Latin style.'

[8] Seneca (the Elder?) quoted in Lactantius, *Inst.* 7.15.14–17; Florus, *praef.*; Ammianus 14.6.3–5.

[9] Funck's titles are worth recording in abbreviated form: *De origine Latinae linguae tractatus* (1720); *De pueritia Latinae linguae tractatus* (1720) [up to the second Punic War]; *De adulescentia Latinae linguae tractatus* (1723) [second Punic War to the times of Cicero]; *De virili aetate Latinae linguae tractatus* (two parts, 1727–30) ['quo maximus cum robore vigor et gloria sermonis Romani'; from the age of Sulla and Cicero to the death of Augustus]; *De imminenti Latinae linguae senectute tractatus* (1736) ['decrescens Romani sermonis vigor'; down to Hadrian's reign]; *De vegeta Latinae linguae senectute commentarius* (1744) [down to the reign of Honorius and the Gothic sack of 410]; *De inerti et decrepita Latinae linguae senectute commentarius* (1750) ['extrema tandem eius linguae calamitas'; from 410 to the death of Charlemagne].

[10] Novati 1891–1911: III. 76–91 (dated to 1 August 1395); Uliari's original letter is published by Campana 1964 (who shows that the date should be 10 July, probably of 1394). I owe my knowledge of this letter to Hernández Lobato 2020: 674–5. For further discussion and contextualisation see Witt 2000: 325–6.

He immediately gains a superior position with a relentless and reasoned rebuke of Uliari for addressing him in the plural (i.e. as *uos*, the polite plural of Romance languages), a practice that he criticises as an ungrammatical and flattering invention of modern times, wholly inappropriate to a personal letter. Uliari had made a favourable comparison of Salutati to Cassiodorus (designated 'inclytum illud eloquentie sidus' by Salutati, p. 79.10). It was Salutati's diplomatic role in charge of the correspondence of the Florentine republic that prompted Uliari's comparison to the author of the *Variae*, public letters for the Gothic kings of Italy, Theoderic and his successors.[11] Salutati was happy to remind readers of the *Variae* and of Cassiodorus' many other literary endeavours, which included private letters, philosophical writings, commentary on the psalms and the translation of the *Historia tripartita*,[12] but he still protested that it was absurd to compare him with the great Cassiodorus. Indeed, he says, there is none of the ancients ('antiquorum') whose shoelaces he is worthy to untie,[13] let alone be preferred to, or viewed as an equal to (p. 79.21–3). For Salutati, antiquity remains unmatched and holds the field ('tenet gradum suum insuperata vetustas et in campo remanet signis immobilibus atque fixis', p. 79.23–5), and whatever modernity's boasts about its own sophistic subtlety (i.e. despite Scholasticism), the wisdom and eloquence of antiquity is supreme, and no contemporary can match the learning of the ancients. That period's flowering of literary studies and eloquence had been one that later ages could not sustain, however much they sought to. He continues (p. 80.1–4):

> Mansit in proximis successoribus similitudo quedam et aliquale vestigium antiquitatis; sed, paulatim ab illa scribendi soliditate discedente posteritate, cum ipso temporis lapsu latenter primum decus illud effluxit, deinde manifestiore dissimilitudine ab eloquentie principe Cicerone discessum est.

> There remained in immediate successors a certain likeness and some sort of trace of antiquity, but as later generations gradually departed from that robustness of writing, with the very passing of time that glory at first stealthily leaked away, and then with a more manifest difference there was a parting of the ways from Cicero, the prince of eloquence.

Over the following pages, Salutati illustrates this thesis with a catalogue of prose writers of Latin, and he begins by describing the glories of the age of

---

[11] Cassiodorus was reasonably widely read in the Middle Ages and the citation is not that surprising (see e.g. Manitius 1935: 319–22).
[12] Novati 1891–1911: III 79. 'Private letters' presumably refers to those Cassiodorus wrote in his own voice as praetorian prefect in *Variae* 11–12. On Salutati's knowledge of Cassiodorus see Ullmann 1963: 221.
[13] Cf. John the Baptist in John 1:27.

## 3 Periodisations

Cicero. Modern readers might be surprised by his admiration for Cicero's correspondents almost as much as Cicero himself, but Salutati had recently unearthed Cicero's letters *Ad familiares*, just as Petrarch had rediscovered the letters *Ad Atticum* half a century earlier, and he was determined to advertise his discovery – and his intimate knowledge of classical Latin authors wholly unknown to his correspondent.[14] The next generation of writers that he lists ('concurrerunt vel potius successerunt his temporibus': these are clearly seen as the 'proximi successores' referred to earlier) are Seneca of Corduba,[15] Valerius Maximus and Livy – and Salutati quotes learned statements of Quintilian and Jerome praising the first and the last and himself says that Valerius can easily count among the 'principes facundie' – even if not quite equal to Cicero (p. 81.6–16). In the next group he places Tacitus (not quite equal to Livy!),[16] and with him Suetonius, Plinius Secundus,[17] the various pseudonymous authors of the *Historia Augusta*, Martianus Capella, Apuleius and Macrobius: authors from whose writings it can be seen how with the passing of time the adornment of phrasing had flourished and how the majesty of the earlier form of language, which had peaked with Cicero, had been diminished.[18] Salutati is clearly not entirely at home with literary chronology, as Capella and Macrobius would certainly belong in his next category, the times of the Theodosian dynasty (i.e. from 379 to 455) and their successors. Cassiodorus heads this list, followed by Ambrose, Symmachus, Jerome, Augustine, Ennodius, Sidonius, Sulpicius Severus, Firmianus (i.e. Lactantius), Orosius, Iulianus (i.e. of Toledo), Ausonius and Cyprian, who revived eloquence or ensured its continuation (again the chronology is approximate). But after these, there was a profound change and a collapse in eloquence. He next names a group of authors who for all their claims to eloquence cannot be compared with the ancient or the middle writers (a list including Ivo of Chartres, Bernard of Clairvaux, Hildebert of Tours, Peter of Blois, Peter Abelard). Finally, Salutati sees something of a revival in his own age, with Albertino Mussato and Geri d'Arezzo, as well as the great luminaries of Florence: he ostentatiously names in passing the great glory

---

[14] p. 80.13–81.6. Salutati asked for a copy of Cicero's letters from Milan in 1392 (Ullmann 1963: 146 (#14), and unexpectedly received the *Ad familiares* (Reeve 1996: 27).
[15] Salutati conflated the two Senecas, but ascribed the authorship of the tragedies to a different person, his first Seneca's brother (Ullmann 1963: 250).
[16] p. 81.16–82.3. Ullmann 1963: 252 shows that Salutati had probably not actually read Tacitus; the position of Livy may have been meant partially as a compliment to his Paduan correspondent.
[17] The Elder and Younger Plinies are here undifferentiated, but later in the letter he does distinguish them.
[18] p. 82.4–10.

of eloquence in the vernacular, Dante, and then Petrarch and Boccaccio, whose works would be celebrated by posterity – but no rightful judgement, he says, can ignore how much they differ from the ancients in their rhetorical skill ('facultas dicendi').[19]

Salutati's letter has gained scholarly interest because of the attempt to move away from the mediaeval respect for the great but somewhat timeless *auctores* of the past towards a categorisation by periods, albeit one that is sometimes imprecise on chronological detail. His vision of literary history shares some features with the taxonomy later used by Ainsworth, though of course his Latinity is far more alive and accomplished than that of Ainsworth or the schoolboy users of the latter's dictionary. Like Ainsworth, albeit in a much more considered way, he has a firm break between antiquity, ending in around the sixth century, and later periods;[20] within antiquity, moreover, he too sees Cicero and his contemporaries as an apogee from which later authors in varying ways decline. There are also considerable differences. Salutati views the Latin tradition as extending to the present, however transformed and different from that of antiquity: even Dante's eloquence in *volgare* is part of it. For all his view of post-Ciceronian stylistic slippage, he has high esteem for several authors disdained by Ainsworth (Valerius Maximus and Apuleius, for example), and above all a much more positive view of high imperial and late antique authors, Ainsworth's Brazen and Iron Ages. Thus, he engages in and rejects as too generous to himself the comparison to Cassiodorus; later in the letter he repeatedly quotes Symmachus as an authority; he cites Jerome in praise of Livy, giving Church Fathers a place that they would be denied by Ainsworth.

Let us turn now to my third vignette. This is a story told in Aulus Gellius about an older contemporary, the bilingual sophist Favorinus of Arles (died *c*. 160). Favorinus encountered a young man who was in love with old words and would bring out ancient and unknown expressions in daily conversations. Favorinus reproached him: men of great antiquity, he said, like Curius, Fabricius, Coruncanius and the three Horatii used to converse with their contemporaries in a plain and lucid manner and did not employ the vocabulary of the ancient colonisers of Italy but of their own time:

'Tu autem, proinde quasi cum matre Euandri nunc loquare, sermone abhinc multis annis iam desito uteris, quod scire atque intellegere neminem

---

[19] p. 84.1–12. On Salutati's attitude to Petrarch see Ullmann 1963: 240–4; Fubini 2003: 95–8, Witt 2000: 315–23; and his letter to Poggio of 17 December 1405 (Novati 1891–1911: IV.1 126–45).
[20] Salutati does appear to have some conception of a middle period, referring to *medii dictatores* (p. 83.9), but these seem to represent authors in as well as after antiquity.

uis quae dicas. Nonne, homo inepte, taces, ut abunde consequaris quod uis? (3) Sed antiquitatem tibi placere ais, quod honesta et bona et sobria et modesta sit. (4) Viue ergo moribus praeteritis, loquere uerbis praesentibus atque id, quod a C. Caesare scriptum est, habe semper in memoria atque in pectore, ut "tamquam scopulum, sic fugias inauditum atque insolens uerbum".' (Gell. *NA* 1.10.2–4)

'But you, as though speaking even now with Evander's mother, use speech that was outmoded many years past, because you want nobody to know or understand what you're saying. You fool! Why not shut up so you can fully achieve what you want? (3) Ah, but you say that you like antiquity for being honourable and good and sober and modest. (4) In that case live by old fashioned morality but speak with words of the present, and keep always in your memory and your heart what was written by Gaius Caesar, how "you should run as from a cliff from an unknown and inappropriate word".'

Salutati held up 'antiquity' as the ideal in our previous passage. So does Gellius' young man. Antiquity, however, is a relative term. Favorinus taught and Gellius wrote amid the archaising tendency of the second century CE: this entailed a fondness for the vocabulary of Latin authors of the third and second century BCE and a rejection of the primacy of Cicero and Virgil. This tendency is found in various ways in Fronto, Apuleius and Gellius himself – and we can presume that the young man exemplifies it to an extreme extent.[21] Favorinus' own Latin style is lost to us, as the surviving works are exclusively in Greek,[22] but in another anecdote we find him strategically losing an argument to the emperor Hadrian, another famous archaiser, again over rare words (SHA, *Hadr.* 15.12–13). But from our knowledge of Latin lexicography and society we can infer that the language of his own times did not mean the everyday speech of ordinary people (what was traditionally called vulgar Latin but is now more often called informal Latin or *sermo cotidianus*, everyday speech, the Latin that existed alongside and at some distance from the literary language).[23] Probably what was actually recommended was the spoken version of the elite language, which was based on the literature of the last generation of the republic and first generation of the empire: Julius Caesar himself (here quoted in his secondary role as grammatical authority) and Cicero were among the major prose figures. It is not clear whether Favorinus' objection was to excessive archaism in itself, or to its presence in speech rather than

---

[21] See e.g. Holford-Strevens 2017.
[22] Editors include Gellius' Latin summaries of Favorinus' views among his fragments, but that may not be indicative of the latter's Latin style.
[23] For discussions of the problems of 'vulgar Latin' and associated concepts, see section 3.

on the page. And we cannot know to what extent Gellius' young man was rebelling against the norms of literary Latin, whether merely choosing vocabulary from less prestigious authors of the third and second centuries BCE, or perhaps going further and varying his syntax as well.

My three vignettes span more than 1500 years. The history of Latin literature is an extraordinarily long one, running from the third century BCE for at least two millennia, as a major stream down to the eighteenth century and in attenuated form down to the present. Amid vast transformations in the world around it, the Latin language – at least in its written form – remained remarkably consistent in its formal features such as vocabulary, accidence and syntax. From a very early stage, readers and writers of Latin, and often its speakers as well, were conscious of a Golden Age in the past and usually looked to it as a fundamental measure – and this was the case even if they did not know it well, did not necessarily seek to rival it, had doubts about the best models (like Gellius' young man), or had qualms of a different nature (like St Jerome imagining God in judgement calling him a Ciceronian, not a Christian, *Ep.* 22.30). Use of Latin may have spread with the Roman conquest of Italy and then of Rome's empire, but long after the western Roman empire ceased to exist individuals who did not identify as Romans still gained a central part of their cultural identity from an education founded on Virgil and other ancient authors and on grammatical works intended to preserve the language.[24] The everyday spoken language, which had always been different to some degree, was eventually replaced by the Romance languages,[25] but in its literary form Latin writers (and speakers) repeatedly looked back to such past models, often queried usages that were not hallowed by them, and in several periods (the Carolingian age, the twelfth century, the Renaissance) made conscious efforts to revive a version of Latin based on them, or at least on a grammar derived from them: think of Salutati's hostility to the use of the polite plural in Latin. This is not to deny that formal Latin developed or that it is possible to observe substantial differences between the Latinity of different periods; but I would suggest that the degree of linguistic continuity and of repeated regression from innovations is far more remarkable than any change.

In other words, even by the second century CE, Latin was – just like Greek, the other lingua franca alongside which it coexisted in the Roman empire – a classical language. It is in one sense the archetypal classical

---

[24] On grammatical and scholarly works up to 800, see the definitive survey of Zetzel 2018.
[25] See n. 28.

language, in that the epithet 'classical' comes from it. As it happens, Gellius has a claim to be the term's originator, as the first author we know of to metaphorically extend the usage of the adjective *classicus*, referring to the social elite of republican Rome, to indicate a group of first-rate authors who should be imitated (*NA* 19.8.15); the usage was revived in something like its modern sense in the Renaissance (it is first attested in the humanist Filippo Beroaldo the Elder).[26] Cognates of *classicus* in modern languages have extended their meaning to refer to a prestigious form of the Latin language, to the whole period of Graeco-Roman antiquity, to prestigious and imitated periods and modes of other literatures (including Greek, Arabic, Persian, Sanskrit and Chinese[27]), as well as to music, dance, art, architecture and physics. The Latin of Gellius' time fits many of the standard definitions of a classical language: a language with a literary canon which provides linguistic and stylistic exemplars, as well as with incipient diglossia, that is to say a differentiation between the formal language and ordinary speech.[28] Salutati's theory that the age of Cicero was the pinnacle of eloquence is hardly original to him. The prestige given to this particular age originates in antiquity, even if the modern name Golden Age does not. The cult of Virgil and his place at the centre of the educational curriculum originates in antiquity. Prose authors of later antiquity themselves treat Cicero as the epitome of style and rhetoric; they quote him directly and by name along with Virgil, Terence and Sallust – these are the four authors dubbed the *quadriga Messii* ('Messius' quartet')[29] – and sometimes prestigious contemporaries like Caesar and Horace; meanwhile they habitually avoid citations of later authors even when it is clear from verbal allusions that they know them. All three of my examples show a belief in some sort of decline from an ideal antiquity (although Gellius' Favorinus provides a stinging critique). The respect for the 'classical' and for 'antiquity' continues among modern readers of Latin, for all the language's very long history.

[26] Rizzo 1986: 389–90; see further Settis 2010. See also Peirano Garrison's chapter, pp. 43–52.
[27] See Gibson and Whitton's introduction, p. 11 n. 67, for some classicists' objections to the term in other cultures. Classicism is also used of prestigious periods of modern European literatures, often as counterpart to Romanticism.
[28] The extent of the diglossia is unknowable, as the exact nature of spoken Latin is also unknowable. It is certainly a simplification to see a straightforward development from *sermo cotidianus* into the Romance languages (see Adams 2016). See further section 3 on linguistic periodisations.
[29] So called in Cassiodorus, *Inst.* 1.15.7, referring to the *Exempla elocutionum*, a work using the four authors to illustrate Latin usage, compiled by Arusianus Messius in Rome in c. 395: see Zetzel 2018: 281–2.

## 2 Periodisation, Latin and Their Problems

Dividing the past into periods is an unavoidable intellectual short cut, a convenient and conventional way of organising and thinking about the past. At the simplest level, I have found myself in this chapter constantly writing down terms like 'early modern' quite without conscious thought, but satisfying myself once I do reflect on it that readers will understand what I mean. Likewise, we have become conditioned to think of the historical past in terms of centuries and of decades and of years beginning on 1 January within the Christian and pre-Christian eras and to associate particular trends with them: 10- or 100-year periods are arbitrary, and no doubt the whole habit is Europocentric and Christianising, but most of us tend to accept the convenience and let it go without worrying excessively.[30] Although periodisation is obviously a major part of the academic study of history, literature and the arts, and indeed of archaeology and geology, periodising labels are not always very exact or very academic: vintage clothing, vintage cars, Old Master paintings, classical music, modern art are none of them precise descriptors. Others can be short and very precise: incunabula, Jacobean architecture, Second Empire furniture, Weimar culture.[31] Labels may have geographical and aesthetic associations as much as chronological ones; they may even be of value for promoting a product (Jacobean applies only in Great Britain; 'modern art' could exclude conservative or academic styles; the designations 'vintage clothing' and 'Old Masters' surely aim at opening wallets). Similarly, vast diversity will be found in the duration of periodisations discussed in this chapter, from massive concepts like antiquity, the Middle Ages, the Renaissance, to narrow and specific periods like neoteric or Neronian literature. Some of these examples, like the Renaissance and neoteric, carry strong aesthetic associations. In general, slippage between political chronology and artforms, and between different artforms, is entirely characteristic of periodisation: reigns, dynasties and political systems are used to designate literature or fine art without necessarily implying any connexion with politics; terms from one form of creative process can shift to another.[32]

---

[30] Theodor Mommsen's *Römische Geschichte* used years *Ab urbe condita* alongside the Christian dating; it is safe to say that his approach has not caught on. The principal way that embarrassment at the Christian dating system is expressed by scholars is the pseudo-secular BCE/CE (used here only because, alas, required by the style guide of this volume). I can better understand the reservations of non-western historians, who have nevertheless mostly adopted the Gregorian calendar for convenience.

[31] Incunabula are defined as European printed books up to 1500 – a case where Christian centuries create a wholly arbitrary break.

[32] Later in this essay I use the term 'baroque', normally reserved for art and music of the seventeenth and eighteenth centuries, to refer to late Roman art-prose.

## 3 Periodisations

There is also potential imprecision concerning the temporal and geographical coverage of particular periodising labels. To return to concepts already discussed, does antiquity refer just to ancient Greek and Roman civilisations? Obviously not, one might have thought, and yet it is a perfectly normal usage to restrict the word in this sense. Especially important for our purposes, does classical Latin literature mean literature from *c*. 250 BCE to 600 CE, or only the first half of that period down to the second century CE? After all, both usages are common.[33] If the former, does it include material by Christians? A further important point to make is that by periodisations we mean not just names and labels for the past but also theories and assumptions about historical change that do not necessarily have a single convenient name – Salutati's literary history in *Ep.* 9.9, discussed in the previous section, is an excellent example.

As for how periodisations arise: we have seen in the three vignettes of the opening section that periodisations tend to be assimilated and passed down by inheritance, without particular thought being given to them or awareness of where they come from or exactitude about the details. It is clear that they are not reached by strictly logical or historical processes; their meaning may carry an ideological charge, and their sense may evolve. The idea that there is an archaic period of Latin literature derives from and takes for granted the values of the later first century BCE and early centuries CE, and characterisations of archaic literature as rough and (if being positive) majestic echo Horace and Ovid: it is not that archaic authors thought of themselves as archaic.[34] The epithet 'neoteric', used to refer to a possible school of mostly lost poets in the late republic, originates in a passing comment of Cicero, but the way that it is used is a construction of relatively modern scholarship and may bear little resemblance to what Cicero meant.[35] The idea both of a mediaeval or middle period and a renaissance in literature are products of the Renaissance itself: if one creates an idea that one's linguistic and literary practice is returning to the ancients, that makes the time in between a middle period.[36] The letter of

---

[33] In other words, 'classical' is often used in opposition to mediaeval, but sometimes in opposition to 'later Roman'/'late antique'/'Christian'. The latter is the usage preferred by Gibson and Whitton in their introduction (pp. 11–14); this chapter seeks to explain why I prefer the former. A similar ambiguity is found with 'classical music', which can be a label both for all western art music since the Renaissance and for the predominant style of the later eighteenth and early nineteenth centuries, associated with Gluck, Mozart and Haydn.

[34] Hinds 1998: ch. 3 on literary history. For the tenacity of such characterisations, see e.g. Jenkyns 2015: 155 on the 'natural ruggedness' of Ennius. On 'archaic' Latin see further section 3.

[35] Cicero, *Att.* 7.2.1. For a confident reconstruction of what Cicero was referring to, see Lyne 1978.

[36] Equivalent 'middle periods' have been identified in other cultures: in Chinese historiography, for example, the end of the Han dynasty in 220 CE is treated as the beginning of such a period, though

Salutati discussed on pp. 99–102 contains an incipient sense of that middle period, but not with a definition we would now recognise.[37] As we have seen, Golden Age and Silver Age are (probably) early modern constructs, even if they have origins in ancient perceptions, but their meaning has arguably been changed with the disappearance from discussion of the following Bronze and Iron Ages. Indeed in the late twentieth century, the epithet 'Silver Latin' was often used by those promoting its study.

If use of periodisation is inevitable, does it do any intellectual harm? It may help here to focus more closely on historical studies. When historians talk of periodisation, it is a commonplace to say that every periodisation is potentially a rip in the fabric of history. The metaphor is of a tapestry or a painted canvas; one might also use the less violent metaphor of periodisation as framing. The implication of the idea of the rip is that by starting to view at one point and not another, there is a risk of a distorted picture of reality, one that cuts out crucial earlier causes or later consequences, and relates the topic of one's interest to some nearby objects while leaving others – perhaps equally close – quite out of account. There will always be a case to make for a different periodisation, one that seeks continuity across the moments seen as turning points. After all, turning points are sometimes obviously arbitrary and even those that are not are debatable.

Why is the award of the title of Augustus in January 27 BCE seen as inaugurating the Roman imperial system, rather than (say) Pompeius' government of Spain through legates in the 50s, Julius Caesar's victory at Thapsus, or any number of other moments in the career of Caesar's heir?[38] Why is the deposition of the emperor Romulus in 476 seen as the end of the western Roman empire? In practice, serious historical accounts of the end of the Roman republic or of the end of Roman power in the west will nuance and question these supposed turning points rather than endorsing them. Studies of the end of the Roman republic do not judder to a halt in January 27 BCE: Syme's classic *The Roman Revolution* (1939), for example, has narrative chapters covering 60 to 23 BCE followed by thematic coverage of the Augustan regime down to 14 CE. And while some major historical works have paused or terminated in or around 476,[39] most historical

---

some scholars dismiss such a periodisation as an inappropriate foreign import. See e.g. Davis and Puett 2015, Holcombe 2017.

[37] See n. 20.

[38] Barnes 2009 points out that most late antique writers saw Julius Caesar as the first emperor, and that Mommsen 1904: v 461 saw Caesar's victory at Thapsus on 6 April 46 BCE as the start of the monarchy.

[39] Otto Seeck's *Geschichte des Untergangs der antiken Welt* (1895–1920) ends in 476. The first three volumes of Gibbon's *Decline and Fall* (published 1776 and 1781) continued for two chapters beyond

research will make clear that the 'fact' (questionable in itself)[40] that the last Roman emperor in the west was deposed in that year is less important than various longer-term trends. These include the weakness of the imperial office in the fifth-century west; the loss of effective imperial control in most western territory outside Italy and southern Gaul in the previous generations; the fact that military matters were already dominated by long-serving Masters of the Soldiers who were often of non-Roman or partially non-Roman backgrounds, indeed often barbarian royalty; that the subsequent rulers of Italy, Odoacer and Theoderic, follow in this pattern and that they governed with the nominal consent of the eastern emperor; that the senatorial elite, at least in Italy, continued to hold the consulate and other high offices. A rational case can be made that in Italy, at any rate, the Roman empire in the west continued by other means in the half-century following 476.[41] Though there remains a good deal of controversy about the nature of the migrations, the processes of shifts in power and ethnic identity across the west, and the question of whether or not scholars should use the word 'Germanic', none of this is particularly new. Gibbon may have paused soon after 476, but he did then continue his narrative.[42] And in the aftermath of the First World War, Henri Pirenne promoted the thesis that the major moment of reorientation in western European culture came not with the Germanic kingdoms but with the Arab conquests of the southern Mediterranean.[43]

Indeed, if one wants a positive example of how periodisation can be modified and nuanced, the period on either side of the ending of Roman rule in the west can serve very well. Over the last half-century, a new paradigm of 'late antiquity' has bridged the scholarly gap between the late Roman empire and what is otherwise called 'the early Middle Ages' in the western Mediterranean and 'early Byzantium' in the east. The term late antiquity comes from art history, and the approach gives attention to religious and cultural history rather than focusing exclusively on politics;

---

that point (discussing monasticism and the reign of Clovis in Gaul) before the 'General Observations on the Fall of the Roman Empire in the West' as interim concluding chapter; the last three volumes appeared only in 1788.

[40] On a pedantic note, Romulus' deposed predecessor Julius Nepos had coins minted for him in the west until his murder in 480, though he remained in exile at Salona in Dalmatia. It is about half a century later, in Constantinople, that we find the first explicit suggestion that 476 marked the end of the western empire (Croke 1983); however, see Harries 1994, showing that 476 was seen at the time as the end of Roman power in Gaul.

[41] O'Donnell 2008.

[42] The most recent and definitive assessment of the migrations is Meier 2019. On Gibbon see n. 39.

[43] Pirenne 1937 (though based on ideas formulated earlier).

it crosses over traditional period divides ('from Marcus Aurelius to Muhammad', as the subtitle of the seminal book in the field has it);[44] it allows the history of Europe, the Mediterranean and the Near East to be viewed in a perspective that goes beyond Roman frontiers and beyond Latin and Greek – indeed, the recent trend is to try to bridge the Eurasian landmass.[45] Coexisting alongside the old periodisations and geographical divisions, the concept of late antiquity helps to challenge them when they may potentially mislead – though traditional views will endure and will sometimes seem more valid.[46] Periodisations can be questioned, invented and revised; topics that have been chronologically or geographically marginalised can be put in the centre. And clearly this is what good historians will try to do in any period.

But for all that, I cannot help feeling that periodisation may still do intellectual harm, for several reasons. First, the fact that historians can argue for new periodisations or nuanced versions of existing ones does not mean that the rest of the world will accept their arguments, however cogent. Secondly, there is an obvious risk that established periodisations that help with grasping the chronology may bring with them an oversimplified view of historical processes; perhaps this is especially the case for students and for amateur enthusiasts, but very few people, including experts, are immune from such influences. To return for a moment to 476 and All That and to the dangers of Memorable Dates: in the popular understanding, at any rate, the landmark date of the last Roman emperor in the west has often blurred into the end of the Roman empire altogether. Not only does it create an idea in the popular imagination of the replacement of the Roman state by barbarian kingdoms as being something akin to a conquest; but more subtly it also helps in the process of occluding the continuation – for another millennium – of the eastern Roman empire, which is given the evocative and orientalising name of Byzantium.[47] The label is established and useful, but has nothing to do with what the Romans of the empire based in Constantinople called themselves.[48]

---

[44] Brown 1971; the subtitle is replaced in later editions by 'AD 150 to 750'.
[45] See Humphries 2017 for a discussion of the trend; Kulikowski 2017: 117–36 illustrates the potential of this approach.
[46] One illustration: the first edition of the *Cambridge Ancient History* (*CAH*, completed in 1939) ended in 324, with Constantine's takeover of the east and the founding rites of Constantinople; what followed had been covered in the *Cambridge Medieval History*, begun in 1911. The second edition of the *CAH* ended in *c.* 600 – unquestionably a far more sensible stopping point, because it includes and looks a little beyond the end of the western empire and reaches a natural pause in the east.
[47] For the 'othering' of the eastern Roman empire and Byzantium as a form of Orientalism, see e.g. Cameron 2003 and Stouraitis 2022.
[48] Namely *Rhōmaioi*, Romans. *Byzantion* and *Byzantioi* were mainly used as an archaic name for the city and inhabitants of Constantinople, especially in Greek classicising historiography.

Thirdly, academic subject boundaries are influenced by inherited periodisations, and not all boundaries are easily crossed. People do things differently in different subjects, and speak different languages. This is not such a great problem for the history of the Roman revolution: whether taught in Classics or history departments, republic and empire will be presented as part of a continuum, often by the same teachers, with the same standard texts and reference works (one caveat, however: in this period on either side of the birth of Jesus, the history and literature of Jews, even if writing in Greek, is often not integrated with Graeco-Roman studies).[49] But my other example, 476 and the collapse of the western empire, may equally be taught as a beginning, an end or a middle, in departments of history, Classics or religion, each with different traditions and emphases. Or perhaps it will be taught in none of them, as being too early, too late or too unfashionable and difficult.

Fourthly, the topic of this chapter is periodisations in literature, and these surely work differently from historical ones – as the vignettes in the first section show. It is true that the literary and historical periodisations are often closely related: for example, 'Renaissance' originally denoted literary and linguistic reform in Latin and the rediscovery of Greek in Italy, but has taken on a much broader historical and art-historical meaning. Periodisations of artforms are more likely to have descriptive and aesthetic connotations; they may be associated with certain movements; in particular they are more likely to be tied up with ideas of a canon. Within the discipline of Classics, literary and historical studies are often remarkably well integrated – it is one of the most admirable features of the discipline[50] – but in all times and languages, most readers of literature focus primarily or wholly on enjoying and interpreting the text before them rather than using it to understand changes in the longer term outside the world of the text; and most scholars of literature, whatever their ideological bent may be, have the same inclination. I shall argue later on that assumptions about periodisation have a profound and unconsidered impact on the study of Latin literature.

---

[49] As Goldhill 2020: 57 points out, 'The Septuagint, the most influential piece of Hellenistic Greek prose, is rarely if ever discussed in Classics departments and even more rarely in courses on Hellenistic prose.'

[50] I am prejudiced by my national and educational background here (see Fuhrer, pp. 457–60). For some legitimate criticisms of this interdisciplinarity as practised (though more applicable to the republic and early empire than Greek or late Roman studies), see Lavan's chapter; see also the editors' introduction, pp. 28–30.

Indeed, Latin literature has its peculiarities that make literary history, especially on the macro-level, even more difficult than in other cultures. As a result of the classicising tendency, there is remarkable linguistic stability in Latin over a very long period, and repeated regression from innovations. This has the result, and can be illustrated neatly by the fact, that there are plenty of works whose dating is very uncertain. Some of these doubtful cases are quite well known and consist of differences of a couple of centuries: was the Christian poet Commodianus third-century, or as late as the fifth?[51] Were the eclogues of Calpurnius Siculus written under Nero or in the third century?[52] Other problems are less well known but involve even greater chronological chasms. Are the so-called Einsiedeln eclogues Neronian or from the fifth century? As for another pastoral poet, Martius Valerius, does he belong to the twelfth century – or the sixth?[53] Is the poem attributed to the first-century satirist Sulpicia that survives among the Bobbio epigrams authentic or a fourth-century imposture?[54] Are the eighty lines of Silius Italicus' *Punica* found in none of the manuscripts and only in the Aldine edition of 1523 the work of the author from the late first century CE or a Renaissance invention?[55] Were the elegies attributed to Sabinus written by a contemporary of Ovid or by a fifteenth-century humanist?[56] To the best of my knowledge, most modern literatures have no problems such as these (attributions might be questioned, but not period). Of course, these problems are mostly soluble and many such problems have been solved: nobody now confuses the poems of the sixth-century elegist Maximian with those of Virgil's friend Cornelius Gallus.[57] And yet, the very existence of these problems suggests that many Latin texts do not straightforwardly carry the stamp of their own times in easily detectable ways.[58]

An important and distinct feature of Latin – to which I shall return repeatedly – is the differential survival of literature from different periods. The texts that do survive from across the two thousand years of Latin are skewed overwhelmingly towards the mediaeval and early modern. Gustav

---

[51] The modern consensus seems to be early: see Heck 1997.
[52] Champlin 1978; Wiseman 1982; Courtney 1987; Horsfall 1997.   [53] Stover 2015 and 2017.
[54] This poem has received astonishingly little attention in comparison to its author's Augustan namesake – perhaps because the idea that it is a fake is already bought in. See Butrica 2006 for the case for authenticity.
[55] Brugnoli and Santini 1995.   [56] Spieß 2012.   [57] See White 2019.
[58] The texts cited here are verse, and that is perhaps suggestive of the constraints of conservative rules of style and metre (and hence the greater ease of imposture or error); but one could add prose texts to the examples. The Neronian date of Petronius is still not universally accepted; the letters attributed to Sallust have been seen as anything from authentic to late antique; the pseudo-Quintilianic declamations have been dated across the second, third and fourth centuries.

Leonhardt reached the estimate that surviving post-Roman Latin texts outnumber those from ancient Rome by more than 10,000 to 1.[59] Although the details of this calculation are left rather vague, including the precise boundaries of antiquity, and although the later texts included are swollen by documentary material in archives, there is no reason to doubt the overall shape of the calculation, even as applied to literary texts.[60] Moreover, the overwhelming majority of texts surviving from Roman antiquity have been edited, most of them many times;[61] plenty of mediaeval and early modern texts remain in manuscript or, in the latter case, have languished in obscurity after one printing. Within antiquity, there is a similar if less dramatic disparity: many more surviving Latin texts come from the fourth century CE and after. Indeed François Dolbeau has observed that the works of Augustine, written between the mid-380s and his death in 430, are longer in total wordcount than all the surviving Latin literature of the republic and the first century CE.[62]

The nature of surviving texts is also different. Later imperial literature is markedly international, while we owe republican and early imperial texts overwhelmingly to writers based in Rome (though most of them did not originate there). In the later empire (and *a fortiori* subsequent periods) works of high literary culture form a lower proportion of what we possess, while many more technical, occasional and popular works survive. There are also whole genres such as the chronicle, the sermon, the hagiography and the commentary which (in what survives) belong almost entirely to late antiquity, and others, like grammatical treatises and letters, that survive disproportionately from that period. Most surviving texts from the early empire, by contrast, are works of high culture. In between, the third century is a period from which remarkably little literary production survives – a phenomenon all the more notable because elite genres such as poetry, history and letters are almost wholly absent.[63]

---

[59] Leonhardt 2013: 2–4.
[60] As Stover in this volume (p. 272) remarks, 'mediaeval Latin defies quantification ... no one even knows the full extent of what survives'.
[61] There may be some late antique texts that have escaped notice (for example, the Gospel commentary of Fortunatianus of Aquileia was only discovered in the twenty-first century, having been considered contemporary with the Carolingian manuscript in which it was preserved: see the *editio princeps*, Dorfbauer 2017). Latin translations of Greek patristic and medical texts are another under-investigated area. For the likelihood of further discoveries see Dolbeau 1998.
[62] Dolbeau 1998: 134. For further discussion of this pattern of survival see sections 7 and 8, and Gibson and Whitton in this volume, pp. 18–20.
[63] Poetry: only Terentianus Maurus and Nemesianus, and perhaps the uncertainly dated Calpurnius Siculus and Commodian; history: nothing that survives; letters: Cyprian and a few pseudonymous Christian items.

In one sense, the linguistic continuity of Latin literature makes things easier for its readers: more or less the same skills are needed to understand texts across two millennia.[64] On the other hand, that bimillennium encompasses vast transformations in other areas: political arrangements and culture, religion, other languages spoken by Latin speakers, education, scientific and technical knowledge. In politics, one moves from the Roman empire through mediaeval Christendom to modern nation states. Quite understandably, few readers or scholars of Latin are comfortable about their ability to contextualise literature across different nations, religions and societies over 2000 years. Most focus on a narrower period, in which they feel more at home. Of course, many scholars and readers do branch out, but even those who do so often focus on texts that have a familiar feel, so that admirers of Roman imperial epic leapfrog late antique and mediaeval poetry to arrive at classicising Renaissance epic, for example.

The tendency for Latinists to stay within the bounds of the familiar is exacerbated by the modern context of Latin studies, which most commonly finds its academic home in a Classics department. Such departments may be to varying degrees inclusive of Greek and Roman history, art and archaeology, philosophy, linguistics – that is the trend in the biggest departments in the Anglophone world; the bigger the department the more branches – or they may be institutes of classical philology whose work is at best loosely connected to whatever other specialists in the Graeco-Roman world the institution may have – as in German-speaking countries, for example.[65] Either way, such departments tend to focus mainly or even exclusively on the languages as means of understanding the ancient Greek and Roman world: they generally consider their main business done by some point between about 400 and 600, and leave (at least the more technical) Christian literature to theologians. In them students are trained, of whom some, with luck, will later go on to teach Latin language and literature in schools; they will aim to get their pupils reading Virgil at an early stage in their proficiency, as teachers have done for two thousand years; and they will teach Latin alongside an understanding of classical civilisation.

---

[64] Of course, writings from different periods can sometimes seem very different, but arguably in style more than language. See Stover's section '*Stilgeschichte*' in this volume, pp. 292–316.

[65] The modern Italian academic system works slightly differently from other countries, with more attention paid to mediaeval and humanist Latin, partly because it is seen as an essential prerequisite for Italian studies. Authors like Salutati are thus studied on a continuum between the classical and the modern; this openness to post-classical Latin also nourishes the outstanding scholarship that comes from Italy on manuscript studies and textual transmission.

This puts Latin from after the period of the Roman empire in an anomalous position (the same applies to Greek). Classics departments occasionally have mediaeval Latinists or neo-Latinists as a luxury (or perhaps, as in North American liberal arts colleges, because the research specialism does not matter to the institution), or have specialists in textual transmission who have a professional interest in later periods. This mean that specialists in Latin of post-Roman, post-antique periods tend – when they succeed in finding employment that allows them to carry out their scholarship, and their odds are surely worse than classical Latin specialists – to be based in other academic departments: history, or mediaeval studies, or religion, or philosophy, or vernacular languages and literatures.[66] There are many fine Latinists in such departments and plenty of Latin being taught in them; and yet Latin itself may be somewhat ancillary. There are of course exceptions in the form of outstanding centres of mediaeval and neo-Latin studies, and in some countries there is a tradition of simply studying Latin in its own right rather than Classics: in those circumstances mediaeval Latin and Neo-Latin have more of a place as topics in themselves. But overall the balance of scholarly preferment and consequently of scholarship in Latin studies is skewed towards antiquity – despite the fact that only a fraction of a percent of surviving Latin actually comes from antiquity. This also amounts to a lost opportunity for mediaeval and early modern studies, where there is a bad need for texts to be edited and translated for the first time, which classically trained Latinists would be well qualified to meet.[67]

Moreover, in Latin studies within antiquity, there is also a skew away from the late antique and Christian, despite the comparatively larger quantities in which these two largely overlapping groups survive. Avoidance of the latter can partly be accounted for by the lie of the disciplinary land: departments of religion take patristics as their territory.[68] Such a division goes back centuries: in my own university the teaching of Latin originally went under the designation 'Humanity', in opposition to Divinity, and there was a Department and a Chair of Humanity, as in other Scottish universities, until recently.

The skew in the canon can be illustrated in countless ways. Take the standard series of texts: the Latin volumes of the Oxford Classical Texts

---

[66] Rigg 1992: 330: 'In most English-speaking Universities the Medieval Latinists have most often been employed by departments of English, for no self-evident reason.'
[67] See Stover's chapter. Rigg 1992: 3–4 is eloquent on the topic.
[68] In many countries we can also observe divisions of such departments, between Catholic and Evangelical theology in Germany, and between Religion and Divinity in the US.

include as many from the first century BCE as from every other period together (see Figure 3.1).[69] With the more comprehensive Loeb Classical Library, other periods are better represented, but the first centuries before and after Christ are still very dominant: there are 13 volumes from the third and second centuries BCE,[70] 62 from the first century BCE, 57 from the first century CE, 20 from the second century, 1 from the third, 12 from the fourth, 16 from the fifth, 1 from the sixth, and 2 from the eighth (the outlier is Bede's *Ecclesiastical History*, presumably included for its relevance to an Anglophone series).[71] The venerable OCT series in particular, because it is slow-moving and texts are only added or replaced when a suitable editor appears, shows the older prejudices against even post-Ovidian poetry: there is no place yet for Lucan or Flavian epic, for example, though Statius' occasional poems are admitted.[72]

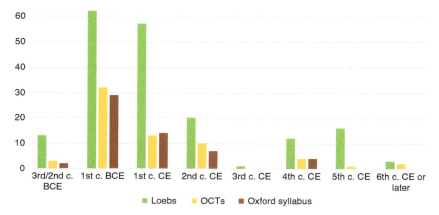

Figure 3.1 Latin Loebs, Latin Oxford Classical Texts and the Oxford Latin syllabus: chronological coverage.

---

[69] I split volumes of Ovid and Tacitus between centuries depending on dates of individual works, dated Juvenal and Persius by the former, and allotted the *Appendix Vergiliana* to the first century CE, and Vegetius and the *Panegyrici Latini* to the fourth. The one sixth/seventh-century author is Isidore of Seville.

[70] Calculation is slightly difficult since the sets called *Remains of Old Latin* and *Fragmentary Republican Latin* cover the same authors and territory, and have multiple authors within each volume; some authors are also hard to date.

[71] I adopted similar counting methods as with the OCTs: the Cato and Varro volume was allotted to the second century BCE, and the *Minor Latin Poets* to the first and fourth centuries CE. In recent years, the Loeb foundation has played a role in supporting the I Tatti Renaissance Library and the Dumbarton Oaks Medieval Library (future bilingual editions of late antique texts will, I understand, go in this series unless they are replacing an existing Loeb edition).

[72] I am not suggesting that there was any systematic determination to keep later authors out (otherwise there would be no Isidore) as much as a failure to conceive that they might be part of mainstream classical literature.

## 3 Periodisations

A similar poll of the Teubner and Budé series, respectively more comprehensive than the OCTs and less commercially driven than the Loebs, would show much less of a skew towards earlier antiquity. A look at teaching texts, however, such as the Cambridge Greek and Latin Classics,[73] would probably show a similar balance to the OCT and Loeb; and this is likely to reflect syllabuses. A similar survey of the undergraduate syllabus of the world's largest Classics department, Oxford (chosen because it is broad and ambitious, publicly available, and rarely changed), eerily echoes the very strong bias of the eponymous university press towards the first centuries before and after Christ.[74]

Or consider standard works, such as dictionaries. The *Thesaurus linguae Latinae*, the world's greatest Latin dictionary, founded in 1896 and currently working on the letters N and R, takes Latin literature down to the sixth century. Later periods are left to have their own dictionaries, often on a geographical basis: for example the *TLL*'s neighbour in the Bavarian Academy of Sciences, the *Mittellateinisches Wörterbuch*.[75] Of the two commonly used dictionaries in English, the older Lewis and Short (1879) goes down to the sixth century, though with the same preference as Ainsworth had had for secular authors; the more recent and respected *Oxford Latin Dictionary* (1968–82) stops at *c*. 200 CE, excluding all Christian authors (even the few writing before 200) and many non-Christians.[76] This is a highly problematic periodisation, as Gibson and Whitton remark in the introduction,[77] but it is not out of keeping with the general picture of a canonical period within the canonical period of antiquity. If we turn to literary histories and handbooks, we find a similar picture. Works which are structured as lists of authors give a more representative pattern. The mighty *Handbuch der lateinischen Literatur der Antike* is the pre-eminent example of this:[78] of its eight

---

[73] On which see Gibson and Whitton in this volume, pp. 19–20, and for statistics Gibson 2021. The results are: third/second century BCE: 7; first century BCE: 28; first century CE: 15; second century: 10; fourth century: 2.
[74] Based on the 2021 Mods and Greats handbooks available via www.classics.ox.ac.uk, counting each set author to be studied in the original once per paper: Cicero, Virgil, Seneca and Tacitus all recur multiple times; the four fourth-century texts (Augustine, Ambrose, Jerome, Symmachus) represent a single optional paper.
[75] Further mediaeval Latin dictionaries, the majority with regional focuses, are listed by Stover in this book, p. 273.
[76] Some post-200 jurists quoted in the *Digest* are explicitly included; other later authors cited seem mainly to be included for quotations of earlier material.
[77] Pp. 11–14. For the intellectual deficiencies of this approach, see the harsh but just review of Goodyear 1983 (also cited by Gibson and Whitton).
[78] The *HLL* is a misleading title for a work projected in eight sturdy volumes, but the title of the French version (*Nouvelle histoire de la littérature latine*) is also misleading, given that the work is

(projected) volumes, the last four cover the period after 284. The fifth volume was published first (1989), in a deliberate attempt to reset the traditional focus on the republic and early empire, while the sixth volume (2020), covering the period 374–430, weighs in at over 1700 pages. Conte's one-volume *History of Latin Literature* (more accurately called *Manuale storico* in the Italian original) also gives balanced coverage of Latin literature of antiquity.[79] But more essayistic volumes tend to follow the biases of their early twentieth-century predecessors:[80] the Latin volume of the *Cambridge History of Classical Literature* (Kenney and Clausen 1982) has 625 pages on Latin literature from its beginnings up to the reign of Trajan (d. 117), and another 109 pages down to Sidonius (d. 479 or after), the last author discussed: each of these periods is roughly 350 years. Much Christian literature is excluded altogether, and while many authors earlier in the work are given individual chapters, Apuleius (perversely placed last)[81] is the only 'later' author to receive such attention.[82] More recently, Oliver Taplin's edited collection, *Literature in the Greek and Roman Worlds* (2000), gave the entire period after the second century only one chapter, an attractive but impressionistic essay by Michael Dewar, framed between Apuleius and Augustine. In Stephen Harrison's edited *Blackwell Companion to Latin Literature* (2005), coverage stops with 'the beginning of Christian Latin literature about AD 200 with Tertullian and Minucius Felix', seen by the editor as 'a major watershed'.[83]

In other words, much of Ainsworth's (and to a lesser extent Salutati's) periodisation of Latin literature still looks relatively familiar in the institutional arrangements and mental furniture of classical studies: a primary focus on Latin of antiquity; within antiquity an avoidance of Christian texts and a focus above all on the so-called Golden and Silver Ages; and within that narrower period on the last part of the Golden Age, as the aesthetic pinnacle. More banally, the focus on vocabulary from 'good

---

organised as a list of authors. The *HLL* has been slowed by its own ambition and also by the sheer quantity of late antique literature. In comparison to the massive two-part volume 6, volumes 4 and 5, covering 117–284 and 284–374 respectively, are well under half its length.

[79] Herzog 1989 (with the editor's 50-page introduction); Berger et al. 2020; Conte 1994.

[80] Duff's two volumes (1909, 1927), specifically devoted to the 'Golden' and 'Silver' Ages, give 27 pages of nearly 1000 to post-Trajanic literature. Rose 1954, Hadas 1952 and Bieler 1980 have proportions of 421:64, 333:113 and 182:17 respectively. Copley 1968, going down only to the end of the second century, devotes nine pages of 358 to the period after Trajan, and concludes with the reflection that 'the Roman idea' was now dead.

[81] See Tony Woodman's critical review (Woodman 1992: 204).

[82] On the forthcoming *Cambridge History of Later Latin Literature*, see n. 200.

[83] Harrison 2005: 2, though he regrets reinforcing the canonical status of the earlier period. Jenkyns 2015 stops with Apuleius.

authors' and Cicero as the stylistic model was part of how I learned Latin prose composition, in a tradition unbroken from Ainsworth's day (and I am not particularly old). Even if prose composition has been dethroned, it is clear that for most classicists, Ciceronian prose is still normative; writings that diverge from it are late, strange, mannered, archaising, Christian ... whatever. It is a striking indication of the longevity of such thinking that 'Golden' and 'Silver' are still comprehensible and the latter at least in common use. It is also revealing that Bronze and Iron Latin, if they were ever used much, are now wholly obsolete and unknown currency, perhaps because 'imperial Latin' or 'later Latin' is still a minority interest on syllabuses, perhaps because specialists would hardly want to use such plainly derogatory terms for their field (one late Latinist uses 'Platinum Latin', a splendid coinage).[84]

The continuity of such patterns of thought is why periodisation matters and, in my view, how it does intellectual harm, by narrowing our horizons and by encouraging a fundamentally unhistorical understanding of literature. How ideas of canons and periods have continued and/or mutated is a fascinating and understudied question. I am not going to attempt to trace the story from antiquity, or even from the Renaissance, to the present. Obviously Gellius' young man could fit into a story of shifting tastes in the ancient world. One might look before Salutati to the literary history of earlier mediaeval *accessus ad auctores*, and go back to the late antique conception of *ueteres*. Or Salutati could be sandwiched more narrowly between Petrarch before him and Poggio and Biondo after him in an attempt to find the origins of the modern idea of antiquity and the development of ideas of Latin literary history. Discussion of Ainsworth could broaden out across Europe to find the origins of the metallic metaphors, and equally one could trace the intellectual history of periodisation in the nearly three centuries since. The selectiveness of my vignettes is surely misleading.[85] But I chose to start with vignettes precisely because tracing a continual intellectual genealogy would be a vast task and well beyond my expertise. Indeed, for reasons I have laid out, few will have the expertise. To grapple seriously with periodisation in Latin literature would

---

[84] Danuta Shanzer devised 'Platinum Latin' as a sponsoring organisation for panels on late antique and mediaeval Latin at the Kalamazoo and Leeds Medieval Congresses from 1998 onwards (personal communication). For a manifesto (without however using the favoured epithet) see Shanzer 2009.

[85] For example, though Ainsworth's disregard of Christian authors is real enough, one should not exaggerate the disconnect between classical and Christian scholarship and teaching in eighteenth and nineteenth-century Britain. Many classicists were also theologians, and many were ordained. On the intellectual connections between the disciplines (with a focus on Greek) see Goldhill 2020.

ideally require understanding of the whole history of Latin literature; of how that history has been written and might be rewritten; of how continuity and change in literature and literary practice are related to historical change and continuity in other areas, such as political arrangements and culture, education, religion, history of language. Even if one aimed only to analyse the periodisation of antiquity, one would still need a good grasp of the history of scholarship since the Middle Ages. The results of the exercise would be interesting, but we might still be no further in thinking how we should best periodise.

Accordingly, in the rest of this chapter, I shall look at different perspectives that have been or could be used to achieve a better sense of historical change and continuity. The sections that follow will cover linguistic change (section 3), metre (4), prose rhythm (5), politics (6), religion (7), and book history (8). Treatment will inevitably be brief, selective and disconnected. I take the unashamed attitude that treating literature as a historical phenomenon is, as a path to understanding, preferable to a purely aesthetic approach, and that periodisations are going to exist anyway, so we may as well seek to improve them. There will be a bias towards the (shorter) first half of the history of Latin literature – antiquity down to around the sixth century – where such expertise as I have is centred, with particular focus on two main areas which have already received attention in this chapter: the time around the end of the republic, and the place of literature from the late Roman world of the fourth and fifth centuries, in our overall understanding of Latin literature.

## 3 The Development of the Language

Might linguistic changes be a path to periodising Latin? This happens, after all, in other languages. For example, Old English, Middle English and Modern English and their various subdivisions represent obviously different stages in the history of the language; and while political change (the Norman conquest) is implicated in the shift from Old to Middle English, the primary division, as far as modern categorisations are concerned, lies in the profound changes in the syntax, accidence and vocabulary of the language itself. But we have already seen the problem in the case of Latin: the fact that Latin became a classical language relatively early on and that certain authors and usages were canonised from the later first century BCE.

If one were to take a passage of Latin prose of the first century BCE or the first couple of centuries of our era, for example Gellius' anecdote about

Favorinus and the young man, any competent Latin writer of the Middle Ages would understand it perfectly well as long as the content permitted (we have endless examples of mediaeval readers interpreting classical literature). Were the mediaeval writer to express such a story in their own words, they might have used some different words and orthography and conceivably different syntax to express the same information and ideas, but the superficial appearance of the text would be more or less the same: most of the individual words, and also, mostly, the accidence and syntax.[86] The counterfactual question of what a writer of the age of Cicero or Seneca or Gellius who tumbled through a time warp would have made of mediaeval Latin is harder to answer. Let us again set aside complications of content; let us also set aside our time traveller's puzzlement at changed spelling, at diphthongs turned to monophthongs, and at palatalisation of consonants. We can speculate that he or she might have found some writers more comprehensible and more attractive than others: an early humanist like Coluccio Salutati was striving to be more classical than earlier Latin writers in the mediaeval *dictamen* (that is, letter-writing) tradition, and most modern Latinists would think he succeeded. Within the letter to Uliari discussed in section 1, I noticed only two words that would have looked out of place in a contemporary of Cicero, *modernus* and *dictator* in the sense of prose writer – both of which are used by late antiquity.[87] Of course, there could be all sorts of nuances apparent to native speakers of Latin of antiquity that would escape Salutati (who, for all his brilliant command of Latin, was ultimately writing and speaking a recreated and reformed language) or modern Latinists.[88] That said, applying the same thought experiment to Old English, Middle English and Modern English leads to a very different result, of a markedly different superficial appearance of the text, a minority of individual words being the same in the different periods, and almost certain mutual incomprehensibility.

The difference arises because, as discussed in section 1, we are dealing with a situation of diglossia. The Latin which displays such considerable continuity is a lingua franca, associated particularly with writing and formal speech; a language not immune to change in pronunciation, orthography and vocabulary, or to regional variation,[89] but prevented

---

[86] In his *Ep.* 40, Enea Silvio Piccolomini, the later pope Pius II, quotes the Gellius story unaltered.
[87] Uliari's own much shorter letter (see n. 10) has one unclassical word, *querelabimur* (which is seemingly in Arnobius).
[88] Modern Latinists might have all sorts of prejudices against mediaeval Latin, but these are surely primarily stylistic rather than linguistic.
[89] Adams 2007.

from diverging too far and brought back into line by a strong gravitational pull from the grammatical tradition and the canon, and by deliberate linguistic reformations in some periods – above all the 'renaissances' of the Carolingian period and at the end of the Middle Ages. The other Latin is a spoken language that always had its differences from literary modes of expression but that increasingly diverged, until it became the various Romance languages – and it is presumably because of the multiplicity of descendants that we do not call Italian or French or Spanish 'modern Latin'.[90] Both the continuity in the formal language, and the divergence between the two, complicate attempts to periodise on linguistic grounds.

Of course, as has already been shown, linguistic diversity is responsible for some existing periodisations and modes of thinking about the history of Latin. On the grandest scale, part of the definition of Renaissance Latin (or humanist Latin, or Neo-Latin) is that it bears the mark of linguistic reformation and an imitation of classical styles that is part of the original concept of the Renaissance. 'Renaissance' has come to have a much wider meaning, but applied to Latin the term carries linguistic expectations, as does 'mediaeval Latin'. In what follows, however, I am going to focus on two of the major linguistic periodisations that are used within antiquity, 'archaic Latin' and 'late Latin' (both of them used in opposition to the third, 'classical Latin').

Archaic Latin is used with somewhat different significance for a linguistic phenomenon and for a literary one; in the former instance beginning with inscriptional texts as far back as the seventh century BCE and fragments of early hymns, in the latter with the rather later phenomenon of earlier Latin literature, running from the later third down to the first century. This rather disparate definition has dissatisfied some linguists.[91] To focus here simply on the literary definition, it is indubitably loose in chronological terms – although the central archaic authors might seem to be Ennius, Plautus, Terence, Cato and Lucilius, the standard collections of early Latin include material right down to the contemporaries of Cicero, and even Lucretius, writing in the 50s BC, is sometimes defined as an archaic writer. Archaism is not solely defined by chronology but also by certain elements in orthography, vocabulary and syntax that subsequently ceased to be mainstream. The norm against which it is defined is the 'classical', and one can see the designation as

---

[90] There are of course descendants of Latin called Ladin, Ladino, Romansh, and Romanian.
[91] Penney 2011: 220, citing Clackson and Horrocks 2007 for dividing into 'archaic' (up to 400) and 'old'.

## 3 Periodisations

a canonisation of the judgement of early writers like Ennius by the Augustans as *hirsutus* ('hairy') or *arte rudis* ('crude in his artistry')[92] – a view later hallowed in remarks such as Ainsworth's that the Romans 'took great cares in polishing their native language'.[93] Later in the history of the literature 'archaic' is replaced by 'archaising', a recurrent reactionary tendency (most literary histories would probably deem the triumviral-era historian Sallust to be 'archaising' rather than 'archaic'). Though Quintilian's reading list of earlier Latin literature involved few pre-Ciceronian authors,[94] the next century would bring the reactionary excesses of the young man rebuked by Favorinus, as well as the likes of the emperor Hadrian, Fronto and Apuleius. Archaising in use of vocabulary, if little else, can be found in the more baroque late antique authors, such as Ammianus Marcellinus or Sidonius;[95] and archaising revivals can be found as late as the early sixteenth century.[96] Elucidating archaism was an important part of the grammatical tradition from the beginning.[97]

The second linguistic periodisation I shall discuss is 'late Latin' (or *Spätlatein*), used of Latin from between about 200 and 600 CE and particularly associated with Swedish scholarship of the first half of the twentieth century.[98] The leading contemporary scholar of this subfield, J. N. Adams, made some acknowledgement of the limitations and problems with this periodisation in a recent chapter discussing the topic. That chapter begins with 'a passage chosen at random' from the pilgrimage narrative from the 380s ascribed to Egeria or Aetheria: the choice of the passage may be random, but the work is not.[99] The renowned philological commentary of Einar Löfstedt (1911) on this text is one of the foundational texts for the study of late Latin. Egeria's narrative is densely packed with unprecedented usages, some of which seem well on the way to the Romance languages, as well as usages only occasionally seen before that may reflect the spoken language.[100] If Adams had selected one of the many other prose writers active in the 380s – Ambrose, Ammianus, Augustine,

---

[92] *Hirsutus*: Propertius 4.1.16, Ovid, *Tr.* 2.259–60; *arte carens / rudis*: Ovid, *Am.* 1.15.19, *Tr.* 2.474.
[93] Ainsworth 1736: xxx, quoted above, p. 97.
[94] Quintilian, *Inst.* 10.1.37–131, discussed by Gibson and Whitton in the introduction, pp. 18–19.
[95] Hertz 1874 on Ammianus; Wolff 2020: 402 on Sidonius; both authors tend to source their archaisms from Plautus, Terence, Gellius and Apuleius.
[96] An entertaining entrée is Mariangelus Accursius' satirical dialogue mocking the archaisers of the Bologna school, *Osci et Volsci dialogus ludis Romanis actus* (Rome, 1513). See Hernández Lobato 2014 for context.
[97] Zetzel 2018: 15–30.   [98] See e.g. Löfstedt 1959.   [99] Adams 2011: 258–63.
[100] Adams' random passage (*Per. Aeth.* 23.1–3) includes *fui ad episcopum* ('I went to see the bishop') and *habebat de ciuitate forsitan mille quingentos passus* ('it was maybe a mile and a half from the city').

Jerome, Symmachus – or perhaps some of the laws so artfully composed by imperial quaestors, he could still have identified linguistic trends characteristic of the period in, say, greater preposition use in place of oblique cases, adverbs replacing the superlative, more participles or new lexis (Christian vocabulary, for example), but it would surely have been with markedly less frequency and without many of the scrunchier examples. The fact is that most prose authors of the later Roman empire, Christian or non-Christian, wrote a version of the standard clausulated art-prose of the period that did not differ much in syntax or vocabulary from the writing of the early empire.

It is not in doubt that there were some real changes in the spoken language in late antiquity that also affected the literary language. But the late Latin periodisation may nevertheless be questionable. First, the existence in greater quantity of texts like Egeria's pilgrimage may simply be a reflection of the far greater number of surviving texts, including those of Christian interest.[101] Second, the connected intellectual project of identifying a separate and markedly different special language (*Sondersprache*) of Christian Latin, proposed by the 'Nijmegen School' (Joseph Schrijnen and Christine Mohrmann) at the same time as Löfstedt was exploring late Latin, has run into the ground and no longer has serious support.[102] A third, more marginal doubt concerns editorial practice. Adams' random passage of Egeria spells the feminine relative pronoun both as *quae* and *que*. In any normal edition of a classical text, such an inconsistency would be ironed out: indeed most editions of Latin texts from Roman antiquity adopt uniform orthography that disregards not only the mediaeval spellings and scribal misspellings of our manuscripts but also the orthographical shifts of antiquity. The third-declension accusative plural in -*is* is often printed in pre-Virgilian poetry, but most editors avoid *deicere* and *formonsus* for *dicere* and *formosus*. Conventional spellings are applied by editors to most late Latin texts, but for some texts which are perhaps regarded as less literary or which come after the end of Roman power, editors are much more susceptible to leaving irregular endings and orthography found in the manuscripts in their texts: the works of Gregory of Tours (later sixth century) are a good and controversial example;[103] chronicles are another type of work often edited diplomatically rather than critically. There is no doubt that authors like Egeria or Gregory diverged

---

[101] See section 2, and the further discussion in section 7.
[102] On Löfstedt's intellectual relationship with and changing views of the Nijmegen School, see Denecker 2018.
[103] Bourgain 2016.

from standard Latin, but there is room to question how far, and each author must be taken on their own terms. In my own work towards a new edition of Ammianus Marcellinus, I have often found that obscure language or unusual forms in the manuscripts have been defended as representative of late Latin, even when they are unparalleled and prose rhythm demonstrates that they are simply scribal errors. In other words, spoken Latin was certainly growing more distant from the literary language in late antiquity, as we can tell from the growing need for grammatical treatises on correct orthography (indeed perhaps the growth of the genre of grammatical writing altogether).[104] But the effect on the language of literature was mainly visible after (indeed, some time after) the empire had ended and in consequence a grammatical and rhetorical education was no longer a requisite for its elites.[105]

It is the general trend of linguistic study of Latin to favour particular sorts of sources that reveal 'informal' Latin: almost a linguists' canon. This includes anything early (Plautus and Terence gain particular attention, presumably because they offer a representation of daily speech); thereafter, either non-literary texts like inscriptions or graffiti, or literary texts that seem to reveal the spoken language and its mutations – the freedmen's speeches in Petronius, the Old Latin Bible, Egeria.[106] By contrast, formal Latin certainly changes, but there are always attempts to match both grammar and style to previous models. The phenomenon of archaic Latin is arguably really a reflection of a process of linguistic standardisation around the first century BCE, which also entails putting certain literary texts at the centre of the canon.[107] Late Latin seems only very partially convincing as a linguistic construct and unconvincing as a literary one, given that it antedates the more substantial changes after the Roman period.[108]

---

[104] For the late antique skew of surviving grammatical works of antiquity see Zetzel 2018.
[105] For an insightful sketch from a literary Latinist's perspective, see Shanzer 2009: 15–17. See John 2018 on education.
[106] Adams' *Anthology of Informal Latin* (2016) gives a personal illustration of this canon, which intersects only occasionally with the literary one. But there are similar preferences in e.g. Clackson and Horrocks 2007. Adams is reluctant (pp. 655–7) to define 'informal Latin' too closely. On the problems of the term 'vulgar Latin', see Clackson in this volume.
[107] For a summary of this generally held view, see e.g. Leonhardt 2013: 56–73; Clackson and Horrocks 2007: 183–228; Adams 2013 and 2016 is more cautious about standardisation and suggests that it is an area meriting further study.
[108] It would be interesting to consider whether the importance given to late Latin and Christian Latin as linguistic periods in the early twentieth century contributed to the unfortunate decision to end the coverage of the *Oxford Latin Dictionary* in 200 CE (see n. 77 and Gibson and Whitton's introduction, pp. 11–13).

For all that, similar usage of Latin in different periods should not hide very different contexts. To write letters in formal Ciceronian Latin is a very different cultural practice both for Cassiodorus in the sixth century and for Salutati in the fourteenth from what it meant for Cicero: for Cicero, a mildly formal version of a first language, universally comprehensible, albeit flecked with Greek code-switching; for Cassiodorus a book language at some distance from spoken Latin, in a court where Gothic was also spoken; for Salutati a book language and an international language presumably incomprehensible to most of his fellow speakers of the Tuscan vernacular.

## 4 Metre

In this section I am going to try using metre (and in the next, and more briefly, prose rhythm) as a means of fleshing out other periodisations of Latin literature. It is a curiosity that although Livius Andronicus' *Odussia*, the first substantial work of known Latin literature (*c.* 240 BCE), was a version of Homer, it was not in Homer's metre. There is no consensus on how the Saturnian metre worked in formal terms, even on whether it was primarily quantitative or accentual.[109] Naevius' epic on the first Punic War was also in Saturnians. But Andronicus also adapted Greek quantitative metres in his tragedies, and was followed by Naevius and Ennius; when Ennius wrote his epic it was in Greek-style quantitative hexameters, and he also write elegiac couplets. The metrical tradition that was followed in virtually all Latin poetry down to late antiquity, and remained dominant thereafter, was thus established.[110]

The versions of Greek metres used by Andronicus, Naevius, Ennius and Plautus shared clear and agreed rules of long and short syllables similar to those of their Greek models. Though prosody would change slightly in detail, in hexameters and elegiacs the fundamentals remain very similar in later Latin writers. In early tragedy and comedy, however, perhaps because of the natural preponderance of long syllables in Latin in comparison to Greek, authors diverged from the practice of Greek predecessors by various licences, including substituting long for short syllables in all but the final metron of both iambic and trochaic metres; they also varied the range of metres. Those writing tragedy in the classical period – only the Senecan corpus survives – abandoned these licences and followed the Greek template. As for comedy, even though Plautus was always read and Terence was one of the most widely read of Latin

[109] The problem is deepened by the uncertainty regarding the Latin word accent in this period. The most recent attempted solution is Mercado 2012. See also Clackson's chapter, pp. 578–82.
[110] Feeney 2016: 59–60 rightly warns against a teleological approach that sees Saturnians as backward.

authors in the Roman empire, admired for his clear conversational Latin,[111] the two authors' metres baffled subsequent generations. Several (not very helpful) guides by grammarians are extant; Rufinus ended his section on comic metres by citing a long list of authorities who insisted that Terence wrote poetry, not prose (*GL* IV 565.1–6). And a further illustration of how alien comic metres were comes in the anonymous fifth-century comedy *Querolus*, which is set out by editors as prose but whose phrases insistently end in cretics, echoing the ending – what perhaps seemed to the author the only fixed feature – of Plautine iambic senarii and trochaic septenarii.[112]

Tellingly, and consistently with the story told elsewhere in this chapter, it is in the second half of the first century BCE that the Roman versions of Greek metres were finally settled. A number of archaisms or (to the classically trained ear) idiosyncrasies of early Latin prosody disappear rapidly. In Ennius' version of Greek metres, final *s* could be elided before another consonant or consonant cluster to produce a short syllable, perhaps reflecting the letter's light pronunciation: so that *fraxinus frangitur* (*Ann.* 6 fr. 9 Skutsch) scans as two dactyls, for instance. In the 50s BCE Lucretius uses this sigmatic ecthlipsis around forty times.[113] But it was already an archaism: his exact contemporary Catullus uses it only once, seemingly as an allusion to Ennius (*Carm.* 116.8).[114] In 46 BCE Cicero (who elides *s* eight times in surviving early poems) describes it as 'bumpkin-like, though formerly elegant' (*subrusticum sed olim politius*, *Orator* 141); and it is never found in Virgil. One could tell a similar story for the archaic first-declension genitive singular in the disyllable -*ai* (e.g. Ennius *siluai frondosai*): common in Lucretius, never in Catullus, thrice in Virgil for archaic effect.[115]

Regularisation is found not just in prosody but in metres too. Catullus was a powerful influence on later authors who wrote in Phalaecian hendecasyllables, but when Pliny the Elder in the dedication to Vespasian of his *Natural History* quoted his fellow Cisalpine's dedication of his poems to Nepos (Catull. 1.3–4), he adapted the metre:

> ... namque tu solebas
> nugas esse aliquid meas putare.
> ut obiter emolliam Catullum conterraneum meum.   (*HN* praef.1)

> ... for you were wont
> To think my trifles not quite worthless
> if I may in passing soften my fellow-countryman Catullus.

---

[111] For ancient scholarship see Zetzel 2018: 253–7.   [112] O'Donnell 1981: 182–212.
[113] Butterfield 2008.   [114] Barchiesi 2005: 335–6.
[115] See Martial, *Epigr.* 11.95 for a parody of both effects; Nethercut 2021: 167–8 argues that Lucretius' usage is a deliberately Ennian archaism.

'Softening Catullus in passing' meant rewriting the line *meas esse aliquid putare nugas*. Catullus allowed a short syllable in first or second position in the hendecasyllable;[116] later practitioners (Martial, Statius, Ausonius, Sidonius) did not. In Catullus, the eleven-syllable line of the sapphic metre (– ᴗ – × – ᴗ ᴗ – ᴗ – –) can have the fourth syllable either long or short: a generation later in Horace it is always long, and subsequent ancient writers of Latin sapphics (including Statius, Ausonius, Paulinus of Nola and Sidonius) uniformly follow Horace.[117]

Other changes in metrical practice take place in the same short period just after 50 BCE in the central metres of hexameter and elegiacs. If one reads the first 100 lines of the fragments of Ennius' *Annales* that include the line ending, the commonest endings are with disyllabic words preceded by a word of at least three syllables or trisyllabic ones preceded by a word of at least two syllables (respectively 31 and 35 times), but he has a great diversity of combinations of words beside that: full five-syllable words taking up the last two feet (*altivolantum, induperator*), spondeiazon lines, final monosyllables.[118]

Table 3.2 *Selected hexameter poets from Ennius to Petrarch: word divisions in the last two feet.*

| first 100 lines of | 3/2 | 2/3 | 2/1/2 | Other |
| --- | --- | --- | --- | --- |
| Ennius, *Annales* | 31 | 35 | 2 | 32 |
| Lucretius | 38 | 43 | 6 | 14 |
| Catullus 62 and 64 | 53 | 32 | 1 | 14 |
| Virgil, *Eclogues* | 52 | 42 | 6 | 0 |
| Lucan | 57 | 37 | 6 | 0 |
| Walter, *Alexandreis* | 42 | 48 | 7 | 3 |
| Petrarch, *Africa* | 52 | 41 | 6 | 2 |

---

[116] Morgan 2010: 65.
[117] Catullus' two poems in sapphics are ignored by Horace at *Carm.* 3.30.13–14, where he claims to be the first to import Aeolian metres into Latin. For a full list of ancient Latin authors of sapphics, and other comprehensive metrical listings, see the invaluable *Musisque deoque* website (www.mqdq.it).
[118] For this exercise I paid no attention to whether the fifth foot started with a word break; for the fragments of Ennius I used Skutsch and counted all lines with a hexameter clausula. For Catullus 62 I counted the refrain only once.

But if one turns to Virgil's first collection of poems, the *Eclogues*, probably completed in around 39 BCE, the pattern is strikingly different. In the first hundred lines, the last two feet only have word divisions before the penultimate and antepenultimate syllables of the line: the three patterns *tegmine fagi* (fifty-two times), *ar-debat Alexin* (forty-two times), and *lentus in umbra* (five times). There are no spondaic fifth feet, no final monosyllables.[119] Go back a mere twenty years before Virgil, and the first 100 hexameters of Lucretius and Catullus show 86 per cent within Virgil's three patterns. But though there would be exceptions – satirists adopted a looser approach to the hexameter, for example – epic poets after Virgil for the most part stuck to his version of the hexameter: the first 100 lines of Lucan, who was in some ways an anti-Virgil, cleave 100 per cent to the same three forms; the equivalent lines in a mediaeval hexameter poem, Walter de Châtillon's *Alexandreis*, and a proto-humanist one, Petrarch's *Africa*, show 97 per cent and 98 per cent adherence to the three Virgilian patterns.[120] In other words, based on this admittedly narrow metrical experiment, we could infer that Virgil's version of the hexameter became the standard one to which authors returned, or, to put it more sensationally, that Virgil's versification has more in common with Petrarch's than that of Lucretius or Catullus – who in other ways influenced him profoundly. This (narrow, metrical) conclusion fits nicely with the canonisation of certain authors and styles in the triumviral and Augustan period, and with the fact that Virgil came to be taught in schools in his own lifetime.

Of course, Ennius, Lucretius and Catullus all continued to be read and to serve to differing degrees as models. It would be wrong too to give the impression that the hexameter remained unchanged ever after: to give a couple of examples, through the rest of the Roman period, authors increasingly preferred to avoid elision, especially of long syllables; and across all metres there were shifts in prosody (for example, final -*o* in the nominative case and in first-person verbs was more often short as the imperial period continued). Nor should we see Virgil alone as responsible for a metrical revolution. In exactly the same years that Virgil wrote, we see the above-mentioned changes in sapphics and hendecasyllables and a similar profound change in the pentameter of the elegiac couplet, usually attributed to Tibullus: a turn towards a final disyllable in contrast to the

---

[119] In fact, the fifth-foot spondee never wholly disappears (it occurs once in the *Eclogues*, in *Eclogue* 4, a poem which imitates metrical features of Catullus 64). The same applies to final monosyllables.
[120] And the exceptions are minor ones (3/1/1 and 1/2/2).

previous generation's great diversity. In the other elegists, the effect is stark. Propertius dramatically changes his practice in favour of the final disyllable after the first book (*c.* 30 BCE); Ovid, whose career began in the late 20s, almost wholly avoids any pentameter ending other than the disyllable; and this preference is persistent in elegiacs thereafter, though not all authors maintain it.[121] So it is rather the case that we can see a number of shifts in metrical practice canonised in the period between about 45 and 20 BCE.

There are good reasons that the patterns at the end of the Latin version of the hexameter and pentameter became uniform in this way: they have to do with the incorporation of quantitative verse into a language with a stress accent.[122] Since the rules of the Latin accent are quite regular, the three Virgilian forms guarantee an accent on the first beat of the final two feet, while the alternatives do not.[123] The fact that Greek contemporaries show no equivalent tendency suggests strongly that this trend is connected to the Latin accent, and a similar trend in prose rhythm, discussed in section 5, provides further confirmation.[124]

It is clear from reading some popular attempts at hexameters, in epitaphs for example, that it was the rhythmical cadence that impressed itself on speakers of Latin in the Roman empire who did not fully understand or had their own versions of prosody: one thinks of funerary inscriptions on tombs or the Christian poet Commodian (probably third-century), where versions of hexameters are found that only loosely resemble the norm.[125] It may be that the rules of metre were always an approximation to the realities of the Latin language, but linguistic changes, including difficulties in distinguishing between long and short vowels, were also certainly

---

[121] Ceccarelli 2018.

[122] Not all linguistic specialists would accept my arguments here. Some scholars take seriously the claims of Latin grammarians that their language had a pitch accent, while others would see these claims as an unconvincing attempt to impose a Greek template on the language. I assume that the latter is correct. For a more sympathetic view of the other side of the argument see Clackson's chapter, pp. 578–82. For a nuanced attempt to understand grammarians' treatment of the Latin accent, see Probert 2019.

[123] I.e. (with bold for accented syllables) **lēntŭs ĭn** | **ŭmbrā**; *ar-*|**dēbăt Ā-**|**lēxĭn**; **tēgmĭnĕ**|**făgī**; as against: *gene-*|*trīx pătrī'* | *nōstrī*; *ĕxŏrī-*|*tŭr sōl*. A similar explanation can be made for the final disyllable in the pentameter. Although the accent on that word will be off the beat, it will cause the accent to fall on the first long of the fourth foot, and of the third too, if there are two additional words in the second hemistich (e.g. **mīlĭtăt** | **ōmnĭs ăm-**|**ăns**).

[124] In fact, Greek underwent major changes in metrical practice in the fifth century under the influence of Nonnus of Panopolis (see Magnelli 2016). A number of these move in the direction of encouraging the accent (now very definitely a stress accent) to coincide with the long syllables of the line, but this was obviously less regular than in Latin given that Greek accents can in principle fall on any of the last three syllables of the word.

[125] See for example the inscribed hexameters of the centurion M. Porcius Iasucthan quoted by Clackson in his chapter, pp. 568–9.

## 3 Periodisations

a factor. As good a Latinist as Augustine acknowledged that he could not hear the differences between long and short vowels (he chose as illustration the first syllable of *cano* – the third word of the *Aeneid* and thus of the Latin curriculum).[126] The surviving verses of as learned a man as Jerome are vitiated by false quantities.[127] In the 370s and early 380s Jerome's employer pope Damasus covered the city with his poems, inscribed with stunning beauty by the calligrapher Filocalus: they celebrated the martyrs in vigorous verse that occasionally deviated from metrical rules.[128] The deviations are themselves indicative. One of Damasus' tics is to lengthen short vowels before the enclitic *-que*: following Christ through the stars, Peter and Paul *aetherios petiere sinus regnāque piorum*, 'made for the lap of heaven and the kingdoms of the blessed'.[129] By the rules of metre, that syllable should be short – but late antique grammarians tell us that the syllable before enclitics always carried the word accent, even if short. Accordingly, it was natural enough for him to treat the syllable as long, simply by applying back the rules of the Latin accent to infer the quantity of the syllable; the greater surprise is how many late antique poets maintained the traditional scansion, despite pronunciation.[130] It is important to be reminded that producing Virgilian verse in a period when the language was pronounced somewhat differently was neither easy nor automatic.

Nevertheless, verse using the rules of scansion as introduced by Ennius and perfected under Virgil remained immensely popular throughout the empire. Rough contemporaries of Damasus like Ausonius, Prudentius, Claudian and Paulinus of Nola produced verse in both hexameters and a great diversity of other traditional but sometimes recherché metres, and preserved metrical norms, and this continues throughout the fifth and sixth centuries. Verse prefaces became a convention, and compositions in multiple metres (polymetry) and alternating prose and poetry (prosimetry) flourished.[131] The most

---

[126] *De musica* 2.1.1; see Adams 2007: 261 for discussion and comparanda (he posits that the ambiguity of the vowel may be a specifically north African phenomenon).

[127] Cameron 2011: 317.

[128] The 'false quantities' are so regular that Alan Cameron used their regularity to support his argument for attributing to Damasus the anonymous *Carmen contra paganos* (Cameron 2011: 312–16); see Trout 2015: 26–38.

[129] *Regnāque piorum* at 20.5, 25.5, 39.8 and 43.5. In the first two cases Damasus could have written *et regna piorum* in accordance with normal prosody (likewise in the others with a little tweaking).

[130] I would surmise that we are dealing with a change of pronunciation that arose by analogy, since the vast majority of forms followed by *-que* or another enclitic would be long by nature or position (e.g. *plerumque*, *plerique*, *plerosque*, etc. occur far more often than *pleraque*).

[131] On prefaces see e.g. Dorfbauer 2010, Pelttari 2014: 45–72; on polymetry Consolino 2017; on *prosimetrum* (for example Boethius, Martianus Capella) and its *longue durée*, see Stover's chapter in this book, pp. 291–2.

influential work in the latter format, Boethius' *Consolation of Philosophy*, has poems in eighteen different metres.

But it is also in the fourth and fifth century that other forms of poetry start to appear. The spread of Christianity among Latin speakers and of scripture in Latin exposed Christians to material that was evidently in some sense poetry, but which had no conventional poetic form: the translations of the psalms and New Testament canticles (the late antique hymn *Te deum laudamus* is sometimes thought to be of this type, but it is in fact in its original form clausulated prose). Still more significantly, the first definitively accentual Latin poems appear. Though this is the beginning of a great tradition, there are relatively few of them. Augustine's *Psalmus contra partem Donati* has an abecedarian structure, so each section begins with the letter of the alphabet following on from the last (a feature with precedents in Hebrew poetry); it presents eight-syllable half-lines with a trochaic feel and use of elision and synizesis (e.g. *ecclesiae* as three syllables). The verse letter written in *c.* 470 by Auspicius of Toul to Arbogastes, count of Trier, presents eight-syllable lines in four-line stanzas, with an iambic feel and maintenance of hiatus without elision (*Austrasian Letters* 23).[132] A possible model for Auspicius can be found in the hymns of Ambrose; though written in quantitative iambic dimeters, they paved the way for later versions of the same metre where accent replaced quantity. A subtler version of the shift seen in Auspicius can be found in the opening of a famous hymn by Venantius Fortunatus:[133]

> Vexilla regis prodeunt,
> fulget crucis mysterium,
> quo carne carnis conditor
> suspensus est patibulo.

The standards of the king advance, the mystery of the cross shines clear, for there in flesh flesh's creator was hung upon a gibbet.

The iambic metre is preserved by the use of the short third and seventh syllables, but in the fourth line we find the second syllable of *patibulo*, short but accented, in a position where there should be a long. This might once have been a solecism, but shows the shift towards accentual poetry that

---

[132] *MGH Epistolae* III 135–7; see Brandes 1905.   [133] *Carmina* 2.6.1–4 (trans. M. Roberts).

would exist alongside quantitative poetry throughout the Middle Ages. Over a century before Fortunatus, Sedulius' tendency towards assonance at middle and end of line has been seen as a precursor of the widespread use of rhyme in later accentual poetry.[134]

The Latin poetry of the Middle Ages presents enormous diversity: not only the coexistence of both quantitative and accentual traditions, but also the significant presence of rhyme including in the 'Leonine' hexameter, macaronic poetry that alternates Latin with the vernacular, and much else.[135] For example, even if much of the best-known accentual poetry develops out of iambs or trochees, it is worth recalling that there were also accentual versions of hexameters and of more exotic metres, such as sapphics or alcaics.[136]

The impression given by Latin metre, then, is of the establishment of quantitative metres in the third century BCE, the canonisation of their rules in the later first century BCE, and the dominance of those rules for the rest of the language's history. Some innovations are first found in late antiquity but primarily associated with the Middle Ages: accentual verse, rhyme and macaronic verses. Mainly, however, the practice of late antiquity is one of continuity even in the face of underlying linguistic change.

## 5 Prose Rhythm

The use of metrical and accentual rhythms in prose tells a similar story of broad continuity amid linguistic change, though the practice is less universal and consistent, and more prone to evolution. Like quantitative metres, metrical clause endings – carefully distinct from those of verse – were first introduced from Greek models in the late republic.[137] Cicero, if not the first Latin user of clausulae, was by far the most influential: his favoured metres at the ends of phrases included the cretic spondee $- \smile - | - \times$, the double cretic $- \smile - | - \smile \times$ (also with a molossus $- - -$ as a substitute for the first cretic), the ditrochee preceded by a cretic or a molossus $- \times - | - \smile - \times$, and the hypodochmiac $- \smile - \smile \times$; variations include the notorious first paeon and spondee $- \smile \smile \smile | - \times$ (as in *esse uideatur*).[138] But even in his

---

[134] Norberg 2004: 31–2.
[135] For macaronic poetry see Stover's chapter, pp. 310–11, 314–15; here too one could argue that there are late antique precedents in the Greek/Latin macaronic verses of Ausonius.
[136] Norberg 2004: 81–129; Rigg 1992: 313–29 usefully illustrates the (fairly representative) metres used in Anglo-Latin poetry in the period 1066–1422.
[137] On the history of scholarship on prose rhythm in antiquity, see e.g. Oberhelman 2003.
[138] In all cases the quantity of the final syllable of the clause is (formally if not aesthetically) indifferent, so what I call spondee is sometimes defined as trochee.

oratory, Cicero's use of standard artistic rhythms is inconsistent in its extent, with some speeches much more and others much less clausulated; his practice varies still more strongly in his letters.[139] The personal and idiosyncratic nature of this practice is well illustrated by the vagueness of Cicero's discussion in his *Orator* 210–36 (the same vagueness can be found in practically all ancient discussions of prose rhythm). Many late republican or early imperial prose writers did not show the same fondness for these Greek rhythms: indeed some – for example, historians like Sallust and Livy – consciously avoided them and exercised their own quite different preferences. Others alternated: the orator Tacitus tends towards Ciceronian clausulae in his *Dialogus*, but when writing as a historian he mostly shuns them.[140]

Move forward a millennium or so, and the practice of prose rhythm was quite different, based on word accent. Modern scholarship refers to the system as *cursus*; the favoured accentual patterns at the end of clauses are (where ó is an accented and ~ an unaccented syllable): 'cursus planus' (ó~~ó~), 'cursus tardus' (ó~~ó~~), and 'cursus velox' (ó~~~~ó~). Some authors also use 'cursus trispondaicus' (ó~~~ó~) and/or 'cursus octosyllabicus' ó~~~~ó~~.

Such a practice is by no means universal, being most consistently used in papal and other chanceries, but appears intermittently throughout Latinate western Europe. For example, *cursus* features in several of the mediaeval prose authors quoted in Justin Stover's chapter (Eugenius, Rather of Verona, Peter Damian) as well in the quotation of Salutati in my section 1.[141] It fell out of favour at the end of the Middle Ages.

The Ciceronian and mediaeval forms of prose rhythm might seem, presented thus, to be wholly different systems (and to match the contrast between quantitative and accentual verse as well). But in fact they are closely related. What stands between them – in the period from roughly 200 to 600, when artistic prose rhythm is arguably more widespread than before – is usually called 'cursus mixtus' (not an ancient name). By the standard story, there was a narrowing down of the metrical clausulae used and a tendency to fit words within them into particular patterns, with the result – thanks to the regularity of the Latin accent – that the word-stress would fall on the first syllable of each foot, just like the trend in verse endings.

---

[139] For a demonstration see Keeline and Kirby 2019: 189–93.
[140] The *Germania*, and speeches in *Agricola* and the *Histories*, are close to the *Dialogus*: Keeline and Kirby 2019: 194–8.
[141] pp. 305, 308–10, 311, 100. Janson 1975 is the standard work on mediaeval prose rhythm, and proposes a methodology of identifying whether prose is influenced by cursus or not.

In Cicero's usage both *iac-**tábit** aud**á**cia* and *coniuratió-**nem** túam **non** uídes* produce double cretic clausulae. In the first the stress accents fall on the first syllables of each cretic (in bold here), and in the latter they do not. The first type, preferred even by Cicero, became overwhelmingly dominant, and double cretics coincided with the so-called 'cursus tardus'. Similarly the cretic spondee led to the 'cursus planus' and a ditrochee preceded by a cretic with a word break between the two feet led to an accent on the first syllable of the first foot and on the second trochee: that is, the 'cursus velox'. The development of accentual rhythm simply arises through the accentual patterns (which usually involve two or four unstressed syllables between the last two stressed syllables)[142] being seen as the primary feature, and the metrical element being weakened or lost. There are problems with the term 'cursus mixtus', beyond anachronism: though many authors did use the mixed system and it was still flourishing in the ornate *Variae* of Cassiodorus or the saints' lives of Venantius Fortunatus in the sixth century, the situation is better seen as a mix of multiple coexisting systems.[143] The preference for clausulae with coinciding ictus and accent is there as early as Cicero, if not so strong as later, and can explain Cicero's use of clause endings which are 'near misses' in metrical terms.[144] An author as late as Sidonius can write with an essentially metrical system.[145] Some authors use clausulae only at some points and not others (for purple passages but not for narrative, for example): this can vitiate statistical attempts to identify practice through sampling. Meanwhile, the use simply of accentual clausulae can be seen as early as Ammianus Marcellinus in *c.* 390, for whom metrical considerations are, if not wholly absent, entirely secondary;[146] a number of other historiographical writers of late antiquity adopt the same system.

The story of Latin prose rhythm is one that tends to be told in descriptions of individual authors or, at best, periods. But it is in some ways a nice illustration of continuity in the writing of prose; and it clearly reflects (at least for the most part) the effects of education and practice rather than blind following of models: Cicero may be a fundamental inspiration for their use of clausulae but he is not normally a direct one. We see a metamorphosing style in the empire, but the use of metrical elements alongside accentual ones lasts many centuries, well beyond the end of the western empire; the appearance of the purely accentual cursus in late antiquity is a new beginning that was

---

[142] The exception is the so-called 'cursus trispondaicus', which derives from paeon 1 + spondee.
[143] The situation is also complicated by a shift to a similar accentual system in Greek art-prose in the fourth century.
[144] Winterbottom 2011 and 2017: 410–11.   [145] Van Waarden and Kelly 2020.
[146] Harmon 1910.

nevertheless compatible with and closely modelled on what went before, and that lasted in various contexts till the end of the Middle Ages. The real break actually comes then. It is an interesting paradox that, as humanists sought to write prose in a reformed 'Ciceronian' style, this did not include restoring Cicero's metrical clausulae and involved the disappearance of rhythmical ones as well. Because prose rhythm was much less widely and less clearly theorised than metre, it was possible for it to be largely forgotten until rediscovered by scholars of the 1880s and 1890s.[147] The comparative lack of reference works suggests that continuity in this field might be seen as evidence for at least some degree of continuity in rhetorical education.

## 6 Politics

Naming literary periods after political arrangements is a very well-established practice, both on the macro-level – for example, republican, imperial, or, indeed, Roman[148] – and on the narrower level of categorising literature according to rulers or dynasties (Augustan, Flavian, etc.). The obvious and widespread assumption is that political systems *should* have a powerful effect on literature: it is implicit, for example, in the designation of the Latin of the later Roman empire by linguists (see section 3) as 'late Latin' – though it is clearly only late in terms of the history of the western Roman state. The presence of an emperor alongside the Roman republican magistrates certainly inaugurates a profound change in attitudes in literature as in life.

Imperial-era Romans built the republic into their sense of their own literary history. Tacitus' *Dialogue about Orators*, a work which adopts the form of the Platonic dialogue as Cicero had transposed it to Rome, confronts the problem of oratory's decline since the age of Cicero. Among the viewpoints expressed by the different speakers (blaming moral laxity, questioning the proposition), the last and most resonant voice, Maternus, stands out, proposing that great rhetoric like Cicero's is the product of disordered times. In a system where decisions are taken by one wise man, great debates – and hence great oratory – are unnecessary (*Dial.* 40–1).[149] Later, in his

---

[147] Among the very earliest studies respectively on metrical and rhythmical clausulae are Wüst 1881 and Valois 1881.

[148] The national Latin literatures of the Middle Ages and early modern period might also be assimilated to this model, though in some cases the state was not strong. For example, the Norman conquest bound Anglo-Latin literature much more closely to the continental mainstream and 1066 therefore marks a starting point for Rigg 1992.

[149] Another speaker, Aper, who attempts interestingly to gainsay the superiority of antiquity, nevertheless proposes a dividing point in 43 BCE, the year of Augustus' first consulship and Cicero's death (*Dial.* 17).

*Annals*, Tacitus reflected that the material from which he could construct his historical account under an autocracy was fundamentally limiting in comparison with those who narrated the earlier deeds of the Roman people: his own effort was narrow and inglorious (*nobis in arto et inglorius labor*, *Ann.* 4.32.2). Without the depth or self-reflection of Tacitus, many other writers see the pre-autocratic past as fundamentally distinct. In the historical examples that Latin poets, declaimers and historians love, republican history – in a heroic mould filtered through Virgil and Livy – offers uncomplicated prestige and is used far more widely than imperial history.[150]

What difference did emperors make? Works written in the reign of the first emperor – indeed early in his reign, as far as it can be defined – are filled with references to him, his putative ancestors and his heirs. This applies not only to obvious works like Virgil's *Aeneid* and Horace's *Odes*, but unlikely ones such as Ovid's *Amores*; and Virgil and Horace, of course, became centrepieces of the teaching curriculum and central models for the future. In the following centuries individual emperors received dedications of numerous works that might surprise (Valerius Maximus' collection of *exempla*, Pliny the Elder's *Natural History*, Volusius Maecianus' treatise on weights and measures), and pious mentions in countless others.

For all that, we might wonder whether it always mattered who the emperor was. Much Augustan literature is intimately linked to the regime, but was this always the case? Much later, Charlemagne might provide another example of a ruler under whom literary and political culture were intimately linked and profoundly changed,[151] but in the Roman period, do individual emperors make a difference? Tacitus calls the regimes of Nerva (96–8) and Trajan (98–117) the rare and happy times in which one could speak one's mind, in contrast to the enforced silence of litterateurs under Domitian (81–96); much the same attitude is found in the Younger Pliny's letters.[152] And yet Domitian's reign saw the complete literary oeuvres of Quintilian and Statius appear, as well as most of Martial and in all probability further epics; and even if Tacitus' focus is on the travails of senators, it seems impossible to see senatorial writing as a different category. Domitian's death prompts no great revival of letters: simply the politically correct condemnations of the immediate past that are expected of the ruling class following a coup d'état in an autocratic system. Tacitus never did get round to a history of Nerva and Trajan's reigns, because historians in his mould

---

[150] Gowing 2005; Nixon 1990.   [151] McKitterick 2008, esp. pp. 292–380.
[152] Tacitus, *Hist.* 1.1.4, *Agr.* 2–3; on a similar implicit narrative in Pliny see Gibson and Morello 2012: 25–6.

never wrote about the current dynasty. When Juvenal remarks that all the hopes of literature rest in Caesar alone (*Sat.* 7.1), it has been seen as a compliment to the new emperor Hadrian. But he is not named, and the idea that the emperor is the sole viable source of literary patronage is both a lie and a cliché: the early imperial period is notable both for senatorial and equestrian authors from across the empire, almost all writing in Rome, and with multiple senatorial patrons if they lacked independent means. The reference to an undifferentiated 'Caesar' is not uncommon: when Jesus asked whose head was on the coin, the Pharisees did not name Tiberius but Caesar.[153] Likewise the everyday references of the two canonical Latin novels to the emperor are to Caesar, not a named individual.[154]

Designating periods by ruling emperors is fashionable, but only selectively applied: as already mentioned, it may be problematic to take it as more than a convenient chronological marker (Victorian literature rarely has much to do with the personality or patronage of its queen). While adjectives to apply to reigns or dynasties can be and are freely created, there are plenty of such micro-periods which are rarely or never given imperial names; in some cases it is ambiguous whether an emperor or a dynasty is denoted (Constantinian, Theodosian, Carolingian). The labels seem only to be attached to certain types of literature: Caesius Bassus' grammatical work, though seemingly dedicated to Nero, does not get dealt with as Neronian literature. Nor does the book of Revelation, for that matter. Sometimes names may well be deployed in an understandable attempt of scholars to give significance to their period of study. It is tempting to wonder whether 'Tiberian literature' might be a label optimistically attempting to claim value for research on the fascinating but unglamorous works of Velleius Paterculus, Valerius Maximus and the Elder Seneca.

Neronian literature, for example, is a popular topic for university courses because it enables the combination of some attractive and important writers, including Lucan, Petronius and Seneca. Themes of doublespeak and theatricality living under tyranny can be brought in, and a poignant backdrop comes from the knowledge of Nero's cultural interests, of the writers' close connections to him, and of Tacitus' accounts of their forced suicides (even if the connection of Tacitus' Petronius to the author of the *Satyrica* is not exactly certain).[155] But beyond the doubts

---

[153] Matthew 22:17–21 = Mark 12:14–17 = Luke 20:22–5.
[154] Petronius 51 (cf. 60.7, Augustus); Apuleius, *Met.* 3.29.
[155] Tacitus, *Ann.* 15.60–3, 15.70; 16.18–19. At the very least we can say that these Petronii were later thought to be the same, since at some point the novelist was designated as 'Arbiter' to match Tacitus' description of the courtier as *elegantiae arbiter* (*Ann.* 16.18.2).

## 3 Periodisations

about whether Petronius and the second-tier figure of Calpurnius Siculus actually are Neronian, one might wonder how far the *Satyrica*, for example, is really illuminated by a Neronian dating: the occasional attempts to see Trimalchio's dinner party as parodying Nero's court are absurd.[156]

One short-term political periodisation which I would want to defend as distinctive, as different from what comes before or after, is 'triumviral' – referring to the second triumvirate and its unravelling, say 43–30 BCE; perhaps we could extend it slightly earlier to take in Cicero's writings under Caesar's rule – is *Pro Marcello* the first imperial panegyric?[157] – and slightly later to take in the *Georgics*. Sallust's historical works would belong to this period, with their use of the past to illuminate more recent problems (the foreshadowing of the rivalries of Caesar and Cato in the *Catiline*, and of Marius and Sulla in the *Jugurtha*). This periodisation characterises the contrast between the earlier poems of Virgil, Horace and (perhaps) Propertius and the later. Virgil's fourth Eclogue of 40 BCE prophesies the boy who will bring the Golden Age, probably gesturing at an unborn son of Antony, or even of Pollio; by the time he completed *Aeneid* 6 in the late 20s, the prophecy was clearly about Augustus (6.791–93). There is an equally stark contrast in the other direction with the political discourse of, say, Catullus.

The most significant changes brought about by political transitions are arguably not dependent on the policies or personalities of individual emperors but on the nature of the state, in which the existence of an emperor is only one aspect. The end of the republic also coincided with a considerable widening of the elite away from the traditional aristocracy; senatorial and elite classes increasingly came from across the western Mediterranean. Latin was increasingly widely taught as the language of law and political power. Literary education across the west, and elites with one foot in Rome and another in the provinces, led to the phenomenon of surviving literature being written by an increasingly international range of authors – at first based almost exclusively in Rome; later, as the empire became more thoroughly Romanised and decentralised, in regional centres as well. Ultimately Latin even competed with Greek as an elite language in the east, particularly in law and government; and by the fourth century an abundance of Latin works are written in the east or by easterners – a phenomenon that continued, at least in Constantinople, until the late

---

[156] Note Lavan's comments (this volume, pp. 819–21) on literary scholars' obsession with reading all early imperial literature as being about the emperor.
[157] See Braund 1998.

sixth century. Equally fundamental are the effects of the disintegration of western empire, even if they were not immediate as far as literary culture was concerned. A version of Roman law continued to apply in the successor kingdoms, but the disappearance of Roman administrative structures in many of them (Italy is a partial exception, as discussed on p. 109) must have weakened the perceived need for a literary education. Existing regional variations grew wider and Latin began to coexist alongside vernaculars, some derived from Latin (perhaps the biggest divide of all). These political changes mark profound changes in literature too, but there are no narrow periodising labels – post-Roman and post-imperial are sometimes used, as Ostrogothic can be in Italy, Vandal in north Africa, or, slightly later, Merovingian in Gaul. The end of Roman literature in Latin, like the end of antiquity, is a fuzzy one.

## 7 Religion

For many Latinists, those who do not venture past Apuleius, religion probably plays little part in ideas of periodisation.[158] For those who go later, it is inevitable, and I use the subtitle with a focus on Christianity. 'What difference did Christianity make?' is a provocative question occasionally asked by historians of later antiquity, with varying answers.[159] Much late Roman social and cultural history as currently practised is more or less indistinguishable from history of Christianity: changes in ideas of wealth, the body and sex are enormous, and undeniably linked to Christianity. In political and military history, the issue is much more debatable. What of literature? As we have already observed, the majority of surviving Latin literature from antiquity is written by late antique Christians, and in most cases the author's religion is integral rather than incidental to the purpose of the text. The business letters of bishops, from Rome and across the west, hagiography and martyrology, biblical exegesis in the form both of sermons and of commentaries, apologetic and heresiology, records of church councils, theological treatises. Beside that, a vast and still not fully tallied quantity of material survives that has been translated from Greek.[160] Christian poetry took the forms of biblical epic, versified saints lives and martyrologies, hymns, apologetic, building epigrams and epitaphs. In the new and already mentioned volume 6 of the

---

[158] Thus Feeney's *Literature and Religion at Rome* (1998) does not deal with Christianity except in so far as it warps our perceptions of earlier religion.
[159] MacMullen 1986 for a provocative and nuanced answer.   [160] See n. 61.

*Handbuch der lateinischen Literatur der Antike*, which covers the period 374–430, a full 1,000 pages out of 1,700 are devoted to Christian prose. And this late antique Christian material survives from a far broader geographical area than most earlier Latin literature. Most of Jerome's output was written in Bethlehem, most of Augustine's in his north African see of Hippo; moreover, in both cases almost all their enormous known output survives.

The shape of literature as it survives is thus transformed by Christianity – even if that is not perceived by all: as has already been discussed, most of this material does not form part of the vista of most Latinists. The whole idea of the classical, however defined, tends in the academy to create its identity by the exclusion of Christian writers (or at least those who are too Christian), and has done so for centuries, as we saw (p. 98) with Ainsworth's dictionary: Christian authors are for other departments, other book series, other dictionaries, other literary histories. (Arguably, the rejection of Christian authors as a subject for classicists has also impinged on the reception of pagan or secular authors from the same period: one popular Latin textbook defines all Latin of antiquity after the Silver Age as the 'patristic age').[161]

In a letter written before he became bishop of Clermont, Sidonius describes an extended house party at the villa of his friend Tonantius Ferreolus (a former Prefect of Gaul who later became an ascetic – even his names are divided between echoing an epithet of Jupiter and that of a local martyr). One set of bookshelves, near the ladies' seats, was dedicated to religious works, the other, by the men's benches, was ennobled by the grandeur of Latin eloquence (*coturno Latiaris eloquii nobilitabantur, Ep.* 2.9.4).[162] The Latin eloquence, however, was divided into authors who exercised similar powers of language (*parilitatem dicendi*) for different purposes, that is Christian and non-Christian authors: Augustine and Varro, Horace and Prudentius. The men of the party discussed Rufinus' translations of Origen (Sidonius gives a trigger warning for the latter's questionable theology), and agreed that they were as fine a translation into elegant Latin as Apuleius' of Plato or Cicero's of Demosthenes. This anecdote flatters the image of both the author (many scholars wonder whether Sidonius even knew Greek)[163] and his class, and Sidonius is of course nothing if not idiosyncratic, and yet the anecdote does give an

---

[161] *Wheelock's Latin* (Wheelock 2011: xxx–xxxv).
[162] The Loeb editor Anderson interprets the passage slightly differently (Anderson 1936: 453 n. 4).
[163] Their doubts are in my view misplaced.

attractive picture of how late antique Christians, even if they saw Christian authors as, theoretically, a different set of shelves in their library,[164] also saw them as part of the same literary ecosystem and appreciated the same learning, lyricism and Latinity. This sort of consciously inclusive mental library, balancing pagans against Christians as earlier Romans balanced Greek and Latin authors, would recur throughout the Middle Ages.[165]

But is the different shape of the literature to survive indicative of fundamental changes? Does Christianity create new genres, or does it rather give them distinct twists, and bring them into greater prominence? Biblical commentary, for example, is surely part of a wider tradition of literary and philosophical commentary; but one might pause before claiming that sermons should be seen as just another type of epideictic rhetoric. Some preachers may have come from such a tradition, but it was certainly not required. In some cases, genres have wrongly been considered intrinsically Christian: chronicle, for example.[166] Christianity brought some linguistic changes, partly through their technical vocabulary (and some secular authors made a show of avoiding Christian technical vocabulary), but more obviously through the use of the bible translations, which reflect both Greek originals with Hebraic influences and everyday speech. It is wrong, however, to consider *sermo cotidianus*, as for example in the pilgrimage narrative of Egeria, as something characteristically Christian.[167]

But at the same time an argument can be made for very significant continuity and adaptation. The Christian apologists of the third and fourth centuries stand in the tradition of Latin sophistic writing.[168] Christian poetry continues to allude to the Virgilian tradition, and as we saw in the metre section, late antiquity was an immensely productive age for Latin lyric; these two phenomena are combined and epitomised in the person of Prudentius, whose designation as the Christians' Virgil and Horace responds to the self-fashioning of his own writing.[169] And turning to more rigorous authors, even Jerome, who claimed to renounce secular reading after that dream in which God judged him for being a Ciceronian, not a Christian (*Ep.* 22.30), did not live up to such claims. Moreover, many of those writing in traditional genres were Christians. It used often to be wrongly alleged that because the majority of Ausonius' oeuvre was not explicitly Christian his adherence should be doubted; more recently

---

[164] See also *Epist.* 4.11.6; *Carm.* 4–5, 7.9.1, 8.11.2  [165] See e.g. Curtius 1953: 260–1.
[166] Burgess and Kulikowski 2013: 7: 'late antique and medieval chronicles ... were the outgrowth of a millennium-old Mediterranean tradition of writing history'.
[167] See e.g. Clackson and Horrocks 2007: 284–92. See also section 3 on the Nijmegen School.
[168] See Volk's chapter.  [169] Lühken 2002.

Ausonius' friend the orator Pacatus, often considered a pagan by default, has been outed as a Christian.[170] An important advance in understanding also comes from the demolition of the idea that pagans struggled to preserve their literature: many of those who commissioned copies of pagan works and subscribed them have been shown to be Christians.[171] Nor is there now any scope, outside potboilers, for the idea that 'pagan' literature was no longer read or was even destroyed because of its paganism.[172] Many supposedly 'pagan' genres stopped being written or read in the end, not because of Christianity but because without an empire to provide a governing class for, traditional grammatical education and the world of *paideia* was weakened.[173]

We can therefore see three main phenomena: first, the establishment and disproportionate spread – and later survival – of Christian forms of writing, of all sorts; secondly, the coexistence, continuity and assimilation of many of the more formal types of writing with earlier Roman writing forms; and thirdly, the establishment of a new set of Christian models (poets like Prudentius; theologians like Augustine, Ambrose, Jerome; popes like Leo I and later Gregory I; but also popular genres like saints' lives). Both continuity and difference deserve notice.

## 8 Book History

For my last case study I turn to an area not habitually used in periodising literature, but which is marked by a succession of profound changes through the history of Latin: books and the physical experience of reading.[174] Those of us who have lived through the vast expansion in the availability of digital publications have learned vividly how shifts in the nature of books, journals and newspapers can change the experience of reading and writing (though also how much – at least in the early stages of a development – can stay the same). There are a variety of shifts in book history that seem certain to have had an impact on literary history: the invention of printing in Europe is one; before that, the diffusion of techniques of paper manufacture in Europe, becoming mainstream in

---

[170] Turcan-Verkerk 2003.  [171] Cameron 2011.
[172] The burning, on Constantine's orders, of Porphyry's anti-Christian works is an outlier – and also fits with earlier Roman practices. That said, one might suspect that the fact that most early mediaeval copyists were Christian clerics or monastics increased the chances of survival of Christian compared to secular literature.
[173] John 2018.
[174] Throughout this section I owe much to repeated discussions with my colleagues Justin Stover and Aaron Pelttari.

the fourteenth century and providing a writing material at a fraction of the cost of parchment; and long before that the waning and disappearance of papyrus from western European markets in the early Middle Ages. But I shall focus here on the great change of the earlier centuries of the Christian era, that from the scroll to the codex.[175]

At its beginning Latin literature, like its Hellenistic models, was recorded by being written in columns on papyrus scrolls (*volumina*), usually of a fairly uniform length. Though there were other ways of circulating shorter items, it was into books, coterminous with the scrolls, that Latin literary works were arranged. These might consist of shorter works brought together, like Virgil's collection of his *Eclogues* or the books into which Cicero's thousands of letters were assembled,[176] or they might be longer works subdivided, like Virgil's *Georgics* and *Aeneid*; but considerable aesthetic attention was given to the ordering and balance of separate parts of individual books – in prose as well as poetry, and arguably even in cases like Cicero's letters, not edited by the author[177] – and to the artful and significant subdivision of longer works. In poetry, careful balancing of line numbers and responsion (to an astonishing degree in some books, like the *Eclogues*);[178] in prose, the beginning and ending of books at significant points, inviting comparison, and collection of works in groups of books, often in regular patterns. Thus the historical work of Livy divides into pentads and decades, that of Tacitus seemingly into hexads.[179] In Tacitus' *Annals*, the opening of book 13 and the third hexad, on Nero, verbally and thematically echoes the opening of the first book and hexad, on Tiberius.[180]

The differences made by the codex are substantial. On the one hand, works are more easily portable, with the contents of multiple scrolls includable in single objects and a larger proportion of the writing surface used than in a scroll. Passages are more easily looked up, bookmarked or found at random – as when Augustine's finger fell upon the passage of Paul that spurred his ascetic conversion (*Conf.* 8.29). But codices, especially

---

[175] For further discussion and bibliography see Squire and Elsner's chapter, pp. 632–52.
[176] We have 845 surviving letters in 37 books (not counting letters by others), and many other books are known to have been lost.
[177] On arrangement in Cicero's letters see Beard 2002, which has inspired much further scholarship (e.g. Martelli 2017).
[178] Rudd 1977: 119–44; for a recent ingenious attempt to unearth some of the intricacies of Virgil's design see Schafer 2017.
[179] See Barnes 1998: 209–12, for the argument that Livy wrote 140, not 142, books.
[180] Tacitus, *Ann.* 1.1.6 ~ 13.1.1. By the reconstruction accepted here, the *Annals* would have taken another two full books to get to Nero's demise from the point at which the text currently breaks off.

## 3 Periodisations

those of parchment,[181] also offer greater luxury, complexity and symbolic worth. Illustrations surely have more effect in a book that can be left open or easily leafed through, like the surviving late antique Virgil codices or Prudentius' *Psychomachia*, for which the illustrations, of battling virtues and vices, can be traced back close to the time of publication.[182] Paratextual headings in red ink were common, but there were also more luxurious possibilities (for example golden letters on a purple background). It is easier in a codex to represent multiple ideas that are not necessary linear: in Latin, Jerome's *Chronicle*, with up to four different columns over a two-page spread representing simultaneous events in different kingdoms, was an influential example, though its models are Greek.[183] A codex can become a significant object that represents the importance of its contents, like the *Theodosian Code* (where the word codex has taken on a sense of definitiveness) or biblical codices – and indeed a link has often, and perhaps overconfidently, been asserted between the spread of Christianity and the diffusion of the codex.[184]

Would it be tempting to claim that there was an age of the codex, a period that was fundamentally different for literature? Perhaps, but there are several significant problems. First is when the codex was adopted. Despite references as early as Martial, the major change was traditionally placed rather late, in the fourth century. In fact, however, the modern consensus is that the codex form was adopted gradually from roughly 100 to 400, as is evidenced by surviving books and book fragments. The earliest surviving manuscript of (parts of) Aulus Gellius, for example, a palimpsested codex now in the Vatican, used to be dated to the late third or fourth century. More recent research has placed it in roughly 180–235 – so perhaps even in Gellius' lifetime.[185] And yet Gellius must also have been transmitted in scrolls, as is evident from the loss of the text of book 8 (only) of the *Attic Nights*. So while there may have been a generation in

---

[181] The shift is often portrayed as being from papyrus scroll to parchment codex, but that is a gross simplification, as argued by Roberts and Skeat 1983: 5–10 (which still has not been replaced as the standard work on the codex). Parchment scrolls and papyrus codices were acceptable forms of book: a famous example of the latter from the fourth century is that containing Cicero's *Catilinarians* 1 and 2, and the Latin poems *Alcestis* and *Psalmus responsorius* (*CLA* 1782).

[182] On the late antique Virgil codices see Squire and Elsner's chapter, pp. 642–51; on Prudentius' *Psychomachia*, see Woodruff 1929.

[183] See Grafton and Williams 2006 on Origen's *Hexapla* and Eusebius' *Chronicle* (Jerome is a supplemented translation of the second section of the latter).

[184] See e.g. Roberts and Skeat 1983: 38–66; recent contributions include Harnett 2017 and Larson and Letteney 2019.

[185] Vatican, Pal. lat. 24 <inf. 7>. See Cavallo and Fioretti 2014 for the dating, accepted in Holford-Strevens 2020: 1 lix, cf. xi–xii.

which the codex clearly became dominant, the two forms certainly coexisted for a long time.

A second reason for caution is that there is a highly plausible correlation between the adoption of the codex and the survival of literary works. We have already seen the number of surviving works from the fourth century rises massively above that for earlier periods, and it is most unlikely that this is simply the result of greater literary production. Rather it has long been assumed that the transfer to the codex was a kind of winnowing process for earlier Latin literature. The codex – particularly the bound, multi-quire, parchment codex – was a securer and longer-lasting format and it was literature preserved in that format that had the chance to survive after the end of the Roman empire in the west. (Some works from the age of the scroll seem to have been knocked around in the process of conversion to codex form: the surviving *liber* of Catullus, for example, looks like the contents of at least three scrolls and there is doubt as to how closely the original arrangement has been preserved;[186] the second book of Propertius is also far longer than one would expect for a single scroll). One implication of the contribution of the codex to differential survival is that some of the perceived differences between late antique and earlier Latin literature may be a mirage: much more ephemeral and utilitarian Latin literature survives from late antiquity. Take the example of historical writing: if one compares the number of Latin historians known in fragmentary or indirect form in the early empire and the late, the earlier period has notably more.[187] And yet in the perhaps more ephemeral form of the abbreviated history we have many from late antiquity (e.g. Eutropius, Festus, the *corpus Aurelianum*, the *Anonymi Valesiani*) – but from the early empire only Velleius and Florus: the difference is of survival. Similarly (as already mentioned), we know that chronicles were produced in the early empire, but they were superseded and all surviving chronicles from antiquity are late.[188] The two classic and artful works of fiction surviving from the early empire, Petronius' *Satyrica* and Apuleius' *Metamorphoses*, are balanced by many later works, usually anonymous and often in multiple recensions, including the Alexander Romance, the story of Apollonius of Tyre, and the various martyr fictions. Similarly, the vast majority of surviving

---

[186] See e.g. Heerink 2009, Schafer 2020.
[187] Contrast the 110 historians of Cornell et al. 2013 (*Fragmentary Roman Historians*, covering 200 BCE to 250 CE (though this includes a few Greek authors) to the 20 attested historians of Van Hoof and Van Nuffelen 2020 (*The Fragmentary Latin Historians of Late Antiquity*, covering the period 300–620).
[188] See n. 166.

grammatical works are late antique, but we know that such works were written plentifully before late antiquity.[189] In other words, elite literature survives from both the early and the late empire, but the everyday, the middlebrow, the functional that survives comes almost solely from late antiquity – helping to create an implied narrative of decline in the quality of literary production. Continuity may have been much greater than it appears to be.[190]

The third reason for caution is that many of the aesthetic effects arising from scrolls, and the habits of careful arrangement into books, do not stop in the later empire, when codex publication must certainly have been the expectation and such divisions did not matter. Ammianus Marcellinus' history follows that of Tacitus in deploying hexads of books of relatively even length and with significant openings and closure. The letters of Ambrose and of Symmachus seem to have been divided into nine books of personal letters and one of imperial or official letters, mimicking the careful arrangement of Pliny the Younger; Sidonius likewise published nine books of letters to friends (there was no western emperor to write a tenth book to by the time he published), with remarkable artistry of arrangement within the books.[191] Poems by Claudian are divided into books, even when they may have been issued simultaneously;[192] many of Prudentius' poems are of recognisable scroll length and one of them, *Contra orationem Symmachi*, is divided into two such books. Augustine's *Confessions* are in thirteen books (a step up from the classic number of twelve). In their length the 'books' of late antique literary works are no longer constrained by the norms of scroll length. For some works, the history of Ammianus and the letters of Sidonius, for example, book lengths are relatively uniform; but in other cases divergences from classical norms arise: the tenth book of Augustine's *Confessions* is nearly four times the length of the second. The aesthetics of arrangement showed itself in new ways: a letter of Augustine discusses how gatherings (*quaterniones*) containing the twenty-two books of his *City of God* can most meaningfully be bound together (*Ep.* 1A in *CSEL* 88). There were of course other long works that were not divided into notional books any more. The idea of book

---

[189] The definitive treatment is Zetzel 2018.
[190] Making it into codex format is not in itself, of course, a sufficient reason for texts to survive: consider how comparatively little survives from the third or even the early fourth century. What survives seems disproportionately to represent the taste of the period just before the disintegration of the western empire. See Kelly 2008: 219–20.
[191] See Gibson 2020.
[192] For example, *De consulatu Stilichonis* 1 and 2 were delivered on the same occasion; *De raptu Proserpinae* 2 and 3 were plausibly issued together. These pairs of books each have only one preface.

divisions continues to exert influence in writing through the Middle Ages, though many works are divided by *capitula* (chapter headings) as well or instead.[193]

Late antiquity therefore coincides with a new beginning in the physical shape of the book, and also in ways of reading;[194] but the ongoing use of 'book divisions' within literary works should warn us against seeing total discontinuity. It might also be worth considering how other sorts of divisions and paratexts within works, such as prefaces, indices and chapter headings, become more frequent alongside the shift to the codex (though they all existed before it). This is an area of study with plenty of scope for further investigation.

## 9 Conclusions

The six perspectives on periodisation explored in this chapter are not, of course, wholly separable from each other. Historical processes cannot neatly be carved into separate provinces, as if religion, say, were distinct from politics – and yet disciplinary divisions, just like periodisations, are a natural, convenient and almost inevitable way of organising thinking, to prevent ourselves being overwhelmed by the sheer complexity of historical causation and change. The production and dissemination of literature is closely bound up with economics and writing technologies, and its ongoing influence with political, linguistic and religious hegemony. (And yet readers can sometimes be reluctant to fit literature into historical processes, perhaps because we are in thrall to the Romantic and not wholly wrong idea that it is a phenomenon arising from individual genius, which must in some sense be arbitrary. Then again, literary works do not always channel the spirit of their times – but readers may try to make works that they admire fit with perceptions of their period, and *vice versa*, however Procrustean the process.)

The perspectives are also selective. Aesthetics and history of education would have been interesting approaches, and I should have liked to have written a section on shifts in models, genres and canons. A model for understanding canon formation in antiquity has been offered for Greek literature in a recent book by Reviel Netz, discussed further in Gibson and Whitton's introduction (pp. 14–16). Some of the methods used by Netz are, alas, unavailable in Latin: we cannot use papyrus finds for systematic

---

[193] On such headings in antiquity, see Schröder 1999: 93–159.
[194] On reading see above all Pelttari 2014.

confirmation of what was read at any particular time; the systematic study of authors cited in particular periods (as Netz does with citations in Athenaeus and Plutarch) would not be representative in Latin as later classical authors are comparatively reluctant to cite post-Augustan authors by name.[195] Library catalogues would be revealing (as they are in Chinese literary history), but we do not have certain examples of them until the Carolingian period. Latin forms part of Netz's coverage, but as an offshoot of Hellenistic literature: this approach is not without point but loses validity over time. A Latin-focused version of his project would begin with how and why Latin literature systematically sought to reproduce Greek models, both by translating ideas and by transposing genres, and would move on to the process by which the Latin versions so transposed themselves took over as models from the originals. A crucial period, once more, would be the last fifty years or so before Christ.[196] And a similar period of both generic innovation and creation of a new set of models would return in the fourth and fifth centuries, the other period highlighted in my case studies. One thing that these perspectives do suggest is how historical change runs faster and deeper in some historical moments, that literature responds to change and is part of it, and perhaps that it is inevitable that such moments will attract special interest.

Periodisations are narratives that are passed down to us. They have usually arisen from an attempt to grasp at something real, but they are never going to be perfect or fully objective, and discussion will not cease as long as Latin is read. Some periodisations will be deeply problematic and deserve to be wholly discredited; others will remain enduringly persuasive even if they are shown to have limitations.[197] In the former category I have argued throughout this chapter against the shrinkage of the classical Latin canon (a phenomenon of only the last few hundred years)[198] that makes dictionaries, syllabi, and often the general knowledge of scholars stop dead in the early empire, in the second century CE. This terminus makes no sense in itself or as part of a wider discipline concerned with ancient Greek and Roman studies, and can only be explained as a way of excluding literature by Christians. On the other hand, I have found some political and

---

[195] Netz 2020, esp. pp. 11–95 and 527–40 on papyri; pp. 547–59 for the calculation of authors in circulation from Plutarch/Athenaeus.
[196] On generic interactions in this period see Harrison 2007.
[197] O'Donnell 2004 has influenced my thinking here.
[198] Curtius 1953: 263: 'It would be a useful task for literary science to determine how the canon of antique authors has changed from 1500 to the present, i.e., how it has diminished.'

linguistic sense in seeing a break in Latin literature at what might be called the end of antiquity, or of the classical world, even if we should look across that break often and for many purposes. Sometimes competing periodisations might be the best way of expressing the complicated reality: the Latin of 300–600 can both belong in a centralised Roman imperial narrative and also be viewed as a period that introduces new models, forms and approaches, with growing regional diversity. Surveys of mediaeval Latin literature that start in this period do so with good reason[199] – or so I would claim.[200]

Instead of unconsciously reproducing past periodisations of Latin literature with all their associated hierarchies, Latinists should be more open in reflecting on where they begin and end their accounts, and why – politics, religion, surviving sources or whatever basis – and thus allow for explicit critique. They should be open to alternative periodisations, to looking beyond the obvious, and to complementing the close reading with the bird's-eye view of the *longue durée*. Indeed on the whole, the prescription is above all that Latinists should be more attuned to the fact that they *have* a *longue durée*. A less chronologically and canonically stunted sense of the duties of the Latinist, as advocated in the editors' introduction, would not only give researchers a new perspective on familiar works and problems, but would lead to different sorts of scholarship: work that looks at broader metrics and takes a more distant view of sets of texts;[201] or applying the familiar close-reading skills to ground-breaking work, in the true sense of the metaphor, on the thousands of texts that have not been translated, have not been edited for centuries, or have not been edited ever. It would be intellectually and materially of benefit to the subjects of Latin studies and Classics, were Latinists to make a full contribution to the study of (all of) Roman antiquity; and to the benefit of the whole humanistic academy were they to consider the millennium of Latin texts of post-Roman, pre-modern Europe as part of their territory.

---

[199] E.g. Norberg 2004. Curtius 1953 (in some aspects at least, but see Vessey 2020 on a late antique blind spot in European literary history).

[200] Aaron Pelttari and I are editing a *Cambridge History of Later Latin Literature* focused on the period c. 100–700. The aim of this coverage is to ensure that the continuities both from early to late empire and from the empire to the post-Roman early mediaeval west are not occluded.

[201] For example, the scope for such an investigation in looking at prose rhythm (see section 5) is enormous: hundreds of texts have not been edited since its rediscovery and attention to clausulation could have wide-ranging implications for both text and interpretation; in some cases it might help in dating.

## References

Adams, J. N. (2007) *The Regional Diversification of Latin 200 BC–AD 200*, Cambridge.
   (2011) 'Late Latin', in Clackson 2011, 257–83.
   (2013) *Social Variation and the Latin Language*, Cambridge.
   (2016) *An Anthology of Informal Latin, 200 BC–AD 900*, Cambridge.
Ainsworth, R. (1736) *Thesaurus linguae Latinae compendiarius, or, A Compendious Dictionary of the Latin Tongue: Designed for the Use of the British Nations*, London. With 2nd edn, 1746.
Anderson, W. B. (1936) *Sidonius: Poems and Letters 1*, Cambridge, MA.
Barchiesi, A. (2005) 'The search for the perfect book: a PS to the new Posidippus', in K. Gutzwiller, ed., *The New Posidippus: A Hellenistic Poetry Book* (Oxford), 320–42.
Barnes, T. D. (1998) *Ammianus Marcellinus and the Representation of Historical Reality*, Ithaca, NY.
   (2009) 'The first emperor: the view of late antiquity', in M. Griffin, ed., *A Companion to Julius Caesar* (Malden, MA), 277–87.
Beard, M. (2002) 'Ciceronian correspondences: making a book out of letters', in T. P. Wiseman, ed., *Classics in Progress* (Oxford), 103–44.
Berger, J.-D., J. Fontaine and P. L. Schmidt, eds. (2020) *Die Literatur im Zeitalter des Theodosius (374–430 n. Chr.)*, 2 vols., Munich (= *HLL* 6).
Bieler, L. (1980) *Geschichte der römischen Literatur*, Berlin.
Bourgain, P. (2016) 'The works of Gregory of Tours: manuscripts, language, and style', in A. C. Murray, ed., *Brill's Companion to Gregory of Tours* (Leiden), 141–88.
Brandes, W. (1905) *Des Auspicius von Toul rhythmische Epistel an Arbogastes von Trier*, Wolfenbüttel.
Braund, S. M. (1998) 'Praise and protreptic in early imperial panegyric: Cicero, Seneca, Pliny', in M. Whitby, ed., *The Propaganda of Power: The Role of Panegyric in Late Antiquity* (Leiden), 53–76.
Brown, P. R. L. (1971) *The World of Late Antiquity: From Marcus Aurelius to Muhammad*, London.
Brugnoli, G. and C. Santini (1995) *L'additamentum Aldinum di Silio Italico*, Rome.
Burgess, R. W. and M. Kulikowski (2013) *Mosaics of Time: The Latin Chronicle Traditions from the First Century BC to the Sixth Century AD. Volume 1: A Historical Introduction to the Chronicle Genre from Its Origins to the High Middle Ages*, Turnhout.
Butrica, J. L. (2006) 'The *fabella* of Sulpicia (*Epigrammata Bobiensia* 37)', *Phoenix* 60: 70–121.
Butterfield, D. (2008) 'Sigmatic ecthlipsis in Lucretius', *Hermes* 136: 188–205.
Cameron, A. D. E. (2011) *The Last Pagans of Rome*, New York.
Cameron, A. M. (2003) 'Byzance dans le débat sur orientalisme', in M.-F. Auzepy, ed., *Byzance en Europe* (Paris), 235–50.

Campana, A. (1964) 'Lettera del cardinale Padovano (Bartolomeo Oliari) a Coluccio Salutati', in C. Henderson Jr, ed., *Medieval and Renaissance Studies in Honor of Bertold Louis Ullmann* (Rome), II 237–54.

Cavallo, G. and P. Fioretti (2014) 'Chiaroscuro: oltre l'angolo di scrittura (secoli I a.C.–VI d.C.)', *Scripta* 7: 29–64.

Ceccarelli, L. (2018) *Contributions to the History of the Latin Elegiac Distich*, Turnhout.

Champlin, E. (1978) 'The life and times of T. Calpurnius Siculus', *JRS* 68: 95–110.

Clackson, J., ed. (2011) *A Companion to the Latin Language*, Malden, MA.

Clackson, J. and G. Horrocks, eds. (2007) *The Blackwell History of the Latin Language*, Malden, MA.

Consolino, F. E. (2017) 'Polymetry in later Latin poems', in J. Elsner and J. Hernández Lobato, eds., *The Poetics of Late Latin Literature* (New York), 100–24.

Conte, G. B. (1994) *Latin Literature: A History* (trans. J. Solodow; rev. D. Fowler and G. W. Most), Baltimore.

Conybeare, C. and S. Goldhill, eds. (2020) *Classical Philology and Theology: Entanglement, Disavowal, and the Godlike Scholar*, Cambridge.

Copley, F. O. (1968) *Latin Literature from the Beginnings to the Close of the Second Century* AD, Ann Arbor.

Cornell, T. J. et al., eds. (2013) *The Fragments of the Roman Historians*, 3 vols., Oxford.

Courtney, E. (1987) 'Imitation, chronologie littéraire et Calpurnius Siculus', *REL* 65: 148–57.

Croke, B. (1983) 'A.D. 476: the manufacture of a turning point', *Chiron* 13: 81–119.

Curtius, E. R. (1953) *European Literature and the Latin Middle Ages* (trans. W. R. Trask), Princeton.

Davis, K. and M. Puett (2015) 'Periodization and "The Medieval Globe": a conversation', *The Medieval Globe* 2: 1–14.

Denecker, T. (2018) 'Among Latinists: Alfred Ernout and Einar Löfstedt's responses to the "Nijmegen School" and its Christian *Sondersprache* hypothesis', *Historiographica Linguistica* 45: 325–62.

Dolbeau, F. (1998) 'Découvertes récentes d'oeuvres latines inconnues (fin IIIe–début VIIIe siècle)', *SEJG* 38: 101–42.

Dorfbauer, L. J. (2017) *Fortunatianus Aquileiensis. Commentarii in Evangelia*, Berlin.

⸻ (2010) 'Die *praefationes* von Claudian und von Prudentius', in V. Zimmerl-Panagl and D. Weber, eds., *Text und Bild* (Vienna), 195–222.

Dryden, J. (1700) *Fables, Ancient and Modern*, London.

Duff, J. W. (1909) *A Literary History of Rome from the Origins to the Close of the Golden Age*, London.

⸻ (1927) *A Literary History of Rome in the Silver Age*, London.

Farrell, J. (2001) *Latin Language and Latin Culture from Ancient to Modern Times*, Cambridge.
Feeney, D. (1998) *Literature and Religion at Rome: Cultures, Contexts, and Beliefs*, Cambridge.
  (2016) *Beyond Greek: The Beginnings of Latin Literature*, Cambridge, MA.
Fubini, R. (2003) *Humanism and Secularization: From Petrarch to Valla*, Durham, NC.
Gibbon, E. (1776–88) *The History of the Decline and Fall of the Roman Empire*, 6 vols., London (cited by original volume and chapter and by pages in the edition of D. Womersley, Harmondsworth, 1994).
Gibson, R. K. (2020) 'Sidonius' correspondence', in Kelly and Van Waarden 2020, 373–92.
  (2021) 'Fifty years of green and yellow: the Cambridge Greek and Latin Classics series 1970–2020', in S. Harrison and C. Pelling, eds., *Classical Scholarship and its History from the Renaissance to the Present: Essays in Honour of Chris Stray* (Berlin), 175–217.
Gibson, R. K. and R. Morello (2012) *Reading the Letters of Pliny the Younger: An Introduction*, Cambridge.
Goldhill, S. (2020) 'The union and divorce of classical philology and theology', in Conybeare and Goldhill 2020, 33–62.
Goodyear, F. R. D. (1983) 'The *Oxford Latin Dictionary*', *Proceedings of the African Classical Associations* 17: 124–36. Reprinted in F. R. D. Goodyear, *Papers on Latin Literature* (London, 1992), 281–7.
Gowing, A. (2005) *Empire and Memory: The Representation of the Roman Republic in Imperial Culture*, Cambridge.
Grafton, A. and M. Williams (2006) *Christianity and the Transformation of the Book: Origen, Eusebius, and the Library of Caesarea*, Cambridge, MA.
Hadas, M. (1952) *A History of Latin Literature*, New York.
Harmon, A. M. (1910) *The Clausula in Ammianus Marcellinus*, New Haven.
Harnett, B. (2017) 'The diffusion of the codex', *ClAnt* 36: 183–235.
Harries, J. D. (1994) *Sidonius Apollinaris and the Fall of Rome*, AD 407–485, Oxford.
Harrison, S. J., ed. (2005) *A Companion to Latin Literature*, Malden, MA.
Harrison, S. J. (2007) *Generic Enrichment in Vergil and Horace*, Oxford.
Heck, E. (1997) 'Commodianus', in K. Sallmann, ed., *Die Literatur des Umbruchs: Von der römischen zur christlichen Literatur 115–283 n. Chr.* (Munich) (= *HLL* 4), 628–37.
Heerink, M. (2009) 'Misconceptions about the art of ancient publishing: Catullus' book of poetry reconsidered', *International Journal of the Book* 6: 95–100.
Hernández Lobato, J. (2014) *El humanismo che no fue*, Bologna.
  (2020) 'Sidonius in the Middle Ages and Renaissance', in Kelly and Van Waarden 2020, 665–85.
Hertz, M. (1874) 'Aulus Gellius und Ammianus Marcellinus', *Hermes* 8: 257–302.
Herzog, R., ed. (1989) *Restauration und Erneuerung: Die lateinische Literatur von 284 bis 374 n. Chr.*, Munich (= *HLL* 5). Translated as *Restauration et renouveau: la littérature latine de 284 à 374 après J.-C.* (Turnhout, 1993).

Hexter, R. (2005) 'From the medieval historiography of Latin literature to the historiography of medieval Latin literature', *Journal of Medieval Latin* 15: 1–24.
Hinds, S. (1998), *Allusion and Intertext: Dynamics of Appropriation in Roman Poetry*, Cambridge.
Holcombe, C. (2017) 'Was medieval China medieval? (Post-Han to mid-Tang)', in M. Szonyi, ed., *A Companion to Chinese History* (Chichester), 106–17.
Holford-Strevens, L. (2017) 'Fronto's and Gellius' *veteres*', in S. Rocchi and C. Mussini, eds., *Imagines antiquitatis: Representations, Concepts, Receptions of the Past in Roman Antiquity and the Early Italian Renaissance* (Berlin), 199–211.
  (2020) *Auli Gelli Noctes Atticae*, 2 vols., Oxford.
Horsfall, N. (1997) 'Criteria for the dating of Calpurnius Siculus', *RFIC* 125, 166–96.
Humphries, M. (2017) 'Late antiquity and world history', *Studies in Late Antiquity* 1: 8–37.
Janson, T. (1975) *Prose Rhythm in Medieval Latin from the 9th to the 13th Century*, Stockholm.
Jenkyns, R. (2015) *Classical Literature*, Harmondsworth.
John, A. (2018) 'A cultural history of education in late antique Gaul'. Unpublished PhD dissertation, University of Edinburgh.
Keeline, T. and T. Kirby (2019) '*Auceps syllabarum*: a digital analysis of Latin prose rhythm', *JRS* 109: 161–204.
Kelly, G. A. J. (2008) *Ammianus Marcellinus: The Allusive Historian*, Cambridge.
  (2018) 'Edward Gibbon and late antique literature', in S. McGill and E. Watts, eds., *A Companion to Late Antique Literature* (Oxford), 611–26.
Kelly, G. A. J and J. van Waarden, eds. (2020) *The Edinburgh Companion to Sidonius Apollinaris*, Edinburgh.
Kenney, E. J. and W. V. Clausen, eds. (1982) *The Cambridge History of Classical Literature. Vol. 2: Latin Literature*, Cambridge.
Keynes, G. (1940) *The Library of Edward Gibbon: A Catalogue of His Books*, London. With 2nd edn, 1980.
Kulikowski, M. (2017) *Imperial Triumph: The Roman World from Hadrian to Constantine AD 138–363*, London.
Larsen, M. D. C. and M. Letteney (2019) 'Christians and the codex: generic materiality and early Gospel traditions', *JECS* 27: 383–415.
Leonhardt, G. (2013) *Latin: Story of a World Language* (trans. K. Kronenberg), Cambridge, MA.
Löfstedt, E. (1911) *Philologischer Kommentar zur Peregrinatio Aetheriae*, Uppsala.
  (1959) *Late Latin*, Oslo.

Lühken, M. (2002) *Christianorum Maro et Flaccus: Zur Vergil- und Horazrezeption des Prudentius*, Göttingen.
Lyne, R. O. A. M. (1978) 'The neoteric poets', *CQ* 28: 167–87. Reprinted in R. O. A. M. Lyne (ed. S. J. Harrison) *Collected Papers on Latin Poetry* (Oxford, 2007), 60–84.
McKitterick, R. (2008) *Charlemagne: The Formation of a European Identity*, Cambridge.
MacMullen, R. (1986) 'What difference did Christianity make?', *Historia* 35: 322–43.
Magnelli, E. (2016) 'The Nonnian hexameter', in D. Accorinti, ed., *Brill's Companion to Nonnus of Panopolis* (Leiden), 351–71.
Manitius, M. (1935) *Handschriften antiker Autoren in mittelalterlichen Bibliothekskatalogen*, Leipzig.
Martelli, F. (2017) 'The triumph of letters: rewriting Cicero in *Ad fam.* 15', *JRS* 107: 90–115.
Meier, M. (2019) *Geschichte der Völkerwanderung: Europa, Asien und Afrika vom 3. bis zum 8. Jahrhundert n. Chr.*, Munich.
Mercado, A. (2012) *Italic Verse: A Study of the Poetic Remains of Old Latin, Faliscan, and Sabellic*, Innsbruck.
Mommsen, T. (1904) *Römische Geschichte*, 8 vols., Berlin.
Morgan, L. (2010) *Musa pedestris: Metre and Meaning in Roman Verse*, Oxford.
Nethercut, J. (2021) *Ennius noster: Lucretius and the Annales*, New York.
Netz, R. (2020) *Scale, Space and Canon in Ancient Literary Culture*, Cambridge.
Nixon, C. E. V. (1990) 'Reading the past in the Gallic panegyrics', in G. Clarke et al., eds., *Reading the Past in Late Antiquity* (Rushcutter's Bay, NSW), 1–36.
Norberg, D. (2004) *An Introduction to the Study of Medieval Latin Versification*, Washington, DC.
Novati, F., ed. (1891–1911) *Epistolario di Coluccio Salutati*, 18 vols., Rome.
Oberhelman, S. (2003) *Prose Rhythm in Latin Literature of the Roman Empire: First Century BC to Fourth Century AD*, Lewiston.
O'Donnell, J. J. (2004) 'Late antiquity: before and after', *TAPhA* 134: 203–13 (abbreviated version of APA Presidential address; fuller version at SCS website, https://classicalstudies.org/sites/default/files/documents/jod.pdf (last accessed 5 April 2021)).
  (2008) *The Ruin of the Roman Empire: A New History*, New York.
O'Donnell, R. D. (1981) 'The *Querolus*, edited with an introduction and commentary', PhD thesis, Bedford College, University of London.
Pelttari, A. D. (2014) *The Space that Remains*, Ithaca, NY.
Penney, J. (2011) 'Archaic and Old Latin', in Clackson 2011, 220–35.
Pirenne, H. (1937) *Mahomet et Charlemagne*, Brussels and Paris.
Probert, P. (2019) *Latin Grammarians on the Latin Accent*, Oxford.
Reeve, M. D. (1996) 'Classical scholarship', in J. Kraye, ed., *The Cambridge Companion to Renaissance Humanism* (Cambridge), 20–46.
Rigg, A. G. (1992) *A History of Anglo-Latin Literature 1066–1422*, Cambridge.

Rizzo, S. (1986) 'Il latino nell'Umanesimo', in A. Asor Rosa, *Letteratura italiana*. v. *Le questioni* (Turin), 379–408.
Roberts, C. H. and T. C. Skeat (1983) *The Birth of the Codex*, Oxford.
Rose, H. J. (1954) *A Handbook of Latin Literature from the Earliest Times to the Death of St. Augustine*, London.
Rudd, N. (1977) *Lines of Enquiry*, Cambridge.
Scaliger, J. C. (1561) *Poetices libri septem*, Lyon.
Schafer, J. K. (2017) 'Authorial pagination in the *Eclogues* and *Georgics*', *TAPhA* 147: 135–78.
 (2020) *Catullus through His Books: Dramas of Composition*, Cambridge.
Schröder, B.-J. (1999) *Titel und Text. Zur Entwicklung lateinischer Gedichtüberschriften, mit Untersuchungen zu lateinischen Buchtiteln, Inhaltsverzeichnissen und anderen Gliederungsmitteln*, Berlin.
Seeck, O. (1895–1920) *Geschichte des Untergangs der antiken Welt*, 6 vols., Berlin.
Settis, S. (2010) 'Classical', in A. Grafton, G. W. Most and S. Settis, *The Classical Tradition* (Cambridge, MA), 205–6.
Shanzer, D. (2009) 'Literature, history, periodization, and the pleasures of the Latin literary history of late antiquity', *History Compass* 7: 1–38.
Spieß, T.-C. (2012) *Die Sabinus-Briefe: Humanistische Fälschung oder antike Literatur? Einleitung – Edition – Übersetzung – Kommentar*, Trier.
Stouraitis, Y. (2022) 'Is Byzantinism an Orientalism? Reflections on Byzantium's constructed identities and debated ideologies', in Y. Stouraitis, ed., *Identities and Ideologies in the Medieval East Roman World* (Edinburgh), 19–47.
Stover, J. (2015) 'Olybrius and the *Einsiedeln Eclogues*', *JRS* 105: 288–321.
 (2017) 'The date of the bucolic poet Martius Valerius', *JRS* 107: 301–35.
Syme, R. (1939) *The Roman Revolution*, Oxford.
Taplin, O., ed. (2000) *Literature in the Greek and Roman Worlds*, Oxford.
Trout, D. (2015) *Damasus of Rome: The Epigraphic Poetry*, Oxford.
Turcan-Verkerk, A.-M. (2003) *Un poète latin chrétien redécouvert: Latinius Pacatus Drepanius, panégyriste de Théodose*, Brussels.
Ullmann, B. L. (1963) *The Humanism of Coluccio Salutati*, Padua.
Valois, N. (1881) 'Étude sur le rhythme des bulles pontificales', *Bibliothèque de l'école des chartes* 42: 161–98 and 257–72.
Van Hoof, L. and P. Van Nuffelen (2020) *The Fragmentary Latin Historians of Late Antiquity (AD 300–620)*, Cambridge.
Van Waarden, J. and G. Kelly (2020) 'Sidonius' prose rhythm', in Kelly and Van Waarden 2020, 462–75.
Vessey, M. (2020) 'Boethius in the genres of the book: philology, theology, codicology', in Conybeare and Goldhill 2020, 149–79.
Wheelock, F. M. (2011) *Wheelock's Latin. Seventh Edition* (rev. R. A. LaFleur), New York.
White, P. (2019) *Gallus Reborn: A Study of the Diffusion and Reception of Works Attributed to C. Cornelius Gallus*, London.
Winterbottom, M. (2011) 'On ancient prose rhythm: the story of the dichoreus', in D. Obbink and R. Rutherford, eds., *Culture in Pieces* (Oxford), 262–76.

(2017) 'The pleasures of editing', *Revue d'histoire des textes* 12: 393–413.
Wiseman, T. P. (1982) 'Calpurnius Siculus and the Claudian civil war', *JRS* 72: 57–67.
Witt, R. G. (2000) *In the Footsteps of the Ancients: The Origins of Humanism from Lovato to Bruni*, Leiden.
Wolff, E. (2020) 'Sidonius' vocabulary, syntax, and style', in Kelly and Van Waarden 2020, 395–417.
Woodman, A. J. (1992) Review of Kenney and Clausen 1982, *LCM* 7: 102–8.
Woodruff, H. (1929) 'The illustrated manuscripts of Prudentius', *Art Studies* 7: 33–79.
Wüst, G. (1881) *De clausula rhetorica quam praecepit Cicero quatenus in orationibus secutus sit*, Strasbourg.
Zetzel, J. E. G. (2018) *Critics, Compilers, and Commentators: An Introduction to Roman Philology, 200 BCE–800 CE*, New York.

CHAPTER 4

# *Author and Identity*

*Alison Sharrock*

## Introduction

What is an author? What do we, as twenty-first-century critics of ancient Roman literature, mean when we use the names 'Cicero', 'Virgil', 'Ovid', 'Pliny'? Or, to ask the same question in another way, is the author 'still dead' in the twenty-first century, that is, where do we envisage the balance of interpretive power sitting as between authors and readers? What we mean when we speak about an author is an issue in literary theory and criticism across the whole of so-called Western tradition: it matters because it is bound up in the question of how much room for manoeuvre there is in interpretation, in what claims we can make about a text when we expect anyone else to be interested in what we say. The value in considering the figure of the author and the nature of authorship is not wholly circumscribed by its contribution to the question of licence and control in interpretation[1] – but it is the primary reason why it causes controversy. The appropriate range of interpretation, of what may validly be said about a text, is particularly problematic for classical Latin literature, where not only are the texts, their authors and original readers very far distant from us, but also there has been in most cases a continuous or near-continuous tradition of interpretation over the intervening centuries, which inevitably changes future readings.[2]

Persona theory has flourished in classical literary criticism since the fall of biographical modes of reading and the questioning of straightforward intentionalism, but it raises thorny problems in hermeneutics and in the ethics of reading. At its simplest level, 'persona' could refer to any character in a literary work, but it has typically been used to describe the speaker in first-person literature and by extension to refer to the image of the author

---

[1] It is a creative theme in its own right, as is shown by the contributions to Fletcher and Hanink 2016 and to Hardie and Moore 2010, as well as in the material/bibliographic turn in classical studies.
[2] Still a classic on this subject is Martindale 1993.

presented in any literary work. I shall argue in this chapter that persona criticism is a valuable mechanism for engaging with ancient texts, but that it comes with the risk of a new form of essentialism which can make reading ancient literature too comfortable; that the entity we call 'the author' is a construct based only in part on the flesh-and-blood person or persons associated with the name in the historical record; that interpretation should be diachronic, dynamic and flexible; that we construct our readings out of material constrained by choices made by flesh-and-blood authors, but that those readings are better understood as hypothetical than as actual intentions; that the actual intentions of flesh-and-blood authors are unknowable and irrelevant in a straightforward sense; that range of meaning depends on purpose in any given reading, which is often but by no means always directed at the reconstruction of readings available to readers contemporary with the original author, but is always a modern reader's reconstruction of an ancient author and reader who is hypothetical, and moreover is not limited to the real author's conscious or even unconscious intention. That this should be so is crucial to the continued vitality of our discipline, as well as being – I hope and believe – true.

There are two related but nonetheless separable aspects to the theory of the author explored in this chapter. One is the image of the self as presented in the work, to which the historical person contributes as raw material to a lesser (e.g. Ovid) or greater (e.g. Cicero) extent. Second is the further question of what, if any, separate entity controls the production of the literary persona. Is it ever possible to get back behind the layers of created personae/avatars/implied authors? Sometimes it is clear that there is an explicit distinction between persona and author (the following are examples of what I am calling 'avatars', but they are also personae in the sense of being characters in a work): Arachne, Daedalus, or Orpheus as Ovid, Umbricius as Juvenal and even character-Cicero as author-Cicero. Sometimes it is extremely likely that there is a difference: Ovid as teacher, Propertius as lover, Virgil as bard. It is probably reasonable to describe these personae as deliberately created by another figure.[3] They are created

---

[3] Joe Farrell's chapter on intertextuality in the revised *Cambridge Companion to Virgil* opens with a perfect example of the kind of plays of different levels of persona with which I am concerned here: 'The *Eclogue* poet is never merely a Roman Theocritus: from time to time, he assumes the identity of his own rustic characters, which in general are also borrowed from Theocritus' *Idylls*, but are modified to suit new purposes in a new context; and he occasionally assumes personae borrowed from other writers, as well. The *Eclogue* poet's reflected and composite persona in turn becomes a model for those of his counterparts, the *Georgic* poet and the *Aeneid* poet. Furthermore, these three poets are themselves distinct characters but also facets of an integrated authorial identity developed over time and satisfyingly whole despite its remarkable composite nature. The issues involved go

by the constructed author, of whom the flesh-and-blood author is only one aspect, and who is constantly subject to change in the process of reading. The flesh-and-blood author played a major role in the creation of the constructed author, but is of himself, or herself, all but entirely unknowable. It is the constructed author whom we invoke when we say 'Ovid' or 'Cicero'.

An important element contributing to the author named as 'Ovid' or 'Cicero', especially visible in authors who have left works in multiple genres, is what I propose to call the super-persona, the big 'I' who transcends the individual work and the individual genre, who is associated with the name, and who actively constructs both continuity and discontinuity in the first-person voices across the corpus. The constructed author is not unreal, but neither is he/she identical with the flesh-and-blood author. For example, both constructed authors 'Ovid' and 'Cicero' really did fall foul of powerful political forces in the first centuries BCE and CE, and (almost certainly) really were exiled/relegated. Likewise, the personae of Cicero or Pliny are not wholly fictional. It is a challenge to say whether the personae of Ovid the teacher, Tibullus and more problematically Ovid the violent lover are wholly fictional. Persona get-out theory enables us to construct them as wholly fictional and thereby to construct an author who knowingly creates the persona of the violent lover in order to encourage us to condemn him. This may well be a rhetorical sleight of hand in modern criticism that should, morally, be nuanced.

The final major theme of this chapter can be summarised under the heading of 'intentionalism'. Many professional classicists will have had the experience of interaction with non-classicists who are rather surprised that it is still possible to do research on classical texts, as 'surely it's all been said by now'. It is my contention that if flesh-and-blood authors had complete control over the meaning of the texts, then all we would be able to do is to repeat their words, which to most of our readers would then be largely unintelligible (so, paradoxically, we would not in fact be repeating them). If they do not have that control, then a simple intentionalism is manifestly unsustainable. If this kind of maximalist or simplistic intentionalism is unsustainable, then it is appropriate to attempt to theorise for the twenty-first century what we mean when we say anything about an ancient text.

---

beyond the formal and the literary. Virgil's intertextual personae are ethical, both in the sense that they each have their own character, and that they represent different patterns of outlook on and behaviour inside and outside the world of the poems. They are also culturally inflected: the kinds of individual who populate Virgil's three major works, the herdsman, the farmer, and the hero, did not mean the same thing to Greek and Roman readers' (Farrell 2019: 299–300).

This is because it is also, I submit, unsustainable to assign all power in the production of meaning to the reader. It is easy to say, and indeed it is a truism, that meaning is only realised in the moment of reception, but it is all too easy to glide over the extent to which reception is constrained by the nature of the thing received, and that the thing received is the product of a human intelligence ('the author'), together with a tradition or multiple traditions. There is, moreover, an issue in the difference between intentional meaning in different contexts, including that between, for example, Ovid writing the *Metamorphoses* and me writing this chapter.[4]

## Persona *Simplex* and Author Complex

I begin the discussion not with the modern critical story of Anderson and Juvenal (on which more later), but with the ancient history of the term 'persona'. While it would be wrong to give overwhelming privilege to the linguistic genesis of a term in exploring its later functions, nonetheless it seems worth noting that classical Latin literature had a concept of persona in which the theatrical metaphor (*persona* = mask)[5] expresses the capacity of a human being to play out different roles and even to 'be' multiple people in different aspects of their lives.[6] *Persona* also comes to mean 'personality/character' and even 'person',[7] without the implications of multiplicity active in the theatrical metaphor, but in all discourses other than legal ones the notion of multiplicity is never far below the surface. Although not every part of the vast range of meanings of *persona* in Latin is active in the modern critical term, the fact that this notion of human beings playing roles has purchase in Roman culture creates a seedbed in which future development of the theory can grow and perhaps claim a degree of authentication from antiquity.

The modern literary-critical persona – that is, the idea that the speaker (and his/her avatars) in a work of literature might be a construct rather than

---

[4] Ovid aimed to communicate something, as well as to write a classic. I aim to communicate something, as well as to fulfil a promise to the editors and to add to my publications list. I may well fail to communicate my intentions about intentionality, and readers may well take different messages from what I say – different from each other and different from, whether better or worse than, what I hoped.
[5] *TLL* x.1 1715.35 quotes Gavius Bassus 2.4.3 on the origin of the term from a theatrical mask.
[6] Gill 1988, Bartsch 2006: 216–29, Littlewood 2015. According to Stoic persona theory, 'appropriate' actions for a moral agent are determined by the four constituent personae of the individual agent: the rational persona imposed by Nature on all humans, one's own character, the persona imposed by circumstance, and the profession of one's choosing.
[7] Including what we would call 'legal person', *TLL* x.1 1720.8–47.

an unmediated reflection of the historical author – arises in the middle of the twentieth century, part of the multifaceted response to Romanticism, to biographical criticism, to the 'confessional' reaction to the new critical reaction to biographism, and to the creative language of personae and masks by poets such as Pound and Yeats, as well as to questioning of the 'self' arising in part out of psychoanalysis.[8] Satire was a particular beneficiary of this development, which injected new life into a genre whose tone and manner were so out of sync with twentieth-century sensibilities. The doctrine of persona enabled the critic to distinguish the various voices employed by satirists from the historical authors themselves, thus enhancing their artistry and rhetorical force while saving their moral blushes. This technique provides a double win: the poet is even cleverer than we thought, but at the same time less nasty.[9] William Anderson was quick to perceive the value in doing for Horace and Juvenal what Mack and others had done for Pope and Swift, thus constituting the vanguard of scholarship on Roman satire to this day.[10] As James Uden puts it: 'The *persona* assumed a unique centrality in scholarship on Juvenal over the next half-century because approaching the satirist in this way seemed to resolve much that is discomforting and unruly in his poetics.'[11] While the satiric community now often expresses some impatience with persona theory, especially with regard to its political implications, it nonetheless remains the dominant mode of reading Roman satire and other first-person genres in Latin literature.

This use of persona theory has spread from exonerating Juvenal from the impotent aggression and violent racism of his satiric speaker into other areas where it can ease the sensibilities of the critic, one effect of which is to make ancient authors more like us (as it makes us like them more). I should stress that it is not my intention to undermine persona theory by pointing

---

[8] For an excellent account of the rise of the persona, as well as the challenges to it and the real difficulties it involves, see Elliott 1982, ch. 1. His assessment of the value, both positive and negative, of persona criticism in exonerating the historical writer is very similar to my own position. With the hindsight of more than a further forty years, I would not agree with Elliott's contention that his project and deconstruction do not speak to each other, indeed are completely unconnected. He makes this case on the grounds that, from what he believes to be the 'poststructuralist' position, his own project is 'an illusion', since 'the self is a construct, constituted entirely by a variety of social and linguistic codes of which it is a mere function' (p. xii). Rather, I would suggest that in the new millennium both persona criticism and deconstruction have undergone both naturalisation (elements of their doctrines are widely accepted) and moderation.

[9] Seminal in this regard was Mack 1951. Elliott 1982: 7–12 is a good source for further information.

[10] Anderson 1964 and 1982, Braund 1996, Freudenberg 2001, Schlegel 2005. Oliensis 1998 prefers the term 'face' to persona in reference to Horace.

[11] Uden 2014: 3.

to its effect in this regard. Awareness that the speaker at any given moment in a work of Latin literature is a more or less fictional construct is extremely valuable in enabling creative and effective readings of ancient works. Moreover, it contributes to an argument that I shall develop in the chapter, which is that not only the speaker but also the author is a construct, (only) part of whose make-up comes from the flesh-and-blood being out of whom the author originates. Nonetheless, in a project designed to reflect on how we read classical texts it is important to note the extent to which persona theory is used to make, and has the effect of making, ancient authors more palatable.[12]

A recent article by Gallia on Juvenal 3 provides good examples of current usage in persona criticism.[13] Much of the paper is focused on the speaker, Umbricius, described as 'persona' both, it seems, as a character in the fictional world of the poem and as an avatar of the satirist.[14] A core question is whether the poor person who has lost everything in a fire is Roman Cordus or Greek Codrus (with its pastoral/Virgilian associations). The problem is that this is the poem of the most extreme anti-Greek prejudice, so it would be odd if the speaker, Umbricius, were to be sympathetic with a Greek. As Gallia says, 'the core issue is one that by now has become a commonplace in Juvenalian scholarship: the poet's creation of satiric personae who present speeches that are full of moralising bombast, but which are also frequently incoherent in ways that draw the attentive listener's approach back onto the speakers themselves'.

Gallia undertakes the common critical move of distinguishing clearly between persona and author. The fact that in this case the persona is an avatar rather than one who holds the author's name is less important than the nature of the distinction made between persona and author:

> The approach to Juvenal's third satire developed here depends upon the reader's acknowledgement of the substantial distance between the position of Umbricius' persona and that of the text's (implied) author. Although Umbricius ostensibly gives a voice to the resentment and outrage of a typical Roman graecophobe, his arguments actually expose the callowness and

---

[12] An interesting nuance on the case that the persona criticism of satire arises considerably from discomfort comes from Harrison 2013, who asks (p. 154): 'is satire more effective if we link its speaker with an apparently real person, or is it more satisfying from a literary perspective if the speaker is an evident artistic creation? Does the evident artificiality of a voice compromise or deconstruct its moralising message?' See also Freudenberg 2005: 28–9, Uden 2014: 4.

[13] Gallia 2016. An addition to the list of satirist's avatars is offered in the person of the 'bully' of Juv. 3, by Moodie 2012.

[14] See Keane 2006, especially pp. 22–5 on what she calls the 'satirist figure', for whom she stresses the dramatic character as well as the familiar distinction between satirist and author.

internal contradictions of this sort of ethnic prejudice ... Taken together, these contradictions cannot be ignored or emended away, and must be regarded as part of the underlying message of the work as a whole.[15]

In this account, we are meant to see the author (rightly qualified as 'implied') as responsible for this exposure and implicitly disagreeing with it. The qualification, however, even though it is easily slipped over in reading, is highly significant: we must consider the possibility that the implied author, that is the author-figure who exposes ethnic prejudice as callow, might be much more visible to twenty-first-century readers than to a first-century audience, although Gallia himself appears to be convinced that the satire implies ancient readers who would be sensitive to and critical of ethnic prejudice.[16] At the same time, we should also heed his counter-example of a modern 'lovable bigot' in an American sitcom, who is intended by his author (in a position, unlike Juvenal, to express his opinion and attempt to impose it on the reception of his work) to be himself the subject of satire, but who is actually more popular with people 'less likely to be in on the joke', a situation which is said to be 'presumably because they identified with the opinions of the character they perceived to be its hero'.[17] Such straightforward, albeit unintended, identification with the views expressed by satirists has a venerable history.

From its earliest days, persona theory has been subject to the accusation that it divorces the poet from his or her poem.[18] Gowers, after a good account of the turn against biography in the reading of Horace, points out that, even though the current emphasis on persona is in many ways right and proper, 'there is some danger in all this of losing sight of the historical figure Horace and his connections with a particular period, the uncertain time of the second triumvirate'.[19] She then offers a nuanced reading of the traces of the historical Horace in *Satires* 1 as 'a kind of anti-autobiography ... in which certain disarming details of Horace's life are exposed ... while other more discreditable, antagonizing, and, indeed,

---

[15] Gallia 2016: 336–7.
[16] Ibid. 340: 'so long as we assume that the problems that have been identified with Umbricius' graecophobia derived from Juvenal's authorial design rather than from modern readers' subjective interactions with his text, it stands to reason that these problems in themselves reveal something about how some Romans might have thought about these issues'. I would suggest that 'Juvenal's authorial design' is something on which we should remain agnostic, except insofar as the author Juvenal is a construct of modern reading.
[17] Gallia 2016: 341.
[18] Highet's 1974 broadside against Anderson and others is an extreme case, bound up in a presumption of biographism.
[19] Gowers 2003: 57.

important aspects ... are apparently concealed'.[20] Her reading partakes in an important development in classical scholarship of recent years, in which New Historicist concerns combine with a post-deconstructionist awareness of the constructedness of all autobiography to explore and expose the two-way interactions between internal personae and external lives in kinds of literature which are far removed from fiction. In a similar vein, Uden argues that 'Juvenal is more than an invisible guiding hand ironising the speaking voices in his poems. The invisibility of Juvenal is not so much a tacit authorial manoeuvre as it is a surface aspect of his text (and a real event in performance).'[21]

Persona theory has been useful to classical scholars in many ways. In addition to its crucial role in the recent history of reading Roman satire, it has also contributed to important developments in responses to love elegy. Here it has combined with late twentieth-century innovations in metapoetics and in feminism to enable the reinterpretation of the elegiac love affair not as simple biography but as programmatic exploration of the poetic process based on exploitation of the female body. Wyke's seminal reading of Cynthia as *scripta puella*, a 'written girl' who is an embodiment of elegy, depends in part on reading the 'I' of Propertius' poetry as a persona – of both lover and poet – rather than a window onto an individual elite Roman male's personal biography.[22] Earlier still, Ovid's *Ars amatoria* invited persona-informed criticism, in which the character of the teacher was regarded as a pompous fool wholly separate from the poet,[23] despite the first-person presentation and the explicit connection with other Ovidian works. Indeed, most readings of Ovid's erotodidactic work in the last century would regard the teacher as to some extent a persona distinct from the poet, which is perhaps unsurprising given that the alternative requires the poem to be taken as real-life instruction, to which there has been strong resistance.

Interpretative expression of a distinction between 'I-the-lover' and 'I-the-poet' is critical in any modern reading of Roman love poetry. Love poetry seems, indeed, to be especially prone to attracting persona-reading, to the extent that even those most dubious about applying the critical category of persona to the ancient world nonetheless acknowledge that it may have some role to play precisely in the area of sexual *mores*.[24] This will be in part because it is in such areas that there are statements from Roman poets in which it is hardest to deny a distinction between 'literature' and

---

[20] Ibid. 60.   [21] Uden 2014: 7–8.   [22] Wyke 1987. See also Keith 1994 and Sharrock 1991.
[23] Durling 1958.   [24] Mayer 2003a, to be discussed further in the chapter.

'life', but I suspect that it has also arisen from a desire to protect the morals of the ancient authors, and additionally because the subjects of love poetry – women, and men of some form of lower status – have tended to be regarded as less closely connected with reality than elite men.[25] As with satire, however, so also with elegy our tendency to construct the speaking lover as wholly other to the designing poet is inclined not only to absolve the poet from blame for attitudes which are out of keeping with contemporary sensibilities but even to laud him (the gendered pronoun is intended here) for exposing the nefarious behaviour and attitudes of the speaking lover. As a result, we may ascribe to the author views which are historically unsustainable, or at very least unknowable. This distinction between speaker and poet is absolutely a valuable mode of criticism, but is nonetheless at risk of too comfortably foreclosing a problem in the ethics of interpretation, if we do not acknowledge the extent to which the 'designing poet' is a construct.

In a recent paper, I explore the challenge of using persona theory to read some of the most uncomfortable parts of Ovid's *Amores*, the story of domestic violence in *Am.* 1.7 and the dramatisation of exploitation by a Roman elite male of an enslaved woman of likely African origin in *Am.* 2.7–8.[26] *Amores* 1.7 is a poem which has discomfited readers for many years, but gains a new degree of difficulty in a world which rightly takes domestic violence more seriously than it did even two or three decades ago. My first question is how modern readers (should) respond to a poet-lover who indulges in self-centred sentimentality about his violence towards his beloved, before callously dismissing its significance. With the parenthesis 'should', I aim to imply both theoretical and moral obligation. Among the strategies regularly used to lessen the reader's discomfort and to make the speaker 'more like us' is the use of persona theory as a kind of 'get out of jail free' card. In my view, the most useful reading of these poems does indeed explore the (nefarious) speaker as a fictional character, but we miss the political force of the poems if we allow ourselves to be seduced by the sparkling brilliance of the poetic deception which these poems play on the reader. I suggest that we ought not to allow persona theory to strip away the violence displayed (and played) by the poems.

---

[25] Sharrock 2000.
[26] Sharrock 2021. The following paragraphs repeat some of the points made there. For recent work on related issues in *Am.* 1.7, see Pasco-Pranger 2012, Drinkwater 2013, Oliensis 2014, Perkins 2015, Turpin 2016: 85–97, Pandey 2018, O'Rourke 2018: 112–18. Greene 1998 remains important. For the diptych, see Watson 1983, Fitzgerald 2000: 63–7, James 1997, Henderson 1991 and 1992, Green 2015, O'Rourke 2018, esp. 112 and 118.

### 4 *Author and Identity*

A brilliant and disturbing aspect of *Am.* 1.7 is its manipulation of the reality-effect by creation of gaps which must be filled by a reader, who is thereby encouraged to seek to find out 'what really happened'. In addition, there are various forms of displacement at work, such as the deflecting of responsibility to the speaker's hands, the engagement of questionably relevant mythological exempla, and rhetorical questions which pose as self-blame but which equally imply doubt as to their own validity. Other techniques which draw the reader into collusion with the speaker and poet include the apparent presence of a third party who is invited to intervene,[27] the application of potential speech to this third person but not to the aestheticised and eroticised victim, and hints which undermine the seriousness of the damage done. So powerful are these effects that, in exploring them in detail, I felt it necessary to comment:

> Just in case anyone is in any doubt, I would like to stress that I am not trying to prove that the dramatic situation of this poem is one in which no physical harm was done. To the contrary, my aim is to show the way in which the poem tempts the reader to think that there is 'no real harm done'.

In my discussion of these poems, I used the term 'Ovid' to apply both to the implied author and to the speaker, because this is what the poem does. *Amores* 1.7, moreover, provides perhaps the most extreme example, other than the exile, of Ovid's creation of a super-persona straddling his different works. As is well known, Ovid 'answers' this poem in his role as teacher of love, when he reflects on this event as an element in his own experience presented in order to caution his pupil that he should be cautious in his dealings with the beloved and not fight with her (*Ars am.* 2.169–72).[28] Ovid thereby offers us another possible way of escaping from the discomfort of the poem – to fill in the gaps by constructing the woman herself as manipulative. One might claim, then, that the woman (in the fantasy, into which this hypothetical reader is being drawn) has made a fuss about nothing and used the situation for her own financial ends. Another way of looking at this move on the part of Ovid and some of his readers, however, is to see it in continuity with a long tradition of blaming women for their victimisation by men. I am inclined to feel that we ought to take this possibility seriously.

As regards the Cypassis diptych,[29] *Amores* 2.7 and 2.8, in which Ovid first denies and then perpetrates his manipulative affair with Corinna's

---

[27] But what was he doing there? Answer – he is the reader.
[28] Except, that is, when it is artistic to do so, cf. *Ars am.* 2.427–62. On the play of personae between *Amores* and *Ars amatoria* see James 1997, Armstrong 2005: 34, Rimell 2006: 83–4.
[29] On the diptych nature, see Kutzko 2006: 169–72.

enslaved hairdresser, I deliberately read from the perspective of the (fictional) women involved. Henderson's difficult but rich discussion of these poems and the nature of reading is important for showing up the complexities of multiple identities in the triangle Ovid – Corinna – Cypassis, where any two may have the possibility for identification which excludes the third.[30] What is most remarkable, I suggest, is that the opportunity for mutuality which appears to gain the least traction is gender. Corinna and Cypassis function as two alternatives for Ovid, but their shared gender is given no chance to create a bond of sympathy between them, despite the fact that they are both victims of the speaker. An additional aspect of the diptych gains greater traction in the modern world, in that we must assume that Ovid and Corinna are 'white', while Cypassis is 'black', these colour-based ethnic identities – modern categories – mapping painfully (for us) onto the statuses of freedom and slavery. The diptych can thus feed usefully into modern intersectional discourses surrounding gender and race. It is an indictment of the potential misogyny in ancient Roman culture that shared gender is given no opportunity to create solidarity between the two women being manipulated by the male lover. It is equally an indictment of the remaining racism in contemporary Western, especially American, culture that Cypassis can stand as a symbol for the struggle of black women to make common cause either with men or with white women.[31]

Although one should remain carefully agnostic, in either direction, about the possibility of historic individuals holding what might seem to be remarkably modern personal opinions, it would surely be anachronistic to hold that the flesh-and-blood Ovid 'intends' a reading of his poems in exactly these terms. Nonetheless, such an interpretation, I suggest, is valid and appropriate from the modern perspective. It is what I would call a form of 'situated reading', which does not require attribution to ancient readers. I shall discuss 'situated reading' on pp. 193–200; what matters here, in order to appreciate the ethical significance of our construction of authors and personae, is that it is sadly likely that most ancient readers, and indeed the vast majority of post-ancient readers, would not perceive major moral difficulties in these poems and would therefore have no reason to keep so fierce a cordon sanitaire between the speaker and the poet as is required by contemporary persona criticism. Moreover, most readers, even if they resist interpreting the poems biographically, are inclined to be seduced away from moral/political judgements by poetic assessments. The Ovidian 'sting

---

[30] Henderson 1991 and 1992.
[31] On this issue with regard to Classics, see in particular Haley 1993.

in the tail' which serves to undermine the 'seriousness' of the violent situation in 1.7 becomes the genius which makes everything all right and makes the speaker's words just a pose.[32]

Enabling a helpful distance between the poet and the character who speaks in the first person is not the only role for persona in the reading of elegy, as indeed in other genres. It contributes also to the construction of the author-speaker of elegy as playing a range of roles, variations in his role as poet. For example, Greene and Keith have both argued persuasively for epic elements in the construction of the elegiac poet-lover, elements which complicate his role as regards both poetics and gender.[33] Oliensis reads the poet of the metapoetic and paratextual *Am.* 1.15 as constituting just as much a persona as the lover of *Am.* 1.14 is generally taken to be.[34] She rightly draws attention to the problem that readers today tend to be comfortable in making a split between the lover and the historical Ovid, but less so between the poet and the flesh-and-blood author. Although it is my impression that many contemporary scholars would, if asked (especially if asked), describe the poet in *Am.* 1.15 as an 'implied author', rather than simply the historical Ovid, nonetheless Oliensis identifies important consequences of the underlying tendency to identify the poet-figure directly with the flesh-and-blood author. To take a simple example, readers tend to take poetic statements in the *Amores* much more seriously than erotic ones. No one would imagine that Ovid really thought that Cupid really stole a foot from him when he had set out to write epic, but most modern critics would be inclined to see the scene created by this conceit in *Am.* 1.1 as a reflection of the historical author. Oliensis ends her discussion with a statement both close to my position and raising issues for it: 'I insist on the difference between Ovid and Naso not because I believe they are entirely disconnected (I am certain they are not) but because I am sure

---

[32] A related matter is the increasing problem in recent years over how to manage the prevalence of rape in Ovid's poetry, and how to present this to students of the '#metoo' generation, on which see James 2012, Liveley 2012 and Gloyn 2013. Richlin's classic 1991 article remains an important contribution to the debate around reading Ovid, including with regard to persona. It was suggested to me by Roy Gibson that the reason why Ovid's treatment of women has tended to be positively represented by our generation of critics, using persona theory to help us in that endeavour, is that we are drawn towards constructing him as 'like us' in part, ironically, because of the pull of the biographical tradition – Ovid in exile, the subversive opponent of Augustus, is very attractive to those who grew up in the second half of the twentieth century.

[33] Keith 1999, Greene 2000, Keith 2008: 74–5.

[34] Oliensis 2014 belongs to a volume on the Roman paratext. Much of that excellent collection offers readings which I would describe as intratextual rather than paratextual in the sense developed by Genette 1997. The distinction is relevant to my present purposes, because the absence of truly (i.e. in Genette's sense) paratextual ancient material for the vast majority of classical literature contributes to the constructed nature of the ancient author.

that it would be a serious mistake to underestimate Ovid's hyperconsciousness of the authorial game into which he has dispatched the poet lover who bears his name.'[35] My concern is that this position risks taking us back to exactly the strong distinction between historical author and poetic persona that over-estimates the extent to which we can get in direct touch with the entity whom we envisage as the historical author pulling the strings.[36]

I have been primarily concerned so far with the most obvious candidates for persona criticism in Latin literature (satire and love poetry). Before widening the discussion into other genres, we should acknowledge and engage with the challenges raised by some classical critics to the very notion of persona. There have been numerous challenges to classical persona theory, in addition to the ethical and political worries explored earlier: scholars of satire, in particular, have been concerned about the overuse of persona criticism and its tendency to produce rather predictable readings;[37] while the most concerted opposition has come from those who regard the concept as anachronistic and regard anachronism as a serious problem. Clay argues for the paucity of distinction, within ancient literary criticism, between poet outside the poem and poet inside the poem, either in rhetorical works or even in explicit statements by the poets themselves, the notable exception being the protestations of erotic poets such as Catullus, Ovid and Martial about their naughty poetry but pious life.[38] He suggests that any ancient theory of the literary persona is to be found 'not in ancient literary criticism but in our increasing awareness of the practice of the poets who created personae within their poetry for their own rhetorical purposes and who created a persona for their reader'.[39] Clay's view appears to be that the literary persona is a fact of literature, practised by Roman poets but not acknowledged by extant ancient critics.

More determinedly anti-persona, as being anachronistic for Roman poetry, is Mayer, who takes the view that 'since persona criticism is an approach to reading texts rather than a theoretical system of literary analysis . . ., and since it is agreed by all that the persona is a consciously created element in a poem . . ., it may be urged that so far as classical poetry

---

[35] Oliensis 2014: 223.
[36] Volk 2005 shows slippage between the persona of poet and of lover in the *Amores*, requiring us to reject the simplistic view of the lover-persona as simply a character on stage unconnected with the poet.
[37] Nappa 1998. The earlier history of opposition to persona criticism in modern literature is well told by Elliott 1982, esp. 13–18.
[38] Clay 1998, Lowrie 2009: 363.   [39] Clay 1998: 39.

## 4 Author and Identity

is concerned the modern reading is misapplied'.[40] His case is that the idea of a distinction between the literature and the life of a poet is contrary to ancient reading practices, ancient audiences assuming that the speaker is the author unless proven otherwise. (He appears to take it as axiomatic that only ancient reading practices are relevant to the reading of ancient texts, despite the impossibility of reconstructing those and the actuality of our reading as twenty-first-century people.) As regards the claims of the poets regarding their (lack of) responsibility for the sexual misdemeanours of their poetic selves, he portrays their denials as simply matters of self-defence. Ovid, in particular, is taken to be trying it on.[41] A complication with Mayer's article is that it slips between an interest in persona and literature as autobiography, two phenomena which, though connected, are not identical. It would be perfectly possible, and is indeed widely perceived in the work of Pliny, for example, for an author to construct a range of personae all of which reflect in some way on autobiographical claims.[42]

With any piece of criticism, one should look at the straw persons being presented. Mayer asks (rhetorically) why, if Horace and his audience had the notion of persona, Horace did not defend himself from the charge of being *nimis acer* in his satirical writing (*Sat.* 2.1.1) by claiming it was the persona who spoke these words, not himself.[43] Mayer implies that persona-critics are claiming that nothing in satire means anything because it is spoken by the satirist not by the flesh-and-blood author. That, however, is not what they are saying. If I were to apply the same technique of the straw person to him, I would say that his argument would mean that Roman readers believed, and we should believe, that Ovid really did have a limb amputated by Cupid.

A theoretically sophisticated contribution to this line of reasoning about reading ancient authors' voices is Whitmarsh's argument, apropos of

---

[40] Mayer 2003a: 57. It does not seem to me necessary that the persona is consciously created by the flesh-and-blood author. Another challenger to the theory is Iddeng 2005, also concerned only with a persona consciously constructed by the flesh-and-blood author. Iddeng argues for a 'flexible I-poet', in which some elements are clearly fictional and others not. Like Mayer, Iddeng concentrates on the absence of explicit statements by poets except in the case of 'a few remarks connected to erotic or lascivious poetry' (194). He rejects any 'reason to assume that the narrator in Tacitus's works of history, Seneca's treatises on philosophy or Pliny the Elder's *Naturalia* is anyone but the author himself' (185–6), to which my answer is that even in these cases the 'himself' is the one the author chooses to show, and one he shows despite himself.
[41] To my surprise, Mayer does not discuss *Am.* 3.12, which could be used to support the notion that common reading practice saw the speaker of love poetry straightforwardly as the poet himself. On the other hand, that is such a magnificent piece of multiple bluffing that it might not have worked quite so well for him.
[42] Henderson 2003 represents this way of reading Pliny, now becoming widely accepted.
[43] Mayer 2003a: 77–8.

Apuleius, that ancient readers and writers do not have a notion of the narrator as separate from the author, and that by pushing the contemporary narratological orthodoxy we miss much of the complex play at work in ancient narrative. He claims that the modern 'easy acceptance of fictional conventions . . . has dulled our sense of the transgressiveness of this kind of speech act'.[44] This is in relation to a case where the narrator of the story is dead, though naturally we do not have to assume that the author is equally so. The fact that we are so comfortable with the split between author and narrator 'does violence to the fictional conventions of the ancient world, foreclosing the complex and unresolved play between the autobiographical and the fictional modes'. This is because ancient autobiography is a mode of speaking in the tradition of impersonation, as with actors, rhapsodes and lexicographers.[45] As a result, a dead speaker is more shocking and unstable than we can feel, with our easy acceptance of a divide between author and narrator. As a challenge to persona theory, this is a timely warning which fits well with my arguments against the 'get out of jail free' card, and also with my suggestions about the super-persona, the 'big I' of Ovid or Cicero outside individual works. Transgressive slippage between the impersonated I and the real author, as discussed by Whitmarsh, is precisely what I consider Ovid to be doing in his plays between genres. It seems to me, then, that Whitmarsh's case (a) is strong against the kind of maximalist and even sometimes mechanical application of narratological theory;[46] (b) enables an effective reading of Apuleius; but (c) does not finally constitute a challenge but rather a contribution to the kind of persona theory I am promoting here.

### The Prose-Writer as Author

Literary theorists of the twentieth century, when the great debates were being set up, were primarily interested in fiction, indeed primarily the novel and the lyric poem (to use the term 'lyric' in the modern loose sense). The twenty-first century, which is the age of the handbook, reflects similar interests, especially when it tells its own histories.[47] These thinkers

---

[44] Whitmarsh 2013: 238.
[45] Whitmarsh 2013: 240: 'fictional autobiography is a form of illusionism. In Augustine's response to Apuleius, the authorial "I" slides fictitiously into the (narratorial) alter ego, even as the reader retains an awareness of the irreducible fictionality of the process.'
[46] Whitmarsh 2013: 244: 'I have argued not that the critical category of the narrator should not exist or does not make sense, but that narratology's automatic compartmentalisation of the narrator as discrete from the author discounts much of the metaleptic play on which pre-narratological fiction depends.' This is a smaller claim than in his opening salvos.
[47] The nature of literature is a huge topic: for a (politicised) discussion see Eagleton 2012.

## 4 Author and Identity

interacted creatively with and learned from the theorists of epistemology and hermeneutics, despite the fact that the biggest names in those areas are not literary critics but philosophers and historians, such as Foucault and Derrida. Anticipating somewhat my discussion of intentionalism (pp. 184–93), I quote a statement by Andrew Bennett, in his analysis of the theory of author:

> Indeed, it might be argued that it is just this sense of a fundamental or constitutive uncertainty of authorial intention that distinguishes literature itself from other discourses, from philosophy, say: it may be that our reading of a poem or other literary text begins, in a certain sense, when we can believe that we have located something that the author didn't fully, consciously, properly intend, or that she intended only in the blink of an eye, in the periphery of a certain vision.[48]

Although such a distinction certainly cannot work in any simple way for ancient texts, it nonetheless resonates with classicists if we change the term slightly to distinguish 'philosophy' from 'poetry'.[49]

The distinctions between fiction and non-fiction in antiquity do not fall into neat lines in the way that has been common in European literature since the early modern period (especially before post-modern challenges widened the scope of the fictional, and the docudrama – and 'fake news' – widened that of the 'factual'). It can be tempting, however, to make a broader distinction in classical scholarship between prose and verse, as a shorthand for the difference between two types of writing, which might then itself seem to fall into a distinction between fiction and non-fiction,[50] and from there into the development of a category of 'literature'. It thus becomes meaningful to claim that a piece of scholarship is taking a work 'seriously as literature', a designation which would only be required when there was some possibility or history of not doing so. Ancient authors themselves, moreover, have a language of distinctions which would make a category of 'literature'. Pliny the Younger's *paulo curatius* (*Ep.* 1.1.1) is a classic case, for his designation of the collection of his letters as entering thereby into a category of literature (rather than ephemera), while the trope of triviality employed especially by epigrammatists shows the sophistication with which play can be made of such categorisation.[51] Ancient writing as it has come down to us is perhaps better thought of as a spectrum,

---

[48] Bennett 2005: 83. [49] Gould 1990 is an important assessment of this issue.
[50] Works such as Apuleius' *Metamorphoses*, Petronius' *Satyrica* and Seneca's *Apocolocyntosis* become a kind of honorary poetry.
[51] For example, Catullus 1.3–4 *namque tu* [i.e. *Cornelius*] *solebas | meas esse aliquid putare nugas*, also in a programmatic opening.

moving from those most obviously literary and fictional (Ovid's *Metamorphoses* would stand at the far left of the spectrum) to works which additionally appear to have, or to have had at some stage in their lives, what I can best categorise as a non-aesthetic purpose. Letters which were actually sent and speeches which were actually delivered would have purposes beyond the aesthetic, although they are mostly not available to us in that form (or only by a leap of imagination). Letters collected and speeches circulated in written form, however, have become literature. These works, nonetheless, also maintain implicit claims for non-fictionality which go beyond those made by Ovid's *Metamorphoses*.[52] We should notice, however, that the *Metamorphoses* is rare for antiquity in the extent of its fictionality. Many poetic works present their content as non-fictional: Lucretius' *De rerum natura* is a polemical example, while Lucan makes a poem out of recent history and Virgil writes an epic with strong historical implications. Ovid's *Fasti* is full of fantasies about interviewing divinities, and full of funny stories that are easy to call fictional, but nonetheless it purports, like all didactic literature (even the *Ars amatoria*), to be about real things.[53]

One of the most important developments in the study of Latin literature over the last few decades is the blossoming of approaches to prose authors which, to use the terms I have suggested, take the works seriously 'as literature', applying to those works the insights gained from the study of verse. Informed also by the post-deconstructionist understanding of the self as a series of roles, critics have come to see how works such as the letters of Pliny or speeches of Cicero display personae which should not be regarded as direct windows onto the inner soul of the author or as straightforward historical sources.[54] Recent scholarship on prose genres, particularly letters, has developed the analysis of the prose persona, for which I offer a few examples.

---

[52] On the other hand, at the level of the text itself it is precisely Ovid who makes claims for the factuality of his work – although we engage with his poetological manipulation of this claim precisely by *not* believing him. Examples are *Am.* 1.9 (*crede mihi*) and 3.12, or the sphragis of the *Metamorphoses*. I think it is fair to say that genres like oratory, philosophy, historiography and technical writing offer themselves as having a more direct relationship with the world of the text than does the *Metamorphoses*. I am conscious of the potential challenges to this claim.

[53] I agree with Whitmarsh 2013 that we lose out if we fail to appreciate the slippages between fiction and non-fiction in ancient literature. Important on the relationship between fiction and falsity in Latin literature is Lowrie 2009, esp. 81–3.

[54] The controversy over this last is discussed in this volume by Myles Lavan. See Roman 2014 on aesthetic autonomy.

## 4 Author and Identity

Henderson, opposing the historically standard transparent reading of Pliny's letters, describes the *Letters* as 'a creative self-dramatisation, a literary stab at self-immortalisation'.[55] His claim (if I understand him correctly) is that not only is the style the man but also the man is the style, so that even the 'real Pliny' is this rhetorical construct. Such an analysis is in keeping with post-modern interpretation of the self as a rhetorical construct. More importantly for my purposes is the fact that the man-as-style is all there is, this is what we can see. We are entitled to see it differently from how Pliny wanted us to see it, as is inevitable with the changes in social mores, but we can only ever talk about the constructed Plinian self.

Tempest claims that it is widely accepted 'that textual analyses will reveal at best how Cicero wanted his audience to perceive him', rather than actual fact, and seeks to explore the mechanisms by which Cicero is able to develop a persuasive self-presentation, which she describes as the construction of 'an ethos of sincerity'. In doing so, she works effectively with the notion of the super-persona which I have suggested is important for many ancient authors. So, for example, 'Cicero's political treatise thus acts as an intertext for the speech, with the result that "Cicero" in the *Pro Marcello* is made to speak like "Cicero", the author of the *De republica*'.[56]

Ash explores the apparent conflict between the image Pliny generally appears to want to betray of himself in the *Letters*, 'as kind and altruistic, fulfilling the obligations of a Roman aristocrat', and on the other hand those relating to Regulus, in which 'the author's voice instead appears malignant and hostile'. Her argument is that Pliny as epistolographer, by setting up Regulus as a target for his own contemporary brand of invective embedded in his letter collection, enhances his own identity as a truly neo-Ciceronian writer. By placing these letters in conjunction with the wider collection and the gentler authorial voice, Ash suggests that Pliny seeks to emphasise the awfulness of Regulus (bad enough to make even Pliny turn

---

[55] Henderson 2003: 115. As he says, the scholarship was rapidly changing in the early years of the millennium: 'in contemporary reception, Pliny's modelling of the self has moved toward the centre of interest in the letters' (124). Other papers in the same volume of *Arethusa* are valuable for the issues with which I am concerned, in particular De Pretis' (2003) debunking of the difference between sincere real letters and insincere constructs, especially in the letters to and about Calpurnia. She reads them as examples of epistolary literature, while remaining agnostic about the 'reality' behind them. Mayer (2003b) there argues for the importance of Pliny the orator in the letters, claiming that Pliny regarded his oratory as the most important thing and his letters as a way to advertise them. Such a reading would be in close connection with my case for the super-persona. Morello (2003) discusses Pliny's mechanism in the cover letters and preparatory letters for works of oratory and others – which is to say very little about them, and which turns out to be a way of eliciting desire to read. Having 'nothing to say' is also a Ciceronian trope.

[56] Tempest 2013: 271.

to invective) and at the same time to demonstrate the mildness of the Plinian character as not someone 'in whom *obtrectatio et liuor* ("disparagement and malice") are ingrained'.[57]

As an example of how two different pieces of Roman literature of different kinds (one verse and one prose, and that at the most apparently practical end of the spectrum) can nonetheless make very similar moves as regards the construction of their persona, I offer the work of Marden Fitzpatrick Nichols on Horace and Vitruvius.[58] Nichols shows how the two authors construct their personae in a similar way to each other and similar to the wider discourse surrounding the right behaviour of the class of *scribae* to which the historical authors may both have belonged. The similarities include moves such as 'rejections of political office, self-promotion and the desire to accumulate wealth' (121), their success being based on good education and good character, and being wanted by important people, rather than by canvassing. It would not be possible to make a clear distinction between Horace and Vitruvius in this way, despite the fact that Vitruvius is writing a work which may have practical purposes in architecture, in addition to aesthetic and rhetorical purposes. Horace in the 'real life' hexameter poems cannot simply be sealed off from lyric Horace: there is a transgeneric Horatian super-persona as for Ovid. For both Horace and Ovid, the super-persona transcends not only the distinctions between texts and metres, but even the distinction between aesthetics and politics. The case of Vitruvius is not much different.

Consideration of persona cannot take many steps without becoming entangled in questions of sincerity, truth and meaning, as will be explored further in this chapter. In an attempt to find some categorisations which will not immediately slip through critical fingers, the next few paragraphs offer thoughts on the difference between more and less fictional works. Lowrie explores Horace's protestations that he did not enjoy reciting in public (*Sat.* 1.4.23, 73–4), as part of her important investigation into the extent to which poetry intervenes in society.[59] Lowrie says: 'it is uncertain whether we can take Horace's satiric statements seriously and whether they pertain to lyric, but the likelihood of recitation is based on current cultural realities rather than anything Horace says'.[60] I quote this statement not in order to enter the debate about recitation itself, but to consider its implications for different kinds of persona. It is the Horace-persona who makes

---

[57] Ash 2013, esp. 211–12.
[58] Nichols 2009. See also Nichols 2017 for a good example of the literary turn in the study of technical writing.
[59] Lowrie 2009: 63–7.  [60] Lowrie 2009: 63.

this claim, in keeping as it is with the rhetoric of the *Satires*. Horace the poet, and in some sense Horace the man (by definition, firstly, and, secondly, by our construction in the act of reading it), intended to write a sentence which says 'I do not enjoy reciting in public' – of this we can be reasonably sure. But this does not mean that Horace the man really did not enjoy reciting in public. Rather, it means that he intended to put this sentence into the 'mouth' of Horace the poet as projected in the *Satires*. It cannot tell us whether Horace the man really did recite in public, with enjoyment or otherwise. What it can tell us is that such a claim was felt, by Horace and probably at least some contemporary readers, to be an appropriate sentiment to express in that (generic and other) context. When Cicero makes any statement in a work like the *Ad familiares*, it may still have more of a rhetorical drive than being a true reflection of his real feelings, but it is closer to being the reflection of the feelings of Cicero the man *that he, man and letter-writer, wants to portray* at that point. With regard to Horace, it is a reflection of what Horace the man wants to portray as the feelings of Horace the poet, which could have nothing to do with Horace the man – except in so far as the interaction between man and poet is one with which poets play. There is, therefore, slightly more clear water between flesh-and-blood and persona for Horace than for Cicero – but only slightly.

A question to which I keep returning is to what extent we can (or should) perceive the difference between the persona as created by Ovid in the *Amores* and Pliny in the *Letters* (in collected form, as we read them). When I read critics' accounts of Pliny the author manipulating the persona of Pliny the letter-writer, I am uncertain as to the extent to which it is any different from Ovid the author (constructed author and super-persona) manipulating the persona of Ovid the lover, or the teacher, or indeed the poet. Could it be that Pliny intends (we are only guessing) the picture of Pliny in the *Letters* to have an effect on the life and position of the flesh-and-blood author, while Ovid does not? That would be ironic, given which author was sent into exile as a result of his work. Just because flesh-and-blood Pliny wants (this is a construction) people to link *Letters* Pliny to himself, whereas flesh-and-blood Ovid might not want people to link *Amores* Ovid to himself (it is easier to construct versions of flesh-and-blood Ovid who would actively not want that, though plenty of senses in which he clearly might), does that make a fundamental difference? If that were the case, I imagine we might want to say that there is a narrower gap between flesh-and-blood Pliny, author Pliny and the persona created in the *Letters* than is the case for Ovid. But perhaps the difference is one of extent rather than nature. To run through the comparison again: flesh-and-blood Pliny creates (that is, contributes to creating, along with associates, traditions and readers) implied author Pliny, who creates personae (which reflect back on flesh-and-blood Pliny, for certain purposes including flesh-and-blood Pliny's social standing). Flesh-and-blood Ovid creates (that is, contributes to creating likewise) implied author Ovid, who creates 'elegiac poet Ovid', who creates personae. In the Ovidian case, there was an extra stage up to this point, which is easiest for moderns to call fiction. As fiction, it would generally have the effect of distancing the various personae from the implied author and thus also from the flesh-and-blood author. But how does my final Plinian parenthesis work in the case of Ovid? It may well be that although for the modern reader the intrusion of a level of fictionality and an extra layer between flesh-and-blood author and persona means that persona does not so obviously reflect back on the author outside the text, but it may well be that this was less true in antiquity. The exile might seem to suggest it.[61]

What about the difference between Ovid and Tacitus? The historian creates an image of himself, a persona in the sense of the best picture of himself as historian, but he is not a fictional character within his own work. Could it be that the most fundamental difference in ancient literature is that between first-person texts and those in which the narrator is relatively invisible – in narratological terms, the distinction between homodiegetic and heterodiegetic texts? Here, however, I need to disagree with the claim of Iddeng that 'we construe the *Annales* as Tacitus' own words, not those of an invented *I*-person'.[62] That is only true in the limited sense in which the narrator of the historical works of Tacitus *is* the constructed author to whom we give that name: 'Tacitus' own words' in the sense of the words of a figure who presents himself as a senatorial historian skilfully laying a hatchet to the imperial project. The person to whom we give the name Tacitus is this constructed persona. Nonetheless, the author who puts himself, or a version of himself, directly into a textual world is playing a different kind of game from cases where the image of the author is only as a narrator or an authority for information which he presents as being part of a factual world. But then what about Virgil in the *Aeneid*? There is, perhaps, a more obviously generic aspect to Virgil's construction of himself as epic poet, but otherwise I am not

---

[61] Why should we think that the writing of fiction causes authors to be immune to real-world consequences? The history of the twentieth century should disabuse us of any such idea.
[62] Iddeng 2005: 186.

convinced that it would be appropriate to make a strong distinction between the Tacitean persona and the Virgilian.

## More Flesh on the Bones of the Constructed Author – and Why We Need It

The implied author is a layer between flesh-and-blood author and narrator, mostly developed for the study of the novel, with considerable overlap also with the literary persona, especially in its super-persona form.[63] I propose a small twist on this tool in the form of the 'constructed author': this is the author as we are able to engage with him/her, an image made up out of the (for Classics, largely unknowable) flesh-and-blood author, other contemporary contributors, and the history of reading (both of the text and of the life of the author) between then and now, possibly even with interventions from interpolators and forgers. Stanley Fish says that all criticism is necessarily biographical in that whatever we say about an utterance, we are necessarily positing a being, with some degree of a biography, to make that utterance,[64] while Uhlig, in a volume in which the contributors were particularly interested in the way biographies and authors work on a two-way street, describes the 'author' as possessed by the text and 'neither fully inside nor outside the text'.[65] Both comments reflect helpfully on my understanding of the constructed author, which I suggest is an image coming into existence only in our reading, through our formulation of it, and subject to change over the critical centuries, but nonetheless with roots in a historical moment.[66] The words out of which the constructed author is made were put together by the flesh-and-blood author, with the

---

[63] The 'implied author' as a critical term was developed by Booth 1961. It has had huge progeny, on the one hand sparking significant theoretical opposition (and defence), and on the other becoming naturalised in literary discourses even among those who do not follow theoretical debates. Although its theoretical origin and development is in narratology and narrative genres, its naturalisation spreads into all forms of writing (and beyond). Many twenty-first-century handbooks offer accounts of the theory of the implied author, among which I recommend Schmid 2009, Bennett 2005: 13–26 and 120–9, and Bennett and Royle 2016: ch. 3. In 2011, the journal *Style* published a special issue (Richardson 2011) devoted to a consideration of the implied author, with sometimes polemical arguments on both sides.
[64] Fish 1991. See pp. 191–3 on hypothetical intentionalism.
[65] Uhlig 2016: 105. See also ibid. 110–11.
[66] Bennett 2005: 120: 'The author of Tess of the D'Urbervilles, for example, is both an individual who lived between 1840 and 1928, trained as an architect, lived most of his life in Dorset, married twice, at different times, two women called Emma (Gifford and Dugdale), and wrote seventeen novels, some forty short stories and more than nine hundred poems. But the author of Tess of the D'Urbervilles is also not that individual, or it is an individual as an empty shell, a hollow man, a man constructed or "performed" in and by the novel.'

help of audiences and an existing and indeed ongoing tradition, in the form of editors, commentators and readers. But as we cannot possibly know exactly what was in the historical author's mind over the period of initial production, any claim that we are reproducing his or her mind has to be at best agnostic. Rather, what we have is the traces left of it in the text, from which we construct the meaning in the terms of the twenty-first century.

Readers in our Western tradition have a very strong desire for originary authors, as the focus for our sense of the need for a text to have an identifiable, authoritative source.[67] Bennett describes authors as made 'in the image of our desire for a transcendent originary unity', while perhaps the most pertinent soundbite from Barthes comes in his statement of the author as the object of desire: 'in the text, in a way, *I desire* the author: I need his figure (which is neither his representation nor his projection) as he needs mine'.[68] As is well known, the ancient book tradition was committed to the 'Big Name' effect, as witnessed by the way in which orphaned plays are ascribed to Plautus in antiquity, juvenilia are identified for Virgil and other great men, authorities are named in scientific and technical work in preference to empirical investigation, and a substantial industry is developed in pseudepigraphy.[69] Peirano Garrison explores the challenge for ancient authors in negotiating the effects of naming within their work.[70] This includes use of the author's name that creates a kind of authority and a claim for authorship, but also one that risks actually suggesting the opposite – that it is forgery, precisely because it protests too much. She names the desire for the 'Big Name' as onymity, and argues that 'because of the reader's desire for the figure of the author, anonymity

---

[67] I make that qualification, 'Western', simply because of my ignorance of the extent to which it is true of other traditions. I would like to mention the situation which I understand to pertain in biblical literature regarding the fluidity of texts and authors, which makes even Homer seems straightforward. McCarthy 2016 gives a taste of the complexity. Late in the preparation of this paper, I read Tom Geue's powerful and entertaining analysis (Geue 2019) of this scholarly desire for the originary author in the classical scholarly tradition which, along with the work of Irene Peirano Garrison discussed in this paragraph, I recommend highly for anyone interested in new ways of thinking about authorship.

[68] Bennett 2005: 35; Barthes 1975: 27. On readers' desire for the author, see also Abbott 2011: 464: 'If it can be argued, as some have, that Booth's cushioning of the word *author* with the word *implied* was in fact a deliberate strategy for avoiding the "intentional fallacy" ..., the continuing argument regarding what exactly the implied author is and what role this concept should play attest to a persistent need to anchor the interpretation of literary texts in some version of an intending source' (emphasis original).

[69] Morrison 2013 on pseudepigraphic letters. See also Bennett 2005: 5.

[70] Peirano Garrison 2013. Her chapter includes an excellent, brief account of the constructed author. See also Peirano Garrison 2014 on the sphragis, and her extended study of pseudepigraphy, Peirano Garrison 2012.

## 4 Author and Identity

can thus never be reduced to a complete lack of onymity.'[71] So, for example, the Song of Iopas in *Aen.* 1 is taken as self-reference to Virgil, via the Homeric Demodocus, but Virgil as poet of nature, hence also the poet of the *Georgics* (and *Eclogues*). Furthermore: 'If they [the audience] are willing to subscribe to this fiction of presence and immediacy, the author's name delivers the illusion of authorial *maintenance* in what is ultimately, however, nothing but a triumph of signification.'[72] In a similar way, Laird shows how ancient commentators' (to us) bizarre interpretations may be better understood in the context of a strong desire for character on their part for Virgil/the poet.[73] We should, however, be careful to distinguish this from Romantic-style understanding of poetry as expression of personal psychology. The Big Name is about authority, not about the self in Romantic terms.

While the practice of name-checking and ascription of works to individual Big Names seems to be prevalent throughout the Western literary tradition, it is increasingly becoming recognised that the highly intertextual and collaborative model of authorship, which we could even call the 'Homeric' mode, is widely relevant to the realities of text-production, in both ancient and modern contexts.[74] The role of critical friends in the production of poetry, as indicated by Horace in *Ars poetica* 426–52, is emblematic of this process, which has been explored in detail by Gurd.[75] Gurd examines the Ciceronian fluidity of textual production, in which revision serves not only, or even primarily, to produce a fixed text, but rather is driven by paedagogic-cognitive goals and social goals.[76] He sees Cicero as aiming at an egalitarian, non-hierarchical relationship between textual agents, which he regards as strongly associated with republicanism.[77]

---

[71] Peirano Garrison 2013: 276.   [72] Ibid. 281.   [73] Laird 2016: 83–4.
[74] Bennett 2005: passim. Recent work on Renaissance theatre has shown the extent to which the UK national hero of poetic genius was actually a genius at teamwork. The case of Bakhtin and his collaborators is also telling in this regard. Indeed, in modern academic research a published piece is hardly ever the work only of the named author. It is very likely to have undergone contributions from colleagues, students and especially editors. Some of the changes required by editors may even be contrary to the wishes of the named author. For ancient authors, see Tarrant 2016: 4–6.
[75] See Gurd 2011, and the bibliographic turn more widely. Gurd's book engages with what he calls the 'new bibliography', in which authorial manuscripts are not seen as witnesses helpful in establishing the exact words of a work but as the traces of an adventure of creation. He argues (p. 3) that ancient authors and readers did not take for granted that a final published version was simply the 'best' or the one that most closely approximated an author's intention. See also Tarrant 2016. McCutcheon 2016 also argues for the radical fluidity of the text of Cicero's letters and the absence of any original.
[76] Gurd 2011: 6.
[77] Ibid. 76: 'Since this circulation for the sake of correction was a social end in itself, we could conclude that these texts offer traces not of literary processes aimed at the production of perfect texts, but of social performances.' A point which he perhaps does not sufficiently acknowledge is the difference made by presence of an item in the collection, which is the only form to which we have access. There

By contrast, Augustus' desire to fix texts is associated with the imperial project and with increasing anxiety among poets over the need for revision. While not all readers will be happy with the extent of Gurd's attribution of (good) fluidity to republicanism and (bad) fixity to imperialism, it is, as he says: 'at least suggestive that the same texts that speak of Augustus's desire to create a library of canonical Roman poets (*Epistles* 2.1.216–18, 2.2.94) also discuss revision in terms metaphorically linked to censorial activity'.[78] Gurd's emphasis on the fluidity of textual production and the involvement of a large number of players is important for any understanding of the author, both as constructed figure and as object of desire.

The identity and singularity of originary authors has had a powerful role to play in the history of textual criticism. Until recently, I blindly espoused the view that textual criticism, contrary to literary interpretation, dealt in absolutes and had as its goal the reconstruction of the author's originally intended and produced text.[79] I hope it will not be regarded as excessively self-reflexive if I quote an early draft of this essay in which I said:

> Despite all the problems of singularity in ownership of texts, of whether the author's last thoughts should carry particular weight, or indeed his first thoughts, nonetheless there is one area of classical scholarship where intentionalism is more necessary and more philosophically meaningful, which is establishing the text. I find it easy to say that, at least for Virgil or Ovid, we are attempting to reconstruct what the poet, or at least the poet and his slave and maybe other collaborators, wrote and authorised to be copied.[80]

Then I read Richard Tarrant's 2016 book and was, frankly, bowled over by a new understanding of the project of textual criticism and its similarity to that of interpretation. Tarrant exposes 'the myth of the recoverable original'[81] which has driven a kind of heroic textual criticism, but which is problematised first by the question of whether a single perfect text (i.e. embodying the author's every desire) ever existed, second by the barriers to reproducing that, and finally by the impossibility of ever knowing whether we have done so.[82] Tarrant argues that textual criticism is better conceived of as

---

is a related problem, which I don't think he manages to deal with, about the extent to which the version we are reading is before or after the revisions it talks about.

[78] Ibid. 102.
[79] On the editing of texts being particularly concerned with intention, see Bennett 2005: 109.
[80] Even at that point, I modified the claim with a note to self: 'But did they? What about multiple recension? And there is value in reading unauthorised but widely circulated textual constructions, such as Cicero's letters to his friends, as powerfully shown by Beard 2002.'
[81] Tarrant 2016: 38.
[82] Ibid. 39: 'Even if we could succeed in completely reconstituting an original, we would have no way of knowing that we had done so.'

being in the business not of absolutes but of rhetoric and persuasion,[83] of producing readings which will gain acceptance by a Fishian interpretative community, but which is unlikely to remain fixed for evermore.[84] It is dealing, therefore, in probabilities. He says: 'No edition of a classical text can be definitive, in part because the possibility of new and convincing conjectures can never be ruled out, but also because in any text of some length there will be places where different editors can reasonably make different choices, either by preferring one manuscript reading to another, or by adopting a conjecture instead of the transmitted reading(s), or by judging the text corrupt and using the obelus.'[85]

The long history of textual criticism is aligned with that of literary criticism in its fetishisation of the author, which is a contributory factor in worries about interpolation of lines and indeed of whole poems, leading to uncertainties over the 'authenticity' of, for example, some of the *Heroides* letters.[86] While it is appropriate that we should as literary critics be aware of and, for the purposes of certain kinds of readings, influenced in our interpretations by current views on the provenance and authenticity of lines and whole poems, for other kinds of readings I would suggest that we should resist worshipping at the altar of authenticity. When it comes to Plautus, I am much less happy to say, as Zwierlein does, that our goal should be to work out what Plautus personally composed. What exactly happened in the first production, which in any case might not be the same as the poet's script, seems to me rather less interesting than engagement with over two thousand years of engagement with the written text (repetition intended).[87] The 'original' is a valid subject for historical investigation, if seriously subject to speculation, but it is barely a literary question. Just as readings are for purposes, so there is critical value in making a wide range of textual variants available to readers. This is not only because we do not know for certain the answer to a question (what the author wrote) which may or may not be in principle fixable, but also because the process of interpretation is part of a long tradition, which includes those variants.[88] No doubt it also includes others now lost to us, which puts textual criticism in the same position as in the case of intertextuality.

---

[83] Ibid. 29: 'since persuasion is fundamentally a rhetorical activity, a suitable next focus of attention is the place of rhetoric in textual criticism'.
[84] Ibid. 69 discusses proof as acceptance by a community in this way.   [85] Ibid. 40.
[86] Bennett 2005: 98 comments on the style of criticism that assigns anything it does not like in a Shakespeare play to 'other writers who have "tampered" with his work'. See also Tarrant 2016: 22.
[87] The enormous subject of Plautine 'authorship' is an industry in its own right.
[88] Tarrant 2016: 150 praises in this regard the Digital Latin Library being developed in Oklahoma (discussed by Kaster and Huskey in this volume).

## Intentionalism and the Range of Interpretation

The issue of the relationship between persona, constructed or implied author and flesh-and-blood author is at heart an issue in the nature of literary interpretation. The question for literary theory is: what is the (appropriate) range of interpretation? This is a crucial matter for a project concerned with questions of how we read and how we should read. If 'we' are established scholars, it is our job to judge what deserves to be published and to be accepted in the university system of examination, but on the other hand we are ourselves subject to that judgement, while also feeling the need to justify our subject, and therefore our jobs, to those who control the funding of higher education and academic publishing. If we are students or more junior scholars, we are trying to learn what kinds of judgements are currently controlling the gateways to an academic future – and in the future how we might be in a position to adapt them. We therefore reasonably want justifications for the boundaries of what we regard as good literary interpretation. While I would stress that those boundaries may be different for readings with different purposes, historicist, ideological, ethical, imaginative, creative and many more, across this range we are always faced with the problem that arises out of the analogy between literature and ordinary communication, which is the extent to which the goal of interpretation is exegesis of the author's intention. As Bennett says apropos of the foundational work of Wimsatt and Beardsley: 'The essay ['Intentional fallacy'] engages with one of the most important and one of the most troubling questions in any attempt to think about literary texts, the question of whether or not our sense of what a text means should be determined by our sense of what the author meant by it.'[89]

When I was a student in the 1980s, there was a rearguard action being fought in which one respected scholar said in a discussion that he wanted to 'defend the right of a Latin poet to mean only one thing by one word'.[90] Readers of a certain age will recognise traces here of the 'theory wars' of the twentieth century. I would suggest that, for Classics at least, the intensity of that battle has eased in the last twenty years, partly by the debunking of the most extreme forms of deconstruction and its balancing by other approaches, and partly by the naturalisation of some of its basic tenets, especially regarding multiplicity of meaning.[91] While more kinds of further

---

[89] Bennett 2005: 76.
[90] As Barthes says, victory to the critic as high priest of the author's meaning: see n. 96.
[91] Fowler 2001: 66: narratology lost some of its popularity at the end of the last century, 'but as with other theoretical positions of recent times that was only because the essential elements of narratological analysis had been absorbed into the reading practice of almost all scholars'.

voices are continuing to make themselves heard, the idea that what we are aiming to do is to reconstruct the author's intention has still a somewhat troubled and interesting continuing existence. Add to this the not infrequently voiced question about 'what has happened to high theory since the millennium' and the impression that we might be living in a 'post-theoretical' age (as if that were possible), and the need to address the question head-on becomes pressing.[92]

The history of the move from author to reader, from intentionalism to interpretation, has been told many times: it is a story of the twentieth century, its ideologies and insecurities, and its relationship with the long nineteenth century, with the Enlightenment and especially with Romanticism. I particularly recommend the account in Andrew Bennett's book on *The Author*.[93] The story usually starts with the modernist poetics of C. S. Lewis and T. S. Eliot, the so-called 'New Criticism' and the seminal articles of Wimsatt and Beardsley on the 'intentional fallacy' and the 'affective fallacy', when critics sought to develop a more objective, even scientific, approach to literature than was previously current.[94] It is a nice irony that a move which can reasonably be described as having begun with attempts at quasi-scientific objectivity developed in such a way that it became subject to the accusation of excessive subjectivity, which was precisely what Wimsatt and Beardsley sought to avoid. The author's death, however exaggerated, was proclaimed by Roland Barthes, whose 'Death of the Author', alluding to Nietzsche's 'Death of God', needs to be understood against the background of monolithic but Romantic literary interpretation still prevalent in the mid-twentieth century.[95] It is not a claim for 'free love', where anything goes in the reading of texts. Barthes sought to lessen the grip of the controlling author-father as an

---

[92] Eagleton 2003, Waugh 2006b.
[93] Bennett 2005. See also Burke 1995, Irwin 2002, Eagleton 2003, Waugh 2006a and Bertens 2014. I have also been greatly stimulated by reading Farrell 2017, whose pro-intentionalist arguments have, despite my multiple points of disagreement, helped me to hone my thoughts on the nature of intention and its role in criticism. Bennett 2005: 2–3 identifies the Romantic period as a turning point in the history of literature. If he is right, a less author-centred reading would actually be more in keeping with antiquity than the traditional, Romantic, approach.
[94] Wimsatt and Beardsley 1946; Wimsatt and Beardsley 1949: 31, 'The Intentional Fallacy is a confusion between the poem and its origins, a special case of what is known to philosophers as the Genetic Fallacy. It begins by trying to derive the standard of criticism from the psychological causes of the poem and ends in biography and relativism. The Affective Fallacy is a confusion between the poem and its results (what it is and what it does), a special case of epistemological skepticism, though usually advanced as if it had far stronger claims than the overall forms of skepticism. It begins by trying to derive the standard of criticism from the psychological effects of the poem and ends in impressionism and relativism.'
[95] Barthes 1977: 142–8.

image for the production and dissemination of literary meaning. He did so against a background of traditional literary criticism in which the critic plays the role of high priest of the author-father-god, acting as controller, rather than proliferator, of meaning.[96] Perhaps the most important development in the twentieth century was the breaking-down not so much of the power of the author but that of the (singular) critic and its replacement by the (potentially multiple) reader.[97] Once the critic – the reader – becomes multiple, once the academy started taking an interest in readers and moved away from the idea that there is only one meaning, which is the author's intention, and to which the critic has privileged access, the balance of power and opportunities for freedom changed.[98] With that change, however, came also ongoing anxiety about the dangers of freedom.

At around the same time, Foucault published a short but important essay in which he interprets the unificatory and originary author as what he calls the 'author-function'.[99] His concentration on the Name contributes to the development of an argument for regarding the author, his 'author-function', not as an ordinary person with a life both outside and inside the text: 'We can conclude that, unlike a proper name, which moves from the interior of a discourse to the real person outside who produced it, the name of the author remains at the contours of text – separating one from the other, defining their form, and characterising their mode of existence.' The language he uses to describe how readers employ the author-function in their responses to texts sits well with my inclination to call the author a 'metaphor', that is, a figurative expression of a process rather than a direct description of historical reality:

> Undoubtedly, this construction is assigned a 'realistic' dimension as we speak of an individual's 'profundity' or 'creative' power, his intentions or the original inspiration manifested in writing. Nevertheless, these aspects of an individual, which we designate as an author (or which comprise an individual as an author), are projections, in terms always more or less psychological, of our way of handling texts: in the comparisons we made, the traits we extract as pertinent, the continuities we assign, or the exclusions we practise.[100]

---

[96] Barthes 1977: 147 'victory to the critic'.
[97] The literature on reader-response theory is vast, it being an umbrella term for a range of different approaches which concentrate on readers, be they literal or hypothetical. A good starting place would be Bennett and Royle 2016: ch. 2.
[98] The narrative of change and development projected in this paragraph is, of course, an oversimplification.
[99] Foucault 1977: 124–38. Homer provides him with an especially illustrative example (122).
[100] Foucault 1977: 127. I am more doubtful about his later claim (138): 'We can easily imagine a culture where discourse would circulate without any need for an author. Discourses ... would unfold in a pervasive anonymity.' Evidence of almost three millennia suggest that society, at least in the

Alongside Barthes and Foucault came the deconstructionist move to language rather than subjects as speakers, with its radical instability and denial of absolutes.[101] Despite the complex philosophical problems involved in the work of Derrida, his interest in communication, in the iterability that makes communication possible but always (already) subject to misunderstanding, his apparent approbation and celebration of multiple meaning, together with his own poetic style, encouraged reception of his work by literary critics. This reception far exceeded the clique of paid-up deconstructionists, becoming softened and normalised into a wider acceptance of multiplicity of interpretation. As an example of how Derridean thought has played into the issues raised in this chapter, I quote Glendinning:

> ... the conception of writing outlined by the argument from iterability does not aim to eliminate ordinary (and hence iterable) talk of meaning and understanding but to criticize the classical conception of meaning – where the only meaning that *is* one would be a meaning that is *one* – embedded in the idea of an event of human speech that would express an ideally pure presence, a pure ideality that would be fully present in the present.[102]

Thomson is also helpful: 'So, contrary to popular belief, deconstruction does not hold that texts mean whatever their readers think they mean. In fact, the opposite: deconstruction calls for as rigorous a reconstruction of what a text says at face value, alongside a compendium of its rhetorical and logical strategies for reinforcing its points.'[103]

One of Derrida's many insights on the issues involved was his stress on the extent to which the problem of meaning and communication in a written text goes back to Plato. He was, of course, not the first philosopher to think about ancient epistemology, but for our purposes he points to something crucial: while it is likely to be true, as many scholars have said, that the move away from naïve intentionalism was a reaction to Romanticism, it is not true that the problem *only* arises from Romantic

---

European tradition, is not comfortable with pervasive anonymity in texts. Geue 2019 explores this discomfort and offers creative alternatives to such a reaction.

[101] A good starting point for the relationship between Derrida and literature is Thomson 2006. Among the many general introductions to Derrida, I would suggest Glendinning 2011.
[102] Glendinning 2011: 74–5.
[103] Thomson 2006: 313. Glendinning 2011: 56: 'It will bear repeating that Derrida's effort to make problematic the traditional Aristotelian – or let's say simply philosophical – conception of language does not mean that he wants simply to affirm the opposite, that plurivocity or polysemia is the essence, or the telos, of language. The intention to oppose polysemia with dissemination does not aim to affirm that everything we say is ambiguous (that every word is characterized by at least two or more meanings), but that polysemia is irreducible in the sense that each and every "meaning" is itself subject ... to more than one understanding.'

notions of the individual genius and his personal subjectivity and psychology. Crucial is Derrida's work on Plato (especially the wonderful image of the silent statues at *Phaedrus* 275d–e) and the problem of writing and presence/absence, with its picture of the written word as an orphaned child cut off from its author-father, unable to control its meaning. Here is the answer to the 'single meaning for single word' problem – although an author might intend a certain connotation for his chosen vocabulary, he is not in a position to control which other connotations might be activated in the minds of his readers.[104] It is worth thinking about those silent statues of the *Phaedrus* when we describe ourselves, using a perfectly appropriate metaphor, as 'interrogating' a text. Only metaphorically do the texts answer us; rather, it is we who provide both question and answer. Writing, moreover, though orphaned, has not lost all the genetic material that it inherited from its author-father.

For all the antiquity, and the imaginative power, of the image of the author-father, it is a constructed image. Many contemporary critics have drawn attention to the Romantic notion of the author as individual genius, against which were marshalled the founding anti-authorial philosophies of literature. This modern critical notion of the Romantic notion of the author is itself a construct. Bennett argues that 'at least since the late eighteenth century, writers and critics have almost obsessively dwelled on the complex interaction of authorial presence and absence, on the way that the centrality of the author is bound up with, is caused by and a cause of, his or her marginality, that authorship indeed is in thrall to the apparitional'.[105] Burke even claims that the modern death of the author is actually in keeping with pre-Romantic notions of authorship, it being the Romantic idea of private consciousness which is the aberration.[106] On the other hand, much contemporary classical criticism resonates strongly with the idea of 'complex interaction of authorial presence and absence'. We have only to think of the epilogue to the *Metamorphoses*, alongside its intertexts such as Ennius, Virgil and Horace living on the lips of men, or on the double bluff that is *Am.* 3.12.[107] Nonetheless, the point still holds that the twentieth-century conception of the nineteenth-century

---

[104] I note that both Derrida and Kristeva publicly lost control of the significance of key vocabulary, including 'deconstruction' and 'intertextuality'. Thomson 2006: 300 attempts to reimpose some control precisely through Derridean polysemy: 'the word "deconstruction" does not point to a single, fixed, definite meaning which stands behind and apart from all its uses; "deconstruction" is one of a potentially infinite series of uses of the same word, in different contexts, to communicate different meanings. Its ideality is inseparable from this repeatability in new contexts, which also means that we can never fully pin down or exhaust its meanings.'
[105] Bennett 2005: 66.   [106] Burke 1995: xvi–xvii.   [107] For Juvenal, Uden 2014.

Romantic author substantially affects the twenty-first-century conception of the ancient author.

Like many in the pragmatist school of reaction to twentieth-century high theory,[108] John Farrell (2017) argues for a 'common sense' reading of intentionalism as the most economic and realistic description of what happens in literary communication and literary criticism. I think he is often overconfident in his estimation of the self-evidence of those 'meanings' he describes as being (obviously, so he implies) the intention of the author under discussion. He and other pro-intentionalist readers, moreover, have a minimalist understanding of 'meaning' which allows them to claim a distinction between fixed, authorially intended 'meaning' and more fluid, multiple and reader-driven 'significance'. This rhetorical sleight of hand feels a bit like cakeism.[109] Nonetheless, Farrell is right to stress that successful verbal communication arises from the intention of the communicator. Three points I would make in response: first, literature is not the same as day-to-day communication, because the context of becoming literature changes the nature of the communication; secondly, the extent to which the surface meaning is self-evident is easy to overstate; and thirdly, I would not deny (nor, I think, does anti-intentionalism deny this)[110] that what an author intends plays a very large role in how we construe his/her sentences, and a substantial role in how we construe the larger structures and meanings of the text.

My quarrel with the pro-intentionalist approach stems in large part from my perception of the invalidity of the slippage its proponents make between day-to-day communication, communication within the world of the text, and communication between the text and the reader. The writing and reading of a work of literature is, indeed, a form of communication, but it is one sufficiently different from private, immediate, ephemeral, day-to-day, interpersonal verbal interaction as to make it problematic to use the one directly to elucidate the other. An author attempts to communicate

---

[108] Mitchell 1985, Hirsch 1967 and 1976 (which, like Farrell, differentiates between fixed, intended 'meaning' and more malleable 'significance').

[109] During the agonies of the Brexit debate, 'cakeism' entered the popular vocabulary from the proverb 'have your cake and eat it', to express the desires of those who want to hold onto two mutually exclusive benefits.

[110] Wimsatt and Beardsley do not ignore or deny that authors have intentions – though Wimsatt archly points out that they may not necessarily have realised their intention: the intention to produce a literary classic does not guarantee the success of the intention. Farrell 2017 would say that this is a difference between artistic intentions and communicative intentions. Producing a literary classic is an artistic intention, which he would regard as quite separate from the communicative intention, which is what creates meaning.

a meaning and a reader attempts to receive that communication by figuring out the author/sender's intentions as far as possible (so far, so ordinary), but the context, barriers, complexities and implications (crucially – what it means *matters* in a very different way in ordinary communication) of the interaction between, for example, Ovid and me are of a different nature from those which pertain in the day-to-day situation. Communications within a work of literature, that is, between the characters, are fictional representations of direct communication, with the result that the act of interpretation from the point of view of a fictional character is a reflection of (though not the same as) the act of interpretation in day-to-day speech, while the act of interpretation on the part of the reader of literature is fundamentally different.[111] This is a difference that goes beyond that which arises from greater distance – it is not just that it is harder to know what the sender means, but that 'what the sender means' no longer has the illocutionary force of private communication. In private communication, the recipient has the option of accepting or rejecting the illocutionary force of many types of speech acts, such as apologies, proposals or promises, but his/her options are otherwise limited. On the other hand, taking a view on the degree of sincerity on the part of the sender matters a great deal. Once a piece of communication becomes literature, however, it has no such direct force, though it may have all sorts of other indirect implications.

Once a piece of communication has become literature, I contend, the nature of communication between sender and recipient changes, with the result that the text becomes especially privileged as regards its capacity to hold multiple meanings. It is particularly easy to see this difference in the case of letter collections, where the discrete parts often have a double life and where a third party – the editor or compiler – enters into the equation. The editor of a collection can, through selection and juxtaposition, create meaning that cannot have been intended by the original author.[112] This is the case, I suggest,

---

[111] Metapoetics constructs an interpretation of an internal character who shares in the kind of reading undertaken by the reader of literature – but is itself an interpretive act of the kind it posits.

[112] Martelli 2017 brings the editor of *Ad fam.* 15 to life as a major player in the construction of Cicero (quotation at 112–13): 'In a remarkable display of his own power to revise textual and historical meaning, the editor has transformed the premise for Cicero's vote of thanksgiving from his military victory over the enemy in Cilicia to his rôle in galvanizing Caesar's enemies into action.' White 2010: 170: 'Readers of the published corpus stand too far away from situations in which the letters were written to catch every nuance of every performance, but as they read letter after letter, they have occasion to recognise more clearly than original readers could that some degree of role-playing always accompanies the writing of his letters.' Beard 2002: 124: 'whatever their origin in the day-to-day world of real-life letter writing, through their collection and publication, through the very editorial practices I have been discussing, through their reading and reception, they were progressively reformulated as a literary collection'.

even when the compiler is the original author's later self. So, for example, for the original recipient of a Ciceronian letter, receiving the letter might very well involve all sorts of guesswork – even paranoia – about things unsaid, about possible double meanings, or it might be taken in a very straightforward, 'prosaic' way, but that reading is itself a personal one – and if it is a crazy one, that does not matter to anyone else. Once the Ciceronian letter enters into a collection and is published (i.e. circulated) as such, it invites and enables a much wider range of responses, including many that could not have been available to the recipient. It does this in part because it has lost illocutionary force, in part because its interpretive community and context have changed.

The approach laid out by Levinson, in a retrospective on a volume devoted to theories of intention and interpretation, may have some value for, and coherence with, actual classical practice. He proposes what he calls 'hypothetical intentionalism', in which the reader attempts to construct meaning for the text (he calls this 'utterance meaning'), taking into account all available information about genre, historical moment, etc. I quote:

> So utterance meaning is logically distinct from utterer's meaning and at the same time is necessarily related to it conceptually: we arrive at utterance meaning by aiming at utterer's meaning in the most comprehensive and informed manner we can muster as the utterance's intended recipients. Actual utterer's intention, then, is not what is determinative of the meaning of a literary offering (or other linguistic discourse) but such intention as *optimally hypothesized*, given all the resources available to us in the work's internal structure and the relevant surrounding context of creation, in all its legitimately invoked specificity. The core of utterance meaning can be conceived of analytically as *our best appropriately informed projection of author's intended meaning* from our positions as intended interpreters.[113]

Such a formulation would connect well with Tarrant's views on the project of textual criticism, discussed on p. 183. It also resonates with actual practice, for example, in the privileging classicists generally give to interpretations based on historical chronology: we tend, albeit not exclusively, to regard the relationship between Ovid's *Metamorphoses* and Statius' *Achilleid* as strongly informed by the fact that Ovid came first. Likewise, we would not usually describe Ovid as referring to Shakespeare, even if we find Shakespeare's reading of Ovid elucidating about something we regard as being 'in the text' of Ovid.[114] There is, then, considerable value in

---

[113] Levinson 1992: 224 (emphasis mostly mine).
[114] Edmunds 2001 is most willing, among theorists of classical intertextuality, to liberate intertextual reading from authorial intention and so from priority. O'Rourke and Pelttari in this volume explore these important issues in much more detail.

thinking about *intendable* meaning, rather than making claims for *intended*. Regarding interpretation as hypothetical reconstruction also fits well with my contention that we should regard the author as a construct, but not as one built randomly out of *undique collatis membris*.

If we emphasise intendable, rather than intended, meaning, we can also allow room to more liberal formulations of authorial activity. There is no need to be afraid to suggest that a structure or thought or other feature that we are perceiving in a text could also be perceived by and therefore intended by the author. There is no need to imagine that saying 'Ovid means' will lead us to naïve biographism, if we remember that 'Ovid' is a construct and his 'meaning' is an act of interpretation. In practice, we regularly make a difference between possibilities that would be open to a person in our author's position and those which would not. We are inclined to call this 'the text's meaning' (like Levinson's 'utterance meaning'). Richard Thomas argues eloquently for traces of later critical responses to the *Aeneid* being already present in the text itself, by which I take him to mean, or at least to imply, that they are potentially intendable by Virgil – and probably, in his heart, he believes they were so intended (as do I).[115]

Hypothetical intentionalism cannot, however, cover all our critical practices. In order to make sense of any piece of literature, we have to posit an intending consciousness, even if we are aware that the outcome we are reading may not be singular in origin (either from a single real person or at a single time) – the simple hypothetical intentionalism would be constrained by everything we know about the circumstances of production of the work; but there are also the kinds of readings that are not constrained by what we know of the time of production, and are therefore not possible as intentions of actual authors, nor (therefore) of the hypothetical intending author, but are readings which are nonetheless usefully identifiable by modern readers. I want to say that feminist readings of Ovid's poetry are 'present in the text itself', but I cannot be more than agnostic over the question of whether flesh-and-blood Ovid meant those elements to be intended. In practice, I think it is unlikely: Ovid intended the *Metamorphoses* to be read by future ages, but he had no idea that his future readers would include female professors employed in international universities, working on computers and exploring his work through the 'Musisque Deoque' website.

When we say that certain possibilities are active in the poem, it would be unnecessarily limiting to claim that all possibilities were actively, or

---

[115] Thomas 2001. Criticism is never emotionally or ideologically neutral.

even unconsciously, intended by the author.[116] To say that the text contains multiple possibilities is perhaps the best figurative expression, even though a text cannot literally intend anything, or even contain anything other than marks on page. The human action which is intentionality and which creates meaning comes in this case from the reader, but not the reader doing whatever she feels like doing: that would be the subjective fallacy 'gone mad'. Rather, it is the intention of a reader constrained by (as well as herself shaping) the history of reading the poem both over the centuries and in the context of contemporary academic debate. I find the Fishian answer of the 'interpretive communities' to be the most plausible and effective control – a right reading is one which is persuasive to others, or is otherwise worth repeating, for a community which, however fuzzy-edged and chrono-dynamic, nonetheless has the critical mass to give value to its judgements.[117]

## Reading Women

Two aspects of feminist criticism are of particular relevance to the issues surrounding personae, authors and readings: the so-called 'gynocriticism'[118] and the practice of 'resisting' reading.[119] The former

---

[116] Even the pro-intentionalist Farrell 2017 accepts the possibility that readers and critics might be more attuned to authors' 'intentions' than the author is him or herself.

[117] It was suggested to me that authorial intention and fixity of meaning are of paramount importance for authors with a strong ideological commitment to what they say. Rather than supporting a pro-intentionalist theory of authorship, however, I would suggest that the issue of committed meaning might be very useful for seeing the role of interpretive communities. The original author (whatever that might mean) of Exodus intended crossing the Red Sea to have a certain meaning, which I presume would be something to do with the validity of Israel as a nation in that particular part of the world, a reading which has considerable resonance with contemporary Israel. Christian authors reinterpreted it, however, as a foreshadowing of baptism, itself a foreshadowing of the death and resurrection of Jesus. It is the interpretive community, in dynamic continuity, which validates these different meanings. Literary scholarship might work to try to uncover plausible personal meanings for the original text, despite massive problems in working out what counts as the 'original text' in this case, but the resultant literary historical reading would only be one among many. On the other hand, at the surface level the story tells how the Israelites crossed over on dry land and the Egyptians were killed. It does not, on the surface level, tell a story about someone who lost his iPhone. What I mean here is that there is no way to make the story 'mean whatever you want it to mean'. The 'story about someone who lost his iPhone' has particular relevance for me, remembering an occasion on which my youngest son accidentally jumped into the sea with his elderly, and not waterproof, iPhone in his pocket. This, however, is not what the crossing of the Red Sea is about.

[118] Showalter 1979 coined the term, while important also is Gilbert and Gubar 1979. This Anglophone movement was related also to the more philosophical and psychological Francophone 'écriture féminine' associated with Cixous, Irigaray, Kristeva and others. There is a good brief account of gynocriticism, including criticisms of its biological determinism, in Plate 2016. See Moi 2002 for a clear account of both the Anglo-American and the French traditions.

[119] Fetterley 1978. Good classical examples include Liveley 1999 and Salzman-Mitchell 2005.

encourages us to concentrate attention on flesh-and-blood female authors, while the latter promotes a reading strategy which identifies and actively opposes an authorial intention in the meaning of a text. For the former, we must consider the attribution or otherwise of poems to Sulpicia; the latter forms an important part of the most extensive kind of situated reading in the classics.

Gynocriticism, generally identified as part of what is known as the 'second wave feminism', sought to move feminist critics away from the male-dominated canon and into exploration of female-authored literature, not only to recover neglected works by women but also to analyse and represent women's writing as an expression of female consciousness which in essence and in mode is different from male, and which constitutes – to appropriate Virginia Woolf's famous phrase – 'a room of one's own'.[120] Like many of the theoretical developments of the twentieth century, gynocriticism has undergone a mixture of debunking and naturalisation in the twenty-first. It has been criticised for biological determinism, for essentialising gender as the category of overwhelming dominance, for exclusions of other identities and for the risk of unhelpful ghettoisation. On the other hand, it made major contributions to the widening of the literary canon in many academic and publishing fields. Latinists are among the most deprived of scholarly groups as regards female-authored texts, with the result that it has been overwhelmingly difficult to widen the canon in this regard. Every extant word from antiquity which can plausibly be assigned to biologically female authorship is seized upon with intense desire, from the poetry of Sulpicia to the birthday invitation found in that outpost of empire now called Hadrian's Wall, but they are very few.[121]

While I entirely understand and support the desire to study texts by women, I am conscious of the challenge to my understanding of 'the author' embodied in such a desire. One might say that the desire to read female-authored texts is an indication of the importance of flesh-and-blood authors, since it is actual bodily female authors who are sought.[122] If it is the

---

[120] Showalter 1977.
[121] See McIntosh Snyder 1989, Hemelrijk 1999, Stevenson 2005, Churchill, Brown and Jeffrey 2002. The anthology of women's writing in Plant 2004 is very limited, especially on the Latin side, from antiquity itself, though the situation improves with the move into mediaeval and especially modern, neo-Latin, writers. On these last see Haskell in this volume; see also O'Rourke and Pelttari in this volume on the fourth-century Christian poet Proba.
[122] By contrast, the other form of what we might call gynocriticism in classical studies is the attempt to extract women's authorship from male authors, as for example Spentzou 2002.

constructed author with whom we are concerned when reading a literary text, does the biological sex of the flesh-and-blood author have any more significance than his or her (unknowable) personal feelings? My answer to this is that it does matter. It matters partly because the political goal of increasing the visibility of women, including women authors and including those from the past, is a separate issue from the theory of literature. In this regard, we could describe a reading based on the biological femininity of the author as especially situated and especially directed towards a particular purpose. That is not to say that all readings should be so. It matters also, moreover, because it is not my contention that the flesh-and-blood author has no relevance to the constructed author: rather, just as the historical moment of the flesh-and-blood author is a relevant factor in the process of reading, so too is any other knowable fact, be it gender, social class, ethnicity or health status.[123]

Almost the only classical Latin woman author whose literary work survives with any degree of reliability and extension is Sulpicia, who names herself as the daughter of Servius ([Tibullus] 3.16.4) and who writes in the persona of a high-status Roman citizen woman and of an elegiac lover-poet in love with a man she calls Cerinthus, drawing on but substantially innovating within the elegiac tradition of Propertius, Tibullus and Ovid.[124] Poems 13–18 of [Tib.] 3 are presented in the voice of Sulpicia and currently widely, though not universally, regarded as female-authored, while poems 8–12 alternate between the voice of a (male) third person on the subject of 'Sulpicia' and the first person associated with that name. This group, sometimes known as the *amicus*-cycle, is generally regarded as of unknown (male) authorship, although arguments have been raised for the Sulpician attribution of the odd-numbered first-person poems and even of

---

[123] These details are the more relevant, I would say, the more reliably they are independently known, as opposed to constructed out of the texts themselves, as is the case for most ancient literary biography. Kletke 2016 pointedly reminds us of the internal nature of all the 'evidence' for the biography of Sulpicia. Keith 2006: 9 makes the point, not sufficiently often acknowledged by the feminist pro-Sulpician critics, that the content of the poems is the life of a fictional persona rather than the autobiography of the flesh-and-blood author.

[124] See the introduction to Fulkerson 2017, especially p. 30, and her general discussion of women writing Latin, pp. 46–53. Fulkerson is carefully agnostic about the authorship and identity of the people involved in the *corpus Tibullianum* (although, as she says, making the best case she can for female authorship), while perceptive in drawing out the extent of the difference between the poetic voice of the Sulpicia poems and conventional elegy. Seminal for appreciation of the differences as well as similarities between the Sulpicia poems and Propertius, Tibullus and Ovid is Hallett 1989.

the whole group.[125] Whether the persona created by poems 8–18 is closely linked to a flesh-and-blood female author of similar biography, or on the other hand arises from a male or female author of different biography, nonetheless Sulpicia's work is remarkable for its exploration of elegiac themes from a female perspective, in which issues of class and social status as well as complicated relations of gender and power are more explicitly foregrounded than either in conventional male-voiced elegy or in the female-voiced elegiac works of Propertius and Ovid.

The history of reading Sulpicia, whatever status that name may have, provides an outstanding example of the extent to which beliefs about authors – the way authors are constructed – affect interpretation, as has been brilliantly argued by Mathilda Skoie.[126] Skoie explores how, over the centuries, commentators' views on the authorship of poems transmitted in the *corpus Tibullianum* changed their responses to those poems: those who believed that the poems presenting the voice of Sulpicia were ventriloquised by a male author regarded them as sophisticated and skilful works of literary artistry, whereas those who took them as authored by a real Sulpicia herself interpreted them as simple (even if delightful in their simplicity). Whether critics think a particular poem is by Sulpicia or by someone (male) else does not affect the words on the page, but it does make a big difference to what critics say about it. Crucially, this applies not only to Skoie's chauvinistic commentators and *Sulpiciae amici*, but also to contemporary feminist critics.[127] The rest of the *corpus Tibullianum* receives far less interest than do the poems plausibly attributable to a female poet.[128]

This is a fascinating and enlightening topic in the history of scholarship and feminism. I want, nonetheless, to hold to the sense that Sulpicia – as much and as little as Tibullus – is an implied author, an author-figure constructed in part out of (we hope) a flesh-and-blood elite woman of the early imperial age, in part out of a long history of reading in which contemporary feminism plays an important role. There is a good deal of

---

[125] See Keith 2006. Recent work has attempted to increase the corpus of Sulpicia: see Hallett 2002, Fabre-Serris 2018. The minimalist, or strongly agnostic, view with regard to female authorship is represented by Hinds 1987, Holzberg 1998, Hubbard 2004, Kletke 2016. Hauser 2016 explores the rhetoric and vocabulary of authorship by women authors, including Sulpicia and Proba – an issue which is at least potentially independent of historical biography. See also Milnor 2002, Batstone 2018.

[126] Skoie 2002 and 2012.   [127] Fulkerson 2017: 52.

[128] Fulkerson 2017 treats the whole book apart from the anomalous 3.7 and includes valuable comment on 'Lygdamus', the other apparently named author in the collection, but it is inevitable, and appropriate, that Sulpicia and the issue of female authorship remain central to her volume.

significance in my throwaway parenthesis in the previous sentence. Stefanie Kletke argues that all the apparently biographical details in the Sulpician poems could be interpreted fictionally and figuratively, in keeping with now conventional approaches to mainstream elegy, and that there is therefore no good reason to believe that the poems are written by a woman.[129] I see the force of these arguments, while at the same time perceiving the risk that they re-enact the erasure of the female agent. Indeed, one might say that for a woman to acquire metaphorical status in *active* mode is quite a significant step in the feminist battle for the symbolic order.[130] Moreover, many contemporary readers, me included, are not unreasonably driven by strong desire not only to recuperate a neglected woman poet, but also to hear an authentic female voice. Is the political importance of releasing a woman's voice so great that it should be allowed to bypass the critical police? Perhaps so, but I am concerned that, even among feminist scholars, the move to assign authenticity to a woman's voice at some more absolute level than that which we acknowledge for male poets might constitute a chauvinist rather than a liberatory act.[131]

I fear that there is a real risk here. Even the most feminist and sympathetic of readers is inclined to interpret Sulpicia's poetry as a more direct window onto authentic female experience than is the case for her male counterparts. If they are reading the author as a woman, scholars are much less inclined to interpret her as developing the persona of a noblewoman in love with an under-specified man, created by the poet who is our constructed author. That is what we do for male authors. Lee Pearcy, after noting that biographically minded critics in the past were excessively interested in identifying the nature of the relationship between Sulpicia and her beloved Cerinthus, then remarks that 'it is now fashionable to take Sulpicia's account of their connection as an example, precious because both rare and authentic, of a woman's voice affirming a transgressive relationship. These questions grow out of an accurate perception that

---

[129] Kletke 2016: 633, 641.
[130] Metaphorical status in *passive* mode is the reading of Cynthia as embodiment of Propertius' poetry, with all the well-known feminist implications of such an identification. It takes considerable interpretative force to keep Sulpicia ranked alongside Propertius, rather than Cynthia. Women's entry into the symbolic system, as active players rather than as blank pages, marked an important development in twentieth-century feminism.
[131] The issue is easier for the pro-intentionalist critic. Irwin 1999: 27–8 decrees that 'the place of the woman author, and with it the place of the author in general, must be preserved', because 'to read texts as if they were authorless and anonymous is to deny part of a feminist agenda'. I hope that even this small snippet will expose the issues of straw persons.

Sulpicia positioned herself against the grain of expectation.'[132] I presume that by calling this woman's voice 'authentic' he means that, differently from the *Heroides* or the female speakers in the *Metamorphoses*, these poems were actually written by a woman and are therefore 'more real'. What he almost says ('positioned herself'), but does not quite say, is that the Sulpicia who speaks is a persona and the Sulpicia who writes is a constructed author who is female, based on a flesh-and-blood author who happens to be also female (or not). He explores the representation of Cerinthus as not just a *puer scriptus* to match the standard elegiac *puella scripta*, but rather as an absence denied the status of primary reader that male elegy (fictionally) gives to the *puella*, while the poet herself (the Sulpicia persona – though Lee does not quite say this) plays a role that is a conglomeration of poet and *puella*. For better, for worse, it seems, Sulpicia cannot be a female colleague on equal terms with the male elegists as regards the construction of personae and implied authors, because gender was far from neutral around the turn of the eras, and that remains so in the contemporary culture that constructs Sulpicia as a poet of substance.

The second aspect of feminist scholarship which has an important bearing on authorship and the nature of reading is 'resistance', in which the critic identifies chauvinistic, masculinist or misogynist structures in the literary texts, exposes them to view and refuses to be mastered by them. This mode of reading, even when not explicitly placed in the tradition of Judith Fetterley and the 'resisting reader', has had a more widespread existence in the criticism of Latin literature than has gynocriticism, for the obvious reason that there are so many more texts with male authors and masculine gender available to resist than there are female authors to celebrate gynocritically. When we undertake a resisting reading, we are not attempting to recreate the author's intention or a reading likely to have been available to contemporary readers, at least not in the terms in which we express it. This kind of reading is one which I would call especially 'situated'. That is, it is a reading which explicitly or implicitly takes a particular stand to ask particular questions of the text under scrutiny. It might, for example, ask the question of what can be extracted from the text by paying particular attention to its female characters, or its subaltern characters or its ethnic and geographical structures. As well as feminist, the reading might be situated in the structures of modern gender and sexuality, or of political theories developed long after antiquity (such as Marxist readings). Such approaches may usefully leak into thought

[132] Pearcy 2006: 33–4.

## 4 *Author and Identity*

experiments like the excellent paper by Ruth Morello, in which she sets up Virgil's Camilla as if in a modern industrial tribunal to explore the quality of her CV.[133] Readings which have the purpose of exploring the text from particular points of view are explicitly not constructions of authorial intention. They may use persona theory to distinguish between levels of speaker and authorial design which claim or at least imply that the author behind the speaker intends the perceived outcome, but they should not be restricted to doing so.[134]

Although in this account of situated readings the critical balance favours a theoretical view that places interpretation more closely with the reader than with the author, nonetheless it seems to me that critics, even when resisting, often present their readings in accordance with the construction of a historical author and reader. In other words, the dissonance caused by the clash between approaches informed by contemporary ideology on the one hand and a desire for originary authors on the other is audible in the golden oldie as to whether Euripides or Ovid is 'a misogynist or a proto-feminist', or indeed, as I have explored recently, whether it is right to describe Ovid as 'sympathetic to women'.[135] Perhaps an acknowledgement of the constructedness of our authors might help us to bring theory and practice better into line with each other. I take the example of a paper of mine in a collection of essays by the *Eugesta* group, concerned with women and war,[136] in which I considered the presentation of female warriors in Roman epic. I argue that Virgil creates a remarkably sophisticated and modern image of the warrior woman, moving away from the standard reification of the warrior woman as an 'Amazon', sexualised and objectified by her Otherness to gendered norms. Although I acknowledge the presence of a link in the text between Camilla and the Amazon woman, I suggest that readers are too quick to seize upon this association and that such a reading is closer to the objectifying gaze of Aeneas on the Amazon breast represented on the temple of Juno than it is to the totality of the representation of warrior women in the poem. By contrast, I argue, Ovid returns the representation of warrior women to the chauvinist norm, from which it never recovers in ancient epic. On this account, it is Virgil, rather than

---

[133] Morello 2008.
[134] Bennett 2005: 89 discusses the so-called New Historicism as creating readings of which original authors could not be aware. This kind of reading, alongside my situated resisting reading, would be the product of a process different from Levinson's hypothetical intentionalism because the latter requires us to create our best guess of what an author with the available historical and cultural resources would be most likely to have meant, whereas the former is open about the fact that it is standing outside the original context.
[135] Sharrock 2020. [136] Sharrock 2015.

Ovid, who is the proto-feminist. I am only willing to espouse that view in so far as the words 'Virgil' and 'Ovid' are constructs. I am fairly sure that neither Virgil nor Ovid could have realised or articulated my description as what they are doing, but it is there in the text, and the activity of 'the author' is a convenient fiction for it.

Another comparison I offer for consideration of feminist readings of ancient authors is between Ovid and Pliny. I attempted earlier (pp. 177–8) to address the question of what difference there is between the persona of Ovid the lover and poet in the *Amores* and that of Pliny the aristocrat, husband, statesman and all the other roles he plays in the *Letters*. I have already suggested that even a distinction between fiction and non-fiction would make no difference to a situated reading. One is no more (and no less) constrained by the intentions of Pliny than by those of Ovid. In practice, however, it may be more tempting for the modern critic to assign the resistant reading to Ovid, and thus the attitudes and beliefs resisted to a persona, than is the case for Pliny. This may be because of a wider gap between persona and author in the case of Ovid, but I think that equally relevant as a cause is the nature of the authorial persona developed over the years by generations of readers. We have constructed Ovid in our own image, but we are much happier to regard Pliny as different from us. Ovid, then, 'intends' the feminist reading in a way that Pliny does not – though in both cases the feminist reading is a modern construct.

I have considered only the feminist stance among potential situated readings, but there are many others to be explored, some of which may turn out to constitute significant developments in the discipline in coming decades. Examples include the eco-critical, post-human and so-called cognitive approaches which have gained purchase in the study of modern literatures and have made minor inroads on Classics. These are explicitly readings for a purpose, deriving from millennial social, scientific and cultural developments.[137] Such readings are clearly not attempts to get at original intentions or even original readers' responses, so of necessity they sit in the eye of the beholder, being undertaken from the point of view of a millennial reader, possibly even as part of a desire to address (or to be seen to address) a real-life contemporary social problem. Their validity as modes of enquiry should not be undermined by their distance from ancient reconstruction, but nor need it diminish the value of historicist approaches.

---

[137] Bertens 2014: 234–5 links this point to millennial post-theoretical concerns.

## Conclusion

In thinking about the issues raised by this chapter, I kept returning to a problem of persona, interpretation and intention, which is also a problem of the nature of literature. When Pliny in the *Letters* makes a claim about his feelings, what do we (what should we) think is happening? Even if it is what Pliny the man (and letter-writer) wants to portray as the feelings of Pliny the man, that does not stop us from interpreting it as deceptive, even self-deceptive, on his part, whether that is as man or as letter-writer, or indeed as compiler. Our interpretation would then be different from his intention, but surely still valid. There are two distinct, albeit related, problems at issue: one is the relationship between the author and the persona, in which we are interested in levels of fictionality; the other is the question of how much control the author has over the range of our reading, of the text irrespective of questions of fictionality. I would like to suggest that in the second case there is no difference between Ovid and Pliny. We can, for example, apply a feminist or a class-based reading to either of them, which the flesh-and-blood authors would not be in a position to formulate. This would apply to any text, and the relationship between that text and the fiction/non-fiction spectrum would make no difference. In the question of persona, there is perhaps a difference, but it is a difference of degree, rather than essence. More importantly, however, Pliny – at whatever level – is a construct.

## References

Abbott, H. P. (2011) 'Reading intended meaning where none is intended: a cognitivist reappraisal of the implied author', *Poetics Today* 32: 461–87.
Anderson, W. S. (1964) 'Anger in Juvenal and Seneca', *University of California Publications in Classical Philology* 19: 127–96.
  (1982) *Essays in Satire*, Princeton.
Armstrong, R. (2005) *Ovid and His Love Poetry*, London.
Ash, R. (2013) 'Drip-feed invective: Pliny, self-fashioning, and the Regulus letters', in Marmodoro and Hill 2013, 207–32.
Barthes, R. (1975) *The Pleasure of the Text* (trans. R. Miller), New York.
  (1977) *Image – Music – Text: Essays Selected and Translated by Stephen Heath*, London.
Bartsch, S. (2006) *The Mirror of the Self: Sexuality, Self-Knowledge, and the Gaze in the Early Empire*, Chicago.
Bartsch, S. and A. Schiesaro, eds. (2015) *The Cambridge Companion to Seneca*, Cambridge.

Batstone, W. W. (2018) 'Sulpicia and the speech of men', in S. Frangoulidis and S. J. Harrison, eds., *Life, Love and Death in Latin Poetry* (Berlin), 85–109.
Beard, M. (2002) 'Ciceronian correspondences: making a book out of letters', in T. P. Wiseman, ed., *Classics in Progress: Essays on Ancient Greece and Rome* (Oxford), 103–44.
Bennett, A. (2005) *The Author, the New Critical Idiom*, Abingdon.
Bennett, A. and N. Royle (2016) *An Introduction to Literature, Criticism and Theory*, 5th edn, London and New York.
Bertens, H. (2014) *Literary Theory: The Basics*, 3rd edn, Abingdon.
Booth, W. C. (1961) *The Rhetoric of Fiction*, Chicago.
Braund, S. M. (1996) *The Roman Satirists and Their Masks*, London.
Burke, S. (1995) *Authorship, from Plato to the Post-Modern: A Reader*, Edinburgh.
Churchill, L. J., P. R. Brown and J. E. Jeffrey, eds. (2002) *Women Writing Latin in Roman Antiquity, Late Antiquity and the Early Christian Era*, New York.
Clay, D. (1998) 'Theory of the literary persona in antiquity', *MD* 40: 9–40.
Drinkwater, M. (2013) '*Militia amoris*: fighting in love's army', in T. S. Thorsen, ed., *The Cambridge Companion to Latin Love Elegy* (Cambridge), 194–206.
Durling, R. M. (1958) 'Ovid as *praeceptor amoris*', *CJ* 53: 157–67.
Eagleton, T. (2003) *After Theory*, London.
    (2012) *The Event of Literature*, New Haven, CT.
Edmunds, L. (2001) *Intertextuality and the Reading of Roman Poetry*, Baltimore.
Elliott, R. C. (1982) *The Literary Persona*, Chicago.
Fabre-Serris, J. (2018) 'Intratextuality and intratextuality in the *Corpus Tibullianum* (3.8–18)', in S. J. Harrison, S. Frangoulidis and T. Papanghelis, eds.,' *Intratextuality and Latin Literature* (Berlin), 67–79.
Farrell, John (2017) *The Varieties of Authorial Intention: Literary Theory Beyond the Intentional Fallacy*, London.
Farrell, Joseph (2019) 'Virgil's intertextual personae', in C. Martindale and F. Mac Góráin, eds., *The Cambridge Companion to Virgil*, 2nd edn (Cambridge), 299–325.
Fetterley, J. (1978) *The Resisting Reader: A Feminist Approach to American Fiction*, Bloomington, IN.
Fish, S. (1991) 'Biography and intention', in W. H. Epstein, ed., *Contesting the Subject: Essays in the Postmodern Theory and Practice of Biography and Biographical Criticism* (West Lafayette, IN), 9–16.
Fitzgerald, W. (2000) *Slavery and the Roman Literary Imagination*, Cambridge.
Fletcher, R. and J. Hanink, eds. (2016) *Creative Lives in Classical Antiquity: Poets, Artists and Biography*, Cambridge.
Foucault, M. (1977) *Language, Counter-Memory Practice: Selected Essays and Interviews* (ed. D. Bouchard; trans. D. Bouchard and S. Simon), Ithaca, NY.
Fowler, D. P. (2001) 'Narrative: introduction', in S. J. Harrison, ed., *Texts, Ideas, and the Classics: Scholarship, Theory, and Classical Literature* (Oxford), 65–9.
Freudenberg, K. (2001) *Satires of Rome: Threatening Poses from Lucilius to Juvenal*, Cambridge.

(2005) 'Introduction', in K. Freudenberg, ed., *The Cambridge Companion to Roman Satire* (Cambridge), 1–30.

Fulkerson, L. (2017) *A Literary Commentary on the Elegies of the Appendix Tibulliana*, Oxford.

Gallia, A. B. (2016) '"Some of my best friends": reading prejudice in Juvenal's third Satire', *CJ* 111: 319–46.

Genette, G. (1997) *Paratexts: Thresholds of Interpretation*, Cambridge.

Geue, T. (2019) *Author Unknown: The Power of Anonymity in Ancient Rome*, Cambridge, MA.

Gilbert, S. and S. Gubar (1979) *The Madwoman in the Attic: The Woman Writer and the Nineteenth-Century Literary Imagination*, New Haven.

Gill, C. (1988) 'Personhood and personality: the four-personae theory in Cicero *De officiis* 1', *OSAPh* 6: 169–99.

Glendinning, S. (2011) *Derrida: A Very Short Introduction*, Oxford.

Gloyn, E. (2013) 'Reading rape in Ovid's *Metamorphoses*: a test-case lesson', *CW* 106: 676–81.

Gold, B. K., ed. (2012) *A Companion to Roman Love Elegy*, Oxford.

Gould, T. (1990) *The Ancient Quarrel between Poetry and Philosophy*, Princeton.

Gowers, E. (2003) 'Fragments of autobiography in Horace *Satires* 1', *ClAnt* 22: 55–92.

Green, F. M. (2015) 'Witnesses and participants in the shadows: the sexual lives of enslaved women and boys', *Helios* 42: 143–62.

Greene, E. (1998) 'Travesties of love: violence and voyeurism in Ovid *Amores* 1.7', *CW* 92: 409–18.

(2000) 'Gender identity and the elegiac hero in Propertius 2.1', *Arethusa* 33: 241–61.

Gurd, S. A. (2011) *Work in Progress: Literary Revision as Social Performance in Ancient Rome*, Oxford.

Haley, S. P. (1993) 'Black feminist thought and Classics: re-remembering, re-claiming, re-empowering', in N. S. Rabinowitz and A. Richlin, eds., *Feminist Theory and the Classics* (New York), 23–43.

Hallett, J. P. (1989) 'Women as same and other in classical Roman elite', *Helios* 16: 59–78.

(2002) 'The eleven elegies of the Augustan poet Sulpicia', in Churchill, Brown and Jeffrey 2002, 45–65.

Hardie, P. R. and H. Moore, eds. (2010) *Classical Literary Careers and Their Reception*, Cambridge.

Harrison, S. J. (2013) 'Author and speaker(s) in Horace's *Satires* 2', in Marmodoro and Hill 2013: 153–71.

Hauser, E. (2016) '*Optima tu proprii nominis auctor*: the semantics of female authorship in ancient Rome, from Sulpicia to Proba', *Eugesta* 6.

Hemelrijk, E. (1999) *Matrona docta: Educated Women in the Roman Elite from Cornelia to Julia*, London.

Henderson, J. G. W. (1991) 'Wrapping up the case: reading Ovid, *Amores* 2.7 (+8) I', *MD* 27: 37–88.

(1992) 'Wrapping up the case: reading Ovid, *Amores* 2.7 (+8) II', *MD* 28: 27–83.

(2003) 'Portrait of the artist as a figure of style: P.L.I.N.Y.'s letters', *Arethusa* 36: 115–25.
Highet, G. (1974) 'Masks and faces in satire', *Hermes* 102: 321–37.
Hinds, S. (1987) 'The poetess and the reader: further steps towards Sulpicia', *Hermathena* 143: 29–46.
Hirsch, E. D. (1967) *Validity in Interpretation*, New Haven.
  (1976) *The Aims of Interpretation*, Chicago.
Holzberg, N. (1998) 'Four poets and a poetess or a portrait of the poet as a young man? Thoughts on book 3 of the *corpus Tibullianum*', *CJ* 94: 169–91.
Hubbard, T. K. (2004) 'The invention of Sulpicia', *CJ* 100: 177–94.
Iddeng, J. W. (2005) 'How shall we comprehend the Roman *I*-poet?', *C&M* 56: 185–205.
Irwin, W. (1999) *Intentionalist Interpretation: A Philosophical Explanation and Defence*, Westport, CT.
Irwin, W., ed. (2002) *The Death and Resurrection of the Author?*, Westport, CT.
James, S. L. (1997) 'Slave-rape and female silence in Ovid's love poetry,' *Helios* 24: 60–76.
  (2012) 'Teaching rape in Roman love elegy, Part II', in Gold 2012, 549–57.
Jansen, L., ed. (2014) *The Roman Paratext: Frames, Texts, Readers*, Cambridge.
Keane, C. C. (2006) *Figuring Genre in Roman Satire*, Oxford.
Keith, A. M. (1994) '*Corpus eroticum*: elegiac poetics and elegiac *puellae* in Ovid's *Amores*', *CW* 88: 27–40.
  (1999) 'Slender verse: Roman elegy and ancient rhetorical theory', *Mnemosyne* 52: 41–62.
  (2006) 'Critical trends in interpreting Sulpicia', *CW* 100: 3–10.
  (2008) *Propertius: Poet of Love and Leisure*, Bristol.
Kletke, S. (2016) 'Why is Sulpicia a woman?', *Mouseion* 13: 625–53.
Kutzko, D. (2006) 'The major importance of a minor poet: Herodas 6 and 7 as a quasi-dramatic diptych', in M. A. Harder, R. F. Regtuit and C. G. Wakker, eds., *Beyond the Canon* (Leuven), 167–84.
Laird, A. (2016) 'Recognising Virgil', in Fletcher and Hanink 2016, 75–100.
Levinson, J. (1992) 'Intention and interpretation: a last look', in G. Iseminger, ed., *Intention and Interpretation* (Philadelphia), 221–56.
Littlewood, C. A. J. (2015) 'Theater and theatricality in Seneca's world', in Bartsch and Schiesaro 2015, 161–73.
Liveley, G. (1999) 'Reading resistance in Ovid's *Metamorphoses*', in A. Barchiesi, P. R. Hardie, and S. E. Hinds, eds., *Ovidian Transformations: Essays on Ovid's Metamorphoses and Its Reception* (Cambridge), 197–213.
  (2012) 'Teaching rape in Roman elegy, Part I', in Gold 2012, 541–8.
Lowrie, M. (2009) *Writing, Performance, and Authority in Augustan Rome*, Oxford.
Mack, M. (1951) 'The muse of satire', *Yale Review* 41: 80–92.
Marmodoro, A. and J. Hill, eds. (2013) *The Author's Voice in Classical and Late Antiquity*, Oxford.
Martelli, F. (2017) 'The triumph of letters: rewriting Cicero in *Ad fam.* 15', *JRS* 107: 90–115.

Martindale, C. (1993) *Redeeming the Text: Latin Poetry and the Hermeneutics of Reception*, Cambridge.

Mayer, R. G. (2003a) 'Persona<l> problems: the literary persona in antiquity revisited', *MD* 50: 55–80.

(2003b) 'Pliny and *gloria dicendi*', *Arethusa* 36: 227–34.

McCarthy, C. (2016) 'Textual criticism and biblical translation', in J. Barclay, ed., *The Hebrew Bible: A Critical Companion* (Princeton), 532–56.

McCutcheon, R. W. (2016) 'A revisionist history of Cicero's *Letters*', *Mouseion* 13: 35–63.

McIntosh Snyder, J. (1989) *The Woman and the Lyre: Women Writers in Classical Greece and Rome*, Carbondale.

Milnor, K. (2002) 'Sulpicia's (corpo)reality: elegy, authorship and the body in [Tibullus] 3.13', *ClAnt* 21: 259–82.

Mitchell, W. J. T., ed. (1985) *Against Theory: Literary Studies and the New Pragmatism*, Chicago.

Moi, T. (2002) *Sexual/Textual Politics: Feminist Literary Theory*, 2nd edn, London.

Moodie, E. K. (2012) 'The bully as satirist in Juvenal's third satire', *AJPh* 133: 93–115.

Morello, R. (2003) 'Pliny and the art of saying nothing', *Arethusa* 36: 187–209.

(2008) '*Segregem eam efficit*: Virgil's Camilla and the scholiasts', in S. Casali and F. Stok, eds., *Servio: stratificazioni esegetiche e modelli culturali/Servius: Exegetical Stratifications and Cultural Models*, Collection Latomus 317 (Brussels), 38–57.

Morrison, A. D. (2013) 'Authorship and authority in Greek fictional letters', in Marmodoro and Hill 2013, 287–312.

Nappa, C. (1998) 'Place settings: *convivium*, contrast, and persona in Catullus 12 and 13', *AJPh* 119: 389–97.

Nichols, M. F. (2009) 'Social status and the authorial personae of Horace and Vitruvius', in L. B. T. Houghton and M. Wyke, eds., *Perceptions of Horace: A Roman Poet and His Readers* (Cambridge), 109–22.

(2017) *Author and Audience in Vitruvius' De agricultura*, Cambridge.

Oliensis, E. (1998) *Horace and the Rhetoric of Authority*, Cambridge.

(2014) 'The paratext of *Amores* 1: gaming the system', in Jansen 2014, 206–23.

O'Rourke, D. (2018) 'Make war not love: *militia amoris* and domestic violence in Roman elegy', in M. R. Gale and J. H. D. Scourfield, eds., *Texts and Violence in the Roman World* (Cambridge), 110–39.

Pandey, N. B. (2018) '*Caput mundi*: female hair as symbolic vehicle of domination in Ovidian love elegy,' *CJ* 113: 454–88.

Pasco-Pranger, M. (2012) 'Duplicitous simplicity in Ovid, *Amores* 1', *CQ* 62: 721–30.

Pearcy, L. T. (2006) 'Erasing Cerinthus: Sulpicia and her audience', *CW* 100: 31–6.

Peirano Garrison, I. (2012) *The Rhetoric of the Roman Fake: Latin Pseudepigrapha in Context*, Cambridge.

(2013) '*Ille ego qui quondam*: on authorial (an)onymity', in Marmodoro and Hill 2013, 251–85.

(2014) 'Sphragis: paratextual autobiographies', in Jansen 2014, 224–42.
Perkins, C. A. (2015) 'The *poeta* as *rusticus* in Ovid *Amores* 1.7', *Helios* 42: 267–85.
Plant, I. M. (2004) *Women Writers of Ancient Greece and Rome: An Anthology*, London and Norman, OK.
Plate, L. (2016) 'Gynocriticism', in N. Naples, M. Wickramasinghe and A. Wong Wai Ching, eds., *The Wiley Blackwell Encyclopedia of Gender and Sexuality Studies* (Hoboken, NJ).
De Pretis, A. (2003) '"Insincerity," "facts," and "epistolarity": approaches to Pliny's epistles to Calpurnia', *Arethusa* 36: 127–46.
Richardson, B., ed. (2011) *Implied Author: Back from the Grave or Simply Dead Again?* (= *Style* 45), DeKalb, IL.
Richlin, A. (1991) 'Reading Ovid's rapes', in A. Richlin, ed., *Pornography and Representation in Greece and Rome* (Oxford), 158–79.
Rimell, V. (2006) *Ovid's Lovers: Desire, Difference and the Poetic Imagination*, Cambridge.
Roman, L. (2014) *Poetic Autonomy in Ancient Rome*, Oxford.
Salzman-Mitchell, P. (2005) *A Web of Fantasies: Gaze, Image, and Gender in Ovid's Metamorphoses*, Columbus, OH.
Schlegel, C. M. (2005) *Satire and the Threat of Speech: Horace Satires 1*, Madison, WI.
Schmid, W. (2009) 'Implied author', in P. Hühn, J. Pier, W. Schmid and J. Schönert, eds., *Handbook of Narratology* (Berlin), 161–73.
Sharrock, A. R. (1991) 'Womanufacture', *JRS* 81: 36–49.
　(2000) 'Constructing characters in Propertius', *Arethusa* 33: 263–84.
　(2015) 'Warrior women in Roman epic', in A. Keith and J. Fabre-Serris, eds., *Women and War in Antiquity* (Baltimore), 157–78.
　(2020) 'Gender and transformation: reading, women, and gender in Ovid's *Metamorphoses*', in A. R. Sharrock, M. Malm and D. Möller, eds., *Ovidian Readings: Transformations of Language, Gender and the Metamorphoses* (Oxford), 33–53.
　(2021) 读者与文本身份政治:女性与男性，读者与文本' [Identity politics: women and men, readers and texts], (trans. Yi Zeng), in J. Liu, ed., 全球视野下的古罗马诗人奥维德研究前沿 [*The New Frontiers of Research on the Roman Poet Ovid in the Global Context*] (Beijing).
Showalter, E. (1977) *A Literature of Their Own: British Women Novelists from Brontë to Lessing*, Princeton.
　(1979) *Towards a Feminist Poetics*, London.
Skoie, M. (2002) *Reading Sulpicia: Commentaries 1475–1990*, Oxford.
　(2012) 'Corpus Tibullianum, book 3', in Gold 2012, 86–100.
Spentzou, E. (2002) *Readers and Writers in Ovid's Heroides: Transgressions of Genre and Gender*, Oxford.
Stevenson, J. (2005) *Women Latin Poets: Language, Gender, and Authority from Antiquity to the Eighteenth Century*, Oxford.
Tarrant, R. J. (2016) *Texts, Editors, and Readers: Methods and Problems in Latin Textual Criticism*, Cambridge.

Tempest, K. (2013) 'An "ethos" of sincerity: echoes of the *De republica* in Cicero's *Pro Marcello*', *G&R* 60: 262–80.
Thomas, R. (2001) *Virgil and the Augustan Reception*, Cambridge.
Thomson, A. (2006) 'Deconstruction', in Waugh 2006a, 298–318.
Turpin, W. (2016) *Ovid, Amores Book 1*, Cambridge.
Uden, J. (2014) *The Invisible Satirist: Juvenal and Second-Century Rome*, Oxford.
Uhlig, A. (2016) 'A poetic possession: Pindar's Lives of the poets', in Fletcher and Hanink 2016, 103–28.
Volk, K. (2005) '*Ille ego*: (mis)reading Ovid's elegiac persona', *A&A* 51: 83–96.
Watson, P. (1983) 'Ovid, *Amores* 2, 7 and 8: the disingenuous defence', *WS* 17: 91–103.
Waugh, P., ed. (2006a) *Literary Theory and Criticism: An Oxford Guide*, Oxford.
Waugh, P. (2006b) 'Introduction: criticism, theory, and anti-theory', in Waugh 2006a, 1–33.
White, P. (2010) *Cicero in Letters: Epistolary Relations of the Late Republic*, Oxford.
Whitmarsh, T. (2013) 'An I for an I: reading fictional autobiography', in Marmodoro and Hill 2013, 233–47.
Wimsatt, W. K. and M. C. Beardsley (1946) 'The intentional fallacy', *The Sewanee Review* 54: 468–88.
  (1949) 'The affective fallacy', *The Sewanee Review* 57: 31–55.
Wyke, M. (1987) 'Written women: Propertius' *scripta puella*', *JRS* 77: 47–61.

CHAPTER 5

# *Intertextuality*

## Donncha O'Rourke and Aaron Pelttari

La parola è come acqua di rivo che riunisce in sé i sapori della roccia dalla quale sgorga e dei terreni per i quali è passata: di questo ho già parlato.

The word is like water from a stream that combines in itself the taste of the rock from which it springs and of the lands through which it has passed; of this I have already spoken.   G. Pasquali 1942: 185

Oratio [*sc.* Marci Calidi] ... primum ita pura erat ut nihil liquidius, ita libere fluebat ut nusquam adhaeresceret; nullum nisi loco positum et tamquam in uermiculato emblemate, ut ait Lucilius, structum uerbum uideres.   (Cic. *Brut.* 274)

The oratorical style of Marcus Calidius was, in the first place, so pure that nothing could be more pellucid; it flowed so freely as to never get bogged down. You could see every word set in its proper place and arranged, as Lucilius says, as though in the wavy design of a mosaic.

> Virgil's happy shades in pure blanched raiment
> Contend on their green meadows, while Orpheus
> Weaves among them, sweeping strings, aswerve...
>           Seamus Heaney, 'Route 110' x

The elucidation of classical language and literature, especially that in Latin, by reference to other languages and literatures, classical and postclassical, has always been a core methodology of philologists, textual critics, commentators, literary critics, ancient historians and philosophers. From the 1960s these constituent disciplines, and that of cultural studies more generally, were confronted with a revolutionary way of thinking about textual interaction, known as intertextuality, that drew a radicalising energy from its roots in structuralism and poststructuralism. Reviewing the history of Latin studies since then, one might well wonder whether any methodology has generated as much heat, or as much scholarship – not all of which, it might be said, is quite so hot.[1]

Before classicists started to take notice of intertextuality, however, intertextuality had already located itself within the Classics. In the essay in which she coined the term, Julia Kristeva took her cue from Bakhtin to contrast the 'monologism' of epic and Aristotelian logic (authoritarian texts in which meaning is tightly controlled) with the 'dialogism' of Socratic dialectic and Menippean satire (poly-vocal and multi-tonal texts that escape the confines of ordinary or official language use in a creative and disruptive Carnival).[2] It was not so much the ideological aspect of intertextuality's embrace of anti-monologism that made its first mark on Classics, however, but rather the semiotic approach that, for all its latent poststructuralist verve, gave to intertextuality a more analytical foundation in structuralism.[3] As if to enact her theory, Kristeva, a Bulgarian writing in French, formulated her theory of intertextuality through her own dialogue with Russian Formalism:

> Bakhtin was one of the first to replace the static hewing out of texts with a model where literary structure does not simply *exist* but is generated in relation to *another* structure. What allows a dynamic dimension to structuralism is his conception of the 'literary word' as an *intersection of textual surfaces* rather than a *point* (a fixed meaning), as a dialogue among several writings: that of the writer, the addressee (or the character) and the contemporary or earlier cultural context.[4]

She continues with the implications of such a multidimensional view of the text:

> Each word (text) is an intersection of word (texts) where at least one other word (text) can be read. In Bakhtin's work, these two axes, which he calls

---

[1] A search on *L'Année philologique* for the terms 'intertext(ual[ity])' in publication titles and abstracts (avoiding double-counting) across all languages in Roman script yields the following hit-rates for each of the following decades: 1970–9: 2; 1980–9: 29; 1990–9: 246; 2000–9: 668; 2010–19: 1116. The figures show the rapid uptake of the terminology of intertextuality (the search did not cover the terminology of 'allusion') in publications (i.e., titles) and/or their reception (i.e., abstracts) in the '80s and '90s, with the explosion of studies since the millennium apparently continuing unabated. A breakdown of national trends, however, presents a slightly more nuanced picture. For publications in English, French, German, Italian and Spanish, respectively, the statistics are: 1970–9: 0, 1, 1, 0, 0; 1980–9: 6, 5, 3, 13, 1; 1990–9: 60, 15, 7, 64, 8; 2000–9: 232, 73, 92, 161, 72; 2010–19: 539, 73, 124, 276, 72. It was thus in Italian scholarship that intertextuality first came to prominence, outstripping the other nationalities up to the end of the 1990s (including the far more ubiquitous Anglophone scholarship); since then it is Anglophone scholarship's fascination with intertextuality (and dominance as *lingua franca* more generally) that continues to expand.
[2] Kristeva 1980: 64–91.
[3] Allen 2011 is a systematic account of how intertextuality is presented by different schools of critical theory.
[4] Kristeva 1980: 64–5 (= 1986: 35–7). All emphasis in the original.

*dialogue* and *ambivalence*, are not clearly distinguished. Yet, what appears as a lack of rigor is in fact an insight first introduced into literary theory by Bakhtin: any text is constructed as a mosaic of quotations; any text is the absorption and transformation of another. The notion of *intertextuality* replaces that of intersubjectivity, and poetic language is read as at least *double*.

As readers trained in a relatively closed set of predominantly literary texts, classicists had evolved an acute sensitivity for the subtle ways in which authors manipulated the literary tradition.[5] At the same time, however, philological and political tensions left them little disposed to overtures from the new theory, and in the following years intertextuality's retreat from intentions and authors would be a recurrent flashpoint in its reception among classicists. Such tensions led many Latinists to treat intertextuality as an aesthetic and pointillist phenomenon rather than, with Kristeva, as the political outcome of the transposition of a system of signs.

The present contribution follows a cluster of retrospectives that have sought to take stock of intertextuality's diffusion through Latin studies, some of them by its chief architects.[6] It is more than forty years since the publication of the pioneering work of Gian Biagio Conte in *Memoria dei poeti e sistema letterario* (1974), and twenty years since Stephen Hinds' *Allusion and Intertext: Dynamics of Appropriation in Latin Literature* (1998) won widespread acclaim as the highpoint of the Anglophone boom in intertextualist study that followed the publication in English of a revised version of Conte's pioneering study.[7] Yet the present moment of introspection may not be a cooling-off phase so much as a lull: the recent retrospectives have shown that there is unfinished business in the theory and practice of intertextuality,[8] and scope for ideological rancour where structuralism and poststructuralism part company.[9] Allusion and intertextuality are not absolutes in a static relation, but

---

[5] For a representative discussion of 'Originalität und Nachahmung', see Kroll 1924: 139–78, with pp. 150–5 on difficult cases of priority.
[6] Citroni 2011, Conte 2014 (translated as Conte 2017), Barchiesi 2015: 115–34, Farrell 2019.
[7] Conte 1986: 32–95. Conte 1986 also incorporates a version of Conte 1984 (Conte 1986: 97–207). Other paradigm-breaking theorisations of intertextuality in Latin studies include Barchiesi 1984 (2015) and 2001, Fowler 1997, Thomas 1999 and Edmunds 2001. Pucci 1998 focuses on the reader; Farrell 1991, Gale 2000 and Nelis 2001 are outstanding studies focused on individual works. Wills 1996 is in a class of its own as a painstaking study of figural repetition as an intertextual phenomenon. Note also Kelly 2008 on historiography, O'Rourke 2012 on elegy, Pelttari 2014 on *Rezeptionsästhetik* and Whitton 2019 for a remarkable new study of Pliny's engagement with Quintilian. For a bibliography on intertextuality, see Coffee 2013.
[8] Barchiesi 2015: 118–19, 128; see also Fowler 1997, esp. pp. 28–32 (= 2000, esp. pp. 130–5).
[9] Conte 2014, esp. pp. 89–95 (= 2017, esp. pp. 51–4).

a dynamic dialectic that, for as long as there are readers, will be a *perpetuum mobile*.[10] Whether we re-read the classics or broaden the canon (a welcome trend that the present volume instantiates), intertextualities and their interpretations are ever-renewable. Recent studies have effected a shift beyond author-centred models of intertextuality to consider other contexts of encounter, such as chronology, space, language and genre,[11] as well as other fuzzier kinds of 'interactivity' within and beyond the medium of text;[12] new research on material and visual texts brings literary intertextuality into intermedial relations that transcend the boundaries of language narrowly defined;[13] and new capacities in the digital humanities are approaching the infinite reach of intertextuality as theorised in the abstract, but in a way that poses new challenges in its practical application.

With the aim of seeing this mosaic from its many *tesserae*, the first two sections of this chapter will consider what difference it makes to pursue a genuinely intertextual approach, in the first case to a passage of Virgil with long-identified parallels in archaic and Hellenistic Greek literature, and in the second to Roman comedies which, as 'translations' of lost Greek 'originals', present a maximal case of intertextuality for which, paradoxically, there is no comparand available. From there, the third section turns to historical differences in intertextual habits, beginning with the practices of self-reflexive annotation especially (though not exclusively) associated with Augustan Latin poetry. The following section moves forward to intertextuality in late antiquity, with examples drawn from cento poetry, from ideas about compilation and from some typological strategies of interpretation. The final section takes up the material and social realities of intertextuality and ends with a consideration of modern and digital methods of reading Latin texts.

## Reading Intertextually

The capacity of intertextuality still to foment unrest and ignite debate is something of a paradox given its move into the mainstream of Latin studies as a reliable, but apparently now quite predictable, way of thinking about how texts interact with each other. If anything, the criticism nowadays tends to be directed not at a few revolutionaries who would liberate the text

---

[10] On the dynamic between allusion and intertext, see Hinds 1998, esp. pp. 17–51.
[11] See Hutchinson 2013.
[12] See the essays collected in König and Whitton 2018, esp. pp. 1–34 for an introduction in which the editors set out 'to restore some of the Kristevan breadth to "intertextuality"' (12 n. 61, cf. 22).
[13] See O'Rourke 2014, Gibson 2014, Squire 2009.

from a straitjacket of authorised reference-points and conservative meaning, but rather at the many who have adopted the terminology of intertextuality as the unreflective vernacular in which they tell a familiar story. Predicates such as 'alludes to', 'looks to', 'reworks', or indeed 'is intertextual with', and so on, are often used interchangeably and in a way that undervalues the dynamic and conceptual force of intertextuality as a separate analytical category that looks beyond static and unidirectional allusion to a multidimensional interaction of texts that each bring their own semiotic systems.

Let us take a well-known and apparently open-and-shut case of allusion from a text that is 'central station' for all intertextual journeys in classical literature – inbound and outbound – and ask: what difference does it make to our reading of Virgil's allusive engagement with Homer to state that Apollo's prophecy of the future supremacy of the Aeneadae in *Aeneid* 3 'is intertextual with' that of Poseidon when he rescues Aeneas from Achilles in *Iliad* 20? After all, the Homeric pedigree of the Virgilian prophecy has been recognised since antiquity, so its investiture with the language of intertextual theory ought to contribute something new, if it is not to be a case of the emperor's clothes. In Macrobius' *Saturnalia* (5.3.8), Eustathius juxtaposes *Iliad* 20.307–8 and *Aeneid* 3.97–8 in a sample of lines that Virgil 'translated almost word-for-word' from Homer (5.3.3 *versus ad verbum paene translatos*):

> Νῦν δὲ δὴ Αἰνείαο βίη Τρώεσσιν ἀνάσσει
> καὶ παίδων παῖδες, τοί κεν μετόπισθε γένωνται.
>
> Hic domus Aeneae cunctis dominabitur oris
> et nati natorum et qui nascentur ab illis.    (Macrob. *Sat.* 5.3.8)[14]
>
> And now the might of Aeneas is lord over the Trojans,
> and so his children's children, and any born thereafter.
>
> Here the house of Aeneas will be lord over all shores,
> and so his children's children and those to be born from them.

Eustathius moves on to his next example without further comment, but it will be clear – as, for example, it was to Knauer – that these lines of the *Aeneid* are heavily invested in a passage of Homer that rescues Aeneas from

---

[14] For *Il.* 20.307 ἀνάσσει the Homeric mss give ἀνάξει, which is yet closer to Virgil's future *dominabitur*.

annihilation and guarantees the survival of his line beyond the destruction of Troy.[15] The momentous importance of the prophecy registers in Servius' extraordinary note ad loc.: *Sane hic uersus Homeri est, quem et ipse de Orpheo sustulit, item Orpheus de oraculo Apollinis Hyperborei* ('Clearly this is a line of Homer which he himself derived from Orpheus, just as Orpheus got it from the oracle of Hyperborean Apollo'). To account for the electrifying effect of the prophecy from a Roman point of view, Servius here engages in an extreme *Quellenforschung* that he attempts to justify in the rest of his note by claiming that the phrase *haec Phoebus* in line 99 is Virgil's knowing acknowledgement of his ultimate source. At the far end of this tradition stands Knauer's monumental *Die Aeneis und Homer*, which explicitly acknowledges its own debt to Macrobius and his long line of successors.[16] Knauer's work marks a significant moment in the understanding of Virgil's 'poetische Technik', but the unidirectional optic of its source criticism is laid bare in the series of diagrams in which all the arrows point from Homer (and in one case Apollonius) to the *Aeneid*.

It is the move beyond the one-way traffic of *Quellenforschung* that enables us to account for the frisson experienced by Servius. The highpoint of the pre-intertextual tradition goes back to Giorgio Pasquali's short but latterly influential essay on 'the art of allusion', first published in 1942.[17] In a nod to Pasquali's earlier *Orazio lirico* (1920), the opening of 'Arte allusiva' stages an exchange featuring *obtrectatores* who accuse the author of suffocating the classics with parallel passages, and a rebuttal encapsulated in the lyrical reflection quoted above as the first epigraph to this chapter. In line with a prominently German recuperation of the 'later' literature of the Hellenistic and Roman periods from a neoromantic prejudice against it, Pasquali saw imitative and allusive writing not as derivative or subordinate, nor as operating within a narrow compass of aims such as emulation, polemic or intellectual display, but as a creative act of recovery and adaptation of earlier or otherwise different literary worlds in new settings and times. In the case of *Aen.* 3.97–8, on this view, we have not so much a translated source as a marked and archaic evocation of a Homeric prophecy solemnly integrated with Virgil's Augustan 'now'. Yet even this explanation is incomplete: the electrifying effect of Apollo's prophecy from

---

[15] Knauer 1964a: 348: 'Die *Aeneis* scheint hier nur die Verwirklichung dieser Voraussage Poseidons ins Unendliche beabsichtigen zu wollen – *imperium sine fine dedi*.'
[16] Knauer 1964a: 62–106 at 67 n. 2, 361–527 at 367.
[17] Pasquali 1942. For an assessment of Pasquali's provenance and influence, see Citroni 2011.

a Roman point of view derives from reading it not only as informed by Homer, as it has been in unidirectional forms of source criticism,[18] but also as itself informing Homer through the prism of Virgil. Pasquali presents one side of this story; it is intertextuality, freed of authorial intention and priority, that fully animates the other side of the allusive art.

It was once again in the Italian tradition that the two intellectual streams of 'arte allusiva' and intertextuality converged, *in primis* in Conte's work on 'poetic memory' and the 'rhetoric of imitation'. The philologist in Conte continued to be interested in the alluding poet, but as theorist he recognised that text-to-text links could not be ascribed to a given set of motivations for the intending subject:[19]

> If poetic memory is reduced to the impulse to emulate, the production of the text will be devoted to the relationship between two subjectivities, and the literary process will center more on the personal will of two opposing authors than on the structural reality of the text.

Shifting the optic in this way from the intersubjective to the intertextual encourages a view not so much of Virgil alluding to Homer to achieve the effect that Pasquali described, but rather of Homer's epic creating the conditions for a Virgilian successor just over the horizon (μετόπισθε, as it were), obligingly stepping into line as a mere prequel to the *Aeneid*.[20] Thought-provoking though this 'flipped' priority is, hypersensitivity against ascribing allusive intention has sometimes resulted in the elision of the author's agency and its replacement with all-too-facile references to how the text functions and even what it intends. In practice, most Latinists find it instinctively difficult to embrace a worldview in which there can be no place for allusive intention or priority among authors operating in a relatively closed system of literary texts and with a high degree of self-consciousness about their tradition.[21] The stark mechanics of Conte's earlier theorisation of intertextuality for Latinists, formulated against the same backdrop of neoromantic prejudice that Pasquali sought to escape, later yielded to the notion of authorial intention as something (re)constructed by the 'ideal' or 'model' reader projected from the text as a model for real 'empirical' readers to follow.[22] If this 'backdoor'

---

[18] Page 1894: 283 ad loc.: 'This and the next line are copied from *Il*. 20.307'; Williams 1962 ad loc.: 'These lines are very closely similar to . . . '
[19] Conte 1986: 27, in the introduction to the English version of Conte 1974 and 1984. On the problems of intentionality see Sharrock in this vol., esp. pp. 184–93.
[20] For this retroactive reconstruction and displacement of the source text, see Hinds 1998: 52–98.
[21] See, however, Edmunds 2001 for a view of intertextuality that gives absolute priority to the reader.
[22] Conte 1986: 30 with n. 13 and 1994: xviii–xx, 133–8. See Hinds 1998: 49–50. For different responses to the (post)structuralist *aporia* about intention, see Heath 2002: 59–97 and Farrell 2005.

intentionalism, as Hinds describes it, is compatible with intertextuality, then we may describe the situation at *Aen.* 3.97–8 ecumenically as follows: the *Aeneid* invites us to read out from it a Virgil who harnesses the intertextual potential of allusion to reconfigure the epic tradition in such a way as to make Homer anticipate and accommodate its successor. To acknowledge this expanded view at every intertextual node would clog scholarly discussion with an intolerable level of verbosity, but the reputation of much work in Latin intertextual studies for a certain dullness would suggest that many of its practitioners have not thought these implications through in the first place.

With preconceptions about intention and priority relaxed, this reading unlocks a potent cultural ideology from Virgil's text. A further positivism that intertextuality looks beyond, also with interpretative and ideological ramifications, is the philological move of isolating allusions from apparently non-referential confluences. One of the more subtle forms of this kind of positivism, but one that still seeks to police the borders between allusion and intertext, was that which distinguished nondescript repetition of language in everyday usage (*Verbrauchsrede*) from repetition that makes language more charged and liable for reuse (*Wiedergebrauchsrede*).[23] Conte developed this distinction by contrasting what he called the 'code model' (the generic matrix in which the text locates itself) with the 'exemplary model' (i.e., a specific locus in the source text by which the target text is informed).[24] Since all texts are intertextual, however, intertextuality in the final analysis requires the reader potentially to relax even these hierarchies of referentiality in favour of a wider network of textual links. As Don Fowler insisted, the difference is made by individual readers, who are able to tell more compelling stories about some of these intertexts than about others.[25] In looking beyond allusive hierarchies, the example of *Aeneid* 3.97–8 makes for an interesting test-case since its linkage to *Iliad* 20.307–8 is marked by strong lexical equivalence, position (the lines conclude the prophecy in each case), and a prophetic register that demarcates the lines from the language of everyday speech (e.g., the polyptota παίδων παῖδες/*nati natorum*).[26] It would be hard to imagine a pair of Greek hexameters that come close to this degree of resemblance, but in the Homeric

---

[23] See Conte 1986: 40–5 (cf. Conte 1974: 17–22) and Wills 1996: 16–17, both expanding on an idea advanced at Lausberg 1966: 47–8.
[24] Conte 1986: 31 and Barchiesi 1984: 91–122, esp. pp. 95–6 (2015: 69–93, esp. pp. 73–4).
[25] Fowler 1997: 19–20.
[26] See further Heyworth and Morwood 2017 ad loc.; on the figural repetition see Wills 1996: 213.

Hymn to Aphrodite Aeneas' mother vouchsafes her son's bloodline in terms that will be familiar to those who have heard or read the *Iliad*:

> Σοὶ δ' ἔσται φίλος υἱὸς ὃς ἐν Τρώεσσιν ἀνάξει
> καὶ παῖδες παίδεσσι διαμπερὲς ἐκγεγάονται· (*Hymn. Hom. Ven.* 196–7)
>
> And you will have a beloved son who will be lord over the Trojans
> and to his children children will be born forever;

Although it was flagged by the Spanish Jesuit Juan Luis de la Cerda (b. 1558), the parallel is rarely acknowledged in commentaries on *Aeneid* 3.97–8.[27] The even closer correspondence of the Iliadic lines, and the place occupied by the Homeric epics in the Virgilian horizon of expectation, appears to have bumped Aphrodite's prophecy off the shortlist of allusions made available to the audience of Apollo's cryptic instruction that the Trojans should seek out their ancient mother (96 *antiquam exquirite matrem*). There is at least one member of that audience, however, for whom the words of Aeneas' mother should be intimately familiar, and his reading is staged for us within the text: it is to Anchises that Aphrodite foretells the future dominion of the Aeneadae in the Homeric hymn, and it is Anchises who now interprets her words as translated, recontextualised and updated in Apollo's prophecy. Perhaps it is his ongoing complicity with that earlier moment of intimate revelation that prevents Anchises, and us with him, from recalling Aphrodite's guarantee of Trojan supremacy as compensation for the mortality which, in the *Aeneid*, he is soon to fulfil.

The possibility of reading *Hymn to Aphrodite* 196–7 into *Aeneid* 3.97–8 suggests that its demotion in the scholarly record since La Cerda marks a regression that might be corrected by the more pluralistic reading strategies that intertextuality encourages – or should encourage.[28] Future commentators on *Aeneid* 3 might, then, wonder what consideration should be given to apparently more remote parallels, such as La Cerda's cross-reference to Aristotle's *Politics* for the idea of *nati natorum*. In its context, the Aristotelian version of the phrase traces the development of the state from originary familial colonies 'that some refer to as weaned on the same milk, children and the children of children' (1252b οὓς καλοῦσί τινες

---

[27] The Virgilian lines were, however, cited by Italian humanist Giorgio Valla (b. 1447) in his commentary on *Hymn. Hom. Ven.* 197: see Thomas 2016: 282. On the enduring value of La Cerda's commentary to Virgilian studies, see Laird 2002.

[28] The *Homeric Hymn to Aphrodite* has, however, been taken to impart an incestuous subtext to Aeneas' encounter with his mother in *Aeneid* 1: see Reckford 1996, Olson 2011, Gladhill 2012: 167 ('intercestuality'), McAuley 2016: 61–2.

ὁμογάλακτας, παῖδάς τε καὶ παίδων παῖδας). If this passage from the start of the *Politics* was available to La Cerda's recall, then so much the more will it have been to that of Virgil's contemporary readers, for whom it will then import into *Aeneid* 3.97–8 and its Homeric intertexts the political theory that is actualised in their own descent from Aeneas' colonial enterprise.[29]

In practice, then, the question of where to draw the line in the chain of text-to-text links is an urgent one, as witnessed in the balance between text and intertextual 'cf. e.g.' that the commentator must strike under every lemma.[30] Such discrimination is not the business of intertextuality in theory, however, as Hinds explains: 'There is no discursive element in a Roman poem, no matter how unremarkable in itself, and no matter how frequently repeated in the tradition, that cannot in some imaginable circumstance mobilise a specific allusion.'[31] Perhaps the best an intertextual philologist can do is to settle for a pragmatic compromise such as that proposed by Monica Gale: 'To put it rather flippantly, I recognize that all texts are intertextual, but I prefer to see some intertexts as more intertextual than others.'[32] The current prominence of such pragmatic approaches might be taken as indirect evidence that intertextuality *in sensu stricto* has no competitors, and may be all the more necessary in the face of the exponential proliferation of the 'cf.' enabled by advances in the digital humanities, to be discussed further on p. 257–61. Increasingly muscular intertext generators such as *Tesserae* renew the question of how to filter the 'more intertextual' from the 'less intertextual' (some might say inert) parallels.

If the question of where to call a halt to intertextual concatenation has proved more complicated than might have been expected in the case of a verbatim calque, then it will be even more complex in cases of looser correspondence. An example is again available in the second half of *Aeneid* 3.97, which conspicuously swerves from Homer's more modest Τρώεσσιν ἀνάξει to Virgil's resoundingly panegyric *cunctis dominabitur oris*: the *Aeneid* has already trained us to understand the house of Aeneas, and the sons of its sons, as the *gens Iulia* which achieves worldwide dominion under Augustus (*Aen.* 1.257–96). The intertextual strategy of this line, it has been suggested, looks beyond the unique *post eventum* prophecy of *Iliad* 20 (and the *Homeric Hymn to Aphrodite*) to that of Callimachus' *Hymn to Delos*, in which the unborn Apollo tells his parturient mother of a 'Saviour' (Ptolemy II Philadelphus) 'under whose crown will come both continents,

---

[29] On Aeneas as colonist, see Horsfall 1989.  [30] See Gibson 2002.  [31] Hinds 1998: 26.
[32] Gale 2000: 5 n. 10.

not unwilling to be ruled (κοιρανέεσθαι) by a Macedonian, and the islands in the sea, as far as the ends of the earth and from where the swift horses carry the Sun' (166–70).[33] This intertextuality produces an irony in the fact that, as Virgil's readers will have appreciated, the Ptolemaic dynasty and world-power predicted by Callimachus' unborn Apollo have now, in the god's maturity, been obliterated by Aeneas' descendant at the Battle of Actium (the site of which Augustus' ancestor will visit after the present detour on Delos). Read as a weft in history's text, then, Virgil's intertextuality with archaic and Hellenistic models documents and, in its own way, enacts the wider geopolitical upheaval of its time.

Here, then, the reach of intertextuality extends beyond the localised encounters in literary texts treated by structuralist philology to embrace the wider discourses with which poststructuralist readers are concerned. It is only in this latter sense that intertextuality can accommodate the way in which the second half of *Aeneid* 3.97, in deviating from the Homeric calque, also registers Virgil's intervention in an ancient debate – recorded by Dionysius of Halicarnassus (1.53.4–5) and Strabo (13.1.53), and audible in what we can reconstruct of Arctinus of Miletus, Hellanicus of Lesbos, Acusilaus of Argos, Sophocles' *Laocoon*, Menecrates of Xanthos, Demetrius of Scepsis – as to whether or not Aeneas left Troy, and where he settled if he did.[34] Dionysius ascribes to an over-literal interpretation of Poseidon's prophecy the view that Aeneas remained in Troy and never travelled to Italy; conversely, Strabo rules that the authority of Homer discredits local histories that posit a connection with the Aeneadae, including tendentious Roman histories that he deems responsible for the variant reading that replaces Homer's Αἰνείαο βίη Τρώεσσιν ἀνάξει ('the might of Aeneas will be lord over the Trojans') with Αἰνείαο γένος πάντεσσιν ἀνάξει ('the family of Aeneas will be lord of all people'). While few would go so far as to suggest that Virgil's *cunctis dominabitur oris* influenced the manuscripts of Homer cited by Strabo,[35] an intertextual perspective on the matter would hear *Aeneid* 3.97 as a voice that rose above a wider conversation in such a way as to cast doubt on the version of the Homeric line that Strabo, as a Greek writing in Rome, found more congenial to his agenda. In this controversy, as in others, our access is limited to a few sound-bites in a web of claims and counterclaims – recorded in poetry, antiquarian and ethnographic research, annotated on texts, and no doubt voiced in schools

---

[33] Barchiesi 1994, esp. pp. 441–2. McNelis and Sens 2016: 180–217, esp. pp. 201–15, argue (against uncertainties of chronology) that Lycophron's *Alexandra* also mediates the Homeric passage to Virgil.
[34] See Smith 1981. [35] So Williams 1962 *ad loc.*; see Horsfall 2006 ad loc.

and, for all we know, aired on street corners – within which the *Aeneid* takes up its own position, not unaware of what may be at stake for its interlocutors. As the Trojans ponder what they have just heard (3.100 *cuncti quae sint ea moenia quaerunt*, 'they all inquire what those walls could be'), Anchises 'turns over in his mind the testimony of men of old' and, simultaneously, plays the role of archivist 'unrolling the records of men of old' (3.102 *ueterum uoluens monimenta uirorum*), albeit to pronounce what is apparently the wrong interpretation, but actually one that has much to commend it.[36] Playing out before us in the text, then, is the construction of an ideology, the formation of a discourse from diverse voices and ideas seeming to converge on a solution already presupposed by the text. The discourse in question, about the facticity of the Trojan migration west, belies the truer situation of Rome's geopolitical drift east, redrawing the map and rewriting cultural capital in the process (*cunctis dominabitur oris*). Intertextuality – in this case, our tuning into and out of interference from the channels over which the *Aeneid* broadcasts itself – charts this process and locates the Roman epic on that map. In view of this reading, it is instructive that Julia Kristeva later compared her theorisation of intertextuality to her own experience of intercultural and intellectual interaction as academic visitor to the USA:[37]

> America seems to me to be a territory that welcomes and even encourages grafts. This personal experience was the first kernel, the permanent basis for my interest in studying phenomena such as cultural and textual interaction, and above all intertextuality.

Viewed as intertextual subjects in the same way as Kristeva views herself, Aeneas and his Homeric author are wayfarers into the Roman west, their story of uncertain integration told in an *Aeneid* which, in its turn, is ambassador of a Roman system of signs that has sought to make them its own.[38]

This interpretation of Apollo's prophecy in *Aeneid* 3 would appear to endorse Kristeva's view of epic as authoritarian monologism.[39] For

---

[36] See Horsfall 2006 *ad loc.*
[37] Kristeva 2002: 8. See ibid. 9 for potential metaphors in and extensions beyond this nexus: 'the concept of intertextuality began resonating with some other concepts that I was working out, namely that of strangeness/hospitality, migrant personalities, and grafts; that of the semiotic/the symbolic and their trans-verbal meaning; then abjection, borderline personalities, and the blurring of object and subject acting out'.
[38] See Hardie 1998: 41: 'The *Aeneid* itself is the monument to the final naturalization on Roman soil of Greek cultural goods transported from the east, a journey parallel to that of its hero Aeneas, from east to west, from the world of Homer to the world of Augustus.' For elegiac dialogue with this reading, see O'Rourke 2011.
[39] Compare Lyne 1987: 2 (but see our n. 42): 'If we hearken to this voice, and to it alone, we find our conventional epic: "objective", credible, univocal.'

carnivalesque dialogism, we can turn instead to the latter-day Aeneas of Juvenal's third Satire: when Umbricius laments that 'for honourable skills there is no place in the City, no reward for toil' (21–2 *artibus ... honestis | nullus in urbe locus, nulla emolumenta laborum*), scant significance might have been accorded to his echo of Helenus' prophetic description of the future Rome later in *Aeneid* 3 (393 *is locus urbis erit, requies ea certa laborum*, 'that shall be the site of the city, that the sure rest from your toils') were it not for the wider intertextual configuration of Umbricius as an Aeneas-in-reverse, leaving a Rome that he sees in a state of physical and social collapse.[40] Yet there is nothing to stop this intertextual channel from back-feeding into the monologist reading of *Aeneid* 3 just offered: in a way that interrupts Virgil's confident promise of Trojan *Nachleben* in Rome, Juvenal insinuates the erased Homeric original back into the text by reversing the trajectory of the Trojans' trans-Aegean ambitions. Such a reading would be resonant especially for those attuned to Virgil's meditations on the transience of empire. In line with this interpretation, the recollection from *Iliad* 20 that Octavian's patron god had led Aeneas to perdition, far from being corrected,[41] could contribute to a wider network of inscrutable and inconsistent behaviour on the part of the Julian family's supporting gods. As Oliver Lyne appreciated, it is intertextuality that guarantees the further voices from which more indignant perspectives on Roman imperialism can be recuperated in the *Aeneid*.[42] It seems possible, then, to side with satire's rebellious streak and to link Umbricius' speech with other passages of Juvenal in which the promise of Virgil's *Aeneid* seems to be subverted in its translation to post-Domitianic Rome (e.g., *Sat.* 2.149–59 is a travesty of the 'Parade of Heroes' in *Aeneid* 6). Then again, dialogistic reading in the opposite direction might equally take Aeneas' precedent as immigrant to ironise Umbricius' racism towards easterners who have overthrown the old order. Intertextuality cuts both ways: a dialogic exposé is open to a rearguard action from its monologist opponent, and vice versa.

Starting out from localised encounters with the text of *Aeneid* 3.97–8, the intertextual reader is ultimately confronted with a proliferation of texts and cultural fields that can only be approached interdiscursively.[43] What

---

[40] See Staley 2000: 87.   [41] So Miller 2009: 108–10.
[42] See Lyne 1987: 2: 'But there are "further voices" ... Devices are exploited to insinuate ramifying meanings and messages for those prepared to listen. Further voices intrude other material and opinions, and these may be disturbing, even shocking. Further voices add to, comment upon, question, and occasionally subvert the implications of the epic voice.'
[43] Fowler 1997: 128–9, though with a bias towards Derridean pantextuality that might be widened to accommodate more 'ocularcentric' cognition such as obtained at Rome: see Squire 2009.

Conte adopted from Kristevan intertextuality was the semiotic account of the reader as a plurality of texts for whom intertextuality 'defines the condition of literary readability'; what he explicitly left behind, on the other hand, following Genette, was the politics of Kristevan intertextuality, 'purifying' it of its ideological import and making it 'a more neutral instrument suited to philological analysis'.[44] The result might be seen as a rather inward-looking form of intertextuality which, despite in principle seeing meaning produced in a system rather than in isolation, has tended not to concern itself with the wider ramifications of the intertextual encounter for literary works as a whole and, in particular, for their participation in the wider discourses of their time, as Kristeva originally proposed in her far more political conception of intertextuality. Likewise, the 'intertextual unconscious' subsequently evolved by Riffaterre and Kristeva, where intertextuality is a kind of double entendre through which the repressed makes its presence felt,[45] has played less of a role than might have been expected in discussion of those further voices that Latinists tend to hear. Some work has bucked this trend,[46] but these studies stand in a certain tension with structuralist intertextuality as first applied in Latin studies. In his retrospective reflection on the evolution of these methodologies in the forty years since the publication of *Memoria dei poeti e sistema letterario*, Conte recants his earlier de-prioritisation of authorial intention only to reaffirm his commitment to a structuralist intertextuality guided by philologically observable features in the text, repudiating as unphilological poststructuralist arbitrariness the 'capricious intertextuality' that would import into the text what cannot directly be observed within it.[47] The excesses include deconstructive readings that ascribe to the text motivations that work against its grain; a focus on 'absences' rather than on what is present in the text; Bloomian 'misprisions' that wilfully take the model amiss; metapoetic readings that ascribe a higher level of meaning to a self-conscious author; and psychoanalytical interpretations that excavate the author's unexpressed and repressed subconscious. For poststructuralist intertextualists these possibilities are inherent in textuality in its fullest expression, such that the positivist's exasperation at the non-philological application of intertextuality will be comparable to Ovid's protest in *Tristia* 2 at the 'misappropriation' of his *Ars amatoria* for purposes more

---

[44] Conte 1986: 29 n. 11.   [45] See Riffaterre 1987.
[46] Political or other ideological intertexts are addressed in e.g. Morgan 1999, Gale 2000, Nelis 2001. For discussion of the latent work done by intertextuality in the psychologies of characters and narrative situations in which they find themselves, see Oliensis 2001 and Schiesaro 2008.
[47] Conte 2014: 63–106, at 95 (= 2017: 35–61, at 54).

transgressive and amoral than he had intended. To accept at face value Ovid's insistence that his good intentions were taken amiss would in itself be to acknowledge that no author can be held accountable for what others will (mis)read into a text;[48] but to suspect that Ovid is being disingenuous legitimates the possibility of the transgressive and amoral reading that *Tristia* 2 ostensibly denies. While philological positivism is a bedrock in the interpretation of classical literature as a highly introspective body of texts, Ovid suggests that some ancient readers, at least, shared a postmodern awareness of its porosity.

Predicates such as 'is intertextual with', then, are freighted – perhaps fraught – with possibilities and responsibilities. As a rule of thumb, its potential to mean 'enters into a reciprocally defining transaction with' should never be neglected. When this transaction has a destabilising effect on the source text – as is commonly felt in respect of Virgil's reading of Homer, or Juvenal's reading of Virgil – it also implicitly acknowledges the authority of the text destabilised. Intertextuality thus gets involved in the formation of canons, just as it plays its part in the construction of genres, in periodisation and in the generation of other powerful discourses.[49] Conte's 'code model', mentioned earlier, gives expression to the role of intertextuality in genre formation, and the example of the epic code shows the ideological power up for grabs in that formation – as in any attempt to reform or deform it. It is intertextuality that enables classicists of all hues to locate their readings within a wider cultural matrix; indeed it would be an interesting thought-experiment to consider how all of the chapters in this book might in some way profit from, or even be redescribed in terms of, the intertextual approaches outlined here.

## *uortit barbare*

Translation, as the reconfiguration of one sign system into another, is the ultimate in intertextuality. The high volume of translations of Greek epic and dramatic poetry by the earliest Latin authors known to us lays the foundations of intertextuality as a self-conscious property of Roman literature from its first beginnings.[50] Many histories, ancient and modern, of Latin literature begin with Livius Andronicus, a Graeco-Roman from

---

[48] See Gibson 1999.
[49] The didactic genre is a particularly active area for the intertextual formation of ideology: see e.g. Schiesaro 1997, Habinek 1997, O'Rourke 2019.
[50] Leo 1913, Feeney 2016. On intertextuality with Greek sources, see Hutchinson 2013; on translation theory, McElduff 2013.

## 5 Intertextuality

Tarentum. The exhibition of his versions of Greek drama on the Roman stage in 240 BCE (Cic. *Brut.* 72) – a year after the First Punic War was concluded – points to the cultural and political potency of Latin literature as an intertextual phenomenon; the same potency necessarily inheres in Livius' most famous work, a 'translation' of the *Odyssey* into Latin saturnians. Its first line is preserved in Aulus Gellius' discussion of the archaic meaning and spelling of the verb *insequi*:

> Offendi enim in bibliotheca Patrensi librum uerae uetustatis Liuii Andronici, qui inscriptus est Ὀδύσσεια, in quo erat uersus primus cum hoc uerbo sine u littera: *uirum mihi, Camena, insece uersutum*, factus ex illo Homeri uersu: Ἄνδρα μοι ἔννεπε, Μοῦσα, πολύτροπον. (Gell. 18.9.5)

> In the library at Patrae I came across a manuscript of Livius Andronicus of genuine antiquity. It was entitled *The Odyssey*, and its first line had our word without the letter *u*: 'Tell me, Camena, about the versatile man', translated from the corresponding verse of Homer: 'Tell me, Muse, about the man of many turns'.

Gellius goes on to explain that *insequi* ('to follow') once meant 'to say' in the same way that ἔπη, the Greek for *uerba* or *uersus*, is said to be related to ἕπεσθαι ('to follow') and εἰπεῖν ('to say'). If *insece* tracks Homer's ἔννεπε with this kind of etymological precision, Gellius' phrase *factus ex illo Homeri uersu* might be taken to recommend an understanding of Livius' intertextuality as unidirectional in its optic. Our fragmentary access to Livius' *Odysia* and to Latin literature of its time should urge caution, however, as might a second look at Gellius' explanation. In his etymologising discussion, the repetition of the noun *uersus* (alongside *uerbum*) is conspicuous in a sentence that introduces a quotation containing the adjective *uersutus*. It is hard to imagine that Gellius failed to pick up on the kind of self-reflexive play on *uertere* (the technical term for 'to translate') with which S. Hinds credits Livius: 'Here in this programmatically loaded context our poet introduces a Ulysses in whom the very linguistic switch to which he owes his textual existence has been made part of his proverbial versatility, has been troped into his πολυτροπία.'[51] There is much at stake when the Latin Camena sings Homer's *Odyssey* to Livius, the Ἄνδρα μοι to Andronicus himself, a Romanised Greek who contributed in his own way to the same cultural appropriation that saw statues of the Muses physically translated to Rome to adorn a shrine set up by Ennius' patron.

---

[51] Hinds 1998: 61–2.

Similar considerations apply in respect of the *fabula palliata*, the Latin play in Greek dress. The extent to which scholarship on Plautus and Terence has debated questions of originality and indebtedness to Greek models may be seen as a function of the kind of intertextual reading the plays demand.[52] Plautus' *uortit barbare* (*Asin.* 11; *Trin.* 19) focalises the act of cultural translation and appropriation from the alien perspective. The loss of the Greek models on which Plautus' Latin plays may be said to be based presents the opposite situation to that which obtains in the case of Livius' *Odyssey*, where it is the source text that survives intact. From this one-sided perspective there resulted a view of Plautus' plays as second-hand derivations of Greek classics, an assumption that held sway until E. Fraenkel's pioneering study of *Plautinisches im Plautus* (1922). The later discovery of a papyrus fragment of Menander's *Dis exapaton*, corresponding to *Bacchides* 494–562, allowed scholars to assess what *uortit barbare* means in practice, and did much to vindicate Plautus as an artist of some originality.[53] Liberated from presumed indebtedness to hypothesised Greek models, Plautine comedy was resituated, especially by the so-called 'Freiburg School', in the Atellan tradition of improvised farce.[54] Yet as far as its intertextuality is concerned, these debates have left the *fabula palliata* in a certain limbo as a hybrid Graeco-Roman genre of, on the one hand, depreciated literary intertextuality and, on the other, heightened connectivity with extempore oral traditions.

A case in point is Plautus' *Menaechmi*: for the Freiburg School, this play is a product of the Italian extempore tradition and entirely independent of any Greek model;[55] others, however, have posited a lost Hellenistic original whose basic outline can be recovered from the rough-and-tumble of its Plautine adaptation.[56] In beginning with a mock-academic disquisition on dramatic convention, the *Menaechmi* itself might be said to offer its own perspective on this debate. The *prologus* appears to bungle a rather pedestrian premise – that poets set their plays in Athens to effect a Greek style (9 *quo illud uobis graecum uideatur magis*) – by pointing out that the present play, set in the Illyrian port of Epidamnus, will be more Sicilian than Attic in its Graecising (11–12 *hoc argumentum graecissat, tamen | non atticissat, uerum sicilicissitat*).[57] This geographical confusion is then resolved in the ensuing *argumentum*, which explains how it has come about that Sicilian

[52] For an overview of these debates see Petrides 2014 on Plautus and Fontaine 2014 on Terence.
[53] Handley 1968, Bain 1979, Anderson 1993: 1–29.
[54] See, e.g., Lefèvre, Stärk and Vogt-Spira 1991.   [55] Stärk 1989.
[56] See Fantham 1968 (= 2011: 3–14) and Gratwick 1993: 23–30.
[57] On the linguistic punning in this line, see Fontaine 2006.

twins separated in childhood have both ended up in Epidamnus. The setting of a play, we are told, is as interchangeable as the parts acted in it (74 *sicut familiae quoque solent mutarier*).[58] The most dramatic interchange afoot here, of course, is the delivery of this analysis in Latin: *apporto uobis Plautum, lingua non manu* (3 'I bring you Plautus – by his tongue, not his hand'). Given this opening elaboration of the *Plautus-uortit-barbare* idea, it might well be wondered what relationship the Roman stage constructs in this play with its Greek twin. While the nature of our response to this question is conditioned by the limited nature of our evidence, it can nevertheless be recognised that it is the play itself that mobilises the debate about its relationship to Greek drama, and that intertextuality must therefore be relevant to its interpretation.

The theory embedded in the *Menaechmi* prologue conditions our reception of the rest of the play. For example, when the Sicilian Menaechmus, mistaken for his Epidamnian twin, is assumed to have lost the plot and decides opportunistically to act the part (832 *adsimilem insanire*), his ensuing 'mad scene' is a representative example of Plautine paratragedy that necessarily brings the whole question of originality and imitation under the spotlight.[59] On one analysis, the scene is pure Plautus, since it is exuberant in ways that no Greek model would have been.[60] Others, however, see the scene's apparent reworking of Euripides' *Herakles mainomenos* (*The Madness of Heracles*) as, on the most straightforward view, directly inherited from Plautus' Greek model.[61] So, for example, A. S. Gratwick comments (ad loc.):

> For the Greek audience, that description of the madness of Hercules was as 'classic' as the prince's pretended madness in Hamlet II. ii is for us. The Greek playwright may have exploited this with more or less specific recollections (imaginary chariot *HF* 862 | *Men.* 947–9; 'is he joking or mad?' *HF* 828 | *Men.* 824–30; mad fit ended by divine intervention, *HF* 1002–9 | *Men.* 870).[62]

Viewing the 'mad scene' through a Plautine lens (*apporto uobis Plautum*) produces a stereotype of Greek culture customised for a Roman audience,

---

[58] Gratwick 1993 transposes lines 72–6 to follow 10.
[59] On Plautine paratragedy, see Manuwald 2014 with further bibliography; for Terence's non-comic intertexts, see the overview by Sharrock 2013 with further bibliography.
[60] Stärk 1989: 105–9, at 107: 'Ein derartiges Götterpotpourri ist den Wahnsinnsszenen des griechischen Dramas fremd.'
[61] Fantham 2011: 15–26 hypothesises that Plautus conflated his model with a medley of Greek mad-scenes adapted for the Roman stage, including that found in his earlier *Mercator*.
[62] Gratwick 1993: 215.

complete with code-switching (835 *Bromie*; 841 *lampadibus*; 854 *Cynospater*; 872 *en Hercle*) and a display of the irrational. At the same time, the possibility of viewing the scene through a Greek lens (*hoc argumentum graecissat*) invites consideration of a model for whose audience this 'Greekness' is no less staged (*adsimilem insanire*), and who may have enjoyed how the comic dramatist exploits the farce so narrowly avoided in Euripides (824 *profecto ludit te hic*; *HF* 952 Παίζει πρὸς ἡμᾶς δεσπότης ἢ μαίνεται; 'Is our master joking with us or is he mad?'). Rather than poking fun at Greek culture, the *Menaechmi* on this view would effect a rapprochement between Greek and Roman entertainment.

In this way, the *Menaechmi* – irrespective of what Greek model may or may not have existed for it – sets up a productive dialogue between the different intertextual positions that may be assumed for the play. In Terence's prologues, too, the issue of direct or mediated imitation crops up as an issue of some significance.[63] At the start of the *Eunuchus* we are told that an anonymous critic identified in antiquity as the contemporary playwright Luscius of Lanuvium has accused Terence of importing into Menander's Urtext a pair of characters from *The Toady* (*Colax*) of Naevius and (i.e., revised by?) Plautus: *exclamat furem, non poetam fabulam | dedisse et nil dedisse uerborum tamen* (23–4 'he shouts that a thief, not a poet, put on the play – but did not put one over him'). In response, the prologue speaker concedes that the scene is borrowed, but adds that Terence was working from Menander's *Kolax* in ignorance of the Latin intermediaries by Naevius and Plautus. Not without sleight of hand, Terence's proxy then rounds on Luscius by claiming, in effect, that a veto on recycling the stock material of the comic repertoire would spell the end of literary production (40–1 *denique | nullumst iam dictum quod non dictum sit prius*, 'in short there is nothing said now that has not been said before') and that one should acknowledge and condone the use by new poets of older material (42–3 *cognoscere atque ignoscere | quae ueteres factitarunt si faciunt noui*). The culminating proviso *si faciunt noui* teases out an argument that is central to the prologue as a whole: Luscius has himself already been condemned for failing to meet the standard of novelty as one 'who, by translating plays well and writing them badly at the same time, has made bad Latin plays out of good Greek ones' (7–8 *qui bene uortendo et easdem scribendo male | ex Graecis bonis Latinas fecit non bonas*). If this can be taken to imply that Luscius' comedy was a slavish imitation, then his own punning claim that Terence's thieving did not deceive him (24 *nil dedisse uerborum*) might

---

[63] On Terence's prologues see Goldberg 1983; Gowers 2004; McElduff 2004; Sharrock 2009: 63–95.

itself be translated literally as he 'gave no sense [lit. 'nothing'] of the words' – that is, is an inaccurate translation. In this way, the prologue to the *Eunuchus* might be said both to generate the scholarly debate that seeks to differentiate between direct and indirect models, and to replace it with a principle of textual interconnection that goes beyond direct verbal correlation. Given the scope for liberal elaboration of source material suggested by the example of Plautus, even in a play as apparently source-less as the *Menaechmi*, it may be significant that the *Eunuchus* is regarded as one of Terence's most Plautine creations.

As with Plautus, the question of Terence's dependence on Greek models, especially Menander, has been much discussed.[64] In an important update to these debates, Michael Fontaine argues that one of the features that may make Terence most Menandrian is his affinity with a Menander who in antiquity attracted such works as Παράλληλοι αὐτοῦ τε καὶ ἀφ' ὧν ἔκλεψεν ἐκλογαί (*Parallel Excerpts of Himself and from Those He Plagiarised*) and the six-volume Περὶ τῶν οὐκ ἰδίων Μενάνδρου (*On Un-Menandrian Elements in Menander*).[65] Indeed, the temptation to read the *Eunuchus* as a play of the imitative type that its prologue critiques is mischievously encouraged by the dependence of its backstage allegations on Terence's prior knowledge of the literary history his *prologus* denies on his behalf.[66] Instructive here is the disclosure in the *Adelphoe* prologue that Terence has interpolated into his version of Menander's original a 'word-for-word' translation of a scene that Plautus' *Commorientes* (*Comrades in Death*) had omitted from its apparently freer version of Diphilus' *Synapothnescontes* (see also *Andr.* 8–16; *Heaut. tim.* 16–18):

> In Graeca adulescens est qui lenoni eripit
> meretricem in prima fabula: eum Plautus locum
> reliquit integrum, eum hic locum sumpsit sibi
> in Adelphos, uerbum de uerbo expressum extulit.
> Eam nos acturi sumu' nouam: pernoscite
> furtumne factum existumetis an locum
> reprehensum qui praeteritu' neglegentiast.  (*Adelph.* 8–14)

In the Greek original there is a youth who kidnaps a prostitute from her pimp in the first act: that scene Plautus passed over without touching it, and

---

[64] For two extremes in the older scholarship, contrast Norwood 1923 with Jachmann 1934; in the middle ground, see Ludwig 1968.
[65] See Fontaine 2014, esp. pp. 551–2. On plagiarism in relation to Greek and Latin literature, see Stemplinger 1912 and McGill 2012.
[66] For this as a limiting take on Terence's originality, see, e.g., Jachmann 1934.

that scene our playwright has adopted in his *Brothers* and given it a word-for-word rendering. That's the play we are about to act, a brand new one: consider carefully whether in your opinion a theft has been committed or a scene has been rescued that was overlooked through carelessness.

These lines characterise Terence as a close reader of Plautine adaptation as well as an innovative adapter (and adopter) of Menander himself, but also as an attentive translator in the process (*uerbum de uerbo expressum extulit*). This paradox is a provocation to the intertextually sensitive audience that the prologue otherwise flatters by inviting it to decide for itself whether the lines have been stolen or rescued. Although we do not have the target and source texts of Plautus and Diphilus with which to compare the lines to which Terence refers (*Adelph*. 155–96), it seems hardly coincidental that the metacritical debate about literary theft centres on a scene about literal theft. In an important article on Terence's prologues, Emily Gowers has shown that in all six cases a reciprocal correlation can be observed between the opening critical debate and the drama that follows: 'Beneath the surface of what looks like abstract discussion of his own literary experiences, Terence is in fact still "telling the plot" of the play in question. Meanwhile, the events of the play as they unfold reflect back an image of the experience the author offers us as preface to the play.'[67] Without pursuing too close a correlation between the literal and literary levels, it can be wondered what view of intertextuality this metadrama might suggest; in view of the later tendency among the Latin elegists to figure their texts as desirable women, it is suggestive that the scene to which Terence has drawn our attention features an adopted (and adapted) son wresting a *meretrix* from her owner so that he may pass her on to his brother.

Just as Terence's prologues map onto his plays, so too did his plays map out the contours of his biographical tradition.[68] As an extrapolation from his work, then, it is instructive to read in his *Vita* that Terence perished in (or died from grief after) a shipwreck in which he was transporting back to Italy 108 plays adapted from Menander (Suet. *Vit. Terent*. 5); no less instructive is the tradition (though Suetonius denies it) that Terence himself was an African shipped to Italy as a prisoner of war (cf. *Anth. Lat*. 487c.1–2 *Natus in excelsis tectis*

---

[67] Gowers 2004: 151.
[68] On this aspect of intertextuality in the ancient *Lives*, see Goldschmidt 2019.

*Karthaginis altae | Romanis ducibus bellica praeda fui*, 'Born in the towering citadel of lofty Carthage, I was war booty for Roman generals'). These narratives of Terence's appropriation of Menander and Rome's appropriation of Terence imbricate Roman intertextuality with Roman imperialism, and vice versa. Graeco-Roman geopolitics might be said to be ever-present in the *fabula palliata*, even in a play as Plautine as the *Menaechmi*. Set in Epidamnus (Dyrrachium), an area that fell under Roman control in Plautus' lifetime, this play has been found to use costume-change and cross-dressing to thematise the anxieties contingent on the Roman world's expanding intercultural horizons:[69] its action is plotted around a Greek dress (*palla*) which Menaechmus filches from his wife and sequesters under his *pallium* for a prostitute who, in turn, hands it over to his twin to be adjusted beyond recognition (426–7 *pallam illam, quam dudum dederas, ad Phrygionem ut deferas, | ut reconcinnetur atque ut opera addantur quae uolo*, 'That dress you gave me just now, take it down to the Phrygian shop to be repaired and have added the bits and bobs I'd like'). Crucially, this romp of cross-cultural confusion concludes with the auction of the Epidamnian Menaechmus' possessions and impending relocation back to the more normative world of Syracuse in the (now Roman) west. In the metatheatre of the *fabula palliata*, costume-change figures the Romanising of Greek literature, stolen and remade as good as new.

## Self-Reflexive Intertextuality

Obvious or maximal cases of intertextuality, such as the calques and translations examined above in Plautus, Terence and Virgil, show that the 'intersection of textual surfaces' is never just an aesthetic feature of the text or an index of literary history, but itself the very process of cultural exchange and appropriation in action. Localised intertextual events will therefore plug into a wider grid of Roman power. The big themes of these works, after all, are empire, immigration, abduction, naturalisation and so on, each a kind of intertextuality in a broad sense, and so each capable of troping intertextuality in a narrower sense. The present section will look at this self-reflexive aspect of intertextuality in itself, building the previous section's metaphors for allusion (e.g., theft) and intertextuality (e.g.,

[69] Dufallo 2013: 21–8.

immigration, costume-change) into a representative (but by no means exhaustive) typology. In its most basic form, this kind of self-reflexive annotation is signalled quite explicitly by markers such as *dicitur* or *fertur* (the so-called 'Alexandrian footnote'),[70] but it has been broadened into a range of more implicit or embedded signals which, though sometimes stretching the limits of credibility, have become virtually routine in the analysis of Latin literary allusion, especially in poetry.[71] Taken together, all of these metaphors can present a composite view of the Roman intertextual imagination in all its variety; and since – as Hinds indicates in an important discussion of the phenomenon – tenor and vehicle might always be reversed,[72] they also present Roman intertextuality as a trope adaptable to any narrative (see example viii below):

i *Repetition* may be variously flagged, for example by forms of *dicere* (e.g., Ovid's Ariadne, faced now with Bacchus' faithlessness, repeats her earlier recriminations against Jason in Catullus 64: *Fast.* 3.473 *'Dicebam, memini, "periure et perfide Theseu!"'*, 'I used to say, I remember, "You lying traitor, Theseus!"', cf. Catull. 64.130–5, 143–4) or *ferre* (e.g., *Aen.* 5.588 *ut quondam Creta fertur labyrinthus in alta*, 'As once in high Crete, it is said, the Labyrinth ...', cf. Catull. 64.112–15 and *Il.* 18.590–2),[73] or by adjectives such as *alius* or *similis* and adverbs such as *rursus* or *iterum* (see again Ariadne at *Fast.* 3.471 *'En iterum, fluctus, similes audite querellas'*, 'See again, waves, hear similar complaints'). As a hallmark of epic language and narrative, repetition is rarely inert in the genre: thus, for example, Virgil's Sibyl predicts 'another Achilles' (*Aen.* 6.89 *'alius ... Achilles'*) and an impending replay of the *Iliad* (93–4 *'causa mali tanti coniunx iterum hospita Teucris | externique iterum thalami'*, '"The cause of such woe for the Trojans? Again a foreign bride and again an alien bedchamber!"').[74]

ii *Memory* may be invoked where the literary tradition is brought to bear on the text: the classic example again is Ovid's Ariadne at *Fast.* 3.473, just quoted.[75] *Recognition* works similarly: the textbook

---

[70] The term was coined by David Ross (1975: 78, footnoting in turn a compact discussion at Norden 1957: 123–4).
[71] Some might say too routine: see Conte 2014: 96–9 (= Conte 2017: 55–7); Barchiesi 2015: 124 is wary but not sceptical.
[72] Hinds 1998: 10–16.
[73] For this example in a discussion of similar cases, see Horsfall 1991: 117–33; see also Horsfall 1990 and 2016: 111–34.
[74] On repetition writ large in the Latin epic tradition see Hardie 1993. On repetition in (and of) Ovid, see the essays collected in Fulkerson and Stover 2016.
[75] Conte 1986: 60–3 (cf. Conte 1974: 38–40); Hinds 1998: 3–4.

example is Lucan's 'recognition' (1.686 *agnosco*) of Priam's decapitated and nameless trunk at *Aen.* 2.557–8 as itself an allusion to Pompey.[76]

iii *Echo* is a particularly marked variety of repetitiveness: the sound-world of Virgil's *Eclogues* is awash with literary resonances, as signalled at *Ecl.* 1.5 *formosam resonare doces Amaryllida siluas* ('you teach the woods to echo "fair Amaryllis"');[77] Ovid's Echo (*Met.* 3) personifies intertextual repetition with self-reflexive remythologising of Lucretius' rational account of the same phenomenon (4.572–94), a passage that itself demythologises the earlier poetry it echoes.[78] Valerius Flaccus stages a complex game of intertextual repetition at *Arg.* 3.596–7 *rursus Hylan et rursus Hylan per longa reclamat | auia: responsant siluae et uaga certat imago* ('"Hylas!", he shouts, "Hylas!", again and again through the trackless expanse: the woods respond and the wandering echo vies with him').[79]

iv *Fama*, as Philip Hardie has shown, tropes the literary tradition as rumour and renown: the House of Fama at Ovid *Met.* 12.39–63 is thus an echo-chamber that 'repeats voices and doubles what it hears' (47 *uocesque refert iteratque quod audit*).[80]

v Made famous in Callimachus' *Aetia* prologue (fr. 1.25–8), *the path* – especially rutted, crowded or conversely never travelled – is itself a well-worn image for poetic (un)originality: so Virgil, explicitly seeking originality in the proem to *Georgics* 3, declares 'I must essay a path ... ' (3.8 *temptanda uia est*); alluding to this passage and its Callimachean model, Propertius follows suit (3.1.14 *non datur ad Musas currere lata uia*, 'there is no broad road to run to the Muses'; cf. 3.3.26 *noua ... semita*); Valerius Flaccus' *auia* at *Arg.* 597 quoted in iii similarly gestures to this paradox in its thick layer of metapoetic symbolism. In prose, too, Quintilian avoids the *uulgarem uiam* at *Inst.* 1.*pr.*3.[81]

vi Along the same lines, following in another's *footprints* figures literary debt to a precursor, as explicitly for Lucretius in respect of Epicurus (3.3–6).[82] In the epilogue to the *Thebaid* Statius apostrophises his epic as a successor to the *Aeneid* (*Theb.* 12.816–17 *nec tu diuinam Aeneida tempta, | sed longe sequere et uestigia semper adora*, 'and do not vie with the divine *Aeneid*, but follow afar and forever revere its footprints')[83]

---

[76] See Hinds 1998: 8–10, updating Narducci 1973.   [77] Breed 2006: 99–100.
[78] See Hardie 1988 and Hinds 1998: 5–8 on Ovid, and Nethercut 2020 on Lucretius.
[79] See Heerink 2015, esp. pp. 7–8, 88–90, 124–5.
[80] Hardie 2012, at pp. 150–77 for Ovid; see also Hardie 2002.   [81] See Whitton 2019: 479.
[82] Konstan 1988.   [83] See Ganiban 2007: 2–3 and *passim*.

in lines that allude to Creusa's relegation at Troy (*Aen.* 2.711 *longe seruet uestigia coniunx*), which in turn looks back to Eurydice at *G.* 4.486–7. See also for example Hor. *Epist.* 1.19.21–2 and (again) Quint. *Inst.* 1.pr.3.

vii The Latin *fons* readily denotes both literal and literary wellsprings. The setting of Calpurnius Siculus' second Eclogue hints at the extent to which its author draws on his Virgilian source: two shepherds meet 'by cool *fontes* and as it happened under the same shade' (5 *ad gelidos fontes et easdem forte sub umbras*); they compete in pastoral resources (34–5 '*Accipe,*' *dixerunt Nymphae,* '*puer, accipe fontes:* | *iam potes irriguos nutrire canalibus hortos*', '"Receive these *fontes,* boy," said the nymphs, "receive them: now with channels you can nourish your well-watered garden"') and go back to the source for new vitality (49–51 *irriguo perfunditur area fonte* | *et satiatur aqua, sucos ne forte priores* | *languida mutata quaerant plantaria terra*, 'the yard is soaked with a drenching *fons* and quenched with water lest with the change of soil the plants droop and seek their former moisture'), apparently with success (88–9 *fontibus in liquidis quotiens me conspicor, ipse* | *admiror totiens*, 'whenever I behold myself in the clear *fontes*, I marvel at myself').

viii The word *silua* ('wood') has occurred enough times above to corroborate it as a synonym for *materia* ('raw material'): Hinds gives a classic discussion of *Aen.* 6.179 *itur in antiquam siluam* ('into the ancient wood they go') as troping the Ennian material about to be logged and recycled (and also of the logging and recycling of Ennian material as troping Aeneas' irruption into pristine Italy).[84]

ix Grafting as a metaphor for intertextuality spreads from *G.* 2.69–82;[85] it reappears in Calpurnius, Columella and Palladius. In describing the cultivation of trees, Virgil attends both to the art required to effect a transplant and to the natural bounty that comes when it produces new fruit.

x Fathers like authors lose control of their offspring, and texts like children can be full of anxiety.[86] Not surprisingly, Roman authors described their literary progeny in familial terms long before Harold Bloom brought such imagery to widespread attention with his *Anxiety of Influence* (1973). Ovid, characteristically, reverses the

---

[84] Hinds 1998: 11–14.
[85] Pucci 1998: 99–108, Clément-Tarantino 2006, Lowe 2010, Henkel 2014.
[86] Hardie 1993: 88–119, Farrell 1999 and O'Sullivan 2009.

trope and describes a weak ancestor, so that his literary predecessor may appear all the more frail and in need of replacement: in a pointed reminder of the master craftsman's failure in the *Aeneid* (6.33 *bis patriae cecidere manus*, 'twice the father's hands failed'), Daedalus' hands tremble in the *Metamorphoses* (*Met.* 8.211 *et patriae tremuere manus*).[87]

xi The motif of exchange, both of song in amoebaean competition and of property or gifts in other contexts, can figure intertextual transference. In Virgil's third Eclogue Damoetas' inheritance of a flock from Aegon (2 *non, uero Aegonis; nuper mihi tradidit Aegon*, cf. Theoc. *Id.* 4.2 οὔκ, ἀλλ' Αἴγωνος· βόσκειν δέ μοι αὐτὰς ἔδωκεν) draws a barbed reaction from Menalcas (5–6 *hic alienus ouis custos bis mulget in hora, | et sucus pecori et lac subducitur agnis*, 'this interloper of a guard milks the sheep twice an hour, draining the life from the flock and the milk from the lambs', cf. *Id.* 4.3, 13) that comments also on Virgil's exploitation of Theocritus.[88] Sometimes these metaphors derive from the world of banking (borrowing or lending), such as Seneca the Elder on Ovid's open borrowing from Virgil (*palam mutuandi*, *Suas.* 3.7).

xii Competitions, spectacles and conflicts within poetry can signal rivalry – with attendant victory, loss or anxiety – in respect of a literary precursor: Anchises' funeral games in *Aeneid* 5 lock Virgil into a contest with *Iliad* 23, except a boat race now replaces the Homeric chariot race (to which, however, Virgil's regatta is compared in the simile at *Aen.* 5.144–7),[89] and the boxing match is more of a brawl, with both Apollonius (*Arg.* 2.1–97) and Theocritus (*Id.* 22.44–134) weighing in.[90] Behind these competitions is the basic idea of *aemulatio* as an implicit theorisation of text reuse.

xiii Since *uertere* is the technical term for translation and troping, metamorphosis and shape-shifters can figure intertextual process: Propertius' Vertumnus at 4.2.47 *formas unus uertebar in omnis* ('I could change my singular self into every form') signals his similarity to Virgil's Proteus (*G.* 4.411 *formas se uertet in omnes*, 'he will change himself into every form'), who for his part has been read as a figure for Virgil's intertextual struggle with Homer.[91]

xiv A particularly suggestive category of metamorphosis is reincarnation or metempsychosis. Lucretius satirises Ennius' self-presentation as

---

[87] O'Sullivan 2009: 470 n. 67.   [88] Farrell 1997: 231–2.
[89] See Nugent 1992, esp. pp. 257–8 and Farrell 1997: 232–3.
[90] Nelis 2001: 8–21, with 9 n. 41 for the Theocritean dimension.
[91] On Proteus in *Georgic* 4, see Morgan 1999: 17–49.

Homer reborn (Lucr. 1.112–26),[92] committed as he is to the Epicurean view that soul and memory are lost upon death, irretrievable even if the atoms of which we are currently constituted were at some point to recombine in the same formation:[93] paradoxically the reconstitution of Ennius' *elementa* ('atoms' but also 'letters') in the *De rerum natura* acknowledges the poet's *Nachleben* through intertextual memory. Virgil marks his inheritance of the epic tradition in the dream in which Hector's ghost hands over to Aeneas the Penates and responsibility for Troy's future (*Aen.* 2.268–97), a scene that remodels *inter alia* Ennius' dream at the start of the *Annales*.[94] More generally, the interplay of voices or characters in a text can figure the various intertextual personae an author might adopt;[95] in accordance with his own theology, Prudentius uses the Christian resurrection as a figure for textual renewal in *Cath.* 3.196–200.[96]

xv *Hospitality*, itself highly intertextual as a 'type-scene' in epic, entails a transaction between host and guest that can stage intergeneric and intertextual exchanges between visiting and receiving texts.[97] The dynamics of ancient hospitality are not necessarily amicable (*hospes*, like ξένος, means 'stranger' as well as 'host' or 'guest', and was semantically close to *hostis*, as demonstrated in the Twelve Tables at Tab. 2.2, 3.7): thus Virgil's Gallus in Eclogue 10 is an elegiac interloper in bucolic;[98] Aeneas' reception by Evander in *Aeneid* 8 tropes Virgil's adversarial reception of Ptolemaic hospitality narratives after Actium.[99] Propertius' generically and intertextually experimental fourth book begins *Hoc quodcumque uides, hospes* (4.1.1 'All that you see here, *hospes*') and features an elegiacised re-run of *Aeneid* 8 in which Hercules seeks to be admitted (4.9.34 *pandite . . . hospita fana*) where he is less than welcome (53 *parce oculis, hospes*).[100]

The evident popularity of this kind of poetological footnoting among readers of Latin poetry is likely to be driven at least in part by the legitimising force it appears to offer in positivistic literary criticism: as with 'stichometric' parallels between texts (see p. 255), the allusion alludes

---

[92] On Ennius and Homer, see Brink 1972: 556–65; on Lucretius and Ennius, see Gale 1994: 107–9.
[93] For a metaliterary reading of this 'palingenesis' in Lucretius, see Schiesaro 1994.
[94] Hardie 1993: 102–3.   [95] See Farrell 2019.   [96] See Pelttari 2019: 216–18.
[97] Harrison 2007, esp. pp. 11–18, evolves a theory of 'generic enrichment' based on a paradigm of hospitality between 'host' and 'guest' texts.
[98] Conte 1986: 100–29 (cf. Conte 1984: 13–42).   [99] See O'Rourke 2017.
[100] Warden 1982; DeBrohun 2003: 118–25, 134–43.

to itself and confirms its presence.[101] It is perhaps for the same reason that self-reflexive annotation is less often connected with the inherently less positivistic category of intertextuality, although there is no special reason why a particular term cannot be mobilised as a metaphor for the phenomenon of textual reuse more generally. If, for example, theft figures allusion as a localised, covert and adversarial operation, immigration and costume-change read intertextuality as a more open (though no less ideological) form of exchange. Moreover, since intertextuality teaches us that all language is recycled, there is no term that under some circumstance could not mobilise a self-reflexive annotation. The ultimate laboratory for this suggestion is the Latin cento, to be discussed in the next section: since, for example, the Medea of Hosidius Geta necessarily speaks a patchwork of Virgilian quotations, everything she says will take on the aspect of a self-annotation, with the result that her reference to Jason's new marriage as *externique iterum thalami* (209), lifted from *Aen.* 6.94 (see i), will seem doubly troped as a repetition of a repetition.

At the other end of the scale of literary self-consciousness, the capacity of intertextual Latin to trope itself might also be tested in a laboratory of non-poetic texts with which 'poetological' reflexivity is less often associated. The closing paragraph of Tacitus' *Agricola* has struck readers as a passage of heightened Latinity. Contemplating how the memory of his father-in-law can best be venerated (46.3 *memoriam uenerari*), the historian has a particular stake in the power of literature over and above other forms of commemoration:

> Quidquid ex Agricola amauimus, quidquid mirati sumus, manet mansurumque est in animis hominum in aeternitate temporum, fama rerum; nam multos ueterum uelut inglorios et ignobilis obliuio obruit: Agricola posteritati narratus et traditus superstes erit. (Tac. *Agr.* 46.4)

> Whatever we have loved in Agricola, whatever we have admired, remains and will remain in the minds of men through everlasting time by the record of his achievements: for oblivion will engulf many of the ancients as though neither fame nor name were theirs; Agricola – his story told and passed on to posterity – will stand enduring.

Enlarging an earlier suggestion, R. G. Austin ventured that the emotive power of this passage owed something to Tacitus' experimentation with prose rhythm: 'The sudden leap to a rarefied atmosphere in the epilogue to the *Agricola* has often been remarked; the Latin seems to speak with a new

---

[101] For this formulation see Hardie 1993: 98–9; see also Smith 1990 on stichometric 'meta-allusion'.

strength, and (as Dr Mackail long ago pointed out) to fall into new rhythms; the reader's heart inevitably quickens at its strange grandeur. To my ear, these rhythms seem curiously lyric.'[102] Indeed, to the examples given by Austin one might add the cretic and iambic sequence of *aeternitate temporum* and the glyconic effected by *nam multos ueterum uelut*. The phrase *superstes erit*, too, is a favourite pentameter ending of Ovid (*Am.* 1.15.42; *Her.* 9.148, 13.164; *Tr.* 1.2.44, 3.7.50), insistently in connection with an individual's *Nachleben* (as also at Mart. *Epigr.* 10.2.10, the only other prior attestation); but its position as the final words of the *Agricola* forges a positional connection with Ovid's claim to literary immortality at the close of *Amores* 1.[103] This is a conclusion 'woven out of commonplaces', then, but also one in which there are certain stand-out features. Its specified interest in memory and oblivion is thematised in a wash of literary association that reinforces Tacitus' valorisation of the commemorative power of literature. The result, almost paradoxically, is a passage that is peculiarly memorable, as may be witnessed in its subtle reproduction by Pliny the Younger in his Tacitean eulogy for his surrogate father Verginius Rufus (*Ep.* 2.1).[104]

We might suspect that Tacitus was conscious of the subtle interplay between allusive borrowing and intertextual echo at the end of the *Agricola* because he puts borrowings to meaningful use elsewhere, too. At *Histories* 2.70, Vitellius visits the fields of Bedriacum near Cremona to review the site of his army's victory over Otho forty days previously (2.39–45); the passage is shot through with irony since, in the next book (3.15–29), Vitellius will suffer a reversal of his fortunes in his defeat by Vespasian's forces on the same site. This is a locale not just of Tacitean intratextuality, however, but of historiographical intertextuality more generally, since the visit to the scene of a battle is a *topos* in the genre (Sall. *Cat.* 61; Livy 22.51.5–9; Tac. *Ann.* 1.61–2; cf. Verg. *Aen.* 2.27–30; Stat. *Theb.* 12.22–37; Lucan 7.787–824, 9.961–99; Sil. *Pun.* 6.1–13). As Timothy Joseph has argued, this very topicality enables Tacitus to thematise the 'regressive repetitiveness' of Roman civil war in the year 69 CE.[105] The historian's insistence precisely here on verbs of viewing and recognition, on revisiting previously trodden *loci* and retracing footsteps, and on the pile-up of raw material exploits

---

[102] Austin 1939: 116, apparently referring to Mackail 1896: 211–12 on Virgilian allusion and prose rhythms in the 'peroratio' ('it anticipates in its cadences the language of the Vulgate and of the statelier mediaeval prose').
[103] See Smith 2002: 30–6.   [104] See Marchesi 2008: 189–99 and Whitton 2013: 80–3.
[105] Joseph 2012: 113–52, at 115. Also on 2.70 see Ash 2007: 270–6 *ad loc*.

## 5 Intertextuality

some of the most familiar metaliterary symbolism in a way that tropes the text's very conventionality into heightened thematic pertinence:

> Inde Vitellius Cremonam flexit et spectato munere Caecinae insistere Bedriacensibus campis ac uestigia recentis uictoriae lustrare oculis concupiuit, foedum atque atrox spectaculum. Intra quadragensimum pugnae diem lacera corpora, trunci artus, putres uirorum equorumque formae, infecta tabo humus, protritis arboribus ac frugibus dira uastitas ... Aderant Valens et Caecina, monstrabantque pugnae locos: hinc inrupisse legionum agmen, hinc equites coortos, inde circumfusas auxiliorum manus: iam tribuni praefectique, sua quisque facta extollentes, falsa uera aut maiora uero miscebant. Vulgus quoque militum clamore et gaudio deflectere uia, spatia certaminum recognoscere, aggerem armorum, strues corporum intueri mirari; et erant quos uaria sors rerum lacrimaeque et misericordia subiret. At non Vitellius flexit oculos nec tot milia insepultorum ciuium exhorruit: laetus ultro et tam propinquae sortis ignarus instaurabat sacrum dis loci. (Tac. *Hist.* 2.70)

> From there Vitellius turned to Cremona and, after watching Caecina's games, conceived a desire to stand on the fields of Bedriacum and survey with his own eyes what was left of the recent victory. A foul and frightful sight it was, nearly forty days since the battle – the mangled bodies, the severed limbs, the rotting shapes of men and horses, the ground infected with disease, the crushed trees and terrible devastation of crops ... Valens and Caecina were there, pointing out spots on which the battle was fought: here the legionary column had burst in, here the cavalry got involved, there the auxiliary troops encircled. Now the tribunes and prefects, each extolling their own deeds, were mixing fiction and fact, or rather amplified fact. The common soldiers, too, turned off from the road with whoops of joy and recognised the scene of their fight, gazing and marvelling at the pile of weapons, the heaps of bodies; and some were struck by the vicissitudes of life's lot, its tears and pity. But Vitellius did not avert his eyes or shudder at so many thousands of unburied citizens; happy, even, and so ignorant of his imminent lot, he offered sacrifice to the gods of the place.

Within this intertextual wasteland, a case can be put – as at the end of the *Agricola* – for more specific reminiscences. In particular, Vitellius' desire to survey all with his eyes (*lustrare oculis*) and failure to bury the dead makes him a would-be Caesar, the monster whom Lucan had portrayed breakfasting at the site of the Battle of Pharsalus and savouring his inability to see the ground for all the carnage heaped upon it (7.794–5 *iuuat Emathiam non cernere terram | et lustrare oculis campos sub clade latentes*). Epic repetition also takes the reader back to an eerie *locus classicus* for the battle-site visit: with ominous implications for Vitellius' insouciant soldiers, the series of deictics (*hinc ... hinc ... inde*) is reminiscent of the Trojans' survey of the deserted Greek camp in *Aeneid* 2 (27–30 *iuuat ire et Dorica castra | desertosque uidere locos litusque relictum: | hic Dolopum manus, hic saeuus tendebat Achilles; | classibus hic locus, hic acie certare solebant*, 'it is a delight to go and see the Doric encampment, the abandoned stations and deserted shore: here Dolopian bands, here cruel Achilles pitched camp; here was the site of their fleet, here they used to fight us in battle').[106] For some Virgilian readers the phrase *sors rerum lacrimaeque* recalls Aeneas' famously ambivalent reception of stories from the Epic Cycle depicted on Dido's Temple of Juno in *Aeneid* 1 (462 *'Sunt lacrimae rerum'*).[107] If that phrase comes to mind, as it seems to do for the more sentimental among Vitellius' troops (*subiret*), it makes a commonplace of the Virgilian passage in which Aeneas wonders where on earth (*Aen.* 1.459 *'Quis iam locus . . . ?'*) has not heard the stories of the cyclical narratives that, like the protagonists in Tacitus' *Histories*, he now recognises and will shortly replay. As at the end of the *Agricola*, then, so here in the *Histories* Tacitus' reader finds the movement between generalised and specific intertextualities – between code and exemplary models, as it were – troped in a range of metaphors that, necessarily, cannot be the reserve of poetic texts.

Poetological double-speak will come naturally to those who recognise allusion as itself a kind of metaphor in which the surface meaning of the text (the tenor) takes on an added dimension through its connection to a term in another semantic network (the vehicle).[108] For students of Latin literature this manoeuvre has the advantage of locating intertextuality within the categories of classical rhetoric.[109] There are many passages of ancient rhetorical discussion that lend themselves to analysis in this way, but one that stands out in the present connection is Cicero's description of the orator Marcus Calidius, from which a quotation serves as this chapter's second epigraph (Cic. *Brut.* 274). Here Cicero explicitly cites Lucilius when comparing Calidius' flowing style to a well-composed mosaic (*tamquam in uermiculato emblemate*) in which no element appears out of place, so much so that even in his metaphors the proper meanings of words did not so much invade an alien context as migrate into their own (*non inruisse in alienum locum sed immigrasse in suum*). If metaphor functions through intertextuality (which is also to say that intertextuality is analogous to metaphor), it is striking that Cicero thinks of the process in

---

[106] Ash 2007: 274 *ad loc.*; Joseph 2012: 149–50.   [107] Ash 2007: 275 *ad loc.*; Joseph 2012: 150–1.
[108] Ben-Porat 1976, esp. pp. 116–21; Conte 1986: 38, 52–7 (cf. Conte 1974: 13–14, 30–5). For further discussion in relation to late antique intertextuality, see Pelttari 2014: 118–21.
[109] See Plett 1999. For other aspects of ancient rhetorical interest in intertextual mimesis, see D'Ippolito 2000.

terms of what is 'alien' and 'immigrant' – themselves metaphors that, as such, are examples of what is to be admired in Calidius. All the more striking, therefore, is Cicero's explicit reuse of Lucilius' mosaic as a further comparand for these stylistic qualities. In this case, too, Cicero has integrated into a new context a metaphor that for Lucilius seems to have meant something rather different: elsewhere Cicero and Quintilian make it clear that Lucilius, not without satirical double standards, used the mosaic analogy to criticise the non-integrative use of Greek lexis in Latin (fr. 84–5 W. *quam lepide lexis compostae ut tesserulae omnes | arte pauimento atque emblemate uermiculato*, 'how charmingly is his *lexis* composed, artfully like all the little squares in a floor's wavy mosaic'),[110] and indeed this is how the analogy is generally employed in a tradition that continued into the Renaissance.[111] From the present passage alone, however, it would be difficult to infer that Cicero has tendentiously misappropriated the Lucilian mosaic. Only with the allusion activated do we appreciate that the mosaic now functions as a positive metaphor not so much for Calidius' flowing style as for Cicero's skill in effecting its seamless immigration into the alien context of the *Brutus*; at the same time, through a kind of intertextual seepage, it also functions as a backhand satire of Calidius, shortly to be confirmed in Cicero's follow-up critique of the orator's inability to move his audience.

For structuralist theories of intertextuality, it may be instructive that Cicero's cross-reference to Lucilius' metaphor, though explicitly footnoted, still entails a disruption to the surface meaning of his text. Conte compares the self-reflexively annotated allusion to simile rather than to metaphor on the grounds that it does not integrate the source with the target text, but the present example shows the potential of the source still to turn around the meaning of its target and so to function as a trope in the same way as allusion does. In this passage, then, the surface discussion of rhetorical tropes draws its energy from a pointed use of allusion and intertextuality. For poststructural theories of intertextuality, too, it is also instructive that Ciceronian intertextuality here dovetails with a theorisation of metaphor. In strongly reader-orientated accounts of the parity of allusion and intertextuality, the analogy with metaphor has been challenged on the grounds that metaphor cannot fly below the radar of a reader's consciousness, whereas allusion and, *a fortiori*, intertextuality might well go undetected.[112] On Cicero's analysis, however, it might be

---

[110] On Lucilius' Greek see Chahoud 2004.
[111] MacPhail 2014: 92–115. See also Fitzgerald 2016: 70–3 on the mosaic as a figure for variety. Hardie 2019: 223–49 treats the limits of applying mosaic imagery to a specifically late antique intertextuality.
[112] Edmunds 2001: 165–6, concluding (p. 166) that 'at best, metaphor is a metaphor for intertextuality'.

countered that much of the language we use is metaphorical in a way that goes unobserved (e.g. in this sentence, 'observation' employs a metaphor of seeing to denote a cognitive process of deduction), such that language use in general, both allusive and intertextual, may be said to carry terms across a semantic gap in the same way as metaphor does. As for Lucilius as impure purist, then, so for Cicero as orator and theorist what matters is mobilising intertextuality and signalling its presence by troping the trope.

## Cento Writing, Compilation and Typological Interpretation

As indicated by the translation movement in Latin literature, historical differences in writing and interpretation have changed how intertextuality was practised and understood over time. In the case of literary models, historical trends are obvious, but also crucial: the subjective counter-historical move of reading Virgil as alluding to Statius has been possible only for those of us who were born after the *Thebaid*; likewise, we now read the *Aeneid* differently because of the input of an entire range of modern poets including Seamus Heaney. As new texts come into existence and old ones fade from view, perspectives shift and certain sensible changes emerge in the web of potential intertexts. In this section, the Latin centos, attitudes to compilation and typological interpretations will serve as examples of how intertextuality has been reshaped by broader trends in literature and writing.

Homeric and Virgilian centos developed from parodic quotations (e.g. Petronius, *Satyrica* 111–12) and mock epic (e.g. *The Battle of the Frogs and the Mice*).[113] Despite the ubiquity of parody, we do not hear anything about centos as such until the second century CE, and that would seem to be the time that Greek and Latin poets first began to write free-standing poems out of the lines and half-lines of their most canonical authors.[114] Twelve of the sixteen surviving ancient centos were collected in Africa in the sixth century and transmitted in the *Codex Salmasianus*, and only two of those are accompanied by any authorial attribution (the *Iudicium Paridis* of Mavortius and the *Epithalamium Fridi* of Luxurius). Of the other four extant centos, Ausonius' *Cento nuptialis* has been well studied, because of the prominence of the poet, his theoretical reflections on cento writing and the explicit sex scene at the end of the poem.[115] The *Cento Probae*, written

---

[113] McGill 2005: xvi–xxv.
[114] See Schottenius Cullhed 2015: 1–2; and Pelttari 2014: 96–8, with further bibliography.
[115] For discussion and further bibliography, see McGill 2005: 92–114, Hinds 2014: 190–6 and Elsner 2017: 178–81.

## 5 Intertextuality

most likely by Faltonia Betitia Proba in the 350s or 360s, is the longest and most ambitious of the centos.[116] The other two, on Christian themes, have separate transmissions.[117] Depending on broader cultural trends, the status of cento writing has risen and fallen over the centuries.[118] Not surprisingly, the cento's stock has soared in recent years with the advent of poststructuralism and the surge of scholarship on intertextuality.[119]

The *Cento Probae* may serve to demonstrate the theoretical questions at stake in understanding such a creative form of textual dismemberment. In terms of its composition, the poem is almost entirely a patchwork of Virgilian quotations. As for its purpose, there is little to support the sometimes prominent idea that Proba wrote the cento as an educational text for her children and as a response to Julian's edict preventing Christians from teaching mythological poetry.[120] In a brisk 694 lines, the poet recounts creation, several stories from the Jewish scriptures and the life, death and resurrection of Jesus. The originality and ambition of Proba's work would have been remarkable no matter how she composed her poem. It is, after Juvencus' *Four Books of the Gospels*, only the second of the so-called scriptural epics. As for the narrative, Proba adapts scripture in some surprising ways, including a re-arrangement of the days of creation and having Mary rather than Joseph visited by an angel warning of Herod's persecution.[121] She describes the goal of the poem in its proem, in which she invokes God the Father and God the Son to assist her labour and, with a self-reflexive nod to the scriptures and almost explicit reference to Moses, sets the stage for her gentle revisions of the Genesis story:

> O pater, o hominum rerumque aeterna potestas,
> da facilem cursum atque animis inlabere nostris,
> tuque ades inceptumque una decurre laborem,
> nate patris summi, uigor et caelestis origo,
> quem primi colimus meritosque nouamus honores,
> iam noua progenies, omnis quem credidit aetas.
> Nam memini ueterum uoluens monumenta uirorum
> Musaeum ante omnes uestrum cecinisse per orbem
> quae sint, quae fuerint, quae mox uentura trahantur.
> (*Cento Probae* 29–37)

---

[116] See Clark and Hatch 1981, Bažil 2009: 115–97, Sineri 2009 and Schottenius Cullhed 2015.
[117] Bažil 2009: 204–23.
[118] Bažil 2009: 17–42 and 231–42; and Schottenius Cullhed 2015: 56–81.
[119] Ground-breaking scholarship includes Desbordes 1979, Salanitro 1981 and Polara 1989. Recent work on the centos by prominent classicists includes Hardie 2007, Hinds 2014 and Elsner 2017.
[120] Schottenius Cullhed 2015: 18–55.   [121] Ibid. 137–88.

> O Father, power eternal of matter and humans,
> give an easy path and descend to our mind;
> and you, the high Father's son, our strength and source
> from heaven, come and together run the labour begun.
> We worship you first, and renew deserved honours;
> now is the new progeny in whom every age has believed.
> For I remember, unrolling the records of ancient men,
> that Musaeus sang, before all others in your world,
> of what is, what has been and what is brought soon to arrive.

Musaeus, the legendary Greek singer whom Virgil had set head and shoulders above his peers in the Elysian fields (*Aen.* 6.667–8), is a cipher for the Hebrew lawgiver Moses. In fact, several of the manuscripts offer variations of *Mosaeum* and *Moysen* in place of the name from the Virgilian hypotext. Although modern editors and scholars have preferred *Musaeum*, most of them take it as a direct reference to Moses via antonomasia.[122] However, the Greek singer should not be dismissed so very hastily, because the confusion of Moses and Musaeus was a powerful form of cultural appropriation. Both Jewish and Christian partisans claimed that Hebraic literature and wisdom were the source of Greek literature and wisdom, and even that Musaeus was the son of Moses, or a variant for him.[123] In this case, Proba would be suggesting that the mythological source of Greek poetry was only a half-forgotten memory of the author of the Hebrew Pentateuch, and Proba's introduction of Musaeus in place of Moses would then be a daring and outrageous attempt to rewrite Greek mythology. Either way, Proba proclaims the priority of her source (*ante omnes*), and she goes on to tell her version of the creation story on the basis of the Mosaic accounts in the book of Genesis, which latterly removes Musaeus from contention as the source for her poetic authority. A destabilising reminder of who was silenced in order to authorise Proba's claim to power lingers in the interplay between Musaeus and Moses.

While focusing on Proba's claims for the priority of her source, we skipped over line 35, which sets the poet's memory against the records of ancient men.[124] By ignoring for as long as possible that each of the lines and half-lines in this passage are taken from Virgil, we have conspired with Proba in her claims to authority. What difference does it make that Proba's text is woven out of pre-existent words and phrases? Naturally, it need not make any difference: although the text can be read as a cento only when its

---

[122] See Schottenius Cullhed 2015: 128–9; and for further references Sineri 2009.
[123] Buchheit 1988.
[124] Regarding an author's 'own voice', cf. Sharrock in this volume, pp. 161–72.

Virgilian hypotext is recognised, Proba is perfectly legible and even provocative on her own.[125] Thus, when Proba says 'I remember' (*nam memini*), there is no sound basis on which to deny her voice as being fully and truly her own. As a radically secondary kind of writing, however, cento poetry demonstrates the strange alchemy that takes place when a text is identified as an intertext. Proba found *nam memini* in *Aen.* 8.157, in a passage in which Evander remembers once meeting Anchises; the second half of her line (*ueterum uoluens monumenta uirorum*) comes from *Aen.* 3.102, in which Anchises recalls his ancestral history. Both halves of the line are self-reflexive annotations, and for good reason: Anchises and Evander are ancestral voices and they are the ones providing Proba with the words to express her own Mosaic authority. In acknowledging her debt to Virgil, Proba confirms these lines of filiation and paternity; Proba reverses those lines when she speaks new meaning into Virgil's old words, thereby claiming the right to be a mosaic poet of tessellated fragments. Rather than simply borrowing vocabulary, Proba accomplishes the interpenetration of two different systems of signs – scriptural and mythological – along with all of the attendant differences in values and points of view that they imply. Her poem is intertextual in every sense of the word.

As for the Virgilian hypotext, a cento that is recognised as a cento invites readings in which every single word is seen as meaningful, even though we might suspect that many were chosen without particular regard for the precise context of their source. An identification of the Virgilian source for each phrase demonstrates the range of possibilities within a fully intertextual poem:

O pater, o hominum rerumque aeterna potestas, (*Aen.* 10.18)
da facilem cursum atque (*G.* 1.40) animis inlabere nostris, (*Aen.* 3.89)
tuque ades inceptumque una decurre laborem, (*G.* 2.39)
nate patris summi, (*Aen.* 1.665) uigor et caelestis origo, (*Aen.* 6.730)
quem primi colimus (*Aen.* 11.786) meritosque nouamus honores, (*Aen.* 8.189)
iam noua progenies, (*Ecl.* 4.7) omnis quem credidit aetas. (*Aen.* 7.680)
Nam memini (*Aen.* 8.157) ueterum uoluens monumenta uirorum (*Aen.* 3.102)
Musaeum ante omnes (*Aen.* 6.667) uestrum cecinisse (*Ecl.* 10.70) per orbem (*Aen.* 1.457)[126]
quae sint, quae fuerint, quae mox uentura trahantur. (*G.* 4.393)

(*Cento Probae* 29–37)

---

[125] On the broader point, see Pelttari 2014: 98–101. The literary status of the cento text is neatly confirmed by a growing number of parallels identified as likely allusions to these secondary texts, for which see McGill 2005: 104–5, Green 2008: 270–2, Bažil 2009: 209–18 and Schottenius Cullhed 2015: 60 and 84–5.

[126] The same phrase appears at line-end in *Ecl.* 8.9, *G.* 1.231, *G.* 1.505, *Aen.* 1.602, *Aen.* 10.783, *Aen.* 11.257 and *Aen.* 11.694. Which, if any, is the hypotext? The question is not rhetorical.

Some of these phrases are more meaningful when their source is recognised, and in others the intertextual source seems entirely inert – it guarantees only that Proba will be read as a secondary author, always mediating between Virgil and the scriptures and never allowed to be her own beginning. To be sure, identifying such non-referential allusions is slippery business (not least when Proteus is in view!), and an interpretable link could always be discovered. Nevertheless, some lines almost advertise their lack of referentiality, the implication being that they were taken without a shadow of concern for their original context. As Scott McGill says, 'Many units in centos are simply too unrelated to the Virgilian contexts from which they derive to generate allusive meaning.'[127] For example, our appreciation of Proba's poem is not much improved by recognising the precise source of the questions in line 37, a passage from near the end of the *Georgics* in which Cyrene teaches Aristaeus about Proteus, who can provide the truth of all things. On the other end of the spectrum, *iam noua progenies* is one of the most recognisable half-lines in all of Virgil; it was even more familiar in late antiquity when Christians were interpreting the fourth Eclogue as a prophecy of the birth of Christ.[128] The contrast between such lines should be seen as part of the game: cento poetry derives a dynamic force from the interplay between apparently inert borrowings and borrowings so obvious that they almost overwhelm the text.

Despite Proba's decision to write as a cento poet, the first lines of her poem are written in her own voice and about herself; only in line 24 does she begin in the full centonic style.[129] The very first words of the poem refer to some now distant past (*Iam dudum* . . .) in which she previously wrote martial poetry; this is something that she now confesses as a mistake. Then, after some criticisms of fame and a *recusatio* of the Aonian Muses (14 *nec libet Aonio de uertice ducere Musas*), Proba announces her beginning with

---

[127] McGill 2005: 26. Hinds asks a rhetorical question along the same lines: 'If some (perhaps the majority) of the recycled phrases reuse Virgilian language in ways that seem to have nothing to do with the original Virgilian context, does that mean that instances where there does seem to be a meaningful engagement with Virgilian context should be seen as mere chance occurrences?' (Hinds 2014: 174). Both McGill and Hinds grapple with Hinds' earlier provocative claim that there is ultimately no such thing as 'a wholly non-negotiable confluence, no such thing as zero-interpretability' (Hinds 1998: 34). On the apparent phenomenon of non-referential allusions in Latin poetry more broadly, see Pelttari 2014: 115–60.

[128] Schottenius Cullhed 2015, 127; and Ziolkowski and Putnam 2008, 487–503.

[129] On the beginning of this poem, see Green 1997.

a series of lines that gradually transition into a continuous cento – insofar as his verses allow, the poet will begin to speak through Virgil:

Hinc[130] canere incipiam (*G.* 1.5). *Praesens, Deus,*[131] erige mentem: (Lucan 8.76)
*Vergilium cecinisse loquar pia* munera Christi (Juvenc. 1.439[132]).
Rem nulli obscuram (*Aen.* 11.343) repetens ab origine pergam, (*Aen.* 1.372)
si qua fides animo,[133] (*Aen.* 3.434) *si uera* infusa per artus (*Aen.* 6.726)
mens agitat molem et *toto*[134] se corpore miscet (*Aen.* 6.727)
spiritus (*Aen.* 6.726) *et* quantum non noxia corpora tardant (*Aen.* 6.731)
terrenique hebetant artus moribundaque membra. (*Aen.* 6.732)
(*Cento Probae* 22–8)

From here will I begin to sing. Be present, God, raise my mind:
I will say that Virgil sang the holy deeds of Christ.
Material known to all will I go through, resuming from the beginning,
if my mind has any confidence, if a true thought is spread
through my limbs and moves their mass and the spirit is infused
in the whole body and insofar as guilty bodies do not cause delay
or earthly limbs cause dullness or mortal members.

Proba's claim that she will begin from the beginning of the story (creation) is already contradicted by her explanation that she will be speaking of Virgil. Her assertion that Virgil sang of Christ enacts her power to bend the text according to her own interpretation. Her appropriation of Lucan and Juvencus demonstrates that her desire to write a cento does not preclude serious engagement with the entire literary tradition. These movements reveal her literary ambition, but her doubts as to the adequacy of her body point to the tension at the heart of intertextuality. She turns to her body and her confidence precisely at the moment when she begins to borrow Virgil's lines – hardly an accident given that the limbs and bodies she mentions are a metapoetic nod to the Virgilian fragments of which her poem subsists.[135] In her hesitancy and doubts about her physical members, Proba expresses the possibility that those fragments might dull her message and delay her spirit. And yet these lines come from the passage in *Aeneid* 6 in which Anchises explains to Aeneas how souls are purified in the afterlife from their bodily imperfections. While the cento poet acknowledges the

---

[130] Fittingly enough, some corruption in line 20 obscures whether Proba will find holy inspiration in the Castalian font, or by rejecting it.
[131] The typography follows that in the edition of Schottenius Cullhed, in which the regular distinction is reversed so that italics indicate the words *without* a known hypotext.
[132] The same phrase appears at line-end in Juvenc. 2.361 and 2.381, and as a textual variant in 4.148.
[133] *Animum* in the hypotext.   [134] *Magno* in the hypotext.
[135] For this interpretation, see Bažil 2009: 121, Hinds 2014: 187–8 and Schottenius Cullhed 2015: 126.

tension between her text and its source, that tension is already inscribed in the source as the residual imperfections imprinted upon a soul by its body. Despite Proba's best efforts at appropriation, the intertext retains its material and bodily presence, with the risk of importing also its original context and meaning.

As an extreme form of intertextuality, the cento allows the author to reflect on his or her own status as an author. Proba uses Virgil's words to make claims for her own authority in her proem, in a proem in the middle (333–45) and in her epilogue (687–94). By way of contrast, Ausonius flamboyantly declares that his lascivious cento was enough to bring disgrace upon Virgil, and he apologises in an epistolary preface for writing his epithalamium in such a manner:

> Piget equidem Vergiliani carminis dignitatem tam ioculari dehonestasse materia. (Auson. *Cento, Ausonius Paulo sal.*)
>
> Distasteful indeed to have brought dishonour upon the worthiness of the Virgilian poem with such light-hearted material.

Because intertextuality operates within a synchronic field, the centonist can claim to dishonour Virgil with a playful poem that undermines his authorial sovereignty. Whether in self-reflexive references to their own treatment of Virgil or in pronouncements of their own authority, Proba and Ausonius reveal their understanding that cento poetry raised serious questions about how poetic authority functions within a fully intertextual world.

The ludic complexity of cento writing underlines a broader trend current in late antiquity, namely a more open acceptance of compilation as an artistic mode of composition. In the preface to his *Saturnalia* and in his appreciation of Virgil's reuse of Greek and Latin material, Macrobius displays a very generous attitude to textual reuse.[136] Isidore, the encyclopaedist and renowned hoarder of information, was more concerned with the final literary product than with its composition. His definition of *compilator* takes the sting out of a word that had been levelled as a charge against Virgil:

> *Conpilator*, qui aliena dicta suis praemiscet sicut solent pigmentarii in pila diuersa mixta contundere. Hoc scelere quondam accusabatur Mantuanus ille uates cum quosdam uersus Homeri transferens suis permiscuisset et conpilator ueterum ab aemulis diceretur. Ille respondit: 'Magnarum esse uirium clauam Herculi extorquere de manu.' (*Etymologiae* 10.44)

---

[136] Pelttari 2014: 25–32, with further references.

Compiler, one who mixes someone else's words with his own, just as paint-sellers grind together different mixtures in a bowl. That Mantuan poet was once accused of this atrocity when he transferred some of Homer's verses and mixed them together with his own and he was called a compiler of the ancients by the jealous. He responded: 'To tear the club of Hercules out from his hand is a matter of great strength.'[137]

'Atrocity' (*scelere*) is melodramatic, presumably because Isidore is ventriloquising this charge through the voice of Virgil's detractors. The example of the artist surely implies no negative judgement, and the parallelism of *suis praemiscet* and *suis permiscuisset* makes it clear that Isidore is presenting Virgil himself as a compiler.[138] While no one would deny that Virgil was the better craftsman, Isidore even allows a certain comparison between the work of the Mantuan poet and his own encyclopaedic compendium, which would of course be cited as an authoritative text for centuries to come. The fact that its being a compilation did not detract in any way from the perceived quality of Isidore's work indicates that intertextuality was regarded as fundamental to writing, rather than as a threat to the unity of the text. In this context, Martin Irvine observed that Isidore's compilation demonstrates how intertextuality functions within communities:

> The compiler sets up a dialogue between prior texts and the interpretive discourse of his own community, isolating or bringing into focus a pattern in the larger network of texts that forms the library. In short, the notion of the *compilator* opens up the question of the intertextual dimensions of writing, both the awareness of this principle by medieval writers and readers themselves and the historical conditions for writing and interpretation that function impersonally and unconsciously.[139]

In general, encyclopaedic collections of knowledge are emblematic of the urge to catalogue and categorise every possible link between known semiotic systems; they derive from the desire to provide a complete map of intertextuality.[140]

In response to accusations that Virgil plagiarised and stole lines from Homer, his defenders have almost always explained that his adaptations were creative and not merely passive borrowings.[141] Thus, with a nod to

---

[137] The wording of Isidore's line apparently derives from Jerome, *Liber quaestionum Hebraicarum in Genesim, praef.* (*CCSL* 72, 1), a passage in which Jerome compares himself to Terence and Virgil to duck malicious charges of plagiarism. The *VSD* (46) reports that Virgil's comment was transmitted by Asconius Pedianus, and Macrobius offers a similar line in *Sat.* 5.3.16.
[138] *pace* Hathaway 1989.    [139] Irvine 1994: 241–2.
[140] On encyclopaedism as it relates to antiquity, see König and Woolf 2013.
[141] On the so-called *obtrectatores Vergilii*, see Ziolkowski and Putnam 2008: 485–6.

Auerbach's work on early Christian figural interpretation, Knauer described Virgil's use of Homer as typological in nature.[142] In general, ancient schools of thought would describe apparently meaningful intertextual relations via allegory or other similar physical explanations. Platonist allegory developed the idea of the symbol as a way to mediate between related texts and an alleged ultimate referent.[143] Stoic models of allegory regarded texts as linked by virtue of their being diverse instantiations of the same essential sayables (*lekta*).[144] Epicurean and Lucretian materialism saw texts and contexts, letters and atoms, as infinite and mutable realities in a co-ordinate and explicable system.[145] Pythagorean ideas of reincarnation would describe poetic memory as a kind of absent presence.[146] As an outworking of their appropriation of the Jewish scriptures, Christians developed typological interpretation as a method of linking the Old and the New Testament, so that a type would be read as the shadow or prefiguration of its fulfilment: for example, forerunners of Christ were seen as finding their fulfilment in his coming.[147] The beginning of Jerome's commentary on Isaiah 7:14 shows the variety of connections that could be created with this kind of intertextual reading:

> PROPTEREA DABIT DOMINUS IPSE VOBIS SIGNUM. ECCE VIRGO CONCIPIET ET PARIET ET VOCABIS NOMEN EIUS EMMANUEL Nequaquam multifarie iuxta apostolum Paulum et multis modis loquetur Deus (cf. Heb. 1:1), nec iuxta alium prophetam in manibus prophetarum assimilabitur (cf. Hosea 12:10); sed qui ante loquebatur per alios, dicet ipse: adsum. De quo et sponsa rogabat in Cantico Canticorum: *Osculetur me osculis oris sui* (Song of Sol. 1:2). *Dominus* enim *uirtutum ipse est rex gloriae* (Ps. 24:10). Ipse descendet in uterum uirginalem et ingredietur et egredietur orientalem portam quae semper clausa est (cf. Ezek. 44:1–2); de qua Gabriel dicit ad uirginem: *Spiritus sanctus ueniet super te, et uirtus Altissimi obumbrabit te; propterea quod nascetur in te sanctum, uocabitur Filius Dei* (Luke 1:35). Et in Prouerbiis: *Sapientia aedificauit sibi domum* (Prov. 9:1). (Jerome, *In Esaiam* 3, 7.14 = *CCSL* 73A, 102–3)
>
> THEREFORE THE LORD HIMSELF WILL GIVE YOU A SIGN. BEHOLD, A YOUNG WOMAN SHALL CONCEIVE AND BEAR

---

[142] Knauer 1964a: 354–9 and 1964b: 81–4; see also Hardie 2019: 209 n. 63. Barchiesi 1984 (= 2015 in English) was essential for demonstrating how imitation is a communicative strategy in the *Aeneid*. Auerbach 1944 is the beginning of modern scholarship on figural/typological interpretation.

[143] Lamberton 1986, Struck 2004.   [144] See especially Long 1992.

[145] The seminal study of Lucretian 'atomology' is Friedländer 1941, arguing that different kinds of wordplay in the *De rerum natura* instantiate the natural connection between signifier and signified. From a large bibliography see especially Armstrong 1995, Schiesaro 1994 and, for an overview, Volk 2002: 100–5.

[146] Hardie 2002: 81–97.   [147] Dawson 2002.

A SON, AND YOU SHALL CALL HIS NAME IMMANUEL. By no means will God speak in many and various ways as according to the apostle Paul (cf. Heb. 1:1); nor as another prophet says will he speak in parables through the prophets (cf. Hosea 12:10); but he who previously spoke through others will himself say, I am present. Concerning whom the bride also pleaded in the Song of Songs: 'He will kiss me with the kisses of his mouth' (Song of Sol. 1:2). For the Lord of virtues he is the king of glory (Ps. 24:10). He will himself descend into the virgin's womb and will enter and exit the eastern gate that has always been closed (cf. Ezek. 44:1–2); concerning her, Gabriel says to the virgin, 'The Holy Spirit will come over you, and the power of the Most High will overshadow you. Therefore, the one to be born in you will be holy; he will be called the Son of God' (Luke 1:35). And in Proverbs, 'Wisdom has built her house' (Prov. 9:1).

The first two references provide justification for Jerome's associative reading of the Hebrew scriptures. The following three citations are meant to show that Christ's advent was expected, glorious and miraculous. The passage from the angel's message to Mary justifies reading the Jewish prophecies as references to a virgin birth. The last passage is a gloss on the Hebrew name Emmanuel, which Jerome had just explained means 'God with us'. Christian interpreters would justify such readings on the basis of their belief that the human authors of scripture were all speaking as mouthpieces of one divine author.[148] Nevertheless, such interpretations were controlled by a reader's understanding of the ultimate goal (*skopos*) of the text. Augustine, for example, defined the *skopos* of scripture as charity, and so this was the ultimate rule that would determine whether he could accept any given interpretation.[149] In this way, interpreters recognised the possibility that intertexts would proliferate without end, and they sought to control against that potential by imposing some definite external limit.

The Christian poet Prudentius demonstrates in a short passage the prospective bounty of proliferating intertextuality. In *Liber apotheosis* 376–80, Prudentius says that Hebrew, Greek and Roman literature are all now tuned to praise Christ.[150] He gives an example of what he means by writing an ecstatic prayer in which almost every word derives from classical sources:

> O nomen praedulce mihi, lux et decus et spes
> praesidiumque meum, requies o certa laborum,
> blandus in ore sapor, flagrans odor, inriguus fons,
> castus amor, pulchra species, sincera uoluptas!     (Prud. *Apoth.* 393–6)

---

[148] Augustine, *De doctrina Christiana* 3.27 (38) and *Conf.* 12.31.42.
[149] Augustine, *De doctrina Christiana* 1.35–8 (39–42).
[150] For a full discussion of this passage, see Heinz 2007: 121–41.

> O name so sweet to me, *light* and *honour* and *hope*
> and *my fortress*, o *certain rest from labours*,
> you're a pleasing *taste in my mouth*, an ardent odour, *a watery fount*,
> *my chaste love*, pleasing beauty, *pure pleasure*!

The phrase *nomen … praedulce mihi* recalls Valerius Flaccus 4.161 (the phrase *dulce decus meum* also appears with *praesidium* in the second line of Horace's first *Ode*, which addresses Maecenas as patron). In the same line, Prudentius takes *o, lux* and *spes* from *Aeneid* 2.281, where Aeneas addresses Hector in a dream. At *Aeneid* 3.393, a line discussed above in reference to Juvenal, Helenus tells Aeneas that he will found his new city in Italy and that *requies ea certa laborum*. At *Georgics* 4.277, Virgil describes a flower (the purple Italian starwort) as having an *asper in ore sapor*. An *inriguus fons* appears at *Georgics* 4.32, although it is in the accusative case in that line. The exact phrase *castus amor* shows up in one of Ambrose's hymns (4.15), a poem by Paulinus of Nola (27.623) and also one of Maximianus' elegies (3.66); these four passages together might point to an earlier, shared poetic source. The phrase *sincera uoluptas* appears in Ovid *Metamorphoses* 7.453. Given all of these parallels, it is reasonable to think that *flagrans odor* and *pulchra species* (the only two phrases unaccounted for) also derived from one poetic source or another, and the intense religious fervour of these lines only underscores the gap between Prudentius' statements and the original contexts of the phrases repurposed. By praying in such language, Prudentius demonstrates his ability to link any two passages of Latin poetry.

Confronted with such endless proliferation, Christian interpreters sought to limit the intertextual field, as did commentators on Virgil's poetry. Servius' formulation of the *intentio* (*skopos*) of the *Aeneid* in the introduction to his commentary is well known: Virgil meant to imitate Homer and praise Augustus through his ancestors (*Intentio Vergilii haec est, Homerum imitari et Augustum laudare a parentibus*, Serv. *Aen.*, *praef.*). The implications and practical utility of setting such a limit ought to be just as well known.[151] Servius' definition is the only justification for any number of interpretations in his commentary, for example his note on *Aeneid* 12.940–1:[152]

> CVNCTANTEM FLECTERE SERMO COEPERAT omnis intentio ad Aeneae pertinet gloriam: nam et ex eo quod hosti cogitat parcere, pius

---

[151] On the preliminary questions addressed before studying philosophical texts in antiquity, see Mansfeld 1994.
[152] For the ideological implications of this note, see Thomas 2001: 111–12.

ostenditur, et ex eo quod eum interimit, pietatis gestat insigne: nam Euandri intuitu Pallantis ulciscitur mortem.

HIS SPEECH BEGAN TO BEND HIM [i.e. AENEAS] HESITATING. All of the intention is directed to the glory of Aeneas. For from his thinking about sparing the enemy, he is shown to be pious; and for killing him he bears a mark of piety. Indeed, from the viewpoint of Evander, he avenges the death of Pallas.

Every contradictory note is excluded from Servius' commentary because he has decided to shut out any model or voice that would not accord with his explanation of Virgil's intention. Such was one prominent reader's response to the endless possibilities presented by the intertextual field of Latin poetry.

## Technologies and Materialisms

The pleasure that comes in recognising a line of Virgil at, say, Trimalchio's villa or in a metrical Saint's Life or in Dylan's songbook is an experience that cuts through every mediation, aural, written or digital. All the same, the shape and texture of a source is part of its reception, which is the moment at which intertextuality is realised. By reconfiguring source criticism as the personal involvement of readers within the textual system, reception studies offer a framework for seeing the historical and material realities of intertextuality without reducing its power or pleasure. In other words, a turn in this last section towards materialism – bookrolls, codices, paratexts, hypertexts and algorithms – should not be confused with some return to a lifeless or inert source criticism.

Because texts are created, read and interpreted within communities, communities are essential for understanding the material realities within which Latin literature has been written and transmitted.[153] In his *Saturnalia*, Macrobius offers a prominent example of such a community. In this text, to which we have already had reason to refer, Macrobius captures the pleasure and the labour of textual scholarship – as such, he offers a kind of looking glass by which to view modern research on Latin intertextuality. In order to set the stage for his happy band of Virgilians to investigate their author's knowledge of Greek and Latin literature, Macrobius as Neoplatonist compares the work of Virgil to the profundity of the universe itself (*Sat.* 5.1.19). A short time later, we see them pulling out

---

[153] For discussion of 'interpretive communities' in the context of reading Latin poetry, see Martindale 1993: 15–16. For theorisations, see Fish 1980 and Stock 1990. For a practical study of reading communities in the second and third centuries CE, see Johnson 2010.

a copy of Virgil to study his Homeric borrowings. Their exchange captures the contingencies and tensions involved in any recognition of intertextuality:

> 'Perge quaeso,' inquit Auienus, 'omnia quae Homero subtraxit inuestigare. Quid enim suauius quam duos praecipuos uates audire idem loquentes? Quia cum tria haec ex aequo impossibilia putentur, uel Ioui fulmen uel Herculi clauam uel uersum Homero subtrahere, quod etsi fieri possent, alium tamen nullum deceret uel fulmen praeter Iouem iacere, uel certare praeter Herculem robore, uel canere quod cecinit Homerus: hic opportune in opus suum quae prior uates dixerat transferendo fecit ut sua esse credantur. Ergo pro uoto omnium feceris si cum hoc coetu communicata uelis quaecumque uestro noster poeta mutuatus est.'
> 'Cedo igitur,' Eustathius ait, 'Vergilianum uolumen, quia locos singulos eius inspiciens Homericorum uersuum promptius admonebor.' Cumque Symmachi iussu famulus de bibliotheca petitum librum detulisset, temere uoluit Eustathius ut uersus quos fors obtulisset inspiceret et, ... (Macrob. *Sat.* 5.3.16–17)

> 'Go on, please,' said Avienus, 'and track down all that he stole from Homer. For what is sweeter than to hear two outstanding poets saying the same thing? Indeed, these three things are considered equally impossible, either to steal from Jove his thunderbolt or from Hercules his club or from Homer a line; and even if it were possible, it would not be fitting for any other except Jove to cast his thunderbolt, or except Hercules to compete with his stick, or to sing what Homer sang. Nevertheless, this one, by aptly transferring into his own work what the prior poet had said, made it so that they were credibly his own. Therefore, you will do us all a favour if you should wish to communicate with this gathering all that our poet borrowed from yours.
> 'Hither then,' said Eustathius, 'with the Virgilian scroll. As I inspect its single passages, I will be reminded more readily of the Homeric verses.' And when, at Symmachus' order, the servant had brought the requested book from the library, he casually unrolled it so as to examine the verses presented by chance; and ...

In the following line, chance leads Eustathius to land on *Aeneid* 1.159–69, although Avienus quickly intervenes (5.4.1) to ask him to begin from the beginning, so that Macrobius can present Virgil's borrowings in a logical order. The element of chance derives from the humanness of the scene presented. Rather than offering a dispassionate treatise on Virgil's poetry, Macrobius constructs a dialogue full of polite remarks and gentle digressions. Evaluative and aesthetic language (*suauius, deceret*) sits alongside constructions of cultural identity ('our' Latin poet contrasted with 'your', i.e. Eustathius', Greek poet) and evidence of the power imbalances between this learned community, their slaves and the wider public. The notion that the two poets are saying the same thing (*idem loquentes*) begs the question of whether any two texts, much less one in Greek and another in Latin, say the same thing. Furthermore, Avienus' desire to hear and Eustathius' inspection of the text make their experiences into auditory and visual interactions. As for the copy of the *Aeneid* opened by Eustathius, it appears to be in the form of a bookroll, or at least such are the implications of *uolumen* and *uoluit*. In his Loeb translation, Kaster notes the incongruity of that phrasing: Eustathius' copy apparently held the entire poem; the book's leaves (*folia*) are mentioned very shortly below (5.4.1); and we would expect a codex because that format had become the norm by the end of the fourth century.[154] Macrobius' old-fashioned language mirrors the conservative and idealising nature of his literary dialogue, the dramatic date of which was fifty years or so prior to its composition around the early 430s. The reason that his characters talk about unrolling a text is that they are traditional figures; the dramatic setup is also just that, a setup. Eustathius' impressive feats of memory are neither the result of happy chance nor the product of the author's own memory. Whether in full or in part, Macrobius culled his knowledge of Virgil's debts from previous scholarly treatises and lists. Thus, books 5 and 6 of the *Saturnalia* are composed of long lists of passages from Virgil juxtaposed with Greek and Latin intertexts; important but succinct commentary and discussion between Macrobius' characters obscure, but do not conceal, the fact that much of this material must have come from previous scholarship, quite possibly from the treatises mentioned in *VSD* 44–6.[155] What else was Macrobius to do in the face of readers like Avienus who wanted to know *all* that Virgil took from Homer? In a remarkable twist (and as noted above), Macrobius' compilation has remained so prominent that Knauer fully cited it as one of the sources for his lists of parallels (see above p. 213). Scholarly attention, social embeddedness and literary reception are all reflected in Macrobius' banquet, which is to say that our own experiences of intertextuality will also reflect our expectations and the material conditions of our interactions with ancient texts.

The stratigraphy of the preceding passage suggests that the story of Latin textuality has more than a few twists and turns. Livius Andronicus must have found Homer in the voluble columns of a papyrus bookroll, the same medium in which he would have left his *Odysia*. It would be conceivable,

---

[154] Kaster 2011: II 245.
[155] On Macrobius' sources, see Kaster 2011: I xlv–liii, with further references.

therefore, to tell a story of Latin literature that ignored Homer's orality and Plato's Myth of Theuth. Indeed, as Latinists access text through reading, their consideration of intertextuality tends to overlook the auditory experience of texts through much of antiquity,[156] and as a result to ignore the many spoken voices still audible in Latin literature. Cicero's speeches, for example, are a vast repository of quotations and allusions, and the provenance of many of these from myth (e.g. the strategic pointers to Orpheus' fate in *Pro Archia*)[157] or the stage (e.g. the comic subplot constructed in *Pro Caelio*)[158] speaks volumes about intertextuality's independence of text in any narrow sense of that word. Sometimes still familiar are Latin *Sprichwörter*, many of which arise from popular philosophy or attract generally ethical affiliation.[159] The principle of justice encapsulated in the motto *suum cuique* ('to each his own'), popularised by Cicero (e.g. *Fin.* 5.23.65; *Leg.* 1.19; *Nat. D.* 3.38; *Off.* 1.15; *Rep.* 3.24), had a complicated biography long before its cynical recasting over the main gate of Buchenwald concentration camp as 'Jedem das Seine'. It withstood its entry into Roman satire in Persius (*Sat.* 5.53), but not in Petronius (40.7 *inde cum **suum cuique** iussisset referri Trimalchio, adiecit: 'etiam uidete, quam porcus ille siluaticus lotam comederit glandem'*, 'Then when Trimalchio had ordered to be served to each his own portion, he added: "See, too, what exquisite acorns that woodland pig has munched"'). From time to time modern readers are even allowed to hear (about) literature's intertextual vitality on the streets of Rome: Suetonius preserves what must be a representative sound-bite in his anecdote about Augustus dressing down a group of down-dressing Romans with an ironic citation of *Aeneid* 1.282 (*Aug.* 40.5 *'En, Romanos, rerum dominos, gentemque togatam!'*, '"Behold! 'Romans, masters of the world, the race of the toga'!"'). There may be more to this repartee than meets the eye if Jupiter's scion here restores to oral banter a phrase that, according to Macrobius (*Sat.* 6.5.15), Virgil derived from a mime of Decimus Laberius.[160] We next hear the Virgilian quip in a two-line epigram on Domitian's toga legislation in which Martial 'retweets' the famous phrase to Augustus' successor (*Epigr.* 14.124), but we will never know how many laughs (or groans) it raised in the intervening years of intertextual recall. If literary texts are liable to (re-)enter political discourse in this atomised way, the reverse is also true: political

---

[156] But scholarship on literacy no longer treats it as mutually exclusive from orality, as exemplified in the papers collected in Johnson and Parker 2009; a seminal work on sound-play in Latin poetry is Ahl 1985.
[157] Steele 2001: 93–5; Pierzak 2015.   [158] Leigh 2004.   [159] Otto 1890.
[160] For discussion, see Panayotakis 2010: 250–1 on fr. 28 and 254 on fr. 29.

slogans have a powerful intertextual vitality ('Forza Italia' converted stadia of football fans into affiliates of a political party, and vice versa). A surviving example from the late Republic is voiced in Virgil's first Eclogue in an exslave's explanation of the reason for his recent visit to the city of Rome: 'libertas' (*Ecl.* 1.27) is witnessed in numismatic and other sources as the watchword for both the Caesarian and Republican sides that clashed at Philippi, a dual claim that enables Virgil's first collection to hedge its bets in its political reception.[161]

The relationship between spoken and written textuality, between memory and monument, is foregrounded in Latin poetry sometimes as a tension or rivalry, sometimes as a collaboration and co-dependency.[162] Jupiter's prophecy of Roman predestination in *Aeneid* 1 reveals a powerful process of entextualising the spoken word (256 *fatur*, 258 *fata*, 261 *fabor*) into the *uolumen* of his and Virgil's written text: 261–2 *fabor enim* ... | *longius et uoluens fatorum arcana mouebo* ('For I will speak ... and unrolling further I will disclose fate's secrets'). Likewise, we have seen Anchises decoding the spoken word of Apollo in the manner of an antiquarian researcher, hinting at the archives that mediate Virgil's poem. The bookroll, with its remorseless series of columns, might at first seem unsuited to non-linear forms of reading or complex intertextuality; yet the acrostics,[163] paratexts[164] and stichometric allusions[165] that we find in Latin poems demonstrate in the most material of ways that texts were conceptualised as radically open assemblages of words. When Lucretius argues in *De rerum natura* 1 that the nature of the universe is spatially infinite, his universal textbook instantiates its argument in the physical continuity of the bookroll beyond a false *finale* in lines 921–50 (the poet's programmatic traversal of the 'trackless paths of the Muses' (*auia Pieridum*), lines repeated in the proem to book 4 as transmitted) into an extended new argument about, precisely, endlessness (952–3 *Nunc age, summai quaedam sit finis eorum* | *necne sit, euoluamus*, 'Come now, let us unroll whether there is an end to their [the atoms'] sum, or not').[166] When Jupiter scrolls through Rome's *imperium sine fine* in *Aeneid* 1, then, his prophecy is intertextual with the infinite *De rerum natura* both as text and text-artefact.

---

[161] See Cucchiarelli in Cucchiarelli and Traina 2012: 149–50 ad loc. [162] See Farrell 2009.
[163] Kronenberg 2018 and Hejduk 2018, both with further references.
[164] On paratextual games in Virgil, Tibullus and Propertius: see Schafer 2017, Wray 2003 and O'Rourke 2014.
[165] For stichometric allusions, see O'Rourke 2012, Lowe 2013 and Lowe 2014. For a late antique example, Claud. *Rapt.* 2.308–11 responds precisely to *Aen.* 6.309–12.
[166] See further O'Rourke 2020.

Lucretian atomism was reconfigured as Christian imperial panegyric by Publilius Optatianus Porfyrius on the pages of the book – surely a single quire codex – which he dedicated to Constantine in 326 and for which, unlike Ovid, he obtained recall from exile.[167] Each page of his book featured a separate poem, usually written on a grid within which individual letters outlined mimetic or symbolic shapes; as though to emphasise the boundless potential of his pages, his *Carmen* 25 eschews figural games in favour of a combinametric format by which the twenty words of the poem can be recombined in a seemingly endless variety of permutations. As demonstrated repeatedly by Optatian's poetry, the adoption of the codex facilitated the non-linear navigation of the text. Thus, although lists of headings had been in use in technical and didactic writing since the Hellenistic period, it was apparently users of the Christian scriptures who first made full use of a format for writing that enabled one to flip directly from one passage to another. Eusebius compiled his Canon tables in the early fourth century; these were lists of correspondences between the Gospels keyed to each paragraph via a complex paratextual apparatus.[168] Each paragraph was annotated in the margins with two different numbers, one pointing back to one of ten separate prefatory lists of correspondences and one permitting the user of those lists to locate individual linked paragraphs. In the later fourth century, the Spanish bishop Priscillian wrote similar tables for the Pauline epistles to link paragraphs on related topics from different books; marginal annotations again allowed the reader to begin either from the prefatory material or directly from a paragraph in the text. Such tools are a perfect expression of the non-linear reading exemplified by Jerome in his commentary on Isaiah 7:14; although the complexities of transmission sometimes meant that later copies of such an apparatus were practically useless, they were the clearest expression of the idea that the written text would be navigated in multiple directions.

The next major leap forward in the technology of text was not until the Renaissance introduction of the printing press, which was crucial in two ways. The printing press facilitated the refinement of the standard or critical text. To be sure, this was a desire of scholarly readers since the Alexandrian Library and before, and the centos, for example, could not have been written without a very widespread understanding of what was the standard Virgilian text; but correcting written copies was a more than

---

[167] On Optatian, see the chapters in Squire and Wienand 2017, especially Bažil 2017, and Squire and Elsner in this volume, pp. 618–40.
[168] Grafton and Williams 2006; Crawford 2019.

*5 Intertextuality*

Sisyphean labour, and at last the ground was not in constant motion. The printing press also allowed authors and editors to exert far more control over their paratexts.[169] Whereas previously the paratextual designs of a Virgil or Propertius might have been lost within a generation, to be recovered only after two millennia, they could finally be reproduced in hundreds or thousands of identical copies. As for the *apparatus criticus* and the *apparatus fontium*, these developed in their modern form only centuries after the introduction of the printing press.

This cursory history of textuality is a contingent precursor to the way we read now. Of course, many of the changes brought by the internet are superficial if not positively harmful, and the material codex remains the best format for many kinds of traditional reading. Nevertheless, as everyone knows, the digital age offers new tools for studying Latin intertextuality. Their promise resounds in the final paragraph of the newly revised *Cambridge Companion to Virgil*:

> Online editions are just the tip of the digital humanities iceberg. Digital tools now expedite different kinds of analysis from stylometrics to intertextuality. With human supervision as necessary, digital tools enable a level of data processing far beyond the ability of a team of Mommsens and Wilamowitzes, and as the methods become more refined they may also revolutionise the way in which we search for phrases and collocations across texts. This said, so far, these digital applications have hugged the shore of what classicists have always done anyway: we have yet to see them fulfil the paradigm-shifting promise of 'macroanalysis' and 'distant reading' as truly radical alternatives to our comfort-zone pursuits, microanalysis and close reading.[170]

Among classicists at least, these tools are far more widely discussed than they are understood, which would not matter so much if it did not lead to the inevitable let-down of realising that digital scholarship is, like all scholarship, a slow and laborious process.

The creation of digital texts[171] in extensive searchable corpora has made it trivially easy to make discoveries about the corpus of extant Latin literature that can impress even the most philological of critics. For example, a simple user-defined search reveals that the phrase *nati natorum* is found before the fourth century only in *Aeneid* 3.98, and that closely cognate phrases do not appear either, that is, *filii filiorum* or either phrase

---

[169] Genette 1987: 9.    [170] Mac Góráin 2019: 476–7.
[171] The production of born-digital scholarly editions is treated in the chapter of Huskey and Kaster in this volume (pp. 541–58), and they explain the crucial role of textual markup in eventually enabling the automated processing of edited texts.

in an oblique case. In order to identify such absences, previous generations had to depend on the memory of an expert, whether the memory of one of Aulus Gellius' sophists or of a latter-day philologist like Mommsen or Wilamowitz. Such discoveries can be used to police the boundary between intertext and allusion, but the sheer abundance produced by most searches is hardly restrictive. Indeed, the search tool in itself allows for radically non-linear forms of reading – a simple search for the string *hic domus*, for example, returns results (besides two other instances in Virgil) in Statius, Silius Italicus, Claudian, Sidonius and Hosidius Geta. Prominent open-access corpora include the Open Greek and Latin Project, Perseus, PHI and *Musisque deoque*; important subscription-based corpora are currently offered by Brepols, De Gruyter and Oxford University Press.[172]

Similarity, not absence, is the goal of the currently available tools used for identifying parallels in Latin texts, whether those parallels are retained by their human readers or merely dumped into the digital void of discarded searches. Among search engines that employ complex algorithms, *Tesserae* stands out; other important tools include *Filum* (from the Quantitative Criticism Lab) and *TRACER*.[173] Whereas a user-defined search depends on having a predetermined question in mind, these tools are designed to find a very broad range of similarities between a source text and a target text. At the time of writing this chapter, a search with *Aeneid* 3 as the target turned up a number of lines in Ovid, Silius Italicus and Claudian that exhibit trivial similarities, but not new intertexts about which one could readily 'tell a story' in the way envisaged by Fowler: for example, *ab illo* was returned as similar to Virgil's line-ending *ab illis* – other sources, of course, could have been added to increase the number of hits. Steady progress is being made to improve all of these tools, and existing algorithms already search for verbal, semantic, sonic, metrical and contextual similarities.[174] Such tools have already been shown capable of reproducing many of the parallels cited in classical commentaries.[175] Because similarities between canonical texts have been well studied already, this kind of tool will probably be most useful for texts that are at the margins of the canon or entirely beyond it.[176]

---

[172] For a recent review of digital resources relevant to Roman studies, see Bagnall and Heath 2018.
[173] http://tesserae.caset.buffalo.edu, www.etrap.eu/research/tracer, http://tools.qcrit.org/filum.
[174] Coffee 2018: 207–8. See also Nelis et al. 2017 and Dexter et al. 2017. Pedecerto (www.pedecerto.eu/) enables searching by metrical similarities.
[175] Coffee et al. 2012, Forstall et al. 2015, Coffee 2018: 208 n. 12.
[176] On Claudian and Lucan, see Coffee and Forstall 2016.

5 *Intertextuality* 259

Although the tools described in the previous paragraph can be used to identify individual passages on which to exercise the kind of close reading long familiar within scholarship on Latin literature, the researchers developing them are already experimenting with forms of so-called 'distant reading', using large-scale patterns to track historical changes unnoticeable from close range.[177] Franco Moretti is a champion of quantitative methods in literary study, and he has viewed one of the most promising features of such methods to be their potential to upset established hierarchies and to open the canon.[178] This is perhaps unlikely in a field like classical Latin in which the extant corpus of texts is so very limited, but if we include extant mediaeval and neo-Latin texts then such methods could in fact radically alter our understanding of Latin intertextuality. Less controversially, Ted Underwood has described the most important advances in digital humanities as a result not of increasingly large digital corpora or of increasingly fast processors, but of the turn towards using data to study hypotheses or statistical models: 'Since a model defines a relationship between variables, a mode of inquiry founded on models can study relationships rather than isolated facts.'[179] He continues: 'Numbers enter the picture not as an objective foundation for meaning somewhere outside history but as a way to establish comparative relationships between different parts of the historical record.'[180] In the past, such large-scale comparisons tested the memory and endurance of even the most intrepid of scholars, but now a model, that is, a formal representation, of the system of Latin intertextuality can be developed and tested in any number of ways.

Memory has always been central to the understanding and practice of intertextuality, which makes it even more noteworthy that new research on human cognition is laying bare some of the most basic ways in which memories are processed in the brain.[181] In antiquity and into the modern era, the art of memory was practised to enable extensive and accurate recall, in rhetoric but also in other fields.[182] In relation to poetic texts, we know less about, and can only guess at, the working methods that produced the first treatises on Virgil's debts to Homer. It seems likely enough, however, that lists were originally composed from memory and then gradually enlarged. Even the Latin centos may have been composed without textual aids, since we hear of some remarkable displays of memory from ancient

---

[177] E.g. Coffee and Forstall 2016; and Dexter et al. 2017.   [178] Moretti 2000 and 2013.
[179] Underwood 2019: xii.   [180] Ibid.
[181] See Sharrock 2018 for an assessment of what cognitive research offers to the study of Latin intratextuality.
[182] Yates 1966; Carruthers 2014. On memory and literacy, see Small 1997.

sources (Xen. *Symp.* 3.6; Dio Chrys. *Or.* 36.9; August. *De anima* 4.7), although there is no way to exclude the possibility that centonists used written lists or concordances of some kind.[183] In his book on *Memory and Intertextuality in Renaissance Literature*, Raphael Lyne highlights the insights to be gleaned from the cognitive sciences for the study of literature. The most compelling aspect of his book is its analysis of two competing explanations of human memory, the one theorising that memory is at root hierarchical and structured and the other that memory is associative and random. Quite possibly, different parts of the mind use one method or the other, and their conjunction may help to explain why self-conscious allusions and also rather unexpected intertexts can both exercise a powerful effect upon their readers. As Lyne explains, a hybrid model of human memory locates both processes within a single mind that unites both associative and conscious processes.[184] In this case, theoretical debates about intertextuality are inscribed within the very structure of the human organism; consequently, Lyne expresses hope that research into the observable practices of intertextuality could even lead to new discoveries in the cognitive sciences.

Amid the many directions that new research will take in the coming years, we draw attention here to a method for digitally presenting intertexts that seems especially promising. As a leap beyond the references in hardcopy footnotes and tables, the introduction of hypertext and with it the World Wide Web has made it possible to re-create in digital form the intertextual networks through which Latin literature is known; an early entrant in this category was *The Vergil Project* (http://vergil.classics.upenn.edu), which in 1995 began work towards publishing the *Aeneid* alongside a suite of commentaries and explanatory aids that include intertextual material. Such projects have lost some of their lustre as digital standards have evolved and led to broken links and inaccessible information published on older websites. A far-reaching innovation that could change how intertextual links are mapped and accessed in the future is the turn towards linked data, also known as the semantic web.[185] Developing an ecosystem for charting Latin intertextuality would be transformative, as highlighted by Neil Coffee in a recent review article: 'Intertext standards could permit editors of digital texts to embed intertextual links that not only take readers to the

---

[183] For the circumstantial evidence regarding memory in this context, see McGill 2005: 10–11, which is the source of the examples cited in the text. Lamacchia thought that written aids were used (1981: ix n. 3); on the Greek side, Usher 1998 treats Eudocia's cento as a continuation of the rhapsodic tradition.
[184] Lyne 2016: 26–7.   [185] See Berners-Lee 2006 and Berners-Lee et al. 2001.

## 5 Intertextuality

connected text and possibly indicate the type of intertextual relationship, but also enable search across entities tagged as intertexts, in order to answer larger-scale questions.'[186] In order to construct a workable map of intertextuality, it will be necessary to create a standard (machine-readable) way of referring to Latin texts,[187] along with standard ways of encoding intertextual links.[188] The trade-off for the time and investment required to build databases of intertextual links is that it would then be possible to search, not only for texts linked to *Aeneid* 3.98, but also for texts linked to those texts and so on as far as you like. Because links identified by human readers could be tagged as such, meaningless intertexts would be easier to filter out: indeed, an obvious first step is to encode the apparatuses of sources and testimonia compiled with much labour by previous editors, for example in editions now out of copyright.[189] Because a database of linked data could be accessed in any direction and connected to other similar databases, the readings and analysis enabled by such collections would not be limited in any way by the original assumptions of our source-critical forebears. Rather than being limited by the assumptions of any single reader, this ever-expanding database would instead approximate the entire field of Latin intertextuality as it has been recognised up to the present day.

In the spirit of recognising the living tradition of Latin literature, we will conclude with a text that is also a translation, that most direct form of intertextuality, hard-coded into Latin literature from its very first engagements with Greek predecessors. The passage from Seamus Heaney quoted as an epigraph to this chapter comes from a poem in which he refigures his life in terms of *Aeneid* 6; in his translation of that book from several years later, we can hear his voice in father Anchises' response to Aeneas' question as to who the figures crowding around the river Lethe are:

> 'Spirits,' Anchises answered,
> 'They are spirits destined to live a second life
> In the body; they assemble here to drink
> From the brimming Lethe, and its water

---

[186] Coffee 2018: 217.
[187] Current projects to enable standard citations include the Perseus Catalog (https://sites.tufts.edu/perseuscatalog), the Canonical Text Services protocol (http://cts.informatik.uni-leipzig.de/Canonical_Text_Service.html) and the Digital Latin Library Catalog (https://catalog.digitallatin.org); the Classical Works Knowledge Base (classics.cornell.edu/cwkb) also provides automated links to digital editions of classical texts.
[188] The schema by which any set of linked data is organised is called an ontology; the project Sharing Ancient Wisdoms developed a model for describing reused text: see Hedges et al. 2017.
[189] This is one of the approaches being pursued in work for the Leipzig Open Fragmentary Texts Series; see Berti, Almas and Crane 2016.

> Heals their anxieties and obliterates
> All trace of memory. For a long time now
> I have looked forward to telling you about them,
> Letting you see them face to face, but most of all
> I wished to call the roll of my descendants, parade
> My children's children, so you could all the more
> Share my joy at your landfall in Italia.' (Heaney 2016: 959–69)

And where is the translator's joy, *his* anxiety, *his* memory? Was it from the time of his school days that *he* looked forward to this roll-call of his ancestors? In such spirits gathered around Lethe, Heaney memorialises the forgetting that precedes recognition, and this is how he communicates the joy found in meeting his poetic father on his own terms. As dreams from the future, Heaney's spirits point us away from Virgil's past and towards the manifold receptions awaiting Latin literature in the years to come. Textual parallels are no longer limited to sources or influences because lines like these are truly sites of intertextuality, always in the middle and never complete.

## References

Ahl, F. (1985) *Metaformations: Soundplay and Wordplay in Ovid and Other Classical Poets*, Ithaca, NY.

Allen, G. (2011) *Intertextuality*, 2nd edn, New York.

Anderson, W. S. (1993) *Barbarian Play: Plautus' Roman Comedy*, Toronto.

Armstrong, D. (1995) 'The impossibility of metathesis: Philodemus and Lucretius on form and content in poetry', in D. Obbink, ed., *Philodemus and Poetry: Poetic Theory and Practice in Lucretius, Philodemus, and Horace* (New York), 210–32.

Ash, R. (2007) *Tacitus Histories. Book 2*, Cambridge.

Auerbach, E. (1944) 'Figura', in *Neue Dantestudien* (Istanbul), 11–71. Revised from E. Auerbach, 'Figura', *Archivum Romanicum* 22 (1938), 436–89.

Austin, R. G. (1939) 'The epilogue to the *Agricola*', *CR* 53: 116–17.

Bagnall, R. and S. Heath (2018) 'Roman studies and digital resources', *JRS* 108: 171–89.

Bain, D. (1979) '*Plautus vortit barbare*: Plautus *Bacchides* 526–561 and Menander *Dis exapatōn* 102–112', in D. West and T. Woodman, eds., *Creative Imitation and Latin Literature* (Cambridge), 17–34.

Barchiesi, A. (1984) *La traccia del modello: effetti omerici nella narrazione virgiliana*, Pisa.

(1994) 'Immovable Delos: *Aeneid* 3.73–98 and the Hymns of Callimachus', *CQ* 44: 438–43.

(2001) *Speaking Volumes: Narrative and Intertext in Ovid and Other Latin Poets* (trans. M. Fox and S. Marchesi), London.

(2015) *Homeric Effects in Vergil's Narrative* (trans. I. Marchesi and M. Fox), Princeton.

Bažil, M. (2009) *Centones Christiani: métamorphoses d'une forme intertextuelle dans la poésie latine chrétienne de l'Antiquité tardive*, Paris.

(2017) '*Elementorum varius textus*: Atomistisches und Anagrammatisches in Optatians Textbegriff', in Squire and Wienand 2017, 341–68.

Ben-Porat, Z. (1976) 'The poetics of literary allusion', *PTL: A Journal for Descriptive Poetics and Theory of Literature* 1: 105–28.

Berners-Lee, T. (2006) 'Linked data', *Design Issues*, www.w3.org/DesignIssues/LinkedData.html.

Berners-Lee, T., J. Hendler and O. Lassila (2001) 'The semantic web', *Scientific American* 284: 34–43.

Berti, M., B. Almas and G. R. Crane (2016) 'The Leipzig Open Fragmentary Texts Series (LOFTS)', in N. Bernstein and N. Coffee, eds., *Digital Methods and Classical Studies,* Special edition of *Digital Humanities Quarterly* 10.2.

Bloom, H. (1973) *The Anxiety of Influence: A Theory of Poetry*, New York.

Breed, B. (2006) *Pastoral Inscriptions: Reading and Writing Virgil's Eclogues*, London.

Brink, C. O. (1972) 'Ennius and the Hellenistic worship of Homer', *AJPh* 93: 547–67.

Buchheit, V. (1988) 'Vergildeutung im Cento Probae', *Grazer Beiträge* 15: 161–76.

Carruthers, M. (2014) *The Book of Memory*, 2nd edn, Cambridge.

Chahoud, A. (2004) 'The Roman satirist speaks Greek', *Classics Ireland* 11: 1–46.

Citroni, M. (2011) '*Arte allusiva*: Pasquali and onward', in B. Acosta-Hughes, L. Lehnus and S. Stephens, eds., *Brill's Companion to Callimachus* (Leiden), 566–86.

Clark, E. A. and D. F. Hatch (1981) *The Golden Bough, the Oaken Cross: The Virgilian Cento of Faltonia Betitia Proba*, Chico, CA.

Clément-Tarantino, S. (2006) 'La poétique romaine comme hybridat féconde. Les leçons de la greffe (Virgile, *Géorgiques*, 2, 9–82)', *Interférences – Ars Scribendi* 4, http://ars-scribendi.ens-lsh.fr/article.php3?id_article=37&var_affichage=vf.

Coffee, N. (2013) 'Intertextuality in Latin poetry', *Oxford Bibliographies Online*, DOI: 10.1093/OBO/9780195389661-0113.

(2018) 'An agenda for the study of intertextuality', *TAPhA* 148: 205–23.

Coffee, N. and C. Forstall (2016) 'Claudian's engagement with Lucan in his historical and mythological hexameters', in V. Berlincourt, L. G. Milić and D. Nelis, eds., *Lucan and Claudian* (Berlin), 255–83.

Coffee, N., J.P. Koenig, S. Poornima, R. Ossewaard, C. Forstall and S. Jacobson (2012) 'Intertextuality in the digital age', *TAPhA* 142: 383–422.

Conte, G. B. (1974) *Memoria dei poeti e sistema letterario. Catullo, Virgilio, Ovidio, Lucano*, Turin.

(1984) *Virgilio: il genere e i suoi confini. Modelli del senso, modelli della forma in una poesia colta e 'sentimentale'*, Milan.

(1986) *The Rhetoric of Imitation: Genre and Poetic Memory in Virgil and Other Latin Poets*, Ithaca, NY.

(2014) *Dell'imitazione: furto e originalità*, Pisa.

(2017) *Stealing the Club from Hercules: On Imitation in Latin Poetry*, Berlin.
Crawford, M. (2019) *The Eusebian Canon Tables: Ordering Textual Knowledge in Late Antiquity*, Oxford.
Cucchiarelli, A. and A. Traina (2012) *Virgilio, le Bucoliche*, Rome.
Dawson, D. (2002) *Christian Figural Reading and the Fashioning of Identity*, Berkeley.
DeBrohun, J. B. (2003) *Roman Propertius and the Reinvention of Elegy*, Ann Arbor, MI.
Desbordes, F. (1979) *Argonautica: trois études sur l'imitation dans la littérature antique*, Brussels.
Dexter, J. P., T. Katz, N. Tripuraneni, T. Dasgupta, A. Kannan, J. A. Brofos (2017) 'Quantitative criticism of literary relationships', *Proceedings of the National Academy of Sciences* 114: E3195–E3204, DOI:10.1073/pnas.1611910114.
D'Ippolito, G. (2000) 'Il concetto di intertestualità nel pensiero degli antichi', *Classica Salmanticensia* 2: 13–32.
Dufallo, B. (2013) *The Captor's Image: Greek Culture in Roman Ecphrasis*, Oxford.
Edmunds, L. (2001) *Intertextuality and the Reading of Roman Poetry*, Baltimore.
Elsner, J. (2017) 'Late Narcissus: classicism and culture in a late Roman cento', in J. Elsner and J. Hernández Lobato, eds., *The Poetics of Late Latin Literature* (Oxford), 176–206.
Fantham, E. (1968) 'Act IV of the *Menaechmi*: Plautus and his original', *CPh* 63: 175–83.
 (2011) *Roman Readings: Roman Response to Greek Literature from Plautus to Statius and Quintilian*, Berlin.
Farrell, J. (1991) *Vergil's Georgics and the Traditions of Ancient Epic: The Art of Allusion in Literary History*, Oxford.
 (1997) 'The Virgilian intertext', in C. Martindale, ed., *The Cambridge Companion to Virgil* (Cambridge), 222–38.
 (1999) '*Aeneid* 5: poetry and parenthood', in C. Perkell, ed., *Reading Vergil's Aeneid* (Norman, OK), 96–110.
 (2005) 'Intention and intertext', *Phoenix* 59: 98–111.
 (2009) 'The impermanent text in Catullus and other Roman poets', in W. Johnson and H. Parker, eds., *Ancient Literacies* (New York), 164–85.
 (2019) 'Virgil's intertextual personae', in F. Mac Góráin and C. Martindale, eds., *The Cambridge Companion to Virgil*, 2nd edn (Cambridge), 299–325.
Feeney, D. (2016) *Beyond Greek: The Beginnings of Latin Literature*, Cambridge, MA.
Fish, S. (1980) *Is There a Text in This Class? The Authority of Interpretive Communities*, Cambridge, MA.
Fitzgerald, W. (2016) *Variety: The Life of a Roman Concept*, Chicago.
Fontaine, M. (2006) '*Sicilicissitat* (Plautus, *Menaechmi* 12) and early geminate writing in Latin (with an appendix on *Men.* 13)', *Mnemosyne* 59: 95–110.

(2014) 'The Terentian reformation: from Menander to Alexandria', in Fontaine and Scafuro 2014, 538–54.
Fontaine, M. and A. C. Scafuro, eds. (2014) *The Oxford Handbook of Greek and Roman Comedy*, Oxford.
Forstall, C., N. Coffee, T. Buck, K. Roache and S. Jacobson (2015) 'Modeling the scholars: detecting intertextuality through enhanced word-level n-gram matching', *Digital Scholarship in the Humanities* 30: 503–15.
Fowler, D. (1997) 'On the shoulders of giants: intertextuality and classical studies', *MD* 39: 13–34. Reprinted in D. Fowler, *Roman Constructions: Readings in Postmodern Latin* (Oxford, 2000), 115–37.
Fraenkel, E. (1922) *Plautinisches im Plautus*, Berlin.
Friedländer, P. (1941) 'Patterns of sound and atomistic theory in Lucretius', *AJPh* 62: 16–34.
Fulkerson, L. and T. Stover, eds. (2016) *Repeat Performances: Ovidian Repetition and the Metamorphoses*, Madison, WI.
Gale, M. R. (1994) *Myth and Poetry in Lucretius*, Cambridge.
  (2000) *Virgil on the Nature of Things: The Georgics, Lucretius and the Didactic Tradition*, Cambridge.
Ganiban, R. T. (2007) *Statius and Virgil: The Thebaid and the Reinterpretation of the Aeneid*, Cambridge.
Genette, G. (1987) *Seuils*, Paris.
Gibson, B. J. (1999) 'Ovid on reading: reading Ovid. Reception in Ovid *Tristia* 2', *JRS* 89: 19–37.
  (2014) 'Paraintertextuality: Spenser's classical paratexts in *The Shepheardes Calender*', in Jansen 2014, 242–61.
Gibson, R. K. (2002) '"Cf. e.g.": a typology of "parallels" and the function of commentaries on Latin poetry', in Gibson and Kraus 2002, 331–57.
Gibson, R. K. and C. S. Kraus, eds. (2002) *The Classical Commentary: Histories, Practices, Theory*, Leiden.
Gladhill, C. W. (2012) 'Sons, mothers, and sex: *Aeneid* 1.314–20 and the *Hymn to Aphrodite* reconsidered', *Vergilius* 58: 159–68.
Goldberg, S. (1983) 'Terence, Cato, and the rhetorical prologue', *CPh* 78: 198–211.
Goldschmidt, N. (2019) *Afterlives of the Roman Poets: Biofiction and the Reception of Latin Poetry*, Cambridge.
Gowers, E. (2004) 'The plot thickens: hidden outlines in Terence's prologues', *Ramus* 33: 150–66.
Grafton, A. and M. Williams (2006) *Christianity and the Transformation of the Book: Origen, Eusebius, and the Library of Caesarea*, Cambridge, MA.
Gratwick, A. S. (1993) *Plautus: Menaechmi*, Cambridge.
Green, R. (1997) 'Proba's introduction to her cento', *CQ* 47: 548–59.
  (2008) 'Which Proba wrote the cento?' *CQ* 58: 264–76.
Habinek, T. (1997) 'The invention of sexuality in the world-city of Rome', in Habinek and Schiesaro 1997, 23–43.
Habinek, T. and A. Schiesaro, eds. (1997) *The Roman Cultural Revolution*, Cambridge.

Handley, E. (1968) *Menander and Plautus: A Study in Comparison*, London.
Hardie, P. R. (1988) 'Lucretius and the delusions of Narcissus', *MD* 20/21: 71–89.
  (1993) *The Epic Successors of Virgil: A Study in the Dynamics of a Tradition*, Cambridge.
  (1998) *Virgil*, Greece & Rome New Surveys in the Classics, Oxford.
  (2002) *Ovid's Poetics of Allusion*, Cambridge.
  (2007) 'Polyphony or Babel? Hosidius Geta's *Medea* and the poetics of the cento', in S. Swain, S. Harrison and J. Elsner, eds., *Severan Culture* (Cambridge), 168–76.
  (2012) *Rumour and Renown: Representations of Fama in Western Literature*, Cambridge.
  (2019) *Classicism and Christianity in Late Antique Latin Poetry*, Oakland, CA.
Harrison, S. (2007) *Generic Enrichment in Vergil and Horace*, Oxford.
Hathaway, N. (1989) '*Compilatio*: from plagiarism to compiling', *Viator* 20: 19–44.
Heaney, S. (2016) *Aeneid Book* VI, London.
Heath, M. (2002) *Interpreting Classical Texts*, London.
Hedges, M., A. Jordanous, K. F. Lawrence, C. Roueché and C. Tupman (2017) 'Computer-assisted processing of intertextuality in ancient languages', *Journal of Data Mining and Digital Humanities*, Special Issue on Computer-Aided Processing of Intertextuality in Ancient Languages, https://hal.archives-ouvertes.fr/hal-01265297.
Heerink, M. (2015) *Echoing Hylas: A Study in Hellenistic and Roman Metapoetics*, Madison, WI.
Heinz, C. (2007) *Mehrfache Intertextualität bei Prudentius*, Frankfurt.
Hejduk, J. D. (2018) 'Was Vergil reading the Bible? Original sin and an astonishing acrostic in the *Orpheus and Eurydice*', *Vergilius* 64: 71–102.
Henkel, J. (2014) 'Vergil talks technique: metapoetic arboriculture in *Georgics* 2', *Vergilius* 60: 33–66.
Heyworth, S. J. and J. Morwood (2017) *A Commentary on Vergil Aeneid 3*, Oxford.
Hinds, S. (1998) *Allusion and Intertext: Dynamics of Appropriation in Roman Poetry*, Cambridge.
  (2014) 'The self-conscious cento', in M. Formisano and T. Fuhrer, eds., *Décadence: 'Decline and Fall' or 'Other Antiquity'* (Heidelberg), 171–97.
Horsfall, N. (1989) 'Aeneas the colonist', *Vergilius* 35: 8–27.
  (1990) 'Virgil and the illusory footnote', *Papers of the Liverpool Latin Seminar* 6: 49–63.
  (1991) *L'epopea in alambicco*, Naples.
  (2006) *Virgil, Aeneid 3: A Commentary*, Leiden.
  (2016) *The Epic Distilled: Studies in the Composition of the Aeneid*, Oxford.
Hutchinson, G. O. (2013) *Greek to Latin: Frameworks and Contexts for Intertextuality*, Oxford.
Irvine, M. (1994) *The Making of Textual Culture: 'Grammatica' and Literary Theory, 350–1100*, Cambridge.
Jachmann, G. P. (1934) 'Terentius Afer', *RE* 5A: 598–650.
Jansen, L., ed. (2014) *The Roman Paratext: Frames, Texts, Readers*, Cambridge.

Johnson, W. (2010) *Readers and Reading Culture in the High Roman Empire: a Study of Elite Communities*, New York.
Johnson, W. and H. Parker, eds. (2009) *Ancient Literacies*, New York.
Joseph, T. (2012) *Tacitus the Epic Successor: Virgil, Lucan, and the Narrative of Civil War in the Histories*, Leiden.
Kaster, R. A. (2011) *Macrobius: Saturnalia*, 3 vols., Cambridge, MA.
Kelly, G. (2008) *Ammianus Marcellinus: The Allusive Historian*, Cambridge.
Knauer, G. N. (1964a) *Die Aeneis und Homer: Studien zur poetischen Technik Vergils, mit Listen der Homerzitate in der Aeneis*, Göttingen.
  (1964b) 'Vergil's *Aeneid* and Homer', *GRBS* 5: 61–84.
König, A. and C. Whitton, eds. (2018) *Roman Literature under Nerva, Trajan and Hadrian: Literary Interactions, AD 96–138*, Cambridge.
König, J. and G. Woolf, eds. (2013) *Encyclopaedism from Antiquity to the Renaissance*, Cambridge.
Konstan, D. (1988) 'Lucretius on poetry: III.1–13', *ColbyQ* 24: 65–70.
Kristeva, J. (1980) 'Word, dialogue and novel', in J. Kristeva, *Desire in Language: A Semiotic Approach to Literature*, New York. Reprinted in T. Moi, ed., *The Kristeva Reader* (New York, 1986), 35–61. Translated from 'Bakhtine, le mot, le dialogue et le roman', *Critique* 239 (1967), 438–61.
  (2002) '"Nous deux" or a (hi)story of intertextuality', *Romanic Review* 93: 7–13.
Kroll, W. (1924) *Studien zum Verständnis der römischen Literatur*, Stuttgart.
Kronenberg, L. (2018) 'Seeing the light, Part II: the reception of Aratus's LEPTĒ acrostic in Greek and Latin literature', *Dictynna* 15, http://journals.openedition.org/dictynna/1575.
Laird, A. (2002) 'Juan Luis de la Cerda and the predicament of commentary', in Gibson and Kraus 2002, 171–203.
Lamacchia, R., ed. (1981) *Hosidius Geta. Medea: Cento Vergilianus*, Leipzig.
Lamberton, R. (1986) *Homer the Theologian: Neoplatonist Allegorical Reading and the Growth of the Epic Tradition*, Berkeley.
Lausberg, H. (1966) 'Rhetorik und Dichtung', *Der Deutschunterricht* 18.6: 47–93.
Lefèvre, E., E. Stärk and G. Vogt-Spira, eds. (1991) *Plautus barbarus: Sechs Kapitel zur Originalität des Plautus*, Tübingen.
Leigh, M. (2004) 'The *Pro Caelio* and comedy', *CPh* 99: 300–35.
Leo, F. (1913) *Geschichte der römischen Literatur. Vol. 1: Die archaische Literatur*, Berlin.
Long, A. A. (1992) 'Stoic readings of Homer', in R. Lamberton and J. J. Keaney, eds., *Homer's Ancient Readers: The Hermeneutics of Greek Epic's Earliest Exegetes* (Princeton), 41–66.
Lowe, D. (2010) 'The symbolic value of grafting in ancient Rome', *TAPhA* 140: 461–88.
  (2013) 'Women scorned: a new stichometric allusion in the *Aeneid*', *CQ* 63: 1–3.
  (2014) 'A stichometric allusion to Catullus 64 in the *Culex*', *CQ* 64: 862–5.
Ludwig, W. (1968) 'The originality of Terence and his Greek models', *GRBS* 9: 169–92.
Lyne, R. (2016) *Memory and Intertextuality in Renaissance Literature*, Cambridge.

Lyne, R. O. A. M. (1987) *Further Voices in Vergil's Aeneid*, Oxford.
McAuley, M. (2016) *Reproducing Rome: Motherhood in Virgil, Ovid, Seneca, and Statius*, Oxford.
McElduff, S. (2004) 'More than Menander's acolyte: Terence on translation', *Ramus* 33: 120–9.
  (2013) *Roman Theories of Translation: Surpassing the Source*, New York.
McGill, S. (2005) *Virgil Recomposed: The Mythological and Secular Centos in Antiquity*, Oxford.
McNelis, C. and A. Sens (2016) *The Alexandra of Lycophron: A Literary Study*, Oxford.
  (2012) *Plagiarism in Latin Literature*, Cambridge.
Mac Góráin, F. (2019) 'Virgil: the future?', in Mac Góráin and Martindale 2019, 472–7.
Mac Góráin, F. and C. Martindale, eds. (2019) *The Cambridge Companion to Virgil*, 2nd edn, Cambridge.
Mackail, J. (1896) *Latin Literature*, 2nd edn, London.
MacPhail, E. (2014) *Dancing Around the Well: The Circulation of Commonplaces in Renaissance Humanism*, Leiden.
Mansfeld, J. (1994) *Prolegomena: Questions to be Settled Before the Study of an Author, or a Text*, Leiden.
Manuwald, G. (2014) 'Tragedy, paratragedy, and Roman comedy', in Fontaine and Scafuro 2014, 580–98.
Marchesi, I. (2008) *The Art of Pliny's Letters: A Poetics of Allusion in the Private Correspondence*, Cambridge.
Martindale, C. (1993) *Redeeming the Text: Latin Poetry and the Hermeneutics of Reception*, Cambridge.
Miller, J. F. (2009) *Apollo, Augustus, and the Poets*, Cambridge.
Moretti, F. (2000) 'The slaughterhouse of literature', *Modern Language Quarterly* 61: 207–27.
  (2013) *Distant Reading*, London.
Morgan, L. (1999) *Patterns of Redemption in Virgil's Georgics*, Cambridge.
Narducci, E. (1973) 'Il tronco di Pompeo', *Maia* 25: 317–25.
Nelis, D. (2001) *Vergil's Aeneid and the Argonautica of Apollonius Rhodius*, Leeds.
Nelis, D., C. Forstall and L. Galli Milić (2017) 'Intertextuality and narrative context: digital narratology?' *HAL*, https://hal.inria.fr/hal-01480773.
Nethercut, J. S. (2020) 'Lucretian echoes: sound as metaphor for literary allusion in *De rerum natura* 4.549–94', in D. O'Rourke, ed., *Approaches to Lucretius: Traditions and Innovations in Reading the De rerum natura* (Cambridge), 124–39.
Norden, E. (1957) *P. Vergilius Maro Aeneis Buch* VI, 4th edn, Stuttgart.
Norwood, G. (1923) *The Art of Terence*, Oxford.
Nugent, S. (1992) 'Vergil's "voice of the women" in *Aeneid* V', *Arethusa* 25: 255–92.
Oliensis, E. (2001) 'Freud's *Aeneid*', *Vergilius* 47: 39–63.
Olson, S. D. (2011) 'Immortal encounters: *Aeneid* 1 and the *Homeric Hymn to Aphrodite*', *Vergilius* 57: 55–61.

O'Rourke, D. (2011) '"Eastern" elegy and "western" epic: reading "orientalism" in Propertius 4 and Virgil's *Aeneid*', *Dictynna* 8, https://journals.openedition.org/dictynna/699.
  (2012) 'Intertextuality in Roman elegy', in B. K. Gold, ed., *A Companion to Roman Love Elegy* (Chichester), 390–409.
  (2014) 'Paratext and intertext in the Propertian poetry book', in Jansen 2014, 156–75.
  (2017) 'Hospitality narratives in Virgil and Callimachus: the ideology of reception', *The Cambridge Classical Journal* 63: 1–25.
  (2019) 'Knowledge is power: dynamics of (dis)empowerment in didactic poetry', in L. G. Canevaro and D. O'Rourke, eds., *Didactic Poetry of Greece, Rome and Beyond: Knowledge, Power, Tradition* (Swansea), 21–52.
  (2020) 'Infinity, enclosure and false closure in Lucretius' *De rerum natura*', in D. O'Rourke, ed., *Approaches to Lucretius: Traditions and Innovations in Reading the De rerum natura* (Cambridge), 103–23.
O'Sullivan, T. M. (2009) 'Death *ante ora parentum* in Virgil's *Aeneid*', *TAPhA* 139: 447–86.
Otto, A. (1890) *Die Sprichwörter und sprichwörtlichen Redensarten der Römer*, Leipzig.
Page, T. E. (1894) *The Aeneid of Virgil*, 2 vols., London.
Panayotakis, C. (2010) *Decimus Laberius: The Fragments*, Cambridge.
Pasquali, G. (1920) *Orazio lirico*, Florence.
  (1942) 'Arte allusiva', *Italia che scrive* 25: 185–7. Reprinted in G. Pasquali, ed., *Stravaganze quarte e supreme* (Venice, 1951), 11–20.
Pelttari, A. (2014) *The Space that Remains: Reading Latin Poetry in Late Antiquity*, Ithaca, NY.
  (2019) 'The reader and the resurrection in Prudentius', *JRS* 109: 205–39.
Petrides, A. K. (2014) 'Plautus between Greek comedy and Atellan farce: assessments and reassessments', in Fontaine and Scafuro 2014, 424–46.
Pierzak, D. (2015) 'Was Cicero's audience aware of how Orpheus died (*Arch.* 19)?', *Scripta Classica* 12: 75–82.
Plett, H. F. (1999) 'Rhetoric and intertextuality', *Rhetorica* 17: 313–29.
Polara, G. (1989) 'I centoni', in G. Cavallo, P. Fedeli and A. Giardina, eds., *Lo spazio letterario di Roma antica. Vol. 3: La ricezione del testo* (Rome), 245–75.
Pucci, J. (1998) *The Full-Knowing Reader: Allusion and the Power of the Reader in the Western Literary Tradition*, New Haven.
Reckford, K. J. (1996) 'Recognizing Venus (1): Aeneas meets his mother', *Arion* 3: 1–42.
Riffaterre, M. (1987) 'The intertextual unconscious', *Critical Inquiry* 13: 371–85.
Ross, D. O. (1975) *Backgrounds to Augustan Poetry: Gallus, Elegy and Rome*, Cambridge.
Salanitro, G. (1981) *Osidio Geta: Medea*, Rome.
Schafer, J. K. (2017) 'Authorial pagination in the *Eclogues* and *Georgics*', *TAPhA* 147: 135–78.
Schiesaro, A. (1994) 'The palingenesis of *De rerum natura*', *PCPhS* 40: 81–107.

(1997) 'The boundaries of knowledge in Virgil's *Georgics*', in Habinek and Schiesaro 1997, 63–89.
(2008) 'Furthest voices in Virgil's Dido', *SIFC* 6: 60–109, 194–245.
Schottenius Cullhed, S. (2015) *Proba the Prophet: The Christian Virgilian Cento of Faltonia Betitia Proba*, Leiden.
Sharrock, A. (2009) *Roman Comedy: Poetics and Playfulness in Plautus and Terence*, Cambridge.
(2013) 'Terence and non-comic intertexts', in A. Augoustakis and A. Traill, eds., *A Companion to Terence* (Malden, MA), 52–68.
(2018) 'How do we read a (w)hole? Dubious first thoughts about the cognitive turn', in S. Harrison, S. Frangoulidis and T. Papanghelis, eds., *Intratextuality and Latin Literature* (Berlin), 15–31.
Sineri, V. (2009) 'Musaeus come Mosè nel centone di Proba', *RCCM* 51: 153–60.
Small, J. P. (1997) *Wax Tablets of the Mind: Cognitive Studies of Memory and Literacy in Classical Antiquity*, London.
Smith, P. M. (1981) 'Aineiadai as patrons of *Iliad* xx and the Homeric *Hymn* to Aphrodite', *HSPh* 85: 17–58.
Smith, R. A. (1990) 'Ov. *Met.* 10.475: an instance of "meta-allusion"', *Gymnasium* 97: 458–60.
Smith, S. J. (2002) 'Tacitus' *Agricola*: Representing Imperial Rome', unpublished PhD dissertation, University of Birmingham.
Squire, M. (2009) *Image and Text in Graeco-Roman Antiquity*, Cambridge.
Squire, M. and J. Wienand, eds. (2017) *Morphogrammata / The Lettered Art of Optatian: Figuring Cultural Transformations in the Age of Constantine*, Paderborn.
Staley, G. (2000) 'Juvenal's third satire: Umbricius' Rome, Vergil's Troy', *MAAR* 45: 85–98.
Stärk, E. (1989) *Die Menaechmi des Plautus und kein griechisches Original*, Tübingen.
Steele, C. E. W. (2001) *Cicero, Rhetoric, and Empire*, Oxford.
Stemplinger, E. (1912) *Das Plagiat in der griechischen Literatur*, Leipzig.
Stock, B. (1990) *Listening for the Text: On the Uses of the Past*, Baltimore.
Struck, P. T. (2004) *Birth of the Symbol: Ancient Readers at the Limits of Their Texts*, Princeton.
Thomas, O. (2016) 'Homeric and/or hymns: some fifteenth-century approaches', in A. Faulkner, A. Vergados and A. Schwab, eds., *The Reception of the Homeric Hymns* (Oxford), 277–99.
Thomas, R. F. (1999) *Reading Virgil and His Texts: Studies in Intertextuality*, Ann Arbor, MI.
(2001) *Virgil and the Augustan Reception*, Cambridge.
Underwood, T. (2019) *Distant Horizons: Digital Evidence and Literary Change*, Chicago.
Usher, D. (1998) *Homeric Stitchings: The Homeric Centos of the Empress Eudocia*, Lanham, MD.

Volk, K. (2002) *The Poetics of Latin Didactic: Lucretius, Vergil, Ovid, Manilius*, Oxford.
Warden, J. (1982) 'Epic into elegy: Propertius 4,9,70 f.', *Hermes* 110: 228–42.
Whitton, C. (2013) *Pliny the Younger. Epistles Book* 11, Cambridge.
  (2019) *The Arts of Imitation in Latin Prose: Pliny's Epistles/Quintilian in Brief*, Cambridge.
Williams, R. D. (1962) *P. Vergili Maronis Aeneidos liber tertius*, Oxford.
Wills, J. (1996) *Repetition in Latin Poetry: Figures of Allusion*, Oxford.
Wray, D. (2003) 'What poets do: Tibullus on easy hands', *CPh* 98: 217–50.
Yates, F. A. (1966) *The Art of Memory*, Chicago.
Ziolkowski, J. M. and M. C. J. Putnam (2008) *The Virgilian Tradition: The First Fifteen Hundred Years*, New Haven.

CHAPTER 6

# *Mediaeval Latin*

*Justin Stover*

### 'Sine finibus'

Mediaeval Latin, as a period of the long history of Latin literature, is beset with obscurity and paradox. As a field it defies boundaries. It admits only of vague periodisation. No one agrees as to where precisely it begins – in the fourth century with the *Itinerarium Egeriae*, in the third with Tertullian and the Latin *passiones*, or in the seventh after the age of Boethius, Cassiodorus, Maximian, Corippus, Venantius had passed? When does it end? Everyone acknowledges that the generations following Lovato Lovati, Albertino Mussato and Petrarch marked some fundamental change in the approach to Latinity, yet millions of pages of what is indisputably mediaeval Latin continued to be written in the universities, courts and chanceries for centuries to follow.[1] As recent work has demonstrated, once one goes beyond the mannered prefaces, the language even of such works as Bacon's *Novum Organum* and Newton's *Principia* is simply mediaeval Latin under a different guise.

Mediaeval Latin defies quantification. No one knows how many Latin texts were written in the millennium between 500 and 1500. No one has any idea what proportion the surviving texts bear to the number originally produced. No one even knows the full extent of what survives.[2] We are fairly certain that what has been put into print or discussed in scholarship represents only a fraction of what remains in manuscript even for this period. The large repertories, which themselves cannot claim to be genuinely comprehensive – such as

---

[*] I would like to thank the editors of this volume for many helpful comments, as well as Aaron Pelttari and Zubin Mistry for reading various drafts. My forays into mediaeval Latin have very much been inspired by Jan Ziolkowski, to whom this chapter is dedicated.
[1] On Neo-Latin, see Haskell in this volume; and on the problems of periodisation in general, see Kelly in this volume.
[2] For some hints on the extent of lost mediaeval Latin literature, see Haye 2016.

Stegmüller's eleven-volume *Repertorium biblicum*, a handlist of biblical commentaries, Lohr's five-volume *Latin Aristotle Commentaries*, or Weijer's *Le travail intellectuel à la Faculté des Arts de Paris: textes et maîtres (ca. 1200–1500)*, in nine volumes – give the impression that the edited and studied texts represent a fraction considerably less than 5 per cent of the whole.[3] And even what has been edited is almost unimaginably vast: the *Repertorium edierter Texte des Mittelalters* of Schönberger and others, which focuses only on philosophy broadly conceived, covers forty thousand editions with brief bibliographic data, in almost five thousand pages.[4] For the later period, after 1500, non-humanistic texts in Latin survive in even greater numbers. Law dissertations written in German-speaking countries between 1650 and 1750, as Leonhardt points out, come to a total of some million pages of texts, a corpus larger than the entire surviving output of Latin antiquity.[5]

Mediaeval Latin defies standardisation. No lexicon can claim to be comprehensive. Most of the modern lexica are based on limited national corpora, such as the recently completed *Dictionary of Medieval Latin from British Sources* (1975–2013), or Bartal's *Glossarium mediae et infimae Latinitatis Regni Hungariae* (1901), or Arnaldi's *Latinitatis Italicae medii aevi lexicon* (1939–64). The only complete lexicon which aims for comprehensiveness remains that begun by Du Cange in 1678 in three volumes, which was expanded and updated until the end of the nineteenth century, when Favre came out with a ten-volume edition from 1883–87. It remains an astonishing work of scholarship, even though it is nowhere near comprehensive of all the Latin words contained in mediaeval texts. Its successor, the *Novum glossarium mediae Latinitatis*, has only managed to cover thus far the words from *la* (the Romance feminine article that is very rarely found in Latin texts) to *potentificus* in twenty-three fascicles from 1972 to the present day. Likewise, no grammar of the Latin of the mediaeval period can claim the comprehensiveness of Kühner–Stegmann: the magisterial five-volume *Handbuch zur lateinischen Sprache des Mittelalters* of Stotz (1996–2004) is more a patient and painstaking catalogue of bewildering linguistic variety than what classicists might think of as a systematic grammar.[6]

---

[3] Stegmüller 1950–80; Lohr 1988–2013; Weijers 1994–2012.
[4] Schönfeld 2011, which continues Schönberger 1994.     [5] Leonhardt 2013: 3–4.
[6] Stotz 1996–2004.

Mediaeval Latin defies stylistic qualification. It is the last period in which Latin remained a living language for the normal business of life, and the first period in which Latin was a fixed, canonised language learned through the study of old books. It is a language, or a phase of a language, marked by both conservatism and innovation. For a thousand years, its rudiments were taught from the same textbook, Donatus' *Ars minor*. Education aimed at reading the same small number of works – the Latin of the vulgate Bible and the liturgy, Virgil, Terence, Statius' *Achilleid*, the *Dicta Catonis*, Boethius, Augustine, Gregory the Great, some Ovid, a little Sallust, a little Cicero. Under such conditions, the language itself could undergo no radical transformation without undermining its raison d'être. And yet this list of texts contains astounding variety and stylistic range, from the evocative broken impressionism of the Latin Septuagint psalter to the charming and supple elegiac couplets of Ovid, from the ponderous and patient ploddings of the *Moralia in Iob* to the glittering *brevitas* of the *Catiline*. This variety of canonical models – of considerably greater range than the models admitted during the Renaissance and later – gives mediaeval Latin its distinctive feel, and ultimately fostered tremendous flexibility and innovation in both style and genre without compromising imitation of the *auctores*.

## The History of Histories of Mediaeval Latin

No single study can claim to trace the history or even the lineaments of so vast a field. The lone exception is Manitius, whose three-volume *Geschichte der lateinischen Literatur des Mittelalters* (1911–31) is the only completed attempt at a continuous literary history of the Latin Middle Ages (only three volumes out of four of Brunhölzl's work of the same name were published before his death in 2014).[7] As valuable as both of these histories are, they are by necessity severely selective, in a way that Conte's *Latin Literature* did not have to be.[8] A history as comprehensive as Conte's (which itself does not cover everything, particularly from late antiquity) would extend to hundreds of volumes, even if it were made up of cursory notices.[9] There is also no agreement as to what sort of texts this imaginary guide would contain. The corpus of Latin works from antiquity is slim enough that most everything can be subsumed

---

[7] Manitius 1911–31; Brunhölzl 1975–2014.   [8] Conte 1994.
[9] See the trenchant comments by Ziolkowski 1996a: 530.

under the category of literature: agricultural manuals sit alongside novels, philosophical commentaries next to bawdy comedies. The only specimens of ancient Latin often excluded from the category of Latin literature are late finds usually based on archaeological discovery, and many are included in Adams' new *Anthology of Informal Latin* (2017).[10] So catholic an approach would hardly suit mediaeval Latin. Even granting the traditional distinction between charters and texts, analogous to the one between diplomatics and palaeography, many texts of the latter category would rarely be considered examples of mediaeval Latin literature. Are the untold masses of commentaries on Peter Lombard's *Sentences* or on the *Corpus Aristotelicum* part of mediaeval Latin literature or not? One could assign them respectively to the history of theology and philosophy. And yet one could not even begin to understand, contextualise and interpret such undoubtedly literary authors as Alan of Lille, Alexander Neckham or Peter Abelard without understanding them. Are the vast troves of sermons part of mediaeval Latin literature?[11] Many of them may indeed be dull and formulaic, but to exclude them as a category would be to fail to mine one of the richest veins of classical rhetorical practice in the postclassical period. It would ignore the most important works of one of the most dextrous and skilled prose stylists of the entire mediaeval period, Bernard of Clairvaux, considered by some Renaissance humanists as the only one to achieve eloquence between Gregory the Great and Petrarch. The fact of the matter is that there is no consistent rule or criterion for determining what counts as literature from the Latin Middle Ages.

Mediaeval Latin has no canon, at least not in the normal sense of the word.[12] What one might term the canon – which really means the texts that most specialists in mediaeval Latin will be familiar with, those that are often taught in surveys, excerpted in anthologies like Harrington's *Medieval Latin*, available in translation in modern languages, and with sufficient scholarship to generate a bibliography – is heterogeneous, and the product of accidental formation.[13] It includes texts which have been read for a very long time, such as the poetry of Venantius Fortunatus (d. c. 600), the histories of Gregory of Tours (d. 594), Isidore's *Etymologiae*, the works of Aldhelm and Bede, some Carolingian productions like the *De laudibus sanctae crucis* of

---

[10] Adams 2017.  [11] Schneyer 1969–90 is a repertory of those from 1150–1350 in eleven volumes.
[12] For comparison, see Peirano Garrison in this volume on canons.  [13] Harrington 1997.

Hrabanus Maurus (pattern poems imitating Optatian), the comedies of Hrotswitha of Gandersheim, some twelfth-century works, such as the love letters of Abelard and Heloise, the *Anticlaudianus* of Alan of Lille, the *Alexandreis* of Walter of Châtillon, the *Architrenius* of John of Hauville, the legendary history of Geoffrey of Monmouth, and the satiric *Speculum stultorum* of Nigel of Canterbury.[14] Other components of this canon are more recent discoveries, like the early mediaeval historical epic, the *Waltharius*, or the German chivalric romance called the *Ruodlieb*, both of which were discovered and printed for the first time in the nineteenth century.[15] Indeed, it was the nineteenth century in which mediaeval secular lyric first came to be printed and appreciated, with the discovery of *Carmina Burana* at the beginning of the century and Thomas Wright's printing of the poetry attributed (almost always falsely) to Walter Map in 1841.[16] Similar is Jakob Grimm's discovery of the beast-poems *Ysengrimus* and *Ecbasis captivi* as well as the narrative tales *Rapularius* and *Asinarius* in the first decades of the century, followed up a few decades later by the poems of the Archpoet.[17] Other now canonical works were not even printed till the end of the century: the *Dolopathos* of John of Altasilva by H. Oesterley in 1873, Bernardus Silvestris' *Cosmographia* by C. S. Barach and J. Wrobel in 1876, *Eupolemius* and the classicising *Sermones* of Sextus Amarcius in 1891 and 1888 by M. Manitius.[18] At least two undoubtedly canonical mediaeval poetic collections were not even printed until the twentieth century, the poems of Hugh Primas by Meyer in 1907 and those of Baudri of Bourgeuil by Phyllis Abrahams in 1926.[19]

All of these are works of sterling quality which richly repay close attention and study. But as a roster or syllabus they represent a mishmash with no internal consistency as to what is included and what is excluded, dependent above all on accidents of the chronology of scholarly study. The *Flosculus* of Rahewin of Freising (d. c. 1175), with its rich reimagining of bucolic (discussed further on pp. 287–8), is as interesting and unusual a poetic project as anything produced in the Middle Ages; and yet

---

[14] On Venantius, see Roberts 2009; on Gregory, see Contreni 2011.
[15] Both are translated by Kratz 1984.
[16] For Map, Wright 1841; and for the *Carmina*, see the new DOML text and translation by Traill 2018.
[17] See Ziolkowski 2007 and 1993.
[18] *Dolopathos*: trans. Gilleland 1981; *Cosmographia*: trans. Wetherbee 2015; *Eupolemius* and Sextus Amarcius: trans. Pepin and Ziolkowski 2011.
[19] Abrahams 1926. The standard edition for Baudri is Tilliette 1996–2000. For Hugh, see the translation by McDonough 2010.

some works, with arguably less intrinsic interest, like the formal eclogues of Warnerius of Basel (d. *post* 1050), have received considerably more scholarly attention. Warnerius is mentioned at least in passing in nearly every survey of mediaeval Latin literature, and has been the subject of at least a couple of dedicated studies; Rahewin's *Flosculus* is mentioned in almost none. This is because Warnerius' two long poems, the *Synodius* and the *Paraclitus*, were edited in 1887 (by Huemer) and 1892 (by Hauréau) respectively, but Rahewin's collection was only fully edited in 1999 (by Deutinger).[20] Indeed, some works of considerable literary and intellectual merit have yet to attract much attention at all. The verse encyclopaedia of the Italian Benedictine Gregorio de Montesacro, the *Peri ton anthropon theopiisis* (*sic*) (*c*. 1228) in some 13,000 hexameters has attracted only a fraction of the scholarship of the nearly contemporary *Anticlaudianus* of Alan of Lille (d. 1202).[21] A strong case can be made for Alan's superior merit, as he is surely one of the most vigorous and original authors of the entire mediaeval period, but this can also be explained by chronological bias, since Gregorio's work was only edited in 2002.[22] The most detailed commentary on the generation of the soul in Plato's *Timaeus* – in the same spirit as Plutarch's *De procreatione animae in Timaeo* – written by one Hisdosus, was only fully edited for the first time in 2016 (by Hicks), this despite the fact that an apophthegm comparing the soul to a spider attributed to Heraclitus found only in this text has long been included – for no particularly compelling reason – among the fragments of the pre-Socratics (Heraclitus fr. 67a Diels, 115 Marcovich).[23] The Levantine historian William of Tyre has been described as one of the best writers of the Middle Ages, and one of its greatest historians, and has been a principal source for crusade history since the Renaissance.[24] And yet his *Chronicon* was critically edited for the first time only in 1986 by R. B. C. Huygens.[25] Other important works are still in wholly inadequate editions: the first text to cite Propertius since antiquity, a strange mystagogic treatise from mid-twelfth-century England entitled the *De septem septenis*, is still only available in an incomplete and wholly inadequate nineteenth-century edition by J. A. Giles.[26] Its thirteenth-century sequel, a treatise abounding in pseudo-antique Hermeticism, called the *De novem scienciis*, is only available in a diplomatic transcription in a doctoral dissertation from 1938.[27]

---

[20] Warnerius: the best edition is Hoogterp 1933. Rahewin: Deutinger 1999.
[21] See Wetherbee's translation of Alan (2013); and for a discussion Curtius 1953: 119–21 and, at much greater length, Simpson 1995.
[22] Pabst 2002.  [23] Hicks 2016.  [24] For example, Hamilton 2000: 6.
[25] On the difficulties of this, see Huygens 1984.  [26] Giles 1848.  [27] Williams 1938.

The huge and hugely influential Latin lexicon of the eleventh-century scholar Papias survives in a substantial number of manuscripts and was printed four times before 1500; contemporary scholarship has only been able to offer a critical edition of the letter A (by V. De Angelis) and a reprint of the 1496 Venice printed edition (1966).[28] Much remains unavailable to scholarship. For example, G. Dinkova-Bruun's survey of biblical poetry of the twelfth and thirteenth centuries lists forty-seven items: nineteen of them are unedited.[29] Astonishingly, the *inediti* include two full versifications of the Bible by known authors, Adam of Barking (*c.* 1200) and Leonius of Paris (d. after 1201) each comprising around 15,000 hexameter lines. Indeed, it is only genre surveys of this sort that can give some picture of how much is unavailable. Carmen Cardelle de Hartmann's 2007 study *Lateinische Dialoge 1200–1400*, for example, lists some 120 dialogues written in Latin in the two centuries under discussion.[30] Only about half have been printed, and some of those only in the sixteenth century or before.

Mediaeval Latin cuts across what are now national and linguistic boundaries, defying conventional conceptions of national literature. Yet, as a discipline, it has been fostered piecemeal, primarily as an adjunct to the project of constructing national literatures. There is no single series for mediaeval Latin comparable to the Bibliotheca Teubneriana, Collection Budé or Oxford Classical Texts, although Brepols' *Corpus Christianorum continuatio medievalis* (*CCCM*), with 374 volumes in print, is coming closer to assuming that role despite its history of hewing closely to theological, devotional and religious texts, and the DOML, with its Loeb-like format, is growing rapidly.[31] Instead, publication of mediaeval Latin has been piecemeal, and in many cases directed by national consciousness. The great *Monumenta Germaniae historica* (*MGH*), founded in 1819, has given the *respublica litterarum* hundreds of high-quality critical editions of texts from late antiquity to the fifteenth century.[32] While the *MGH* has interpreted its mandate broadly, that national mandate still constricts the sort of texts for which editions are commissioned. A number of similar projects sprang up in other countries. Britain, for example, had the *Rolls Series* which printed some 253 volumes between 1853 and 1911, albeit not all of them containing Latin texts, and J. A. Giles' *Patres ecclesiae Anglicanae*, for which he edited thirty-four volumes between 1837 and 1843. The British Academy still sponsors the *Auctores Britannici medii aevi*, which has

---

[28] De Angelis 1977. On the manuscripts of Papias, see Zonta 1960.    [29] Dinkova-Bruun 2007.
[30] Cardelle de Hartmann 2007.
[31] The early history of the *CCCM* is discussed by Hendrix 1993.    [32] See Knowles 1960.

published since 1969 some thirty-eight volumes containing critical editions of mostly philosophical texts by mediaeval British authors. In Italy, the *Fonti per la storia d'Italia* have since 1900 published hundreds of editions of mediaeval Latin texts relevant to Italian history, inspired by the *Rerum italicarum scriptores* of Ludovico Antonio Muratori issued in twenty-eight volumes between 1723 and 1751. Many smaller such series exist, such as the *Corpus philosophorum Danicorum medii aevi*, which since 1955 has produced some sixteen volumes of Latin editions of mediaeval philosophers from Denmark. These initiatives at their origin were fuelled by more than a little Romantic nationalism, particularly the *Monumenta* and Muratori's *Scriptores* both undertaken to provide Latin *fontes* for the history of nations which did not yet exist. And yet as a mode of organising (not to mention funding) scholarship, national initiatives make a certain intuitive sense in a general way.[33] In particular cases, however, it can introduce misunderstanding. Anders Sunesen, for example, archbishop of Lund from 1201–28, composed a verse hexaemeron inspired by his theological studies in Paris, extant in a single manuscript now in Copenhagen (E don. var. 155 4°, available online).[34] It has received considerable attention, an *editio princeps* in 1892 by M. Cl. Gertz, a second deluxe two-volume edition by S. Ebbesen and L. B. Mortensen (1985–8) and a modern-language translation (Danish, by Schepelern),[35] as well as several dedicated studies.[36] Contrast that with the attention paid to the *Planctus Evae* of Henry of Augsburg, a verse Genesis with an hexaemeron, from about a century earlier. In 1891, about a quarter of the poem was published in a Gymnasium programme by Huemer.[37] The rest was not printed until the 1956 edition by Colker published in a journal.[38] Anders' poem is listed in the major repertories, such as Stegmüller's *Repertorium biblicum* (no. 1332) and Schönberger's *Repertorium edierter Texte* (2890–10); Henry's is listed in neither. This discrepancy cannot by any means be chalked up to merit – literary or philosophical – or contemporary relevance. Henry is as good a poet as Anders, and in terms of intellectual history, his ideas are more original than those of Anders, whose theology very much follows lines laid down by Stephen Langton at Paris.[39] Nor can we blame simple chronology, since Huemer's and Gertz's edition came out about the same time. Instead, it must be

---

[33] Cf. Fuhrer in this volume on national traditions in classical scholarship.
[34] http://www5.kb.dk/permalink/2006/manus/638/eng/.   [35] Schepelern 1985.
[36] Ebbesen and Mortensen 1985–88; on Anders, see the papers in Ebbesen 1985.   [37] Huemer 1891.
[38] Colker 1956.   [39] See Ebbesen and Mortensen 1985.

due to the fact that Henry is one of quite a few eleventh-century authors from German-speaking lands, and by no means the most important, whereas Sunesen's poem has to be regarded as one of the 'national monuments' (Ebbesen) of Danish literature.[40] This is just one example – and many, many more could be adduced. While not a major problem – it is not that Anders deserves less attention, but rather that Henry deserves more – it does illustrate the potential distortions introduced by pursuing the study of a designedly international and cross-linguistic literature like mediaeval Latin along national lines.

✳✳✳

This introduction has been deliberately apophatic. At least at our current stage of scholarship, we cannot pin down the elusivity of mediaeval Latin literature through the usual means, defining it through periodisation or linguistic and literary analysis, by genre or canon or place. To attempt to do so requires one to disregard whole categories of evidence and sources, and any results obtained give not just a partial picture but a misleading one. Hence I shall not attempt here to retread ground that has been covered elsewhere, and give my own (partial, misleading) survey of so vast a field. Instead, I shall illustrate two separate ways of looking at mediaeval Latin without the pretence of a universal survey: *microstoria* and *Stilgeschichte*. While both have weaknesses, these two approaches complement one another. For the first, we will explore how to write a *diachronic* history through the lens of genre, epic in particular, and bucolic, and assess how such histories taken together can help trace the outlines of a broader literary history. For the second, we will look *synchronically* at the different stages in Latin style from late antiquity to the Renaissance. While the first approach tends to abstract individual authors from their own historical context to put them in an ideal frame, linking each to their own literary models and successors, the second ignores that ideal frame, and tries to uncover the links contemporary authors have with one another in their way of approaching and using the Latin language, untrammelled by national or generic boundaries.

### *Microstorie*

Exploring microhistories means looking at mediaeval Latin as having not one, single, architectonic history, but untold numbers of histories,

---

[40] Ebbesen 2012.

each formulated under its own distinctive principles.[41] In social and cultural history, the practice of *microstoria* often entails a close examination of those margins of society which are ignored or elided in larger-scale histories.[42] In a similar way, applying the principle to literary history can help shed light on the more obscure corners of the library which canonical histories tend to ignore. Take genre. One way to write about mediaeval Latin would be to look at one specific genre through a long diachronic frame, only bringing in material from outside the genre as it is relevant to help us illuminate our primary subject. The advantage of this approach is that it frees us from arbitrary chronological and national distinctions, while restricting the material that has to be covered to a more manageable scope, and putting the works by authors both major and minor, known and unknown, identified and anonymous, on a level footing. Even so, there are challenges: genre is not unproblematic in classical literature, problems extensively explored in contemporary classical scholarship,[43] and those problems grow even larger in following the genres from the classical period to the Middle Ages.[44]

Say we wanted to write the history of mediaeval Latin epic poetry.[45] The first thing that might be noticed is the fact that epic is not a single thing in the Middle Ages, even if we do restrict our enquiry to extended hexameter narrative. Instead, epic comprises several distinct streams or sub-genres or branches. For the first branch, we might look at classically themed epic, starting from the ancient sources (Virgil, Ovid, Statius, the *Ilias Latina*) and their late antique successors (Claudian, Ausonius), through the sixth century (Dracontius). We arrive then in the Middle Ages proper, where texts like the *Iliads* of Simon Chèvre d'Or and Joseph of Exeter and the anonymous *Historia troyana Daretis Frigii* can be examined next to the *Alexandreis* of Walter of Châtillon and the later *Troilus* of Albertus von Stade, and conclude perhaps with the *Africa* of Petrarch.[46] In parallel, we could look at historical epics from Lucan to Corippus in the sixth century, continue to the

---

[41] The *loci classici* for the concept of microhistory are Ginzburg 1993 and Levi 1991. To my (very limited) knowledge, it is not used elsewhere for literary history.
[42] See Raggio 2013.    [43] Farrell 2003 is a good place to start.    [44] See Rigg 2015.
[45] For the best overview, see Ziolkowski 1996b and Schaller 1993.
[46] Simon Chèvre d'Or: the most recent edition is Peyrard 2007; see also Boutemy 1947. Joseph of Exeter: Gompf 1970, with translation by Rigg 2005. *Historia troyana Daretis Frigii*: Stohlmann 1968. *Alexandreis*: ed. Colker 1978, trans. Townsend 1996, with a book-length study by Lafferty 1998. Albertus von Stade: ed. Gärtner 2007. Petrarch: ed. Festa 1926, with the study of Bernardo 1962.

Carolingian period with *Karolus Magnus et Leo Papa* and Abbo Cernuus' *Bella Parisiacae urbis*, and on to the Crusader epics of the eleventh and twelfth centuries.[47] The twelfth century also sees a rich harvest of contemporary historical epic produced in Italy, by authors such as William of Apulia (*Gesta Roberti Wiscardi*).[48] We could take this strand perhaps up to the *De obsidione domini Canis Grandis de Verona* of Albertino Mussato.[49] As a third strand, we would need to examine biblical epic, starting with its origins with Juvencus, and proceeding through Marius Victor, Arator, Avitus, Severus Episcopus and the rest,[50] up to the poetry of the eleventh, twelfth and thirteenth centuries just mentioned, authors like Henry of Augsburg, Anders Sunesen, Leonius of Paris, Peter Riga, including the considerable amount of material still only found in manuscript. As a fourth strand, we would have to look at the rich tradition of epic hagiography – which itself goes back to the ancient genre of verse biography.[51] Starting from such disparate sources as the two Paulini, of Pella and Petricordia, continuing through to Venantius and Bede, and dwelling on extraordinary productions like the *Passio S. Thebeorum* of Sigebert of Gembloux, Hildebert of Lavardin's *Vitae S. Mariae Aegyptiacae*, and Nigel of Canterbury's *Passio S. Laurentii*.[52] (We could go a step further and include the 'anti-hagiography', in Tolan's phrase, of Embrico of Mainz's *Vita Mahumeti*.)[53] A final strand could include allegorical poetry, tracing a history from the *Psychomachia* of Prudentius to *Eupolemius* and the *Anticlaudianus* and the *Architrenius*, concluding perhaps with at least a glance at Dante's (non-Latin) *Commedia*.

All of these different strands of mediaeval Latin epic have a common stock in ancient Latin epic. Indeed, it is precisely the status of the *auctores* – the authoritative ancient authors – which provided generic coherence and stability throughout the mediaeval period. As Jan Ziolkowski put it, *imitatio* was the highest form of compliment in mediaeval Latin culture, and in that sense we can begin to understand the whole history of mediaeval Latin epic as

---

[47] *Karolus Magnus*: ed. Hentze et al. 1999, with the studies in Godman et al. 2002.
[48] See Bayerle 2012.   [49] Edited in Gianola 1999.
[50] A good overview is Green 2006; McBrine 2017 provides a bridge from the late-antique epics to the early mediaeval.
[51] For example, Phocas' verse life of Virgil, on which see McGill 2017 and Harrison 2017.
[52] On verse hagiography, see in general Tilliette 1989.   [53] Tolan 1996.

*imitatio* of Virgil, Ovid, Lucan, Statius, Prudentius and Claudian.[54] But we cannot end there.

Each of these different strands would bring unique challenges. To understand the Trojan epics, for example, one would have to examine minutely sources a classicist would not normally consider suitable: Dictys Cretensis' *Ephemerides*, which claims to be a Latin translation of a Phoenician account of the war supposedly written by one of the Greek combatants, a companion of Idomeneus, king of Crete; and Dares Phrygius, which purports to be a translation made by Cornelius Nepos and addressed to Sallust of an account of the war by the Trojan Dares, a priest of Hephaestus (cf *Il*. 5.9–10 ἦν δέ τις ἐν Τρώεσσι Δάρης ἀφνειὸς ἀμύμων | ἱρεὺς Ἡφαίστοιο).[55] (In reality, both are probably late antique Latin productions, Dictys a translation of a Greek text, fragments of which are preserved on papyrus, and Dares perhaps an original Latin composition.) One would also need to look at other mediaeval Latin prose sources for the war, some of which preserve ancient information independently, such as the Rawlinson *Excidium Troiae*, the *Origo Troianorum*, and Guido of Colonna's *Historia destructionis Troie* (1287).[56] One would also need to look at the emerging national legends associated with the Trojan diaspora in both Latin and vernacular texts, and the burgeoning harvest of Trojan romances, such as Benoît de Saint-Maur's *Roman de Troie* (written between 1155 and 1160) or Chaucer's *Troilus and Criseyde* (c. 1385).[57] Likewise, to chronicle the Alexander epics one would have to immerse oneself in the major ancient Latin sources – Curtius Rufus and Julius Valerius, in addition to minor works like the *Itinerarium Alexandri* or the Metz Epitome – in addition to thoroughly sounding the ancient and early mediaeval sources for the Alexander Romance, and not just those in Latin and Greek.[58]

The history of mediaeval Latin biblical epic, by contrast, would entail a completely different set of contiguous fields. One would have to know the Bible in the most intimate detail, obviously, but this means not only the Vulgate translation, but the various Vetus versions as well. One would also have to have a very firm grasp on the whole patristic tradition of exegesis, which includes not only the four Latin doctors – Ambrose, Jerome, Augustine and Gregory – and the minor Western exegetes, but

---

[54] Ziolkowski 2001.
[55] On the circulation of Dares, along with some manuscripts of the (neglected) *Origo Troianorum*, see Favrier D'Arcier 2006.
[56] See, for a general guide, Atwood 1937 and Yavuz 2015. [57] See Desmond 2016.
[58] See the essays in Zuwiyya 2011.

also the Greek Fathers whose works were available in Latin translation, such as Origen, John Chrysostom and John of Damascus. From that foundation, one would have to traverse the width and breadth of mediaeval exegesis, with de Lubac's magisterial two-volume *Exégèse médiévale: les quatres sens de l'Écriture* (1959) providing the road map and travel guide. Of course, exegesis by itself is simply an abstraction, *fides sine operibus*. And so to round out our auxiliary disciplines, one would have to turn to sermons, perhaps with something like Kienzle's *The Sermon* (2000) providing a starting point, especially since biblical poetry shared with sermons an essentially paedagogical and hortatory didactic function.

Allegorical epic would share some background with biblical epic, but require additional specialised sources. To do justice to the allegorical tradition, one would need to seriously investigate the Latin philosophical exegetical tradition. One would need a firm grounding in what might be the earliest philosophical commentary in Latin to survive, Calcidius' translation and commentary on Plato's *Timaeus*, followed up by Favonius Eulogius' brief discourse on Cicero's *Dream of Scipio*, Macrobius' massive commentary on the same, and Martianus Capella's allegorical introduction to the liberal arts, and the vast field of ancient Virgil scholarship, not just Servius' commentary – which is of course essential – but Fulgentius' explicitly allegorical *Expositio Virgilianae continentiae secundum philosophos moralis* as well.[59] Mediaeval theory and practice of hermeneutics is just as necessary, entailing traversing the commentaries of such twelfth-century masters as Bernard of Chartres on Plato, William of Conches on Plato, Macrobius and Boethius, and Bernardus Silvestris on Virgil and Martianus, which provide the essential background to Alan's *Anticlaudianus*.[60] At least a cursory glance at later mediaeval vernacular productions – most of all the *Roman de la rose* and Dante's *Commedia* – would round out a full treatment of Latin allegorical epic.[61]

So too would the other strands of this enquiry require investigation of other fields. In all cases, however, heavy demands would be put on our intrepid enquirer: he or she would have to make free use of sources

---

[59] On Calcidius and his influence: Dronke 2008 and the text and translation by Magee 2016; Macrobius: Caiazzo 2002, trans. Stahl 1952; Martianus: trans. Stahl and Johnson 1977; the mediaeval commentaries are surveyed and translated into Italian in Ramelli 2006. On mediaeval *Vergiliana*, see Ziolkowski and Putnam 2008.

[60] A good introduction to these authors can be found in Dronke 1988; the twelfth-century hermeneutic tradition is ably traversed in Bezner 2005. Much of the work of discovering and editing the commentaries of William of Conches was done by E. Jeauneau.

[61] Two worthwhile general guides to the allegorical tradition are Dronke 1986 and Treip 2015.

which are only available in manuscript; keep one eye on the vernacular tradition, not only as parallel and derivative to the Latin tradition, but in some cases as the source of the Latin texts; and have that same eye keep the Greek tradition in sight, and not only the ancient Greek tradition, but the contemporary Byzantine tradition as well.

### Generic Microhistory: Mediaeval Bucolic Poetry

The principle of microhistory can be applied even more productively to slighter genres. Consider the *tenuis Musa* of bucolic. Latin literature offers a slim but virtually unbroken 1,500-year history of pastoral poetry, starting from Virgil. His *Eclogues* have always been read, and the slim but important line of authors that follow in antiquity, Calpurnius Siculus, Nemesianus, Olybrius (the author of the *Einsiedeln Eclogues*), Endelechius, the centonist Pomponius, testify to the enduring attraction of his rustic strains.[62] The last two show how flexibly bucolic could adapt to innovation: Endelechius, who taught rhetoric in Rome, and is mentioned in a subscription to Apuleius' *Metamorphoses* dated 395 and 397, writes a Christian allegory with cowherds named Buculus, Aegon and Tityrus, but not in hexameters, but rather asclepiads.[63] Pomponius, of uncertain date but at least of the same era, cashed in on the elite vogue for centos – witness the obscene Virgilian cento of Ausonius, the pious one of the aristocratic Proba and the pious Homeric cento of the Empress Eudocia – by writing a Christian centonic bucolic. In the sixth century, we find two, or even three, rewritings of Virgil's bucolic corpus. Two are wholly lost. From Cassiodorus, we know that Boethius wrote bucolic: *condidit et carmen bucolicum*, as he says (*Anecdoton Holderi* 7). This probably means that Boethius wrote bucolic divided into individual *eclogae*, but it is impossible to be sure. We also know from the Lorsch library catalogue that one Severus Episcopus (tentatively identified as the bishop of Malaga who died before 602) composed ten bucolics, four georgics and a twelve-book Gospel epic.[64] Sadly, only a few folios of the last survive, so we cannot say anything definite about his bucolic poetry. We do, however, have one collection surviving seemingly entire, albeit in a single thirteenth-century manuscript (and

---

[62] See for example Mayer 2006 and Karakisis 2011. For the identification of the author of the *Einsiedeln Eclogues*, see Stover 2015.
[63] On both of these, see Barton 2000 and O'Hogan 2016: 99–108.   [64] See Stover 2020.

a sixteenth-century copy of it). The four eclogues of Martius Valerius imitate successively the first, second, third and sixth of Virgil's *Eclogues*, and hew closely to bucolic convention.

The other prolific sixth-century poets – Ennodius at the beginning of the century, and Venantius Fortunatus at the end – never write formal bucolic, although individual poems of theirs are strongly marked by the influence of the bucolic tradition. The florescence of letters in the Carolingian period, whether or not we call it a Renaissance, sees renewed cultivation of the *Musa agrestis*.[65] Alcuin composed a couple of short, formal bucolic poems, including the famous *Conflictus* between winter and spring, which manages to merge the emerging genre of *Streitgedicht* with the Virgilian song contest. Winter and Spring personified are the singers, but Daphnis sits in the audience and Palaemon is the judge.[66] The other Carolingian formal bucolics are the miniature *Libri* of Modoinus, who styled himself Naso. The *Libri Nasonis* are structured as two long bucolic poems, bookended by an elegiac prologue and epilogue addressed to Charlemagne. Like Calpurnius, Olybrius and, to a lesser degree, Virgil before him, Modoin uses bucolic – still with its traditional trappings of fields shaded by oaks, springs, hills, characters like Micon and Meliboeus – as a mode for reflection on Empire. Under Charlemagne, the promise of the fourth Eclogue is fulfilled: 'the lamb hastens to the wolf, the fiercest bear convenes with the sheep in a pious peace' (2.41–2).[67] The other Carolingian poet to make use of the pastoral mode was Paschasius Radbertus, who wrote a pastoral dialogue between two nuns called Galathea and Phillis, lamenting the death of Adalard of Corbie (d. 827). The inspiration is Virgil's fifth Eclogue, from which Paschasius took the name Phyllis.

But it was not Modoinus' *Libri* or Paschasius' pastoral elegy which would shape the later bucolic tradition, but another written some decades later, called the *Eclogue of Theodulus*.[68] In it, an Athens-born shepherd named Pseustis, making a tune on his pipe, happens upon the shepherdess Alithia playing the lyre she inherited from David her forefather. This naturally leads to a singing contest: Pseustis proposes stakes, and Alithia points out that *mater Phronesis* is standing by to serve as a judge. They begin – and for more than three hundred lines

---

[65] On Carolingian pastoral, see Mosetti Casaretto 2001.
[66] On the *Conflictus*, see Zogg 2017. Alcuin's authorship is only probable, not certain.
[67] The first book of Modoinus is translated in Godman 1985: 190–7 and discussed in Godman 1987.
[68] On Theodulus, see Mosetti Casaretto 1997.

they trade quatrains, Pseustis offering an ancient mython, Alithia topping with a biblical story with much the same moral. Who Theodulus was – the German equivalent would be Gottschalk – and when he wrote is still debated. But not debatable is the influence of his poem. By the twelfth century, the *Ecloga Theoduli* had become a standard school work, incorporated into the so-called *Liber Catonianus* with the *Dicta Catonis* and Statius' *Achilleid*, and extant in countless manuscripts.[69] This influence extended to formal imitation. The *Synodus* of the eleventh-century cleric Warnerius of Basel, a formal bucolic, is deeply marked by Theodulus' influence.[70] In it, Sophia describes the *locus amoenus* she finds herself in and proposes a song contest between Thlepsis and Neocosmus. Thlepsis, or 'tribulation', begins with an anecdote in seven lines from the Old Testament; Neocosmus responds with a linked anecdote from the New Testament, or Christian history, again in seven verses. After some three hundred lines, the sun goes down, and Sophia calls a halt to the day's contest. The next day they pick up again, until at last after some 540 verses total, Sophia draws the conclusion to a close. Sophia is an innovative character – hardly a passive judge like Virgil's Palaemon and Theodulus' Phronesis. She actively gets involved in the contest, interrupting the songs to bestow admiration and praise. At the end, she tells them both how much more they could have done, fashioning a series of paired monostichs and distichs on other parallel anecdotes they could have adduced.

Around the middle of the twelfth century, bucolic underwent a revival in Bavaria. The historian Rahewin of Freising, who authored the continuation of the more famous chronicle of his predecessor Otto of Freising, also composed a poetic collection he called the *Flosculus*.[71] It is divided into four parts, the first two versifications of a scholastic summa like the sentences of Peter Lombard. The remaining two parts consist of a prologue, or *Apollogeticum*, and a long bucolic poem of 332 hexameter lines, written in the first person. *Forte die quadam solus residens meditabar* ('One day I chanced to sit alone and sing'), he begins, and the subject of his meditation is his *curae* (cf. *Carm. Einsid.* 2.1). Rahewin transforms Virgil's poetic *otium* into a mental affliction (*ut curae crucient, dissolvant ocia mentem*, 'that

---

[69] See Green 1982. There is even an extant eleventh-century commentary on it, by Bernard of Utrecht (ed. Huygens 1977).
[70] Walther 1920: 9608. On Warnerius, see Ziolkowski 1991.   [71] Ed. Deutinger 1999.

cares torture the mind, relaxation slackens it'), and seeks urgent solace (9–10). Three characters appear to him: *Philosophia consolans*, the Lady Philosophy of Boethius' *Consolatio*, Apollo with his lyre and Pan with his pipe. Philosophia sings first (lines 16–59 should be assigned to Philosophia in Deutinger's edition), about the subjects of philosophy; Pan goes next with a straightforward theogony (66–98). Apollo responds with a euhemeristic account of the gods, focusing on physical interpretations – such as that Juno is air and Jupiter is fire, and they are said to be siblings and spouses due to the adjacency of the two elements (101–56).[72] So the debate between the two of them continues, in a free-flowing, non-symmetrical verse, until at last Apollo abruptly closes the exchange and the poem. (It is quite likely that the poem is imperfect at the end.)

At about the same time as Rahewin, further to the south the monk Metellus of the monastery of Tegernsee was embarking on one of the most ambitious literary projects of the twelfth century, a six-part rewriting of a large corpus of ancient poetry by Horace and Virgil into pious poems celebrating St Quirinus, Tegernsee's patron.[73] After imitating Horace's *Odes* for the first four parts, the fifth embarks on a sequence of ten bucolics, each modelled after the corresponding Eclogue of Virgil. Metellus' curious art can best be appreciated through examples. The first bucolic, unsurprisingly a dialogue between one Melibeeus and a Tytirus, begins: *Tytire, tu magni recubans in margine stagni* ('You, Tytirus, reclining on the shore of a great lake', 1.1). Metellus has only changed four words of Virgil's first line (*Tityre, tu patulae recubans sub tegmine fagi*, 'You, Tityrus, reclining under the cover of a spreading beech', *Ecl.* 1.1), but thereby effectively transports the bucolic scene to the shores of the Bodensee, the *magnum stagnum*. Metellus transforms Virgil's second Eclogue into Corydon's praise of a beautiful cow, which he has promised to St Quirinus but which he is loath to give up: *Rusticus est Coridon, nec munera providet are* ('Coridon is rustic, and does not look to gifts for the altar', 2.35) slyly adapts Virgil's *Rusticus es, Corydon; nec munera curat Alexis* ('You are rustic, Coydon, and Alexis cares not for your gifts', *Ecl.* 2.56). With just two words, Metellus transforms the lover's *munera* into pious offerings for an interceding saint. Or at the beginning of the song contest in Metellus' third, Dametas sings *Principium Deus est, orbem Deus ambit et implet* ('God is the beginning; God embraces and fills the world', 3.70), which keeps the essential word *principium* from Virgil (*Ab*

---

[72] This can be fruitfully compared with contemporary discussions in such texts as the mythography of Alberic of London (Third Vatican mythographer), the anonymous *De natura deorum*, William of Conches, *Glosae super Macrobium* and Bernardus Silvestris, *Commentum in Martianum Capellam*.
[73] Ed. Jacobsen 1965.

*Iove principium Musae, Iovis omnia plena*, 'From Jove is the beginning of the Muse, of Jove all things are full', *Ecl.* 3.60), while correcting its heterodox theology.

With Rahewin and Metellus, formal bucolic slips again beneath the surface, only to re-emerge in dramatic fashion some 170 years later in the bucolic epistle of Dante to Giovanni de Virgilio, which inaugurates the rich tradition of Renaissance bucolic from Boccaccio to Sannazaro and beyond.[74]

In broad outlines, at least, that is roughly the story of mediaeval bucolic, on the basis of the seminal studies of P. G. Walsh (1976) and P. Klopsch (1985), a story told in both general treatments of mediaeval literature (e.g. Worstbrock 1999) and in diachronic surveys of bucolic (e.g. Cooper 1977 and Kegel-Brinkgrove 1990).[75] Still, it has never been told quite this way: Rahewin's *Flosculus* was only edited in 1999, and Martius Valerius has only been correctly dated since 2017 (although Dolbeau intimated the date thirty years earlier).[76]

But it is, nonetheless, not wholly satisfying. What are we to make of something like this?

1. Declinante frigore,
picto terre corpore
tellus sibi credita
multo reddit fenore.
Eo surgens tempore
nocte iam emerita
resedi sub arbore.

2. Desub ulmo patula
manat unda garrula,
ver ministrat gramine
fontibus umbracula,
qui per loca singula
profluunt aspergine
virgultorum pendula.

3. Dum concentus avium
et susurri fontium
garriente rivulo
per convexa montium
removerent tedium,
vidi sinu patulo
venire Glycerium . . .

5. Frons illius adzima,
labia tenerrima.
'Ades,' inquam, 'omnium
michi dilectissima,
cor meum et anima,
cuius forme lilium
mea pascit intima.

6. In te semper oscito,
vix ardorem domito;
a me quicquid agitur,
lego sive scriptito,
crucior et merito,
ni frui conceditur,
quod constanter optito.'

7. Ad hec illa frangitur,
humi sedit igitur.
Et sub fronde tenera,
dum vix moram patitur,
subici compellitur.
Sed quis nescit cetera?
Predicatus vincitur.

---

[74] On Dante's bucolic, see Raffa 1996 and Witt 2000: 221–3; for translation and commentary, one still must rely on Wicksteed and Gardner 1902. For a survey of the later tradition, see Velli 1992.
[75] See also Skafte Jensen 1997.   [76] See Dolbeau 1987 and Stover 2017.

As the chill was waning, and the earth's body became adorned with colour, the soil returned its loan with interest. Arising at that time when night retired, I took a seat under a tree. (2) Under the spreading elm, a babbling brook trickles, spring offers shade on grass by the springs, which flow by every place with a splash, which dripped from the bushes. (3) As the symphony of birds and whispers of springs, and the jabber of the stream, down the slope of the hills, took away my weariness, I saw Glycerius coming, with her prominent breasts ... (5) Her brow was unblemished, her lips most tender. 'You're here,' I said, 'my favourite of all, my heart and soul, lily, whose beauty sustains me inwardly. (6) I gape at you, barely able to control my passion. If I read or write, whatever I try to do, I am tormented, and rightly so, if I am not allowed to enjoy what I constantly long for.' (7) At this, she was broken, and sat upon the ground, and under the tender branches, as she could scarcely brook a delay, she was forced to lie down [i.e. be a subject]. But who doesn't know the rest? A predicate is attached!'

This was written by Walter of Châtillon (the author of the *Alexandreis* discussed on p. 281) in the twelfth century, and represents mediaeval lyrical style at its summit. It is also clearly pastoral, situated in a *locus amoenus* with all its conventional accompaniments, springtime, trees, water, birds and the like, indeed with a textual resonance of the opening of Virgil's first in the word *patula*. The very name of Glycerium was learnedly pilfered from Servius' commentary on Virgil's *Eclogues* (cf. Glyceranus in *Carm. Einsid.* 2).[77] Indeed, its frank sexuality makes it closer in spirit to the bucolic tradition from Theocritus to Nemesianus than the pious and pedantic poems of Rahewin and Metellus, although Walter too is not without his pedantry (witness the grammatical euphemism at the end). And yet generically, we would assign this poem not to bucolic but rather to 'pastourelle', a vernacular genre, and it is clearly in the same tradition as an Occitan poem like *L'autrier, a l'issida d'abriu* of the troubador Marcabru (*c.* 1130).[78] It is not my intention here to delve into the vexed and disputed question of the origins of pastourelle, and the relationship between Latin and vernacular examples of the genre. It is beyond my competence to address whether, for example, Marcabru's 'Trobiei la sotz un fau ombriu' ('I found her under a beech tree's shadow') has anything to do with Virgil's *sub tegmine fagi*.[79] Instead, I would only

---

[77] This source is not mentioned in the learned comments by Bate 1983: 23–4.
[78] No. XXIX in the edition of Gaunt, Harvey and Paterson 2000. On the generic problem of Walter's poem, see Tilliette 2016.
[79] See De Conca 2009: 9.

suggest that Walter's use of Virgil's bucolics is undoubtedly deliberate – no one can doubt Walter's intimate familiarity with the entire Virgilian corpus – and that he viewed his lyric pastoral as part of the tradition of Virgilian bucolic. Hence a full treatment of mediaeval Latin bucolic would need to look beyond formal bucolic to pastourelle, both Latin and vernacular, to paint a full picture of the *Musa rustica* in the Middle Ages.

## The History of Mediaeval Latin Genres

I do not pretend that this is any great critical innovation. Even if no one has called them microhistories, approaching the development of mediaeval Latin literature through genre (broadly or narrowly conceived) has been a common approach in scholarship throughout the twentieth century and beyond. Starting with poetry, we could read the two classic surveys by Raby, *A History of Christian Latin Poetry* (1927, with 2nd edition 1953) and the two-volume *History of Secular Latin Poetry* (1934). The latter study has a replacement in Joseph Szövérffy's four-volume *Secular Latin Lyrics and Minor Poetic Forms of the Middle Ages* (1992–5), which covers some 5,000 poems from the tenth to the fifteenth century; its utility, however, is marred by the difficulty in accessing it, and the frequent lapses in editorial oversight. Less ambitious, more focused histories have been more successful. For example, just for Latin hymnody – and we have thousands of mediaeval Latin hymns surviving, many of them collected in the fifty-five-volume *Analecta hymnica medii aevi*, edited by Dreves and Blume from 1886 to 1922 – we have Szövérffy's indispensable two-volume *Annalen der lateinischen Hymnendichtung* (1964–5), and a host of his other studies. For biblical epic, we have the extraordinary work by Dinkova-Bruun, which over the course of a number of studies provides the lineaments of a general history of the genre.[80] For love lyric, there is the extraordinary *Medieval Latin and the Rise of the European Love Lyric* by Dronke (1965–6). For the mixed genre – prosimetrum or Menippean satire – we are in the unusually fortunate position of having two general guides – a huge and minutely detailed repertory by Pabst, and a lively analytic investigation by Dronke.[81] Pabst discusses some 131 (mostly Latin) prosimetric texts from Menippus to Jean Gerson in detail. This makes prosimetrum one of the smaller genres

---

[80] Especially Dinkova-Bruun 2007 and 2008. See also the essays in Stella 2001.  [81] Dronke 1994.

from the Middle Ages in terms of the number – albeit not the importance – of surviving texts. Yet a real history still takes some 1,100 pages. It is true, as Shanzer has pointed out, that Pabst's study could be condensed considerably without compromise,[82] but this example still illustrates how vast an adequate survey of all mediaeval Latin literature would have to be. (Indeed, that number, 131, represents approximately the total number of authors discussed in the Latin volume of the *Cambridge History of Classical Literature*, as listed in Drury's 'Appendix of authors and works' at the end of the volume.)[83]

What all of these generic surveys, or microhistories, have in common is their humility. They do not purport to be exhaustive. They are provisional, summations of the current state of knowledge, but open to revision as new texts are discovered and further work is done. Looking at epic or bucolic or prosimetrum or hymns in the Middle Ages opens for us little windows into the vast library of mediaeval Latin literature. While perhaps frustratingly narrow, such microhistories can give us insights into the *longue durée* of mediaeval Latin with a greater verisimilitude than a broader history can provide. And by reading as many of them as possible together, we can catch at last some glimpse of the whole.

## *Stilgeschichte*

The best, or at least the most engaging, history of postclassical Latin literature before Manitius is found in a novel. In Joris-Karl Huysmans' novel *À rebours* (1884), the syphilitic protagonist Jean Floressas des Esseintes is a libertine, a decadent, an aesthete. He possesses an extraordinary library, whose shelves unfurl an 'anticanon' of Latin literature.[84] It is not just a library: in Huysmans' narration, it is a history of literature from the perspective of style. Des Esseintes rejects and despises the authors of the so-called Golden Age, not finding a single author to his taste until Petronius and the Christian poet Commodian (whom he dates to the middle of the third century):

> These stilted, gloomy verses, with their whiff of the feral, full of everyday terms, of words with their original sense distorted, appealed to him and interested him even more than the style (for all that it was over-ripe and already green with rot) of the historians Ammianus

[82] Shanzer 1996.   [83] *CHCL* II 799–935.
[84] The phrase is Hexter's (2015: 33). See also McGill 2018.

## 6 Mediaeval Latin

Marcellinus and Aurelius Victor, of the letter-writer Symmachus or of the compiler and grammarian Macrobius; he even preferred them to the genuinely scanned lines, and the many-faceted, magnificent language that came from the pens of Claudian, of Rutilius and of Ausonius. These last three were at that time, the masters of the art; they filled the dying Empire with their cries: the Christian Ausonius with his *Cento nuptialis* ... Rutilius, with his hymns to the glory of Rome ... Claudian – a kind of avatar of Lucan ... a poet forging dazzling, sonorous hexameters, and amid showers of sparks beating out his epithets with staccato blows of his hammer ... Santus Burdigalensis [*viz.* Endelicius], who, in an eclogue imitated from Virgil, shows the shepherds Aegon and Buculus lamenting the ailments that plague their flocks ... He much preferred browsing through the *Psychomachia* of Prudentius, the inventor of the allegorical poem, a form which was to enjoy a long run of popularity in the Middle Ages, and he enjoyed dipping into the works of Sidonius Apollinaris, whose correspondence, studded with witticisms, conceits, archaisms, and enigmas, he found enticing ...

Des Esseintes' interest in the Latin language remained undiminished, now that it hung like a completely rotted corpse, its limbs falling off, dripping with pus, and preserving, in the total corruption of its body barely a few firm parts, which the Christians took away to steep in the brine of their new idiom ...

Years went by; the Barbarian tongues began to systematize themselves, to emerge from their sclerosis, to develop into true languages; Latin, saved from the cataclysm by the cloister, remained confined to the convents and the presbyteries; here and there a handful of poets sparkled, cold and deliberate: the African Dracontius, with his *Hexameron*, Claudius Mamertus with his liturgical verses, Avitus of Vienne ...

The centuries that followed were represented on Des Esseintes' shelves by just a scattering of works. Nevertheless, he did have, for the sixth century, Fortunatus, Bishop of Poitiers, whose hymns and whose *Vexilla regis*, carved out of the old carcass of the Latin language and seasoned with the aromatic spices of the Church, haunted him on particular days; Boethius, old Gregory of Tours, and Jornandes [*leg.* Jordanes] ... the low Latin of the chroniclers such as Fredegarius and Gregory of Tours ... the legend of St Columba by the cenobite Jonas and that of the blessed Cuthbert, composed by the Venerable Bede ... the lives of St Rusticula and St Radegunde, the first related by Defensor, Synodite of Ligugé, the second by the modest and artless Baudonivia, a nun of Poitiers.

There were, however, a number of singular works of Anglo-Saxon literature, written in Latin, that he found more enticing: the entire series of enigmas by Aldhelm, Tatwine, and Eusebius ... His enjoyment lessened as these two centuries drew to a close; by and large he took little pleasure in the ponderous works of the Carolingian Latinists, the Alcuins and Einhards, being content, as far as examples of ninth-century Latin were concerned . . . with the poem on the siege of Paris by Abbo le Courbé, and with the *Hortulus*, the didactic poem written by the Benedictine Walafrid Strabo, in which the chapter in honour of the pumpkin, symbol of fruitfulness, filled him with delight . . .

. . . his Latin library stopped at the beginning of the tenth century. For in fact the quaintness, the complicated artlessness of Christian Latin had likewise come to an end . . .[85]

The genius of Huysmans' *Stilgeschichte* is that it takes the pose toward later Latin literature typical since the Renaissance – decline, decay, decadence – and turns them into virtues. It is true, as McGill puts it, that:

The vision of literary history it provides is refracted through [Des Esseintes] and must be colored by what Huysmans lets us know about him. Thus, we should consider his sense of Latin literature to be, like Des Esseintes himself, rebellious and thrilling in its novelty, but also willfully contrarian, alienated, and even perverse.[86]

The Latin of the Middle Ages is certainly not classical, but for Des Esseintes, it has value precisely because it does not ape Cicero and Virgil. In describing it, Huysmans is making what was then a radical claim: works of mediaeval Latin literature deserve attention not only for their content, as monuments of historical, or philosophical or theological importance, which is the view implicit in the great national or ecclesiastical collections of mediaeval Latin literature, from the *Monumenta* to the *Rolls Series* to the *Patrologia*, but as works of literature and specimens of Latin style. Fifteen years after Huysmans, style would form the basis of one of the first attempts at a continuous history of Latin literature since the Renaissance, Eduard Norden's *Die antike Kunstprosa vom VI. Jahrhundert v. Chr. bis in die Zeit der Renaissance* (1898). Unlike Huysmans' Des Esseintes, however, for whom anticlassicism was the chief attraction of late Latin, the classicist Norden was primarily concerned (in the later parts of the study) with tracing the persistence of the classical style through the late antique and mediaeval periods. The difference between Huysmans and Norden can be seen at a glance in their treatments of Charlemagne's biographer Einhard. Self-consciously imitating Suetonius, Einhard managed what was at times a tolerable facsimile of the style of ancient historiography. Indeed, in Norden's judgement, there are in his works passages of which Caesar or Livy would not be ashamed, such as this:[87]

---

[85] Huysmans 1998: 28–33.　[86] McGill 2018: 90–1.　[87] Norden 1898: II 749.

> Cum enim assiduo ac poene continuo cum Saxonibus bello certaretur, dispositis per congrua confiniorum loca praesidiis, Hispaniam quam maximo poterat belli apparatu adgreditur; saltuque Pyrinei superato, omnibus, quae adierat, oppidis atque castellis in deditionem acceptis, salvo et incolomi exercitu revertitur. (Einhard, *Vita Karoli* 9)

> While he was carrying out the war with the Saxons persistently, indeed almost continuously, he established garrisons at appropriate places and set out for Spain with the greatest military force he could muster. After crossing the Pyrenees he received the submission of every town and fortification that he approached and his army came back safe and sound.[88]

Huysmans' Des Esseintes will have none of this, taking 'little pleasure in the ponderous works of the Carolingian Latinists, the Alcuins and Einhards'.

Norden, in turn, inspired one of the most important and engaging surveys of later Latinity, Erich Auerbach's *Literatursprache und Publikum in der lateinischen Spätantike und im Mittelalter* (1958). Auerbach's goal is to trace the influence of what he calls the *sermo humilis*, or the distinctive contribution of Latin Christianity, and particularly the vulgate Bible, to Latin style, what Huysmans had called *la saumure de leur nouvelle langue* ('the brine of their new language'). But for Auerbach it is precisely this which gives vitality and freshness to some mediaeval Latin literature. Neither a hunter for linguistic perversity like Huysmans' Des Esseintes, nor possessed of Norden's censorious classicism, Auerbach found his heroes in authors like Augustine, Caesarius of Arles and Bernard of Clairvaux. As for Einhard, Auerbach grudgingly acknowledged his skill in depicting the political events of Charlemagne's reign, but judged his efforts a failure as soon as he turned to matters of personality and character:

> It was not possible in Suetonian Latin, to show how men lived in the Carolingian period, how they looked and moved, and above all how they spoke and reacted. The rhythm is wrong, the words are wrong, and the sentence structure is incompatible with the structure of a genuine Carolingian sentence of conversation ... His Latin is correct, it may even be said to be relatively elegant, but it is lifeless.[89]

There are considerable advantages to pursuing the history of mediaeval Latin literature through the standpoint of style. Stylistic trends flow across generic and national boundaries. Stylistic change in Latin literature tends

---

[88] Trans. Noble 2009: 29–30.   [89] Auerbach 1965: 119.

to move according to a broad dialectic, providing a general overview of a period without needing to discuss the innumerable individual works.

## Mannerism

The key driver of stylistic change in the Middle Ages is mannerism (*Manierismus*), or an author's deliberate decision to turn his or her work into an intellectual puzzle. Mannerism means finding the most difficult and convoluted way of saying the simplest thing – *la naïveté compliquée*, the 'complicated artlessness', that charmed Des Esseintes. It can manifest in many ways: sometimes it is merely when 'syntax is simple, vocabulary fantastic in the extreme' (Winterbottom); sometimes the syntax itself collapses under its own weight, often both.[90] It is the spectre that haunts the history of mediaeval Latin, and one way to understand the history of the literature is through the progressive emergence, eclipse and reappearance of mannerism. Such an enquiry offers a counterpoint to Auerbach, who traced the development of the *sermo humilis* against the constant threat of mannerism – unfailingly denigrated with the usual descriptors, 'decadent', 'obscure', 'arid', 'unctuous', 'self-satisfied', 'degenerate', 'absurd', 'ornamental', 'rigid', 'sterile', 'pedantic' and so on. One could equally examine the history the other way around. The *Stilgeschichte* of postclassical Latin up to the Renaissance offers a dialectic of mannerism.

Certainly, mediaeval readers read a small number of books intensively and repeatedly.[91] But those works included not just the psalms and the *Moralia* and the *Aeneid*. Indeed, as pointed out in the introduction, what gives mediaeval Latin its vitality is the diversity of its stylistic models. While Latin studies since Petrarch has tended to narrow the range of the Latin authors accepted as models of style, mediaeval writers could choose to follow a bewildering variety of models. Like Pope's Bentley, they had no qualms in quarrying the arid technical remains of antiquity:

> For me, what Virgil, Pliny may deny,
> Manilius or Solinus shall supply:
> For Attic phrase in Plato let them seek,
> I poach in Suidas for unlicens'd Greek.
>
> (*Dunciad* 4.225–8)

---

[90] Winterbottom 1977.
[91] Essential on monastic reading is Leclercq 1982. On the difference between 'intensive' and 'extensive' reading, see, inter alia, Darnton 1986 and Engelsing 1974.

Mediaeval scholars read, re-read, meditated on, taught and commented on Martianus Capella, Macrobius' commentary, Boethius' *Arithmetica*. Understanding the Latinity of these works is essential to understanding mediaeval Latin as a literary language.

Everyone may know that Martianus Capella's *De nuptiis Philologiae et Mercurii* is a prosimetric encyclopaedia of the liberal arts, composed toward the end of antiquity and immensely influential in the Middle Ages. Not everyone tries to actually read it. Here is how *Astronomia* is introduced by Satira in the eighth book, with Martianus' own response:

> Astrigerae iam sedis iter cursumque polorum
> et sacra multiuagos qua tollunt sidera flexus
> dicere tempus adest. Video splendescente pulsu
> icta corusciferi subitum laquearia caeli.
> Illinc bis septem solitus seruare Triones
> pastor Hyperborea resplendet luce Bootes,
> hinc, qua deuexo tellus subducitur axe,
> ignoto Canopos sese infert fulgidus astro.
> Phoebeos pariter currus rapidosque meatus
> et toties uariae flammantia cornua lunae,
> quin etiam medios quos nectunt culmina circos
> obliqua, et rutilis qua se rapit orbita signis,
> cernere iam uideor: tu fingere ludicra perstas
> uiliaque astriloquae praefers commenta puellae?

> Talia adhuc canente Satura, uetitus ille ac durissime castigatus denuo me risus inuasit. 'Euge,' inquam, 'Satura mea, an te poetriam fecit cholera? Coepistine Permesiaci gurgitis sitire fontes? Iamne fulgores praeuides et uultus deorum? Vbi illud repente discessit, quod irrisoria semper lepidaque uersutia inter insana [semper] deridebas uatum tumores, dicabulis cauillantibus saleque contenta nec minus [poetarum] rhetorum cothurno inter lymphatica derelicto? Et quod rabido feruebas cerebrosa motu, ac me Sileni somnum ridentem censorio clangore superciliosior increpabas?' (Martianus, *De nuptiis* 8.808–9)

> 'The time is now at hand to speak of the path of the starry sphere, the course of the poles and of the region where the hallowed planets trace their diverse and winding courses. I see the canopy of heaven gleam, now struck by a bolt of lightning from the sky. From one direction, Herdsman Bootes, brilliant in the northern light, is wont to watch the Septentriones [Ursa Major and Ursa Minor]; in the other direction, where the earth verges out of sight beneath the inclined sky, bright Canopus ranges imperceptible. And now I think I see Phoebus' team, swiftly coursing, and the blazing horns of the ever-changing moon; and what is more, the middle circle that is bound by the diagonal girdle, along which a path is

traced by glittering planets. You would rather fashion cheap and silly fictions than listen to a girl discoursing on the stars.'

As Satire was reciting these lines, I succumbed again to the mood to banter, despite her prohibitions and stern rebukes. 'A fine performance, my Satire', I said. 'Has your choler made a poet out of you? Have you begun to thirst for Permessian waters? Are you already anticipating the flashing countenances of the gods? What has suddenly happened to your ever-ironical and subtle contempt for the bombast and conceits of the poets, whereby you content yourself with chaffing and witticisms while consigning their poetry to the realms of absurdity? Is there any reason to rage madly at me and to chide me in a superior and contemptuous way for being amused at the slumbering Silenus?'[92]

An author like Tacitus might use what one might call tortured Latinity, but he does it with a point, for psychological layering, for innuendo, to mirror the political complexity of the early Empire; his 'asymmetrical, often jarring syntax ... highlights pretext, juxtaposes truth and falsehood, and emphasizes the discordant relationship between events' (Hammer).[93] But what need is there for a rather basic introduction to the liberal arts to deploy what can only be described as obfuscation? The answer can only be that the stylistic effect is its own goal. It is not the case that Martianus wanted simply to pass along the rudiments of the arts, but that he wanted to do so in such way that would dazzle his readers and give them the satisfaction of working out exactly what he was trying to say.

It was not just Martianus. Many influential authors of the late fifth and early sixth centuries composed works tinged with mannerism, including Boethius (who was even more widely read than Martianus), Macrobius, Cassiodorus and Fulgentius in prose, and Dracontius, Merobaudes and Martius Valerius in verse. Martius, for example, ends the elegiac prologue to his bucolic with a sequence of lines consisting of two or three words:

> Fortunatorum diffamavere tropaea
>     indelimatis plurima carminibus,
> commemoraverunt praetermittenda frequenter,
>     praetermiserunt commemorabilia,
> decantaverunt inconsummabiliora
>     formidandorum proelia caelicolum.
> Excusabuntur natura pauperiores:
>     dormitaverunt irreprehensibiles.     (Martius *pr.* 13–20)

---

[92] Trans. Stahl 1977: 316–17.   [93] Hammer 2014: 356.

They disgraced the many trophies of those upon whom fortune had smiled in unpolished song. They often commemorated things that should have been passed over, and passed over things that ought to be commemorated. They sang the matchless battles of the terrible gods. Those poorer by nature will be excused: the blameless have fallen asleep.

Toward the end of the sixth century, however, Auerbach's *sermo humilis* and its analogues were in the ascendant. Gregory the Great, Isidore of Seville, Martin of Braga and Venantius Fortunatus, different as they may be, are all marked by clarity. Even a work like the *Historia Francorum* of Gregory of Tours, which is not necessarily particularly clear to us, was appreciated in its own day for its *rusticitas*, its easy accessibility to the unlearned.[94] As an example, consider the discussion of *disciplina* and *ars* at the beginning of Isidore's *Etymologiae*:

> Disciplina a discendo nomen accepit: unde et scientia dici potest. Nam scire dictum a discere, quia nemo nostrum scit, nisi qui discit. Aliter dicta disciplina, quia discitur plena. Ars vero dicta est, quod artis praeceptis regulisque consistat. Alii dicunt a Graecis hoc tractum esse vocabulum ἀπὸ τῆς ἀρετῆς, id est a virtute, quam scientiam vocaverunt. (Isid. *Etym*. 1.1.1–2)

> *Disciplina* gets its name from *discere* ['to learn'], and for this reason it can also be called *scientia*, knowledge. For *scire* comes from *discere*, since no one has knowledge unless he learns. Alternatively, *disci-plina* is derived from the fact that a *pleni*tude is learned. *Ars*, by contrast, is so called, because it is constituted by narrow (*artus*) rules and regulations. Others say that this word is taken from the Greeks, ἀπὸ τῆς ἀρετῆς, that is, from virtue, since they called it a science.

Whatever one thinks about the linguistic prowess on display or the (lack of) originality (cf. *TLL* 11 656.6–44 [Klotz]), there is no question that Isidore's Latin is clear, indeed as clear as any specimen of Latin of any century. One might be tempted to attribute the clarity to genre, but that does not suffice. Consider the following from an Easter homily by Gregory the Great, keeping in mind that homily of all Christian genres was the one most indebted to ancient rhetorical theory:

> Sed Maria, cum fleret, inclinavit se, et prospexit in monumentum. Certe iam monumentum vacuum viderat, iam sublatum Dominum nuntiaverat; quid est quod se iterum inclinat, iterum videre desiderat? Sed amanti semel aspexisse non suffict, quia vis amoris intentionem multiplicat inquisitionis. Quaesivit ergo prius, et minime invenit; perseveravit ut quaereret, unde et contigit ut inveniret, actumque est ut desideria

---

[94] This is also true of Fortunatus; see Roberts 2016.

> dilata crescerent, et crescentia caperent quod invenissent. (Greg. Magn. *Hom*. 25.2)

> But as Mary [Magdalene] wept, she bent over and looked at the tomb. Certainly she had already seen that the tomb was empty, she had already announced that the Lord had been taken away. Why then did she bend over again, desire again to see? For one who loves, to have seen just once does not suffice, since the power of love multiplies the intention of the one seeking their beloved. Thus she sought first, and did not find. She kept on seeking, and so came to find, and it happened that her desire increased as its fulfilment was delayed, and as it increased it obtained what it sought.

This is more rhetorical than Isidore, to be sure, but no less clear. Indeed, it is precisely its clarity that gives it its power. In this respect, it illustrates precisely what Auerbach found so compelling about the *sermo humilis*.

The following century and a half, widely excoriated as the Dark Age, saw a transformation of Latin style. Just a few years after Isidore's death in 636, the monastic *littérateur* Jonas of Bobbio composed his life of St Columbanus, the Irish founder of Bobbio.[95] From the preface of the first book, it is very clear that we are worlds away from Gregory or Isidore:

> Rutilantem atque eximio fulgore micantem sanctorum praesulum atque monachorum patrum solertia nobilium condidit vitam doctorum, scilicet ut posteris alma redolerent priscorum exempla. Egit hoc a saeculis rerum sator aeternus, ut suorum famulorum famam commendaret perennem utque praeterita gesta linquerent futuris exempla et de praecedentium meritis vel imitando exemplo vel memoriae commendando ventura sobolis gloriaretur. (1.1)

> The skill of renowned learned men has preserved the radiant life, shining with an extraordinary splendour, of the leading saints and noble fathers of monks so that the nourishing examples of these ancient men might emit their perfume to future generations. The Eternal Creator of things did this from the beginning of time, so that He might commend the everlasting fame of His servants and that their past deeds might leave examples to the future, and that by imitating the example of the merits of their predecessors and committing it to memory a future generation might rejoice.[96]

To put it simply, many monks and ecclesiastics have written biographies to give posterity models to follow. God ordained this, so that the

---

[95] On Jonas, see O'Hara 2018.  [96] Trans. O'Hara and Wood 2017: 93.

memory of those who served him would last forever, and for the sake of those who would come after. Jonas undoubtedly believed that his mannered rendering of this fairly simple notion was rhetorically effective. He probably considered it a proper *captatio benivolentiae*, establishing for his readers his scholarly *bona fides*. It may also have been inspired by his subject. We have a number of pieces attributed to St Columba, Columbanus' contemporary and fellow Irish monk, one of them an abecedarian hymn that begins:

> Altus prosator, vetustus
> dierum et ingenitus
> erat absque origine
> primordii et crepidine
> est et erit in saecula
> saeculorum infinita;
> cui est unigenitus
> Christus et sanctus spiritus
> coaeternus in gloria
> deitatis perpetua. (*Altus prosator* 1–10)

> Lofty creator, ancient of days, unbegotten, without origin of beginning and foundation, he was and is and will be unto boundless ages of ages, to whom the only-begotten is Christ and the Holy Ghost is coeternal, in the endless glory of godhead.

Here the mannerism extends from the broad level of poetic form – abecedarianism is necessarily mannered; compare the lipogrammatic abecedarianism of Fulgentius' *De aetatibus* – to poetic diction, with words like *prosator* and *crepidine*. Off-putting, perhaps, but at least it is relatively comprehensible. That is not the case with a later Irish composition, the *Hisperica famina*, whose ridiculously mannered title (*hisperica* < *Hibernia+Hesperia*) is an accurate guide to the contents. See the opening:

> ampla pectoralem suscitat uernia cauernam
> mestum extrico pulmone tonstrum
> Sed gaudifluam pectoreis arto procellam arthereis
> Cum insignes sophie speculator arcatores
> Qui egregiam urbani tenoris propinant faucibus linpham
> Vipereos que litteratur plasmant syllogismos (*Hisperica famina* 1–6)[97]

---

[97] Ed. Herren 1974: 64.

> Ample jubilation swells the caverns of my breast and scorching grief I pluck from my lungs, and I imprison in the arteries of my chest a beating storm of joy, when I behold the famous lords of wisdom who down their throats swallow the glorious liquor of an urbane culture who weave the vipery syllogisms that men of letters understand.[98]

Translation can transmit the sense of the Latin, but not the exoticism of the words. The roughly contemporary works of the Anglo-Saxon abbot and bishop Aldhelm show many of the same features, if less extreme.[99]

> Iamdudum ad pontificale proficiscens conciliabulum, fraternis sodalium catervis comitatus, almitatis vestrae scripta meae mediocritati allata satis libenter suscipiens, erectis ad aethera palmis, immensas Christo pro sospitate vestra gratulabundus impendere grates curavi, quo stylo non solum ecclesiastica promissorum votorum foedera, quae fida pollicitatione spopondistis, ubertim claruerunt, verum etiam melliflua divinarum studia Scripturarum sagacissima sermonum serie patuerunt. (*Prosa de virginitate* ch. 1, p. 229 Ehwald)

> Some time ago, while proceeding to an episcopal council accompanied by brotherly throngs of associates, I received most pleasurably what had been written by your Grace to my humble self and, with hands extended to the heavens, I took care joyously to extend immense thanks to Christ on behalf of all your welfare. In your writing, not only were the ecclesiastical compacts of your sworn vows – which you had pledged with a solemn promise – abundantly clear, but also the studies of Sacred Scriptures, which drip with honey, were manifest in the extremely subtle sequence of your discourse.[100]

A particular feature of Aldhelm's work is that it demonstrates the applicability of the mannered aesthetic to poetry as well as prose. Consider the opening of his verse *De virginitate*:

> Omnipotens genitor, mundum ditione gubernans,
> Lucida stelligeri qui condis culmina coeli,
> Nec non telluris formas fundamina verbo,
> Pallida purpureo pingis qui flore vireta,
> Sic quoque fluctivagi refrenas caerula ponti,
> Mergere ne valeant terrarum littora lymphis,
> Sed tumidos frangant fluctus obstacula rupis;     (*Carmen de virginitate* 1–7)

---

[98] Trans. Rand 1931: 137. A more literal translation can be found in Herren 1974: 65.
[99] The classic study is Orchard 1994.
[100] Trans. Lapidge and Herren 1979: 59, with modifications.

## 6 Mediaeval Latin

> Almighty Progenitor, guiding the world by Your rule, Who are creator of the shining heights of the star-filled heaven, Who also formed the foundations of the earth by Your Word; You Who paint the pale greensward with purple blossom and restrain the azure surface of the wave-wandering sea so that the shores of the land are not submerged by water, but rather that obstacles of rocks may break the swollen waves ...[101]

The connection of all these authors to Insular milieux has led scholarship to invent a stylistic category called Hiberno-Latin (not to be confused with Hiberno-Latin as a geographic convenience). It has also been called the 'hermeneutic style' on the grounds that its dominant characteristic is the use of obscure diction derived from glossaries called *Hermeneumata*. But the case becomes muddled once one takes a broader look at sixth-, seventh- and eighth-century literature. A contemporary of Columba, Dynamius of Marseilles, wrote Latin prose of much the same flavour as Jonas:

> Quantum aestifero solis ardore defesso vel longinqui itineris a vastitate quassato gelida limpha, dum ariditatem temperat, restinguit desideria sitientis, ita mihi vestrarum epistularum elocutio, cum incolomitatis vestrae indicia rettulit, gaudiorum incrementa nutrivit; quia, quotiens crebra recordatione dulcia affectionis vestrae vota commemoro, desideria pectoris publicare suspiriis non desisto, pro eo, quod ille corporali fraudatur intuitu, qui de cordis non absentatur arcano. (*Epistolae austrasiacae* 12.1)[102]

> Just as when one is wearied by the roasting heat of the sun or shattered by the vastness of a long journey, cold, clear water, as it moderates thirst, extinguishes the desire of the one who thirsts, so too the eloquence of your letters to me, when it brings evidence that you are well, nourishes the growth of my joys, since, as often as I recall with frequent recollection the sweet promise of your affection, I cannot hold back the desires of my heart to burst forth in sighs, for the one who, though deprived from my bodily sight, is not absent from the secret chamber of my heart.

His wife Eucheria composed a charming epigram, a specimen of 'cultivated precocity' displaying a 'delight in mannerism' (Dronke).[103] The elegiacs posit a series of adynata, an impeccably classical poetic device, but in a language far removed from Horace or Virgil:

> Aurea concordi quae fulgent fila metallo
>     setarum cumulis consociare uolo.

---

[101] Trans. Lapidge and Rosier 1985: 108.
[102] = *MGH Epist.* III 435. On Dynamius, see Norberg 1991.
[103] Dronke 1984: 28. See also Marcovich and Georgiadou 1988.

> Sericeum tegmen, gemmantia texta Laconum,
>     pellibus hircinis aequiperanda loquor.
> Nobilis horribili iungatur purpura burrae;
>     nectatur plumbo fulgida gemma graui ...   (vv. 1–6)
>
> The threads of gold, shining with the glitter of the concordant metal, I want to put together with the heaps of bristles; a silken garment, a Spartan cloak wrought with gems, I want to put on the same level with goatskins. Let a noble purple tunic be attached to an awful shaggy rag. Let a shining gem be affixed to a piece of heavy lead.[104]

The snobbery comprehends not just style but content, coming to the devastating conclusion:

> Haec monstra incertis mutent sibi tempora fatis:
>     rusticus et seruus sic petat Eucheriam!   (vv. 31–2)
>
> Let these beasts exchange their way of life for an uncertain fate: then only may a countryman and a serf come to woo Eucheria![105]

Traces of mannerism can be found everywhere. In the third quarter of the seventh century, Chrodobertus (Robert), bishop of Tours, wrote a letter to the Abbess Boba (St Beuve of Reims):

> Si futuri temporis cautela, largiente Christi gratia, inhibeatur et culpa non iteretur, quatinus multis fletibus diebus et noctibus, publicae et occulte, ieiuniis et orationibus, gemitibus, suspiriis, laboribus, obedientia et taciturnitate, humilitate et caritate preterita deleatur, non sunt querenda aut numeranda annorum tempora ad agendam penitentiam, sed fortitudo cuiuslibet temporis vel momenti conpungtionis, timoris sui et amoris Dei ex toto cordis desiderio.[106]
>
> If one is restrained by concern for the time to come, by the gift of Christ's grace, and the fault is not repeated, such that by much weeping through days and nights, both in public and private, by fasting and prayers, by groans, sighs, labours, obedience and silence, by humility and charity, the past fault is blotted out, the duration of the years for doing penance are not to be examined or counted, but only the fortitude of fear of oneself and the love of God at each time and moment of sorrow, from the whole desire of the heart.

---

[104] Trans. Marcovich and Georgiadou 1988: 166.   [105] Ibid. 167, with modifications.
[106] *Ep. aev. Mer. coll.* 16 = *MGH Epist.* III 462.

## 6 Mediaeval Latin

One could equally look at some of the prose of Eugenius of Toledo, such as this period from a letter to Isidore's executor Braulio:

> Quid aut taliter signatis remedii, aut his possit pro correctione praeberi, me fateor ignorare; sed a te de his illuminari me postulo, qui divinae sapientiae maiori lumine pollens, et legis sanctae quotidie meditationi deserviens, latebrosas nigrorum cordium factiones et vehementer insequeris, et prudenter invenis, et acute dissolvis. (*Ep.* 1.3, *PL* 87, 403)

> I confess that I am ignorant as to what can be offered as a remedy to those who anointed in this way, or for their correction, but I ask to be enlightened by you on these matters, since you are mighty in the greater light of divine wisdom, and daily devote yourself to meditation on the holy law, and you doggedly search out the shadowy factions of black hearts, and cleverly find them, and sharply remove them.

The persistence of mannerism across Europe in the seventh century defies attempts to locate specific cultural conditions which fostered it. Certainly in the South there were still remnants of the machinery of rhetorical education,[107] and certainly in Ireland, scholars approached Latin as a language to be learned from books, a code even. But none of the explanations can comprehend the whole. The fact is simply that throughout the seventh century, and beyond, writers were still drawn to mannerism, readers still enjoyed it, and these readers were found dispersed across the Latin world. Aldhelm, for example, may have known the *Versus Eucheriae*.[108]

Understood this way, it makes sense that the important sea-change in Latin style comes not with the Carolingians but with an Insular author who never set foot beyond Britain. The Latinity of Bede has long been praised, and even a cursory glance at the opening of the *Historia ecclesiastica* is enough to understand why:

> Historiam gentis Anglorum ecclesiasticam, quam nuper edideram, libentissime tibi desideranti, rex, et prius ad legendum ac probandum transmisi, et nunc ad transcribendum ac plenius ex tempore meditandum retransmitto; satisque studium tuae sinceritatis amplector, quo non solum audiendis scripturae sanctae uerbis aurem sedulus accommodas, uerum etiam noscendis priorum gestis siue dictis, et maxime nostrae gentis uirorum inlustrium, curam uigilanter impendis. (*praef.*)

---

[107] The classic study is Riché 1976.  [108] Orchard 1994: 207.

> The ecclesiastical history of the English, which I recently had set forth, I did both first very gladly send to you at your desire, my king, for you to read and assess first, and now do send it to you again, that you may have it copied and may more fully at your leisure consider it: and I cannot but highly commend your unfeigned zeal, not only to give diligent ear to the words of Holy Scripture, but also exercise a watchful care to know of things done or spoken by worthy men before your time, and specially of our own country.[109]

This is not the simple Latin, or *sermo humilis*, of Gregory or Isidore, but it is not mannered. The achievement of Bede was a complex but clear Latinity deploying registers appropriate to his subject.[110] The literary florescence of the following period – in the late eighth and ninth centuries – continues on this track. Deliberately, it seems; the leading light of that movement, Alcuin of York, was himself a student of one of Bede's pupils. We have already seen specimens of Carolingian prose and poetry, by Modoin, Paschasius and Einhard. Perhaps they can be criticised, with Auerbach or Des Esseintes, as lifeless, although I confess to knowing no objective measure for linguistic vitality. At the very least, from the perspective of *Stilgeschichte*, they may be understood not merely as classical revivals, but also as reactions against mannerism.

But the tides changed. At the very end of the ninth century, Abbo of St Germain wrote an epic account of the Viking siege of Paris that he had himself witnessed in 885. It is prefaced with a letter to one brother Gozelin which can only be described as highly mannered:[111]

> Tuae admodum mihimet acceptissimę germanitatis affectio sibimet dudum destinari crebro poposcit, ut bellorum Parisiacę polis, precellentissimi quoque principis ab examine regni hucusque Odonis, nostro genitum labore codicellum didicit, tam contigui studiosa ingenioli quam fraterni insuper non inmemor flagri. (*Bella Parisiacae urbis, pr.*)

> The love of your kinship, most acceptable to me – your love that is enthusiastic for your kin's little intellect and not unmindful of brotherly love – when it learned that a little book of the wars of the city of Paris and also of Odo, the most outstanding prince up to now since the origin of the kingdom, had been born from our labour, often desired that it be sent.[112]

This contrasts with the style of the actual text at least of the first two books, which is mostly very clear and written under the predominant influence of

---

[109] Trans. King 1930, with substantial modifications.
[110] See Hays 2015: 224–7, who analyses another passage of the *Historia ecclesiastica*.
[111] Ed. von Winterfeld 1899: 77. An English translation is offered by Adams and Rigg 2004.
[112] Trans. Adams and Rigg 2004: 18.

ancient epic. Consider, for example the brief speech of the Viking king to Gozelin (Jocelyn, bishop of Paris, not Abbo's addressee):

> O Gozline, tibi gregibusque tuis miserere,
> ne pereas; nostris faveas dictis, rogitamus;
> indulge, siquidem tantum transire queamus
> hanc urbem – tangemus eam numquam; sed honores
> conservare tuos conemur, Odonis et omnes. (1.40–4)

> O Gozelin, show pity to yourself, your flocks,
> Lest you should die. Obey our words, that's all we ask.
> Indulge our wish: allow us only to pass through
> This town, which we will never touch. We'll do our best
> To save you honours, and all those of Odo too.[113]

When, however, we move to the third book, written specifically for a clerical audience (*clericorum decus*) and for students (*tirunculorum effectus*), we are right back into the world of Martianus and the *Hisperica famina*:

> Clerice, dipticas lateri ne dempseris umquam.
> Corcula labentis fugias ludi fore, ne te
> laetetur foedus sandapila neque toparcha.
> Machia sit tibi, quo ierarchia, necque cloaca.
> Non enteca nec alogia, verum absida tecum
> conmaneat, mentes, acrimonia, non quia mordet. (3.1–6)

> O cleric, never take the diptychs from your side;
> Flee from being the leader of the sliding game, lest
> The filthy bier and the toparch rejoice in you.
> Let your battle be where hierarchy, not the sewer, is.
> Let not the money chest nor banqueting but clear
> Severity stay with you, since it does not bite
> The mind.[114]

Tellingly, the first two books of Abbo's poem achieved almost no mediaeval circulation. The third book was wildly popular, and particularly so in England. The following century and a half would see the triumphant return of mannerism in both poetry and prose.[115]

---

[113] Trans. Adams and Rigg 2004: 23.    [114] Trans. Adams and Rigg 2004: 63.
[115] A counterpart to Abbo from this period would be Atto of Vercelli, in the mid-tenth century, who composed a double version of his prose work, one simple and one mannered. See the analysis in Hays 2015: 227–9, who makes the connection to works like the *Hisperica famina*, without, however, using the term mannerism.

The Latin of tenth-century England has been well studied, particularly in regard to the 'hermeneutic style'.[116] It is well known that virtually the entire Latin literary output of pre-conquest England after the ninth century is written with a tortuous – perhaps torturous – mannerism. But mannerism flourished everywhere in Europe where literary Latin was written. In 981, the monk Walther of Speyer prefaced his verse life of St Christopher (*Vita et passio Sancti Christophori martyris*) with a description of his own education:

> At postquam prima sicienti fauce saliva
> Imbibit alphabetum notularum docta tenore,
> Syllabicas recta rugas plicuisse rubrica,
> Nuda mihi clausas tribuit psalmodia mammas
> Terpsicoreque suam docuit me texere pallam,
> Donec bis tropicos repetivit Apollo meatus.                    (12–17)[117]

> And after the first saliva in the thirsty mouth had drunk of the alphabet, learned in the shape of characters to fold the creases of syllables with the right rubric, naked Psalmody offered her still closed-up breasts to me, and Terpsichore taught me to weave her mantle, until Apollo had twice made his wandering journey between the tropics.

In other words, Walther studied chant after grammar for two years. This work has been described as having an 'artificial and overladen classicizing style of poetry' (Jaeger) – an observation that might hold if one thinks of Martianus, Macrobius and Boethius as the real classics.[118] In prose, the best example of tenth-century mannerism on the continent can be found in the incomprehensible works of Rather of Verona.[119] An irascible ecclesiastic from the territory of Liège, Rather's career ranged all over Europe. Driven from the sees of Verona (twice) and Liège, he wandered from Provence to Bavaria and the Rhineland. Along the way he composed an extraordinary corpus of Latin works in a highly personal style. One specimen will suffice. On 29 July 966, Rather mounted his pulpit in Verona and delivered an extraordinary sermon:

> Cum enim eo quo indignus attollor officio debitorem me utriusque fore non nesciam ritus, id est ut et domino in membris suis, hoc est sanctae matris ecclesiae debeam filiis ministrare, ob hoc tamen a contemplando eo numquam cessare sed in lege eius meditari die ac nocte, et neutrum horum me

---

[116] The *locus classicus* is Lapidge 1975.   [117] Ed. Vossen 1962: 36.   [118] Jaeger 1994: 63.
[119] On Rather and his inimitable style, see Reid 1981.

## 6 Mediaeval Latin

perspiciam agere, sed econtra non me solum sed et omnes mihi commissos, precipue uere magis necessarios, corrumpendo, eum die noctuque (quamuis in eum nulla cadat passio) ad iracundiam prouocare, quid de me dicere, quid ualeo cogitare (et ut turpia subsidens honesta solum, prohibita licet, depromam) si in lege Dei ut debitorem me fore non nescio die <non> meditor et nocte, Catullum numquam antea lectum, Plautum quando iam olim lego neglectum, musicam quando sepe rogatus expono, cum nequeam (primo aritmetico scilicet cassatus auxilio), milites quando meos ad prelium ob Cesaris cogo preceptum, quando illos mitto uenatum? (*Sermo de Maria et Martha* 4)

I am aware that in the office to which I am unworthily raised I am obliged to live both kinds of life, that is, that I should both minister to the Lord in his members (i.e. the sons of the Holy Mother the Church) and yet never cease from contemplating Him, but meditate on His law day and night, and I see that I do neither of these things, but on the contrary, by corrupting not only myself but also all those entrusted to me, and particularly those of my brotherhood, provoke Him day and night to anger, though no passion affects Him. What then can I say, what can I think of myself (to omit the shameful acts and to mention only the honourable, though forbidden, ones), if I do not meditate – as I am well aware that I ought – day and night on the law of God, when I read some Catullus never read before and Plautus long neglected, when I often expound music in response to a request (though quite unable to do so, as I lack the first help of mathematics), when I marshal my soldiers for war following Caesar's orders and send men out hunting?[120]

This is a passage well known to classical scholars, as it is the only secure testimonium to the reading of Catullus in the Middle Ages. Many are content to paraphrase it – an unsurprising choice, given the passage's relentless recursiveness and dizzying grammar. One can only imagine the bafflement of the Veronese hearing it delivered orally. He found one appreciative ear, at least, a millennium later, in Auerbach, who described his work with a period not unworthy of Rather himself:

Rather is always expressive, and unquestionably the mannerism of his language is something more than learned ornamentation, namely an authentic reflection of his nature: as far as I know, he is the first author of the Middle Ages in whom mannerism became a genuine style, but it was rooted in his being, which he could not have expressed any other way.[121]

---

[120] Trans. Kiss 2015: 6. A translation of Rather's works – on which Kiss based his own rendering – can be found in Reid 1991.

[121] Auerbach 1965: 143. Compare the original (1958: 107): 'Doch ausdrucksvoll, wie schon gesagt, ist Rather immer, und es ist ganz unbezweifelbar, daß der Manierismus seiner Sprache nicht nur eine gelehrte Ornamentierung, sondern die eigentliche Form seines Wesens ist: der erste Schriftsteller

Mannerism extends beyond mere lexical and syntactic choices. It can also involve the use of innovative and artificial literary forms, such as the anti-abecedarian composition of Fulgentius mentioned earlier. In this period, leonine verse (hexameter with internal rhyme) became widespread – one of the earliest and most influential examples was the *Ecloga Theoduli* (discussed on pp. 286–7). Hucbald of St Amand (d. 930) composed a tautogrammatic poem in praise of bald men of 136 hexameter lines in which every word begins with C, beginning *Carmina, clarisonae, calvi cantate, Camenae* ('Sing, far-sounding Muses, songs for bald men'). This period sees the earliest macaronic poetry, or poetry which freely mixes Latin and the vernacular. A composition from Canterbury in praise of Aldhelm dating from this period contains a bizarre blend of Old English and mannered Latin:[122]

>                     Etiam nusquam
> ne sceal ladigan    labor quem tenet
> encratea,    ac he ealneg sceal
> boethia    biddan georne
> þurh his modes gemind    micro in cosmo,
> þæt him drihten gyfe    dinams on eorðan,
> fortis factor ...                                    (*Aldhelm* 12–17)

> Never indeed must mastery excuse the one whom work occupies, but ever he must eagerly ask for aid in his mind's thought in the microcosm, that the Lord, the mighty maker, grant him power ...[123]

Further examples of macaronic poetry, this time with German, can be found in the *Carmina Cantabrigiensia*.[124]

The eleventh century saw a gradual stylistic change. A little more than a century after Abbo had composed his third book of the *Bella Parisiaca* for students, a schoolmaster of Liège, named Egbert, composed an hexameter medley specifically for students, entitled the *Fecunda ratis*, or *Well-Laden Ship*.[125] It opens with a couplet ever so slightly tinged by mannerism:

> Lintris foeta iocis diversa aplustria portat,
> cuius Prora nitet vario distincta colore.        (*Fecunda ratis* 1.3–4)

---

des Mittelalters, so viel ich weiß, bei welchem das Manierierte zum eigentlichen Stil wird, weil es aus seinem Dasein entspringt, diesem Dasein entspricht und allein fähig ist, es auszudrücken.'

[122] See Lapidge 1975: 83.    [123] Trans. Orchard 1994: 292, modified.    [124] Ed. Ziolkowski 1994.
[125] Ed. and trans. Babcock 2013.

> My ship teeming with riddles carries diverse rigging; its 'Embellished Prow' shines with manifold color.[126]

The text, however, immediately sails into monostich proverbs modelled on the *Dicta Catonis*, written in a register of Latin we would recognise as suitable for beginners. In prose too, the change is perceptible. Compare a sermon by Peter Damian (d. 1072) with the sermon by Rather:

> Non igitur nobis avaritiae ardor incandeat; non iracundiae nos furor impellat. Non in nobis flamma libidinis aestuet; non turpis cogitatio pulchram animae nostrae coram Deo speciem foedet. Non nos terrenae facultatis abundantia in superbiam erigat; non tenacitas misericordiae viscera pauperibus claudat. Vigeat in nobis perpetua castitas, humilitas, patientia, sobrietas, iustitia cum pietate, severitas cum mansuetudine. (*Serm.* 73, *PL* 144, 866b)

> Let not, then, the heat of avarice set us aflame, let not the madness of anger drive us. Let not the flame of lust grow hot within us, let not disgraceful thoughts defile the beauty of our soul in the sight of God. Let not the accumulation of earthly power stiffen us into pride, let not stubbornness choke off the depths of our mercy for the poor. In us may there flourish ceaseless chastity, humility, patience, sobriety, justice with devotion, severity with tenderness.

In Peter Damian, we can recognise both the influence of classical rhetorical theory, and the vigorous Latinity of the vulgate Bible, combining clarity with rhetorical power.[127] It is for this reason that he has been described as 'one of the best Latinists of his age, and one of the greatest writers of the Latin Middle Ages'.[128] In poetry, the Loire valley poets – Marbod of Rennes, Baudri of Bourgeuil and Hildebert of Lavardin, active around the end of the eleventh century and into the beginning of the twelfth – developed a mature and classical poetic style, which did not avoid the formal innovations of the Middle Ages entire, and made no attempt to avoid common unclassical words. One example will suffice. Baudri wrote a poem describing his own poetry to one Robert, written probably before 1107, in response to a request for a poem:

> Carmen inurbanum nulla fornace recoctum
>     misi mitto iterum, quod tibi rus sapiat.
> Rus colimus, mulgemus oves, armenta minamur,

---

[126] Trans. Babcock 2013: 9.
[127] On Peter Damian, see the classic study Leclercq 1960; and his rhetoric, see Schönbeck 1998 and Yolles 2009.
[128] Leclercq 1960: 172.

>    urbis rus nobis abstulit officium.
> Nos fora nescimus, nescimus castra subire,
>    ruris delicias nos numeramus oves.
> Quiquis in urbe manet, novit quicquid fit in orbe
>    urbs prior agnovit quicquid in orbe novum.
> Nos avium varia laetemur garrulitate,
>    nos voces ovium novimus atque boum. (vv. 1–10) [129]

> I have sent you and again I send not a city poem, one distilled in no furnace, but one which savours of the country for you. I live in the countryside, I milk my sheep, I drive my herds. The country has exempted me from the city's obligations. I don't know the courts, I don't know how to enter military service. I count my sheep as the countryside's pleasures. Whoever sticks to the city knows whatever is going on in the world – the city knows what's new in the world first. I am delighted by the different chirpings birds make. I know the voices of my sheep and my cows.

There are many ways one could describe this poem; mannered is not one of them. There are quite a few reasons why the twelfth century has been described as a Renaissance, some of them more valid than others. But the most obvious one is because of style. Many twelfth-century writers strove to imitate the Latin classics, both prose and poetry. Norden found the prose of John of Salisbury notable for its imitation of classical style.[130] John's near contemporary and fellow Englishman, William of Malmesbury, has received similar analysis at the hands of Winterbottom.[131] But focusing just on the most classical authors risks a distortion of perspective. The real genius of the twelfth century was developing a Latin that could express extremely complex ideas in clear terms. In poetry, for example, Adam of St Victor (d. 1146) could encode complex theological ideas into perfectly balanced rhythmic strophes suitable for singing. Take, for example, a bit of a sequence for the feast of Pentecost:

> Panes legis primitivi
> sunt sub una adoptivi
>    fide duo populi.
> Se duobus interiecit
> sicque duos unum fecit
>    lapis, caput anguli. (13.5 p. 53 Gauthier)

---

[129] Hilbert 1979: no. 251. See Szövérffy 1992–5: II 169.   [130] Norden 1898: 717.
[131] Winterbottom 2017.

> The two breads of the old law are the two peoples, joined by adoption, under one faith. He, the cornerstone, joins them both, and so makes the two one.

Any attempt to put this into a language other than Latin must either choose theological fidelity or poetic effect. In Adam's hands, the two are one. In terms of style, then, there is little daylight between Adam and the goliardic poets. The Archpoet achieves a similar complexity in simplicity, such as in his famous 'confession':[132]

> Tercio capitulo memoro tabernam.
> illam nullo tempore sprevi neque spernam,
> donec sanctos angelos venientes cernam
> cantantes pro mortuis 'requiem eternam'.
>
> Meum est propositum in taberna mori,
> ut sint vina proxima morientis ori.
> tunc cantabunt letius angelorum chori:
> 'Sit deus propitius huic potatori.'
>
> On the third count, I list the tavern. At no time have I spurned it, nor will I, until I see the holy angels coming, singing *requiem aeternam* for the dead. It is my plan to die in the tavern, so wine might be at my lips as I expire. Then the choirs of angels will sing in greater exultation, 'May God have mercy on this drinker!'

Beneath the facile and glittering surface run deep currents of parody of liturgy and sacramental theology, and the Archpoet is no more an easy poet than Adam.

The scholastics were the masters of this art: it is often said that Thomas Aquinas, for example, is easier to read in Latin than in translation, so closely is the structure of the thought wedded to the structure of the language. The stylistic development of the Latin language is at least as important a factor in the tremendous intellectual and philosophical achievements of the later Middle Ages as the translation of the *Corpus Aristotelicum* into Latin. As a language Latin became explosively productive: if one needed to discuss the concepts of 'this' and 'that', *haecceitas* and *illeitas*, 'thisness' and 'thatness', were ready at hand. If one wanted to have a serious ontological discussion – the kind that Seneca wished he could have in Latin (*Ep.* 58) – one could readily distinguish between *ens*,

---

[132] On the Archpoet, see Godman 2014.

*esse, essentia, essentitas, essentialitas* and *entitas*, and that without even bringing in *exsistentia, subsistentia, essentificatio, quidditas* and *substantia*. One cannot but note a touch of manneristic whimsy in the philosophical vocabulary of the Majorcan theologian Raymond Llull (d. 1315); for example, from *De ascensu*:

> Considerat intellectus passiones, quas habet Deus respectu ad nos, secundum quod nos sumus peccatores, sicut: incredibilitas, intimibilitas, iniustificabilitas, ignorabilitas, inrecolibilitas, inamabilitas, ingratibilitas, inlaudabilitas, blasphemabilitas, inhonorabilitas, periurabilitas; et sic de multis aliis, quas longum esset narrare. (d.6)

> The intellect considers the passions which God has with respect to us, insofar as we are sinners, such as: inability-to-be-believed, inability-to-be-feared, inability-to-be-justified, inability-to-be-known, inability-to-be-recalled, inability-to-be-loved, inability-to-be-rejoiced-over, inability-to-be-praised, ability-to-be-blasphemed, inability-to-be-honoured, ability-to-be-perjured, and so too regarding many other qualities, which would take too long to enumerate.

Indeed, as we move from the twelfth into the later thirteenth and fourteenth centuries it is hard not to notice a sort of recurrence of mannerism. We can do nothing more than present a few gleanings, since in this period the amount of surviving literature becomes so vast and the nature of it so varied that generalisations are far less useful than in the preceding centuries.

Formal innovations and experiments can be found in poetry. Macaronic poetry, for example, takes on new life. Take this example from England:

> *Alas, my hart will brek in thre;*
> *Terribilis mors conturbat me.*
>
> Illa iuventus that is so nyse
> Me deduxit into vayn devise;
> Infirmus sum, I may not rise –
>     Terribilis mors conturbat me.
>       *Alas, my hart etc.*
>
> ...
>
> Queso iam the Trynité:
> 'Duc me from this vanité
> In celum, ther is joy with the' –
>     Terribilis mors conturbat me.
>       *Alas, my hart etc.*     (*Illa iuventus* 1–7, 23–7)

Alas my heart will break in three; dreadful death confounds me. That youth which is so foolish has led me into vain device. I am weak, I may not rise – dreadful death confounds me. *Alas, my heart etc.* .... Now I beg the Trinity: 'Lead me from this vanity into heaven, there is joy with thee' – dreadful death confounds me. *Alas, my heart etc.*

Also from England is an extraordinary poem written entirely in a perverse Latinity which deliberately transposes morphology, *Quondam fuit factus festus*:

Abbas dixit: ut senectus
ego bipsi cum affectus.
Vadi queri promtum lectus
ubi sum iacencia.

Dixit abbas serviatis:
Date vinum nostris fratris.
Bene legunt et cantatis
Ad nostra solempnia.

Dixit prior ad abbatis:
bene bibunt, habent satis.
Non est bonum ebriatis;
eant ad claustralia.

Unus cano iuniorum,
bonus lectus et cantorum,
irascatus ad priorum
dixit, 'Ista folia!'

The Abbot said: 'As an old man, I have drunk with gusto. Go and look for a bed where I can lie down.' The Abbot said to the servants: 'Give wine to our brothers. They have read and sung well at our solemnities.' The prior said to the Abbot: 'They have drunk well and had enough. It is not good to get drunk – let them go back to the cloister.' One of the younger cantors, skilled in reading and singing, grew angry at the prior and said, 'What folly!' (translated as if correct Latin forms were employed)

From its first publication, this poem has been described as *Spottlatein*, or mock-Latin, but the fact that every word in it is a valid Latin word, suggests something more is going on.[133] Some six centuries earlier the mysterious grammarian Virgilius Maro had described twelve different kinds of Latinity, the eighth of which, called *belsavia*, exhibits all the features found in *Quondam fuit*.[134]

Belsauia, hoc est peruersa, cum casus nominum modusque uerborum transmutat, cuius exempla sunt hec, ut lex, hoc est legibus, et legibus, hoc est lex, et rogo, hoc est rogate, et rogant, hoc est rogo. (*Epit.* 15)

*Belsavia*, or perverse, is when the cases of nouns and the moods of verbs are switched around. Examples of this are these: *lex* means *legibus*, and *legibus* means *lex*, and *rogo* means *rogate* and *rogant* means *rogo*.

---

[133] Most recently Rigg 2015: 279.
[134] The best edition of Virgilius Maro is Löfstedt 2003; the most detailed study is Law 1995.

I do not suggest any genetic relationship between Virgilius and the *Quondam fuit*, even though Virgilius did find at least one appreciative reader in thirteenth-century England.[135] Both are products, however, of a parallel aesthetic, and the *Quondam fuit* can be appreciated as a specimen of a sort of mannerism. It was not written for those who lacked Latin grammar; on the contrary, it can only be appreciated for its art by readers who understand what the Latin ought to say.

*Quondam fuit* was only published in 1908, and so there is no way Huysmans could have put it into Des Esseintes' library. It is also not the sort of composition Auerbach was apt to comment on, and we can have little doubt as to what Norden would have thought about it. Nonetheless it stands as a peculiar monument of some of the trends that characterise some of the literature of the whole mediaeval period, bringing together a mannerist aesthetic in a popular and new poetic form shot through with parody and satire. It is a mediaeval composition and, unlike some, could not have been written in any other age.

### The Legacy of Mediaeval Latin Style

As an overview of *Stilgeschichte*, I recognise that one could find the foregoing analysis perverse, with its omission or cursory treatment of the canonical texts of mediaeval Latin, such as they are, and its emphasis on mannerism instead of classicism or the *sermo humilis*. Nonetheless, it provides a flexible enough framework into which many mediaeval works of many different ages can be securely placed, and its emphasis on mannerism and the enduring legacy of the late Roman authors tries to respect and understand what mediaeval writers and readers themselves considered to be good Latin.

It also points to the enduring legacy of mediaeval Latin literature. The intellectual complexity of the metaphysical poets of the seventeenth century, such as John Donne and Richard Crashaw, owes much to the way in which style was wedded to thought in mediaeval Latin, particularly scholastic philosophy and hymnody.[136] A similar aesthetic to mediaeval mannerism marks some of the defining works

---

[135] A protégé of Robert Grosseteste, on whom I have a study in preparation.
[136] On Donne, see Kortemme 1933; Crashaw even translated several famous mediaeval hymns: see Claydon 1960.

## 6  Mediaeval Latin

of literary modernism – a fact rendered less surprising, perhaps, by Huysmans' evident interest in non-classical modes of Latinity. Eliot's *Waste Land* is a renewal of macaronic and centonic poetics, both types of mannerism. It is a poem written to be *studied* as much as read – witness, after all, Eliot's own explanatory footnotes – just as Alan of Lille's *Anticlaudianus* was equipped with a full-scale commentary just a few years after his death by his student Ralph of Longchamps, and Boccaccio composed notes for his own (Italian) *Teseida*.[137] But the most obvious debtor to the traditions of mediaeval mannerism is the (appropriately enough) Irish novelist, James Joyce, who repurposes the eschatologically rich language of the *Altus prosator* for scatological ends in *Finnegans Wake*:

> Primum opifex, altus prosator, ad terram viviparam et cunctipotentem sine ullo pudore nec venia, suscepto pluviali atque discinctis perizomatis, natibus nudis uti nati fuissent, sese adpropinquans, flens et gemens, in manum suam evacuavit (highly prosy, crap in his hand, sorry!), postea, animale nigro exoneratus, classicum pulsans, stercus proprium, quod appellavit deiectiones suas, in vas olim honorabile tristitiae posuit, eodem sub invocatione fratrorum geminorum Medardi et Godardi laete ac mellifue minxit, psalmum qui incipit: Lingua mea calamus scribae velociter scribentis: magna voce cantitans (did a piss, says he was dejected, asks to be exonerated), demum ex stercore turpi cum divi Orionis iucunditate mixto, cocto, frigorique exposito, encaustum sibi fecit indelibile (faked O'Ryan's, the indelible ink).[138]

Whatever Joyce's reading consisted of, he has caught the spirit of mannered Latin, not just with the obvious nod to Columba, but with the unsteady syntax, the obscure vocabulary (*vivipara* and *cunctipotens*), the use of a Greek word (*perizoma*) where an obvious Latin word would do (*cingulum*), with the wrong case ending, too, probably to rhyme with *discinctis*, the pun on *nates* – *nati*, the superfluous subjunctive in *fuissent*, the general nonsense of a reflexive object of *adpropinquans*, and so on.

These are mere soundings in deep and unexplored waters – the post-mediaeval reception of mediaeval Latin literature – a subject which, despite its central place in Curtius' *European Literature and the Latin Middle Ages*, is even more obscure and neglected than the

---

[137] Ralph: ed. Sulowski 1972; Boccaccio: see Schnapp 1992.
[138] Joyce 1939: 185. Boyle 1966 offers a translation.

history of mediaeval Latin itself. It is a sea vast beyond all reckoning: Ziolkowski's recent *The Juggler of Notre Dame and the Medievalizing of Modernity* follows the wake of a single mediaeval Latin story across nineteenth- and twentieth-century literature and culture in some 2,500 pages.[139] But perhaps when that story is written – if ever – it is what is distinctively *mediaeval* about mediaeval Latin – the playfulness and love of language it displays, its unabashed intellectualism, its addiction to formal and verbal experimentation, its parsimonious union of word and thought, in a word, its *oulipisme* – which will be found to have left the richest legacy.[140]

## 'A Rival Aesthetic'

The thirteenth and fourteenth centuries, or perhaps, more accurately the *Duecento* and the *Trecento*, with which we concluded the survey above, also bring what is conventionally considered the end of mediaeval Latin. At the end of the thirteenth century, a Paduan notary named Lovati Lovato and his circle of friends exchanged with each other poetic epistles which have been dubbed the foundation of humanistic Latin. It is not hard to see why. In one letter he describes visiting a witch, who prepared for him a potion:

> Postmodo secrete Circeas aggerat herbas,
>     quas dederat Pindos, Othris, Olimpus, Athos,
> quas Anthedonii gustarunt intima Glauci.
>     Nec desunt monti gramina lecta Rubro,
> nec que te refovent ictam serpente, Galanthi,
>     nec Florentini stamina fulva croci.
> Additur his mirre facinus, gummique Sabeum
>     et que cum casiis cinnama mittit Arabs.  (*Ep.* 4.83–90)

> Afterwards, she secretly piles up the herbs of Circe which Pindos, Othrys, Olympus, and Athos had provided for her, and which the belly of Anthedonian Glaucus had tasted. Nor are the herbs collected from Mount Rubrus lacking, nor those which renew you, Galanthis, struck by the serpent, nor the tawny fibres of the Florentine crocus. To these are added the working of myrrh and Sabaean gum and twigs of cinnamon, which, with cinnamon bark, the Arabs send.[141]

---

[139] Ziolkowski 2018.   [140] See Hexter 2015 and Uden 2018.
[141] Trans. Sisler 1977: 85, with modifications.

The extent of Lovato's knowledge of ancient Latin poetry has been overstated (there is no real evidence he knew Propertius or Statius' *Silvae*, for example). Nonetheless, there can be no doubt that this poetry imitates Ovid and Horace in a way that is more intimate than almost any mediaeval examples. But this can also be understood as a new mannerism, challenging readers to pick out the allusions, sending them scurrying to other books to find the geographic and mythological references. A quick glance at some of Lovato's other poetry confirms this impression, such as this one addressed to Mussato (the Asellus of the poem; Lovato himself is Lupus):

> Dulcis Aselle Lupo, virtutis amator ephebe,
> Qua potes, adversis obstantia pectora praebe,
> Te decet esse virum. Seu clamat copia bebe,
> Si quid habes pulcrum chordis impelle, rebebe,
> Si nihil aut nostri carmen tibi displicet, ebe,
> Sive latere velis clipeum collectum in hebe,
> Cum reliquos hebetent turpia, turpis hebe.  (*Carm.* 27.12–18, p. 21 Padrin)

> Ass sweet to the wolf, young lover of virtue, in which you excel, set your chest athwart adversity – manhood becomes you. Or if your talents cry out bleating, if you have anything fine, play it on the strings, bleat it again, if my poem does not displease you at all, bleat it out, or if you wish to hide the trophy you have gained in your youth, while wantonness dulls your contemporaries, as a wanton man be dulled.[142]

*Ebe* must be one of the most challenging two-syllable rhymes in Latin – Lovato handles it with aplomb. The conventional explanation that examples like this represent Lovato's degeneration back into 'mediaeval taste', a concession 'to a contemporary and rival aesthetic'.[143] But how rival is the aesthetic? Witt characterises Lovato's classicising poems as follows:

> This is learned poetry, densely interspersed with ancient poetic fragments and mythological and biblical reminiscences ... The intensely referential verses of Lovato's poems must have delighted his audience, charmed by familiar literary associations set in a new context and intrigued about the origin of some of the expressions and imagery – in fact drawn from rare ancient texts – classical in character but unfamiliar.[144]

---

[142] Translation mine. I am grateful to Gavin Kelly for a number of suggestions. Witt 2000: 104 wrongly suggests that some of the words are nonsense.
[143] Witt 2000: 104.  [144] Ibid. 97.

What Witt is saying – even though he never uses the term – is that readers would have been attracted to Lovato's mannerism. I do not see any reason why those same readers would not be delighted by Lovato's *-ebe* poem. And so from its origins, humanistic, or protohumanistic, poetry looks a lot like yet another manifestation of mannerism. Further evidence can be found in Dante. In the second decade of the fourteenth century, Giovanni de Virgilio sent Dante a poem, gently suggesting that he ought not be writing allegorical poetry in the vernacular but rather Latin epic on contemporary events. The style of Giovanni's poem is definitely mannered:

> Pieridum vox alma, novis qui cantibus orbem
> mulces letifluum, vitali tollere ramo
> dum cupis, evolvens triplicis confinia sortis
> indita pro meritis animarum, sontibus Orcum,
> astripetis Lethen, epiphoebia regna beatis,
> tanta quid heu semper iactabis seria vulgo,
> et nos pallentes nihil ex te vate legemus? (*Ecl.* 1.1–7)

> Sacred voice of the Pierides, which sweetens the world awash in death with new songs, as you long to raise it up with the bough of life, unfurling the boundaries of the triple fate established according to each soul's deserts, Orcus for the guilty, Lethe for those who sought the stars, and for the blessed, the kingdoms beyond the sun [viz. the three cantos of the *Commedia*], why alas will you throw such weighty and serious matters to the common rabble, while we who are pale with study read nothing of your poetry?[145]

Dante responded to this provocative condemnation of his vernacular poetic project in a curious fashion, with a poem *à clef*, in the form of the most authentically Virgilian bucolic the world had seen at least since late antiquity, with himself as Tityrus and Giovanni as Mopsus, in a poem rightly seen as a landmark of protohumanist verse:

> Tunc ego sub quercu meus et Meliboeus eramus.
> Ille quidem, cupiebat enim consciscere cantum,
> 'Tityre; quid Mopsus, quid vult? Edissere,' dixit.
> Ridebam, Mopse; magis et magis ille premebat.
> Victus amore sui, posito vix denique risu,
> 'Stulte, quid insanis?' inquam. 'Tua cura capellae
> te potius poscunt, quamquam mala cenula turbet . . .'. (*Ecl.* 2.4–10)

---

[145] Translation mine, but I benefited from Wicksteed and Garland 1902: 147.

My dear Meliboeus and I were then under an oak tree. He said to me – for he wanted to know my song – 'Tityrus, what does Mopsus want? Tell me.' I smiled, Mopsus; he urged me more and more. Overcome at last by my affection for him, with effort at last I hid my smile, and said, 'Foolish man, why are you raving? The goats in your care are asking for you, although your meagre poor repast is troubling you . . .'.

Dante answered the mannerism of Giovanni – whose verse is redolent most of all of Boethius – with a mannerism of his own, a learned facsimile of Virgil. The kind of readers who would appreciate Giovanni's poem and Dante's response are not two different categories of readers and the aesthetics that characterise them are not two different aesthetics, but one. In the same way, both varieties of Lovato's poetry are united by a single aesthetic which could have been appreciated by the same audience.

Of course, I am only speaking here of the very beginnings of humanistic Latin. There is no doubt that a stylistic and aesthetic revolution would take place over the following decades, and that the literary Latin of the Renaissance is not just another mode of mediaeval Latin. Later humanists would themselves point to Lovato and Dante as precursors to their own movement, but this was conditioned by their own views of the Latinity of the Middle Ages. In their view eloquence died perhaps with Augustine, perhaps with Gregory the Great, and was only reborn in the Italy of the *Trecento*. Hence Witt is not wrong to characterise revivalist Neo-Latin as a 'rival aesthetic' to mediaeval Latin, but it was not so at the earliest stages. The Latin poetry of Lovato and Dante has its roots in the very traditions of style their successors attempted to displace.

Nonetheless, it is important to keep a wide perspective, for more than a century after Petrarch, humanistic Latin was not the only kind of literary Latin in use. In many – if not most – corners of the Latin world, what we would instantly recognise as mediaeval Latin remained in full flower. Far from Italy, for example, Piotr Wilhelmi from Grudziądz, a town on the Vistula south of Gdańsk, then part of the Baltic *Deutschordenstaat*, produced a remarkable collection of poetic compositions set to music, in an itinerant career which took him across central Europe over the first half of the fifteenth century.[146] A glance at some of the incipits, or openings, of his compositions is instructive: *Prodigiis eximiis, Praeconia etroclita,*

---

[146] On Piotr, see Gancarczyk 2006. The edition is Černý 1993. Most of the attention paid to Piotr since his rediscovery had been in musicology, but for a recent examination of his compositions as Latin poetry in the context of late mediaeval aesthetics, see Awianowicz 2017.

*Problemata enigmatum, Praedulcis eurus turbinis, Praelustri elucentia, Phoebus ecclipsi tumuli, Phonicorum ethicorum.* One example:

> Psalmodium exileratum
>     triphariali resono
> verum stipantes Dei natum
>     promemus vite consono
>
> ut per ipsum a scelesti
>     liberemur scoria
> et defuncti in celesti
>     collocemur gloria.

> Gathered round the true son of God, we will offer hymns of joy in threefold harmony befitting his life, that through him we might be freed from the slag of evil and after death come together in the glory of heaven.

The first thing one might note is that this is not the Latin of his humanist contemporaries, like Pier Paolo Decembrio, or Panormita, or Enea Silvio Piccolomini (whom Piotr may well have known). This is instead the Latin of the *Altus prosator*, Abbo of St. Germain, or Walther of Speyer. At the same time, Piotr was alive to new possibilities, particularly those offered by composition for polyphonic settings. For example, a composition about a monk named Andreas Ritter, entitled *Probitate eminentem*, demonstrates the literary and aesthetic potential of polyphonic poetry.[147] One specimen:

> Is sanctam vitam comitatur
> et morum rectitudinem
> amplexatur, veneratur
> iustorum sanctitudinem ...
>
> Et in templo est devotus,
> pro veniaque supplicat;
> quando bibit bonos potus,
> verba non multiplicat.
>
> Non est lentus, sed festinus
> divina ad obsequia; ...                (vv. 9–12, 17–26)

> He pursues a holy life, and embraces uprightness of character, and venerates the holiness of the just ... And he is devoted in church, and begs God for

---

[147] On this poem and its interpretation, see Gancarczyk 2016.

pardon. When he quaffs a good drink, he does not multiply his words. He is not slow but swift to God's service; ...

While the first voice sings these strophes, the second voice corroborates the sentiments:

> Hic non advertit mulieres
> viventes incomposite,
> sed puellas mente meras
> diligit theorice ...
>
> Raro manet in tabernis,
> pro se et suis cogitans
> lacrimatur, pro eternis
> devote deum rogitans.
>
> In bibendo, comedendo
> observat temperanciam; ...

> He pays no attention to women who live dissolutely, but he esteems pure-minded girls in a Platonic way ... He rarely spends time in taverns; he sheds tears when he thinks of himself and his own, devoutly beseeching God for eternal life. In drinking, in eating, he keeps to moderation; ...

So far, rather unremarkable both in content and poetic quality. The sting in the tail is what the text means when the two parts are read together:

> Is sanctam vitam comitatur,  hic non. Advertit mulieres
> et morum rectitudinem.       Viventes incomposite
> amplexatur, veneratur.       Sed puellas mente meras,
> iustorum sanctitudinem,      diligit theorice ...
>
> Et in templo est devotus     raro. Manet in tabernis,
> pro veniaque supplicat       pro se et suis cogitans.
> Quando bibit bonos potus,    lacrimatur; pro eternis
> verba non multiplicat        devote deum rogitans
>
> Non est lentus, sed festinus in bibendo, comedendo.
> Divina ad obsequia           observat temperanciam ...

> That man pursues a holy life, this one does not. He takes note of women and the uprightness of their characters. He embraces and venerates those who live dissolutely, but esteems girls of pure mind and the holiness of the just – in theory ... He is rarely devout in church. He spends his time in taverns, and begs for favour, thinking only of himself and his own. When he quaffs a good drink, he weeps. When he is devoutly asking God for eternal life, he does not multiply

his words. He is not slow, but quick to drink and to eat; but when it comes to the worship of God, he keeps to moderation ...

While the satire and parody on display here is of a piece with late mediaeval aesthetics – consider the *Quondam fuit* or the works of Chaucer or Boccaccio in the two generations preceding – the use of polyphonic layering to provide new and deeper meanings comes from mediaeval liturgical practice, and particularly the use of tropes to the ordinary chants of the Mass to comment on and expand upon the set liturgical texts.[148] It also tells us something about Piotr himself, and his playful approach to text. An alert reader might note as well that the *Psalmodium exileratum*, as well as every one of the incipits mentioned, has the acrostic sequence *P – E – T*. Piotr emerged from the obscurity that surrounds most popular Latin poets of the late Middle Ages due to the marvellous discovery by Černý in 1975 that he indulged in the mannerist game of signing his compositions with the acrostic *Petrus* (and one with a full *Petrus Wilhelmi de Grudencz*), as in the first six words of the *Psalmodium*.[149]

The lesson of this brief pilgrimage to fifteenth-century central Europe is that mediaeval Latin sensibilities and mediaeval Latin style persisted long after humanism took root. It is a tragedy, and one whose effects are still felt today, that even when scholars in the sixteenth century began to move away from a rigid aesthetic approach to Latin style and to historicise the language, understanding how it changed and developed over time from old Latin all the way up to 'Silver Latin', they were never able to historicise the development of Latin after antiquity.[150] It remained simply Gothic barbarism. And yet the reasons for this pose are not hard to grasp: all the way into the sixteenth century, as Piotr and the continuing manuscript circulation of his poetry for decades after his death testify, mediaeval Latin offered (in Witt's phrase) 'a contemporary and rival aesthetic', a living tradition of a Latin literature that was inspired by, but not subject to, the style of Cicero and Virgil.

*Postscript*

This is a time of transition in Mediaeval Latin studies. Eight of the scholars whose work appears in this essay, and all of them leading lights in the field, passed away as it was in preparation: A. G. Rigg (1937–2019), Peter

---

[148] See in general on tropes and liturgical poetry, Iversen 2010.  [149] See Černý 1975.
[150] Stok 2016 offers an excellent overview of one of the first humanist attempts to periodise Latin, that by Perotti, toward the end of the fifteenth century.

Godman (1955–2018), Richard Sharpe (1954–2020), Peter Dronke (1934–2020), Fr Édouard Jeauneau (1924–2019), Peter Stotz (1942–2020), Ronald Witt (1932–2017) and Marvin Colker (1927–2020). *Tantus labor non sit cassus.*

### References

Abrahams, P. (1926) *Les oeuvres poétiques de Baudri de Bourgueil (1046–1130)*, Paris.
Adams, A. and A. G. Rigg. (2004) 'A verse translation of Abbo of St. Germain's *Bella Parisiacae urbis*', *Journal of Medieval Latin* 14: 1–68.
Adams, J. N. (2017) *An Anthology of Informal Latin*, Cambridge.
Atwood, E. B. (1937) 'The *Excidium Troie* and medieval Troy literature', *Modern Philology* 35: 115–28.
Auerbach, E. (1958) *Literatursprache und Publikum in der lateinischen Spätantike und im Mittelalter*, Bern.
  (1965) *Literary Language and Its Public in Late Latin Antiquity and in the Middle Ages* (trans. R. Manheim), London.
Awianowicz, B. (2017) 'Texts by Petrus Wilhelmi de Grudencz in the context of the late medieval *Ars poetriae*', *Muzyka* 2017: 41–54.
Babcock, R. G. (2013) *The Well-Laden Ship. Egbert of Liège*, Cambridge, MA.
Barton, M. (2000) *Spätantike Bukolik zwischen paganer Tradition und christlicher Verkündigung: das Carmen de Mortibus Boum des Endelechius*, Trier.
Bate, K. (1983) 'Ovid, medieval Latin, and the pastourelle', *Reading Medieval Studies* 9: 16–33.
Bayerle, H. (2012) 'Speech genres in the twelfth-century Latin historical epics of Italy', in *Donum natalicium digitaliter confectum Gregorio Nagy septuagenario a discipulis collegis familiaribus oblatum* (online at: http://nrs.harvard.edu/urn-3:hul.ebook:CHS_Bers_etal_eds.Donum_Natalicium_Gregorio_Nagy.2012.)
Bernardo, A. (1962) *Petrarch, Scipio and the Africa: The Birth of Humanism's Dream*, Baltimore.
Bezner, F. (2005) *Vela Veritatis: Hermeneutik, Wissen und Sprache in der Intellectual History des 12. Jahrhunderts*, Leiden.
Boutemy, A. (1947) 'La version parisienne du poème de Simon Chèvre d'Or sur la guerre de Troie', *Scriptorium* 1: 267–88.
Boyle, R. (1966) '*Finnegans Wake*, page 185: an explication', *James Joyce Quarterly* 4: 3–16.
Brunhölzl, F. (1975–2014) *Geschichte der lateinischen Literatur des Mittelalters*, Munich.
Caiazzo, I. (2002) *Lecture médiévales de Macrobe. Les Glosae Colonienses super Macrobium*, Paris.
Cardelle de Hartmann, C. (2007) *Lateinische Dialoge 1200–1400: Literaturhistorische Studie und Repertorium*, Leiden.
Černý, J. (1975) 'Petrus Wilhelmi of Grudencz – an unknown composer of the "Age of Dufay"', *Musica antiqua. Acta scientifica* 4: 91–103.

Černý, J., ed. (1993) *Petrus Wilhelmi de Grudencz Magister Cracoviensis. Opera musica*, Krakow.
Claydon, M. (1960) *Richard Crashaw's Paraphrases of the Vexilla regis, Stabat mater, Adoro te, Lauda Sion, Dies irae, O gloriosa domina*, Washington, DC.
Colker, M. L. (1956) 'Heinrici Augustensis *Planctus Evae*', *Traditio* 12: 149–230.
  (1978) *Galteri de Castellione Alexandreis*, Padua.
Conte, G. B. (1994) *Latin Literature: A History* (trans. J. B. Solodow, rev. D. P. Fowler and G. W. Most), Baltimore.
Contreni, J. (2011) 'Gregorius Turonensis', *CTC* 9 (Washington, DC), 55–72.
Cooper, H. (1977) *Pastoral: Medieval into Renaissance*, Ipswich.
Curtius, E. R. (1953) *European Literature and the Latin Middle Ages* (trans. W. Trask), Princeton.
Darnton, R. (1986) 'First steps towards a history of reading', *Australian Journal of French Studies* 23: 5–30.
De Angelis, V., ed. (1977–78) *Papiae Elementarium littera A*, Milan.
De Conca, M. (2009) 'Marcabru. Lo vers comens cant vei del fau (BdT 293.33)', *Lecturae tropatorum* 2: 1–38.
Desmond, M. (2016) 'Trojan itineraries and the matter of Troy', in R. Copeland, ed., *The Oxford History of Classical Reception in English Literature: Volume 1: 800–1558* (Oxford), 251–68.
Deutinger, R. (1999) *Rahewin von Freising: Ein Gelehrter des 12. Jahrhunderts*, Hannover.
Dinkova-Bruun, G. (2007) 'Biblical versification from late antiquity to the middle of the thirteenth century: history or allegory?', in W. Otten and K. Pollman, *Poetry and Exegesis in Premodern Latin Christianity: The Encounter between Classical and Christian Strategies of Interpretation* (Leiden), 315–42.
  (2008) 'Rewriting Scripture: Latin biblical versification in the later Middle Ages', *Viator* 39: 263–84.
Dolbeau, F. (1987) 'Les *bucoliques* de Marcus Valerius sont-elles une œuvre médiéval?', *MLatJb* 22: 166–70.
Dreves, G. M. and C. Blume (1886–1926) *Analecta hymnica medii aevi*, 55 vols., Leipzig.
Dronke, P. (1965–6) *Medieval Latin and the Rise of the European Love Lyric*, 2 vols., Oxford.
  (1984) *Women Writers of the Middle Ages: A Critical Study of Texts from Perpetua to Marguerite Porete*, Cambridge.
  (1986) *Dante and Medieval Latin Traditions*, Cambridge.
  (1988) *A History of Twelfth-Century Western Philosophy*, Cambridge.
  (1994) *Verse with Prose from Petronius to Dante: The Art and Scope of the Mixed Form*, Cambridge, MA.
  (2008) *The Spell of Calcidius: Platonic Concepts and Images in the Medieval West*, Florence.
Ebbesen, S. (2012) 'Andreas Sunonis', in *Medieval Nordic Literature in Latin* (online at https://wikihost.uib.no/medieval/index.php/Andreas_Sunonis).

Ebbesen, S., ed. (1985) *Anders Sunesen. Stormand, teolog, administrator, digter*, Copenhagen.
Ebbesen, S. and L. Mortensen (1985) 'A partial edition of Stephen Langton's *Summa* and *Quaestiones* with parallels from Andrew Sunesen's *Hexaemeron*', *CIMAGL* 49: 25–244.
 (1985–88) *Andreae Sunonis filii Hexaemeron*, 2 vols., Copenhagen.
Engelsing, R. (1974) *Der Bürger als Leser. Lesergeschichte in Deutschland 1500–1800*, Stuttgart.
Farrell, J. (2003) 'Classical genre in theory and practice', *New Literary History* 34: 383–408.
Favrier D'Arcier, L. (2006) *Histoire et géographie d'un mythe: la circulation des manuscrits du 'De excidio Troiae' de Darès le Phrygien (VIIIe–XVe siècles)*, Paris.
Festa, N., ed. (1926) *Petrarca, L'Africa, edizione critica*, Florence.
Gancarczyk, P. (2006) 'Petrus Wilhelmi de Grudencz (b. 1392) – a central European composer', *De musica disserenda* 2: 103–12.
 (2016) '*Probitate eminentem/Ploditando exarare*: Petrusa Wilhelmiego de Grudencz – środkowoeuropejska inkarnacja motetu izorytmicznego', in P. Gancarczyk, ed., *Ars musica and Its Contexts in Medieval and Early Modern Culture* (Warsaw), 255–70.
Gärtner, T. (2007) *Albert von Stade. Troilus*, Hildesheim.
Gaunt, S., R. Harvey and L. Paterson, eds. (2000) *Marcabru: A Critical Edition*, Cambridge.
Gianola, G. (1999) *Albertini Muxati. De obsidione domini Canis Grandis de Verona ante civitatem Paduanam*, Padua.
Giles, J. A. (1848) *Joannis Saresberiensis, postea epsicopi Carnotensis, opera omnia*, 5 vols., London.
Gilleland, B. (1981) *Johannes de Alta Silva, Dolopathos, or the King and the Seven Wise Men*, Birmingham, NY.
Ginzburg, C. (1993) 'Microhistory: two or three things that I know about it', *Critical Inquiry* 20: 10–35.
Godman, P. (1985) *Latin Poetry of the Carolingian Renaissance*, Norman, OK.
 (1987) *Poets and Emperors: Frankish Politics and Carolingian Poetry*, Oxford.
 (2014) *The Archpoet and Medieval Culture*, Oxford.
Godman, P. et al., eds. (2002) *Am Vorabend der Kaiserkrönung: Das Epos 'Karolus Magnus et Leo Papa' und der Papstbesuch in Paderborn 799*, Paderborn.
Gompf, L. (1970) *Joseph Iscanus, Werke und Briefe*, Leiden.
Green, R. P. H. (1982) 'The genesis of a medieval textbook: the models and sources of the *Ecloga Theoduli*', *Viator* 13: 49–106.
 (2006) *Latin Epics of the New Testament: Juvencus, Sedulius, Arator*, Oxford.
Hamilton, B. (2000) *The Leper King and His Heirs: Baldwin IV and the Crusader Kingdom of Jerusalem*, Cambridge.
Hammer, D. (2014) *Roman Political Thought: From Cicero to Augustine*, Cambridge.
Harrington, K. (1997) *Medieval Latin* (rev. J. Pucci), Chicago.

Harrison, S. J. (2017) 'The *Vita Phocae*: literary context and texture', in A. Powell and P. Hardie, eds., *The Ancient Lives of Virgil: Literary and Historical Studies* (Swansea), 73–92.
Haye, T. (2016) *Verlorenes Mittelalter: Ursachen und Muster der Nichtüberlieferung mittellateinischer Literatur*, Berlin.
Hays, G. (2015) 'Prose style', in Hexter and Townsend 2015, 217–38.
Hendrix, G. (1993) 'The *Continuatio mediaevalis* of the *Corpus Christianorum*', *Scriptorium* 47: 95–106.
Hentze, W. et al., eds. (1999) *De Karolo rege et Leone papa: Der Bericht über die Zusammenkunft Karls des Grossen mit Papst Leo III. in Paderborn 799 in einem Epos für Karl den Kaiser*, Paderborn.
Herren, M. (1974) *The Hisperica Famina 1: the A-Text*, Toronto.
Hexter, R. (2015) 'Canonicity', in Hexter and Townsend 2015, 25–47.
Hexter, R. and D. Townsend, eds. (2015) *The Oxford Handbook to Medieval Latin Literature*, Oxford.
Hicks, A. (2016) 'Hisdosus Scholasticus, *De anima mundi Platonica*: an edition', *Mediaeval Studies* 78: 1–64.
Hilbert, K. (1979) *Baldricus Burgulianus. Carmina*, Heidelberg.
Hoogterp, P.-W. (1933) 'Warnerii Basiliensis Paraclitus et Synodus', *AHMA* 8: 261–433.
Huemer, J. (1891) 'Zur Geschichte der mittellateinischen Dichtung: Heinrici Augustensis *Planctus Evae*', *Jahresbericht über das k.-k. Staatsgymnasium im II. Bezirke in Wien für das Schuljahr 1890/91*: 1–8.
Huygens, R. B. C. (1977) *Bernard D'Utrecht. Commentum in Theodolum (1076–1099)*, Spoleto.
  (1984) 'Editing William of Tyre', *SEJG* 27: 461–73.
  (1986) *Willemi Tyrensis Archiepiscopi Chronicon*, Turnhout.
Huysmans, J.-K. (1998) *Against Nature* (trans. M. Mauldon), Oxford.
Iversen, G. (2010) *Laus angelica: Poetry in the Medieval Mass* (trans. W. Flynn, ed. J. Flynn), Turnhout.
Jacobsen, P. C. (1965) *Die Quirinalien des Metellus von Tegernsee*, Leiden.
Jaeger, C. S. (1994) *The Envy of Angels: Cathedral Schools and Social Ideas in Medieval Europe, 950–1200*, Philadelphia.
Joyce, J. (1939) *Finnegans Wake*, London.
Karakisis, E. (2011) *Song Exchange in Roman Pastoral*, Berlin.
Kegel-Brinkgrove, E. (1990) *Echoing Woods: Bucolic and Pastoral from Theocritus to Wordsworth*, Amsterdam.
Kienzle, B. (2000) *The Sermon*, Turnhout.
King, J. E. (1930) *Bede. Ecclesiastical History*, Cambridge, MA.
Kiss, D. (2015) 'The lost *Codex Veronensis* and its descendants', in D. Kiss, ed., *What Catullus Wrote: Problems in Textual Criticism, Editing and the Manuscript Tradition* (Swansea), 1–28.
Klopsch, P. (1985) 'Mittellateinische *Bukolik*', in *Lectures médiévales de Virgile. Actes du colloque de Rome (25–28 octobre 1982)* (Rome), 145–65.

Knowles, M. D. (1960) 'Presidential address: great historical enterprises III. The *Monumenta Germaniae Historica*', *Transactions of the Royal Historical Society* 10: 129–50.
Kortemme, J. (1933) *Das Verhältnis John Donnes zur Scholastik und zum Barock*, Münster.
Kratz, D. (1984) *Waltharius and Ruodlieb*, New York.
Lafferty, M. K. (1998) *Walter of Châtillon's Alexandreis: Epic and the Problem of Historical Understanding*, Turnhout.
Lapidge, M. (1975) 'The hermeneutic style in tenth-century Anglo-Latin literature', *Anglo-Saxon England* 4: 67–111.
Lapidge, M. and M. Herren (1979) *Aldhelm: The Prose Works*, Cambridge.
Lapidge M. and J. Rosier (1985) *Aldhelm: The Poetic Works*, Cambridge.
Law, V. (1995) *Wisdom, Authority and Grammar in the Seventh Century: Decoding Virgilius Maro Grammaticus*, Cambridge.
Leclercq, J. (1960) *St. Pierre Damien: ermite et homme d'Église*, Rome.
  (1982) *The Love of Learning and the Desire for God: A Study of Monastic Culture* (trans. C. Misrahi), New York.
Leonhardt, J. (2013) *Latin: Story of a World Language* (trans. K. Kronenberg), Cambridge, MA.
Levi, G. (1991) 'On microhistory', in P. Burke, ed., *New Perspectives on Historical Writing* (Cambridge), 93–113.
Löfstedt, B. (2003) *Virgilius Maro Grammaticus: opera omnia*, Munich.
Lohr, C. (1988–2013) *Latin Aristotle Commentaries*, 5 vols., Florence.
Lubac, H. de (1959) *Exégèse médiéval: les quatres sens de L'Écriture*, 2 vols., Paris.
Magee, J. (2016) *Calcidius: On Plato's Timaeus*, Cambridge, MA.
Manitius, M. (1911–31) *Geschichte der lateinischen Literatur des Mittelalters*, 3 vols., Munich.
Mantello, F. M. and A. J. Rigg, eds. (1996) *Medieval Latin: An Introduction and Bibliographical Guide*, Washington, DC.
Marcovich, M. and A. Georgiadou (1988) 'Eucheria's *Adynata*', *ICS* 13: 165–74.
Mayer, R. (2006) 'Latin pastoral after Vergil', in M. Fantuzzi and T. Papanghelis, eds., *Brill's Companion to Greek and Latin Pastoral* (Leiden), 451–66.
McBrine, P. (2017) *Biblical Epics in Late Antiquity and Anglo-Saxon England: Divina in Laude voluntas*, Toronto.
McDonough, C. (2010) *The Arundel Lyrics: The Poems of Hugh Primas*, Cambridge, MA.
McGill, S. (2017) 'Larger than life: the elevation of Virgil in Phocas' *Vita*', in Powell and Hardie 2017, 93–114.
  (2018) 'Reading against the grain: late Latin literature in Huysmans' *À rebours*', in S. Schottenius Culhed and M. Nairn, eds., *Reading Late Antiquity* (Heidelberg), 85–104.
Mosetti Casaretto, F. (1997) *Theodulus. Ecloga. Il canto della verità e della menzogna*, Florence.

(2001) 'Il genere pastorale e la Bibbia: ambiguità dell'imaginario e ridefinizione cristiana del modulo narrative in epoca carolingia', in Stella 2001, 339–58.

Noble, T. F. X. (2009) *Charlemagne and Louis the Pious: The Lives by Einhard, Notker, Ermoldus, Thegan and the Astronomer*, Philadelphia.

Norberg, D. L. (1991) 'Dyname Patrice de Marseilles', *Journal of Medieval Latin* 1: 46–51.

Norden, E. (1898) *Die Antike Kunstprosa vom VI. Jahrhundert V. Chr. bis in die Zeit der Renaissance*, Leipzig.

O'Hara, A. (2018) *Jonas of Bobbio and the Legacy of Columbanus*, Oxford.

O'Hara, A. and I. Wood (2017) *Jonas of Bobbio. Life of Columbanus, Life of John of Réomé, and Life of Vedast*, Liverpool.

O'Hogan, C. (2016) *Prudentius and the Landscapes of Late Antiquity*, Oxford.

Orchard, A. (1994) *The Poetic Art of Aldhelm*, Cambridge.

Pabst, B. (1994) *Prosimetrum: Tradition und Wandel einer Literaturform zwischen Spätantike und Spätmittelalter*, 2 vols., Cologne.

(2002) *Gregor von Montesacro und die geistige Kultur Süditaliens unter Friederich II. Mit text- und quellenkritischer Erstedition der Vers-Enzyklopädie Peri ton anthropon theopiisis (De hominum deificatione)*, Stuttgart.

Pepin, R. and J. M. Ziolkowski (2011) *Sextus Amarcius, Sermones. Eupolemius*, Cambridge, MA.

Peyrard, S. (2007) 'L'*Ilias* de Simon Chèvre d'Or: édition critique et commentaire' Diplôme d'archiviste paléographe, École nationale des chartes, Paris.

Powell, A. and P. Hardie (2017) *The Ancient Lives of Virgil: Literary and Historical Studies*, Swansea.

Raby, F. J. E. (1927) *A History of Christian Latin Poetry: From the Beginnings to the Close of the Middle Ages*, Oxford.

(1934) *A History of Secular Latin Poetry*, 2 vols., Oxford.

Raffa, G. P. (1996). 'Dante's mocking pastoral Muse', *Dante Studies* 114: 271–91.

Raggio, O. (2013) 'Microstoria e microstorie', in *Il Contributo italiano alla storia del Pensiero – Storia e Politica* (*Treccani* online), www.treccani.it/enciclopedia/microstoria-e-microstorie_(altro)/.

Ramelli, I. (2006) *Tutti i commenti a Marziano Capella. Scoto Eriugena, Remigio di Auxerre, Bernardo Silvestre e anonimi*, Milan.

Rand, E. K. (1931) 'The Irish flavour of *Hisperica famina*', in W. Stach and H. Walther, eds., *Studien zur lateinischen Dichtung des Mittelalters*, Dresden.

Reid, P. L. D. (1981) *Tenth-Century Latinity: Rather of Verona*, Malibu.

(1991) *The Complete Works of Rather of Verona*, Binghamton, NY.

Riché, P. (1976) *Education and Culture in the Barbarian West, Sixth through Eighth Centuries* (trans. J. J. Contreni), Columbia, SC.

Rigg, A. G. (2005) *Josephus Iscanus, Daretis Phrygii Ilias*, Toronto.

(2015) 'Crossing generic boundaries', in Hexter and Townsend 2015, 265–83.

Roberts, M. (2009) *The Humblest Sparrow: The Poetry of Venantius Fortunatus*, Ann Arbor, MI.

(2016) 'Venantius Fortunatus and Gregory of Tours: poetry and patronage', in A. C. Murray, ed., *A Companion to Gregory of Tours* (Leiden), 35–59.
Schaller, D. (1993) 'La poesia epica', in *Lo spazio letterario del Medioevo, 1: Il Medioevo latino*, 1.11.9–42, Rome.
Schepelern, H. D. (1985) *Anders Sunesøns Hexaëmeron gengivet på danske vers*, Copenhagen.
Schnapp, J. (1992) 'A commentary on commentary in Boccaccio', *South Atlantic Quarterly* 91: 813–34.
Schneyer, J. B. (1969–90) *Repertorium der lateinischen Sermones des Mittelalters für die Zeit von 1150–1350*, 11 vols., Münster.
Schönbeck, O. (1998) 'Peter Damian and the rhetoric of an ascetic', in M. W. Herren, C. J. McDonough and R. G. Arthur, eds., *Latin Culture in the Eleventh Century*, 2 vols. (Turnhout), vol. 2, 350–70.
Schönberger, R. (1994) *Repertorium edierter Texte des Mittelalters aus dem Bereich der Philosophie und angrenzender Gebiete*, Berlin.
Schönfeld, A. et al. (2011) *Repertorium edierter Texte des Mittelalters aus dem Bereich der Philosophie und angrenzender Gebiete*, 2nd edn, Berlin.
Shanzer, D. (1996) Review of Pabst 1994, *Speculum* 71: 749–52.
Simpson, J. (1995) *Sciences and the Self in Medieval Poetry: Alan of Lille's Anticlaudianus and John Gower's Confessio amantis*, Cambridge.
Sisler, W. P. (1977) 'An edition and translation of Lovato Lovati's *Metrical Epistles*', unpublished PhD dissertation, Johns Hopkins University.
Skafte Jensen, M. (1997) 'Petrarch's farewell to Avignon: *Bucolicum carmen* VIII', in M. Pade, H. R. Jensen and L. W. Pedersen, eds., *Avignon and Naples: Italy in France, France in Italy in the Fourteenth Century* (Rome), 69–82.
Stahl, W. H. (1952) *Macrobius: Commentary on the Dream of Scipio*, New York.
Stahl, W. H. and W. Johnson (1977) *Martianus Capella: The Marriage of Philology and Mercury*, New York.
Stegmüller, F. (1950–80) *Repertorium biblicum medii aevi*, 11 vols., Madrid.
Stella, F., ed. (2001) *La scrittura infinita. Bibbia e poesia in età medievale e umanistica*, Florence.
Stohlmann, J. (1968) *Anonymi historia Troyana Daretis Frigii. Untersuchungen und kritische Ausgabe*, Wuppertal.
Stok, F. (2016) 'Niccolò Perotti e la costruzione dell'arcaico', in A. Setaioli, ed., *Apis matina. Studi in onore di Carlo Santini* (Trieste), 679–92.
Stotz, P. (1996–2004) *Handbuch zur lateinischen Sprache des Mittelalters*, 5 vols., Munich.
Stover, J. (2015) 'Olybrius and the *Einsiedeln Eclogues*', *JRS* 105: 288–321.
(2017) 'The date of the bucolic poet Martius Valerius', *JRS* 107: 301–35.
(2020) 'Window allusion in Latin bucolic: the case of Martius Valerius', in C. Burrow, S. Harrison, M. McLaughlin and E. Tarantino, eds., *Imitative Series and Clusters from Classical to Early Modern Literature* (Berlin), 121–37.
Sulowski, J. (1972) *Radulphus de Longocampo. In Anticlaudianum Alani commentum*, Wrocław.
Szövérffy, J. (1964–65) *Annalen der lateinischen Hymnendichtung*, 2 vols., Berlin.

(1992–95) *Secular Latin Lyrics and Minor Poetic Forms of the Middle Ages: A Historical Survey and Literary Repertory from the Tenth to the Late Fifteenth Century*, Concord, NH.

Tilliette, J.-Y. (1989) 'Les modèles de sainteté du IXe au XIe siècle, d'après le témoinage des récits hagiographiques en vers métriques', in *Santi e demoni nell'alto medioevo occidentale (secoli v–xi)*, 2 vols. (Spoleto), 381–406.

(1996–2000) *Baudri de Dol, Carmina*, 2 vols., Geneva.

(2016) 'Poésie latine et tradition courtoise (... ou pas). Note sur la chanson d'amour O 17 (*Declinante frigore*) de Gautier de Châtillon', in *La rigueur et la passion. Mélanges en l'honneur de Pascale Bourgain* (Turnhout), 329–46.

Tolan, J. (1996) 'Anti-hagiography: Embrico of Mainz's *Vita Mahumeti*', *Journal of Medieval History* 22: 25–41.

Townsend, D. (1996) *The Alexandreis of Walter of Châtillon: A Twelfth-Century Epic*, Philadelphia.

Traill, D. (2018) *Carmina Burana*, 2 vols., Cambridge, MA.

Treip, M. (2015) *Allegorical Poetics and the Epic: The Renaissance Tradition to Paradise Lost*, Lexington.

Uden, J. (2018) 'Nineteenth- and twentieth-century visions of late antique literature', in S. McGill and E. Watts, eds., *A Companion to Late Antique Literature* (Malden, MA), 627–42.

Velli, G. (1992) '"*Tityrus redivivus*": the rebirth of Vergilian pastoral from Dante to Sannazaro (and Tasso)', in C. Lucente, ed., *The Western Pennsylvania Symposium on World Literatures. Selected Proceedings 1974–1991: A Retrospective* (Greensburg, PA), 107–18.

Vossen, P. (1962) *Der Libellus Scolasticus des Walther von Speyer*, Berlin.

Walsh, P. G. (1976) 'Pastor and pastoral in medieval Latin poetry', *Papers of the Liverpool Latin Seminar* 1: 157–69.

Walther, H. (1920) *Der Streitgedicht in der lateinischen Literatur des Mittelalters*, Munich.

Weijers, O. (1994–2012) *Le travail intellectuel à la Faculté des Arts de Paris: textes et maîtres (ca. 1200–1500)*, 9 vols. (vol. 9 with M. Calma), Turnhout.

Wetherbee, W. (2013) *Alan of Lille: Literary Works*, Cambridge, MA.

(2015) *Bernardus Silvestris: Poetic Works*, Cambridge, MA.

Wicksteed, P. H. and E. G. Gardner (1902) *Dante and Giovanni del Virgilio*, Westminster.

Williams, K. F. (1938) 'The *Liber de novem scienciis*', unpublished PhD dissertation, University of Chicago.

Winterbottom, M. (1977) Review of Herren 1974, *CR* 27: 196.

(2017) 'Words, words, words ...' in R. Thomson, E. Dolman and E. Winkler, eds., *Discovering William of Malmesbury* (Woodbridge), 203–18.

Winterfeld, P. von, ed. (1899) *Abbonis Bella Parisiacae Urbis. MGH Poetae* IV (Berlin), 72–122.

Witt, R. G. (2000) *In the Footsteps of the Ancients: The Origins of Humanism from Lovato to Bruni*, Leiden.

Worstbrock, F. J. (1999) 'Vergil', in *Die deutsche Literatur des Mittelalters. Verfasserlexicon. Volume 10* (Berlin), coll. 262–4.
Wright, T. (1841) *The Latin Poems Commonly Attributed to Walter Mapes*, London.
Yavuz, N. K. (2015) 'Transmission and adaptation of the Trojan narrative in Frankish history between the sixth and tenth centuries', unpublished PhD dissertation, University of Leeds.
Yolles, J. (2009) 'The rhetoric of simplicity: faith and rhetoric in Peter Damian', unpublished MA thesis, Amsterdam University.
Ziolkowski, J. M. (1991) 'Eupolemius', *Journal of Medieval Latin* 1: 1–45.
  (1993) *Talking Animals: Medieval Latin Beast Poetry, 750–1150*, Philadelphia.
  (1994) *The Cambridge Songs (Carmina Cantabrigiensia)*, New York.
  (1996a) 'Toward a history of medieval Latin literature', in Mantello and Rigg 1996, 503–36.
  (1996b) 'Epic', in Mantello and Rigg 1996, 547–55.
  (2001) 'The highest form of compliment: *imitatio* in medieval Latin culture', in J. Marenbon, ed., *Poetry and Philosophy in the Middle Ages: A Festschrift for Peter Dronke* (Leiden), 293–307.
  (2007) *Fairy Tales from Before Fairy Tales: The Medieval Latin Past of Wonderful Lies*, Ann Arbor, MI.
  (2018) *The Juggler of Notre Dame and the Medievalizing of Modernity*, 6 vols., Cambridge.
Ziolkowski, J. M. and M. C. J. Putnam (2008) *The Virgilian Tradition: The First Fifteen Hundred Years*, New Haven.
Zogg, F. (2017) 'Palaemon and Daphnis in a medieval poem: the Vergilian challenge of the *Conflictus Veris et Hiemis*', *Vergilius* 63: 125–40.
Zonta, B. (1960) 'I codici GLPV dell'*Elementarium Papiae*: un primo sondaggio nella tradizione manoscritta ed alcune osservazioni relative', *SCO* 9: 76–99.
Zuwiyya, D., ed. (2011) *A Companion to Alexander Literature in the Middle Ages*, Leiden.

CHAPTER 7

# *Neo-Latin*

*Yasmin Haskell*

The parameters of the field of Neo-Latin studies were first set in the second half of the last century in continental Europe, but scholars of many disciplines, all over the world, have long engaged, out of necessity or curiosity, with Renaissance and post-Renaissance Latin texts. This chapter takes a snapshot of the field at an exciting point in its history and considers what specialists and non-specialists in this literature have to gain from more explicit disciplinary dialogue.

## Portrait of the Neo-Latinist as a Young Woman

The editors have invited me to open with a reflection on my own intellectual journey to Neo-Latin, as a classicist who has strayed from the true path. They were struck by a remark I made at a meeting for contributors to this volume about a sense that the conversations I have with neo-Latinists being different from those I have with classicists, even with 'receptionists'. In some ways this chapter is an attempt to account for that difference, if not that straying. At the risk of disappointing readers with the prospect of full initiation into the neo-Latin mysteries, though, I share my story here simply as an heuristic device, with no pretensions to exemplarity. The reasons I took the neo-Latin road in Australia, thirty years ago, as an itchy-footed, not-quite classicist, will not necessarily be the same as those attracting many talented young scholars to the field today, from different disciplinary bases and different parts of the world. I nevertheless welcome the opportunity to take stock of the general progress of Neo-Latin studies at the end of the second decade of the twenty-first century, and to reflect on what has changed since I was last asked to do so, coincidentally some twenty years ago. Then, responding to a position paper by the Swedish neo-Latinist, Hans Helander, in a special issue of *Symbolae Osloenses* devoted to 'Neo-Latin studies: significance and prospects', I concluded with a rather naïve glance towards the internet as a possible virtual home for the nomadic *Respublica neolatina*.[1] While the internet has since yielded many unexpected treasures for our field, not least Google Books, it is interesting to reflect that many of the challenges of identity and visibility for researchers and teachers of Renaissance and post-Renaissance Latin have persisted.

\*\*\*

As a Classics undergraduate in Sydney, Australia, I found myself floating around the library of the Theosophical Society one day, perhaps seeking inspiration for my Sanskrit homework, when I stumbled across a copy of Frances Yates' *Giordano Bruno and the Hermetic Tradition* (1964).[2] The title re-activated a childhood memory. On a visit to Italy I had seen Ettore Ferrari's haunting statue of the cowled Renaissance heretic in Rome's Campo de' Fiori. Someone must have told me the story of Bruno being burnt at the stake as a 'martyr to science', and now Yates' book began to fire my imagination with hermetic sparks between the ancient authors I had been studying in Latin and Greek and the development of modern thought – free thought, no less! It was from Frances Yates that I first learned about the movement of Renaissance humanism, the Neoplatonic academy of Florence, the classical tradition and the mythical Warburg Institute. Another Frances (Muecke) facilitated my conversion to what I didn't realise at the time was 'Neo-Latin' when she agreed to supervise a then rather irregular Classics honours dissertation, on the influence of Lucretius on Giordano Bruno. After commencing doctoral work in Australia – in the bad old pre-internet days when one had to wait for months for interlibrary loans to arrive from Europe and North America – I attended a Neo-Latin conference in Cambridge, UK, and there, more or less, found 'my' people. I recall a paper by Lisa Jardine in which she casually described her encounters with this or that manuscript or first edition of Erasmus and I thrilled at the thought of modern scholars physically handling the books and letters of the authors they studied. It was not long after that I, too, got to pore over illuminated manuscripts in the Vatican library – another heady experience that made the Renaissance and classical past seem more present and stereoscopic than it ever had in Australia, where, *pace* our Sydney University motto, 'same mind under a different constellation' (*sidere mens eadem mutato*), the eponymous *mens* was usually understood to be that of Oxbridge rather than Rome or

---

[1] Haskell 2001.
[2] Giordano Bruno, I did not yet know, was a *de facto* patron saint of the Theosophists. One of their founders, Annie Besant, claimed to be his reincarnation.

Athens. Later, as a research fellow in Cambridge, I volunteered as secretary for the small but flourishing Cambridge Society for Neo-Latin Studies, which, under its indefatigable president, Philip Ford, hosted a visiting speaker series and annual international symposium. In the early days I do not recall many Cambridge classicists attending those events – Philip Hardie was an exception to the rule – but shortly before I returned to Australia in 2003 Cambridge had launched its first neo-Latin paper under the aegis of the Faculty of Modern and Medieval Languages.

No doubt Bruno's ashes would be flying in their unmarked grave if they knew that their teenaged convert had gone on, via a PhD in Renaissance Latin and Italian didactic poetry, to a career largely focused on the culture of the early modern *Jesuits*. (The Jesuit cardinal Robert Bellarmine, after all, was one of the chief inquisitors at Bruno's trial for heresy.) Yet the Jesuits were not only the most prolific composers of Latin didactic poetry in early modern times, some of it even modelled on Lucretius, but their missionary and humanistic adventures from the Americas to Asia gave me freedom to roam far beyond the walls of 'old world' Classics. As a student I had found that reading Plato, Lucretius, Virgil and Ovid by the lights of their Renaissance readers Ficino, Pontano, Marullus, Palingenio, Bruno and Fracastoro somehow intensified the colour of the classical authors for me. Some thirty years later those *recentiores* take their place in a palimpsest of many layers through which the classical authors are still discernible, if sometimes less vivid – but when I tease apart the tissues of this dense intertextual palimpsest I now do so as a 'neo-Latinist'. What should be clear, I hope, from this brief intellectual autobiography, is that my journey from Classics to Neo-Latin was entirely serendipitous. There was no obvious career path for an Antipodean neo-Latinist back then. Even today, to call oneself a neo-Latinist is to invite puzzlement and false assumptions, for example that neo-Latinists are or should be competent mediaevalists (some, of course, are). I was very fortunate to secure an externally funded position in 'Latin humanism' in a Classics department in Australia and to have enjoyed, over the years, many collaborative research and teaching opportunities through a discipline group in 'Medieval and Early Modern Studies'. While ostensibly employed to broaden the curriculum, however, I have sometimes found it challenging to wrap neo-Latin teaching around a traditional Classics curriculum. This chapter will therefore conclude with a few suggestions for introducing Neo-Latin to undergraduates, especially classicists; a quick census of available texts and tools, physical and digital; and a cautious wave in the direction of a neo-Latin 'canon'.

In the following sections I begin by plotting the parameters of Neo-Latin first as an historical idiom and discourse, then as a modern research field. I proceed to indicate two possible access points for classicists who are curious about the neo-Latin cult: genre and emotions. If genre is an obvious choice of focus, emotions perhaps requires further explanation. It is first necessary to know that Neo-Latin has long benefitted from its ancillary usefulness to other fields – perhaps especially historical, but also philosophical and scientific. A research project at the University of Münster led by Karl Enenkel, for example, proposes that the neo-Latin commentary offers 'an extremely complex exegesis that systematically unlocks the classical texts for diverse disciplines and practices of knowledge, such as medicine, geography, zoology, agriculture, hunting, horsemanship and so on' and in this way 'fundamentally differs from the modern practice in classical philology'.[3] We shall return to this mixed blessing of Neo-Latin's utility at the end of our chapter. In attending to 'emotions' I am less interested, for present purposes, in mining early modern Latin texts for word histories[4] than in confronting the old bugbear of the artificiality and presumed lack of authenticity of Neo-Latin as a *literary* medium. In the process, I hope to shine some light on what might be distinctive about it *vis-à-vis* its classical and vernacular cousins. My approach therefore subtends history of emotions and one with which classical Latinists will be even more familiar: the discussion of intertextuality in Roman literature. In this chapter I follow the broadest definition of 'Neo-Latin' as announced in the preamble to the newly relaunched *Humanistica Lovaniensia*, one that embraces 'neo-Latin language, literature and culture from the fourteenth to the twenty-first century'.

## Authority and Alterity: Neo-Latin and Its More or Less Civil Wars

The Italian humanists of the fourteenth and fifteenth centuries strained to listen to the ancients over the crackle of the centuries, to understand antiquity as *another* culture, as much as they appropriated and sometimes fetishised aspects of it.[5] Learning to write and speak as the ancients did was

---

[3] The New Management of Knowledge in the Early Modern Period: The Transmission of Classical Latin Literature via Neo-Latin Commentaries. Cf. Martin Korenjak's ERC project at the University of Innsbruck, '*Nova Scientia*: Early Modern Science and Latin'.
[4] See Champion et al. 2016; Marr et al. 2019.
[5] Especially the Rome-based humanists, Pomponio Leto, Biondo Flavio, Angelo Colocci and friends, with their antiquarian pursuits and revivalist games. For background, see Rowland 1998. There has been resurgence of interest in these figures – poets, topographers, creative anachronists . . . – in recent years. See: www.repertoriumpomponianum.it/ and www.repertoriumblondianum.org, and Pade

at the heart of the Renaissance humanist enterprise.[6] Neo-Latin studies are essentially concerned with this attempt and its consequences – in literature, ideas and institutions – over the past 600 years. While it is true, then, that most historians of early modern philosophy, theology, science and medicine, of education, universities, politics, economics and diplomacy will need to come to grips with texts *in Latin*, what makes (some of) us more or less card-carrying neo-Latinists is an additional concern for what the language, or *choice* of language, brings to our understanding of those texts. In the case of Spinoza, for example, the use of Latin has a not inconsiderable bearing on the interpretation of his core philosophical ideas.[7] And what of the *cultural* meanings of Latin? What were the social and political valences it assumed or shed in the course of the centuries after the Renaissance? What did it allow writers to express and in which contexts? What or whom did it obscure or exclude? In her provocative *Latin or the Empire of a Sign* (2001),[8] Françoise Waquet sought to probe the darker recesses of Latin's historical subconscious from the sixteenth to the twentieth centuries, and declared the language, or at least its 'sign', 'dead of exhaustion',

> but certainly not exhaustion of the language itself which had been dead since at least the eighteenth century. On that end, historians and neo-Latin literature specialists are in agreement, although their explanations are markedly divergent. In the historians' view, 'the decline of Latin was due not to those opposed to the classical heritage, but to its own promoters, the humanists, whose insistence on the classical norm ended by turning Latin into a dead language'. The vitality of Latin – mediaeval Latin – had been irremediably broken by the humanist restoration, and neo-Latin, 'a reconstitution by committee', had subsequently lived an artificial, specious existence; its death was in some sense written into its very renewal. Neo-Latin specialists support an opposite point of view, hinged on fifteenth- and sixteenth-century works and writings of literary type: the decline and death of Latin had nothing to do with the humanists; indeed they had given it new life, or at least prolonged its existence, until its reduction to the school and university eventually proved fatal. No matter from our point of view. The exhaustion of which Latin dies in the 1960s was not exhaustion of the language. *Latin disappeared because it no longer meant anything to the*

---

2015. Biondo's major works *Italy Illuminated* and *Rome in Triumph* may be consulted in the I Tatti editions of White 2005–16 and Muecke and Pincelli 2016. See also Mazzocco 2016; Campanelli and Muecke 2017.

[6] It is beyond the scope of this chapter to provide even a snapshot of the state of scholarship on Renaissance Latin humanism, but for the origins of the movement see Witt 2000 and 2012.

[7] On Spinoza's Latinity see e.g. Kajanto 2005; Van Rompaey 2015. Other major early modern philosophers who wrote principally in Latin include Descartes, Newton, Leibniz and Wolff.

[8] Translated from Waquet 1998.

*contemporary world. All that it had once embodied – a certain idea of humanity, a form of discrimination, a system of power, a universal outlook, with an underlying conception of society, its order, its standards – no longer carried meaning, or was being said differently, and the hegemonic cultural model to which it referred was now victoriously rivalled.*[9]

Waquet's book has not been without its modern humanist critics, although the battle lines drawn here between 'neo-Latin literature specialists' and 'historians' may lack meaning for many younger researchers, at least outside of France. Nevertheless, by throwing down the gauntlet, Waquet has undeniably generated some useful and necessary conversations over the past twenty years.

Was (Neo-)Latin always so hegemonic and monosemic, or did the meaning of the 'sign' change when it was posted outside of Europe, or when it was (over-) written by Chinese, Japanese, indigenous Americans, women, even the enslaved? In the wake of Waquet's book neo-Latinists have increasingly moved to chart humanist Latin's voyages of discovery beyond Europe, and its relationship with its various 'others'.[10] The best-known example of African Latin is the epic on the battle of Lepanto by Juan Latino, a son of slaves who taught at the University of Granada in the sixteenth century.[11] But what of Latin by the 'other sex'? One might infer from Waquet that Latin was never a language for the ladies,[12] yet Jane Stevenson's landmark *Women Latin Poets* (2005) has amply demonstrated the error of such an assumption.[13] It is true that those women who were able to acquire a Latin education, and to progress to a level at which they could produce Latin (and/or Greek) verse, *were* exceptional, and that, as Stevenson says, 'they demonstrate that in a very wide variety of contexts, élite culture in Europe has included individual women's voices while denying the rights of women in general' (5). But if they are relatively rare, women Latinists of the early modern period vastly outnumber those

---

[9] Waquet 2001: 273 (my emphasis). [10] For a selection of responses see Haskell and Ruys 2010.
[11] See Wright 2016. The text of Latino's *Austrias* is available in Wright, Spence and Lemons 2014: 288–405. On the Latin thesis defending slavery by former slave J. C. Capitein, see Parker 1999. For the free-born Jamaican Latin poet, Francis Williams (*c.* 1700–70), see Gilmore 2005. On neo-Latin writing *about* Africans, see Gilmore 2009, 2010 and 2011.
[12] Cf. Jardine 1983 and 1985. Waquet's chapter on 'social status' in Knight and Tilg 2015 includes a short section on 'women's long road to Latin' which stands in curious contrast to Diana Robin's preceding chapter on 'gender', that tells the remarkable story of women's successful penetration into the early modern neo-Latin world, often through mutual assistance (363–77). On women writers' networks cf. Stevenson 2014.
[13] Surprisingly, the call to scholarly arms of Stevenson's book has not yet been answered, in spite of her furnishing a generous checklist (more than 100 pages) of women Latin poets of all periods. This includes 'every manuscript and edition of each poet that I have been able to find: this is not mere pedantry, but an expression of the principle that the circulation and reception history of writing tells one important things about it' (Stevenson 2005: 9).

whose writings survive from antiquity and the Middle Ages, and it is also significant that not a few of them succeeded in exercising their soft Latin power on an international stage. The seventeenth-century Dutch poet, painter and polyglot Anna Maria van Schurman (1607–78) published a *Dissertatio de ingenii muliebris ad doctrinam, & meliores litteras aptitudine* (1638) which was translated into several European languages, including English as *The Learned Maid or, whether a Maid May Be a Scholar* (1659).[14] The English–Czech poet Elizabeth Jane Weston (1582–1612) used Latin poetry for strategic self-fashioning and fund-raising after the disgrace and death of her father, the notorious Elizabethan alchemist, Edward Kelley.[15]

Neo-Latin is, of course, inextricable from the history of classical scholarship itself, and from the development of modern classical philology. A (very) partial selection of milestones: Lorenzo Valla's (1407–57) explosive dating of the 'Donation of Constantine' in the fifteenth century and Isaac Casaubon's of the Corpus Hermeticum in the seventeenth;[16] the rediscovery of Lucretius' *De rerum natura* by Poggio Bracciolini (1380–1459) in 1417 and the ensuing flurry of editorial and creative activity around that prodigiously seminal text;[17] Ermolao Barbaro's (1454–93) critical work on the Elder Pliny and Justus Lipsius' (1547–1606) on Tacitus;[18] Joseph Justus Scaliger's (1540–1609) adjustment of the geographical and chronological boundaries of the classical world to accommodate the civilisations of the ancient Near East,[19] and the extraordinary Virgilian commentary (1608, 1612, 1617) by Spanish Jesuit Juan Luis de la Cerda, still cited by modern editors.[20] Greek scholarship was also transmitted in Latin, of course, from the *Commentarii linguae Graecae* (1529) of Guillaume Budé to Friedrich August Wolf's 1795

---

[14] She achieved celebrity for her collection of Hebrew, Greek, Latin and French writings (van Schurman 1650). Such was her reputation that the prominent French scholar Pierre Daniel Huët (1630–1721) recorded his visit to the *muliebris gloria sexus* in Utrecht in his verse epistle to Johannes Capellanus, *Iter Suecicum*, on his journey from Caen to Stockholm (IJsewijn 1990–8: 11 55).

[15] Kelley worked for the Emperor Rudolph II in Prague but fell steeply out of favour after 1591 when he killed a member of the court. See Cheney and Hosington 2000: xiii.

[16] Valla's text is available in Bowersock's I Tatti Renaissance edition (Valla 2007).

[17] Greenblatt's *Swerve* (2011) probably overstates the impact of the *De rerum natura*, but that book, together with the 2017 anniversary, seems to have set in motion a chain of re-evaluations of the early modern Lucretius, including Passanante 2011; Palmer 2014; Paladini 2015; Norbrook, Harrison and Hardie 2016; Hardie, Prosperi and Zucca 2020. See also Brown 2010; Prosperi 2004; Longo 2004.

[18] Ruysschaert 1949; De Landtsheer 1998 and 2013.

[19] I.e. in his *De emendatione temporum* (Paris, 1583). See Grafton 1983–93. The significance of the publication of the (massive!) correspondence of Scaliger, edited by Botley and Van Miert (2012) is explored in a useful review article by Haugen 2014. About two thirds of Scaliger's letters are in Latin.

[20] See Laird 2002, who writes that this 'magisterial work displays a refined sense of Virgil's role in Augustan society and in the Greco-Roman literary tradition. At the same time La Cerda's commentary highlights the importance of its subject in his own time: for education and intellectual exploration in various fields (science, language, ethnography), as well as for poetic and literary

*Prolegomena ad Homerum*. 'Classical' philological skills remain important for neo-Latinists in their work as editors, translators, commentators and attributors; and neo-Latinists, like classicists, acquire expertise in the style of their predilected authors.[21] That said, while the humanist idiom is for all intents and purposes 'classical', the contemporary neo-Latinist is often less concerned than the classical traditionalist or receptionist with texts and genres as continuations or appropriations of *ancient* texts and genres – or, for that matter, in what Renaissance readers can reveal to us about our contemporary readings of ancient texts[22] – than as vehicles or affordances for early modern literature and thought. The neo-Latinist looks sideways as much, if not more, than she looks backwards – to vernacular and other *recentiores*.

The question of Neo-Latin's relationship with its, as it were, imperfect pasts, with late and mediaeval Latin, is less straightforward than might be assumed. In its early Renaissance phase, to be sure, the new-old Latin describes a strong ideological swing away from the scholastic usage of the late-mediaeval universities.[23] From Petrarch on, the war on 'barbarism' leads to what can sometimes seem an excruciatingly pedantic obsession with classical lexis and stylistic propriety, one that is often unedifyingly bound up with humanists' interpersonal squabbles and jockeying for attention and favour.[24] Yet the 'old' scholastic (philosophical) Latin continued to evolve through the Renaissance and after. The *lingua franca* of the early modern *Respublica litterarum* was, unsurprisingly, not always as classically correct as it was for the likes of Valla, Perotti, Politian, Bembo, Agricola, Erasmus and others who made their living as the teachers and

---

innovation. La Cerda combines erudite antiquarianism with occasional displays of another kind of exegesis – contemporary cultural and ideological commentary' (171).

[21] It was, above all, for his specialist knowledge of Milton's Latin that John Hale, author of two monographs on Milton's languages (1997 and 2005) and editor of a collection of the Latin writings (1998), was invited to join a multidisciplinary team (with Gordon Campbell and Thomas Corns) to assess the manuscript of the *De doctrina Christiana*, in the aftershock of William Hunter's 1991 impugning of Milton's authorship.

[22] Charles Martindale's challenge in *Redeeming the Text*: 'The "weak" thesis is that numerous unexplored insights into ancient literature are locked up in imitations, translations and so forth ... The "strong" thesis is that our current interpretations of ancient texts, whether or not we are aware of it, are, in complex ways, constructed by the chain of receptions through which their continued readability has been effected' (1993: 7). See, however, Kallendorf 2007 for the application of Martindale's approach to neo-Latin epic in imitation of Virgil.

[23] See Moss 2003 and 2010, arguing for nothing less than a cognitive revolution sparked by humanist Latin.

[24] See D'Amico 1983; Fantazzi 2014. Tunberg 1997 has shown that even dyed-in-the-wool Ciceronians were not really as orthodox as they believed themselves to be, in his assessment of the style of the Flemish wunderkind Christophe de Longueil (1488–1522), who was initially feted, then hounded out of Renaissance Rome.

gatekeepers of style.[25] Thus humanist poet and reformer Aonio Paleario (1500–70) consciously code-switches, in his *Actio in pontifices Romanos* (published posthumously in 1600), to a more modest, theological Latin which eschews:

> ornaments of speech, which on another subject might have pleased me, but on the subject of Christ, who has no need for such supports, do not please in the least ... I shall therefore assume a lean and humble style, and I would happily have adopted the vernacular to discuss these matters, were it not that I am addressing men of whom not a few are ignorant of Italian, whereas they all know Latin.[26]

And Paleario's contemporary Giordano Bruno was no humanist language purist in his Latin philosophical poetry, where he affects a spontaneity of expression and an indifference to the opinion of the 'grammarians'.[27]

It is true that in 1629 the Barberini pope and poet Urban VIII enlisted the help of four Jesuits, Famiano Strada, Tarquinio Galluzzi, Girolamo Petrucci and Matthias Sarbiewski, to 'tidy up' the Roman Breviary, but of course humanists never conspired to throw out *all* post-classical Latin literature with the barbaric bathwater of late-mediaeval scholasticism. The curtain never fell on the Fathers of the Church,[28] and neo-Latinists, especially those concerned with Renaissance and Reformation authors, cannot afford to ignore them, nor the works of Prudentius, Boethius and many others.[29] Erasmus' 1506 poem to the physician Guillaume Cop on the troubles of old age – all the more poignant for his relative youth at the time of composition – is in its 'autobiographical elements, so captivating to the modern reader ..., modelled above all on Prudentius' *Praefatio*'.[30] As for mediaeval writers, the genre and theme of Aeneas Silvius Piccolomini's (later Pope Pius II) epistolary novel, *Historia de duobus amantibus sive*

---

[25] See Bury 2005; Giglioni 2015.
[26] '... dicendi ornamenta, quae in alia causa fortasse me delectassent [sed] in ea quae Christi est, qui istis adiumentis non eget, minime delectant ... Tenue itaque et humile dicendi genus sequar et libenter profecto lingua vulgari et patria de his agerem ... nisi apud eos sermo esset, quorum nonnulli Italice nesciunt, Latine omnes sciunt' (my translation from text cited in IJsewijn 1990–8: II 417).
[27] He cultivates a 'virile' Lucretian style that parallels his imitation of the literary rebel Pietro Aretino in the vernacular (see Haskell 1998a). Cf. the Latin of mathematician, astrologer and polymath Girolamo Cardano (1501–76), for which he claimed divine inspiration, and which was also highly idiosyncratic.
[28] See Backus 1997 and 2014; Cortesi 2006. Cf. Bejczy 2001 on Erasmus and the Middle Ages.
[29] Sacré's short but useful chapter on student verse from the Brussels college (Sacré 1996b) remarks the often recherché meters employed by budding poets, some of which are traced back not to the usual classical suspects but to late antique writers including Boethius.
[30] Vredeveld, in his introduction to the *CWE* edition of Erasmus' poetry (Erasmus 1993: xlvii).

*Euryalus et Lucretia* was indebted to the mediaeval 'love story' of Heloise and Abelard.[31] One of Giordano Bruno's forerunners in Latin philosophical verse, the humanist paedagogue Marcello Palingenio Stellato (c. 1500–51), seems to have been as much influenced by twelfth-century allegorical epic in his *Zodiacus vitae* (Venice, 1536; Basel, 1543) as he was (undoubtedly) by Lucretius.[32] It is true that in their *Ratio studiorum* ('code of studies') of 1599, the Jesuits seemingly left little room for the teaching of non-classical authors in their humanistic schools, yet their creative reception of late antique and mediaeval Christian literature, especially in their sacred verse, is as undeniable as their exploitation of those *classical* texts that were also technically off limits.[33] Indeed, Jesuit diplomat, bibliographer and book-censor Antonio Possevino (1533–1611) furnished a long list of Christian Latin writers from late antiquity through to his own day in his guide for right-reading Counter-Reformation Catholics, *Bibliotheca selecta de ratione studiorum* ... (Rome, 1593).[34] In his recent edition of Jesuit Francesco Benci's (1542–94) epic *Quinque martyres* ([Venice, 1591]; Rome, 1592), on the martyrs of Cuncolim in Southern India, Paul Gwynne has highlighted the influence of Juvencus and Prudentius, in addition to the usual epic suspects (Virgil, Ovid, Lucretius, Lucan, Statius), as well as more recent neo-Latin ones (e.g. Marco Girolamo Vida).[35]

Moreover, if the neo-Latin world ideally shared a common, revived classical, language, there was plenty of stylistic variation within its borders, from strict Ciceronianism, to the mixed style favoured by Florentine humanist, Angelo Poliziano (1454–94), to the spare and cryptic prose of Flemish political theorist, Justus Lipsius (1547–1606), crafted from Seneca and Tacitus, to the rhetorical 'silver' colours of baroque German Jesuits Jacob Bidermann (1578–1639) and Jacob Balde (1604–68), to the archaising 'Oscan' affectations of some sixteenth- and seventeenth-century

---

[31] IJsewijn 1990–8: II 248; Morrall 1988.

[32] There is a modern edition with French translation by Chomarat (Stellato 1996). The 'mediaeval' Palingenius, in turn, enjoyed a vigorous posthumous reception in Protestant countries through the sixteenth and seventeenth centuries. See e.g. Lepri 2015.

[33] E.g. Ovid's amatory didactic, which was exploited not only by Jesuit teachers as a model for poems on e.g. civility and anger management, but imitated by schoolboys in collaborative poems on the art of friendship. See Haskell 2015, 2011 and 2003: 273–90 for the *De vita urbana* (Rome, 1725) of Francesco Grimaldi.

[34] *Elenchus aliquot poetarum, qui vel de rebus sacris, vel certe haud obscoenis scripserunt: Quive de recto poesi usu egerunt* ('De poesi, et pictura', liber XVII, caput XXIX).

[35] Gwynne 2018. See also Gwynne 2016: 5 n. 6, pointing out that as well as editions of Homer, Lucan, Silius Italicus, Statius and Valerius Flaccus, editions of early Christian epicists Juvencus, Sedulius and Arator (sixth century), and Sannazaro's *De partu Virginis*, were awarded as prizes for composition in the ancient languages at the Jesuits' Roman college in the sixteenth century. Cf. Benci 1591: 250–6, 318–24.

antiquarians.[36] All of these had their contemporary detractors and parodists, most famously and devastatingly Erasmus in his *Ciceronianus*, attacking the cult of Cicero in the Roman Curia.[37] In the dialogue's opening joke, Erasmus deflates the unfortunate Nosoponus' Ciceronian pretensions by diagnosing him with a terrible mental illness:

BULEPHORUS: Quem video nobis procul in extrema porticu deambulantem?
  Nisi parum prospiciunt oculi, Nosoponus est vetus sodalis, et studiorum σύντροφος.
HYPOLOGUS: An hic est ille Nosoponus, olim congerronum omnium lepidissimus, rubicundulus, obesulus, Veneribus & Gratiis undique scatens?
B. Is ipse est.
H. Vnde haec nova species? Larvae similior videtur, quam homini. Num quis hominem habet morbus?
B. Habet gravissimus.
H. Quis obsecro? Num hydrops?
B. Interius malum est, quam in cute.
H. Num novum hoc leprae genus, cui vulgus hodie scabiei nomine blanditur?
B. Et hoc interior haec lues.
H. Num ptysis?
B. Penitius insedit malum, quam in pulmone.
H. Num phthisis, aut icteris. [*sic*]
B. Est quiddam iecore interius.
H. Fortasse febris in vaenis et corde grassans.
B. Febris est, et non febris, interius quiddam adurens quam si febris in vaenis aut corde grassetur. Sed desine frustra divinare, novum mali genus est.
H. Nondum igitur habet nomen?
B. Apud Latinos nondum, Graeci vocant Zelodulean.
H. Nuper accidit, an χρόνιον est malum?
B. Annos jam plus septem eo tenetur miser. Sed heus conspecti sumus...

from *Ciceronianus, sive de optime dicendi dialogus* (= *ASD* 1–2: 606)

BULEPHORUS: Who's that I see strolling about down there at the end of the arcade? Unless my eyes have lost their sharpness, it's our old friend and fellow student, Nosoponus.
HYPOLOGUS: Nosoponus? The fellow who once used to be the life and soul of our set, rosy-cheeked, a bit on the plump side, diffusing charm and amiability in every direction?
B: The very same.

---

[36] See IJsewijn 1990–8: II 412–19. For the critique of Lipsius' style see Fullenwider 1984. On Bidermann's grisly, almost Marinesque, epic on the massacre of the innocents, see Hess 2000 and Haskell 2013b.
[37] See Knott's useful introduction, 1986: 324–36. (For the critical Latin text, *ASD* 1–2: 599–710, at 606.) See also DellaNeva 2007.

H: But whatever has made him look so different? He's more like a ghost than a human being. Is he suffering from some disease?
B: Yes, a very serious one.
H: Whatever is it? Surely not dropsy?
B: No, it's a malady that goes deeper into the skin.
H: You don't mean that new sort of ulcerating disease, the scab, as people euphemistically call it nowadays?
B: No, this is eating him away deeper than that.
H: Perhaps he's got a fever affecting his veins and heart?
B: Yes, it is a fever, but then it isn't: it's something that burns deeper down than any fever raging in the veins and heart – something with its source in the brain, in the depths of the mind. But stop making wrong guesses, it's a new sort of illness.
H: Hasn't it got a name yet then?
E: Not a Latin one; the Greeks call it *zelodulea*, 'style addiction'.
H: Did he catch it recently, or has he had it a long time?
B: It's had the poor fellow in its grip for more than seven years. I say, we've been spotted ... (trans. Knott in Erasmus 1986: 342)

Erasmus uses Greek medical language here for comic effect. He was, in fact, far less sceptical of the medical profession than his humanist precursor, Petrarch,[38] and of course Erasmus was as much a devotee of Greek as of Latin antiquity. It is worth underlining that many humanists and 'neo-Latinists', from Ficino to Poliziano, Turnèbe to Budé, were also *de facto* 'neo-Hellenists' and sometimes original writers of Greek.[39]

## Diversity and Decline: Sunset on the Empire of the Sign?

But what of *regional* linguistic variation? This is most obvious in the 'macaronic' writing that bubbled up in Italy in the fifteenth century. There were certainly mediaeval precedents for mixing Latin and the vernacular but the Renaissance rebranding went viral, aided no doubt by print.[40] Who could resist humble peasant fare (*macaronea*) served up as high literature, and the guilty pleasures of semi-learned over-consumption?

---

[38] See Struever 1993 on Petrarch's *Invective contra medicum*, and Marsh's I Tatti edition of the anti-scholastic *Invectives* (2004).
[39] See e.g. Botley 2010 and 2012; Lamers 2018. It is interesting that Politian's Greek nemesis, Michael Marullus, chose *Latin* as the medium for his pagan *Hymni naturales* – and indeed for his poetry in imitation of the Greek anthology (Haskell 1998c). For the intellectual culture of Byzantine émigrés in Renaissance Italy, see Lamers 2015. Note, however, that 'Neo-Hellenism' has nationalistic connotations in contemporary usage and is not a straightforward counterpart to 'Neo-Latin'.
[40] For mediaeval macaronic, see Stover in this volume.

From northern Italy the macaronic craze spread to every part of Europe and even America – though one suspects there will have been many cases of spontaneous generation. Not the first, but probably the most accomplished, example of Italian macaronic verse is the picaresque epic *Baldus* by Teofilo Folengo (four versions were published in 1517, 1521, *c.* 1536 and 1552, the language becoming progressively more 'classical').[41] The opening lines will give a taste of Folengo's earthy and exuberant style, but also illustrate the impossibility of fully savouring it if one is unfamiliar with the vernacular idiom (picked out in italics):

> Phantasia mihi plus quam *fantastica* venit
> historiam Baldi *grassis* cantare Camoenis,
> altisonam cuius phamam nomenque *gaiardum*
> terra tremat baratrumque metu sibi *cagat adossum*.
> Sed prius *altorium* vestrum *chiamare bisognat*,
> o *macaronaeam* Musae quae funditis artem.
> An poterit *passare* maris mea *gundola scoios*,
> quam *recomandatam* non vester *aiuttus* habebit?
> Non mihi Melpomene, mihi non *menchiona* Thalia,
> non Phoebus *grattans chitarinum* carmina dictent;
> *panzae* namque meae quando ventralia penso,
> non facit ad nostram Parnassi *chiacchiara pivam*.
> *Pancificae* tantum Musae doctaeque sorellae,
> Gosa, Comina, Striax Mafelinaque, Togna, Pedrala,
> *imboccare* suum veniant *macarone* poetam
> dentque *polentarum* vel quinque vel octo *cadinos*. (*Baldus* 2–3, my emphasis)

A fantasy, more fantastic than ever, has come to me: to sing with the fat Muses the story of Baldo, whose high-sounding fame and valiant name make the earth tremble, and the underworld beshit itself in fear. Yet first I must call for your aid, oh Muses, you who ladle out the Macaronic arts. Would my gondola be able to brave the sea reefs without the help of your patronage? Not for me Melpomene, or that chump Thalia, or Apollo scratching his little guitar. Let them not dictate verses to me, for when I think of the innards of my belly, the chatter of Parnassus will not do for my pipes. Only the paunchy Muses, those learned sisters – Gosa, Comina,

---

[41] I cite Mullaney in Folengo 2007, who points out in her introduction that Folengo's masterpiece is extraordinary for its time, as it thumbs its nose at cardinal Bembo's contemporary programme of reforming the Italian literary language. For critical text and extensive notes, see Folengo 1997. On macaronic neo-Latin verse and prose more widely, see IJsewijn 1990–8: II 136–8. On the diglossia of the 'tenth Muse', New Spanish nun and literary prodigy, Sor Juana de la Cruz (1648–95), see Romero (2013).

Striax, Mafelina, Togna and Pedrala – may come to ply their poet with macaroni and give him five platters, or eight, full of polenta. (Mullaney)

Much of the humour here is linguistic and derives from the overlaying of vernacular lexis with classical morphology, the alternation of Greek and Latin orthography (*phamam* for *famam* with perhaps a pinch of a pun on *famem*?) and scatological bathos (*cagat* = 'shit').[42] The language of the beautiful and mysterious Aldine incunable *Hypnerotomachia Polifili*, a mixture of Tuscan and Roman dialects festooned with Latin, represents the other side of this macaronic coin, gently deflating humanist pretensions, and is comparable with the poetry known as 'fidenziana' (after Camillo Scroffa's *Canti di Fidenzio Glottocrisio Ludimagistro*).[43] Many other forms of polyglossia were practised in the early modern period, from dictionaries, textbooks and translations through to emblem books and satirical pamphlets.[44] Verbeke has observed that 'mixed-language and multilingual texts from the early modern period acted as "ambassadors of Babel", as eloquent emissaries of the polyglot world that was early modern Europe (and beyond). Latin was clearly still an important part (or perhaps the most important part) of this polyglot world.'[45]

Beyond Europe, Laird has detected the signs of Nahuatl rhetorical and mnemotechnical modes in the writing of indigenous Latinists from sixteenth-century New Spain.[46] In a Japanese Latin writer of the same period, 'Miguel' Gotō, Watanabe finds formal polish but a lack of authenticity.[47] In 1582 Alessandro Valignano, Jesuit Visitor to the Indies, dispatched four noble Japanese Christian youths to the courts of Europe to drum up publicity for the mission. Had this Tenshō embassy returned to

---

[42] The macaronic sauce of the satirical *Allegoria. Protheus felicitatis et miseriae Cechicae. Staroceska zeme* (1715), by Jesuit priest, Jan Florian Hammerschmidt (1652–1735), proved too rich for my neo-Latin doctoral intern Ewelina Drzewiecka (Jagellionian University, Cracow), who found it difficult to decipher even with the assistance of a Czech native speaker.

[43] On Scroffa see most recently Trifone 2019. I thank Dario Brancato for confirming that the style of the *Hypnoteromachia* is 'highly artificial' and that 'this particular mix was used specifically to make fun of the Latin language' (*per litteras*).

[44] E.g. the war of Dutch and Latin verse satires launched in 1746 by the cocky student-poet Gerard Nicolaas Heerkens, in which bilingual puns are let fly in a series of semi-pseudonymous pamphlets attacking the literary establishment of Groningen. See Haskell 2013a: 33–70.

[45] Verbeke 2015: 27–40, at 36.

[46] Laird 2010. On missionary linguists, Latin and Amerindian languages see Laird 2019. On an early modern translation of Aesop into Nahuatl *via Neo-Latin*, and the false inferences of some modern commentators about indigenous departures from the original, Laird 2017.

[47] Watanabe 2018.

less stony political ground eight years later, the Latin dialogue commissioned by Valignano from Portuguese Jesuit Duarte de Sande, purportedly based on the boys' own travel journals, might have fertilised a new generation of Japanese Latinists.[48] Valignano had wanted it rolled out as a textbook in Japanese seminaries, but its blatant Eurocentrism would have made it dangerously conspicuous at this time.[49] The language kept alive by 'hidden Christians' during Japan's long period of *sakoku* was Latin in spirit but hardly in the letter (*orasho* = *oratio*, *abe Maruya* = *ave Maria*). While very little Latin written by early modern Chinese has been documented to date, we know that Chinese Christians collaborated with Jesuits – notably Matteo Ricci with blessed 'Doctor Paulus', the eminent Christian scholar-official Xu Guangqi (1562–1633) – to translate Latin works into Chinese.[50] Golvers points to paedagogical materials prepared to instruct Chinese in Latin, such as Jesuit Figurist Joseph Henri Marie de Prémare's (1666–1736) unpublished Latin grammar, *De Romana lingua dialogus*, so it is reasonable to conclude that 'a number of Chinese came to speak and write Latin actively'.[51] The handful of missionary anecdotes reproduced by Waquet, lamenting poor Chinese pronunciation of Latin – for example 'not only do they speak like parrots without understanding anything but they cannot even pronounce words that parrots can pronounce' – should be taken with a grain of salt. They are certainly not evidence of any inherent lack of aptitude for the Latin language.[52]

Within Europe itself there were periodic perceptions and assertions of regional variation in Latin, but these seem to have more to do with prevailing cultural–political winds than with the detection of linguistic

---

[48] For Latin text and translation see de Sande 2012.
[49] For early modern Latin education in Japan and missionary reports of Japanese aptitude for the language, see Taida 2017.
[50] Jesuit translations of the Confucian Classics were immensely important for bringing knowledge of Chinese culture and philosophy to Europe, beginning with the *Confucius Sinarum philosophus, sive, Scientia Sinensis latine exposita* (Paris, 1687) by Philippe Couplet (1623–93), Christian Herdtrich (1625–84), Prospero Intorcetta (1625–96) and Francis Rougemont (1624–76). See Meynard 2011 and 2015. A later project, also very influential, was the *Sinensis imperii libri classici sex* (Prague, 1711) by the Flemish Jesuit François Noël (1651–1729). For translations from Latin into Chinese, see Po-chia Hsia 2007; Meynard and Pan 2020.
[51] 'Among the few extant testimonials are the Latin letters that Michael Shen Fuzong wrote to Thomas Hyde from London, the Latin diary of André Ly, and several recently edited *testimonia* or witness accounts sent by Chinese Christians to Rome' (Golvers 2015: 570). Cf. von Martels 2014: 861, who, citing Standaert 2001, mentions the Chinese seminarians educated at the Neapolitan Jesuit *Collegio Cinese* in Naples and one Philippe Stanislas Kang, who apparently earned a reputation for his excellent Latin verses.
[52] Waquet 2001: 54, citing Bontinck 1962. The success of Mr Junyang Ng at the Wenli Academy (Zhuli) in training young Chinese students to oral Latin fluency makes me suspicious of some of these historical reports.

contamination by local vernaculars (at least in the more literary echelons of Neo-Latinity). Standards of Latinity – its supposed purity, decline or desuetude in different nations and times – are associated with sporadic panics about moral and cultural decadence. The eighteenth-century Groningen physician and lifelong Francophile Gerard Nicolaas Heerkens (1726–1801) took aim at frivolous modern French literature in his 1790 Latin poem on the health of scholars. Heerkens fantasises that his bête noire Jean le Rond d'Alembert (among other *philosophes*) is jealous because France used to produce serious writers – Latin ones, of course – who were eagerly snapped up by the international book trade:

> ... prius omnia, Galli
> Quae dederant, populos sparsa per orbis erant.
> Praeterito quidquid vix Gallia scripserat aevo,
> Mox pavit Batavos terque quaterque typos.
> Quid modo Germano, Batavoque recuditur orbe,
> Quam Latium si quod Gallia prodit opus?
> Scripta Poligniacus, sua vix Vanierius edit,
> Anglus, et haec Ubius, moxque Batavus amat.
> Idne Dalambertus ferat, et sua quisquis amari
> Sola, vel a lingua censet amanda sua?
> Gallica jure placet, nec et altera notior orbi.
> Sed minus unde legi nunc sua scripta facit?
> Quid, calamistratis pascam mea pectora nugis?
> Frivola, res nullas, jamque pudenda sequar?
> Quid video scribi, via Jacobaeaque vendit,
> Illa novit fluvii plenaque ripa libris?
> Si pauca excipias, data nuper et optima, quaeque
> Et nimio et vano pars aliena dabat;
> Estne, quod ad Batavos bene sana mente reportem?
> Meque relecturum vel semel ipse putem?
> Quotque locis illis scripta aurea, caraque terris,
> Verae mirata est Gallia laudis amans!
> Tanta fuit clades, Veterum contemnere linguas!
> Tanta fuit, nugas et nova monstra sequi!

Before, everything the French published was spread to all peoples of the globe. In the past, whatever France wrote would go through three or four Dutch editions. What else was printed in the German and Dutch worlds until recently, if not Latin books from France? Polignac and Vanière had scarcely published their works before an Englishman, a German and soon enough a Dutchman was mad for them. Could d'Alembert bear this? Or anyone who thinks only *his* writings should be loved, or are only worthy of love if in *his* language? The French language is nice, I won't deny, nor is there another throughout the world. But why does France now render her own literature less read? What, should I feed my soul on flowery rubbish? Should I seek out the trivial, mere bagatelles, and now the shameless? The stuff I see being written and hawked in the rue Saint-Jacques, or what the Quai des Grands Augustins, overflowing with books, has become acquainted with? With a few recent and fine exceptions, and the books some have published against this excess and vanity, is there anything I, in my right mind, could take back to the Dutch? Anything I would consider reading again, even once? And how many golden writings, dear to the world, has France, the lover of true praise, admired in those places [sc. 'bouquinistes']? It has been such a disaster, this contempt for the ancient languages, such a disaster to chase after nonsense and monsters of novelty![53]

By the time Heerkens (self-)published these lines he was an older man, reflecting on a lifetime of travels and people-watching between the Netherlands, Paris and Italy. In Paris as a young medical student he had met Voltaire, who quizzed him on the then hot topic of the modern pronunciation of Latin. The issue would be provocatively canvassed by d'Alembert in his 1767 essay on the 'harmony of languages'. On more than one occasion the Encyclopaedist had gleefully deflated the pretensions of modern Latin poets – a proxy for the hated Jesuits.[54] D'Alembert's remarks provoked a swift response from an Italian, Girolamo Ferri, in a series of Latin letters to his learned compatriots, *Pro linguae Latinae usu epistolae adversus Alambertium* (Faenza, 1771), which in turn inspired the Jesuit poet and essayist Giambattista Roberti (1719–86) to muse on the innate superiority of *Italian* Latinists in a letter to his fellow Bolognese, Francesco Maria Zanotti (1692–1777). Roberti, better known for his light-hearted vernacular poems on worldly topics such as modern fashion and strawberries – could not resist a dig at contemporary Spanish and Spanish-American writers, including some of his unfortunate Jesuit brethren. He was answered in the stunning *Dissertatio ludicro-seria* by Jesuit exile in Italy, Diego Abad:[55]

> Nunc jam singula qualia breviter perstringamus. Portento mihi eris, si quod Arpini, aut Veronae natus es, propterea jam tibi quasi haereditario quodam

---

[53] Heerkens 1790: 25–6.
[54] 'Why spend six years learning a dead tongue? I am far from disapproving the study of the language in which writers like Horace and Tacitus wrote; this study is absolutely essential for a knowledge of their admirable works; but I believe that it is sufficient to arrive at understanding them and that the time spent on Latin composition is time wasted' (d'Alembert and Mallet 2003).
[55] See Kerson 1991. Abad was the author of an extraordinary didactic religious epic, *De Deo deoque homine* (Cesena, 1780). See Valenzuela 1974 and Laird 2004.

> jure putes deberi Tullianam in dicendo divinitatem, aut Catullianam dulcitudinem et simplicitatem. Oportebat totidem haberemus Catullos et Cicerones, quot sunt Veronenses et Arpinates. Quod si re vera ita est, infelicitatem meam accuso. Nam cum annos jam decem in Italia versatus sim, beatissimam hanc Ciceronum et Catullorum multitudinem necdum mihi videre contigit. Quo Ciceronis aut Catulli similis quantum fieri potest, aut rursus quantum fieri potest dissimilis sis, nihil attinet ubinam locorum aut gentium natus sis. Turcae hac nostra aetate sunt inertissimi, et infacundi, et inelegantes, et a Musarum commercio alienissimi. Et tamen illorum multi inibi locorum nati sunt, ubi Socrates, Plato, Demosthenes, Sophocles, Pindarus, Homerus.

> Let us now briefly glance over what Roberti's points are, one at a time. You will be a source of astonishment to me if, because you were born in Arpinum or Verona, you should think on that account there is due you Ciceronian divineness in oratory, or Catullan sweetness and simplicity by a sort of hereditary right. It would then be proper to have as many Catulluses and Ciceros as there are Veronese and Arpinians. But if this is so in truth, I reproach my misfortune. For although I have lived for ten years now in Italy, it has not been my lot to observe this most blessed throng of Ciceros and Catulluses. To the extent you may be as similar as possible to Cicero and Catullus, or again, as dissimilar as possible, has nothing to do with where you were born, or of what nationality you are. In our time, the Turks are wholly inactive, ineloquent and unpolished, and very remote from any commerce with the muses. And yet many of them were born in the same places as Socrates, Plato, Demosthenes, Sophocles, Pindar, and Homer. (trans. Kerson 1991: 395)

The narrative of decline of Latin as the *lingua franca* of early modern Europe is usually pegged to the rise of the vernaculars as viable learned languages, the suppression of the Jesuits and the end of the *ancien régime*.[56] Reports of Latin's death in the eighteenth century, especially in the further reaches of her early modern empire, are, however, premature. Even if raw numbers of Latin publications were falling off,[57] the passion with which the Latin language was cultivated and defended in this period makes the 'Latin Enlightenment' a compelling focus for further research.[58] In Italy, for example, one can almost speak of a second Renaissance in

---

[56] In her anthology of Jesuit poetry Thill 1999 brings the blade down on Jesuit Latin at the end of the seventeenth century, apparently unaware of the wealth of eighteenth-century Jesuit Latin in Italy and the Americas. See Kaiser 1984 and Mertz, Murphy and IJsewijn 1989.
[57] See Burke 2007. But see Bertiau 2017: 2 for a rally in publication of neo-Latin poetry from the middle of the eighteenth century.
[58] For the concept, see Haskell 2013a, and Verhaart and Brockliss 2023.

the eighteenth century, one that has gone relatively unremarked, even by neo-Latinists, until quite recently.[59] Many questions remain as to where and how Latin continued to be used in the eighteenth century, and for what cultural and counter-cultural purposes.[60] After all, even d'Alembert, in the 'Preliminary Discourse' to the *Encyclopédie*, had conceded the necessity of Latin for scholarship and science, as much as he mocked it as a medium for modern poetry.[61] How do writers using Latin and networks map (or not) onto those using the vernaculars?

The writing of Latin from the nineteenth and first half of the twentieth century is even less well charted, but is gradually emerging into view. Latin poetry experienced a second wind in nineteenth-century Italy, fanned by the international *Certamen poeticum Hoeufftianum*.[62] Giovanni Pascoli (1855–1912), who died just two years before the outbreak of World War I, was for many years the most decorated talent in this competition.[63] The *Certamen* attracted entries on major world events, such as British atrocities in the Second Anglo-Boer War.[64] Bertiau has recently surveyed the rich neo-Latin literature of nineteenth-century Europe, a challenge to the assumption that the language was abandoned as a literary medium for serious poetry.[65] De Sutter has thrown a searchlight on the Latin of the early part of the twentieth century[66] and Lamers, Reitz-Joosse and Sacré have unearthed disquieting material from the period of Italian fascism.[67]

And so we arrive at our own times and the Latin compositions of contemporary authors. *Certamina Latina* are still regularly held in Italian

---

[59] See Campanelli and Ottaviani 2007; Campanelli 2008, 2013 and 2014.
[60] E.g. during the so-called 'Ibero-American Enlightenment', in which the leading light was Jesuit father José Rafael Campoy (1723–77). See Laird 2014: 828–30.
[61] 'The use of the Latin language, which we have shown to be ridiculous in matters of taste, is of the greatest service in works of philosophy, whose merit is entirely determined by clarity and precision, and which urgently require a universal and conventional language' (d'Alembert 2009 [1751] n.pag.). See also Bianco 1996.
[62] Founded by Jacob Hendrik Hoeufft (1756–1843) and organised annually by the Royal Netherlands Academy of Arts and Sciences from 1845.
[63] See Murru and Filos 1980; Fera, Gionta and Morabito 2006; Fera 2017. See also the useful website 'Giovanni Pascoli nello specchio delle sue carte: l'archivio e la casa di Giovanni e Maria Pascoli a Castelvecchio': www.pascoli.archivi.beniculturali.it/.
[64] See Van Binnebeke 2018.
[65] Bertiau 2017. See also Bertiau and Sacré 2020; Sacré 1996a; Bicknell 1996 (on Walter Savage Landor); Szörényi 1976; Krüssel 2011–15 1 (on Napoleonic war poetry); Jalabert 2015; Sanzotta 2019.
[66] See De Sutter 2019b and, on the Titanic, 2019a. See also Giustiniani 1979.
[67] On Italian fascist Latin see Fedeli 1977; Lamers, Reitz-Joose and Sacré 2014; Lamers and Reitz-Joose 2015 and 2016; Lamers, Reitz-Joose and Sanzotta 2019; Agbamu 2019.

secondary schools and universities.[68] Beyond the paradoxically popular Latin translations of (especially British and American) children's literature,[69] more or less serious neo-Latin writing continues to be published in a few boutique venues.[70] Francisco José Cabrera, for example, is a well-regarded contemporary Mexican neo-Latin poet.[71] It is admittedly difficult to get the necessary perspective on such writing – where to place it, perhaps as 'world literature'? – for the simple reason that its audiences are vanishingly small. And yet, to be fair, how many writers of the early modern period, let alone of the eighteenth and nineteenth centuries, ever expected their poems to be read beyond a coterie of learned peers? Much of the post-mediaeval literature of the British Isles circulated in manuscript, and occasional verses were the social media of the early modern world.[72] In 1999 the Belgian 'Harundine' collective published *Tonight They All Dance: 92 Latin and English Haiku*, which, if not in its verse form, recalls in its collaborative creation the ephemeral productions of so many early modern neo-Latin poets, in college, university or academy settings.[73]

## Neo-Latin as a Modern Research Field

The use of 'neo-Latin' to describe post-Renaissance Latin literature is attested from the later eighteenth century,[74] and academic monographs on the subject from at least the nineteenth,[75] but Neo-Latin was staked out as a modern research field only in the last third of the twentieth, with the launch of the journal *Humanistica Lovaniensia* in 1968, the inaugural conference in Leuven of the International Association of Neo-Latin Studies in 1971,

---

[68] The 2019 *Certamen Latinum 'Nova Humanitas'* at the University of Rome, La Sapienza, was won by Nicolò Campodonico for his Horatian satire, 'Nova Musica', a dinner party debate about the merits of 1950s and contemporary Italian popular music.
[69] Among the more enjoyable is the *Cattus petasatus*, one of a series of Dr Seuss books translated by Jennifer Morrish Tunberg and Terence Tunberg (2000).
[70] See Sacré, Tusiani and Deneire 2006; Deraedt 2016, for her neo-Latin poem on the terrorist attacks in Brussels of 22 March 2016. The older Latin language journals *Melissa* and *Vox Latina* have been joined, e.g., by the open-source *Vates* (from 2010), a 'journal of new Latin poetry' edited by M. Walker (https://vatesblog.wordpress.com/blog).
[71] Cabrera 2012 and 2016.
[72] On occasional verse, see Moul 2017: 7–9. For the techniques which facilitated the rapid production of neo-Latin occasional verse, see Gwynne and Schirg 2018.
[73] Ed. Sacré and Smets; English translations by Herman Servotte in Sacré, Smets and Servotte 1999. On the collaborative efforts of schoolboy poets in the old Society of Jesus, see Haskell 2019a.
[74] 'Johann Gottfried Herder speaks of *Neulatein* and *neulateinischen* [*sic*] poems and poets in a number of works from the 1760s onwards', Knight and Tilg 2015: 1; cf. IJsewijn 1990–8: 1 27, of Johannes Dominicus Fuss (1782–1860), professor of Latin at Liège, using 'neolatinus' much as we use 'neo-Latin'.
[75] E.g. Vissac 1862.

and the 1977 publication by its first president, Jozef IJsewijn, of the *Companion to Neo-Latin Studies*.[76] Since then, Neo-Latin has enjoyed a relatively healthy presence in northern Europe – especially Germany, the Low Countries, Austria and Scandinavia – where classical scholars such as Walther Ludwig, Reinhold Glei, Stephan Heilen, Stefan Tilg, Martin Korenjak, Thomas Haye, Marc Laureys, Karl Enenkel, Dirk Sacré, Claudia Schindler, Hans Helander and Minna Skafte Jensen have held university chairs that explicitly incorporate humanist or Neo-Latin.[77] In recent years the Ludwig Boltzmann Institute for Neo-Latin Studies in Innsbruck, Austria, has done much to foster international and interdisciplinary research and to support early career neo-Latin scholars – even if, inevitably, many will rebrand themselves as classicists, comparativists or historians to secure permanent jobs. Prominent neo-Latin scholars and groups of scholars are also to be found scattered across southern and eastern Europe and in the Baltic states.[78] It is worth pointing out that national, regional, and sometimes parochial, interests continue to drive (and fund) much neo-Latin scholarship.[79] In Italy, 'neo-Latinists' in our sense of the word (since 'neolatino' = 'Romance') have overwhelmingly concentrated their attentions on Italian Renaissance humanism and are not usually attached to Classics departments.[80] That said, Italian academics who were educated at a *liceo classico* or even *liceo scientifico* are well equipped to deal with neo-Latin texts at a reasonably advanced level. This is in fact the case for the majority of Italian scholars *in the humanities*, even more so for early modernists, many of whom are *de facto* 'neo-Latinists' when they need to be.[81]

---

[76] Revised and expanded in collaboration with his student and successor, Dirk Sacré (IJsewijn 1990–8).
[77] For example the Heidelberg Seminar for Medieval and Neo-Latin Philology added 'Neo-Latin' to its name in 1973. The relative uptake of Neo-Latin by different European nations might be calibrated with their receptiveness to Latin studies more broadly, for which see Fuhrer in this volume.
[78] For Croatia, see the digital text library edited by Neven Jovanović, *Croatiae Auctores Latini* (CroALa), at http://croala.ffzg.unizg.hr/. An interesting experiment was recently conducted by scholars from Croatia and the Tyrol to compare the neo-Latin corpora of two historically unconnected regions; see Jovanović, Luggin, Špoljarić and Šubarić 2018.
[79] This is not necessarily a bad thing, as rich printed and manuscript holdings in state and institutional collections inevitably demand the attention of those who have sustained access to them. See Vratović and Gortan 1969–70; Mikołajczak 1998; Korenjak, Schaffenrath, Šubarić and Töchterle 2012; Trofymuk 2014. For Scandinavia, see e.g. Skafte Jensen 1995 and 2004; Helander 2004; and the Database of Nordic Neo-Latin Literature (https://www.cdnl.dk/dbnnl/dbnnl_search.htm).
[80] 'Neo-Latinists' Francesco Tateo, Silvia Rizzo, Vincenzo Fera, Davide Canfora and Maurizio Campanelli, for example, are all professors of 'Lettere'.
[81] Italian early modern religious, intellectual and scientific historians work regularly and comfortably with neo-Latin material, including literary texts.

Neo-Latin is entering an era of greater confidence in the Anglophone world, with the recent publication of three major English-language handbooks (Brill, Oxford and Cambridge).[82] It is, of course, far from a new presence on the British and Irish academic scene. The neo-Latin flame has been kept alive for decades by scholars in a handful of British institutions and departments, from the Warburg Institute to the University of Warwick;[83] in Ireland, the Centre for Neo-Latin Studies at the University of Cork has been in operation now for over twenty years. Yet it was only in 2004 that the 'Society for Neo-Latin Studies' was formed as the national association in the UK, aiming to 'foster dialogue among scholars from different disciplines working on neo-Latin literature, support the next generation of scholars and encourage teaching of this material'. The upscaling of neo-Latin research in the UK has been made possible by large grant funding, for example from the Leverhulme Foundation and AHRC. For example, 'Latin poetry in English manuscript verse miscellanies, c. 1550–1700', led by Victoria Moul (University College London), is transforming our understanding of post-mediaeval English literary history through the systematic survey of Latin verse in manuscript miscellanies.[84] Moul has memorably described Latin as the 'dark matter' of early modern English literature – and, importantly for the history of that literature, it does not always proceed *pari passu* with trends and genres in the vernacular.[85] From a later period, John Gilmore's (University of Warwick) 'Oriental poetry, Latin scholarship & the European Enlightenment' calibrates Sir William Jones' (1746–94) Latin accounts of 'Oriental' poetry, especially in the *Poeseos Asiaticae Commentariorum Libri Sex* (1774), with his shorter and more familiar English *Essay on the Poetry of the Eastern Nations* (1772). For all the interdisciplinary consciousness-raising of such projects, however, it

---

[82] Bloemendal, Ford and Fantazzi 2014a and 2014b; Knight and Tilg 2015; Moul 2017.
[83] See Reid and McOmish 2016; Houghton and Manuwald 2013; Burnett and Mann 2005; Binns 1990 and 1974. See also Moul 2016.
[84] As Moul 2018: 257 reports, in a chapter on her initial findings: 'Throughout this period, the manuscript circulation of verse remained an important element of English literary culture, with many well-known poets of this period, such as George Herbert and John Donne, circulating their verse only or largely in manuscript. For this reason, manuscript verse miscellanies and personal notebooks have received considerable scholarly attention, but almost exclusively in terms of the English verse that they contain. In practice, literary culture throughout this period was bilingual: the enormous quantity of post-medieval Latin verse in manuscript has, however, received no systematic scholarly study, and is often poorly catalogued, or not catalogued at all.'
[85] Moul 2018 and 2021. In particular, she has found 'substantial evidence of non-classical metrical innovation in the seventeenth century, including significant numbers of polymetric, rhyming and "free" Latin verse' (2019: 262). These early results add important detail to the picture sketched in IJsewijn 1990–8: II 15–20 and 423, who comments on the classical conservatism of neo-Latin poetry and a general lack of metrical experimentation.

would be premature to claim that Neo-Latin has become mainstream in the UK and Ireland.[86] Given the linguistic obstacles it presents even for Classics undergraduates – the necessity of reading not just reams of untranslated Latin but also in several modern languages – the neo-Latin path is perhaps less likely to be taken than, say, that of classical reception studies.

The health of Neo-Latin in the United States is more difficult for me to gauge. While a handful of American neo-Latinists, or at least scholars with more than a passing interest in neo-Latin texts, are known *as* or to classicists,[87] Neo-Latin has a less visible institutional footprint in Northern America than in many parts of Europe. It may be significant that the International Association of Neo-Latin Studies has only ever convened once on that continent (Toronto). In North America, neo-Latin scholarship has typically clustered around canonical vernacular writers (Petrarch, Erasmus, More, Milton) and neo-Latinists have most often found perches in departments of English, modern European languages (especially Italian), comparative literature, history, religion, and history and philosophy of science. The Italian Renaissance remains a primary focus, and it is telling that the series once billed as Neo-Latin's answer to the Loeb Classical Library is the I Tatti *Renaissance* Library, edited by an Italian Renaissance historian, James Hankins. The twice-yearly bulletin of 'Neo-Latin News', produced for the American Society for Neo-Latin Studies by Craig Kallendorf, and since 2021, by Patrick M. Owens, is a section of 'Seventeenth-Century News', the official organ of the Milton Society of Northern America and the Milton Section of the Modern Language Association.[88] Whether for reasons of disciplinary tradition, institutional structures and hiring priorities, or perhaps because its own home-grown neo-Latin literature is relatively sparse and late compared with that of Europe (with the exception of New France),[89] Neo-Latin remains a somewhat niche area in North America. By contrast, Neo-Latin studies have seen steady growth in *Latin* America since at least the 1990s, where there are now several major hubs of activity (especially in Mexico, but also Argentina, Peru, Chile and Brazil). The neo-Latin literature from colonial

---

[86] We can also mention the AHRC Research Network in Baroque Latinity, led by Jacqueline Glomski and Gesine Manuwald (University College London), and the new series of neo-Latin texts and studies to be published by Bloomsbury.
[87] E.g. Julia Haig Gaisser, Charles Fantazzi, John Miller, Michael Putnam.
[88] It is true that there has been a sprinkling of neo-Latin sessions at recent conferences of the Society for Classical Studies and of the Renaissance Society of America, although it might be noted that the majority of panels at the RSA 2018 in New Orleans were populated by Northern European scholars.
[89] Thus Blair 2014: 'Overall, Neo-Latin writings from North America are relatively sparse and of unremarkable quality' (834). Contrast Cottier and Westra 2015.

New Spain and Brazil is extraordinarily rich, and runs from the sixteenth century through to the present.[90] The work of modern scholars from this part of the world is still less well known to the global neo-Latin community than it should be.[91]

We might at this point distinguish the study of early modern Latin texts for the purposes of literary and historical scholarship from the 'living' Latin movement, which, perhaps more than Neo-Latin *stricto sensu*, has flourished discreetly in the United States for several decades now under the aegis of the University of Kentucky's Latin summer school, the *Conventiculum Lexintoniense*, directed by Terence and Jennifer Tunburg and Milena Minkova.[92] For comparison, an ambitious project of revival of the ancient languages has borne startling fruit at the Accademia Vivarium Novum (AVN) in Frascati, Italy, where students from all over the world, including Malawi, Egypt, Columbia, Chile, Mexico, Hungary, Singapore and China are taught to converse and write in classical Latin and Greek and have already produced an impressive series of graduate dissertations in Latin.[93] Such initiatives reveal an interesting paradox. One suspects that not a few modern university professors of Classics would find it difficult to match the Latin fluency, oral or written, of some of the advanced students of the AVN, and yet its graduates are by no means all destined for or even seeking careers as academic classicists. A halfway house between such 'active'[94] Latinity, qua revival of the ideals and methods of Renaissance

---

[90] For useful overviews, see Laird 2015 and 2014 (pointing out, however, that much nineteenth- and twentieth-century Latin was connected to repressive, conservative politics, e.g. the Jesuit José Luis Velasco's Horatian ode hailing General Franco's conquest of Madrid). See also Romero 1981.

[91] E.g. Ignacio Osorio Romero, Tarcisio Herrera Zapién, Roberto Heredia Correa, Mauricio Beuchot, Felipe Reyes Palacios, José Quiñones Melgoza, Miguel Castillo Didier, Walter Hanisch Espíndola, Marcela Suárez, Alfredo Fraschini, Luis Ángel Sánchez, Marcos Carmignani, Guillermo De Santis, Matías Robbio Fernández, Mariana and Elena María Calderón, Leonardo Waisman, Rodrigo Gonçalves, Artur Costrino, Maria Cecília de Miranda Nogueira Coelho, Erika Valdevieso. (I am grateful to Maya Feile Tomes for providing this list of names.)

[92] Since 2000 a graduate certificate in Latin studies, *taught in Latin*, has been offered through the University of Kentucky's Institute for Latin Studies, providing the closest thing to a Neo-Latin 'qualification' in North America. The three-semester course is 'aimed at students who need strong Latin skills for any academic discipline in which Latin is important, including not only classics, but also history, philosophy, theology, and a wide variety of fields in literatures and languages' (https://mcl.as.uky.edu/latin-institute).

[93] The AVN is exclusively male, in part because of Italian government rules against mixed residential accommodation for minors. I am informed that a nearby residence is currently being prepared to receive female students.

[94] The director of the AVN, Luigi Miraglia, has little patience with the up-dating of the language pursued by some in the 'living' Latin movement. See his 2013 lecture to the *Athenaeum illustre* in Amsterdam, 'De causis corruptae institutionis Latinæ', available on YouTube.

humanism, and the academic study of Latin texts for modern historical research and literary analysis, is the approach taken by University of Cork's MA in Renaissance Latin Culture. Designed primarily for historians who need to read early modern Latin texts, the Cork course teaches Latin from textbooks of the period, and requires students to speak it, for the purposes of what might best be described as a sort of experimental cognitive archaeology.

*∗∗*

The fact that increasing numbers of Anglophone classicists are beginning to dip their toes into neo-Latin waters[95] should probably be attributed to a growing awareness of the very existence of this literature, partly in consequence of its heightened visibility in digital libraries such as Perseus,[96] to conversations with colleagues who have worked with neo-Latin texts, and to a more expansive attitude to the Latin canon in *all* periods,[97] rather than to any sought engagement with Neo-Latin as a 'discipline'. That is, one suspects that the interest of classicists is more often piqued by their personal discovery of neo-Latin texts, in the context of exploring the reception of *classical* authors, than by curiosity about the work and research agendas of self-defined and specialist neo-Latinists. Of course, many classicists, myself included, stumbled upon Neo-Latin in just this way, even if some of us wandered off and never entirely returned to the Classics fold. But it is important to recognise that others have come to the field from different disciplinary bases. The late Philip Ford, Professor of French and Neo-Latin at the University of Cambridge, was a modern linguist and *seiziémiste*. Speakers at the annual conferences organised by the Cambridge Society for Neo-Latin Studies from the 1990s regularly included Renaissance and Reformation scholars, art historians, historians of the book, of scholarship, of early modern science, medicine and music and so on. With so many disciplines of origin, is it possible to identify any

---

[95] E.g. Stephen Hinds, Gideon Nisbet, Michael Putnam, John Miller, Helen Lovatt, Martin Dinter, Mary Beard and others. Others, such as Philip Hardie, Julia Haig Gaisser and Andrew Laird, have had a longer involvement with the field without ever wholly 'defecting' to it.

[96] 'Humanist and Renaissance Italian Poetry in Latin' (www.perseus.tufts.edu/hopper/collection?collection=Perseus:collection:PDILL); cf. 'Italian Poetry in Latin' (http://mizar.unive.it/poetiditalia/public). Other online libraries of neo-Latin materials include the German 'CAMENA – Latin Texts of Early Modern Europe' (https://mateo.uni-mannheim.de/camenahtdocs/camena_e.html); 'De Heinsius-Collectie', for Dutch Latin verse and prose (https://let.leidenuniv.nl/Dutch/Latijn/Heinsius.html); the 'Database of Nordic Neo-Latin Literature' (https://www.cdnl.dk/dbnnl/dbnnl_search.htm); and Dana Sutton's 'Analytic Bibliography of On-line Neo-Latin Texts': (https://philological.bham.ac.uk/bibliography/index.htm), which currently runs to 63,210 entries. Cf. the sub-collection of hypertext critical editions by Sutton and others at https://philological.bham.ac.uk/library.html.

[97] On the canon, see Peirano in this volume.

intellectual common ground for neo-Latinists as we enter the third decade of the twenty-first century?

A first and obvious answer, as foreshadowed in the previous section, is the historical period(s) of our research, beginning with the Italian Renaissance and on through the Reformation, Enlightenment and even nineteenth and twentieth centuries. But to say that a neo-Latinist is a historian, critic, editor or translator of early modern, modern and/or contemporary Latin texts does not really say much about our typical concerns and approaches. Some of us specialise in major authors and their milieux; others have more longitudinal interests in the role of Latin in a range of post-classical institutional, professional and confessional contexts: schools, universities, religious orders, traditions of science, philosophy, law, art, medicine, the *Respublica litterarum*.[98] For those of a more philological bent, it is worth noting that neo-Latin literature often permits, indeed *demands*, quite different kinds of analysis from Roman literature. Consider, for example, that nearly every early modern schoolboy was a Latin 'poet' and that many (perhaps too many ...) persevered in the habit. The sheer volume of sources available in manuscript and print can be daunting if we are panning for literary gold, but is, of course, an open invitation to mine literary *corpora* – themselves embedded in a wealth of contextual material, including paratexts, variant versions, letters, paedagogical documents, theoretical reflection and commentary, even on their performance[99] ... – for the sorts of cross-sectional cultural and historical information unavailable to most classicists.

It has to be admitted that a lot of neo-Latin scholarship to date, including literary scholarship, has amounted to more or less sophisticated surveying. The question of what is distinctive about Neo-Latin as a literary idiom is rarely, if ever, posed. How is neo-Latin intertextuality different from that between classical Latin authors, or classical to vernacular? Does it arise from or produce different cognitive or affective experiences for writers and readers? What is the significance of the fact that neo-Latin poetry is 'fitted together', more or less consciously, from the literal *stuff* of ancient

---

[98] See, e.g. the new online Belgian *Journal of Latin Cosmopolitanism and European Literatures* (*JOLCEL*), which 'aims to be a platform for research on the dynamic role of Latin as a cosmopolitan language within European literary history. With a dialogical format, the journal seeks to perform the academic discussion on what shapes European literary identity.'

[99] For the reading and performance of Latin poetry, 1500–1700, see the essays collected in Isebaert and Smeesters 2013.

poetry, that is, out of bits and pieces of Lucretius, Virgil, Horace, Ovid, et al.?[100] D'Alembert put his finger on this (for him, sore) point in his 1767 essay on the 'harmony of languages':

> 'But,' someone will say, 'you cannot deny, at least, that a writer who uses only whole phrases drawn from the best Latin authors in his works does not write well in that language.' First, is it possible to use only phrases borrowed from elsewhere in a modern Latin work, without having to mix in at least something of one's own, which can then ruin everything? Secondly, let's suppose that we use only such phrases – I deny that we can still flatter ourselves that we write well in Latin. Indeed, a writer's true merit consists in having his own style; but the merit of a Latinist such as this would be to have a style that did not belong to him, and which was, as it were, a *cento* of twenty different styles. Now, I ask, what we should think of such a farrago?[101]

While d'Alembert's answer is characteristically mischievous,[102] we might respond with more seriousness that the special 'merit' of a neo-Latin poet resides, paradoxically, in his or her ability to reanimate the ancient Latin matter as a medium for contemporary thought and feeling. The 'success' of the neo-Latin poem, moreover, depends on the classical intertext(s) remaining simultaneously alive *and* dead, Schrödinger's cat-style. A neo-Latin text might even implant false memories of an ancient one, as when the Victorian Roger Cholmeley, in his Oxford prize poem on the Stone Age, almost makes us believe that Lucretius had spoken the language of Charles Darwin and Edward Tylor.[103] It is because the neo-Latin idiom

---

[100] Haskell 2017.

[101] 'Mais, dira-t-on, vous ne pouvez disconvenir au moins qu'un écrivain qui n'emploierait dans ses ouvrages que des phrases entières tirées des bons auteurs latins, n'écrivît bien en cette langue. Premièrement, est-il possible qu'on n'emploie absolument dans un ouvrage latin moderne, que des phrases empruntées d'ailleurs, sans être obligé d'y mêler du moins quelque chose du sien, qui sera capable de tout gâter? En second lieu, je suppose qu'on n'emploie en effet que de pareilles phrases; et je nie qu'on puisse encore se flatter de bien écrire en latin. En effet, le vrai mérite d'un écrivain est d'avoir un style qui soit à lui; le mérite au contraire d'un latiniste tel qu'on le suppose, serait d'avoir un style qui ne lui appartînt pas, et qui fût, pour ainsi dire, un *centon* de vingt styles différents. Or je demande ce qu'on devrait penser d'une pareille bigarrure?' (text from https://obvil.sorbonne-universite.fr/corpus/critique/alembert_harmonie-langues; my translation).

[102] 'The reader might reply, together with the philosopher to whom someone wanted to introduce a young man who knew all of Cicero by heart: "I have his book." One could also cite what M. de Fontenelle said: "In my youth I composed some Greek verses, some even as good as Homer's – because they were his"' ('Le lecteur peut dire alors comme ce philosophe, à qui on voulait présenter un jeune homme qui savait tout Cicéron par cœur; il répondit, *j'ai le livre*. On peut citer aussi ce que disait M. de Fontenelle: *J'ai fait dans ma jeunesse des vers grecs, et aussi bons que ceux d'Homère, car ils en étaient*'; my translation).

[103] Haskell 2009.

is capable of sparking such quantum leaps of intertextual energy – sometimes, as here, across millennia – that it seems to demand a different critical toolkit from that used to analyse ancient literature or even vernacular appropriations of ancient texts.

More generally, the relationship of Neo-Latin to parallel or emerging modern European literatures is a perennial theme in the scholarship; the discussion has already moved well beyond the identification and criticism of Latin writings by 'star' vernacular authors.[104] Classicists may be unsurprised to learn that Renaissance poets Lodovico Ariosto and Torquato Tasso wrote Latin verse.[105] But if the lost Latin epigrams of John Donne turn up one day in manuscript we should not necessarily expect them to be great.[106] In *The Judgment of Palaemon*, Philip Ford has plotted the fertile bilingual literary culture of Renaissance France and demonstrated that the Pléiade poets picked up the neo-Catullan style not from Catullus himself but from contemporary neo-Latin poets.[107] Indeed, Moul warns that the classical receptionist who spots the Catullan intertexts in the (English) lyrics that first appeared in Ben Jonson's *Volpone* (reprinted as poems 5 and 6 in his 1616 collection, *The Forest*) may miss the point that Jonson is alluding to this *neo-Latin* tradition: 'The theme is not in fact less but much more hackneyed than it appears to the modern reader who earnestly notes the parallel with Catullus ... The lyrics are meant to sound beautiful, but also unoriginal almost to the point of pastiche.'[108]

Many 'canonical' neo-Latin writers were truly bilingual talents: Petrarch, Boccaccio, Politian, Sannazaro, Bruno, Milton, Campion,

---

[104] Castor and Cave 1984; Taylor and Coroleu 1999; Föcking and Müller 2007; Hass and Ramminger 2010; Thurn 2012 and 2014; Ford 2013; Deneire 2014a and 2014b; Bloemendal and Verbeke 2015; Refini 2017; Schaffenrath and Winkler 2019.
[105] For the Latin poetry of Torquato Tasso, see Pavone 1968; for Ludovico Ariosto, see the I Tatti edition by Looney and Possanza (Ariosto 2018); Luccioli 2019. Thurn 2014: 292–3 reminds us that 'dominating trends certainly influenced Neo-Latin poetic productions such as the Petrarchan style, the Tasso-influenced epic, and perhaps even Dante. Lesser known is the fact that – despite sometimes merely regional popularity – nearly ever genre in the vernacular had found its way into Neo-Latin poetry ... The German *Zeitungslied* (historical ballad), the tradition of the *Kontrafaktur* (parody), and the *Narrenschelte* (fool's literature) had their counterparts in Latin poems in Germany, just as the Tuscan *laude*, the Spanish *Romance*, the Catalan *Tautogrammata*, English ballads, and Hungarian historic battle poems were influential as well.'
[106] While Samuel Johnson produced some beautiful Latin poems (Rudd 2005) – see his poignant recollection of a traumatic swimming lesson – the Latin verse of Jesuit Gerard Manley Hopkins is underwhelming. On Johnson see Rudd 2000 and 2012. For Hopkins see Wyatt 1997.
[107] The vernacular classicism of Marot was, conversely, as influential on French neo-Latin poets in the first half of the sixteenth century as it was on French.
[108] Moul 2017: 4–5. See O'Rourke and Pelttari in this volume on intertextuality.

Herbert, Crashaw, Marvell, Kochanowski, Pascoli.[109] Others, perhaps surprisingly, were not: Marullus,[110] Pontano, Vida, Erasmus, Owen, Balde, Sarbiewski.[111] The fact that a writer did not publish literary works in the vernacular should not, however, be taken as evidence that he or she was insulated from its influence.[112] In her 2017 Cambridge doctoral thesis, Maya Feile Tomes convincingly indicated thematic, and even precise verbal, traces of Spanish poets, including Alonso de Ercilla (1533–94), in the Columbus epic *De invento novo orbe inductoque illuc Christi sacrificio* (1777) by exiled Ibero-American Jesuit, José Emmanuel Peramás (1732–93) – in spite of the fact that vernacular models are *not* confessed in the poem's preface (as are Lucretius, Virgil, Horace, Ovid, the Renaissance neo-Latin poets Fracastoro and Sannazaro, and Jesuits Jacques Vanière and Tommaso Ceva).[113]

Speaking of Columbus, Peramás' is only the last (or latest?) identified in a series of neo-Latin epics on the discovery of the 'New World', beginning with Girolamo Fracastoro's epyllion in the third book of his didactic epic *Syphilis sive de morbo gallico* (Verona, 1530).[114] Feile Tomes' salvaging of Peramás' 'lost' Columbus poem from the *mare magnum* of the internet is emblematic of the rapid pace with which the neo-Latin world is revealing itself to us in the digital age.[115] In fact, neo-Latin scholarship has, from the earliest pioneering surveys of Jozef IJsewijn through to the latest Brill, Oxford and Cambridge handbooks, evinced an almost compulsive cartographic spirit, and the extent and co-ordinates of both the sources and the 'discipline' are still – perhaps perpetually? – being negotiated.[116] Hence

---

[109] See especially Hale 1997. The *Complete Poetry* of George Herbert has been recently released in an excellent English–Latin edition by John Drury and Victoria Moul (Herbert 2015). On Pascoli see n. 63.

[110] Michael Marullus (c. 1458–1500), after all, was Greek, as he frequently announced in his Latin poetry!

[111] Maciej Kazimierz Sarbiewski's Latin writings were an international sensation and the 'Sarmatian Horace' was frequently translated *into* the vernacular. See Fordónski and Urbánski 2008.

[112] Thurn 2014: 292–3 points e.g. to Ugolino Verino's (1438–1515) epic *Carlias*, inspired, as the poet himself declares, by Homer, Virgil and Dante, but which also cribs Italian *romanzi cavallereschi*. Cf. Thurn 2002: 753, suggesting that Verino, in turn, was a minor influence on Ariosto's *Orlando furioso*.

[113] For this poem, see Feile Tomes 2015a, 2015b and 2015c.

[114] For the others, see Hofmann 1994 and Schaffenrath's edition of Jesuit Ubertino Carrara's *Columbus. Carmen epicum* (2004).

[115] A world that James Hankins has dubbed a 'lost continent' (2001).

[116] See n. 82. I once warned that neo-Latinists were in danger of developing a 'Columbus complex': 'In the past when classicists moonlighted as Neo-Latinists they ran the risk of being seen as dabblers and dilettantes. Today we run that risk again when we turn our classical telescopes on so many enticing New Worlds, worlds which our mere mastery of the Latin language seems to reveal to us' (Haskell 2001: 48–9).

long chapters in the *Macropaedia* volume of the Brill *Encyclopedia* on Neo-Latin *and* music, the visual arts, architecture, mathematics, astrology and astronomy, alchemy, patristics, pornography, not to mention the even more miscellaneous shorter entries in the *Micropaedia*.[117] While this panoply of topics can seem bewildering and messy to those unfamiliar with the field, classicists will at least recognise many of the literary genres that are routinely surveyed: epic, lyric, didactic, pastoral, elegy, epigram, letters (prose and verse), drama, dialogue, novel, satire. Having taken our bearings on Neo-Latin as an historical discourse and modern discipline, then, we now turn to genre as a handy compass for classicists looking to navigate the choppy seas of neo-Latin writing.

## Purity and Hybridity: Neo-Latin Genres

But looks can be deceiving. Neo-Latin versions and hybrids of classical genres have developed under the influence of Christian and vernacular traditions, and under diverse and discrete historical conditions.[118] Moreover, a classicist's nose for what a classical genre *is* may lead her in circles when searching for its descendants in the early modern literary record. Take epic, for example. Moul has pointed to a surprising blind-spot in scholarship on the reception of Claudian in early modern England, where an important sub-genre of political panegyric-epic emerged in English in response to Claudianic poems of the Cromwellian poet laureate Payne Fisher (1616–93). Thus, where we don't find Virgilian epic, we find Claudian, who, as Moul reminds, was 'a classic of the medieval classroom', excerpted in school readers, his influence 'perceptible in many works of epic and short epic, such as Jacopo Sannazaro's *De partu Virginis*'.[119] Again, the classicist may be curious about the reception of 'their' ancient author in

---

[117] Bloemendal, Ford and Fantazzi 2014a and 2014b.
[118] E.g. Špoljarić 2018 proposes an idiosyncratic epideictic sub-genre of Dalmatian humanist *orationes in creatione ducis*, advancing local and regional agendas; Luggin 2018 limns the features of a distinctively Tyrolian sub-genre of Menippean satire. For a macroscopic view of neo-Latin Menippean satire, see De Smet 1996.
[119] Moul 2019: 25. She writes that Fisher's verse, 'unVirgilian in style, draws upon a very wide range of classical and late antique models, including Lucan, Statius, Silius Italicus, Valerius Flaccus and Prudentius, as well as earlier neo-Latin poets such as George Buchanan and Mantuan (Baptista Spagnuoli), and even works (by John Milton, Caspar Barlaeus and Charles I) published within the previous decade' (ibid. 23). For contemporary reception of Claudian on the continent, see Berlincourt 2013.

different historical periods – hence the obligatory chapter on the reception of Virgil or Ovid, Cicero or Seneca, in the Middle Ages, Renaissance, Victorian England or the colonial Americas, in so many modern companions and handbooks. As rich and interesting as these case studies may be, it makes little sense to compare – to take an admittedly extreme example – Giordano Bruno's voluminous cosmological trilogy *De minimo*, *De monade* and *De immenso* (Frankfurt, 1591) with Roger Cholmeley's bijou Victorian prize poem on the 'Stone Age', no matter how much they are both formally indebted to Lucretius' *De rerum natura*. More useful, perhaps, are micro-historical explorations of how a classical genre is adopted and transformed in more or less intellectually or institutionally demarcated cultural milieux.[120]

There are a handful of neo-Latin-born genres, such as the emblem book,[121] printed commonplace book,[122] the *hodoeporicon* (humanist travel poem),[123] psalm and Biblical paraphrase,[124] the *Colloquia scholastica* popularised by Erasmus (though predating him),[125] the multilingual *tumuli/tombeaux* of Renaissance France and the *alba amicorum/Stammbücher* of early modern Germany.[126] Others are offcuts or outgrowths of classical models, such as the *Somnia* of Vives, Lipsius, Kepler and others, transformed beyond recognition from Cicero's dream of Scipio, the various supplements and continuations of ancient texts,[127] and all manner of Christianised *Eclogues*,[128]

---

[120] On Ovidian verse letters, for example, see Eickmeyer 2012 and Manuwald 2015.

[121] The literature on emblem books is immense, from Alciati's *Emblematum libellus* (Augsburg, 1531) through to the *Imago primi saeculi Societatis Jesu* (Antwerp, 1640). For the latter, see O'Malley 2015.

[122] Moss 1996. See now MacPhail's fascinating study of the dynamics of reception of Renaissance commonplaces in Latin and vernacular, from the humanist *sylvae*, repositories of paroemial raw material, to their setting as literary gems by Erasmus and others (2014).

[123] Wiegand 1984; Enenkel and De Jong 2019.   [124] Green 2014.

[125] Some are available through Perseus, and a small collection archived at web.archive.org/web/20190405153208/http://www.stoa.org/colloquia/, including the fascinating *Ad exercitia linguae Latinae dialogi* (1554), describing the city of Mexico, by Francisco Cervantes de Salazar (1514?–75), rector of the newly founded Royal and Pontifical University of Mexico from 1553.

[126] Ludwig 2006a and 2006b.

[127] Most famously Maffeo Vegio's (1407–58) thirteenth book of the *Aeneid*, but also supplements to Livy, Quintus Curtius, Tacitus and Petronius. See IJsewijn 1990–8: II 5–6.

[128] The Christian eclogues of Carmelite Baptista Spagnuoli Mantuanus (Mantuan) (1447–1516) and the piscatorials of Jacopo Sannazaro (1458–1530) are well known and were much imitated. Nautical eclogues become fashionable in the age of discovery. IJsewijn reports that the sailors of Flemish Jacobus Sluperius (1532–82) are to be found 'singing in such exotic places as Cuba and among its cannibals' (*Poemata*, Antwerp, 1575); the Scotsman Joannes Leochaus (Leech) (c. 1590–c. 1630) added a series of viticultural eclogues, *Vinitoriae*, to his *Bucolicae, Piscatoriae* and *Nauticae* (*Musae priores*, London, 1630) (IJsewijn 1990–8: II 63). To these we might add the didactic eclogues on friendship by French Jesuit Jacques Vanière (1664–1739); see Haskell 2015.

*Heroides*[129] and dramatic forms.[130] Catullus' kiss poems spawned a long-lived sub-genre, the *Basia*, in the erotic poetry of Erasmus' contemporary, Janus Secundus ([Jan Everaerts] 1511–36), whose intertextual entanglements with Roman love poetry are perennially entertaining, if not titillating, for classicists.[131] Neo-Latin love poetry spreads over a much wider field than Roman elegy, however, and cannot be appreciated solely in reference to the latter. It encompasses the pornographic (e.g. the louche hendecasyllables of Giovanni Gioviano Pontano on his encounters with the prostitutes of Baiae, and the even more obscene *Hermaphroditus* by the founder of the humanist Neapolitan Academy, Antonio Beccadelli),[132] the domestic (the same Pontano's poems *De amore conjugali*, Michael Marullus' austere marriage proposal to 'Neaera', George Herbert's 'Memoriae matris sacrum'),[133] and also the sacred, from the emblematic to the didactic (e.g. Hermann Hugo's *Pia desideria* (Antwerp, 1624), Tommaso Ravasini's *De arte amandi B. Mariam Virginem libri iii* (Modena, 1706) and Gaetano Corrazza's *De arte bene amandi sive de diligendo Deo libri iii* (Rome, 1724)).

As for the quintessentially classical genre of epic, myriad are the neo-Latin knock-offs designed to look like the *Aeneid*, but some are almost unrecognisable as the Virgilian epics they purport to be. The arresting opening lines of Jesuit Jacob Bidermann's *Herodiados libri iii* (1622), on the massacre of Bethlehem, metapoetically prime us not only for the horrors of biblical baby-slaughter but for a *sparagmos* of Virgil's poem itself:

> Infandas acies, *Iraeque* pudenda profanae
> Bella, *Palastinos* vetito populata nepotes
> Agmine: Et undantes lactenti sanguine Cunas,
> Maternique sinus ululata *Biennia*, cantu
> Promere Musa iubet.                                    (*Herodias* Book 1, §1)
>
> Unspeakable troops, shameful wars of profane rage, laying waste to Palestinian grandchildren with your forbidden army, and cradles running

---

[129] From Helius Eobanus Hessus (1488–1540) to the Jesuits, for whose efforts in this genre see Eickmeyer 2012.
[130] See Fontaine's edition of Joannes Burmeister's Plautine plays (2015). The baroque German poet Joannes Burmeister of Lüneburg (1576–1638) wrote several Christian 'inversions' of Plautus, ingeniously transforming pagan plays into biblical comedies. The bibliography on neo-Latin drama is vast, but much of it is captured in Bloemendal and Norland 2013, a compendious history of periods and regions. In spite of the volume's title ('early modern Europe'), Barea's chapter (2013) covers 'neo-Latin drama in Spain, Portugal and Latin America'.
[131] See Endres 1981; Price 1996; Wright 1930.
[132] See Coppini 1990 and 2009; O'Connor 2001; Pontano 2006. See also Enenkel 2014: 491–3.
[133] I Tatti Renaissance edition by Roman (Pontano 2014).

with milky blood, and two years at the mother's breast filled with howling: this the Muse orders me to set forth in song.

Like many of his confrères, Bidermann composed in prose and verse across a variety of genres, including drama.[134] The *Cenodoxus*, his early smash-hit play on the legend of St Bruno, a possible inspiration for Goethe's *Faust*, was first performed in Augsburg in 1602 and remains popular in Germany to this day.[135] Though published much later, the epic *Herodias* was drafted in the same early period of Bidermann's career; parallels between the climactic damnations of Cenodoxus and Herod have been indicated by Hess.[136] Indeed, if the *Cenodoxus* is, as Bidermann proclaims, a 'comico-tragedy', the *Herodias* might be described as a tragedo-epic, of which Herod is the Senecan anti-hero.[137] The twelve-book martyr epic *Pacieicis* (Coimbra, 1640) by Portuguese Jesuit Bartolomeu Pereira is woven from Virgilian threads, though heavily embroidered with marvels and monsters from later sources such as Camões' *Lusiads*.[138] We have no evidence that Pereira himself composed plays, but a residue of Jesuit 'multimedia' performance certainly seems to permeate his epic poem. The personified virtues and vices which do battle over the souls of the protagonists ('Love of Life', 'Purity', 'Blind Love', 'Fame', 'Vainglory', 'Faith', 'Heresy', 'Piety', 'Impiety' and 'Constancy'), reminiscent as they are of Prudentius' *Psychomachia* and even Ovid, regularly stride the Jesuit stage. The interpenetration of rhetorical, dramatic and visual (emblematic and ekphrastic) modes is a hallmark of Jesuit Latin poetry. In the eighteenth century,

---

[134] In addition to the plays for which he is most famous, collected in the posthumous *Ludi theatrales sacri* (Munich, 1666), Bidermann composed three books each of *Heroum epistolae* (Antwerp, 1630) and *Heroidum epistulae* (1638), *Silvulae hendecasyllaborum* (Rome, 1634), theological works, a biography of Ignatius of Loyola and a prose *Utopia*, for which see Schuster 1984.

[135] The story of the self-satisfied doctor of Paris who pronounces himself 'accused', 'judged' and 'damned' on his funeral bier was treated by several Jesuit playwrights. It is generally accepted that Bidermann was obliquely criticising the neo-Stoic doctrine of Justus Lipsius and his friend Langius (Charles de Langhe) in this play. See Sinn 2007; Gier 2005; Hess 1976 and 2000; Best 1975; Tarot 1963. English translation in Dyer and Longrigg 1975.

[136] Hess 2000: 188–9. Thus Herod's anxious dreams in the second book recall those of Cenodoxus (act 3, scene 1); the chorus of demons rejoicing at Cenodoxus' comeuppance (act 4, scene 7) recall the infernal reckoning in the third book of *Herodias*. Nevertheless, Herod is dispatched to Hell in the closing lines of the poem in Virgilian terms: *Ipse diu obluctans oculisque immanè retortis, | Multa gemens Stygias è corpore fugit in undas* ('He, struggling long, and monstrously rolling his eyes, groaning much, quit his body and fled to the Stygian waters' (cf. *Aen.* 12.951–2).

[137] See Haskell 2013b. For more on the Jesuits' use of Virgil and undermining of the *Aeneid*'s secular imperial ideology, see Haskell 2010.

[138] See Klecker 2002. On the influence of Camões, see Urbano 2005: 80, 83.

Pierre Brumoy, SJ (1668–1742), author of the influential *Théâtre des grecs* (1730), rendered the passions as dramatic allegories in his twelve-book Latin didactic poem, *De motibus animi*.[139]

Neo-Latin didactic poetry is an example of a genre that is for the most part grown from classical rootstocks, principally Virgil's *Georgics*, but also from Lucretius, Ovid and, to a lesser extent, Horace and Manilius.[140] The range and complexity of its subjects, however, is greatly enlarged *vis-à-vis* those ancient models, and presents new challenges and opportunities for virtuosic versification.[141] Modern machines, from the bilge-pump to the barometer, the electrical harpsichord to the airship, are the objects of extended technical ekphrases. In the age of printing, the more scientifically demanding poems are published with explanatory footnotes or endnotes, even technical diagrams, to assist the reader.[142] Ovid's elegiac didactic poems on loving give rise to various poems on the arts of *living*, from anger management to good manners to the health of scholars (though Virgil's *Georgics* is the template for more than one on education and *cultura animi*). To what genre, finally, should we assign Gerard Nicolaas Heerkens' ornithological portraits, *Aves Frisicae* (Rotterdam, 1788), penned during the poet's retirement in the Groningen countryside? Most of these delightful natural-historical specimens, initially published in serial form in the *Journal des sçavans*, are in elegiacs. Heerkens draws inspiration from Ovid (and from a clutch of French avian georgics published earlier in the century) but the form and feeling of his semi-didactic, semi-descriptive poems is unparalleled in antiquity. The poet programmatically combines personal observation and experiment, bird-catchers' tales and book learning, to create a new form, if not genre, of neo-Latin 'eco-poetry', infused with both scientific and scholarly curiosity and an almost proto-Romantic sensibility.[143] While Heerkens' bird poems may not have attracted any immediate imitators, didactic poetry in Latin did not die back as quickly as it did in the European vernaculars during the Romantic period. If anything, it seems to have rallied in the

---

[139] See Haskell 2019a. Brumoy was professor of mathematics at the Collège Louis-le-Grand (Paris) and editor of the Jesuit Journal of Trévoux.
[140] See Charles-Alphonse Dufresnoy, *De arte graphica* (Paris, 1668), edited with introductory essays and commentary by Allen, Haskell and Muecke (Dufresnoy 2005); see also Ludwig 2008.
[141] Surveyed in Haskell 2014.
[142] E.g. Roger Boscovich's notes to Benedict Stay's *Philosophiae recentioris libri* x (1755–92). See Korenjak 2019. For Stay's Lucretian poem and the 'school' of Roman Jesuit didactic it inspired, see Haskell 2003, especially 189–244.
[143] For discussion of this work, see Haskell 2013a: 179–98. For another genre-bending 'didactic' collection, see Moul 2013 and 2015 on Abraham Cowley's *Plantarum libri* (1668).

nineteenth century.¹⁴⁴ But if epigram also endured, and short-form inscriptions and riddles bloomed, Giustiniani has reported the fading of other traditional neo-Latin genres in this period, such as the satire, eclogue, ode and elegy.¹⁴⁵ It would be wrong to infer a general retreat into formalism and intellectualism – plenty of nineteenth-century Latin poetry is infused with Romantic spirit – but a view has persisted, from at least the earlier part of the twentieth century,¹⁴⁶ that neo-Latin literature is, *ipso facto*, artificial and passionless. We address this misconception in the following section.

### Artificiality and Authenticity: Neo-Latin Emotions

No-one could accuse Petrarch or Erasmus of faking feeling in their Latin letters. Ego-writing in Latin was shaped in many genres, from poetry to letters, diary to dialogue.¹⁴⁷ The eighteenth-century Dutch physician, scholar and poet G. N. Heerkens shared in-jokes and private emotions with his closest friends in Latin correspondence – his letters in French and Italian to great men are comparatively restrained, and he wrote in Dutch rarely, on more mundane topics. Long beyond the maturation of the vernaculars, then, Latin continued to bind men and women in thick affective webs of education and experience.

The notion that neo-Latin poetry is somehow less authentic or affectively compelling than vernacular writing goes back at least to Leo Spitzer's article, 'The problem of Renaissance Latin poetry' (1955):

> We are able now to grasp the main problem which presented itself to neo-Latin poets in general: how to give the flavour of new personal emotion to the traditional Latin vocabulary? It was one thing to attempt to write philosophical treatises or letters in the style of Cicero, satires in that of Martial, tragedies in that of Seneca, and even eclogues in Virgilian fashion; it is another to find a Latin medium of expression

---

[144] Bertiau 2017 mentions, e.g. Diego Vitrioli, who won the *Certamen poeseos latinae (Hoeufftianum)* in 1845 for his poem on swordfish fishing in Sicily (*Xiphias* [1845] 1998) and the Swiss Pierre Esseiva, who versified Angelo Secchi's meteorograph in his poem *Urania* (1870). Cf. Jalabert 2015: I 135–42.

[145] Giustiniani 1979: 12–13, reported in Bertiau 2017: 420, who expresses some hesitation about this conclusion as the data is incomplete.

[146] See Lewis 1990: 21.

[147] E.g. Olimpia Morata's (1526–55) dialogue *Lavinia Ruverensis Ursina et Olympia Morata colloquuntur*, to her friend Lavinia della Rovere (1521–1601), written during a period of separation from her German husband, represents a 'fonte preziosa per i numerosi spunti autobiografici e come testimonianza del sorgere di una nuova coscienza a seguito alle esperienze dolorose vissute' (Saracco 2012). The Ibero-American Jesuit, José Manuel Peramás, wrote *two* diaries of exile, one in Spanish, the other in Latin. See Fúrlong Cárdiff 1952; Suárez 2009.

for the unique, immediate, personal emotions, especially the emotions of love, that most generic feeling of mankind that, wrongly or rightly, is conceived by us as requiring the most personal expressions. The words we normally use in our vernaculars in order to render what has moved us deeply have grown with us during our lives and have thus acquired close affinity to our feelings: we have been tender, we have been sad; when this happens, something in us says the words 'tender' and 'sad' – and with these words we become still tenderer or sadder.[148]

I have touched on the issue of 'artificiality' in this chapter and elsewhere – the mosaic construction of neo-Latin poetry out of tiles of ancient verse[149] – but here I should like to focus on its supposed unsuitability for the expression of 'personal emotion', an assumption that lingers to this day among philologists and historians.[150] Peter Burke, for example, echoes Spitzer when he suggests that 'neo-Latin poets faced a serious problem when it came to expressing and communicating emotions, because they were writing in a language which for writer and reader alike was devoid of the associations of childhood'.[151] In fact, Latin was deeply embedded in the childhoods of early modern writers, who learned not just to read but to write and *perform* it, in emotionally charged settings of praise and humiliation, competition and camaraderie.[152]

The attractions of neo-Latin verse *vis-à-vis* the vernacular were memorably captured by Renaissance poet Joachim du Bellay (1522–60) in an elegy comparing Latin as the pleasing mistress to his plain French wife:

> Gallica Musa mihi est, fateor, quod nupta marito:
> Pro Domina colitur Musa Latina mihi.
> Sic igitur (dices) praefertur adultera nuptae?
> Illa quidem bella est, sed magis ista placet.[153]

---

[148] Spitzer 1955: 137.
[149] Haskell 2017: 33, for the metaphor of tessellation used by Milanese Jesuit poet and mathematician, Tommaso Ceva.
[150] Cf. Moul: 'The belief that neo-Latin literature is austerely impersonal, concerned only with public life and even then limited to the static recasting of classical elements, remains oddly persistent, despite the wealth of evidence to the contrary', whereas 'in many instances the most personal material is found in Latin: this is true, for instance, of Thomas More, as it is of George Herbert, John Milton and even Thomas Hobbes' (2017: 13 and n.).
[151] Burke 1991: 37.
[152] For the lifelong literary-emotional communities established in Jesuit schools through competitive Latin composition, see Haskell 2019a. For English examples, see the collected Latin prize poems of schools such as Winchester, Eton and Berkhamstead from the seventeenth through nineteenth centuries.
[153] Du Bellay 1558: 'Cur intermissis gallice latine scribat', 3.

> My Muse is French, I admit, because she is married to me; I cultivate a Latin one as my mistress. What, you will say, is the paramour preferred to the wife? The one is nice, but I like the other more.

Modern French poetry was still in its infancy; du Bellay's compatriot Pierre Ronsard turned to neo-Latin writers of the Italian Renaissance, notably Michael Marullus (1458?–1500), as models for his French hymns and love poetry.[154] Marullus himself – Greek refugee in Italy, mercenary soldier, husband to Alessandra Scala, linguistic prodigy and daughter of the Chancellor of Florence – wielded *Latin* verse to project an image of himself as melancholy Constantinopolitan exile and brave patriot, one that perfectly matches his 'profile picture', the seductively sombre Botticelli portrait of 1497 that adorns nearly all modern editions of this author. Indeed, so successful was Marullus in communicating his Greek patriotic emotions in the Latin idiom that John Sparrow once effused, 'if we are looking for a writer to whom that language [Latin] came with absolute naturalness, and who used it in poetry with the greatest effect when ... he was uttering his inmost feelings, we may turn to Michele Marullo'.[155]

Of course, these neo-Latin poetic emotions are not unmediated (are poetic emotions ever?). The Platonic longing for fatherland that Marullus everywhere professes in his *Epigrammata et hymni* (1509) is constructed in such a way as to deflect attention from more difficult, perhaps more shameful emotions. Through the defensive flourish of Ovidian and Lucretian feints, under the philosophical fortitude of the adult 'exile', it is possible to glimpse the fears and humiliation of Marullus the child *refugee*.[156] Two centuries later another exile in Italy, the Portuguese former Jesuit, Emmanuel de Azevedo, published a collection of Latin verse on the suppression of the Society of Jesus with the triumphant title, *Heroum libri iv & Ad heroas epistolae* (1789); in a preliminary autobiographical note, however, Azevedo offers a telling alternative description of these poems: *Tristia*. The juxtaposition of epic and verse epistles (to his fellow exiled Jesuits) within the same volume carries over into a subtle generic mixing of epic and elegiac voices within individual poems. Azevedo alternates elegiac grief over the traumatic expulsion of the

---

[154] See Ford 1997. In the 'Preliminary discourse' to the *Encyclopédie* (2009 [1751]), d'Alembert sneered that Ronsard had 'created a barbarous jargon, bristling with Greek and Latin; but fortunately he made it so unrecognizable that it became ridiculous'.
[155] Sparrow 1960: 388.     [156] See Haskell 1998c.

American Jesuits from their homelands (in his four-book 'Virgilian' epic) with 'heroic' epistolary exhortations to his brothers to remain united in captivity (in his 'Ovidian' letters). The volume is dedicated to Catherine the Great's favourite, General Potemkin, and looks to the survival of the Society of Jesus in Russia (which is figured as a reverse Tomi to the Papal States, where Azevedo endures the spiritual frigidity of his own exile).[157] By exploiting the vocabulary and tropes of ancient literature, then, neo-Latin writers could find the means to express (and indeed *strategise*) emotions with at least as much authenticity as when they wrote in the vernacular.

The third poem of Girolamo Fracastoro's (1478–1553) *Carminum liber*, to Giovanni Battista della Torre, on the premature deaths of his own two sons, is a tour-de-force of philosophical self-consolation, a Neoplatonic sermon on earthly transience that openly retraces Virgil's tribute to Lucretius at the end of *Georgics* 2.[158] Fracastoro – a physician and natural philosopher as well as Latin poet and literary theorist – regrets that the boys will never reach the age at which he had hoped to induct them, with the help of his friend, into poetry and the secrets of nature:

> *Fortunate senex*, si natorum ore referri
> fata sinant, ut nata chao antiquissima rerum
> materies, visi correpta cupidine pulchra,
> arserit, atque deum thalamo complexa, iugarit
> corpora prima. Quibus Discordia nata hymenaeis
> et divisa locis: suprema petiverit ignis
> purior, et nitidis vicinus sederit astris;
> quem iuxta per inane amplum se fuderit aer;
> ima autem tellus vasto circum obruta ponto
> constiterit; quam dudum hinc inde agitantibus undis
> substerni late campi, deformia arva
> paulatim apparere supra, et concrescere montes
> coeperunt, procul et nudas ostendere cautes,
> mox nemora, et virides undis mirantibus ornos.
> Montanis tum speluncis et rupibus altis
> Exsiluere udae formoso corpore nymphae,
> In viridi flavos siccantes litore crines.
>     *O fortunatum nimium*, si numina tantum
> haec mihi servassent, si non casura dedissent.     (vv. 30–47, my emphasis)

Happy the old man whom fate allows to see in the faces of his children how elementary nature was anciently born out of chaos and how it burned with

---

[157] See Haskell 2016.   [158] Text and translation from Gardner's I Tatti edition (2013: 190–7).

love as it beheld beauty and embraced it in the chambers of the gods, thus begetting the first corporeal forms. From this union discordant elements were born in divers places, as a purer fire rose to the heavens and sat, a neighbour, among the gleaming stars. And hard by, the air rolled forth through the great emptiness. The earth stood below, overrun by the vast sea. While the waves churned all around for a great age, gradually the fields began to spread out and shapeless plains appeared. And the waters looked on astonished as mountains arose, revealing rough and naked cliffs and woods and leafy ash trees. Then the watery nymphs, with their graceful forms, began to emerge from their mountain caves and lofty cliffs, drying their golden hair by the verdurous shore. O how happy I should have been if fate had reserved these things for me, rather than giving them, only to take them away!

In this cosmogonic reverie, Fracastoro recalls not only Virgil's first Eclogue (*fortunate senex*, *Ecl.* 1.46 and 51) and especially second Georgic (*o fortunatos nimium, sua si bona norint*, 2.458), but, more generally, the atmosphere of Ovid's 'Creation' (*Met.* 1) and of his own Lucretius-fretted didactic poem, *Syphilis*, which sublimates fear and disgust at the venereal epidemic of his time into *wonder* at nature's workings and the discovery of a 'new world'.[159] But the Lucretian crescendo at the end of the poem to della Torre is gloomier, for all its philosophical fortitude. We are transported to the dire finale of *DRN* 2, on the exhaustion of the earth and the fruitless efforts of the aged ploughman:

> Interea curas numeris Musasque levemus,
> Batte, animos, quando rerum mortalis origo est,
> Quando etiam vitae norunt vasta aequora finem.
> Scilicet et quondam veniet, labentibus annis,
> illa dies, cum iam curvo sub vomere Taurus
> *insudet terramque gravis praevertat arator*,[160]
> nunc ubi caeruleae rostris spumantibus undae
> sulcantur, verruntque citae freta longa carinae.   (vv. 88–95, my emphasis)

Until such time, Battista, let us lighten our sorrows with poetry and our souls with song, seeing that the origin of nature is mortal, that even the vast seas will know an end to life. For that day will come, in the course of years, when the ox will sweat under the curved plough and the heavy ploughman

---

[159] Christopher Whitton also detects an echo of Dido's *'felix, heu nimium felix, si litora tantum | numquam Dardaniae tetigissent nostra carinae'* (*Aen.* 4.657–8).
[160] Cf. Lucretius: *iamque caput quassans grandis suspirat arator | crebrius, in cassum magnos cecidisse labores, | et cum tempora temporibus praesentia confert | praeteritis, laudat fortunas saepe parentis* (2.1164–7); *una dies dabit exitio, multosque per annos | sustentata ruet moles et machina mundi* (5.96–7).

will turn the earth, where now the blue waves are plied by churning prows and swift ships sweep the distant seas.

The *gravis arator* ploughs a melancholy furrow over this poem's conclusion, deeper for the uncanny *adunaton* of subsiding seas (a reversal of Ovid's flood).[161] And while the Lucretian *una* [*illa*] *dies* would be recuperated by other neo-Latin poets for the Last Judgement, Fracastoro does *not* look to resurrection in his peroration, but denies permanence even to his beloved Eridanus (the river Po, elsewhere a source of his poetic inspiration), and to majestic mountain ranges which also succumb to old age and death, 'since that first moment when nature and a new universe experienced their wedding night and the birth of the discordant elements' (*ex quo materies thalamos primosque hymenaeos, | atque elementa novus sensit discordia mundus*, vv. 99–100). These final lines, capped by the oxymoronic *discordia mundus*, serve as an almost gnostic *sphragis* to the poem. Surface meanings are troubled by intertextual and intellectual turbulence – Virgil, Lucretius, Christian Platonism, materialism – and the philosophical poet seems to succumb to a deep undertow of personal grief.[162] In the hands of the best writers, then, Neo-Latin can be a peculiarly subtle medium for conveying affective complexity.

## Future-Proofing Neo-Latin: Teaching, Texts, Canons and Computers

Neo-Latin is a field into which students of Classics may stumble happily at graduate level, but for historians of early modern science, medicine, philosophy, diplomacy, etc., it can be more of a necessary reckoning than a calling. Françoise Waquet dreamed of a future for Latin teaching which provided:

> the means to read Latin fluently: that is what the primary objective of Latin teaching should be. Not so much to read the classics – which, as Diderot remarked, have been translated and retranslated a hundred times – as to have access to those wellsprings of our own culture, the Fathers of the Church and the *Corpus juris*, along with the colossal mass of documents … that contains much of the record of our ancestors' lives and thought through

---

[161] *Occupat hic collem, cumba sedet alter adunca | et ducit remos illic, ubi nuper arabat: | ille supra segetes aut mersae culmina uillae | nauigat, hic summa piscem deprendit in ulmo* (Ov. *Met.* 1.293–6).

[162] Michael Marullus also shades Neoplatonic mysticism with Lucretian pessimism in his *Hymni naturales*, especially in his long hexameter hymn to the Sun.

the Middle Ages and into the modern era. One can only hope that Latin will finally become a speciality in the full sense of the word.[163]

Classicists may blanch at the notion that we can dispense with Latin (or Greek) for ancient-world studies and rely solely on translations, but it is of course *possible* to be a classical receptionist and write on, for example, contemporary literature, drama, film or philosophy, without regular recourse to original texts in the ancient languages. Waquet's brave new world of Latin for historians is, however, a fantasy as far as Neo-Latin is concerned, because that 'colossal mass of documents', for the most part untranslated, will yield only its most superficial meanings to scholars lacking a decent command of the classical sources from which it is mortised. To continue her (Joseph de Maistre's) metaphor, a basic knowledge of Latin might allow us to (roughly) decode the sign, but we will miss many of its more subtle and even crucial significations.[164]

So how to make undergraduates aware of Neo-Latin and equip them with the tools to explore a field that borders now on European languages, now intellectual history and history of science, and now comparative literature and (post-)colonial studies? While it is impossible to prescribe a single method for all disciplines and institutional structures, I recommend incorporating one or two key neo-Latin texts into upper-level language or literature units for Classics students, even for those with limited prior knowledge of ancient texts. Since many undergraduate Classics majors in the English-speaking world are now adult beginners, devoting even half of a precious semester to neo-Latin authors might seem dangerously profligate. Nevertheless, the reading of Renaissance texts can be an excellent and economical way to introduce Classics students to key topics in the history of scholarship and literary history, and to initiate more complex conversations about reception and intertextuality, race and gender. Value may be added to a class on Virgil's *Georgics*, for example, by studying the fourth book in conjunction with the third book of Fracastoro's *Syphilis*, a conveniently detachable epyllion (c. 420 lines) on the first European encounter with indigenous Americans. Fracastoro's multilayered Latin epic-didactic poem invites us to triangulate the fourth Georgic with selected passages from *Aeneid* 3, 6 and 8 (and Lucretius) and

---

[163] Waquet 2001: 274.
[164] E.g. what IJsewijn 1990–8: II 3 has called 'microscopic' imitation, 'which affects a smaller part of a work, ranging from a paragraph to a single line or a typical figure or expression. The opening chapter of Seneca's satire *Apocolocyntosis* was closely imitated by Lipsius in his *Somnium* (1581) including the humorous definition of the time when the event described is supposed to have taken place.'

to calibrate the Renaissance poet's optimistic fantasy of intercultural conviviality with later, more problematic, literary colonial encounters.[165] This, as it were, *hysteron-proteron* approach, in which a classical text (here the *Aeneid*) is discovered for the first time *after* a 'derived' one (here Fracastoro's Columbus epyllion), can be paradoxically gratifying for students, who find themselves reading the 'original' with relative ease, almost as if predigested. It is also a teaching point for Martindale's 'strong thesis' of classical reception (see n. 22). In general, Italian Renaissance texts, such as those available in the I Tatti series, seem best suited to this approach because of their relative proximity to classical models.

With more time to play with, for example at master's level, one can afford to be more ambitious.[166] The Society for Neo-Latin Studies has produced a small, free online anthology of extracts from Giovanni Gioviano Pontano in the fifteenth century through to Walter Savage Landor in the nineteenth, 'for the use of teachers of Latin everywhere, and we hope that the range of texts and authors will be particularly valuable to tutors, students and researchers working on neo-Latin sources. The anthology is aimed at postgraduate students, and includes texts of varying levels of difficulty, so that individual tutors can select texts for their own paedagogical purposes.'[167] A larger selection is provided in a pair of printed anthologies from the new Bloomsbury Neo-Latin series, one of British and another (!) of European neo-Latin literature, which also includes some British writers.[168] Other recent collections include Rose Williams' *Latin of New Spain* (Bolchazy-Carducci, 2015), Mark Riley's *The Neo-Latin Reader: Selections from Petrarch to Rimbaud* (Sophron Editor, 2016) and Milena Minkova's *Florilegium recentioris Latinitatis* (Leuven University Press, 2018), the latter entirely in Latin. But while the neo-Latin neophyte may be fascinated by the shoals of exotic fish swimming through these readers,

---

[165] E.g. myths of literary acculturation and agricultural exploitation in a poem on the cultivation of chocolate by seventeenth-century Neapolitan Jesuit, Tommaso Strozzi, *De mentis potu sive de cocolatis opificio*, in *Poemata varia* (Naples, 1689), which was influenced by Fracastoro. See Haskell 2003: 70–117. Time permitting, one might explore the use of Fracastoro's myths by another Latin physician-poet, Raphael Thorius, in his popular didactic poem on the medicinal powers of tobacco, *Hymnus tabaci* (London, 1626). (I am grateful for Alexander Winkler for pointing out this influence.) Thorius' poem is available in Mark Riley's hypertext edition, with introduction, notes and English translation, at www.philological.bham.ac.uk/thorius/.
[166] For a semester-long Neo-Latin unit some years ago I made selections from the letters of Petrarch, the *Colloquies* of Erasmus, Vives' *Education of a Christian Woman*, the 'Ovidian' exile poetry of Michael Marullus and Elizabeth Jane Weston, the *Basia* of Janus Secundus, Milton's *Epitaphium Damonis*, Fracastoro's *Syphilis* and some baroque religious verse.
[167] At https://warwick.ac.uk/fac/arts/ren/snls/snls_teaching_anthology/.
[168] Hadas, Manuwald and Nicholas 2020; Houghton, Manuwald and Nicholas 2020.

she will find, when she tries to reel one or two in for closer inspection, that critical editions and commentaries are elusive – even for some of the major authors mentioned in this chapter. The humanist Lorenzo Bonincontri's (1410–91) Lucretian and Manilian poems have been scrupulously edited by Stephan Heilen, whereas Pontano's astrological didactic masterpiece, *Urania*, a work of greater literary interest, and celebrated in its day, has never been translated into a modern European language (and only since this chapter was drafted, Pontano's georgic *De hortis Hesperidum*, on citrus trees).[169] Several series of neo-Latin texts and translations have sprouted and withered over the years, but there is no equivalent of the OCT, Teubner or even Loeb Classical Library for our field.[170] The 'I Tatti Renaissance Library' covers only the Italian Renaissance and has gaps.[171]

The question of a neo-Latin canon has been deferred to the end of our chapter because its definition depends to a large extent on one's disciplinary or even national starting point. Beyond the Italian Renaissance 'classics' of Petrarch, Pontano, Sannazaro, Marullo, Vida and Fracastoro, a Grand Tour of British neo-Latin authors[172] would usually include Thomas More, George Buchanan, George Herbert (1593–1633), Abraham Cowley (1618–67), John Milton (1608–74), Andrew Marvell (1621–78) and Thomas Hobbes (1588–1679).[173] German students might be served up the classics of 'their' Reformation, such as humanist drinking poets Eobanus Hessus (1488–1540) and Vincentius Obsopoeus (1485–1539), or a rich banquet of baroque Jesuits such as Jacob Bidermann (1578–1639), Jacob Balde (1604–68) and Johannes Bisselius (1601–62).[174] It is notable that most modern neo-Latin anthologies are of poets, but even here we are skimming the surface if we compare the vast early modern (national) compilations by

---

[169] Bonincontrius 1999; Goddard 1991; Haskell 1998b; Roman 2022.
[170] Others that have stayed the distance are 'Noctes neolatinae: neo-Latin texts and studies' (Georg Olms Verlag) and the 'Bibliotheca latinitatis novae' (Leuven University Press). The 'Supplementa humanistica Lovaniensia' (Leuven University Press) occasionally publishes neo-Latin editions. Newer arrivals include the 'Officina neolatina' (Brepols), 'Jesuit Neo-Latin library' (Brill), and the recently announced 'Early-modern texts and anthologies' (Bloomsbury).
[171] A modern edition and translation of Giovanni Aurelio Augurello's intriguing and influential Renaissance alchemical poem *Chrysopoeia* recently appeared with Brill (not, as we might have expected, from I Tatti): Soranzo 2019.
[172] See Bradner 1940 and Binns 1974 and 1990.
[173] Johanna Luggin's authoritative new edition of Hobbes' *De mirabilibus Pecci carmen* (2016) has a German translation.
[174] The literature on Balde alone is immense, but see e.g. Burkard 2006 and Lefèvre 2017. For Bisselius' *Deliciae veris* see Bisselius 2013. See also the POEMATA section of the University of Mannheim's CAMENA website ('Corpus automatum multiplex electorum neolatinitatis auctorum'): www2.uni-mannheim.de/mateo/camenahtdocs/camena_e.html.

Janus Gruter and others.[175] The Jesuits produced a number of more or less in-house poetic anthologies, including the *Parnassus Societatis Jesu* (Frankfurt, 1651), of which only the first section, on 'heroic' verse, was published – and runs to 823 pages.

Which texts urgently need to be edited, translated or furnished with commentaries? Philologists are perhaps not always best placed to judge the extrinsic interest of their neo-Latin darlings, nor how to present them for the benefit of a wider scholarly community. Moreover, different skills must be gleaned, sometimes on the job, for bespoke projects: a nose for libraries and archives, and now digital collections; a familiarity with hands, printers and book histories; a sensitivity not just to classical allusions, but to biblical, post-classical and vernacular influences; an awareness of different intellectual and religious traditions, including those beyond Europe. Some level of interdisciplinary collaboration is inevitable. Keith Sidwell has called for neo-Latin editions to be produced not in isolation but from 'texts associated with wider projects, where historical and cultural analysis can move hand in hand with the task of editing', citing large grant-funded projects or centres such as his own 'Renaissance texts of Ireland' or the Ludwig Boltzmann Institute for Neo-Latin Studies in Austria:

> In all of these cases, the production of critical editions runs parallel with more broadly historical and cultural commentary, to provide a platform for better understanding of the wider context within which these Latin texts were produced, as well as to facilitate access to the most important of them to non-Latinists who are students of their contemporary culture.[176]

There is certainly merit in this idea, and much to be learned and fun to be had in team projects, which are becoming increasingly common due to research funding trends. Unfortunately, the preparation of scholarly commentaries, let alone translations, is not generally supported by national research councils. When it is, it is often deemed ancillary, not to say inferior, to monograph publication. For this reason, one must guard against the unwitting exploitation of early career researchers when recruiting them as willing labourers in the neo-Latin vineyard.

But we may wonder, finally, whether neo-Latinists are forever to serve as handmaidens to our home or host disciplines, uncovering the 'lost' Italian

---

[175] E.g. *Delitiae CC Italorum poetarum coll. Ranutius Gherus* [*Ianus Gruterus*], 2 vols. (Frankfurt, 1608); *Delitiae C poetarum Gallorum coll. Ranutius Gherus*, 3 vols. (Frankfurt, 1609); *Delitiae poetarum Germanorum coll. A.F.G.C.*, 6 vols. (Frankfurt, 1612); *Carmina illustrium poetarum Italorum*, 11 vols. (Florence, 1719–26); *Delitiae poetarum Scotorum huius aevi illustrium* (Amsterdam, 1637); *Delitiae poetarum Hungaricorum* ... à Ioh. Philippo Pareo, 2 vols. (Frankfurt, 1619).
[176] Sidwell 2017: 397–8.

Renaissance, the Latin backstory to modern English, Irish, Scottish, French, Spanish, Portuguese (...) literatures, the Latin in the margins of early modern religious and colonial history. In spite of the proliferating handbooks, a general coordinated history of neo-Latin literature is an obvious desideratum – one that would, of necessity, be the work of many hands and probably several generations. There is no space to review here the many useful suggestions for editing neo-Latin texts available in IJsewijn and the respective chapters in the Brill, Oxford and Cambridge handbooks: suffice it to say that one size does not fit all.[177] The view of Wolfgang Schibel – librarian, digital humanist and long-term contributor to the CAMENA ('Latin texts of early modern Europe') project – strikes me as sensible: in most cases, there is no need to 'establish' a neo-Latin text, since autographs were usually destroyed at the time of printing – often by the author himself. Indeed, sometimes very different versions of the 'same' work circulated in print, as early modern authors tinkered with their compositions.[178] While physical editions, translations and commentaries certainly have their place and uses, a more pressing need is to build on and coordinate the various existing libraries of texts, to future-proof them and open them up, as far as possible, to collaborative scholarly intervention.[179] The pioneering approach of the CAMENA project seems to me exemplary in providing access not only to photographs of the early editions, but to machine-readable text, and for 'presenting the old editions in their original form ... [facilitating] access to specific content by converting to e-text their tables of contents, headings, argumenta, end indexes, and by linking every entry to the image page it refers to'.[180] Not only are the texts more navigable than, for example, those of Gallica and Google Books, but their intellectual architecture is usefully exposed, since:

> humanist writing reflects ways of collecting and storing information while reading; we may assume that contemporary indexing corresponds to these working procedures.

---

[177] IJsewijn 1990–8 devotes some pages to editorial procedure (II 460–75). See also Rabbie 1997. The format of Gwynne's Brill edition of Francesco Benci's four-book epic, *Quinque martyres* (Gwynne 2018), or the Droz edition of C.-A. Dufresnoy's (relatively short) *De arte graphica*, with several introductory essays and appendices (Dufresnoy 2005), would be unwieldy and uneconomical for longer works.

[178] G. N. Heerkens' poem on the health of scholars exists in a one-book (1749) and three-book version (1790). See Haskell 2013a: ch. 2.

[179] CAMENA (n. 96), funded by the Deutsche Forschungsgemeinschaft, provides texts and biographies for the major German neo-Latin poets (as well as collections of early modern political and historical, epistolary and encyclopaedic sources), as well as the ITALI collection of Italian Renaissance poets, sponsored by the Istituto italiano per gli studi filosofici: www2.uni-mannheim.de/mateo/camenahtdocs/itali.html. See also the online collections mentioned in nn. 78 and 96.

[180] www2.uni-mannheim.de/mateo/camenahtdocs/itali.html#02.

The valorisation of original indexing materials thus paves the way to new research into the habits of humanist reading, memorising, teaching and writing. By comparing a large quantity of these paratexts, we may be able to trace traditions, commonplaces, debates and references.[181]

The situation is of course more complicated for manuscript verse, letters, diaries and the like. In spite of the various local and multinational surveys of printed neo-Latin literature conducted over the years since IJsewijn's *Companion* one suspects that many unpublished treasures still languish in archives and attics from Europe to the Americas, not to mention East Asia.[182] The future of Neo-Latin is undoubtedly digital, but *what* remains to be digitised lies tantalisingly beyond my powers of scholarly clairvoyance.[183]

## References

Abad, Diego José (1974) *Poema heróico* (Cesena, 1780) (trans. B. F. Valenzuela), Mexico City.
Agbamu, S. (2019) 'The Arco dei Fileni: a fascist reading of Sallust's *Bellum Iugurthinum*', *Classical Receptions Journal* 11: 157–77.
Alciati (1531) *Emblematum libellus*, Augsburg.
d'Alembert, Jean-Baptiste le Rond (1751) 'Discourse Préliminaire', *Encyclopédie ou Dictionnaire raisonné des sciences, des arts et des métiers*, vol. 1, Paris.
   (1767) 'Sur l'harmonie des langues, et en particulier sur celle qu'on croit sentir dans les langues mortes; et à cette occasion sur la latinité des modernes', *Mélanges* v 523–68. Reprinted in *Œuvres de d'Alembert*, IV.1 (Paris, 1822) 11–28. http://obvil.sorbonne-universite.fr/corpus/critique/alembert_apologie-etude/.
   (2009) 'Preliminary Discourse' (trans. R. N. Schwab and W. E. Rex), *The Encyclopedia of Diderot and d'Alembert Collaborative Translation Project*, Ann Arbor. http://hdl.handle.net/2027/spo.did2222.0001.083. Trans. of d'Alembert 1751.
d'Alembert, Jean-Baptiste le Rond and Edme-François Mallet (2003) 'College [abridged]', *The Encyclopedia of Diderot and d'Alembert Collaborative*

---

[181] Ibid.
[182] Or are hiding in plain sight in libraries, e.g. the Latin documents from presidential papers showcased in the Library of Congress' online 'guide to neo-Latin materials written outside of Europe during the sixteenth to nineteenth centuries': https://guides.loc.gov/neo-latin/introduction.
[183] At the time of revising this chapter I was made aware of a call for prospective editions of early modern Latin texts to be hosted by the Digital Latin Library (https://digitallatin.org/), a joint initiative of the Society for Classical Studies, the Medieval Academy and the Renaissance Society of America; also, an online conference in April 2021 on digital Neo-Latin studies, organised by Neven Jovanović (Zagreb), Marc Laureys (Bonn) and Alexander Winkler (Berlin/Halle) under the auspices of the International Association of Neo-Latin Studies, with sessions on 'OCR, digital editions and corpora', 'text mining and stylometry', 'linked texts and data' and 'digital humanities and digital teaching of Neo-Latin'.

*Translation Project* (trans. by N. S. Hoyt and T. Cassirer), Ann Arbor. https://quod.lib.umich.edu/d/did/did2222.0000.144/.

Ariosto, Ludovico (2018) *Latin Poetry* (ed. D. Looney and M. Possanza), Cambridge, MA.

Backus, I. (2014) 'Patristics', in Bloemendal, Ford and Fantazzi 2014b, 733–45.

Backus, I., ed. (1997) *The Reception of the Church Fathers in the West: From the Carolingians to the Maurists*, 2 vols., Leiden.

Barea, J. P. (2013) 'Neo-Latin drama in Spain, Portugal and Latin America', in Bloemendal and Norland 2013, 545–631.

Bejczy, I. (2001) *Erasmus and the Middle Ages: The Historical Consciousness of a Christian Humanist*, Leiden.

du Bellay, J. (1558) *Poematum libri quatuor*, Paris.

Benci, Francesco ([1591] 1592) *Quinque martyres*, [Venice] Rome.

   (1591) *Carminum libri quatuor Eiusdem Ergastus et Philotus dramata*, Ingolstadt.

Berlincourt, V. (2013) 'Commenting on Claudian's "political poems", 1612/1650', in K. A. E. Enenkel, ed., *Transformations of the Classics via Early Modern Commentaries* (Leiden), 125–50.

Bertiau, C. (2017) 'Neo-Latin literature in nineteenth-century Europe: an overview', *History of European Ideas* 43: 416–26.

Bertiau, C. and D. Sacré (2020) *Le latin et la littérature néo-latine au XIXe siècle: pratiques et représentations*, Turnhout.

Best, T. W. (1975) *Jacob Bidermann*, New York.

Bianco, L. A. (1996) 'Latin et langues vivantes dans l'*Encyclopédie*', *Recherches sur Diderot et sur l'Encyclopédie* 20: 141–7.

Bicknell, T. (1996) '*Calamus ense potentior est*: Walter Savage Landor's poetic war of words', *Romanticism on the Net* 4. http://id.erudit.org/iderudit/005730ar.

Bidermann, Jacob (1630) *Heroum epistolae*, Antwerp.

   (1634) *Silvulae hendecasyllaborum*, Rome.

   (1638) *Heroidum epistulae*, Antwerp.

   (1666) *Ludi theatrales sacri*, Munich.

   (1975) *Cenodoxus* (ed. and trans. D. G. Dyer and C. Longrigg), Edinburgh.

Binns, J. (1974) *The Latin Poetry of English Poets*, London and Boston.

   (1990) *Intellectual Culture in Elizabethan and Jacobean England: The Latin Writings of the Age*, Leeds.

Bisselius, Johannes (2013) *Deliciae veris – Frühlingsfreuden. Lateinischer Text, Übersetzung, Einführungen und Kommentar* (ed. L. Claren, J. Eickmeyer, W. Kühlmann and H. Wiegand), Berlin.

Blair, A. (2014) 'North America', in Bloemendal, Ford and Fantazzi 2014b, 833–48.

Bloemendal, J., P. Ford and C. Fantazzi, eds. (2014a) *Brill's Companion to the Neo-Latin World: Micropaedia*, Leiden.

   (2014b) *Brill's Companion to the Neo-Latin World: Macropaedia*, Leiden.

Bloemendal, J. and H. B. Norland, eds. (2013) *Neo-Latin Drama and Theatre in Early Modern Europe*, Leiden.

Bloemendal, J. and D. Verbeke, eds. (2015) *Bilingual Europe: Latin and Vernacular Cultures – Examples of Bilingualism and Multilingualism ca. 1300–1800*, Leiden.

Bonincontrius, Laurentius (1999) *De rebus naturalibus et divinis. Zwei Lehrgedichte an Lorenzo de' Medici und Ferdinand von Aragonien* (ed. S. Heilen), Stuttgart and Leipzig.

Bontinck, F. (1962) *La lutte autour de la liturgie chinoise aux XVIIe et XVIIIe siècles*, Louvain.

Botley, P. (2010) *Learning Greek in Western Europe, 1396–1529: Grammars, Dictionaries and Student Texts*, Philadelphia.

 (2012) 'Greek epistolography in fifteenth-century Italy', in J. Glucker and C. Burnett, eds., *Greek into Latin: From Antiquity until the Nineteenth Century* (London), 187–205.

Botley, P. and D. van Miert, eds. (2012) *The Correspondence of Joseph Scaliger (1540–1609)*, 8 vols., Geneva.

Bradner, L. (1940) *Musae Anglicanae: A History of Anglo-Latin Poetry, 1500–1925*, London.

Brown, A. (2010) *The Return of Lucretius to Renaissance Florence*, Cambridge, MA.

Burkard, T., ed. (2006) *Jacob Balde im kulturellen Kontext seiner Epoche: Zur 400. Wiederkehr seines Geburtstages*, Regensburg.

Burke, P. (1991) '*Heu domine, adsunt Turcae*: a sketch for a social history of post-medieval Latin', in P. Burke and R. Porter, eds., *Language, Self and Society: A Social History of Language* (Oxford), 23–50.

 (2007) 'Translations into Latin in early modern Europe', in P. Burke and R. Po-Chia Hsia, eds., *Cultural Translation in Early Modern Europe* (Cambridge), 65–80.

Burnett, C. and N. Mann, eds. (2005) *Britannia Latina: Latin in the Culture of Great Britain from the Middle Ages to the Twentieth Century*, London.

Bury, E., ed. (2005) *Tous vos gens à Latin: le latin, langue savante, langue mondaine (XIVe–XVIIe siècles)*, Geneva.

Cabrera, F. J. (2012) *Quetzalcóatl y el paraíso de Tamoanchan: dos poemas neolatinos*, Mexico City.

 (2016) *Exaltación guadalupana = Laus guadalupensis: tradición y recepción clásico-moderna*, Mexico City.

Campanelli, M. (2008) 'Settecento Latino II', *L'Ellisse. Studi storici di letteratura italiana* 3: 85–110.

 (2013) 'Settecento Latino III. L'inflazione dei poeti e il monte di Testaccio in un'epistola di Contuccio Contucci', *L'Ellisse. Studi storici di letteratura italiana* 8: 159–95.

 (2014) 'Settecento Latino IV. Due frammenti della preistoria poetica di G. B. Casti', *L'Ellisse. Studi storici di letteratura italiana* 9: 101–14.

Campanelli, M. and A. Ottaviani (2007) 'Settecento Latino I', *L'Ellisse. Studi storici di letteratura italiana* 2: 99–133.

Campanelli, M. and F. Muecke, eds. (2017) *The Invention of Rome: Biondo Flavio's Roma triumphans and Its Worlds*, Geneva.
*Carmina illustrium poetarum Italorum* (1719–26), 11 vols., Florence.
Carrara, Ubertino, SJ (2004) *Columbus. Carmen epicum* (ed. and trans. F. Schaffenrath), Innsbruck.
Castor, G. and T. Cave (1984) *Neo-Latin and the Vernacular in Renaissance France*, Oxford.
Champion, M., R. Garrod, Y. Haskell and J. Ruys (2016) 'But were they talking about the emotions? *Affectus, affectio* and the history of emotions', *Rivista storica italiana* 128: 521–53.
Cheney, D. and B. Hosington, eds. (2000) *Elizabeth Jane Weston: Collected Writings*, Toronto.
Coppini, D. (1990) *Antonius Panormita. Hermaphroditus*, Rome.
  (2009) 'The comic and the obscene in the Latin epigrams of the early fifteenth century', in S. de Beer, K. A. E. Enenkel and D. Rijser, eds., *The Neo-Latin Epigram: A Learned and Witty Genre* (Louvain), 83–102.
Cortesi, M., ed. (2006) *'Editiones principes' delle opere dei padri greci e latini*, Florence.
Cottier, J.F. and H. Westra (2015) 'North America', in Knight and Tilg 2015, 541–56.
Couplet, Philippe, SJ, Christian Herdtrich SJ, Prospero Intorcetta SJ and Francis Rougemont SJ, eds. (1687) *Confucius Sinarum philosophus, sive, Scientia Sinensis latine exposita*, Paris.
D'Amico, J.F. (1983) *Renaissance Humanism in Papal Rome: Humanists and Churchmen on the Eve of the Reformation*, Baltimore.
de la Cerda, Juan Luis, SJ, ed. (1608) *Bucolica et Georgica argumentis: explicationibus notis illustrati*, Lyon.
  (1612) *P. Virgilii Maronis Aeneidos sex libri priores: argumentis, explicationibus notis illustrati*, Lyon.
  (1617) *P. Virgilii Maronis Aeneidos libri sex posteriores: argumentis, explicationibus notis illustrati*, Lyon.
De Landtsheer, J. (1998) 'Justus Lipsius (1547–1606) and Lucius Annaeus Seneca', *Annales Societatis litterarum humaniorum regiae Upsaliensis*, 217–38.
  (2013) 'Annotating Tacitus: the case of Justus Lipsius', in K. Enenkel, ed., *Transformations of the Classics via Early Modern Commentaries* (Leiden) 279–326.
de Sande, Duarte (2012) *Japanese Travellers in Sixteenth-Century Europe: A Dialogue Concerning the Mission of the Japanese Ambassadors to the Roman Curia (1590)* (ed. and trans. J. F. Moran and D. Massarella), London.
De Smet, I. (1996) *Menippean Satire in the Republic of Letters 1581–1655*, Geneva.
De Sutter, N. (2019a) 'A modern myth in classical dress: the Titanic disaster in contemporary Latin verse', *New Voices in Classical Reception Studies* 13.

(2019b) 'Through Vergil's eyes: the *Certamen Hoeufftianum* and the revival of figures from antiquity in the Latin poetry of the First World War', *Futuro Classico* 5: 45–91.

*Delitiae C poetarum Gallorum coll. Ranutius Gherus* (1609), 3 vols., Frankfurt.

*Delitiae CC Italorum Poetarum coll. Ranutius Gherus [Ianus Gruterus]* (1608), 2 vols., Frankfurt.

*Delitiae poetarum Germanorum coll. A.F.G.C.* (1612), 6 vols., Frankfurt.

*Delitiae poetarum Hungaricorum . . . à Ioh. Philippo Pareo* (1619), Frankfurt.

*Delitiae poetarum Scotorum huius aevi illustrium* (1637), 2 vols., Amsterdam.

DellaNeva, J., ed. (2007) *Ciceronian Controversies. English Translation by Brian Duvick*, Cambridge, MA.

Deneire, T. (2014a) 'Neo-Latin and the vernacular: prose', in Bloemendal, Ford and Fantazzi 2014b, 275–85.

Deneire, T., ed. (2014b) *Dynamics of Neo-Latin and the Vernacular: Language and Poetics, Translation and Transfer*, Leiden.

Deraedt, F. (2016) 'Post Bruxellensem ictum tromocraticum', *Melissa* 191: 1–3.

Dufresnoy, Charles-Alphonse (2005) *De arte graphica* (ed. with introductory essays and commentary by C. Allen, Y. Haskell and F. Muecke), Geneva.

Eickmeyer, J. (2012) *Der jesuitische Heroidenbrief. Zur Christianisierung und Kontextualisierung einer antiken Gattung in der frühen Neuzeit*, Berlin and Boston.

Endres, C. (1981) *Johannes Secundus: The Latin Love Elegy in the Renaissance*, Hamden, CT.

Enenkel, K. A. E. (2014) 'Neo-Latin erotic and pornographic literature', in Bloemendal, Ford and Fantazzi 2014b, 487–501.

Enenkel, K. A. E. and J. L. de Jong, eds. (2019) *Artes apodemicae and Early Modern Travel Culture, 1550–1700*, Leiden.

Erasmus, Desiderius (1986) 'The Ciceronian: a dialogue on the ideal style' (trans. B. I. Knott), in *Collected Works of Erasmus*, vol. 28 (Toronto), 323–448.

(1993) *Poems* (trans. C. H. Miller, ed. and annotated H. Vredeveld), = *Collected Works of Erasmus*, vol. 85, Toronto.

Esseiva, Pierre (1870) *Urania: Carmen didascalicum*, Amsterdam.

Fantazzi, C. (2014) 'Imitation, emulation, Ciceronianism, anti-Ciceronianism', in Bloemendal, Ford and Fantazzi 2014b, 141–53.

Fedeli, P. (1977) 'Studio e uso del latino nella scuola fascista', in *Matrici culturali del Fascismo* (Bari), 209–24.

Feile Tomes, M. (2015a) 'News of a hitherto unknown neo-Latin Columbus epic – part I: José Manuel Peramás's *De invento novo orbe inductoque illuc Christi sacrificio* (1777)', *IJCT* 22: 1–28.

(2015b) 'News of a hitherto unknown neo-Latin Columbus epic – part II: José Manuel Peramás's *De invento novo orbe inductoque illuc Christi sacrificio* (1777)', *IJCT* 22: 223–57.

(2015c) 'Further points on Peramás: an *erratum* and two *addenda*', *IJCT* 22: 383–9.

Fera, V. (2017) *Pascoli e le vie della tradizione: atti del convegno internazionale di studi: Messina, 3–5 dicembre 2012*, Messina.

Fera V., D. Gionta and E. Morabito, eds. (2006) *La poesia latina nell'area dello Stretto fra Ottocento e Novecento*, Messina.
Ferri, G. (1771) *Pro linguae latinae usu epistolae adversus Alambertium*, Faenza.
Föcking, M. and G. M. Müller, eds. (2007) *Abgrenzung und Synthese. Lateinische Dichtung und volkssprachliche Traditionen in Renaissance und Barock*, Heidelberg.
Folengo, T. (1997) *Baldo* (ed. with critical text, trans. and extensive notes, index and glossary by M. Chiesa), Turin.
  (2007) *Baldus* (ed. and trans. A. E. Mullaney), Cambridge, MA.
Fontaine, M. (2015) *Joannes Burmeister: Aulularia and Other Inversions of Plautus*, Leuven.
Ford, P. (1997) *Ronsard's Hymnes: A Literary and Iconographical Study*, Binghamton, NY.
  (2013) *The Judgment of Palaemon: The Contest Between Neo-Latin and Vernacular Poetry in Renaissance France*, Leiden.
Fordónski, K. and P. Urbánski, eds. (2008) *Casimir Britannicus: English Translations, Paraphrases, and Emulations of the Poetry of Maciej Kazimierz Sarbiewski*. Revised and expanded edn, London.
Fracastoro, G. (2013) *Latin Poetry* (ed. J. Gardner), Cambridge, MA.
Fullenwider, H. F. (1984) 'Die Kritik der deutschen Jesuiten an dem lakonischen Stil des Justus Lipsius im Zusammenhang der jesuitischen Argutia-Bewegung', *Rhetorica* 2: 55–62.
Fúrlong Cárdiff, G., ed. (1952) *José Manuel Peramás y su Diario del destierro*, Buenos Aires.
Gier, H. ed. (2005) *Jakob Bidermann und sein 'Cenodoxus': Der bedeutendste Dramatiker aus dem Jesuitenorden und sein erfolgreichstes Stück*, Regensburg.
Giglioni, G. (2015) 'Philosophy', in Knight and Tilg 2015, 249–62.
Gilmore, J. (2005) 'The British empire and the neo-Latin tradition: the case of Francis Williams', in B. E. Goff, ed., *Classics and Colonialism* (London), 92–106.
  (2009) '*Aethiopissae*: the classical tradition, neo-Latin verse and images of race in George Herbert and Vincent Bourne', *Classical Receptions Journal* 1: 73–86.
  (2010) '*Sub herili venditur hasta*: an early eighteenth-century justification of the slave trade by a colonial poet', in Haskell and Ruys 2010, 221–39.
  (2011) 'John Barclay's "Camella" poems: ideas of race, beauty and ugliness in Renaissance Latin verse', in D. Orrells, G. K. Bhambra and T. Roynon, eds., *African Athena: New Agendas* (Oxford), 277–92.
Giustiniani, V. (1979) *Neulateinische Dichtung in Italien 1850–1950: Ein unerforschtes Kapitel italienischer Literatur- und Geistesgeschichte*, Tübingen.
Goddard, C. (1991) 'Pontano's use of the didactic genre: rhetoric, irony and the manipulation of Lucretius in *Urania*', *Renaissance Studies* 5: 250–62.
Golvers, N. (2015) 'Asia', in Knight and Tilg 2015, 557–73.
Grafton, A. T. (1983–93) *Joseph Scaliger: A Study in the History of Classical Scholarship*, 2 vols., Oxford.

Green, R. P. H. (2014) 'Poetic psalm paraphrases', in Bloemendal, Ford and Fantazzi 2014b, 461–9.

Greenblatt, S. (2011) *The Swerve: How the Renaissance Began*, New York.

Gwynne, P. (2016) 'Francesco Benci and the origins of Jesuit neo-Latin epic', in R. Maryks, ed., *Jesuit Distinctiveness* (Leiden), 4–23.

(2018) *Francesco Benci's Quinque martyres: Introduction, Translation and Commentary*, Leiden.

Gwynne, P. and B. Schirg, eds. (2018) *The Economics of Poetry: The Efficient Production of Neo-Latin Verse, 1400–1720*, Oxford, Bern, Berlin, Brussels, New York and Vienna.

Hadas, D., G. Manuwald and L. R. Nicholas, eds. (2020) *An Anthology of European Neo-Latin Literature*, London.

Hale, J. K. (1997) *Milton's Languages: The Impact of Multilingualism on Style*, Cambridge.

(1998) *John Milton, Latin Writings: A Selection*, Assen.

(2005) *Milton's Cambridge Latin: Performing in the Genres 1625–1632*, Tempe, AZ.

Hankins, J. (2001) 'The lost continent: neo-Latin literature and the rise of modern European literatures', *HLB* 12: 1–92.

Hardie, P. R., V. Prosperi and D. Zucca, eds. (2020) *Lucretius Poet and Philosopher: Background and Fortunes of De rerum natura*, Berlin.

Haskell, Y. (1998a) 'The masculine muse: form and content in the Latin didactic poetry of Palingenius and Bruno', in C. Atherton, ed., *Form and Content in Didactic Poetry* (Bari), 117–44.

(1998b) 'Renaissance Latin didactic poetry on the stars: wonder, myth, and science', *Renaissance Studies* 12: 495–522.

(1998c) 'The *Tristia* of a Greek refugee: Michael Marullus and the politics of Latin subjectivity after the fall of Constantinople (1453)', *PCPhS* 44: 110–36.

(2001) 'The Columbus paradigm – or complex? – in Neo-Latin studies', *SO* 76: 47–51.

(2003) *Loyola's Bees: Ideology and Industry in Jesuit Latin Didactic Poetry*, Oxford.

(2009) 'Back to the stone age: virtual Roman realities in Victorian Britain', in P. C. Hummel, ed., *Epilanguages: Beyond Idioms and Languages* (Paris), 129–47.

(2010) 'Practicing what they preach? Virgil and the Jesuits', in J. Farrell and M. Putnam, eds., *A Companion to Vergil's Aeneid and Its Tradition* (Chichester), 203–16.

(2011) 'Early anger management: Seneca, Ovid, and Lieven De Meyere's *De ira libri tres* (Antwerp, 1694)', *IJCT* 18: 136–65.

(2013a) *Prescribing Ovid: The Latin Works and Networks of the Enlightened Doctor Heerkens*, London.

(2013b) 'Child murder and child's play: the emotions of children in Jakob Bidermann's epic on the massacre of the innocents (*Herodiados libri iii*, 1622)', *IJCT* 20: 83–100.

(2014) 'The classification of neo-Latin didactic poetry from the fifteenth to nineteenth centuries', in Bloemendal, Ford and Fantazzi 2014b, 437–48.

(2015) 'Arts and games of love: genre, gender and friendship in eighteenth-century Jesuit poetry', in S. Broomhall, ed., *Ordering Emotions in Europe, 1100–1800* (Leiden), 225–44.

(2016) 'Suppressed emotions: the heroic *Tristia* of Portuguese (ex-)Jesuit, Emanuel de Azevedo', *Journal of Jesuit Studies* 3: 42–60.

(2017) 'Conjuring with the Classics: neo-Latin poets and their pagan familiars', in Moul 2017, 17–34.

(2019a) '*Latinitas Jesu*: neo-Latin writing and the literary-emotional communities of the Old Society of Jesus', in I. G. Županov, ed., *The Oxford Handbook of the Jesuits* (Oxford), 553–74.

(2019b) 'Performing the passions: Pierre Brumoy's *De motibus animi* between dramatic and didactic poetry', in Y. Haskell and R. Garrod, eds., *Changing Hearts: Performing Jesuit Emotions between Europe, Asia and the Americas* (Leiden), 43–62.

Haskell, Y. and J. F. Ruys, eds. (2010) *Latinity and Alterity in the Early Modern Period*, Tempe, AZ.

Hass, T. A. and J. Ramminger, eds. (2010) *Latin and the Vernaculars in Early Modern Europe* (= *Renæssanceforum* 6), www.njrs.dk.

Haugen, K. (2014) 'Joseph Scaliger's letters: collaborator, teacher, impresario', *History of Universities* 18: 105–47.

Heerkens, G. N. (1790) *De valetudine literatorum*, 2nd expanded edn, Groningen.

Helander, H. (2004) *Neo-Latin Literature in Sweden in the Period 1620–1720: Stylistics, Vocabulary and Characteristic Ideas*, Uppsala.

Herbert, G. (2015) *Complete Poetry* (ed. and trans. J. Drury and V. Moul), London.

Hess, G. (1976) 'Spectator-Lector-Actor. Zum Publikum von Jacob Bidermanns Cenodoxus', *Internationales Archiv für Sozialgeschichte der deutschen Literatur* 1: 30–106.

(2000) '*Der Mord auff dem Papier* oder: Herodes in Augsburg', in G. Hess, ed., *Der Tod des Seneca: Studien zur Kunst der Imagination in Texten und Bildern des 17. und 18. Jahrhunderts* (Regensburg), 145–65. Reprinted in Gier 2005, 169–89.

Hobbes, T. (2016) *De mirabilibus Pecci carmen* (ed. J. Luggin), Hildesheim, Zürich and New York.

Hofmann, H. (1994) '*Adveniat tandem Typhis, qui detegat orbes*: Columbus in neo-Latin epic poetry (16th–18th centuries)', in W. Haase and R. Meyer, eds., *The Classical Tradition and the Americas. Vol. 1: European Images of the Classical Tradition and the Americas* (Berlin), 420–656.

Houghton, L. B. T. and G. Manuwald, eds. (2013) *Neo-Latin Poetry in the British Isles*, London.

Houghton, L. B. T., G. Manuwald and L. R. Nicholas, eds. (2020) *An Anthology of British Neo-Latin Literature*, London.

IJsewijn, J. (1990) 'Poetry in a Roman garden: the *Coryciana*', in P. Godman and O. Murray, eds., *Latin Poetry and the Classical Tradition: Essays in Medieval and Renaissance Literature* (Oxford), 211–31.
  (1990–8) *Companion to Neo-Latin Studies*. With D. Sacré, 2 vols., Leuven.
  *Imago primi saeculi Societatis Jesu* (1640), Antwerp.
Isebaert, L. and A. Smeesters, eds. (2013) *Poésie latine à haute voix (1500–1700)*, Turnhout.
Jalabert, R. (2015) 'Les vers latins en France au XIXe siècle', 3 vols., unpublished PhD dissertation, Université Paris-Sorbonne.
Jardine, L. (1983) 'Isotta Nogarola: women humanists – education for what?', *History of Education* 12: 231–44.
  (1985) '*O decus Italiae virgo*, or the myth of the learned lady in the Renaissance', *The Historical Journal* 28: 799–819.
Jovanović, N., J. Luggin, L. Špoljarić and L. Šubarić, eds. (2018) *Neo-Latin Contexts in Croatia and Tyrol: Challenges, Prospects, Case Studies*, Vienna, Cologne and Weimar.
Kaiser, L. (1984) *Early American Latin Verse 1625–1825: An Anthology*, Chicago.
Kajanto, I. (2005) 'Spinoza's Latinity', in F. Akkerman and P. Steenbakkers, eds., *Spinoza to the Letter: Studies in Words, Texts and Books* (Leiden), 35–54.
Kallendorf, C. (2007) *The Other Virgil: Pessimistic Readings of the Aeneid in Early Modern Culture*, Oxford.
Kerson, A. L. (1991) 'Diego José Abad, *Dissertatio Ludicro-Seria*', *HumLov* 40: 357–422.
Klecker, E. (2002) 'Ein Missionar auf den Spuren des Aeneas. Die *Paciecis* des Bartholomaeus Pereira SJ (Coimbra 1640)', in D. Briesemeister and A. Schönberger, eds., *De litteris neolatinis in America meridionali, Portugallia, Hispania, Italia cultis* (Frankfurt), 99–112.
Knight, S. and S. Tilg, eds. (2015) *The Oxford Handbook of Neo-Latin*, Oxford.
Korenjak, M. (2015) 'Short mythological epic in neo-Latin literature', in M. Baumbach and S. Bär, eds., *Brill's Companion to the Greek and Latin Epyllion and Its Reception* (Leiden), 519–36.
Korenjak, M., F. Schaffenrath, L. Šubarić and K. Töchterle, eds. (2012) *Tyrolis Latina: Geschichte der lateinischen Literatur in Tirol*, 2 vols., Vienna.
Krüssel, H. (2011–15) *Napoleo Latinitate vestitus: Napoleon Bonaparte in lateinischen Dichtungen vom Ende des 18. bis zum Beginn des 20. Jahrhunderts*, 2 vols., Hildesheim, Zürich and New York.
Laird, A. (2002) 'Juan Luis de la Cerda and the predicament of commentary', in R. K. Gibson and C. S. Shuttleworth Kraus, eds., *The Classical Commentary: Histories, Practices, Theory* (Leiden), 171–203.
  (2004) '*Selenopolitanus*: Diego José Abad, Latin, and Mexican identity', *StudUmanistPiceni* 24: 231–7.
  (2010) 'Latin in Cuauhtémoc's shadow: humanism and the politics of language in Mexico after the conquest', in Haskell and Ruys 2010, 169–200.

(2014) 'Latin in Latin America', in Bloemendal, Ford and Fantazzi 2014b, 821–32.
(2015) 'Colonial Spanish America and Brazil', in Knight and Tilg 2015, 525–40.
(2017) 'A mirror for Mexican princes: reconsidering the context and Latin source for the Nahuatl translation of Aesop's Fables', in B. Taylor and A. Coroleu, eds., *Brief Forms in Medieval and Renaissance Hispanic Literature* (Newcastle), 132–67.
(2019) 'American philological associations: Latin and Amerindian languages', *TAPhA* 149: 117–41.
Lamers, H. (2015) *Greece Reinvented: Transformations of Byzantine Hellenism in Renaissance Italy*, Leiden.
Lamers, H., ed. (2018) 'Constructing Hellenism: studies on the history of Greek learning in early modern Europe', introduction to special issue of *IJCT* 25.3: 201–15.
Lamers, H. and B. Reitz-Joosse (2015) '*Lingua lictoria*: the Latin literature of Italian fascism', *Classical Receptions Journal* 8: 1–37.
(2016) *The Codex Fori Mussolini: A Latin Text of Italian Fascism*, London.
Lamers, H., B. Reitz-Joosse and D. Sacré (2014) 'Neo-Latin literature – Italy: fascism (1922–1943)', in Bloemendal, Ford and Fantazzi 2014a, 1091–5.
Lamers, H., B. Reitz-Joosse and V. Sanzotta, eds. (2019) *Studies in the Latin Literature and Epigraphy of Italian Fascism*, Leuven.
Lefèvre, E. (2017) *Jakob Baldes 'Expeditio Polemico-Poetica' (1664). Eine satirische Verteidigung der lateinischen und neulateinischen Literatur. Einführung, Text, Übersetzung, Kommentar*, Berlin.
Leochaus [Leech], Johannes (1630) *Musae priores*, London.
Lepri, V. (2015) '*Hic liber libenter legitur in Polonia*: mapping the popularity of the *Zodiacus Vitae* between the sixteenth and seventeenth centuries', *Odrodzenie i Reformacja w Polsce* 59: 67–93.
Lewis, C. S. (1990) *Poetry and Prose in the Sixteenth Century*, Oxford.
Longo, S. G. (2004) *Savoir de la nature et poésie des choses: Lucrèce et Epicure à la Renaissance italienne*, Paris.
Luccioli, F. (2019) 'Ariosto *latine redditus*: early modern neo-Latin rewritings of the *Orlando Furioso*', in F. Schaffenrath and A. Winkler, eds., *Neo-Latin and the Vernaculars: Bilingual Interactions in the Early Modern Period* (Leiden), 113–29.
Ludwig, W. (2006a) 'Das *Album amicorum* als Bestandteil der humanistischen Kultur', in *Traditio Classicorum. Auf dem Wege zur Gründung des Centre for the Classical Tradition. Reden und Beiträge anläßlich der Beendigung der Lehrtätigkeit von Karl August Neuhausen an der Universität Bonn* (Bonn), 19–33.
(2006b) *Das Stammbuch als Bestandteil humanistischer Kultur. Das Album des Heinrich Carlhack Hermeling (1587–1592)*, Göttingen.

(2008) 'Unbekannte emblematologische Jesuitendichtung: Das horazisierende Lehrgedicht *De arte symbolica ad Erastum* (1701) des Jacobus Boschius aus Sigmaringen', *NLJ* 10: 195–261.

Luggin, J. (2018) 'Macrohistory or microhistory? The Tyrolean Menippean satire as a regional literary genre', in Jovanović, Luggin, Špoljarić and Šubarić 2018, 107–18.

Mack, P. and J. North, eds. (2015) *The Afterlife of Ovid*, London.

MacPhail, E. (2014) *Dancing Around the Well: The Circulation of Commonplaces in Renaissance Humanism*, Leiden.

Manuwald, G. (2015) 'Letter-writing after Ovid: his impact on neo-Latin verse epistles', in Mack and North 2015, 95–114.

Marr, A., R. Garrod, J. Ramon Marcaida and R. Oesterhoff, eds. (2019) *Logodaedalus: Word Histories of Ingenuity in Early Modern Europe*, Pittsburgh, PA.

Martindale, C. (1993) *Redeeming the Text: Latin Poetry and the Hermeneutics of Reception*, Cambridge.

Mazzocco, A., ed. (2016) *A New Sense of the Past: The Scholarship of Biondo Flavio (1392–1463)*, Leuven.

Mertz, J. J., SJ, J. P. Murphy SJ and J. IJsewijn, eds. (1989) *Jesuit Latin Poets of the 17th and 18th Centuries: An Anthology of Neo-Latin Poetry*, Chicago.

Meynard, T., SJ (2011) *Confucius Sinarum philosophus (1687): The First Translation of the Confucian Classics*, Rome.

  (2015) *The Jesuit Reading of Confucius. The First Complete Translation of the Lunyu (1687) Published in the West*, Leiden.

Meynard, T., SJ, and D. Pan, ed. and trans. (2020) *Giulio Aleni: A Brief Introduction to the Study of Human Nature*, Leiden.

Mikołajczak, A. W. ([1998] 2005) *Łacina w kulturze polskiej* [= *Latin in Polish Culture*], Warsaw.

Morrall, E. J. (1988) *Aeneas Silvius Piccolomini (Pius II) and Niklas von Wyle: the Tale of Two Lovers Eurialus and Lucretia*, Amsterdam.

Moss, A. (1996) *Printed Commonplace-Books and the Structuring of Renaissance Thought*, Oxford.

  (2003) *Renaissance Truth and the Latin Language Turn*, Cambridge.

  (2010) 'Other Latins, other cultures', in Haskell and Ruys 2010, 19–34.

Moul, V. (2013) 'Horatian Odes in Abraham Cowley's *Plantarum Libri Sex* (1668)', in Houghton and Manuwald 2013, 87–104.

  (2015) 'The transformation of Ovid in Cowley's herb garden: books 1 and 2 of the *Plantarum libri sex* (1668)', in Mack and North 2015, 221–32.

  (2016) 'Neo-Latin poetry, 1500–1700: an English perspective', *Oxford Handbooks Online* https://doi.org/10.1093/oxfordhb/9780199935338.013.16.

  (2017) *A Guide to Neo-Latin Literature*, Cambridge.

  (2018) 'Neo-Latin metrical practice in English manuscript sources, c. 1550–1720', in S. Tilg, ed., *Neo-Latin Metre* (Tübingen), 257–75.

  (2021) 'England's Stilicho: Claudian's political poetry in early modern England', *IJCT* 28: 23–50.

Muecke, F. and M. A. Pincelli, eds. (2016) *Rome in Triumph, Books* I–II, Cambridge, MA.
Murru, F. and G. P. Filos (1980) *Alla riscoperta della didattica del latino in Italia nel Settecento e nell'Ottocento*, Rome.
Noël, F., SJ (1711) *Sinensis imperii libri classici sex*, Prague.
Norbrook, D., S. Harrison and P. Hardie, eds. (2016) *Lucretius and the Early Modern*, Oxford.
O'Connor, E. (2001) *Antonio Panormita: Hermaphroditus*, Lanham, Boulder, New York and Oxford.
O'Malley, J. W., SJ, ed. (2015) *Art, Controversy, and the Jesuits: The Imago primi saeculi (1640)*, Philadelphia.
Pade, M., ed. (2015) *Vitae Pomponianae: Lives of Classical Writers in Fifteenth-Century Roman Humanism* (= *Renæssanceforum* 9), www.njrs.dk.
Paladini, M. (2015) *Lucrezio e l'epicureismo tra Riforma e Controriforma*, Naples.
Palmer, A. (2014) *Reading Lucretius in the Renaissance*, Cambridge, MA.
Parker, G. (1999) *The Agony of Asar: A Thesis on Slavery by the Former Slave, Jacobus Elisa Johannes Capitein, 1717–1747*, Princeton.
Passanante, G. (2011) *The Lucretian Renaissance: Philology and the Afterlife of Tradition*, Chicago.
Pavone, F. (1968) *I carmi latini del Tasso*, Catania.
Po-chia Hsia, R. (2007) 'The Catholic Mission and translations in China 1583–1700', in P. Burke and R. Po-chia Hsia, eds., *Cultural Translation in Early Modern Europe* (Cambridge), 39–51.
Pontano, G. G. (2006) *Baiae* (ed. and trans. R. G. Dennis), Cambridge, MA.
 (2014) *On Married Love* (ed. and trans. L. Roman), Cambridge, MA.
 (2022) *Eclogues. Garden of the Hesperides* (ed. and trans. L. Roman), Cambridge, MA.
Porteman, K., ed. (1996) *Emblematic Exhibitions of the Brussels Jesuit College (1630–1685)*, Turnhout.
Possevino, A., SJ (1593) *Bibliotheca selecta de ratione studiorum* . . ., Rome.
Price, D. (1996) *Janus Secundus*, Tempe, AZ.
Prosperi, V. (2004) *Di soavi licor gli orli del vaso: la fortuna di Lucrezio dall'Umanesimo alla Controriforma*, Turin.
Rabbie, E. (1997) 'Editing neo-Latin texts', *Editio* 10: 25–48.
Refini, E. (2017) 'By imitating our nurses: Latin and the vernacular in the Renaissance', in W. Caferro, ed., *The Routledge History of the Renaissance* (Abingdon and New York), 46–61.
Reid, S. J. and D. McOmish, eds. (2016) *Neo-Latin Literature and Literary Culture in Early Modern Scotland*, Leiden.
Romero, I. O. (1981) 'Jano o la literatura neolatina de Mexico', *HumLov* 30: 124–55.
Romero, M. E. (2013) 'El uso diglósico del latín en los villancicos a San Pedro Nolasco de Sor Juana Inés de la Cruz', *Auster* 18, http://sedici.unlp.edu.ar/handle/10915/51470.

Rowland, I. (1998) *The Culture of the High Renaissance: Ancients and Moderns in Sixteenth-Century Rome*, Cambridge.
Rudd, N. (2000) 'Notes on the Latin poems of Samuel Johnson', *Translation and Literature* 9: 215–23.
  (2012) 'Samuel Johnson's Latin poetry', in Houghton and Manuwald 2013, 105–24.
Rudd, N., ed. (2005) *Samuel Johnson: The Latin Poems*, Lewisburg, PA.
Ruysschaert, J. (1949) *Juste Lipse et les Annales de Tacite. Une méthode de critique textuelle au XVIe siècle*, Leuven.
Sacré, D. (1996a) 'La poésie néo-latine en France au xixe siècle', in G. Cesbron and L. Richer, eds., *La réception du latin du xixe siècle à nos jours: actes du colloque d'Angers des 23 et 24 septembre 1994* (Angers), 66–77.
  (1996b), 'Formal aspects of the Brussels emblem verses: reconnaissance of the terrain', in Porteman 1996, 47–53.
Sacré, D., M. Smets and H. Servotte, eds. and trans. (1999) *Tonight They All Dance: 92 Latin and English Haiku*, Wauconda, IL.
Sacré, D., J. Tusiani and T. Deneire, eds. (2006) *Musae saeculi* xx *Latinae*, Brussels and Rome.
Sanzotta, V., ed. (2019) *Una lingua morta per letterature vive: il dibattito sul latino come lingua letteraria in età moderna e contemporanea*, Leuven.
Saracco, L. (2012) 'Olimpia Fulvia Morato', in *Dizionario biografico degl'Italiani* 76. www.treccani.it/enciclopediaolimpia-fulvia-morato_(dizionario-biografico)/.
Scaliger, J. (1583) *De emendatione temporum*, Paris.
Schaffenrath, F. and A. Winkler, eds. (2019) *Neo-Latin and the Vernaculars: Bilingual Interactions in the Early Modern Period*, Leiden.
Schuster, M., ed. (1984) *Jakob Bidermanns Utopia. Edition mit Übersetzung und Monographie*. Bern, Frankfurt and New York.
Scroffa, C. (1981) *I cantici di Fidenzio. Con appendice di poeti fidenziani* (ed. P. Trifone), Rome.
Sidwell, K. (2017) 'Editing neo-Latin literature', in Moul 2017, 394–407.
Sinn, C. (2007) 'The figure in the carpet: metadramatical concepts in Jacob Bidermann's *Cenodoxus* (1609)', in G. Fischer and B. Greiner, eds., *The Play within the Play: The Performance of Meta-Theatre and Self-Reflection* (Amsterdam and New York), 61–75.
Skafte Jensen, M. (1995) *A History of Nordic Neo-Latin Literature*, Odense.
  (2004) *Friendship and Poetry: Studies in Danish Neo-Latin Literature*, Copenhagen.
Sluperius, J. (1575) *Poemata*, Antwerp.
Soranzo, M., ed. (2019) *Giovanni Aurelio Augurello (1441–1524) and Renaissance Alchemy: A Critical Edition of Chrysopoeia and Other Alchemical Poems, with an Introduction, English Translation and Commentary*, Leiden.
Sparrow, J. (1960) 'Latin verse of the High Renaissance', in E. F. Jacob, ed., *Italian Renaissance Studies: A Tribute to the Late Cecilia M. Ady* (London), 354–409.

Spitzer, L. W. (1955) 'The problem of Latin Renaissance poetry', *Studies in the Renaissance* 2: 118–38.
Špoljarić, L. (2018) 'Power and subversion in the ducal palace: Dalmatian patrician humanists and congratulatory orations to newly elected doges', in Jovanović, Luggin, Špoljarić and Šubarić 2018, 81–104.
Standaert, N. (2001) *Handbook of Christianity in China, Vol. 1: 635–1800*, Leiden.
Stellato, M. (1996) *Le Zodiaque de la vie (Zodiacus vitae, 1534)* (ed. J. Chomarat), Geneva.
Stevenson, J. (2005) *Women Latin Poets: Language, Gender, and Authority, from Antiquity to the Eighteenth Century*, Oxford.
  (2014) 'Women writers' networks', in Bloemendal, Ford and Fantazzi 2014a, 1202–4.
Strozzi, T., SJ (1689) *De mentis potu sive de cocolatis opificio*, in *Poemata varia*, Naples.
Struever, N. (1993) 'Petrarch's *Invective contra medicum:* an early confrontation of rhetoric and medicine', *Modern Language Notes* 108: 659–79.
Suárez, M. A. (2009) 'La literatura neolatina del siglo XVIII y el exilio: la obra de Rafael Landívar y José Peramás', in R. Casazza et al., eds., *Artes, ciencias y letras en la América colonial* (Buenos Aires), 1–17.
Szörényi, L. (1976) 'Poésie latine entre 1770 et 1820', *Neohelicon* 4: 271–302.
Taida, I. (2017) 'The earliest history of European language education in Japan: focusing on Latin education by Jesuit missionaries', *Classical Receptions Journal* 9: 566–86.
Tarot, R., ed. (1963) *Jakob Bidermann, Cenodoxus: Abdruck nach den 'Ludi Theatrales' mit den Lesarten der Kelheimer und Pollinger Handschrift*, Tübingen.
Taylor, B. and A. Coroleu (1999) *Latin and Vernacular in Renaissance Spain*, Manchester.
Thill, A. (1999) *La lyre jésuite: anthologie de poèmes latins (1620–1730)*, Geneva.
Thorius, R. (1626) *Hymnus tabaci* (ed. M. Riley), https://philological.cal.bham.ac.uk/thorius/.
Thurn, N. (2002) *Kommentar zur Carlias des Ugolino Verino*, Munich.
  (2012) *Neulatein und Volkssprachen: Beispiele für die Rezeption neusprachlicher Dichtung Europas im 15.–16. Jh.*, Munich.
  (2014) 'Neo-Latin and the vernacular: poetry', in Bloemendal, Ford and Fantazzi 2014b, 287–302.
Trifone, P. (2019) 'La Maschera ambigua del pedante: Fidenzio e il suo linguaggio', in A. Sorella and P. Ortolano, eds., *Il personaggio nella letteratura italiana* (Florence), 67–74.
Trofymuk, M. (2014) *Латиномовна література України (XV–XIX ст.): жанри, мотиви, ідеї* [= *Latin Literature in Ukraine (15th–19th c.): Genres, Motifs, Ideas*], Lviv.
Tunberg, J. M. and T. Tunberg (2000) *Cattus petasatus*, Wauconda, IL.
Tunberg, T. (1997) 'Ciceronian Latin: Longolius and others', *HumLov* 46: 13–61.

Urbano, C. (2005) 'The *Paciecidos* by Bartolomeu Pereira, SJ: an epic interpretation of evangelization and martyrdom in 17th-century Japan,' *Bulletin of Portuguese–Japanese Studies* 11: 61–95.
Valenzuela, B. F. (1974) *Diego José Abad. Poema heroico. Introducción, versión y aparato crítico*, Mexico City.
Valla, L. (2007) *On the Donation of Constantine* (ed. and trans. G. W. Bowersock), Cambridge, MA.
van Binnebeke, X. (2018) 'The *Certamen poeticum Hoeufftianum* and the Second Anglo-Boer War (1899–1902)', in A. Steiner-Weber and F. Römer, eds., *Acta conventus neo-latini Vindonobensis* (Leiden), 163–72.
van Rompaey, C. (2015) 'Language and meaning in the *Ethics*. Or, why bother with Spinoza's Latin?', *Parrhesia* 24: 336–66.
van Schurman, A. M. (1650) *Opuscula Hebraea Graeca Latina et Gallica, prosaica et metrica*, Utrecht.
Verbeke, D. (2015) 'Neo-Latin's interplay with other languages', in Knight and Tilg 2015, 27–40.
Verhaart, F. and L. Brockliss, eds. (2023) *The Latin Language and the Enlightenment*, Liverpool.
Vissac, J. A. (1862) *De la poésie latine en France au siècle de Louis XIV*, Paris.
Vitrioli, D. ([1845] 1998) *Xiphias: Epigrammata: Elegiæ*, Reggio Calabria.
von Martels, Z. (2014) 'Asia', in Bloemendal, Ford and Fantazzi 2014b, 849–61.
Vratović, V. and V. Gortan (1969–70), *Hrvatski latinisti: Croatici auctores qui latine scripserunt*, Zagreb.
Waquet, F. (1998) *Le latin ou l'empire d'un signe*, XVIe–XXe siècle, Paris.
  (2001) *Latin or the Empire of a Sign: From the Sixteenth to the Twentieth Centuries* (trans. J. Howe), London.
  (2015) 'Social status', in Knight and Tilg 2015, 379–92.
Watanabe, A. (2018) 'From Coimbra to Nagasaki: an overview of Jesuit Neo-Latin in early modern Japan', in P. Gwynne and B. Schirg, eds., *The Economics of Poetry: The Efficient Production of Neo-Latin Verse, 1400–1720* (Oxford, Bern, Berlin, Brussels, New York and Vienna), 387–408.
White, J. A. (2005–16) *Biondo Flavio: Italy Illuminated*, 2 vols., Cambridge, MA.
Wiegand, H. (1984) *Hodoeporica: Studien zur neulateinischen Reisedichtung des deutschen Kulturraums im 16. Jahrhundert. Mit einer Bio-Bibliographie der Autoren und Drucke*, Baden-Baden.
Williams, R. (2015) *Latin of New Spain*, Mundelein, IL.
Witt, R. G. (2000) *In the Footsteps of the Ancients: The Origins of Humanism from Lovato to Bruni*, Leiden.
  (2012) *The Two Latin Cultures and the Foundation of Renaissance Humanism in Medieval Italy*, Cambridge.
Wright, E. R. (2016) *The Epic of Juan Latino: Dilemmas of Race and Religion in Renaissance Spain*, Toronto.
Wright, E. R., S. Spence and A. Lemons, eds. (2014) *The Battle of Lepanto*, Cambridge, MA.

Wright, F. A. (1930) *The Love Poems of Joannes Secundus: A Revised Latin Text and an English Verse Translation, Together with an Introductory Essay on the Latin Poetry of the Renaissance*, London.
Wyatt, W. S. (1997) 'Notes on the Latin poems of Gerard Manley Hopkins', *Translation and Literature* 6: 83–8.
Yates, F. (1964) *Giordano Bruno and the Hermetic Tradition*, Chicago.

CHAPTER 8

# *Reception*

*James Uden*

More than any other avenue of classical research, the study of reception connects the ancient world to how we live our lives, and why we think the things we do. It has become a familiar name for that part of the discipline committed to examining the role that Greek and Roman texts, images and ideas have played in subsequent cultures, and continue to play in contemporary life. While studies of the classical tradition were a familiar presence in previous generations, the greatly expanded place given to reception in the discipline's structure and self-perception is one of the major shifts in the field over the past three decades, and work in this area is now a key component in paedagogy and public-facing scholarship as well as research. This chapter provides an accessible overview of classical reception studies, its history in debates over the role of the reader and the nature of interpretation, and its current transformation into a more diverse conception of 'Global Classics'. While I argue here for the vital importance of reception studies to the future of classical scholarship, I also examine the limitations of the concept of reception itself, questioning whether the name adequately communicates the breadth and ambition of current work in the area. At its best, the word categorises and unifies an important strain of research, a term of institutional organisation rather than genuine intellectual self-description. At its worst, it risks dulling the ideological force of our analyses, classing as 'reception' acts and images that might better be described as instances of challenge, appropriation, resistance or rebellion.

Despite having become a familiar component of the discipline, the position of reception studies is in many ways far from central. It is true that a large number of outlets are now dedicated to receptions

---

* My thanks to the editors for their invitation, my fellow contributors for commenting on a draft, Joseph Rezek for sharing unpublished material, and Peter J. Schwartz and Katharina Volk for their assistance and advice.

research, including journals (*Classical Receptions Journal*, *The International Journal of the Classical Tradition*), book series (Oxford's *Classical Presences*, Cambridge's *Classics After Antiquity*, Bloomsbury's *Classical Receptions in Twentieth-Century Writing* and *IMAGINES – Classical Receptions in the Visual Performing Arts*) and professional organisations (the Classical Receptions Studies Network; the Society for Early Modern Classical Reception). The term is increasingly found in job advertisements and on department websites in the USA, and as a classification for work in the Research Excellence Framework (REF) in the UK.[1] Yet assumptions of institutional acceptance are belied by the more complex realities of hierarchy within the discipline. In my experience, few young classicists go on the job market, at least in the USA, listing reception studies as their primary research area, because it would raise inevitable questions about their capability to teach the main line of language and literature courses in Latin and Greek.[2] Books devoted to a post-classical period are frequently scholars' second projects – I admit to this myself – after a book on a classical period or author. With these hierarchies unshaken, it is no doubt riskier for a junior than a senior scholar to undertake work in classical reception, and that senior scholar is likely only to have been formally trained in Greek and Latin, not in the 'other' field of research. In the USA, a tenure case based primarily on publications in reception would almost certainly raise the sort of questions about disciplinary fit and measures of achievement that a body of research in a traditional area would not. From this perspective, Charles Martindale's call in *Redeeming the Text* (1993) for us to reconceive of *all* classical scholarship as a form of reception still seems radical, and pointedly unrealised. Reception may be familiar now as a subsection of the discipline, but its institutional acceptance cannot be taken for granted. It still has the air of being many classicists' second jobs.

Yet in many ways reception studies could be the best face for the discipline as a whole, given its range, diversity, responsiveness to political critique and capacity to challenge the associations of cultural elitism and insularity that 'Classics' – as long as it is so called – will always accrue. Debates over the homogeneity and Eurocentrism of the

---

[1] The publication of the *Oxford History of Classical Reception in English Literature* (2012–19), under the general editorship of David Hopkins and Charles Martindale, is another milestone.
[2] For the UK perspective on the job market's marginalisation of reception studies, see Richardson 2017; and on the persistent bias against reception scholars as 'real' classicists, Rankine 2019: 353.

canon that were fought in the 1980s and 1990s have recently been renewed in a paedagogical context in waves of general education reform and continuing controversies over Great Books programmes in the United States.[3] But reception studies is, or at least is potentially, unmoored from any canon, not limited to the Western literary tradition, and not restricted to particular modes of cultural production, 'high' or 'low'. As Emily Greenwood (2016: 42–3) writes, the emergence of reception as a prominent part of the discipline 'marks a shift away from a fixed and hierarchical classical tradition, which emphasised a single lineage traced through European culture to the present day, to an unruly, uncanonical, and unpredictable series of encounters and responses to Greek and Roman Classics in diverse cultures and contexts'. A large number of recent volumes consider the reception of the Greek and Roman world outside of Europe[4] and in popular culture.[5] Its premise of investigating links between eras and cultures offers unique opportunities in the classroom to connect what is familiar to what is new, or to explore similarities and differences between students' own cultural traditions.[6] Even areas that have previously been lamented as blind spots are now being filled, such as the reception of late antique Latin literature.[7] But a bias towards certain subjects remains. Philip Hardie (2013: 193) has observed the tendency for reception scholars to 'gravitate to modernity, the nineteenth to the twenty-first centuries'. I would add a tendency to focus on poetry and drama over prose. Michael Squire (2015) has drawn attention to a different sort of blind spot, arguing that reception scholars overemphasise written texts at the expense of visual art and material culture.

Reception is simply too broad and varied a field of scholarship to describe in one chapter, so it has been impossible to be comprehensive here. I have focused on Rome and Latin literature specifically, aiming to give a sense of exciting critical developments and suggesting some ways forward. For the case studies in the latter half of this chapter,

---

[3] See Peirano in this volume on the context of these debates.
[4] Torlone, Munteanu and Dutsch 2017 on East and Central Europe; Parker 2017 on South Africa; Burton, Perris and Tatum 2017 on New Zealand; Laird and Miller 2018 on Latin America; Johnson 2019 on Australia; Renger and Fan 2019 on East Asia; and see also my section later in this chapter on 'Global Classics'.
[5] See e.g. the volumes edited by Rogers and Stevens 2015, 2017, 2018; on television and video games, Lowe and Shahabudin 2009; on children's literature, Hodkinson and Lovatt 2018; on rock music, Fletcher and Umurhan 2019.
[6] Friedman 2013; Bakogianni 2018. [7] Formisano and Fuhrer 2014; Culhed and Malm 2018.

I have drawn examples from my own research in the eighteenth century, but I do so more as an admission of the limits of my own expertise than as a claim for any special status of texts in that era. Indeed, quite the opposite: I argue in the section on 'Global Classics' that some of the most exciting current work in reception moves beyond English-language writing and beyond Europe. After a section examining the background of the term 'reception', the three subsequent sections pursue three specific claims. First, allusions to antiquity frequently occur within a broader cultural matrix of challenge and contestation. A critical classical reception practice needs to pay attention to voices that challenge the values accorded to classical literature, as well as to voices that embrace them. Second, a focus on the history of education can help us see classical allusion as a social challenge rather than simply a submission to prevailing literary or cultural norms. 'Classicising' – a word that too often suggests literary ornamentation rather than dynamic intellectual work – can signal a rebellion against societal prejudices about the proper boundaries of knowledge. Third, the study of reception is at its most vital as a mode of communication outside Classics, whether to the public, to students or to scholars in other fields. The more reception is perceived as a 'subfield' of Classics, the less impact its insights will have.

## Background: Hermeneutics and Reception Theory

Anglophone Classics draws its theoretical master-term 'reception' (*Rezeption*) from Hans Robert Jauss and the so-called School of Konstanz, and through Jauss from the broader philosophical tradition of hermeneutics. As Charles Martindale and Lorna Hardwick emphasised in influential early accounts of reception for classical scholars, Greece and Rome offers a particularly fertile ground for studying the processes of textual reinterpretation from one author to the next, given classical writers' obsessive allusions to literary tradition and competitive referentiality. Antiquity is itself a hothouse for the study of classical reception.[8] Modern philosophical debates about the nature and practice of interpretation have also been convincingly traced to

---

[8] Martindale 1993; Hardwick 2003. Hardwick in particular classifies as reception an array of phenomena that we might group under an array of other analytical headings: canon formation, translation, intertextuality, cultural memory (*exempla*), paedagogy (*paideia*). Porter (2008: 494–5) correctly predicted reception within antiquity as a growth area of research; see e.g. Hardie 2009, Goldschmidt and Graziosi 2018, Goldschmidt 2019.

classical antiquity, to debates enacted in ancient rhetoric, grammar and early Christianity.[9] But the hermeneutical tradition from which Jauss drew his ideas has its own origin in the Protestant thought of nineteenth-century Germany. Without the aid of centralised Church authority to help decide vexed points of scriptural exegesis, Protestant ministers of the seventeenth and eighteenth centuries looked to a growing body of treatises to guide biblical interpretation, and these treatises led in turn to a body of philosophical texts in the nineteenth century that grappled with the role of the interpreter in determining meaning.[10] Twentieth-century hermeneutics continues to examine the active role of the individual in construing meaning. As Martindale has observed, though, such debates about the role of the interpreter appear infrequently in scholarship on classical reception, which tend towards more conventional forms of literary history. There is little of the drive of philosophical hermeneutics towards investigating the place of the reader's own beliefs, and rarely an impulse to dissolve the boundaries between subject and object, interpreter and text. As it has developed in classical scholarship, reception studies is to some extent at odds with the philosophical tradition to which it owes its name.[11]

Key for the School of Konstanz was the work of Hans-Georg Gadamer (1900–2002), whose *magnum opus* was *Truth and Method* (*Wahrheit und Methode*, 1960) – a somewhat misleading title, since Gadamer offers no singular or objective method for interpretation. For Gadamer, understanding is fundamentally dialectical. The reader must bring the historical text back to life by pulling it into a process of dialogue with the present, and thereby becoming sensitive to the questions to which the text is an answer.[12] Gadamer rejects any firm separation of reader from text, since the mental background that the reader brings to the process of interpretation is the product of accumulated tradition, a tradition that the historical text has itself helped to construct. 'History does not belong to us,' he writes; 'we belong to it' (2004: 278). Gadamer also does not argue that the reader should aspire to any objective or presupposition-less position from which to

---

[9] Bruns 1992; Eden 1997.   [10] Palmer 1969: 34–8.
[11] As the editors of this volume suggest to me, a parallel might be drawn with the movement away from a more radical notion of Kristevan intertextuality – a component of all textual meaning – to a more familiar use of intertextuality in classical scholarship; see O'Rourke and Pelttari in this volume. On the continuing utility of Jauss' ideas for biblical interpretation, see Evans 2014.
[12] Gadamer 2004: 363.

interpret meaning. Rather, the prejudices (*Vorurteile*) that each reader brings to the interpretation of an historical text are both inevitable and desirable, since they constitute the present situation from which a contemporary person can and should enter into dialogue with the past. In order to reach the point of understanding, though, a point of connection needs to be reached between the worldview of the text and that of the reader, a process which Gadamer calls the 'fusion of horizons' (*Horizontverschmelzung*).[13] By engaging in a dialogical process of question-and-answer with the text, we reach a point at which the horizon of the reader and the horizon of the text – the range of what each can 'see' from its vantage point in history – begin to overlap. Gadamer rejects research into the prior meanings of text as irrelevant to this process, and indeed as a failure to bring the written work back into living dialogue with the present. We must instead *apply* the ideas of the historical text to the present, since understanding is 'always application' (2004: 308). As Gadamer and his interpreters freely acknowledge, this model fits theological or juridical interpretation better than it does the reading of literature, since in those cases the reader does indeed seek the wisdom of an authoritative text to solve a spiritual or legal problem in the present.[14]

It is worth noting that despite the importance of Gadamer's ideas for reception theory, his conception of understanding has been criticised on several fronts. Jürgen Habermas argued that Gadamer's idealised vision of free dialogue between individuals and tradition ignores the fact that tradition has itself frequently been shaped by force rather than consensus, and that appeals to tradition have long been a convenient way to mask expressions of power.[15] The collaborative ideal between present and past underplays the social and cultural forces that have shaped the discourses from which we make meaning. Feminist thinkers have similarly critiqued Gadamer's insistence that individuals 'belong' to history. Whose history? Far from willingly entering into dialogue with tradition, a feminist or queer reader may justifiably want to resist or challenge its 'wisdom' as a force that has historically repressed, persecuted or excluded them. While Gadamer specifically rejects the negative representation of prejudices – he dismisses this as an unwelcome legacy of the Enlightenment's praise of reason over tradition (Gadamer 2004: 272–3) – other thinkers have been less willing to assume the inevitability of prejudices shaping

---

[13] Ibid. 305.   [14] Palmer 1969: 236.   [15] Habermas 1985: 316.

understanding, or to valourise them as a necessary dialogic partner for understanding in the present.[16] Marie Fleming has also critiqued the model of 'fusion of horizons' in Gadamer's thought, arguing that it reduces readers to abstract instantiations of the period they inhabit rather than individuals characterised by differences of power, gender and class. His model of interpretation, she argues (2003: 116), dissolves 'all traces of concrete individuality, the site of differences, otherness, embodiment, and history'. In the call to fuse the horizons of present and past, opposing values of challenge and difference are downplayed or erased.

Gadamer's student Hans Robert Jauss developed many of his ideas, but with an explicit focus on literary interpretation, and with a key distinction: for Jauss, the history of a text's reading is not an antiquarian occupation severed from contemporary concerns, but lies at the heart of our aesthetic and hermeneutic project. In his inaugural lecture at the University of Konstanz from 1967, 'Literary History as a Provocation to Literary Theory' (*Literaturgeschichte als Provokation für die Literaturwissenschaft*), Jauss presents his ideas as a counter to both Marxist and formalist modes of literary analysis.[17] Both fail to grasp the full historicity of texts, he argues, reducing literary works (respectively) to the means of their production or to formal categories such as metre or genre. Like Gadamer, Jauss emphasises that meaning is fundamentally dialectical; it emerges through a process of dialogue between the world of the text and that of the reader. But rather than emphasising a single encounter in the present, Jauss argues that the full potential of a literary work is disclosed across time, in the successive series of readings from the work's origin to today.[18] The literary work establishes a 'horizon of expectation' (*Erwartungshorizont*) for its initial audience, appealing to their presuppositions based on their knowledge of synchronic factors (is this text similar to others of the era?) and diachronic factors (is this text like others in its genre?). Some texts aim merely to satisfy their readers' expectations. Others challenge them, thereby forcing a sideways shift in readers' horizon of expectation, and leading to the broadening or alteration of that horizon in the next generation of readers.[19] Hence

---

[16] Code 2003a: 6.   [17] Jauss 1982: 3–45.
[18] So Jauss 1982: 20, on the relationship between aesthetics and literary history: the 'understanding of the first reader will be sustained and enriched in a chain of receptions from generation to generation; in this way the historical significance of a work will be decided and its aesthetic value made evident'.
[19] Jauss 1982: 23–8.

a work of literature which might seem dissonant or strange in its initial context is sometimes later discovered as a classic; its challenges have led to a broadening of readers' horizon of expectation, and so the entirety of its qualities and achievements can only be realised in the fullness of time. Jauss' boldness consists partly in describing reception as a mode of *aesthetics*. Rather than understanding the aesthetic qualities of a work in terms of its formal features or its mimesis of the culture around it, his conception of *Rezeptionsästhetik* (reception-aesthetic, usually translated into English as 'aesthetic of reception') assesses literature according to the degree to which it has challenged or confirmed its readers' expectations, a process studied historically by reconstructing the ongoing dialogue between readers and text.

The influence of the School of Konstanz in Anglophone scholarship split along disciplinary lines. The work of another student of Gadamer, Wolfgang Iser, arrived earlier and made a deeper impact in English literary studies, where it helped to create what became known as 'reader-response criticism'. (Iser was himself a professor of English literature, and participated in the translation of his own texts from German into English.) Iser also adopts the language of 'horizon', though on the micro-level of the reading experience. Each sentence, he writes, 'opens up a particular horizon, which is modified, if not completely changed, by succeeding sentences' (1974: 278). When we read a text, we create a world, and that world will vary in its details from reader to reader. In visualising the hero of a novel, for example, the outlines are established by the author (he is blond, green-eyed, wears a tuxedo), but each reader will shade in the details differently and create a slightly different picture of the character in their minds. Thus there is often a sense of disappointment when we see the film version of the novel: the potential multiplicity of the literary text has been reduced to a singularity, and the role that our own imagination can play has been correspondingly diminished.[20] Iser describes moments of indeterminacy in the text as 'gaps' that each reader is invited to fill (1974: 283). In much the way as two people looking at the same set of stars might trace out the pattern of different constellations in the night sky, so 'the "stars" of a literary text are fixed; the lines that join them are variable' (282). Reader-response theory was a critical battlefield in the early 1980s, and Iser quickly came under fire from Stanley Fish, who attacked the distinction between

---

[20] Iser 1974: 283.

determinacy and indeterminacy by asserting that *every* detail in a text is subject to interpretation.[21] Yet Iser's ideas are still productively invoked by classical scholars in describing the dynamics of ancient texts, since Greek and Roman authors frequently depend upon their audience to supply part of their texts' meaning from a knowledge of literary and mythical tradition. As Sharrock (2018: 29) says, 'Latin poets seem to be particularly interested in gaps, including back stories, alternative versions, and missing expectations'.

These debates were translated most influentially to Latin literary studies in Charles Martindale's bracing and still-important *Redeeming the Text: Latin Poetry and the Hermeneutics of Reception* in 1993, a work that was cited frequently in classical scholarship in the decades that followed, particularly for the statement in its opening pages: 'Meaning ... is always realized at the point of reception.'[22] The book was by no means a call to institute a new section of the discipline called 'reception studies'. *Redeeming the Text* instead aimed to dislodge the naïve hermeneutic assumptions of classicists working in the mainstream of Latin literature, by emphasising the Gadamerian point that there can be no pure or unmediated access to the classical text. The desire to peel back the layers to access the 'original' meaning of Virgil or Horace is an illusory task, since our reading of their texts is inescapably shaped by the preconceptions of our own period. Martindale challenges the idea of Jauss that the process of reception reveals or discloses the potential of the ancient work. How could its future meanings have all been there already? Instead, he argues (with reference to Derrida) that traces of previous readings inhere in our current readings. Hence, for example, 'no reading of Homer, at least in the West, has been, or *could be*, wholly free of a vestigial Virgilian presence' (1993: 8). He encourages Latinists to abandon the historicist approach to ancient literature, the desire to

---

[21] Fish 1981: 7 ('the stars in a literary text are not fixed; they are just as variable as the lines that join them'). In *The Return of the Reader* (1987), Nancy Freund already announced the end of reader-response criticism, stating that it has 'a past rather than a future' (p. 10). Yet critical theories that enjoy a frantic career in English literary studies can frequently count on a longer lifespan in other parts of the humanities.

[22] The phrase was originally made a condition (1993: 3): '*Meaning*, could we say, *is always realized at the point of reception*; if so, we cannot assume that an "intention" is effectively communicated within any text' (italics original). The book was one in a trio (with Hardie 1993 and Kennedy 1993) that inaugurated the series *Roman Literature and its Contexts* (edited by Denis Feeney and Stephen Hinds), which did more than any other in the 1990s and 2000s to shape the critical notions of a generation of Latinists.

see Virgil as he 'really' was, and embrace a new critical self-consciousness regarding our own position within the tradition. Martindale's book is itself self-conscious in its appeals to the tradition of philosophical hermeneutics (especially Gadamer and Jauss), right down to the theological implications of its title and its use of scriptural interpretation as a paradigm for understanding the relationship between reader and text.[23] That relationship, again in accordance with the tradition of German hermeneutics, is frequently presented by Martindale in interpersonal terms. He imagines our reading of the Classics variously as a human encounter, a domestic argument and an erotic tryst.[24]

The phrase 'meaning is realised at the point of reception' was repeated regularly by Latinists. Stephen Hinds called it an 'axiom' in *Allusion and Intertext* in 1998, and William Batstone called it the 'founding claim of reception study' in 2006.[25] Yet the version of reception described in *Redeeming the Text* differs significantly from the field of reception studies as it later evolved. Although Martindale argues that every reading of classical literature produces a new version of the text, he ends up returning to a very specific set of readings – the Western canon – and calling for a renewed faith in the writers of the past. By reading Virgil or Lucan through Milton, Dante or Eliot, he says, we can 'bypass twentieth-century criticism' (1993: 55). The book's democratising conviction that every exercise of understanding is a fresh production of meaning sits oddly with its hierarchical conclusion that some understandings are richer and more worthy of study than others.[26] Dante may of course be a 'better' reader of Virgil than a contemporary scholar, but if this is the criterion of what we read and study, it should be obvious how limited and conservative the field would become. Martindale's Gadamerian vision of reception as

---

[23] See esp. Martindale 1993: 103–4.
[24] Martindale 1993: 32 (reading is 'an encounter'); 91 ('dialogue, like love, requires at least two participants'); 105 (the reconciliation between power and freedom is like that which occurs in 'millions of homes' every day). R. E. Palmer's influential theoretical overview, *Hermeneutics* (1969), similarly imagines interpretation as a 'loving union' between text and interpreter (at 244).
[25] Hinds 1998: 49; Batstone 2006: 14.
[26] This hierarchical point was reiterated more strongly later. Cf. Martindale 2006: 11: 'Already a classics student is far more likely to spend time analyzing *Gladiator* than the *Commedia* of Dante. I find this trend worrying ... [W]e form ourselves by the company that we keep, and ... material of higher quality is better company for our intellects and hearts than the banal and the quotidian'. Again (2013: 176): 'Classics is more alive to my thinking in Joyce's *Ulysses* or the poetry of Seamus Heaney than in *Gladiator*...'. For a response to Martindale from a scholar of Classics and film, see Winkler 2000: 12–13.

intimate dialogue with tradition is equally distant from the aims of the field as it is currently constituted, which seeks to include representations of Greek and Roman civilisation mediated by translation, adaptation in art and film, and popular culture. Few Latinists will deny the pleasure of reading an ingenious close reading of an ancient text we know well, or the paedagogical usefulness of using such close readings to explain or expose new aspects of the ancient text. But as a theoretical model, the figurative representation of reception as a direct, interpersonal relationship between ancient author and modern reader excludes, in reality, the range and vitality of contemporary appropriations of ancient images and ideas. Scholars who work in this area have tuned their ears to hear a wider crowd of voices, each of whom is more or less empowered and eager to interact directly with Greek and Latin texts.

As Martindale's own interests turned to transhistorical notions of value and beauty in subsequent years, he increasingly critiqued the 'collapse' of reception into 'cultural studies', which focuses on the historical context of a work's production to the exclusion of literary or aesthetic questions about the work itself.[27] Yet a critical attention to the forces that have shaped our perception of Latin texts is a natural and even necessary consequence of accepting Martindale's argument for the historical situatedness of any act of interpretation.[28] In an important recent essay, Patrice Rankine argues for the fallacy of appeals to 'purely' philological readings of texts, the claim that we could read Virgil or Horace without our vision of both the poet and ourselves being shaped by larger historical and cultural forces. The dream of seeing the text in its antique purity – a dream that Martindale attacked as hermeneutically naïve – is also politically naïve, Rankine argues, since it is one that has traditionally been used to exclude certain participants. The incapability of women and people of colour to attain a state of philological purity has been asserted throughout the history of Classics as a discipline, and thus 'classics, and especially philology at its essence', has never been a 'neutral and disinvested test of intelligence'.[29] If meaning is realised at the point of reception, then our study of that reception can and should involve self-consciousness

---

[27] Martindale 2005: 124; 2006: 9. Lorna Hardwick's *Reception Studies* (2003) already took a strikingly different tack, elevating public performance over private reading as the paradigmatic act of classical reception, and stressing that reception 'is and always has been a field for the practice and study of contest about values and their relationship to knowledge and power' (at 11).
[28] So also Harloe 2010: 17.   [29] Rankine 2019: 352–3; and see p. 415–22 in this chapter.

about the forces that have shaped those exercises of critical judgement. On this model, reception is not a flight from aesthetics to cultural politics but a fresh investment in analysing their interconnection. This in turn raises a new question: is our current term of choice the best way of achieving that goal?

## The Limits of 'Reception'

In Germany, the term *Rezeption* has the ring of an earlier critical era, and other phrases are currently used to denote the study of classical texts in later cultures (compare *Transformationen der Antike*, the title of a book series published by De Gruyter). Among Anglophone classicists, the word's breadth and popularity have long been accompanied by disputes about its usefulness. While 'reception' is not inaccurate as a literal rendering of Jauss' *Rezeption* (or perhaps rather *Rezeptionsgeschichte*), the English word is more common and less markedly academic than the German *Rezeption*, and Hans Robert Jauss himself joked that it was more likely to evoke the language of the hotel business than literature for non-speakers of German.[30] If 'reception' is to be more than simply a contemporary rebranding of the classical tradition or the *Nachleben* of Greek and Roman texts, then what additional meaning does it bring? Or to put it the opposite way, what presumptions or limitations does the term import when we are analysing the role that classical texts played in later cultures? In this section, I outline a series of objections that have been lodged against the phrase 'classical reception', and argue that we should be mindful of its limitations as a master-term for our analyses when we use it.

The metaphorical association of reception with an interpersonal relationship carries with it certain theoretical baggage. To speak of one text receiving another evokes a process of voluntary communication between two equal participants – unsurprisingly, since, as we have seen, our critical notion of reception has its origins in a hermeneutical tradition that conceptualises interpretation as a dialogue between reader and text. But that model of interpersonal communication fits encounters between two authors far better than it

---

[30] Jauss 1980: 15, cited at Holub 1984: 1 ('Le mot allemand "Rezeptionsästhetik" suggère malheureusement un malentendu fatal: en français et en anglais, on ne rencontre le mot *réception* que dans le langage de l'hôtellerie!').

does interactions between authors and anything broader: cultural discourses, ideologies, social structures, political movements. 'Reception' is an awkward metaphor for understanding the role of classical texts in structuring ideology or discourse, a process that is anything but voluntary, interpersonal or intentional. No matter how congenial imagery of talking, exchanging, giving or receiving is to liberal conceptions of civic discourse, in this context it risks eliding power differences by feigning a sort of ontological equality between reader and tradition. To speak of an individual 'receiving' the classics also risks underplaying the authority of a tradition when it is mobilised as part of cultural norms. Reception is a convenient label for classicists' work on Cavafy, for example, but it hardly captures the force of Greek and Roman history upon that poet's life and work, the overwhelming pressure exerted by the past upon articulations of his personal and sexual identity.[31] Here the word 'tradition', even if it falsely implies a unified lineage of ancient thought, at least communicates the idea that individuals are faced with ideas that have cultural power and cachet, so that the adaptation of ancient ideas is a confrontation or co-option of time-bound forces much larger than themselves.[32] Gadamer's insight that individuals are themselves shaped by the historical texts they seek to interpret is important and bears repeating. An author's choice to refer to certain classical texts may overshadow the fact that fundamental aspects of his or her identity might already have been structured by ideas drawn from those texts, or others in the tradition.

This raises another problem: the question of attitude or motivation that an individual brings to the classical text. When we talk of one author 'receiving' another, it is hard to escape a specific metaphorical image: the image of a host admitting a guest into his or her space. The image implies willingness and presupposes a sort of voluntary acceptance. Stephen Harrison makes the imagery of hospitality explicit when he is describing the relationship between what he calls the 'receiving' and the 'visiting' genres in Latin poetry: 'In what follows I will sometimes use the metaphor of hospitality to describe this relationship: in this sense the dominating genre of the text is the "host" which entertains the subordinate genre as a "guest".'[33]

---

[31] See e.g. Jeffreys 2015: 159–68; Orrells 2011 on antiquity and modern sexual identities.
[32] On the opposition between tradition and reception see pp. 428–33 in this chapter; also Hardwick 2003: 2.
[33] Harrison 2007: 16. On this aspect of the metaphor, see the analysis by O'Rourke 2017, who argues that the particular quality of ancient hospitality – a relationship between strangers, not between friends – allows for a more aggressive conceptualisation of reception.

The passivity suggested by the image of the author as benign host has commonly been lamented. Reception, writes Simon Goldhill, is 'too *passive* a term for the dynamics of resistance and appropriation, recognition and self-aggrandisement' of successive contests over the nature of Hellenism.[34] By evoking an act of hospitality, the image fits authors who eagerly allude to the classical tradition better than those who are forced to confront it as part of a system that they wish to challenge. In order to achieve a complete picture of the later influence of classical works, the full range of responses they engendered – awe, fear, horror, suspicion; even boredom, contempt – are as crucial to their history as appreciation or affirmation. In *Leviathan* (1651), Hobbes compares the reading of Greek and Roman authors to the bite of a rabid dog; the ancients, he says, infect the modern populace with the venom of their mistaken notions of liberty.[35] Edward Young's *Conjectures on Original Composition* (1759), a pivotal text for the English Romantics, imagines Virgil and Horace as demons: writers must exorcise them, as Constantine did pagan spirits, if they are ever to produce their own original literary works.[36] Larry Norman's *The Shock of the Ancient* (2011) explores the emotions of horror and repulsion, as well as love and intimate connection, inspired by canonical Greek and Roman texts in the seventeenth-century French *Querelle des Anciens et des Modernes*. In short: the Classics have always been something to be confronted, not just received. The history of resistance against and within classical texts is integral to a full picture of their afterlife.

A different but related problem of attitude relates to our tendency to idealise or identify with the authors we study. One particular danger for classical receptions scholars is that of transforming artists, film-makers and writers of all eras into classicists or proto-classicists like ourselves, influenced by the same texts as us, caught up in a formalist circle of allusion and intertext, fired by a familiar desire to engage with an unchanging body of works. Usually the assumption that a writer or artist must have known this or that ancient text, even when shaky or 'fuzzy', helps our case.[37] Part of the regular business of making an argument in reception studies is the statement (and

---

[34] Goldhill 2002: 297, emphasis original. Also Wood 2012: 171: 'the word "reception" suggests an unenviable state of passivity'. Whitmarsh 2006: 115 makes a different objection to the term, arguing that it implies a completed process, rather than the constant 'shuffling back and forth' of meaning between readers and texts.
[35] Hobbes 1996: 226; on this passage, Skinner 2008: 140–2.
[36] Young 1759: 77–8. On Young's Gothic vision of antiquity, and on the legacy of antiquity as a spectral 'haunting' of modernity, see Uden 2020.
[37] On 'fuzzy' connections, see Hardwick 2011.

frequently the overstatement) of an author's awareness or interest – or even desire or love – for 'our' texts as classicists. Yet it is all too easy to project our attitudes, our professional enthusiasm for Greece and Rome, onto other generations and disciplines. That sort of critical idealisation is an alienating aberration to scholars working on the same material from other disciplinary perspectives, and in any case risks underplaying the matrix of contestation and challenge in which references to antiquity have frequently taken place.[38] We need a study of the uses of antiquity not burdened by the recuperative instinct that so easily slides into critical self-representation.

Scholars have also raised a number of objections to the imagery of dialogue between reader and text with which reception theory has long been associated. The image has raised some basic questions, since it is, after all, an imaginative construct. What does it really mean to have dialogue with a text? Or, as Katherine Harloe (2010: 18) puts it: 'How strong a notion of agency would we need to attribute to such works in order for the comparison to hold?' Is this merely a way of justifying our own interpretive decisions with a false sense of to-and-fro? Jonathan Culler (1982: 74–5) has argued against the tendency of theories of reading to dissolve into a sort of 'monism', in which every aspect of the reading process takes place in the reader's own mind; for, if we are not interacting with something other than ourselves, he argued, how can we learn from what we read? Yet we might equally argue that the personification of the books as dialogue partners is mystificatory and overly abstract, and that it risks eliding aspects of the material, social and commercial circumstances of reading. The book itself has no voice: it is a physical object that must be produced and bought; its meaning is mediated through conventions of printing and formatting; we cannot simply 'speak' to it but learn to decipher its signs, a process that requires labour, time and expense; and so on.[39]

Margaret Litvin, in her study of twentieth-century readings of *Hamlet* in the Arabic world, raises a different concern about both 'reception' and 'dialogue'. These terms, she argues, tend to imply a two-party interaction (source culture and receiving culture), which imposes a misleading linearity on what are often multidirectional

---

[38] See Matzner 2016 on the particularly close personal connection between critic and the object of study in reception research.
[39] This is not to exclude the *desire* that a text might let us hear a voice: S. Butler 2015.

phenomena. For the communities she studies, *Hamlet* has become a 'global text', no longer specifically English but interpreted through adaptations in French and through the prism of German literary criticism. Rather than 'writing back' to the coloniser by transforming an English text, then, she demonstrates that Arabic intellectuals sought to participate in a kaleidoscopic discourse deliberately unmoored from any desire for the original.[40] Litvin's critical reflections could benefit analyses of responses to classical works, which similarly take place in a shifting and complex set of cultural and literary frames, recording a crowd of voices rather than a singular and unidirectional conversation with the ancient world.

## Resisting Antiquity

In the remaining sections of this chapter, I alternate between theoretical discussion and close readings of particular authors and works. In the close readings, I do not abandon reception but try to balance it with a sense of *resistance* to the classical – although I am aware that 'classical' is itself a word too often 'poorly defined and theorised' (Greene 2013: 81). Here I mean the invocation of the classical as a challenge to its power, but the classical as more than individual words or images – the classical as a mode of cultural authority, as something that has come down through time and has accumulated weight and force along the way.[41] Resistance suggests a confrontation with something different and bigger than oneself. Of the three case studies, Mary Wollstonecraft resists the authority of classical *exempla* as part of her declaration of a rational modernity not bound to the inherited structures of the past. Anna Letitia Barbauld inhabits new and unexpected subject positions *within* Roman poetry in order to challenge assumptions about what a woman of her period should say or do or know. Erasmus Darwin uses allusions to Ovid's *Metamorphoses* in his botanical writing to underline the limitations of myth in describing the universe, asserting an epistemological distinction between 'Imagination' and 'Science' that he sees as fundamental for the exploration of the new. True, a capacious interpretation of reception to mean any sort of contact with a prior text or idea would include all of these

---

[40] Litvin 2011, esp. pp. 6–8, 58–9.
[41] See Goff 2005: 11: 'because classics bears with it the weight of tradition and authority, it can easily be pressed into service as a *sign* of tradition and authority in general'.

examples. A guest can be received badly or well. But resistance suggests a mode of reference to the past that does not idealise or romanticise the classical world, nor does it sentimentalise its continuing presence as a partner for personal communication and affection. It is a mode of questioning or challenge, either *of* antiquity or *through* antiquity, against literary, social and political forces that wield lasting power.

### Case Study 1: Mary Wollstonecraft

The two great polemical works by the feminist pioneer Mary Wollstonecraft, *A Vindication of the Rights of Men* (1790) and *A Vindication of the Rights of Woman* (1792), are products of the anxious, early period of responses to the French Revolution in England, a period of intellectual upheaval and reassessment of all aspects of the civic life, from the family to the state.[42] After the Bastille fell on 14 July 1789, Edmund Burke vigorously condemned the revolutionaries in his *Reflections on the Revolution in France* (1790). Liberal thinkers rushed to respond to Burke and defend what had become pejoratively known as 'French principles'. Among the over fifty responses published were the classic works of political theory *The Rights of Man* (1791) by Thomas Paine and *Political Justice* (1793) by William Godwin (later the husband of Mary Wollstonecraft, and the father of Mary Shelley). But the first response was Wollstonecraft's *A Vindication of the Rights of Men* (1790), written at furious speed and published less than a month after Burke's work appeared. That was followed, after the sensational success of the first tract, by *A Vindication of the Rights of Woman* two years later. Both of these works explicitly reject emotional rhetoric – what Wollstonecraft calls memorably 'the drapery of factitious sentiments' – and yet are also highly rhetorical, full of vivid images and pointed maxims.[43] Characteristic of their period, they reflect a sense of a dramatic temporal breach, a consciousness that the modern is, and must be, very different from the inheritances of the past. They also express a deep suspicion of 'sensibility' and the aesthetic, sharpened by a sense of political betrayal by Burke, who had acquired fame decades earlier by theorising influentially about aesthetics and the sublime.[44]

---

[42] Wollstonecraft 1993; all citations are to this edition. On the context, Butler 1984.
[43] Wollstonecraft 1993: 231.
[44] In *A Philosophical Enquiry into the Origin of Our Ideas of the Sublime and the Beautiful* (1757) [= Burke 2015].

Wollstonecraft's works encode a mode of what we might call resistant allusion, which interrogates the connection between inherited political power and classical words and ideas even as she is citing them. The image of the Roman empire is one of the structuring metaphors for her analysis of gender and power, but her invocation of classical ideas is consistently accompanied by critique. As a test case for reflection upon the limits of classical reception studies, she offers a paradigm of a resisting reader whose attention was drawn to structures of authority more than specific texts, and who aimed to speak against the power of antiquity rather than speaking with it.

Wollstonecraft's vision of the Classics was shaped by her views on educational reform.[45] One of the cornerstones of the *Vindication of the Rights of Woman* is the advocacy for day schools that would educate girls and boys together, and would train women not merely in taste and politeness but rigorously to think for themselves. She allows that young people of 'superior abilities, or fortune' might be taught the 'dead and living languages', but 'reading, writing, arithmetic, natural history and some simple experiments in natural philosophy' form the basic curriculum in the more egalitarian schools she envisions, where 'boys and girls, the rich and poor, should meet together'.[46] The classical images that appear intermittently in Wollstonecraft's prose are therefore the traces of a learned discourse whose influence she seeks to question. Indeed, at stake for Wollstonecraft in the reverence paid to Greece and Rome are core questions of individual autonomy and responsibility. Repeatedly throughout the *Vindications* she associates the rhetoric of men such as Burke with an unreflective obeisance to classical authority. 'I perceive, from the whole tenor of your *Reflections*', she tells him cuttingly, 'that you have a mortal antipathy to reason', since the entire result of the argument is that we should 'reverence the rust of antiquity'.[47] Like other writers who supported abolition, she attacks the 'servile reverence for antiquity' that underlay arguments for the slave trade, which was sanctioned by 'our ignorant forefathers', but 'outrages every suggestion of reason and religion'.[48] Any argument from inheritance or custom is a failure of individual rationality; 'reverence for superiors or antiquity', she asserts, is 'reason at second-hand'.[49] Burke's call to faith in tradition suggests to Wollstonecraft that he has relinquished the greater duty of considering for himself the moral

---

[45] On Wollstonecraft's views on education in the context of her political thought, see Sapiro 1992: 237–49.
[46] Wollstonecraft 1993: 253.    [47] Ibid. 8.    [48] Ibid. 13.    [49] Ibid. 30.

integrity of society's beliefs. 'I am not accustomed', she says, 'to look up with vulgar awe'.[50]

Wollstonecraft particularly takes aim at moral reasoning founded on the examples of previous generations, and in particular at the convention of apotheosising the heroes of Greece and Rome as a standard of political action in the present. In *Reflections on the Revolution in France*, Burke chastised revolutionaries for their failure to imitate a 'more early race of ancestors':

> Under a pious predilection for those ancestors, your imaginations would have realized in them a standard of virtue and wisdom, beyond the vulgar practice of the hour: and you would have risen with the example to whose imitation you aspired. Respecting your forefathers, you would have been taught to respect yourselves.[51]

Philip Ayres has described Burke's habitual invocation of ancient examples in his oratory: he frequently cast himself in the role of Cicero and his political opponents as contemporary avatars of Verres or Catiline.[52] In Wollstonecraft's response to this passage of the *Reflections*, she begins by deflating attempts to ennoble the present by constant reference to antiquity. The morality or immorality of ancestors has little bearing on the behaviour of their descendants – although, she concedes, it might be maintained that the Romans' origin in Romulus' asylum was consistent with their later savagery and lack of civility (they were 'private robbers' who 'became public predators', glorying in the 'vicious elegance' of the amphitheatre).[53] But she also doubts whether recursion to ancient example is a sound basis for moral thought at all. A principle that would be praiseworthy for an artist – to study carefully the 'noble models of antiquity, till your imagination is inflamed' – is an insecure and dangerous principle for ethical or political thought. To base the new civic structures in France on 'the *imagined* virtues of their forefathers' would not be a rational foundation for a political system; it would merely assent uncritically to the inequities of the past.[54]

Yet in fact the Roman empire is pervasive as a metaphor in *A Vindication of the Rights of Woman*, and is fundamental in structuring its vision of the enforced relationship between men and women. In a much-quoted phrase, Wollstonecraft assured readers that she did not wish women 'to have

---

[50] Ibid. 17.  [51] Burke 1993: 36.
[52] Ayres 1997: 42–6. Cf. Sachs 2010: 60: Burke alludes to Roman literature to 'consolidate a consensus among the governing elite and to position himself within it'.
[53] Wollstonecraft 1993: 40.  [54] Ibid. 40–1.

power over men; but over themselves'.[55] The beauty system, she argues, turns women into either 'abject slaves or capricious tyrants', encouraging them either to assume a position of weakness and subordination, or to exercise control by physical attractiveness and sexual charms.[56] This undesirable social control is represented – in a choice of metaphor clearly shaped by the political situation in France – as a decadent imperialism, a corrupt empire doomed to fall. She laments that women, taught the arts of allurement from a young age, are 'bred up with a desire for conquest', taught to wield 'the iron sceptre of tyranny', intoxicated with the 'insipid grandeur and slavish ceremonies' of domestic rule.[57] At times the connection with Rome is explicit. A 'woman of fashion', she writes, 'is not a more irrational monster than some of the Roman emperors, who were depraved by lawless power'. Female sexual jealousy resembles Cato's desire to expand Rome in the period of the Republic by crushing Carthage, 'not to save Rome, but to promote its vain-glory'.[58] More often, it exists as traces in the negative paradigm of empire. We have to catch Rome's reflection indirectly, as part of broader invocations of concepts of tyranny and rule. The classical world is here less a target of specific allusion than a mobile structure of thought through which Wollstonecraft articulates her powerful rejection of gender norms. Rome is simultaneously a metaphor of enormous rhetorical productivity and a metonym for the paradigms that progressive thinkers aimed to reject.

Are Wollstonecraft's writings works of classical reception? Aspects of her thought certainly become visible through attention to classical ideas. Yet to speak of the work as 'receiving' the classical risks misdescription on a number of fronts. Her writing stands apart deliberately from classicising rhetoric such as Burke's – indeed it is largely motivated by rebellion against it – and it rejects the classical examples and narratives that shored up aristocratic power in her age. Her proto-feminist ideal was, to use Ronald Paulson's word, an aspiration towards the 'unmythical'.[59] Wollstonecraft's suspicion of the seductions of sensibility clearly differentiates her from the poets and dramatists who adapted classical ideas in the Romantic writing of her decade. Her motivations are political, not aesthetic. Her references are rarely to specific texts, but instead to systems she traces back to antiquity: exemplary ethics, slavery and empire, gender norms.

---

[55] Ibid. 133.   [56] Ibid. 113.   [57] Ibid. 169, 175, 223.   [58] Ibid. 111, 277.   [59] Paulson 1983: 55.

Wollstonecraft's work, in short, emerges as a challenging test case: it is not a work of reception so much as rejection, of resistance to the classical, and yet it is also an indirect testament to the cultural force of the Roman world in her era. But if classicists remain drawn only to writers whose enthusiastic affection for ancient writers most resembles their own, we will miss the opportunity to foster a critical as well as an appreciative mode of reception studies – one that could include thinkers like Wollstonecraft, who hold such a vital place in the history of ideas.

### Reading for Exclusion

In a famous article published in 1959, Walter J. Ong described Latin language learning in the Renaissance as a rite of passage, a puberty ritual which offered male students admittance to a separate and privileged environment. For boys learning Latin in the Renaissance, he wrote, the 'cleavage between the vernacular world and the Latin world' coincides with the 'division between family life and a certain extra-familial life, and with a division between a world in which women had some say and an exclusively male world'.[60] For most of its history – and, many argue, still today – classical education has constituted what Ong calls a 'marginal environment', limited by barriers of gender, geography, race and class.[61] Penelope Wilson, writing about women writers of the eighteenth century, calls the study of Latin and Greek an 'exclusion zone', observing that the 'relationship of women writers with the classics is a complex and essentially agonistic one'.[62] Much recent work in classical reception studies has sought to emphasise these barriers as part of a candid acknowledgement of the forces that have shaped the legacy of classical literature, and to draw out, therefore, the spirit of challenge with which many writers and artists approached their own experiments in classical adaptation and allusion.

Yet classicists working in other periods also need to confront a different misapprehension, one familiar to anyone who has worked on classical material in new periods and fields. This misapprehension associates Latin automatically with what is conservative, stifling and obscure, and the vernacular with the democratising of literary culture,

---

[60] Ong 1959: 108; on the gender division in Renaissance classical education, Stevenson 2015.
[61] On the history of social exclusion in the teaching of classical languages from antiquity to the present, see the essays in Archibald, Brockliss and Gnoza 2015; Morley 2018.
[62] Wilson 2012: 497.

with freedom, imagination, anti-elitism and the other values of the modern liberal academy. Jürgen Habermas' description of the development of the bourgeois public sphere, culminating in the expansion of print in the eighteenth century and the creation of new spaces for private citizens to engage in debate outside the control of the state, has been particularly influential in this respect. According to this still-dominant narrative, the tyranny of Latin was broken by the expansion of newspapers, coffee-houses and circulating libraries, which fostered a new, middle-class readership according prestige to vernacular history and language rather than to the aristocratic preserve of the classical languages.[63] The model has many problems: the public sphere was not exclusively monolingual; periodical writers and readers still made recourse to classical literature; people still aspired to learn Latin and Greek. The sense of extreme distance between Latin and vernacular languages is more a product of modern disciplinary politics than the realities of literary production in the period Habermas described, since, as many scholars of classical reception have shown, Roman literature retained its imaginative and expressive powers long after the use of Latin is supposed to have 'broken down'.[64] The task of classicists working on later periods is therefore one of balancing different objectives: to acknowledge the barriers that long excluded certain readers and writers of Latin, or imposed additional and extraordinary burdens on their acquisition of classical knowledge, while also showing that allusions to Latin literature could communicate a range of different emotions and ideas. This is what I call here 'reading for exclusion'. When we are reading allusions to antiquity in the work of writers to whom classical education was denied, a focus on education can help us cast those moments – however conventional – as a *rebellion* against, rather than a capitulation to, expectations of gender, class and race. Every demonstration of classical erudition potentially tells its own story about why and how the author came to that knowledge.

---

[63] Habermas 1989 (original text 1962).
[64] For a representative example of the Habermas-derived model, see e.g. Kramnick 1999: 21, 43: the 'linguistic foundation [of the public sphere] could not be Latin, the cosmopolitan script of the old aristocracy ... During the late seventeenth and early eighteenth century uniform Latinity breaks down as the cultural capital of the elite classes and variously cultivated vernaculars take its place.' Marilyn Butler's analysis in *Mapping Mythologies* (written in 1984 but published posthumously) encapsulates similar assumptions: 'by the eighteenth century, classicism was now too familiar, and above all too much the main plank of aristocratic education, to retain its radical force among the educated population at large ...' (M. Butler 2015: 13).

For a woman of Wollstonecraft's generation, Latin learning was a difficult attainment, and one of questionable propriety. In the eighteenth century and earlier, modern languages were seen as appropriate accomplishments for women, but the classical languages were taught in schools traditionally restricted to male students. If a woman did have classical learning, she risked being seen as an intruder on traditionally masculine ground. A striking example is a celebrated member of the 'Bluestocking' circle of learned women, Elizabeth Carter (1717–1806). She was taught classical languages by her father as a child and then followed a punishing routine as an adult, waking every morning between four and five o'clock to read, and keeping herself awake with tea, coffee, snuff and wet towels around her head. Her most famous work, the first complete English translation of the lectures of Epictetus (1758), won her condescension and suspicion as well as acclaim. Samuel Johnson quipped that she could 'make a pudding as well as translate Epictetus', and another man said more bluntly that he would only subscribe to a work of female scholarship if it were a 'treatise of œconomy for the use of the ladies'.[65] Her reputation was made earlier, though, in a celebrated Latin poetic exchange that marked her as an invader in a jealously guarded male preserve. By the late 1730s, the precociously talented Carter had won some early fame as a poet of learning. In 1738, a Latin epigram was published in *Gentleman's Magazine* – anonymously, although almost certainly by Johnson – commemorating a visit by the twenty-one-year-old Carter to Alexander Pope's gardens at Twickenham:

> Elysios *Popi* dum ludit laeta per hortos
>     En auida lauros carpit *Elisa* manu.
> Nil opus est furto. Lauros tibi, dulcis *Elisa*,
>     Si neget optatas *Popus*, *Apollo* dabit.

> While happy Eliza sports in Pope's Elysian groves,
>     Look! – she snatches the laurel with a greedy hand.
> There is no need for theft. Sweet Eliza, if Pope should deny you
>     the laurel you desire, Apollo will give it to you.[66]

The epigram's ostensible compliment is undercut by its overtones of appropriation and theft. By imagining Carter 'snatching' the laurel – the phrase alludes to a line from Virgil's second Eclogue – the poet represents her erudition as an encroachment on the exclusion zone of

---

[65] Boswell 1887: I 142; Pennington 1807: 143.
[66] *The Gentleman's Magazine*, July 1738, p. 372, with my translation.

masculine learning.[67] The epigram set off a flurry of back-and-forth in the periodical's pages, including one translation of the Latin epigram that picks up on the allusive potential of the laurel tree. It imagines Carter not as a nymph but as the male god Apollo in the first book of Ovid's *Metamorphoses*, in violent and farcical pursuit of the innocent Daphne ('Cease, lovely thief! my tender limbs to wound, / Cry'd *Daphne* whisp'ring from the yielding tree').[68] Carter responded in an epigram, written in Latin, humbly pleading that Pope's 'laurel' was too lofty for her and would only droop on her brow.[69] Scholarly work on contemporary women's writing and classical literature has shown how the discovery of new and silent voices in ancient texts can still constitute a continuing mode of transgression.[70] This narrative of female movement into forbidden space has its prehistory in the anxious contestation of the spaces of proper knowledge in earlier eras – in snatching the laurel from a bounded garden.

In the nineteenth century, classical education in women became more familiar and even desirable, and training in Latin became more widespread in schools and colleges. Class, however, remained a formidable barrier. As Hurst (2006: 53) writes, the 'classics were an irrelevance to working-class women who came from an environment where the struggle to read the Bible or English literature was difficult enough'. In his work on the history of classical education in the UK, Christopher Stray has done more than any other scholar to demonstrate in detail how the study of the classics became a means of 'social closure'.[71] Knowledge of Latin and Greek, long a symbol of the educated elite, became an attractive marker of social status among an aspiring middle class in the UK throughout the nineteenth century, but its cultural prestige was bounded by a number of factors. Entrance to public schools, 'seedbeds of social exclusion', was increasingly regulated by written entrance examinations, which were largely based on classical learning.[72] This in turn led to the spread of preparatory schools for families who could afford the fees, while

---

[67] *Ecl.* 2.54: *et uos, o lauri, carpam* ... ('And you, o laurel, I will snatch ...').
[68] *The Gentleman's Magazine*, August 1738, p. 429. For a nuanced reading of this exchange and its role in Carter's career, see Wallace 2003.
[69] *The Gentleman's Magazine*, August 1738, p. 429.
[70] Note, e.g., Theodorakopoulos 2012: 149: 'When it comes to the classical tradition ... women are indeed transgressing into a territory they have not previously owned.' Cf. Balmer 2012 on transgression as the key mode for a modern female poet engaging with Greek and Latin literature; Cox 2018: 175–8.
[71] Stray 1998, 2015.   [72] Stray 1998: 12.

local schools with non-classical curricula were established for those families who could not.[73] While the quotation of ancient Greek in casual conversation remained for most people a scholarly affectation or an eccentric obscurity, Latin quotations were a more accessible, 'semi-public field', which nonetheless functioned as a marker of education for the socially elite (or those who aspired to be so).[74] In a sense, the content of classical learning was irrelevant to its usefulness as a dividing social line. Stray quotes Lord Macaulay, who argued that if Greek were replaced with Cherokee on examinations for the East India Company, the exams would still be able to distinguish the 'superior man' for the job.[75] Yet Henry Stead and Edith Hall have shown that Greek and Latin language and literature were in fact an object of closer interest for working-class readers and theatre audiences than has generally been assumed, and icons from antiquity could be recruited for progressive as well as conservative causes. 'The dominant classes may have had the master key to the Classics', they write, 'but this means neither that others could not gain entrance to the classics ... nor that some did not make it their life's work to cut and distribute new keys, promoting access to all areas'.[76]

The same metaphor of crossing into bounded space finds expression in a different educational debate across the Atlantic about the appropriateness of classical education for African Americans. 'This is a study in transgression and transcendence', begins Michele Valerie Ronnick in her introduction to the autobiography of William Sanders Scarborough, the first Black member of the Modern Language Association and one of the first Black members of the American Philological Association (APA, and now the Society for Classical Studies). The outlines of Scarborough's successful career look misleadingly ordinary for a professional classicist: he wrote a Greek textbook, *First Lessons in Greek* (1881), published over twenty papers in the journal of the APA (*TAPhA*), and rose to the position of President of Wilberforce University in Ohio. But born into slavery in Macon, Georgia, 1852, he was forced to face, like other Black scholars of the period, the humiliating prejudice that his erudition was either an embarrassment or an impossibility. His success as a philologist was in fact the

---

[73] Ibid. 36, 52.
[74] Ibid. 79. The distinctive focus of Richardson 2013 is on the failure of hopes for social mobility through classical learning.
[75] Stray 1998: 53, citing Keith 1922: 11 253. Note that Macaulay was defending the place of Greek in the examinations, not attacking it. See further Vasunia 2013: 201–3.
[76] Stead and Hall 2015: 4; also McElduff 2006.

product of extraordinary struggle, as recent scholars have emphasised.[77] Scarborough's later career was witness to a broader educational debate about the relevance of classical education for African American students, which is associated primarily with the opposing figures of Booker T. Washington and W. E. B. Du Bois. Washington advocated for practical education and a focus on economic advancement. Du Bois, in his seminal *The Souls of Black Folk* (1903) and other writings, defended the importance of classical education and the equal right of Black students to cultivate the mind. Du Bois' critical engagement with Cicero, Ovid and other Roman authors is evident in his own writing, which looks to antiquity 'not merely for ideals to imitate, but for questions to debate, and for habits of thought that compel us to recognise and reconsider our assumptions about the present'.[78]

At the very origins of the African American literary tradition is an earlier figure of obvious interest to classicists, the remarkable Phillis Wheatley (c. 1753–84), who published the first book of poetry by a Black American writer, *Poems on Various Subjects, Religious and Moral* (1773).[79] Wheatley was born in West Africa and transported to Boston on the *Phillis*, the source of her first name. She learnt English at prodigious speed and made 'some progress in Latin' according to John Wheatley, identified as 'the Master who bought her' in a notice attached to the opening of her book. The classical imagery through which Wheatley expresses herself, with its apparently conventional appeals to the Muses and the Graeco-Roman gods, was long seen as a disappointingly opaque lens through which to view the subject of *real* interest to modern critics: her own experiences and emotions as an enslaved woman. Yet the wave of re-evaluation of Wheatley has stressed the boldness of her subtle inversion and transformation of classical paradigms and the scope of her poetic output, which includes an epyllion retelling the anguished story of Niobe in Ovid's *Metamorphoses*.[80]

Her book begins with 'To Maecenas', in which she blends Virgilian pastoral with Horace's praise of his patron in the first of the *Odes*. Wheatley

---

[77] See Ronnick's introduction in Scarborough 2005: 1–22; Cook and Tatum 2010: 93–107.
[78] Fertik and Hanses 2019: 9. This introduction to a special issue of the *International Journal of the Classical Tradition* on Du Bois' classicism offers a helpful orientation to current debates about Black classicism.
[79] Text in Wheatley 1989.
[80] 'Niobe in Distress for her Children Slain by Apollo, from Ovid's *Metamorphoses*, Book VI, and from a View of the Painting of Mr. *RICHARD WILSON*' (Wheatley 1989: 98). On the poem's reshaping of Ovid: Thorn 2008; Cook and Tatum 2010: 35–47. Wheatley also owned copies of Pope's *Iliad* and *Odyssey*: see Rezek 2020.

## 8 Reception

had written in her preface that her poems were the products of her 'leisure Moments'.[81] Yet the very notion of leisure for an enslaved woman is immediately put under question at the beginning of this programmatic poem, in which it is the free Maecenas, not the poet herself, who enjoys pastoral *otium* ('Maecenas, you, beneath the myrtle shade, / Read o'er what poets sung, and shepherds played').[82] Wheatley moves through a series of classical poetic figures in distinctly personal and bodily terms: a 'deep-felt horror thrills through all my veins' when she reads Homer, she writes; 'ardors' arise in reading Virgil; and Terence, finally (out of chronological order), is 'one alone of *Afric*'s sable race' who was accorded 'grace' by the Muses, language redolent not of inspiration but of manumission.[83] In the penultimate stanza, she declares her own intentions:

> Thy virtues, great *Maecenas*! shall be sung
> In praise of him, from whom those virtues sprung:
> While blooming wreaths around thy temples spread,
> I'll snatch a laurel from thine honour'd head,
> While you indulgent smile upon the deed.[84]

'I'll snatch a laurel'. In Yopie Prins' book on women learning Greek in the Victorian era, she describes the need to read female writers engaging with classical literature in more than biographical terms, as participants in a broader 'recurring narrative of desire that has its own conventions'.[85] It is hard to miss here the adoption by Wheatley of the same image that was used to describe Elizabeth Carter's entrance into the male garden of poetic activity, with the same overtones of transgression and theft. In other ways, the story we hear is completely distinct. The image of benign supervision ('you indulgent smile upon the deed') gains a new and more literal force in Wheatley's poems, since it appears immediately after the preface by her slaveholder, which verifies and permits her pursuit of literary activity. The image of 'snatching' the laurel resonates with the experience of classical education for a Black person of Wheatley's era, since before the Civil War enslaved people would have had to acquire their learning in Latin from their owners 'through stealth', not through any formal schooling.[86] The verb has an even more fundamental and

---

[81] Wheatley 1989: 45.  [82] Ibid. 49; see Cook and Tatum 2010: 13–24.
[83] Ibid. 49–50; on this representation of Terence, Bennett 1998: 67–8.  [84] Wheatley 1989: 50.
[85] Prins 2017: 243.
[86] 'Through stealth': Ronnick, in Scarborough 2005: 6. Many readers have assumed that Corydon, the speaker of the Virgilian line to which the image refers (*Ecl.* 2.54), was himself enslaved (see Leigh

painful resonance within the poetry book, since in a later poem, in a rare moment of direct autobiographical description, Wheatley says that she was herself 'snatch'd', stolen from her family in Africa by 'seeming cruel fate'.[87] Her embodiment of this poetic convention is in fact a radical realignment of the classical poet's voice, and an expression of her own unique subject position.

What does it mean for classicists working on later eras to read for exclusion? It is a way of making meaning out of allusions to the ancient past, even – or especially – where the author does *not* appear to be speaking in personal terms, but merely inserting her or himself into the familiar tropes of classical texts. By emphasising the struggles and exclusions of classical learning during the period in which the author was writing, and incorporating the realities of education into our interpretation of aesthetic tropes, even apparently conventional allusions communicate a particular and ungeneralisable stance towards the norms of that era. That stance could be an expression of conformity, the reassertion of an expected coherence between mind, expression, reading patterns, intelligence, body, skin colour, gender, class. Or it could rebel. The rebelling voice, sometimes loudest to those who are familiar with classical texts, should also be heard.

### *Case Study 2: Anna Letitia Barbauld*

In a long footnote in *A Vindication of the Rights of Woman*, Wollstonecraft had criticised Anna Letitia Barbauld for parroting masculine language and ideas. In 'To a lady, with some painted flowers' (1773), Barbauld had written:

> Flowers to the fair: to you these flowers I bring,
> And strive to greet you with an earlier spring.
> Flowers sweet, and gay, and delicate like you;
> Emblems of innocence, and beauty too.[88]

The final couplet of Barbauld's poem is the antithesis of Wollstonecraft's argument, though a foreshadowing of Wollstonecraft's political metaphor:

> Nor blush, my fair, to own you copy these;
> Your best, your sweetest empire is – to please.

---

2016: 416 on the history of this question), which would give additional pertinence to Wheatley's allusion.
[87] Wheatley 1989: 83.
[88] McCarthy and Kraft 1994: 77. The poem was first published in Barbauld's collection, *Poems* (1773).

Wollstonecraft despaired that even a learned woman such as Mrs Barbauld could perpetuate a system of ideas that robs women of their dignity, which classes them with 'the smiling flowers that only adorn the land'.[89] By unthinkingly replicating the cultural association of women with beauty and the private sphere, the poem contributes to male society's empire over women. 'This has ever been the language of men', wrote Wollstonecraft, 'and the fear of departing from a supposed sexual character, has made even women of superior sense adopt the same sentiments'.[90]

Although Wollstonecraft omits it from her quotation of the poem in *A Vindication of the Rights of Woman*, 'To a lady, with some painted flowers' in fact begins with lines quoted from Virgil's second Eclogue, the famous homoerotic account of the shepherd Corydon's unsatisfied yearning for the boy Alexis. When Barbauld imagines bringing flowers to the unnamed Lady, she puts herself in the position of Corydon in that poem, who enumerates the flowers he imagines as gifts for his ungrateful lover.[91] The striking epigraph, with its suggestions of queer eroticism, has aroused surprisingly little comment from contemporary scholars, although we know that the homoerotic theme of this particular poem of Virgil was a point of difficulty for eighteenth-century readers.[92] If Wollstonecraft noticed Barbauld's quotation at all, she presumably saw it as a textual ornament of little weight, much like the painted flowers themselves. But I take Barbauld as my next case study to prove a more general point. Given that knowledge of the classical has always involved the emplacement of a writer in a cultural hierarchy, *no* classical allusion, even the most apparently conventional or trite, is merely 'decorative' or inert. Each classical reference tells a story about education, confirming or challenging assumptions about how or why that learning was acquired. Nor is the use of the classical necessarily a means of reasserting the oppressive aspects of that hierarchy; for if Wollstonecraft engages in resistance against the classical, Barbauld articulates her ideals of compassion and empathy from *within* the

---

[89] Wollstonecraft 1993: 122.  [90] Ibid.
[91] *Ecl.* 2.45–6 *tibi lilia plenis | ecce ferunt nymphae calathis* ('look, the nymphs bring you lilies in full baskets').
[92] Fredericksen 2015: 433–6. He quotes the botanist John Martyn in his edition of the *Eclogues* (1749: 27): 'some indeed have ventured to affirm, that this whole Eclogue is nothing but a warm description of pure friendship: but I fear an impartial reader will be soon convinced, that many of the expressions are too warm to admit of any such interpretation'.

classical, rejecting Rome's association with empire and control, and finding her learned voice through complex allusion to Latin texts.

Paedagogy formed the constant backdrop of Barbauld's life and writing. She spent her early years at the Dissenting academies in Kibworth and Warrington (the 'Athens of the North'), where her father taught. Later in life, she and her husband directed the Palgrave Seminary in Suffolk. These schools were attended only by boys. Nonetheless, Barbauld acquired strong convictions regarding the importance of learning for herself and other women, convictions fostered also by the liberal orientation of her branch of Protestantism (Unitarian Dissent), which put a particular emphasis on education. She maintained throughout her writing that even classical learning – typically reserved for men – was a desirable attainment for women. Greek and Roman authors, she wrote in one essay for young female readers, are 'so frequently referred to both in books and conversation, that a person of cultivated mind cannot easily be content without obtaining some knowledge of them'.[93] Yet despite being raised in as congenial an environment for learning as was possible in the period, Barbauld faced significant barriers. A later biographer tells us that her father long resisted teaching her Latin despite her 'earnest desire' to learn, and he only relented when she at length 'overcame his scruples'.[94] Domestic instruction was the only available route for women's classical learning, and it depended on women having someone willing and able to teach them. Indeed, when Barbauld herself was asked to establish a college for female students, she declined, arguing that the 'best way for women to acquire knowledge, is from conversation with a father, a brother or a friend ... and by such a course of reading as they may recommend'. Women's 'thefts of knowledge', she observed with bitter irony, must be regulated with 'Spartan' severity, since any public display of learning is 'punished with disgrace'.[95] When Barbauld displays her classical knowledge, then, it is no hollow or outmoded literary device. It is a point of contact with a charged paedagogical debate about what women can and should know, and how they can come to know it.

Her poetry revolves insistently around the contrast between big and small: trees and flowers, Muses and insects, ideas and objects. Barbauld describes, often in grand terms, a world of miniature things. 'Embryo

---

[93] Barbauld 1826: 73.   [94] Aikin 1825: 1 x.
[95] Aikin 1825: 1 xv. These comments have disappointed later readers; McCarthy 2001 argues that Barbauld aimed only to protect her time, not to object to the principle of schooling for women.

schemes' emerge in the laboratory of the scientist Joseph Priestley in one poem, like matter from chaos – recalling the opening of Ovid's *Metamorphoses* – and like new-born babes, ready to be clothed in print.[96] In another poem, the 'proud giant of the beetle race' flashes his horns, as Barbauld attempts to describe the myriad 'atom forms of insect life'.[97] Frequently she sets the grand trappings of classical literature and myth against the modern, domestic and everyday. 'Come, Muse, and sing the dreaded *Washing-Day*', she announces, reimagining from a child's eye-view the epic struggles of laundry day: of 'dirt and gravel stains / hard to efface, and loaded lines at once / snapped short'.[98] In another poem, two chimney ornaments carry out a poetic dialogue in which one boasts of holding the 'lamp of Science', fed with Attic oil from the 'stores of Greece and Rome'.[99] It is not by coincidence that Barbauld projects images of learning onto ordinary domestic objects, since, as for other learned women of her period, her own classical learning came, unavoidably, from within the home.

Barbauld's most beloved poem in her own time, 'The mouse's petition', subtly proposes the reinterpretation of a canonical work of Roman literature in a distinctly compassionate and anti-imperialist mode. 'The mouse's petition' again shows Barbauld's close observation of a world of miniature beings. Joseph Priestley, the man credited with the discovery of oxygen, was experimenting with noxious gases one evening when Barbauld visited. There she saw a mouse in a trap, ready to be used as a test subject in one of Priestley's experiments with 'different kinds of air'.[100] The poem is spoken by the mouse, petitioning for its freedom:

> Or, if this transient gleam of day
> Be *all* of life we share,
> Let pity plead within thy breast
> That little *all* to spare.[101]

---

[96] 'An inventory of the furniture in Dr. Priestley's study', vv. 39–42: 'A mass of heterogeneous matter, / A chaos dark, nor land nor water; – / New books, like new-born infants, stand, / Waiting the printer's clothing hand –' (McCarthy and Kraft 1994: 39).

[97] 'To Mrs. P[riestley], with some drawings of birds and insects', vv. 114–15, 104 (McCarthy and Kraft 1994: 8–9).

[98] 'Washing-Day', vv. 8, 25–7. The description of this domestic task in an epic setting is, of course, already in Homer (*Od.* 6.85–95). In *The Authoress of the Odyssey* (1897), Samuel Butler notoriously used the 'washing day episode' as the cornerstone for his argument that Nausicaa herself wrote the *Odyssey*; see Porter 2018: 239–50.

[99] 'Lines for Anne Wakefield on her wedding to Charles Rochemont Aikin, with a pair of chimney ornaments in the figures of two females seated with open books', vv. 5–8 (McCarthy and Kraft 2002: 151).

[100] McCarthy and Kraft 1994: 36–7; the quotation is from Barbauld's footnote.

[101] Vv. 37–40 (McCarthy and Kraft 1994: 37).

'Little *all*': the phrase captures in miniature Barbauld's characteristic juxtaposition between the big and the small. A tiny mouse makes a grand appeal for its life, appealing by a series of moralising tropes to the virtues of mercy and the community of all things. The mouse even reminds its tyrannical master that it may contain the soul of a brother, since, 'as ancient sages taught', mind shifts 'thro' matter's varying forms, / In every form the same'. Moreover, the Latin epigraph to the poem is *Parcere subiectis, et debellare superbos* ('to spare the humbled, and war down the proud'), drawn from Anchises' foundational statement of the mission of Roman civilisation in Virgil's *Aeneid* (6.853). Many scholars have observed that Barbauld's poem reaches beyond its immediate context by including words and ideas that carried particular weight in the liberal political arguments of her period, and the mouse's cry for freedom could resonate with any number of contemporary discourses: the treatment of the colonists in America, oppression of Dissenting Protestants in England, the cruelty of the slave trade (Barbauld spoke out publicly for the abolitionist cause).[102] Wollstonecraft frequently invoked the image of Rome as a mutable symbol for oppression of all kinds, describing Rome's empire endlessly reproduced in culture and society, in domestic tyranny, class oppression and national belligerence. Other writers of the eighteenth century used precisely this quotation as a positive endorsement of force: in Richardson's *Clarissa* (1747), for example, the villainous Lovelace invokes the same line of Virgil to symbolise his own imperious control, naturally stressing the second half of Anchises' injunction.[103] Barbauld, however, puts stress on the first half of the quotation. She invokes the spectre of Rome as part of a call for mercy, not control, finding within antiquity a model for her own compassionate ethical and political philosophy.

What, finally, of the 'sweetest empire' that Barbauld attributed to a woman in 'To a lady, with some painted flowers', the poem to which Wollstonecraft objected? Barbauld is not, despite Wollstonecraft's statements, legislating any general ideal for female behaviour. For readers of Virgil, the quotation from the second *Eclogue* subtly creates an imagined (or real?) context of seduction and disappointed love for the poem's praise of female delicacy and

---

[102] For political readings of the poem, see Ross 1994: 98–101, Myers 1995: 275–6.
[103] 'Many and many a pretty rogue had I spared, whom I did not spare, had my power been acknowledged and my mercy been in time implored. But the *debellare superbos* should be my motto, were I to have a new one' (Richardson 1985: 165). See Weinbrot 2005: 287: 'Lovelace images himself as the triumphant imperial state imposing its will and law.'

sweetness. In Eclogue 2, the lovelorn Corydon pledges gifts of flowers to Alexis, comparing his own rusticity to the beauty and sophistication of his beloved. Barbauld inserts herself here into the shepherd Corydon's role.[104] Once the Virgilian context is remembered, it seems impossible to imagine that Barbauld is articulating some kind of universal ideal. Indeed, the qualities for which Barbauld praises this particular lady are ones that she herself lacked. 'I know myself remarkably deficient in gracefulness of person, in my Air and manner', she wrote, 'and in the easy graces of conversation, deficient even amongst those of my own rank, much more amongst those who move in so much a higher Sphere'.[105] Whether there was any real situation behind the text or it was a teasing exercise with the erotic ambiguities of the pastoral mode, we do not know. We should leave open the possibility, though, that Barbauld is using the fragment of Virgil's homoerotic poem to give expression to a queer desire that she would have forsworn or never explicitly named in English. Far from dictating what a woman should say or do, the classical frame hints tantalisingly at what a woman might not have been able to say at all.

The 'classicising' moments of an author such as Barbauld tend to be viewed by modern critics as less connected to personal experience and less expressive of the poet herself. If we view her allusions within the contemporary cultural drama of classical education and its exclusions, though, these moments seem far less conventional and trite, and articulate something more challenging. To write in the classical mode is no withdrawal from reality. It is a demonstration of Barbauld's own passions and an expression of her identity as a learned writer. The charge of Wollstonecraft, therefore, that Barbauld had merely imitated the 'language of men', underplays the extent to which her classicising celebrates the work of having acquired that learning in the first place, and in doing so contests expectations of a 'proper' level of education for women. This is her empire. It is not a space of conquest or control. It is a space of intellectual labour, formidable challenge and hard-won achievement.

---

[104] Barbauld's desire to cast herself and her world in pastoral dress places her in the eighteenth-century culture of masquerade described by Castle 1995, which allowed for an imaginative escape from the restrictions of the self, and temporarily gave women the 'essentially masculine privilege of erotic object-choice' (p. 93). On the importance of the pastoral genre for female engagements with the classics, see Wilson 2012: 504.

[105] McCarthy 2001: 377. DeRosa 2016: 225–6 points to the prominence of imitation in the poem (the 'painted' flowers, flowers as 'emblem', the woman as 'copy') to argue that Barbauld highlights the artificiality of codes of gentility and female behaviour, making her closer in spirit to Wollstonecraft than has generally been assumed.

## Global Classics

The study of classical reception has long been envisioned as a movement beyond the study of the classical tradition. 'Tradition' – the word is formed from the Latin *tradere*, to 'hand down' – presupposes a unified body of knowledge handed down from one generation of author and artist to the next. It is easily reified: it is all too often '*the* classical tradition', a set of common values.[106] The idea of a unified Greek and Latin corpus or tradition is, as any classicist knows, a gross simplification of what was in fact a varied set of dialects and linguistic forms in antiquity, a highly dispersed array of sites of literary production, and a set of texts disparate in its ideological allegiances and ethical orientations. Tradition also implies direction. Knowledge moves from a centre (Europe) and is handed down to successive generations, which exist at an ever-increasing distance from the source. On the other hand, 'reception' as a metaphor emphasises individual encounters with antiquity. Its appeal has been to allow for a much less predictable mapping of the diffusion of Greek and Roman knowledge, so that, for example, adaptations of classical ideas in the art and literature of China, the Caribbean and Central and South America can be interpreted as equally significant visions of the ancient world. To cast such interactions as participation in a shared cultural tradition would be to misrepresent the political and aesthetic contexts in which encounters with European antiquity take place. Reception, then, usefully highlights the breaks and fissures in the history of ideas rather than a genealogy of direct descent. Yet the more diffuse and global the study of antiquity becomes, the more strain it puts in the conception of reception itself as a unified scholarly field with a common set of assumptions, shared critical touchstones and common methodological training.

In *Borges' Classics: Global Encounters with the Graeco-Roman Past* (2018), Laura Jansen sets an invigorating agenda for 'Global Classics'. A number of qualities mark this study apart from commonly accepted conventions of receptions research. First, it is decentred. It maps a new mental geography that expands beyond Europe and includes encounters with antiquity across the globe without imposing

---

[106] Cf. the force of the plurals in the title of Laird and Miller's *Antiquities and Classical Traditions in Latin America* (2018), and its opening sentence: 'Antiquities and classical traditions in Latin America are not confined to those of Greece and Rome.'

a hierarchy of centre and periphery. Instead, each site of classical allusion is its own centre, with its own 'local, multi-local and global preoccupations and goals'.[107] Second, it emphasises interactions with ancient texts and ideas in fragments rather than wholes. Allusion to isolated phrases or quotations, partial knowledge of an ancient figure or text, the juxtaposition of detached objects in radically different, local contexts – all of these represent the global experience of antiquity better than the transmission of a unified tradition or the desire to identify entirely with ancient knowledge or ideas. Third, 'Global Classics' disrupts our familiar conception of chronology. It reminds us of the co-existence of different eras of knowledge in any one particular time. This aspect of Jansen's model is particularly germane to the subject of her book, the Argentine writer Jorge Luis Borges, whose fantastic narratives create a temporal universe in which literary time often turns back on itself, inverting the usual order of original and copy.[108] This sense of temporal co-existence is equally strong in Shane Butler's conception of 'Deep Classics', which encourages us to develop a mode of reading comparable to the study of a cross-section of rock in geological research, in which the traces of different time periods appear simultaneously as a series of temporal strata. The object is not to get back to a single source or origin – a near-impossible task, since it is silted over by so many layers of classical reuse – but to incorporate the weight and expanse of those layers, as broad as they are deep, into our reading of any ancient object or text.[109]

These potential models for a future 'Global Classics' demonstrate clear affinities with other movements. The comparative study of the dynamics of Graeco-Roman literature and the literature of China, for example, has been pioneered by scholars such as Alexander Beecroft (2010) and Wiebke Denecke (2014), who stress the need to move beyond the constraints of direct influence and embrace a far more global – indeed, planetary – scope of analysis for literary interactions. This work has come not out of Classics *per se*, but out of comparative literature, and particularly from its split into World Literature, a body of critical work that seeks to avoid imposing Eurocentric theoretical paradigms, canons and chronologies on the many

---

[107] Jansen 2018: 122. Greenwood 2016: 43 proposes an 'omni-local' category for 'Greek and Roman classical texts that circulate widely in different historical and cultural contexts'; cf. Torlone, Munteanu and Dutsch 2017, who adopt Greenwood's term in their survey of Eastern and Central European receptions of classical texts (p. 10).
[108] Jansen 2018: 107–10.  [109] Butler 2016a.

various centres of global literary production.[110] As classical reception moves potentially towards 'Global Classics', it should lead us to similar questions about hierarchies of centre and periphery, the dominance of particular canons, and the prioritising of aesthetic engagements with antiquity. In this context, 'reception' itself seems increasingly an insular critical paradigm, since its use is predominant only in English-language scholarship and it is not widely recognised as a critical term in cognate fields such as English, history and film studies.[111]

There is also evidence that even scholars from other fields who *are* familiar with classical reception work are wary of some of its implicit presumptions. John Levi Barnard's *Empire of Ruin* (2018) is a particularly sophisticated and thoughtful example. His study examines the ways in which African American authors and artists from the eighteenth to the twentieth-first centuries subverted hegemonic, classicising visions of America as the 'new Rome', by insistently associating the classical legacy with slavery, decadence and ruin. These subversive strategies are partly textual and literary, as for example in the works of Phillis Wheatley, for whom 'the concept of freedom provides a center of gravity on which almost every classical reference can be grounded', and of the satirist Charles Chesnutt, who sets out to reorient the archive of Western, classical culture 'from the perspective of the oppressed and enslaved'.[112] But Barnard also studies more oblique strategies for resisting the classicising rhetoric of power in the United States, as for example when images or narratives of the kidnapping of free people to be sold in the South are juxtaposed visually or in narratives with the neoclassical Capitol building in Washington, DC.[113] At the beginning of the study, Barnard, a scholar of American literature rather than a classicist, acknowledges the foundational and important work done by classical reception scholars who have studied the pioneering careers of Black scholars, or who have explored the adaptation of Graeco-Roman texts in African American literature. But that work tends to have assumed, Barnard writes, a 'certain type of affirmative appropriative relationship between Black writers and classical tradition', focusing on the ways in which the classical tradition proved empowering or useful to writers of colour. Barnard does not doubt that Greek and Latin languages and texts sometimes held that function. His research aims to uncover, though, 'a specific and pointedly critical strain' in the adaptation of classical ideas by African American writers and artists. The subjects of his study are less

---

[110] Damrosch 2003.
[111] Willis 2018: 3, 31 remarks on the term's lack of use in an equivalent sense in other fields.
[112] Barnard 2018: 43, 121.   [113] Ibid. 69–75.

## 8 Reception

interested in participating in any classical legacy than in diagnosing the connection between neoclassical imagery and political power, the role that evocations of the ancient past played in the system that 'underlies and authorises the regime of oppression and enslavement'.[114]

In conversation, a colleague of mine once summed up the difference between our university's departments of Religion and Theology in this way: one studies religion from the outside, and the other from the inside. Does something similar exist in the division between those studying the legacy of classical texts inside and outside of Classics departments? Is classical reception studies, in other words, only for believers? The question is not meant to undermine the work done, for example, by Barbara Goff and Phiroze Vasunia on colonialism and the classical tradition – work that more than meets the call for a politically engaged classical reception studies.[115] Yet Barnard's academic self-positioning does suggest a perception, at least, that classicists' work speaks less well to those who seek to approach the same material in a more critical spirit. Examples could be added of recent books that study the appropriation of ancient ideas without identifying as works of 'classical reception' (or even using that phrase). Jared Hickman's *Black Prometheus* (2017), for example, examines how the character of Prometheus became coded as Black in abolitionist writings of the Romantic period, and how his bondage became a symbol of racial struggle. Caroline Miriam Jacobson's *Barbarous Antiquity* (2014) examines the ways in which early modern writers blend characters and motifs from classical texts with words and images drawn from trade in the Levant, thereby accentuating the 'Eastern' elements of the antique world. The fact that scholars of other disciplines are producing this invigorating work is encouraging, but why do these scholars not identify as scholars of classical reception? We should be sceptical of a field of work that encourages conversation mostly among ourselves. Is it simply a difference of classification and citation habits within different departments and fields? Does it reflect the challenges of genuine interdisciplinary conversation? Or is there an actual or perceived intellectual distinction in the work being done by classical reception scholars and work on the same legacy by scholars in other fields?

One way to lessen the risk of insularity is to encourage classicists to communicate as much as possible across disciplines, and to subject that work to refereeing processes outside the field. That would involve working not as classical reception scholars at home within that sub-discipline, but as classicists abroad, working seriously within the disciplinary frameworks of

---

[114] Ibid. 8.   [115] Goff 2005; Vasunia 2013.

medieval studies, Romanticism, critical theory, film studies and so on. It is hard work. Testing the credibility of one's findings against scholarship in different fields is a high bar, in part because it necessitates learning new scholarly conventions and new bodies of scholarship as well as surmounting the initiation rituals of a new field. It also takes time, and any investment of time in a particular area of research without 'output' entails considerable risk in the modern academy. Ruby Blondell makes a similar point in relation to the study of Classics and film:

> Few classicists have the leisure to acquire real expertise in even one of the many fields bearing on the interpretation of screen texts (fields including not only cinema and television studies but the study of twentieth and twenty-first century social history and popular culture); but this does not free us from the obligation to approach such texts, as best we can, on their own terms, and not just as comparanda for ancient narratives. (Blondell 2016: 283)

If we are working on post-classical periods and media, our work has to speak to specialists in those fields, and be judged credible by them.[116] By engaging deeply and seriously with work outside of Classics, we stand a chance of gaining an audience outside the field. We also stand to transform the centre and periphery of Classics itself, reconceptualising work on Latin literature in later periods as part of the core of the discipline.[117] An investment in serious work in other scholarly areas can help expand ideas of what the field as a whole can and should do.

One potential aspect of that interdisciplinary work, and one illustrated in this chapter's final case study, is a movement away from aesthetic receptions, and an emphasis instead on more varied uses and reuses of ancient texts in different discourses. The transformation of ideas from Roman literature in scientific texts, for example, is a necessary and established element of Neo-Latin;[118] and the boom in work on Lucretius by scholars of the Renaissance and the Enlightenment is a promising expansion of attention.[119] Yet the study of the transformation of Roman literature in later mathematical, astronomical, philosophical and medical thought has stayed on the outskirts

---

[116] Martindale 2006: 9: 'Research on, say, the Victorians must be credible to Victorianists as well as classicists.' Cf. Keen 2018, writing both as a classicist and a scholar of science fiction: it is 'possible to be credible as both – but the work has to be done' (p. 14).

[117] As Güthenke and Holmes 2018 helpfully observe, the ideal of complete competence in all of classical literature and its afterlife is impractical. Instead, each scholar should work to bring different points of knowledge into productive contact, as part of a network rather than a 'self-constituting whole' (p. 70).

[118] See Haskell 2005, for example, for an overview of the neo-Latin didactic poem as a pervasive early modern form of information technology.

[119] So, e.g., Greenblatt 2011; Passannante 2011; Kramnick 2012.

of classical reception studies, which still tends to be conceptualised primarily around aesthetic interactions with antiquity. Classical 'reception' is, again, an uneasy heading for this sort of work, if it implies that the receiving of ancient literary texts was these writers' primary goal. To study classical allusions in scientific or philosophical texts is to analyse the routes through which an author has travelled to arrive at somewhere new entirely. Yet by continuing to broaden the range of texts studied by classicists – with diligent attention to critical work on those texts by scholars in other disciplines – classicists can show how widespread Greek and Latin was as a conceptual resource for writers and artists. The benefit is a global vision not only of classical material, but of the range of opportunity of our own work.

### Case Study 3: Erasmus Darwin

When Erasmus Darwin published *The Loves of Plants* (1789), an exuberant versification of Linnaeus' sexual system of plant classification, he explicitly cast the poem as Ovid's *Metamorphoses* in reverse. The Roman poet had transformed gods and humans into plants. Darwin, however, would give poetic life to vegetation, visualising their vibrant world of promiscuous eroticism. His grandson, Charles Darwin, would later quote a journal entry written by his grandfather at age sixteen, in which he says that his journal is so stuffed full of Greek and Latin 'translation, verses, themes' that it would be 'perfectly unintelligible to any but Schoolboys' (another telling reflection of the gender division underlying classical education), and *The Loves of Plants* is certainly an extraordinary chapter in the reception of Ovid's poem.[120] But Darwin's use of antiquity is fundamentally forward-looking. He aims not to encourage rereading of Ovid, or to help readers see what was already there in the original poem. He uses the ancient models to illustrate and generate new knowledge, enlisting, according to his poem's advertisement, 'Imagination under the banner of Science'. Darwin consistently emphasises the inadequacy of the poetic imagination to describe the reality of his observations, recalling the memory of myths and characters only to expose their imprecision as a means of describing the natural world. While *The Loves of Plants* luxuriates in the licensed eroticism of Ovidian myth, this grand and bizarre poem is premised above all on the *mismatch* between myth and science – a mismatch which, for Darwin, is the vital seed of modernity itself.

As well as cataloguing the different reproductive processes of his plants, the 1700-line poem also includes descriptions of recent discoveries in physics

---

[120] Cited in Hassler 1973: 29.

and engineering, anecdotes drawn from historical and travel narratives, a series of prose interludes theorising about the relationship between poetry and other arts, and a rousing indictment of the slave trade, all supplemented by Darwin's loquacious footnotes and endnotes. The 'love' of the poem's title is between the male (stamen) and the female (pistil) parts of the plant. Since Linnaeus' classes were based upon the number and position of stamens in each plant – anywhere between one and twenty (or more) – it is easy for Darwin to turn plant reproduction into a sex comedy. *Genista* or dyer's broom, for example, has ten stamens and one pistil, so Darwin writes: 'sweet blooms GENISTA in the myrtle shade, / and *ten* fond brothers woo the haughty maid'.[121] Linnaeus' *Systema Naturae* was written, of course, in Latin, and the classicising imagery of *The Loves of Plants* is no doubt inspired partly by the references to the ancient pantheon in that work.[122] Thus Galatea, riding a dolphin and inspiring love from all who see her, is used to describe the movement of seaweed spores.[123] The Adonis genus of plants, each flower of which contains many stamens and pistils, is the site of a wild, promiscuous 'marriage', presided over by the god Hymen ('As round his shrine the gaudy circles bow, / and seal with muttering lips the faithless vow').[124] These sexual aspects of botany were profoundly disturbing to conservative readers, especially because flowers and plants had traditionally been coded as feminine spheres of knowledge. The conservative polemicist Thomas James Mathias claimed that Darwin's poems 'debauched' their (implicitly female) readers, seducing them 'in filmy, gawzy, gossamer lines, / With lucid language, and most dark designs'.[125]

Indeed, Darwin's proem seems calculated to generate moral alarm. The voice of the proem flits from *persona* to *persona*, hovering over an ambiguous and ever-changing space. At first he is a hawker advertising a magic trick to a reader and ushering us into some magical space, an 'inchanted garden'. Then the space we are led to imagine is a woman's boudoir (a 'lady's dressing-room'); the poet is a pimp, comparing the plants in his poem to a series of beautiful women he has invited the reader (a man, or still a woman?) to admire. I print

---

[121] Darwin 1789: 5. On Linnaeus' sexual system, see Morton 1981: 268–9. It is currently replaced by the so-called Angiosperm Phylogeny Group (APG) system of plant classification.
[122] Heller 1945 and 1971. Haskell 2013 is an innovative account of the 'Latin Enlightenment', the understudied network of scientists, philosophers and theologians communicating in Latin throughout Europe in the eighteenth century. See further Haskell in this volume.
[123] Canto 1.354–72 (Darwin 1789: 34–6); cf. Ovid, *Met.* 13.738–879.
[124] Canto 4.387–406 (Darwin 1789: 164–5).
[125] Mathias 1798: 56–7. He claimed that the poem was decadent in both style and content; it 'is to England', he wrote, 'what Seneca's prose was to Rome'.

the entirety of the proem here, complete with Darwin's quirky, excitable typography:

> GENTLE READER!
> Lo, here a CAMERA OBSCURA is presented to thy view, in which are lights and shades dancing on a whited canvas, and magnified into apparent life – if thou art perfectly at leisure for such trivial amusement, walk in, and view the wonders of my INCHANTED GARDEN.
> Whereas P. OVIDIUS NASO, a great Necromancer in the famous Court of AUGUSTUS, did by art poetic transmute Men, Women, and even Gods and Goddesses into Trees and Flowers; I have undertaken by similar art to restore some of them to their original animality, after having remained prisoners so long in their respective vegetable mansions; and have here exhibited them before thee. Which thou may'st contemplate as diverse little pictures suspended over the chimney of a Lady's dressing-room, *connected only by a slight festoon of ribbons*. And which, though thou may'st not be acquainted with the originals, may amuse thee by the beauty of their persons, their graceful attitudes, or the brilliancy of their dress.
> FAREWELL[126]

In the middle is Ovid. The erotic aspects of the scene fit his reputation well: he is, after all, the poet not only of the *Metamorphoses* but of the *Ars amatoria* and the *Amores*, and would be the 'tutor' of Byron's Don Juan.[127] The wondrous reversal of Ovid in *The Loves of Plants* is likened in the proem to the experience of the camera obscura, a staple of early modern optic technology, in which an observer looks through a peephole lens in a darkened room and sees an image inverted on a screen. As Priestman (2013: 49) observes, the description of Ovid as a 'necromancer' in Augustus' court conjures a sense of 'fairytale wonder rather than the weary recognition of the site most often visited in any well-to-do boy's classical education'. The comparison with the camera obscura also gives the ancient text a startlingly new frame. In one of the literary-critical interludes in the poem, Darwin further likens the structure of Ovid's *Metamorphoses* to the fashion of the 'show box', a miniature moving panorama, in which a strip of prints was wound on rollers so that the viewer could scroll through them, and the images appeared to move sequentially before the viewer's eyes.[128] The comparison with these illusionistic technologies suggests a particularly modern vision of Ovid's antique epic. Its ever-moving

---

[126] Darwin 1789: v–vii; on this proem, Priestman 2013: 46–50.   [127] Vance 1988: 217.
[128] Darwin 1789: 83: the images 'succeed each other amusingly enough, like prints of the London Cries, wraped [*sic*] upon rollers, with a glass before them. In this at least they resemble the monsters in Ovid's *Metamorphoses*' An example of the sort of object Darwin describes is in the Cotsen Children's Library at Princeton: https://blogs.princeton.edu/cotsen/2016/09/curators-choice-a-moving-panorama-of-london-cries/.

mythological narratives are imagined as discontinuous, flickering images, flashes of imagination rather than legacies of tradition or learning.

When Darwin is describing each particular plant, his allusions to Ovid do not depend on any one-to-one correspondence between natural processes and classical myth. Instead he moves by a chain of loosely connected imagery rather than strict logic, allowing his reader's memory to fill in the gaps. When he comes to madder (*Rubia tinctorum*), for example, Darwin compares the colour of the roots to a witch stirring up magic in her cauldron ('With nice selection modest RUBIA blends, / Her vermil dyes, and o'er the cauldron blends').[129] The roots were cultivated for their red colour, which, Darwin tells us, will stain the bones of pigs or chickens red if they feed on the plant. Darwin then imagines men dying a white fleece red; a sexual image, since these 'four favour'd youths' represent the four stamens of the madder reproducing with the one pistil.[130] Finally, the combination of witch and fleece leads the poet to Medea, and he pauses to retell in nine lines Ovid's account of Medea boiling the body of Aeson in her cauldron in order to rejuvenate him.[131] Why Medea? The associative connections are never particularly tight. We might be tempted to look for some sophisticated allusion to the herbs and other plants mentioned by Ovid in his narrative, but a more childlike delight in the sound of the words – madder/Medea – is likely Darwin's launching point. Nonetheless, the sinister associations of the Medea character do lead Darwin to a new and different conception of the plant's physical structure. In a discursive note at the bottom of the page, he speculates about why plants grow substances of particular colours, since they appear to be unrelated to the aim of camouflage in the colour patterns of animals. He postulates that they could instead serve as a weapon. 'The colouring materials of vegetables … seem given to it as a defence against the depredations of insects or other animals, to whom these materials are nauseous or deleterious.' Although he personifies the madder plant initially as 'modest', blushing and beautiful, the imagistic connection to the sinister witch Medea seems to lead to a new botanical theory: her dyes are poisons. In later poems, Darwin articulated the idea that ancient myths could be read allegorically, as describing or predicting scientific theories.[132] Here there is no clear sense of whether myth or theory is logically

---

[129] *Canto* 1.321–2 (Darwin 1789: 31).
[130] *Canto* 1.325 (Darwin 1789: 31). The sexual overtones of the colour combination of red and white are familiar from the *Metamorphoses*: Rhorer 1980.
[131] *Canto* 1.329–38 (Darwin 1789: 32); cf. Ovid, *Met.* 7.159–293.   [132] Priestman 2013: 141–3.

prior. The poet dramatises the two emerging together, and moving, in no precise or complete fashion, towards clarity.[133]

Medea returns later in the poem in Darwin's description of the *Impatiens* (touch-me-not) genus, which shoots its seed capsules in a process botanists call 'explosive dehiscence'. Darwin writes:

> With fierce distracted eye IMPATIENS stands,
> Swells her pale cheeks, and brandishes her hands,
> With rage and hate the astonish'd groves alarms,
> And hurls her infants from her frantic arms.[134]

The image of infanticide leads once more to Medea. This time Darwin tells her entire narrative – exile from native soil, jealousy and murder of Creusa, inner struggle and then killing of her children, escape on the winged chariot – across forty-four lines of gaudy, grandiose verse, not sparing readers her story's horrors:

> Thrice with parch'd lips her guiltless babes she press'd,
> And thrice she clasp'd them to her tortur'd breast;
> Awhile with white uplifted eyes she stood,
> Then plunged her trembling poynards in their blood.[135]

In one of his literary-critical prose interludes in *The Loves of Plants*, Darwin had discussed the line between the Tragic and the Horrid, and his expatiation on the Medea story reads as an exemplification of his literary ideas. Like any good tragedian, he can evoke 'distress' in his audience through horrid scenes, but also mingle 'the bitter cup of true Tragedy with some sweet consolatory drops' of pity, endearing his audience to the tragic heroine while at the same time inspiring pleasure in their knowledge that 'the scenery is not real', and they can awake from the scene as 'from a distressful dream'.[136] What about the seed capsules? Given that explosive dehiscence is a biological means of increasing the chance of plant reproduction, no reader can fail to notice that Medea's infanticide is a very vague analogy. Yet here too the inexactness is the point, since Darwin draws a line between the free semantic play of Imagination and the necessary precision of Science. If a poet's simile too exactly resembles its subject, he says, then it becomes 'ratiocination', systematic reasoning, and it has lost the picturesque quality that makes it poetry.[137]

---

[133] Ascribing a precise cause to this phenomenon of protective colouration would become a prominent point of argument in the evolutionary debates of the nineteenth century: Evans 1965.
[134] *Canto* 3.131–4 (Darwin 1789: 98–9). [135] *Canto* 3.167–70 (Darwin 1789: 101).
[136] Darwin 1789: 86–7.
[137] Ibid. 84; cf. Priestman 2013: 48 on Darwin's gendered dichotomy between 'loosely dressed Imagination and strict reason'.

Just so, the 'monsters of Ovid's *Metamorphoses* have entertained the world for many centuries', despite their deviation from nature as we know it.[138] Darwin may enlist Imagination under the banner of Science, but the distance between the two remains one of his basic principles.

If one of the tasks of reception studies is to ask what role the Classics have played in various later cultures and eras, texts like *The Loves of Plants* can help to diversify our answers. In part, the appeals to classical mythology have the same benefit as appeals to botany in the Romantic era: they allow a writer to explore modes of sexuality that would otherwise have been taboo in eighteenth-century society. Darwin's never-ending array of Naiads and Nymphs create an imagined world of eternal erotic opportunity – a timeless place that exists seductively alongside modern conventions and restraints. It was always possible to step out sideways into that parallel universe and explore modes of coupling otherwise forbidden by the moral policing of contemporary society. The fact that Darwin presents his poem both as an inversion of Ovid's *Metamorphoses* and as like the 'diverse little pictures' of a 'Lady's dressing-room' also suggests that, despite the gendering of classical education in the period that restricted formal instruction of Latin in schools to boys – or because of it? – Ovid too could represent what was forbidden and erotic. When you have made your way inside Naso's 'inchanted garden', through the gates and into its inner sanctum, there is Latin. Not the dead matter of schoolboys' lessons but the mystic medium of the necromancer's art, Latin literature too was able to conjure the fantasy of an eroticised ancient past.

The links drawn in *The Loves of Plants* between biology and metamorphosis are part of a long line of scientific thought. Goethe came independently to plants through Ovid in his didactic poem *Die Metamorphose der Pflanzen* (1790), although later he eagerly read Darwin's works.[139] In later eras, Marjorie Garber has explored the persistence with which writers – beginning with Erasmus' grandson Charles – cast evolutionary theory as a mode of metamorphosis. In order to communicate the ideas of evolution, scientists and poets drew connections between the processes of evolutionary adaptation and the much faster and externally imposed transformations described in Ovid's epic.[140] When we study classical reception in texts like these, we are not observing a backwards glance towards the past. We study

---

[138] Darwin 1789: 50.
[139] King-Hele 1986: 169–71. On the conceptual indebtedness to Ovid in Goethe's poem, Pfau 2010.
[140] Garber 2017: 23–6. See also Beer 2009: 104, who nonetheless draws an important distinction: while Ovidian metamorphosis is premised on the eternal transformation of matter from one thing into another, evolution inevitably involves extinction.

the role of Greece and Rome in looking forward, in the discovery of something new in society, in the universe or in ourselves.

## Conclusion

Too often reception study is given a marginal or secondary position in the discipline, but its call to explore and interrogate the connections between ancient texts and broader historical systems is crucial to the future of Classics. Ideally reception would not be seen as a field or subfield at all, but simply a way of doing work on ancient texts, a mode of scholarship that is conscious of its own situatedness in history and ideology, the cultural forces implicated in the transmission of ancient ideas, and the impact that Greek and Roman culture has had on the private and public lives of others. In this chapter I have suggested a number of ways that we might go about this sort of study: by balancing reception with resistance and challenge in our analyses of later references to the antique world; by 'reading for exclusion', drawing out a story about classical education from each allusion to a Latin or Greek text; and by embracing a vision of 'Global Classics', challenging straightforward notions of centre and periphery in understanding the circulation of ideas.

As I have suggested throughout this chapter, though, the word 'reception' itself has certain limitations, and its origins in the hermeneutical tradition lie at an oblique angle to the field as it has developed. Which word is better? While reception has largely been favoured by contemporary scholars over the 'classical tradition' because that phrase imposes a false unity on a heterogeneous group of texts, and because it implicitly limits our focus to the study of those regions and cultures in which Greece and Rome did indeed congeal into a coherent tradition, the phrase does make more transparent the power dynamics involved in an individual person invoking a set of texts and ideas that have accrued historical and cultural weight.[141] Terms like 'appropriation' and 'use' are also useful if they allow an ethical component in analyses of cases in which Greeks and Roman texts have been manipulated for pernicious political or moral ends, although, as Basil Dufallo (2018: 13) notes, such judgements are necessarily tied to our own position in time and ideology: 'nothing prevents today's "use" from becoming tomorrow's "abuse", and vice versa'. Ultimately, though, the search for one single word to cover such a diverse set of cultural phenomena is misleading, especially if it suggests the existence of some *essence* unique to

[141] See e.g. Goff 2005: 9 on the study of classical texts in African education systems, where 'Latin is simply one more language'. Silk, Gildenhard and Barrow 2014 retain 'tradition' over 'reception' but for a quite different reason, arguing that 'reception' is insufficiently expressive of the value accorded to Greece and Rome (pp. 5, 217–23).

the Greek and Roman past, some exceptional quality that distinguishes allusion to those cultures from references to ancient and authoritative traditions in other parts of the world. The provocation of work in this area lies precisely in its ability to connect us to other histories, other knowledge. Rather than somehow diluting or compromising the 'core' linguistic and interpretive skills of a classicist, we are reminded of the capacity of those skills to travel – so long as classicists have the humility and diligence to learn the principles of the new field first. Ultimately, the institutional success of reception as a name for this work may have held out an illusory promise of its equal ability to describe the range of our potential research. Rather than searching for a label or a theory that would capture any essence of Greek and Roman antiquity in later eras, perhaps it is time to embrace the area's promise of diversity and emphasise difference.

## References

Aikin, L., ed. (1825) *The Works of Anna Laetitia Barbauld*, 2 vols., London.
Archibald, E. P., W. Brockliss and J. Gnoza, eds. (2015) *Learning Latin and Greek from Antiquity to the Present*, Cambridge.
Ayres, P. (1997) *Classical Culture and the Idea of Rome in Eighteenth-Century England*, Cambridge.
Bakogianni, A. (2018) 'Classical reception for all? Performance pedagogy in the twenty-first century', *CW* 112: 615–26.
Balmer, J. (2012) 'Handbags and gladrags: a woman in transgression, reflecting', *Classical Receptions Journal* 4: 261–71.
Barbauld, A. L. (1773) *Poems*, London.
  (1826) *A Legacy for Young Ladies*, London.
Barnard, J. L. (2018) *Empire of Ruin: Black Classicism and American Imperial Culture*, Oxford.
Batstone, W. (2006) 'Provocation: the point of reception theory', in Martindale and Thomas 2006, 14–20.
Beecroft, A. (2010) *Authorship and Cultural Identity in Early Greece and China*, Cambridge.
Beer, G. (2009) *Darwin's Plots: Evolutionary Narrative in Darwin, George Eliot, and Nineteenth-Century Fiction*, 3rd edn, Cambridge.
Bennett, P. (1998) 'Phillis Wheatley's vocation and the paradox of the "Afric muse"', *Publications of the Modern Language Association* 113: 64–76.
Blondell, R. (2016) 'Classics and cinema', *CR* 66: 282–4.
Boswell, J. (1887) *The Life of Samuel Johnson* (ed. G. B. Hill), 6 vols., New York.
Bruns, G. L. (1992) *Hermeneutics Ancient and Modern*, New Haven.
Burke, E. (1993) *Reflections on the Revolution in France* (ed. J. G. Mitchell), Oxford.

(2015) *A Philosophical Enquiry into the Origin of Our Ideas of the Sublime and Beautiful* (ed. P. Guyer), Oxford.
Burton, D., S. Perris and J. Tatum, eds. (2017) *Athens to Aotearoa: Greece and Rome in New Zealand Literature and Society*, Wellington.
Butler, M. (1984) *Burke, Paine, Godwin, and the Revolution Controversy*, Cambridge.
(2015) *Mapping Mythologies: Countercurrents in Eighteenth-Century Poetry and Cultural History*, Cambridge.
Butler, S. (2015) *The Ancient Phonograph*, New York.
(2016a) 'Introduction: on the origin of "Deep Classics"', in Butler 2016b, 1–19.
Butler, S., ed. (2016b) *Deep Classics: Rethinking Classical Reception*, London.
Castle, T. (1995) *The Female Thermometer: Eighteenth-Century Culture and the Invention of the Uncanny*, New York.
Code, L. (2003a) 'Introduction: why feminists do not read Gadamer', in Code 2003b, 1–36.
Code, L., ed. (2003b) *Feminist Interpretations of Hans-Georg Gadamer*, University Park, PA.
Cook, W. and J. Tatum (2010) *African American Writers and Classical Tradition*, Chicago.
Cox, F. (2018) *Ovid's Presence in Contemporary Women's Writing: Strange Monsters*, Oxford.
Culhed, S. S. and M. Malm, eds. (2018) *Reading Late Antiquity*, Heidelberg.
Culler, J. (1982) *On Deconstruction: Theory and Criticism after Structuralism*, Ithaca, NY.
Damrosch, D. (2003) *What Is World Literature?*, Princeton.
Darwin, E. (1789) *The Botanic Garden, Part II: Containing The Loves of the Plants*, London.
Denecke, W. (2014) *Classical World Literatures: Sino-Japanese and Greco-Roman Comparisons*, Oxford.
DeRosa, R. (2016) 'A criticism of contradiction: Anna Leticia Barbauld and the "problem" of nineteenth-century women's writing', in S. Shifrin, ed., *Women as Sites of Culture: Women's Roles in Cultural Formation from the Renaissance to the Twentieth Century* (London), 221–32.
Dufallo, B. (2018) 'Introduction: "Roman error", dangerous and inspiring', in B. Dufallo, ed., *Roman Error: Classical Reception and the Problem of Rome's Flaws* (Oxford), 1–14.
Eden, K. (1997) *Hermeneutics and the Rhetorical Tradition: Chapters in the Ancient Legacy and Its Humanist Reception*, New Haven.
Evans, M. A. (1965) 'Mimicry and the Darwinian heritage', *JHI* 26: 211–20.
Evans, R. (2014) *Reception History, Tradition, and Biblical Interpretation: Gadamer and Jauss in Current Practice*, London.
Fertik, H. and M. Hanses (2019) 'Above the veil: revisiting the classicism of W. E. B. Dubois', *IJCT* 26: 1–9.
Fish, S. E. (1981) 'Why no one's afraid of Wolfgang Iser', *Diacritics* 11: 2–13.

Fleming, M. (2003) 'Gadamer's conversation: does the other have a say?', in Code 2003b, 109–32.
Fletcher, K. F. B. and O. Umurhan, eds. (2019) *Classical Antiquity in Heavy Metal Music*, London.
Formisano, M. and C. S. Kraus, eds. (2018) *Marginality, Canonicity, Passion*, Oxford.
Formisano, M. and T. Fuhrer, eds. (2014) *Décadence: 'Decline and Fall' or 'Other Antiquity'?*, Heidelberg.
Fredericksen, E. (2015) 'Finding another Alexis: pastoral tradition and the reception of Vergil's second *Eclogue*', *Classical Receptions Journal* 7: 422–41.
Freund, E. (1987) *The Return of the Reader: Reader-Response Criticism*, London.
Friedman, R. (2013) 'A reformed classical pedagogy', *Classical Receptions Journal* 5: 226–37.
Gadamer, H.-G. (2004) *Truth and Method*, 2nd revised edn (trans. J. Weinsheimer and D. G. Marshall), London.
Garber, M. (2017) *The Muses on Their Lunch Hour*, New York.
Goff, B., ed. (2005) *Classics and Colonialism*, London.
Goldhill, S. (2002) *Who Needs Greek? Contests in the Cultural History of Hellenism*, Cambridge.
Goldschmidt, N. (2019) *Afterlives of the Roman Poets: Biofiction and the Reception of Latin Poetry*, Cambridge.
Goldschmidt, N. and B. Graziosi, eds. (2018) *Tombs of the Ancient Poets: Between Literary Reception and Material Culture*, Oxford.
Greenblatt, S. (2011) *The Swerve: How the World Became Modern*, New York.
Greene, R. (2013) *Five Words: Critical Semantics in the Age of Shakespeare and Cervantes*, Chicago.
Greenwood, E. (2016) 'Reception studies: the cultural mobility of Classics', *Daedalus* 145: 41–9.
Güthenke, C. and B. Holmes (2018) 'Hyperinclusivity, hypercanonicity, and the future of the field', in Formisano and Kraus 2018, 57–74.
Habermas, J. (1985) 'On hermeneutics' claim to universality', in K. Mueller-Vollmer, ed., *The Hermeneutics Reader* (New York), 294–319.
  (1989) *The Structural Transformation of the Public Sphere: An Inquiry into a Category of Bourgeois Society* (trans. T. Burger), Cambridge, MA.
Hall, E. and H. Stead (2015) 'Introduction', in Stead and Hall 2015, 1–19.
Hardie, P. (1993) *The Epic Successors of Virgil: A Study in the Dynamics of a Tradition*, Cambridge.
  (2009) *Lucretian Receptions: History, the Sublime, Knowledge*, Cambridge.
  (2013) '*Redeeming the Text*, reception studies, and the Renaissance', *Classical Receptions Journal* 5: 190–8.
Hardwick, L. (2003) *Reception Studies*, Cambridge.
  (2011) 'Fuzzy connections: classical texts and modern poetry in English', in J. Parker and T. Matthews, eds., *Tradition, Translation, Trauma: The Classics and the Modern* (Oxford), 39–60.
Harloe, K. (2010) 'Can political theory provide a model for reception? Max Weber and Hannah Arendt', *Cultural Critique* 74: 17–31.

Harrison, S. (2007) *Generic Enrichment in Vergil and Horace*, Oxford.
Haskell, Y. (2005) 'Didac-tech? Prolegomena to the early modern poetry of information', in S. Zielinski and S. M. Wagnermaier, eds., *Variantology 1. On Deep Time Relations of Arts, Sciences and Technologies* (Cologne), 209–22.
  (2013) *Prescribing Ovid: The Latin Works and Networks of the Enlightened Dr Heerkens*, London.
Hassler, D. M. (1973) *Erasmus Darwin*, New York.
Heller, J. L. (1945) 'Classical mythology in the *Systema Naturae* of Linnaeus', *TAPhA* 76: 333–57.
  (1971) 'Classical poetry in the *Systema naturae* of Linnaeus', *TAPhA* 102: 183–216.
Hickman, J. (2017) *Black Prometheus: Race and Radicalism in the Age of Atlantic Slavery*, Oxford.
Hinds, S. (1998) *Allusion and Intertext: Dynamics of Appropriation in Roman Poetry*, Cambridge.
Hobbes, T. (1996) *Leviathan* (ed. R. Tuck), Cambridge.
Hodkinson, O. and H. Lovatt, eds. (2018) *Classical Reception and Children's Literature: Greece, Rome and Childhood Transformation*, London.
Holub, R. (1984) *Reception Theory: A Critical Introduction*, London.
Hurst, I. (2006) *Victorian Women Writers and the Classics*, Oxford.
Iser, W. (1974) *The Implied Reader: Patterns of Communication in Prose Fiction from Bunyan to Beckett*, Baltimore.
Jacobson, M. I. (2014) *Barbarous Antiquity: Reorienting the Past in the Poetry of Early Modern England*, Philadelphia.
Jansen, L. (2018) *Borges' Classics: Global Encounters with the Graeco-Roman Past*, Cambridge.
Jauss, H. R. (1980) 'Esthétique de la réception et communication littéraire', in Z. Kostantinovic, M. Naumann and H. R. Jauss, eds., *Literary Communication and Reception: Proceedings of the IXth Congress of the International Comparative Literature Association* (Innsbruck), 15–26.
  (1982) *Toward an Aesthetic of Reception* (trans. T. Bahti), Minneapolis.
Jeffreys, P. (2015) *Reframing Decadence: C. P. Cavafy's Imaginary Portraits*, Ithaca, NY.
Johnson, M., ed. (2019) *Antipodean Antiquities: Classical Reception Down Under*, London.
Keen, T. (2018) 'More "T" vicar? Revisiting models and methodologies for classical receptions in science fiction', in Rogers and Stevens 2018, 9–17.
Keith, A. B., ed. (1922) *Speeches and Documents on Indian Policy 1750–1921*, 2 vols., Oxford.
Kennedy, D. F. (1993) *The Arts of Love: Five Studies in the Discourse of Roman Love Elegy*, Cambridge.
King-Hele, D. (1986) *Erasmus Darwin and the Romantic Poets*, New York.
Kramnick, J. B. (1999) *Making the English Canon: Print-Capitalism and the Cultural Past, 1700–1779*, Cambridge.
  (2012) 'Living with Lucretius', in H. Deutsch and M. Terrall, eds., *Vital Matters: Eighteenth-Century Views of Conception* (Berkeley), 13–38.

Laird, A. and N. Miller, eds. (2018) *Antiquities and Classical Traditions in Latin America*, Chichester.
Leigh, M. (2016) 'Vergil's second *Eclogue* and the class struggle', *CPh* 111: 406–33.
Litvin, M. (2011) *Hamlet's Arab Journey: Shakespeare's Prince and Nasser's Ghost*, Princeton.
Lowe, D. and K. Shahabudin, eds. (2009) *Classics for All: Reworking Antiquity in Mass Culture*, Cambridge.
Martindale, C. (1993) *Redeeming the Text: Latin Poetry and the Hermeneutics of Reception*, Cambridge.
  (2005) *Latin Poetry and the Judgement of Taste: An Essay in Aesthetics*, Oxford.
  (2006) 'Introduction: thinking through reception', in Martindale and Thomas 2006, 1–13.
  (2013) 'Reception – a new humanism? Receptivity, pedagogy, the transhistorical', *Classical Receptions Journal* 5: 169–83.
McCarthy, W. (2001) 'Why Anna Letitia Barbauld refused to head a women's college: new facts, new story', *Nineteenth-Century Contexts* 23: 349–79.
McCarthy, W. and E. Kraft (1994) *The Poems of Anna Letitia Barbauld*, Athens and London.
  (2002) *Anna Letitia Barbauld: Selected Poetry and Prose*, Peterborough, ON.
McElduff, S. (2006) 'Fractured understandings: towards a history of classical reception among non-elite groups', in Martindale and Thomas 2006, 180–91.
Martyn, J. (1749) *Pub. Virgilii Maronis opera*, London.
Mathias, T. J. (1798) *The Pursuits of Literature: A Satirical Poem*, 7th edn, London.
Matzner, S. (2016) 'Queer unhistoricism: scholars, metalepsis, and interventions of the unruly past', in Butler 2016b, 179–201.
Morley, N. (2018) *Classics: Why It Matters*, Cambridge.
Morton, A. G. (1981) *History of Botanical Science*, London.
Myers, M. (1995) 'Of mice and mothers: Mrs. Barbauld's "New Walk" and gendered codes in children's literature', in L. W. Phelps and J. A. Emig, eds., *Feminine Principles and Women's Experience in American Composition and Rhetoric* (Pittsburgh), 255–88.
Norman, L. (2011) *The Shock of the Ancient: Literature and History in Early Modern France*, Chicago.
Ong, W. J. (1959) 'Latin language study as a Renaissance puberty rite', *SPh* 56: 103–24.
O'Rourke, D. (2017) 'Hospitality narratives in Virgil and Callimachus: the ideology of reception', *Classical Receptions Journal* 63: 118–42.
Orrells, D. (2011) *Classical Culture and Modern Masculinity*, Oxford.
Palmer, R. T. (1969) *Hermeneutics: Interpretation Theory in Schleiermacher, Dilthey, Heidegger, and Gadamer*, Evanston, IL.
Parker, G., ed. (2017) *South Africa, Greece, Rome: Classical Confrontations*, Cambridge.
Passannante, G. (2011) *The Lucretian Renaissance: Philology and the Afterlife of Tradition*, Chicago.
Paulson, R. (1983) *Representations of Revolution (1789–1820)*, New Haven, CT.
Pennington, M. (1807) *Memoirs of the Life of Mrs. Elizabeth Carter*, London.

Pfau, T. (2010) '"All is leaf": difference, metamorphosis, and Goethe's phenomenology of knowledge', *Studies in Romanticism* 49: 3–41.
Porter, J. I. (2008) 'Reception studies: future prospects', in L. Hardwick and C. Stray eds., *A Companion to Classical Receptions* (Malden, MA), 469–81.
  (2018) 'Homer in the gutter: from Samuel Butler to the Second Sophistic and back again', in Formisano and Kraus 2018, 231–62.
Priestman, M. (2013) *The Poetry of Erasmus Darwin: Enlightened Spaces, Romantic Times*, London.
Prins, Y. (2017) *Ladies' Greek: Victorian Translations of Tragedy*, Princeton.
Rankine, P. (2019) 'The Classics, race, and community-engaged or public scholarship', *AJPh* 140: 345–59.
Renger, A.-B. and X. Fan, eds. (2019) *Receptions of Greek and Roman Antiquity in East Asia*, Leiden.
Rezek, J. (2020) 'Transatlantic traffic: Phillis Wheatley and her books', in D. S. Lynch and A. Gillespie, eds., *The Unfinished Book* (Oxford), 288–302.
Rhorer, C. C. (1980) 'Red and white in Ovid's *Metamorphoses:* the mulberry tree in the tale of Pyramus and Thisbe', *Ramus* 9: 79–88.
Richardson, E. (2013) *Classical Victorians: Scholars, Scoundrels, and Generals in Pursuit of Antiquity*, Cambridge.
Richardson, L. (2017) 'Teaching the classical reception "revolution"', *Council of University Classical Departments Bulletin* 46 (n.pag.).
Richardson, S. (1985) *Clarissa, or the History of a Young Lady* (ed. A. Ross), Harmondsworth.
Rogers, B. R. and B. E. Stevens, eds. (2015) *Classical Traditions in Science Fiction*, Oxford.
  (2017) *Classical Traditions in Modern Fantasy*, Oxford.
  (2018) *Once and Future Antiquities in Science Fiction and Fantasy*, London.
Ross, M. B. (1994) 'Configurations of feminine reform: the woman writer and the tradition of dissent', in C. S. Wilson and J. Haefner, eds., *Re-envisioning Romanticism: British Women Writers, 1776–1837* (Philadelphia), 91–110.
Sachs, J. (2010) *Romantic Antiquity: Rome in the British Imagination, 1789–1832*, Oxford.
Sapiro, V. (1992) *The Vindication of Political Virtue: The Political Theory of Mary Wollstonecraft*, Chicago.
Scarborough, W. S. (2005) *The Autobiography of William Sanders Scarborough: An American Journey from Slavery to Scholarship* (ed. M. Ronnick), Detroit.
Sharrock, A. (2018) 'How do we read a (w)hole? Dubious first thoughts on the cognitive turn', in S. Harrison, S. Frangoulidis and T. D. Papanghelis, eds., *Intratextuality and Latin Literature* (Berlin), 15–34.
Silk, M., I. Gildenhard and R. Barrow (2014) *The Classical Tradition: Art, Literature, Thought*, Chichester.
Skinner, Q. (2008) *Hobbes and Republican Liberty*, Cambridge.
Squire, M. (2015) 'Theories of reception', in C. Marconi, ed., *The Oxford Handbook of Greek and Roman Art and Architecture* (Oxford), 637–61.

Stead, H. and E. Hall, eds. (2015) *Greek and Roman Classics in the British Struggle for Social Reform*, London.
Stevenson, J. (2015) 'Women writers and the Classics', in P. Cheney and P. Hardie, eds., *The Oxford History of Classical Reception in English Literature, Vol. 2 (1558–1660)* (Oxford), 129–46.
Stray, C. (1998) *Classics Transformed: Schools, Universities, and Society in England, 1830–1960*, Oxford.
—— (2015) 'Classics and social closure', in Stead and Hall 2015, 116–37.
Theodorakopoulos, E. (2012) 'Women's writing and the classical tradition', *Classical Receptions Journal* 4: 149–62.
Thorn, J. (2008) '"All beautiful in woe": gender, nation, and Phillis Wheatley's "Niobe"', *Studies in Eighteenth-Century Culture* 37: 233–58.
Torlone, Z. M., D. L. Munteanu and D. Dutsch, eds. (2017) *A Handbook to Classical Reception in Eastern and Central Europe*, Malden, MA.
Uden, J. (2020) *Spectres of Antiquity: Classical Literature and the Gothic, 1740–1830*, Oxford.
Vance, N. (1988) 'Ovid and the nineteenth century', in C. Martindale, ed., *Ovid Renewed: Ovidian Influences on Literature and Art from the Middle Ages to the Twentieth Century* (Cambridge), 215–32.
Vasunia, P. (2013) *The Classics and Colonial India*, Oxford.
Wallace, J. (2003) 'Confined and exposed: Elizabeth Carter's classical translations', *Tulsa Studies in Women's Literature* 22: 315–34.
Weinbrot, H. D. (2005) *Menippean Satire Reconsidered: From Antiquity to the Eighteenth Century*, Baltimore.
Wheatley, P. (1989) *The Poems of Phillis Wheatley* (ed. J. D. Mason), 2nd edn, Chapel Hill, NC.
Whitmarsh, T. (2006) 'True histories: Lucian, Bakhtin, and the pragmatics of reception', in Martindale and Thomas 2006, 104–15.
Willis, I. (2018) *Reception*, London.
Wilson, P. (2012) 'Women writers and the Classics', in D. Hopkins and C. Martindale, eds., *The Oxford History of Classical Reception in English Literature, Vol. 3: 1660–1790* (Oxford), 495–518.
Winkler, M. M. (2000) *Cinema and Classical Texts: Apollo's New Light*, Cambridge.
Wollstonecraft, M. (1993) *A Vindication of the Rights of Woman and a Vindication of the Rights of Men* (ed. J. Todd), Oxford.
Wood, C. S. (2012) 'Reception and the Classics', in W. Brockliss, P. Chaudhuri, A. H. Lushkov and K. Wasdin, eds., *Reception and the Classics* (New Haven, CT), 163–73.
Young, E. (1759) *Conjectures on Original Composition*, London.

CHAPTER 9

# *National Traditions*

*Therese Fuhrer*

## Preliminary Remarks

The concept of 'tradition' presupposes the existence of a historically definable development. This chapter will examine the often diverse modern developments in the field of Latin studies in different periods and in different countries and institutions. The attribution of such divergences to specific 'nations' should certainly not be seen in terms of ethnic groups but rather of cultural-political and even 'imagined' or 'abstract' communities.[1] It has nothing at all to do with nationalism and nationalistic differences such as were developed and strongly promoted – even in universities and in classical scholarship – in the nineteenth and early twentieth centuries. Nevertheless, thanks to its geographical focus on ancient Rome, Italy and in the Mediterranean area,[2] Latin studies have a strong West European flavour.[3] This means that the history and the status of Latin studies in the schools and universities in which it is taught are decisively shaped by its relationship to western culture.[4] The export of Latin studies outside Europe first had colonial and missionary motivations, then educational and political ones. Today this process is continued by academic and personal exchanges, for example by organisations such as the 'Fédération Internationale des Études Classiques' (FIEC), which has helped to ensure that Latin studies play a prominent role within the internationally connected scientific and scholarly community.[5]

---

[*] I am grateful to Paul Knight for translating this chapter from German.
[1] Cf. Anderson 1983; James 1996.
[2] The discussion about the name of the 'Roman Society' is indicative. In 1909, Oxford classical archaeologist Percy Gardner proposed that it be called the society 'for Latin or Italian Studies'. Stray 2010: 3.
[3] On the discussion of the role of Latin in the definition of European identity, cf. Bulwer 2018: 67: 'Classics is *the* European subject. Educated Europeans across the whole region are more likely to read Ovid or Virgil at school than the canon of accepted authors from another country.'
[4] However, this was also the reason why Latin studies usually played second fiddle to ancient Greek and to Hellenistic studies.
[5] Paschoud 1996.

However, distinct and organically developed national traditions continue to exist, as does the traditional West European embedding of this subject. This also means that Classical studies are still, to some extent, guided by the legacies of European elite education and the nineteenth-century colonial context, disadvantaging and marginalising not only certain (e.g. non-male, non-white, non-western-centric) groups of scholars and students and other (e.g. religious, racial) minorities, but also, by defining an aesthetic superiority of a selection of 'Great Books', a quite wide range of texts.[6] On the other hand, the centrality of the Classical tradition and the repository and colonial mindset of its ideas have been challenged by counter-narratives, especially in countries and at universities where ethnic and gender diversity are of central importance.[7]

Depending on the embedding of the subject in its environment and on the financial and human resources available, the conditions vary in which Latin studies have developed and will develop. In one respect these differences have an effect – sometimes a major one – on the formation of traditions. As Latin studies are a minor subject in schools and universities in most countries, it depends to a considerable extent on individual academic personalities and on decisions in the wider educational context. In specific circumstances that are difficult or precarious for the subject, a tradition may not be able to develop, at least not continuously, or it may quickly come to an abrupt end. In some countries mentioned in this chapter, such as Turkey and Japan, we cannot strictly speak of a tradition of Latin studies. It would be more accurate to talk in some cases of the adoption or appropriation of tradition by eminent academics who have provided important and characteristic impulses in a specific country and over a certain period but were unable to permanently establish a national tradition per se.

The language in which Latin studies are taught or in which specialist literature is written is a critical factor. Academic papers continue to be written in journals in a wide spectrum of national and supra-regional languages but English-language publications are now becoming increasingly dominant: English has become a kind of lingua franca even in Classics. This facilitates scholarly exchanges but also makes access to and by non-English publications more difficult. Latin studies have a long tradition in Italy, France, Spain and Germany and can still afford to accept and even to promote doctoral and post-doctoral work and specialist literature in their respective languages. However, they are increasingly

---

[6] Cf. Irene Peirano Garrison in this volume, also James Uden, at pp. 396–7.    [7] See also p. 475.

confronted with the problem that their research findings are not widely known in Anglophone countries.[8]

The history of classical philology is well researched, from its beginnings and through the various phases of its history from classical times to the modern era.[9] Most of these studies have a specific focus, for example on politically and ideologically distinct phases,[10] on various disciplines in classical scholarship,[11] on scholars who have established, dominated or developed a tradition,[12] or on geographical areas in which specific traditions have emerged.[13] Here I propose to give a – more or less brief – overview of the historical traditions of Latin studies in European countries, the wider Mediterranean region, Russia, the USA and Canada, Latin America, Africa, Australia and New Zealand, Japan and China.[14] I will also attempt to analyse the diverging methods and research issues in Latin studies resulting from different institutional conditions and personal constellations (Section 1).

The next step examines a number of case studies in an effort to determine the extent to which historically developed or characteristic 'national' differences impinge – often even up to the present – on research in Latin studies and on its results (Section 2).

The following remarks also contain a performative element. I am the only author in this volume who has not studied and taught primarily in Anglophone schools and universities. Having spent twenty years teaching and researching in the German-speaking region, I cannot deny my own

---

[8] Rubel 2019.
[9] Sandys 1903–8; Gudemann 1909; Wilamowitz 1921; Pfeiffer 1968 and 1976 (without the twentieth century); Hentschke and Muhlack 1972; Lehnus 2012; Lanza and Ugolini 2016/2022; Flashar et al. 1979 on the nineteenth century; Reverdin 1980 of the nineteenth and twentieth centuries. In 2019 there appeared the first issue of the open access academic journal *History of Classical Scholarship*, based in Newcastle.
[10] National Socialism: Wegeler 1996. Communism: Karsai et al. 2013; Movrin and Olechowaka 2016.
[11] Fontaine et al. 1993 (Patristics and Late Antiquity Research); cf. the chapters on Mediaeval Latin and Neo-Latin in this volume.
[12] E.g. Brink 2010 on Bentley, Porson and Housman; Butterfield and Stray 2009 on Housman; Jocelyn 1997 on Brink; Arrighetti et al. 2014 on Pasquali; Conte 1966 on Klingner; Verhaart 2020. See also *Brill's New Pauly* Suppl. 6, *History of Classical Scholarship – A Biographical Dictionary* (2012).
[13] Arrighetti et al. 1989 invited philologists from thirty-five countries to present their national philologies (Greek and Latin), of which I will refer to those who focus on Latin studies (but see the criticism of Lloyd-Jones 1990: 459: 'to assess the value of the contribution made to philology by one's own country during one's own century is an uncommonly difficult thing to do'). See also Stray 1998 on England; Winterer 2002 on the USA; Flashar 1995 and Espagne and Maufroy 2011 on Germany; Bers and Nagy 1996 on East Europe; Movrin and Olechowaka 2016 on communist countries.
[14] The term 'country' in the sense of nations that are distinguishable from one another in cultural, political and geographical terms is the basis of the lemmata in the six volumes on the 'Classical Tradition' of *Brill's New Pauly* (*DNP* vols. 13 to 15.1–3, 'History of Reception and Scholarship').

typical national (that is, Swiss and German) background. This is evident from the way in which I compile and critically evaluate the material. I hope that in doing so I will not justify the criticisms directed by American philologist Paul Shorey in 1919 at German pedantry and research into *quisquiliae*.[15]

## 1 Historical Outline

### General Remarks

The Latin language was fundamentally important up to the nineteenth century in every culture based on the West European model. It was an essential tool for political, diplomatic, legal, clerical and even social communication and therefore enjoyed a high status in school and university education, from the nineteenth century onwards increasingly in combination with classical Greek. Latin studies are therefore a crucial element in the educational history of European countries and – as a result of colonialisation – of certain countries in other continents.[16] The Latin schools, cathedral schools and Jesuit schools, organised and financed by ecclesiastical and secular authorities, played a particular role here, their influence depending on the cultural and denominational traditions of the countries concerned. A solid grounding in and use of the Latin language were a feature – often a distinguishing feature – of an elite that was, and aspired to be, Eurocentric. Latin was their lingua franca until the nineteenth century.[17]

The educational reforms of the nineteenth century, together with those after the Second World War and again in the 1960s, led to changes that were detrimental to the classical languages. An active command of the Latin language, Latin as a compulsory requirement for university entrance, Latin as a scholarly language for doctoral and post-doctoral dissertations, were no longer essential targets in school curricula. This in turn led to new emphases in university courses. Latin was regarded more and more as a dead language. In the case of classical, late classical and mediaeval Latin, the language became an object of editorial, historical-linguistic or literary classical-philological research.[18] As classical philology became an

---

[15] Cf. p. 497.   [16] Cf. p. 477.
[17] This development is described in detail for most of the national traditions by Waquet 2001.
[18] On the historical development of Latin from a literary language to a dead language and finally on its role as the subject of academic research, cf. the remarks by Farrell 2001, ch. 4: 'The life-cycle of dead languages'; also ibid. ch. 4 and ch. 5 on (biomorphic) metaphors.

academic discipline and universities were founded in the nineteenth century, national classical research institutions (academies, institutes, seminars) were founded, and large-scale and/or long-term projects were established, most of which have survived into the twenty-first century.[19] The increasing number of research articles went hand in hand with the development of publishing that also followed, and to some extent still follows, national traditions (series, encyclopaedias, dictionaries, textbooks, companions). Latin was and is regarded as part of classical philology in most universities and academic institutions but depending on national linguistic and cultural-historical interests, national and regional emphases and orientations now predominate.

Four factors help to explain the continuing relatively high status of Latin studies in individual countries: (1) the importance of the teaching of classical languages, especially Latin, in schools;[20] (2) the political and cultural-historical significance of the national language and other modern foreign languages in competition with the classical languages; (3) interest in educational reform, notably the role of technology and of natural sciences in competition with the classical languages; (4) the cultural, religious and political embedding of traditional Roman antiquity and of the Latin language and of the corresponding educational subjects in a national tradition. Geographical and – linked to this – cultural-historical national differences can be observed since the seventeenth and eighteenth centuries and these traces are visible even in the present. There are also notable differences in the pronunciation of Latin that are not solely attributable to the phonetic nuances of individual modern languages and the inevitably audible dialectal accents but also stem from variously defined pronunciation rules resulting from school traditions.[21]

The following overview of the history of Latin studies in individual countries and/or regions will consider whether or to what extent institutional and personal factors played a major part in the development of national traditions of Latin teaching culture in schools and universities.

### *German-Speaking Countries*

In German-speaking countries, the new humanism and the efforts of Wilhelm von Humboldt and Johann Joachim Winckelmann helped to

---

[19] See the list in *DNP* 15.1 (2001) 656–722 s.v. 'Nationale Forschungsinstitute'; Holtermann 1999: 808–9.
[20] Holmes-Henderson et al. 2018 provides a good overview of the present situation in the teaching of classical languages at schools in Europe and Latin America.
[21] Waquet 2001: 160–71; Stotz 1999, esp. 357 on the national traditions. On the French pronunciation cf. Waquet 2000: 58; on the much-debated English practice Stray 2018: 249–51 ('manliness and accuracy').

ensure that the classical languages dominated school curricula.[22] Latin remained the language of scholarship in German universities until the nineteenth century. Goethe obtained his doctoral degree at Strasbourg University by writing a dissertation and taking a viva in Latin. Even in the twentieth century, Greek specialist Rudolf Kassel (born 1926) wrote his dissertation at Mainz University in Latin.[23]

By the 1930s, German classical philology and hence Latin studies had achieved a leading position compared to other countries thanks to the large number of universities with outstanding specialists and the big research 'enterprises' at the Berlin Academy.[24] However, as a considerable number of these scholars were Jewish and many were dismissed from their posts and forced to emigrate, the quality of scholarship in Latin studies diminished and the German lead was irrevocably lost.[25] The dismissals resulting from the de-Nazification process after the Second World War led for a while at least to a further reduction in the number of classical philologists working at German universities.[26]

Switzerland was one of the beneficiaries of the involvement of Latin studies in German politics. In 1939 the prominent Latinist Eduard Norden

---

[22] Holtermann 1999: 807–8. Cf. van Bommel 2015 and the review by Landfester 2018.

[23] Johann Wolfgang Goethe, *Positiones juris quas auspice deo inclyti jurisconsultorum ordinis ... defendet I. W. G.*, Strasbourg 1771 (his famously unsuccessful doctoral dissertation); Rudolf Kassel, *Quomodo quibus locis apud veteres scriptores Graecos infantes et parvuli pueri inducantur describantur commemorentur*, dissertation Mainz 1951.

[24] Ludwig 1986: 217: 'This assertion [i.e. that 'at that time no other country produced such a large number of outstanding scholars in this subject'] may easily lead to accusations of nationalistic prejudice. However, a close investigation of the facts will show that this accusation is unjustified.' According to Pollock 2009, German classical philology had already passed its zenith with Wilamowitz's scathing review of Nietzsche's *Geburt der Tragödie*, as the chance was missed to move away from positivistic and bloodless erudition – what Nietzsche, himself a student of Ritschl, called 'ant labour' ('Ameisenarbeit') – towards a lively, humanistic, education-oriented culture. Holtermann 1999: 810; Latacz 2002: 268–71; King 2017: 1–2; Güthenke 2020: 189–93. In fact, Wilamowitz himself often complained about Mommsen's idea of a (mainly German) 'Großbetrieb der Wissenschaft', 'big business of scholarship'; Calder 1994: xxi; Hose 2009.

[25] Professors specialising mainly in Latin studies included the following: Eduard Norden (Berlin, emigrated to Zurich), Eduard Fraenkel (Freiburg to Oxford), Georg Rohde (Marburg to Ankara), C. O. Brink (Technical University of Munich to Oxford, Manchester and Cambridge), Otto Skutsch (Technical University of Munich to St Andrews and London), Willy Morel (independent scholar, Frankfurt to Cambridge and London); Friedrich W. Lenz (born Levy, from Minden/Westphalia to Florence, Yale and Austin, Texas). Otto Regenbogen in Heidelberg and Rudolf Helm in Rostock were forced to resign or to take early retirement. Ludwig Bieler left Vienna for Northern Ireland (cf. Watson 1989: 984–5). Cf. Ludwig 1986: 224, quoting Lloyd-Jones: 'in the 30s the great benefactor of classical studies in this country was Adolf Hitler, who gained for us a group of distinguished scholars from the continent'. On scholars teaching at Oxford, cf. Crawford et al. 2017.

[26] Rudolf Till in Munich, recalled to the University of Erlangen in 1958; Hans Oppermann in Strasbourg, reappointed to a professorship at the University of Hamburg in 1959; Ulrich Knoche in Hamburg, returned to the University in 1950. Cf. Malitz 1998; P. L. Schmidt 2001.

was appointed to the chair at Zurich. He died there in 1941. In 1932 Latinist Harald Fuchs (died 1985) was appointed to the chair at Basel. Fuchs had already become disillusioned with German politics and had dissociated himself from his mentor Werner Jaeger and Jaeger's notions of the German contemporary movement oriented towards an idealised antiquity and Renaissance Italy, known as 'Third Humanism'.[27] After the Second World War a German diplomat, Baron Kurd von Hardt (died 1958), invested his fortune in an estate in Vandœuvres near Geneva 'dedicated to reconciling Europeans through the study of their common heritage, classical culture'; in 1949 this became the 'Fondation Hardt'.[28]

The reasons why Latin studies in Germany always played second fiddle to Greek studies were also political. Already under Kaiser Wilhelm II, the nationalist appropriation of classical antiquity was gathering strength, a process which had a stronger impact on Greek than on Latin studies. For many years the philhellenism and (ahistorical) classicism espoused by Johann Gottfried Herder, Winckelmann, Friedrich August Wolf and the Göttingen School (Christian Gottlob Heyne) was dominant.[29] It was inspired to a large extent by the confrontation with militarily superior Napoleonic France and with 'Latin' culture.[30] Wilhelm von Humboldt's notion that a spiritual affinity existed between Hellenes and Germans,[31] and the neoclassicism that emerged in the circle around the poet Stefan George, exerted a powerful influence on German national consciousness and on the academic presuppositions of German classical philology into the 1930s.[32] This philhellenism was in turn a central feature of the Third Humanism advocated by Werner Jaeger. Although several leading exponents of philhellenism emigrated to the USA for political reasons, they did not have an ideological impact: the national ideology of the USA certainly did not wish to be influenced by German modes of thinking.[33]

---

[27] Jaeger himself preferred the term 'humanism', probably in order to avoid any association with the expression 'Third Reich'; see Näf 2017; Horn 2018. On the critical attitude of the Nazi Classics professors such as Hans Drexler (d. 1984) towards any form of 'classical humanism', see Roche 2017: 241–3.
[28] www.fondationhardt.ch/en/la-fondation_en. Cf. Näf 2002: 1149.
[29] Fornaro 1999: 795–802; Latacz 2002: 262–3; Schmidt 2002: 299–300 and 30–6; Güthenke 2020: 21–47.
[30] Holtermann 1999: 806–7; von Ungern-Sternberg 2017, and see the contributions in Espagne and Maufroy 2011.
[31] W. von Humboldt to Goethe: this, he says, is a 'fundamental truth' ('eine Grundwahrheit'); Stiewe 2011.
[32] Habermehl and Seidensticker 1999: 818; Stiewe 2011; Thomas 2001: 248–50.
[33] Schmidt 2002: 313; Landfester 2017.

It was only towards the end of the nineteenth century and in the first half of the twentieth century that Latin studies acquired greater prestige. One reason for this was the increased interest in Roman research: in the 1930s and the 1940s, 'Römertum' ('Romanness') became the focus of ideologically coloured research promoted by Hans Oppermann (d. 1982), Rudolf Till (d. 1979), Ulrich Knoche (d. 1968) and Viktor Pöschl (d. 1997).[34] However, this rise in the scholarly status of Latin studies is also attributable to the influence of Eduard Norden (d. 1941), Richard Heinze (d. 1929) and Friedrich Klingner (d. 1968), who increasingly seceded from the dominant primacy of Greek studies.[35] Norden promoted interest in the history of Roman science and religion; Klingner produced seminal articles on Latin authors of late antiquity and of the early Christian period (Boethius, Prudentius). He influenced German Latin studies both as an editor (see pp. 485–7) and, inspired by the hermeneutic methods and life philosophy of Wilhelm Dilthey, in his methodologically somewhat unsystematic interpretations of Virgil.[36]

In linguistic philology, the stringent historical-critical exegetical methods of Karl Lachmann (d. 1851) in Berlin, the Göttingen School of philology and the founding of the Bonn School under Friedrich Ritschl (d. 1876), with its emphasis on exegesis, now gained the ascendancy. Göttingen was notable for its tradition of exegetical and especially of 'Wortphilologie',[37] whose leading representatives were Friedrich Leo (d. 1914), Jacob Wackernagel (d. 1938) and their student Günther Jachmann, who taught in Cologne from 1925 and died in 1979. With his interest in Old Latin, Ritschl inspired German research on Plautus, bolstering the self-assurance and methodological sensitivity of German Latin studies.[38] Ritschl's influence was also palpable in the work of Leo, Jachmann and Fraenkel. In response to the (narrowed reception of) text-philological positivism and historicism of Ritschl's Bonn School,[39] the Bonn 'Dioscuri' Hermann Usener (d. 1905) and Franz Bücheler (d. 1908) focused on classical history, thus raising awareness of the processes by which texts

---

[34] On 'Römertümelei' ('Romanomania') and its relationship to contemporary 'Deutschtümelei' ('Germanomania') see Schmidt 1995: 166–81; Schmidt 2002: 314–20. On Oppermann see Malitz 1998; Thomas 2001: 241–6 and 250–1.
[35] Schmidt 2002: 305–10.
[36] In this context, see the judgement of Conte 1966: 486–92. Cf. Schmidt 1995: 158–62.
[37] In *DNP* the German term 'Wortphilologie' (which includes textual criticism, editorial philology and linguistics) is translated as 'grammatical-critical text philology' and 'philology of the word', as opposed to 'Sachphilologie' (antiquarian, historical, cultural and anthropological studies). See Landfester 2002.
[38] Schmidt 1995: 121; Güthenke 2020: 108–9.   [39] Schmidt 2002: 304.

are transmitted.[40] Germany was now, during the last two decades of the nineteenth and at the beginning of the twentieth century, becoming the Mecca of classical philology, in Latin studies with Lachmann in Berlin, Leo and Jachmann in Göttingen, Ritschl and Bücheler in Bonn. But at the same time the strengths of German editorial philology, the trust in method, developed into what Housman called 'its naive faith in methodological thoroughness and routine', or, in the words of the originally German student and scholar C. O. Brink, 'mechanical scholarly routine'.[41] German conjectural criticism was thought conservative, too timid with emendations; Housman was dismissive of 'the troop of little dogs which trotted at [Buecheler's] heels'.[42]

The positivistic tendency, which was further strengthened in the twentieth century as a result of the competition between linguistic and antiquarian philology,[43] is still evident, and productive in a number of lexicographical projects influenced by Ritschl's interests in the history of language. It should be stressed, though, that from their inception these projects have involved a high degree of international cooperation.[44] They include the *Thesaurus linguae Latinae* (Munich),[45] the *Mittellateinisches Wörterbuch* (Munich), the editorial project *Monumenta Germaniae historica* (Berlin, Munich), the *Corpus inscriptionum Latinarum* and *Carmina epigraphica* (Berlin) and the Bibliotheca Teubneriana Latina.[46] During the period of the partition of Germany, there were two versions of this last, one published in Leipzig in East Germany, the other in Stuttgart. As a result, there were a number of duplications in the editions (see pp. 470 and 487–8). An important feature of German Latin studies in the post-war period is the increasing interest in classical Christian literature. At the suggestion of Franz Joseph Dölger (d. 1940), a scholar of religion and church history, his students (including the Leiden Latinist Jan Hendrik Waszink, d. 1990) founded the *Reallexikon für Antike und Christentum (RAC)*.[47] The recourse to antiquity and Christianity, following the defeat of Germany and the condemnation of National Socialism with its

---

[40] Schmidt 1995: 125–31; Schmidt 2002: 303–5; Güthenke 2020: 122–8.
[41] Cf. the quotations on p. 485 with n. 213.  [42] Cf. Tarrant 2016a: 23.
[43] Cf. Schwindt 2003: 1308 on F. A. Wolf's role in establishing this dichotomy between 'Wort-' and 'Sachphilologie' (see n. 37); Holtermann 1999: 809–10 on the Boeckh–Hermann dispute on this issue.
[44] Schmidt 1995: 121–2; Schmidt 2002: 302.  [45] Krömer 2001: 143–9.
[46] As a result of the international backgrounds of the editors, the Bibliotheca Teubneriana enjoys considerable international standing; cf. Reeve 2000: 203–4: 'the oldest series of classical texts still current and since the war the most international'.
[47] Fürst 2002: 198.

invocation of Germanic origins, represented a return to the classical occidental roots of modern culture, which was regarded as an interaction between Roman and Christian elements.[48] Since 1866 the *Corpus scriptorum ecclesiasticorum Latinorum* (*CSEL*) has published critical edition of Latin Christian authors, now in Salzburg (previously in Vienna).[49]

Since the period of the Brothers Grimm, mediaeval studies and hence Latin philology of the Middle Ages became university subjects.[50] The Bonn Romanist Ernst Robert Curtius (d. 1960) established the study of the Latin Middle Ages within Literary Studies. Prominent representatives of this new development were Ludwig Traube (d. 1907), first professor of mediaeval Latin in Munich, and Paul von Winterfeld (d. 1905) in Berlin. However, in the German academic tradition, mediaeval Latin is usually institutionally separate from classical Latin, as part of mediaeval studies, which has traditionally regarded itself as a different branch of knowledge.

Linguistic competence in high school teaching and the focus on grammatical and stylistic formalism continue to influence strongly (and in some instances to dominate) academic teaching at German universities.[51] Latin prose composition ('Stilübungen') still plays a major role, on the grounds that students should learn to write Latin sentences for their future pupils to practise. The use of the 'direct method'[52] to enable pupils to achieve levels of active competence is one of the arguments advanced in favour of this emphasis, though this is rather controversial for so-called dead languages. It can be argued that at university level German–Latin translation is only valuable as a way of consolidating grammar; if it is too prominent in the curriculum this reduces the time available for study of the Latin texts themselves and for literary analysis.[53] One could argue that this

---

[48] Schöllgen 2018: 648: 'In the 1950s the RAC represented a means of underlining the dissociation from the national socialist past and of creating a new identity based on Greek and Roman classical antiquity and on Christianity. This was probably the main motive behind the financial support provided by the international banks who wanted in this way to underline that they had turned away from their "brown" past and had returned to the fold of Western culture.'

[49] Schmidt 2002: 302; Schmidt-Dengler 2003: 1293.

[50] See the chapter by Justin Stover in this volume.

[51] Fornaro 1999: 794; Holtermann 1999: 809: 'the analysis of content is restricted by the dominance of a grammatical-stylistic formalism'. See also Landfester 2018: 114: 'Language training took the place of general education to the detriment of literary education' (my translation); Landfester argues that the high value attached to active language competence in German schools is a continuation of 'old humanist teaching' – which is in fact alien to the new humanist education movement. Cf. Raeburn 1999: 120 on the traditional emphasis on Latin prose composition at British universities which has now disappeared from the academic curricula.

[52] On experience with the 'direct approach' and teaching Latin for language acquisition, normally associated with modern languages, in American schools: see Hunt 2018b. Cf. Raeburn 1999: 121.

[53] On opposition to Latin prose composition, ongoing since the 1970s, cf. Stroh 2001: 93.

grammar-based focus is responsible for the still rather conservative orientation of German research in this field. Another possible cause is the continuing strong position of Latin in high schools (the gymnasium) and – within Classics – in universities. This in turn means that the pressure to secure academic funding is not as challenging as elsewhere – above all in British universities, where intense competition has spurred academics to peak performance.

## United Kingdom

In the UK, a classical education and knowledge of classical languages was, until the early twentieth century at least, part of the undisputed ideal of the British gentleman (not of women).[54] Reminiscences of learning Latin grammar are frequently found in autobiographical descriptions and accounts, for example in William Shakespeare's *The Merry Wives of Windsor* (1602),[55] William Hazlitt's *On the Conduct of Life or Advice to a Schoolboy* (1822),[56] James Boswell's *Life of Johnson* (1927)[57] and Winston Churchill's *My Early Life* (1930).[58] The reading of texts from classical antiquity played a major role in the school curriculum, forming the basis for English literary production even for writers without a university degree, such as Shakespeare.[59]

Thanks to this tradition, Latin held a strong position in British schools until the 1960s, but the utilitarian ideas of educational reformers meant that it then disappeared almost completely from school curricula – at the latest by 2004 when the New Labour's Higher Education Act (ch. 8) to

---

[54] Waquet 2001: 214–5 with a quotation from *The Times* of 1866 by Robert Lowe: Latin is 'an indispensable part of the education of a gentleman'. Stray 2018: 243–57 and 326–47.
[55] Bate 2008: 79: 'Grammar meant Latin grammar. From dawn to dusk, six days a week. All the year round.'
[56] E.g. in *Table Talk or Original Essays*, vol. 2, Paris 1825: 'You were convinced the first day that you could not learn Latin, which now you find easy. Be taught from this, not to think other obstacles insurmountable, that you may meet with in the course of your life, though they seem so at first' (p. 287); but also: 'Though you are master of Cicero's *Orations*, think it possible for a cobbler at a stall to be more eloquent than you' (p. 275).
[57] Stray 2018: 243–4.
[58] Ch. 1 'Childhood', in which 'The author, aged five' describes his first Latin lesson and the declension table for the word *mensa*. When Winston asks the teacher about the meaning of the vocative form 'o table', the teacher threatens to punish him for impertinent behaviour; this is followed by the comment: 'such was my first introduction to the classics, from which, I have been told, many of our cleverest men have derived so much solace and profit'. Cf. Waquet 2001: 140–1 who describes school Latin as 'a cross children had to bear'; ibid. 130–45 contain similar testimonies and anecdotes from schools in other countries.
[59] Bate 2008: 92–8 and 141–57 (chapter 9: 'Shakespeare's Small Library').

monitor and regulate 'fair access' to higher education in England came into force.[60] In recent years new perspectives in the teaching of Latin have opened up, thanks in particular to the use of initiatives such as 'Classics for All'[61] and 'Classics in Communities', a partnership scheme between the Universities of Oxford and Cambridge.[62] A number of prominent politicians joined forces in 2010 to press for the reintroduction of classical languages in the school curriculum. These advocates included former British Prime Minister, at that time Conservative MP, Boris Johnson, Old Etonian and Oxford classicist. Johnson argued that otherwise Greek and Latin would be in danger of becoming the 'fodder of the independent sector' (not least the elite public schools).[63] Sheila Lawlor, director of the think tank 'Politeia', also stressed the importance of Latin teaching for the General Certificate of Secondary Education, which is usually taken at the age of sixteen.[64] Prominent academics such as Cambridge Latinist David Butterfield also spoke out in favour of the project.[65] Christopher Pelling, then Regius Professor of Greek at Oxford, stressed the benefits of teaching Latin, referring to experiences in the USA, where Latin helped to improve the literacy, oracy and intercultural understanding of students learning the language.[66] However, these moves were also criticised as part of a 'right-wing educational agenda'.[67] Theoretically at least, a degree of success was achieved in 2013, when Latin and classical Greek were for the first time included in the list of languages for primary schools. In 2021, the Department for Education launched a £4 million Latin Excellence Programme for teaching Latin in state schools, now transformed into a 'levelling-up' programme in forty state schools.[68]

The history of Latin studies at universities has been equally dramatic. In the Augustan era around the beginning of the eighteenth century, the 'Battle of the Books' (Jonathan Swift, 1704) broke out. This was the British version of the 'Querelle des anciens et modernes', a dispute between traditionalists and modernists about the importance of classical antiquity

---

[60] Searle et al. 2018.   [61] https://classicsforall.org.uk.   [62] Holmes-Henderson 2016.
[63] Quoted from 'Mayor urges London state schools to teach Latin', BBC News website 17.3.10 (http://news.bbc.co.uk/1/hi/england/london/8571662.stm). See Hunt 2018a. The inclusion of Latin in state school curricula was proposed among others by Toby Young, author, journalist and founder of the West London Free School, and Harry Mount, journalist and author of a popular Latin textbook which proved an unlikely bestseller at Christmas time (Mount 2008).
[64] Lawlor 2013.   [65] Butterfield 2013b. See also Hunt 2018a.   [66] Pelling and Morgan 2010.
[67] The view of Beard 2012. This negates the claims still being made in the 1960s that training in classical languages could help to overcome class distinctions (see also Waquet 2001: 207–8 and 228–9).
[68] TES magazine online 14.04.2022.

## 9 National Traditions

for their own cultural activities.[69] One of the leading modernists was Richard Bentley (d. 1742), an outstanding classicist and a friend of Isaac Newton. His advocacy of methods of conjectural criticism and of the basic right to make linguistic and content-based amendments to the original texts led to an improvement in the scholarly stringency of classical philology and particularly of Latin studies.[70] A. E. Housman (d. 1936) adopted and critically evaluated Bentley's 'enlightened' approach,[71] and the development of critical editorial methods since the nineteenth century was further enriched by the application of scholarly criteria to philological editions and of rational faculties to appreciate classical literature. This remains a characteristic feature of British Latin studies and is exemplified in the OCTs and in the Oxford and Cambridge series of commentaries (see pp. 483–4 and 493–4).

Two German scholars whose work illustrated the different traditions of their country of origin also played a significant role in the history of British Latin studies.[72] Eduard Fraenkel (d. 1970), who, together with Eduard Norden, was the leading Jewish-German Latinist of the time, was appointed to a fellowship at Trinity College, Cambridge and then in 1935 to the post of Corpus Christi Professor at Oxford, a choice that met with the approval – with some reservations – of Housman, the leading Latinist in England. At Oxford, Fraenkel moved away from a primarily philological and editorial focus towards a method of textual interpretation based on literary and cultural history approaches.[73] Charles Oscar Brink (d. 1994), who was born as Karl Oskar Levy, studied in Berlin and, on the advice of Werner Jaeger, in Oxford. In Munich he worked on the *TLL* and for the *RE*, but he had to leave Germany in 1938 because of his Jewish origin. He worked for a while on the *OLD* project and taught at several British universities. In 1954 he was appointed Kennedy Professor of Latin at Cambridge. His work on classical literary theory, in particular his monumental edition with commentaries of Horace's literary letters combines typically German lexicographic scholarship with the methods of British conjectural criticism in the tradition of Housman.[74]

---

[69] Baumann 2003: 811–14.
[70] Brink 2010: 4 calls Bentley 'the Newton of European philological and literary studies'.
[71] Konstan and Muecke 1993: 183; Landfester 2002: 252. Housman himself, in his inaugural lecture at University College London (1892), challenged the supposed utility of science, especially of astronomy (Sutton 2018).
[72] On the multifarious facets of national characteristics on the one hand and ethnic background on the other, see Stray 2014 and 2017; Elsner 2017.
[73] Farrell 2005; Ludwig 1986: 222, quoting Lloyd-Jones: 'his influence somehow created an amalgam of German classical philology and English classical scholarship which combined much of what was best in both'.
[74] Jocelyn 1997. On the antiquarian, lexicographic and philological tradition of German scholarship cf. p. 455.

The primacy of philology and of linguistic competence that characterised Latin studies at the elite universities of Oxford and Cambridge was so strong even in the late 1960s that a knowledge of Latin was a requirement for anyone wishing to study any subject at English universities. When this 'obstacle' was removed,[75] the impact on the position of Latin in schools was immediate – and of course negative. On the other hand, perhaps the movement away from the old primacy of linguistic competence led to a strengthening of Latin studies in institutes of ancient history outside Oxbridge. It is noteworthy that the cultural history orientation of British Latin studies was established by the British School at Rome. The Society for the Promotion of Roman Studies in London was founded in 1910 and continues to play a prominent role in this field, not least in publishing the *Journal of Roman Studies*.[76] It seems to me that British Latin research as a whole has benefited from its stronger cultural history focus and its links to other specialist disciplines. It may also be the case that the British government's insistence on social relevance and on 'impact beyond academia',[77] although hard to accept for many philologists, has had a stimulating effect on the formulation of research questions and also on the manner in which research literature is written.[78]

*Ireland*

The Irish tradition of Latin studies is more strongly influenced by mediaeval Latin ecclesiastical and monastic scholarship. The prohibition of Catholic schools in 1695 and the exclusion of Catholic pupils from state secondary schools led to the formation of the so-called hedge schools, in which Latin played a leading part.[79] Trinity College Dublin, the first university in Ireland, closely following but also competing with the Oxford and Cambridge model, barred non-Protestant students from taking degrees until the end of the eighteenth century. Only afterwards did the study of Classics and of Latin studies become open to all students, regardless of their religious or denominational affiliations. On the other hand, Latin is virtually absent from school curricula today.

---

[75] On the collapse of compulsory Latin cf. Raeburn 1999: 120; Stray 2018: 241–2 and 265.
[76] Stray 2010.   [77] Searle et al. 2018.
[78] Examples of this trend are Roy Gibson's analysis, entitled *Excess and Restraint* (2007), of the description of erotic experience in Roman poetry and elegies, (Danish) Henriette van der Blom's *Cicero's Role Models* (2010), (German) Ingo Gildenhard's study of Cicero's rhetoric as 'creative eloquence' (2011) and Victoria Rimell's *Closure of Space in Roman Poetics* (2015).
[79] Poppe 2000: 645.

The 'Dublin School' of Classics in particular played a leading role in the formation of the Irish national identity in Latin studies, demarcating itself with considerable humour and self-irony from the German tradition of classical philology. Perhaps its most prominent representative was Robert Yelverton Tyrrell who founded the journal *Hermathena* at Trinity College Dublin in 1873. In 1901 Tyrrell was one of the original fellows of the newly founded British Academy. He was also the co-founder of the classical-philological satirical magazine *Kottabos*, which parodied, among others, Theodor Mommsen and contemporary research on Virgil.[80] Tyrrell's research on Cicero's letters, which he produced at first alone and later in conjunction with his Dublin colleague Louis Claude Purser (Tyrrell 'n' Purser, 1879–1901), marked a milestone in Latin studies at the time.

Another notable feature of the Irish university system is that mediaeval Latin is often studied in conjunction with Old English.[81] This may be because from the Middle Ages to the present classical culture has been a major element in national identity formation.[82] The reception of classical antiquity, more often than in other national traditions, has gone hand in hand with a process of transformation: Greek and Roman works were freely translated and assimilated into Gaelic literature up to the nineteenth century.[83] In the 1930s, the works of Ovid were placed on the index of banned books by the Irish Censorship Board.[84] In 1994 Seamus Heaney, whose creative output ranged from poetry to interpretations of classical texts, was the president of the Classical Association of Ireland, and in the following year he was awarded the Nobel Prize for Literature. Heaney's verse translation of the sixth book of Virgil's *Aeneid*, which he himself wanted to be a 'poetic remaking' of the book, appeared in 2016, three years after his death (2013); after having long been rumoured, this publication was a major event.[85] Heaney was steeped in Catholic Latin-based traditions at St Columb's College in Derry and subsequently at Queens University Belfast.[86] It is reported that his last words to his wife were *noli timere*, a quotation from the Vulgate version of the Christmas story in Matthew 14:27.

## France

The French tradition of the editing of philological texts was established by Guillaume Budé and Henri Estienne in the heyday of French humanism in

---

[80] Beard 2002: 106–7. [81] Wright 1993.
[82] On the formation of the 'Irish classical self' see O'Higgins 2017, esp. ch. 2.
[83] Stanford 1976: 74; Watson 1989. [84] Poppe 2000: 645–6. [85] Harrison 2019.
[86] See the introduction in Harrison et al. 2019: 6–8.

the sixteenth century. In the seventeenth century, philhellenic classicism was overshadowed by increasing interest in Roman history and culture, by means of which French philologists sought to underline their difference from the German academic tradition.[87] The Jesuit colleges, where the future cultural elite of the monarchy were trained in 'grande éloquence', played a leading part here. Rhetoric dominated the teaching programme and pupils trained their rhetorical skills by declaiming the works of prominent Latin authors. The model par excellence here was Cicero, whose ideas of rhetorical and philosophical education shaped the aristocratic ideal of the 'honnête homme'. Routines and mechanisms of learning Latin were elaborated; they included mnemonic poems, tables, 'déclinographies' and other learning methods which continued to be used in Latin teaching until the 1960s.[88] Admittedly the authority of classical culture and of its strict canon had been questioned during the quarrel of the ancients and moderns, but it was not until the Enlightenment in the eighteenth century that the Jesuit colleges, with their emphasis on Latinate declamation and style, began to lose ground to French as the language of pure reason.[89]

In the nineteenth century the increasing importance of Classical studies in university syllabuses in France led to the promotion of auxiliary scholarly disciplines such as epigraphy (which occupied a prominent position in the Académie des Inscriptions et Belles-Lettres), palaeography and codicology.[90] In addition a number of translation projects were launched, such as that of literary historian Desiré Nisard (d. 1888), who founded the 'Collection des auteurs latins avec traduction en français' (1838–50). This tradition continued in the twentieth century with the *Année philologique* founded by Latinist Jules Marouzeau, an institution that worked together with several international branches from the outset.[91] In 1920 the first bilingual Budé editions with commentaries appeared (*Collection des Universités de France/CUF*)[92] and 1959 saw the first publications in the Érasme series of texts with commentaries (*Collections de textes latins et grecs commentés*). The production of editions and translations of a wide range of

---

[87] Petitmengin 1983 and (including non-classical German philological scholars) Petitmengin 1992; P. L. Schmidt 2001; von Ungern-Sternberg 2017. On the 'scholarly war between a "French" tradition – here represented by Le Clerc and Dacier – and an Anglo-Dutch approach, to which Burman, Bentley, and their intellectual predecessors, such as Graevius and Van Broekhuizen, belonged', see Verhaart 2020: 89–90.
[88] Waquet 2000: 59–60.    [89] Rommel 2000: 44–5.    [90] Schmitz 2003a: 1256–7.
[91] On the 'tension between patriotic sentiment and promotion of internationalization . . . transpired throughout Marouzeau's career' see Hilbold 2019, esp. 175.
[92] These editions are now available to a wider public in the *Classiques en poche* editions.

classical authors and the broad cultural interest in the classical period did not prevent French educational policy-makers from drastically reducing the role of classical languages in the grammar school curriculum.[93]

Interest in late antique Christian literature and in mediaeval Latin literature was and remains a characteristic feature of French Latin studies.[94] In the seventeenth century C. D. Du Cange (d. 1688) founded the *Glossarium ad scriptores mediae et infimae Latinitatis*. In the nineteenth century the ultra-Catholic royalist Jean-Paul Migne (d. 1875) initiated a new edition of the Church Fathers, the *Patrologiae cursus completus*. Bypassing the book trade, he took advantage of the most recent advances in printing technology to compile this work from a huge mass of different corpora, which, partly with the aid of grants from the Catholic Church, he quickly made available to the reading public. In 1844–5 he published the *Patrologia Latina*, the works of the Latin Church Fathers up to 1216, in 221 volumes. As for works of Greek authors up to 1439 (*Patrologia Graeca*), he published these first in Latin translation (eighty-five volumes, 1856–7), then in Greek with Latin translations (165 volumes, 1857–8).[95] This publishing coup by the Abbé Migne was achieved partly at the cost of philological accuracy, but subsequent editions using more up-to-date methods of editorial criticism have attempted to compensate for these failings.[96] In the 1930s the Jesuit order in Lyons proposed the idea of a bilingual version of these works. The realisation of the project was delayed by the outbreak of the Second World War but the work was finally published in the German-occupied north of France under the series title *Sources Chrétiennes (SC)*.[97]

Compared with these antiquarian and editorial projects, the theologically oriented cultural anthropology of philologist Jean-Pierre Vernant (d. 2007), social historian Pierre Vidal-Naquet (d. 2006) and ethnologist

---

[93] Bulwer 2018, referring to the reforms in 2016: 'The result of this is seen by the teachers concerned to mean a severe cut to the hours available for Latin; the present regular timetable allocation of a certain number of hours per week would be replaced by the introduction of cross-curricular project work which will cover a number of different topics and areas and will be available for study of the ancient world.'

[94] Fontaine et al. 1993.

[95] See also the novelistic description by Bloch 1995, which is still read and appreciated even by specialists.

[96] The *Patrologia Latina* has been available electronically since 1993. See p. 456 for the *CSEL* in Austria and the *CCL* in Belgium.

[97] Of the texts in the *SC* only about a third are in Latin and about 50 per cent in Greek. In 2018 the seventy-fifth anniversary of this project was celebrated with a conference on the subject of 'L'apport grec et latin à la culture européenne' in Athens.

Claude Lévy-Strauss (d. 2009) represented a markedly different approach.[98]

### Italy and the Mediterranean

The self-image of Latin studies in Italy today is still indebted to the work of the Renaissance humanists,[99] who made ground-breaking contributions not only in the history of the Classical tradition but also in linguistic history, as well as rhetorical and stylistic analysis. Latin held – and has continued to hold until recently – a strong position in the school curriculum and at universities. In the fascist period (1922–43), Latin studies was given an ideologically based and exaggerated role in the school curriculum, and classical Latin played a pivotal role also as a literary and epigraphic language.[100] The imported ideas of Third Humanism along the Berlin–Rome axis played a part in this over-valuation.[101]

The discovery of the palimpsests with Plautus' comedies in 1815 and Cicero's *De re publica* in 1819 by librarian Angelo Mai in the Bibliotheca Vaticana gave a spectacular impetus to Italian editorial philology. This was the period of the establishment of Latin studies at universities and the Napoleonic founding of the Scuola Normale Superiore di Pisa. Latin studies in the nineteenth century were bolstered as a result of political accusations that Greek studies were excessively Germanophile. Consistent broadsides at – conservative, but methodically authoritarian – German conjectural criticism, which was dismissed as an aberration ('una aberrazione tedesca'),[102] had been a characteristic feature of Italian textual philology in the nineteenth century. This German-Italian controversy prompted Giorgio Pasquali (d. 1952) to found the *Editiones Paravianae* in Turin, with the declared aim of purging the Latin texts of German conjectures.[103] Hellenist Pasquali had studied in Göttingen with Friedrich Leo among others.[104] He was a corresponding member of the Göttingen and Bavarian Academies of Science, a close friend of Eduard Fraenkel and in regular contact with Ulrich von Wilamowitz-Moellendorf, even

---

[98] Schmitz 2003a: 1257; Schmitz 2003b: 1301.
[99] Cessi 1930: 63: 'Per avere una completa storia della Filologia classica in Italia si dovrebbe cominciare proprio dai nostri umanisti.'
[100] On the role of 'Fascist Latinity' see Lamers et al. 2020.   [101] Cf. p. 453 with n. 27.
[102] Kenney 1974: 48.   [103] Doblhofer 1992: 5.
[104] Arrighetti 2014; Bossina 2016: 277–82. The connection with his late Italian colleague probably prompted Fraenkel to edit the *Ausgewählte Kleine Schriften* ('Selected minor writings') of their former teacher Friedrich Leo (d. 1914). This was published in the series *Edizioni di storia e letteratura* several decades after Leo's death (Rome, 1960).

participating in the famous meeting with Thomas Mann organised by the latter in Florence.[105] In 1930 he was offered a professorship of Latin at the University of Hamburg which he turned down in 1931.[106] Yet he distanced himself from the strongly positivistic German source criticism, opposing it with the concept of 'arte allusiva' – a notion that also distanced itself from Benedetto Croce's aesthetics.[107] He also criticised the editorial principles formulated by Paul Maas.[108] In contrast to the primarily philological methods of Pasquali, Augusto Rostagni (d. 1961) practised a type of Latin studies with a marked literary-theoretical, theological and comparatist orientation.[109] He was one of the first Italian philologists to insist on the originality of Latin literature compared to Greek.[110]

A notable feature of Italian philology is its self-assured awareness of its own history and of its influential personalities; the long list of Italian representatives of Latin studies, both in terms of methods and interests, can be summarised as a continuing history of outstanding (primarily male) scholars and their successors or rivals.[111]

In recent years educational policy has made efforts to increase the number of universities and a number of new professorships for Latin studies have been created. This has meant that the funds available have to be shared among a smaller number of institutes and this has led to reductions. Under the Berlusconi government it was possible to limit the damage thanks to the commitment of Latinist Alessandro Schiesaro, professor at La Sapienza in Rome (now at the Scuola Normale di Pisa), who was then also a secretary in the Ministry of Education. Further cuts are to be expected under the present regime.

The status of Rome and of Italy as the cradle of Latin and of Latin studies practically guarantees that there will continue to be keen interest in the subject at Italian universities and among young scholars and schoolteachers. For European Latinists, Italy remains the country in which 'it all began' and it will therefore remain the prime destination for study trips and research visits. The country's international institutes, its libraries with mediaeval manuscripts and Renaissance printed books, and the summer schools of the Schola Latina or the Villa Vergiliana of the Virgilian

---

[105] Guida 2014; Bossina 2017, esp. 256–8, and Pasquali himself in his *Storia dello spirito tedesco nelle memorie d'un contemporaneo* (1953).
[106] Lohse 2014: 1–2 with n. 5 (because his wife could not stand the climate in Hamburg).
[107] De Martino 2014.
[108] In his *Storia della tradizione e critica del testo* (Pasquali 1934). Bossina 2016: 289–301.
[109] Lana 1989: 1154–5.   [110] Gatti 2012.
[111] Zetzel 2015: 'Italian scholarship is conscious of its own history in a way that American scholarship rarely is.'

Society,[112] will ensure that it remains a powerful magnet for everyone interested in Latin studies.

In Spain and Portugal, the teaching of Latin at Jesuit colleges and grammar schools has played a major role in the general curriculum.[113] Following the process of secularisation during the nineteenth century, Latin studies are now mainly confined to the academic sphere.[114] These countries have produced an impressive series of editions and academic journals.[115] Historical linguistics as well as editorial philology and textual commentaries remain one of the particular strengths of Latin studies in both countries.

In the republic of Malta, Latin studies have traditionally had a British flavour and even since independence from the UK the subject continues to play a surprisingly important role, perhaps because it functions as a distinguishing feature of the non-African population.[116]

Classical philology in Greece naturally focuses on Greek and Byzantine studies, with the result that Cicero's *De re publica*, a classical Latin text generally regarded as fundamental to European culture, has only recently been completely translated into modern Greek. Many other centrally important classical Latin texts remain untranslated and are therefore scarcely known.[117] The latest trends in educational policy have been rather uneven: the ministry's decision to abolish Latin in schools by 2020 and to replace it with sociology have been reversed by the opposition of the Panhellenic Union of Philologists, and Latin is being gradually reinstated in the Greek school curriculum, becoming again part of the national exams.[118] By contrast, the annual conferences on 'Trends in Classics' in Thessaloniki offer a stimulating occasion in which topics on Latin language and literature are regularly discussed.

### *The Netherlands, Belgium and Scandinavia*

In the sixteenth century, the flowering of Dutch humanism associated with the name of Erasmus led to the publication of numerous printed editions

---

[112] https://scholalatina.it; www.vergiliansociety.org/villa/. Attempts have even been made to resuscitate Latin as a spoken language, for example in Luigi Miraglia's 'Accademia Vivarium Novum', the 'Certamen Ciceronianum' and the 'Certamen Viterbiense della Tuscia'. On similar 'festivals' cf. Stroh 2001: 96–8.
[113] López Férez 2003: 106–19 and de Oliveira 2002.
[114] On the present situation of Latin in Spanish schools see Bulwer 2018: 'Spain has a long tradition of classics teaching, a language based on Latin and a dedicated teaching force. However, pressure has been placed on teaching of classics in schools after the transition to democracy in the 1980s.'
[115] For example the re-organised *Exemplaria Classica* based in Huelva.      [116] Serracino 2018.
[117] Bulwer 2018.
[118] See the report of the online newspaper *I Kathimerini* of 5.9.2018: www.ekathimerini.com/232297/article/ekathimerini/news/anger-over-scrapping-of-latin-classes.

and translations, including the works of early Christian Latin authors such as Augustine and Jerome. Louvain,[119] Bruges, Antwerp and the Leiden School, with outstanding Latinists such as Justus Lipsius, Joseph Scaliger, Daniel Heinsius and Hugo Grotius, emerged as powerhouses for the printing and publication of classical texts.[120] Latin remained the dominant university language until the revolution in 1830, and even at the newly founded universities Latin studies initially remained strong in institutional and personnel terms. The main research interests, continued and refined well into the twentieth century, focused on Old Latin, systematic linguistics and Christian literature. Notable exponents of this approach were Josef Schrijnen (d. 1938) and Christine Mohrmann (d. 1988) who both taught at the Catholic University of Nijmegen, producing a series of studies on 'Old Christian Latin'.[121] Thanks to the *Corpus Christianorum* ('Series Latina' and 'Continuatio Mediaevalis') edition project of the Brepols publishing house, Belgium has established itself as a centre of Latin studies with a focus on early Christian authors.[122] Belgian philologist J. IJsewijn (Louvain, d. 1998) is considered 'the founding father of modern Neo-Latin studies',[123] and these continue to play a prominent part in teaching and research in the Netherlands, Belgium and Luxembourg. After the Second World War and the re-opening of the Vrije Universiteit Amsterdam and the University of Nijmegen, which had been closed by the National Socialists,[124] the dominance of editorial philology was somewhat reduced, but it remains strong in commentary projects such as Cicero *De oratore* in Amsterdam, Apuleius in Groningen and Ammianus Marcellinus in Amsterdam and Utrecht, as well as the research centres for Old Christian and mediaeval authors (Leiden, Utrecht, Louvain, Ghent). The tradition in systematic linguistics is still quite dominant, now with a focus on discourse pragmatic aspects of Latin (Amsterdam). The establishment of national research schools for Classical studies in the Netherlands (OIKOS) and in Ghent (Belgium) has now led to a greater emphasis on postgraduate education.[125] This may be one of the reasons

---

[119] On the teaching of Latin in the 'Leuven Collegium Trilingue' (1517–1797) and Erasmus' three-step plan for learning Ciceronian Latin cf. Feys and Sacré 2018.
[120] Heesakkers and Tournoy 2001: 988–9; Heesakkers 2001: 994–1001; Verhaart 2020: 44–50.
[121] Heesakkers 2001: 1011.    [122] Sacré 2001: 1034.    [123] Rummel and Kooistra 2007: 96.
[124] Their plans to establish, with the assistance of Cologne University, a 'Germanic university' in Leiden failed. Heesakkers 2001: 1012.
[125] The Dutch Research Council is supporting the project 'Anchoring Innovation' with a total of €18.8 million from 2017 to 2027. Latin studies also benefit from this, as the OIKOS group of Dutch classical scholars receives part of this funding.

why the number of university graduates in Classics has significantly increased in recent years.[126]

In the Scandinavian countries, the nationalist ideologies with their emphasis on national folklore started to erode the primacy of classical culture during the nineteenth century.[127] However the tradition of Latin studies in these countries remains intact – in contrast to the fate of Greek – and Latin continues to be taught in grammar schools. There is a traditionally strong emphasis on linguistic studies.[128] In Denmark, Johan N. Madvig (d. 1886), working with German-speaking colleagues J. C. von Orelli (Zurich), K. G. Zumpt (Berlin) and Lachmann, developed fundamental principles in stemmatics and the definition of the archetype.[129] He made philological history with his commentated editions of Cicero (1839) and Lucretius (1825). In Sweden, Einar Löfstedt (d. 1955), founder of the Swedish school of Late Latin syntax and stylistics, together with his student Bertil Axelsson (d. 1984), made substantial contributions to Latin philology. Harald Hagendahl (d. 1986) is outstanding with his studies on the 'Latin Fathers'.[130] Both in Norway and Finland the main emphasis was clearly on linguistic research. Finland also specialises in Latin linguistics, especially onomastics (F. Kajanto, H. Solin and O. Salomies are the leading exponents here)[131] and in the active teaching of language. The Finnish broadcasting company produces a weekly programme entitled 'Nuntii Latini',[132] which is also available in electronic form. It also broadcasts rock and pop songs translated into Latin, in close collaboration with academic activities and with the 'Conventus Internationalis Academiae Latinitati Fovendae' that was held at the University of Jyväskylä in 1997.[133]

*Eastern Europe*

In eastern European countries the status of Latin since the period of humanism has developed in different directions depending on its role in diplomacy and education and in connection with historical-linguistic and hence to some extent nationalistic factors. In the recent period of socialism,

---

[126] Bulwer 2018: this is increased from 6,000 to 10,000 in the past twenty years.
[127] There was some resistance in seventeenth-century Sweden, where King Gustaf Adolf admonished the professors in Uppsala to lecture in Swedish – without success. The Swedes considered themselves the new Romans, embodying Roman virtues and mastering Latin. Lindberg 2002: 1115–20.
[128] Norberg 1989.   [129] Torresin 1999: 680.   [130] Norberg 1989: 752.   [131] Vainio 1999: 1151.
[132] https://yle.fi/nuntii; https://areena.yle.fi/1-1931339 (with glossary). See Stroh 2001: 98.
[133] Bulwer 2018; Farrell 2001: 109–10, who argues that the prominence of 'Latinitas viva' in Finland can be attributed to the fact that Finnish is not an Indo-European language.

Classics was dismissed as ideologically irrelevant. Academic work in Latin studies in Poland and in the former East Germany (GDR) were exceptional in some respects. After the fall of the Iron Curtain and the Berlin Wall, institutes and seminars of classical philology with a long-standing tradition in the subject were re-opened. Since then, Latin studies in Eastern Europe has experienced a renaissance.

In the GDR, Classical institutes were re-opened after the war, following the de-Nazification of the teaching staff. By the year 1946, classical philology was being taught at the five universities of Berlin, Halle, Jena, Leipzig and Rostock. The case of Latinist Johannes Stroux, who had previously taught in Strasbourg, Basel, Kiel, Jena and Munich and from 1935 in Berlin, illustrates the extent to which a university career and hence the continued existence and development of Latin studies in Germany depended on political connections and circumstances. Because of his hostility to National Socialism and his good contacts with the controlling officers of the Soviet Military Administration in Germany, Stroux was appointed Vice-Chancellor of Berlin University in 1945. At Stroux's suggestion, the name was then changed to Humboldt University. He also became president of the German Academy of Sciences in Berlin, which in 1972 was renamed the Academy of Sciences of the GDR. Until his death in 1954, Stroux occupied a leading position in German academic policy. In his academic capacity he sent Josef Stalin a congratulatory letter on his seventieth birthday in which he praised the 'visionary clarity' ('seherische Klarheit') with which Stalin had understood and had determined the course of history. This telegram had not been authorised by the Academy. This provoked its West German members, who subsequently rejected his invitation to the 1950 Academy anniversary; Stroux subsequently resigned from the Academy.[134] On the other hand, he made notable contributions to Latin studies. Classical corpus projects such as the *Corpus inscriptionum Latinarum*, the *Lexicon mediaevalis Latinitatis* and the *Carmina epigraphica* were continued at the Berlin Academy, and the journals *Philologus*, *Klio* and *Das Altertum* were revived; in all of these Johannes Stroux played a substantial role.[135] In 1947 the East German Socialist Unity Party called for the inclusion of Marxist teaching in the university programme.[136] At this point a number of Berlin University professors moved to the newly founded Free University in West Berlin or to other West German universities. Friedrich Klingner for example

---

[134] Stroh 2016: 116–17.   [135] Dummer 1999: 684–6.
[136] Dummer 1999: 681; Gavrilov 2002: 1026.

moved to Munich. However, the Schadewaldt student and Hellenist Johannes Irmscher, a former member of the Nazi party, enthusiastically implemented the ideology in his research and in his activity as an unofficial collaborator of the Ministry of State Security ('Stasi').[137]

Thanks to the location of the headquarters of the Teubner Verlag in Leipzig and the publication of a series of major editions of Latin authors (see pp. 487–8) by East European scholars such as the Hungarian Latinist István Borzsák (d. 2007), Latin studies in the universities always had a certain status and international reputation.[138] It is worth mentioning that the official history of the B. G. Teubner publishing company states that the confiscation of the Leipzig branch in 1952 and the move to Stuttgart in 1955 marked the end of the East German company. The fact that the International Thesaurus Commission proposed to continue cooperation with the Leipzig operation is still regarded as an illegal act.[139] However, the politically motivated publishing policy was unable to prevent the highly successful work of 'East Teubner' (see p. 455).

In Poland, Latin was used as a language of everyday communication even in non-aristocratic circles for much longer than in other European countries, even in West Europe. Among the Polish aristocracy, Polish came second after Latin as a national language. Until the end of the eighteenth century a mixed (macaronic) form of the two languages was used.[140] For the Polish aristocracy and later for the intellectual elite of the post-war era up to 1989, Roman culture and Latin language and literature symbolised a sense of belonging to West Europe and its system of values and to the Catholic Church. It also represented a means of communication that could not be censored. University teaching and research in Latin studies was dominated by personalities such as Tadeusz (Theodor) Zieliński (d. 1944), who after holding professorships in St Petersburg, Rostock (Greek) and Warsaw moved to Germany in 1939.[141] The libraries in all Polish universities with the exception of Kraków were completely destroyed during the Second World War.[142]

Whereas in the GDR the grand old German tradition and in Poland the Catholic Church saved the Classical studies in at least some universities,

---

[137] Stark 2016. [138] Cf. the quotation from Reeve 2000 in n. 46 (p. 455).
[139] Krämer 2011: 59–60: 'Until 1990 the Leipzig Teubner operations were continued illegally and important publishing rights belonging to the Stuttgart company were stolen and used ... This meant that the International Thesaurus Commission tolerated the claim of the confiscated Leipzig operation' (my translation).
[140] Axer and Kolendo 2002: 398; Waquet 2001: 41–7. [141] Plezia 2002: 405–6.
[142] Plezia 2002: 406.

other East European universities were less fortunate. In the schools of the former Czechoslovakia the teaching of classical languages almost completely disappeared. In the Czech Republic the renaissance of Latin studies was supported by the re-opening of the Centre for Greek, Roman and Latin studies at the Czech Academy of Science in Prague with its journals *Listy filologické* and *Eirene*. At the department of Greek and Latin studies at Charles University, there is a strong orientation towards the Prague linguistic circle and its structuralist theory, with tight connections to the Amsterdam School of discourse pragmatics. At present, the full range of Greek and Latin philology is represented in the Czech universities of Prague, Brno and Olomouc. Another encouraging development is that Latin studies are now being taught at the recently founded University of South Bohemia in Budejovice.[143]

For many years Classics in Hungary benefited from Austria-Hungary's promotion of the social elites, for whom a knowledge of Latin was a sign of their superior status. Latin also served as a medium in which members of the elite from the diverse and culturally heterogeneous regions of the Austro-Hungarian monarchy could communicate in a 'universal', neutral language.[144] In the wake of the university reform implemented in 1848–50 on the Prussian model, classical philology became a separate subject. Its founder is generally considered to be Emil Thewrewk von Ponor (d. 1917), who had studied in Vienna with Johannes Vahlen and in Berlin and Leipzig with Friedrich Ritschl and Theodor Mommsen.[145] Von Ponor's German background is indicated by the fact that he translated not only Homer's *Iliad* and Virgil's *Aeneid* but also Tacitus' *Germania*. Nevertheless, in his linguistic and musicological research he stressed the importance of Hungarian as well as motifs of gipsy music and Hungarian and folk songs, for example in correspondence with Franz Liszt.

The Romanian Institute of Classical Studies (Societatea di Studii Clasice) headed by Eugen Cizek (d. 2008) remained intact even under Ceaucescu, albeit with 'din Republica Socialistă România' appended to its title. To this day, the reference to classical Latin and Roman culture – together with an awareness of the 'barbaric' influence of Dacian – is a key element in the process of formation of a national identity, which explains why the status of Latin studies in schools is being positively reconsidered.[146]

The neo-Latin national literature of the early modern period is now a principal focus of research in the Baltic States.[147]

---

[143] Hošek 2003.  [144] Waquet 2001: 96–7.  [145] Ritoók 2003: 755.  [146] See Piatkowski 2002.
[147] Gavrilov 2002: 1028–9 (on the situation up to 1991); Jönsson and Vogt-Spira 2017.

## North America

From the outset, libraries with the works of classical authors and Classical education as a marker of status played a major role in the southern states of the New World and in New England.[148] A network of centrally organised Latin schools or grammar schools based on the British model was soon established. Perhaps the most notable was the Boston Latin School, founded in 1635, a year before the foundation of Harvard College in neighbouring Cambridge. The teachers were British clergymen from Oxford and Cambridge whose task was to teach the children of the colonial elite to write and speak Latin. The Puritans and Quakers supported the Latin schools because of their role in studying the Bible. Certain authors were given canonical status, partly for economic and pragmatic reasons, as a selective approach was adopted to the import of books from Europe.[149] However, these tendencies ran counter to Benjamin Franklin's insistence on strictly utilitarian forms of knowledge.

The period of the Revolution and of independence from the colonial power Britain (eighteenth century) was also a golden age for the reception of Classics in North America, a reception which also promoted a puritanical and typological view of history. The newly founded USA, according to the second President, John Adams, identified itself with classical Greece, with the ideal of liberty and with ethical and ideological liberalism, whereas London was seen as the counterpart of stern, cruel and violent ancient Rome. By contrast, the Roman Cincinnatus and his relinquishment of power were a typological model for George Washington, and John Adams regarded Cicero as an exemplar of the republican virtue of selflessness.[150]

The classical languages were a central element in the school curriculum until the Civil War in the 1860s.[151] At the start of the nineteenth century, classical philology was introduced at Harvard, and in 1819 Edward Everett (d. 1865), who had studied in Göttingen, became the first professor of Greek Studies.[152] Other Ivy League universities such as Princeton and Yale followed suit in the second half of the nineteenth century. The professionalisation of classical philology did not really begin until Basil L. Gildersleeve (d. 1924), 'the father of American ancient philology',

---

[148] On the history of Latin studies in the USA see Calder 1994 and 1998; Buschendorf 2003.
[149] See e.g. Richard 2010 on 'Vergil and the Early American Republic'.
[150] George Washington was called by Byron 'Cincinnatus of the West'. The mixed constitution of Rome, which Thomas Jefferson adopted as the basis of the American constitution, is that described by Polybius (Cicero's *De re publica* was not discovered until 1819). Buschendorf 2003: 833–9.
[151] On the situation of Latin in today's schools, see Hunt 2018b.  [152] Buschendorf 2003: 859.

appeared on the scene.[153] Gildersleeve had studied in Berlin, Bonn (with Ritschl) and Göttingen. From 1856 he taught Greek and Latin at the University of Virginia and in 1878 he moved to Johns Hopkins University. Gildersleeve founded the North American tradition of text-oriented classical philology which in the early stages was influenced by the German tradition.[154] At Harvard, Latinist Edward K. Rand (d. 1945), who had been a student of Ludwig Traube in Munich, began the 'Harvard Servius' in 1915.[155]

As the study of Classics progressed at American universities, a growing sense of national independence emerged, yet always together with a strong awareness of the European roots.[156] At the time of the First World War this movement went hand in hand with a certain resentment *vis-à-vis* German scholarship. The emancipation of US Classical scholarship is associated with the name of the Hellenist Paul Shorey (d. 1934) who had studied in Leipzig, Bonn and Munich, receiving his doctorate in Munich in 1884. After his return to the USA, he held professorships at Bryn Mawr and at Chicago, actively promoting the development of Classical studies in American universities. He frequently and publicly spoke out against German academic practice, notably in a speech to mark the fiftieth anniversary of the American Philological Association in 1919. In this speech he clearly dissociated himself from English classical scholarship as 'brilliantly amateurish' and from the German tradition of 'abuse of conjecture and the pyramiding of hypothesis'.[157] He portrayed this tradition as the epitome of a positivist, pedantic, rule-bound obsession with trivia.[158] Even today, this perception has not entirely disappeared.[159]

---

[153] Buschendorf 2003: 860; Ross 1989: 295–6.
[154] Ross 1989: 297: 'historically the model for our philology has been German'. On the development of Gildersleeve's philological research, in which he gradually moved away from interest in grammar, cf. Winterer 2002: 130–1 and 154; Holtermann 2002: 330: 'practically all leading Classical philologists of North America had studied in Germany and established the seminar concept in American universities'.
[155] Ross 1989: 304: 'during the golden age of the German-style research seminars in this country'; cf. Farrell 2005: 98–9. The Harvard Servius was completed over a century later by Charles E. Murgia and Robert Kaster in 2018 (see S. Huskey and R. Kaster in this volume).
[156] In the editorial statement of the February issue of *Classical Review* 3 (1889), p. 1, the newly established American Philological Association was announced with the conclusion that 'for a fruitful study of Greek and Roman antiquity the practical judgment of the English is no less needful than the unwearied research and the daring speculation of the Germans, or the lucidity and mental vivacity of the French', Stray 2018: 181. But cf. Calder 1994: xxii: 'Nationalism plays no role in our classical scholarship. Whether non-Greek blood flowed in Alexander's veins or whether there is Jewish influence on Vergil's *Eclogue* 4, or whether Agricola was French or the Thracians Bulgarians are just scholarly questions of no more emotional import than whether Euripides' *Electra* precedes Sophocles'.'
[157] Kopff 1994; Stray 2018: 181.   [158] Ludwig 1986: 229–30.
[159] Ross 1989: 299–304 complains 'that there is still no such thing as "American philology", that there is no sign that the "national style" Gildersleeve called for at the beginning of the century has ever appeared'; cf. ibid. 310: the 'imposition of German philology . . . has not been a success'. See Hallett

James Loeb (d. 1933) is an unusual and notable figure on the US Classical scene. He became interested in classical antiquity during his studies at Harvard. In the course of visits to Europe, he built up a considerable network of classicists and publishers. Impressed by the achievements of the French school of classical philology, which had promoted the translation of classical authors (see p. 462), he decided to establish a bilingual series that would make the best texts of Greek and Latin authors, 'from Homer to the Fall of Constantinople', available to a wider public in English translation. He collaborated on the project with the French archaeologist Samuel Reinach, recruiting a number of prominent philologists from the UK and the USA as translators and co-editors.[160] The Loeb Classical Library (LCL) is today published by Harvard University Press, which is now aiming to update the older volumes with new or revised translations.[161]

The seizure of power by the National Socialists in Germany in the 1930s led to the emigration of a number of prominent classicists to the USA, virtually all of them Hellenists.[162] A notable representative of Latin studies was Hellenist Hermann Fränkel (d. 1977), whose Sather Lectures on 'Ovid: a poet between two worlds' demonstrated his credentials as a Latinist with a strong cultural history bent. Another prominent Latinist was Friedrich W. Lenz (born Levy, d. 1969), who from 1939 taught at Yale, Georgetown and Austin, Texas, and edited the Teubner editions of Ovid, Tibullus and Seneca. A protégé of Giorgio Pasquali, he was a representative of the conservative tradition of editorial philology and textual criticism. On the whole the impact of German émigrés at US universities was rather limited.[163]

The history of Latin studies in Canadian universities is similar in many respects to developments in the USA. Classical languages were a central element of the academic institutions founded in the nineteenth century, such as King's College (1827), which later became the University of Toronto. A professorship of Classics was established at McGill College

---

1997: 127 on the 'differences between American and European education in classics': 'it is precisely these differences between me and my European counterparts which have caused me to harbour feelings of scholarly inadequacy. Ours is a generalist rather than a specialist system, one which prides itself on giving rather than foreclosing academic options'; but also ibid. 131: 'we have no need to injure ourselves further by regarding our differences from Europeans as proof of our inferiority to them. Nor do we need to hurt our European colleagues, as Shorey would have had us do, by spotlighting their scholarly shortcomings'.

[160] Stewart 2000 and Salmen 2000. This is the subject of a research project by Mirte Liebregts in Nijmegen entitled 'Behind the red and the green: A socio-cultural history of the Loeb Classical Library'.

[161] Stewart 2000: 104.    [162] A list can be found in Ludwig 1986: 232–4.
[163] Ludwig 1986: 231–2.

in Montreal in 1834. From the outset, teaching was officially bilingual. Accordingly the Classical Association of Canada is also known as 'La Société canadienne des Études classiques'. However the nature of exchanges between students and teachers from diverse linguistic backgrounds and the demands of the research dialogue mean that English tends to dominate.

North America is also the region in which ethnic diversity in the profession has been the subject of most debate. Classicists of colour remain a distinct minority, but efforts continue to diversify the field, with organisations and societies such as the Mountaintop Coalition, the Asian and Asian American Classical Caucus, and Eos (on African receptions of ancient Greece and Rome) playing an active part.[164] Attention in this area has only been increased by the 'Black Lives Matter' movement, as also in the UK, where the under-representation of ethnic minorities is an increasingly live topic.[165]

Classical philology in the USA and Canada follows the British model, which means that Latin studies are generally integrated into Classics departments. This in turn means that they are required to place more emphasis on cultural than on philological aspects in teaching and research. The so-called Harvard School became a powerhouse of research on Virgil, allegedly in response to the consequences of the Vietnam War (see pp. 499–500). Culture-historical and sociological theories such as gender studies, feminist studies and post-colonial studies were adopted more rapidly into Latin studies in the USA and Canada than in other countries.[166] The availability of translations in Loeb editions, which meet the most exacting standards of scholarship, and hence easier access to classical texts, promotes the tendency to teach the subject under the heading of 'classical civilisation' or 'Classics in translation', but the cultural studies orientation also provides fresh perspectives and insights (see p. 483). The LCL project continues to create a demand for philological work and for the corresponding competence. In view of the historical dominance of the British and German traditions in

---

[164] www.mountaintopcoalition.org, www.aaaclassicalcaucus.org, www.eosafricana.org. See also J. Uden in this volume, p. 418, on the nineteenth-century background.

[165] As Tobias Reinhardt tells me, in 2017 members of the Oxford Classics Faculty participated in student-led decolonisation initiatives, challenging the traditional geographical and ethnic boundaries of Classics and divisions such as East and West. Cf. Barnard 2017, but also the dissenting voices of Zuckerberg 2018 and Hallett 2019.

[166] This development may be seen in analogy to the transformation of the American Philological Association/Society for Classical Studies over the past half-century and the more prominent role played by classicists of previously marginalised backgrounds; see Hallett 2019.

editorial philology, it should be stressed that the LCL is an 'area of excellence' for North American Latin studies. This is reflected in a series of new editions in the OCT series in which American Latinists (Wendell Clausen, Robert Kaster, Cynthia Damon) and other scholars from North American universities (Shackleton Bailey of British origin, Richard Tarrant of New Zealand origin) play a leading part.

### Australia and New Zealand

The first secondary schools in Australia and New Zealand naturally provided Latin teaching on the British model, and knowledge of Latin was a compulsory requirement for admission to all Australian universities. The requirement was only dropped after the Second World War. During the 1970s it looked likely that Latin would disappear completely from the Australian school curriculum. However, the importing of Latin textbooks from England – the Cambridge Latin Course and the Oxford Latin Course – revived interest in the subject and reversed the negative trend. In recent years, the position of classical languages in schools has even become stronger. In 2016 they were once again included in the Australian curriculum.[167]

Those who founded and continued the tradition of classical philology in the Australian universities were British graduates.[168] It was also quite common for Australian and New Zealand graduates to continue their studies at Oxbridge and, less frequently, in Germany. Latinist F. A. Todd (d. 1944) was awarded a bursary to study in Leipzig and Jena; his pupil G. P. Ship (d. 1980) held a scholarship at Emmanuel College, Cambridge. Both graduated from the University of Sydney and held, successively, the chair of Latin there.[169] The British influence is still prevalent in Antipodean Latin studies, especially in the ongoing production of philological and culturally oriented commentaries.[170] There have recently been efforts to come to terms with the colonial past of Classical studies and to emphasise the specificity of Antipodean antiquity.[171]

---

[167] Matters 2018. [168] Barsby 1995; Jocelyn 1989.
[169] Jocelyn 1989: 560–3. It is noteworthy that K. F. Quinn, who graduated from Victoria University College in Wellington, took a second bachelor's degree at Emmanuel College, Cambridge after the Second World War; see Jocelyn 1989: 568–70.
[170] Notably by Frances Muecke (Horace); Paul Roche (Lucan); Robert Cowan (Statius); Lindsay and Patricia Watson (Juvenal); Anne Rogerson (*Aeneid* 8, planned for the Cambridge 'Green and Yellow' series).
[171] See the essays in Johnson 2019.

## 9 National Traditions
### Western Classics in ...

Outside Europe and the Anglophone world, the study of Greek and Roman Classics was generally the privilege of an elite who were keen to appropriate the West European culture that they had encountered in different phases of their history.

Latin studies have always enjoyed a high status in Latin America, thanks to their influence on the respective national languages and cultures.[172] The Latin schools and Jesuit schools in which Latin was intensively taught began to operate from the beginning of the colonial period. During the independence movements of the nineteenth century, Latin authors were frequently invoked as part of the formation of national identity.[173] Several researchers at Brazilian universities have established regular formal contacts with German Latinists, a fact which reflects the recent history of immigrants to Brazil from European countries, especially Germany.[174] Especially since the FIEC conference in Ouro Preto in 2004, efforts to strengthen the position of Classics at Brazilian universities have been intensified.[175] After a hiatus of fifty years, interest in Classical studies at schools is now increasing. A group of lecturers and students at the University of São Paulo started the 'Projeto Minimus' in 2013 with the aim of introducing the subject in the first years of secondary school.[176]

Marburg Latinist Georg Rohde (d. 1960), a former student of Eduard Norden, emigrated to Turkey in 1935 to take up the chair of Greek and Latin language at Ankara University established by Kemal Atatürk. He made a major contribution, overseeing translations of classical authors into Turkish, producing textbooks for Latin and Greek and working hard to build up the library.[177] In 1949 he left Ankara to take up the first professorship of Latin at the Free University of Berlin. At the moment the main focus of Classics and ancient history in Turkey is on classical archaeology and epigraphics, both subject areas – still with the support of the Turkish

---

[172] See the essays in Laird and Miller 2018 and in Feil et al. 2021.
[173] Gonzales de Tobia 2001: 35.
[174] To take one example, Jürgen Paul Schwindt (Heidelberg University) and Isabella Tardin Cardoso (Campinas University) are collaborating on a project on the Theory of Philology (www.uni-heidelberg.de/fakultaeten/philosophie/skph/theorie-der-philologie/).
[175] Several new academic journals have been founded: *Classica*, founded in 1988, is the official publication of the Sociedade Brasileira de Estudos Clássicos (SBEC). It has now been joined by *Letras Clássicas* since 1996, *Nuntius Antiquus* (2008) and *Revista Caletroscópio* (2012). Konstan et al. 2001.
[176] Cunha Corrêa 2018. The 'Classics for All' programme in the UK also played a part here (see p. 458 with n. 61).
[177] Ludwig 1986: 221.

authorities – staffed mainly by European and North American research teams. Latin studies do not play any part in these subject areas.[178]

Classical philology in Russia still benefits from structures established in the period of national classicism in the eighteenth century. German philologist and Orientalist Gottlieb S. Bayer (d. 1738) established Classical studies at the Academy of Sciences in St Petersburg as part of the effort to 'open a window onto Europe'.[179] The Halle philologist Heinrich K. Eichstädt, an admirer of Richard Bentley, became a professor at the Imperial Russian University of Moscow. Students of the Alexander Nevsky seminars in St Petersburg were enthusiastic practitioners of '*loqui Latine*'.[180] Following the foundation of universities in the Baltic regions, classical languages made rapid advances. German philologists August Nauck (d. 1892) and Lucian Müller (d. 1898) were actively involved in this upswing.[181] However, during the 1871 school reforms, Classics were subjected to severe criticism, as they were seen as an instrument of German-inspired conservatism. Classical philologists were persecuted during the 1917 October Revolution and into the 1920s. Josef Stalin's efforts to reintroduce Latin in schools were unsuccessful because of the lack of trained teachers. The chairs of classical philology in Moscow, Leningrad and Tbilisi remained in place during the communist period and in 1989, thanks to the existing structures, contacts with western universities were rapidly re-established.[182] One result of this was the foundation of the Bibliotheca Classica in St Petersburg, an independent research centre, editing the journal *Hyperboreus*.[183] However the tradition of the classicistic orientation of Russian Classics and their embedding in Russian Orthodox culture meant that Greek studies were the main beneficiary of this process.

In the African states the tradition of Latin studies is naturally associated with the acculturation processes of the colonial era and hence it has proved difficult to maintain continuity. The French-founded schools and universities in the Maghreb countries and in central African states such as Senegal attracted a large number of productive Latinists. The most prominent example is the Augustine specialist André Mandouze (d. 2006), a student of Henri-Irénée Marrou (d. 1977), who, like Marrou, taught at the University of Algiers founded in 1909. Both scholars were actively engaged from 1946 onwards in the struggle against colonialism. Since independence from France, Latin studies in the Maghreb states have struggled, particularly in comparison with archaeological and cultural-historical research,

---

[178] Sinanoğlu 1989, esp. col. 581.　[179] Frolov 2004.　[180] Gavrilov 2002: 1018.
[181] Gavrilov 2002: 1022.　[182] Pachenko 1992.　[183] Gavrilov 2002: 1030; Schwindt 2003: 1310.

9 *National Traditions* 479

which is increasingly focused on Tunisia (above all Carthage).[184] The *Revue Africaine des Études Latines* is published by the Ausonius publishing house in Bordeaux. The main impetus for Latin studies today comes from South Africa, where the British tradition is dominant. The Classical Association of South Africa has had a strong international presence since it was re-established in 1956 (the original foundation was in 1927).[185] It is interesting from a German perspective that chairs in the South African universities have frequently been held by German Latinists (Gregor Maurach in Pretoria, Bernhard Kytzler in Durban). The dispute between German Latinist Heinz Hoffmann, former lecturer at the University of South Africa in Pretoria, and Jo-Marie Claassen, professor in Stellenbosch, on the issue of the historicity or fictionality of Ovid's exile in Tomi became a minor international cause célèbre. There are flourishing exchanges with Germany, thanks in particular to the support of the Alexander von Humboldt Foundation. A South African Latinist from Stellenbosch of Afrikaans origin told me that she still felt 'Calvinistically challenged' and therefore continued to cultivate an unusually wide-ranging international network.

Latin was first introduced to Japan through the activities of Christian missionaries in the sixteenth century. However, after the prohibition of the Christian religion in the middle of the seventeenth century, Latin studies became a thing of the past. At the end of the nineteenth century, the Samurai were expropriated and banished. The Japanese educational canon was again open to western culture and literature. Dairoku Kikuchi (d. 1917), who later became Japanese minister of education, obtained outstanding results in Latin studies at University College School and went on to study Classics at Cambridge. The German-Russian philosopher Raphael von Koeber (d. 1923) taught at the University of Tokyo, where he played an influential role in strengthening the academic presence of Latin studies in Japan. The first professorship in Classics was established in Kyoto in 1939 and its first incumbent was Tanaka Hidenaka (d. 1974), a student of von Koeber and the pioneer of classical philology in Japan.[186]

The history of Latin studies in China is also closely bound up with Christian missionary activity in the country. In the nineteenth century,

---

[184] Thus Ammar Mahjoubi, emeritus Professor of Ancient History at the University of Tunis, in an article dated 17 December 2016 in the Tunisian Journal *Leaders*: 'L'éradication de la langue et culture latines au Maghreb'. See also Schwindt 2003: 1309.
[185] The Association publishes *Acta Classica* (founded 1958), one of the most internationally renowned academic journals. Dominik 2003.
[186] Kubo 1989; Dettmer 2000; Jacob 2016.

classical missionary schools and seminaries were established in Shanghai and in Wuhan, where Latin was taught and in some instances used as the language of tuition. This tradition was interrupted during the Cultural Revolution in the 1960s but it was resumed in the 1980s. However, western Classics remains marginal in China in cultural and academic terms.[187]

## Summary and Prospects

It is not always easy to attribute the various research interests in Latin studies to 'national' schools. The focus on the study of religion which originated in the French tradition of cultural anthropology, primarily in Greek studies, has now become international and is strongly represented in Latin studies.[188] The Afrocentrist discourse developed by Martin Bernal in the USA[189] has been taken up in the UK by scholars interested in 'Black Romans' and the 'Black presence in Roman Britain'.[190] Research on Roman philosophy, late antique (including early Christian) Latin literature, the history of Roman science and Latin specialist literature cannot be assigned to specific 'national' schools.

Throughout the world, Latin studies are associated with the study of classical Roman history and are inextricably linked to the role of the Christian church.[191] This double embedding in the pagan-classical and in the ecclesiastical sphere gave the Latin language an exceptional impetus. The process of colonisation and the use of Latin in diplomatic communication between nation states have further reinforced the status of the language at the international level. This all-encompassing pre-eminence – political, ecclesiastical and legal – has also strengthened the western European educational institutions in which Latin has been taught since the classical period, first as a native language and later as the language of scholars and of the clergy. As the means of communication used by clergymen, lawyers and teachers, Latin permeated national cultures and their languages, even at the level of everyday interaction, in which Latin tags are still present in modern languages.[192]

---

[187] Mutschler and Mittag 2008; Scheidel 2009.
[188] Above all in the work of Jörg Rüpke, from the Tübingen School of Hubert Cancik.
[189] Cf. Ronnick 2010 on 'Vergil in the Black American Experience' and most recently the critical view of Barnard 2017, offering a counter-narrative on the reception of the classical tradition ('Black classicism').
[190] Pirker 2010. Cf. J. Uden in this volume (pp. 419–20 and 430–1).    [191] Waquet 2001: 41–79.
[192] My English neighbour (the translator of the present chapter) Paul Knight mentioned a number of Latin tags commonly used in English such as *ad nauseam, ad infinitum* and *vice versa*. When speaking German I sometimes use expressions such as *corpus delicti, in nuce, in dubio pro reo, stante pede* and *carpe diem*, but I have noticed that they are not always understood.

In the nineteenth century, Latin studies were strongly promoted in European universities and educational centres, and it was from there that their influence spread and deepened in non-European institutions. The position and promotion of Latin studies in German, English, Italian, French and Spanish universities have had a clear multiplying effect: central European universities with large Classics departments were and are more likely to attract young Latinists as well as senior scholars from home and abroad. This in turn meant that the cultural, confessional and political characteristics of a given country, the national characteristics that emerged at an early stage and continue to exert a certain influence, have receded in importance to a large extent at the academic level. This may be an essential feature of all efforts to achieve academic objectivity. But in the case of classical Greek and Latin, this certainly also means that the European, especially the West European, tradition has had the greatest influence on individual academic disciplines.

This tradition, naturally enough given its Mediterranean location, defines the subject and plays a leading role in the development of philological methods, the evaluation and analysis of literature. This may be a cause for concern. However, it is clear that interest in Latin language and literature remains intact even outside Europe, a fact which affirms the quality of its forms and contents as well as its linguistic relevance. A tendency can be observed to burst free of traditions and to raise questions about which traditions and methods should dominate the scholarly study of Latin language and literature. The answers to this central question tend to vary of course, but they are not determined by national or ideological schools of thought.

## 2 Priorities and Traditions in Research from the Nineteenth to the Twenty-First Centuries

As Latin studies became institutionalised and professionalised from the nineteenth century onwards, the differing status of Latin in schools and universities in individual countries and regions led to varying priorities in research. These national differences are still discernible today.[193] The majority of initiatives and activities in the field of classical philology – and hence of Latin studies – remain chiefly the preserve of West European and North American universities. How far this picture will change in the coming decades is an open question and certainly ripe for challenge;

---

[193] Schwindt 2003: 1311–19.

expertise and intellectual potential are available worldwide, thanks to the initiatives of individual scholars and international networks. The traditional division between linguistic and antiquarian philology (p. 454) has been completely replaced by textual criticism, historical linguistics and 'literary studies'. In the latter, theory tends to dominate. However, in contrast to 'modern philologies', with their clear division between linguistics and literature, the distinction between philological and literary scholarship in Classics has not been particularly significant. More recently, though, this distinction has come into sharper focus.[194]

In the UK, editorial philology and philological commentaries are central areas of research, thanks mainly to series produced by major British publishers such as Cambridge University Press, Oxford University Press, Routledge and others (even though the editors are not always British nationals).[195] New ideas and trends are also emerging in linguistics, literary criticism, cultural history and increasingly also in reception studies[196] as a result of close informal cooperation between Classics departments and possibly also in response to the government's insistence that research should have an 'impact beyond academia'. In some instances this has even led to a latter-day revival of the 'battle of the books' between hardline philologists on the one hand and literary and cultural scholars on the other. Similar tendencies are observable in the Netherlands and Belgium, given their alignment to British discourse. By contrast, their attachment to their humanistic tradition means that they give greater priority to Neo-Latin research. In German-speaking countries, the philological tradition of the new Bonn School (below, pp. 492–3) and positivistic source criticism (p. 465) have remained strong, but since the 1960s efforts have been made to introduce literary discussion methods and theory formation, particularly in the reception research of the Konstanz School, which Manfred Fuhrmann introduced into Latin studies.[197] Its counterpart is the American 'reader response criticism'.[198] In southern Europe, historical linguistics as well as editorial and commentary philology remain prominent. Latin studies in France have been shaped by structural anthropology and the religious studies of the Paris School, with its strong

---

[194] See the chapter by James Clackson in this volume.
[195] Kenney 1989: 640–1. In addition to the edition and commentary series (pp. 493–6), small-format and popular series such as 'Roman Literature and Its Contexts' (CUP), 'Classical Foundations' (Routledge) and 'Oxford Approaches to Classical Literature' (OUP) should also be mentioned.
[196] The 'Society for the Classical Tradition' was founded in Boston in 1988 and had a broad impact. But cf. the criticism by Martindale 2002: 144–5. On this, see James Uden's chapter in this volume.
[197] On Fuhrmann and Konstanz reception aesthetics see Schmidt 2002: 322; Edmunds 2005: 6–7.
[198] Schwindt 2003: 1313–14.

orientation towards Greek literature. On the other hand, the French tradition of Budé bilingual editions with commentaries – now often with translations only – creates opportunities to edit the works of 'marginal' authors, making them more easily accessible for teaching and research purposes. Possibly due to the obligation to teach 'Great Books' undergraduate courses, classicists at northern American universities have concentrated their research mainly, but certainly not always, on major authors.[199] Teaching and research – perhaps an echo of previous criticisms of German-language research and of the anti-positivistic approach of the new criticism – tend to align strongly with modern literary studies,[200] with different focuses, as for example of identity and diversity research. In recent times, Latin studies in the UK and USA have also been marked by a strong theoretical interest in linguistics and semantics.[201]

Is it possible to detect and to describe lines of development within existing national traditions in Latin studies and across these traditions as a result of academic exchanges? International networks are still being intensified and exchanges of junior and senior researchers are promoted by a series of high-level exchange programmes[202] and by the considerable number of conferences. Nevertheless – and this applies to Classics as a whole – research in English, German and other languages tends to operate in parallel lines (clearly with more potential for cross-communication), with the exception of text digitisation projects. Nevertheless, it seems likely that national traditions will continue to be cultivated and to have an impact, with the positive effect that considerable diversity and also a kind of equilibrium of methods and approaches results.[203] In the following pages an attempt will be made to illustrate these developments by means of selected case studies.

### Textual Criticism and Editorial Philology

The Oxford Classical Texts and the Bibliotheca Teubneriana occupy pride of place in Latinist edition philology. The OCT editions are traditionally

---

[199] On the problematic issue of defining canons and 'Great Books', see Irene Peirano Garrison's chapter in this volume.
[200] For an exception see Martindale 2002.
[201] E.g. Adams 2008; Dickey and Chahoud 2010; Devine and Stephens 2013; J. Clackson in this volume.
[202] The Alexander von Humboldt Foundation and the Feodor-Lynen scholarship are both explicitly designed to internationalise German scholarship and exchanges with the USA. Schmitz 2003b: 1298–9; Schwindt 2003: 1310–11; Calder 1994: xxxiv–xxxv.
[203] An overview of the situation and tendencies of Latin studies in different countries and within national traditions is given by Schwindt 2003: 1307–22.

less conservative, with a slimmer apparatus criticus.[204] The Teubners, like the majority of South European series (for example the Italian *Corpus Scriptorum Paravianum* or *Bibliopolis*, the *Collection des Universités de France*), typically contain a more comprehensive apparatus.[205] The Loeb Classical Library under editor George Goold has increased its ambition and quality since the 1970s.[206] For some time now OCTs have permitted English prefaces rather than Latin. In the BT the Latin preface was not challenged until 2017.[207]

In the following three examples, I will attempt to show how certain methodological decisions in textual criticism can be attributed to national influences and schools or even to outstanding individuals ('heroes').[208] The principle of (self-)attribution to a national tradition goes hand in hand with reverence for certain academics and a professed allegiance to the philological methods that they adopted.[209] For British editors the 'heroic critic' of Latin texts is clearly Housman,[210] while in Germany the list is headed by Lachmann, followed by a number of further scholar-heroes such as Leo, Jachmann, Ritschl, Bücheler and Zwierlein.[211] The line that stretches back to Bentley and to Housman is continued in British philology and hence in Anglo-American philology generally. However, this approach, as we can see in Propertius philology, also has its exponents in

---

[204] Reeve 2000: 204.   [205] On the Italian editorial tradition see Reeve 2000: 204–5.
[206] Reeve 2000: 200.
[207] Augustine, *Contra Academicos, De beata vita, De ordine* (ed. Therese Fuhrer and Simone Adam 2017) has an English preface. In a personal communication Heinz-Günther Nesselrath, a member of the BT scientific committee, bemoaned the 'fall' of the rampart, and others continue to prefer Latin (e.g. Deufert's Lucretius, 2019) The issue was raised much earlier in the Anglophone world, with the OCT Sophocles edited by Lloyd-Jones and Wilson in 1990. See Reeve 2000: 196, who ridicules the often poor or incorrect Latin of *praefationes*; also Tarrant 2016a: 140–1 and 157. Tarrant himself continues to use Latin (as in his Ovid *Metamorphoses*, 2004), to maintain consistency with the Latin apparatus criticus.
[208] Following the lead of Tarrant 2016a: 18–29 ('the heroic editor').
[209] In other disciplines too, the field of textual scholarship and editorial theory has been shaped differently by national traditions, mainly Anglo-American and continental. Fraistat and Flanders 2013: 4–6 (and in their volume, the chapters on 'Anglo-American editorial theory' by K. Sutherland and on 'Continental editorial theory' by G. Lernout).
[210] Hübner 2010: 6–8 goes to the heart of the matter when he says: 'For everyone interested in Manilius, the crucial question is: "What do you think of Housman?" Housman's arrogance in individual cases is often criticised in England but his overall achievement as an editor and a commentator is seldom questioned.' He refers to J. B. Hall, 'who raised the issue of nationalism, referring to an "anti-Housman lobby" in Germany'.
[211] Tarrant 2016a: 22 quotes Don Fowler, who praised Zwierlein as 'one of the few modern scholars to bear the weight of sustaining the German Great Tradition'. On the other hand, Tarrant 2016a critically comments on the methodological loyalty and 'fidelity' in connection with Zwierlein's students. It is relevant in our context that Tarrant is a US scholar of New Zealand origin and displays a certain distance *vis-à-vis* the British tradition.

Germany and, with some modifications, in Italy.[212] The critical confrontation with the German tradition was initiated mainly by Housman, who contrasted his own rational approach to text-critical issues to what he considered to be the weakness of German editorial philology: its naive faith in methodological thoroughness and routine.[213]

*a)   Horace: German Conservatism versus British Conjectural Criticism*
The history of the critical editions of Horace's poetry graphically illustrates the persistence of national traditions in editorial philology to the present day. The starting point is the 1711 edition of Horace by Richard Bentley, Master of Trinity College, Cambridge. Bentley's method of 'divinatio' and of *per te sapere aude,* together with his numerous amendments and conjectures in the printed text, provided material for criticism or at least critical discussion for all subsequent editors of Horace.[214]

The history of modern critical editions of Horace text was initially dominated by the conservative German school. It begins with the two-volume Teubner by Ritschl students Otto Keller and Alfred Holder (1864–70, with 2nd edn 1899–1925), in which the manuscript tradition is meticulously documented. Such a 'recensio codicum' subsequently became fundamental for all later editors of Horace. The edition by Friedrich Vollmer (1907, 2nd edn 1912), a student of Leo and Wilamowitz, dividing the manuscripts in three groups, does not make significant amendments to the text. It is this version – with about twenty-four conjectures[215] – on which the slightly less conservative BT edition by Friedrich Klingner (1939, 4th edn 1959) is based.

---

[212] See pp. 488 and 491. More recently, German (Hans-Christian Günther) and Italian (the later work of Giancarlo Giardina) as well as French (Gautier Liberman) and Spanish (Antonio Ramírez de Verger) editors align themselves with the Bentley–Housman tradition, as Tarrant 2016a: 22 points out.
[213] Brink 2010: 171–2: 'By the time when Housman established his own position, during the last two decades of the 19th century, the great merits of procedure German scholarship had tended to give way to a certain complaisant trust in method ... Housman often expressed his admiration for the achievements of earlier German scholarship. But, precisely because of his adherence to rationality and scholarship, he saw the dangers in rationality misapplied, that is, mechanical scholarly routine.' Cf. ibid. 188: 'the two adversaries are best described as contemporary sciolism, especially Victorian, and mechanical methodizing, or science overshooting its mark, especially towards the end of the century in Germany'.
[214] See Brink 2010: 66–72 on the 700 to 800 changes of the common readings; Konstan and Muecke 1993: 179–80 say that there are 'nearly seven hundred ... of which under two hundred were conjectures, the rest having some manuscript support, though not necessarily the best'. On Bentley's exchange with the Dutch philologist and editor of Petronius Pieter Burman and their common impact on the 'new self-consciousness of philologists', see Verhaart 2020: 94–119.
[215] Tarrant 2016b: 300.

The first British reaction came in 1901 in the form of a pared-down OCT by E. C. Wickham, followed by a second edition, revised by H. W. Garrod, in 1912. This version has never played a significant role in philological research on Horace.[216] The same can also be said of the Budé edition by François Villeneuve (1927–34) and for the 1957 *editio Paraviana* by Massimo Lenchentin de Gubernatis, which once again provided detailed documentation of the manuscript tradition. A second edition, revised by Domenico Bo, was published in 1960.

This meant that, 250 years after Bentley, the Horace text and its tradition had now been meticulously but unspectacularly documented and/or edited. However, the position advocated by conservative continental European scholars, namely that the existing text was correctly edited and that Bentley's amendments could not be justified,[217] was itself soon called into question.[218]

The two most recent Horace Teubners are a testimony to German publishing history as well as to the British and continental European philological traditions.[219] The Klingner edition (1950) had been subjected to a great deal of criticism because of its clearly mistaken interpretation of the manuscript tradition.[220] It was followed in 1985 by a West (Stuttgart) Teubner by D. R. Shackleton Bailey (d. 2005) in which conjectural criticism in the Bentley tradition again reared its head with a vengeance.[221] The critical apparatus in accordance with the British method is extremely pared down, documenting almost exclusively the amendments to the tradition. In line with Housman's verdict that certain interpolated verses should not be excluded, Shackleton Bailey retains a number of passages previously bracketed in the editorial consensus.[222] In about forty instances the amendments are based either on the editor's judgement or on older conjectures, particularly those in Bentley's 1711 edition.[223] In some cases he revived or even rescued Bentleian conjectures that were not even

---

[216] Tarrant 2016b: 292–3; Harrison 2016. But cf. n. 224.
[217] Lenchantin de Gubernatis, quoted by Borzsák 1984: v.
[218] Tarrant 2016b: 300–1 with reference to Paul Maas, C. O. Brink, Josef Delz, D. R. Shackleton Bailey and his own planned OCT; compare this opinion with Tarrant 1983: 185.
[219] According to Doblhofer 1992: 15: 'In Borzsák and Shackleton Bailey there is an encounter between continental European (mainly German) and Anglo-Saxon tradition' (my translation). Cf. Tarrant 2016a.
[220] Tränkle 1993; Harrison 1995: 1–2; Tarrant 2016b: 316.
[221] Delz 1988: 501: 'Bentley and Housman would congratulate him' (my translation).
[222] For example in *Sat.* 10.1–8 (in spite of the critical note in his apparatus) and *Carm.* 3.11.17–20. Tarrant 2016b: 313–15, with a reference to Housman ('"the coward's remedy" of athetesis').
[223] Shackleton Bailey has frequently been referred to as 'Bentley *redivivus*', for example by Delz 1988: 495 (cf. Krämer 2011: 6); Doblhofer 1992: 3.

## 9 National Traditions

mentioned by Klingner and Borzsák, as for example *Campum* for *populum* (codd.) in *Epist.* 1.6.59:[224] *Si bene qui cenat bene uiuit, lucet, eamus | quo ducit gula, piscemur, uenemur, ut olim | Gargilius, qui mane plagas, uenabula, seruos | differtum transire Forum Campumque iubebat* (*Epist.* 1.6.56–9).[225]

The impact of Shackleton Bailey's edition of Horace was all the more sensational[226] because in the previous year (1984) an extremely conservative edition by the Hungarian scholar István Borzsák (d. 2007) had been published by East Teubner (Leipzig). This edition contained a substantial apparatus, including many *quisquiliae* of the manuscript tradition, but only a small number of modern conjectures. In his expansive critical apparatus to the passage just quoted he mentions the rather uninteresting variants *uiuit bene* from the scholia to Persius (56), *ueneremur* from the ninth-century Harleianus 2725 and a fifteenth-century manuscript that had it *ante rasuram* (57), and *gragilius* in four manuscripts (58).

The criticisms of each of these editions reflect the opposition between the respective academic schools: Borzsák's meticulous approach to the manuscript tradition of the text is contrasted with the 'exaggerated admiration for Bentley and Brink'. Opponents of conservatism responded by endorsing the critical-sceptical 'revival of certain neglected insights' by Shackleton Bailey, lambasting 'the indiscriminate mass of useful and useless information' in Borzsák's edition, which was seen as the nadir of East Teubner editorial history and hence of continental European editorial philology.[227]

Ultimately the conservative German tradition of Keller/Holder and Klingner and the British conjectural-critical method of Shackleton Bailey can be seen as opposites.[228] The new edition by the US philologist Richard Tarrant, to be published by OCT, will, in the editor's words, represent a halfway house between these extremes and will perhaps rise

---

[224] Tarrant 2016b: 304 calls it one 'of Bentley's most brilliant and convincing alterations'. Yet he is also critical, pointing out that in the more recent English-language commentaries on Horace the Teubner by Shackleton Bailey does not play a central role and even lags behind the editions of Klingner, Wickham and Brink (Tarrant 2016b: 316–17).

[225] 'If he who feasts well, lives well, it is day: let us go where our appetite leads us: let us fish, let us hunt, as did some time Gargilius who ordered his toils, hunting-spears, slaves, early in the morning to pass through the crowded forum and the Campus Martius.'

[226] Tränkle 1993: 17: 'ein Paukenschlag' ('a bombshell'). Tränkle counts 450 passages in which Shackleton Bailey's edition differs from Klingner's.

[227] The quotations are found in Doblhofer 1992: 15 and Tarrant 2016b: 293 (cf. Tarrant 2016a: 68). Cf. also Delz 1988: 495.

[228] The reservations about the athetesis of interpolations which characterises Shackleton Bailey's 'Horace' are in line with Housman's practice (Brink 2010: 178–9).

above these national traditions – although not in the sense of the 'middle position' advocated by Tränkle in 1993.[229]

### b) *Propertius: Continental Erudition versus British 'divinatio'*

The differences between national traditions and methods are even more pronounced in recent Propertius philology. The national differences and the resultant – often virulent – controversy started in the British camp. In the nineteenth century a large number of international editors had created a situation described by J. S. Phillimore in his 1910 OCT with the often-quoted remark: *quot editores, tot Propertii*.[230] After two Loeb editions by E. A. Barber (1905 and 1912), the same scholar edited a – still rather conservative – OCT in 1953. In his second OCT edition of 1960, Barber adopted the text-critical considerations in Shackleton Bailey's *Propertiana* (1956), which meant that he was now moving closer to the British tradition.[231]

A further step in the history of the *Propertii* was marked by the two Teubners by R. Hanslik (Leipzig, 1979) and P. Fedeli (Stuttgart, 1984, corr. 1994 and 2006). The difference between these two editions – in contrast to the Horace Teubners – is that Hanslik in the East Teubner edition sticks to the 'English tradition of Bentley and Housman'[232] while Fedeli in the West Teubner follows the conservative continental European method.[233]

It is noteworthy that the conservative editors of Propertius, the early Barber and Fedeli, are seasoned antiquarian and philological experts. This erudition is evident in their commentaries (H. E. Butler and E. A. Barber: 1933; P. Fedeli: book 1, 1918; book 2, 2005; book 3, 1985; book 4, 1965 and, with R. Dimundo and I. Ciccarelli, 2015). The critical apparatus – even in Barber's second OCT – is packed with information.[234] This runs contrary

---

[229] Tränkle 1993: 26; Tarrant 2016b: 292 and 301. Tarrant plans to present the sequence of the *corpus* (usually arranged by genre) chronologically, based on the date of writing or publication (2016b: 320). This will fly in the face of all previous traditions. The plan to make an 'apparatus plenus' electronically available is undoubtedly appropriate.

[230] Cf. e.g. Butrica 1997: 176; Tarrant 2006: 45–55; Tarrant 2016a: 105–6.

[231] Shackleton Bailey strongly questioned the reliability of the traditional text and underlined the urgent need for amendments; Tarrant 2016a: 106.

[232] According to his (conservative) reviewer Antonio La Penna (1982, quoted by Tarrant 2016a: 22) who compares Hanslik's edition with those of Shackleton Bailey and G. P. Goold.

[233] For this he was severely reprimanded by Stephen Heyworth; cf. Tarrant 2016a: 106–7. Fedeli 1986 describes this kind of criticism as 'philological terrorism'. Cf. also Butrica 2006: 'Fedeli simply leaps from Lachmann to the present.' Fedeli for his part does not pull any punches when criticising Housman and Goold (e.g. Fedeli 2006: 16–17). Another example of European continental conservatism is the edition and commentary of book 4 by Éric Coutelle in the Belgian monograph series Éditions Latomus (2015).

[234] Fedeli's Teubner is even hypertrophic, in the words of my Basel teacher Joseph Delz to me and to participants in a seminar on Propertius.

to the principles of Housman, who insisted that the intellect should play a primary role in decisions about the constitution of the text and that precisely for this reason textual transpositions were permitted.[235] Shortly after publication of the commentary by Butler and Barber, Housman wrote a review in which he bemoaned the editors' dependence, even in textual matters, on their German predecessor, the commentated version by M. Rothstein based on the old positivist tradition. He added that a new edition was urgently needed.[236]

Housman's expectations were perhaps only satisfied with the publication of texts by the general editor of the LCL G. P. Goold (LCL, 1990) and Oxford Latinist Stephen Heyworth (OCT, 2007), who wrote his doctorate on the manuscript tradition. These editions were produced after mutual consultation[237] and both invoke Housman's project for an edition of Propertius (just before his death in 1936 he gave instructions for his first draft of this edition to be burned).[238] Heyworth had the opportunity to consult Housman's unpublished notes in the Oxbridge libraries where he worked. Heyworth often adopts Housman's opinions, accepting forty-seven of his conjectures (including transpositions). He also mentions many of his reflections in the apparatus criticus and in his philological commentary entitled *Cynthia*.[239] The invocation of the often cutting and provocative Englishman may have prompted Goold and Heyworth, relying on the divinatory method, boldly to alter the traditional text in several places and to provoke criticism. Heyworth consistently follows the principle that any alteration – conjectures, atheteses, transpositions – of the (defective) text may be justified by cogent arguments.[240] He has therefore produced a text that is quite different from all previous editions, including that of Goold,[241] not least by dislocating in the printed text all bracketed verses to the end of the poem.

The most spectacular example is Elegy 3.7, whose 'chaos ... exceeds that of all other poems in Propertius'.[242] Heyworth's large-scale transpositions and bracketing of two distichs (21–4) creates a neat progression and continuity of thoughts. Yet the extensive changes allow the methodological

---

[235] Brink 2010: 179–80. On Housman's divinatory faculty see Kenney 1974: 128–9.
[236] Housman 1934: 136: 'a new edition ought to raise itself high above the level of intelligence, attention, and scholarship to which we have been accustomed'.
[237] Goold 1990: ix and Heyworth 2007: xii.   [238] Heyworth 2009: 11.
[239] Heyworth 2007: xi and xii with n. 4. See also Luck 2009: 250, who in his bilingual edition (German–Latin, Zurich, 1964) follows the Housman line.
[240] This principle is explained by Canadian Latinist Butrica 1997.   [241] Tarrant 2016a: 105–23.
[242] Goold 1990: 22.

conclusion that there are still other possibilities to understand the poem's structure and train of thought.[243]

In some cases Heyworth appears to be even less sceptical than the allegedly conservative critics. In 2.34, another much studied elegy, his scepticism is rather directed against older critics as Vulpius (1710), Lachmann (1816) or Lucian Müller in the old Teubner (1870); he also steps back behind the editions of Barber, who divided it into two poems (vv. 1–14 and 25–94), and Fedeli, who transposes verses 51–4 between 46 and 47. Heyworth keeps the transmitted order of verses with the exception of the two couplets 77–80, which he inserts after line 66.[244] Unlike Butrica, who alleged 67–84 to be an interpolation in the archetypal text, Heyworth brackets only the couplet 83–4.[245] The reason lying behind these seemingly conservative decisions may be conveyed by two examples in verses 31–40, where Propertius recommends to his addressee Lynceus to write small-scale poetry in the Alexandrian, not in the grandiose tragic or epic, style. The text in line 31, which Fedeli in his apparatus assesses as 'locus uexatissimus, mea sententia prorsus deperditus' (*tu †satius memorem musis† imitere Philitan*), and in line 39, where Barber and Fedeli put cruces (respectively †*non amphiareae prosint tibi fata quadriga*† and †*non amphiareae prosint tibi*† *fata quadrigae*), is easy to restore according to Heyworth; he prints: *tu potius memorem Musis imitere Philitan* (31) and *Amphiaraëae nil prosint fata quadrigae* (39).[246] The only conjectures Heyworth makes in the transmitted text of Elegy 2.34 seem to be rather unspectacular, namely to read *sic* instead of *haec* in each of verses 85, 87 and 89 (*sic quoque ... ludebat ... Varro*; *sic quoque ... cantarunt scripta Catulli*; *sic etiam ... confessa est pagina Calui*).[247] This is a neat idea to avoid repetition of *haec* in 81 which, after relocating 77–80 after 66 and after deleting the couplet of 83–4, must refer to Virgil's *Eclogues*, which is not the case for the references to the erotic poetry of Varro, Catullus and Calvus (and Gallus and Propertius) in the following and final couplets (85–94).[248] These samplings prove the point that even the most sceptical critics can decide to accept

---

[243] Tarrant 2016a: 79–80.
[244] Against Günther 1997: 32 and Tarrant 2006: 62, who still deem the relocation of 2.34.47–50 after 54 'patently correct' (Günther).
[245] Heyworth 2007: 278–9. In addition he suspects 7–8.
[246] Heyworth 2007: 563: 'You should rather imitate with your Muses the unforgetting Philitas' (31); 'the fate of the chariot of Amphiaraus would be of no benefit'.
[247] Heyworth 2007: 'So too did Varro play ...; so too did the writings of ... Catullus sing; so too confessed the page of ... Calvus ...'.
[248] Heyworth 2007: 279.

difficult readings in the transmitted text if 'divinatio' reveals them to be sound and allowing a genuine appreciation of Propertius as a poet.[249]

Heyworth makes suggestions for further amendments in his copious appendix, in which he describes his edition as a proposal for a *conceivably* best text and therefore as a reminder to the academic community to continue working on the text. His appeal had an impact also on conservatist editors like Fedeli who in his commentary on Propertius, book 4 (2015, with Dimundo and Ciccarelli) adopts a series of conjectures and transposition proposed by Heyworth, who was his severest critic.[250]

Nevertheless, the sceptical openness in classical editing, guided by the critic's judgement on the authenticity of the author's style, may still be regarded as typically Anglo-Saxon[251] but it has had a considerable impact even on continental European Propertius philology. My former Freiburg colleague Hans-Christian Günther (d. 2023), whose *Quaestiones Propertianae* align with the Housman tradition, proposing numerous transpositions and atheteses, admitted to me that he consistently had to revise his own proposals for text transpositions, and was glad to do so. This principle also informs the editorial practice of the Italian Giancarlo Giardina, whose recent editions (2000 and 2010) each contain alterations to the traditional text and thus more radical amendments to the text than those of his British colleagues. However, because Giardina 'normalises' Propertius' Latin, his changes are less spectacular than those of the Housman camp.[252] This is another respect in which differences between the British and continental European tradition can be discerned. However, Giardina does not appear to be as conservative as his compatriot Fedeli, who seeks whenever possible to preserve the manuscript tradition. Giardina's method is to revise the manuscript tradition by means of linguistic normalisation. In doing so, Giardina paradoxically displays affinities with Lachmann, who in his 1816 edition of the text of Propertius sought to rescue the text from what he considered to be older (even mediaeval) linguistic extravagances. In the

---

[249] On this methodological issue and the disagreement between the different philological traditions cf. Tarrant 2016a: 111.

[250] Cf. n. 233.

[251] On the method and principle of 'divinatio', see I. Peirano Garrison in this volume (p. 58): it 'rests on the [critic's] loving identification with the author'. Cf. also Goold 1990: xi: 'In my 1987 article ... as in a later article (1989), I comment on the failure of scholars to admit and retract their mistakes publicly; I feel certain that it was a reluctance to do so which was chiefly responsible for Housman's abandoning his Propertian aspirations.'

[252] O'Rourke 2011: 'Paradoxically, many of Giardina's adventures will produce a less adventurous Propertius, at the cost (some may feel) of what is most characteristic of the poet'; irreconcilable to Tarrant 2016a: 108: 'Giardina's propensity to conjecture makes Heyworth look timid by comparison.'

nineteenth century we also find the diametrically opposed opinion of British scholar J. P. Postgate, who in his *Select Elegies* of 1881 argued that Propertius' language was in fact bold and extravagant and that interventions in the text should bear this principle in mind.[253] Postgate subsequently 'changed sides' and in 1894 published an 'orderly' text containing numerous text transpositions, thus provoking Housman's wrath.[254] Nevertheless the discussion of the particularity of Propertius' poetic language – not just the issue of the manuscript tradition – initiated by Postgate was taken up in North America. US scholar Richard Tarrant strongly advocates the view that deviations from the law of a 'graceful and elegant style' do not constitute grounds for alterations to the text or for assuming that the readings are corrupt. On the contrary, the often difficult and awkward Latin is an indication of quality and should be interpreted as 'a positive source of expressive power'.[255] Could this linguistic as well as literary conception of poetry help to bridge the gulf between British and continental scholarship?

*c) Seneca and Lucretius: The German Tradition of Interpolationist Criticism*
The history of the Horace and Propertius Teubners shows that editions are not necessarily tied to national traditions. Admittedly, the duplication of the two Horace texts – which appeared almost simultaneously – can be attributed to the politics of the division of Germany. However there are numerous other examples that illustrate a blending of national traditions. In this respect, the Teubner editions are more open than OCTs.[256] The Oxford edition of Seneca's tragedies was produced by Otto Zwierlein, a student of Rudolf Kassel. He was the fourth German editor in succession to Hellenists Hermann Diels, Wilamowitz and Kassel. Zwierlein was only the second non-British-trained Latinist to edit works in the OCT series.[257] With his stringent attention to diagnosing interpolations and

---

[253] On Lachmann's and Postgate's differing approaches, cf. Butrica 1997: 176–7, esp. p. 177: 'Most Propertian scholars now belong to one of two irreconcilable camps.'

[254] On criticism of his colleagues at University College London, see Fedeli 2006: 18; Hopkinson 2009.

[255] Tarrant 2016a: 111. He argues that 'the degree of difficulty in Propertius' writing is greater than is allowed by Goold and Heyworth'.

[256] See also Reeve 2000: 203–4. In this respect the OCT was more conservative. The first female OCT editor was Dutch scholar Maaike Zimmermann in 2012 (Apuleius' *Metamorphoses*), followed in 2015 by Cynthia Damon of the USA (Caesar's *Civil War*), both editing Latin texts. Cf. the remarks of S. Huskey and R. Kaster in this volume.

[257] There was a Belgian editor in the nineteenth century, Du Pontet, editor of the pseudo-Caesarean *Commentarii*. It was originally planned that Swedish Latinist Bertil Axelson should edit the Seneca tragedies in conjunction with Gunnar Carlsson. Zwierlein completed the job on the basis of their preliminary work.

his continuation of the methods of authenticity criticism ('Echtheitskritik') developed by Jachmann and Ritschl, Zwierlein founded a Bonn School of his own.[258] So it seems paradoxical that his edition of the Senecan plays is almost completely free of (allegedly) interpolated material. This is due to the fact that for Seneca's tragedies he rejects the tradition of stage productions ('performability') and thus of 'falsification' by actors' interpolations designed to heighten dramatic effects. The critical apparatus is accordingly pared down, in keeping with the British OCT tradition.[259] Zwierlein's Plautus edition would certainly have turned out very differently and it is highly probable that he would have rejected a large number of verses if he had been able to realise the project outlined in his critical-exegetical Plautus commentaries.

In 2019 Markus Deufert, a German scholar who positions himself in the interpolationist school, published his Teubner edition of Lucretius. The editor states that he has applied the methods of criticism developed by the nineteenth-century Lucretius expert Eichstädt, by Lachmann and by his teacher Zwierlein.[260] The British tradition is represented by the OCT text due to be published and edited by David Butterfield, a student of Michael Reeve. Butterfield distances himself from the aims of German interpolation study, remaining faithful to the Housman tradition of conjectural criticism.[261] The Latinist scholarly community will then be able to compare two editions that vary in an almost exemplary way according to their editors' 'national tradition'.

## Philological Commentaries

In all national traditions a contrast can be observed between monumental, philological-critical commentaries and those primarily addressed to a student audience. The differences also depend on the place of publication

---

[258] Tarrant 2016a: 23: 'His approach (which explicitly recalls that of nineteenth-century predecessors such as Friedrich Ritschl and J. L. Ussing) provoked reactions ranging from outright dismissal to partial acceptance' (referring to Gratwick 1993 and Jocelyn 1993 and 1996).

[259] However, his pared-down apparatus criticus is time-consuming and unnecessarily complicated because of the numerous references to Zwierlein's previously published text-critical discussions. Cf. the criticism in Reeve 2000: 203.

[260] Deufert 2018: 200–2; cf. also Butterfield 2014. However in several cases Deufert does not make the emendations announced in his *Prolegomena* (Deufert 2017); cf. Deufert 2018: v.

[261] Butterfield 2013a: 2–3, 2014 and 2016. Cf. Tarrant 2016a: 31, who criticises the 'overtones of illegitimacy' and suggests that 'the shadowy figure of the interpolator is often depicted as a would-be forger'. For Housman's attitude to interpolation research, see n. 222. It would not be fair to assign the much criticised edition by E. Flores (2002: books 1–3 and 5–6; 2004: book 4) to the Italian conservative tradition; cf. the criticism of Deufert 2005 and Tarrant 2016a: 132 and 148.

and the language concerned, which is sometimes dictated by the publishers.[262] There is a clear dichotomy between, on the one hand, the Cambridge 'orange series',[263] the 'Oxford red' commentaries[264] or the series 'Groningen commentaries on Apuleius'[265] and, on the other hand, the Cambridge 'green and yellow' series, the (red) Macmillan commentaries, or the 'Aris & Phillips Classical Texts' series with commentaries on texts translated into English.

Developments in the commentary tradition are reflected in the shift of emphasis from the positivist enthusiasm for collecting material that characterised the nineteenth century to a growing interest in philological and literary questions in recent decades. For Latin studies in the German-speaking region, the most notable example of the former type is the 'Weidmann'sche Reihe' of commentaries on Caesar, Livy, Propertius, Horace and Ovid. They were designed for use in schools but from the outset they also satisfied academic standards.[266] The Latin commentary by Swedish academic Madvig on Cicero's *De finibus*, on the other hand, is a good example of a philological commentary that dispenses almost completely with factual explanations. A philological focus characterises British commentaries, for example the monumental Oxford 'reds' by Robert N. Ogilvie (d. 1981), Stephen P. Oakley and John Briscoe on Livy, who not only provide a wealth of factual information but also complement the text editions (OCT and Teubner). The commentaries that concentrate mainly on text-critical issues document the different schools of editorial philology outlined above.[267] There is also a category of commentaries with a more literary slant, usually consisting of a substantial introduction,

---

[262] The Heidelberg series is mostly written in German (published by Winter); also worth mentioning are the Phaedrus commentaries by Ursula Gärtner (C. H. Beck, Munich). The De Gruyter series of 'Texts and Commentaries' and the ARCA series from Francis Cairns Publications are multilingual. The following series are all in English: the Macmillan series, OUP commentaries, the 'Cambridge Greek and Latin Classics' ('green and yellow') and CUP's orange 'Classical Texts and Commentaries', and the Dutch Apuleius commentaries.

[263] Gibson 2016.

[264] Henderson 2006 (with Stray 2007 and Kraus 2008). It is interesting that Fraenkel's 'red' commentary on Aeschylus' *Agamemnon* can still be called 'a Teutonic monster' (Stray 2016).

[265] Also worth mentioning are Andrew Dyck's commentaries on Cicero's *De officiis* (1997) and *De legibus* (2003), published by the University of Michigan press.

[266] Wilamowitz is regarded as the leading exegete of an approach in which philological study of the text is combined with content-based, interpretative and cultural-historical considerations, the most notable example being his commentary on Euripides' *Herakles* (Berlin, 1889).

[267] Such as Zwierlein on Plautus and Seneca Tragicus, of Deufert on Lucretius, of Heyworth on Propertius and of Damon on Caesar's *Bellum ciuile*. Cf. Deufert 2018: v, in the preface to his commentary: 'In line with the Lachmann tradition of Lucretius commentary, this study focuses almost exclusively on textual criticism leaving aside the other problems, particularities and beauties of the poem that deserve commentary' (my translation).

a reading text and a translation, as for instance David West or Hans-Peter Syndikus on Horace's *Odes*. Commentaries of this kind cannot be easily assigned to national traditions.

Commentaries are a rather sober genre, so it is interesting to note that they are enjoying a revival in Latin studies. This seems to be coupled with the general level of research interest in given authors. As these research interests are in turn linked to national traditions, accordingly different tendencies can be observed here too. This can be illustrated by looking at commentaries on the corpus of Seneca tragedies, where in recent years much has been published in the field of literary studies, particularly performance studies. In the German-speaking region, apart from the commentary by Otto Zwierlein (Mainz, 1986), which focuses on text-critical questions, the most outstanding commentary is the monumental *Oedipus* (Heidelberg, 1994) by the Austrian scholar Karlheinz Töchterle (Austrian Minister of Education and Science in 2011–13).[268] A large number of commentaries have been published in Italian, most of them concentrating on linguistic and stylistic phenomena and clearly addressed to undergraduate students and school pupils.[269] In recent years a whole raft of philological and literary commentaries on Seneca have been published in the Anglophone world, starting with the Cambridge ('orange') *Agamemnon* by Richard Tarrant (1976) and continuing with the work of A. J. Boyle, mostly published by Oxford.[270] The *Troades* may serve as a case in point: in 1982 Elaine Fantham published a running commentary with Princeton University Press. This was followed by a commentary by A. J. Boyle addressed to a student readership. Both works focus on textual interpretation and on the question of performance – to which they provide different answers. The revised Groningen University dissertation by Atze Keulen was published in English in 2001. In its thoroughness it meets the requirements of the Dutch tradition of commentary.[271] The Italian commentary by Franco Caviglia (Rome, 1981) is also worth mentioning, although it is intended mainly for use in schools.

Commentaries on Juvenal are also noteworthy. Historical and text-critical editions with commentaries were published by Ludwig Friedländer (1895) and Ulrich Knoche (1950), representing the antiquarian

---

[268] Schmidt-Dengler 2003: 1293.
[269] Especially noteworthy here is Averna 2002 (4th edn 2014) on the (pseudo-)Senecan *Hercules Oetaeus*.
[270] *Phaedra* (1987); *Troades* (1994); *Oedipus* (2010); *Medea* (2014); *Thyestes* (2016); *Agamemnon* (2019); also the pseudo-Senecan *Octavia* (2008).
[271] Cf. the commentary on Apuleius *Metamorphoses* 11 by Wytse Keulen et al. (Leiden/Boston 2015).

and text-historical approach of German Latin studies; in English J. E. B. Mayor produced his massive *Thirteen Satires of Juvenal* (1867, 4th edn 1886).[272] These were followed by general commentaries by John Ferguson (1979, for students) and Edward Courtney (1980, scholarly). In recent years, commentaries have been published on individual satires or books.[273] This development reflects the considerable and growing interest in the literary genre of Roman satire in Latin studies, particularly in the Anglophone world. I would even go so far as to argue that a certain affinity between the English language and literature and the satirical style of writing with its concepts of deject, abject and non-object plays a significant part here.[274]

Another development is worth noting here. The need for auxiliary texts to explicate the Latin language and its context(s) has existed since the classical period, but in recent years this need has not only increased but has also shifted: there seems to have emerged, particularly in Anglophone commentaries, a tendency to focus on grammar and syntax and therefore to provide more information for a student readership.[275] This should, however, not be a cause for lamentation but can rather be seen as a prerequisite for ensuring that Latin texts are read and understood and continue to be the subject of Latinist research.

*Literary Studies*

The foregoing remarks on commentaries to Seneca Tragicus and Juvenal also identify a tendency that has now clearly emerged and that can be observed in the history of the subject and in research literature as a whole. In Anglophone countries in particular, but increasingly also in Italy, France and Germany, Latin studies have adopted approaches and perspectives derived from theoretical discourses in modern languages and literatures.[276] The influence of narratology, performance studies and intertextuality research is particularly notable; this last contains

---

[272] Mayor omitted *Satires* 2, 6 and 9, considered too offensive.
[273] By Susanna Morton Braund (1996); Biagio Santorelli (2012 and 2013); Lindsay Watson and Patricia Watson (2014).
[274] This is reflected in literary studies on Juvenal (Kirk Freudenburg, Susanna Braund, Maria Plaza, David Larmour, James Uden, Christopher Nappa).
[275] E.g. Heyworth and Morwood 2011; Owen and Gildenhard 2013; Heyworth and Morwood 2017; Ash 2017. On this tendency cf. Ash 2002: 288 and 292; Bartera 2016: 130.
[276] The term 'literary studies' distinguishes such work from text-philological and editorial-philological research. The distinction proposed by Jocelyn 1989 between philology and Classics separates textual philology from Classical studies in the wider sense.

considerable input from the Italian tradition ('arte allusiva')[277] as well as from rhetoric, formal semantics, semiotics, poetics and hermeneutics.[278]

Alongside this is a further tradition which remains influential, one in which texts are regarded not only as literary and aesthetic products but are primarily read as important cultural-historical evidence and as sources that can provide insights into discourses and phenomena in the classical Roman world. This tradition is older, dating back to the positivist and antiquarian research into *Realien* that was prevalent in West European countries in the nineteenth century and was, and still is, promoted institutionally in universities and research centres. The theory deficit that characterised this positivist research tradition has now been overcome. In recent studies, textual analysis is informed by methods and theories of the history of ideas, history of mentalities, gender studies and cultural anthropology.[279] National tendencies remain observable but are by no means as significant as they were for example in the early twentieth century, when Paul Shorey criticised 'specifically German' pedantry.

Two examples will, I think, illustrate the way in which historical and political 'national' tendencies strongly influenced approaches to texts and authors for many years. The examples I have chosen are those of Horace and of Virgil, in particular interpretations of the *Aeneid*.

*a) Horace: Patriotic, Positivist and Theoretical Traditions*

The question of where to place Horace and his works politically played a major role in German and Italian literary studies in the twentieth century.[280] Richard Reitzenstein made a powerful impact on the German school in a lecture which he gave to the Philological Association in Jena in 1921. In it, he stressed Horace's 'service' to the West and described the poet's 'idea of the greatness of the state' and 'the duty of the state'. A further example of this 'German national' ideology, in which the educated bourgeoisie reacted to the events of Versailles and Weimar, can be found in the Horace commentary by Adolf Kiessling (1884–9), revised by Richard Heinze. First published in 1901, it received a fourth edition in 1914 and

---

[277] Pasquali's concept (cf. Bossina 2016: 301) was systematically developed by G. B. Conte and A. Barchiesi and taken up in the Anglophone world. Cf. Schmidt 2002: 323: 'It is at this point that the greatest distance between German and Italian or American Latin Studies seems noticeable, where intertextuality is systematically developed (G. B. Conte, A. Barchiesi) and ways are sought out of the impasse of Deconstruction' (with reference to Galinsky 1992).
[278] Schwindt 2003: 1311–16.
[279] On these tendencies in US Latinist scholarship see Habinek 2005; Edmunds 2005.
[280] Cf. the overviews by Doblhofer 1992; Holzberg 1994; Harrison 1995.

a further seven by 1930.[281] In his commentary on the *Roman Odes*, Kiessling refers to the 'singer' who pointed the way to the fulfilment of 'duty to the Fatherland'. By describing Augustus as the exalted 'Führer' (p. 248), he presents Horace as a prophet of the Third Reich. In humanistic education in German grammar schools in the inter-war period, Horace was seen as a mediator of 'Roman values'.[282] German research on Horace after the Second World War can be interpreted as a kind of counter-reaction to the political and 'Führer-ideological' monopolisation of the poet. This approach is exemplified in monographs by Walter Wili and Hildebrecht Hommel, whose interpretations hark back to the interpretations of German classicism and romanticism. They read Horace's texts as pure poetry of experience, allowing them to interpret them as historical and (auto)biographical documents.[283] The attempts to favour an immanent reading of the work at the expense of temporal and biographical interpretations are exemplified in articles by Viktor Pöschl, Carl Becker and Friedrich Klingner. To today's readers these articles come across as attempts by the scholars to distance themselves from the fascist and National Socialist monopolisation of the poet.

Attempts to exploit the methods developed in modern literary studies – particularly in American 'New Criticism' – for the interpretation of Horace's poetry emerged in the 1960s, especially in Italian and Anglophone research. Eduard Fraenkel's *Horace* (1957; German translation 1963) made a major contribution to Anglophone literary studies,[284] but in his efforts to show Horace moving from an overtly political to a more ethical stance as his poetry develops, Fraenkel remains heavily indebted to 'Wilamowitzian source positivism'.[285] His views were refuted not by the British academic world but by the Italian scholar Antonio La Penna, who objected to Fraenkel's harmonisation of the 'voices' and, invoking Benedetto Croce's aesthetics, criticised the historicist tendency of German research.[286] The positivist research tradition is also represented in the commentaries on the *Odes* by Robin Nisbet and Margaret Hubbard (and Niall Rudd), who continue the source- and draft-oriented research of Pasquali and Fraenkel but also discuss formal issues – hence the (often negative) judgements with which they seek to objectify the poetic quality of the *Carmina*.[287] By contrast, in the more recent Anglophone commentaries which are being produced with impressive

---

[281] Harrison 2016: 71–5.   [282] Holzberg 1994: 292–4; Schmidt 2002: 314–20; Roche 2017: 247.
[283] See the criticism by Holzberg 1994: 296.   [284] Doblhofer 1992: 26–8; Harrison 1995: 5-6.
[285] Holzberg 1994: 295. But cf. Hose 2009: 473 and see above n. 266.
[286] Harrison 1995: 6 and 9; Doblhofer 1992: 5–6 and 27.
[287] Harrison 1995: 3; Doblhofer 1992: 19–21, with the critical remark on p. 21 about 'self-enamoured erudition' ('eine in sich selbst verliebte Gelehrsamkeit'); Harrison 2016: 76–81.

frequency,[288] theory-based textual interpretations are given greater prominence. This can be said for research on Horace in general and independent of national traditions.[289]

b) *Virgil: Father of Western Culture – Optimist or Pessimist?*
Positions in Virgil research, especially with regard to the question of the temporal and political relevance of the *Aeneid*, reveal the persistence of national traditions.[290] During the inter-war period in the twentieth century, in the wake of the 'German Vergilian renaissance' led by Richard Heinze and Eduard Norden, international research revered Virgil as the 'father of Western culture',[291] but diametrically opposed positions emerged in some instances after 1945. On the one hand we have the so-called 'pessimistic' tendency of Anglo-American interpreters, who regard the poem either as the expression of an inwardly torn authorial voice (the 'two voices theory') or as a great lament for the victims of violence and war and therefore interpret it as critical of Augustus or at least as ambivalent.[292] Diametrically opposed to this is the German or European research perspective, which in its hardest form views the *Aeneid* as an 'optimistic', affirmative, pro-Augustan or even propagandistic epic.[293] In research articles on the *Aeneid*, the position of American research, often referred to as the 'Harvard School',[294] is often seen as

---

[288] I.e. the commentaries on individual books in the series 'Cambridge Greek and Latin Classics' ('Green and Yellows') and in 'Aris & Phillips Classical Texts'.
[289] The collection of essays in the *Cambridge Companion to Horace* (2007) edited by Stephen Harrison with contributions by scholars from Italy, UK, Ireland, USA, Denmark and Australia – but, alas, not from German-speaking countries – gives a good impression of this.
[290] Cf. the detailed overview by E. A. Schmidt 2001; Thomas 2001: 222–59; Tarrant 2012: 16–30.
[291] Harrison 1990: 3–4, referring to the German author (*Vergil. Vater des Abendlandes*, 1931) Theodor Haecker (d. 1945) whose Catholic-conservative interpretation focuses on 'Vergil's imperial and Augustan theology as the foundation of Constantine-Christian political theology' (Habermehl and Seidensticker 1999: 818); cf. Kennedy 1997: 38–9.
[292] See Tarrant 2012: 16–17: 'the terms "optimist" and "pessimist" … are at best a crude shorthand to describe positions that may be quite subtle, but the basic opposition they denote is a real one in contemporary Virgilian scholarship'; ibid. 27: 'Ambivalence … coheres well with the poem's period of gestation.' On Virgil being ambivalent toward Augustus cf. Thomas 2001, *passim*, esp. ch. 1 ('Virgil and Augustus').
[293] Wlosok 1973: 129 = 1990a: 279 and *passim*: 'German and English representations of Vergil'; Harrison 1990: 8: the 'traditional/German view'; E. A. Schmidt 2001: the 'German approach/ interpretation'; cf. Galinsky 1988. Cf. Suerbaum 1981: 76: 'It could be called the German school after its leaders V. Pöschl and K. Büchner' (my translation). The first proponents of this view are indeed Pöschl 1950 (translated in 1962) and Buchheit 1963; most strongly committed to this view are Binder 1971 and Hans-Peter Stahl 2015, who studied in Kiel and Münster and now teaches in the USA. But the term 'European' is also current (with reference to the influence of T. S. Eliot); cf. Thomas 2001: 223: 'the European reception' and ibid. 247: the 'strongly European and strongly Augustan Virgil'. The 'optimistic' view is also shared by the US scholar Otis 1963.
[294] Coined by Johnson 1976; cf. Thomas 2001: 224–5.

a specific response to the racial unrest and the Vietnam War in the 1960s.[295] However the German tradition, too, is not without reference to the historical experiences of its representatives.[296] Viktor Pöschl, who served as an SS officer and was on the losing side in the Second World War, produced a symbolistic interpretation of the characters and events and their figurative representation in the epic narrative, seeing it as a sequence of victories and defeats. He argues that the conflicts in which victors and defeated enemies such as Turnus are involved are invested with meaning and hence symbolically ennobled. Karl Büchner (d. 1981) developed the still-prominent teleological interpretation on the basis of Pöschl's argument.[297] In line with T. S. Eliot's claim, at the founding of the Virgilian Society, that Virgil is the main exponent of the western tradition, Pöschl saw his work on the *Aeneid* as re-establishing communication about a world of values common to all, and hence as a means of overcoming the insecurities in post-war German society.[298] Pöschl's book on Virgil was influential in several respects, not least because the symbolist approach he adopted provided pessimistic American research with a key to hear and to understand the hidden voice of the empirical author.

More recently, 'optimistic' and 'pessimistic' readings have broken away from historically determined modes of understanding and hence from specific national traditions.[299] This is most evident in articles in which authors seek to employ a soberly factual and theory-driven approach. Italian scholars for example, following the lead of the quasi-structuralist and editorial-philological works of Gian Biagio Conte, now increasingly

---

[295] Thomas 2001: 224: 'my own views ... were very much formed by reading Virgil in the context of a culture troubled by the exercise of power in Vietnam'. Glei 1990: 333–4; Harrison 1990: 5. A more critical view is that of E. A. Schmidt 2001: 154–6, in particular 156: 'the Vietnam War is not to be seen as the direct reason for or the cause of the pessimistic interpretation of the *Aeneid*. It should rather be understood as a catalyst that made traditional American mistrust of a strong state and of imperialism enter into the understanding of Vergil's poem'.

[296] See Wlosok 1973: 132–3 = 1990a: 282; Wlosok 1990b; Suerbaum 1981: 85; Harrison 1990: 4–5; Glei 1990: 333; E. A. Schmidt 2001. On the role of Wlosok, cf. E. A. Schmidt 2001: 150–67; Thomas 2001: 259: 'a post-war German (woman) whose voice validates and affirms the German Augustan Virgil of an earlier generation'.

[297] In the *RE* article of 1958; cf. Wlosok 1973: 133–4 = 1990a: 28; Thomas 2001: 256 on Pöschl, Klingner and Büchner and their 'optimistic Virgil whose views were synonymous with those of the state and Augustus its leader'.

[298] Harrison 1990: 4, referring to Pöschl 1950: 10–11 = 1962: 12; cf. ibid. 4: '... to support Eliot's view of the Aeneid as an assertion of the fundamental values of Western civilization, seen as relevant to the post-war reconstruction of German society at the time he wrote'. Cf. also Suerbaum 1981: 75–6; Kennedy 1997, esp. 40–1 on the meaning of the term 'tradition' in Eliot's *What Is a Classic?* (1945).

[299] Cf. Harrison 1990: 17–19 on the three Anglophone studies by R. D. Williams (1983, as showing affinities to the 'Harvard School'), P. Hardie (1986, as a positive view of the poem) and R. O. A. M. Lyne (1987, as a 'challenging version of the dark view'). Tarrant 2012: 16–17 criticises the dichotomy between optimistic and pessimistic views (cf. above n. 292).

focus on the analysis of language, style and intertextuality.[300] Taking up a central aspect of positivist research, the *Enciclopedia Virgiliana*, together with recent German and American studies, has shown renewed interest in *Realien* and motives and has exploited the notion of the 'spatial turn' in spatial semantics, with beneficial results for Virgil research.[301]

### Translation Series

Translation series also contribute to the national and perhaps also language-dependent development of Latin studies. Some of the series meet high scholarly standards, especially in the case of bilingual editions and editions with commentaries. This applies to the Loeb series in Anglophone countries, the Budé series in France, the Fondazione Lorenzo Valla and the Biblioteca Universale Rizzoli in Italy, the Tusculum and Edition Antike series in Germany and in some cases also to the Reclam Universalbibliothek.[302] The issue of the status of affordable monolingual or bilingual series, usually in the popular paperback format, is also instructive. In Italy this has increasingly led to the wider accessibility of works by non-canonical authors such as Vegetius.[303] Translation projects are often a central (but by no means exclusive) component of research in countries that cannot boast a long and generously promoted 'humanist' tradition. Even in countries where the study of classical languages has so far played a central part, the language acquisition phase in schools and/or universities is constantly being reduced, and hence the role of 'Classics in translation' is gaining importance. The 'frame of readership' is becoming more similar in the different countries. In the twenty-first century, Latin studies will face the challenge of how to deal with this development and this is likely to bring various national traditions closer together.

### Digitisation

Digitisation has logically led to the even greater *inter*nationalisation of national research activities. In Latin studies this applies to the *TLL* (which in the 'Thesaurus Commission' was 'international' in nature from its inception);[304]

---

[300] Cf. Conte 2016 in the afterword to his Teubner editions; also Harrison 1990: 16–17.
[301] The article by Skempsis in Skempsis and Ziogas 2014 was written in Göttingen; that of Kondratieff was published in the USA in 2014.
[302] See e.g. Calanchini 2015. [303] See the remarks of I. Peirano Garrison in this volume.
[304] www.thesaurus.badw.de/en/project.html. The executive secretary of the project tells me that in 1931 the German Reichsregierung presented five volumes of the *TLL* to the Italian Foreign

the 'Library of Latin Texts', formerly the 'CETEDOC Library of Christian Latin Texts', in Turnhout (Belgium); the 'Ancient World Online' (AWOL) project produced by the 'Library of Digital Latin Texts' in Göttingen; the DLL financed by the Society for Classical Studies in the USA; the 'Perseus Digital Library' run by Tufts University; the Würzburg-based 'Corpus Augustinianum Gissense' and the digitised version of the *Patrologia Latina* published in the UK.

The scenario for commentary literature outlined earlier in this chapter probably also applies to non-lexicographical Latinist research: the digitisation of older commentaries has led to an interconnection of information on classical texts, thus creating the possibility of 'a gigantic ... cross-indexed reference work'.[305] The easy availability of research literature from all periods thanks to media networks has not only made synergies possible but has also internationalised knowledge. The idea of combining a critical edition with an electronic version of an 'editio maior', or at least of an apparatus plenus which could be regularly updated, is a fascinating prospect.[306]

### Social Media and Popularisation: the Future of Latin Studies?

As already stated, Latin studies in Anglophone countries are under greater pressure than elsewhere to ensure that the results of research are not confined to academic researchers and teachers but are also made accessible to a wider public. Authors such as Mary Beard, Martha Nussbaum and Robin Lane Fox have helped to increase the popularity of Latin literature, history and culture. Social media have assumed the role of disseminators of knowledge, and academic evaluation systems ensure that this output is subject to constant quality control. The future of academic communication, which now takes place largely via the internet, will probably be increasingly determined by blogs and platforms such as Twitter. The (desired) result is a greater visibility of subjects and of discussions that do not necessarily have to be novel or progressive per se; there is no reason why they

---

Secretary, Dino Grandi, when he came to Berlin, as a gift to the Duce. The series of donations was continued in the following years, but, nevertheless, in 1936 Italy refused to cooperate with the Germans in this respect.

[305] Heslin 2016: 495; cf. McCarty 2002; Anderson 2016; Goldberg 2016: 519 on Heslin's vision of a 'universal variorum'.

[306] Tarrant 2016b: 319 on his planned Horace edition (see also n. 229). On the perspectives of digital editing see S. Huskey and R. Kaster in this volume.

should not even be material-oriented or conservative-positivist in their world view.

Does this openness and democratisation of knowledge create opportunities for Latin studies more easily to disregard national borders? Two factors tend to militate against this: first, the lingua franca of international, universally and permanently accessible communication is and is highly likely to remain English.[307] Secondly it should not be assumed (or even necessarily wished) that centuries-old, nationally based differences in approaches to the subject and to its methods and purposes should be completely forgotten and rendered redundant. Nevertheless I am inclined to answer the question with considerable optimism – partly because the generation of our students has no choice but to study and to communicate via the internet and media platforms and also because the subject itself – Latin language and literature – does not change in content or in form and therefore retains its supra-national relevance.

## References

Adams, J. N. (2008) *Bilingualism and the Latin Language*, Cambridge.
Albrecht, A., L. Danneberg and S. De Angelis, eds. (2017) *Die akademische 'Achse Berlin-Rom'? Der wissenschaftlich-kulturelle Austausch zwischen Italien und Deutschland 1920 bis 1945*, Berlin.
Anderson, B. (1983) *Imagined Communities*, London.
Anderson, P. J. (2016) 'Heracles' choice: thoughts on the virtues of print and digital commentary', in Kraus and Stray 2016, 483–93.
Arrighetti, G. (2014) 'Pasquali rittratista', in Arrighetti et al. 2014, 1–28.
Arrighetti, G. et al., eds. (1989) *La filologia greca e latina nel secolo* XX: *atti del congresso internazionale, Roma, consiglio nazionale delle ricerche . . . 1984*, 3 vols., Pisa.
  (2014) *Giorgio Pasquali sessant'anni dopo. Atti della giornata di studio (Firenze, 1 ottobre 2012)*, Florence.
Ash, R. (2002) 'Between Scylla and Charybdis? Historiographical commentaries on Latin historians', in Gibson and Kraus 2002, 269–94.
  (2017) *Tacitus, Annals Book* XV, Cambridge.
Averna, D. (2002) *Lucio Anneo Seneca, Hercules Oetaeus. Testo critico, traduzione e commento*, Rome. With 4th edn, 2014.
Axer, K. and J. Kolendo (2002) 'Poland I. Reception history A. Literature 5. Significance of the Latin language and classical culture' = 'Polen I. Rezeptionsgeschichte A. Literatur 5. Bedeutung der lateinischen Sprache und der antiken Kultur', *DNP* 15.2: 398–9.

---

[307] In spite of Rubel 2019.

Barnard, J. L. (2017) *Empire of Ruin: Black Classicism and American Imperial Culture*, Oxford.
Barsby, J. (1995) 'Latin studies in New Zealand', in *Acta selecta Octavi Conventus Academiae Latinitati Fovendae* (Rome), 683–95.
Bartera, S. (2016) 'Commentary writing on the *Annals* of Tacitus', in Kraus and Stray 2016, 114–35.
Bate, J. (2008) *Soul of the Age: The Life, Mind and World of William Shakespeare*, London.
Baumann, U. (2003) 'United Kingdom II. The modern period' = 'United Kingdom II. Neuzeit', *DNP* 15.3: 797–822.
Beard, M. (2002) 'Ciceronian correspondences: making a book out of letters', in T. P. Wiseman, ed., *Classics in Progress* (London), 103–44.
  (2012) 'Saving Latin from the Tory party', *Times Literary Supplement*, 22.06.2012. Available online: www.the-tls.co.uk/saving-latin-from-the-tory-party/.
Bers, V. and G. Nagy, eds. (1996) *The Classics in East Europe: from the End of World War II to the Present*, American Philological Association Pamphlet Series, Worcester, MA.
Binder, G. (1971) *Aeneas und Augustus: Interpretationen zum 8. Buch der Aeneis*, Meisenheim am Glan.
Bloch, R. H. (1995) *God's Plagiarist: Being an Account of the Famous Industry and Irregular Commerce of the Famous Abbé Migne*, Chicago.
van Bommel, B. (2015) *Classical Humanism and the Challenge of Modernity: Debates on Classical Education in 19th-Century Germany*, Berlin.
Borzsák, I. (1984) *Quinti Horati Flacci opera*, Leipzig.
Bossina, L. (2016) 'Giorgio Pasquali e la filologia come scienza storica', in D. Lanza and G. Ugolini, eds., *Storia della filologia classica* (Rome), 277–314.
  (2017) 'I rapporti tra Italia e Germania nella filologia classica (1920–1940)', in Albrecht, Danneberg and De Angelis 2017, 229–304.
Braund, S. M. (2002) *Latin Literature*, London and New York. Revised as S. M. Braund, *Understanding Latin Literature* (Abingdon and New York, 2017).
Brink, C. O. (2010) *English Classical Scholarship: Historical Reflections on Bentley, Porson, and Housman*, revised edn, Cambridge.
Buchheit, V. (1963) *Vergil über die Sendung Roms. Untersuchungen zum Bellum Punicum und zur Aeneis*, Heidelberg.
Bulwer, J. (2018) 'Changing priorities in Classics', in Holmes-Henderson et al. 2018, 67–88.
Buschendorf, C. (2003) 'United States of America', *DNP* 15.3: 833–75.
Butrica, J. L. (1997) 'Editing Propertius', *CQ* 47: 176–208.
  (2006) Review of P. Fedeli, *Properzio, Elegie, Libro II. Introduzione, testo e commento*, Cambridge 2005, *BMCRev* 2006.03.25.
Butterfield, D. (2013a) *The Early Textual History of Lucretius' De rerum natura*, Cambridge and New York.

(2013b) 'Why learn Latin?', in D. Butterfield et al., *Latin for Language Lovers: Ancient Languages, the New Curriculum and GCSE* (London), 4–5.

(2014) '*Lucretius auctus*? The question of interpolation in *De rerum natura*', in J. Martínez, ed., *Fakes and Forgers of Classical Literature: Ergo decipiatur!* (Leiden), 15–42.

(2016) 'Some problems in the text and transmission of Lucretius', in Hunter and Oakley 2016, 22–53.

Butterfield, D. and C. Stray, eds. (2009) *A. E. Housman: Classical Scholar*, London.

Calanchini, P. (2015) *Cicero, De fato – Über das Schicksal*, Stuttgart.

Calder, W. M., III (1994) 'Classical scholarship in the United States: an introductory essay', in W. W. Briggs, Jr, ed., *Biographical Dictionary of North American Classicists* (Westport, CT and London), xix–xxxix.

(1998) *Men in Their Books: Studies in the Modern History of Classical Scholarship* (ed. J. P. Harris and R. Scott Smith), Hildesheim.

Cessi, C. (1930) Review of G. Gervasoni, *Studi e ricerche sui Filologi e la Filologia classica fra il 700 e l'800 in Italia*, Bergamo 1929 – *Linee di storia della Filologia classica in Italia. Parte I: sino ai filologi settentrionali della prima metà dell'800*, Florence 1929, *Aevum* 4: 62–5.

Conte, G. B. (1966) 'Uno studioso tedesco di letteratura latina: Friedrich Klingner', *CS* n.s. 5: 481–503.

(2016) *Critical Notes on Virgil*, Berlin.

Crawford, S. et al., eds. (2017) *Ark of Civilization: Refugee Scholars and Oxford University, 1930–1945*, Oxford.

Cunha Corrêa, P. (2018) 'Reintroducing Classics in a Brazilian public school: project Minimus in São Paulo', in Holmes-Henderson et al. 2018, 55–66.

De Martino, D. (2014) 'Pasquali maestro di italianisti: il caso di Lanfranco Caretti', in Arrighetti et al. 2014, 97–114.

Delz, J. (1988) Review of D. R. Shackleton Bailey, ed. *Q. Horati Flacci opera* (Stuttgart 1985), *Gnomon* 60: 495–501.

Dettmer, H. A. (2000) 'Japan', *DNP* 14: 721–2.

Deufert, M. (2005) Review of *Titus Lucretius Carus. De rerum natura. Edizione critica con introduzione e versione a cura di Enrico Flores. Volume primo (Libri I–III)* (Naples 2002), *Gnomon* 77: 213–24.

(2017) *Prolegomena zur Editio Teubneriana des Lukrez*, Berlin.

(2018) *Kritischer Kommentar zu Lukrezens 'De rerum natura'*, Berlin.

Devine, M. and L. D. Stephens (2013) *Semantics for Latin: An Introduction*, Oxford.

Dickey, E. and A. Chahoud, eds. (2010) *Colloquial and Literary Latin*, Cambridge. With 2nd edn, 2016.

Doblhofer, E. (1992) *Horaz in der Forschung nach 1957*, Darmstadt.

Dominik, W. J. (2003) 'South Africa' = 'Südafrika', *DNP* 15.3: 342–6.

Dummer, J. (1999) 'GDR 1. Classical studies' = 'DDR 1. Die klassischen Altertumswissenschaften', *DNP* 13: 681–89.

Edmunds, L. (2005) 'Critical divergences: new directions in the study and teaching of Roman literature', *TAPhA* 135: 1–13.
Eliot, T. S. (1945) *What Is a Classic?*, London.
Elsner, I. (2017) 'Pfeiffer, Fraenkel, and refugee scholarship in Oxford during and after the Second World War', in Crawford et al. 2017, 25–49.
Espagne, M. and S. Maufroy, eds. (2011) 'La philologie allemande, figures de pensée. Denkfiguren der deutschen philologischen Tradition. Philology in Germany: figures of thought', *Revue Germanique Internationale* 14 (n.pag.).
Farrell, J. (2001) *Latin Language and Latin Culture from Ancient to Modern Times*, Cambridge.
  (2005) 'Eduard Fraenkel on Horace and Servius, or, texts, contexts, and the field of "Latin studies"', *TAPhA* 135: 91–102.
Fedeli, P. (1986) 'Sul modo di costituire il testo di Properzio', *RFIC* 114: 238–50.
  (2006) 'The history of Propertian scholarship', in H.-C. Günther, ed., *Brill's Companion to Propertius* (Leiden), 3–21.
Feile, T. et al., eds. (2021) *Brill's Companion to Classics in the Early Americas*, Leiden and Boston.
Feys, X. and D. Sacré (2018) '*Regina linguarum*: the teaching of Latin at the Collegium Trilingue, 16th–18th Century', in J. Papy, ed., *The Leuven Colloquium Trilingue 1517-1797: Erasmus, Humanist Educational Practice and the New Language Institute Latin-Greek-Hebrew* (Leuven), 103–28.
Flashar, H., ed. (1995) *Altertumswissenschaft in den 20er Jahren. Neue Fragen und Impulse*, Stuttgart.
Flashar, H. et al., eds. (1979) *Philologie und Hermeneutik*, Göttingen.
Fontaine, J. et al. (1993) *Patristique et antiquité tardive en Allemagne et en France de 1870 à 1930. Influences et échanges: actes du colloque franco-allemand de Chantilly (25–27 octobre 1991)*, Paris.
Fornaro, S. (1999) 'Germany III. Up to 1806' = 'Deutschland III. Bis 1806', *DNP* 13: 792–805.
Fraistat, N. and J. Flanders (2013) 'Introduction: textual scholarship in the age of media consciousness', in N. Fraistat and J. Flanders, eds., *The Cambridge Companion to Textual Scholarship* (Cambridge), 1–15.
Frolov, E. (2004) 'The first steps of St. Petersburg classical scholarship: an academician Gottlieb Siegfried Bayer (1694–1738). Classical scholarship in modern Russia', *Hyperboreus* 10: 10–21.
Fürst, A. (2002) 'Patristic theology/Patristics' = 'Patristische Theologie/Patristik', *DNP* 15.2: 197–203.
Galinsky, K. (1988) 'The anger of Aeneas', *AJPh* 109: 321–48.
  (1992) 'The current state of the interpretation of Roman poetry and the contemporary critical scene', in K. Galinsky, ed., *The Interpretation of Roman Poetry: Empiricism or Hermeneutics?* (Frankfurt), 1–40.
Gatti, P. L. (2012) 'Rostagni, Augusto', *DNP Suppl.* 6: 1082–3.
Gavrilov, A. (2002) 'Russia' = 'Russland', *DNP* 15.2: 1014–30.
Gibson, R. K. (2016) 'Fifty shades of orange: Cambridge classical texts and commentaries', in Kraus and Stray 2016, 346–75.

Gibson, R. K. and C. S. Kraus, eds. (2002) *The Classical Commentary: Histories, Practices, Theory*, Leiden, Boston and Cologne.
Gildenhard, I. (2011) *Creative Eloquence: The Construction of Reality in Cicero's Speeches*, Oxford.
Glei, R. (1990) 'Von Probus zu Pöschl: Vergilinterpretationen im Wandel', *Gymnasium* 79: 321–40.
Goldberg, S. M. (2016) 'The future of antiquity: an afterword', in Kraus and Stray 2016, 512–23.
Gonzales de Tobia, A. M. (2001) 'Latin America' = 'Lateinamerika', *DNP* 15.1: 20–47.
Goold, G. P. (1990) *Propertius Elegies*, Cambridge, MA.
Gratwick, A. S. (1993) Review of O. Zwierlein, *Zur Kritik und Exegese des Plautus I: Poenulus und Curculio* (Mainz, 1990), *CR* 43: 36–40.
Gudemann, A. (1909) *Grundriss der Geschichte der klassischen Philologie*, Berlin. 2nd edn, Darmstadt 1967.
Günther, H.-C. (1997) *Quaestiones Propertianae*, Leiden.
Güthenke, C. (2020) *Feeling and Classical Philology: Knowing Antiquity in German Scholarship, 1770–1920*, Cambridge.
Guida, A. (2014) 'Firenze maggio 1925: l'incontro di Thomas Mann con Wilamowitz, Pasquali, e Snell', in Arrighetti et al. 2014, 37–57.
Habermehl, P. and B. Seidensticker (1999) 'Germany v. The 20th century (after 1918)' = 'Deutschland v. 20. Jahrhundert (ab 1918)', *DNP* 13: 817–28.
Habinek, T. (2005) 'Latin literature between text and practice', *TAPhA* 135: 83–9.
Hallett, J. P. (1997) 'Writing as an American in classical scholarship', in J. P. Hallett and T. Van Nortwick, eds., *The Personal Voice in Classical Scholarship* (London), 120–52.
  (2019) 'Expanding our professional embrace: the American Philological Association/Society for Classical Studies 1970–2019', *TAPhA* 149: 61–87.
Hardie, P. R. (1986) *Virgil's Aeneid: Cosmos and Imperium*, Oxford.
Harrison, S. J. (1995) 'Some twentieth-century views of Horace', in S. Harrison, ed., *Homage to Horace: A Bimillenary Celebration* (Oxford), 1–16.
  (2016) 'Two-author commentaries on Horace', in Kraus and Stray 2016, 71–83.
  (2019) 'Heaney as translator: Horace and Virgil', in Harrison et al. 2019, 244–62.
Harrison, S. J., ed. (1990) *Oxford Readings in Vergil's Aeneid*, Oxford.
  ed. (2001) *Texts, Ideas, and the Classics: Scholarship, Theory, and Classical Literature*, Oxford.
  ed. (2007) *The Cambridge Companion to Horace*, Cambridge.
Harrison, S. J. et al., eds. (2019) *Seamus Heaney and the Classics: Bann Valley Muses*, Oxford and New York.
Hazlitt, W. (1825) *Table Talk or Original Essays*, vol. 2, Paris.
Heck, E. and E. A. Schmidt, eds. (1990) *Res humanae – res divinae. Kleine Schriften*, Heidelberg.

Heesakkers, C. L. (2001) 'Netherlands and Belgium 11. The northern Netherlands after 1575' = 'Niederlande und Belgien 11. Die nördlichen Niederlande nach 1575', *DNP* 15.1: 994–1015.

Heesakkers, C. L. and G. Tournoy (2001) 'Netherlands and Belgium 1. The low countries to 1575' = 'Niederlande und Belgien 1. Die alten Niederlande bis 1575', *DNP* 15.1: 985–94.

Henderson, J. (2006) *'Oxford Reds': Classic Commentaries on Latin Classics*, London.

Hentschke, A. and U. Muhlack (1972) *Einführung in die Geschichte der klassischen Philologie*, Darmstadt.

Heslin, P. (2016) 'The dream of a universal variorum: digitizing the commentary tradition', in Kraus and Stray 2016, 494–511.

Heyworth, S. J. (2007) *Cynthia: A Companion to the Text of Propertius*, Oxford.
(2009) 'Housman and Propertius', in Butterfield and Stray 2009, 11–28.

Heyworth, S. J. and J. H. W. Morwood (2011) *A Commentary on Propertius, Book 3*, Oxford.
(2017) *A Commentary on Vergil, Aeneid 3*, Oxford.

Hilbold, I. (2019) 'Jules Marouzeau and *L'Année philologique*: the genesis of a reform in classical bibliography', *History of Classical Scholarship* 1: 174–202.

Holmes-Henderson, A. (2016) 'Teaching Latin and Greek in primary classrooms: the classics in communities project', *Journal of Classics Teaching* 33: 50–3.

Holmes-Henderson, A. et al., eds. (2018) *Forward with Classics: Classical Languages in Schools and Communities*, London and New York.

Holtermann, M. (1999) 'Germany IV. The 19th century to 1918' = 'Deutschland IV. 19. Jahrhundert, bis 1918', *DNP* 13: 806–17.
(2002) 'Philological seminar' = 'Philologisches Seminar', *DNP* 15.2: 328–31.

Holzberg, N. (1994) 'Horaz und seine "Deutsche Schule"', *Lampas* 27: 290–330.

Hopkinson, N. (2009) 'Housman and J. P. Postgate', in Butterfield and Stray 2009, 175–91.

Horn, C. (2018) 'Werner Jaeger's *Paideia* and his "Third Humanism"', *Educational Theory and Philosophy* 50: 682–91.

Hose, M. (2009) '"... und Pflicht geht vor Neigung": Ulrich von Wilamowitz-Moellendorff und das Leiden am Großbetrieb der Wissenschaft', in A. Baertschi and C. G. King, eds., *Die modernen Väter der Antike. Die Entwicklung der Altertumswissenschaften an Akademie und Universität im Berlin des 19. Jahrhunderts* (Berlin and New York), 445–80.

Hošek, R. (2003) 'Czech Republic v. History of the study of antiquity A. Classical philology and ancient history' = 'Tschechien v. Geschichte der Altertumswissenschaften A. Klassische Philologie und Alte Geschichte', *DNP* 15.3: 638–43.

Housman, A. E. (1934) 'Review: Butler and Barber's Propertius: H. E. Butler and E. A. Barber, *The Elegies of Propertius*', *CR* 48: 136–9. Reprinted in J. Diggle and F. R. D. Goodyear, eds., *The Classical Papers of A. E. Housman, Vol. 3: 1915–1936* (Cambridge, 1972), 1234–9.

Hübner, W. (2010) *Manilius, Astronomica Buch* v. *Band 1: Einführung, Text und Übersetzung*, Berlin.
Hunt, S. (2018a) 'Getting Classics into schools? Classics and the social justice agenda of the UK coalition government, 2010–2015', in Holmes-Henderson et al. 2018, 9–26.
  (2018b) 'Latin is not dead: the rise of communicative approaches to the teaching of Latin in the United States', in Holmes-Henderson et al. 2018, 89–108.
Hunter, R. and S. Oakley (2016) *Latin Literature and Its Transmission: Papers in Honour of Michael Reeve*, Cambridge.
Jacob, F. (2016) 'Western classics in modern Japan (German)', *CUNY academic works summer 7–12*: http://academicworks.cuny.edu/qb_pubs/32.
James, P. (1996) *Nation Formation: Towards a Theory of Abstract Community*, London.
Jocelyn, H. D. (1989) 'Australia – New Zealand: Greek and Latin philology', in Arrighetti et al. 1989, 543–78.
  (1993) 'Zur Kritik und Exegese des Plautus. I: *Poenulus* und *Curculio* by Otto Zwierlein', *Gnomon* 65: 122–37.
  (1996) 'Zur Kritik und Exegese des Plautus. II: *Miles gloriosus* by Otto Zwierlein', *Gnomon* 68: 402–20.
  (1997) 'Charles Oscar Brink (1907–1994)', *PBA* 94: 319–54.
Johnson, M., ed. (2019) *Antipodean Antiquities: Classical Reception Down Under*, London and New York.
Johnson, W. R. (1976) *Darkness Visible: A Study of Vergil's Aeneid*, Berkeley, Los Angeles and London.
Jönsson, A. and G. Vogt-Spira, eds. (2017) *The Classical Tradition in the Baltic Region: Perceptions and Adaptations of Greece and Rome*, Hildesheim, Zürich and New York. 2nd edn, 2018.
Karsai, G. et al., eds. (2013) *Classics and Communism: Greek and Latin behind the Iron Curtain*, Ljubljana.
Kennedy, D. (1997) 'Modern receptions and their interpretative implications', in C. Martindale, ed., *The Cambridge Companion to Virgil* (Cambridge), 38–55.
Kenney, E. J. (1974) *The Classical Text: Aspects of Editing in the Age of the Printed Book*, Berkeley, Los Angeles and London.
  (1989) 'Great Britain: Latin philology', in Arrighetti et al. 1989, 619–49.
Keulen, W. et al. (2015) *Apuleius, Metamorphoses 11*, Leiden and Boston.
King, C. G. (2017) 'Einführung', in C. G. King and R. Lo Presti, eds., *Werner Jaeger: Wissenschaft, Bildung, Politik* (Berlin), 1–4.
Kondratieff, E. J. (2014) 'Future city in the heroic past: Rome, Romans, and Roman landscapes in *Aeneid* 6–8', in A. M. Kemezis, ed., *Urban Dreams and Realities in Antiquity: Remains and Representations of the Ancient City* (Leiden), 165–228.
Konstan, D. and F. Muecke (1993) 'Richard Bentley as a reader of Horace', *CJ* 88: 179–86.

Konstan, D. et al. (2001) 'The Classics in the Americas', *CB* 77: 209–44.
Kopff, E. C. (1994) 'Shorey, Paul', in W. W. Briggs, ed., *Biographical Dictionary of North American Classicists* (Westport, CT), 582–4.
Krämer, H. (2011) *Die Altertumswissenschaft und der Verlag B. G. Teubner*, Leipzig.
Kraus, C. (2008) 'The "Oxford Reds"' (review of Henderson 2006), *CR* 58: 122–5.
Kraus, C. and C. Stray, eds. (2016) *Classical Commentaries: Explorations in a Scholarly Genre*, Oxford and New York.
Krömer, D. (2001) 'Lexicography III. Thesaurus linguae Latinae' = 'Lexikographie III. Thesaurus Linguae Latinae', *DNP* 15.1: 143–9.
Kubo, M. (1989) 'Japan: Greek and Latin philology', in Arrighetti et al. 1989, 669–84.
Laird, A. and N. Miller, eds. (2018) *Antiquities and Classical Traditions in Latin America*, Hoboken, NJ.
Lamers, H. et al., eds. (2020) *Studies in the Latin Literature and Epigraphy of Italian Fascism*, Leuven.
Lana, I. (1989) 'Italia. La filologia latina nel secolo XX', in Arrighetti et al. 1989, 1141–67.
Landfester, M. (2002) 'Philology I. Greek A–B' = 'Philologie I. Griechisch A–B', *DNP* 15.2: 237–55.
  (2017) 'Werner Jaegers Konzepte von Wissenschaft und Bildung als Ausdruck des Zeitgeistes', in C. G. King and R. Lo Presti, eds., *Werner Jaeger: Wissenschaft, Bildung, Politik* (Berlin), 5–50.
  (2018) Review of van Bommel 2015, *Gnomon* 90: 109–14.
Lanza, D. and G. Ugolini (2016) *Storia della filologia classica*, Rome. Translated as *History of Classical Scholarship: From Bentley to the 20th Century*, Berlin and Boston, 2022.
La Penna, A. (1982) Review of R. Hanslik (1997), *Sexti Propertii Elegiarum libri* IV, *Gnomon* 54: 515–23.
Latacz, J. (2002) 'Philology I. Greek C–D' = 'Philologie I. Griechisch C–D', *DNP* 15.2: 255–78.
Lawlor, S. (2013) 'Latin GCSE: aims and means', in *Latin for Language Lovers: Ancient Languages, the New Curriculum and GCSE* (London), 2–3.
Lehnus, L. (2012) *Incontri con la filologia del passato*, Bari.
Lindberg, B. (2002) 'Sweden' = 'Schweden', *DNP* 15.2: 1115–20.
Lloyd-Jones, H. (1990) 'Twentieth century philology', *CR* 40: 459–62.
Lohse, G. (2014) 'Bruno Snell und Hermann Fränkel. Zu einem Berufungsverfahren an der Universität Hamburg 1930/31', *A&A* 60: 1–20.
López Férez, J. A. (2003) 'Spain I. History of scholarship' = 'Spanien I. Wissenschaftsgeschichte', *DNP* 15.3: 102–27.
Luck, G. (2009) 'Lessons learned from a master', in Butterfield and Stray 2009, 247–54.
Ludwig, W. (1986) 'Amtsenthebung und Emigration Klassischer Philologen', *Würzburger Jahrbücher* 12: 217–39. First published in *Berichte zur Wissenschaftsgeschichte* 7 (1984), 161–78.
Lyne, R. O. A. M. (1987) *Further Voices in Virgil's Aeneid*, Oxford.

Malitz, J. (1998) 'Römertum im "Dritten Reich": Hans Oppermann', in P. Kneissl and V. Losemann, eds., *Imperium Romanum. Studien zu Geschichte und Rezeption* (Stuttgart), 519–43.

Martindale, C. (2002) 'Classics, theory, and thought' (review of Harrison 2001 and Braund 2002), *Arion* 10: 141–55.

Matters, E. (2018) 'Classics in Australia: on surer grounds?', in Holmes-Henderson et al. 2018, 47–54.

McCarty, W. (2002) 'A network with a thousand entrances: commentary in an electronic age?', in Gibson and Kraus 2002, 359–402.

Mount, H. (2008) *Amo, amas, amat ... and All That: How to Become a Latin-Lover*, London.

Movrin, D. and E. Olechowaka, eds. (2016) *Classics and Class: Greek and Latin Classics and Communism at School*, Warsaw and Ljubljana.

Mutschler, F.-H. and A. Mittag, eds. (2008) *Conceiving the Empire: China and Rome Compared*, Oxford.

Näf, B. (2002) 'Switzerland' = 'Schweiz', *DNP* 15.2: 1120–56.

(2017) 'Werner Jaeger, der Dritte Humanismus und Italien', in Albrecht, Danneberg and De Angelis 2017, 203–27.

Norberg, D. (1989) 'Danemark, Finlande, Norvege, Suede', in Arrighetti et al. 1989, 745–62.

O'Higgins, L. (2017) *The Irish Classical Self: Poets and Poor Scholars in the Eighteenth and Nineteenth Century*, Oxford.

de Oliveira, F. (2002) 'Portugal' = 'Portugal', *DNP* 15.2: 516–26.

O'Rourke, D. (2011) Review of G. Giardina (ed.), *Properzio. Elegie*, Pisa and Rome 2010, *BMCRev* 2011.06.48.

Otis, B. (1963) *Virgil: A Study in Civilized Poetry*, Oxford. 2nd edn, Ann Arbor, MI, 1995.

Owen, M. and I. Gildenhard (2013) *Tacitus, Annals, 15.20–23, 33–45: Latin Text, Study Aids with Vocabulary and Commentary*, Cambridge.

Pachenko, D. (1992) 'Teaching the classics: private education in the USSR', *Brown Classical Journal* 8 (Suppl.).

Paschoud, F. (1996) 'Le cinquantième anniversaire de la FIEC. Exposé présenté le 22 août 1997 à Varsovie lors de la 24ᵉ assemblée générale des délégués de la FIEC', *Eos* 84: 5–17.

Pasquali, G. (1934) *Storia della tradizione e critica del testo*, Florence. 2nd revised edn, Florence, 1962.

(1953) *Storia dello spirito tedesco nelle memorie d'un contemporaneo* (ed. M. Romani Mistretta), Florence. Reprinted Milan, 2013.

Pelling, C. and L. Morgan (2010) *Latin for Language Learners: Opening Opportunity for Primary Pupils*, London.

Petitmengin, P. (1983) 'Deux têtes de pont de la philologie allemande en France, le Thesaurus linguae Graecae et la "Bibliothèque des auteurs grecs" (1830–1867)', in M. Bollack et al., eds., *Philologie et herméneutique au 19e siècle*, II (Göttingen), 76–107.

(1992) 'La bibliothèque de l'École normale supérieure face á l'érudition allemande au XIXe siècle', *RS* 113: 55–68.
Pfeiffer, R. (1968) *History of Classical Scholarship: From the Beginnings to the End of the Hellenistic Age*, Oxford. 2nd edn 1978. Translated as *Geschichte der klassischen Philologie. Von den Anfängen bis zum Ende des Hellenismus*, Munich, 1970 (with revised edn 1978).
  (1976) *History of Classical Scholarship: From 1300 to 1850*, Oxford. 2nd edn 1978. Translated as *Die klassische Philologie von Petrarca bis Mommsen*, Munich, 1982.
Piatkowski, A. (2002) 'Romania III. History of classical studies' = 'Rumänien III. Geschichte der Altertumswissenschaften', *DNP* 15.2: 1010–14.
Pirker, E. U. (2010) '"Black Romans" – Die Antike im öffentlichen Diskurs um eine "schwarze" britische Geschichte', in H.-J. Gehrke and M. Sénécheau, eds., *Antike, Archäologie und Öffentlichkeit: Für einen neuen Dialog zwischen Medien und Wissenschaft* (Bielefeld), 103–22.
Plezia, M. (2002) 'Poland II. History of scholarship A. Classical philology' = 'Polen II. Wissenschaftsgeschichte A. Klassische Philologie', *DNP* 15.2: 404–7.
Pollock, S. (2009) 'Future philology? The fate of soft science in a hard world', *Critical Inquiry* 35: 931–61.
Poppe, E. (2000) 'Ireland' = 'Irland', *DNP* 14: 641–8.
Pöschl, V. (1950) *Die Dichtkunst Virgils. Bild und Symbol in der Aeneis*, Innsbruck.
  (1962) *The Art of Vergil: Image and Symbol in the Aeneid*, Ann Arbor, MI (trans. of Pöschl 1950).
Postgate, J. P. P. (1881) *Select Elegies of Propertius*, London.
Raeburn, D. A. (1999) 'Ancient languages, teaching of II. Great Britain' = 'Altsprachlicher Unterricht II. Großbritannien', *DNP* 13: 120–2.
Reeve, M. D. (2000) '*Cuius in usum?* Recent and future editing', *JRS* 90: 196–206.
Reverdin, O. (1980) *Les études classiques aux XIXe et XXe siècles. Leur place dans l'histoire des idées*, Vandœuvres.
Richard, C. J. (2010) 'Vergil and the early American republic', in J. Farrell and M. C. J. Putnam, eds., *Vergil's Aeneid and Its Tradition* (Malden, MA), 355–65.
Rimell, V. (2015) *The Closure of Space in Roman Poetics: Empire's Inward Turn*, Cambridge.
Ritoók, Z. (2003) 'Hungary II. History of classical studies' = 'Ungarn II. Geschichte der Altertumswissenschaften', *DNP* 15.3: 754–9.
Roche, H. (2017) 'Classics and education in the Third Reich: *Die Alten Sprachen* and the Nazification of Latin- and Greek-teaching in secondary schools', in H. Roche and K. N. Demetriou, eds., *Brill's Companion to the Classics, Fascist Italy and Nazi Germany* (Leiden), 238–63.
Rommel, B. (2000) 'France III. 16th–18th century' = 'Frankreich III. 16.–18. Jh.', *DNP* 14: 27–54.
Ronnick, M. V. (2010) 'Vergil in the Black American experience', in J. Farrell and M. C. J. Putnam, *Vergil's Aeneid and Its Tradition* (Malden, MA), 376–403.

Ross, D. O., Jr (1989) 'United States: Latin philology', in Arrighetti et al. 1989, 295–314.
Rubel, A. (2019) 'Quo vadis *Altertumswissenschaft*? The command of foreign languages and the future of Classical studies', *CW* 112: 193–223.
Rummel, E. and M. Kooistra (2007) *Reformation Sources: The Letters of Wolfgang Capito and His Fellow Reformers in Alsace and Switzerland*, Toronto.
Sacré, D. (2001) 'Netherlands and Belgium III. The southern Netherlands after 1575' = 'Niederlande und Belgien III. Die südlichen Niederlande nach 1575', *DNP* 15.1: 1016–36.
Salmen, B. (2000) 'James Loeb – Leben und Wirken', in *James Loeb 1867–1933: Kunstsammler und Mäzen* (Munich), 17–72.
Sandys, J. E. (1903–8) *A History of Classical Scholarship*, 3 vols., Cambridge, MA. 2nd edn, New York, 1958. 3rd edn, New York, 1964.
Scheidel, W., ed. (2009) *Rome and China: Comparative Perspectives on Ancient World Empires*, Oxford and New York.
Schmidt, E. A. (2001) 'The meaning of Vergil's *Aeneid*: American and German approaches', *CW* 94: 145–71.
Schmidt, P. L. (1995) 'Zwischen Anpassungsdruck und Autonomiestreben: Die deutsche Latinistik vom Beginn bis in die 20er Jahre des 20. Jahrhunderts', in Flashar 1995, 115–82.
  (2001) 'Latin studies in Germany, 1933–1945: institutional conditions, political pressures, scholarly consequences', in Harrison 2001, 285–300.
  (2002) 'Philology II. Latin' = 'Philologie II. Lateinisch', *DNP* 15.2: 278–327.
Schmidt-Dengler, W. (2003) 'Austria III. 20th century' = 'Österreich III. 20. Jahrhundert', *DNP* 15.3: 1292–7.
Schmitz, T. (2003a) 'France IV. 19th and 20th century' = 'Frankreich IV. 19. und 20. Jahrhundert', *DNP* 15.3: 1253–73.
  (2003b) 'Philology I. Greek' = 'Philologie I. Griechisch', *DNP* 15.3: 1297–1307.
Schöllgen, G. (2018) 'Franz Joseph Dölger-Institut zur Erforschung der Spätantike', in T. Becker and P. Rosin, eds., *Die Natur- und Lebenswissenschaften. Geschichte der Universität Bonn*, vol. 4 (Göttingen), 646–9.
Schwindt, J. P. (2003) 'Philology II. Latin' = 'Philologie II. Lateinisch', *DNP* 15.3: 1307–22.
Searle, E. et al. (2018) 'Widening access to Classics in the UK: how the impact, public engagement, outreach and knowledge exchange agenda have helped', in Holmes-Henderson et al. 2018, 27–46.
Serracino, C. (2018) 'The gateway to honour: a history of Classics at the University of Malta from 1800 to 1979', unpublished PhD dissertation, Universities of Malta and Oxford.
Shackleton Bailey, D. R. (1956) *Propertiana*, Cambridge.
Sinanoğlu, S. (1989) 'Turchia. La filologia classica', in Arrighetti et al. 1989, 579–89.
Skempis, M. and I. Ziogas, eds. (2014) *Geography, Topography, Landscape: Configurations of Space in Greek and Roman Epic*, Berlin.

Stahl, H.-P. (2015) *Poetry Underpinning Power. Vergil's Aeneid: The Epic for Emperor Augustus*, Swansea.
Stanford, W. B. (1976) *Ireland and the Classical Tradition*, Dublin.
Stark, I. (2016) 'Johannes Irmscher's unofficial activity for the state security of the German Democratic Republic', in Movrin and Olechowaka 2016, 257–90.
Stewart, Z. (2000) 'Gründung und Geschichte der Loeb Classical Library', in *James Loeb 1867-1933. Kunstsammler und Mäzen* (Munich), 99–106.
Stiewe, B. (2011) *Der 'Dritte Humanismus'. Aspekte deutscher Griechenrezeption vom George-Kreis bis zum Nationalsozialismus*, Berlin and New York.
Stotz, P. (1999) 'Pronunciation II. Latin' = 'Aussprache II. Latein', *DNP* 13: 353–8.
Stray, C. (1998) *Classics Transformed: Schools, Universities, and Society in England, 1830–1960*, Oxford.
  (2007) Review of Henderson 2006, *JRS* 97: 309–10.
  (2010) '"Patriots and professors": a century of Roman studies, 1910-2010', *JRS* 100: 1–31.
  (2014) 'Eduard Fraenkel: an exploration', *SyllClass* 25: 113–72.
  (2016) 'A Teutonic monster in Oxford: the making of Fraenkel's Agamemnon', in Kraus and Stray 2016, 39–57.
  (2017) 'Eduard Fraenkel (1888–1970)', in Crawford et al. 2017, 180–99.
  (2018) *Classics in Britain: Scholarship, Education, and Publishing, 1800–2000*, Oxford and New York.
Stroh, W. (2001) 'Living Latin' = 'Lebendiges Latein', *DNP* 15.1: 92–9.
  (2016) '*Vitae parallelae*: on Classical studies which took place (or could have taken place) in the Federal Republic of Germany (FRG) and German Democratic Republic (GDR) up until 1989', in Movrin and Olechowaka 2016, 113–22. Originally published in Latin as V. Stroh, 'Vitae parallelae', *Vox Latina* 50 (2014): 54–61.
Suerbaum, W. (1981) 'Gedanken zur modernen Aeneis-Forschung', *AU* 24: 67–103. Reprinted in C. Leidl and S. Döpp, eds., *In Klios und Kalliopes Diensten. Kleine Schriften von Werner Suerbaum* (Bamberg, 1993), 309–45. Published in Italian as *Riflessioni in margine alla moderna critica dell'Eneide*, trans. M. Martina (Trieste, 1985).
Sutton, D. A. (2018) *Introducing A. E. Housman (1859–1936): Preliminary Studies*, Newcastle.
Tarrant, R. J. (1983) 'Horace', in L. D. Reynolds, ed., *Texts and Transmission: A Survey of the Latin Classics* (Oxford), 182–6.
  (2006) 'Propertian textual criticism and editing', in H.-C. Günther, ed., *Brill's Companion to Propertius* (Leiden), 45–65.
  (2012) *Virgil. Aeneid Book* XII, Cambridge.
  (2016a) *Texts, Editors, and Readers*, Cambridge.
  (2016b) 'A new critical edition of Horace', in Hunter and Oakley 2016, 291–321.
Thomas, R. F. (2001) *Virgil and the Augustan Reception*, Cambridge.
Torresin, G. (1999) 'Denmark' = 'Dänemark', *DNP* 13: 679–81.

Tränkle, H. (1993) 'Von Keller-Holder zu Shackleton Bailey. Prinzipien und Probleme der Horaz-Edition', in O. Reverdin and B. Grange, eds., *Horace* (Vandœuvres), 1–29.
Vainio, R. (1999) 'Finland' = 'Finnland', *DNP* 13: 1148–52.
van der Blom, H. (2010) *Cicero's Role Models: The Political Strategy of a Newcomer*, Oxford.
Verhaart, F. (2020) *Classical Learning in Britain, France, and the Dutch Republic, 1600–1750*, Oxford.
von Ungern-Sternberg, J. (2017) *Les chers ennemis. Deutsche und französische Altertumswissenschaftler in Rivalität und Zusammenarbeit*, Stuttgart.
Waquet, F. (2000) 'France V. History of the teaching of Latin' = 'Frankreich V. Geschichte des Lateinunterrichts', *DNP* 14: 54–61.
  (2001) *Latin or the Empire of a Sign: From the Sixteenth to the Twentieth Centuries* (trans. John Howe), London and New York. Translation of *Le latin ou l'empire d'un signe*, XVIe–XXe siècle, Paris, 1998.
Watson, G. (1989) 'Ireland: Greek and Latin philology in the twentieth century, II', in Arrighetti et al. 1989, 983–1002.
Wegeler, C. (1996) '... *wir sagen ab der internationalen Gelehrtenrepublik'. Altertumswissenschaft und Nationalsozialismus. Das Göttinger Institut für Altertumskunde 1921–1962*, Vienna.
von Wilamowitz-Moellendorff, U. (1921) *Geschichte der Philologie*, Leipzig. 2nd edn, Stuttgart, 1998. Translated as *History of Classical Scholarship* (ed. H. Lloyd-Jones), Baltimore, 1982.
Williams, R. D. (1983) *The Aeneid of Virgil. Edited with Introduction and Notes*, 2 vols., New York.
Winterer, C. (2002) *The Culture of Classicism: Ancient Greece and Rome in American Intellectual Life 1780–1910*, Baltimore and London.
Wlosok, A. (1973) 'Vergil in der neueren Forschung', *Gymnasium* 80: 129–51.
  (1990a) 'Vergil in der neueren Forschung', Heck and Schmidt 1990, 279–301 (reprint of Wlosok 1973).
  (1990b) '*Aeneas vindex*: ethischer Aspekt und Zeitbezug', in Heck and Schmidt 1990, 419–36.
Wright, C. D. (1993) *The Irish Tradition in Old English Literature*, Cambridge.
Zetzel, J. (2015) Review of Arrighetti et al. 2014, *BMCRev* 2015.04.07.
Zuckerberg, D. (2018) *Not All Dead White Men: Classics and Misogyny in the Digital Age*, Cambridge, MA.

CHAPTER 10

# *Editing*

*Samuel J. Huskey and Robert A. Kaster*

Virtually all editions of ancient Latin texts have for centuries been founded on the same premise: that the text being edited is a singular entity, produced by one specific person at a specific time.[1] The identity of the creator might be in doubt or unknown, and we might not be able to place the time of creation more precisely than within a more or less general range. But unless they are editing a text like the pseudo-Acronian scholia to Horace – transmitted only in multiply revised and reconstituted forms – all editors aim to recreate 'the author's original', the text as it existed when it first began to circulate in antiquity. In some cases the concept of an author's original is unproblematic: we know that soon after Cicero defended Publius Sestius in March, 56 BCE he put a written version of the speech into circulation. In other cases – the *Aeneid* being the most obvious – it would be absurd to say that the text entered circulation in a form its creator found satisfactory, and the very idea of 'the author's original' is at least fraught. Yet even in that case, and in many others in which we simply do not know whether or not the author's original existed in the relevant sense, an editor must proceed as though it did, for down any other route methodological chaos lies.

But whereas editing the typical ancient Latin text entails the same basic premise and goal, every edition represents a unique theory, if by 'theory' we mean a structure of ideas used to organise and understand a given set of data. There are three reasons why this is so. There is the obvious fact that the data mainly relevant to editing a text are the words that the text comprises, and different texts comprise different words. But, second, it is highly unlikely that

---

[*] We wish to thank the Andrew W. Mellon Foundation's Scholarly Communications Division for supporting the development of the Digital Latin Library and its Library of Digital Latin Texts, and the University of Oklahoma for being the institutional home of the project.
[1] Authors occasionally did produce different versions of the same work – thus Ovid's successive five-book and three-book versions of *Amores* – but each of those was a singular entity which in principle could be edited as such (in fact, the three-book version so completely superseded the original that the latter has left not a trace); for argument that evidence of more than one authorial 'recension' can be found in the correspondence between Ausonius and Paulinus of Nola, see Dolveck 2015: 151–62.

any two editions of the same text would base themselves on exactly the same sets of data. And even were that unlikely event to come to pass, it is inconceivable – humans being humans and, in particular, scholars being scholars – that two editors would independently generate exactly the same structure of ideas to organise and understand those data. Expressly recognising that an edition represents a unique and highly personal theory should help us to recognise in turn that any edition is an exercise, not in establishing the incontrovertible truth, but in using the data available to produce the most plausible approximation of an elusive 'author's original'.[2]

Finding, understanding and presenting the available data in that sort of probabilistic exercise form the subject of this chapter's first part. We begin with the different categories of data on which editors typically rely, and then consider how the data are collected. Next we examine how editors survey the data they have collected and build theories to organise and explain them: here we glance back at the ways in which editorial methods have developed since the fifteenth century and briefly summarise the 'stemmatic method'. Our last topic is the 'critical apparatus', in which editors display selections from their data that they believe especially deserve editorial and readerly scrutiny, typically because in certain passages there are discrepancies in the text's documentary record: the apparatus both displays the judgements a given editor has made and invites readers to evaluate those judgements.

We conclude the chapter's first part by discussing a complex text – the Servian commentaries on Virgil – that in fact challenges some of the premises and methods we describe, not because the concept of an 'author's original' is irrelevant to the text but because our ability to reconstitute that original is compromised by the ways in which the text has been transmitted: for reasons that will emerge, this text might in fact be best represented not by a traditional printed edition but by the sort of digital critical edition that is the subject of the chapter's second part.

Here we discuss the development of digital critical editions, with particular focus on the Library of Digital Latin Texts (LDLT), a joint project of the Digital Latin Library, the Society for Classical Studies, the Medieval Academy of America and the Renaissance Society of America. We begin by discussing the terms 'digital critical edition', 'scholarly digital edition' and 'digital edition' and their application to a wide variety of products, from simple text documents to interactive, multimedia resources. We show that the addition of the word 'digital' often signals a departure from editorial practice as the first part of this

---

[2] Damon 2016: 202–3 stresses that every edition represents a theory, and that the theory is distilled in the edition's critical apparatus, the subject of our third section (p. 530).

chapter explains it. That is, the power of digital technology to process large amounts of data and visualise it in new and interesting ways leads to thoughts of applications and interfaces that somehow obviate the need for editors and editing. In opposition to this view, we argue that the explosion in the availability of data related to texts makes editing and editors all the more important, lest readers drown in information coursing through the firehose.

Next we discuss how traditional critical editions may be seen as databases. The data model that has been in use for centuries has a schema for encoding textual data with symbols, abbreviations and standard formats for typography and page layout. As data models go, the traditional critical edition is remarkably flexible and effective. It can accommodate prose and poetry, fragmentary texts, texts in multiple languages, texts in multiple versions and a variety of ancillary materials. It also runs on a stable platform – the codex – that has undergone centuries of testing and development, and that is relatively inexpensive and simple to produce.

We then take up efforts to adapt this model for use with modern technology. Even considering the extraordinary scholarly achievements of the last two centuries, humans have limitations when it comes to storing and processing large amounts of information – two things computers do exceptionally well. Using examples from a text currently in preparation, the Servian commentaries mentioned in the first part of the chapter, we demonstrate some of the basic concepts of encoding textual data according to the LDLT's guidelines. We also address some of the common misperceptions about the technical barriers surrounding digital editing, and we survey some of the current efforts underway to facilitate entry into the field.

We conclude by returning to the argument that the purpose of a critical edition, traditional or digital, is to present a carefully curated, well-organised dataset that reflects the considered judgement of a scholar with deep familiarity of the issues and problems associated with a text and its tradition. The fact that digital critical editions can also provide guided access to primary and secondary source materials, or even the editor's own research materials, is all the more reason to embrace digital critical editions.

## Part One: The Edition as Text

### Gathering the Data

Every classical Latin (and Greek) text must be constituted, not from one or more copies that come from the author's own hand, but from later copies and other evidence that typically postdate the author's by centuries.[3] All these data can be divided into two categories: the 'direct' tradition constituted by the surviving ancient, mediaeval or humanist manuscripts; and the 'indirect' tradition, constituted by quotations, references and allusions in other ancient and (in some cases) mediaeval texts. The former will receive most of our attention, but the importance of the latter should be understood as well. In the case of the ten authors – all but one of them poets – for whose work some version of an ancient commentary survives, the commentaries' lemmata and the comments themselves provide important evidence of the texts that circulated in antiquity, in most case centuries before the oldest extant manuscripts.[4] Many more texts were quoted in one or another learned compilation produced by Aulus Gellius, Nonius Marcellus, grammarians and others: for example, in the *Index scriptorum* found in the last of the seven volumes of Keil's *Grammatici Latini* (1855–80), citations of Horace run to just over twelve columns; of Terence, over fourteen; of Cicero, fifteen; and of Virgil, more than seventy-two – in fact, an intelligible text of the *Aeneid* could probably be constituted from the lemmata of the Servian commentaries and the grammarians' citations alone.[5] Beyond Cicero and Sallust, who were read in the schools, prose authors tend to benefit less from robust indirect traditions, though there are exceptions: for example, Einhard modelled his *Vita Karoli Magni* (c. 828?) on Suetonius' life of Augustus and drew extensively from the lives of the eleven other Caesars Suetonius treated, and his imitation at least once provides a text superior to that of the direct tradition.[6]

---

[3] In Part One, first-person pronouns and the like refer to Robert Kaster; in Part Two, to Samuel Huskey. For the ground covered in Part One there is no better guide than the expert and elegant survey in Tarrant 2016; West 1973 is also excellent, if more austere, while the final chapter of Reynolds and Wilson 2013 (4th edn, 1st edn 1968) is a concise classic. Tarrant 1995, Reeve 2000, and De Nonno 2010 offer *tours d'horizon* of Latin editing from different perspectives, each with further references; Reeve's reviews of editions of classical texts (listed at Hunter and Oakley 2016: 322–38) provide an education in the field. Reynolds 1983a has been the indispensable guide to the transmission of classical Latin texts for more than a generation; it will soon be updated by the larger and more inclusive *Oxford Guide to the Transmission of the Latin Classics* being edited by Justin Stover. Other fundamental work will be cited as it becomes pertinent to the subjects of the sections that follow.

[4] Zetzel 2018: 253–77 efficiently surveys the ten – Terence, Cicero, Virgil, Horace, Ovid, Germanicus, Persius, Lucan, Statius and Juvenal – with further references; for the Servian commentaries on Virgil, see the final section of Part One (p. 537).

[5] Given well-known patterns of commentary and citation, the early books would fare better than the later. Other authors well represented in Keil's index include Plautus (6.5 columns), Lucan (just over 4), Sallust (4) and Juvenal (3.5), the popularity of Lucan and Juvenal reflecting the renewed interest in their texts from the late fourth century on; by contrast, consider the relative neglect of Ovid (not quite 2 columns), Statius (1.75), Lucretius (just over 1), Catullus (1/3) and Caesar (1/4).

[6] See Kaster 2016a: 120 (on *Aug.* 80 *claudicaret*).

But the direct and indirect traditions do not exhaust the resources that editors must take into account. To take another example from Suetonius' life of Augustus: it is clear that among his sources was the great inscription we know as the *Res gestae Divi Augusti*, and that familiarity allows us to restore at least the sense of a passage where a lacuna is found in all the extant manuscripts; similarly, a graffito at Pompeii restores the correct reading in a line of Propertius that the manuscripts get wrong.[7] On a different front, no editor of Virgil would ignore his use of Homer or Catullus, and no editor of Statius would ignore his relation to Virgil. And so on: the sources and parallels that must be controlled are as varied as the texts that are to be edited. But for most texts there is a further resource that relieves the editor of the need to reinvent the wheel: the great mass of scholarship that has grown up around the texts over the course of the past 500 years, especially the work of earlier editors and commentators (fortunate is the editor whose text was once the province of a Casaubon) and other scholars who addressed blemishes (real or apparent) in the transmitted text.[8]

But for virtually all texts the manuscripts form the centre of an editor's attention,[9] in numbers and configurations that cover a vast range of possibilities, from texts that owe their existence to a single surviving manuscript (e.g. Tacitus' *Annals* and *Histories*) to those represented by many hundreds of manuscripts (e.g. the Virgilian corpus, Ovid's *Metamorphoses*). The editor's first task, therefore, is to determine where on that continuum her text lies – how many extant manuscripts are there? – so that she can devise a plan to gather their data. To a certain extent she can rely on previous editions (with luck, someone reliable has done a thorough and convincing job before), but in most cases due diligence requires a thorough survey of the many excellent catalogues, both print and online, that now exist:[10] the aim is to identify as

---

[7] Suetonius: see Wardle 2014: 321, and Kaster 2016a: 105–7, on *Aug.* 43.1 *histriones* \* \* \* *non*. Propertius: see Heyworth 2007a: 455, on *CIL* IV 1894 and Prop. 4.5.47–8 *pulsat*.

[8] Arriving at anything like a complete tally of emendations proposed for a given text is one of the most daunting aspects of editing, even though electronic resources have vastly facilitated bibliographic surveys. Producing a repertory of conjectures of the sort that Margarethe Billerbeck and Mario Somazzi compiled for the Senecan tragedies (2009) is a generous and noble act, but most texts lack such resources; equally generous and noble, and more promising as a path to the future, is Dániel Kiss' 'online repertory of conjectures on Catullus' (2013, 2017), which can be updated *ad lib*.

[9] An exception: the sole source of Velleius Paterculus' history, a lost manuscript from Murbach, is most securely known from the edition that Beatus Rhenanus based upon his copy of it (now also lost) and J. A. Burer's careful collation of the Murbach manuscript with that edition: Reynolds 1983b.

[10] A complete accounting is impossible, but some high points should be noted. Munk Olsen 1982–2009 (with supplements in *RHT* 1991, 1994, 1997, 2000, 2002, 2007), an exhaustive survey of classical Latin manuscripts down through the twelfth century, has eased the labour and improved the lives of all who work with these texts. There are many up-to-date printed catalogues of important collections, among which the complete catalogue of the classical Latin manuscripts of

many of the surviving manuscripts as possible before deciding which will be the centre of attention, then settling down to the job of collation, comparing a manuscript's text word by word with that of a modern printed edition and noticing variations.[11]

Here human frailty imposes significant limitations on the process, since proper collation is slow and painstaking work.[12] Where the text is of moderate length and the number of manuscripts is manageable (both adjectives being left to subjective definition), the editor should feel obliged to collate all the surviving books. Otherwise, and in most circumstances, the editor will proceed selectively, with the goal of casting her net widely enough to snare all variant readings transmitted from antiquity. To quote Richard Tarrant on his experience editing Ovid's *Metamorphoses*:

> From a logical standpoint, complete collation is the only defensible approach, but in most cases that is a counsel of perfection rather than

the Vatican Library by Elisabeth Pellegrin and others (1975–2010) is a crown jewel. Resources for investigating national collections are available online for Germany (www.manuscripta-mediaevalia.de/), Italy (https://manus.iccu.sbn.it/), the Netherlands (www.mmdc.nl/), Austria (https://manuscripta.at), Switzerland (www.codices.ch/) and France (http://medium.irht.cnrs.fr/, with information on the collections of many other nations), as are catalogues of collections in major libraries, including the Bodleian Library (www.bodley.ox.ac.uk/dept/scwmss/wmss/online/online.htm), the British Library (https://searcharchives.bl.uk/), the Vatican Library (www.mss.vatlib.it/guii/console?service=scan) and the Bibliothèque nationale de France (https://archivesetmanuscrits.bnf.fr/). Online digitised images of manuscripts are available from the Bibliothèque nationale de France (https://gallica.bnf.fr/), the Vatican Library (https://digi.vatlib.it/), the Biblioteca Medicea Laurenziana (http://mss.bmlonline.it/), the British Library (www.bl.uk/manuscripts/), select libraries in Switzerland (www.e-codices.unifr.ch/), and the Bibliothèque virtuelle des manuscrits médiévaux (sponsored by the Institut de recherche et d'histoires des textes: https://bvmm.irht.cnrs.fr): the list is doubtless becoming longer as I write.

[11] In the case of any given manuscript the editor will ultimately decide both that most of those variations are surely or probably wrong (the modern edition is correct, or at least more probably correct) and that some of them are in fact correct (the modern edition is wrong), but at the stage of collation such decisions lie in the future: noting variations is all that initially matters, for reasons to be made plain presently.

[12] Collating thoroughly the eighteen manuscripts I decided to use for my edition of Suetonius took three years, during which I devoted to the job all time not required by other obligations, six or more usually seven days a week. Collating with equal thoroughness the 207 other manuscripts I identified would obviously have been beyond my capacity, or the capacity of any one (sane) person. Quite possibly there will come a time when optical character recognition technology will make it possible for all the many different hands found in mediaeval Latin manuscripts to be scanned swiftly and read accurately by machines (though distinguishing original from corrected readings will be a more daunting challenge), and when other algorithms will do the job of analysing and organising the machines' output along the lines described in the next section on p. 523 (sophisticated cladistic software is already used for similar purposes in phylogenetics and other sciences, in comparative mythology and folklore and in historical linguistics; on its still rudimentary application to classical texts, Tarrant 2016: 152–3). But the perfection of these technologies is not imminent; and even when the collection and organisation of the data have been reliably mechanised, 'at the heart of the process will always be the scholar who applies his or her fallible judgement to the improvement of a text that can never be recovered' (Tarrant 2016: 156).

a feasible policy. For the *Metamorphoses*, I decided to collate in full all extant manuscripts written before 1200 (which happens to be the cut-off point of Birger Munk Olsen's indispensable catalogue ...),[13] and to rely on samplings for manuscripts after that date; in all I looked at nearly 300 manuscripts, most of them in a highly selective way ... In practice, therefore, editors generally cross their fingers and hope that the manuscript evidence they have assembled contains all or almost all [ancient] readings.[14]

My own experience editing Macrobius' *Saturnalia* and Suetonius' *De vita Caesarum* (*DVC*) tracks Tarrant's very closely. Both texts enjoyed significant but still relatively modest circulation in the ninth through thirteenth centuries, with the number of surviving manuscripts weighted toward the beginning of that period for Macrobius, toward the end for Suetonius, until their popularity exploded in the fourteenth and, especially, fifteenth centuries.[15] For the *Saturnalia* I collated and used fifteen of the earlier manuscripts and examined another dozen thoroughly enough to determine that they contributed nothing useful not found in the other fifteen;[16] for the *DVC* I collated eighteen of the nineteen manuscripts surviving from the ninth through thirteenth centuries and examined just over 100 of the later books, most of them in specifically targeted ways.[17] In other words, I crossed my fingers and hoped: for though it seems very unlikely, it is not impossible that one or more of the later books provides evidence of an independent line of transmission not attested in the older books – after all, Ermanno Malaspina has recently demonstrated that two fifteenth-century manuscripts of Cicero's *Lucullus* must ultimately be derived from a lost twelfth-century copy that represented an independent branch of the tradition.[18] But I contemplate that possibility with equanimity: if it turns out that my hope was misplaced, it will mean that progress has been made.

---

[13] On Munk Olsen cf. n. 10.
[14] Tarrant 2016: 55–6. I have here substituted 'ancient' for the phrase 'potentially archetypal': on the meaning of 'archetype', see p. 524.
[15] Sixty manuscripts of the *Saturnalia* – more than half the total number extant – were written in the fifteenth century; in the case of the *DVC*, more than 160 of 225.
[16] At Kaster 2010: 85–102, I discuss the dozen manuscripts of the *Saturnalia* eliminated from consideration.
[17] I did not collate the nineteenth survivor among the earlier manuscripts because it had previously been shown to be a copy of another extant early manuscript (Dunston 1952, on London, BL Egerton 3055, s. XII$^{2/2}$; for the criterion of elimination, see p. 527). The later books that I examined include all those of the fourteenth century save one and all but three of the fifteenth-century books that can be dated to the period before 1470, when the first printed editions began to appear: I was primarily aiming to identify the earliest attestations of good humanist corrections that previous editors had ascribed to undifferentiated '*recentiores*'.
[18] Malaspina 2015 and 2019. The twelfth-century manuscript in question belonged to the great historian of mediaeval England William of Malmesbury, who also played an important role in the transmission of Suetonius' *DVC*: see next section at n. 49.

## *Organising and Understanding the Data*

Once the manuscripts have been collated, with their divergent readings entered in a spreadsheet or some other medium affording a synoptic view, the editor must decide what it all means: in other words, he must build a theory that explains the data. Approaches to this part of the job, especially, evolved slowly from the early modern era on. In the time of the first printed books it was not uncommon for an edition to be based upon a single manuscript, which was often whatever manuscript happened to be closest to hand.[19] The practice of seeking out and comparing the readings of a variety of manuscripts became increasingly common from the sixteenth century on, so that in the editions of scholars like Pieter Burman the elder and Franz Oudendorp in the mid-eighteenth century one expects to see notes that contain references to half a dozen different books.[20] But such sources were cited without a synoptic view of the transmission, and so without a sense of what it meant, in terms of the history of the text as a whole, when manuscript A offered one reading and manuscript B had another. It was not until the nineteenth century that editors of classical texts, influenced especially by developments in the editing of the New Testament, began to devise a method – most commonly known, misleadingly, as the 'method of Lachmann' – for tracing the history of their texts and understanding how the data offered by one manuscript might be related to the data offered by another.[21] The method, which editors have continued to ponder and refine, included all the steps so far described and, most importantly, the step that is the subject of this section.

Central to any attempt to build a theory for one's edition, then, is a clear conception of the text's history; and central to that conception is the distinction between 'closed' and 'open' traditions.[22] In a closed tradition,

---

[19] In the case of Suetonius' *DVC* it is clear that the first printed editions were heavily influenced by a remote corner of the tradition represented by the manuscripts **FBE**, with the result that what became the print vulgate was significantly shaped by sources no editor today, knowing the tradition's history, would even cite: see pp. 528–31 on the stemma of the *DVC*.

[20] Richard Bentley collated a number of manuscripts of the *DVC*, including the oldest and best, for an edition that was never realised: his collations survive in the margins of his copy of Gronovius' edition of 1698, now British Library 687.c.6 (see Preud'homme 1902).

[21] On 'the genesis of Lachmann's method' see Timpanaro 2005 (first published in 1963 as 'La genesi del metodo del Lachmann'; the English translation includes bibliography of recent work on pp. 234–9). The label 'Lachmann's method' arose from Karl Lachmann's successful application of the method in his edition of Lucretius published in 1850; for a glimpse of the 'New Stemmatics' movement – dedicated to 'analysis [that] aims to obtain as comprehensive a view as possible of the relations among the witnesses, . . . [that is] based, as far as possible, on all data, [and that uses] quantitative tools, typically computer-based' – see www.textualscholarship.org.

[22] On the logical principles pertinent to a closed tradition, discussed more fully, the classic work is Maas 1927 (Engl. trans. Maas 1957); see also Reeve 1986 and 2007. The classic work on open traditions, Pasquali 1971 (first edn 1952), was developed from a review of Maas (Pasquali 1929).

manuscripts descend in discrete lines of transmission from a single source intermediate between the author's original and the extant manuscripts. The single intermediate source, or 'archetype', can be defined as the latest copy of the text, extant or (more usually) hypothetically reconstructed, absent which no subsequent copies would exist.[23] Discrete lines of transmission result when (for example) books A and B are copied independently from the archetype, C is copied from A, D from B, E from C, F from D, and so on. Since it is virtually impossible for a text of any length to be copied by hand with perfect accuracy, the texts of A and B will deviate – largely in different ways – from the text of the source; A's innovations will be passed to C, which will add some innovations of its own and pass the whole lot on to E, and so similarly from B to D to F; and the lines of transmission will remain discrete so long as none of the books ACE comes into contact with any of the books BDF – if, that is, a reader does not compare C with B and enter some of the latter's innovations in the former, or copy some of D's innovations into E, in the process known as 'contamination' (a more neutral term might be 'blending'). If these basic conditions are satisfied, the closed tradition's manuscripts, and the patterns of innovation that they reveal, can be used (as we will soon see) to reconstruct the archetype, by tracing the patterns of innovation from the lower reaches of the tradition upward to the source.

By contrast, when an editor sees that the basic conditions of a closed tradition do not obtain – when there is not a single source more recent than the author's original standing between the latter and the extant manuscripts, or when the lines of transmission do not remain discrete – she knows that she is dealing with an 'open' tradition. That is the position of any editor of Virgil (to cite the most obvious example) or Lucan, among others.[24] In the case of Virgil, we have several surviving ancient capital manuscripts that have no clearly traceable relation to one another; it is all but certain that other ancient manuscripts, now lost, reached the Middle Ages, were copied, and propagated new lineages before they perished; and it is the consensus that there is no common source of the ancient and mediaeval tradition more recent than the version that Varius and Tucca reportedly put into circulation after Virgil's death.[25] But even if there

---

[23] This is a slight variation on the two-part definition proposed at Reeve 1985: 201.
[24] On the tradition of Lucan see Housman 1926: v–xviii, Gotoff 1971, Håkanson 1979, Tarrant 1983.
[25] Note, however, that Courtney 1981 and 2002–3 offered substantial arguments for a fourth-century archetype (in the most recent critical edition the verdict is *non liquet*: Conte 2009: xiv–xv, with other references).

were a more proximate common source, it is perfectly clear that both in antiquity and in the Carolingian age copies of Virgil's poetry were so frequently and vigorously compared with one another, and altered as a result of the comparison, that the lines of transmission are thoroughly blurred. In such a tradition, any reading can in principle appear in any manuscript: thus while we know that among the three most substantially preserved ancient manuscripts of Virgil the Mediceus and the Palatinus are generally more reliable than the Romanus, the best reading might at any moment surface in the latter. In any given case, the quality of the specific reading is more important than the overall quality of the manuscript in which it is found, and the editor must proceed one case at a time, weighing the divergent readings that present themselves.

Open traditions are far from rare, and the more commonly a text was read in antiquity and the early Middle Ages, the more open its tradition is likely to be.[26] But a striking number of classical Latin texts do survive because a single ancient copy reached the Middle Ages and served as a source of other copies, which then followed paths of transmission sufficiently distinct to allow us to speak of a closed tradition. To see how that kind of tradition is identified, and how it can be used, we can consider first a hypothetical case, intentionally simplified for the purpose at hand, then an actual, and fairly typical, example of the type.

Imagine for a moment that Abraham Lincoln's Gettysburg Address chanced to survive in only four handwritten copies – A, B, C and D – each plainly written by a different hand, none of them the distinctive hand of Lincoln himself.[27] If we found that each ended with the words '. . . shall not', we would have to infer either that Lincoln left the speech unfinished (we are reliably informed that is not the case); or that exactly the same disastrous error was committed repeatedly by coincidence (in favour of which are the odds vanishingly slim); or that it occurred in one of our copies and was introduced intentionally into the others by one or more misguided attempts at correction;[28] or that all four copies derive this error from a defective common

---

[26] West 1973: 37–47, describes a method for selecting manuscripts in an open tradition that maximises the likelihood that all traditional (i.e. ancient) variants will be taken into account.
[27] This and the next three paragraphs are based on Kaster 2016b: 113–15. Perhaps ironically, given the tenor of this account, we do not in fact know the precise words of the text that Lincoln delivered, though none of the variations found in the several extant versions involves the famous words quoted in the examples that follow: for an accessible account, see Wills 1992: 191–203; for the earliest version in Lincoln's own hand, see www.ourdocuments.gov.
[28] Since so-called correctors do sometimes introduce absurdities into texts, such a thing could in principle happen. But this alternative is nonetheless much less likely than the next, and in this case it would not materially alter the general picture of the tradition that emerges: see n. 31.

source, or archetype, intermediate between themselves and the text Lincoln delivered.[29] If, further, we found that A and D ended with the words 'government of the people, by the people, for the people shall not', but B and C closed with 'government of the pebble, by the pebble, for the pebble shall not', we might begin to suspect that B and C are more closely connected to each other than either is to A or D, descending from a more proximate common source, an 'offspring' of the archetype, that had received the textual blot bequeathed by its 'parent' and added a large stain of its own.

Now suppose that further comparison tends to bear out this initial impression. B and C share not only that distinctive error at the end but also a number of other readings that – because they seriously distort the sense or produce mere gibberish – cannot be what Lincoln intended: so they both begin with the phrase 'Seven score and four years ago ...', and halfway through they have Lincoln assert that 'we can not hollow this ground'. Not only that, but A and D similarly share variant readings that can only count as errors: toward the beginning we find 'testing whether that nation, or any nation so, can long endure', and toward the end, 'these dead shall have died in vain'. We would then be justified in supposing that our four manuscripts constitute two distinct branches, each descending separately from the defective archetype.

The next question needing an answer is this: if the members of one branch (AD or BC) are more closely related to each other than they are to the remaining copies, what is the nature of that relationship? Here again the shared gross errors of each pair are the key, as we consider which of two patterns these agreements follow. I say 'which of two' because in fact when any two manuscripts share a number of errors, two patterns are the most likely to emerge:[30]

- if in any given pair of manuscripts – A and D, say – the two share a number of indubitable errors and each has further such errors of its own, then in all likelihood they descend, independently of each other, from a common source: their shared errors are owed to that source, and the peculiar errors of each are the tokens of their mutual independence; on the other hand,
- if in any given pair of manuscripts – B and C, now – C has all the indubitable errors of B and differs from B only in having further such errors of its own, then in all likelihood C is a copy (or a copy of a copy ...) of B.

---

[29] Note, however, that if all four ended with the words 'shall not perish', we might never suspect corruption and certainly could never prove it.
[30] 'Most likely' must be stressed: on the ways in which less likely patterns can (and no doubt sometimes do) lurk undetected in plausible stemmata, see the remarks at West 1973: 34–6, and the next n.

The discussion so far, then, can be summarised in the stemma shown in Figure 10.1, a graphic representation of our theory showing how we think all our copies' data can best be organised and interpreted (by convention, ω = the archetype).³¹

Here ω is the defective archetype of our hypothetical Gettysburg Address, α the source of A and D's shared errors that distinguish them from B and C, and B the source of the common errors that distinguish both B and C from A and D. In using this stemma to reconstruct the archetype, we first eliminate C, which has no value for this purpose, since the only thing it can be presumed to offer that is not already found in B is more innovation relative to the archetype.³² From that point on, we can infer that we have the text of ω whenever we find one of three patterns of agreement: when the texts of A, D and B all agree, of course, but also when AB agree against D or DB agree against A. In each of the latter two cases, the text shared by the two independent manuscripts is presumptively derived from their common source, while the text of the third is presumptively a departure from the archetype. ('Presumptively', in both instances, not because it is certainly the case but because that is just the more likely state of affairs: any editor is a more or less cautious gambler.) But where A and D stand together and apart from B, the archetype's text cannot, strictly, be determined, and we are left to decide which of the two readings – AD's or B's – Lincoln himself is more likely to have written: here the decision is based (for example) on our knowledge of how Lincoln used English ('people', not

Figure 10.1 Gettysburg Address: hypothetical stemma.

---

³¹ Note that if the error with which we began – the corrupt predicate at the end of the Address – had in fact first occurred in **B**, only to be noticed by a deeply foolish reader who then introduced it into α (see n. 28), the error would again appear in all four manuscripts, giving the same impression as the archetypal error we have posited. But that would simply demonstrate that a probabilistic method cannot control for the actions of fools: we would still be justified in positing a bifurcated tradition, and each manuscript would still occupy the same place in the stemma (we would be similarly justified if the error originated in α and was introduced into **B**).

³² Discarding **C** as useless for reconstructing the archetype does not necessarily mean discarding it entirely: its singular innovations might, for example, include a scribe or reader's conjectural corrections that repair inherited defects, and of course the editor would choose to print the corrections, not the defects. But in terms of reconstructing the manuscripts' descent, any such correction is as much an error – a failure to reproduce the book's source exactly – as the worst sort of gibberish.

'pebble'), or on our knowledge of the occasion on which he spoke (19 November 1863, therefore 'Four score and seven years'), or on our sense of what he is likely to have said on that occasion ('these dead shall *not* have died in vain').

The same principles can be illustrated from a text more complex (though certainly not more profound) than Lincoln's 272 words, Suetonius' *DVC*, all 200-odd surviving manuscripts of which owe their existence to a single book that emerged in north central France no later than the early ninth century. We can be reasonably confident of the location and date because the oldest surviving copy (M = Paris, BNF lat. 6115) was copied at Tours by 820, and because the tradition of the text was concentrated in north central France until the end of the eleventh century. And we know that it was a single book for the same reason that we know it was a very bad book: every extant copy of the work shares with all the rest a very large number of identical defects so gross and so numerous that a single common source is the only plausible explanation. In it, for example, the *DVC*'s original eight-book structure (*Suda* T.895) – one each for the first six lives, then one for Galba, Otho and Vitellius and one for the three Flavian *principes* – had been effaced, leaving the impression (made plain in the incipits and explicits of some early manuscripts) that each life constituted an independent book. Far worse, as much as a full gathering of eight folia was missing from the beginning, and with it the dedication to Suetonius' patron Gaius Septicius Clarus that Ioannes Lydus had seen 300 years earlier in Constantinople (*De mag.* p. 92.6–10 Bandy) and the beginning of the life of Julius Caesar, who appears nearly full grown at age sixteen in the first surviving sentence; and there were besides many other shared lacunae and corruptions, so numerous that my edition contains roughly 700 readings that would not have stood in the archetype, or about one correction every 100 words.

It is almost equally clear that two discrete lines of transmission descended from that very bad book, one (α) comprising nine manuscripts of predominantly French origin, the other (β) comprising ten manuscripts written on one side or the other of the English Channel in the generations following the Norman Conquest of Britain. Each of these branches is distinguished from the other by a large number of errors that are both uncorrected and 'uncorrectable': errors that by their nature could not be corrected (e.g. omissions) or in some cases even detected (e.g. transpositions of word order that violate Suetonian norms, substitutions of synonyms that did not enter Latin until well after Suetonius' day) absent comparison with an unrelated manuscript, and that accordingly tend to reappear in the base texts of any closely related books. α and β, in turn, each gave rise to sub-branches of their own. From α there descend $α_1$ (which includes the oldest copy, M),[33] V,[34] and $α_2$ (five manuscripts dating from the late eleventh century to the second half of the twelfth),[35] each with its own set of uncorrected 'uncorrectables'. β yields two similarly distinct sub-branches, $β_1$ (three manuscripts written in England between the beginning of the twelfth and beginning of the thirteenth centuries)[36] and $β_2$ (seven manuscripts of predominantly French origin).[37] When arranged graphically to illustrate their relationships and chronological range, these clusters of manuscript produce the stemma at Figure 10.2.

There was some contact between the two branches (indicated by the dotted lines), from G to β and from β to some members of $α_2$.[38] But it was not such as to blur the basic structures that can be discerned, and in the case of the α manuscripts the contamination can be easily controlled: it affects N and S most thoroughly but L not at all, and it appears in P only as corrections (that is, we see the hand responsible for the contamination at work), leaving the base text clearly visible and allowing L and P's uncorrected text to serve as authentic representatives of the family, so that ONS can be set aside. Other trimming is possible, too: among the β-manuscripts A, the much younger and much more corrupt partner of K, is not needed to represent η, a job that KQ do well enough on their own; and FBE are all descendants of D and so can be set aside, since they give us no access to the archetype's text that is not provided by D. Once these

---

[33] The other member of this branch is **G** = Wolfenbüttel, HAB 4573 (s. xi$^{3/4}$): from Eichstätt in Bavaria, **G** is the geographical outlier among the α-manuscripts, which otherwise were written in France; it also happens to be the only manuscript of this branch that cannot yet be consulted online in digital form.

[34] Vatican, BAV lat. 1904 (s. ix$^{1/2}$): the next oldest manuscript, it is unfortunately lacking for the second half of the work.

[35] **L** = Florence, BML Plut. 68.7 (s. xii$^{2/2}$); **P** = Paris, BNF lat. 5801 (s. xi/xii); **O** = Florence, BML Plut. 66.39 (s. xii med.); **N** = Vatican, BAV Reg. lat. 833 (s. xii$^{2/2}$); and **S** = Montpellier, Fac. de médecine 117 (s. xii med.).

[36] **R** = London, BL Royal 15 C. iii (s. xii in.); **H** = London, BL Royal 15 C. iv (s. xiii in.); **C** = Oxford, Bodl. Lat. class. d. 39 (s. xii$^{3/4}$).

[37] **A** = Soissons, Bibl. mun. 19 (s. xiii); **K** = Cambridge, UL Kk.5.24 (s. xii$^{2/2}$); **Q** = Paris, BNF lat. 5802 (s. xii med.); **D** = (Durham, Cath. Libr. C.III.18 (s. xi ex.); **F** = Florence, BML Plut. 64.8 (s. xii$^{2/2}$); **B** = Paris, BNF lat. 6116 (s. xii med.); and **E** = San Marino, Huntington Libr. HM 45717 (s. xii ex.).

[38] On this contact, and the reasons why we know it passes from **G** to β and from β to $α_2$, not the other way around, see Kaster 2016a: 33–40.

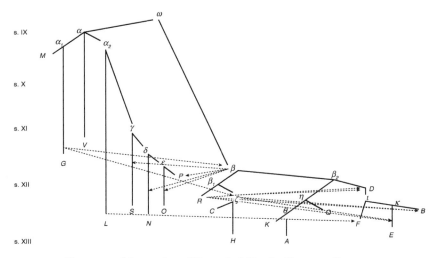

Figure 10.2 Manuscripts of Suetonius' *De uita Caesarum*. Stemma.

adjustments are made, we have a fairly handy working stemma that is shown at Figure 10.3.

Applying this understanding of the tradition according to the principles demonstrated here (i.e. the agreement of, say, $α_1$V against $α_2$ – or, after V is lost, $α_1$L against P – reveals α, $αβ_2$ against $β_1$ reveals ω, and so on) it is possible in all but a relative handful of cases to reach a clear view either of the division in the tradition or, more commonly still, of the archetype itself. Of course, with a text as corrupt as the one the archetype provided, a great deal of work still remains, to attempt to bridge the centuries between the early ninth century and (in this case) the early second century, when Suetonius sent the *DVC* on its way to Gaius Septicius Clarus.

### *Presenting the Data*

But we can draw a curtain over that work, and the countless decisions it entails, because the work and decisions alike are peculiar to whichever text is under consideration, whereas in this part of the chapter I have focused on aspects of editing that are the concern of all editors. Not least among these is the preparation of the critical apparatus, the part of the edition where the editor lays her cards on the table and says, in effect, 'Here is my evidence: don't you agree with my

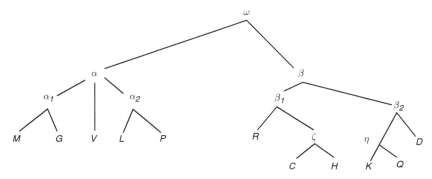

Figure 10.3 Manuscripts of Suetonius' *De uita Caesarum*. Working stemma.

understanding of it?' The claim and the question are not put in so many words, of course: the apparatus, in its compressed format, is a kind of code.[39] But if the editor is competent and thoughtful, the code's meaning should become evident to a careful reader with moderate effort, and its aims should always be the same, whatever the peculiarities of the text at issue: it is where the editor fulfils her basic obligation to present the documentary basis, and the implied or express justification, of the text she has printed;[40] and it gives the reader the chance to respond to the question, 'Don't you agree with my understanding of it?', by answering, 'No'.

We can begin with the distinction between a 'skinny apparatus' and a 'fat apparatus'.[41] The distinction is familiar to anyone who has turned from a typical apparatus in an Oxford Classical Text edition, where the words *brevi ... adnotatione critica instruxit* appear on virtually every title

---

[39] On 'decoding the apparatus' see briefly Damon 2016: 210–12.
[40] Since not even the most capacious apparatus of a printed edition allows an editor to explain every controversial decision, editors commonly publish their critical notes independently: the OCT series now encourages editors to write companion monographs, a practice begun by Hugh Lloyd-Jones and Nigel Wilson for their edition of Sophocles (1990, supplemented by Lloyd-Jones and Wilson 1997) and continued most recently by Heyworth 2007a (Propertius), Kaster 2010 (Macrobius, *Saturnalia*), Damon 2015 (Caesar, *De bello civili*), Wilson 2015 (Herodotus) and Kaster 2016a (Suetonius, *DVC*); and the practice has been extended to the Teubner series with Deufert 2017 and 2019. The apparatus of a digital edition could of course accommodate such material in several different ways.
[41] Also known as 'minimalist' and 'maximalist': on the distinction, see the chapter on 'presenting the text' in Tarrant 2016: 124–44. The examples that follow are adapted from a video presentation, 'Constructing the Critical Apparatus', that I recorded for the DLL's video library on editorial techniques (https://digitallatin.org/digital-latin-library/video-library/kaster).

page,[42] to a typical edition in the Bibliotheca Teubneriana, where the apparatus sometimes occupies more of the page than the text. I can illustrate the difference here with two versions of an apparatus to poem 7 of Catullus:

quaeris quot mihi basiationes
tuae, Lesbia, sint satis superque.
quam magnus numerus Libyssae harenae
lasarpiciferis iacet Cyrenis
oraclum Iouis inter aestuosi                                5
et Batti ueteris sacrum sepulcrum;
aut quam sidera multa, cum tacet
nox furtiuos hominum uident amores:
tam te basia multa basiare
uesano satis et super Catullo est,                          10
quae nec pernumerare curiosi
possint nec mala fascinare lingua.

VII 1 quot α : quod *V*     4 lasarpici feris al. fretis *X*, lasarpici fecis *O*     tyrenis *O* tyrrenis *ut uidetur G1*, tyrenis al. cyrenis *Rmg*     5 oradum *V* : *corr.r*     6 batti *ed. Rom.* : beati *O*, beati al. beari *X*     9 basia] basiei *O*, basiei al. basia *X*

hoc carmen uersui 5.13 adiunxit Herrmann 1957 et 1957a 677, qui uersus hoc ordine posuit: 5.1–13, 7.11–12, 7.1–10 | 1 quot *MS. 8 a. 1412* : quod *OGR* | michi *OGR*     2 nostrae *D.F.S. Thomson 2009*     3 libisse harene *O* : lybisse arene *G* : libisse arene *R*     4 asarpiciferis *MS. 8 a. 1463* : lasarpici fecis *O* :lasarpici feris *GR* (al' fretis *R2G2*) : laserpiciferis *Calphurnius 1481, prob. Vossius 1684* : laserpitiferis *Muretus 1554* : lasserpiciferis *Trappes-Lomax 2007 49* | iaces *O* | al' cyrenis *R2m1G2* : tyrenis *OR* : tyarenis *G* (a *del. G2*)     5 oraclum *MSS. 45, 47 et 56 a. 1465 ca.* : oradum *OR* : ora dum *G* : hora dum *MS. 1 a. 1451* : oraculum *ed. Bipontina 1783* | aestuosum *Baehrens 1885*     6 batti *ed. Mediol. 1475, ed. Rom. 1479 ca., MS. 15 ante a. 1479* (bati *iam manus prima ut uid. in MS 122 a. 1460 conscripto*, bachi *MS. 52. a. 1467*) : beati *OGR* : al' beari *G1R2* | sacri *MS 15 ante a. 1479* | sepulcrum *OGR*     7 sydera *OG* | nocet (*cfr. Varro L.L. 6.6*) *Herrmann 1957 et 1957a 677*     9 al' basia *G1R2* : basiei *OGR*     10 catulo *O* | satis, haud super *Barthius* († 1658) 1827 114     11 7.11–12 post 5.13 transp. *Herrmann 1957 et 1957a 677* | euriosi *OGR, corr. R2*     12 possunt *MS. 15 ante a. 1479* | maga *manus prima in marg. MS. 129a ca. a. 1450 scribens* : maha 'Exemplar manu exaratum quod olim fuit Hieronymi Commelini' teste Vossio 1684 : male *dub. Sillig 1823*

---

[42] The adjective *brevi* is appropriately omitted from the title page of S. J. Heyworth's OCT of Propertius (2007b).

The first example, from Roger Mynors' OCT of 1958, is austere even by the standards of that series. It has entries for only five of the poem's twelve lines, and those entries are almost entirely confined to the data found in the three manuscripts (OGR) most proximately derived from the archetype (V).[43] Most strikingly – in view of the fact that Catullus' corpus requires and has received more post-archetypal emendation per hundred lines than any other text of classical Latin poetry with the possible exception of Propertius – the apparatus registers only two emendations: the obvious correction of *quod* to *quot* in line 1, from a Bolognese manuscript written in 1412, and the more learned replacement of the archetype's *beati* with *Batti* in line 6, from one of the incunabula. It includes no proposal made in the subsequent four and a half centuries: at the very least, then, the apparatus conveys the misleading impression that the text of Catullus has been found to be not so problematic after all.

The second example represents the sum of the entries for the poem in Dániel Kiss' exhaustive online repertory of the conjectures that have been made since the *editio princeps* of Catullus was printed in 1472. It thus includes everything that Mynors left out (and of course any suggestions made since the late 1950s), and as a repository of information on the corpus it is invaluable. But it is not something, I think, that many readers would actually want to encounter at the bottom of the page. There plainly must be some middle ground between misleading austerity and exhaustive overload, something that would omit information that serves no ordinary reader's interests – for example, the archetype's *michi* in line 1, the four different misspellings of *oraclum* in line 5, or the fantastic textual gymnastics of Ludwig Herrmann from 1957 – while incorporating more information worth a reader's time and thought, like Baehrens' suggestion of *aestuosum* in line 5.

I do not, however, intend to further explore this particular middle ground here but leave it to readers to work out the puzzle for themselves (*quot lectores, tot apparatus?*). Instead, I will show how I approached a similar issue while preparing the critical apparatus for my edition of Suetonius' *DVC*. The following is a fairly run-of-the-mill passage from the life of Julius Caesar, in which Suetonius chronicles some of Caesar's sexual adventures (*Iul.* 52), followed by the unfiltered data gleaned from the

---

[43] **O** = Oxford, Bodl. Canon. class. lat. 30 (s. xiv); **G** = Paris, BNF lat. 14137 (an. 1375); **R** = Vatican, BAV Ottob. lat. 1829 (s. xiv ex.). **X** = the common ancestor of **GR**, and the agreement of **XO** yields **V**, the lost *codex Veronensis* that surfaced in Catullus' *patria*; **r** is a correcting hand in **R**.

eighteen manuscripts I collated. The text is that of Maximilian Ihm's *editio maior* of 1907, the *comparandum* for my collations:

> Dilexit et reginas, inter quas Eunoen Mauram Bogudis uxorem, cui maritoque eius plurima et immensa tribuit, ut Naso scripsit, sed maxime Cleopatram, cum qua et conuiuia in primam lucem saepe protraxit et eadem naue thalamego paene Aethiopia tenus Aegyptum penetrauit, nisi exercitus sequi recusasset. quam denique accitam in urbem non nisi maximis honoribus praemiisque auctam remisit filiumque natum appellare nomine suo passus est. 2. quem quidem nonnulli Graecorum similem quoque Caesari et forma et incessu tradiderunt. M. Antonius adgnitum etiam ab eo senatui adfirmauit, quae scire C. Matium et C. Oppium reliquosque Caesaris amicos; quorum Gaius Oppius, quasi plane defensione ac patrocinio res egeret, librum edidit, 'non esse Caesaris filium quem Cleopatra dicat'. 3. Heluius Cinna tr. pl. plerisque confessus est habuisse se scriptam paratamque legem quam Caesar ferre iussisset cum ipse abesset, uti uxores liberorum quaerendorum causa quas et quot uellet ducere liceret. at ne cui dubium omnino sit et impudicitiae et adulteriorum flagrasse infamia, Curio pater quadam eum oratione omnium mulierum uirum et omnium uirorum mulierem appellat.[44]

> 1. et (1°) *om.* S[ac]  Eunoen] et e- H[ac], eunen FBE  cui maritoque eius] –que *om.* S[ac], cuius marito CH  plurima et] plurimaque N  ut *om.* V  Naso] vasa MGVLSPONRCHAKQDFBE  *super* Cleopatram *ss.* dilexit AK  conuiuia] –uiua R[ac]  lucem saepe protraxit] saepe l- p- O, l- p- saepe N  thalamego MGVL[ac] : t(h)alamoque SP[ac]O[c]NRCHAKQDFBE (thalamoquego L[c], thalameque P[c], thala ego O[ac])  paene] poene M  recusasset] recussa- F[ac]  accitam] asciam N, acitam Q  auctam] actam KQD[ac]  appellare] appllae N, appellari CH  similem *post* Caesari *repet.* H[ac]  2. incessu] incensu N  adgnitum MVP[ac]O : agnitum GLSP[c]NRCHAKQDFBE  adfirmauit quae NRCHAKQDFBE : -mauitque MGVLS[c]PO (-mauit Sac)  Mattium] martium CH,

---

[44] 'He had affairs with queens, too, among them the Moor Eunoe, wife of Bogud, and to her and her husband he presented a very great number of huge gifts, as Naso wrote; but above all there was Cleopatra, with whom he often caroused until dawn and sailed up into Egypt in the same cabin cruiser almost as far as Ethiopia – and would have reached it had not the army refused to follow. He subsequently summoned her to Rome and sent her back loaded with the greatest honours and rewards and allowed her to give her son his name. 2. Indeed, some Greek writers have handed it down that he resembled Caesar in both his physical form and his gait. Mark Antony affirmed to the senate that Caesar even acknowledged the boy as his own, as Gaius Matius and Gaius Oppius and the rest of Caesar's friends knew. Of these Gaius Oppius published a book titled 'Cleopatra says he's Caesar's son – but he's not', as though the matter stood in need of vigorous defence. 3. Helvius Cinna, a tribune of the plebs, admitted to a large number of people that he had a law, drafted and ready, that Caesar had bade him carry when Caesar himself was absent, to the effect that it was allowable for Caesar to have whatever wives he wished, and in any number, for the sake of producing children. But lest anyone be in any doubt that he was seared by the disgraceful reputation he had for sexual immorality, the elder Curio, in a certain speech, calls him "a man to every woman and a woman to every man".' In the apparatus, a siglum in the form 'L[c]' = 'L corrected,' 'L[ac]' = 'L before (*ante*) correction'.

marcium E  Oppium] appium M, opium E  egerit] geret Q  edidit *bis* S$^{ac}$  Cleopatra dicat MGVLSPONF$^c$ : de Cleopatra dicant RCHAKQDFBE  3. Heluius] Kel- LSPON paratamque *om.* E$^{ac}$  ferre] ferri CH  quas] quos PO  quot] quod M  uellet MGVRAKQDFBE : uellent LSPON, uellet quis CH  at] ad M, ac CH  eum *post* impudicitiae *add.* RCHAKQDFBE(-diticiae O)  adulteriorum] aduter- R$^{ac}$  flagrasse] –set M$^{ac}$, fragrasse RF$^{ac}$, flaglasse ADF$^{ac}$  eum oratione] o- e- CH  uirum *inter* omnium *et* mulierum *coll.* N$^{ac}$  uirum] uirorum M$^{ac}$

This display clearly would fall under the 'maximalist' heading of the sort familiar from some Teubner editions, but as far as the establishment of the text is concerned, the amount of chaff it contains far exceeds the amount of wheat. There are, for example, the many *singularia*, innovations in individual manuscripts that can simply be called errors, since they stand no chance whatever of being what Suetonius wrote; the readings of FBE, the three descendants of D that add nothing to our knowledge of the archetype that D itself does not provide; and the readings of ONS, the contaminated manuscripts of the α₂ family that tell us nothing about α₂ that we cannot learn from LP. There are, to be sure, reasons why such data would be worth cataloguing, for a full accounting of the text's documentary basis or for students of mediaeval orthography and those interested in tracking scribal habits at particular times or places. But the appropriate place for such data would be one or more appendices in the edition, a separate article, or a website associated with the edition; and of course in a digital edition of the kind projected in Part Two, individual readings can be tagged in various ways to give readers maximally flexible control over the kinds of data they want to display. But to be true to its name, the critical apparatus should be dedicated to the places where editor and reader must act as critics, and so should chiefly provide the information necessary for the judgements they have to make.

As a next step, then, we can strip away the *singularia*, the readings of unhelpful manuscripts, and assorted bits of flotsam (e.g. the inept superscript gloss, *dilexit*, found above *Cleopatram* in AK). For further economy and clarity, we can substitute for the Roman *sigla* of individual manuscripts the Greek *sigla* of the lost books from which they were derived (α, α₁, and so on: see the 'working' stemma in Figure 10.3) and thus make plain how the tradition's basic building blocks are deployed in this segment. The result is an apparatus I would call neither 'skinny' nor 'fat', but 'sleek' and, most important, legible:

1. Naso] vasa ω  thalamego α₁VL$^a$c : t(h)alamoque P$^{ac}$β (thalamoquego L$^c$, thalameque P$^c$)  auctam] actam β₂ (*recte* D$^c$)  appellare] appellari ζ  2. adgnitum MVPac :

agnitum GLPcβ    adfirmauit quae β :-mauitque α    Cleopatra dicat α : de Cleopatra dicant β    3. Heluius] Kel- α₂    ferre] ferri ζ    uellet α₁Vβ : uellent α₂, uellet quis ζ    at] ac ζ    eum *post* impudicitiae *add.* β

If I then add some information not derived from the principal manuscripts and make my final decisions on the text to print, the result is this:[45]

1. Naso *Princeton Firestone Library Kane 44* (*an. 1433*) : vasa ω    thalamego α₁VL^ac : t(h)alamoque P^ac β (thalameque L^c, thalameque P^c)    auctam] actam β₂ (*recte* D^c)    appellare] appellari ζ (*e coniect. Marzullo 2006, 88 n. 13*)    2. adgnitum MVP^ac : agnitum GLP^c β    • adfirmauit, quae scire β : -mauitque s- α, adfirmauit scireque *Glar. 1560* (*Annot. 13*), adfirmauit idque s- *Modderman 1892, 44*    Cleopatra dicat α : de Cleopatra dicant β    3. Heluius] Kel- α₂    ferre] ferri ζ    uti] ut ei *Büch.*    quas et quot uellet (*Lipsius 1585a, 115*)] q- et 3q- uellent α₂, quis *post* uellet *inser.* ζ, *post* quas *Oudendorp*    • ac ζ *Basil. 1518 al.* (cf. *Cal. 37. 3, Claud. 15. 4, 29. 1*) : at ω (ad *M*), atque *Ven. 1471 al.*    eum *post* impudicitiae *add.* β

This version includes some further philological background: for example, I note that a contemporary scholar not long ago independently made the same plausible conjecture, *appellari*, as the person responsible for the early twelfth-century book ζ, the source of the manuscripts CH ('independently', since ζ was not known before my edition), and I cite conjectures made by Henricus Glareanus and H. C. Modderman that are useful diagnostically, in helping to clarify what the issues in the passage are, even if I decided that they are not correct. I was also able to identify the earliest attestation of a correction, near the start of the passage, that replaces the archetype's nonsensical *vasa* with the name of the historian (Marcus Actorius) Naso, an obscure figure cited earlier in this life (*Iul.* 9.3), where the full form of his name appears:[46] thanks to an alert reader, it ended up at this point in a book of stunning beauty written in 1433 and now housed in my own university's library.[47] Finally I decided, near the end of the passage, to adopt *ac ne cui dubium . . . sit* in place of the archetype's *at ne . . .* (or the *atque ne . . .* of some early printed editions), because *ac ne . . .* is what Suetonius writes elsewhere, never *at ne . . .* or *atque ne . . .*, combinations that are scarcely more common (absent *quidem* after *ne*) in classical Latin more generally. It was Erasmus who first printed *ac*, no doubt his

---

[45] As I explain in the OCT's preface, the symbol '•' placed before two entries here signals that I discuss these passages in my companion monograph (Kaster 2016a: 73–4).
[46] Nothing is known of Naso beyond Suetonius' citations: see Cornell 2013: 1 390.
[47] For a description of Princeton Kane MS. 44 and color plates of its miniatures of the twelve Caesars, see Skemer 2013: 11 99–103, with plates 4–7.

own emendation, in his edition of 1518, from which most later editors (*'al.'*) adopted it. It happens, however, that Erasmus was anticipated, three centuries earlier, by the person responsible for ζ; it also happens that this is only one of sixty-four good corrections of the archetype's text – a simply astonishing number – for which ζ is the earliest source. I could discover the nature of that book and its impact on the text, and ultimately discover the identity of the person responsible for it, simply because I was the first editor to collate both manuscripts C and H and so see the sort of text that their common source presented; and I was the first editor to collate both manuscripts simply because such resources are far more accessible today – remotely, across thousands of miles – than they were over a century ago when the last critical edition of the *DVC* was produced.[48] I cannot say how Erasmus would have received the news that he had been anticipated (the grammarian Aelius Donatus, in comparable circumstances, said, 'Pereant qui nostra ante nos dixerint!'), but perhaps any pique he might have felt would have been assuaged by learning that his predecessor was William of Malmesbury, the most learned man in the Europe of his day.[49]

## *A Contrary Case*

At the beginning of the chapter we wrote that the editing of classical texts assumes that each text is a singular entity produced by a specific person at a specific time, and the methods I have described are appropriate to texts that match that assumption, despite the fact that the crisp and sharp picture thus implied can at times be blurred around the edges: for example, the presence in a tradition of 'author's variants' – more than one possible reading left in the text and margins of an author's copy – would introduce a new layer of complexity, although the presence of such readings is more easily posited than demonstrated.[50] But to close this part of the paper and provide a transition to the next, I put before you a very well-known and commonly used text – Servius' commentary on the poetry of Virgil – that challenges the original premise more directly and fundamentally.

The commentary is doubly distinguished: it is one of very few ancient commentaries on a classical Latin text to survive essentially intact;[51] and it

---

[48] On the impact of such improvements cf. Kaster 2016a: vii–viii.
[49] On the nature of ζ's extraordinary text, and the discovery of William's identity, see Kaster 2016b: 122–35.
[50] On author's variants, see (e.g.) Reeve 1969, Haslam 1978: 61–5, Langlois 1997, Goffaux 2003, with the work of Dolveck on Ausonius cited in n. 1.
[51] Tiberius Claudius Donatus' *Interpretationes Vergilianae* and the commentary on the *Eclogues* falsely ascribed to Probus are two others (my thanks to Jim Zetzel for his comments on this point).

was transmitted in two radically different forms. There is the original commentary created by the *grammaticus* Servius early in the fifth century (sometimes called the 'vulgate Servius'), emphasising grammar and syntax; and a greatly enlarged version ('Servius Auctus') produced in the seventh century, when a reader ('the Compiler') blended his copy of Servius with much ancient lore from other sources, including the massive variorum commentary produced by Aelius Donatus in the fourth century and used by Servius himself in the fifth.[52]

In effect, then, the commentary represents not one but two 'author's originals' – one of them the text put into circulation by Servius, the other the blended text (DS) that the Compiler created – and reconstituting both should, in principle, be a plausible goal. It has certainly been the goal of editors from the nineteenth century, when Georg Thilo produced the first modern edition, down to the edition of the commentaries on *Aeneid* 9–12 that the late Charles Murgia left mostly finished at his death in 2013, and which I completed and have seen into print.[53] The goal is certainly plausible in the case of the commentary of Servius the *grammaticus*, which is largely transmitted as a unitary entity in the manuscripts, along lines that are often complex but nonetheless traceable.[54] Whether the goal of reconstituting the Compiler's original text in a standard edition is attainable, or even whether that is the best way to conceive of the goal in practice, is quite a different matter.

For one thing, DS has no full and stable form in any manuscript: to confine ourselves to the *Aeneid*, one book preserves DS for *Aeneid* 1–6 but it is more Servius than DS in *Aeneid* 3–6 (it lacks eight gatherings besides: C = Kassel, Universitätsbibl. Poet. Fol. 6, s. ix); another manuscript preserves

---

[52] Besides 'Servius Auctus' the second version is also known as 'Servius Danielis' (after Pierre Daniel, who first published a copy of this version in 1600) and 'DS', the designation used here; the many places where the text of DS overlaps with that of Macrobius' *Saturnalia* (written c. 430), to the exclusion of Servius, almost certainly represent material taken independently from Donatus' work (see Marinone 1946 and Santoro 1946). Goold 1970 provides the most vivid introduction to the versions' differences; other important accounts include Timpanaro 1986: 143–76, 2001: 119–38 (on the Servian commentaries and the text of Virgil), Marshall 1997, Pellizzari 2003, Delvigo 2011, Bouquet and Méniel 2011 (on the reception of Servius), and Murgia and Kaster 2018: xi–xx (overview of the tradition); Casali and Stok 2008, Stok 2013: 51–314, and Garcea, Lhommé and Vallat 2016 collect essays on diverse Servian topics.

[53] Murgia and Kaster 2018, which was to be the last of the five-volume 'Harvard Servius' initiated by E. K. Rand in the 1920s to replace Thilo's edition: the commentaries on *Aen.* 1–2 appeared in 1946 (vol. 2 = Rand et al. 1946, reviewed fiercely but justly in Fraenkel 1948 and 1949); those on *Aen.* 3–5 in 1965 (vol. 3 = Stocker et al. 1965). The volume on *Aeneid* 6–8 is being completed by James Brusuelas, E. Christian Kopff and Dirk Obbink, but the commentaries on the *Bucolics* and *Georgics* have been abandoned.

[54] Most thoroughly explained in Murgia 1975.

DS for *Aeneid* 3–12 but is more Servius than DS in *Aeneid* 6–7 (F = Paris, BNF lat. 7929 + Bern, Burgerbibl. 172, s. IX, from Fleury, lacking after 12.819); while the earliest known fragment of this material has excerpts from DS on *Aeneid* 3.561–5.638 and 7.710–8.713 that – being fuller than the versions transmitted in C and F – suggest that whatever it is that we have is at best a redacted version of what the Compiler produced.[55] More fundamentally, what the Compiler produced was regarded and treated, not as a unitary entity to be copied and preserved, but as a resource to be used, excerpted, augmented and altered according to the needs of the user – much as the Compiler himself had done – with every use effectively producing a new commentary. That is what we see happening, for example, in the 'Virgil of Tours' (T = Bern, Burgerbibl. 165), a magnificent manuscript of the first half of the ninth century in whose paratextual spaces multiple hands inscribed excerpts from DS and from other sources like Nonius Marcellus and Isidore of Seville.[56] It is what we see happening in other manuscripts where a predominantly Servian text is blended with DS material,[57] and indeed it is what we see happening in C and F, where a DS text is blended with, and sometimes overwhelmed by, material taken from Servius. In these cases, in effect, the sort of work that the Compiler himself did is being repeated time and again, and uniquely each time.

James Zetzel has trenchantly summarised this state of affairs:[58]

> Continuous commentaries, like the vulgate Servius or the *Commentum Cornuti* on Persius or Pseudo-Asconius on Cicero might be said to aim at textuality: they are designed to be stable texts. But stability, in this realm, does not last; and the majority of exegetical manuscripts represent snapshots of a tradition in flux: personal texts, possibly, or at least idiosyncratic manuscripts that were written at a particular time for a particular purpose or person, but texts that also provide invaluable evidence for the traditions on which they draw ... What, then, is one to do? It is possible, indeed it is desirable, to edit the vulgate Servius carefully, with the full evidence of the manuscripts ... But DS cannot be edited – at least, not on paper, in

---

[55] The fragment is Marburg, Hess. Staatsarch., Frag. 319 Pfarrarchiv Spangenberg (Depositum) Hr Nr. 1, a bifolium written in Anglo-Saxon minuscule in southwest England (s. VII/VIII): see Marshall 2000.
[56] On the character of **T** see Savage 1925; in Murgia and Kaster 2018 **T** and another manuscript like it (**v** = Vatican, BAV lat. 1570, s. $x^{1/2}$) are reported in two different ways, the DS material in a separate critical apparatus, the apparently non-DS material in an appendix.
[57] For example, **Pa** = Paris, BNF lat. 7959 (s. $IX^{2/4}$) and other members of the 'Tours group', on which see Savage 1934: 170–90.
[58] Zetzel 2004: 7–8, with detailed discussion of these issues in Zetzel 2005.

anything short of a hexapla ... What can be done, however, is a virtual edition: with a few well-chosen clicks of a mouse to switch the text from Servius to [DS] to the abridged manuscripts to the Virgil of Tours, and to construct an overlapping apparatus that is relevant to all of them, and to be able to track both the varying history of individual notes and the collective shape imposed upon them in each commented manuscript.

Zetzel's vision of a virtual edition provides a good segue to the second part of this chapter, on editing in the digital age, because it illustrates a fundamental problem with discussions about, and conceptions of, digital editions. It is to this problem that we now turn.[59]

## Part Two: The Edition as Database

In fact we are working on a digital edition of the Servian commentaries on *Aeneid* 9–12, using the materials originally gathered for the printed edition, but our primary concern is to represent the data accurately so that other scholars who specialise in information visualisation, human–computer interaction and interface design can build the sorts of tools that will realise Zetzel's vision. But we need to be clear that what that vision describes is not itself an edition. Rather, it is one among many possible applications of the data in an edition. Our aim in the second part of this chapter is to demonstrate that, although the activity and goals of editing are fundamentally the same whether the product is a traditional printed volume or a database, an editorial approach based on a digital paradigm can lead to new ways of experiencing and understanding texts and allow us to advance beyond the current state of the art, in which digital editions are often unique, idiosyncratic and prone to obsolescence.[60]

---

[59] Reaching this point, I noticed that seventy-odd scholarly works are cited in our notes, by sixty-four different scholars, only six of them women: Margarethe Billerbeck, Monique Bouquet, Marie Louise Delvigo, Marie-Karine Lhommé, Elisabeth Pellegrin and Cynthia Damon, the last only the second woman to produce an edition for the OCT series, trailing the first – Maaike Zimmerman, the editor of Apuleius (2012) – by just three years. It is fair to say that this reflects the way things stand in the field of textual criticism more generally, and I am unhappy to think that this state of affairs differs only marginally from the one that obtained when I began my graduate studies fifty years ago. That state of affairs, and the reasons for it, lie far beyond the remit of this chapter, yet are highly pertinent to the place that the craft of editing has in Latin studies today: I hope that occasions will be found for thoughtful discussion of the issue.

[60] On the ephemeral nature of many digital editions, see Del Turco 2016: 228, 'While manuscripts may have lasted hundreds of years, it is discomforting to note how the life span of a digital facsimile/edition is sometimes less than 4–5 years.' See also McGann 2013: 286, 'most – nearly all – websites created in html will not outlive their creators, and the duration of the materials may well be much shorter even than that'. The importance of ensuring the permanence of all digital resources intended

## Digital Editions

The terms 'digital critical edition', 'scholarly digital edition', 'digital edition' and the like currently apply to a wide variety of products, from simple text documents to interactive, multimedia resources. One has only to browse through the *Catalogue of Digital Editions* to see how capacious the term 'digital edition' is.[61] The criteria for inclusion in the catalogue are broad:[62]

> We primarily look for digital editions and digital *scholarly* editions (by which we mean editions with a strong critical component) but people are also beginning to submit digital archives, textual collections where some texts are treated in more detail, etc. It's worth noting that people define their projects in various ways (e.g. a project may define itself as a database when in fact it might be more of a digital archive) using different terms synonymously. This makes it difficult to pick what should be included in our list or not. The line of inclusion in our catalogue is a little blurry but it reflects the fuzziness that comes with these projects.

To bring some clarity to that fuzziness, the catalogue offers a number of filters for browsing the projects. The filters are based on Sahle's efforts to refine the terminology for this area of scholarship, but I reproduce them here as they appear on the *Catalogue of Digital Editions*' website:[63]

- **Scholarly**: 'An edition must be critical, must have critical components – a pure facsimile is not an edition, a digital library is not an edition';
- **Digital**: 'A digital edition can not be converted to a printed edition without substantial loss of content or functionality – vice versa: a retrodigitised printed edition is not a Scholarly Digital Edition (but it may evolve into a Scholarly Digital Edition through new content or functionalities)';
- **Edition**: 'An edition must represent its material (usually as transcribed/edited text) – a catalog, an index, a descriptive database is not an edition.'

Without applying any filters, 261 entries are available for browsing as of this writing. Applying all three filters reduces the number only a little, to 202. Even then, the file format, platform, encoding standards and other details vary significantly from entry to entry. To be fair, the catalogue is descriptive, not prescriptive, and its overall goal is to understand the many ways of representing texts in a digital format. Consequently, the application of Sahle's taxonomy is generous.

---

for scholarly use is among the leading themes of the survey of 'Roman studies and digital resources' in Bagnall and Heath 2018.
[61] Franzini et al., https://dig-ed-cat.acdh.oeaw.ac.at/.  [62] https://dig-ed-cat.acdh.oeaw.ac.at/faq/.
[63] Sahle 2013: 157–280.

In his own work, Sahle offers the following prescriptive definition: 'Scholarly digital editions are scholarly editions that are guided by a digital paradigm in their theory, method and practice.'[64] Understanding what is meant by 'digital paradigm' is therefore key to the rest of this chapter. Given the negative examples that he uses to support his definition (e.g. 'a digitised edition is not a digital edition'[65]), it is clear that he means to describe a concept, not a specific instantiation of a digital edition. The key idea is that a digital edition cannot be rendered in a print format without the loss of crucial functionality. Clickable hyperlinks, resizable images, dynamic visualisations and other common aspects of digital editions simply do not function on the printed page, and if they are essential to the argument of an edition, then their loss would indeed be significant. However, if those features are essential to the argument, it seems likely that we are dealing not necessarily with an edition, but with a resource for experiencing the edition's text and materials. In other words, Sahle's taxonomy is more relevant to the features of a platform for using an edition than to the edition itself. Similarly, when he describes a product that presents not a specific version of a text, but several versions meant to be viewed and manipulated dynamically, he is referring to a way of experiencing a text or texts, not to a particular edition of those texts. Indeed, Sahle's definition of digital edition could apply to what Heslin describes as a 'universal variorum', in which users have unmediated access to a set of diplomatic transcriptions of witnesses. In this extreme vision of a digital edition, the editor is reduced to a mere reporter, a collector of information:[66]

> The job of the editor should now be not to decide on the text, but to marshal all of the evidence in such a way for the reader to manipulate conveniently. The reader ought to be able to see instantly the text as reported by any given witness or previous editor, not as a collection of variants reported against the editor's text, but in its own right. The editor could still give his or her preferred text, but as one option among many, which the reader could change at will.

The sort of product described by Heslin may be empowering and liberating for the handful of readers who have the background and understanding of a text (texts?) and its (their?) historical context(s).[67] It certainly cannot be implemented outside of a digital paradigm, at least not easily. But such

---

[64] Sahle 2016: 28.  [65] Ibid. 27.  [66] Heslin 2016: 503.
[67] The question marks and singular/plural forms here are meant to reflect the theoretical approach, taken by Sahle and Heslin, that problematises the notion of a single authoritative text. For a provocative introduction to and survey of this point of view, see Apollon and Bélisle 2014.

a product is a research tool, not a unified argument about a text, based on the experience and considered judgement of an editor or editors.

If, on the other hand, we consider that a digital paradigm may simply be a specific way of approaching the information associated with a critical edition – not only the preface, text, apparatus and other materials that appear in the printed edition, but also the by-products of the editor's research (e.g. notes, collation tables, transcriptions, correspondence, images, etc.) – then the kind of editing described in the first part of this chapter will continue to be not just a viable approach to Latin textual scholarship, but a vital one. Accordingly, in the rest of this chapter, I will argue that the digital paradigm makes editors and their craft more important than ever; for however protean, dynamic or interactive a digital product might be, if it is not based on sound textual scholarship and the careful application of an editorial theory, it will be of limited use, at least for research purposes, and its contribution to scholarship will not survive the demise of the technologies that deliver it.

### The Digital Paradigm

The shift into a digital paradigm begins with examining the traditional data model for critical editions. Much of the information in a critical edition is communicated through visual cues such as page layout, typographical conventions and special abbreviations. Humans must interpret all of those cues correctly to understand an editor's argument about the text, and they often have to rely on their long experience of accepted conventions to do that, since editors make assumptions about their readers' acquaintance with the format and layout of critical editions. Otherwise, every critical edition would include not only a preface, but also a primer on the conventions of textual criticism. Because those conventions are so well established by tradition, users of critical editions are able to make subtle adjustments to accommodate the different ways publishers deploy those conventions. One publisher might use italic type for manuscript sigla, but another one might use boldface or roman type. One might require editors to use a particularly terse format for their annotations, but another might allow for greater expressiveness. Experienced readers often adapt quickly to these differences precisely because the underlying data model is both well established and flexible.

Machines, however, need explicit instructions for processing information. They might be able to follow instructions for displaying a word-processing file in a way that looks like a critical edition, but the typographical conventions that have meaning for humans are literally just bits of textual data to a machine. The example of a traditional critical apparatus from Kaster's edition of Suetonius, as printed on p. 536 here, is instructive:

> 1. Naso *Princeton Firestone Library Kane 44 (an. 1433)* : vasa ω    thalamego α₁VL^ac : t(h)alamoque P^ac β  (thalamoquego L^c, thalameque P^c)    auctam] actam β₂ *(recte* D^c*)*  appellare] appellari ζ *(e coniect. Marzullo 2006, 88 n. 13)*    2. adgnitum MVP^ac : agnitum GLP^c β   • adfirmauit, quae scire β : -mauitque s- α, adfirmauit scireque *Glar. 1560* (*Annot. 13*), adfirmauit idque s- *Modderman 1892, 44*    Cleopatra dicat α : de Cleopatra dicant β    3. Heluius] Kel- α₂    ferre] ferri ζ    uti] ut ei *Büch.*    quas et quot uellet (*Lipsius 1585a, 115*)] q- et q- uellent α₂, quis *post* uellet *inser.* ζ, *post* quas *Oudendorp*   • ac ζ *Basil. 1518 al.* (cf. *Cal. 37. 3, Claud. 15. 4, 29. 1*) : at ω   (ad M), atque *Ven. 1471 al.*    eum *post* impudicitiae *add.* β

Human readers who have been trained to read a critical apparatus will know, first of all, that this block of text is related in complex ways to a block of text presented in a different location. They will understand that a word followed by a single right square bracket is a reference to a lemma in the edition's text (e.g. appellare]), and in the absence of that symbol they will know how to distinguish a lemma (adgnitum) from a variant reading (agnitum) from a group of sigla for manuscripts (MVP^ac or GLP^c β). They will also know that P^c means 'the reading of P after it was corrected' and that β stands not for a particular manuscript, but for the hyparchetype of a branch of manuscripts. Even better, they can distinguish different kinds of blank spaces: a gap of several spaces indicates the termination of one entry and the beginning of another, but a single space separates two words in a phrase. It will also be apparent to them that *recte* is the editor opining on the quality of a particular reading. A computer, on the other hand, would 'see' all of these different runs of text only as strings of characters and spaces.

Given how effective and productive human readers have been and continue to be in using printed critical editions, it is no wonder that the shift to a digital paradigm in editing and using critical editions has been slow. Even though Latin scholars have been using networked computers for decades, it is still the case that the vast majority of Latin texts on the internet lacks a critical apparatus. A principal reason is that it is difficult to reproduce a traditional critical apparatus in an online format. There is also the matter of whether it is worth the considerable time and effort it takes to encode the data, considering that relatively few readers will pay close attention to the critical apparatus. On the other hand, the accessibility of a digital critical apparatus could cause more readers to consult it. Concerns about copyright have also led some to believe that the text of an ancient author is in the public domain, but the critical apparatus is the editor's intellectual property. Of course, that view betrays a misunderstanding of the nature of a critical edition's text, but that is a different matter. All of this highlights the tension that naturally arises during a transition from one paradigm to another, when we recognise the potential in the new approach while cleaving to the familiar one. It can be seen in skeuomorphism, the school of design that gave us digital calendars that appear to have spiral bindings and pages that need to be 'flipped'. The mimicking of real-world objects in a digital interface may make for comfortable and familiar engagements, but it places limits on what can be achieved with a shift to a digital paradigm that makes better use of the underlying technology.

Consider that most scholarship today is produced on a digital platform such as a word-processing program. Most of those programs still force users to think in terms of physical objects like pages with fixed dimensions, and that orients us toward the codex platform for final publication. The digital paradigm, however, can lead us away from thinking about digital and print media in binary terms. From a more traditional point of view, one might wonder, for example, in what ways a digital edition is better or worse than a codex. But on the digital paradigm, the codex is one of many platforms available for working with an edition's data. That is, a codex is a platform for delivering information, just as a website, a visualisation application or a digital file format is a platform for delivering information. Those platforms have their strengths and weaknesses that make them more or less suitable for certain uses. As a storage and delivery mechanism, centuries have shown that the codex is portable, durable and reliable, and it remains relatively inexpensive to produce and easy to maintain. On the other hand, the codex format presents information only in a static format that cannot be easily rearranged, edited or displayed in novel ways, but those are all things that digital platforms are able to do. The digital paradigm aims to make an edition's data available in a variety of formats, to be used on a variety of platforms, including the codex.

If we think of a digital edition not in terms of a platform for publishing and interacting with data, but as data alone, then it becomes a matter of selecting the platform that best suits a particular use. It should not matter if a reader prefers to use a codex for one task and a visual interface for another, as long as the data in the edition remain citable so that references point to the same things regardless of the platform.[68]

---

[68] On the importance of a persistent and stable system for citation, see Smith 2009. Canonical Text Services (CTS, Blackwell and Smith 2014) is currently the gold standard for citation in digital

Calling the information in critical editions 'data' is the first step toward thinking about a critical edition not as a book, but as a set of information. It is also the first step toward thinking about how digital methods and tools might be developed for and applied to those data. Another important step is thinking about computers as a new kind of reader, one that excels at rapidly ingesting, processing and outputting large amounts of information. If a computer has instructions for distinguishing a lemma from a variant reading from a group of manuscript sigla, it can obey commands, for example, to swap variant readings in and out of the text, to filter certain kinds of information into or out of the apparatus criticus, to calculate statistics about the degrees of difference between variant readings, or to visualise the text and apparatus as a graph or a storyline, among other things.

The longevity of an edition produced according to this paradigm is without doubt a concern. When I wrote my dissertation sixteen years ago, I used a database program to organise my notes and bibliography. That program and its file format did not survive an upgrade to the computer's operating system, so that work has been more or less lost to me, except as a PDF that I saved as a backup. I could probably rebuild the database, but it would take more effort than I care to invest. Had I written all of those notes on index cards, they would still be usable, provided that they had been stored in a safe place. Although it is unlikely that future scholars would have any interest in my notes, this personal story does illustrate the problem of long-term preservation of data for future use. I can go to my university's library and find critical editions published decades, if not centuries, ago. If a database that I created less than two decades ago is unusable today, why should I have any confidence that digital editions produced today will be of any use in a decade?

The answer to that question depends on the digital edition. If it is bound to a proprietary presentational format and a specific technology or technologies, then it, like my dissertation research database, is liable to rapid obsolescence. But if a digital edition is a set of data stored in an open, non-proprietary format and published in a widely accessible, version-controlled repository, it is much more likely to survive rapid changes in technology. One such approach is to use Extensible Markup Language, or XML.

---

media, particularly for classical literature. For an overview of CTS, see Tiepmar and Heyer 2017. Distributed Text Services (https://github.com/distributed-text-services/specifications), currently in development, seeks to build and expand on the capabilities of CTS.

In XML, right- and left-facing angle brackets distinguish kinds of information, much as the original word processors required users to type <b> and </b>, for example, to indicate where boldface type should begin and end. Indeed, XML is the format used by many modern word-processing applications.[69] But word-processing programs are concerned mostly with visual styles and page layout. An interactive experience of a text requires a different model, one concerned not with layout, but with meaning, which is why we use the term *semantic encoding* to describe the work of making the visual cues of a traditional edition mean something to a machine.[70]

The Text Encoding Initiative (TEI) has developed a model, or schema, for using XML to represent texts of various kinds (e.g. prose, poetry, drama, documentary texts, manuscripts, speeches, etc.) in XML.[71] Individuals and groups have adapted the TEI's model for their own purposes. EpiDoc, for example, is a customisation of TEI XML for the purpose of representing inscriptions, papyri and manuscripts in digital form.[72] The next section examines how the DLL has incorporated many of Epidoc's techniques and approaches into its own customisation, designed specifically for representing the information in critical editions of Latin texts. In partnership with the Society for Classical Studies, the Medieval Academy of America, and the Renaissance Society of America, the DLL will publish new editions encoded in this way in a series called the Library of Digital Latin Texts (LDLT).

## *The Library of Digital Latin Texts*

The DLL's encoding guidelines translate the data model for traditional critical editions into a digital format.[73] Editions published in the LDLT may include a preface, descriptions of manuscripts and other source materials, a bibliography, a list of sigla, an edited text and an apparatus criticus. They may also have an apparatus fontium, an apparatus testium, an apparatus for parallel passages, various indices and brief textual commentary. The encoding guidelines include instructions for using XML to represent all of these parts of an edition. For example, here is the first section of the passage from Suetonius *Iul.* 52 printed on p. 534 as it might be encoded for the LDLT:

```
<p n="52" >
  <seg n="1" >Dilexit et reginas, inter quas Eunoen Mauram
```

---

[69] The 'x' in Microsoft Word's file extension '.docx', in fact, stands for 'XML'.
[70] For more on encoding meaning, see Huitfeldt 2014 and Pichler and Bruvik 2014.
[71] www.tei-c.org/index.xml.
[72] Elliott, Bodard, Cayless et al. 2006–17.   [73] Huskey and Cayless 2018.

Bogudis uxorem, cui maritoque eius plurima et immensa tribuit, ut
```
  <app>
   <lem source="#Princeton44">Naso</lem>
   <rdg wit="#ω">vasa</rdg>
  </app>
```
scripsit, sed maxime Cleopatram, cum qua et conuiuia in primam lucem saepe protraxit et eadem naue
```
    <app>
        <lem wit="#αι #V #Lac">thalamego</lem>
        <rdg wit="#Pac #β #Lc #Pc" xml:id="rdg-52.1-thalamoque">t(h)alamoque</rdg>
            <witDetail wit="#Lc" target="#rdg-52.1-thalamoque">thalamoquego</witDetail>
            <witDetail wit="#Pc" target="#rdg-52.1-thalamoque">thalameque</witDetail>
    </app>
```
paene Aethiopia tenus Aegyptum penetrauit, nisi exercitus sequi recusasset ...
```
  </seg>
</p>
```

Aside from the addition of XML elements and attributes, the major difference from a traditional edition is that variant readings are encoded alongside their lemmata within the main text of the edition. That is one outcome of operating on the digital paradigm. Readers of traditional critical editions are used to thinking of the text and the apparatus as two different things, since they appear on different parts of the page. Indeed, this perceived difference leads some readers to ignore the critical apparatus altogether, since its placement at the bottom of the printed page implies that it is of secondary importance at best.[74] Since an XML document is, in fact, a database, it is good practice for like data to be encoded and stored together.[75]

This example shows only the minimal encoding required to capture the information in the print version of the text. Because the encoded version is

---

[74] Keeline 2017: 349 reports hearing students refer to the critical apparatus as the 'crapparatus', for example.

[75] The TEI guidelines, in fact, list three methods of linking the critical apparatus to the text (www.tei-c.org/release/doc/tei-p5-doc/en/html/TC.html#TCAPLK) either in-line or in a separate location in the same file or another file. The LDLT uses the 'parallel segmentation method' in which variant readings are encoded at the place of variation within the text. In all methods, critical apparatus data are encoded together.

not restricted to what can be printed on a page, other data could be made machine-readable. For example, *Eunoen Mauram Bogudis uxorem* could be encoded as follows:

```
<persName ref="#Eunoen">Eunoen</persName> Mauram
<persName ref="#Bogudis">Bogudis</persName> uxorem
```

The values of the 'ref' attributes would point to a list of people encoded elsewhere in the edition, and that list could include links to more information about those people elsewhere on the internet. One might also consider encoding *Mauram* as a reference to Mauretania, which could be included in a similar list of places, perhaps with a link to the data available at Pleiades, https://pleiades.stoa.org. Encoding names and places increases the amount of information that can be read and processed by machines, creating more avenues for research on the text and its contexts. For example, queries can be executed against encoded names and places to generate visualisations of social and geographical relationships. It would be trivial, for example, to generate a map of all of the places mentioned in the text or a certain section of the text, if that data had been encoded. Moreover, if several texts are encoded according to uniform guidelines, it becomes possible to generate maps and lists and other visualisations of data within an entire corpus.

It is important, however, to bear in mind that maps, social graphs and other visualisations are examples of uses of an edition's data; they are not the edition itself. Whether or not to encode certain kinds of information, and in some cases *how* to encode certain kinds of information, ought to be matters for the editor to decide, just as the editor must decide which variant readings to report in a critical apparatus. After all, editing is often about making decisions concerning what matters most for understanding a text. From a purely text-critical point of view, the names of people and places can be the source of much difficulty. Having an unambiguous identifier to make the distinction between one Gnaeus Calpurnius Piso and another Gnaeus Calpurnius Piso, for example, could be useful. But is it an editor's duty to enhance an edition of Cicero's epistles with prosopographical and geographical tags? Does that same sort of information add much of interest to an edition of Calpurnius Siculus' bucolic poetry? Or is that a matter for a different kind of scholarship and a different kind of scholarly product, one that uses a carefully encoded text as the foundation for a study in the visualisation of geographical references? After all, an edition conceived on the digital paradigm can be the basis for further encoding of data by other scholars wishing to study specific kinds of information – provided that the data are freely available for reuse (as they ought to be).

## Two Case Studies

The rest of this chapter will focus on two examples of editors who are making the transition from the traditional to the digital paradigm. One of them happens to be my co-author Robert Kaster; the other is Cynthia Damon. Both of them have been involved in the DLL project since its beginning. The goal of this discussion will be to show that the skills, processes and activities described in the first part of this chapter still apply in the digital realm; the shift is in the way editors think about and approach their information.

It is fair to say that when Damon and Kaster began to advise the DLL project, they were operating on the traditional paradigm. Both of them were working on editions for the venerable OCT series at the time. Although they used computers in the course of their work, they were not thinking in terms of editions as databases. As they learned more about text encoding and data modelling, however, their perspective changed, and they began to operate on a digital paradigm. Even if they did not write any XML code, their main contributions to the DLL project have been in the development of encoding guidelines for LDLT editions. Figuring out the minimum requirements for encoding the information in a traditional edition was straightforward, since it involved applying the existing TEI standard to a particular use case. Input from Damon and Kaster during that process was invaluable, to be sure, but when we began looking at implementing the guidelines, their respective contributions were essential.

With regard to the requirement to encode LDLT editions in XML, both Damon and Kaster echoed the concerns expressed by participants in our user studies. Given the choice between using a familiar word processor to prepare a text for a traditional publisher and learning how to use new software to encode a text as a database for publication on an unfamiliar platform, most editors will opt for the familiar path, however interested they might be in the possibilities of digital editions. It is not difficult to understand why. Although XML is not particularly difficult to learn, encoding texts can be tedious and repetitive work. For example, during the development of the encoding guidelines, the DLL team manually encoded an existing edition of Calpurnius Siculus' bucolic poetry. Although it is a relatively short text at seven poems, or a total of 758 lines of poetry, the digital version occupies over 15,000 lines of XML, and it took over a year of effort by a team of students and scholars.[76] Of course, much

---

[76] Number of lines is not the most meaningful metric to use, since lines and white space are used to make XML more readable for humans. The same edition could have been written on a single, very long line of XML. Nevertheless, the number of lines does give a certain sense of scale.

of that time was spent analysing the data and developing patterns for the encoding guidelines, but the amount of time required to encode a text properly is not trivial. To provide another example, I manually encoded the first thirty-three paragraphs of Damon's edition of the *Bellum Alexandrinum* mostly to see how long it would take. The time per paragraph varied from a few minutes to over an hour, depending on the number and complexity of the apparatus entries. In all, it took just over fourteen hours to encode thirty-three paragraphs of text, and most of that time was spent on repetitive tasks.

My experience with manually encoding texts made it abundantly clear that the potential for introducing new errors into a text is high when bored humans are doing the work. That prompted me to begin working on a method for automating much of the repetitive work. The goal was to find a way for editors to deliver their editions to the DLL in plain text files (i.e. not marked up in XML) for processing, encoding and formatting by DLL staff. Having a stable data model for critical editions in place allowed us to write scripts to match patterns in those text files and translate them into the corresponding XML.

For example, Damon uses traditional notation to indicate a crux at *BAlex* 2.5: †obiectis†. The script uses Regular Expressions to find any text surrounded by † and replace † with the corresponding XML elements for tagging a crux (i.e. <sic>).[77] It contains similar instructions for other commonly used symbols and abbreviations.

Our success with automating the encoding of the main text of an edition led us to try using the same techniques on the critical apparatus. Since the critical apparatus contains much more complex information, it presented some challenges, but the process is a good example of working within the digital paradigm. Prior experience told us that the vast majority of entries in any apparatus criticus follows a reliable pattern: reference number (to a paragraph, section and/or line number); lemma (often only in cases where the reference is ambiguous in printed editions, but always in our digital model), sigla for witnesses (i.e. manuscripts and early editions) to the lemma, sources (i.e. modern editions, commentaries, etc.) for the lemma, annotations on the lemma (e.g. cross-references to other passages),

---

[77] Regular Expressions (also known as 'regex') make it possible to search for patterns instead of specific strings of text. For example, the regex to search for a word or phrase surrounded by the character '†' is †([a-zA-Z(\s)?]*)†. That means, 'Find every instance of a word or phrase (comprising any combination of the lower and upper cases of the alphabet and, optionally, a space) surrounded by the character †.' It is possible to replace the '†' with its XML equivalent while leaving the captured group (i.e. the word or phrase) in place.

and, occasionally, more general comments; the pattern is roughly the same for variant readings. Regular patterns are good candidates for automation, since computers excel at following instructions and completing repetitive tasks. Accordingly, I made a database that had a row for each entry in the apparatus criticus and columns for the different kinds of information just listed, and I wrote a program that gave specific instructions for iterating over each row and encoding the information in each column. I tested this method on a couple of sections of Damon's *BAlex* and found that it took the computer a couple of seconds to encode what took me over half an hour to do manually. Virginia K. Felkner, an undergraduate in Letters and Computer Science at my home university, has developed my prototype into a much more robust application that handles a variety of texts, including prose, poetry and dramatic texts.[78]

The downside to this method is that the critical apparatus has to be in a tabular format for the script to work. Persuading editors to work in that format could be difficult, but Damon has found much to like about it. For example, it helps with organisation of material because it is much easier to verify information when it is in discrete columns than when it is presented as connected strings of text. It is also easier to involve students in the work of assembling the data for a critical edition. Damon has had success using this method with graduate students and undergraduate students in a seminar on textual criticism.[79] Even though she and her students do not encode the text and critical apparatus in XML, they are thinking about and treating the information as data, which means that they are operating on the digital paradigm.

Automating the encoding process has also had the effect of bringing into sharp focus the difference between writing XML and making an original scholarly contribution through textual encoding. That is, marking up a text in XML does not necessarily qualify as scholarly activity, especially if the same work can be automated and completed accurately and in a fraction of the time it would take a trained scholar to do it. As it stands, however, the current automation scripts can handle only about ninety per cent of a critical edition's text and apparatus. Even if that percentage increases as we perfect our methods, there will always be unique problems in a text that cannot be documented and explained without the application of critical thought and experienced

---

[78] The scripts are available in a code repository at https://github.com/DigitalLatin/automation.
[79] See Damon 2018, the abstract of a paper delivered at the 2018 annual meeting of the Society for Classical Studies, for more information.

judgement.[80] These are the places where automation fails and where scholars must decide on the best method for capturing the issue through the application of the encoding guidelines. Issues and problems such as these will often become apparent during the creation of the tabular apparatus criticus. If an entry does not fit neatly into the table's columns, the editor will know that it will require special attention in the encoding process, either directly or in consultation with someone more comfortable with marking up texts.

It is fitting to end this section with a discussion of my co-author's tentative transition to working on a digital edition. One of his recent projects has been to finish the work Charles Murgia had done on Servius' commentary on *Aeneid* 9–12.[81] The final volume of the so-called 'Harvard Servius' series, it had been conceived and prepared for publication as a printed book with a traditional text and critical apparatus long before the DLL came into existence. At the time of Murgia's death, the edition was not yet complete, so Kaster finished the work following the original model, and the Society for Classical Studies (SCS) published the volume in print through its relationship with Oxford University Press. Since the SCS is also affiliated with the DLL project, and since Kaster has been involved with the DLL from the beginning, the SCS has authorised Kaster to prepare a digital version of the edition for publication in the LDLT. For this reason, the project offers a good view into the transition from a traditional to a digital model. It also highlights Kaster's main scholarly contribution to the project: a taxonomy for classifying variant readings.

'Prepare a digital version of the edition' means much more than 'send the word-processing files to Sam'. The digital edition will differ from the printed edition in significant ways. As we have explained, it will be a database, not a digitised book, so users will be able to work with the information in ways not possible with words printed on a page. To transform the existing files into encoded data, Kaster worked with a student at Princeton (Rafail Zoulis) to parse the apparatus criticus into the tabular format that I have described. I am working with Felkner (mentioned earlier) to turn that information and the rest of the text into valid XML.

All of that effort is concerned with converting existing information into a different format, and the final product could justly be called a 'digital

---

[80] On the prospects for mechanising other stages in the production of a critical edition, see n. 12: the conclusion of Tarrant 2016 quoted there is valid here as well.
[81] Murgia and Kaster 2018.

version of the edition', but the final product is projected to have an added component that will further distinguish it from the book published in 2018: a detailed analysis of the variant readings.

As we have seen, most of the information included in a traditional printed critical apparatus can be separated into discrete types: location, lemma, variant reading, references to sources, annotations and general comments. Depending on the publisher's guidelines regarding the space devoted to the critical apparatus, editors must make decisions about the kinds of variants to report. Consequently, to save space, and to avoid overwhelming readers, editors often omit variants of a purely orthographical nature, for example, however useful that information might be to some readers. But in a digital edition, where the primary concern can be the quality of the data and metadata, not the presentation or visualisation of it, space on a printed page is only a constraint if a user wishes to format the data for print. Editors, however, are free to expand their work to include information that might be of interest to different kinds of readers.[82] If that information is classified in some way, filters can be designed to allow readers some degree of control over the critical apparatus. Kaster's contribution to the DLL's encoding guidelines was to develop a taxonomy of variants for just that purpose.

The following is a list of available terms in Kaster's taxonomy, with their definitions:

- **Lexical**: the reading differs from the lemma by offering an entirely different lexeme.
- **Morphological**: the reading differs from the lemma in its grammatical form.
- **Ordinal**: the reading differs from the lemma by changing the order in which units (letters, words, phrases, sentences, lines) occur.
- **Orthographical**: the reading differs from the lemma only in spelling (i.e. not in any grammatically significant way).
- **Syntactic**: the reading differs from the lemma in its grammatical construction or arrangement.
- **Subtractive**: the reading differs from the lemma in omitting some unit of text through oversight, erasure or some other cause.

---

[82] Tarrant 2016: 153 remarks, 'the most important contribution of electronic data recording to classical editing is the ability to transcend the limits of traditional book format and to generate a truly comprehensive apparatus'. Murgia's Servius lends itself particularly well to this aspect of the digital environment, since in conceiving the Harvard Servius E. K. Rand aimed to report every reading of every manuscript used, including what most editors regard as orthographical trivia, and Murgia largely (if somewhat reluctantly) continued the practice.

- **Additive**: the reading differs from the lemma in adding some unit of text through oversight, intentional insertion or some other cause.
- **Segmentational**: the reading differs from the lemma in altering divisions between words or other units of text.
- **Metrical:** the reading differs from the lemma in its adherence to relevant metrical principles (in the case of poetic texts).

Use of the taxonomy is optional, and it should be noted that many of the terms are not mutually exclusive, so more than one could be applied to the same reading (e.g. lexical and ordinal). Editors opting to use the taxonomy are encouraged to include in the preface to the edition an explanation of how they have applied the taxonomy. As I write this, we are still making decisions about the scope of use for the taxonomy of variants in Kaster's digital version of Murgia and Kaster 2018, but I can offer an example of how the edition's data could be enriched.

The printed edition's critical apparatus has the following at 10.865:

dominos Teucros Σ dominor teucris F

Presenting the information as pairs of words makes some sense, but Kaster's analysis of variants requires a finer distinction:

```
<app>
  <lem wit="#Σ">dominos</lem>
  <rdg wit="#F" ana="#orthographical">dominor</rdg>
</app>
<app>
  <lem wit="#Σ">Teucros</lem>
  <rdg wit="#F" ana="#morphological">teucris</rdg>
</app>
```

That is, *dominor* is an orthographical variant of *dominos*, and *teucris* is a morphological variant of *Teucros*. Since the taxonomy terms must be applied to specific words, it is not possible to encode *dominor teucris* as a single variant of *dominos Teucros*. Otherwise, *dominor teucris* would be labelled as an orthographical, morphological variant. Although that is true, it is more accurate to label *dominor* as the orthographical variant and *teucris* as the morphological variant.

Editors have always used some sort of classification system to determine what to put into their editions. That is implicit, for example, when West decrees 'Variants of a merely orthographical nature should be omitted unless they represent real alternatives (οἰκῆσαι : οἰκίσαι) or unless manuscript evidence is involved.'[83] But it has been neither practical nor practicable to use an explicit classification system in a printed edition. Even if it had been possible, it is difficult to imagine how useful that information might be in a static format. But when that information is available for processing, it is intriguing to imagine the applications. Here are some possible results of queries executed on an encoded edition:

- A count of the different types of variants
- A list of all of the readings of a certain type in a particular manuscript
- A view of all of the variant readings, sorted by type, and the manuscripts in which they appear
- A display of instances of a certain type of variant in a particular combination of manuscripts

It is also possible to use the data as the basis for charts, graphs and other visualisations, including displays optimised for interactive reading on a screen. It is even possible to format the data for use in a print-optimised viewing environment – otherwise known as a traditional printed edition, which leads us back where this part of the chapter started.

All of the things mentioned in the previous paragraph are just potential uses of the data in an edition; consequently, no one of them can be singled out as the edition itself. This is a difficult concept because we are so used to equating a critical edition with the bound paper format we use in our work. Moreover, editors have become so accustomed to that format that they naturally allow its physical characteristics to influence their decisions about what to include and what to omit. Even so, we do not expect editors themselves to select the typeface and design the layout any more than we expect them to source the paper, sew the binding, market the product and ship it to consumers. Why, then, is there an expectation that creators of digital editions should be responsible not only for the data in a digital edition, but also for the implementation of the database(s) and the design of user interfaces with all of the features that have come to be expected of 'digital editions'?

The answer is that the expectation is unreasonable. Damon, Kaster and other editors should not have to learn XML, XSLT, HTML, Javascript, CSS, Linux, Apache, MySQL, PHP, Python and all of the other technologies that can go into the making of a digital product, any more than they should be expected to master the scholarly disciplines of Human

---

[83] West 1973: 86.

Computer Interaction, Data Scholarship or Information Visualisation. To expect textual critics to master all of those subjects in addition to the techniques and methods of textual criticism is to misunderstand not only the value of editing, but also the legitimacy of those other subjects as fields of scholarly endeavour in and of themselves.

This is not a generational issue. It is not the case that younger scholars will take to working with technologies more easily just because they have grown up using digital devices. If anything, their apparent facility with technology has more to do with developments in interface design and information visualisation than with their innate abilities as so-called 'digital natives'. Instead, textual critics, regardless of their age, should do textual criticism, but they should do it according to the digital paradigm, not only so that their work will no longer be constrained by the physical limitations of a particular format, but also so that their data will be available to scholars in other fields. This means that textual critics should continue to apply the principles articulated in the first part of this chapter, but with a broader view of the potential uses of the data. They might include more variant readings in their apparatus criticus than they would have on the print paradigm. They might take the time to highlight the geographical references in the text. They might classify readings or tag the people mentioned in the text with universal identifiers. Whatever they do, the goal should be an expertly compiled and curated set of data that makes a new contribution to scholarship on the text.

As for delivering that scholarship to users, the LDLT will be the outlet for publishing critical edition datasets. The learned societies that are the DLL's partners in this endeavour will accept proposals for editions according to policies and procedures that they establish for the series. Proposals that pass review will be entered into a database of current projects, each with its own horizon for publication. Publication will be in the form of a valid, well-formed XML document encoded according to the DLL's guidelines. That document, along with any ancillary or archival materials the editor may wish to make available, will be available on an open licence in a version-controlled repository.

The DLL has developed a reading environment that highlights the digital nature of editions in the LDLT and makes them available for human readers.[84]

---

[84] The reading environment is the scholarly project of Hugh Cayless. It is an implementation of the CETEIcean application (https://github.com/TEIC/CETEIcean) that he developed for displaying unmodified TEI documents in a web browser.

This reading environment includes features familiar from other sites, such as the ability to click on words to see definitions and morphological analysis, but it also includes some innovations, such as the ability to click on variant readings to swap them into and out of the main text for evaluation *in situ*. The DLL has also developed a number of more sophisticated data visualisations to highlight the potential of editions created on the digital paradigm.[85] Work is also underway to provide the data in a format suitable for print-on-demand as a traditional critical edition. The point of these efforts is to demonstrate that interfaces, visualisations and other uses of critical edition data are scholarly projects in and of themselves. Separating the content of critical editions from its many uses and applications and publishing that content as version-controlled, structured data in an open format will go a long way to guarding against obsolescence and toward preserving the scholarly contribution of LDLT editions for use with applications yet to be developed.

\* \* \*

To sum up this chapter's argument: in the foreseeable digital future, there will still be human editors. They will continue to use their expertise to gather the data relevant to their texts, construct theories explaining those data and achieve the most probable approximation of the artefact that the ancient author produced; and those texts will still be made widely available in forms that are readable by other humans. But organising the data in a carefully structured way that is also readable by machines – in short, as a database – will also allow humans to analyse, represent, experience and understand the ancient texts in some ways that are fundamentally new.

## References

Apollon, D. and C. Bélisle (2014) 'The digital fate of the critical apparatus', in Apollon, Bélisle and Régnier 2014, 81–113.
Apollon, D., C. Bélisle and P. Régnier, eds. (2014) *Digital Critical Editions*, Urbana, IL.
Bagnall, R. S. and S. Heath (2018) 'Roman studies and digital resources', *JRS* 108: 171–89.
Billerbeck, M. and M. Somazzi (2009) *Repertorium der Konjekturen in den Seneca-Tragödien*, Leiden.

---

[85] These visualisations are the scholarly work of my colleague Christopher Weaver, a professor in the School of Computer Science at the University of Oklahoma. He and his students have developed visualisation techniques for use in his Improvise visualisation application (www.cs.ou.edu/~weaver/improvise/).

Blackwell, C. and N. Smith (2014) 'The Canonical Text Services protocol, version 5.0.rc.1', http://cite-architecture.github.io/cts_spec/.
Bouquet, M. and B. Méniel, eds. (2011) *Servius et sa réception de l'Antiquité à la Renaissance*, Rennes.
Casali, S. and F. Stok, eds. (2008) *Servio: stratificazioni esegetiche e modelli culturali / Servius: Exegetical Stratifications and Cultural Models*, Collection Latomus 317, Brussels.
Conte, G. B., ed. (2009) *P. Vergilius Maro: Aeneis*, Berlin.
Cornell, T. J., ed. (2013) *The Fragments of the Roman Historians*, 3 vols., Oxford.
Courtney, E. (1981) 'The formation of the text of Vergil', *BICS* 28: 13–29.
  (2002–3) 'The formation of the text of Vergil – again', *BICS* 46: 189–94.
Damon, C. (2015) *Studies on the Text of Caesar's 'Bellum civile'*, Oxford.
  (2016) 'Beyond variants: some digital desiderata for the critical apparatus of ancient Greek and Latin texts', in Driscoll and Pierazzo 2016, 201–18.
  (2018) 'The editor(s) in the classroom', https://classicalstudies.org/annual-meeting/149/abstract/editors-classroom.
Del Turco, R. Roselli (2016) 'The battle we forgot to fight: should we make a case for digital editions?', in Driscoll and Pierazzo 2016, 219–38.
De Nonno, M. (2010) 'Transmissional history and textual criticism', in A. Barchiesi and W. Scheidel, eds., *The Oxford Handbook of Roman Studies* (Oxford), 31–46.
Delvigo, M. L. (2011) *Servio e la poesia della scienza*, Pisa.
Deufert, M. (2017) *Prolegomena zur Editio Teubneriana des Lukrez*, Berlin.
  (2019) *Titus Lucretius Carus. De rerum natura libri* VI, Berlin.
Dolveck, F. (2015) *Paulini Nolani carmina*. Corpus Christianorum. Series Latina, 21, Turnhout.
Driscoll, M. J. and E. Pierazzo, eds. (2016) *Digital Scholarly Editing*, Cambridge.
Dunston, A. J. (1952) 'Two manuscripts of Suetonius' *De vita Caesarum*', *CQ* 2: 146–51.
Elliott, T., G. Bodard, H. Cayless et al. (2006–17) *EpiDoc: Epigraphic Documents in TEI XML*, http://epidoc.sf.net.
Fraenkel, E. (1948 and 1949) 'Review of Rand et al. 1946', *JRS* 38: 131–43, 39: 145–54. Reprinted in E. Fraenkel, *Kleine Beiträge zur klassischen Philologie* (Rome, 1964), 2.339–90.
Fraistat, N. and J. Flanders, eds. (2013) *The Cambridge Companion to Textual Scholarship*, Cambridge.
Franzini, G., P. Andorfer and K. Zaytseva (2016–) *Catalogue of Digital Editions: The Web Application*, https://dig-ed-cat.acdh.oeaw.ac.at/.
Garcea, A., M.-K. Lhommé and D. Vallat, eds. (2016) *Fragments d'érudition: Servius et le savoir antique*, Spudasmata 168, Hildesheim.
Goffaux, B. (2003) 'Mémoire et citation poétique dans l'*Histoire Auguste*', *REL* 81: 215–31.
Goold, G. P. (1970) 'Servius and the Helen episode', *HSPh* 74: 101–68.
Gotoff, H. C. (1971) *The Text of Lucan in the Ninth Century*, Cambridge, MA.

Håkanson, L. (1979) 'Problems of textual criticism and interpretation in Lucan's *De bello civili*', *PCPhS* 25: 26–52.
Haslam, M. W. (1978) 'Apollonius Rhodius and the papyri', *ICS* 3: 47–73.
Heslin, P. (2016) 'The dream of a universal variorum: digitizing the commentary tradition', in C. A. Kraus and C. A. Stray, eds., *Classical Commentaries: Explorations in a Scholarly Genre* (Oxford), 494–511.
Heyworth, S. J. (2007a) *Cynthia: A Companion to the Text of Propertius*, Oxford.
Heyworth, S. J., ed. (2007b) *Sexti Properti elegos*, Oxford.
Housman, A. E., ed. (1926) *M. Annaei Lucani Belli Civilis libri decem*, Oxford.
Huitfeldt, C. (2014) 'Markup technology and textual scholarship', in Apollon, Bélisle and Régnier 2014, 157–78.
Hunter, R. and S. P. Oakley, eds. (2016) *Latin Literature and Its Transmission: Papers in Honour of Michael Reeve*, Cambridge.
Huskey, S. J. and H. Cayless (2018) *Guidelines for Encoding Critical Editions for the Library of Digital Latin Texts*, https://digitallatin.github.io/guidelines/LDLT-Guidelines.html.
Ihm, M., ed. (1907) *C. Suetoni Tranquilli De vita Caesarum libri* VIII, Leipzig.
Kaster, R. A. (2010) *Studies on the Text of Macrobius' 'Saturnalia'*, Oxford.
  (2016a) *Studies on the Text of Suetonius' 'De uita Caesarum'*, Oxford.
  (2016b) 'Making sense of Suetonius in the twelfth century', in A. Grafton and G. Most, eds., *Canonical Texts and Scholarly Practices: A Global Comparative Approach* (Cambridge) 110–35.
Keeline, T. (2017) 'The apparatus criticus in the digital age', *CJ* 112: 342–63.
Keil, H., ed. (1855–80) *Grammatici Latini*. 7 vols., with a supplement edited by H. Hagen, Leipzig.
Kiss, D. (2013, 2017) *Catullus Online: An Online Repertory of Conjectures on Catullus*, www.catullusonline.org.
Langlois, P. (1997) 'Le texte d'Ausone en face de la théorie des "variantes d'auteur"', *Latomus* 56: 142–53.
Lloyd-Jones, H. and N. G. Wilson (1990) *Sophoclea: Studies on the Text of Sophocles*, Oxford.
  (1997) *Sophocles: Second Thoughts*, Göttingen.
Maas, P. (1927) *Textkritik*, Leipzig.
  (1957) *Textual Criticism*, Oxford.
Malaspina, E. (2015) 'In Anglia invenitur: come Guglielmo di Malmesbury leggeva e soprattutto correggeva Cicerone nel XII secolo', in P. De Paolis, ed., *Dai papyri al XX secolo: l'eternità di Cicerone*, Studi e ricerche del Dipartimento di Lettere e Filosofia 13 (Cassino) 31–52.
  (2019) 'A tradição manuscrita do Lucullus de Cícero: do Corpus Leidense a William de Malmesbury e à fortuna no período humanístico', in I. T. Cardoso and M. Martinho, eds., *Cícero: obra e recepção* (Coimbra), 19–53.
Marinone, N. (1946) *Elio Donato, Macrobio, e Servio*, Vercelli. Reprinted in N. Marinone, *Analecta graecolatina* (Bologna, 1990), 193–264.

Marshall, P. K. (1997) *Servius and Commentary on Virgil*, Asheville, NC.
  (2000) 'The Spangenberg Bifolium of Servius', *RFIC* 128: 192–209.
McGann, J. (2013) 'Coda: why digital textual scholarship matters; or, philology in a new key', in N. Fraistat and J. Flanders, eds., *The Cambridge Companion to Textual Scholarship* (Cambridge), 274–88.
Munk Olsen, B. (1982–2009) *L'Étude des auteurs classiques latins aux XIe et XIIe siècles*, 4 vols., Paris.
Murgia, C. E. (1975) *Prolegomena to Servius 5: The Manuscripts*, Berkeley.
Murgia, C. E. and R. A. Kaster, eds. (2018) *Serviani in Vergili Aeneidos libros IX–XII commentarii*, Oxford.
Mynors, R. A. B., ed. (1958) *C. Valerii Catulli Carmina*, Oxford.
Pasquali, G. (1929) 'Review of Maas 1927', *Gnomon* 5: 417–35, 498–521.
  (1971) *Storia della tradizione e critica del testo*, 2nd edn, Florence.
Pellegrin, E. (1975–2010) *Les manuscrits classiques latins de la Bibliothèque vaticane: Catalogue*, 3 vols., Paris.
Pellizzari, A. (2003) *Servio: storia, cultura e istituzioni nell'opera di un grammatico tardoantico*, Florence.
Pichler, A. and T. M. Bruvik (2014) 'Digital critical editing', in Apollon, Bélisle and Régnier 2014, 179–99.
Preud'homme, L. (1902) 'Première étude sur l'histoire du texte de Suétone, *de vita Caesarum*', *Bulletin de la classe des lettres et sciences morales et politique et de la classe des beaux-arts* 3: 299–328.
Rand, E. K. et al., eds. (1946) *Servianorum in Vergilii carmina commentariorum editionis Harvardianae volumen 2: Quod in Aeneidos libros I–II explanationes continet*, Lancaster, PA.
Reeve, M. D. (1969) 'Author's variants in Longus?', *PCPhS* 15: 75–85.
  (1985) 'Archetypes', *Sileno* 11:193–201.
  (1986) 'Stemmatic method: "Qualcosa che non funziona"?', in P. Ganz, ed., *The Role of the Book in Medieval Culture*, Bibliologia 3 (Turnhout), 57–9.
  (2000) '*Cuius in usum?* Recent and future editing', *JRS* 90: 196–206.
  (2007) 'Reconstructing archetypes: a new proposal and an old fallacy', in P. J. Finglass, C. Collard and N. J. Richardson, eds., *Hesperos: Studies in Ancient Greek Poetry Presented to M. L. West on His Seventieth Birthday* (Oxford), 326–40.
Reynolds, L. D., ed. (1983a) *Texts and Transmission: A Survey of the Latin Classics*, Oxford.
  (1983b) 'Velleius Paterculus', in Reynolds 1983a: 431–3.
Reynolds, L. D. and N. G. Wilson (2013) *Scribes and Scholars: A Guide to the Transmission of Greek and Latin Literature*, 4th edn, Oxford.
Sahle, P. (2013) *Digitale Editionsformen: Zum Umgang mit der Überlieferung unter den Bedingungen des Medienwandels. Teil II: Befunde, Theorie und Methodik*, Norderstedt.
  (2016) 'What is a scholarly digital edition?', in Driscoll and Pierazzo 2016, 19–40.
Santoro, A. (1946) 'Il Servio Danielino e Donato', *SIFC* 20: 79–104.

Savage, J. J. H. (1925) 'The scholia in the Virgil of Tours, Bernensis 165', *HSPh* 36: 91–164.
  (1934) 'The manuscripts of Servius's commentary on Virgil', *HSPh* 45: 157–204.
Skemer, D. (2013) *Medieval and Renaissance Manuscripts in the Princeton University Library*, 2 vols., Princeton.
Smith, N. (2009) 'Citation in classical studies', *Digital Humanities Quarterly* 3.1 (n.pag.).
Stocker, A. F. et al., eds. (1965) *Servianorum in Vergilii carmina commentariorum editionis Harvardianae volumen 3: Quod in Aeneidos libros III–V explanationes continet*, Oxford.
Stok, F., ed. (2013) *Totus scientia plenus: percorsi della esegesi virgiliana antica*, Pisa.
Stover, J. A., ed. (in preparation) *The Oxford Guide to the Transmission of the Latin Classics*, Oxford.
Tarrant, R. J. (1983) 'Lucan', in Reynolds 1983a, 213–18.
  (1995) 'Classical Latin literature', in D. C. Greetham, ed., *Scholarly Editing: A Guide to Research* (New York), 95–148.
  (2016) *Texts, Editors, and Readers: Methods and Problems in Latin Textual Criticism*, Cambridge.
Tiepmar, J. and G. Heyer (2017) 'An overview of Canonical Text Services', *Linguistics and Literature Studies* 5: 132–48.
Timpanaro, S. (1986) *Per la storia della filologia virgiliana antica*, Rome.
  (2001) *Virgilianisti antichi e tradizione indiretta*, Florence.
  (2005) *The Genesis of Lachmann's Method* (ed. and trans. G. W. Most), Chicago.
Wardle, D. (2014) *Suetonius: Life of Augustus*, Oxford.
West, M. L. (1973) *Textual Criticism and Editorial Technique Applicable to Greek and Latin Texts*, Stuttgart.
Wills, G. (1992) *Lincoln at Gettysburg: The Words that Remade America*, New York.
Wilson, N. G. (2015) *Herodotea: Studies on the Text of Herodotus*, Oxford.
Zetzel, J. E. G. (2004) 'In Rand's margins – from Fraenkel's review to a postmodern Servius'. Paper presented in the panel 'Whither the APA/Harvard Servius?' at the 135th Annual Meeting of the American Philological Association (San Francisco, 5 January 2004), www.academia.edu/35776337/In_Rands_Margins_From_Fraenkels_Review_to_a_Post-modern_Servius.
  (2005) *Marginal Scholarship and Textual Deviance: The 'Commentarium Cornuti' and the Early Scholia on Persius*. BICS Supplement 84, London.
  (2018) *Critics, Compilers, and Commentators: An Introduction to Roman Philology, 200 BCE–800 CE*, Oxford.
Zimmerman, M., ed. (2012) *Apulei Metamorphoseon libri* XI, Oxford.

CHAPTER 11

# Latin Literature and Linguistics
## James Clackson

### What Linguists Want

Whereas many Latinists have written articles or books with titles containing the phrase 'an interpretation', I am unaware of any work by a classical linguist that styles itself as 'an interpretation'. No one has written 'an interpretation' of the uses of the Latin perfect, the meaning of *sacer*, the form of the accusative plural or the pronunciation represented by Latin consonantal *u*. Linguists are as keen as anyone else to better their understanding of Latin, but generally see themselves in the positivist tradition of scientists, elucidating underlying truths about the language, rather than contributing to an ongoing discourse. Among themselves, linguists can be heard sometimes describing the latest theories of their literary colleagues as 'not even wrong', borrowing a favourite put-down from the sciences for work which does not have a falsifiable hypothesis, or dismissing literary studies as 'the usual blah blah'.[1] The vocabulary of grammars and works on the Latin language (whether from the perspective of a traditional or modern linguistic approach) encourages linguists to think of language as a self-contained system which is governed by absolutes: the *law* of the antepenultimate, the *rules* for sequence of tense, *mistakes* of diction and *incorrect* Latinity. In English, we talk of speakers 'knowing Latin' in the same way that it is possible to know the dates of Augustus or the stages of the *cursus honorum*; there is a general idea, shared at some level by most linguists, that this linguistic knowledge belongs somewhere in the realm of solid fact, rather than in abstraction, shifting interpretative frameworks and ideologies. Linguists working on the prehistory of Latin (thought to be essential, as we shall see, for the interpretation of a number of Latin forms) openly reify the hypothetical construct of a reconstructed parent language

---

[*] The late Ian Du Quesnay read an earlier version of this chapter and gave many helpful comments and corrections. For this, and much else, I am hugely in his debt.
[1] 'The usual blah blah that characterizes so many literary studies' (Katz 2003: 193).

of Latin (usually the so-called Proto-Indo-European, but sometimes other constructs such as Proto-Latin or Proto-Italic are used). Other linguists, who may themselves even be slightly sceptical about these reconstructed languages, are nevertheless happy to operate with other hypothetical entities, such as Vulgar (or sub-elite) Latin, Classical Latin or colloquial Latin. The apparent certainties with which many linguists operate and their often easy and hasty dismissal of different interpretative approaches would probably be off-putting to the outsider, if outsiders were able to venture far enough into linguistic works to read them and were not blocked near the entry by the thickets of technical terms and examples from other languages.

In order to illustrate the ways literary scholars and linguists differ in their approach, I start this chapter with the discussion of how critics, commentators and linguists have set about explaining an oddity in a poem of Catullus. This broadens then to a wider discussion around conceptions of literary language and its place among the registers of Latin. I then map certain points along the borders between literary and linguistic studies where there is most interaction – sometimes fruitful exchange, but occasionally raids into each other's territory or indeed skirmishing: versification and metre; lexicography, etymology and semantic study; grammatical accounts of Latin and the relationship of literary texts to the changing nature of the Latin language. Finally, digitisation of texts, better search facilities and new approaches to language allied to research on human cognition help to give some sense of how the borderlands between literary and linguistic study might evolve in future years.

## How Many Venuses? Catullus 3.1

Catullus' lament for Lesbia's pet sparrow (poem 3) is widely read by those in the early stages of learning Latin. The poem is short, the language is elevated but largely straightforward, the subject and wit are engaging. But in the opening line there is a potential stumbling block: *Lugete, o Veneres Cupidinesque*, 'Mourn, o Venuses and Cupids'. This is not the only time that the collocation *Veneres Cupidinesque* occurs in Catullus; at 13.12 the two deities are also given in the plural and function as the subject of the verb *donauerunt* 'gave'. At 36.3, however, Lesbia is said to have made a vow to a singular Venus and Cupid, *sanctae Veneri Cupidinique* 'blessed Venus and Cupid'. No Latin writer before Catullus mentions more than one Cupid and there is certainly only one goddess Venus, so why does Catullus use the plural?

Most classicists, faced with this question, would turn to one or more of the existing commentaries for the answer.[2] Many commentaries on Catullus have been produced (Konstan 2014 'highly recommends' eleven), ranging from guidance for the beginning Latinist to detailed discussions of textual problems. Robinson Ellis (1876: 7), the earliest commentator included in Konstan's list, was already able to interlace four different reasons for Catullus' plurals. Ellis first noted that Cicero mentioned four Venuses and three Cupids in his *De natura deorum* (3.59) and so Catullus 'would thus be speaking with strict accuracy'. He counters this explanation with the observation that Lesbia herself makes a vow to *sanctae Veneri Cupidinique* at 36.3; Ellis consequently suggests that Catullus 'merely pluralizes this, without any special reference to the various forms of the goddess and her son'. He then offers a third account: *Cupidines* stood in for the Ἔρωτες who were mentioned with Venus by Hellenistic poets and the 'first outline of the expression may have been *Venus Cupidinesque*'. The change to the plural *Veneres* was brought about 'to make the expression symmetrical'. As a final flourish, Ellis noted that the plural would suggest the meaning of Graces, 'thus combining in one Κύπρις and the Χάριτες'.

Ellis' idea that the plural *Veneres* occurred by 'attraction' to *Cupidines* was taken up and extended by K. P. Schulze (1882: 205), but given short shrift by the next monumental commentator, Emil Bährens (1885: 82). Bährens also rejected the idea that the poet used the plural to display his learning ('sterili cum doctrina'), either about the number of epithets of Venus or the different incarnations of the goddess. Instead he furthered the idea that the plural was to be taken to include the Graces.[3] Merrill's school edition, first published in 1893 but republished as recently as 2014, gives some grudging respect to the 'attraction' explanation and has the courtesy to mention both Schulze and Ellis by name (1893: 6). He thinks a more likely explanation is the result of the 'conception of the character of Venus and of Lesbia'. Lesbia is said to have possessed *omnes Veneres* at 86.6, which Merrill takes to subsume 'mental as well as physical endowments'. He subsequently explains *Cupidines* as the extension of the Greek notion of Ἔρωτες, which he supports with parallels from later Latin poets. The

---

[2] On the so-called 'hit-and-run' use of commentaries to find the answer(s) to a specific question, see Ash 2002: 274; Kraus 2002: 11, 18; Gibson 2015: 266.

[3] Bährens failed to give any credit to Ellis for this idea, citing only Schulze for the 'attraction' theory. The failure to attribute observations to Ellis did not go unnoticed: 'Any one who takes the trouble to examine this work, will see how greatly its author is indebted to my pages, and how little acknowledgment he has made of his debts' (Ellis 1889: xii).

scholarly edition of Kroll was more favourable to the 'attraction' theory.[4] Kroll also mentioned yet another linguistic explanation, originally put forward by Eduard Schwyzer (1903), which I will discuss more fully on pp. 571–3.

Commentaries in English after Kroll repeat many of the earlier possible explanations for the plurals, sometimes pruning or refining the references to other classical texts. Fordyce (1961: 90), following Kroll, was able to supply a fragment of Callimachus which describes the multiplicity of Venus (fragment 200a Pfeiffer), and Quinn (1970: 97) added a reference to Pausanias' discourse on Aphrodite in Plato's *Symposium*, where the goddess is said to have two forms, *Pandemos* and *Uranios*. Commentators in the second half of the twentieth century further follow Ellis in his reluctance to commit to any single explanation. Having cited the 'attraction' explanation, the possible allusion to Callimachus and the identification of Venus and the Graces, Fordyce declared that none of these was 'entirely convincing': 'with characteristic extravagance (and not without thought for his metre; it is sometimes too lightly assumed that poets are above such considerations) Catullus has chosen to turn both into indefinite plurals – all the powers of Charm and Desire are there'. Quinn (1970: 97) wondered whether the phrase might be a 'proverbial expression or traditional jingle', while also stating that the idea that there was more than one Aphrodite 'seems to have become a commonplace of Alexandrian mythology'. Forsyth (1986: 111) viewed *Veneres Cupidinesque* as 'a "poetic plural" (with the added incentive of the meter)'. This view is continued by Thomson (1997: 208), who thought that 'the Latin habit of mind, which gave to so many abstract nouns (e.g. *fides, Fides*) a divine embodiment, implies that the regular and the personified use of such nouns lie close together, and could not always be distinguished ... Consequently, it seems quite natural to use plurals even when personification is required.' The forthcoming commentary of Monica Gale, in contrast, drops the idea of indefinite or poetic plurals and reverts to the idea of pairing of Graces and Erotes in Greek poetry, also identifying 'learned allusion here to scholarly arguments about multiple, homonymous deities'.[5]

As has often been observed, it is the nature of the classical commentary to be tralaticious,[6] and my quotations in the previous paragraph exemplify this if nothing else. The passing down of a range of opinions, with

---

[4] Kroll 1968: 5–6, but note that the first edition of this commentary was printed in 1923.
[5] I am grateful to Monica Gale for giving me sight of her unpublished work.
[6] Kraus 2002: 16, Kraus and Stray 2015a: 9.

occasional promotion or dismissal of one of them, encourages a multiplicity of interpretations. Literary scholars of the last 150 years have, in general, been comfortable with a poet who might use an expression such as *Veneres Cupidinesque* for a range of different effects. The attentive commentary reader can also detect different national traditions, or witness the growth, bloom and decay of particular interpretative frameworks.[7] Hence Merrill's 'conception of character' morphs into Fordyce's 'indefinite plural', Forsyth's 'poetic plural' and Thomson's 'abstract'. Dictionaries are also tralaticious and sometimes the interplay between commentary and dictionary can lead to apparent confirmation of the commentator. Thus the *Oxford Latin Dictionary*, which itself sought to avoid the tralaticious tendency through a 'fresh reading of the sources' and a new collection of slips, does cite the Catullus passage (s.v. *Venus*$^1$ 1) but with the brief annotation '(*pl., poet.*)', possibly reflecting Fordyce's commentary.[8] The *OLD*, however, puts paid to Merrill's attempts to link the plural at 86.6 with the *Veneres Cupidinesque* phrase, since this is allocated to sense 3, 'the quality of attracting sexual love, charm'.

To see how Catullus' use of the plural is judged by a linguist, we can turn to an unpublished paper given by Timothy Barnes (Barnes 2016). Despite the title of the paper, only one page of the seven-and-a-half-page handout is devoted to the phrase *Veneres Cupidinesque*. Barnes first gives full citations of Catullus 3.1–2 and 13.11–14 (the two passages with *Veneres Cupidinesque*), followed by poem 36, which has the singular *Veneri Cupidinique*. He notes that the divine names when pluralised stand alongside each other and that *Cupidines* never occurs in Catullus in the plural on its own, *Veneres* only once (86.6). Barnes gives three interpretations that are to be rejected. First the idea that '*Veneres* = Venus and Venus-like goddesses (e.g. *Gratiae*/Χάριτες) and a plurality of *Cupidines*/"Ερωτες'. Second, Fordyce's suggestion that there are 'indefinite plurals', and thirdly the idea that Venus is 'attracted' into the plural through its pairing with *Cupidines*. Barnes does not think any of these explanations are adequate, since they do not take into account the fact that Catullus gives the same phrase in the dative as *Veneri Cupidinique*, 'a clear indication that the poet intended a pair of two individuals'. Barnes accordingly sets out the 'answer' as that given by Schwyzer, which was mentioned (and dismissed) by Kroll, but otherwise ignored by commentators, although perhaps discernible in

---

[7] See Fuhrer in this volume on different national traditions.
[8] For Fordyce's role in the composition of the *OLD* see Henderson 2006: 91–2 and 2010: 159–60. I give an outline of the *OLD* entry later on in this chapter.

Quinn's remark about a 'traditional jingle'. I shall set out Schwyzer's theory in detail below, but before I do it is worth pausing to consider how linguists can come so quickly to a single 'right' answer, discounting or ignoring the other explanations.

For Barnes and I suspect many other linguists, appeals to 'allusion' are not cogent in cases where the same phrase recurs in different passages. Is there also an allusion to Callimachus at 13.12, where again the phrase refers to animate divine beings, but not at 36.3? How would it be possible to falsify this notion that Catullus is 'alluding' to an earlier poet or philosopher?[9] Similarly, the commentators' rather vague notions of a 'poetic plural' which would seem natural to an ancient Roman cut little ice. Poets avoid using plural for singular when referring to persons or deities and even though gods and goddesses can stand in place of substances or abstracts (as *Ceres* for wheat, food or bread, *Bacchus* for wine), in this passage Venus and Cupid are not abstracts, but represented as individuals, with the ability to mourn.[10]

In general, linguists tend to fight shy of the implication that 'poetic' language is a free-for-all, where any grammatical 'rule' may be broken in order to fit the demands of metre.[11] Indeed, to show some of the difficulties involved in the notion of 'poetic' features, it is possible to point to Latin poetry composed by individuals who were probably not native speakers, such as the hexameter verses inscribed in 222 CE by the centurion Marcus Porcius Iasucthan at the Roman outpost known as Bu Njem in the Sahara desert.[12] The initial lines from Iasucthan's poem (lines 7–12 of the inscription) recording the exploits of his legion, the Third Augustan, in building a gate are as follows:

> omnes praeteriti cuius labore uitabant
> rigido uigore iuuenum tertia augustani fecerunt
> creto consilio hortante parato magistro
> iuncta uirtus militum paucorum uelocitas ingens
> usui compendio lapides de longe adtractos chamulco
> sub arcata militum uirtus funib(us) cannabinis strictis

---

[9] See further O'Rourke and Pelttari in this volume on intertextuality.
[10] For discussions of the range and extent of the different types of plurals for singular in Latin, including the poetic plural, see Löfstedt 1956: 1 27–65; and the useful summary of the poetic plural in Coleman 1999: 75.
[11] For some attempts to categorise 'poetic language' and registers, see Maurach 1995, Coleman 1999, Ferri 2011.
[12] Iasucthan's poetry is discussed in depth by Adams 1999, whose account I largely follow here. I am grateful to Ian DuQuesnay for comments on and discussion of the text and translation.

## 11 *Latin Literature and Linguistics* 569

The labour (*labore* = *laborem*) of which (i.e. the *restitutio*) all (our) predecessors avoided (that) with firm vigour of the warriors the third Augustans did by after a plan had been formed, encouraged by Paratus (?) the magister, linked (were?) the valour of a few soldiers (and) vast speed, by a saving of effort to the normal practice, (the plan was that) stones drawn from afar by traction engine, under the arches, the valour of the soldiers, with hempen ropes drawn tight.

For readers wondering how this could be considered a hexameter, I shall return to the metre of this poem later in this chapter. For the moment it is worth noting just a couple of the many unusual syntactic features. In the phrase *tertia augustani* Iasucthan seems to have confused two idioms, the *tertia legio Augusta* 'third Augustan legion' and *tertiani augustani* 'the third Augustans'.[13] After the main verb in the second line, the next four lines run on with no main verb, but two phrases in the ablative, two in the nominative (*uirtus militum, uelocitas ingens*), followed by what might be an accusative and infinitive clause after *creto consilio* (*lapides de longe adtractos chamulco*) and then another nominative (*militum uirtus* again). Iasucthan is clearly incompetent and his command of Latin limited, but it is not impossible that, in the words of Adams (1999: 123), 'he may have been deliberately seeking originality of expression on the grounds that that is what a poet should attempt'. To a speaker such as Iasucthan, who might well have come across Latin hexameter verse in his training in basic literacy,[14] in poetry perhaps anything seemed permissible. We could assume that educated and literate Romans had the same view, but this seems unlikely, given that the licences that Iasucthan takes are not found in Latin poetry that survives through the manuscript tradition before the end of the Empire. A view that poetic syntax is a free-for-all does not allow us to distinguish the incompetents from the masters.

Returning to Catullus, in considering the anomalous plurals *Veneres Cupidinesque* linguists prefer to seek an explanation which tallies with the singulars *Veneri Cupidinique* in poem 36. In order to understand what Catullus might be doing with this phrase and how his first listeners may have understood him, indeed, to have a sense of what sounded 'natural' to native speakers of Latin, linguists, like literary scholars, look for parallels. The search for parallels is, however, of a different order to that of the literary critic. On the one hand, the linguist's parallels are far beyond the dreams of the most ardent intertextualist, ranging through the entire

---

[13] Adams 1999: 111 n. 16.
[14] For the survival of lines of Virgil in educational contexts see Clackson 2011a: 241–2, Dickey 2012c: 15.

diachrony of Latin and further afield, to other languages and textual traditions. On the other, the linguist would claim that the parallels have to be more 'exact' than those of the literary critic, since they are instances of a linguistic 'fact'. No 'fuzzy logic' or 'exact inexactitude' (Hinds 1998: 50) here. The linguist, as far as possible, avoids the question of authorial intention by ignoring the role of the author.[15] If possible, an oddity in the text is preferably explained by reference to a linguistic universal, or a general principle of the way Latin works, or as a feature of the diachrony of the language, whether a survival from earlier stages or harbinger of what is to come. In any corpus language, especially where much of the received text is open to emendation, it is of course possible to find possible parallels (or dismiss them) for many anomalous constructions. Catullus' plural *Veneres* could be paired, Fordyce (1961: 93) and others have noted, with the plural *soles* at *Culex* 351 *soles et sidera cuncta* ('suns and all the stars'); giving an apparent parallel for the attraction of a singular *sol* to the plural by the presence of the plural *sidera*. Finding a parallel does not guarantee the permissibility of a construction, any more than the apparent lack of one condemns it, but it does at least give the linguist the opportunity to search for the general truth rather than a particular interpretation. Furthermore, parallels allow linguists the chance to explain the construction, rather than name it – and that is their ultimate goal.

Much of the research on the linguistics of the classical languages takes place within a historical and comparative paradigm enabling scholars to cast their nets in a very large pool to fish for parallels. Latin, like all languages, was not static, but changed considerably over its long period of attestation, a feature that was noticed as early as Polybius, who stated that the language of the earlier Romans differed so much from that of his day that it was difficult to understand (3.22.3). Since Saussure, most researchers into linguistics have split the analysis of a language into the synchronic and the diachronic, the first looking at how the language fits together as a system, the second at how it changes in time.[16] The Latin grammatical oddity of one time may reflect a commonplace of earlier Latin, or be a harbinger of what is to come. To take a familiar example, the conjugation of *memini* 'I remember' as a perfect has no good synchronic explanation; it can however be explained diachronically by

---

[15] Linguists are consequently not, in general, troubled by distinctions between the flesh-and-blood author, persona and the like, as discussed by Sharrock in this volume.
[16] Saussure's lectures on general linguistics were published from his students' notes after he died (de Saussure et al. 1985 [1916]). Matthews 2001 is a good account on the impact of Saussure's thought on the field of linguistics.

considering the origins of the Latin perfect.[17] In this case, the knowledge of the origin of the form does not add anything to our understanding of Latin texts; the translation of *memini* is unchanged.

The case of *Veneres Cupidinesque* is more complex. Here specialist knowledge of the history of Latin is required in order to engage with Schwyzer's proposed explanation (Schwyzer 1903). (Here one might note that the failure of this interpretation to become incorporated into the Anglophone commentary tradition may reflect differences in the training of professional classicists in the German-speaking world, where literary scholars are perhaps more likely to have been required to take courses in historical linguistics as part of their first or higher degree.) There is, I am sorry to say, no sweet honey to alloy the bitter taste of historical linguistics in what is to follow, but I can promise that this interpretation does have the potential to impact on our understanding of Catullus as a poet and his use of different registers and sources. There is comparatively little surviving Latin before Catullus, other than the plays of Plautus and Terence; it is possible that *Veneres Cupidinesque* is an archaism, which survived only in the register of invocations to the gods, apparently a particularly favourable locus for the conservation of features which had been superseded in other areas of the language.[18]

The linguist's search for parallels leads first to the comparison of *Veneres Cupidinesque* with other divine pairs in the Roman pantheon. First, consider Ceres and her daughter Persephone, who can be referred to by the plural *Cereres*, an idiom that is unrecorded in the *OLD* s.v. *Ceres*, since it occurs in no literary text,[19] but for which the *TLL* gives a number of inscriptional examples, including the formulaic phrase *sacerdos Cererum*. The same idiom seems to occur in the republican period in an epithet written of a priestess written in Paelignian, a sister-language to Latin, once spoken in the central Apennines east of Rome.[20] Paelignian is only attested epigraphically in a small number of texts, almost entirely associated with funerary monuments, written in the Latin alphabet in the second to first

---

[17] Weiss 2009: 409. For an extensive treatment of the prehistory of the Latin perfect, see Meiser 2003.
[18] Compare the survival of old forms of third-declension genitive singulars in -*us*, which are disproportionately associated with divine names such as *Venerus* for *Veneris*: *CIL* 1² 2536, 1² 2297, x 3776, x 3777, x 5191 and possibly 1² 2885, accepting the restoration [*Ven*]*erus poc(o)lom* (Adams 2007: 40–4).
[19] See Lavan in this volume for what is counted as 'literary'; like Lavan, I take the literary to comprise texts which survive in the manuscript tradition, although I do not count the work of commentators, such as Servius, or grammarians or educational material as 'literary'.
[20] Paelignian is now normally classed as a variety of Oscan, as in Rix 2002. See Clackson 2015b and Fortson 2017 for recent overviews of the dialectal array of the Italic languages.

centuries BCE.[21] The seven-line priestess' epithet from Corfinium, the longest Paelignian text known, is still not perfectly understood. One of the female titles which features on the stone is *cerfum sacaracirix,* usually rendered in English as 'priestess of Ceres and Persephone' (Crawford et al. 2011: 268). It is clear that *cerfum* is a genitive plural, most likely the Paelignian equivalent to *Cererum*.[22] Latin inscriptions provide another example of a divine pair referred to by the plural of one name, the twins Castor and Pollux, who are named as *Castores*.[23] The plural *Castores* also appears in some late literary works including the poetry of Ausonius; Servius' note on Virgil *Georgics* 3.89 makes it clear that the plural of either brother could serve for them both:

> Certe ideo Pollucem pro Castore posuit, quia ambo licenter et Polluces et Castores uocantur; nam et ludi et templum et stellae Castorum nominantur.
>
> Without doubt he consequently puts *Pollux* in place of *Castor*, since both can be called *Polluces* or *Castores*; indeed, both the games and the temple and the stars are named 'of the *Castores*'.

In Latin, the use of a plural form of one member of a divine pair is a marginal phenomenon, but, as the Paelignian example shows, a similar rule seems to operate in closely related languages on the Italian peninsula. Grammatically, this use of a plural is sometimes termed an 'elliptical' plural, which is found in other nouns in Latin, particular those referring to kinship terms. Hence *patres* can mean 'mother and father' (*OLD* s.v. *pater* 1e), *fratres* 'brother and sister' (*OLD* s.v. *frater* 1b), *mariti* 'husband and wife' (*OLD* s.v. *maritus*² 1b), *soceri* 'father-in-law and mother-in-law' (*OLD* s.v. *socer* 1b). The same phenomenon is also observed in other ancient members of the Indo-European family, Greek and Sanskrit. The best Greek example is the dual Αἴαντε, literally 'the two Ajaxes', but shown by Wackernagel (1877) to refer to the pair of the Greater Ajax and his brother Teucer at *Iliad* 13.46 and elsewhere. Greek also has elliptical plurals for relationship terms such as πατήρ (LSJ s.v. A VII.2) and ἀδελφός (LSJ s.v. A1) and for other words, such as ἵππος, used in the plural or dual for 'team of chariot horses, horses and chariot' (LSJ s.v. A1). Scholars of ancient Greek epic are more used to gaining insights from Indo-European linguistics than their Latin counterparts, owing to the numerous oddities of Homeric grammar which can be attributed to survivals of earlier speech patterns. Wackernagel's statement

---

[21] See Crawford et al. 2011: 267–8 for text and bibliography of this inscription, with further discussion in Martzloff 2016: 387–9.
[22] Weiss 2017: 372 gives a different explanation of this word.
[23] See *TLL* s.v. *Castor* for references.

about dual Αἴαντε has found its way into the Anglophone commentary tradition as well as the German.[24]

In Sanskrit the elliptical plural and elliptical dual is well attested, but here the usage goes further than that of either Greek or Latin. Indeed, it is the Sanskrit parallels that best explain the Catullan usage. The Sanskrit pattern can be illustrated by Mitra and Varuna, two gods who frequently appear together in the earliest Sanskrit hymns. When spoken of together, it is possible to use just the name of one god in the dual number to refer to the pair, hence *Mitrā́* or *Váruṇā*, just as Servius says that *Castores* or *Polluces* are possible ways to refer to Castor and Pollux (as already noted by Wackernagel; Latin, of course, does not have a dual number and so must use the plural). In early Sanskrit the divine pair Mitra and Varuna can also be named in a different way, with a double dual featuring both gods: *Mitrā́ Váruṇā*. In the Castor and Pollux example, the Roman equivalent of this would be *Castores Polluces* or *Castores Pollucesque*. Schwyzer (1903) recognised that this pattern would neatly explain why we appear to have plurals in *Veneres Cupidinesque*; this is just a survival of an inherited way of naming two closely related divinities, by marking them both as non-singular entities. Catullus may therefore have taken a very ancient construction, surviving only in the religious register, to add to the bathos of his lament. The historical background and the survival of similar forms in related languages and non-literary Latin can thus be used as parallels to Catullus' Latin, which would otherwise be lost from the record.

It is worth noting some of the hidden moves in the linguistic account I have sketched out. First, linguists are, for the most part, happy with the idea that speakers of languages can preserve words or even constructions from earlier stages of the language, even when they are apparently nonsensical in the contemporary language. The analogy between linguistic evolution and evolution in the natural world goes back as far as Darwin (if not further) and linguists readily take up evolutionary metaphors and frameworks (Croft 2000). However, spoken languages are unlike evolving entities in the natural world since they do not have any existence independent of speakers. New learners of a language create the language afresh in their brains and speakers are generally intolerant of anomalies unsupported by frequent usage or parallel structures. For linguistic fossils to survive into the works of a poet such as Catullus, the linguist has to assume some medium outside of the normal transmission of language from speaker to speaker, such as an unrecorded special register of religious language, as we have done in this case. Such a hypothesis is not impossible, but it is not normally explicitly

---

[24] Leaf 1902: 6, Willcock 1984: 204, Janko 1992: 48.

labelled as a hypothesis and it cannot easily be falsified (it is 'not even wrong'). A further sleight of hand from the linguist concerns what counts as good evidence. Linguists, who may be sceptical about the reliance on parallel passages from Plato or Hellenistic poets to account for Catullus' language, are far readier to take as cogent a parallel from a priestess' epitaph written in the imperfectly understood language Paelignian (and one that is itself contested by other linguists). Next to nothing is known about the context in which the Paelignian text was created; it appears to be written in an idiom that is significantly different from the language of other Paelignian funerary inscriptions.[25] If for linguists, as we shall see shortly, the primary focus of research is the spoken language, where do literary registers fit in?

This rather lengthy discussion of Catullus 3.1 has served to exemplify the different approaches and different tool-kits employed by the linguist and the literary scholar. As shall become clearer throughout this chapter, my constructions of 'the linguist' and the 'literary critic' are, to a certain extent, creatures of straw and many scholars might think them caricatures rather than reflections of reality. There is, moreover, a genuine difference between the style and rhetoric of literary critics and linguists which does reflect an underlying contrast in the goals of study and I shall explore this difference in the next section. Linguists are wary of multiple explanations for the same phenomenon, and suspicious of accounts which rely on repeated independent creations of the same output. In this case, there is little tolerance given to any suggestion that Catullus' *Veneres Cupidinesque* could be both an allusion to Callimachus and the continuation of a Latin traditional phrase. Linguists generally cite the principle of Occam's razor with approval.[26] What counts as a good explanation is one that gives a general statement about the language, which fits in with the accepted model for Latin development and history, not one that relies upon a particular quirk of a particular author at a particular stage.

## Literary Language and the Latin Language

Linguists are trained from early on to understand that their objective is a description of a language, or some feature of the language under investigation. Since the nineteenth century, there has been discussion and debate

---

[25] For a recent account of the different registers of Paelignian literary texts, see Clackson 2015a: 75–7. See Fisher 2014: 1–5 for the distinction between 'literary allusion' and the comparison of 'traditional collocations' which may occur in poetry, or in other 'systems of non-poetic discourse' in particular focused around ritual. Fisher's conception of 'literary allusion' is, like that of many linguists, fairly rudimentary.
[26] See for example Hock 1991: 538–40.

about how best to achieve this and what constitutes the 'language' that is the object of study. Nearly all (but not all – note maverick voices such as Harris 2000) agree that the fundamental form of language is spoken language and that written language is a secondary phenomenon, although with the possibility that written constructions or spelling pronunciations may be fed back into speech. Linguists studying classical languages, or indeed any language no longer spoken, are constantly reminded of the inadequacy of their evidence. Discussions of the so-called 'bad data' problem in historical linguistics frequently cite a passage of one of the most eminent scholars in linguistics, William Labov, which is worth repeating yet again here:

> The fundamental methodological fact that historical linguists have to face is that they have no control over their data; texts are produced by a series of historical accidents ... the great art of the historical linguist is to make the best of this bad data – 'bad' in the sense that it may be fragmentary, corrupted or many times removed from the actual productions of native speakers. (Labov 1972: 100)

Subsequent discussions of the 'bad data' problem have stressed that written evidence may have some advantages over spoken for the elucidation of linguistic facts; moreover, it is a misnomer to think of any usable data as 'bad'.[27] Nevertheless, the label 'bad data problem' has stuck. Furthermore, linguists identify a distinction between instances of language production and an abstract, underlying system (very broadly, the distinction goes back to Saussure's separation of *parole* from *langue*).[28] Individual utterances or texts are of themselves only revealing insofar as they can give information about the language system that produced them. The emphasis on the descriptive carries with it a widespread belief among linguists that no single form of language is inherently more complex, more correct or 'better' (or worse) than any other. Literary language is consequently not considered to be more privileged *per se* than other types of language and is seen as likely to be further removed from speech than other written registers, owing to the pressure to conform to existing models. For linguists, the failure to find a good Latin literary parallel to the construction *Veneres Cupidinesque* discussed earlier on is not a problem for its interpretation,

---

[27] See the excellent discussion of the responses to Labov's 'bad data' challenge in McDonald 2015: 37–9.
[28] For discussion of Saussure's distinction between *langue* and *parole*, see Matthews 2001: 11–13, for the enduring influence of the distinction in linguistics, ibid. 143.

because there are inscriptional parallels, both in Latin and Paelignian, combined with the metalinguistic comments of Servius. Indeed, these non-literary sources may be closer to the linguist's desired spoken Latin, providing more secure parallels than literary works could. Finally, since literary Latin is transmitted to us via a manuscript tradition, linguists cannot be sure whether the written forms in any manuscript, let alone as given in a printed text, are those used by the ancient author, not a later corruption.

Literary language is therefore a difficult source to use for the elucidation of the form of Latin of most interest to the hard-core linguist. The search for spoken Latin is made through looking through or beyond the surviving works of Latin literature. By 'looking through' I refer both to the way that some passages of Roman literature apparently allow us to see beyond the screen of literary language, with direct representations of the language of individuals through citations or presentations of speech. The most famous example is of course the speeches of the freedmen in Petronius' *Satyrica*, which present a striking contrast to the literary Latin of the framing narrative (I shall be looking in more detail at another example of supposed colloquial speech from Catullus later in this chapter).[29] Works written by those with less experience of education, particularly in the imperial period, may also in part reveal what is going on in the spoken language, underneath the suffocating crust of the 'dead landscape of literary Latin' (Palmer 1954: 149). The concern of the linguist with spoken language does not only manifest itself with respect to non-standard texts and in tracing the evolution of Latin over time, but it can be seen in the recent *Oxford Latin Syntax* (Pinkster 2015), which aims to replace the reference grammar for syntax that most literary scholars still rely upon (Kühner, Stegmann and Thierfelder 1966). Pinkster's syntax accordingly gives a greater proportion of space to examples from Plautus, which represents spoken interactions, than Kühner, Stegmann and Thierfelder (32.3% of all citations against 9.4%), downplaying the contribution of more 'literary' texts, the Augustan poets and Livy (7.7% of all citations against 15.5%; figures from Clackson 2017).

For the description of the language of a literary text, many linguists make an assumption (sometimes explicit, often not) about the spoken

---

[29] For recent orientations for the language of the freedmen in Petronius, see Adams 2003b, Boyce 1991 and Leiwo 2010.

Latin prevalent at the time of the author, then attributing other accretions present in the text to other factors. Education, the persistence of literary norms, generic considerations, Greek models and socially prestigious forms are all held to account for departures from presumed spoken Latin. A familiar example, again taken from Catullus, is the use of the nominative and infinitive in place of the native accusative and infinitive in the opening lines of poem 4, on the model of the Greek construction:

> Phaselus ille, quem uidetis, hospites
> ait fuisse nauium celerrimus.
>
> The pinnace you see, my friends, says that she was once the fleetest of ships.
> (trans. F. W. Cornish 1988, revised by G. P. Goold)

In recent linguistic discussions of the accusative and infinitive construction in Latin, this passage and the parallel nominatives and infinitives in Horace and Martial are not mentioned, presumably because they are viewed as ephemeral interferences of the language, having no significance for the syntactic analysis of Latin.[30] The principle of Occam's razor is again at work here. No one knows for sure whether nominative and infinitive constructions were in fact a feature of the everyday speech of some Romans at some point in time, but it is easier for the syntactician to hypothesise a Latin grammar without the construction.[31]

For many linguists working in the historical or Indo-European framework, their study of Latin may not even be as a means to find out about the linguistic system of Latin, but as a means to uncover more about the nature of the Indo-European parent language, reconstructed through comparison of the daughter languages. Latin is attested later than Greek, Sanskrit or Anatolian languages, but still has a large and accessible body of text from before the Christian era and has an important contribution to make to Indo-European texts. Other historical linguists may be more interested in tracing the relationship between Latin and its siblings from the Italian peninsula,

---

[30] Recent accessible discussions include Horrocks 2011: 138–41 and Oniga 2014: 290–301. This passage is, however, mentioned in works dealing with Greek syntactic influence on Latin, Coleman 1975 and Calboli 2009. Calboli declares that 'it was quite incompatible with the nature of Latin to use the nominative *celerrimus* instead of the accusative *celerrimum*' (Calboli 2009: 130).

[31] Textual considerations are also relevant here, given that the nominative and infinitive construction in this passage is actually an editorial emendation to the transmitted text *ait fuisse nauium celerrimum*. The basis for the emendation is the parallel in *Catalepton* 10: *ait fuisse mulio celerrimus*, where the accusative *mulionem celerrimum* would not scan (Fordyce 1961: 100). See Butrica 2007 for a survey of the history of the transmission of the text of Catullus.

Oscan, Paelignian and the rest, or using the evidence of Latin to help interpret a South Picene inscription or an Umbrian tablet.

## The (Un)naturalness of Metre

Poets are held to be even further removed from their native Latin language than other literary figures, owing to the constraints of metre, which imposes rhythmic patterns which may be alien to everyday speech. Hence much recent work on Latin word order has concentrated solely on Latin prose texts, ostensibly on the grounds that in verse the 'natural' word-order patterns have been disrupted.[32] A further problem is the fact that the bulk of the surviving metres of Roman verse are transfers from Greek; moreover, the ancient grammarians discussed and described Latin metres in Greek terms. Livius Andronicus employed what seems to have been a native metre, the saturnian, for his translation of the *Odyssey*, but adapted Greek metres for his dramatic works. After Ennius pioneered the writing of epic in Greek hexameters, saturnians were doomed, even if they hung around in the productions of archaising poets and provincial epitaphs (Morgan 2010: 286–300).

If the metres of Latin poetry are foreign imports, does that make Roman metrical practice even further removed from real speech? Scholars have given different answers to this question. One view makes much of the supposed fact that Greek had a 'pitch accent', whereby the accentual contour of a word was made prominent through modulation of the pitch of the voice, but that Latin had a 'stress accent', in which one syllable in any accented word was pronounced louder. As encapsulated by Allen (1973: 337–40), this difference of 'phonological type' led to an artificial situation. Speakers of Latin were supposed to have had difficulty in picking out the syllable-timed metres of Greek, unless habituated through long exposure to Greek poetry. Moreover, accustomed as a Roman was to stress patterns, 'it is possible that the untaught speaker would have been aware of quantitative differences only in so far as they were connected with the placement of accent; so that in final syllables, for example, quantity might mean nothing to him' (Allen 1973: 339).[33] In order to make it easier for Romans to pick out

---

[32] See Spevak 2010, Danckaert 2012 and Spevak 2014. Compare the more nuanced remarks of Devine and Stephens 2006: 567, who argue that certain word orders permitted in verse but not found in (Ciceronian) prose may be continuations of an earlier stage of the language.

[33] Allen's claim that Romans would be unlikely to hear differences of vowel quantity in the final syllable of words is countered by the bulk of Latin verse in which long and short vowels preserve their original quantity in final position. Note also that the apparent indifference to quantity at verse-end

the metre, poets thus had to smuggle stress back into the hexameter line. According to the theory, they did this by aiming for a correlation between stress and the first position in the verse foot (what is now termed the ictus, although this is a modern use of the term)[34] at the end of the hexameter line, giving native speakers something to hold on to, with a recognisable line-end TUM-ti-ti TUM-tum. As has long been observed, there is a gradual move from Ennius to Virgil towards a correlation between the first position in the foot and a stressed syllable in the last two feet of the hexameter, with a corresponding decrease in the co-incidence of first position and stress placement in the first four feet.[35] Later in the history of Latin, as the language changed and vowel length ceased to be distinctive, writers of hexameter verse kept the correlation between accent placement and ictus in the last two feet of the hexameter. This helps to understand the attempts at verse by Iasucthan in the Libyan desert cited earlier. Although the lines are impossible to scan quantitatively, if read accentually and ignoring all original vowel lengths then the last two feet generally work out: *labóre uitábant*; *augustáni fecérunt*; *paráto magístro*; *uelócitas íngens*; *adtráctos chamúlco*; *cannábinis stríctis*. This tendency is found in epigraphic poems, in Commodian and other Christian poets and hymnographers.[36]

There are still many adherents, particularly among Anglophone and German-speaking classical scholars, to the theory that the differing accentual systems of Greek and Latin led to a tension between metre and stress patterns that is 'the essence of the expressive power of the Latin hexameter' (Morgan 2010: 334 n. 181). In his influential handbook *Vox Latina*, Allen used the correlation between ictus and accent in the final two feet of the hexameter as the clinching argument for a Latin stress accent (Allen 1978: 86). Many of the linguistic underpinnings of the argument are, however, looking pretty shaky if not already collapsed. It is now accepted that Romans, certainly in the Augustan period and probably also later, did

does not offer any support for Allen's view, since, as noted by Fortson (2008: 101), Quintilian records that heavy final syllables at verse-end were more satisfying to the ear than light ones (9.4.93).

[34] On the meaning of *ictus* in the grammarians, see *TLL* s.v. VII.1 167.63–72 and Stroh 1990: 99. The modern use of the term stems from Gottfried Hermann's *Handbuch der Metrik* (1799), with antecedents in Richard Bentley's edition of Terence (see Stroh 1990: 88 for full references).

[35] See Allen 1973: 337–8 for figures and references and Probert 2019: 40–4 for examples and discussion.

[36] For analysis of Iasucthan's metrical practice and its relationship to *carmina epigraphica* and Christian verse, see Adams 1999: 113–18 and Zeleny 2008: 75–8 for ample references to work on accentual Latin verse. For discussion and examples of other *carmina epigraphica* see Allen 1973: 346–7; of Commodian's versifying, Beare 1957: 242–7.

not read hexameter or any verse stressing the first element of every foot (i.e. the so-called ictus).[37] The dichotomy between 'stress-accent' and 'pitch-accent' languages, although maintained in many modern works on Greek and Latin prosody and metre, is now looking decidedly uncertain.[38] Better descriptions of the accentual systems of living languages reveal that languages once thought of as 'stress-accent' also use pitch as one of the ways to give prominence to a syllable; Probert shows that the Latin grammarians' description of the Latin accent, although using Greek terminology, is alive to the differences between the languages. What about the correlation between first position in the foot and word-accent in the last two feet of the hexameter? This can be explained by the rules for the assignment of Latin word-stress (the co-called law of the penultimate), which is sensitive to syllable weight, with the consequence that Latin word-stress and ictus will automatically align if stressed monosyllables and quadrisyllabic words are avoided at the end of the line. The increase in lines which show a correlation, from 92.8% in Ennius to 98.8% in Virgil, may reflect an avoidance of quadrisyllables and monosyllables as much as a desire to make sure that the audience recognises a hexameter rhythm.

The notion that the Greek metres are in some way at variance with the natural shape of Latin relies also on scholars' conception of what the saturnian actually is. The metre is attested in too small a number of lines to enable thorough analysis.[39] It is clear that later Roman grammarians, perhaps even some of its composers, did not understand its structure. The presence of alliteration and assonance in a number of saturnian lines called to mind the early metres used in Germanic verse, with some seeing parallels to Old Irish verse.[40] Parsons 1999 and Mercado 2012 have worked out schemata which explain the metre to be basically accentual, with two metra in each half line. Both schemata meet the possible objection, however, that

---

[37] The literature on this is enormous, with various different schools taken up in different national traditions (compare Fuhrer in this volume). For useful discussions see in particular Allen 1973: 341–6, Stroh 1990, Boldrini 1999: 22–4 and Zeleny 2008: 60–74. A final possible argument in favour of the effect of ictus on the pronunciation of verse might be found in Virgil's practice of *brevis in longo* scansions, which are more frequent at the first element rather than the second of a foot. Recent work by Thompson and Zair 2019 shows that this is not statistically significant, and the apparent preference for lengthening of short syllables in the first element of the foot may just reflect the constraints imposed by the hexameter form.

[38] Allen 1973 has been fundamental to many classicists working on ancient pronunciation, see for example Zeleny 2008: 32, even though Allen's phonological theories are now very outdated. See Probert's illuminating discussion based on more recent work on phonology (2019: 18–35).

[39] Mercado 2012: 56 counts 114 examples, of which 37 are attested epigraphically and so completely textually secure.

[40] Cole 1969 followed by e.g. Gasparov 1996: 69–70.

they would permit a large number of possible word-sequences to make the grade as a saturnian.[41]

The surviving record of Latin's Italic siblings, Faliscan, Oscan, South Picene and the rest, include inscriptions where the diction and word order suggest that the language is marked in some way, as was shown earlier in the case of the Paelignian priestess' epitaph. Could these texts be metrical as well? There have been several attempts to detect their underlying poetic forms and, indeed, to link their metres to the Latin saturnian or to other early Latin *carmina* such as the hymns of the Arval brethren or the Salian priests.[42] Possibly shared metrical patterns offer one approach to uncover a native Italic tradition of verse; another is to look for shared formulae and relate collocations found in early Latin poets to those attested in the scattered and scanty epigraphical remains of the speakers of Italic languages (such was the mission of Fisher 2014). These studies are still very much in their infancy, but in the absence of enough of the right sorts of texts for the comparison, it is unlikely that they have a flourishing life ahead of them.[43]

Even if we were confident that we could understand the saturnian metre perfectly, it would be unlikely to change the way we read and interpret the Latin metres borrowed from Greek. Whatever the earlier verse forms of the Romans were, the Greek metres, first adopted at a time when the Latin stress accent was itself undergoing changes, became fully naturalised in Latin. Caesar's soldiers composed verses for him in trochaic septenarii derived from a Greek model (Suet. *Iul.* 49, 51 and 80), but now fully Latinised; it is true that sometimes in these verses the stress and the verse beat collide perfectly, but in the others they do not.[44] Although the hexameter and other classical Latin metres were not 'native', they were not completely at variance with Latin phonological structures. Some features of Greek verse, such as the variation between short and heavy syllables before clusters with *l* and *r*, were not part of native Latin phonology, but could be assimilated without too much difficulty (see Sen 2015: 91). It is true that from the end of the first century CE, as changes affected the Latin system of accent and quantity, Latin versification became increasingly removed from the spoken language (as is shown by the attempts to

---

[41] This is a criticism Mercado makes of Parsons, although in his own analysis of early Latin prose samples there is also a high number of false positives (Mercado 2012: 203–5).
[42] The fullest recent attempt is given in Mercado 2012: 259–332, who gives abundant references to earlier work on the topic, see also Mercado 2018.
[43] See Farrell 2017 for a sceptical review of Fisher 2014: 'I believe that this book contains not a single dispositive, conclusive or irrefutable argument.'
[44] For discussion of these and other 'popular verses' see Beare 1957: 169–92.

write hexameters by Marcus Porcius Iasucthan, mentioned on p. 568). Yet in the late Republic and early Empire poets and audiences seem to have been remarkably adept at picking out different metres, with, as Morgan 2010 shows, an awareness of their associations.

## Standard Latin

When linguists approach the language of literary productions, they do so with an analytical framework which is largely based on the sociolinguistic concept of a standard language. Since the 1960s linguists have been better at finding ways to talk about linguistic norms, including those in their description of language. The notion of a standard language has become widespread in discussions of language variation and language history. A standard language is the term used to refer to the form of language that is viewed as correct by speakers and writers, bolstered by educational practices and with some form of official sanction.[45] When speakers and writers depart from the standard by using non-standard forms or expressions (for which a standard alternative is available), they may do so for various reasons. It may be that they have not received adequate education in the standard, reverting to usages of their native idiolect that they have not learnt to suppress or replace, or it may be a semi-conscious reaction against the standard, in order to assimilate to (or represent the speech of) a particular social group. For Latin, the standard language model seems to work well; it tallies to a certain extent with what ancient writers themselves seem to say about the Latin language. Take for example the earliest surviving definition of *Latinitas* as found in the anonymous *Ad Herennium*:

> Latinitas est quae sermonem purum conseruat ab omni uitio remotum. Vitia in sermone, quo minus is Latinus sit, duo possunt esse: soloecismus et barbarismus. soloecismus est, cum in uerbis pluribus consequens uerbum superiori non adcommodatur. Barbarismus est, cum uerbis aliquid uitiose efferatur. (4.17)

> It is Correct Latinity which keeps the language pure and free of any fault. The faults in language which can mar its Latinity are two: the Solecism and the Barbarism. A solecism occurs if the concord between a word and one before it in a group of words is faulty. A barbarism occurs if the verbal expression is incorrect. (text and translation after Caplan 1954: 269–71)

---

[45] The fundamental work on the rise of standard languages is Joseph 1987. For the application of the concepts of standard languages and standardisation to Latin, see Müller 2001, Clackson and Horrocks 2007, Clackson 2011a and 2015c.

The concerns of the author of the *Ad Herennium* about which forms are to be avoided and which to be used have already occurred in earlier surviving Latin authors, notably in surviving fragments of Lucilius, whose linguistic prescriptions included spelling rules and approved lexical usages.[46] Not much definite survives directly from the republican period, but since Lucilius' strictures were repeated by later grammarians,[47] it is likely that many other grammatical statements also reflect prescriptive rules of this date. Other statements about *Latinitas* and of linguistic usage in Rome usually follow the same paradigm that we see in the *Ad Herennium*, with the two overlapping categories of pure and fault-free (see the collection of material in Müller 2001). In the *Ad Herennium* faults are largely seen as syntactic, but their names (*soloecismus, barbarismus*) also show that they are considered impure. Late grammarians and other writers sometimes contrast usages characterised as *Latine* with those which are heard in speech or said by the *uulgus*.[48]

The ancient separation between approved, pure Latinity and the stigmatised, impure, barbarian or vulgar seems to reflect the same conceptual division that has been proposed by modern linguists between a standard language and non-standard varieties; linguists have consequently begun to speak about Classical Latin in the same terms as a standard language. Many works on the Latin language contrast Classical Latin with Vulgar Latin, a term which corresponds to the phrase *sermo uulgaris* which is attested already in Cicero (although not used in the modern sense) and which connects to the grammarians' stigmatisation of terms which are in use among the *uulgus*.[49] This picture is supported by the contrast between the speeches of the freedmen in Petronius' *Satyrica* and the surrounding narrative (and the speeches of other characters). However, opinions about the nature of Vulgar Latin are confused, with (*a*) some scholars using the term to refer to a social dialect of Latin, principally the speech of the uneducated, (*b*) others to refer to the ancestor of the Romance languages (assumed to be the direct descendent of the spoken language

---

[46] On Lucilius' grammatical and orthographic pronouncements, see Chahoud 2019; for wider discussion of his own language, see Pezzini 2018 and Poccetti 2018.

[47] Thus Lucilius' distinction between *intro* and *intus* (1215–17) is reprised by Quintilian (1.5.50) and the grammarian Charisius (Chahoud 2019: 62).

[48] See further Zetzel 2018: 49–55 for the intellectual context of the definitions of *Latinitas* given in the *Ad Herennium* and in other later republican writers, and Zetzel 2019 for particular consideration of the definitions of *Latinitas* attributed to Varro.

[49] For definitions of 'Vulgar Latin', see Väänänen 1981: 3–6, Herman 2000: 1–8 and Adams 2013: 3–22; my summary of different views of what constitutes Vulgar Latin by different scholars largely follows Adams.

of the lower classes and hence concomitant with (*a*)) and (*c*) some taking it to mean forms which are stigmatised by the grammarians or which are generally avoided in literary texts, although known through other sources to have been present in speech. Many writers on the Latin language, habituated by the discipline of linguistics to deal with hypothetical constructs, have been content to employ the term Vulgar Latin as a rather nebulous, abstract entity, a convenient fiction.[50] Even those who have generally avoided the term Vulgar Latin have often replaced it with other catch-all terms, such as 'sub-elite Latin', which are equally insubstantial.[51] There is, however, a growing recognition that there is not just one 'Vulgar Latin', but non-standard Latin comprised a range of varieties, across different areas and social groups, but also over time.

The concentration on the dichotomy between Classical and other types of Latin and the extension of the standard language model to the ancient world have perhaps led some linguists to accept without too much reflection the idea that there is a single, monolithic Classical Latin, which is generally used by literary authors. Variations within literary Latin are often seen to be cases of surface interference, either through generic or stylistic considerations, through influence from 'colloquial' or other types of language, or through a gradual adoption of diachronic changes into the literary language.[52] Of course, once anything which does not fit with the conception of a classical language has been explained away as a special case or a stylistic quirk of the author, the classical language will remain monolithic. The process of purifying the poets of barbarisms is one that has taken place continuously since the creation of the texts. The manuscript tradition of Catullus, which has *ait fuisse nauium celerrimum* at 4.2, shows just one example of this purification at work in the textual tradition (if this is not just banal assimilation to *nauium*). It is worth asking whether the standard language model is really so applicable to Classical Latin as it appears. Modern standard languages are reinforced by widespread or mass literacy, printing and mass reproduction of the written word and nearly universal education. Roman sources reveal that scholars and teachers were keen on the idea of purity of language and the avoidance of faults, but this ideology is not always played out at the level of texts. Adams 2013 has shown in detail how many writers, even the 'best authors', do not adhere to the

---

[50] Something recognised even by authors of books entitled *Vulgar Latin*: 'every generalisation made about Vulgar Latin ... is an abstraction' (Herman 2000: 8).
[51] See, for example, the index entry in Clackson and Horrocks 2007: 324 'Vulgar Latin: *see* Latin in late antiquity and the early middle ages, Proto-Romance, sub-elite Latin'.
[52] See the earlier discussion of the nominative and infinitive at Catullus 4.1–2 as an example.

grammarians' strictures (and, consequently, to the rules that appear in modern school grammars) as closely as might be expected. There was clearly considerable variation within what we think of as Classical Latin.[53] The calls for purity of language and the existence of debates about the nature of correct language tend to be taken at face value by linguists, but these need to be examined in their wider cultural and linguistic context. Judgements and statements about language are often not what they appear to be, but declarations of allegiance to or distance from other figures (compare Cicero's criticisms of Mark Antony's language in the *Philippics* – these are not really statements about language, but about power).[54] Other statements about linguistic choices, often transmitted to us stripped from their context, may have functioned differently at their time of utterance. For example, Gellius 1.10.4 attributes to Julius Caesar the statement *tamquam scopulum, sic fugias inauditum atque insolens uerbum* ('you should avoid the novel or unusual word as a mariner avoids a reef'), although Caesar's own vocabulary does contain words which are rare in attested Latin and which do not occur in surviving works before him (for example the Greek loans *hippotoxota* and *malacia*). Caesar's strictures may originally have been used against a political rival, rather than a statement of his own practice.[55] Linguists and classical scholars are starting to look more closely at the relationship between the strictures on language purity or style and the practices of authors in their own works, with closer attention to how ideas about language tie in with wider philosophical or cultural concerns of the age.[56]

## What Linguists Can Do for Literary Critics

The mechanism of human language has been likened to plumbing in a house (Sampson and Babarczy 2013: 300). Speakers rely on language to communicate, as home-owners rely on plumbing for their daily needs, but neither group needs to know how the system works in detail to enjoy the benefits; when everything is going well explanations are neither interesting nor necessarily welcome. Literary scholars are sometimes in the position of home-owners calling in the plumbers to fix a leak. For some observers,

---

[53] As also with later stages of Latin; see Stover in this volume.
[54] For citation and discussion of the passage (*Phil.* 3.22), see Clackson 2015a: 40.
[55] On Caesar's writings on language, see Pezzini 2017, with pp. 182–3 for the relationship between Caesar's own practice and his grammatical strictures.
[56] See, for example, Williams 2015 on Seneca, Chahoud 2016 on Varro, as well as Pezzini 2017 on Caesar.

linguists haven't even been that much help: 'up to now, linguistic evidence has enabled editors to invent unattested forms of archaic Latin to try making sense of passages garbled in transmission, but has not contributed much else' (Farrell 2017: 385). Farrell's caustic comment about the utility of linguists to the study of literature is of course directed at the supposedly meagre rewards from the scholarship into the prehistory and origins of Latin; presumably he would be more charitable about the support for Latinists from grammars and dictionaries and perhaps even from works on variation and sociolinguistics. In this section of the chapter I will look more closely at three areas in which work on linguistics might be consulted by literary critics (broadly: dictionaries, grammars and monographs or other studies dedicated to a particular topic of Latin linguistics) and give some indications about the benefits (and perhaps also perils) for the user.

### *Venus in the Lists: Latin Dictionaries*

Lexicographers are not the same as linguists, even though linguists may take employment as lexicographers while seeking university posts. The British linguist famous for his part in the decipherment of Linear B, John Chadwick, served on the staff of the *Oxford Latin Dictionary* before taking up a post in Classical Linguistics at Cambridge in 1952.[57] The editors of the *Oxford Latin Dictionary* were not chosen for their linguistic experience, but for a combination of qualities including lexicographic experience and 'character'.[58] Chadwick's own account of lexicographic method reflects the training he received from J. M. Wyllie, who in turn was trained by William Craigie, editor of the *Oxford English Dictionary* (Chadwick 1996: 5). Chadwick's description of lexicographic method is revealing:

> The lexicographer confronted by a pile of examples illustrating a particular word must begin by assuming that he does not know its meaning. He is thus in the same position as the cryptographer engaged in breaking a code-book. He must determine the meaning by reference to the context. If enough examples are available, he will in due course discover what meanings will fit all contexts; if some offer a wide range of possibilities, others will narrow it down, until a satisfactory definition emerges. (Chadwick 1996: 20)

[57] Henderson 2010: 146. In 1948, one of those involved in the *OLD* thought Chadwick 'our one safe man' (ibid. 165).
[58] Henderson 2010, Stray 2012.

The lexicographer is viewed almost as an impartial observer of the process as the definition 'emerges' from the material. The meanings of a word are seen as fixed, but unknown, much as the values of the Linear B signs were to modern scholars before the decipherment of Michael Ventris. It may take some clever deductive work to find a sense or a range of sense to fit all the different contexts, but that sense is 'discovered' rather than created by the lexicographer. In actual fact the lexicographer has a more active role in the process of creating a semantic framework in which to fit the attestations of a single word and plays a part in shaping the definition. Rather than cryptographer, a better analogy for the lexicographer is an art historian reconstructing an ancient fresco from a few fragments. While the surviving pieces could at first be interpreted as a boy gathering saffron, subsequent research might rearrange them to give a picture of a monkey cavorting among lilies.[59]

The dictionary accounts of the Latin word *Venus*, already encountered above, give some indications of the possible interpretations offered by lexicographers. Lewis and Short's dictionary[60] gives the following schema of meanings:

I. *the goddess of Love; the goddess Venus*
B. Transf.

    1. *Love, sexual love, venery*
    2. Like the Engl. *love*, to denote a *beloved object, beloved*
    3. *Qualities that excite love, loveliness, attractiveness, beauty, grace, elegance, charms*
    4. *The planet Venus*
    5. *The highest throw* at dice, when each of the dice presented a different number, *the Venus throw*.

Compare the outline of the *Oxford Latin Dictionary*, set out in condensed form:

1. A goddess of Italian origin, identified by the Romans with Aphrodite, the goddess of sexual love and generation . . .

    b. (transf. of a woman who inspires love in one).
    c. (in refs. to Julius Caesar . . .).

---

[59] The example is taken from the Gilliérons' initial restoration of a Minoan fresco in the palace of Knossos; see Chi, Herschman and Lapatin 2017: 19.
[60] Lewis and Short 1879, hereafter L&S; for its history and reception, see Stray 2012: x.

2. (applied to, or used in the names of var. things associated with the goddess Venus):

   a. The planet Venus . . .
   b. the best throw in dicing with *tali* . . .
   c. *aues -eris*, doves.
   d. *pecten -eris*, a plant . . .
   e. *-eris crines*, a precious stone . . .
   f. *portus -eris*, a harbour in Gallia Narbonensis . . .
   g. (see quot.).[61]

3. The quality of attracting sexual love, charm.

   b. (without sexual connotation) charm, grace.

4. Sexual activity or appetite, sexual intercourse; (pl.) amours.

   b. (among animals).

When seen side by side, even without the citations, the superiority of the *OLD* is immediately apparent. The *OLD* is clearer in its distinction of Venus as the goddess of sexual love, more accurate in its placement of the use of *Venus* for the beloved as a transferred employment of the goddess' name, rather than as a semantic extension of 'love'. The *OLD* gives a larger number of better citations (L&S do not cite a single example from Catullus, for example, whereas *OLD* cites 3.1 and 86.6), explaining them more cogently. The classical scholar's third principal source of dictionary reference, the *Thesaurus linguae Latinae*, has not yet reached V and cannot be compared with the *OLD* or L&S (nor would space allow it if the entry did exist!). Although conceived of and executed on a much larger scale than either of its rivals, the *TLL* is itself not free from errors or misleading statements, particularly in the earlier instalments.[62]

The *OLD* is by no means perfect. Its rather coy definition 'amours' under 4 is only exemplified by one line of Propertius (2.10.7) *aetas prima canat Veneres, extrema tumultus* (translated by G. P. Goold as 'Let a poet's first years sing of love, his last of conflicts'). As Goold's translation shows, *Veneres* in this passage need not signify 'amours' (or 'affairs'): 'love' or 'sex' seem equally plausible. Indeed, one could also take the word as an instance of *OLD* sense 1b 'his loves' or 3a 'charms', or indeed ask whether there is an

---

[61] A citation from Paul's epitome of Festus which explains the meaning of *Venus* in a fragment of Naevius (30a Warmington) to mean 'vegetables'.
[62] See Clackson 2016: 76 for an example of the *TLL*'s treatment of the Greek loanword *duas*.

allusion to Catullus 3.1. Does it make sense to nail down the meaning of *Veneres* in that particular line? As has been observed at least since Dr Johnson, wittily recapped by Henderson (2010: 141–3), word-meanings are inherently unstable and changing, perhaps particularly so in the language of poets. It is difficult to blame the editors of the *OLD* for decisions such as allocating a separate sense to *Veneres* in Propertius 2.10.7; the possible range of sense of a particular Latin word, particularly a culturally loaded term such as *Venus*, will inevitably be disputed as long as there are readers around to dispute.

The editors of the *OLD* should, however, be held to account for their neglect of the diachronic element in Latin lexical semantics. The Publisher's Note to the first edition of the *OLD* (Glare 2012: viii–ix) asks readers' indulgence for the chronological ordering of the senses and the brevity of the etymological notes. The impression is given that such things are distractions from the main business of the dictionary. As was noted on p. 572, explanations which rely on an appeal to Indo-European origins of Latin words or constructions are more likely to be taken up by students of early Greek poetry than by Latinists. The reasons for this are not difficult to find. The Greek epic tradition is attested much earlier than even the first very fragmentary Latin inscriptional texts; furthermore the oral transmission of verse means that some Greek poetic formulae might be even older. Hellenists who want to understand the compositional techniques of the Homeric bards cannot avoid some sort of confrontation with the fate of digamma and the dialectal array of ancient Greek, whereas even those studying Livius Andronicus and Ennius do not need to dirty their hands with the details of rhotacism or vowel weakening. To neglect the history, or indeed the prehistory, of a Latin word is, however, short-sighted.

The nature of the formation and composition of the vocabulary of Latin and Greek is one good reason to pay attention to word history. In Greek, as Clarke noted in an influential work on the Greek lexicon, 'the internal structure of the lexicon is strongly *associative*. Much of the basic word-stock falls into families of linked words which share a transparent relationship with each other' (Clarke 2010: 131). Greek γίγνομαι, γένος, γόνιμος, κασίγνητος, εὐγένεια (and dozens of other words) can be immediately recognised as related and all connected through a semantic core of 'birth' and reproduction. Etymologies accordingly play a significant part in scholarly accounts of the Greek literature and in the interpretation of Greek texts. The importance of etymology is enhanced if one follows the view, as set out in Clarke 2010 and Clarke 2019, that word-families of this type can be linked to a 'prototypical' sense of the underlying lexical root from which these forms all derive. The 'prototype' theory of meaning derives from cognitive approaches to linguistic categorisation, which suggest that humans relate possible different instantiations to a single prototypical concept.[63] An animal is judged as a 'dog', a colour as 'blue' or an emotion as 'anger' through reference to prototypical notions of what a dog is, what blue is and what behavioural traits constitute 'anger'.[64]

The Latin lexicon is, like that of Greek, associative, but the language has undergone changes which sometimes cloud the relationship between related terms; furthermore the Romans did not follow the Greek exuberance for forming compounds (except under the influence of Greek models).[65] Latin cognates to the Greek word family given above include *gigno*, *genus*, *(g)natus*, *natio* and *natura*, but the links between them are more difficult to unpick and sometimes the task may be made even more complicated for the non-expert by reference to an etymological dictionary. Consider, for example, the student of Catullus faced with the problem of *Veneres* in Catullus 3.1, who might turn to the most recent etymological dictionary of Latin, de Vaan (2008: 663). The entry reads as follows:

*Venus -eris* [f. r] 'goddess Venus, love, charm'
**Attestation:** (Naev.+; nom.sg. *CIL venos*)
**Derivatives:** *venustus* 'attractive, charming' (Pl.+), *venustulus* 'charming' (Pl.), *invenustus* 'unattractive' (Pl.+), *venustās* 'charm, grace' (Pl.+), *venerius* 'of Venus, erotic', *venerārī/e* 'to worship, pay homage' (Naev.+), *venerātiō* 'adoration' (Varro+).
**Reconstruction:** Proto-Italic wenos- [n.].
Proto-Indo-European *uenh₁-os [n.] 'desire'.
**Cognates:** Italic O. ϝενζηι [dat.sg.] f., borrowed from Latin.
Indo-European see s.v. *vēnor*.

The material is attractively set out, with the relationship to other words such as *uenustus* and *ueneror* made clear. The reader may recall the second line of Catullus poem 3, *et quantum est hominum uenustiorem*, which suggests that the association of words was still transparent to the ancient

---

[63] Work on cognitive theory has impacted on Classics more widely than in semantics, see for a recent collection of papers Meineck, Short and Devereaux 2019 and for bibliography the material available at https://cognitiveclassics.blogs.sas.ac.uk. I am grateful for this information to Michael Carroll, whose forthcoming book *Metaphor and the Creation of Meaning in Aeschylean Tragedy* will apply a cognitive framework to Aeschylean metaphor.

[64] For prototype semantics, see Rosch 1978, Taylor 2004, Geeraerts 2010. Geeraerts 1997 and Clarke 2010 show how prototype semantics can be applied to language diachrony. For applications to Latin, see Short 2013 and Short et al. 2016. Devine and Stephens 2012 is concerned with semantic properties for sentences, not lexical semantics.

[65] The reduction in productivity of compounding is shared with Latin's sibling languages of ancient Italy, see Heidermans 2002. For an attempt to argue that the influence of Greek on Latin compounding is overstated, see Whitehead 2011.

ear. The entry in de Vaan might perhaps inspire a desire to look into the Indo-European background, even to venture as far as the entry for *vēnor* (de Vaan 2008: 662). Here the origin of the verb is given as follows:

Proto-Italic wēn-o/ā- 'hunting' ≫ wēnā-je/o- 'to hunt'.
Proto-Indo-European *(H)u̯enh₁- / *(H)unh₁- 'desire'.

A longer list of cognate forms is supplied:

Hit. u̯en-*ᶻⁱ* / uu̯an- 'to copulate' < *h₁/₃uenh₁-; Skt. *vánate* (RV) [3s.med.], *vañchati* [3s.act.], aor. *vanáti* 'to love, desire', *vā́ má-* 'sweet, precious, noble, beautiful', YAv. *vaṇtā-* [f.] 'beloved one, wife'; (?) Alb. *ũ(n)* [m.] (Geg), *uri* [f.] (Tosk) 'hunger' < *un-; Go. *wens* 'hope' [i], OIc. *ván*, OE *wān* 'supposition, opinion' < *u̯enH-; OHG *wunscen* 'to wish'; Go. *winnan* 'to suffer', OIc. *vinna* 'to labour, overcome' < *u̯enh₁ -; ToA *wañi*, ToB *wīna* 'joy' < PIE *u̯ēnh₁ -, *unh₁ -.

and there is a paragraph of further discussion:

Probably a denominative verb to an adj. *wēno-* 'searching, hunting' or a noun *wēnā-* 'hunt', which must themselves be derivatives from a PIE root noun with a long vowel which is also seen (albeit thematised) in Germanic. The PIE root had final *-h₁ if the Hittite verb is cognate. Kloekhorst 2008: 999f. reconstructs an initial laryngeal, too, on the strength of the Hit. spelling *ú-*.

For the Indo-Europeanist, this material is gold-dust. There is full citation of cognate forms, which the expert will understand are linked through recognised correspondences with the Latin terms, showing the effect of successive waves of regular sound changes from the reconstructed parent. The list of cognates includes very welcome references not just to the Geg and Tosk varieties of Albanian, but also to Tocharian A and B (too often omitted in etymological dictionaries). Furthermore, the reconstruction of a potential PIE root noun with a long vowel (the so-called 'lengthened grade') is exciting.[66] The presence of a root-final and perhaps a root-initial laryngeal is important for the understanding of Italic sound changes from PIE.

The Latinist, on the other hand, may feel disappointed by de Vaan's learning. It is interesting that *uenor* is somehow connected to the name of Venus (a relationship that even ancient etymologists did not guess at, Maltby 1991: 635), but there is not enough guidance on how exactly this whole family

---

[66] The Indogermanische Gesellschaft held a three-day conference on 'The lengthened grade in Indo-European' in Leiden in July 2013.

of words are connected for someone who neither knows nor cares what a laryngeal is. Furthermore, there are some potentially misleading indications of the attestations of the word in the other languages of Italy. We are told that 'Proto-Italic' had a neuter noun wenos- [n.] and an adjective wēn-o/ā- 'hunting', from which a verb wēnā-je/o- 'to hunt' is derived, although the only other cognate given in any other language is the Oscan borrowing ϝευζηι from Latin (which is not translated).[67] The non-linguist might be forgiven for thinking that etymology has been little help in the search for a better understanding of the semantics of the Latin word Venus and is perhaps left uncertain about what this tells us about the Italic background to Roman religion.[68]

This conclusion would be unfortunate, since in fact Latin etymology can offer rewards, if you know where to look. Turn, for example, to the account of *Venus* given in Ernout and Meillet (1959: 721–2):[69]

1. l'amour physique, l'instinct, l'appétit ou l'acte sexuel ...
2. qualités qui excitent l'amour, grâce, séduction, charmes ...
3. personnifié et divinisé, *Venus* « déesse de l'amour » ... par suite « objet aimé comparable à Venus (fr. « déesse »), belle, amante »
4. coup de dès favorable.

Ernout and Meillet select 'sexual love' as the base meaning, since this has an exact correspondent in a Sanskrit word, *vanas-*, meaning 'desire' (as they detail later in the article). Ernout and Meillet reveal a wider Latin word family than even de Vaan, since they connect *uenenum* 'magical herb' or 'poison' (with an original sense of 'love potion'). Ernout and Meillet were not aware of, or did not mention, the Hittite, Albanian and Tocharian cognate forms, but their account can be enriched by including these words in the consideration of the original meaning, which can be assumed to have been something like 'sexual desire, sexual hunger'. This accounts for the erotic connotations of the word in the oldest surviving Indo-European languages, Hittite and Sanskrit. In languages attested later on, the sexual element seems to have given way to more general senses of longing and wanting. As Krostenko (2001: 40–51) has shown, Latin *uenustus*, derived from the original 'sexual desire' sense of the word *uenus*, also originally included an erotic element (not mentioned in the *OLD* entry s.v.), but, as

---

[67] Not everyone has agreed about the Latin origin of the Oscan ϝευζηι; for an alternative view, see Poccetti 2008. I am grateful to Nicholas Zair for bringing this article to my attention.
[68] See also Krostenko 2001: 40–2.
[69] See further Katz 2010: 34–5 for an assessment of de Vaan 2008.

it became a culturally charged term in the late Republic, the sexual connotations are sometimes downgraded or suppressed.

It is possible, following the lead of Clarke (2010), to attempt to capture some of the semantics of the Latin word *Venus* through a diagram (Figure 11.1). A representation of the prototypical semantics of a word might just consist of a circle around the prototypical concept, with arrows leading to instantiations. With the word Venus, I have suggested that the original prototypical meaning is 'sexual desire', but that one particular instantiation of this, as the deity associated with sexual desire, has become a new prototypical sense of the word.

Indeed, the association with a goddess has had the effect that it has changed the gender of the word from neuter to feminine, the gender appropriate for female beings and of other deities which arose from abstracts such as *Fides* and *Salus*.[70] The new prototypical meaning has pulled the earlier concept of 'sexual desire' along with it, so that the now feminine noun carries both senses, 'sexual desire' and 'goddess of Italian origin'. Ancient speakers of Latin did not have access to the history of the

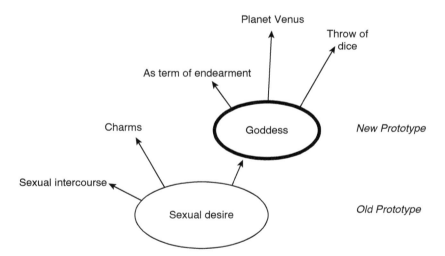

Figure 11.1 Semantic map of *Venus*.

---

[70] See Krostenko 2001: 40 n. 67, who offers the parallel of *Cupido*, originally a feminine noun which becomes a masculine deity; Corbeill 2015: 112 notes that the neuter noun *termen* gives rise to the male god *Terminus*.

language, so this etymological account was unknown to them, but it can help modern readers of Catullus to understand how the relationship between the abstract and personified senses of the word fit together. *Venus'* semantic range is much more akin to pairs such as *fides/Fides*, *spes/Spes* or *salus/Salus*, where modern editions helpfully mark off the divinity with a capital, than to the extended use of *Bacchus*, for example, to mean 'wine'. It is possible to look at Latin semantics without recourse to etymology, but giving space to etymology can lead to a richer appreciation of the language.

### Comparing Latin Grammars with Respect to the Accusative

Most scholars working on Latin texts will be aware of the advantages and disadvantages of the competing triad of Latin dictionaries, the *OLD*, L&S and the *TLL*. The comprehensive offering of the *TLL* makes it less easy for day to day use, the range and ease of access of L&S (especially through the web or in the form of the app) is offset by its inaccuracies and omissions. It is easy to carry across a similar approach to Latin grammars. In order to find out about the inflectional endings of nouns, verbs or pronouns readers can refer to Greenough et al. (1903), Gildersleeve and Lodge (1895), Kühner and Holzweissig (1912) or Neu and Wagener (1892–1905), depending on how much information is needed.[71] For syntax, there is a similar array of grammars – Greenough et al. (1903) and Gildersleeve and Lodge (1895) again, Hofmann and Szantyr (1965) and Kühner, Stegmann and Thierfelder (1966) – and two stand-alone works devoted just to syntax, Woodcock (1959) and Pinkster (2015). Woodcock's work styles itself as a 'New Latin Syntax', but its arrangement, labelling of categories and concerns largely follow the lead of earlier grammars. Pinkster (2015) follows his pioneering work *Latin Syntax and Semantics* (Pinkster 1990), which for the first time described Latin in a modern functional linguistic framework.[72]

Although, from a linguist's point of view, Pinkster's *Oxford Latin Syntax* avoids the excessive jargon of many current linguistic models (de Melo 2017: 405) this might be small comfort to readers who find themselves confronted with terms such as 'illocutionary force' or 'verb frames', which encode significantly different concepts than encountered in traditional

---

[71] Leumann 1977 and Weiss 2009 are excellent resources for the information they give on history and development of Latin.
[72] As discussed earlier, Pinkster's model of functional grammar privileges the use of language as a communicative tool.

grammars. Furthermore, most Latinists will find that it is not possible to find their way around Pinkster's syntax with the ease with which they can move between, say, Woodcock and Kühner–Stegmann. Gripes about the difficulty of finding topics or understanding Pinkster's new *Syntax* may to some extent be assuaged by the production of the second volume, which promises an even more copious index. There is, however, a fundamental problem that most, if not all, Latinists will have been taught using the precepts of traditional grammar and using textbooks which do not yet make use of the terminology of functional grammar. It is difficult to adopt a 'hit-and-run' approach to grammars such as the *Oxford Latin Syntax*, if you don't already know the jargon. Furthermore, given the speed with which different theories of syntax have risen and fallen since the advent of a paradigm of 'Universal Grammar' with Chomsky's *Syntactic Structures* (1957), it would be easy to forgive a sceptical approach to putting on the grammarian's new clothes too quickly.[73] The difficulty for literary scholars in dealing with the new generation of 'linguistically informed' works on Latin grammar again reveals the fundamental difference of their approach to the linguist. Whereas the linguist wants to know the landscape of Latin as a whole, the literary critic is often more interested in just getting from A to B.

To illustrate the changing nature of the grammatical framework in Pinkster (2015), let us consider another example from Catullus, from the description of Ariadne in poem 64, lines 64–5:

> non contecta leui uelatum pectus amictu,
> non terete strophio lactentis uincta papillas
>
> nor was her breast veiled by the covering of her light raiment, nor her milk-white bosom bound with the smooth girdle (trans. F. W. Cornish, revised by G. P. Goold)

The reader who encounters these lines may notice the accusative case of *pectus* and *papillas*, possibly with a vague memory of the 'accusative of respect'. Recalling the Greek construction of the *Phaselus ille* poem, an alert student may wonder whether this is another example of Greek influence on Latin syntax. Perhaps Gildersleeve and Lodge is nearest on the shelf and easiest to consult. A search in the index for 'accusative of respect' leads quickly to section 338: 'The Accusative of the object affected sometimes specifies that *in respect to which* the statement of a passive or intransitive

---

[73] Matthews 2001: 96–117 provides a useful overview of the development of Chomsky's thought and Universal Grammar.

verb, or an adjective, applies.'[74] That looks straightforward enough, but then the reader looks down the page to the following notes, which first explain the Greek origin of the construction, but next state: 'Different is the Accusative with **induor**, *I don*; **exuor**, *I doff*; **cingor**, *I gird on myself*, and other verbs of *clothing* and *unclothing*, as well as *passives*, where the Subject is also the Agent; in which verbs the reflexive or middle signification is retained. These uses are poetical or post-classical.' Which leaves the reader unsure whether the Catullus example belongs under the same heading or not and no wiser about whether it should count as a Greek influence or not. Woodcock provides a page on 'Poetic uses of the Accusative under the influence of Greek' (1959: 13–14), which gives three types: first, the accusative after adjectives; second, with passive participles and occasionally finite verbs, denoting the part of the body affected, as *femur tragula ictus*, 'struck in the thigh with a javelin'; and, third, after verbs of clothing, although the example given here is *indutus pallam* 'clothed with a robe'. The use of a verb of clothing with the part of a body in the accusative is not mentioned. Turn next to Kühner, Stegmann and Thierfelder, who devote six pages (1966: 1 285–92) to 'der Akkusativ der Beziehung (unter griechischem Einfluß)'. Here there is a careful grouping of a large number of examples, including the citation of the phrase 'terete strophio lactentes *uincta* papillas'.[75] The Catullan passage is classed under the section of verbs of adornment, crowning, cloaking and covering and their opposites, construed with the accusative of the part of the body. The grammar seems most interested in whether the verb in these constructions should be classed as 'Middle' or 'Passive' (the latter, apparently) and it remains unclear to what extent this is to be classed as 'griechischer Einfluß'.

Let our hypothetical and by now bemused student now take the plunge into Pinkster. There is no comforting chapter on 'the uses of the accusative', so the first point of call is the index. Under 'accusative case', the first appropriate entry is *accusativus Graecus*, which directs the reader to three separate pages (244, 267 and 1076); a little further down 'Greek accusative' gives two other pages, 242 and 264. Chasing up these references, the intrepid scholar finds the Catullus passage cited on page 266, in the section 'Verbs in the autocausative passive governing an accusative object'. Here 'autocausative' is a new term which refers to verbs 'used when the subject is to some extent actively engaged in the process in which it is involved (as

---

[74] Gildersleeve and Lodge 1895: 215 (emphasis original).
[75] Kühner, Stegmann and Thierfelder 1966: 1 289, at 4b; the reference is given as 'Catull. 64.64 ff'.

a patient)' (260). We are also told that the autocausative is often referred to as a middle. Clothing is clearly an example of such a process; Ariadne would herself have fastened her breasts in a bra. Pinkster tells us that the Catullan example is 'in all likelihood a literary extension: in this type of expression the body or body-part functions as the object of the autocausative passive form' (265), giving a reference to the still useful account in Coleman (1975). Those still with strength might further discover another section of Pinkster, 'The use of nouns and noun phrases in the accusative as respect adjuncts' (915–17), embedded in Chapter 10, entitled 'Satellites', which deals with 'the use of the accusative for the part of the body that is affected by some action or process'. In this section we find examples such as Lucretius' *tremit artus* 'trembles in his limbs' (3.489) and Virgil's *picti squalentia terga lacerti* 'lizards spangled on their scaly backs' (*Georgics* 4.13), which look to be closer to the Greek accusatives of respect (and which the exhausted reader might just remember from their occurrence in Woodcock 1959: 13).

The journey through Pinkster's *Syntax* might leave a few literary critics feeling that they have gained an insight into the complexity of the constructions which they had thought of as 'accusative of respect' and are now better able to make distinctions between accusatives of body parts after autocausative passives and 'true' respect accusatives. They are now able to compare and contrast accusatives of respect with other ways to form 'respect adjuncts' in Latin (which Pinkster shows is the best categorisation of certain ablative phrases, prepositional phrases and adverbs) while tracking the rise and fall of constructions over the life of the language. Others might feel that they have eventually found a rather muted positive answer to the original question about possible Greek influence. A third group might have first looked at Fordyce's long note on these lines of Catullus (1961: 287), where many of the same citations found in the grammatical works occur (grammars are no less tralaticious than commentaries). Fordyce states:

> This poetic idiom probably had a native origin in the use of the verb in the middle voice (expressing an origin done in relation to the agent himself) with a direct object . . . In *contecta pectus, vincta papillas*, and similar phrases, the object is a part of the agent's own body . . . the participial 'middle' idiom seems to have become confused with a much wider poetic use taken from the Greek, that of the 'accusative of respect', with verbs, active or passive, and adjectives.

Fordyce's account is certainly superior to that of Kühner, Stegmann and Thierfelder.[76] It seems to cover the same ground as Pinkster and makes the

---

[76] 'Of course he is sloppy and wilful, but Fordyce could wind up getting *something* dead right about Catullus' (Henderson 2010: 109).

same careful distinction between accusative after the middle (Pinkster's 'autocausative') and other accusatives of respect, perhaps more clearly showing the way a native Latin construction could have become muddled and extended in poetic language with Greek influence. In this instance 'hit-and-run' readers may have gained as much, possibly more, from looking at a commentary than Pinkster or indeed any of the Latin grammatical works, but the grammars still have the edge for giving the overview of the entire system.

## The Sociolinguistics of Vowel Lengths

Linguistic studies of Latin have enjoyed an extraordinary flourishing in the twenty-first century. Consider the number of books devoted to linguistic topics which have received reviews in the *Journal of Roman Studies*: in the 1990s only four were reviewed, in the 2000s eleven and in the years from 2010 to 2015 a further ten. This does not of course exactly reflect the number of books written, but it does indicate the growth in the subject and its impact upon Latin studies more widely. Among the books written on linguistic topics since the year 2000 it is worth drawing especial attention to the substantial contributions of J. N. Adams,[77] which have opened up new avenues of research, even beyond the confines of Latin linguistics.

The recent work on aspects of Latin grammar, pronunciation and the sociolinguistics of spoken and written language have revealed quite how much we now know about Latin. For a demonstration of what we can do with this work, consider another short passage from Catullus, two lines of which appear to contain a representation of speech. At Catullus 10.25–6 the following words are put into the mouth of Varus' girlfriend, who is described as a *scortillum* ... *non sane inlepidum neque inuenustum* ('a bit of a whore, not completely unamusing nor unsexy') at 10.2–3. Her utterance, coming after Catullus' boast that he has his own sedan chair, is introduced in the preceding line by the comment *ut decuit cinaediorem*, literally 'as suited someone more like a *cinaedus*', translated 'like the shameless hussy she was' by Cornish (revised Goold).

> 'Quaeso,' inquit, 'mihi, mi Catulle, paulum
> istos commoda: nam uolo ad Serapim
> deferri.'

---

[77] In particular the monumental quartet Adams 2003a, 2007, 2013 and 2016. Note also that many shorter studies, such as Adams 2003b and 2003c, have had widespread influence.

'Please,' says she, 'dear Catullus, do lend me those slaves you speak of for a moment, for I want to be taken to the temple of Serapis.' (trans. F. W. Cornish, adapted)

Although there is only a small amount of direct speech represented in Catullus (discounting the inset speeches in the longer poems and the complete poems in the voice of a character), much recent work on various aspects of the Latin language helps to assess the tone of this speech: is it, to use Nisbet's terms (1978: 94) 'absurdly peremptory' or 'silkily imperious' (or indeed, neither of these)? We can now consult works on Latin terms of address (Dickey 2002), on Latin requests and politeness formulae (Risselada 1993, Dickey 2012a and 2012b) and on the representation of the speech of women (Adams 1984, Barrios-Lech 2016), even on Latin particles (Kroon 1995), all of which go some way towards providing an answer. A literal translation of *quaeso* followed by an imperative might give the impression that the speech is peremptory or imperious but comparison with other Latin texts shows that the imperative is used in requests by those who have no power (not even that of sexual allure) over the addressee. In Cicero's letters *quaeso* is attached more frequently to requests to intimate acquaintances than to others, and it is therefore appropriate to translate it as 'please' in context. The use of a polite modifier ('please') and the personal pronoun with the vocative are both appropriate markers of female speech (although none of these features is exclusive to the speech of women, indeed, in comedy *quaeso* is more frequently placed in the mouths of men). The particle *nam* can also be shown to be more at home in direct speech than in narrative.

However, the feature of these lines that has most attracted the attention of textual critics is the scansion of the imperative *commoda* as a dactyl.[78] Imperatives in the Latin first conjugation have long vowels and the shortening of final long vowels in words of this shape is unexpected.[79] The history of final long vowels in Latin is quite complicated; we have already seen that over the history of the language long vowels, when not under the accent, were perceived as short, thus allowing Iasucthan to hear a hexameter ending in collocations such as *augustani fecerunt* and *parato magistro*. We also know that the distinction made in Latin between long and short vowels in any position in the word was lost in the later history of

---

[78] See Nisbet 1978: 93–4, Dominicy 2015: 630–2. I assume that *commoda* is not here a neuter plural of the adjective *commodus*, which would probably require a corresponding change to *quaeso* to *quaero* in the preceding line, as Nisbet 1978: 94 suggested.

[79] See n. 33 for discussion of Allen's claim (1973: 339) that Roman hearers did not distinguish final vowel length.

the language, as can be seen from study of the Romance languages.[80] In disyllabic words with light first syllable, long final vowels were shortened already by the time of Plautus through a diachronic process known sometimes as *brevis brevians* or iambic shortening. This is why the Latin word for 'I', *ego*, has a short final vowel in contrast with its Greek cognate ἐγώ.[81] In scansion of Plautus and Terence, it is still possible to find differences between for example *amo* 'I love' (scanned with short final *o*) and *dīcō* 'I say' (scanned as a spondee). By the end of the Republic analogy to other, non-iambic forms has restored a long final vowel to most verbs in the first person singular present, and to the nominative singular of nouns, although it is still possible to find, for example, *homo* for *homō* 'human' in Lucretius (6.652) and *scio* (and *nescio*) are regularly scanned with a short final vowel in Latin verse. In the imperial period, shortenings of final vowels start to spread no matter what the shape of the word, so that Propertius can scan *findo* as a trochee (3.9.35) and Seneca can place *uincendo* in the first position of a iambic line (*Troades* 264). All of these examples show the shortenings of final *o*, where there was little possibility of confusion between different morphological forms. In contrast, short and long final *a* make a difference to meaning in first declension nouns, with a correspondingly greater pressure to keep the short and long vowel distinct. The grammarian Sacerdos, writing in the second half of the third century CE, implies that shortening of the final vowel of *causā* is a feature of the speech of the uneducated;[82] this provides the first unequivocal example of the loss of distinctive vowel length in final *a*.

Catullus' scansion of *commodā* with short final *a* consequently stands out in literary works that survive in manuscript.[83] Could it be a very early example of vowel shortening at the end of a word? Is it possible that Catullus has represented the loose woman as using loose 'colloquial speech', as some commentators have suggested?[84] There is a lack of parallels

---

[80] Loporcaro's recent book (2015) on vowel shortenings in Latin and the Romance languages pays comparatively little attention to the late Latin situation, but others have made up the gap; for example, Mancini 2019 deals with the difficult question of the interpretation of the grammarians' comments on vowel length.

[81] For a quick synopsis of iambic shortening see Weiss 2009: 126–8; for a lengthy discussion Fortson 2008: 176–258.

[82] *GL* VI 493.20–6, with discussion in Leppänen and Alho 2018: 472; the passage is not mentioned in Mancini's 2019 survey. For a useful summary of the shortenings of vowel length in final syllables across the history of Latin, see Adams 2013: 49–50.

[83] In Plautus words of cretic shape sometimes show shortening of a final vowel when in passages of anapaests (Questa 2007: 99–100), but it seems unlikely that Catullus would have extended this metrical licence.

[84] For references to possibly colloquial features in poem 10 as a whole, see a doubtful Jocelyn (1999: 360–7).

in contemporary 'literary' poetry, but in the epigraphic record it is possible to find similar phenomena in the century following Catullus. Consider the following elegiac couplet from Pompeii, *CIL* IV 1516 (= *CLE* 955):

> hic ego nu[nc f]utue formosa(m) fo[r]ma puella(m)
>     laudata(m) a multis, set lutus intus erat.[85]
>
> I just fucked a girl here, shapely in her shape, praised by many, but on the inside she was mud.

The parallel between the vowel shortening on the street wall and in the speech of the louche woman is intriguing. Varus' girlfriend doesn't shorten the final vowels of *quaeso* or *deferri*, but the disappointed Pompeiian punter also keeps a long vowel in a final open syllable of the first person singular verb *futui*.[86] It would not be unlikely that some speakers varied their speech, sometimes preserving an etymologically long vowel in final syllable, sometimes shortening it. Without further examples closer in time to Catullus, it would be a bold linguist who ruled definitively on the question of whether this is a specific example of linguistic characterisation. The issue does, however, show some of the possible avenues for future study.

## New Corpora and the Linguist

I have already stressed in this chapter the importance of the search for parallels in linguistic research; the construction and availability of electronic databases of Latin have changed the field dramatically. Anyone reading through journals of over a century ago is struck by the amount of space given to the publications of parallels to the meanings of a word or the incidence of a grammatical construction, information which is now available almost instantly from a number of different online corpora and databases.[87] There is a smaller, but rapidly growing, amount of Latin text available in electronic form with grammatical tagging attached, which

---

[85] To scan the first line, the final syllable of the ablative *forma* must be scanned short. An adjacent verse, *CIL* IV 1517, has its first line *hic [ego] nu(n)c futue(i) formosam fo[.]e puellam*, leading Buecheler to suggest *forte* (restored in *CIL*'s text) also in this verse (*CLE* 955 ad loc.).
[86] Here written *futue*, with the outcome of the original diphthong *ei* represented by *e*, a spelling attested already in the late third century BCE. For discussion of this spelling in the imperial period see Adams 2007: 442–3 and Zair in press.
[87] Examples include the Perseus Digital Library (www.perseus.tufts.edu, currently (December 2022) with ten million words; see Bamman and Crane 2008), the Latin Library (www.thelatinlibrary.com, with eighty-seven million words), the Library of Latin Texts (www.brepols.net, with more than 150 million words) and the Bibliotheca Teubneriana Latina (www.degruyter.com, with over thirteen million words).

shows the syntactic relationship between all the words in a text.[88] It is possible now not just to call up all instances of a Latin word (in all its inflected forms), but also to find all examples of gerundives in Cicero's letters to Atticus, or all subordinate clauses in the Vulgate. Linguists now pay attention to frequency of usage in a way that was rare a hundred years ago – witness the reliance on statistics to describe tenses, pronouns and case usage in Pinkster (2015) and the use of text corpora to analyse stylistics (Passarotti and Cantaluppi 2016), to track language change in very different ways (e.g. Danckaert 2017, McGillivray 2014, Pezzini 2016) or to make numerous other investigations into the Latin language. The last published collection of papers from the biennial Colloquium on Latin Linguistics (Poccetti 2016) contained thirteen papers reliant on statistical analyses of some kind on corpora of Latin data. The availability of quantitative data for Latin, which can be mapped, manipulated and tested with statistical tools for correlations or abnormalities, further feeds into the linguist's self-identification as a scientist. It can also give false confidence in the statistical results, particularly when care is not taken to consider the nature of the texts from which the evidence is taken, or the framework in which the data is initially analysed.

As an example, consider a recent investigation into the loss of long and short vowels in republican Latin recently undertaken by Giovanna Marotta, on the basis of a new database of Latin inscriptions (Marotta 2015). As we have seen in the discussion of the scansion of *commoda* at Catullus 10.25, the distinction between long and short vowels would eventually be lost in Latin. As vowel length ceased to be distinctive, short and long vowels merged. In most varieties of spoken Latin, an original short *i* merged with long *e* and an original short *u* merged with long *o*. The results of this can be seen in modern Romance languages such as Italian, where the continuation of Latin *pira* 'pear', *pera*, rhymes with the continuation of Latin *sēra* 'late', *sera*, with the meaning shifted in Italian to 'evening'.[89] In Marotta's survey, a new corpus of republican inscriptions was examined in an attempt to detect the first occurrences of these changes. The conclusion reached suggested that mergers between short *i* and long *e*, short *u* and long *o*, had already taken place in some spoken registers during the republican period, on the basis of written forms such as *fece* for *fecit* and

---

[88] Examples include the Latin Dependency Treebank (Bamman and Crane 2006; 53,000 words), the *Index Thomisticus* Treebank (Passarotti 2007; 138,000 words) and the PROIEL Project treebank (Haug and Jøndal 2008; 90,000 words). See further McGillivray and Kilgarriff 2013.

[89] See most recently Leppänen and Alho 2018 on these changes and the extensive discussion in Adams 2013: 37–70.

*pocolom* for *poculum*, which were interpreted as the efforts of poorly educated speakers confusing the vowels (Marotta 2015: 56). The claim is supported by statistics culled from the corpus, shown to be significant using chi-squared tests (ibid. 47–8). If this were right, we would then be in a stronger position to argue that Catullus might really be imitating everyday speech by shortening the final vowel of *commoda*. Here, however, the statistics are misleading, since the spellings Marotta takes to be innovatory are generally understood in fact to represent more archaic forms, maintained in script through archaic spelling practices.[90] The inclusion of percentages and numbers of occurrences is not enough to prove a theory.

## Conclusion: Literary and Linguistic Approaches

It would be in the nature of surveys of the kind of this chapter to call at the end for a closer engagement between linguists and literary critics, with a plea to open up a mutual dialogue between the two constituencies. This might, however, imply that there is a larger gap between linguists and literary scholars than really exists. It is no longer possible to write that 'textual critics, philologers and literary critics shake their fists at each other from opposite sides of a channel, over which as a rule they do not adventure', as Postgate did over a hundred years ago (1908: 3, probably with his tongue in his cheek). It is true that in some countries and some universities there have been, and still are, historical divisions in the departments where linguists and literary scholars work, but the gradual attrition of the academic posts devoted to Latin studies has had the effect of forcing those that remain into a closer unity. Few early career scholars in Classics can now afford the luxury of being seen to be too partisan. In this chapter I have deliberately used the term 'linguist' not 'philologist', because it would have been less easy to attribute the attitudes I have described to a philologist (not least because of a transatlantic confusion about what philologists are). Several Latinists have comfortably straddled any divide that there is between linguistic and literary research and would be proud to be described as working in sense 1 of the *OED*'s definition of philology, 'Love of learning and literature; the branch of knowledge that deals with the historical, linguistic, interpretative, and critical aspects of literature; literary or classical scholarship.' Bob Coleman, my own supervisor, published extensively on Latin linguistics and also wrote a 'Green and Yellow'

---

[90] Leppänen and Alho 2018: 466. On the archaising spellings and changes to Latin vowels in the middle to late Republic, see Weiss 2009: 116–24.

on Virgil's *Eclogues*; indeed, it is possible to call to mind several other scholars, several younger than me, who move comfortably between textual editing, criticism and linguistic research.[91] Some literary critics have followed the recent 'linguistic turn' in cultural studies.[92] Literary scholars have also made and continue to make important contributions on aspects of the Latin language. Most linguists working on a Latin author or text will at least look up what the commentators say about its interpretation, just as most literary scholars will consult grammars and secondary literature to understand a Latin usage.

At the same time, the discipline of linguistics itself is becoming more and more fissiparous. If linguists do not shake their fists at literary critics from opposite sides of a channel, it might be because the syntacticians are too busy moaning about their colleagues the phonologists, or the historical linguists are trying to avoid talking to the pragmaticians. The silos set up between the sub-departments of linguistics are maintained even among Latinists. The publication of the proceedings of the seventeenth Colloquium on Latin Linguistics (Poccetti 2016) has already been mentioned; the fifty-four papers in the volume range from syncope to generative syntax, from prehistory to the Renaissance, with a diversity of approach and linguistic framework that are bewildering even for the trained linguist. There are more jobs in linguistics departments than Classics departments, with many of the early career scholars in Latin trying to show that they are also good optimality theorists or evolutionary phonologists, minimalist syntacticians or followers of LFG. On closer inspection some of the work done in these fields may explain the same phenomena in different ways, sometimes appearing more appropriate for advancing a general theory than the knowledge of Latin. Spevak (2010: 2–6) surveys work on Latin word order under the headings 'the traditional approach', 'the typological approach', 'the generative approach' and 'the pragmatic approach' (the last of which subsumes 'functional grammar').[93] Here perhaps we might find the linguist's equivalence for the literary scholar's penchant for studies entitled 'interpretation', since these different traditions really do offer 'interpretations' of largely congruent sets of data according to the theoretical orientations of their authors.

There will always be some literary scholars who, whether through their own aptitude or as a reflection of their training, will be more predisposed to

---

[91] Names available from the author on request.
[92] For example Krostenko 2001, Farrell 2001 and Corbeill 2015.
[93] The most recent work on Latin word order, Devine and Stephens 2019, combines a generative syntactic approach with pragmatics.

including linguistic material in their reading about Latin and others who will fight shy. Despite the encouragements of reviewers, perhaps few literary scholars will read through the entirety of Pinkster's *Latin Syntax* or Adams on bilingualism, regionalism or social variation, but that does not mean these works are neglected, any more than the fact that few will read through the entirety of Ellis, Bährens or Fordyce on Catullus indicates that these are ignored. Of course, work which relies heavily on a theoretical framework or which abounds in neologisms and technical vocabulary is likely to be avoided by any but the in-group, whether it concerns Latin phonology or syntax on one hand, or post-structuralist approaches on the other. The academic world is witnessing increasing specialisation and a rapid growth of publications coupled with a diminishing level of grammatical training and knowledge. The luxury of studying or working in an environment where it is possible to walk down the corridor and knock on the door of an 'expert' willing to spend fifteen minutes to advise on the best recent account of the gerund is something that fewer people enjoy (if indeed anyone still does). There is a corresponding growth in works which attempt to make some of the linguistic advances more accessible to the non-linguist.[94] Once the literary specialist realises the different ways in which linguists frame their arguments and their different aims, they might find some things of use and possibly also of interest.

## References

Adams, J. N. (1984) 'Female speech in Latin comedy', *Antichthon* 18: 43–77.
   (1999) 'The poets of Bu Njem: language, culture and the centurionate', *JRS* 89: 109–34.
   (2003a) *Bilingualism and the Latin Language*, Cambridge.
   (2003b) 'Petronius and new non-literary Latin', in J. Herman and H. Rosén, eds., *Petroniana: Gedenkschrift für Hubert Petersmann* (Heidelberg), 11–23.
   (2003c) '"*Romanitas*" and the Latin language', *CQ* 53: 184–205.
   (2007) *The Regional Diversification of Latin 200 BC–AD 600*, Cambridge.
   (2013) *Social Variation and the Latin Language*, Cambridge.
   (2016) *An Anthology of Informal Latin 200 BC–AD 900*, Cambridge.
Adams, J. N. and R. G. Meyer, eds. (1999) *Aspects of the Language of Latin Poetry*, Oxford.
Adams, J. N. and N. Vincent, eds. (2016) *Early and Late Latin: Continuity and Change*, Cambridge.

---

[94] See, for example, Janson 2004, Ostler 2007, Clackson and Horrocks 2007, Katz 2010, Clackson 2011a, Oniga 2014, Leonhardt 2013, Clackson 2015a, Ringe 2018.

Allen, W. S. (1973) *Accent and Rhythm: Prosodic Features of Latin and Greek: a Study in Theory and Reconstruction*, Cambridge.
　(1978) *Vox Latina: A Guide to the Pronunciation of Classical Latin*, 2nd edn, Cambridge.
Ash, R. (2002) 'Between Scylla and Charybdis? Historiographical commentaries on Latin historians', in Gibson and Kraus 2002, 269–94.
Bährens, E. (1885) *Catulli Veronensis liber*, volumen alterum, Leipzig.
Bamman, D. and G. Crane (2006) 'The design and use of a Latin dependency treebank', in J. Hajič and J. Nivre, eds., *Proceedings of the Fifth International Workshop on Treebanks and Linguistic Theories (TLT 2006)* (Prague), 67–78.
　(2008) 'Building a dynamic lexicon from a digital library', in *Proceedings of the 8th ACM/IEEE–CS Joint Conference on Digital Libraries (JCDL 2008)*, Pittsburgh.
Barnes, T. (2016) 'Veneres Cupidinesque', unpublished handout from paper delivered at the 35th East Coast Indo-European Conference, Athens, GA, 6–8 June 2016.
Barrios-Lech, P. (2016) *Linguistic Interaction in Roman Comedy*, Cambridge.
Beare, W. (1957) *Latin Verse and European Song: A Study in Accent and Rhythm*, London.
Boldrini, S. (1999) *Prosodie und Metrik der Römer* (trans. from Italian original by Bruno W. Häuptli), Stuttgart and Leipzig.
Boyce, B. (1991) *The Language of the Freedmen in Petronius' Cena Trimalchionis*, Leiden.
Breed, B. W., R. Wallace and E. Keitel, eds. (2018) *Lucilius and Satire in Second-Century BC Rome*, Cambridge.
Butrica, J. L. (2007) 'History and transmission of the text', in M. B. Skinner, ed., *A Companion to Catullus* (Malden, MA), 13–34.
Calboli, G. (2009) 'Latin syntax and Greek', in P. Baldi and P. Cuzzolin, eds., *New Perspectives on Historical Latin Syntax. 1: Syntax of the Sentence* (Berlin), 65–193.
Caplan, H. (1954) *[Cicero] Rhetorica ad Herennium*. Cambridge, MA.
Chadwick, J. (1996) *Lexicographica Graeca: Contributions to the Lexicography of Ancient Greek*, Cambridge.
Chahoud, A. (2016) 'Varro's Latin and Varro on Latin', in R. Ferri and A. Zago, eds., *The Latin of the Grammarians: Reflections about Language in the Roman World* (Turnhout), 15–31.
　(2019) 'Lucilius on Latin spelling, grammar, and usage', in Pezzini and Taylor 2019, 46–78.
Chi, J., R. Herschman and K. D. S. Lapatin (2017) *Restoring the Minoans: Elizabeth Price and Sir Arthur Evans*, Princeton and Oxford.
Clackson, J. (2011a) 'Classical Latin', in Clackson 2011b, 236–56.
　(2015a) *Language and Society in the Greek and Roman Worlds*, Cambridge.
　(2015b) 'Subgrouping in the Sabellian branch of Indo-European', *TPhS* 113: 4–37.
　(2015c) '*Latinitas*, Ἑλληνισμός and standard languages', *SSL* 53: 309–30.

(2016) 'The language of a Pompeian tavern: submerged Latin?', in Adams and Vincent 2016, 69–87.
(2017) Review of Pinkster 2015, *BMCRev* 2017.12.43.
Clackson, J., ed. (2011b) *A Companion to the Latin Language*, Malden, MA.
Clackson, J. and G. Horrocks (2007) *The Blackwell History of the Latin Language*, Malden, MA.
Clarke, M. J. (2010) 'Semantics and vocabulary', in E. J. Bakker, ed., *A Companion to the Ancient Greek Language* (Oxford), 119–33.
  (2019) 'Looking for unity in a dictionary entry: a perspective from prototype theory', in C. Stray, M. Clarke and J. T. Katz, eds., *Liddell and Scott: The History, Methodology, and Languages of the World's Leading Lexicon of Ancient Greek* (Oxford), 247–67.
Cole, T. (1969) 'The Saturnian verse', *YClS* 21: 1–74.
Coleman, R. G. G. (1975) 'Greek influence on Latin syntax', *TPhS* 74.1: 101–56.
  (1999) 'Poetic diction, poetic discourse and the poetic register', in Adams and Meyer 1999, 21–93.
Corbeill, A. (2015) *Sexing the World: Grammatical Gender and Biological Sex in Ancient Rome*, Princeton and Oxford.
Cornish, F. W., J. P. Postgate, J. W. Mackail and G. P. Goold (1988) *Catullus, Tibullus, Pervigilium Veneris*, 2nd edn, Cambridge, MA.
Crawford, M. C., et al. (2011) *Imagines Italicae*, London.
Croft, W. (2000) *Explaining Language Change: An Evolutionary Approach*, London.
Danckaert, L. (2012) *Latin Embedded Clauses: The Left Periphery*, Amsterdam.
  (2017) *The Development of Latin Clause Structure*, Oxford.
De Melo, W. D. C. (2017) Review of Pinkster 2015, *JRS* 107: 405–7.
Devine, A. M. and L. D. Stephens (2006) *Latin Word Order: Structured Meaning and Information*, Oxford.
  (2012) *Semantics for Latin*, Oxford.
  (2019) *Pragmatics for Latin: From Syntax to Information Structure*, Oxford.
Dickey, E. (2002) *Latin Forms of Address: From Plautus to Apuleius*, Oxford.
  (2012a) 'The rules of politeness and Latin request formulae', in P. Probert and A. Willi, eds., *Laws and Rules in Indo-European* (Oxford), 313–28.
  (2012b) 'How to say "please" in Classical Latin', *CQ* 62: 731–48.
  (2012c) *The Colloquia of the Hermeneumata Pseudositheana. Vol. 1*, Cambridge.
Dominicy, M. (2015) 'Catulliana', *CQ* 65: 628–54.
Ellis, R. (1876) *A Commentary on Catullus*, Oxford.
  (1889) *A Commentary on Catullus*, 2nd edn, Oxford.
Ernout, A. and A. Meillet (1959) *Dictionnaire étymologique de la langue latine. Histoire des mots*, 4th edn, Paris.
Farrell, J. (2001) *Latin Language and Latin Culture*, Cambridge.
  (2017) Review of Fisher 2014, *CR* 67: 385–7.
Ferri, R. (2011) 'The language of Latin epic and lyric poetry', in Clackson 2011b, 344–66.
Fisher, J. (2014) *The Annals of Quintus Ennius and the Italic Tradition*, Baltimore.
Fordyce, C. J. (1961) *Catullus: A Commentary*, Oxford.

Fortson, B. (2008) *Language and Rhythm in Plautus: Synchronic and Diachronic Studies*, Berlin and New York.
  (2017) 'The dialectology of Italic', in J. S. Klein, B. D. Joseph, M. Fritz and M. Wenthe, eds., *Handbook of Comparative and Historical Indo-European Linguistics. Vol. 2* (Berlin and Boston), 836–58.
Forsyth, P. Y. (1986) *The Poems of Catullus: A Teaching Text*, Lanham, MD.
Gale, M. (forthcoming) *Catullus*, Cambridge.
Gasparov, M. L. (1996) *A History of European Versification*, Oxford.
Geeraerts, D. (1997) *Diachronic Prototype Semantics*, Oxford.
  (2010) *Theories of Lexical Semantics*, Oxford.
Gibson, R. (2015) 'Fifty shades of orange: Cambridge Classical Texts and Commentaries', in Kraus and Stray 2015b, 346–75.
Gibson, R. and C. S. Kraus, eds. (2002) *The Classical Commentary: History, Practices, Theory*, Leiden.
Gildersleeve, B. L. and G. Lodge (1895) *Gildersleeve's Latin Grammar*, 3rd edn, London.
Glare, P. W. (2012) *The Oxford Latin Dictionary*, 2nd edn, Oxford.
Greenough, J. B., G. L. Kittredge, A. A. Howard and B. L. D'Ooge (1903) *Allen and Greenough's New Latin Grammar for Schools and Colleges*, revised edn, Boston and London.
Harris, R. (2000) *Rethinking Writing*, London.
Haug, D. T. T. and M. L. Jøndal (2008) 'Creating a parallel treebank of the old Indo-European Bible translations', in *Proceedings of Language Technologies for Cultural Heritage Workshop (LREC 2008)* (Marrakech), 27–34.
Heidermans, F. (2002) 'Nominal composition in Sabellic and Proto-Italic', *TPhS* 100: 185–202.
Henderson, J. (2006) *'Oxford Reds': Classic Commentaries on Latin Classics*, London.
  (2010) 'A1-ZYTHUM: DOMIMINA NUSTIO ILLUMEA, or out with the *OLD*', in Stray 2010, 139–76.
Herman, J. (2000) *Vulgar Latin* (trans. R. Wright), Pennsylvania.
Hermann, G. (1799) *Handbuch der Metrik*, Leipzig.
Hinds, S. (1998) *Allusion and Intertext: Dynamics of Appropriation in Roman Poetry*, Cambridge.
Hock, H. H. (1991) *Principles of Historical Linguistics*, 2nd edn, Berlin and New York.
Hofmann, J. B. and A. Szantyr (1965) *Lateinische Grammatik Bd. 2. Lateinische Syntax und Stilistik*, Handbuch der Altertumswissenschaft: Abt. 2, T. 2, Bd. 2, 3rd edn, Munich.
Horrocks, G. (2011) 'Latin Syntax', in Clackson 2011b, 118–43.
Janko, R. (1992) *The Iliad: A Commentary. Vol. IV: Books 13–16*, Cambridge.
Janson, T. (2004) *A Natural History of Latin*, Oxford.
Jocelyn, H. D. (1999) 'The arrangement and the language of Catullus' so-called polymetra with special reference to the sequence 10–11–12', in Adams and Meyer 1999, 335–75.

Joseph, J. E. (1987) *Eloquence and Power: The Rise of Language Standards and Standard Languages*, London.
Katz, J. T. (2003) Review of Krostenko 2001, *CPh* 98: 193–9.
  (2010) '*Nonne lexica etymologica multiplicanda sunt?*', in Stray 2010, 25–48.
Konstan, D. (2014) 'Catullus', *Oxford Bibliographies*, www.oxfordbibliographies.com.
Kraus, C. S. (2002) 'Introduction: reading commentaries/commentaries as reading', in Gibson and Kraus 2002, 1–28.
Kraus, C. S. and C. Stray (2015a) 'Form and content', in Kraus and Stray 2015b, 1–18.
Kraus, C. S. and C. Stray, eds. (2015b) *Classical Commentaries: Explorations in a Scholarly Genre*, Oxford.
Kroll, W. (1968) *C. Valerius Catullus herausgegeben und erklärt*, 5th edn, Stuttgart.
Kroon, C. (1995) *Discourse Particles in Latin: A Study of nam, enim, autem, vero and at*, Amsterdam.
Krostenko, B. A. (2001) *Cicero, Catullus, and the Language of Social Performance*, London and Chicago.
Kühner, R., and F. W. Holzweissig (1912) *Ausführliche Grammatik der lateinischen Sprache. Bd. 1. Elementar-, Formen- und Wortlehre*, Hannover.
Kühner, R., C. Stegmann and A. Thierfelder (1966) *Ausführliche Grammatik der lateinischen Sprache. Teil 2. Satzlehre*, 4th edn, Hannover.
Labov, W. (1972) 'Some principles of linguistic methodology', *Language in Society* 1: 97–120.
Leaf, W. (1902) *The Iliad. Edited with Apparatus Criticus, Prolegomena, Notes, and Appendices. Vol. 11: Books XXIII–XXIV*, 2nd edn, London.
Leiwo, M. (2010) 'Petronius' linguistic resources', in E. Dickey and A. Chahoud, eds., *Colloquial and Literary Latin* (Cambridge), 281–90.
Leonhardt, J. (2013) *Latin: Story of a World Language* (trans. K. Kronenberg), Cambridge, MA.
Leppänen, V. and T. Alho (2018) 'On the mergers of Latin close-mid vowels', *TPhS* 116: 460–83.
Leumann, M. (1977) *Lateinischen Laut- und Formenlehre*, 5th edn, Munich.
Lewis, C. T. and C. Short (1879) *A Latin Dictionary: Founded on Andrews' Edition of Freund's Latin Dictionary*, Oxford.
Löfstedt, E. (1956) *Syntactica. Studien und Beiträge zur historischen Syntax des Lateins. 1. Über einige Grundfragen der lateinischen Nominalsyntax. 11. Syntaktisch-stilistische Gesichtspunkte und Probleme*, 2nd edn, 2 vols., Lund.
Loporcaro, M. (2015) *Vowel Length from Latin to Romance*, Oxford.
McDonald, K. (2015) *Oscan in Southern Italy and Sicily: Evaluating Language Contact in a Fragmentary Corpus*, Cambridge.
McGillivray, B. (2014) *Methods in Latin Computational Linguistics*, Leiden.
McGillivray, B. and A. Kilgarriff (2013) 'Tools for historical corpus research, and a corpus of Latin', in P. Bennett, M. Durrell, S. Scheible and R. J. Whitt, eds., *New Methods in Historical Corpus Linguistics*, Tübingen.
Maltby, R. (1991) *A Lexicon of Ancient Latin Etymologies*, Leeds.

Mancini, M. (2019) 'The use of the past to explain the past: Roman grammarians and the collapse of quantity', in M. Cennamo and C. Fabrizio, eds., *Historical Linguistics 2015: Selected Papers from the 22nd International Conference on Historical Linguistics, Naples, 27–31 July 2015* (Amsterdam), 28–51.

Marotta, G. (2015) 'Talking stones: phonology in Latin inscriptions', *SSL* 53: 39–63.

Martzloff, V. (2016) 'Les quantificateurs latins *omnis* et *omnes*: origine et grammaticalisation', in Poccetti 2016, 378–94.

Matthews, P. (2001) *A Short History of Structural Linguistics*, Cambridge.

Maurach, G. (1995) *Lateinische Dichtersprache*, Darmstadt.

Meineck, P., W. M. Short and J. Devereaux, eds. (2019) *The Routledge Handbook of Classics and Cognitive Theory*, Abingdon and New York.

Meiser, G. (2003) *Veni Vidi Vici. Die Vorgeschichte des lateinischen Perfektsystems*, Munich.

Mercado, A. O. (2012) *Italic Verse: A Study of the Poetic Remains of Old Latin, Faliscan and Sabellic*, Innsbruck.

  (2018) 'From Proto-Indo-European to Italic meter', in D. Gunkel and O. Hackstein, eds., *Language and Meter* (Leiden), 253–66.

Merrill, E. T. (1893) *Catullus*, Boston.

Morgan, L. (2010) *Musa pedestris: Metre and Meaning in Roman Verse*, Oxford.

Müller, R. (2001) *Sprachbewußtsein und Sprachvariation im lateinischen Schrifttum der Antike*, Munich.

Neu, C. F. and C. Wagener (1892–1905) *Formenlehre der lateinischen Sprache*, 4 vols., Berlin and Leipzig.

Nisbet, R. G. M. (1978) 'Notes on the text of Catullus', *PCPhS* 24: 92–115.

Oniga, R. (2014) *Latin: A Linguistic Introduction* (trans. from Italian original by N. Schifano), Oxford.

Ostler, N. (2007) *Ad infinitum: A Biography of Latin*, London.

Palmer, L. P. (1954) *The Latin Language*, London.

Parsons, J. (1999) 'A new approach to the Saturnian verse and its relation to Latin prosody', *TAPhA* 129: 117–37.

Passarotti, M. (2007) 'Verso il lessico Tomistico biculturale. La treebank dell'*Index Thomisticus*', in R. Petrilli and D. Femia, eds., *Il filo del discorso. Intrecci testuali, articolazioni linguistiche, composizioni logiche. Atti del XIII Congresso Nazionale della Società di Filosofia del Linguaggio* (Viterbo), 187–205.

Passarotti, M. and G. Cantaluppi (2016) 'A statistical investigation into the corpus of Seneca', in Poccetti 2016, 684–706.

Pezzini, G. (2016) 'Comic lexicon: searching for submerged Latin from Plautus to Erasmus', in Adams and Vincent 2016, 14–46.

  (2017) 'Caesar the linguist: the debate about the Latin language', in L. Grillo and C. B. Krebs, eds., *The Cambridge Companion to the Writings of Julius Caesar* (Cambridge), 173–92.

  (2018) 'Lucilius and the language of the Roman *palliata*', in Breed, Wallace and Keitel 2018, 162–83.

Pezzini, G. and B. Taylor, eds. (2019) *Language and Nature in the Classical Roman World*, Cambridge.
Pinkster, H. (1990) *Latin Syntax and Semantics*, London and New York.
  (2015) *The Oxford Latin Syntax. Vol. 1: The Simple Clause*, Oxford.
Poccetti, P. (2008) 'Notes de linguistique italique. Nouvelle serie. 5. Une nouvelle inscription osque et le nom de *Venus*', *REL* 86: 24–36.
  (2018) 'Another image of literary Latin: language variation and the aims of Lucilius' Satires', in Breed, Wallace and Keitel 2018, 81–131.
Poccetti, P., ed. (2016) *Latinitatis rationes: Descriptive and Historical Accounts for the Latin Language*, Berlin and Boston.
Postgate, J. P. (1908) 'Flaws in classical research', *PBA* 3: 1–54.
Probert, P. (2019) *Latin Grammarians on the Latin Accent: The Transformation of Greek Grammatical Thought*, Oxford.
Ringe, D. (2018) *An Introduction to Grammar for Language Learners*, Cambridge.
Risselada, R. (1993) *Imperatives and Other Directive Expressions in Latin: A Study in the Pragmatics of a Dead Language*, Amsterdam.
Rix, H. (2002) *Sabellische Texte. Die Texte des Oskischen, Umbrischen und Südpikenischen*, Heidelberg.
Rosch, E. (1978) 'Principles of categorization', in E. Rosch and B. B. Lloyd, eds., *Cognition and Categorization* (Hillsdale, NJ), 27–48.
Questa, C. (2007) *La metrica di Plauto e Terenzio*, Urbino.
Quinn, K. (1970) *Catullus: the Poems*, London.
  (1973) *Catullus: the Poems*, 2nd edn, London.
Sampson, G. and A. Babarczy (2013) *Grammar without Grammaticality: Growth and Limits of Grammatical Precision*, Berlin.
de Saussure, F. et al. (1985 [1916]) *Cours de linguistique générale*, critical edition by T. de Mauro, Paris.
Schulze, K. P. (1882) 'Zu Catullus', *Neue Jahrbücher für Philologie und Pädagogik (Jahrbücher für classische Philologie)* 125: 205–14.
Schwyzer, E. (1903) 'Varia zur griechischen und lateinischen Grammatik 3. Veneres Cupidinesque', *IF* 14: 28–31.
Sen, R. (2015) *Syllable and Segment in Latin*, Oxford.
Short, W. (2013) 'Latin *de*: a view from cognitive semantics', *ClAnt* 32: 378–405.
Short, W. et al., eds. (2016) *Embodiment in Latin Semantics*, Amsterdam and Philadelphia.
Spevak, O. (2010) *Constituent Order in Classical Latin Prose*, Amsterdam.
  (2014) *The Noun Phrase in Classical Latin Prose*, Leiden and Boston.
Stray, C. (2012) 'The *Oxford Latin Dictionary*: a historical introduction', in Glare 2012, x–xvii.
Stray, C., ed. (2010) *Classical Dictionaries: Past, Present and Future*, London.
Stroh, W. (1990) 'Arsis und Thesis, oder: Wie hat man lateinische Verse gesprochen?', in M. von Albrecht und W. Schubert, eds., *Musik und Dichtung: Neue Forschungsbeiträge, Viktor Pöschl zum 80. Geburtstag gewidmet* (Frankfurt), 87–116.
Taylor, J. R. (2004) *Linguistic Categorization*, 3rd edn, Oxford.

Thompson, R. J. E. and N. Zair (2019) 'Irrational lengthening in Vergil', *Mnemosyne* 74: 577–608.
Thomson, D. F. S. (1997) *Catullus, Edited with a Textual and Interpretative Commentary*, London.
de Vaan, M. (2008) *Etymological Dictionary of Latin*, Leiden.
Väänänen, V. (1981) *Introduction au latin vulgaire*, 3rd edn, Paris.
Wackernagel, J. (1877) 'Zum homerischen Dual', *Zeitschrift für vergleichende Sprachforschung auf dem Gebiete der Indogermanischen Sprachen* 23: 302–10. Reprinted in J. Wackernagel, *Kleine Schriften* I (Göttingen, 1953), 538–46.
Weiss, M. (2009) *Outline of the Historical and Comparative Grammar of Latin*, Ann Arbor, MI.
  (2017) 'An Italo-Celtic divinity and a common Sabellic sound change', *ClAnt* 36: 370–89.
Whitehead, B. N. (2011) 'The alleged Greek influence on Latin compounding: theoretical and applied perspectives in comparative grammar', in R. Oniga, R. Iovino and G. Giusti, eds., *Formal Linguistics and the Teaching of Latin*, Newcastle, 215–25.
Willcock, M. M. (1984) *The Iliad of Homer. Edited with Introduction and Commentary. Vol.* II: *Books* XIII–XXXIV, Bristol.
Williams, G. (2015) 'Style and form in Seneca's writing', in S. Bartsch and A. Schiesaro, eds., *The Cambridge Companion to Seneca* (Cambridge), 135–49.
Woodcock, E. C. (1959) *A New Latin Syntax*, London.
Zair, N. (in press) 'Old-fashioned spelling in the Roman Empire', in V. Belfiore, E. Dupraz and T. Roth, eds., *Writing Conventions and Pragmatic Perspectives*.
Zeleny, K. (2008) *Itali Modi. Akzentrhythmen in der lateinische Dichtung der augusteischen Zeit*, Wiener Studien Beiheft 32, Vienna.
Zetzel, J. E. G. (2018) *Critics, Compilers and Commentators: An Introduction to Roman Philology, 200 BCE–800 CE*, Oxford.
  (2019) 'Natural law and natural language in the first century BCE', in Pezzini and Taylor 2019, 191–211.

CHAPTER 12

# Latin Literature and Material Culture
## Michael Squire and Jaś Elsner

The decision to include a chapter on 'material culture' in a *Critical Guide to Latin Literature* bears witness to a fundamental truth: without 'material culture' there would be no 'Latin literature' to speak of.[1] The study of Latin is predicated on a series of physical survivals. Sometimes, albeit comparatively rarely, Latin texts are transmitted on scraps of ancient papyrus rolls or early parchment codices.[2] More often, they are preserved through Carolingian, later mediaeval and Renaissance manuscripts – that is, by scribes who copy a text from one material context to another, thereby providing a principal source for later printed editions.[3] At other times, Latin texts come to us via epigraphic means[4] – whether inscribed as grand monumental declarations in stone, marble or metal (consider Augustus' *Res gestae*, which survives only epigraphically),[5] or else as wholly

---

[*] The authors would like to thank both the anonymous readers and also the two wholly non-anonymous editors for all their suggestions on earlier drafts of this chapter. We are also grateful to the other contributors to this volume for giving us so much to think about during the first airing of the chapter during a workshop at Emmanuel College, Cambridge in May 2018. Last but not least, we thank the dedicatee of the book at large: for his kindness, and above all intellectual inspiration. Both of us owe John Henderson more than we could ever convey.

[1] For a recent championing of the point, see Petrovic 2019. At the same time the decision signals a shift towards a more material-centred account of literature in classical studies and more widely. On this so-called 'material turn', see especially Miller 2005, Bennett 2010 and Miller 2013; for related work in the field of classics, see e.g. Porter 2011, Platt 2016 and 2018 (with more detailed bibliography) and Gaifman and Platt 2018 along with the other chapters in Gaifman, Platt and Squire 2018. Fundamental is the work of Platt forthcoming.

[2] Bagnall 2009 offers a wide-ranging introduction to papyrology; on the form of the 'ancient book', see especially Johnson 2009, along with pp. 632–52 here. For a database of extant fragments of ancient bookrolls, papyrus codices and parchment codices (dating from the fourth century BCE to eighth century CE), see the Leuven Database of Ancient Books founded by William Clarysse in 1998 (www.trismegistos.org/ldab/): of the 16,506 items 2,162 are in Latin.

[3] Cf. Kaster and Huskey in this volume.

[4] The thirty-five essays in Bruun and Edmondson 2015 now offer an excellent guide; cf. e.g. Schmidt 2004, Lassère 2011 and Cooley 2012.

[5] See e.g. Cooley 2009; specifically on the inscriptional nature of the *Res gestae*, cf. Elsner 1996a. One might compare here whole corpora of epigrams that are preserved through the archaeological record – not least the

more humble graffiti.[6] Our opening list could be extended. But the central point remains: the study of Latin – however 'philological' or 'literary critical' our approach – is necessarily grounded in the material realm.

As we explore in this chapter, the physical objects that mediate Latin texts form just part of the contribution that material culture makes to Latin literature, and vice versa. Still, it seems right to begin with the materiality of Latin texts because this aspect is so easily overlooked. In disciplinary terms, Latin language and literature are often studied in isolation from the 'stuff' of the Roman material world: there is a residual tendency to conceptualise (and abstractify) Latin texts in 'purely' literary terms – to think of literary works as Oxford Classical Texts, Teubners or Loebs in the library, for example, or to equate inscribed Roman objects with the taxonomised entries of the *Corpus inscriptionum Latinarum* (where Latin inscriptions are systematically stripped from the material objects that mediate them).[7] Here the delineation of Latin literature as a self-standing field of academic enquiry has gone hand in hand with the rise of separate disciplinary specialisations. When it comes to the study of Latin, as with the study of Greek, texts are conventionally the preserve of classical philologists. Material remains, by contrast, are dispensed – some would say relegated – to the field of classical archaeology.[8]

---

epigraphic poetry of Damasus of Rome in the fourth century CE (cf. Trout 2015). Courtney 1995 provides a useful anthology and translation of selected Latin epigraphic poems (with introductory survey of earlier corpora at pp. 7–10), albeit without illustration of the materials included; crucial here is the *Carmina Latina epigraphica* (*CLE*), stemming back to an anthology by Franz Bücheler and Ernst Lommatzsch (for a historiographic and bibliographic survey, see Schmidt 2015: esp. 769–71).

[6] On the importance of this material within the study of Latin philology and linguistics, see Clackson in this volume. Ancient graffiti have spurred a particularly lively bibliography in recent years: e.g. Benefiel 2010 and 2016; Baird and Taylor 2012; Sears, Keegan and Laurence 2013; Keegan 2014; Benefiel and Keegan 2016; Petrovic, Petrovic and Thomas 2019. Particularly important within the study of Latin literature has been the contribution of graffiti to an understanding of Roman 'literary culture' and the early reception of Latin authors like Ovid and Virgil: e.g. Gigante 1979, Franklin 1991 and Milnor 2014; cf. Liddell and Low 2013.

[7] For the complaint, compare e.g. Koortbojian 1996: 317, n. 8; Hope 1997: 251; Blanshard 2007: 20–1. On the way in which 'any serious effort to make ancient poetry legible ... must reconstruct, at least in part, its material effort as written text', see e.g. Butler 2011 (quotation from p. 5), along with Butler 2002, and the fundamental contribution of Habinek 2009. More generally on the history of the *CIL* and other epigraphic corpora, see Bruun 2015.

[8] On the disciplinary history of classical archaeology (and various disciplinary takes about its future), see e.g. Snodgrass 1987 (focussed on Greek materials), Shanks 1996, Sichtermann 1996: esp. 9–27, and Dyson 2006; cf. most recently Lichtenberger and Raja 2017, Nevett and Whitley 2018. Von den Hoff 2019: 9–43 offers one of the most scintillating recent introductions to the field, at least as practised and envisioned in Germanophone countries; Millett 2007 offers a solid introduction from a specifically Roman perspective (and with a view to the subject as practised in the UK). One might compare here chapters in this volume on the sub-disciplinary relationships between the study of Latin literature and ancient history (Lavan), linguistics (Clackson) and philosophy (Volk).

## 12 Latin Literature and Material Culture

In the UK, at least, those specialising in Roman material and visual culture usually share an institutional home with scholars of Latin language and literature:[9] they are most often housed in collective departments of 'Classics'. Yet despite studying the same timeframe ('Roman antiquity'), and for all the similarity in historical topics, there is still relatively little cross-fertilisation between critical approaches, questions and working methods. Those charged with interpreting the Roman material record have certainly looked to literary materials, most often raiding ancient texts for titbits of contextualising historical information. Consider how Latin sources have informed understandings of individual 'artists' in the Graeco-Roman world,[10] for example, or how literary texts have structured scholarly approaches to the Roman house (not least the domestic displays of visual materials in the late Republic and early Empire).[11] By the same token, extracted sources have helped to direct historical approaches to the archaeology of the Roman villa;[12] ever since August Mau and his pioneering work in the late nineteenth century, moreover, scholars have devised a whole system for analysing the 'Four Styles' of Pompeian wall-painting on the basis of a single passage of Vitruvius.[13] The problem here is not the absence of

---

[9] On different national frameworks, see Fuhrer in this volume. For discussions of the disciplinary status quo of classical archaeology in Britain, cf. Elsner 2007a, with further comments and bibliography in Squire 2011: 372–81. Those varying institutional frameworks are important. In Germany, for example, the study of Klassische Archäologie is formally segregated from Klassische Philologie, and fields like epigraphy and numismatics are the traditional reserve of Alte Geschichte: for overviews of the disciplinary history, see above all Marchand 1996, along with Sichtermann 1996: esp. 9–27, Hölscher 2002: esp. 11–15, 73–5, and von den Hoff 2019: esp. 10–11. On Francophone traditions, see Lissarrague and Schnapp 2000. On the history of classical archaeology in North America, see e.g. Dyson 1998: while it is true that, in the USA, as opposed to the UK, specialists in Roman art and archaeology more often belong to art history as opposed to Classics (or else have dual appointments), many of the same disciplinary tensions recur (cf. e.g. Donohue 2003: esp. 4: 'The study of ancient art exists uneasily in a disciplinary no-man's land. Within art history it holds a marginal position; within textually based disciplines it is seen as irrelevant; and within many forms of archaeology it is variously condemned as effete, exclusive, destructive, or simply lacking validity').

[10] Consider here a recent project like Kansteiner et al. 2014, albeit structured around 'Greek' rather than 'Roman' artists (and revising Overbeck 1868; cf. Squire 2015d). For 'sources and documents' on 'the art of Rome', see Pollitt 1983, along with e.g. Becatti 1951 and Chevallier 1991.

[11] For the importance of texts in approaching the art and archaeology of the Roman house, see e.g. Wallace-Hadrill 1994: 3–16, Hales 2003: esp. 11–93, Nevett 2010: esp. 19–21 and Bergmann 2012. Cicero's letters to Atticus have been particularly influential on scholarly approaches to the selection and display of sculptural subjects within the home: fundamental is Marvin 1993; cf. e.g. Neudecker 1988: esp. 8–18; Bounia 2004: 290–306; Bravi 2012: 21–7; Rutledge 2012: 59–64.

[12] For an-up-to-date survey, see now the essays in Marzano and Métraux 2018b, esp. Marzano and Métraux 2018a and Rothe 2018.

[13] Cf. Mau 1899: 466–74 on Vitr. *De arch.* 7.5, along with Mau 1882. Among countless discussions (each with further bibliography), see e.g Stewart 2004: 74–92, Platt 2009: 51–7 and Lorenz 2015. One might compare here the range of literary discussions that have informed scholarly approaches to the historical functions, display contexts and representational choices of Roman sculpted portraiture (cf. e.g. Lahusen 1983 and 1985; Pékary 1985; cf. also Fejfer 2008).

scholarly intersection between the work of archaeologists and Latinists. In so far as this chapter has a polemic, rather, it is that research into Latin literature and Roman material culture has tended to focus on matching up historical details rather than shared cultural history: there has been insufficient critical reflection about points of collusion and coalescence, and a lazy reliance on (sub)disciplinary boundaries no longer fit for purpose.[14]

The problem is further exacerbated by the variety of fields encompassed within the 'material culture' of our title. Now, to speak of 'Latin literature' is itself to talk in broad-brush terms – across a large chronological span and broad geography, but also across a wide range of literary genres and forms, which in turn nurture different sorts of working methods. For all its diversity, however, Latin literature is still defined around a common language.[15] The situation with Roman material culture is rather more complex. Quite apart from the difficulties of defining the 'Roman',[16] the term circumscribes a wholly miscellaneous range of extant physical remains, and from across the vast geographical expanse of the Roman Empire: it encompasses not only objects housed in museums and galleries (including those heralded as 'art'),[17] but also – among other things – excavated sites and buildings, and for that matter the data of archaeological field survey and geophysics. In many cases, those who study Roman culture consequently find themselves nursing multiple – and sometimes divergent – disciplinary loyalties. While often housed in departments of Classics, scholars of Roman material culture would sometimes label themselves 'archaeologists' or 'art historians' first

---

[14] Cf. Squire 2022. The argument has sometimes been made that this institutionalised 'parallel world' of classical archaeology and classical philology is rooted in the cultural horizons and practices of Graeco-Roman antiquity: see e.g. Small 2003: 27–8, arguing that 'the dominant pattern [in antiquity] is one of artists and writers pursuing independent and parallel worlds with only occasional intersections'. For one recent foray into the relevance of 'images' for 'classicists', see Coleman 2015, with Squire 2013d.

[15] This is not to deny the contested areas of overlap between Greek and Latin literary traditions – the place of Greek in a 'Roman' world where even a Roman emperor like Marcus Aurelius or Julian might choose to write in Greek rather than Latin: cf. Goldhill in this volume.

[16] The quintessential 'Romanness' of Roman material culture (and of Roman art in particular) has long been contested. The debates owe much to key disciplinary figures such as Johann Jakob Bernoulli, Alois Riegl, Franz Wickhoff and Ranuccio Bianchi-Bandinelli. Ultimately, though, they descend from the legacy of Johann Joachim Winckelmann, who defined 'Roman' art in terms of its aesthetic inferiority to the 'Greek'. For an introduction and bibliographic survey, see Elsner 2004; cf. e.g. Brendel 1979 (adapted from an article first published in 1953); Kampen 2003; Stewart 2004: esp. 2–4; Brilliant 2008; Marvin 2008: esp. 2–9; Hallett 2015. The important point to emphasise is that, despite a strong disciplinary impetus to segregate the two (especially in the Anglophone world), distinctions of 'Greek' and 'Roman' material culture do not align with the classical philological paradigms of segregating Greek language and literature from the Latin (cf. Squire 2011: 372–5, with reference also to different national traditions).

[17] For an introduction to the disciplinary tussles between 'art history' and 'archaeology' in the field of Roman material culture, cf. Squire 2011: 375–7 (with further bibliography). More generally on the delineation of 'art' as a meaningful category of historical analysis when it comes to both Greek and Roman antiquity, see the essays in Platt and Squire 2010, with further comments in Platt and Squire 2017a.

and foremost. Some might go still further. Given that many specialists come – and increasingly so – from academic backgrounds other than that of Classics, it is perhaps inevitable that the study of Latin literature is at times deemed secondary, if not alien, to their day-to-day research. Indeed, if Latinists define themselves around mastery of a language and its literature, a number of specialists in Roman material culture might seem in danger of appearing wholly peripheral to that field: in the twenty-first century, training in Roman material culture does not always involve knowledge of Latin. Crowded curricula – not to mention ever-expanding bibliographies and areas of scientific method – mean that, when it comes to training the next generation, choices about paedagogical priority must always be made: how to balance learning Latin grammar, for example, against a working understanding of geophysical survey.

By exploring just some of the tensions, parallels and points of contact between the study of Latin literature and Roman material culture, our aim in this chapter is to survey – and to challenge – this status quo. Rather than focus on the contribution of literary texts to the study of Roman art and archaeology,[18] our concern here is with the role of material culture within Latin studies (broadly conceived). Why should scholars of Latin language and literature concern themselves with ancient objects? How might the study of Roman physical remains inform an understanding of Latin prose and poetry? Can an understanding of Roman material culture learn from Latin texts, or does too close a disciplinary affiliation risk a 'text-hindered' approach (whereby the evidence of written sources ends up obfuscating rather than illuminating the study of material and visual forms)? How, in short, should we hope to balance these different perspectives? And with a view to broader issues of working method, in what ways do scholarly attitudes towards Roman material remains align with – or indeed deviate from – disciplinary approaches to interpreting Latin language and literature?

In navigating these and other questions, the discussion that follows will integrate a variety of both 'literary' and 'material' case studies, and across an extensive chronological span (broadly speaking, from the late Republic to the fourth century CE – but also including late antiquity, with reference to issues of Carolingian and mediaeval reception). We will look, along the way, to a plurality of Latin texts, in prose and verse alike. But we will also be examining a miscellany of material media – among them, wall-paintings, mosaics, free-standing statues, sculptural reliefs and manuscripts.

To furnish our survey with a concrete structure, we have organised the chapter around seven interconnecting topics. The first section begins by

---

[18] For one overview here, see Squire 2022.

returning to the materiality of Roman texts, introducing the picture-poems of one particular late antique writer by way of an example ('Texts and objects'). Our opening case study leads to cultural ideas about words and images in the Roman world ('*Vt pictura poesis?*'), and not least to the artefactual nature of manuscripts in both roll and codex ('The matter of the page'). Late antique 'illustrated' manuscripts – in particular, parchment codices that feature tables, frontispieces and miniature depictions, thereby transforming written script into knowing visual apparition, for a variety of practical and interpretive ends – also introduce a topos that recurs in the three sections that follow: namely, the rhetorical phenomenon of 'ecphrasis', premised on the idea of exploiting language to summon up a figurative sight for a hearing or reading audience. While ecphrasis has been much discussed in recent years ('Reading as seeing'), we argue, scholars remain reluctant to look across landscapes of art and text: there is a residual blindness to what we label the 'cyclical' dynamics between visual and verbal media in the Roman world ('Ecphrastic circles'). The point leads to a broader analysis of words and images displayed in a shared environment, as well as some of the conceptual underpinnings in Roman rhetoric ('Rhetorical juxtapositions'). By way of conclusion, the final section introduces variables of education, learning and literacy ('Beyond the "elite"?'). While any study of 'Latin literature and material culture' must always be attuned to a wide spectrum of responses, we argue, the point in no way contradicts the underlying mantra of our chapter: texts cater to a plurality of readers, just as materials will always solicit a plurality of responses, but there can be no denying the intrinsic materiality of Latin texts, no less than the inherent textuality of the Roman visual environment.

## Texts and Objects

Figure 12.1 provides one way to launch into these questions. What we see here is a single poem by an early fourth-century Latin poet named Publilius Optatianus Porfyrius – 'Optatian' for short.[19] Of course, it is not the material text that Optatian wrote: our picture is taken from a sixteenth-century edition of Optatian's works, edited by Marcus Welser and published in Augsburg in 1595. Welser's edition – featuring twenty-one poems in total – was the second

---

[19] The best edition of Optatian's poems remains Polara 1973 (Polara labels the 'altar' poem discussed here as *Carmen* 26). After centuries of neglect, Optatian has received renewed scholarly attention in recent years: in addition to the essays collected in Squire and Wienand 2017, see e.g. Levitan 1985; Ernst 1991: esp. 95–142; Rühl 2006; Hose 2007: esp. 548–51; Hernández Lobato 2012: esp. 307–11; Pelttari 2014: esp. 75–84; Squire 2017; Körfer 2019. On Optatian's significance for approaching the 'preposterous poetics' of late antiquity, see now Goldhill 2020: esp. vii–xxii.; for further discussion, see also the chapters by O'Rourke and Pelttari and by Goldhill in this volume.

## 12 Latin Literature and Material Culture

version of Optatian's works to be printed: it appeared five years after Pierre Pithou's *editio princeps* of 1590. Importantly, though, Welser's edition was the first to typeset Optatian's works with an eye to their physical layout on the page. The example that we have illustrated is a case in point. Pithou's 1590 edition had not in fact included this poem. When it came to the poet's other *carmina*, however, Pithou had printed the various texts as straightforward lines of verse, featuring them alongside additional *epigrammata et poemata vetera*.[20] Welser did something different. As Figure 12.1 demonstrates, he laid out the constituent letters of the poem in a grid. In doing so, Welser's typesetting sought to translate – into a new, printed medium – some of the materialist concerns that gave rise to Optatian's original corpus in the fourth century (and which continued to play a role during the late antique, earlier Carolingian and mediaeval transmission of the corpus).[21] By varying the number of letters in each line, Optatian exploited the materiality of writing to summon up a mimetic impression of the object with which his poem engaged: the outer frame of the letters evokes and constructs the figurative outline of a Roman altar.[22]

We cannot be sure about the original display of Optatian's poem in the fourth century. Prior to Welser's 1595 edition, manuscripts had rendered it in a variety of ways. In the ninth century, a Carolingian scribe – possibly copying an earlier manuscript version – marked out the framing altar-shape through a pair of red lines, using the same colour for the poem's first verse (which is presented in monumental capitals – until the scribe appears to have run out of space, in the final part of the opening line) (Figure 12.2).[23] Another manuscript, this time housed in Bern and dating from the sixteenth century, does not set the poem in a pictorial frame, but still pays careful attention to the increasing and decreasing length of verses (Figure 12.3).[24] A third – from a sixteenth-century manuscript in Wolfenbüttel – wrote out

---

[20] The sole exception is Pithou 1590: 243, which lays out the text of Optatian's 'water-organ' poem (*Carmen* 20); occasionally Pithou also marked out the acrostichs (e.g. Pithou 1590: 231: *Carmen* 12) and telestichs (e.g. Pithou 1590: 231: *Carmen* 13).

[21] For a brief introduction to the presentation of Optatian's poems in extant manuscripts, see Squire 2017: 73–84 (with more detailed bibliography).

[22] Within the corpus of extant poems attributed to Optatian, this 'altar' is one of three poems laid out in the shape of the object evoked: two additional poems relate to a set of pan-pipes (*Carmen* 27) and a water-organ (*Carmen* 20). For discussion, and analysis of their relationships to earlier Greek picture-poems (see n. 37), see e.g. Helm 1902: 43–4; Levitan 1985: 255; Polara 1987: 163–5, 1991: 295–301; Ernst 1991: 98–108; Rühl 2006: 76–7; Bruhat 2009: 102–3; Wienand 2012: 361–2; Pelttari 2014: 76–7; Squire 2017: 35–40; Kwapisz 2017 (revised in Kwapisz 2019a: 89–111).

[23] For details of the Codex Palatinus Latinus 1713 (dating from the ninth century), see http://digi.ub.uni-heidelberg.de/diglit/bav_pal_lat_1713/0022 (our image is taken from fol. 10v.); on the manuscript, see Squire 2017: 73–4, n. 51.

[24] Fig. 12.3 is taken from Codex Bernensis 148 (fascicule 58, fol. 2v.) – labelled manuscript F by Polara 1973.

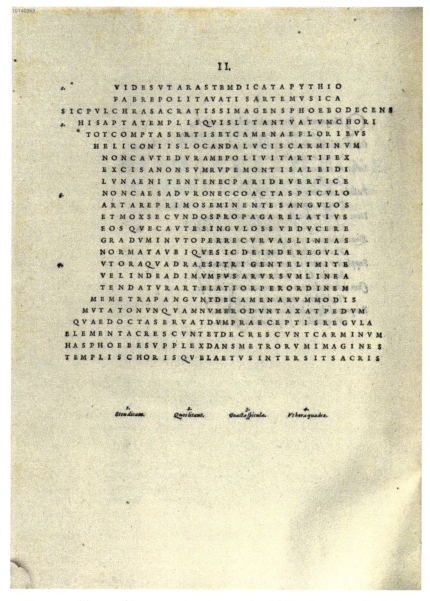

Figure 12.1 Typographic presentation of a poem by Publilius Optatianus Porfyrius (*Carm.* 26) – as published in P. Welser (1595), *Publilii Optatiani Porphyrii panegyricus dictus Constantino Augusto*, Augsburg, p. 5. Photograph by Michael Squire.

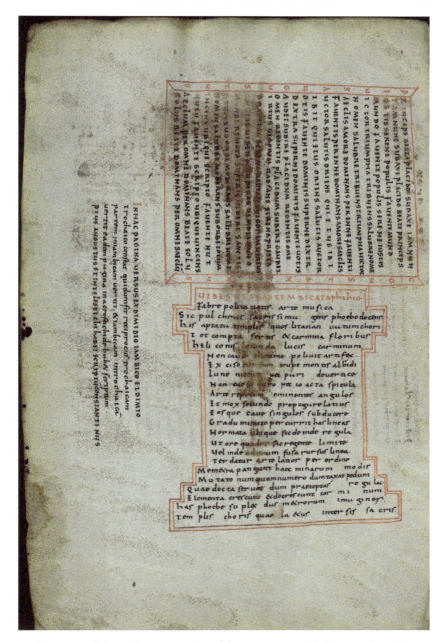

Figure 12.2 Manuscript presentation of the same poem, with *Carm.* 13 above, in Codex Palatinus Latinus 1713 (fol. 10v.; Biblioteca Apostolica, Vatican), ninth century. © Biblioteca Apostolica Vaticana (Vaticano).

the text in elegant Roman square capitals (so-called *capitalis quadrata*), precisely after the manner of an inscription, and encased it in a red frame (Figure 12.4).[25] How these various layouts compare with Optatian's earlier presentation of the text is not known. Still, we can be sure that the physical arrangement of letters and lines was of pivotal importance. The metrical poem can be 'read', of course – its words lend themselves to verbal

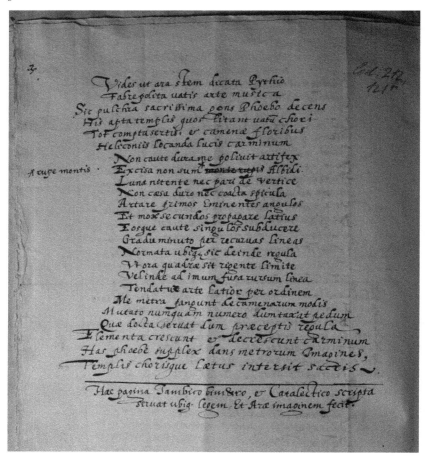

Figure 12.3 Manuscript presentation of the same poem in Codex Bernensis 148 (fascicule 58, fol. 2v.; Bern, Burgerbibliothek), sixteenth century. Note the scribal error and incorrect correction in line 8. Photograph by Johannes Wienand.

[25] Figure 12.4 is taken from Codex Augustaneus 9 Guelferbytanus (Wolfenbüttel, Herzog August Bibliothek, folio 2v.) – labelled manuscript W in Polara 1973. Cf. http://diglib.hab.de/wdb.php?dir=mss/9-aug-4f&distype=thumbs.

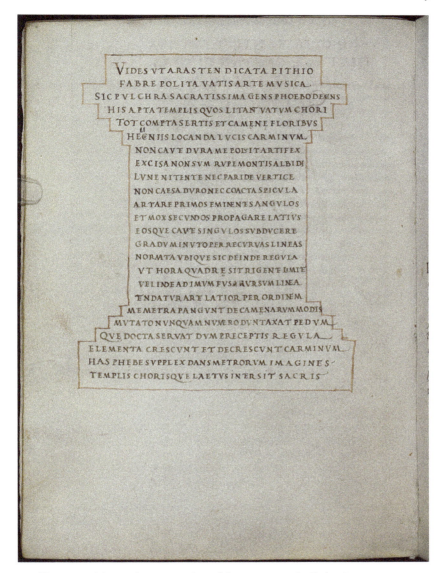

Figure 12.4 Manuscript presentation of the same poem in Codex Augustaneus 9 Guelferbytanus (fol. 2v.; Wolfenbüttel, Herzog August Bibliothek), sixteenth century. © Herzog August Bibliothek, Wolfenbüttel.

decipherment, as indeed to oral recitation (to be incanted in iambic trimeters). But the feat of Optatian's poem simultaneously lies in its artefactual form, taking its lead from honorific inscriptions, not least the monumental texts of Imperial monuments.

As readers engage with the words of the text, they find it taking up that material point of reference. Here is the Latin poem of *Carm.* 26 (in more familiar typographic presentation, complete with word breaks indicated), and an initial attempt at English translation:[26]

> Vides ut ara stem dicata Pythio,
> fabre polita vatis arte musica;
> sic pulchra sacris sim agens, Phoebo decens,
> his apta templis, quis litant vatum chori,
> tot compta sertis et Camenae floribus, 5
> Heliconiis locanda lucis carminum.
> Non caute dura me polivit artifex,
> excisa non sum rupe montis albidi
> Lunae nitente nec Pari de vertice,
> non caesa duro nec coacta spiculo 10
> artare primos eminentes angulos
> et mox secundos propagare latius
> eosque caute singulos subducere
> gradu minuto per recurvas lineas,
> normata ubique sic deinde regula, 15
> ut ora quadrae sit rigente limite,
> vel inde ad imum fusa rursum linea
> tendatur arte latior per ordinem.
> Me metra pangunt de Camenarum modis,
> mutato numquam numero dumtaxat pedum; 20
> quae docta servat dum praeceptis regula,
> elementa crescunt et decrescunt carminum.
> Has, Phoebe, supplex dans metrorum imagines
> templis chorisque laetus intersit sacris.

You see how I stand, an altar consecrated to the Pythian god, polished by the craft of the musical art of the poet. May I become a participant, no less fair in the sacrifices, suitable for Phoebus and fitted for these temples in which the choruses of poets make their acceptable gifts, adorned with so many woven flowers of the Muse, fit to be placed in the Heliconian groves of song. No workman polished me with sharp tool; I was not hewed out of the white rock of the mountain of

---

[26] Our translation has benefitted greatly from that of Kwapisz 2017: 174 (itself adapted after that of Glanville Downey, in Boultenhouse 1959: 72); for useful notes, including on debates about the corruption of the third verse, see Polara 1973: II 159–62. An Italian translation can be found in Polara 2004: 219–23, while Bruhat 1999: 490 provides a French translation.

Luna, nor from the shining peak of Paros. It was not because I was cut or forced with the hard chisel to hold back my edges as they attempt to grow and then, in the succeeding portion, let them spread more broadly. Cautiously I force each edge to be drawn in, line by line, by tiny steps, in lines turning in, thus following on, regulated everywhere by the measure, so that my margin, within the limit which rules it, is that of a square. Then again, continuing on to the bottom, my line, spreading more broadly, is artfully stretched according to the plan. I am composed of the measures whose rhythm the Muses beat out, and the number of feet is never changed. As the rules of the learned principle keep these measures unchanged, it is the letters of the poem that increase and decrease. Phoebus, may the supplicant who offers these metrical pictures take his place joyfully in your temples and your sacred choruses.

The verses of this 'altar' are dedicated to a series of metapoetic reflections, all the while musing on the material fabric of textual form. The opening verse drives home the trope: if Optatian begins by addressing his audience in the second person singular, the first word expressly casts the reader in the role of viewer (*Vides ut ara stem* – 'you *see* how I stand as an altar ...').[27] The second line further develops the thinking, this time capitalising on a shared Roman language for discussing both literary and monumental craftsmanship: in highlighting the underlying *ars* of his text, Optatian establishes his work as a feat of verbal and visual dexterity alike.[28] Still more revealing are verses 7–22. Here the poet embarks on an elaborate description of his working method: on the one hand, he draws a distinction between his literary medium and the carving of stone; on the other, he explains how his creation achieves its monumental semblance – namely, by varying the number of letters in each line (*elementa crescunt et decrescunt carminum*, v. 22).[29] Throughout, this

---

[27] Optatian here plays on an older literary conceit. Of course, the invocation that the reader should 'look' was a mainstay of literary epigram, especially Greek epigrams on visual subjects (cf. e.g. Rossi 2001: 17, n. 13). Here though, the visual form of the poem literalises the literary trope, turning the poem into an actual picture to be viewed. Optatian was not the first to relish the conceit, translating into Latin a game that had already been played out in earlier Greek picture-poems (cf. n. 37): on the one hand, the phrase *uides ut ara stem* takes its lead from Besantinus' *technopaegnion* in an altar-shape (ἐς γὰρ βωμὸν ὁρῆς με, 'you see me as an altar', *Anth. Pal.* 15.25.7); on the other, his decision to open with the trope of viewing adapts the opening line of Simias' earlier picture-poem on the Wings of Eros, with its imperative call that the reader should 'look upon me' (λεῦσσέ με, *Anth. Pal.* 15.24.1).

[28] On the importance of Greek *technê* and Latin *ars* as a critical trope for discussing both the visual arts and poetry, cf. e.g. Squire 2011: 111–21 (with further bibliography); for the etymology, cf. most recently Schatzberg 2018: 16–28.

[29] The significance of the claim lies in Optatian's adjustment to the working principle of extant Greek *technopaegnia* (cf. n. 37). Already from the third century BCE onwards, Simias and his successors had forged their picture-poems by varying the number of metrical feet in each verse. By contrast, Optatian relies on a variation in the number of letters: each line is isometric, but consists of an expanding or decreasing quantity of lettered *elementa*. On Optatian's rhetoric of *elementa*, and its resonance with an 'atomistic' view of language (whereby, in the words of Sergius, 'the letter alone cannot be split' – *littera sola non habet quo soluatur*), as well as contemporary ideas of visual form, cf. Squire 2017: 82–98.

pictorial-poetic 'iconotext' – heralded in v. 23 as *imagines metrorum* (literally, 'images of metres') – is staked on a rhetorical parallel between a physically crafted artefact and a poetically fashioned text: each time Optatian talks of 'polish' and 'measures', or for that matter introduces ideas about rules, colour and shine, he falls back on a rhetorical parallel between writing a text and the manufacture of physical objects. One might add that this studied meditation on textual and artefactual making plays out against earlier poetic evocations of the natural environment, not least through the opening allusion to Horace's famous 'Soracte Ode' (*Carm.* 1.9.1–2 *Vides ut alta stet nive candidum | Soracte*, 'you see how Soracte stands, white with deep snow'):[30] in both its form and allusive texture, Optatian's composition pays homage to the physical world and its literary evocation, only to deny its own 'cutting' from the 'white rock of the mountain of Luna' and 'shining peak of Paros' (vv. 8–9 *excisa non sum rupe montis albidi | Lunae nitente nec Pari de vertice*) – references to marble from both Italian Carrara and the Greek Cycladic island of Paros.

In pitching the resources of poetry against those of material monuments, our opening poem draws on a time-honoured topos of Latin literature. By the fourth century, Optatian could look back to a long-standing Roman analogy between the crafting of written texts and physical objects: among numerous parallels, one might think again of Horace, and his famous boast at the end of his third book of *Odes*, in which he claimed to 'have completed a monument more lasting than bronze' (*exegi monumentum aere perennius*, 3.30.1),[31] or else of Livy's recurrent analogy between the monumental rise of Rome and his own literary monument in the *Ab Urbe condita*.[32] Optatian's altar poem is staked on an audience recognising that topos, no less than appreciating the rich intertextual fabric of the whole. Importantly, though, it is also premised on the reader's recognition of its physical referent: to understand the text, audiences must bring to it a knowledge of the material world around them, and of altars and sacred precincts in particular.

Seen from this perspective, Optatian's poem demonstrates one very concrete way in which Roman material culture could seep into the composition of Latin literary texts. But, to reverse the thinking, it can also serve to showcase the role that Latin texts play in Roman material culture. Throughout the Roman world, altars – like other works of monumental sculpture, including architectural arches, erected portraits and funerary memorials – were inscribed with letters. In each case, moreover, writing constituted a visual

---

[30] For the intertextual allusion, see Polara 1973: 1 105 and Kwapisz 2017: 182–3.
[31] Cf. most recently Kirichenko 2018: esp. 135–6.
[32] Fundamental here is Jaeger 1997. On the development of Greek literary critical ideas which inform the Latin trope, cf. e.g. Benediktson 2000: esp. 12–40.

as much as a verbal sign: inscribed letters were themselves constitutive of monumentality. In exploiting language to evoke the physical form of an altar, Optatian understood the significance of this Roman 'epigraphic habit' (as it has been dubbed):[33] he recognised the integral role that inscriptions could play in the design, appearance and function of Roman objects. Just as the figural form of the altar evokes a performative context for reading the text (including the sacred rhythms of choric recitation and dance: vv. 4–5, 23–4),[34] so the individual letters of the poem construct a material frame: the written page is transformed not just into an object, but rather into a site of epigraphic display.[35] To put the point more strongly, we might say that Optatian evokes his material referent precisely through his recourse to a writerly medium: for all their constituent value as verbal units of words, feet and metrical lines, the letters also function as iconic markers – they inscribe the idea of monumentality in their own written right.

## *Vt pictura poesis?*

It is worth pausing here to note how Optatian evokes not just an altar, but also an *image* of an altar. Indeed, by dedicating itself to 'metrical pictures' (*metrorum imagines*, v. 23), the poem underscores its representation of a sculpted object via a two-dimensional pictorial medium – an *imago*, or rather a pluralistic series of elemental *imagines*. Optatian's letters here literalise a long-standing Roman figurative analogy between painting and poetry – the idea, as Horace famously put it, of *ut pictura poesis* ('as is painting, so is poetry', *Ars P.* 361).[36] No less importantly, Optatian's poem stands in a long tradition

---

[33] MacMullen 1982, with e.g. Beltrán Lloris 2015: 141–5. For some preliminary comments on the monumental and visual aspects of Roman inscriptions, see e.g. Ireland 1983; Williamson 1987; Horsfall 1989a; 1989b; Meyer 1990; Corbier 1991: 115–16; 2006: esp. 9–128; Elsner 1996a; Woolf 1996; Cooley 2002; Squire 2009: esp. 148–9.

[34] On the role that Roman altars themselves play in offering a 'present reiteration of sacrificial performance', see Moser 2019: 9.

[35] Cf. Rühl 2006: 91, discussing the proposed use of *capitalis quadrata* script in Optatian's poems, rather than the sorts of *scriptio continua* standardly used in manuscripts.

[36] On the Horatian maxim, see e.g. Hardie 1993 and Benediktson 2000: 127–39; on its rich western reception, see e.g. Hagstrum 1955 and Barkan 2013. The Horatian analogy appears to stretch back to a maxim of Simonides: according to Plut. *Mor.* (*De glor. Ath.*) 346F (= Simon. fr. 190b Bergk), 'Simonides relates that a picture is a silent poem, and a poem a speaking picture' (ὁ Σιμωνίδης τὴν μὲν ζωγραφίαν ποίησιν σιωπῶσαν προσαγορεύει, τὴν δὲ ποίησιν ζωγραφίαν λαλοῦσαν); cf. e.g. Carson 1992, Sprigath 2004 and Squire 2013a: esp. 161 (on the debt to Homeric ecphrasis). The Simonidean maxim finds numerous echoes in Roman rhetoric – not least *Rhet. Her.* 4.39 (*poema loquens pictura, pictura tacitum poema debet esse*). Both the Simonidean and Horatian maxims have been fundamental to modern aesthetic criticism about the relationship between 'images' and 'texts': central is Lessing's 1766 essay on *Laocoon* – centred around the eponymous statue-group and the description of Laocoon's death in the second book of the *Aeneid* – which set out to compare and above all to differentiate between 'poetic'

```
Ὁλὸς οὔ με λιβρὸς ἱρῶν
Λιβάδεσσιν οἷα κάλχη
Ὑποφοινίηισι τέγγει·
Μαύλιες δ' ὕπερθε πέτρης Ναξίης θοούμεναι
Παμάτων φείδοντο Πανός· οὐ στροβίλωι λιγνύι
Ἰξὸς εὐώδης μελαίνει τρεχνέων με Νυσίων.
Ἐς γὰρ βωμὸν ὁρῆις με μήτε γλούρου
Πλίνθοις μήτ' Ἀλύβης παγέντα βώλοις,
Οὐδ' ὃν Κυνθογενὴς ἔτευξε φύτλη
Λαβόντε μηκάδων κέρα,
Λισσαῖσιν ἀμφὶ δειράσιν
Ὅσσαι νέμονται Κυνθίαις,
Ἰσόρροπος πέλοιτό μοι·
Σὺν οὐρανοῦ γὰρ ἐκγόνοις
Εἰνάς μ' ἔτευξε γηγενής,
Τάων ἀείζωιον τέχνην
Ἔνευσε πάλμυς ἀφθίτων.
Σὺ δ', ὦ πιὼν κρήνηθεν, ἥν
Ἴνις κόλαψε Γοργόνος,
Θύοις τ' ἐπισπένδοις τ'ἐμοὶ
Ὑμηττιάδων πολὺ λαροτέρην
Σπονδὴν ἄδην. ἴθι δὴ θαρσέων
Ἐς ἐμὴν τεῦξιν· καθαρὸς γὰρ ἐγώ
Ἰὸν ἰέντων τεράων, οἷα κέκευθ' ἐκεῖνος,
Ἀμφὶ Νέαις Θρηικίαις ὃν σχεδόθεν Μυρίνης
Σοί, Τριπάτωρ, πορφυρέου φὼρ ἀνέθηκε κριοῦ.
```

Figure 12.5 Typographic presentation of an 'altar' epigram attributed to Besantinus (*Anth. Pal.* 15.25). Typesetting by Christine Luz (reproduced by kind permission).

of texts written in the pictorial shape of the things they evoke. Already in the first century BCE, a neoteric poet named Laevius is known to have composed a poem in the shape of a bird, a self-conscious Latin response to a Greek tradition of picture-poems (so-called *technopaegnia*): six such poems are preserved in the fifteenth book of the *Palatine Anthology*, including two Imperial Greek poems that were also laid out in the form of altars (e.g. Figure 12.5).[37] In the archaeological record, too, we find examples of individual words – and sometimes whole poems – written out as iconic shapes. In Pompeii (as elsewhere), it was fairly common for graffito-names to be drafted into figurative pictures, often playing on their

and 'painterly' representational modes (for an English translation of the text, see Lessing 1984; for an introduction, see Lifschitz and Squire 2017 – along with the other essays in the same edited volume).

[37] On Laevius' *Pterygium Phoenicis* (Morel 1963: 60–1, fr. 22), see Ernst 1991: 95–6, along with Courtney 1993: 119, 136–7 and Kwapisz 2019a: 54–88. For a detailed commentary on the six extant Greek picture-poems (*Anth. Pal.* 15.21–2, 24–7), see now Kwapisz 2013: 59–190, along with the earlier work of Strodel 2002. There has been a surge of scholarly attention over the last few years: Ernst 1991: 54–94; Guichard 2006; Männlein-Robert 2007: 140–54; Luz 2008, 2010: 327–53; Kwapisz 2013: 3–56; Squire 2011: esp. 231–5; 2013c: 98–107; Pappas 2013; Kwapisz 2017 (especially on the relationship with Optatian).

Figure 12.6 Latin graffito in the image of a snake, from Pompeii IV.5 (*CIL* IV 1595): *[Ser]pentis lusus si qui sibi forte notauit, | Sepumius iuuenis quos fac(it) ingenio, | Spectator scaenae siue es studiosus e[q]uorum: | Sic habeas [lanc]es se[mp]er ubiq[ue pares]* ('If anyone has by chance noticed the snaking games, which the young Sepumius skillfully makes, may you always – wherever you are, whether a spectator of the theatre or fond of horses – maintain your impartiality'). After *CIL* IV 1595.

suggested iconic associations.[38] Occasionally, we also find longer, metrical texts inscribed with a view to subjects evoked – as with a pair of elegiac couplets from Pompeii, written in ludic serpentine shape (Figure 12.6).[39]

The interplay in Optatian's artefact between text, object and picture finds an ancestry in precisely the sorts of objects that the poem evokes. Most often, Roman altars combined epigraphic texts and visual imagery without commenting on the assemblage. Occasionally, though, the choice of images was thematised in the accompanying inscription. A famous case is the cinerary grave altar of a certain 'T. Statilius Aper', dating to around 120 CE and today in the Capitoline Museums (Figure 12.7).[40] The central image – below a framed female bust in the pediment (presumably of Aper's wife, Anthis

---

[38] Cf. e.g. Langner 2001: esp. 27–9, 79–83; Clarke 2007: 44–9; Milnor 2014: esp. 26–8; Benefiel and Sypniewski 2016.

[39] *CLE* 927/ *CIL* IV 1595 (from Pompeii IV.5). See caption to Figure 12.6. For discussions, see Wojaczek 1988: 248–52; Courtney 1995: 328–9, no. 120; Ernst 2002: 232–3; Keegan 2014: 214–15; Milnor 2014: esp. 26–8.

[40] Rome, Musei Capitolini: inv. MC0209. See Kleiner 1987: 213–16, no. 83. For discussion, see Koortbojian 1995: 35, n. 46; 1996: 229–31; Elsner 2006: 303–5; Squire 2009: 173–5.

Figure 12.7 Early Hadrianic funerary altar of T. Statilius Aper (displayed in the Musei Capitolini, Rome). Photo: Reproduced by kind permission of the Institut für Klassische Archäologie und Museum Klassischer Abgüsse, Ludwig-Maximilians-Universität, Munich.

Orcivia) – shows a togate male, with scroll in his left hand, standing beside a dead boar; to the left are the remains of a second human figure (perhaps a slave or freedman, or originally a winged personification of death). A large prose inscription at the base of the altar – its most visible writing – records the object's dedication not only to Aper (who died in the twenty-third year of his life), but also to his wife, their freedmen and to the descendants of those freedmen, naming Aper's parents (Statilius Proculus and Argentaria Eutychia) as the dedicators of the monument.[41] Between the figurative panel and that lower epigraph, is a second inscription. The text is inscribed as if it were written in prose, consisting of three smaller lines. When readers verbally engage with these letters, however, they find four metrical hexameters. Here, again represented in the sort of typographic form with which we are familiar in the twenty-first century, is the text of that inscription:

> Innocuus Aper ecce iaces non uirginis ira,
> nec Meleager atrox perfodit uiscera ferro:
> mors tacita obrepsit subito fecitq(ue) ruinam
> quae tibi crescenti rapuit iuuenile[m] figuram.
>
> Behold, harmless Aper, you lie here not because of the anger of the maiden [Diana], nor has fierce Meleager pierced your flesh with his sword. Silent death crept up on you suddenly, and wrought the destruction which snatched away your young figure while you were still growing.

Where Optatian's fourth-century poem exploits writing to summon up an image of a monument, this real-life altar constructs its memorial around the knowing juxtaposition of imagery and inscription. Just as Optatian would look to the iconic potential of writing, moreover, so too this epigram draws on the figurative potential of a name: much is staked on an onomastic pun – the fact that, in Latin, the name 'Aper' means 'Boar'.[42] In its opening address to *innocuus Aper*, the epigram at first appears to refer to the boar featured in the

---

[41] *CIL* VI 1975 = *CLE* 441; cf. Courtney 1995: 374, no. 17. This biographic text comments upon Aper's career as an architect (*mensor aedificiorum* – hence the scroll held in his left hand and the box of tools to his side), and upon the career of his father as an *accensus velatus* (a member of a corporation with civic, military and religious functions). The prose inscription reads: *T(ito) Statilio Vol(tinia) Apro mensori | aedificior(um) vixit ann(is)* XXII *m(ensibus)* VIII *d(iebus)* XV | *T(itus) Statilius Vol(tinia) Proculus | accensus velatus et Argentaria | Eutychia parentes filio optumo et | Orciviae Anthidi uxori eius sibiq(ue) et suis | libertis libertabus posterisque eorum.*

[42] Quintilian, albeit in a very different context, explicitly comments on the visual suggestiveness of the name, observing how the 'origin of the name can be fixed in our memory' (*id memoriae adfigatur unde sunt nomina, Inst.* 11.2.31). For related visual onomastic puns in Roman Imperial funerary monuments, cf. Riti 1977 (with 1973–4 on Greek instances of the same phenomenon), together with Courtney 1995: 374. For another supposed instance of the same onomastic pun (in Plin. *Ep.* 1.6, with a suggested nod to the Aper of Tacitus' *Dialogus*), see Whitton 2019: 465–6, with n. 269.

sculpted imagery above. No sooner does the poem establish an analogy between words and images, however, than it proceeds to undercut it: the real subject of the lament is not the boar (*aper*) depicted in the panel above, but rather the youth that stands beside him (*T. Statilius Aper*). Indeed, while the epigram associates Aper with the 'harmless boar' slain by Meleager, the visual schema more closely connects him with that boar's victorious mythical assailant.[43]

Much more could be said about Optatian's altar poem, no less than about its various literary, material and visual-cultural contexts. But what makes this case study so rich in the context of our chapter is its powerful demonstration of the shared culture to which Latin literature and Roman objects belong. The same goes for the Aper monument – an example drawn this time not from the world of literary texts looking towards objects, but rather of material culture featuring epigraphic writing. However much, in either case, institutional frameworks would have us segregate 'literary' from 'material' cultures, dispensing them to separate specialists, these are categories of modern academic convenience – and ultimately, we would argue, of limited benefit: if our aim is to understand the shared parameters of literary and material cultures in the Roman world, the disciplinary distinctions that we draw hinder as much as they help.

## The Matter of the Page

Optatian's poem demonstrates something else besides: it shows how the production of Latin literature was itself conditioned by the objecthood of the written text. To appreciate the point, it is important to remember that the fourth century – the period in which Optatian was writing – witnessed one of the most seismic technological shifts in the western history of the book: a transition from a reliance on papyrus scrolls to the widespread use of the codex.[44] The rise of this codex form was a major event in the reception of Latin (no less than Greek) literature – a spectacular

---

[43] As such, the imagery seems to nod to the popularity of Meleager in contemporary funerary monuments – a favourite subject of sarcophagi from the early Antonine period (cf. *LIMC* VI.1: 433, s.v. 'Meleagros'; Koortbojian 1996: 325–6, nn. 78–9; Zanker and Ewald 2004: 346–55). The figurative rendering of Aper on this altar finds parallels in this sarcophagus iconography (see *LIMC* VI.1: 422–3, nos. 71–6, s.v. 'Meleagros', esp. no. 75).

[44] For further discussion, see also Kelly in this volume. On 'the pragmatics of reading' scrolls, see Johnson 2010: 17–31, along with Johnson 2004 (both with further bibliography). On the rise of the codex form, see especially Roberts and Skeat 1983, Harris 1991, Blanck 1992: 75–101, Cavallo 1997, Mazal 1999: 125–51, Stanton 2004 and Schipke 2013: esp. 143–52; cf. Engels and Hofmann 1997: 67–76, Cavallo 2010 and Johnson 2009: esp. 267 (with references). On the luxury codices of late antiquity, see Mazal 1999: 95–8 (mentioning Optatian on 96), Mratschek 2000, and Zimmerman 2001. Schipke 2013 now provides the most detailed overview of 'das Buch in der Spätantike' – albeit without reference to Optatian.

feat in fostering new possibilities for criticism and commentary (consider, for example, the systematic commentary on Virgil that Servius composed in the early fifth century).[45] It is all too often overlooked that, before the development of the codex, it was not possible to fit more than a single book of the works of a major writer on a roll of papyrus; there could be no collected Virgil – for that matter, no gathered text of the *Aeneid* as a single object – before this move towards the much more capacious and easily indexible codices of late antiquity.[46] We will look here both at Latin poetry created with the new codex-medium in mind (like the works of Optatian) and at earlier literature, such as the plays of Terence or the poems of Virgil, adapted to the codex form. In these cases, of classic authors, codices not only preserved and collected entire corpora, reinterpreting and potentially illustrating them for a new era, but they also adapted (often in ways we cannot always or fully ascertain) – and hence to some extent preserved – patterns of the material presentation of texts: by late antiquity, these patterns had the potential to include all manner of visual commentaries, forging new modes of presentation in the now almost entirely lost world of the high-level literary papyrus.

Whatever the original form of the anthology that Optatian composed, it seems clear that his individual poems were designed for presentation in a bound volume rather than within a continuous scroll.[47] The format had a profound impact upon Optatian's literary form. Within Optatian's extant corpus, each poem is conceptualised as a discrete entity, most likely laid out on a single folio. This mode of display helped fuel the rise of Optatian's favourite – and wholly innovative – form of poetic composition: the so-called *carmen cancellatum*, or 'gridded poem'. Figure 12.8, illustrating a page from a sixteenth-century manuscript now housed in Wolfenbüttel, provides a neat example of the genre, which would spur all manner of later imitations, especially in the ninth and tenth centuries.[48]

As with Optatian's altar poem, the individual letters are laid out with attention to their spatial arrangement: in this case, the vertical span of the

---

[45] On Servius, see e.g. Fowler 1997 and Bouquet, Méniel and Ramires 2011.
[46] The precise chronology of this shift from scroll to codex has been much debated. Suffice it to say here that earlier authors had already commented on the synoptic qualities of the codex and its new capacities for canonisation: particularly important here is Martial's late first-century sequence of epigrams on the miniatured 'greats' of Greek and Latin literature, as presented in codex form (see Roman 2001: esp. 130–8 on Martial 14.183–96, published in 84–5 CE, along with e.g. Prioux 2008: 311–28 and Squire 2011: 279–83).
[47] Cf. Ernst 1991: 141; 2002: 59–60; Wienand 2012: 364; Squire 2017: 33–5; Körfer 2019: esp. 95–102, 146–7. Discussions here have noted not only Optatian's multiple references to *paginae* (3.33, 3.iv, 4.2, 4.9, 7.11, 8.i, 9.13, 19.4, 19.35), but also his delineation of *charta* (1.7).
[48] Fundamental on Optatian's reception is Ernst 1991: esp. 143–842; for a brief survey, see Squire 2017: 76–84 (with further literature in 78 n. 62). For text and attempted English translation of the poem (*Carmen* 19), see Squire 2015a (with further bibliography at 106–7 n. 40).

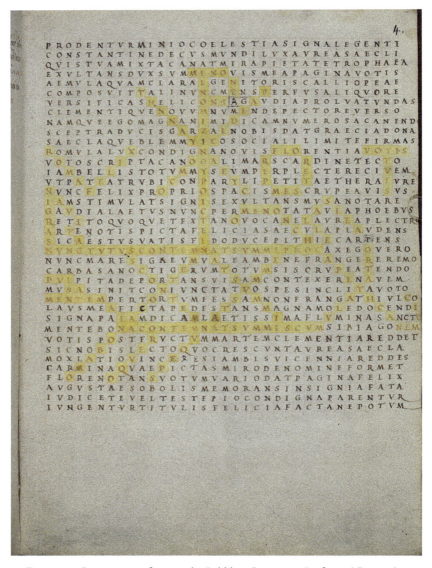

Figure 12.8 Presentation of a poem by Publilius Optatianus Porfyrius (*Carm.* 19) – in Codex Augustaneus 9 Guelferbytanus (fol. 4r.; Wolfenbüttel, Herzog August Bibliothek), sixteenth century. © Herzog August Bibliothek, Wolfenbüttel.

poem stretches to 37 hexameters, with each line consisting of between 35 and 38 lettered units. That gridded arrangement of letters tenders an opportunity to draw out patterns within the internal fabric of the text: the poem morphs into a pictorial field – a mosaic made up of lettered *tesserae* that can spell out additional words and pictures.[49] In the upper section can be found three epigraphic apparitions, inscribing the poem with the letters *VOT* (a decidedly epigraphic abbreviation for the 'vows' – *vota* – as mentioned in vv. 4, 12, 13, 26, 31 and 35);[50] likewise, the text contained within those letters yields an additional cryptic message (*Roma felix floret semper votis tuis*, 'blessed Rome is forever flourishing under your vows'). Still more remarkable are the pictorial patterns in which this inscription finds itself. We see here a ship, complete with oars below, ramming spike to the left, tiller to the lower right and mast and sail above. As readers navigate their way around the shape, they can trace no fewer than five Latin hexameters, two of them readable in a variety of different directions.[51] The pictorial-poetic achievement is crowned with a still more dizzying feat of lettered dexterity – a *Greek* elegiac couplet, hidden in the transliterated constituent *Latin* letters that comprise the ship's chi-rho and tiller:

τὴν ναῦν δεῖ κόσμον, σὲ δὲ ἄρμενον εἰνὶ νομίζιν
θούροις τείνομενον σῆς ἀρετῆς ἀνέμοις.

One must think that the ship is the world, and that you are the hoisted rigging, tautened by the strong winds of your virtue.[52]

Such experiments with textual display were themselves bound up with the technological innovations of the codex. There is certainly a history to Optatian's writerly games: in literary terms, his so-called *uersus intexti* ('interwoven verses') take their lead from the practices of poetic acrostichs

---

[49] Fundamental on the analogy between late antique poetry and mosaics is Roberts 1989: 57, 70–3; cf. now the important intervention of Hardie 2019: esp. 223-49, along with the essays in Hartman and Kaufmann 2023. More specifically on the parallels between Optatian's poetry and contemporary fourth-century mosaics, see Bruhat 1999: 136–41 (on the analogies between mosaic patterns and the geometric shapes of poems 7, 12, 18, 21, 22 and 23), and Squire 2017: 82–98 on Optatian's 'poetry in pieces'.

[50] An alternative interpretation has been proposed: namely, that *VOT* should be understood as an acronym for *Victor Orbis Terrarum* (for bibliography, see Squire 2015a: 111, n. 49). The two interpretations are not, of course, mutually exclusive – and in any case there is surely a game of epigraphic abbreviation at play.

[51] *Nigras nunc tutus contemnat, summe, procellas* ('Let him now defy the black storms in safety, o great one'); *Nauita nunc tutus contemnat, summe, procellas* ('Let the sailor now defy the storms in safety, o great one'); *Tutus contemnat summis cumulata tropaeis* ('Let him defy in safety even that which is piled high with greatest trophies'); *Pulsa mente mala contemnat, summe, procellas* ('With ill intent cast aside, o great one, let him defy the storms'); *Spe quoque Roma bona contemnat, summe, procellas* ('With good faith, let Rome also defy the storms, o great one').

[52] For discussion, cf. Squire 2015a: 104–21 and Körfer 2019: 205–17, along more generally with Squire 2017.

and telestichs,[53] while this 'gridded' mode takes us to so-called *stoichēdon* inscriptions, as well as to 'palindrome square' Latin inscriptions found across the geographical spread of the Roman Empire (e.g. Figure 12.9).[54] Other parallels might be cited, including graffiti turning marine-sounding names into naval form, as with ten early Imperial examples from Rome and Pompeii (Figure 12.10). And yet the radical innovations of Optatian's designs only make sense against the backdrop of the material book: as vehicle for displaying written script, the codex fashioned not only new practices of reading, but also new modes of conceptualising writing.

As Optatian himself seems to have recognised, the medium of the codex also lent itself to new sorts of visual embellishment. The way in which Optatian incorporates images into his poems might be associated with a particular development in fourth-century book production: a new mode of setting miniature paintings alongside literary texts. The extent to which earlier papyrus scrolls had juxtaposed narrative texts with miniature paintings has been much debated:[55] a handful of literary references suggest that some earlier Latin works were occasionally accompanied by images;[56] likewise, a small number of extant papyrus fragments, combining Greek texts with painted imagery, give some indication of the possible form that such scrolls might have taken.[57] But the parchment codex lent itself to pictorial elaboration in a way that fragile scrolls had not: quite apart from the durability of vellum folios, the fact that the pages of a codex are kept flat (rather than rolled up) meant that precious miniatures could now be protected between the covers of a book. Optatian's own corpus of writing brilliantly demonstrates the sorts of experimentation that would result. Although we of course lack earlier manuscripts of the poet's *oeuvre*, the ramifications of this shift are nicely reflected in later versions of Optatian's poems. Consider, for example, a ninth-century Vatican manuscript that features all kinds of embellishments

---

[53] On the history of Greek and Latin acrostichs, the two most important overviews are Vogt 1966 and Courtney 1990; cf. Luz 2010: 1–77, Squire 2011: 224–6 (with references to other discussions), Katz 2013: esp. 4–10 and Kwapisz 2019b.

[54] Ernst 1991: 429–59 provides a thorough introduction; cf. Guarducci 1965; Dencker 2011: 577–82; Habinek 2009: 133; Squire 2011: 216–19.

[55] Fundamental are Weitzmann 1947 and 1959, postulating a tradition of illustrated papyrus scrolls dating back to Hellenistic Alexandria; for sceptical responses, see Squire 2009: 122–39 and 2011: esp. 127–39. Cf. Geyer 1989: 29–104; Blanck 1992: 102–12; Small 2003: 118–54.

[56] The most famous example is Varro's first-century BCE *Imagines*: according to the Elder Pliny, Varro's text set biographies of some 700 celebrities (in fifteen papyrus rolls) alongside representations of their respective portraits (*HN* 35.11: cf. Geyer 1989: 29–32; Horsfall 1994: 80–1; Small 2003: 131–4). It is also clear that ancient technical treatises (among them Vitruvius' *De architectura*) could be accompanied by images: cf. Small 2003: 121–9, along with Stückelberger 1994.

[57] Cf. in particular Nisbet 2011 on *P. Oxy.* 2331 – a fragmentary Greek poem on the labours of Heracles. Turner 1987: 137 saliently lists just seven extant instances of papyrus texts accompanied by images.

Figure 12.9 'Palindrome square' inscription from Ostia, second century CE: the letters can be read across both a horizontal and vertical axis (*Roma | olim | Milo | Amor*: 'Rome – once – Milo – love'). Drawing by Michael Squire (after Guarducci 1965: 265, fig. 8).

alongside the red lettering and framing of the intertextual verses – including varieties of foliage (foll. 3r., 7r., 8r., 9r., 13r., 14r., 16r.), the provision of crosses (13r., 13v.) and the monumentalising of crosses within the intertextual verses by the provision of stepped bases – as if the poems were themselves erected as objects in a civic setting or in a church (9r. (Figure 12.11), 12r.).[58] This kind of embellishment, which ultimately became the visual elaboration of initials and

---

[58] For the manuscript, see http://digi.ub.uni-heidelberg.de/diglit/bav_pal_lat_1713/0035. The poem illustrated in Figure 12.11 (*Carm.* 3) purports to portray the face of the Emperor Constantine, setting the present pictorial-poetic artefact against the painted portraits crafted by Apelles (cf. Squire 2016c). In this case, the two cruciform shapes that make up the pattern of the *uersus intexti* are embellished with additional designs at their ligatures; the central cross is set on a stepped base, almost as if it were mounted on an altar.

638  MICHAEL SQUIRE AND JAŚ ELSNER

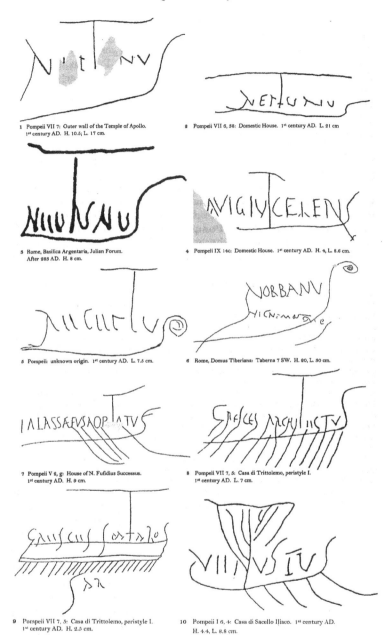

Figure 12.10  Selection of ten name-graffiti in the shape of ships, from early Imperial Rome and Pompeii. Reproduced by kind permission of Jane Heath (after Langner 2001, Tafeln 1–2).

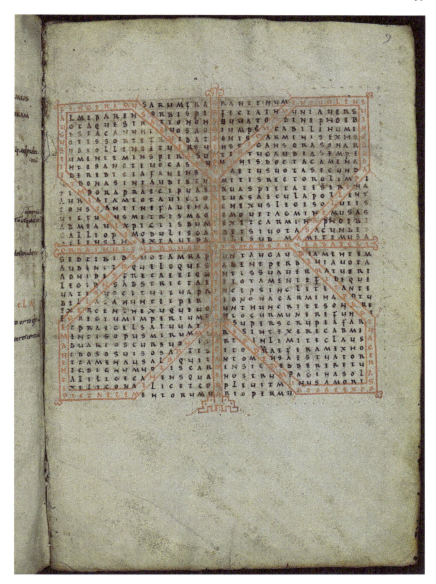

Figure 12.11 Presentation of a poem by Publilius Optatianus Porfyrius (*Carm.* 3) – in Codex Palatinus Latinus 1713 (fol. 9r.; Biblioteca Apostolica, Vatican), ninth century. © Biblioteca Apostolica Vaticana (Vaticano).

letters within the texts of illuminated mediaeval manuscripts, may well go back to the fourth century itself – that is, if we assume that manuscripts like this one were accurately copied from earlier exemplars.

The rise of the codex brought with it a period of immense creativity in the visualisation of a written corpus. But two issues strike us as particularly important, both of which are dependent upon (and in turn influence) the artefactual nature of a book as an elaborate stitching together of expensive vellum parchment sheets: first, the question of frontispieces; and second, new possibilities of depicting scenes alongside the run of any given text.

In the early fourth century, Constantine's biographer Eusebius, bishop of Caesarea, devised a scholarly system for the textual imbrication of the four Gospels into a single unit.[59] It consisted of a prefatory letter to Carpianus, which explained what he had done and served as instructions to the reader about how to use the model; and a series of tables showing the parallels where two or more gospels described the same event, typically placed within arcaded arches (drawn on the page and subsequently subject to very rich illustration), and numbered according to marginal annotations enumerating chapter and verse throughout the text of the four Gospels. These innovations allowed on the one hand for comparisons to be made, and on the other for tabular parallels to be checked.[60] Effectively, at the very inception of the codex form, Eusebius provided not only a model of running reference and indexing whose descendants remain in force today (much more precise than pagination), while also supplying a paratextual and commentarial explanation (actually couched in a brief, simple and helpful epistolary form) for how to make best use of what his scholarship had supplied.[61] The pattern of canon tables and enumeration as well as the Letter to Carpianus were translated into all the languages into which the Gospels themselves were known, appearing – often with wonderful pictorial embellishment in the framing arcades – in early Gospel books in Greek, Latin, Syriac, Arabic, Armenian, Georgian and Ethiopian. A remarkable recent discovery – the Ethiopic Garima Gospels – has illumination on pages whose vellum has been carbon-dated to the fifth and sixth centuries (e.g. Figure 12.12).[62] Beyond Christianity, Eusebius' interventions were paradigms for practical and organisational aids in the kinds of

---

[59] Key contributions include Grafton and Williams 2006: 194–200; Wallraff 2013: 25–37; Crawford 2019; Crawford 2020.
[60] The classic discussion – dated, perhaps, but fundamental – remains Nordenfalk 1938. See also Wessel 1976–7; Nordenfalk 1982 and 1984: 96–104; Sevrugian 2004.
[61] On paratexts, see Genette 1997, with e.g. Jansen 2014b and Crawford 2019: esp. 21–33.
[62] See McKenzie and Watson 2016; for some discussion of the problems and the date, see Elsner 2020a: 109–11.

Figure 12.12 Garima Gospels ms I (AG I, foll. 11r. and 12r. in current binding), opening of the first and second canon tables in the form of aedicules with finely painted architecture and birds on parchment. Date contested – but perhaps as early as the sixth century. Photograph by Michael Gervers, published by kind permission of Judith McKenzie.

collected volumes that integrated works which once occupied many rolls of papyrus. Thus the question of the unity of the Gospels is not only a significant theological one, but a very practical and material affair: for the first time, in the velum codex (whose cost but also longevity was in an entirely different category from the papyrus roll), it was possible to collect a whole text – in one volume the four Gospels, the entire Bible including the Old Testament, the corpora of an ancient writer (the twelve books of the *Aeneid*, or for that matter the collected work of a single author – like the *Eclogues*, *Georgics* and *Aeneid* of Virgil, or the six surviving plays of Terence), or the collections of ancient lore and law (by many authors) that were key to the running of the state (such as the rules about land measurement in the *agrimensores* or the legal codices of Theodosius).

The pattern of prefatory images – to mark both the beginning of a collected written corpus and the beginnings of individual sections –

swiftly became key to the nature of luxury books.[63] In the richly illuminated Carolingian manuscript known as the Vatican Terence (Vat. lat. 3868),[64] we see an author portrait in a square frame surrounding an *imago clipeata* that stands on an altar-like base supported by two actors in masks (fol. 2r., Figure 12.13); this is followed by a fine aedicule flanked by coloured columns with torus mouldings and delicately traced flutes, containing shelves holding theatrical masks (fol. 3r.). The author portrait introduces the entire collection of plays by Terence, while the aedicule – like those at the beginning of the other plays – is a prefatory image for the play that follows (the *Andria*).[65] That this set of forms belongs to the late antique prototype of this manuscript is certain:[66] they appear in the same order in the pen-drawn versions of another ninth-century manuscript (Codex Parisinus 7899).[67] The aedicule with shelved masks becomes a repeated frontispiece motif for different plays within the collection – in the Vatican Terence marking the *incipits* of the *Eunuchus* (fol. 35r.), *Adelphoe* (fol. 50v.), *Hecyra* (fol. 65r.) and *Phormio* (fol. 77r.). There is little doubt that these aedicules are prefatory in function. And there is the possibility (unprovable of course) that they represent forms which antedate the fourth-century collection of the six plays of Terence into a single codex (the presumed prototype of these ninth-century versions), and may have appeared in the papyrus rolls of individual plays.

The richness of such prefatory visual invention is striking. It features pictorial summaries at the opening of books in a series of late antique or early mediaeval manuscripts. One might cite, for abbreviated narrative cycles in pictorial form, the prefatory panel of six pictures framed in red before the third Georgic in the fifth-century Vatican Virgil (fol. 1r.),[68] or the Passion cycle in the sixth-century St Augustine Gospels (now in Corpus Christi College, Cambridge, Figure 12.14), which is part of the

---

[63] See Elsner 2020a, on which the following discussion partly draws.
[64] https://digi.vatlib.it/view/MSS_Vat.lat.3868.
[65] Cf. Jones and Morey 1931: 32 and Wright 2006: 8.
[66] For an attempt to construct the prototype, which the author dates to sometime around 400 CE in Rome, see Wright 2006: esp. 206–24.
[67] BN lat. 7899: http://gallica.bnf.fr/ark:/12148/btv1b84525513/f1.image. There are later versions in two further illustrated Terence mss: Basilicanus H.19 in the Vatican (tenth century), foll. 9v. and 10, and Bodleian Auct. F. 2.13 in Oxford (twelfth century) foll. 2v. and 3.
[68] On the 'Vatican Virgil' (Codex Latinus 3225), presenting the *Georgics* and *Aeneid* along with fifty miniatures, see Wit 1959, with Stevenson 1983, Geyer 1989: 205–32 and Wright 1993. Compare also Biblioteca Apostolica Vaticana (hereafter BAV), MS Vat. lat. 3225, fol. 1r.: see https://digi.vatlib.it/view/MSS_Vat.lat.3225. This page (fol 1r., the first surviving page of the ms) is now poorly preserved. For a range of fine seventeenth-century copies including several purchased for the 'dal Pozzo paper museum', see Claridge and Herklotz 2012: 335–51.

Figure 12.13 The Vatican Terence (BAV, MS Vat. lat. 3868) fol. 2r., ninth-century copy (c. 825) of an Italian original of the fifth century. Prefatory image for the whole codex with a portrait of the author in an *imago clipeata* held by two figures in actors' masks. Photograph: Reproduced by kind permission of the Institut für Klassische Archäologie und Museum Klassischer Abgüsse, Ludwig-Maximilians-Universität, Munich (after Claridge and Herklotz 2012: 36).

prefatory matter to Luke (fol. 125r.).[69] This latter arranges twelve images of the Passion drawn from all four Gospels (starting from the entry to

---

[69] Cambridge, Corpus Christi College, Parker Library, ms 286, fol. 125r.: see https://parker.stanford.edu/parker/catalog/mk707wk3350 and Wormald 1954: 2–5 (for arrangements of prefatory matter) and 11–16 (for the rectangular miniature).

Figure 12.14 The Augustine Gospels (Cambridge, Corpus Christi College, Parker Library, ms 286) fol. 125r., sixth-century codex, probably made in Italy. Prefatory image before the introduction to Luke's Gospel with twelve labelled scenes illustrating the Passion from the Entry to Jerusalem to the Carrying of the Cross. Photo: Reproduced by kind permission of the Institut für Klassische Archäologie und Museum Klassischer Abgüsse, Ludwig-Maximilians-Universität, Munich (after Williams 1999, plate IV).

## 12 Latin Literature and Material Culture

Figure 12.15 The Roman Virgil (BAV, MS Vat. lat. 3867) fol. 6r., late fifth or sixth century, probably made in Italy. Headpiece of the third Eclogue, showing the poem's three speakers – Palaemon, the judge of a poetic contest (left), between Menalcas and Damoetes. The speakers are named as a rubric heading to the poem, beneath the miniature, but this title serves as a poor caption to the picture since the names do not align with the figures that represent them. Photo: Reproduced by kind permission of the Institut für Klassische Archäologie und Museum Klassischer Abgüsse, Ludwig-Maximilians-Universität (after Wright 2001: 17).

Jerusalem at top left and ending with Jesus carrying the Cross at bottom right) within a grid inside a faux-marble frame. Such prefatory pictorialism includes single summary images, such as the pictorial idylls that preface the first, third, fifth and seventh Eclogues (foll. 1r., 6r. (Figure 12.15), 11r. and 16v.) and the wonderful double page spread at the start of the third Georgic (foll. 44v. and 45r. (Figure 12.16)) in the fifth- or sixth-century Roman Virgil (also in the Vatican Library).[70] In the odd-numbered Eclogues of the Roman Virgil, all introducing poetic dialogues, the artist frames the speakers within the poem (three in fol. 6r. which prefaces the third Eclogue), with their names written in red capitals below the images as if they were a caption. The shepherds sit on rocks in the countryside among their sheep and goats, flanked by a rustic shelter to the right and foliage at both ends. Rather than setting out the described narrative pictorially (as in the Augustine Gospels'

---

[70] On the 'Roman Virgil' (Codex Latinus 3867), presenting sections from the *Eclogues*, *Georgics* and *Aeneid*, with nineteen extant miniatures, see Liversidge 1997: 92–3; and Wright 2001 – together with https://digi.vatlib.it/view/MSS_Vat.lat.3867.

Figure 12.16 The Roman Virgil (BAV, MS Vat. lat. 3867) fol. 45r., late fifth or sixth century, probably made in Italy. Headpiece of the third Georgic. Photo: Reproduced by kind permission of the Institut für Klassische Archäologie und Museum Klassischer Abgüsse, Ludwig-Maximilians-Universität (after Wright 2001: 23).

Passion cycle), the Roman Virgil gives us the *mise en scène* to evoke the poetic setting. Likewise, prefatory imagery is strongly characterised, as we have already seen in the case of Terence, by author portraits (Figure 12.17), which would become the ancestors of the rich mediaeval tradition of illuminating images of the Evangelists. The fine pen-drawn author portrait of a bearded figure with an open scroll seated in an aedicule with triangular pediment and shell design from the Codex Arcerianus now in Wolfenbüttel (fol 67v.), a fifth- or sixth-century version of the Roman *corpus agrimensorum*, was painted as frontispiece to the collected florilegia of Agennius Urbicus, of whom the figure may be intended as a portrait. This may itself reflect

Figure 12.17 Codex Arcerianus (Herzog August Bibliothek at Wolfenbüttel, Cod. Guelf. 36.23A) fol. 67v., fifth or sixth century, perhaps Italian. Author portrait in an aedicule as the frontispiece to the florilegia of Agennius Urbicus. © Herzog August Bibliothek, Wolfenbüttel.

a fourth-century prototype of the prefatory aedicule and is our earliest combination of the prefatory visual types of architecture and author.[71] This seated type of author portrait became the most common – one thinks of the images of Virgil at the openings of *Eclogues* 2, 4 and 6 in the Roman Virgil,[72] or the great Luke miniature of Augustine Gospels.[73]

This variety of prefatory visual strategies seeks to reveal different aspects of the written work that follows, commenting visually, as it were, on the textuality contained by the book. An author portrait evokes the human touch behind the text – its authorship and speaking voice; so too prefatory arches and arcades (which often contained titles or contents as in the sixth-century Ashburnham Pentateuch, fol. 2r.)[74] were a visualisation of the threshold and the concomitant spatial exploration which entering a book constitutes for a reader as she or he traverses the pages. The pictorial vignette – what might be deemed a kind of reverse ecphrasis, in that the text or a segment of it is visualised as image[75] – is an anticipatory hint of the text's drama (almost like a trailer for a cinematic film or television series today). Some books – for example the *Eclogues* in the Roman Virgil – varied the kinds of frontispiece by alternating between synoptic pictorial summaries and author portraits. The architectural image, in particular, like the altar of Optatian's poem, focalises the *artefactual* nature of the book as something *constructed* of parchment or papyrus – carefully treated, rolled or stitched, inscribed and painted on.

Beyond the prefatory, the possibilities of illustration – in a variety of forms from full-page inserts via part-page pictures to marginalia – enabled a realm of intermedial commentary and visualisation between text and image.[76] The Vatican Virgil, for example – especially for its presentation of the *Aeneid* – creates a kind of visual commentary through the illumination of particular episodes that heighten and highlight some passages at the expense of others and appears in direct contiguity with them, either written immediately before or after the image. Illustration is particularly rich in the abandonment and death of Dido (foll. 39v., 40r. – these two being a full opening of two pages – and 41r.)[77] and in Aeneas' trip to the Underworld

---

[71] See Carder 1978: 130–6, 198–201; Butzmann 1970: 28–30, 42–3.
[72] Rome, Vatican Library ms Vat. lat. 3867 foll. 3v., 9r., 14v.: Wright 2001 remains fundamental.
[73] Cambridge, Corpus Christi College, Parker Library, ms 286, fol. 129v.: see Wormald 1954: 2–3, 5–11. One might note in passing that the Christian tradition appears not to have preserved the *imago clipeata* model of author portrait, as for example in the lost late antique manuscript of Terence, copied in the ninth century and now in Rome, Vatican Library ms Vat. lat. 3868, fol. 2r. (cf. Wright 2006: 6–7).
[74] For the ms see Paris, Bibliothèque nationale de France (hereafter BnF), MS Nouv. acq. lat. 2334 with von Gebhardt 1883 and the fine digitised facsimile at http://gallica.bnf.fr/ark:/12148/btv1b53019392c/f4.image; cf. Sörries 1993: 26–33. On this page see Rickert 1986: 32–92 and Verkerk 2004: 125–83.
[75] On the rhetorical trope of ecphrasis, pp. 652–8.
[76] On the Vatican Terence in this context see Dodwell 2000: 1–100.   [77] Wright 1993: 38–43.

## 12 Latin Literature and Material Culture

(foll. 47v., 48v. and 49r. – another full opening, 52r. and 53v.).[78] Images here mark pauses and crescendos in the narrative thrust of a lengthy work. We do not know enough about patronage or the circumstances of production to have a sense of whether emphasis on these subjects indicates an effort to claim a Roman classic for some kind of Christian interpretation (by stressing issues of lust, temptation and sin in the Dido episode, or for that matter the visualisation of a Judaeo-Christian 'hell'), or whether an alternative pagan model for the illuminated codex from that of the Bible is being proposed. In any case, though, the images do more than alleviate the process of reading the text: they direct the reader to particular sections, as a kind of emblematic signal to the subject-matter, through pictures.

Let us take as an example fol. 71r. (Figure 12.18). This shows a fine landscape image with sea, sky and rocky hills immediately above the text of *Aen.* 9.117–25 (omitting v. 121, as do all the early manuscripts):

>         . . . et sua quaeque
> continuo puppes abrumpunt uincula ripis
> delphinumque modo demersis aequora rostris
> ima petunt. Hinc virgineae (mirabile monstrum)
> reddunt se totidem facies pontoque feruntur.
> Obstipuere animis Rutuli, conterritus ipse
> turbatis Messapus equis, cunctatur et amnis
> rauca sonans reuocatque pedem Tiberinus ab alto.

> At once each ship tore off its moorings from the bank: they dived down to the depths of the water, plunging in beak-first as dolphins do. Then, a miracle to see, in maiden form they resurface: the same number as before, now swimming in the sea. The Rutulians were amazed; Messapus himself was stricken with terror, his horses afraid. The stream, murmuring loudly, is stayed, and Tiberinus turns back his footsteps from the sea.

The image not only captures the scene in the text, but also glosses it with an act of interpretive visualisation. Virgil's impressionistic evocation of the miracle – in which Cybele turns the prows of the Trojan ships into nymphs, so as to move with their own agency and escape the Rutulian attack – is made visual, with the naked nymphs rendered as the beaks of the ships. Messapus (labelled in the centre of the scene on a white charger) is confounded as he gallops – riding away from the portent at the same time as turning back to gaze upon it – while Turnus, also labelled on a brown horse, rides away and turns towards Messapus. Unfortunately the original facing page of this opening is now lost, although clearly we know the text. In this case, the

---

[78] Ibid. 48–57.

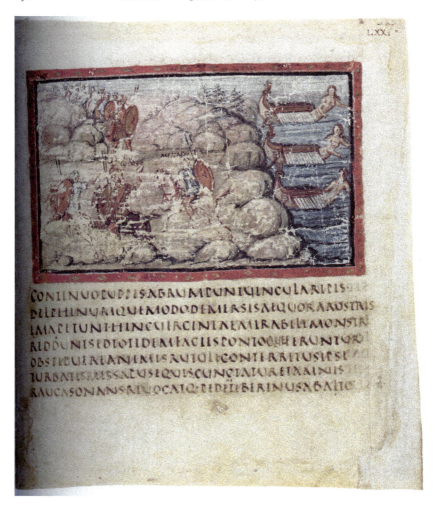

Figure 12.18 The Vatican Virgil (BAV, MS Vat. lat. 3225) fol. 71r., perhaps early fifth century, from Rome. Illumination painted on vellum immediately above the text of *Aeneid* 9.118–25 (omitting v. 121) and illustrating the passage written below. The miniature shows the Trojan ships turning miraculously into nymphs and sailing away as the Rutulians watch in fear. Photo: Reproduced by kind permission of the Institut für Klassische Archäologie und Museum Klassischer Abgüsse, Ludwig-Maximilians-Universität, Munich (after Wright 1993: 71).

## 12 Latin Literature and Material Culture 651

image casts Virgil's account of the specific episode under the distant gaze of a birds' eye perspective. If the poet focuses on individuals, including a deal of direct speech (notably between Cybele and Jove, *Aen.* 9.77–106, and Turnus' address rallying his troops after the shock of the miracle, *Aen.* 9.128–58), the painting does something else: it turns Virgil's rhetorical focalisation around the speeches of divine and heroic characters into a broad landscape vision, one in which even the named heroes on their horses, let alone the receding column of foot soldiers, are subordinate to the larger vision of sea, rocky shoreline and mainland boulders (not to mention the bare-breasted, nymph-fronted ships).[79] What in the poem is an act of divine agency by Cybele (mirroring a long pattern of divine interventions in the epic as a whole) becomes a picture of human beings on the earth, reacting to the portent of the ships becoming nymphs in the sea. Effectively, the painter has cast an entirely different and wider-focused eye on the narrative than the poet implies, raising the land- and seascape (the former hardly present in the poetry at all) to the main pictorial event.

As material objects, illuminated codices like the Vatican and Roman Virgil risk falling between the cracks of disciplinary specialisation. While the texts reproduced in such manuscripts are studied by scholars of Latin literature (for instance, in making the editorial decision to excise *Aen.* 9.121 on the grounds of being a later addition, *because* it appears in no early manuscript), their pictures have generally been seen to belong to late antique art. In Optatian's case, the adverse effects of such disciplinary segregation are felt even more acutely. If Optatian's creative brilliance lies in bridging the fields of 'Latin literature' and 'material culture', his *oeuvre* has received remarkably little attention from philologists,[80] and still less from those interested in early fourth-century art and iconography.[81] In all this, we also need to be wary of the traditional Classicist's dismissal of late antique responses (including pictorial illustration) to earlier classic texts: the commentatorial options and hints offered to us by

---

[79] See Wright 1993: 70–1.
[80] According to the assessment of one prominent Latinist (Courtney 1990: 5), Optatian's works 'have lost all contact with reality and do not merit discussion'. Helm 1959: 1928 offers a typical twentieth-century assessment: 'Publilius Optatianus Porfyrius … ist der Verfasser hirnverbrannter Versspielereien, bei denen man ebenso staunen muß, daß ein Mensch auf derartige mühselig ausgetüftelte Künsteleien seine Zeit vergeuden und sie für Poesie halten konnte, wie daß er damit bei einem Kaiser Beifall zu finden vermochte.'
[81] Bardill 2012 provides a case in point – discussing the 'divine emperor of the Christian golden age' with just passing references to Optatian (pp. 104, 275, 302). Particularly important is Optatian's testimony about the development of symbolic schemes like the chi-rho (emblazoned in *Carm.* 8, 14, 19 and 24: cf. Squire and Whitton 2017, with further comments in Garipzanov 2018: 57–60): in discussing the Constantinian significance of the chi-rho motif (Bardill 2012: 159–202, 220–2), Bardill omits reference to Optatian altogether.

the corpus of late antique scholarship on earlier ancient literature preserve a series of responses to those works closer to their original resonance and reception than our own reactions, even if they are moderated by the arrival of new interpretative models sanctioned by Christianity.

What might the study of Latin literature gain from an appreciation of these material trappings? Quite apart from understanding how changing cultures of the book could affect literary production (and vice versa), attending to the physical presentation of Latin texts reminds us that the act of readerly interpretation was a sensory as well as cognitive affair.[82] More than that, recent work is beginning to show just how crucial a role the physical layout of a text played for ancient writers and readers alike: the extent to which Latin poets could exploit column-breaks of a scroll for semantic effect,[83] for example, the way in which authors of Latin prose paid careful attention to the spacing of their texts (including its literal and metaphorical centres),[84] or how other technologies were exploited to navigate readers around the material frame of a work.[85]

## Reading as Seeing . . .

It is not the case that scholars have entirely overlooked the way in which Latin authors could self-consciously engage with the material realm. Taking their lead from the burgeoning field of 'image and text' studies in the late twentieth century, especially in comparative literary circles,[86] recent studies have put particular store on one way in which Latin authors engaged with the physical world around them: namely, by describing in prose or verse the forms and effects of visual stimuli. 'Ecphrasis' is the Greek rhetorical term that ancient commentators used to delineate the

---

[82] For the 'sensory turn' in Classics, see for example the volumes in the Routledge 'Senses in Antiquity' series, along with e.g. Toner 2014, Betts 2017 and Platts 2020, esp. 1–22.

[83] See especially Schafer 2017 (on how the text of Virgil's *Eclogues* and *Georgics* 'mimetically responds to and comments on its column-breaks, investing the column and surrounding margins with figurative valences', 136); cf. e.g. Wray 2003: 239 (on Tibullus 1.1), O'Rourke 2014 (on the fourth book of Propertius' *Elegies*) and Williams 1992 and Jansen 2014a (on Ovidian elegy).

[84] See, for instance, Whitton 2015: esp. 111–31 on the spacing of Pliny the Younger's *Epistles* (emphasising how 'mediality is one (more) important, meaningful facet of the text', 129); cf. also Gibson 2014, along with Bodel 2015a: 20–42, on the 'paratextual' importance of the Younger Pliny's 'index'.

[85] Cf. e.g. Schröder 1999: 93–159 on the indexes not only of the Elder Pliny and Columella, but also Hyginus, Vegetius, Palladius, Isidorus, Cassiodorus and Augustine. Specifically on the example of Pliny's *Natural History*, cf. Carey 2003: 17–40, Naas 2002: 171–34 and Doody 2010: esp. 120–3.

[86] Among the most important contributions were Krieger 1967 and 1992, Mitchell 1986, Heffernan 1993, Hollander 1995 and Boehm and Pfotenhauer 1995. In Classicist circles, see particularly the pioneering volumes of Goldhill and Osborne 1994 and Elsner 1996b; cf. e.g. Newby and Leader-Newby 2007 on inscriptions, James 2007 and Eastmond 2015 on late antique and Byzantine materials.

phenomenon, and scholarship on Latin ecphrastic literature has flourished over the last thirty years in particular.[87] Our aim in exploring the phenomenon of ecphrasis here is to survey just some of the ways that this work has come to influence the study of 'Latin literature and material culture', while also pointing to some possible future directions.

Like the word itself, ideas of ecphrasis came to Latin literature through a Greek critical lens.[88] While the history of ecphrasis stretches to the very beginnings of Greek literature (taking its lead from Homer's description of the shield of Achilles in the eighteenth book of the *Iliad*),[89] our most detailed extant discussions of it are preserved in a series of Imperial Greek rhetorical handbooks, or *Progymnasmata*.[90] Approaching ecphrasis within the broader framework of epideictic declamation, Theon, Hermogenes, Aphthonius and Nikolaus all provide strikingly similar definitions. According to Theon, in a gloss that recurs among other *Progymnasmata*-authors,[91] ecphrasis amounts to a 'descriptive speech which brings the subject being shown before the eyes with visual vividness' (ἔκφρασίς ἐστι λόγος περιηγηματικὸς ἐναργῶς ὑπ' ὄψιν ἄγων τὸ δηλούμενον).[92] As a special sort of 'descriptive speech' (λόγος περιηγηματικός), ecphrasis was understood to transform the described subject – as something figuratively 'being shown' (τὸ δηλούμενον) – into an almost physical apparition 'before the eyes' (ὑπ' ὄψιν). Like other commentators, Theon is somewhat elusive about how this transformation takes place. But a single adverb is used to describe the process: ἐναργῶς ('with visual vividness'). This concept of *enargeia* was evidently key to

---

[87] For some introductory overviews, see Elsner 2002; Squire 2009: esp. 139–46; Squire 2015b; Zeitlin 2013. Still fundamental are Friedländer 1912 (with a selective inventory of relevant passages); Palm 1965–6; Hohlweg 1971: 36–42. A landmark article on Latin ecphrasis was Fowler 1991 (reprinted alongside two other influential chapters in Fowler 2000: 37–107); more recently see Dufallo 2013.

[88] More generally on the relationship between Greek and Latin literary traditions, see Goldhill in this volume.

[89] *Il.* 18.478–608. The bibliography is immense: see e.g. Lynn-George 1988: 174–200; Becker 1995; Francis 2009; d'Acunto and Palmisciano 2010; Lecoq 2010; de Jong 2011; Squire 2013a (with further bibliography in p. 183 n. 1). Thein 2021 offers a pioneering study of the Homeric passage and both its Greek and Latin reception.

[90] Webb 2009 provides the most detailed analysis, supplementing her earlier studies – including Webb 1997a, 1997b, 1999 and 2000. Much has also been written about the social, intellectual and paedagogical contexts of these handbooks: e.g. Bartsch 1989: 7–14; Anderson 1993: 47–53; Boeder 1996: 29–41; Webb 2001: esp. 294–5; Webb 2009: 39–59; Goldhill 2007: 3–8. For the extracted passages in Greek and English translation, see Webb 2009: 197–211; the texts themselves can be found in Patillon and Bolognesi 1997: 66–9; Rabe 1913: 22–3; Rabe 1926: 36–41; Felten 1913: 67–71.

[91] Although Theon's *Progymnasmata* is still often regarded as the earliest handbook, the dates have been much debated (see e.g. Heath 2002–3). Whatever the chronology, the definition of ecphrasis cited here was repeated by other rhetoricians: Hermogenes even acknowledged the formulaic gloss by adding 'as they say' before his own ensuing explanation (ὡς φασίν: *Prog.* 10.47 = Rabe 1913: 22).

[92] *Prog.* 118.7 (= Patillon and Bolognesi 1997: 66).

rhetorical ideas about ecphrasis, and the word (whether as noun or adverb), is found amid all extant *Progymnasmata* discussions.[93] Indeed, according to Hermogenes, *enargeia* was one of two 'virtues' of ecphrasis, working alongside *saphêneia* ('clarity').[94] 'Ecphrasis is an interpretation that almost brings about seeing through hearing', Hermogenes adds (τὴν ἑρμηνείαν διὰ τῆς ἀκοῆς σχεδὸν τὴν ὄψιν μηχανᾶσθαι);[95] the elements of ecphrasis, to quote Nikolaus, 'bring the subjects of the speech before our eyes and almost make speakers into spectators' (ὑπ' ὄψιν ἡμῖν ἄγοντα ταῦτα, περὶ ὧν εἰσιν οἱ λόγοι, καὶ μονονοὺ θεατὰς εἶναι παρασκευάζοντα).[96]

There can be no doubt that this Greek rhetorical framework, like the Greek literary tradition that stands behind it, informed Latin literary ideas of descriptive evocation. Although he does not use the word ecphrasis *per se*, Quintilian at times echoes the critical thinking reflected in the *Progymnasmata*, above all in discussing the importance of *uisiones* ('visions') in Roman oratory: what Greek rhetoricians call *phantasiae*, writes Quintilian, are the 'means through which images of things that are absent are represented to the mind (*per quas imagines rerum absentium ... repraesentantur animo*), so that we seem to view them with our eyes and to have them present before us'.[97] The same nexus of ideas about ecphrasis recurs in all manner of other Latin contexts, too. To cite one instance, consider how the Younger Pliny introduces the framework in the fifth book of his *Epistles*, framing his famous description of his 'Tuscan' villa around the trope (*Ep.* 5.6.42–4). Referring to Homer's description of the shield of Achilles, as well as to Virgilian description of the shield of Aeneas (while also comparing Aratus' grand but short evocation of the whole universe in his *Phainomena*), Pliny declares an ecphrastic intention 'to set the entire villa before your eyes' (*totam uillam oculis tuis subicere*).[98] So familiar was this rhetorical framework, indeed, that we even find it lampooned. A case in point can be found in Petronius' *Satyrica*, which features a scene of Eumolpus and Encolpius responding to the paintings displayed in a *pinacotheca*: appealing to his high-brow readership, Petronius knowingly sends up pretensions of artistic attribution, aesthetic

---

[93] On *enargeia*, see Webb 2009: esp. 87–130; cf. Zanker 1981; Otto 2009; Sheppard 2014: 19–46; Squire and Elsner 2017. For parallel comments about *enargeia* in the context of Greek scholiastic commentaries, especially on Homer, cf. Rispoli 1984; Manieri 1998: esp. 179–92; Meijering 1987: 29–52; Nünlist 2009: esp. 153–5, 194–8.

[94] *Prog.* 10.49 (Rabe 1913: 23). [95] *Prog.* 10.48 (Rabe 1913: 23). [96] Felten 1913: 70.

[97] *Inst.* 6.2.29–30: cf. Goldhill 2007: 3–5 and Webb 2009: esp. 93–6, along more generally with Henderson 1991, Vasaly 1993 (on Cicero) and Scholz 1998. Cf. Lausberg 1998: 359–66, nos. 810–19 (on *euidentia* in Roman rhetoric).

[98] For discussion, see Chinn 2007: esp. 278; Squire 2011: 353–5; Goldhill 2012: 99–101.

criticism, the limits of mimetic imitation and even – in a verse pastiche of Virgil and Seneca, staged around a painting of the sack of Troy or *Troiae Halosis* – poetic traditions of responding to paintings (*Sat.* 83–90).[99]

The rhetoric of ecphrasis also returns us to Optatian's fourth-century experiments with the materiality of poetic form. In his altar poem (Figures 12.1–4), for example, the opening invocation that the reader should *see* the monument evoked (*uides*) literalises the trope of ecphrastic visualisation. Something similar might be said of Optatian's naval grid-poem (Figure 12.8). Once again, the very first word of the poem is staked on an idea of 'bringing forth' a vision via the medium of words: 'the heavenly signs will be made manifest to the reader in red cinnabar' (*prodentur minio caelestia signa legenti*, *Carm.* 19.1).[100] Just as rhetorical theories of ecphrasis were staked on the promise of 'seeing' through 'hearing', Optatian here pitches the resources of verbal description against the effects of vision, all the while blurring any straightforward distinction between the two. What is so special about such 'art painted in letters/characters' (*arte notis picta*, v. 20), we are told, is its capacity to summon up actual images: the 'Muse permits the weaving of a ship that she has made visible' (*uisam contexere nauem Musa sinit*, vv. 25–6). To put the point more strongly, we might say that Optatian takes the idea of ecphrastic vision, oriented around *enargeia*, and materialises the metaphor of 'seeing' through the physical apparitions of his texts: where rhetoricians had theorised ecphrasis as an art of *almost* seeing through hearing, his poems now forge actual apparitions on the page.[101]

In the twenty-first century, as readers of this volume will know full well, scholarship on ancient ecphrasis is booming, and among Latinists and Hellenists alike. Still, there remains a general tendency to approach the phenomenon in exclusively literary terms. As rhetorical trope, ecphrasis

---

[99] On the passage, and the rhetorical framework of ecphrasis that informs it, see especially Slater 1987; Elsner 2007b: 177–99; Baier 2010; Dufallo 2013: 177–205.

[100] Quite apart from the allusion to rhetorical theories of ecphrasis, or the deliberate ambiguity of Optatian's *signa* here, we might note how the talk of *caelestia signa* echoes Lactantius' talk of the celebrated *caeleste signum* that Constantine is said to have observed shortly before the battle of the Milvian bridge in October 312 (*De mort. pers.* 44.5) – and in the context of a poem that comes complete with a chi-rho mast and sail (cf. Figure. 12.8).

[101] Although concerned with the promise rather than failures of ecphrastic vision, the *Progymnasmata* were well aware of the underlying fictitiousness. For Hermogenes, ecphrasis is about '*almost* (σχεδόν) seeing through hearing' (Hermogenes 10.48 = Rabe 1913: 23), just as Nikolaus talks of 'all but [μονονού] making the audience into spectators' (Nikolaus = Felten 1913: 70). In the words of Simon Goldhill, 'rhetorical theory knows well that its descriptive power is a technique of illusion, semblance, and of making to appear' (Goldhill 2007: 3; cf. Becker 1995: 28). Much later, in his ninth-century commentary on Aphthonius' *Progymnasmata*, John of Sardis would further develop the point: 'even if the speech were ten thousand times vivid [κἂν γὰρ μυριάκις ἐναργὴς εἴη ὁ λόγος], it would be impossible [ἀδύνατον] to bring "the thing shown" or ecphrasised itself before the eyes' (= Rabe 1928: 216; cf. Webb 2009: 52–3).

was defined around an idea of visuality. Ironically, though, the literary workings of ecphrasis are most often discussed without reference to the visual realm with which ancient authors engaged.

The field of Roman visual culture has a key potential contribution to make here. As many scholars have emphasised, the *Progymnasmata* understood ecphrasis to encompass a wide variety of subjects: it was by no means restricted to works of art alone.[102] But there can be no doubt that, in a tradition descending from Homer, Greek and Latin writers recognised the description of artworks as a paradigmatic example of ecphrasis. The materials surviving in the archaeological record consequently help us to see the visual cultural vistas with which ecphrasis was understood to engage. No less importantly, material cultural perspectives can inform our understanding of the underlying critical framework. A case in point comes in Roman depictions of the shield of Achilles – that is, Roman visual engagements with classical literature's most canonical example of a verbally described object. We know of six paintings from Pompeii that take up the Homeric subject, in each case depicting the moment when Hephaestus (always shown to the left) shows the shield that he has fashioned to Thetis (on the right).[103] Although the actual imagery of the shield differs between the paintings (and all in fact leave the iconographic details poignantly vague), it is significant that most paintings transform the tableau into a scene of verbal explication: with rod in hand, a figure is sometimes shown talking Thetis through the visual details. Rhetorical definitions of ecphrasis are consequently turned on their head: while viewers now see the shield through the painting, the imagery

---

[102] Webb 2009: 61–86; cf. Webb 1999; James and Webb 1991: 6. Theon, Hermogenes, Aphthonius and Nikolaus all distinguish between what they call ecphraseis of 'deeds' (*pragmata*), 'persons' (*prosôpa*) and 'places' (*topoi*), while also talking about the interrelated categories of 'times' (*chronoi*: Theon, Hermogenes, Nikolaus) and 'opportunities' (*kairoi*: Hermogenes, Aphthonius). Some authors list additional subjects: Theon includes descriptions of how something came about (*tropoi*), Aphthonius introduces 'speechless animals and plants' (*aloga zôa kai ... phyta*), and Nikolaus cites the example of 'festivals' (*panêgyreis*). Nikolaus (writing towards the end of the fifth century) is the only author to mention descriptions of 'statues, paintings and the like' (Felten 1913: 69). As we have argued at greater length elsewhere, however, there can be little doubt that Graeco-Roman writers and readers would have recognised the description of art as the classic instance of ecphrastic practice (Elsner 2002: 2–3; Squire 2013a: esp. 157–8).

[103] For discussions, see Brendel 1980: 74–80; Hardie 1985: 18–20; Gury 1986; Balensiefen 1990: 56–9; Hodske 2007: 216–18; Squire 2013a: 169–70. Compare also Squire 2018 on the Younger Philostratus' ecphrastic description of a painting showing the shield of Achilles in his *Imagines*. The most recent discussion is Heslin 2015: 161–5, suggesting that each 'humble domestic painting' might be 'a domestic visual quotation of part of a public visual cycle in Pompeii that imitated a fictional ecphrasis in Virgil's *Aeneid* that was inspired by a visual monument in Rome in which there was a cycle of Hellenistic paintings that illustrated the text of Homer's *Iliad*, which itself contained an ecphrasis of the shield' (322); for a response, cf. Squire 2016a.

12  *Latin Literature and Material Culture*      657

Figure 12.19  Wall-painting from the Casa di Sirico (Pompeii VII.1.25), first century CE. Reproduced by kind permission of the Institut für Klassische Archäologie und Museum für Abgüsse Klassischer Bildwerke, Ludwig-Maximilians-Universität, Munich.

points to an absence of words – it depicts a verbal explanation that viewers are unable to hear. One painting, from the Casa di Sirico (Figure 12.19), goes even further in its refractive medial games: what viewers see in this case is the reflection of Thetis as she looks at it – that is, an absolute and categorical absence of the famous Homeric text, but a portrayed projection of the viewing subject. A similar sort of critical inversion is at play on

Figure 12.20 Obverse of *Tabula Iliaca* 4 N (= Rome, Musei Capitolini, Sala delle Colombe, inv. 83a). Photograph by Michael Squire, by kind permission of the Direzione, Musei Capitolini, Rome.

two so-called 'Iliac tablets', both early Imperial in date and found in the immediate proximity of Rome, which transform the Homeric ecphrasis back into three-dimensional material object.[104] In the best surviving example,

---

[104] See Squire 2011: 303–70 and Squire 2013a: 165–79.

## 12 Latin Literature and Material Culture

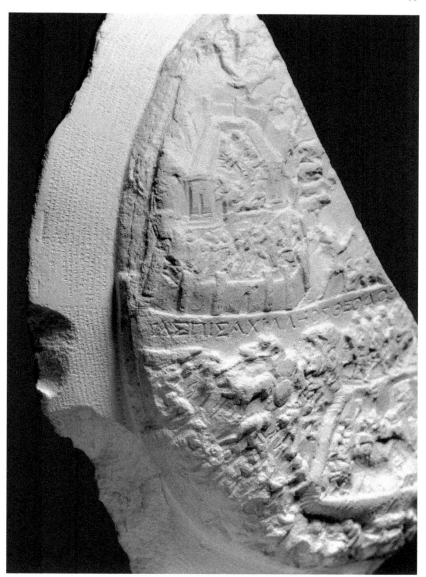

Figure 12.21 Plaster cast of the same tablet (*Tabula Iliaca* 4 N), as housed in the Archäologisches Institut und Sammlung der Gipsabgüsse, Göttingen (inv. A1695). The first three columns of text (from an original total of ten) can be seen here: *Il.* 18.483–92 (top), 493–504 (middle) and 505–19 (bottom); a fourth column, (on the damaged part of the rim at the bottom) was inscribed with vv. 533–45. Photograph by Stefan Eckardt, reproduced by kind permission.

Homer's 'great and mighty' shield is rescaled into an object that is just 17.8 cm in diameter (Figure 12.20). Despite that miniature scope, the outer rim – measuring just 2 cm – is inscribed with the full span of the Homeric passage, originally meandering around the shield in ten columns (*Il.* 18.483–557) (Figure 12.21). The movement from object to text and back consequently finds its counterpart in the epigraphic presentation of the Homeric ecphrasis, albeit in letters that measure less than one millimetre in height: the object tenders the promise of reading the Homeric passage, we might say, while rendering that text in such a way as to be illegible to the naked eye.[105]

## Ecphrastic Circles

Material case studies like these at once respond and contribute to ancient critical thinking about ecphrasis. It is for this reason that they deserve attention from Latinists: they help paint a picture of the historical and intellectual framework in which Latin ecphrasis itself operated. At the same time, the very nature of ecphrasis muddies our academic distinctions between 'Latin studies' and 'material culture': as rhetorical trope, it prompts us to look at texts through a visual cultural prism, no less than to read Roman art through a Latin literary lens.

To demonstrate the point, we turn to one of the best-known ecphrastic passages of all Latin literature: Virgil's description of the Carthaginian temple images in the opening book of the *Aeneid* (1.453–93). Of course, we are dealing here with a single example. But it seems appropriate to focus on Virgil for two reasons: first, on account of the self-reflexivity with which the *Aeneid* exploited material objects to consider its own literary ancestry and poetic fabric; and second, because of its profound influence on the ensuing Latin literary tradition.[106]

The passage is sufficiently famous to require little introduction. After arriving at Carthage, Aeneas quickly stumbles upon a sheltered grove. Concealed in a great mist, he finds local artists constructing a 'great temple for Juno' (*templum Iunoni ingens*, 1.446). The description of the scenes adorning the temple provides the poet with an opportunity for a literary 'flashback' – a brief recap of the Greek epic prehistory from which the *Aeneid* descends.

---

[105] For a transcription of the text – our earliest ancient presentation of these Homeric lines – see Squire 2012. To claim that the 'text is easily legible with a magnifying glass' (Horsfall 1979: 33) would be to lose sight of the intermedial games.

[106] Since the late twentieth century, Virgilian ecphrasis has attracted a burgeoning bibliography – e.g. Boyd 1995; Barchiesi 1997 and 2005: 294–300; Bartsch 1998; Putnam 1998 and 2001; Smith 2005; Elsner 2007b: 78–87. Among the most important passages are the Virgilian descriptions of the Carthaginian temple reliefs (*Aen.* 1.453–93); the silver-gilt dishes (1.630–2); the embroidered cloak given to Cloanthus (5.250–7); the bronze doors made by Daedalus at Cumae (6.20–37); Latinus' cedar-wood statues (7.177–91); the shield of Turnus (7.789–92); the shield of Aeneas (8.626–728); and Pallas' sword-belt (10.495–505).

namque sub ingenti lustrat dum singula templo,
reginam opperiens, dum quae fortuna sit urbi
artificumque manus inter se operumque laborem          455
miratur, uidet Iliacas ex ordine pugnas,
bellaque iam fama totum uolgata per orbem,
Atridas Priamumque et saeuum ambobus Achillem.
constitit, et lacrimans 'quis iam locus' inquit 'Achate,
quae regio in terris nostri non plena laboris?          460
en Priamus! sunt hic etiam sua praemia laudi;
sunt lacrimae rerum et mentem mortalia tangunt.
solue metus; feret haec aliquam tibi fama salutem.'
sic ait, atque animum pictura pascit inani,
multa gemens, largoque umectat flumine uultum.          465
namque uidebat uti bellantes Pergama circum
hac fugerent Graii, premeret Troiana iuuentus,
hac Phryges, instaret curru cristatus Achilles.
nec procul hinc Rhesi niueis tentoria uelis
adgnoscit lacrimans, primo quae prodita somno          470
Tydides multa uastabat caede cruentus,
ardentisque auertit equos in castra, prius quam
pabula gustassent Troiae Xanthumque bibissent.
parte alia fugiens amissis Troilus armis,
infelix puer atque impar congressus Achilli,          475
fertur equis, curruque haeret resupinus inani,

For standing beneath the huge temple Aeneas scans each individual object while he waits for the queen. As he marvels at the prosperity of the city, the handicraft of the artists, and the labour of their works, he sees the Iliac battles laid out in order and the wars whose fame had now spread across the whole world – the sons of Atreus and Priam, and Achilles merciless to both. He stands still and weeps: 'What place is there now, Achates,' he says, 'what land on earth that is not full of our labour? See, there is Priam! Even here does virtue have its due reward: events find their tears, and mortality touches the heart. Let go your fears: this fame will bring you some salvation!'

So he speaks and feasts his mind on the empty picture with many a sigh, dampening his face in a stream of tears. For he saw how, here at one point, the Greeks fled as they were fighting around Troy, the Trojan youth hard on their heels, and at how, there at another, the Trojans fled, with plumed Achilles pressing them hard in his chariot. Not far away, he recognises through his tears the snowy-canvassed tents of Rhesus to which, betrayed in their first sleep, the blood-stained son of Tydeus [Diomedes] laid waste in a great massacre, turning his fiery horses away to his

lora tenens tamen; huic ceruixque comaeque trahuntur
per terram, et uersa puluis inscribitur hasta.
interea ad templum non aequae Palladis ibant
480 crinibus Iliades passis peplumque ferebant,
suppliciter tristes et tunsae pectora palmis;
diua solo fixos oculos auersa tenebat.
ter circum Iliacos raptauerat Hectora muros,
exanimumque auro corpus uendebat Achilles.
485 tum uero ingentem gemitum dat pectore ab imo,
ut spolia, ut currus, utque ipsum corpus amici,
tendentemque manus Priamum conspexit inermis.
se quoque principibus permixtum adgnouit Achiuis,
Eoasque acies et nigri Memnonis arma.
490 ducit Amazonidum lunatis agmina peltis
Penthesilea furens, mediisque in milibus ardet,
aurea subnectens exsertae cingula mammae,
bellatrix, audetque uiris concurrere uirgo.

camp before they could taste Trojan fodder, or drink from the river Xanthus. In another part is Troilus, his armour lost in flight – unhappy boy, and an unequal match for Achilles: he is dragged along by his horses, clinging face-up to the empty chariot, but still clasping the reins; his neck and hair trail along the ground, and the dust is inscribed with the shaft of his spear. Meanwhile the Trojan women were pressing along with their streaming hair to the temple of unjust Pallas Athena, carrying the sacred robe, mourning in suppliant guise and beating their breasts with their hands: with averted face the goddess kept her eyes fixed upon the ground. Three times had Achilles dragged Hector round the walls of Troy, and now he was selling the lifeless body for gold. Then above all Aeneas heaves a mighty groan from the depths of his heart as he viewed the spoils, the chariot, the very corpse of his friend, and Priam stretching out his unarmed hands. Himself, too, he recognised, in close combat with the Greek chiefs, and the Eastern ranks, and the armour of black Memnon. The raging Penthesilea leads the crescent-shielded ranks of Amazons, resplendent among her thousands; a golden girdle is fastened beneath her exposed breast – a female warrior who dares, a maiden, to do battle with men.

## 12 Latin Literature and Material Culture 663

A great deal has been written about this passage, and not least about its relationship to literary and rhetorical traditions of ecphrasis.[107] For one thing, Aeneas' teary-eyed response to this imagery has been seen to reconfigure Odysseus' reaction to Demodocus' song about Troy in the *Odyssey* (8.83–92, 521–30). For another, there is clear significance in the reader's seeing these images through the eyes of Aeneas – so that the audience's view of the Greek literary canon is re-focalised through the epic protagonist of the Latin poem. Like Aeneas, who stands motionless before the images (*constitit*, v. 459), the description has also been understood as enacting a programmatic 'stilling' of the narrative:[108] inserted close to the beginning of the poem, the passage provides a moment for circumspective reflection, allowing readers to review the poetic space into which the *Aeneid* inscribes itself.[109]

But a material cultural perspective can open up some additional literary perspectives. For whatever else we make of the passage, we can be sure that Virgil was responding to actual sorts of objects – and that those materials were in turn familiar to the *Aeneid*'s earliest readership.[110] By around the late first century BCE, painted cycles of Greek epic seem to have been a favourite subject for visual display: according to Vitruvius, 'battles of Troy or Odysseus' wanderings through landscapes' were a particularly popular theme in contemporary wall-painting (*Troianas pugnas seu Vlixis erratione per topia*, 7.5.2); in Petronius' *Satyrica*, we even hear of Trimalchio emulating the fashion – adorning his home with wall-paintings of the two Homeric epics (albeit setting them beside images of gladiatorial games, *Sat.* 29.4).[111] Four related cycles also survive in the archaeological

---

[107] For discussions of the passage, see *inter alios* Williams 1960; Johnson 1976: 99–105; Dubois 1982: 32–5; Clay 1988: esp. 201–3; Leach 1988: 311–18; Lowenstam 1993; Barchiesi 1994: 114–24; Boyd 1995: esp. 76–84; Laird 1996: 87–94; Bartsch 1998: 326–9; Putnam 1998: 23–54; La Penna 2000; Beck 2007; Elsner 2007b: 79–82; Kirichenko 2013; Petrain 2014: 44–8; Squire 2014: 387–94 and Squire 2016b; Heslin 2015: 261–78; Pandey 2018: 16–19.

[108] Fundamental is Fowler 1991: esp. 31–3.

[109] Importantly, the passage also looks forwards and backwards to the narrative frame of the *Aeneid*. The fact that these scenes adorn a temple dedicated to Juno frames the description in relation to the goddess' anger that directs the action of Virgil's poem (*Aen.* 1.4 *Iunonis ob iram*). The individual vignettes forge suggestive analogies between the protagonists of Greek epic and those in Virgil's own poem: the fate of Troilus 'pre-picts' that of Pallas, for example, while the figure of Penthesileia might have us think not only of Camilla, but also of Dido (whose inauspicious arrival into the poem's action follows immediately after this description, at vv. 490–3).

[110] The discussion that follows draws selectively on Squire 2014 and 2016b. Cf. also Barchiesi 1994: 117; Leach 1988: 321 and La Penna 2000: 3–4.

[111] The Elder Pliny also refers to a series of paintings on the Trojan War displayed in the Portico of Philip (*HN* 35.144) – discussed at length by Heslin 2015. On Homeric themes in extant wall-painting, see Santoro 2005, along more generally with Squire 2011: esp. 74–85 (with further bibliography); cf. Stefanou 2006: especially 51–176 on Homeric themes in Roman Imperial mosaics.

record: one set of frescoes from a mid-first-century BCE villa on the Esquiline in Rome (with its so-called 'Odyssey landscapes'),[112] and three from Pompeii (all relating to Iliadic subjects, and including one in painted stucco).[113] It is worth noting that Virgil does not in fact specify a painterly medium: he – or for that matter his audiences – might have had sculptural reliefs in mind.[114] As such, the described visual subjects also take us to objects like the *Tabulae Iliacae*, sculpted in or around Rome during the late first century BCE or early first century CE.[115] We have already mentioned these 'Iliac tablets' in connection with the Homeric shield of Achilles. But of the twenty-two extant marble reliefs, most in fact relate to epic cyclical themes: many lay out the stories of Greek epic in a series of miniature vignettes and friezes, inviting audiences to put together their constituent visual parts in satisfying or meaningful sequence (cf. Figures 12.24–5).[116]

---

[112] The fullest publication is Biering 1995. Cf. Schefold and Jung 1989: 350–7, Coarelli 1998, Andreae 1999: 242–57 and O'Sullivan 2007 (with detailed review of bibliography on pp. 500–4); Petrain 2013: 149–52.

[113] All three cycles – unearthed during excavations along the Via dell'Abbondanza in 1919 – are published in Aurigemma 1953. One comes from the Casa di Octavius Quartio (also known as the Casa di Loreius Tiburtinus), Pompeii 11.2.2. The other two come from the eponymous rooms of the Casa del Criptoportico and Casa del Sacello Iliaco, which at one stage formed a single house (Pompeii 1.6.2 and 1.6.4). More detailed discussions of all three friezes – with more detailed bibliographic references – can be found in Squire 2015c; cf. also Schefold 1975: 129–34, Brilliant 1984: 60–5, Croisille 2005: 154–65 and Pollard 2018.

[114] Cf. e.g. Leach 1988: 312–13 and Boyd 1995: 81–3.

[115] For three monograph discussions, see Valenzuela Montenegro 2004, Squire 2011 and Petrain 2014.

[116] The 'choose-your-own-adventure' element is important (Squire 2011: 127–96). These sorts of wall-paintings and reliefs, we would argue, framed larger cultures of early Imperial Roman visual and readerly interpretation– cultures that were dynamically shaped by (and which in turn themselves dynamically shaped) the contemporary political landscape, and late into 'late antiquity'. We have both in different ways been advocating this cultural historical point for some time, and from a visual critical perspective informed in part by Late Republican and Imperial Latin texts (cf. Elsner 1995: esp. 1–14, 247–87; Elsner 2007b; Squire 2013e: esp. 270–2; cf. e.g. Platt 2009 and Squire 2011: esp. 383–4; all these works respond in different ways to the fundamental account of Zanker 1989, and the important response of Wallace-Hadrill 1989). Unwittingly, it seems, recent work has converged around a related literary and political cultural viewpoint, albeit with minimal reference to Roman art and archaeology: exploring how 'poets read and respond to Augustus' public image as represented in well-known signs, monuments and rituals', for example, a recent monograph has argued that Augustan writers learned to train 'their literary gaze on such symbols . . .', so as thereby to 'explore the degree to which imperial signs and power rely on audience participation' (Pandey 2018: 1–38, quotations from 5). As a result, Pandey concludes, 'political authority' was shown to 'depend on a mutually constitutive relationship with a judging audience' (6). In many ways this work is to be welcomed. What continues to frustrate us, however, is the assumption that visual and material cultures play a wholly passive role, as compared with the active political dynamics of 'Latin literature'. What we would emphasise – as demonstrated via the following analysis – is that early Imperial attitudes towards readerly interpretation were themselves shaped by the contemporary material realm; moreover, that viewing – no less than reading! – must always constitute a political act. We hope that if we make the point often – and loud – enough, scholars of Latin literature might finally reckon with the point . . .

So how might these materials enrich an understanding of Virgilian ecphrasis, and how might the *Aeneid*'s description in turn inform an approach to contemporary Roman objects and imagery? To begin answering those questions, it is necessary to note one significant aspect of Virgil's description: the organisation of the described depictions into a specific narrative sequence.[117] Virgil begins by telling how Aeneas scans each individual tableau (*lustrat . . . singula*, v. 453). As the passage proceeds, however, we find those separate scenes being spun into an intricate whole; indeed, Virgil underscores the point by introducing the idea of arrangement, or *ordo*, emphasising how Aeneas 'sees the Iliac battles laid out in order' (*uidet Iliacas ex ordine pugnas*, v. 456). The account that follows encompasses a panoply of Greek Epic Cyclical scenes, including events described in the *Iliad*, as well as in the lost *Cypria* (the story of Troilus: vv. 469–73) and *Aethiopis* (the references to Penthesilea and Memnon: vv. 489–93). And yet the narrative organisation of those described scenes violates chronology, rearranging episodes out of their established literary sequence. Most conspicuous is the reference to Troilus' death (vv. 474–8) between descriptions of Diomedes' slaughter of Rhesus (vv. 469–73) and of the Trojan women supplicating Athena (vv. 466–8): an event bound up with the pre-Iliadic *Cypria* is here sandwiched between episodes drawn from the *Iliad* (10.465–525, 6.297–310), which are themselves evoked in reverse Homeric order.

A similar concern with *ordo* recurs in our material comparanda. Consider, first of all, the Iliadic frieze in the oecus of the Casa di Octavius Quartio at Pompeii. The room – intended as a space for intimate dining, looking out onto the elaborate pergola and garden of the house – combines two separate painted cycles: a large frieze relating to the life of Heracles above (at a height of c. 80 cm), and a smaller Iliadic frieze below (c. 20 cm).[118] Both friezes stretch around all four walls of the room, interrupted by two doorways in its southern and western sides. Significantly, both cycles also proceed in different – and multiple – directions: if the aim is to put the scenes back into chronological order, viewers must snake across the various walls, eschewing any single mode of linear interpretation (Figure 12.22). Were they to begin the Iliadic frieze with the scene relating to the first book, located in the room's southwest corner, audiences might then proceed across the southern

---

[117] See above all La Penna 2000: 4–7, albeit with a lesser interest in contemporary material visual culture.
[118] On the house, cf. *PPM* 3: 42–108. For the oecus and its painted cycles, see Aurigemma 1953: 971–1008; Bianchi-Bandinelli 1955: 29–30; Brilliant 1984: 60–1; Croisille 1985 and 2005: 161–5; Clarke 1991: 201–7; de Vos 1993; Coralini 2001: 165–73, no. P.038; Coralini 2002; Lorenz 2013; Squire 2014: 374–86.

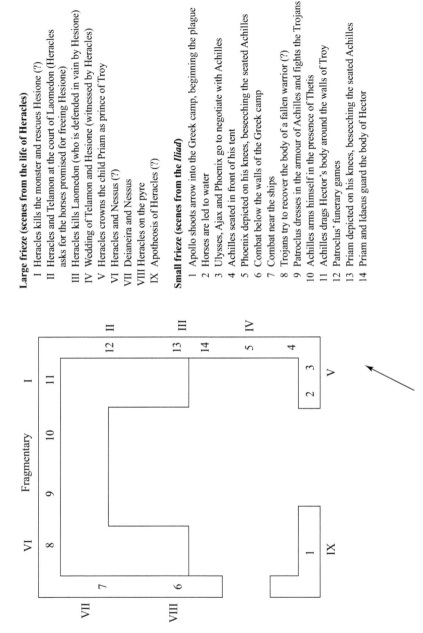

Figure 12.22 Diagram showing the arrangement of scenes in the two lateral friezes of 'oecus h' in the Casa di Octavius Quartio (Pompeii II.2.2). The room measures 5.05 m by 5.25 m, and was likely decorated c. 70 CE. Diagram by Michael Squire (largely following the identifications of Aurigemma 1953: 971–1027 and Coralini 2001: 165–73).

Figure 12.23 Reconstruction drawing of the east wall of the same *oecus*, showing the Heracles frieze above, and the smaller Iliadic frieze below. Photograph reproduced by kind permission of the Archiv, Institut für Klassische Archäologie und Museum für Abgüsse Klassischer Bildwerke, Ludwig-Maximilians-Universität, Munich (after Aurigemma 1953: 975, fig. 990).

doorway and take up the story on the east wall. But, to follow the Iliadic sequence of events, they must then jump across to the west wall, advancing now in a clockwise rather than anticlockwise direction. The decidedly 'jumbling' effect is clearest to see on the eastern wall (Figure 12.23). While the Heraclean scenes of the upper frieze here proceed from left to right, the lower Iliadic frieze is ordered from right to left. Towards the right-hand corner, Achilles can be seen sulking in his tent, and next to him is a depiction of Phoenix's embassy to Achilles (as described in *Iliad* 9). Still further to the left are then scenes drawn from the final books of the *Iliad*. In order to weave the epic episodes into an Iliadic sequence, viewers have consequently to rove back and forth – whether metaphorically, or physically – across the room.[119]

Such painterly games with spatial and narrative arrangement find a sculptural counterpart in the Iliac tablets. Consider the most famous example: the so-called *Tabula Iliaca Capitolina* in Rome (Figure 12.24).[120] In this case, viewers are presented with a much larger – albeit, in physical terms, a marvellously miniature – panorama of the Trojan epic cycle.[121] The left-hand section is lost, but the compositional rationale of the tablet is clear (Figure 12.25): at the centre is a scene of the fall of Troy, bringing together different moments in the story within its single cityscape; on either side are two sets of friezes, relating to the first twelve books of the *Iliad* (to the left), and the final twelve books (to the right). At the top of the tablet, a continuous frieze stretches from the upper left to the upper right, combining subjects from the first and last books of the *Iliad*. At the bottom, positioned between the friezes dealing with the *Iliad*'s central books, are two additional bands, this time relating to other Greek epic cyclical works – the *Aethiopis* and *Little Iliad*. Greek inscriptions accompany the sculpted images throughout: observe, most conspicuously, the two inscribed stelai (of which only one now survives) either side of the central scene, providing a miniature verbal synopsis of the visualised story.

In its form and composition, the Capitoline tablet directly parallels the *Iliacas ex ordine pugnas* described by Virgil. For those minded to approach

---

[119] By publishing the individual scenes in their Iliadic sequence rather than according to their physical arrangement in the room, Aurigemma 1953: 971–1008 significantly underplays the complexity of the arrangement. Classical archaeologists still seem unable to appreciate the rhetorical ruse of order that is at play: e.g. Pollard 2018: 289, n. 11 ('The distorted chronology of the *Iliad* frieze is the subject of much discussion; the reason for its snaking path around the room is never convincingly explained').

[120] Musei Capitolini, Sala delle Colombe, inv. 316: cf. Mancuso 1909; Maras 1999: esp. 17–67; Valenzuela Montenegro 2004: 22–149; Squire 2011: 387–90 (with indexed references to more detailed discussions in the book); Petrain 2014: esp. 3–8. The tablet's inscriptions can be found in *IG* 14: 328–33, no. 1284 (with corrections and translations in Petrain 2014: 188–204).

[121] The tablet measures just 25 × 30 × 1.5 cm; its original width must have been around 40 cm.

the object in Virgilian terms, an additional iconographic prompt might even invite reflection about its potential relationship with the *Aeneid*: at the literal and metaphorical fulcrum of the object, after all, Aeneas can be seen fleeing Troy – so that, just as in the Carthaginian scenes that Virgil describes his protagonist as seeing, Aeneas is shown 'mixed in' among the other scenes (*permixtum*, v. 489).[122] Here, just as in Virgil's passage, the juxtapositions raise questions about how an audience should structure singular scenes into a narrative whole. Where should a viewer begin, or for that matter end? How is the single horizontal band, stretching from the beginning to the end of the *Iliad*, to be reconciled with the vertical arrangement of the intervening books? At which point should the *Aethiopis* and *Little Iliad* friezes be situated in the story (positioned as they are between the Iliadic bands), or for that matter the central scene of Troy's fall?[123] As if to underscore such questions, a Greek elegiac couplet – inscribed towards the bottom of the tablet – expressly refers to issues of arrangement:

[τέχνην τὴν Θεοδ]ώρηον μάθε τάξιν Ὁμήρου
ὄφρα δαεὶς πάσης μέτρον ἔχῃς σοφίας.

Understand [the *technê* of Theod]orus so that, knowing the order of Homer, you may have the measure of all wisdom.

The epigram's talk of 'the order of Homer' (τάξιν Ὁμήρου) directly parallels Virgil's rhetoric of *ordo*, and in the context of closely related subjects. But just as the *Aeneid*'s opening ecphrasis goes on to complicate the references to *Iliacas ex ordine pugnas*, the phrasing here proves wholly ambiguous. For does this genitive work subjectively ('the arrangement of Homer', referring to the narrative order of Homer's original poem)? Or should we understand it objectively ('an arranging of Homer' – that is, as a reference to the new spatial order imposed on Homer by the so-called 'Theodorean' artist)?[124] As

---

[122] For discussion of this and other appearances of Aeneas on the tablet, see Squire 2011: 59, 148–58, 242–3. More generally on the relationship between the *Aeneid* and the tablet, cf. Valenzuela Montenegro 2004: 387–91. It is worth noting the parallel pivotal position of a related schema of Aeneas in the painted cycle of the Casa del Criptoportico in Pompeii: cf. Squire 2015c: 532–7 (with further bibliography).

[123] On the games with order on this and other tablets, cf. Squire 2011: 127–96. Although the reverse of the *Tabula Capitolina* is uninscribed, other tablets developed the games on their verso sides: seven tablets are inscribed with so-called 'magic square' inscriptions, laid out in a lettered grid (cf. Squire 2011: 197–246). While the gridded form anticipates the spatial arrangements of Optatian's poems, these letters can in fact be read in multiple directions, yielding a title for the literary subjects depicted. But the underlying rationale – 'to seize the middle letter [*gramma*] and proceed however you like' (as an accompanying hexameter inscription on two such tablets instructed) – is as pertinent to the obverse as it was to the reverse side of the tablets.

[124] For analysis of the inscription, see Squire 2011: 102–21, further developed in Squire 2014: esp. 353–73; cf. also Petrain 2014: 49–68.

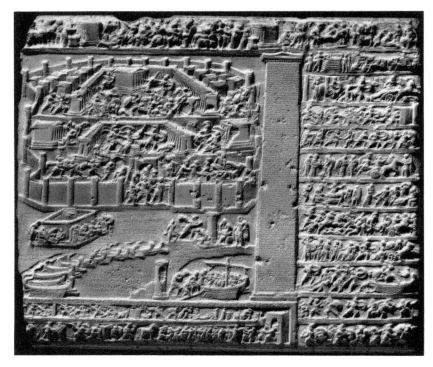

Figure 12.24 Fragmentary obverse side of the *Tabula Iliaca Capitolina* ('Capitoline Iliac tablet'/*Tabula Iliaca* 1 A: Rome, Musei Capitolini, Sala delle Colombe, inv. 316), late first century BCE or early first century CE. Height: 25 cm; width: 30 cm; depth: 1.5 cm. Photograph by Michael Squire, reproduced by kind permission of the Direzione, Musei Capitolini, Rome.

with our Pompeian Iliadic cycle, the *Tabulae Iliacae* raise questions of arrangement, while providing no straightforward answers about the 'order' viewing audiences are instructed to 'understand'. In both their subjects and their formal composition, our two material comparanda share a common critical framework with Virgil's literary evocation.

Now, it would be misguided to draw any *direct* relationship between Virgilian epic and the painted and sculptural material that we have introduced. Although the quantity of surviving Iliac tablet fragments suggests that they were a major genre of early Imperial art, there would be little to be gained in speculating as to whether Virgil might have seen such objects; by extension, we can only guess what proportion of early Imperial viewers

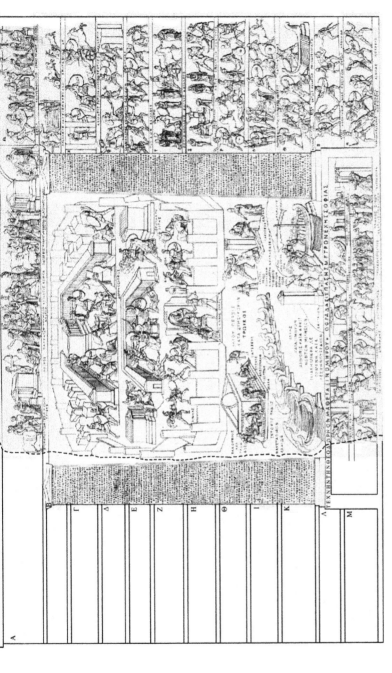

Figure 12.25 Reconstruction of the same tablet in complete state, showing the arrangement of epic cyclical scenes. At the centre of the tablet is a scene of the fall of Troy, complete with an inscribed stele to the right summarising Books 7 to 24 of the *Iliad*. To the right are friezes drawn from *Iliad* 12–24; on the tablet's missing left-hand side would have been friezes relating to the first twelve books, complete with a second inscribed stele. The frieze relating to the first book of the *Iliad* extends across the top of the tablet, leading directly to the frieze of Book 24. The two lower central friezes below relate to two lost Greek Epic Cyclical poems (the *Aethiopis* and the *Little Iliad*). Reconstruction by Michael Squire.

might have approached the object in 'Virgilian' terms, homing in on the central figure of Aeneas. Even greater caution is needed when it comes to the Casa di Octavius Quartio frieze, which was most likely painted in around 70 CE (that is, almost a century after Virgil's death).[125] In each case, we must satisfy ourselves with general sorts of connections between literary and material media.[126] But we can nonetheless be sanguine that both belong to a common cultural framework: those who read Virgil's account of Aeneas viewing these images were themselves also viewers of contemporary Roman art; likewise, the meanings that Roman viewers constructed from material objects could in turn be shaped by the landscapes of literary culture.[127]

## Rhetorical Juxapositions

What we are advocating here is a mode of critical enquiry that stretches across areas of disciplinary specialisation. In describing the viewing of material objects, the phenomenon of literary ecphrasis drives home the point in a very concrete way: if Latin texts can help in reconstructing theories and practices of Roman seeing, so too can material objects help us to understand the conceptual framework that Roman authors and readers brought to the composition and reception of Latin literature. This circularity – from visual stimulus to text, and back again – is fundamental to the dynamics of ecphrasis. But it is ill served by the practice of treating 'Latin literature' and 'material culture' each in hermetic isolation from the other.

---

[125] On the dating of the room, see the bibliography cited by Coralini 2001: 172.

[126] Because of the limited evidence available to us, in other words, surviving materials must usually be used to advance arguments about the sorts of objects that might have informed a particular literary passage. We would therefore distance our approach from that of Heslin 2015, who touches upon the same Virgilian passage (cf. Squire 2016a). Heslin reads Virgil's description as 'staging a very concrete parable of interpretation', based on a close 'parallel with the decorative scheme of the Portico of Philippus' (278), which is deemed 'the Museum of Augustus in that it was the home of the Muses in Rome' – and seat of the *Collegium Poetarum*.

[127] This is not to deny the importance of thinking about the social audiences to which material objects catered: we have to proceed from formal analysis to arguments about their intended or actual audiences. In our eyes, though, there can be no doubting that the *Tabulae Iliacae* catered to a highly elite and learned audience (cf. Squire 2011: esp. 67–94, *pace* e.g. Horsfall 1979 and Mcleod 1985). The situation with the painted Iliadic cycle in the Casa di Octavius Quartio is more complex: Mayer 2012: 199–203 has suggested (in our view, quite short-sightedly) that these scenes catered to the *petite bourgeoisie* of what he anachronistically labels the Pompeian 'middle-classes', arguing that the room 'shows a remarkable disinterest in telling a myth in anything resembling one of its literary versions' (p. 203).

## 12 Latin Literature and Material Culture

The circular relationship between Roman material and literary cultures is especially conspicuous in the case of ecphrastic texts displayed alongside the objects to which they pertain. In combining words with objects, often with explicit commentaries on that juxtaposition, many of the examples so far discussed in this chapter demanded that audiences slip and slide between reading and viewing: consider, for example, not only the two Iliac tablets that we have illustrated (Figures 12.20, 12.24), but also the poems of Optatian (Figures 12.1–4, 12.8, 12.11), or for that matter the funerary altar of T. Statilius Aper (Figure 12.7). The phenomenon also takes us to epigrams inscribed alongside the works to which they refer. The practice of responding to objects in epigram – a literary genre originating in its inscribed material objects – was of course nothing new. Already in the Hellenistic period, we know that collections of Greek epigrams could be assembled into self-contained anthologies, circulating in isolation from the monuments to which they purportedly referred.[128] But the very gesture of placing inscribed texts alongside the objects described monumentalises the two-ways dynamics between seeing and reading: the ecphrastic movement from objects to words here finds its counterpart in a flow of traffic in the opposite direction, as audiences strive to combine an interpretation of verbal and visual media.

All sorts of Roman media might be cited here – from wall-paintings inscribed with responses in verse,[129] through poems inscribed on single statues,[130] to whole sculptural complexes juxtaposed with short epigrammatic ripostes.[131] Given our preceding discussion of a passage from the first book of the *Aeneid*, however, a fourth-century mosaic from a Romano-British villa in

---

[128] On the origins and development of the Greek genre, see e.g. Goldhill 1994; Bing 1998: esp. 29–35; Gutzwiller 1998: esp. 47–114; Meyer 2005: 25–126; Bettenworth 2007; Day 2007; Tueller 2008; Baumbach, Petrovic and Petrovic 2010; Squire 2010 and 2013b. For the inception of self-standing ecphrasis in the Latin epigrammatic tradition, especially Statius' *Silvae* and Martial, see e.g. Newlands 2002: esp. 28–43 and Nauta 2002: 102–4.

[129] In terms of Latin epigrams that accompany wall-paintings, we know of only one example from Pompeii – a poem composed on an image of Pero shown breastfeeding her father in room 6 of the Casa di M. Lucretius Fronto (v.4.11): see *PPM* 3: 1005, no. 78a–b, 1006, no. 81, with Courtney 1995: 277–8, no. 56, Elsner 2007b: 155, Sauron 2009: 252–60 and Milnor 2014: 109–12. For the Greek examples inscribed in the Casa degli Epigrammi (Pompeii v.1.18) and the so-called 'Casa di Properzio' in Assisi, see Prioux 2008: 25–140, Squire 2009: 176–89, 239–93 and Squire 2013f. Compare also Thomas 1995.

[130] Consider, for example, Neudecker 1988: 68, 159, no. 17 (a Latin epigram inscribed on a herm from a villa at Casale Maruffi (Frattochie)), with further comments in Dillon 2000: 38 and Stewart 2003: 255–6. One could also compare the Greek epigrams accompanying herms of Homer and Menander found in the Villa Aeliana in Rome (outside the Porta Trigemenia): Bowie 1989: 244–7 and Prioux 2008: 123–49.

[131] Such is the case with the grotto of an Imperial villa at Sperlonga. Later in the grotto's history (probably in the late third century CE), a ten-line Latin hexameter inscription seems to have been

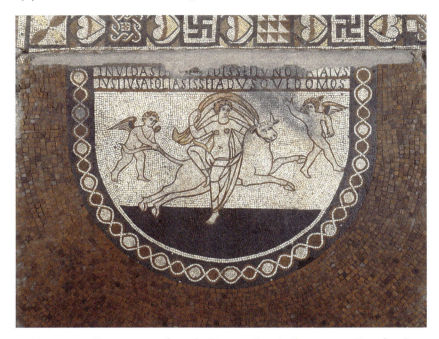

Figure 12.26 Europa mosaic from the Roman villa at Lullingstone in Kent, fourth century CE. Photograph reproduced by kind permission of the Archiv, Institut für Klassische Archäologie und Museum für Abgüsse Klassischer Bildwerke, Ludwig-Maximilians-Universität, Munich.

Lullingstone might provide a fitting case study (Figure 12.26). The section of the mosaic illustrated here forms part of a larger triclinium complex, set around a circling sigma couch: at the centre is the figure of Europa, shown astride a bull, framed by Cupids to the left and right. Above is a single Latin elegiac couplet:[132]

> Inuida si t[auri] uidisset Iuno natatus
>     iustius Aeolias isset adusque domos.
>
> If jealous Juno had seen the swimming bull, more justly would she have approached the house of Aeolus.

displayed alongside the earlier assemblage of monumental sculptural groups: see Squire 2009: 202–38.

[132] The inscription is *RIB* 2447.9. For discussions, see e.g. Toynbee 1964: 262–5; Llewellyn 1988: 155–65; Wattel-de Croizant 1995: 191–4; Lancha 1997: 285–6, no. 120; Scott 2000: 123–4; Leader-Newby 2007: 190–3; Squire 2009: 169–71. On the context of the mosaic in the villa, cf. Meates 1955.

It is the circularity between words and images that strikes us as significant. Audiences are expected to bring to the mosaic a knowledge of both Graeco-Roman iconography and the Latin literary canon: on the one hand, the imagery requires them to recognise the subject as the rape of Europa (who goes unnamed in the inscription, despite the reference to *tauri . . . natatus*, literally the 'swimmings of the bull'); on the other, the Latin inscription nods not only to one of the opening episodes of the *Aeneid* (the storm that Juno persuades Aeolus to bring about so as to delay Aeneas), but also to the poetry of Ovid – not least through its ironic take on 'jealous Juno' and the whimsically unreal conditional frame.[133] Crucially, however, the combination of inscribed epigram with pictorial subject broadens the referential scope of both verbal and visual elements. Indeed, the importance of viewing to each and every act of reading of the epigram is itself underscored in the reference to Juno's sight – or rather, the reference to her *failure* to see, couched in the pluperfect subjunctive of the opening conditional protasis (*uidisset*). Quite apart from the pun on Juno's reported jealousy (the fact that she is *inuida*), the talk of seeing pitches the audience's physical view of the mosaic in front of them against its alleged invisibility to the goddess.

The play between image and text in this ecphrastic realm hints beyond 'intertextuality' to a world of 'inter-textual-pictorial' play, one in which images (and their *tituli*) could evoke famous texts, while famous texts might evoke well-known visual types.[134] Fundamental to this world is a shared culture of education in rhetoric and memory, which extended as much to material as to literary artefacts. As is repeatedly demonstrated by ancient writers' uses of examples from the visual arts to illustrate aspects of rhetoric, or to demonstrate its workings, there was a clear awareness (at least among Graeco-Roman intellectuals) of the associations between rhetoric and the visual arts – even if we possess no extended ancient rhetorical analysis dedicated exclusively to those arts.[135] To cite just one conspicuous instance of this intersection, the art of memory as taught by rhetorical theorists was founded on mentally visualising an environment like 'a house . . . public buildings, a long journey, the ramparts of a city, or even pictures', and walking through or scanning them in the imagination

---

[133] Cf. Toynbee 1962: 262: 'the lines would have been meaningless to anyone who did not know his Virgil'. On the Ovidian resonance of the inscription, see Barrett 1978: 309–13.
[134] Famous examples in Roman poetry include Ariadne in Propertius 1.3 or the range of monuments evoked by Ovid (see Boyle 2003): much rich discussion in Jenkyns 2013.
[135] See Pollitt 1974: 58–63; Benediktson 2000: 87–61; Tanner 2006: 250–4; Elsner 2014.

(Quint. *Inst.* 11.2.21).[136] The precision-training of remembering the visual specifics of a house, building, cityscape or picture in their inter-relations, and then placing particular symbols at given spots so as to jog the memory as a speaker delivers his discourse, served to align the flow of speech with the movement through imagined and memorised spaces: inevitably, such conceptual alignment had an impact on the kinds of visual environments that were created for people whose education was dominated by this kind of training.[137] So too, it follows, such frameworks fundamentally inform the ways in which visual types resonated against each other in the experience of viewing the paintings within a Roman house.[138] The fact that a house and its decoration, or for that matter the details of any given picture, were always potentially a material image of the speech, the secret of whose delivery lay in their mental visualisation, built a shared dynamic between visual environment and rhetoric in the Roman world, which meet most specifically in the imaginative space of *phantasia* where the orator or artist visualises what it is he will create (whether in the medium of words or pigment or carved stone).[139] When he wanted to make the case for the orator grasping his topic 'not with the eye or ear or any of the senses but with the mind and the imagination', Cicero used the example of Pheidias: 'while making the image of Jupiter or Minerva,' Cicero tells us, 'Pheidias did not look at any person whom he was using as a model, but in his own mind there dwelt a surpassing vision of beauty; at this he gazed and all intent on this he guided the artist's hand to produce the likeness of the god' (*Orator* 8–9).[140] Writing about a century and a half later, and in a speech actually delivered at Olympia, the sophist Dio Chrysostom expanded on this model by staging an interrogation of Pheidias, asking whether his statue of Zeus was appropriate to the deity and composing a speech given by Pheidias in response to this which compares the sculptor's *phantasia* of the god with that of the poet Homer.[141]

---

[136] The prescriptive texts are *Rhetorica ad Herennium* 3.27–40, Cicero, *De oratore* 2.351–60 and Quintilian, *Institutio oratoria* 11.2.11–21. Substantive discussions include Yates 1966: 1–26; Blum 1969; Carruthers 1990: 71–5; Small 1997: 81–116; Baroin 2010; Squire 2014: 401–16.

[137] See the discussions by Rouveret 1989: 303–79; Bergmann 1994; Elsner 1995: 76–87; Baroin 1998.

[138] See Bergmann 1994 and Elsner and Squire 2017.

[139] The key ancient discussions for our purposes are Quint. *Inst.* 6.2.29 and Philostratus, *Vita Apollonii* 6.19. On *phantasia* and art, see e.g. Perry 2005: 151–7; Tanner 2006: 283–95; Platt 2006: 245–9.

[140] For similar versions of this trope: Seneca, *Controversiae* 10.5.8; Plotinus, *Enneads* 5.8.1; Philostratus, *Vita Apollonii* 6.19.

[141] Dio Chrysostom, *Oratio* 12.44–6, 49–85. Cicero's *Orator* is usually dated to 46 BCE and Dio's *Olympic Oration* (*Oratio* 12) was delivered in 97 CE. For the trope, see Pernot 2011.

Beyond the high flights of *phantasia*, the exempla of artists and visual practice are a major paradigm by means of which the writers of rhetorical treatises illustrated and clarified what they were saying. When Cicero wanted to show how models of surpassing excellence in rhetoric (like Demosthenes) encourage emulation by later and perhaps lesser orators, he used the example of how artists are inspired by the works of painters like Protogenes and Apelles, or for that matter sculptors such as Pheidias and Polyclitus (*Orator* 1.5). To exemplify the eclecticism of the authors he draws on in writing a textbook on rhetoric, Cicero invokes the anecdote of the many beautiful women who together served as models for Zeuxis' painting in the temple at Croton (*De inventione* 2.1–5).[142] So too, when rhetoricians like Cicero and Quintilian came to make the argument that rhetoric (and indeed all the arts) showed a progressive development from crude beginnings to perfection, they turned to an art-historical narrative about the rise of representation from crude schematism to the heights of naturalism (most familiar to us from Pliny's *Natural History*).[143] Arguably in these passages ancient 'art history', perceived as the movement from winter to spring,[144] becomes a foundational, even a programmatic, model for rhetoric itself.

## Beyond the 'Elite'?

So far this chapter has colluded in a commitment to the elite and highly sophisticated uses of Latin as 'literature'. But of course Latin was a spoken language, and one available well below the literate classes; likewise, entry to the epigraphical record was not the sole prerogative of the richest or most educated.[145] A significant recent thrust within classical archaeology, and indeed within archaeology generally, has been to resist what have been

---

[142] In Cicero, many beautiful women provide the elements for an ideal painted image; in Lucian, *Imagines* 1–10 many beautiful images (both statues and paintings) provide the elements for an ideal mental portrait from which to identify a supremely beautiful (real) woman: see Maffei 1986; Vout 2007: 213–39 and Cistaro 2009: 69–112. On the Zeuxis legend, see especially De Angelis 2005 with full earlier bibliography; cf. also Barkan 2000; Hunter 2009: 111–20; Mansfield 2007: 7, 12–21.

[143] See Cic. *Brut.* 70 and Quint. 12.10.3–9. The passage from Quintilian is an extended piece of potted art history, particularly interesting for being sandwiched between a discussion of style (sculptural and rhetorical, at 12.10.1–2) and a parallel progressive account of the rise of Roman rhetoric (12.10.10–15). See Pollitt 1974: 81–4 and Squire 2013c: 364–6 (with further bibliography); cf. also Aelius Aristides, *Oration* 2.118.

[144] In the elegant characterisation of Bryson 1984: 7.

[145] On the issue, see especially Clackson in this volume. We would only add that low levels of literacy put an even greater onus on the *visual* workings of inscriptions (cf. Harris 1989; Humphrey 1991; Corbier 2006: 77–90; Woolf 2009; Bodel 2015b).

described as 'text-assisted' and even 'text-hindered' realms of material culture, favouring instead areas where no literary frame or reference exists to bias the modern viewer towards the kinds of elite concerns that were inevitably shared by the kinds of people who were able to write or to read. By the same token, even the art history of the Roman world – which has inevitably been concerned with the luxury productions of the elite in both the private and public spheres – has shown considerable interest in the products and visual cultures of so-called 'ordinary' Romans, including freedmen and slaves, and from across the length and breadth of the Roman empire.[146] As our chapter has repeatedly stressed, this is a world where the materiality of writing works significantly *as* visual sign.[147]

Since altars have been a leitmotif of our chapter, following our opening genuflection to Optatian, let us therefore close with what one might call a 'degree zero' altar. Stone altars, shaped something like the altar in Optatian's poem 26 (or for that matter those of earlier Imperial Greek picture-poems: e.g. Figure 12.5), are ubiquitous in the Roman world. Indeed, we have already encountered a particularly elaborate example of the genre in the altar of T. Statilius Aper (Figure 12.7). Often without an archaeological provenance, such objects stand in forgotten corners of museums and storerooms: they constitute a vast cache of material – a cache that bears witness to the practices of ancient religion,[148] albeit one which, at least on first impression, may also seem to be of limited relevance to a specialist in Latin language and literature. Materially speaking, the shape of these objects speaks to a sacred function fundamental to ancient life. In addition, the Roman altar typically has a carving of a *patera* or flat bowl for pouring libations on its right side and an *urceus*, a jug or pitcher for pouring liquid into the patera, on the left.[149] Such objects may or may not have other visual adornment but – if the altar has a funerary function – normally it has the letters DM (for *dis manibus*, 'to the gods below', or spirits of the dead), as well as the name of the deceased.[150]

---

[146] The literature is large, and includes e.g. Clarke 2003 (whence the phrase 'ordinary Romans'); Mayer 2012 (Roman 'middle classes', mentioned in n. 127); Joshel and Hackworth Petersen 2014 (slaves); Hackworth Petersen 2006 (freedmen); D'Ambra and Métraux 2006. On the need to be sensitive to regional variation, and above all 'local' viewpoints (again, often removed from the elite views of so many 'centrist' Roman Imperial writers), see e.g. Scott and Webster 2003; Hales and Hodos 2010; Alcock, Egri and Frake 2016.

[147] For instance, see, on art and inscriptions, Newby and Leader-Newby 2007; on funerary inscriptions and monuments, Carroll 2006.

[148] See the discussion of Adrych and Dalglish 2020: esp. 51–8, 72–3, 79–80.

[149] These accoutrements of the altar go back way into Greek antiquity: see Gaifman 2018.

[150] On funerary altars see: Altmann 1905; Boschung 1989; Dexheimer 1998. More broadly on Roman altars and their archaeological contexts, cf. Cavallero 2018.

Crucially, it is the combination of texual formula with formulaic visual decoration that appears to have determined a viewer's understanding of what the object was.

In the Museo Chiaramonti in the Vatican can be found a large collection of such pieces. The worked marble block known as 'T. 34' is in many ways like other examples of the genre: the funerary altar was once in the Giustiniani Collection, and it has the added distinction of having once been owned by the sculptor Antonio Canova (Figure 12.27).[151] This particular altar has a sculpted *urceus* on the left side, tipped slightly forward as if ready to pour, and a *patera* on the right. Importantly for our purposes, the front also boasts a finely carved inscription set back within a cleanly chiselled frame:

DM
AMABILI
CONIVGI
BELLICVS
THALAMVS
B. MERENTI FECIT.

To the gods below. Bellicus Thalamus rightly made [sc. me, or this altar] for his beloved wife.

Both the first line (DM) and the last – often abbreviated BMF (literally 'made [it] for so and so who deserved it well') – are repeated epigraphic formulae across the corpus of funerary altars. The middle section names the donor. Without specifying the name of his wife, this central part also marks the occasion and cause of the commemorative dedication: how Bellicus Thalamus established the altar for his *amabilis coniunx*. The object is simple but distinctive in its form and decoration. The writing that the object carries is central to both aspects, while also being key to defining function. Indeed, it is the writing – the formulae, the abbreviations and the specific naming of dedicatee or and his relationship to the honorand – that confers individuality and identity to the piece. No less importantly, the writing places the object within a genre of material culture with particular religious agency in Roman social life: here the inscribed text – in the extent of its workmanship, and placement as the main face of the altar – becomes its principal decorative feature.

It is not clear that Roman viewers would have needed to be able to read the letters (and especially formulae like DM or BMF) for them to

---

[151] *CIL* vi 11509; Andreae et al. 1995, vol. 3, plate 804, no. T. 34 and p. 68.

Figure 12.27 Marble funerary altar from Rome, Museo Chiaramonti, Vatican. Photograph reproduced by kind permission of the Archiv, Institut für Klassische Archäologie und Museum für Abgüsse Klassischer Bildwerke, Ludwig-Maximilians-Universität, Munich (after Andreae et al. 1995: 111, plate 804, no. T. 34).

understand their overarching significance. Although the inscription plays a key role in particularising the object, it is possible to understand the altar – as a commemoration of the dead, or as the receptacle of offerings on behalf of the deceased – without deciphering the text. One might do well to remember how in Petronius' *Satyrica*, for example, a former slave named Hermeros, despite his modest education, boasts of 'knowing letters in stone' (*lapidarias litteras scio*, 58.7).[152] Effectively, in objects of this kind, epigraphy is no less a form of image than the carvings of patera and pitcher which underwrite the function of our altar as a locus of libation. Together, image and text are the markings that make the object do the cultural work for which it was intended, without any great pretentiousness or high complexity of sophistication. Crucially, it is the very combination of the two – and in the context of a recognisable everyday object – that enables the kinds of play in which Optatian delighted: for all its superlative literary sophistication and its author's position as Consul at the pinnacle of society, the poetry of Optatian takes its lead from altogether more 'ordinary' objects.

The altar of Bellicus Thalamus – a simple object, one of many, near-identical in form to numerous others and yet an individual memorial to a deceased woman and the mark of a man's grief – may seem far removed from the sophisticated literary play of Optatian's poem with which our chapter began. Ultimately, though, the object shares more with the poem than figural form alone. Just as Optatian's altar poem shifts at once into the first person (*stem*, v. 1), our final case study announces itself as the thing made by a particular person – Bellicus Thalamus – in commemoration of his beloved wife: the object asserts its identity as the material connection between a triangle of subjects – Thalamus, his wife and the viewer who reads the inscription. This same material placement between social actors – the quintessence of the simplest inscriptional information that characterises Roman altars – is at the heart of Optatian's poetics, which addresses the viewer in the first line (*uides*, 'you see'), names its honorand (the Pythian god, Phoebus), ironically turns the altar itself into the first-person speaking subject, and no less ironically refuses to name its maker/dedicator (that is, the poet himself). Optatian's opening word, *uides*, throws the onus onto the respondent: it challenges audiences – as inscribed altars (and for that matter all inscribed monuments) always do – to see and to read at one and the same time.

In all this, the voices of Optatian's poem playfully extend and reconfigure the normal inscriptional claims of altars such as the one in the Museo Chiaramonti: this visual–verbal creation channels in its form and discourse some of the fundamental forces of the material backdrop to which it knowingly refers. The point seems an appropriate one on which

---

[152] Cf. Corbier 1987: 58–9; Horsfall 1989b: 202–6.

to conclude: whether we are dealing with high literary creations, or else cultural artefacts that might appear wholly more humble in origin, Latin texts can never be separated from the material medium that they occupy.

## References

Adrych, P. and D. Dalglish (2020) 'Writing the art, archaeology and religion of the Roman Mediterranean', in Elsner 2020, 51–80.
Alcock, S. E., M. Egri and J. F. D. Frake, eds. (2016) *Beyond Boundaries: Connecting Visual Cultures in the Provinces of Ancient Rome*, Los Angeles.
Altmann, W. (1905) *Die römischen Grabaltäre der Kaiserzeit*, Berlin.
Anderson, G. (1993) *The Second Sophistic: A Cultural Phenomenon in the Roman Empire*, London.
Andreae, B. (1999) *Odysseus: Mythos und Erinnerung*, Munich.
Andreae, B. et al. (1995) *Bildkatalog der Skulpturen des Vatikanischen Museums 1: Museo Chiaramonti*, Berlin.
Aurigemma, F. (1953) 'Appendice: tre nuovi cicli di figurazioni ispirate all'Iliade in case della Via dell'Abbondanza in Pompei', in V. Spinazzola, ed., *Pompei alla luce degli scavi nuovi di Via dell'Abbondanza (anni 1920–23)* (Rome), II 867–1008.
Bagnall, R., ed. (2009) *The Oxford Handbook of Papyrology*, Oxford.
Baier, T. (2010) 'Eumolpe et Encolpe dans une galerie d'art', in É. Prioux and A. Rouveret, eds., *Métamorphoses du regard ancien* (Paris), 191–204.
Baird, J. and C. Taylor, eds. (2012) *Ancient Graffiti in Context*, London.
Balensiefen, L. (1990) *Die Bedeutung des Spiegelbildes als ikonographisches Motiv in der antiken Kunst*, Tübingen.
Barchiesi, A. (1994) 'Rappresentazioni del dolore e interpretazione nell'*Eneide*', *A&A* 40: 109–24.
  (1997) 'Virgilian narrative: b, Ecphrasis', in C. Martindale, ed., *The Cambridge Companion to Virgil* (Cambridge), 271–81.
  (2005) 'Learned eyes: poets, viewers, image makers', in K. Galinsky, ed., *The Cambridge Companion to the Age of Augustus* (Cambridge), 281–305.
Bardill, J. (2012) *Constantine: Divine Emperor of the Christian Golden Age*, Cambridge.
Barkan, L. (2000) 'The heritage of Zeuxis', in A. Payne, A. Kuttner and R. Smick, eds., *Antiquity and Its Interpreters* (Cambridge), 99–110.
  (2013) *Mute Poetry, Speaking Pictures*, Princeton.
Baroin, C. (1998) 'La maison romaine comme image et lieu de mémoire', in C. Auvray-Assayas, ed., *Images romaines* (Paris), 177–91.
  (2010) *Se souvenir à Rome: formes, représentations et pratiques de la mémoire*, Paris.
Barrett, A. A. (1978) 'Knowledge of the literary classics in Roman Britain', *Britannia* 9: 309–33.
Bartsch, S. (1989) *Decoding the Ancient Novel: The Reader and the Role of Description in Heliodorus and Achilles Tatius*, Princeton.

(1998) '*Ars* and the man: the politics of art in Virgil's *Aeneid*', *CPh* 93: 322–42.
Baumbach, M., A. Petrovic and I. Petrovic, eds. (2010) *Archaic and Classical Greek Epigram*, Cambridge.
Bausi, A., B. Reudenbach and H. Wimmer, eds. (2020) *Canones: The Art of Harmony. Canon Tables of the Four Gospels*, Berlin.
Becatti, G. (1951) *Arte e gusto negli scrittori latini*, Florence.
Beck, D. (2007) 'Ecphrasis, interpretation, and audience in *Aeneid* 1 and *Odyssey* 8', *AJPh* 128: 533–49.
Becker, A. S. (1995) *The Shield of Achilles and the Poetics of Ekphrasis*, Lanham, MD.
Beltrán Lloris, F. (2015) 'The "epigraphic habit" in the Roman world', in Bruun and Edmondson, eds., 131–48.
Benediktson, D. T. (2000) *Literature and the Visual Arts in Ancient Greece and Rome*, Norman, OK.
Benefiel, R. (2010) 'Dialogues of ancient graffiti in the House of Maius Castricius at Pompeii', *AJA* 114: 59–101.
  (2016) 'The culture of writing graffiti within domestic spaces at Pompeii', in Benefiel and Keegan 2016, 80–110.
Benefiel, R. and P. Keegan, eds. (2016) *Inscriptions in the Private Sphere in the Greco-Roman World*, Leiden.
Benefiel, R. R. and H. M. Sypniewski (2016) 'Images and text on the walls of Herculaneum: designing the ancient graffiti project', in A. Felle and A. Rocco, eds., *Off the Beaten Track: Epigraphy at the Borders* (Oxford), 29–48.
Bennett, J. (2010) *Vibrant Matter: A Political Ecology of Things*, Durham, NC.
Bergmann, B. (1994) 'The Roman house as memory theatre: the House of the Tragic Poet in Pompeii', *Art Bulletin* 76: 225–56.
  (2012) 'Housing and households: the Roman world', in S. Alcock and R. Osborne, eds., *Classical Archaeology*, 2nd edn (Malden, MA), 228–48.
Bettenworth, A. (2007) 'The mutual influence of inscribed and literary epigram', in Bing and Bruss 2007, 69–93.
Betts, E., ed. (2017) *Senses of the Empire: Multisensory Approaches to Roman Culture*, London.
Bianchi-Bandinelli, R. (1955) *Hellenistic-Byzantine Miniatures of the Iliad (Ilias Ambrosiana)*, Olten.
Biering, R. (1995) *Die Odyseefresken vom Esquilin*, Munich.
Bing, P. (1998) 'Between literature and the monuments', in M. A. Harder, R. F. Regtuit and G. C. Walker, eds., *Genre in Hellenistic Poetry* (Leuven), 21–43.
Bing, P. and J. S. Bruss, eds. (2007) *Brill's Companion to Hellenistic Epigram Down to Philip*, Leiden.
Blanck, H. (1992) *Das Buch in der Antike*, Munich.
Blanshard, A. (2007) 'The problems with honouring Samos: an Athenian document relief and its interpretation', in Newby and Leader-Newby 2007, 19–37.
Blum, H. (1969) *Die antike Mnemotechnik*, Hildesheim.
Bodel, J. (2015a) 'The publication of Pliny's *Letters*', in Marchesi 2015, 13–108.
  (2015b) 'Inscriptions and literacy', in Bruun and Edmondson 2015, 745–63.

Boeder, M. (1996) *Visa est Vox: Sprache und Bild in der spätantiken Literatur*, Frankfurt.
Boehm, G. and H. Pfotenhauer, eds. (1995) *Beschreibungskunst – Kunstbeschreibung. Ekphrasis von der Antike bis zur Gegenwart*, Munich.
Borg, B., ed. (2015) *A Companion to Roman Art*, Malden, MA.
Boschung, D. (1989) *Antike Grabaltäre aus den Nekropolen Roms*, Bern.
Boultenhouse, E. L. (1959) 'Poems in the shape of things', *Art News Annual* 28: 64–83.
Bounia, A. (2004) *The Nature of Classical Collecting: Collectors and Collections, 100 BCE–100 CE*, Farnham.
Bouquet, M., B. Méniel and G. Ramires, eds. (2011) *Servius et sa réception de l'antiquité à la Renaissance*, Rennes.
Bowie, E. (1989) 'Greek sophists and Greek poetry in the Second Sophistic', *ANRW* II.33.1: 209–58.
Boyd, B. W. (1995) '*Non enarrabile textum*: ecphrastic trespass and narrative ambiguity in the *Aeneid*', *Vergilius* 41: 71–92.
Boyle, A. (2003) *Ovid and the Monuments: A Poet's Rome*, Bendigo, Victoria.
Bravi, A. (2012) *Ornamenta urbis: opere d'arte greche negli spazi romani*, Bari.
Brendel, O. (1979) *Prolegomena to the Study of Roman Art*, New Haven. Adapted from 'Prolegomena to the study of Roman art', *MAAR* 21 (1953), 7–73.
  (1980) *The Visible Idea: Interpretations of Classical Art* (trans. M. Brendel), Washington, DC.
Brilliant, R. (1984) *Visual Narratives: Story-Telling in Etruscan and Roman Art*, Ithaca, NY.
  (2008) 'Forwards and backwards in the historiography of Roman art', *JRA* 21: 7–24.
Bruhat, M.-O. (1999) 'Les *carmina figurata* de Publilius Optatianus Porfyrius: la métamorphose d'un genre et l'invention d'une poésie liturgique impériale sous Constantin', unpublished PhD dissertation, Paris IV (Sorbonne).
  (2009) 'Les poèmes figurés d'Optatianus Porfyrius: une écriture à contraintes, une écriture de la contrainte', in F. Toulze-Morisset, ed., *Formes de l'écriture, figures de la pensée dans la culture gréco-romaine* (Lille), 101–25.
Bruun, C. (2015) 'The major corpora and epigraphic publications', in Bruun and Edmondson 2015, 66–77.
Bruun, C. and J. Edmondson, eds. (2015) *The Oxford Handbook of Roman Epigraphy*, Oxford.
Bryson, N. (1984) *Tradition and Desire: From David to Delacroix*, Cambridge.
Butler, S. (2002) *The Hand of Cicero*, London.
  (2011) *The Matter of the Page: Essays in Search of Ancient and Medieval Authors*, Madison, WI.
Butzmann, H. (1970) *Corpus Agrimensorum Romanorum. Codex Arcerianus A der Herzog-August-Bibliothek zu Wolfenbüttel (Cod. Guelf. 36.23A)*, Leiden.
Carder, J. (1978) *Art Historical Problems of a Roman Land-Surveying Manuscript*, New York.

Carey, S. (2003) *Pliny's Catalogue of Culture: Art and Empire in the Natural History*, Oxford.
Carroll, M. (2006) *Spirits of the Dead: Roman Funerary Commemoration in Western Europe*, Oxford.
Carruthers, M. (1990) *The Book of Memory*, Cambridge.
Carson, A. (1992) 'Simonides painter', in R. Hexter and D. Seldon, eds., *Innovations of Antiquity* (New York and London), 51–64.
Cavallero, F. (2018) *Area sacrae: tipi, nomi, atti, funzioni e rappresentazioni degli altari Romani*, Rome.
Cavallo, G. (1997) 'Du volumen au codex: la lecture dans le monde romain', in G. Cavallo and R. Chartier, eds., *Histoire de la lecture dans le monde occidental* (Paris), 85–114.
  (2010) 'Libri, lettura e biblioteche nella tarda antiquitá: un panorama e qualche riflessione', *AntTard* 18: 9–19.
Chevallier, R. (1991) *L'artiste, le collectioneur et le faussaire: pour une sociologie de l'art romain*, Paris.
Chinn, C. (2007) 'Before your very eyes: Pliny *Epistulae* 5.6 and the ancient theory of ekphrasis', *CPh* 102: 265–80.
Cistaro, M. (2009) *Sotto il velo di Pantea: imagines e pro imaginibus di Luciano*, Messina.
Claridge, A. and I. Herklotz (2012) *The Paper Museum of Cassiano dal Pozzo: Classical Manuscript Illustrations*, London.
Clarke, J. R. (1991) *The Houses of Roman Italy, 100 BC–AD 250: Ritual, Space, and Decoration*, Berkeley.
  (2003) *Art in the Lives of Ordinary Romans*, Berkeley.
  (2007) *Looking at Laughter: Humor, Power, and Transgression in Roman Visual Culture, 100 BC–AD 250*, Berkeley.
Clay, D. (1988) 'The archaeology of the Temple to Juno at Carthage', *CPh* 83: 195–205.
Coarelli, F. (1998) 'The Odyssey frescoes of the Via Graziosa: a proposed context', *PBSR* 66: 21–37.
Coleman, K. M., ed. (2015) *Images for Classicists*, Cambridge, MA.
Cooley, A. E., ed. (2002) *Becoming Roman, Writing Latin? Literacy and Epigraphy in the Roman West*, Ann Arbor, MI.
Cooley, A. E. (2009) *Res gestae Divi Augusti: Text, Translation and Commentary*, Cambridge.
  (2012) *The Cambridge Manual of Latin Epigraphy*, Cambridge.
Coralini, A. (2001) *Hercules domesticus. Immagini di Ercole nelle case della regione vesuviana (1. secolo a.C.–79 d. C.)*, Naples.
  (2002) 'Una stanza di Ercole a Pompei: la sala del doppio fregio nella Casa di D. Octavius Quartio (ii 2,2)', in I. Colpo, I. Favaretto and F. Ghedini, eds., *Iconografia. Studi sull'Immagine. Atti del Convegno (Padova, 30 maggio–1 giugno 2001)* (Rome), 331–43.
Corbier, M. (1987) 'L'écriture dans l'espace public romain', in *L'Urbs: espace urbain et histoire (1er siècle av. J.-C.–iii siècle ap. J.-C.)* (Rome), 27–60.

(1991) 'L'Écriture en quête de lecteurs', in Humphrey 1991, 99–118.
  (2006) *Donner à voir, donner à lire: mémoire et communication dans la Rome ancienne*, Paris.
Courtney, E. (1990) 'Greek and Latin acrostics', *Philologus* 134: 1–13.
Courtney, E., ed. (1993) *The Fragmentary Latin Poets*, Oxford.
  (1995) *Musa lapidaria: A Selection of Latin Verse Inscriptions*, Atlanta, GA.
Crawford, M. (2019) *The Eusebian Canon Tables: Ordering Textual Knowledge in Late Antiquity*, Oxford.
  (2020) 'Do the Eusebian canon tables represent the closure or the opening of the biblical text? Considering the case of the Codex Fuldensis', in Bausi, Reudenbach and Wimmer 2020, 17–28.
Croisille, J.-M. (1985) 'La frise d'Héraklès de la Maison de Loreius Tiburtinus à Pompéi et la tradition épique', in M. Renard and P. Laurens, eds., *Hommages à Henry Bardon* (Brussels), 89–99.
  (2005) *La peinture romaine*, Paris.
d'Acunto, M. and R. Palmisciano, eds. (2010) *Lo scudo di Achille nell'Iliade. Esperienze ermeneutiche a confronto*, Pisa.
D'Ambra, E. and G. P. R. Métraux, eds. (2006) *The Art of Citizens, Soldiers and Freedmen in the Roman World*, Oxford.
Day, J. W. (2007) 'Poems on stone: the inscribed antecedents of Hellenistic epigram', in Bing and Bruss 2007, 29–47.
De Angelis, F. (2005) 'L'Elena di Zeusi a Capo Lacinio. Aneddoti e storia', *Rendiconti dell' Accademia dei Lincei* ser. 9, 16: 151–200.
de Jong, I. (2011) 'The shield of Achilles: from metalepsis to mise en abyme', *Ramus* 40: 1–14.
de Vos, M. (1993) 'Heracle e Priamo. Trasmissione di potere: mitologia e ideologia imperiale', in A. Mastrocinque, ed., *Ercole in Occidente. Atti del colloquio internazionale Trento, 7 marzo 1990* (Rome), 81–9.
Dencker, K. P. (2011) *Optische Poesie: Von den prähistorischen Schriftzeichen bis zu den digitalen Experimenten der Gegenwart*, Berlin.
Dexheimer, D. (1998) *Oberitalische Grabaltäre: Ein Beitrag zur Sepulkralkunst der römischen Kaiserzeit*, Oxford.
Dillon, S. (2000) 'Subject selection and viewer reception of Greek portraits from Herculaneum and Tivoli', *JRA* 13: 21–40.
Dodwell, C. (2000) *Anglo-Saxon Gestures and the Roman Stage*, Cambridge.
Donohue, A. A. (2003) 'Introduction', in M. Fullerton and A. A. Donohue, eds., *Ancient Art and Its Historiography* (New York), 1–12.
Doody, A. (2010) *Pliny's Encyclopaedia: The Reception of the Natural History*, Cambridge.
DuBois, P. (1982) *History, Rhetorical Description and the Epic*, Cambridge.
Dufallo, B. (2013) *The Captor's Image: Greek Culture in Roman Ecphrasis*, Oxford.
Dyson, S. (1998) *Ancient Marbles to American Shores: Classical Archaeology in the United States*, Philadelphia, PA.
  (2006) *In Pursuit of Ancient Pasts: A History of Classical Archaeology in the Nineteenth and Twentieth Centuries*, New Haven.

Eastmond, T., ed. (2015) *Viewing Inscriptions in the Late Antique and Medieval World*, Cambridge.
Elsner, J. (1995) *Art and the Roman Viewer: The Transformation of Art from the Pagan World to Christianity*, Cambridge.
  (1996a) 'Inventing imperium: texts and the propaganda of monuments in Augustan Rome', in Elsner 1996b, 32–53.
  (2002) 'Introduction: the genres of ekphrasis', *Ramus* 31: 1–18.
  (2004) 'Foreword', in T. Hölscher, *The Language of Images in Roman Art* (trans. A. Snodgrass and A. Künzl-Snodgrass) (Cambridge), xv–xxxi.
  (2006) 'Art and text', in S. Harrison, ed., *A Companion to Latin Literature* (Oxford), 300–18.
  (2007a) 'Archéologie classique et histoire de l'art en Grande-Bretagne', *Perspective* 2007: 231–42.
  (2007b) *Roman Eyes: Visuality and Subjectivity in Art and Text*, Princeton.
  (2014) 'Art and rhetoric in Roman culture: introduction', in J. Elsner and M. Meyer, eds., *Art and Rhetoric in Roman Culture* (Cambridge), 1–34.
  (2020a) 'Beyond Eusebius: prefatory images and the early book', in Bausi, Reudenbach and Wimmer, eds., 99–132.
Elsner, J., ed. (1996b) *Art and Text in Roman Culture*, Cambridge.
  ed. (2020b) *Empires of Faith in Late Antiquity: Histories of Art and Religion from India to Ireland*, Cambridge.
Elsner, J. and M. J. Squire (2017) 'Sight and memory: the visual art of Roman mnemonics', in M. J. Squire, ed., *Sight and the Ancient Senses* (London), 180–204.
Engels, L. J. and H. Hofmann (1997) 'Literatur und Gesellschaft in der Spätantike: Texte, Kommunikation und Überlieferung', in L. J. Engels and H. Hofmann, eds., *Spätantike, mit einem Panorama der byzantinischen Literatur* (Wiesbaden), 29–99.
Ernst, U. (1991) *Carmen figuratum: Geschichte des Figurengedichts von den antiken Ursprüngen bis zum Ausgang des Mittelalters*, Cologne.
  (2002) *Intermedialität im europäischen Kulturzusammenhang. Beiträge zur Theorie und Geschichte der visuellen Lyrik*, Berlin.
Fejfer, J. (2008) *Roman Portraits in Context*, Berlin.
Felten, J., ed. (1913) *Nicolaus, Progymnasmata*, Leipzig.
Fowler, D. P. (1991) 'Narrate and describe: the problem of ecphrasis', *JRS* 81: 25–35.
  (1997) 'The Virgil commentary of Servius', in C. Martindale, ed., *The Cambridge Companion to Virgil* (Cambridge), 73–87.
  (2000) *Roman Constructions: Readings in Postmodern Latin*, Oxford.
Francis, J. A. (2009) 'Metal maidens, Achilles' shield and Pandora: the beginnings of "ekphrasis"', *AJPh* 130: 1–23.
Franklin, J. L., Jr. (1991) 'Literacy and parietal inscriptions of Pompeii', in Humphrey 1991, 77–98.
Friedländer, P. (1912) *Johannes von Gaza und Paulus Silentarius. Kunstbeschreibungen Justinianischer Zeit*, Leipzig.
Gaifman, M. (2018) *The Art of Libation in Classical Athens*, New Haven.
Gaifman, M. and V. J. Platt (2018) 'Introduction: from Grecian urn to embodied object', in Gaifman, Platt and Squire 2018, 403–19.

Gaifman, M., V. J. Platt and M. J. Squire, eds. (2018) *The Embodied Object in Classical Antiquity* (= *Art History* 41.3), Oxford.
Garipzanov, I. (2018) *Graphic Signs of Authority in Late Antiquity and the Early Middle Ages, 300–900*, Oxford.
Genette, G. (1997) *Paratexts: Thresholds of Interpretation*, Cambridge.
Geyer, A. (1989) *Die Genese narrativer Buchillustration. Der Miniaturenzyklus zur Aeneis im Vergilius Vaticanus*, Frankfurt.
Gibson, R. (2014) 'Starting with the index in Pliny', in Jansen 2014b, 33–55.
Gigante, M. (1979) *Civiltà delle forme letterarie nell'antica Pompei*, Naples.
Goldhill, S. D. (1994) 'The naïve and knowing eye: ecphrasis and the culture of viewing in the Hellenistic world', in Goldhill and Osborne 1994, 197–223.
  (2007) 'What is ekphrasis for?', *CPh* 102: 1–19.
  (2012) 'Forms of attention: time and narrative in ecphrasis', *The Cambridge Classical Journal* 58: 88–114.
  (2020) *Preposterous Poetics: The Politics and Aesthetics of Form in Late Antiquity*, Cambridge.
Goldhill, S. D. and R. Osborne, eds. (1994) *Art and Text in Ancient Greek Culture*, Cambridge.
Grafton, A. and M. Williams (2006) *Christianity and the Transformation of the Book: Origen, Eusebius, and the Library of Caesarea*, Cambridge, MA.
Grewing, F., B. Acosta-Hughes and A. Kirichenko, eds. (2013) *The Door Ajar: False Closure in Greek and Roman Literature and Art*, Heidelberg.
Guarducci, M. (1965) 'Il misterioso "quadrato magico": l'interpretazione di Jérome Carcopino e documenti nuovi', *ArchClass* 17: 219–70.
Guichard, L. A. (2006) 'Simias' pattern poems', in M. A. Harder, R. F. Regtuit and G. C. Wakker, eds., *Beyond the Canon* (Leuven), 83–9.
Gury, F. (1986) 'La forge du destin: à propos d'une série de peintures pompéiennes du IVe style', *MEFRA* 98: 427–89.
Gutzwiller, K. (1998) *Poetic Garlands: Hellenistic Epigrams in Context*, Berkeley.
Habinek, T. (2009) 'Situating literacy in Rome', in Johnson and Parker 2009, 114–41.
Hackworth Petersen, L. (2006) *The Freedman in Roman Art and Art History*, Cambridge.
Hagstrum, J. (1955) *The Sister Arts: The Tradition of Literary Pictorialism and English Poetry from Dryden to Gray*, Chicago.
Hales, S. (2003) *The Roman House and Social Identity*, Cambridge.
Hales, S. and T. Hodos, eds. (2010) *Material Culture and Social Identities in the Ancient World*, Cambridge.
Hallett, C. H. (2015) 'Defining Roman art', in Borg 2015, 11–33.
Hardie, P. (1985) '*Imago mundi*: cosmological and ideological aspects of the shield of Achilles', *JHS* 105: 11–31.
  (1993) '*Ut pictura poesis*? Horace and the visual arts', in N. Rudd, ed., *Horace 2000: A Celebration. Essays for the Bimillennium* (London), 120–39.
  (2019). *Classicism and Christianity in Late Antique Latin Poetry*. Oakland, CA.
Harris, W. V. (1989) *Ancient Literacy*, Cambridge, MA.

(1991) 'Why did the codex supplant the book-roll?', in J. Monfasani and R. G. Musto, eds., *Renaissance Society and Culture: Essays in Honor of Eugene F. Rice Jr* (New York), 71–85.
Hartmann, J. and H. Kaufmann, eds. (2023). *A Late Antique Poetics? The Jeweled Style Revisited*, London.
Heath, M. (2002/3) 'Theon and the history of the *Progymnasmata*', *GRBS* 43: 129–60.
Heffernan, J. (1993) *The Museum of Words: The Poetics of Ekphrasis from Homer to Ashberry*, Chicago.
Helm, N. W. (1902) 'The *carmen figuratum* as shown in the works of Publilius Optatianus Porfyrius', *TAPhA* 33: 43–9.
Helm, R. (1959) '29: Publilius Optatianus Porfyrius', *RE* 23.2: 1928–36.
Henderson, I. (1991) 'Quintilian and the Progymnasmata', *A&A* 37: 82–99.
Hernández Lobato, J. (2012) *Vel Apolline muto: estética y poética de la antigüedad tardía*, Bern.
Heslin, P. (2015) *The Museum of Augustus: The Temple of Apollo in Pompeii, the Portico of Philippus in Rome and Latin Poetry*, Los Angeles.
Hodske, J. (2007) *Mythologische Bildthemen in den Häusern Pompejis. Die Bedeutung der zentralen Mythenbilder für die Bewohner Pompejis*, Stendal.
Hohlweg, A. (1971) 'Ekphrasis', in K. Wessel and M. Restle, eds., *Reallexikon zur byzantinischen Kunst* (Stuttgart), II 33–75.
Hollander, J. (1995) *The Gazer's Spirit: Poems Speaking to Silent Works of Art*, Chicago.
Hölscher, T., ed. (2002) *Klassische Archäologie: Grundwissen*, Stuttgart.
Hope, V. (1997) 'Words and pictures: the interpretation of Romano-British tombstones', *Britannia* 28: 245–58.
Horsfall, N. (1979) 'Stesichorus at Bovillae?', *JHS* 99: 26–48.
  (1989a) '"The uses of literacy" and the *Cena Trimalchionis* I', *G&R* 36: 74–89.
  (1989b) '"The uses of literacy" and the *Cena Trimalchionis* II', *G&R* 36: 194–209.
  (1994) 'The origins of the illustrated book', in B. Katz, ed., *A History of Book Illustration: Twenty-Nine Points of View* (Metuchen, NJ), 60–88.
Hose, M. (2007) 'Konstantin und die Literatur – oder: Gibt es eine Konstantinische Literatur?', *Gymnasium* 114: 535–58.
Humphrey, J. H., ed. (1991) *Literacy in the Roman World*, Ann Arbor, MI.
Hunter, R. (2009) *Critical Moments in Classical Literature: Studies in the Ancient View of Literature and its Uses*, Cambridge.
Ireland, R. (1983) 'Epigraphy', in M. Henig, ed., *A Handbook of Roman Art* (London), 220–33.
Jaeger, M. (1997) *Livy's Written Rome*, Ann Arbor, MI.
James, L., ed. (2007) *Art and Text in Byzantine Culture*, Cambridge.
James, L. and R. Webb (1991) '"To understand ultimate things and enter secret places": ecphrasis and art in Byzantium', *Art History* 14: 1–17.
Jansen, L. (2014a) 'Modern covers and paratextual strategy in Ovidian elegy', in Jansen 2014b, 262–81.
Jansen, L., ed. (2014b) *The Roman Paratext: Frame, Text, Readers*, Cambridge.
Jenkyns, R. (2013) *God, Space and the City in the Roman Imagination*, Oxford.
Johnson, W. A. (2004) *Bookrolls and Scribes in Oxyrhynchus*, Toronto.

(2009) 'The ancient book', in Bagnall 2009, 256–81.

(2010) *Readers and Reading Culture in the High Roman Empire: A Study of Elite Communities*, Oxford.

Johnson, W. A. and H. N. Parker, eds. (2009) *Ancient Literacies: The Culture of Reading in Greece and Rome*, Oxford.

Johnson, W. R. (1976) *Darkness Visible*, Berkeley.

Jones, L. and C. Morey (1931) *The Miniatures of the Manuscripts of Terence*, Princeton.

Joshel, S. J. and L. Hackworth Petersen, eds. (2014) *The Material Life of Roman Slaves*, Cambridge.

Kampen, N. B. (2003) 'On writing histories of Roman art', *Art Bulletin* 85: 371–86.

Kansteiner, S. et al., eds. (2014) *Der Neue Overbeck: Die antiken Schriftquellen zu den bildenen Künsten der Griechen*, 5 vols., Berlin.

Katz, J. T. (2013) 'The Muse at play: an introduction', in Kwapisz, Petrain and Szymański 2013, 1–30.

Keegan, P. (2014) *Graffiti in Antiquity*, London.

Kirichenko, A. (2013) 'Virgil's Augustan temples: image and intertext in the *Aeneid*', *JRS* 103: 65–87.

(2018) 'How to build a monument: Horace the image-maker', *MD* 80: 121–63.

Kleiner, D. E. E. (1987) *Roman Imperial Funerary Altars with Portraits*, Rome.

Koortbojian, M. (1995) *Myth, Meaning and Memory on Roman Sarcophagi*, Berkeley.

(1996) '*In commemorationem mortuorum*: text and image along the "street of tombs"', in Elsner 1996b, 210–33.

Körfer, A.-L. (2019) *Kaiser Konstantin als Leser: Panegyrik, Performance und Poetologie in den Carmina Optatians*, Berlin.

Krieger, M. (1967) 'The ekphrastic principle and the still movement of poetry; or *Laokoön* revisited', in P. W. McDowell, ed., *The Poet as Critic* (Evanston, IL), 3–26.

(1992) *Ekphrasis: The Illusion of the Natural Sign*, Baltimore, MD.

Kwapisz, J. (2013) *The Greek Figure Poems*, Leuven.

(2017) 'Optatian and the order of court riddlers', in Squire and Wienand 2017, 165–90.

(2019a) *The Paradigm of Simias: Essays on Poetic Eccentricity*, Berlin.

(2019b) 'The *technê* of Aratus' *leptê* acrostich', *Enthymema* 23: 374–89.

Kwapisz, J., D. Petrain and M. Szymański, eds. (2013) *The Muse at Play: Riddles and Wordplay in Greek and Latin Poetry*, Berlin.

Lahusen, G. (1983) *Untersuchungen zur Ehrenstatue in Rom. Literarische und epigraphische Zeugnisse*, Rome.

(1985) *Schriftquellen zum römischen Bildnis.* 1: *Textstellen, von den Anfängen*, Bremen.

Laird, A. (1996) '*Ut figura poesis*: writing art and the art of writing in Augustan poetry', in Elsner 1996b, 75–102.

Lancha, J. (1997) *Mosaïque et culture dans l'Occident romain (1er–ive s.)*, Rome.

Langner, M. (2001) *Antike Graffitizeichnungen. Motiv, Gestaltung und Bedeutung*, Wiesbaden.
La Penna, A. (2000) 'L'ordine delle raffigurazioni della guerra Troiana nel tempio di Cartagine (*Aen.* 1.469–493)', *Maia* 52: 1–8.
Lassère, J.-M. (2011) *Manuel d'épigraphie romaine*, 3rd edn, 2 vols., Paris.
Lausberg, H. (1998) *Handbook of Literary Rhetoric: A Foundation for Literary Study* (trans. M. T. Bliss, A. Jansen and D. E. Orton), Leiden.
Leach, E. W. (1988) *The Rhetoric of Space: Literary and Artistic Representations of Landscape in Republican and Augustan Rome*, Princeton.
Leader-Newby, R. (2007) 'Inscribed mosaics in the Roman empire: perspectives from east and west', in Newby and Leader-Newby 2007, 179–99.
Lecoq, M. (2010) *Le bouclier d'Achille: un tableau qui borge*, Paris.
Lessing, G. E. (1984) *Laocoön: An Essay on the Limits of Painting and Poetry* (trans. E. A. McCormick), Baltimore.
Levitan, W. (1985) 'Dancing at the end of the rope: Optatian Porfyry and the field of Roman verse', *TAPhA* 115: 245–69.
Lichtenberger, A. and R. Raja, eds. (2017) *The Diversity of Classical Archaeology*, Turnhout.
Liddel, P. and P. Low, eds. (2013) *Inscriptions and Their Uses in Greek and Latin Literature*, Oxford.
Lifschitz, A. and M. J. Squire (2017) 'Introduction: rethinking Lessing's *Laocoon* from across the humanities', in A. Lifschitz and M. J. Squire, eds., *Rethinking Lessing's Laocoon: Antiquity, the Enlightenment, and the 'Limits' of Painting and Poetry* (Oxford), 1–57.
Lissarrague, F. and A. Schnapp (2000) 'Tradition und Erneuerung in der klassischen Archäologie in Frankreich', in A. H. Borbein, T. Hölscher and P. Zanker, eds., *Klassische Archäologie. Eine Einführung* (Berlin), 365–82.
Liversidge, M. J. H. (1997) 'Virgil in art', in C. Martindale, ed., *The Cambridge Companion to Virgil* (Cambridge), 91–104.
Llewellyn, N. (1988) 'Illustrating Ovid', in C. Martindale, ed., *Ovid Renewed: Ovidian Influences on Literature and Art from the Middle Ages to the Twentieth Century* (Cambridge), 151–66.
Lorenz, K. (2013) 'Split-screen visions: Heracles on top of Troy in the Casa di Octavius Quartio in Pompeii', in H. Lovatt and C. Vout, eds., *Epic Visions* (Cambridge), 218–47.
  (2015) 'Wall painting', in Borg 2015, 252–67.
Lowenstam, S. (1993) 'The pictures on Juno's temple in the *Aeneid*', *CJ* 87: 37–49.
Luz, C. (2008) 'Das Rätsel der griechischen Figurengedichte', *MH* 37: 22–33.
  (2010) *Technopaignia: Formspiele in der griechischen Dichtung*, Leiden.
Lynn-George, M. (1988) *Epos: Word, Narrative and the Iliad*, Basingstoke.
McKenzie, J. and F. Watson (2016) *The Garima Gospels*, Oxford.
Mcleod, W. (1985) 'The "epic canon" of the Borgia table: Hellenistic lore or Roman fraud?', *TAPhA* 115: 153–65.
MacMullen, R. (1982) 'The epigraphic habit in the Roman Empire', *AJPh* 103: 233–46.

Maffei, S. (1986) 'Le *Imagines* di Luciano: un "patchwork" capolavori antichi. Il problema di un metodo combinatorio', *SCO* 36: 147–64.
Mancuso, U. (1909) 'La "tabula iliaca" del Museo Capitolino', *Memorie dell' accademia dei Lincei* 5.14: 661–731.
Manieri, A. (1998) *L'immagine poetica nella teoria degli antichi*, Pisa.
Männlein-Robert, I. (2007) *Stimme, Schrift und Bild: Zum Verhältnis der Künste in der hellenistischen Dichtung*, Heidelberg.
Mansfield, E. C. (2007) *Too Beautiful to Picture: Zeuxis, Myth and Mimesis*, Minneapolis, MN.
Maras, D. F., ed. (1999) *La Tabula Iliaca di Bovillae*, Boville.
Marchand, S. (1996) *Down from Olympus: Archaeology and Philhellenism in Germany, 1750–1970*, Princeton.
Marchesi, I., ed. (2015) *Pliny the Book-Maker: Betting on Posterity in the Epistles*, Oxford.
Marvin, M. (1993) 'Copying in Roman sculpture: the replica series', in E. d'Ambra, ed., *Roman Art in Context: An Anthology* (Englewood Cliff), 161–88.
  (2008) *The Language of the Muses: The Dialogue between Greek and Roman Sculpture*, Los Angeles.
Marzano, A. and G. P. R. Métraux (2018a) 'The Roman villa: an overview', in Marzano and Métraux 2018b, 1–41.
Marzano, A. and G. P. R. Métraux, eds. (2018b) *The Roman Villa in the Mediterranean Basin: Late Republic to Late Antiquity*, Cambridge.
Mau, A. (1882) *Geschichte der decorativen Wandmalerei in Pompeji*, Berlin.
  (1899) *Pompeii: Its Life and Art*, London.
Mayer, E. (2012) *The Ancient Middle Classes: Urban Life and Aesthetics in the Roman Empire 100 BCE–250 CE*, Cambridge, MA.
Mazal, O. (1999) *Geschichte der Buchkultur. Band 1: Griechisch-römische Antike*, Graz.
Meates, G. W. (1955) *Lullingstone Roman Villa*, London.
Meijering, R. (1987) *Literary and Rhetorical Theories in Greek Scholia*, Groningen.
Meyer, D. (2005) *Inszeniertes Lesevergnügen. Das inschriftliche Epigramm und seine Rezeption bei Kallimachos*, Stuttgart.
Meyer, E. A. (1990) 'Explaining the epigraphic habit in the Roman Empire: the evidence of epitaphs', *JRS* 80: 74–96.
Miller, D., ed. (2005) *Materiality*, Durham, NC.
Miller, P. N., ed. (2013) *Cultural Histories of the Material World*, Ann Arbor, MI.
Millett, M. (2007) 'What is classical archaeology? Roman archaeology', in S. E. Alcock and R. Osborne, eds., *Classical Archaeology* (Malden, MA and Oxford), 30–52.
Milnor, K. (2014) *Graffiti and the Literary Landscape in Roman Pompeii*, Oxford.
Mitchell, W. J. T. (1986) *Iconology: Image, Text, Ideology*, Chicago.
Morel, W., ed. (1963) *Fragmenta poetarum Latinorum epicorum et lyricorum praeter Ennium et Lucilium*, 2nd edn, Stuttgart.
Moser, C. (2019) *The Altars of Republican Rome and Latium: Sacrifice and the Materiality of Roman Religion*, Cambridge.

Mratschek, S. (2000) '*Codices vestri nos sumus*: Bücherkult und Bücherpreise in der christlichen Spätantike', in A. Haltenhoff and F.-H. Mutschler, eds., *Hortus litterarum antiquarum. Festschrift für Hans Armin Gärtner zum 70. Geburtstag* (Heidelberg), 369–80.
Naas, V. (2002) *Le projet encyclopédique de Pline l'Ancien*, Rome.
Nauta, R. (2002) *Poetry for Patrons: Literary Communication in the Age of Domitian*, Leiden.
Neudecker, R. (1988) *Die Skulpturenausstattung römischer Villen in Italien*, Mainz.
Nevett, L. (2010) *Domestic Space in Classical Antiquity*, Cambridge.
Nevett, L. and J. Whitley, eds. (2018) *An Age of Experiment: Classical Archaeology Transformed (1976–2014)*, Cambridge.
Newby, Z. and R. Leader-Newby, eds. (2007) *Art and Inscriptions in the Ancient World*, Cambridge.
Newlands, C. (2002) *Statius' Silvae and the Poetics of Empire*, Cambridge.
Nisbet, G. (2011) 'An ancient Greek graphic novel: *P. Oxy.* XXII.2331', in G. Kovacs and C. W. Marshall, eds., *Classics and Comics* (Oxford), 27–41.
Nordenfalk, C. (1938) *Die spätantiken Kanontafeln: Kunstgeschichtliche Studien über die eusebianische Evangelien-Konkordanze in den vier ersten Jahrhunderten ihrer Geschichte*, Göteborg.
  (1982) 'Canon tables on papyrus', *DOP* 36: 29–38.
  (1984) 'The Eusebian canon tables: some textual problems', *The Journal of Theological Studies* 35: 96–104.
Nünlist, R. (2009) *The Ancient Critic at Work: Terms and Concepts of Literary Criticism in Greek Scholia*, Cambridge.
O'Rourke, D. (2014) 'Paratext and intertext in the Propertian poetry book', in Jansen 2014b, 156–76.
O'Sullivan, T. (2007) 'Walking with Odysseus: the portico frame of the Odyssey landscapes', *AJPh* 128: 497–532.
Otto, N. (2009) *Enargeia: Untersuchung zur Charakteristik alexandrinischer Dichtung*, Stuttgart.
Overbeck, J. (1868) *Die antiken Schriftquellen zur Geschichte der bildenden Künste bei den Griechen*, Leipzig.
Palm, J. (1965–6) 'Bemerkungen zur Ekphrase in der griechischen Literatur', *Kungliga Humanistiska Vertenskaps-Samfundet i Uppsala* 1: 108–211.
Pandey, N. B. (2018) *The Poetics of Power in Augustan Rome: Latin Poetic Responses to Early Imperial Iconography*, Cambridge.
Pappas, A. (2013) 'The treachery of verbal images: viewing the Greek technopaegnia', in Kwapisz, Petrain and Szymański 2013, 199–224.
Patillon, M. and G. Bolognesi, eds. (1997) *Aelius Théon, Progymnasmata*, Paris.
Pékary, T. (1985) *Das römische Kaiserbildnis in Staat, Kult und Gesellschaft, dargestellet anhand der Schriftquellen*, Berlin.
Pelttari, A. D. (2014) *The Space that Remains: Reading Latin Poetry in Late Antiquity*, Ithaca, NY.
Pernot, L. (2011) 'Phidias à la barre', in L. Pernot, ed., *La rhétorique des arts. Actes du colloque tenu au Collège de France sous la présidence de Marc Fumaroli, de l'Académie française* (Paris), 11–35.

Perry, E. (2005) *The Aesthetics of Emulation in the Visual Arts of Ancient Rome*, Cambridge.
Petrain, D. (2013) 'Closing the ring: epic cycles in the Tabulae Iliacae and other Roman visual narratives of the Trojan war', in Grewing, Acosta-Hughes and Kirichenko 2013, 143–68.
  (2014) *Homer in Stone: The Tabulae Iliacae in Their Roman Context*, Cambridge.
Petrovic, A. (2019) 'The materiality of text: an introduction', in Petrovic, Petrovic and Thomas 2019, 1–25.
Petrovic, A., I. Petrovic and E. Thomas, eds. (2019) *The Materiality of Text – Placement, Perception, and Presence of Inscribed Texts in Classical Antiquity*, Leiden.
Pithou, P. (1590) *Epigrammata et poemata vetera*, Paris.
Platt, V. J. (2006) 'Making an impression: replication and the ontology of the Graeco-Roman seal stone', *Art History* 29: 233–57.
  (2009) '"Where the wild things are": locating the marvellous in Augustan wall painting', in P. Hardie, ed., *Paradox and the Marvellous in Augustan Literature* (Oxford), 41–74.
  (2016) 'The matter of classical art history', *Daedalus* 145: 5–14.
  (2018) 'Of sponges and stones: matter and ornament in Roman painting', in N. Dietrich and M. J. Squire, eds., *Ornament and Figure in Graeco-Roman Art: Rethinking Visual Ontologies in Classical Antiquity* (Berlin), 241–78.
  (in press) *Epistemic Objects: Making and Mediating Classical Art,* Oxford.
Platt, V. J. and M. J. Squire (2017a) 'Framing the visual in Greek and Roman antiquity: an introduction', in Platt and Squire 2017b, 1–99.
Platt, V. J. and M. J. Squire, eds. (2010) *The Art of Art History in Graeco-Roman Antiquity* (= *Arethusa* 43.2), Baltimore, MD.
  (2017b) *The Frame in Classical Art: A Cultural History*, Cambridge.
Platts, H. (2020) *Multisensory Living in Ancient Rome: Power and Space in Roman Houses*, London.
Polara, G. (1973) *Publilii Optatiani Porfyrii Carmina*, 2 vols., Turin.
  (1987) 'Optaziano Porfirio tra il calligramma antico e il carme figurato di età medioevale', *InvLuc* 9: 163–73.
  (1991) 'Le parole nella pagina: grafica e contenuti nei carmi figurati latini', *VetChr* 28: 291–336.
  (2004) *Optaziano Porfirio: carmi*, Turin.
Pollard, A. (2018) 'Gladiators and circus horses in the *Iliad* frieze in Pompeii's Casa di D. Octavius Quartio?', *JRA* 31: 285–302.
Pollitt, J. J. (1974) *The Ancient View of Greek Art: Criticism, History and Terminology*, Cambridge.
  (1983) *The Art of Rome, c. 753 BC–AD 337: Sources and Documents*, Cambridge.
Porter, J. (2011) *The Origins of Aesthetic Thought in Ancient Greece*, Cambridge.
  (2008) *Petits musées en vers. Epigramme et discours sur les collections antiques*, Paris.
Putnam, M. (1998) *Virgil's Epic Designs: Ekphrasis in the Aeneid*, New Haven.

(2001) 'The ambiguity of art in Virgil's *Aeneid*', *PAPhS* 145: 162–83.
Rabe, H., ed. (1913) *Hermogenis Opera*, Leipzig.
  (1926) *Aphthonius Progymnasmata*, Leipzig.
  (1928) *Ioannis Sardiani Commentarium in Aphthonii Progymnasmata*, Leipzig.
Rickert, F. (1986) *Studien zur Ashburnham Pentateuch*, Bonn.
Rispoli, G. M. (1984) 'φαντασία ed ἐνάργεια negli scolî all'*Iliade*', *Vichiana* 13: 311–39.
Riti, T. (1973–4) 'L'uso di "immagini onomastiche" nei monumenti sepolcrali di età greca: alcune testimonianze epigrafiche, archeologiche e letterarie', *ArchClass* 25–6: 639–60.
  (1977) 'Immagini onomastiche sui monumenti sepolcrali di età imperiale', *Atti dell'Accademia Nazionale dei Lincei: Rendiconti* 21: 257–396.
Roberts, C. H. and T. C. Skeat (1983) *The Birth of the Codex*, London.
Roberts, M. (1989) *The Jeweled Style: Poetry and Poetics in Late Antiquity*, Ithaca, NY.
Roman, L. (2001) 'The representation of literary materiality in Martial's *Epigrams*', *JRS* 91: 113–45.
Rossi, L. (2001) *The Epigrams Ascribed to Theocritus: A Method of Approach*, Leuven and Paris.
Rothe, U. (2018) 'The Roman villa: definitions and variations', in Marzano and Métraux 2018b, 42–59.
Rouveret, A. (1989) *Histoire et imaginaire de la peinture ancienne (v e siècle av. J.-C.– 1er siècle ap. J.-C.)*, Paris.
Rühl, M. (2006) 'Panegyrik im Quadrat: Optatian und die intermedialen Tendenzen des spätantiken Herrscherbildes', *Millennium* 3: 75–102.
Rutledge, S. H. (2012) *Ancient Rome as a Museum: Power, Identity, and the Culture of Collecting*, Oxford.
Santoro, S. (2005) 'I temi iliaci nella pittura pompeiana', in G. Burzacchini, ed., *Troia tra realtà e leggenda* (Palma), 97–123.
Sauron, G. (2009) *Dans l'intimité des maîtres du monde. Les décors privés des Romains*, Paris.
Schafer, J. K. (2017) 'Pagination in the *Eclogues* and *Georgics*', *TAPhA* 147: 135–78.
Schatzberg, E. (2018) *Technology: Critical History of a Concept*, Chicago.
Schefold, K. (1975) *Wort und Bild. Studien zur Gegenwart der Antike*, Mainz.
Schefold, K. and F. Jung (1989) *Die Sagen von den Argonauten, von Theben und Troia in der klassischen und hellenistischen Kunst*, Munich.
Schipke, R. (2013) *Das Buch in der Spätantik. Herstellung, Form, Ausstattung und Verbreitung in der westlichen Reichshälfte des Imperium Romanum*, Wiesbaden.
Schmidt, M. G. (2004) *Einführung in die lateinische Epigraphik*, Darmstadt.
  (2015) 'Carmina Latina Epigraphica', in Bruun and Edmondson, eds., 764–82.
Scholz, B. (1998) '*Sub oculos subiecto*: Quintilian on ekphrasis and enargeia', in V. Robillard and E. Jongeneel, eds., *Pictures into Words: Theoretical and Descriptive Approaches to Ekphrasis* (Amsterdam), 73–99.

Schröder, B.-J. (1999) *Titel und Text: Zur Entwicklung lateinischer Gedichtüberschriften. Mit Untersuchungen zu lateinischen Buchtiteln, Inhaltsverzeichnissen und anderen Gliederungsmitteln*, Berlin.
Scott, S. (2000) *Art and Society in Fourth-Century Britain: Villa Mosaics in Context*, Oxford.
Scott, S., and J. Webster (2003) *Roman Imperialism and Provincial Art*, Cambridge.
Sears, G., P. Keegan and R. Laurence, eds. (2013) *Written Space in the Latin West, 200 BC to AD 300*, London.
Sevrugian, P. (2004) 'Kanontafeln', *Reallexikon für Antike und Christentum* 20: 28–42.
Shanks, M. (1996) *Classical Archaeology of Greece: Experiences of the Discipline*, London and New York.
Sheppard, A. (2014) *The Poetics of Phantasia: Imagination in Ancient Aesthetics*, London.
Sichtermann, H. (1996) *Kulturgeschichte der klassischen Archäologie*, Munich.
Slater, N. W. (1987) 'Against interpretation: Petronius and art criticism', *Ramus* 16: 165–76.
Small, J.-P. (1997) *Wax Tablets of the Mind: Cognitive Studies of Memory and Literacy in Classical Antiquity*, London.
  (2003) *The Parallel Worlds of Classical Art and Text*, Cambridge.
Smith, A. (2005) *The Primacy of Vision in Virgil's Aeneid*, Austin, TX.
Snodgrass, A. (1987) *An Archaeology of Greece: The Present State and Future Scope of a Discipline*, Berkeley.
Sörries, R. (1993) *Christlich-Antike Buchmalerei im Überblick*, Wiesbaden.
Sprigath, G. K. (2004) 'Das Dictum des Simonides: Der Vergleich von Dichtung und Malerei', *Poetica* 36: 243–80.
Squire, M. J. (2009) *Image and Text in Graeco-Roman Antiquity*, Cambridge.
  (2010) 'Reading a view: poem and picture in the Greek anthology', *Ramus* 39: 73–103.
  (2011) *The Iliad in a Nutshell: Visualizing Epic on the Tabulae Iliacae*, Oxford.
  (2012) ''Ἀσπὶς Ἀχιλλῆος Θεοδώρηος καθ' Ὅμηρον: an early imperial text of *Il.* 18.483–557', *ZPE* 182: 1–30.
  (2013a) 'Ekphrasis at the forge and the forging of ekphrasis: the shield of Achilles in Graeco-Roman word and image', *Word & Image* 29: 157–91.
  (2013b) 'Invertire l'ekphrasis: l'epigramma ellenistico e la traslazione di parola e immagine', *Estetica: studi e ricerche* 2013: 109–36.
  (2013c) '*Ars* in their "I"s: authority and authorship in Graeco-Roman visual culture', in A. Marmodoro and J. Hill, eds., *The Author's Voice in Classical and Late Antiquity* (Oxford), 357–414.
  (2013d [publ. 2018]) (Review of Coleman 2015), *Hermathena* 195: 77–83.
  (2013e) 'Embodied ambiguities on the Prima Porta Augustus', *Art History* 36: 242–79.
  (2013f) 'Picturing words and wording pictures: false closure in the Pompeian Casa degli Epigrammi', in Grewing, Kirichenko and Acosta-Hughes 2013, 169–201.

(2014) 'The *ordo* of rhetoric and the rhetoric of order', in Elsner and Meyer 2014, 353–417.
(2015a) 'Patterns of significance: Publilius Optatianus Porfyrius and the figurations of meaning', in R. Green and M. Edwards, eds., *Images and Texts: Papers in Honour of Professor E. W. Handley, CBE, FBA* (London), 87–120.
(2015b) 'Ecphrasis: visual and verbal interactions in ancient Greek and Latin literature', *Oxford Handbooks Online*, DOI: 10.1093/oxfordhb/9780199935390.013.58.
(2015c) 'Running rings round Troy: re-cycling the epic circle in Hellenistic and Roman visual culture', in M. Fantuzzi and C. Tsagalis, eds., *A Companion to the Epic Cycle* (Cambridge), 496–542.
(2015d) '*Ars revixit?* In search of the ancient artist', *JRA* 28: 522–36.
(2016a) '*Ignotum per ignotius:* Pompeii, Vergil, and the "Museum of Augustus"', *JRA* 29: 598–606.
(2016b) '*Iliacas ex ordine pugnas*: ordering time and space in Virgilian ecphrasis', *Lampas* 49: 223–51.
(2016c) 'How to read a Roman portrait: Optatian Porfyry, Constantine and the *uultus Augusti*', *PBSR* 84: 179–240 and 359–66.
(2017) 'POP art: the optical poetics of Publilius Optatianus Porfyrius', in J. Elsner and J. Hernández Lobato, eds., *The Poetics of Late Latin Literature* (Oxford), 25–100.
(2018) 'A picture of ekphrasis? The Younger Philostratus and the Homeric shield of Achilles', in A. Kampakoglou et al., eds., *Gaze, Vision, and Visuality in Ancient Greek Literature* (Berlin), 290–348.
(2022) 'Text & image', in N. Elkins and L. Cline, eds., *Oxford Handbook of Roman Imagery and Iconography* (New York), 51–91.
Squire, M. J. and J. Elsner (2017) 'Homer and the ekphrasists: text and picture in the Elder Philostratus' Scamander (*Imagines* 1.1)', in J. Bintliff and K. Rutter eds., *The Archaeology of Greece and Rome: Studies in Honour of Anthony Snodgrass* (Edinburgh), 57–100.
Squire, M. J. and C. L. Whitton (2017) '*Machina sacra*: Optatian and the lettered art of the Christogram', in I. Garipzanov, C. Goodson and H. Maguire, eds., *Graphic Signs of Identity, Faith, and Power in Late Antiquity and the Early Middle Ages* (Turnhout), 45–108.
Squire, M. J. and J. Wienand, eds. (2017) *Morphogrammata/The Lettered Art of Optatian: Figuring Cultural Transformations in the Age of Constantine*, Paderborn.
Stanton, G. (2004) 'The early Christian preference for the codex', in C. Horton, ed., *The Earliest Gospels: The Origins and Transmission of the Earliest Christian Gospels. The Contribution of the Chester Beatty Gospel Codex P45* (London), 40–9.
Stefanou, D. (2006) *Darstellungen aus dem Epos und Drama auf kaiserzeitlichen und spätantiken Bodenmosaiken. Eine ikonographische und deutungsgeschichtliche Untersuchung*, Munster.
Stevenson, T. B. (1983) *Miniature Decoration in the Vatican Virgil: A Study in Late Antique Iconography*, Tübingen.

Stewart, P. (2003) *Statues in Roman Society: Representation and Response*, Oxford.
  (2004) *Roman Art*, Oxford.
Strodel, S. (2002) *Zur Überlieferung und zum Verständnis der hellenistischen Technopaegnien*, Frankfurt.
Stückelberger, A. (1994) *Bild und Wort: Das illustrierte Fachbuch in der antiken Naturwissenschaft, Medizin und Technik*, Mainz.
Tanner, J. (2006) *The Invention of Art History in Ancient Greece: Religion, Society and Artistic Rationalisation*, Cambridge.
Thein, K. (2021) *Ecphrastic Shields in Graeco-Roman Literature: The World's Forge*, London.
Thomas, E. (1995) 'Zum Zeugniswert griechischer Beischriften auf römischen Wandgemälden der späten Republik und frühen Kaiserzeit', *MNIR* 54: 110–23.
Toner, J., ed. (2014) *A Cultural History of the Senses in Antiquity*, London.
Toynbee, J. M. C. (1962) *Art in Roman Britain*, Cambridge.
  (1964) *Art in Britain under the Romans*, Oxford.
Trout, D. (2015) *Damasus of Rome: The Epigraphic Poetry*, Oxford.
Tueller, M. A. (2008) *Look Who's Talking: Innovations in Voice and Identity in Hellenistic Poetry*, Leuven.
Turner, E. G. (1987) *Greek Manuscripts of the Ancient World*, 2nd edn (revised by P. J. Parsons), London.
Valenzuela Montenegro, N. (2004) *Die Tabulae Iliacae. Mythos und Geschichte im Spiegel einer Gruppe frühkaiserzeitlicher Miniaturreliefs*, Berlin.
Vasaly, A. (1993) *Representations: Images of the World in Ciceronian Oratory*, Berkeley.
Verkerk, D. (2004) *Early Medieval Bible Illumination and the Ashburnham Pentateuch*, Cambridge.
Vogt, E. (1966) 'Das Akrostichon in der griechischen Literatur', *A&A* 13: 80–95.
von den Hoff, R. (2019) *Einführung in die Klassische Archäologie*, Munich.
von Gebhardt, O. (1883) *The Miniatures of the Ashburnham Pentateuch*, London.
Vout, C. V. (2007) *Power and Eroticism in Imperial Rome*, Cambridge.
Wallace-Hadrill, A. (1989) 'Rome's cultural revolution', *JRS* 79: 157–64.
  (1994) *Housing and Society in Pompeii and Herculaneum*, Princeton.
Wallraff, N. (2013) *Kodex und Kanon: Das Buch im frühen Christentum*, Berlin.
Wattel-de Croizant, W. (1995) *Les mosaïques représentant le mythe d'Europe (Ier–VIe siècles). Évolution et interprétation des modèles grecs en milieu romain*, Paris.
Webb, R. (1997a) 'Mémoire et imagination: les limites de l'enargeia', in C. Lévy and L. Pernot, eds., *Dire l'évidence: philosophie et rhétorique antiques* (Paris), 229–48.
  (1997b) 'Imagination and the arousal of emotion in Greco-Roman rhetoric', in S. M. Braund and C. Gill, eds., *The Passions in Roman Thought and Literature* (Cambridge), 12–127.
  (1999) 'Ekphrasis ancient and modern: the invention of a genre', *Word & Image* 15: 7–18.
  (2000) 'Picturing the past: uses of ekphrasis in the *Deipnosophistae* and other works of the Second Sophistic', in D. Braund and J. Wilkins, eds., *Athenaeus and His World: Reading Culture in the Roman Empire* (Exeter), 218–26.

(2001) 'The *Progymnasmata* as practice', in Y. L. Too, ed., *Education in Greek and Roman Antiquity* (Leiden), 289–316.
  (2009) *Ekphrasis, Imagination and Persuasion in Ancient Rhetorical Practice and Theory*, Farnham.
Weitzmann, K. (1947) *Illustrations in Roll and Codex*, Princeton.
  (1959) *Ancient Book Illumination*, Cambridge, MA.
Welser, P. (1595) *Publilii Optatiani Porphyrii Panegyricus dictus Constantino Augusto*, Augsburg.
Wessel, K. (1976–7) 'Kanontafeln', *Reallexikon zur byzantinischen Kunst* 3: 927–68.
Whitton, C. L. (2015) 'Grand designs: unrolling Epistles 2', in Marchesi 2015, 109–43.
  (2019) *The Arts of Imitation in Latin Prose: Pliny's Epistles/Quintilian in Brief*, Cambridge.
Wienand, J. (2012) *Der Kaiser als Sieger. Metamorphosen triumphaler Herrschaft unter Constantin I*, Berlin.
Williams, G. D. (1992) 'Representations of the book-roll in Latin poetry: Ovid, *Tr.* 1.1.3–14 and related texts', *Mnemosyne* 45: 178–89.
Williams, J., ed. (1999) *Imaging the Early Medieval Bible*, University Park, PA.
Williams, R. D. (1960) 'The pictures on Dido's temple', *CQ* 10: 145–51.
Williamson, C. (1987) 'Monuments of bronze: Roman legal documents on bronze tablets', *ClAnt* 6: 160–83.
Wit, J. (1959) *Die Miniaturen des Vergilius Vaticanus*, Amsterdam.
Wojaczek, G. (1988) 'Schlüssel und Schlange: Zwei figurale Texte aus Antike und Mittelalter', *WJA* 14: 241–52.
Woolf, G. (1996) 'Monumental writing and the expansion of Roman society in the early Empire', *JRS* 86: 22–39.
  (2009) 'Literacy or literacies in Rome', in Johnson and Parker 2009, 46–68.
Wormald, F. (1954) *The Miniatures of the Gospels of St Augustine*, Cambridge.
Wray, D. (2003) 'What poets do: Tibullus on "easy" hands', *CPh* 98: 217–50.
Wright, D. (1993) *The Vatican Vergil: A Masterpiece of Late Antique Art*, Berkeley.
  (2001) *The Roman Vergil and the Origins of Medieval Book Design*, London.
  (2006) *The Lost Late Antique Illustrated Terence*, Vatican.
Yates, F. A. (1966) *The Art of Memory*, 2nd edn, London.
Zanker, G. (1981) 'Enargeia in the ancient criticism of poetry', *RhM* 124: 297–311.
Zanker, P. (1989) *The Power of Images in the Age of Augustus* (trans. A. Shapiro), Ann Arbor, MI.
Zanker, P. and B. C. Ewald (2004) *Mit Mythen leben. Die Bilderwelt der römischen Sarkophage*, Munich.
Zeitlin, F. (2013) 'Figure: ekphrasis', *G&R* 60: 17–31.
Zimmermann, B. (2001) '"Illustrierte Prachtcodices": Bücherluxus in der Spätantike', in F. Alto Bauer and N. Zimmermann, eds., *Epochenwandel? Kunst und Kultur zwischen Antike und Mittelalter* (Mainz), 45–56.

CHAPTER 13

# *Philosophy*

Katharina Volk

## The Problem with Roman Philosophy

Some of the most famous products of Latin literature are works of philosophy. Some of the most famous works of philosophy are written in Latin.

Really?

Many Latinists would probably agree with the first statement, on the basis of Lucretius' *De rerum natura* and the philosophical corpora of Cicero and Seneca. By contrast, if any philosophers concur with the second statement at all, they are probably thinking of such mediaeval and early modern thinkers as Aquinas, Descartes or Spinoza, but not of any ancient authors. Philosophy plays a large role in Latin literature; Latin literature does not play a large role in the history of philosophy. Why?

It was not always like this. In the early modern period, Roman philosophical writers were held in the highest esteem. Cicero – whose *De officiis* was the first book of pagan antiquity to appear in print (1465) – was a revered guide not only to good Latinity but also to practical ethics; Seneca inspired the Neo-Stoic movement; and Lucretius served as a subversive source for both corpuscular physics and the Epicurean way of life. Over the course of the centuries, however, a number of developments combined to lead to a devaluation of Roman thought: Cartesian rationalism with its discounting of time-honoured *auctores*; the rediscovery of Greek philosophy in its original language; and, especially in Germany, an aesthetics informed by Idealism and Romanticism, which considered Roman culture inferior to that of the Greeks.

In addition, the establishment of philosophy as a modern university subject in the nineteenth century contributed to a view of the field's

---

[*] My thanks for feedback and support go to the editors as well as my fellow volume authors, in particular James Uden, who has contributed in many ways to improving this chapter. I am further grateful to Gareth Williams and Jim Zetzel for reading and commenting on various drafts and to Yelena Baraz, Monica Gale and Nathan Gilbert for sharing not only their expertise but also unpublished material.

history as an abstract process, one in which ideas take shape and interact in a timeless space inhabited by past and contemporary philosophers alike.[1] What is relevant is the originality and, as it were, quality of a given argument, the way it stands up to scrutiny and improves on earlier approaches. By these criteria, most Roman philosophy – based, as it is, on Greek Hellenistic thought – is bound to appear to be derivative and second rate. Since at the same time, however, the works of Lucretius, Cicero and Seneca are our main sources for Stoic and Epicurean doctrine, owing to the loss of most of the Greek material (a fact that in itself might lead one to reconsider the narrative of Roman inferiority), these texts have been mined for information and often studied as mere doxography.

While there have been calls for decades to take Roman philosophical writing more seriously – an important milestone is the two *Philosophia togata* volumes edited by Jonathan Barnes and Miriam Griffin in 1989 and 1997 – there has just recently begun a marked acceleration and proliferation of study on the topic. All of a sudden, there is such a thing as 'Roman' (or even 'Latin') philosophy, the subject of edited volumes, an *Oxford Bibliographies* commented bibliography and an Oxford University Press *Handbook*.[2] There now exists at least one organisation dedicated specifically to the study of Roman thought, and publishers, too, are getting on the bandwagon by creating special series for the growing number of publications on the subject.[3]

The context of this development is, on the one hand, the ongoing re-evaluation, within the history of philosophy, of Hellenistic and post-Hellenistic thought, which has, in a kind of trickle-down effect, led to a new appreciation of Roman authors as well. Thus, Harald Thorsrud, Raphael Woolf and Brad Inwood, among others, have demonstrated in recent publications that Cicero and Seneca ought to be taken seriously as philosophers, even by the standards of the 'timeless ideas' approach

---

[1] On the ways in which the history of philosophy has often been written by philosophers, and on alternative approaches, see Rorty, Schneewind and Skinner 1984 (as well as the papers in the volume to which that piece is the introduction), Catana 2016, Smith 2016, Marenbon 2018.
[2] Volumes: Williams and Volk 2016 (subtitle: *Studies in Latin Philosophy*), Vesperini 2017, Müller and Mariani Zini 2018; bibliography: Reydams-Schils 2011; handbook: Garani, Konstan and Reydams-Schils 2023.
[3] Organisation: Arbeitsgemeinschaft 'Philosophie in Rome' of the Gesellschaft für Antike Philosophie; series: 'Philosophy in the Roman World' (Routledge), 'Roman Philosophy' (University of Pennsylvania Press), 'Cicero' (De Gruyter). As the field is developing quickly, the information in this and the preceding note makes no claim to completeness.

I have described.[4] On the other hand, scholars – in keeping with the general cultural turn of the field of classics – are increasingly considering philosophical practices at Rome as a broader phenomenon that needs to be studied in context.[5] The latter is the approach the present chapter will take as well.

Studying the history of philosophy with an eye to philosophical content, value and truth implies asking the question, 'What does it mean to us?' – that is, How do the arguments relate to other arguments with which we are familiar?, How (if at all) do they advance our understanding of thought and reality? or perhaps even, How can they help us live a better life? By contrast, I want to ask, 'What did it mean to them?' Why did Romans of the middle and late Republic begin to read Greek philosophy and travel to Greece to study with philosophers there? Why did Lucretius and Cicero decide to write philosophy in Latin? Why did Horace include Epicurean sentiments in his *Odes*? Why did the Stoic Seneca also compose gory tragedies? Why did Marcus Aurelius keep a philosophical diary? Why did the novelist Apuleius insist on being called a *philosophus*? And why was Augustine thinking of pagan philosophy while penning his theological works? All of these questions seem to me to be relevant to a properly understood *history* of philosophy, but they appear to be largely irrelevant to the history of *philosophy* as generally practised. Admittedly, none of them has to do with whether the works of the likes of Cicero and Lucretius make important contributions to philosophy. On the contrary: perhaps the answers to these questions will even provide good reasons why, by the criteria usually employed, they do not.

This chapter, then, will consider Roman philosophical practices and writings in context, taking into account their historical, cultural, social, political and literary background and viewing them, not philosophically as expressive of timeless ideas, but historically as products of a specific time and place. Instead of modern concepts, it will employ actors' categories, trying to explain choices of behaviour or argument with reference to the Romans' own intellectual vocabulary rather than in terms that conform to our ways of thinking. My aim is to get at the specificity of Roman philosophy and to ask whether there is indeed something distinctive

---

[4] Thorsrud 2009: 84–101, Woolf 2015, Inwood 2005. Note, though, that even the most committed apologists often remain equivocal about the ultimate philosophical significance of the authors they study (see e.g. Woolf 2015: 2: 'Cicero is no Plato or Aristotle').

[5] Some scholars working on ancient philosophical thought and practice see such discontinuity between their subject and the modern concept of 'philosophy' that they use the term *philosophia* instead (Trapp 2007, Vesperini 2012); while I have some sympathy for this approach, I will not adopt it here.

about philosophy practised at Rome and especially – given the purview of this volume – philosophy written in Latin. Here it is important not to fall into easy stereotyping. 'The Romans' have often enough been maligned as practical sorts adept at bridge- and empire-building but unsuited for, and uninterested in, the finer points of philosophical inquiry. While I believe that there are arguments to be made for particular Roman interests and intellectual preferences, these do not amount to anything like a national character, and in what follows, the focus will be on individual authors and texts, not 'Roman philosophy' as a whole. In addition, as my discussion of writers and works through the centuries will demonstrate, Roman philosophical thought and practice changed over time: Apuleius lived in a different world from Cicero, had different questions and came up with different answers.

Even so, there are two general observations to be made that hold for much of the philosophy that was practised and written at Rome and that set this chapter in the history of philosophy apart from many others. First, for many Romans philosophy was not so much an intellectual pursuit as a way of life.[6] From their earliest encounters with Greek thought, the Romans were enthusiastic about philosophy – David Sedley has even spoken of 'the great Roman love-affair with philosophy' (2010: 702) – and keen on gaining their own knowledge of the subject matter. However, the men who eagerly adopted Stoicism, Epicureanism or various forms of Platonism did not on the whole do so with the intention of intervening in philosophical debates or coming up with new ideas and arguments. Their purpose was to apply the teachings of philosophy to their own circumstances and, by following the precepts of one school or eclectically choosing from many, ideally to achieve that final goal, the good life.

As a corollary – and this is my second observation, which moves from philosophical practice to philosophical writing – most of the works of Roman philosophy were written by non-philosophers, something that fundamentally distinguishes them from the bulk of the western philosophical corpus. Authors like Cicero, Seneca and Marcus Aurelius were devotees of philosophy as an art of life before they embarked on penning their own philosophical works (the case of Marcus being extreme in that he did not intend his *Meditations* for publication at all). This 'amateur' status of much Roman philosophical writing has its basis in the social and

---

[6] The question whether ancient and especially (post-)Hellenistic philosophy was primarily concerned with promoting a way of life (rather than an intellectual system) has been much and controversially discussed, esp. in the wake of the fundamental works of Foucault 1986 and Hadot 1995 and 2002; see recently Chase 2013 and Sellars 2017.

ethnic background of its authors. As Harry Hine has shown in an important article (2016), such philosophical writers as Cicero and Seneca tend not to refer to themselves as *philosophi* even while speaking of their pursuit as *philosophia* and *philosophari*. The reason for this is that in their society, 'philosophers' were Greek professionals, men with affiliations to individual schools who taught philosophy and often also published their own interventions in philosophical debates. By contrast, Lucretius was an otherwise unknown poet; Cicero was a statesman and orator; Seneca was an imperial tutor, courtier and backroom politician; and Marcus Aurelius was himself an emperor. None of them considered himself a philosopher, none wrote for philosophers, and none (one assumes) was read by philosophers, at least not until long after their own time. While their work may qualify as philosophy, and while they are today often conventionally referred to as philosophers,[7] their social status as well as their interests and intentions set them apart from professional philosophy as understood both in their own times and today.[8]

In this chapter, I combine a chronological framework with a thematic focus on seven different aspects of Roman philosophising. After a brief historical narrative of the *Roman adoption of Greek philosophy* in the second century BCE, I use Lucretius as a case study for the *Latinisation of Greek thought*, before considering Cicero as an example of the *political and cultural uses of philosophy* in the late Republic.[9] I then step briefly outside the chronological framework to explore a few of the many and diverse appearances of *philosophy in Latin poetry* – evidence of both the saturation of the Roman cultural imaginary with philosophical ideas and the fact that Latin philosophical writing was by no means restricted to genres traditionally viewed as philosophical. Moving on into the Empire, I first discuss Seneca as a proponent of *philosophy as a way of life and form of therapy* (here Marcus Aurelius will make a cameo appearance) and then consider the *social practices and self-representation of philosophers*, using as evidence both Apuleius and Aulus Gellius. The chapter concludes with

---

[7] Compare e.g. the title of Morford 2002: *The Roman Philosophers*.
[8] As Hine 2016: 21–3 shows (compare Trapp 2017a), the definition of philosophy shifts in the High Empire: as we will see below, the second-century CE declaimer and novelist Apuleius explicitly identifies as a *philosophus*, perhaps the only Latin philosophical writer to do so (ironically, he may be the one least likely to be considered a 'philosopher' by modern scholars).
[9] Throughout, I am largely bracketing works of political philosophy as such, the topic of Michèle Lowrie in this volume – though as Lowrie reminds us, political thought at Rome was firmly embedded in public discourse as a whole and not cordoned off into specific genres of speech or writing.

a look at the *Christianisation of philosophy* in late antiquity, nodding to Tertullian and Jerome before focusing on Augustine.

## Philosophy Comes to Rome

Like many cultural practices and nearly all literary genres, philosophy was a Greek import into Rome.[10] Following the foundation of the major philosophical schools in fourth-century Athens, philosophy established itself throughout the Greek world as a subject of study, genre of writing and way of life. When, in a well-known but still remarkable development, the Romans, late-comers to the Mediterranean scene, decided, as it were, to model their own emerging high culture on that of their sister civilisation,[11] they adopted and adapted – among epic and tragedy, rhetoric, astronomy and astrology, the conspicuous consumption of the visual arts and numerous other fields of study, artistic endeavours and lifestyle choices – many of the philosophical theories and practices of their eastern neighbours. Among the *artes* that, in the famous words of Horace (*Epist.* 2.1.156–7), *Graecia capta* in her cultural counter-conquest brought to boorish Latium, philosophy was but one of many.

As every Latinist knows, the Romans' typical approach to their Greek models involved not only *imitatio* but also *aemulatio*, testifying to that profoundly Roman mixture of a cultural inferiority complex with a flair for one-upmanship.[12] This held true for philosophy just as for, say, oratory or lyric poetry. 'Greece has been superior to us in learning and every genre of writing', admits Cicero at the beginning of the first book of his *Tusculan Disputations*, only to add that 'it was easy for them to win, given that we were not competing'.[13] It is true that there has not hitherto been any Latin philosophical writing worth mentioning – but if the Romans are to put their minds to it, it is clear that they will equal or even surpass the Greeks.

---

[10] There is no satisfying general history of Roman philosophy. Morford 2002, Maurach 2006 and Maso 2012 are very basic, and the reader is better served with the discussions of specific periods by Garbarino 1973 (second century BCE; cf. also Dutsch 2014), Rawson 1985: 282–97 (late Republic) and Trapp 2007 (Empire). See also Vesperini 2012, a more idiosyncratic take on the second/first century BCE.

[11] On this phenomenon, see Denecke 2014, Feeney 2016 and Simon Goldhill in this volume. While the Romans' use of the Greeks as a 'reference culture' was a complex, drawn-out development and hardly a one-time conscious decision, one of the striking aspects of Roman cultural self-fashioning is the very insistence on the part of Roman authors on having entered this fertile but fraught relationship with the Greeks consciously and on purpose.

[12] See O'Rourke and Pelttari in this volume.

[13] Cic. *Tusc.* 1.3 *doctrina Graecia nos et omni litterarum genere superabat; in quo erat facile uincere non repugnantes*.

'It has always been my opinion', Cicero avers, 'that our people either came up with everything more cleverly than the Greeks, or otherwise improved those things they had taken over from them, provided they considered them worth their effort'.[14] The Romans may be imitators but they are not second-raters: if Greece had Homer and Demosthenes, Rome countered with Virgil and Cicero. It was a competition (as is apparent e.g. from Quintilian's parallel literary histories in *Institutio oratoria* 10), just as it was a passing-on of traditions, a cultural relay-race in which the Romans saw themselves as taking over the baton from the Greeks.

However, in this process of acculturation, in which the Romans became Hellenised only in turn to Romanise the Greek modes of thought and expression they had taken onboard, philosophy was different in important aspects from other Greek cultural practices or genres of writing. Any inspired Ennius or Virgil could undertake to become the Roman Homer, because any talented Roman could be a poet (whether it would have been socially feasible and economically viable for him to make poetry a career is another matter). By contrast, a Roman could not simply become a philosopher. A philosopher was a professional, he belonged to a particular school, he made his living by teaching and writing – and he was a Greek. By contrast, as mentioned above, Romans did not call themselves *philosophi* until the second century CE, however much they were engaged in philosophical study or even writing.[15] Within the contest for cultural supremacy in which the Romans liked to see themselves engaged, philosophy was not a discipline in which they met the Greeks in their own arena. Instead, they carved out their own niche for philosophy, one that was pronouncedly Roman.

There is evidence of Roman awareness of matters philosophical from an early age.[16] According to Pliny the Elder, the Senate during the Samnite Wars erected a statue of Pythagoras, in response to a Delphic oracle that had advised them to put up the images of both the wisest of the Greeks and the bravest (Alcibiades was chosen for the latter role).[17] This surprising notice fits with the well-attested Roman conviction of a close

---

[14] Cic. *Tusc.* 1.1 *meum semper iudicium fuit omnia nostros aut inuenisse per se sapientius quam Graecos aut accepta ab illis fecisse meliora, quae quidem digna statuissent in quibus elaborarent* (cf. also *De or.* 1.14–15, 197).

[15] There are a few exceptions but – tellingly – these are nearly always jokes or other non-straightforward uses; see Hine 2016.

[16] See the classic work of Garbarino 1973 for a collection of evidence and detailed discussion of most of the material treated in this section.

[17] Plin. *HN* 34.26, cf. Plut. *Num.* 8. Pliny does not specify the date; the Samnite Wars lasted from 343 to 290 BCE.

and long-standing connection between Rome and Pythagoreanism, a belief that finds its emblematic expression in the legend of the encounter between Pythagoras and king Numa Pompilius.[18] As later authors such as Cicero realised, this tale involves a chronological impossibility and belongs to the larger phenomenon of Pythagorean myth-making that renders the history of this philosophical sect so difficult to disentangle.[19] Even so, Rome's geographical proximity to southern Italy and the Pythagorean communities and teachers there makes contact and influence perfectly plausible, and we find signs of Roman familiarity with Pythagorean doctrine from the early second century onward.

Most famously, Ennius – himself a native of southern Italy – in the dream narrative at the beginning of his *Annals* presents his own poetic vocation and emulation of Homer in terms of the Pythagorean theory of metempsychosis: he has the Greek poet's shade declare that his soul has passed into the body of his Roman successor and deliver a lecture 'on the nature of things' into the bargain (*Ann*. 1.2–11 Skutsch). In the proem to Book 7, Ennius claims for himself *sophia* 'wisdom' (which he explicitly glosses with Latin *sapientia*) and calls himself *dicti studiosus* 'a student of language', thus presenting himself as a true *poeta doctus* who is both *philo-sophos* and *philo-logos*.[20] The poet's learning and philosophical interests are in evidence also in his *Epicharmus* and *Euhemerus*, two works that, as far as we can tell from the fragments, offered two different rationalising approaches to traditional religion. The *Epicharmus*, based on maxims ascribed to the eponymous fifth-century Sicilian comic writer, explained divinities allegorically as natural forces, while the *Euhemerus*, following the work of the Hellenistic author of the same name, maintained that the gods were just great men who had merited worship through their outstanding achievements.

Even aside from the hyper-intellectual and thoroughly Hellenised Ennius, Latin literature from its very beginning demonstrates Roman familiarity with philosophers and their practices, as well as with some philosophical content. While one needs to keep in mind that archaic tragedy and comedy are based on Greek originals and that references to philosophy in Roman plays will often have been taken over from their sources, the Roman dramatists would presumably not have retained such content if they had not believed that it would mean something to their Roman audience. For example, Plautus would not repeatedly have used the

---

[18] On Roman Pythagoreanism, both real and imagined, see Volk 2016. [19] See Burkert 1961.
[20] *Ann*. 7.211 Skutsch *sophiam, sapientia quae perhibetur*; 7.209 Skutsch *dicti studiosus*. See further Habinek 2006.

terms *philosophus* and *philosophari* to skewer self-important verbosity and aspirations to cleverness if he had not thought that his audience would find this funny. References by name to particular philosophers and schools (Thales, Socrates, Platonism and Cynicism occur in Plautus and Terence) must have rung a bell, as surely did allusions to well-known philosophical tenets.

In comedy, of course, philosophers are good for a laugh. Plautus is especially parodic, but Terence too can play that game, as when he has his parasite Gnatho found a school for men of similar exploitative aspirations: his followers will henceforth – on the model of *philosophorum ... disciplinae* – be known as *Gnathonici* (*Eun.* 263–4). On a more serious note, both tragedy and comedy reflect on the role of philosophy in society: in Terence's *Andria*, philosophy is described as a pursuit of *adulescentuli* in the same breath as enthusiasm for dogs and horses (55–7), while in an Ennian tragedy, the hero Neoptolemus declares that for a military man such as he is, it is appropriate to *philosophari – sed paucis* (fr. 147 Manuwald).

In both the comic and the tragic universe, human beings wonder about the world's moral order: Do the gods uphold justice? Is everything ruled by blind fate? How should we act, and if we act well, will we be rewarded? Often such musings do not rise above popular moralising, but occasionally they show affinity to the ways in which philosophy tackles these same questions or even appear to allude to the answers given by particular schools. Thus, references to the eternal *uoluptates* of the gods or to their lack of engagement in human affairs smack of Epicureanism, while the humorous claim that a man who is *sapiens* is the 'only king' very much seems to be a persiflage of a well-known Stoic paradox.[21] At least some members of the early second-century dramatic audience at Rome must have been able to pick up on these allusions, something that attests to an acquaintance with philosophy, however superficial.

As the century progressed, so did Roman familiarity with Greek thought and culture, a development accelerated by Rome's gradual conquest of the Hellenic world. Increasingly, Greek philosophers were active in the city itself, whether they settled there permanently or sojourned only for a time. The most famous such visit occurred in 155, when – trying to win the senate's support in a legal dispute – Athens sent as ambassadors the Stoic Diogenes of Babylon, the Peripatetic Critolaus and the Academic Carneades. When not busy negotiating, the visitors gave public lectures

---

[21] *Voluptates*: Ter. *An.* 959–60; non-engagement: Enn. fr. 117 Manuwald; *sapiens*: Ter. *Phorm.* 403–6.

to an enthusiastic audience of young Romans, with Carneades creating a particular stir by discoursing, on two subsequent days, first in favour of justice and then against it.[22] This demonstration of sceptical methodology reportedly so alarmed the conservative elder Cato that, in order to protect Roman youth from such subversion, he made sure that the Athenian business was dealt with in a speedy fashion and the ambassadors left the city as quickly as possible. There are also examples of more systematic expulsions of philosophers: in 161, Greek philosophers and rhetors were ordered to leave Rome, while in 154 (?), two Epicureans, Alcius and Philiscus, were expelled for 'teaching pleasure' (Ath. 12.68).

Such isolated conservative measures, however, were unable to stop the Romans' eager embrace of philosophy and its practitioners. In a pattern that was to continue into the first century and beyond, Roman aristocrats began to study with and befriend Greek philosophers, who enjoyed their patrons' hospitality while at Rome and might reciprocate by dedicating some of their work to them. Thus, Scipio Africanus the Younger was close to the Stoic Panaetius, as was Scipio's nephew, Q. Aelius Tubero, who also had friendly relations with another Stoic, Hecato. (Tubero raised some eyebrows when organising the funeral banquet for Scipio and keeping it unusually austere – something in agreement with his Stoic principles but not with Roman custom; Cic. *Mur.* 75–6). Scipio's relative Tiberius Gracchus was friends with the Stoic Blossius of Cumae, while T. Albucius, an extreme philhellene, embraced Epicureanism and even settled in Athens after being exiled in a case *de repetundis*.

Albucius' Graecomania was ridiculed by his contemporaries, and we find in Lucilius' *Satires* (88–94 Marx) the poetic version of an incident in which Q. Mucius Scaevola riled Albucius by addressing him with the Greek *chaere, Tite*, a greeting that was gleefully taken up by a chorus of amused bystanders. Lucilius, whose life spans most of the century, provides an excellent gauge for the spread of philosophical knowledge and interest among his contemporaries. While many of his fragments sadly lack context, there were clearly parodies of philosophical life and aspirations (witness the case of Albucius) as well as humorous references to both cosmological and ethical doctrines. However, the satirist apparently also engaged in moralising reflections of his own, as in the famous *uirtus* fragment quoted by Lactantius.[23] There, a speaker addressing a certain

---

[22] Lactant. *Div. inst.* 5.14.3–5 and *Epit.* 50.5–8; Plut. *Cat. Mai., Min.* 22–3. The recent suggestion of Powell 2013 that this episode was invented by Cicero seems highly unlikely.
[23] Lucilius 1326–38 Marx = Lactant. *Div. inst.* 6.5.3. For discussion, see McDonnell 2006: 123–8 and, on the fragment's philosophical background, Görler 1984, Lévy 2017.

Albinus provides an extended definition of what *uirtus* is – basically, to know what is appropriate in each situation and to act accordingly – in a manner that submits a traditional Roman concept to a new style of inquiry inspired by Greek philosophy.

What is especially striking about the fragment is the stress on knowledge, with the word *scire* occurring three times (1328, 1329, 1331): it is a tenet of Greek ethics going back to Plato that only action based on true understanding can be called virtuous (doing the right thing by chance is not good in the moral sense). In addition, there are pronounced similarities to Cicero's discussion of duty in *De officiis*, a work based in large part on the treatise Περὶ τοῦ καθήκοντος of Lucilius' contemporary, and frequent visitor to Rome, Panaetius.[24] Thus, Lucilius defines *uirtus*, among other things, as the knowledge of 'what is beneficial [and what] honourable' (*utile quid sit, honestum*, 1329), the same two ethical criteria found in Panaetius and Cicero. Lucilius further posits a hierarchy of duties, stating that the obligation to one's *patria* comes first, followed by that to one's parents; only after having taken care of those two can one justifiedly look after one's own *commoda* (1337–8). This is similar to Cicero's division: he puts *patria* and *parentes* first, followed by *liberi* and *domus* (*Off.* 1.58); it seems likely that Panaetius proposed a gradation along similar lines. What we find in Lucilius' fragment, then, is the first extant extended philosophical disquisition in Latin literature, one that is informed by a specific Greek (in this case, Stoic) doctrine while focusing on a topic of central importance to Roman identity. The subsequent history of Latin philosophical writing would follow similar patterns.

## From Greek Darkness to Latin Light

The first philosophical doctrine to find systematic expression in Latin was that of Epicurus:[25] some time in the late second or early to mid-first century, a certain C. Amafinius wrote about Epicurean physics (and ethics?) in a number of books. Cicero – ever scornful of Epicureanism and intent on elevating his own role as a pioneer of Latin philosophical writing – is dismissive of Amafinius' style and that of two other Epicurean authors, C. Rabirius and Catius Insuber, but has to admit that they were successful in gaining a readership.[26] In

---

[24] Already Lactantius triangulates Lucilius, Panaetius and Cicero (*Div. inst.* 6.5.4).
[25] On Roman Epicureanism and its representatives, see Castner 1998, Benferhat 2005, Gilbert 2015.
[26] Cic. *Acad. post.* 5; *Tusc.* 4.6; *Fam.* 15.19.2. For testimonia and fragments, see Garbarino 2003.

fact, Cicero worries, Epicureanism has become so fashionable that its adherents 'have occupied all of Italy'.[27]

Ciceronian hyperbole aside, it appears indeed to be the case that in the late Republic, Epicureanism was the philosophical school most popular among the educated Roman elite.[28] By this time, upper-class Romans typically received some philosophical training as part of their education, studying with Greek philosophers both at home and abroad, and increasingly declared their own allegiance to specific philosophical schools.[29] Cicero, for example, identified as an Academic Sceptic, the younger Cato was a Stoic, and Brutus adhered to the so-called Old Academy of Antiochus. By far the largest group of mid-century Roman philosophy enthusiasts, however, were Epicureans, among them Cicero's friend Atticus, Caesar's assassin Cassius and L. Calpurnius Piso Caesoninus, Caesar's father-in-law, Cicero's bête noire and the patron of the Epicurean philosopher and epigrammatist Philodemus.

Piso has been tentatively identified as the owner of the so-called Villa dei Papiri in Herculaneum, a Roman villa destroyed at the eruption of Vesuvius in 79 CE, in the ruins of which the remnants of an extensive Epicurean library have been discovered. Works of Philodemus are foremost among the carbonised papyrus scrolls that are being deciphered and edited in an ongoing scholarly process, and we know from other sources that Philodemus, a native of Syria, settled on the Bay of Naples, where he taught and socialised with his Roman students and patrons. Another Epicurean, Siro, taught in nearby Naples, counting among his pupils the poets Virgil and Horace. This geographical concentration has given rise to the term Campanian Epicureanism, a phenomenon that is perhaps best understood in social (rather than philosophical) terms: apparently, well-to-do Romans liked to follow up on their Epicurean interests while enjoying

---

[27] *Tusc.* 4.7 *Italiam totam occupauerunt.*
[28] See Sedley 2009. The idea, occasionally found in scholarship, that Epicureanism appealed especially to the lower classes is based on Cicero's biased polemic against the Epicurean disdain for learning and elegant writing, and seems unlikely; see Gilbert 2015: 51–2.
[29] School affiliation was clearly important to philosophically interested Romans of the late Republic, as is evident from Cicero's decision to have individual members of the Roman elite argue for the doctrines of different schools in his dialogues. In less genteel circumstances, a man's adherence to a specific school could lay him open to attack and abuse, as seen in Cic. *Mur.* 58–66, 74–7; *Vat.* 14; *Pis.* passim (targeting, respectively, a Stoic, a Pythagorean and an Epicurean – all Roman senators). During the Empire, too, commitment to philosophy normally entailed allegiance to a school; thus Trapp 2007: 13 writes that 'to declare for *philosophia* was necessarily to declare for a particular kind of *philosophia*, and to identify that kind not by reference to its subject-matter, but by reference to a great thinker, or group of thinkers, from the past'.

their *otium* in a popular vacation spot famous for both its Greek culture and its easy living.

It is in this context of Roman enthusiasm for Epicureanism that Lucretius wrote his *De rerum natura*, a masterpiece of Latin poetry and one of the most influential texts of antiquity.[30] Composed in the mid-50s BCE, it is not the very first Latin work of philosophy (we have seen that there already existed Epicurean treatises, and Cicero was writing his *De re publica* at about the same time); however, both its scope and its poetic form set *De rerum natura* apart. Writing about Epicureanism in verse was itself a daring move in light of the fact that Epicurus himself disapproved of poetry, considering it a waste of time like all the liberal arts and not conducive to the clear expression of truth; such later Epicureans as Philodemus (himself a poet) had a more conciliatory attitude but viewed poetry primarily as entertainment.[31] Lucretius is thus engaged in two connected but distinct projects of translation: he renders Greek philosophy in Latin, while also transforming Epicurean prose into poetry.

The poet reflects on both tasks in a famous self-referential passage.[32] He begins by describing his state of Muse-inspired enthusiasm:

>            ... sed acri
> percussit thyrso laudis spes magna meum cor
> et simul incussit suauem mi in pectus amorem
> Musarum, quo nunc instinctus mente uigenti
> auia Pieridum peragro loca nullius ante
> trita solo. Iuuat integros accedere fontis
> atque haurire, iuuatque novos decerpere flores
> insignemque meo capiti petere inde coronam,
> unde prius nulli uelarint tempora Musae.                (Lucr. 1.922–30)

... but great hope of fame has struck my heart with a sharp thyrsus and at the same time struck into my breast sweet love for the Muses. Inspired by this, with a keen mind, I now roam through the pathless realm of the Pierides, never before trodden by any foot. It is pleasing to approach untouched fountains and drink there; it is pleasing to gather new flowers

---

[30] As points of entry to the ample scholarship on Lucretius, see Gale 2007, Gillespie and Hardie 2007, Campbell 2011.
[31] See Volk 2002: 94–5, with references.
[32] Lucr. 1.921–50 ~ 4.1–25. Like all first-person statements in poetry, such programmatic utterances cannot be taken as straightforward expressions of the historical author's intentions (compare Sharrock in this volume). In my discussion here as elsewhere, I am eliding this problem, being more interested in what can be and is being said in a particular historical and cultural context than in any individual's personal commitment (which is at any rate irrecoverable).

and seek for my head a garland of fame from a spot whence the Muses have wreathed as yet no one's brow.

Lucretius stresses his originality with the help of such Callimachean images as the untrodden path and untouched fountain.[33] The novelty of his enterprise lies not only in his poem's philosophical subject matter and poetic form (cf. vv. 931–4), but also in its linguistic innovation: the pathless realm is that of philosophical poetry in Latin, and the new garland harks back to an earlier mention of 'our Ennius, who first brought down from Helicon a crown of everlasting leaves, to win widespread fame among the Italian tribes of men'.[34] Just as Ennius earns fame for bringing a new genre (hexameter poetry) to Italy, Lucretius wins a crown for his annexing another virgin poetic territory for the Latin language.

The poet's choice of Latin is thus implicitly presented as part of the Roman project of rivalling the Greeks by adopting their forms of cultural expression. As for his choice of poetry, so unorthodox within Epicureanism, Lucretius provides an explanation by means of a celebrated simile:

> Sed ueluti pueris absinthia taetra medentes
> cum dare conantur, prius oras pocula circum
> contingunt mellis dulci flauoque liquore,
> ut puerorum aetas inprouida ludificetur
> labrorum tenus, interea perpotet amarum
> absinthi laticem deceptaque non capiatur,
> sed potius tali facto recreata ualescat,
> sic ego nunc, quoniam haec ratio plerumque uidetur
> tristior esse quibus non est tractata, retroque
> uulgus abhorret ab hac, uolui tibi suauiloquenti
> carmine Pierio rationem exponere nostram
> et quasi musaeo dulci contingere melle.   (1.936–47)

But just as doctors, when they attempt to administer bitter medicine to children, first smear the sweet, golden liquid of honey around the rims of their cups, so that the unsuspecting age of the children be cheated as far as the lips and meanwhile drink up the bitter draught of wormwood, and though deceived be not harmed, but rather be healed in such a way and grow well again – thus I now, since this doctrine often seems quite repulsive to those who have not tasted it, and people shrink back from it, have wanted to expound our doctrine to you in sweet-speaking Pierian song and, as it were, drench it in the sweet honey of the Muses.

---

[33] On Lucretius' Callimacheanism, see Kenney 1970, Donohue 1993.
[34] Lucr. 1.117–19 *Ennius ut noster cecinit, qui primus amoeno | detulit ex Helicone perenni fronde coronam, | per gentis Italas hominum quae clara clueret.*

Strikingly self-confident, Lucretius wastes no time on arguing that it is possible or acceptable to convey Epicureanism in verse. It is his far more ambitious claim that philosophy is in fact taught more effectively through the medium of poetry, which by a touch of the Muses' honey renders the bitter medicine of Epicurus enjoyable and sweet.

In his linguistically as well as generically original approach to Epicurean teaching, Lucretius employs the format of didactic poetry, a previously ill-defined genre, which gains a new identity precisely through the innovations of *De rerum natura*.[35] Greek authors had long used lengthy hexameter poems to impart theoretical or practical knowledge, developing a rhetorical frame in which the teacher-poet explicitly instructs some student figure(s) in the art or science in question. The genre had made its way to Rome, where we find around the time of Lucretius intriguing evidence for what appear to be other didactic poems on topics of natural philosophy: we hear about the *Empedoclea* of a certain Sallustius as well as of Egnatius' *De rerum natura*, and there is reason to believe that Lucretius knew Cicero's version of Aratus' *Phaenomena*, the first of many Latin translations of this immensely popular work.[36] However, before Lucretius' time most didactic poems had been short, humbly occupying a lower place in the poetic hierarchy that was dominated by the grand hexameter genre par excellence, heroic epic. By contrast, Lucretius composed a didactic poem of truly epic proportions and aspirations, taking as his stylistic model the 'Roman Homer', Ennius himself.

*De rerum natura* is thus a daring blend of many traditions: the philosophical prose writing of Epicurus, which furnished the content; the didactic poetry of Empedocles and Aratus, which offered the precedent for writing poetry about nature as well as the didactic frame; and the epic of Ennius, which provided the archaising language and sublime monumentality. Exhibiting the typically Roman penchant for self-conscious metapoetic reflection that we have already observed, Lucretius himself maps out his place in these varied traditions, all the while stressing his own originality. Thus, of the major models for Lucretius' poetic form, Ennius is celebrated for his poetic achievement but taken to task for his false ideas about the afterlife, as seen in his dream-encounter with Homer (Lucr. 1.117–26), while Empedocles both receives extravagant praise for the

---

[35] On *De rerum natura* as a didactic poem, see Volk 2002: 69–118.
[36] Egnatius: Macrob. *Sat.* 6.5.2 and 12; Sallustius: Cic. *QFr.* 2.10.3. For testimonia and fragments, see Garbarino 2003 and cf. Kruschwitz and Schumacher 2005: 100–9. On the influence on Lucretius of Cicero's *Aratea*, see Gee 2013: 81–109.

'songs of his divine mind' (1.731) and comes in for heavy criticism for his mistaken theory of the elements (1.734–829).

Epicurus himself is extolled throughout the work as the man whose mind broke through the 'flaming ramparts of the world' (1.73) to gain knowledge of the way things really are and as the benefactor of mankind who has brought light into darkness and taught us about life's true goods (3.1–2). Lucretius presents himself as following in the footsteps of his master, imitating him without any ambition to equal his achievement:

> Te sequor, o Graiae gentis decus, inque tuis nunc
> ficta pedum pono pressis uestigia signis,
> non ita certandi cupidus quam propter amorem
> quod te imitari aueo; quid enim contendat hirundo
> cycnis, aut quidnam tremulis facere artubus haedi
> consimile in cursu possint et fortis equi uis? (3.3–8)

> You I follow, o glory of the Greek race, and put down my firm footsteps now on the tracks left by you, not so much desirous of competition as out of love, because I wish to imitate you. For how could a swallow vie with swans, or what could kids with trembling limbs achieve in a race to match themselves against the power of a strong horse?

In describing his relationship to his philosophical source in terms of literary *imitatio* and *aemulatio*, Lucretius makes Epicurus sound as though he were himself a poet: he is the swan with whom the Lucretian swallow cannot hope to compete. Lucretius thus daringly assimilates Epicurus to Empedocles and Ennius, presenting all three of his models as 'poets' *de rerum natura*, who provide the inspiration for Lucretius' own ambitious project.[37]

For all their inimitable superiority, however, it turns out that there is one way in which Epicurus' teachings can still be improved upon: the 'discoveries of the Greeks' are *obscura*, dark and difficult (1.136), something that can fairly be said of not only Epicurus' subject matter (as *corpora caeca*, the atoms are inaccessible to sense perception) but also his writing style. It is thus Lucretius' task to sing 'light songs about a dark subject matter' or even 'to throw light' on Greek obscurity 'with Latin verses'.[38] Latin may just be a better medium for explaining the workings of nature than Greek, and poetry may be more effective than prose.

---

[37] Compare Volk 2002: 105–16.
[38] Lucr. 1.933–4 *obscura de re ... lucida ... | carmina*; 1.137 *illustrare Latinis uersibus*. On philosophical translation from Greek to Latin in Lucretius and beyond, see also Goldhill in this volume.

Not that the poet's task is easy. Lucretius stresses the difficulty of translation, pointing out that in his text, 'many subjects need to be expressed in new words on account of the poverty of the language and the novelty of the topic'.[39] Facing the double task of creating not only a Latin philosophical vocabulary but also one that is suitably poetic, Lucretius neither simply borrows Greek expressions nor replaces them with new Latin technical terms. His treatment of the atoms provides a striking example of this practice; rather than using *atomos* as a loanword or settling on a single Latin translation, Lucretius employs a multitude of poetic designations:

> ... rerum primordia pandam,
> unde omnis natura creet res auctet alatque,
> quoue eadem rursum natura perempta resoluat,
> quae nos materiem et genitalia corpora rebus
> reddunda in ratione uocare et semina rerum
> appellare suemus et haec eadem usurpare
> corpora prima, quod ex illis sunt omnia primis.   (1.55–61)

> I will unfold the first-beginnings (lit. 'warp-threads') of things, from which nature creates, increases and nourishes everything and into which nature resolves them again at their demise. In the course of our explications, we are accustomed to call them 'matter' and 'birth-giving bodies' and also name them 'seeds of things' and refer to the same as 'first bodies', since all things arise from them as the first.[40]

The result is a richly textured vocabulary that manages to express the atoms' manifold roles and aspects: their materiality (*materies, corpora*), their primary nature (*primordia, corpora prima*) and their ability to give rise to all other bodies (*genitalia, semina*). At the same time, the implications of some of these terms are such as to threaten to undermine the poem's Epicurean physics: the image of 'seeds' might conjure up an organically grown universe at odds with the Epicurean random collision of matter, while the 'warp-threads' carry dangerous associations of a cosmic designer. Readers have been divided over whether Lucretius is consciously and daringly employing such 'hostile' vocabulary for poetic and didactic effect or whether the poet himself is unable to control the subversive

---

[39] Lucr. 1.138–9 *multa nouis uerbis praesertim cum sit agendum | propter egestatem linguae et rerum nouitatem*. Cf. the references, in 1.832 and 3.260, to *patrii sermonis egestas*, 'the poverty of the mother [lit. father] tongue'. On the Roman idea that Latin is a 'poorer' language, see Fögen 2000 and compare the beginning of the following section.

[40] Lucr. 1.55–61. On Lucretius' creation of a Latin philosophical vocabulary, see Sedley 1998: 35–61, with discussion of atomic terminology on 38–9.

language he has unleashed.[41] Whatever the case may be, Greek philosophy has not crossed into a new language and culture unchanged, but has become transformed: in the course of becoming both Latinised and poeticised, it has undergone subtle but often significant shifts of meaning.[42]

## A Substitute for Politics

While Lucretius presents his Latinisation of the 'obscure discoveries of the Greeks' in the metaphoric language of Roman poetic self-positioning, his contemporary and fellow linguistic pioneer Cicero reflects more explicitly on the role and reception of Latin philosophical writing in the Roman literary marketplace. In the preface to the first book of *De finibus*, he responds to critics who hold that philosophy, being a genuinely Greek genre and pursuit, should not be written in Latin.[43] Pointing out their inconsistency (Why do they enjoy other forms of Latin literature, e.g. drama, that are likewise derived from the Greek?, *Fin.* 1.4–5), he accuses them of a lack of not only patriotism but also culture: 'I at least feel that those who don't know our own literature are not sufficiently educated.'[44] Contrary to popular perception (and, we may add, Lucretius' strategic claim), 'the Latin language is not only not poor but even richer than the Greek'.[45] And as for Cicero's own Latin version of philosophy, it is anything but a verbatim translation:

> Nos non interpretum fungimur munere, sed tuemur ea quae dicta sunt ab iis quos probamus eisque nostrum iudicium et nostrum scribendi ordinem adiungimus. (*Fin.* 1.6)
>
> I don't proceed like a translator, but preserving what has been said by the authors of whom I approve, I add to it my own judgement and order of writing.

Just as the light and sweetness of Lucretius' Latin verse enhance his Greek source, Cicero's Latin rewriting creates a new text informed by his own style and judgement.[46]

---

[41] See Schrijvers 1978, Gale 1994, Kennedy 2002, Campbell 2003, with Volk 2011: 107–9.
[42] On the philosophical implications of some of Lucretius' translation choices, see Reinhardt 2016.
[43] Compare also *Acad. post.* 3–12.
[44] *Fin.* 1.5 *mihi quidem nulli satis eruditi uidentur quibus nostra ignota sunt.*
[45] *Fin.* 1.10 *Latinam linguam non modo non inopem, ut uulgo putarent, sed locupletiorem etiam esse quam Graecam.*
[46] Owing to the thematic structure of my chapter, the remainder of this section focuses on the politics of Cicero's philosophy rather than on his contribution to the creation of a Latin philosophical discourse. Recent contributions on this topic, esp. Cicero's innovations in the format of the philosophical dialogue, include e.g. Schofield 2008, Blyth 2010–11, Müller 2015, Brittain 2016.

When Cicero wrote *De finibus* in the first half of 45, he had already published an extensive treatment of political philosophy (*De re publica*, 51 BCE)[47] and had recently embarked on a monumental philosophical 'encyclopaedia', a series of works intended as a systematic introduction to all aspects of philosophy.[48] He was also, at this point, looking back on a political career that had encompassed popular acclaim as one of Rome's best orators, a quick rise through the *cursus honorum*, a turbulent consulship, exile and return, the successful administration of a province and participation (on the losing side) in a civil war. Why would a man like this, a leading Roman senator, choose to write about philosophy, an activity for which there was – both among his social class and in Rome in general – very little precedent?

Cicero provides a number of explanations in the extensive prefaces to his dialogues, which have accordingly received much scholarly attention.[49] Like Lucretius, he presents himself as engaged in a cultural project of claiming for Latin literature areas that have previously been the sole purview of the Greeks: 'up to now, philosophy has lain fallow [at Rome] and lacked the light of Latin literature'.[50] Creating a Latin philosophy will redound not only to the fame of its creator but also, crucially, to the greater glory of Rome:

> Ipsius rei publicae causa philosophiam nostris hominibus explicandam putaui, magni existimans interesse ad decus et ad laudem ciuitatis res tam grauis tamque praeclaras Latinis etiam litteris contineri. (*Nat. D.* 1.7)
>
> I thought that I ought to expound philosophy to our people for the sake of the commonwealth itself, in the belief that it makes a great difference for the excellence and glory of the citizenry if such important and outstanding matters are treated in Latin writing as well.

---

[47] *De legibus*, conceived as a companion piece to *De re publica*, is often placed in the 50s as well; however, the work was apparently not published in Cicero's lifetime, and the date of its composition remains unclear.
[48] For comprehensive treatments of Cicero's philosophical thought and works, see MacKendrick 1989, Gawlik and Görler 1994, Woolf 2015. I discuss Ciceronian philosophising, with special attention to its social and political aspects, in Chapters 3 and 4 of Volk 2021.
[49] See Schmidt 1978–9, Habinek 1994, Kurczyk 2006: 335–46, Gildenhard 2007: 45–63, 79–88 and (esp. on *Tusc.*) 89–207, Baraz 2012.
[50] *Tusc.* 1.5 *Philosophia iacuit usque ad hanc aetatem nec ullum habuit lumen litterarum Latinarum*; cf. *Div.* 2.4 *nullum philosophia locum esse pateremur qui non Latinis litteris illustratus pateret*. In both passages, note the imagery of light, reminiscent of Lucretius.

On numerous occasions, Cicero thus claims that he is doing a service to his fellow citizens – just as he did during his public activity as senator and magistrate.[51]

But therein lies the rub. As Cicero acknowledges again and again in the works of the 40s, he would not be writing philosophy if he were able to play an appropriate political role in a well-functioning republic. As he spells out in his introduction to the second book of *De divinatione* (45 BCE), it was the 'dire disaster of the commonwealth' – that is, the Civil War and Caesar's dictatorship – that 'provided [his] motivation for expounding philosophy'.[52] Cicero envisages the role of philosophy as twofold: on the one hand, philosophical study and writing provide him with a form of self-therapy that offers consolation and coping mechanisms in a time of public and private crisis;[53] on the other hand, the senator deprived of his erstwhile political influence conceives of his philosophical work as a continuation of his politics by other means.[54] Writing just after the assassination of Julius Caesar and assessing his philosophical output so far, Cicero asserts:

> In libris enim sententiam dicebamus, contionabamur, philosophiam nobis pro rei publicae procuratione substitutam putabamus. (*Div.* 2.7)

> In my books I have been giving speeches in the senate and addressing the assembly, considering philosophy my substitute for administering the republic.

His books, he claims, have been the means by which he has been able to fulfil his political functions as a senator, acting as a veritable substitute for the actual adminstration of the *res publica*.

What does Cicero mean by presenting his philosophical works as political interventions? He does not explain, and there is more than one possible answer. We may view the cultural service already discussed (claiming Greek philosophy for Rome) as a political act in its own right. In addition,

---

[51] *Acad. Pr.* 6 *ut plurimis prosimus enitimur*; *Tusc.* 1.5 *ciuibus nostris prosimus*; *Div.* 2.1 *prodesse quam plurimis*; 2.7 *prodessemus ciuibus nostris qua re cumque possemus*. Cf. also *Fin.* 1.10 *ut sint opera studio labore meo doctiores ciues mei*; *Div.* 2.1 *optimarum artium uias traderem meis ciuibus*.

[52] *Div.* 2.6 *mihi quidem explicandae philosophiae causam attulit casus grauis ciuitatis*. Cicero here provides an explanation specifically for his philosophical work of the 40s, on which I focus in what follows; however, political dissatisfaction seems to be a motivating factor also behind the writings of the 50s (see *De or.* 1.1–3; unfortunately, the preface of *De re publica* is fragmentary, and the parts we possess do not touch on the genesis of the work).

[53] See *Acad. post.* 11; *Tusc.* 5.5, 121; *Nat. D.* 1.9; *Div.* 2.7; *Off.* 3.4. In addition to his political trauma, Cicero was deeply affected by the death of his daughter Tullia in February 45. On philosophy as therapy, see pp. 728–33.

[54] On the politics of Cicero's philosophical writings of the 40s, see Bringmann 1971, Strasburger 1990, Wassmann 1996, Baraz 2012, as well as Gildenhard 2007 specifically on *Tusc.*

the philosophical teachings Cicero imparts can be seen as attempts to shape his peers into a philosophically informed, virtuous ruling class able to move beyond, and avoid in the future, the divisions and depravations of the political present. Such a didactic intention may be discerned in *De re publica*, with its extended discussion (now nearly entirely lost) of the perfect statesman, and is made explicit in some of the works written after the Ides of March, where Cicero presents himself as a teacher specifically of the Roman youth. Finally in a position openly to decry Caesar's dictatorship, the author sees himself on a mission to provide traditional Roman ideals such as friendship or the *honestum* with a sound philosophical footing: readers of *De amicitia* and *De officiis* will never again be able to claim, for example, that loyalty to a friend trumps duty to the *res publica* (for what if the friend is a tyrant, like Caesar?).[55]

The political charge of the works written under Caesar's rule is much more difficult to discern. In the *Academica*, *De finibus*, *Tusculanae disputationes* and *De natura deorum*, Cicero provides fairly straightforward introductions to the teachings of various schools on logic, ethics and physics, and despite scholarly attempts to view these works as openly partisan and anti-Caesarian,[56] they contain few direct political observations. I suggest elsewhere that Cicero is making a political point precisely by creating a 'Caesar-free space', one in which the author and like-minded friends can engage in philosophical debate both on the page – in Cicero's stylised dialogues, in which there is no Caesarian interlocutor in sight – and in their real-life urbane exchanges of opinions, texts and dedications (not incidentally, most of the works of this period are dedicated to Brutus).[57]

However, both at this time of crisis and throughout his life, Cicero viewed philosophy not just as an ersatz politics but as a genuine inspiration for and guidance in his own private and public life. In the preface to *De natura deorum*, he makes the following strong claim:

> Et si omnia philosophiae praecepta referuntur ad uitam, arbitramur nos et publicis et priuatis in rebus ea praestitisse quae ratio et doctrina praescripserit. (*Nat. D.* 1.7)
>
> And if all philosophical precepts apply to life, then I think that in both public and private affairs I have lived up to what reason and teaching prescribed.

While one might debate whether Cicero always succeeded in following *ratio et doctrina*, we have excellent evidence for his attempts to do so. The

---

[55] See *Amic.* 35–43; *Off.* 3.19 and compare Cicero's correspondence with Matius (*Fam.* 11.27–8). On the issue of friendship, see Griffin 1997; on the politics of *De officiis*, see Long 1995.
[56] See esp. Strasburger 1990, Wassmann 1996. [57] See Volk 2021, ch. 4.

over 900 letters of his correspondence provide an invaluable source for his serious engagement with philosophical doctrine and his use of philosophical reasoning in deciding on courses of political action.[58] This is especially evident in the letters to Atticus from 49/48, when Cicero was trying to make up his mind as to whether to follow Pompey or Caesar into the Civil War. Either *imperator* miserably failed to live up to the ideal of the virtuous statesman laid out in *De re publica* (see e.g. *Att.* 10.4.4), and Cicero accordingly found himself between a rock and a hard place.

As a follower of the New – that is, Sceptical – Academy, Cicero was in the habit of debating all issues *in utramque partem* and ultimately choosing what he considered the most plausible (though not necessarily true) option.[59] We find this method again and again in the letters, where we have the unique opportunity to observe close up a significant historical actor apply his philosophical convictions and habits of thought to his own public actions. However, while Cicero may have been unusually or even obsessively self-reflective, he was by no means the only late-Republican politician with a philosophical bent. The Civil War engulfed a whole generation of philosophically trained and interested Romans, and not a few of them drew on the teachings of their respective schools to motivate and justify their actions.

We thus find the avowed Epicurean Cassius explaining to Cicero why virtuous political activity is fully in keeping with Epicurus' teaching: according to the hedonistic calculus, the pursuer of virtue will reap pleasure in the end (*Fam.* 15.19.2–3). Was it this kind of reasoning that ultimately inspired Cassius to take a leading role in Caesar's assassination? Perhaps, though not all Epicureans felt that the road to *ataraxia* led through dangerous political exertion. Cicero's Epicurean friend Atticus, for example, pointedly eschewed a political career, preferring the less fraught life of an *eques*.[60]

At the other end of the philosophical spectrum, we have the Younger Cato, arch-conservative gadfly and, according to Cicero, a *perfectus Stoicus* (*Parad. Stoic.* 2). It is attractive to view his political rigidity as influenced by his Stoic convictions: the Stoic wise man will exercise his virtue by pursuing what he knows to be the right course of action, without regard for public opinion or even his chances of success. When more cautious men

---

[58] See Boyancé 1936: 302–4, Michel 1977, Brunt 1986, Boes 1990, Griffin 1995 and 1997, Leonhardt 1995, Gildenhard 2006, Baraz 2012: 44–95, McConnell 2014, Gilbert 2015.
[59] On Cicero's Scepticism, see Woolf 2015.
[60] There has been hot scholarly debate about the perceived unorthodoxy of the fact that so many Roman Epicureans had political careers, apparently violating Epicurus' injunction to 'live hidden'. See Erler 1992, Roskam 2007, Armstrong 2011, Fish 2011. On Cassius, see Gilbert 2015: 163–283. On Atticus, see Benferhat 2005: 98–169 and Gilbert 2022.

like Cicero called it a day after Pompey was defeated at Pharsalus, Cato carried on the Civil War until his forces were roundly beaten at Thapsus. Rather than suing for Caesar's pardon, Cato committed a philosophical suicide openly modelled on the death of Socrates, thus cementing his own legend as both Republican martyr and Stoic *sapiens*. Once the republic had fallen for good and an autocratic system of government became entrenched at Rome, it was not the sceptical sometime survivor Cicero but the doctrinal freedom fighter Cato who became a prime model for philosophical politics at Rome.[61]

## The Muses of Philosophy

Having reached the watershed between Republic and Empire, I will for a moment deviate from this chapter's chronological framework and consider in this section some manifestations of philosophy in a perhaps unexpected place: Latin poetry. Let us begin with a young poet who in the mid-first century BCE leaves university to attach himself to a teacher of philosophy, inviting his friends to join him:

> Nos ad beatos uela mittimus portus
> magni petentes docta dicta Sironis,
> uitamque ab omni uindicabimus cura.   ([Verg.] *Catal.* 5.8–10)

> We are setting sail for the blessed harbour, seeking the learned words of great Siro, and will free life from every care.

It is none other than Virgil who in this pseudepigraphic fiction abandons his rhetorical training at Rome to move to Naples and study with the Epicurean Siro.[62] Embracing the philosophical life, however, requires a significant change:

> Ite hinc, Camenae, uos quoque ite iam sane,
> dulces Camenae (nam fatebimur uerum,
> dulces fuistis).   (vv. 11–13)

> Go away, Muses, you too go away already, sweet Muses (for to tell the truth, you were sweet).

---

[61] On Cato's suicide and its influence, see Griffin 1986, Hill 2004: 6–7, 64–71, 186–7, Edwards 2007: 1–5, 113–160, Rauh 2018.

[62] On Siro, see p. 711. *Catal.* 5 has often been taken as a poem by Virgil himself, but I am working on the assumption that it is a work of pseudepigraphy from the first century CE. That Virgil studied with Siro is attested in the *Vitae* and commentary tradition, and I consider the connection genuine fact. On the poem and its Epicurean background, see Clay 2004 and Keith 2018.

Poetry is not admitted to the blessed harbour of philosophy – or so it would seem. In an unexpected twist, the poem ends by revoking the goodbye to the Muses immediately after it has been issued. They are allowed in through the backdoor, as long as they change their ways:

> et tamen meas chartas
> reuisitote, sed pudenter et raro. (vv. 23–4)
>
> But still, come back to my pages, but modestly and rarely.

Poetry and philosophy can fruitfully coexist, it seems, but it takes a certain accommodation between the two. Young Virgil here imagines Muses sufficiently chastened and serious to fit his new Epicurean life; in reality, however, Latin poetry does not always treat philosophy *pudenter*. Roman poets of all periods adopt, adapt, subsume, subvert, embrace and parody philosophical elements, attesting both to the cultural significance of philosophy at Rome and to the creative energy of the Latin discourse that kept transforming it.

By the mid-first century BCE, as we have seen, philosophy had become a recognisable part of Roman high culture. Greek philosophers were teaching Roman aristocrats in the city and the Italian countryside; learned authors were penning philosophical works in Latin; and at least certain intellectually and ethically committed individuals were trying to live their own lives according to the philosophical prescriptions of the schools to which they subscribed. At the same time, however, philosophy had extended its reach beyond the rarefied villas of Cicero and his peers and had become part of the general cultural imagination or even, so to speak, of pop culture.[63] Poetry offers a prime example for this embeddedness of philosophy in Roman culture:[64] texts that are not, or at least not in the first place, intended to convey philosophical doctrine provide an excellent indication of just how much philosophy was out there.

In what follows, I examine a number of poetic passages from the late Republic and early Empire with a view to demonstrating the range of Latin poetic uses of philosophy.[65] Poets may refer to a philosophical doctrine in passing, including as a joke; employ philosophical argument for their own purposes as something that is 'good to think with'; openly espouse or

---

[63] On non-elite Roman philosophising, see Zetzel 2016.
[64] On the notion of embeddedness, see Michèle Lowrie in this volume.
[65] For a collection of papers on philosophy in various Latin poets, see Garani and Konstan 2014; bibliography on individual authors will be given in the course of my discussion.

promote philosophical teaching; reject or parody philosophical doctrine or otherwise discuss philosophers and philosophical life, not always approvingly. The spectrum of responses extends from the casual to the committed, and from acceptance to resistance, and encompasses not only the field of ethics but that of natural philosophy as well.[66]

As an example of the covert use of philosophical argument, so deeply fused into a text that it has hardly ever been noticed, consider one of the most famous poems of Catullus, *carmen* 76.[67] This heart-rending cry of the lover *in extremis*, who implores the gods to free him from the *pestis* and *pernicies* (v. 20) of his love for an unworthy woman (presumably Lesbia), is structured around two conditional clauses: (i) *if* there is any pleasure (*uoluptas*, v. 1) for someone who remembers his past good deeds, then Catullus will reap many joys (*multa ... gaudia*, vv. 5–6), given that he has been *pius* (v. 2) and has behaved absolutely impeccably in his love affair. Since, however, his love is not requited, he needs to free himself from his attachment and stop being miserable – though he knows that this is extremely difficult. Hence, (ii) *if* it is in the nature of the gods to take pity on human beings, he prays to them to save him from his affliction, asking them in this fashion at least to reward his *pietas* (v. 26).

The two propositions Catullus considers are central to Epicurean teaching. The Epicureans *do* believe (i) that there is pleasure in the recollection of past good things and that this is efficacious in alleviating present pain.[68] They do *not* believe (ii) that the gods take pity on humans, reward them for their good deeds or indeed interfere with their lives in any manner. The proper Epicurean response to Catullus' plight would be for the lover to cut his losses, remember with pleasure his own good conduct and move on –

---

[66] For reasons of space, I here concentrate on ethics, but note the following discussions of natural philosophy in Latin poetry. On Virgil: Hardie 1986, Farrell 2014 (and see Armstrong et al. 2004 on various aspects of Epicureanism in Virgil); on Ovid's *Metamorphoses*: Hardie 1995, Volk and Williams 2022: 145–247; on Manilius: Volk 2009: 216–58; on Lucan: Lapidge 1979, Loupiac 1998; on Senecan tragedy: Rosenmeyer 1989, Schmitz 1993.

[67] I have not seen the following interpretation in print, though note that Yelena Baraz put forth some of the same ideas in an oral presentation at Columbia University in 2016. Booth 1997 discusses possible philosophical influences on the poem, both Stoic and Epicurean, but ultimately considers them insignificant; for a more positive assessment, see Powell 1990: 199–202. For more on Catullus and Epicureanism, see Gale 2022 (with some remarks on poem 76, esp. an enlightening comparison of lines 13–14 with Lucr. 4.1146–50) and Uden 2021. I thank Professors Baraz, Gale and Uden for discussion and for giving me access to unpublished material.

[68] Of course, the Epicureans advocate remembering past pleasures rather than past good deeds, but given that they also believe in the coincidence of virtue and pleasure (*Kyriai doxae* 5), *benefacta* should produce pleasure in both execution and recollection. At any rate, the word *uoluptas*, prominently placed at the end of line 1 (as in Lucretius' poem), immediately lends the idea of pleasure through recollection – and the poem as a whole – a distinctly Epicurean flavour.

except that a good Epicurean would presumably never have let things come to such a pass and, as Lucretius advises (4.1058–1191), would not have become ensnared in obsessive love in the first place. Catullus, by contrast – though he never pronounces on the truth of his two conditionals – appears in the course of the poem to move away from the Epicurean point of view toward a more traditional hope in divine assistance. The recollection-of-*benefacta priora* approach is clearly not working for him, and all he can do is entrust himself to the pity and justice of the gods, hoping that they are indeed in the business of reciprocating human *pietas*.

Catullus' poem makes perfect sense to a reader without any knowledge of Epicureanism, and it is not in the first place a reflection on philosophical doctrine as such. Instead, philosophy is woven into the text, structuring and reinforcing the poem's train of thought – like Catullus' amatory epigrams in general, the poem proceeds on a high level of abstraction, despite its expressions of strong emotion – in a way that the poet's learned contemporary readers would have found familiar. Any educated Roman would have known about those two Epicurean truisms, or at least would have been aware that a rational person is supposed not to fall victim to destructive passion. Philosophy, Epicurean or otherwise, billed itself as medicine of the soul, but Catullus appears to buck the trend and suggest that only the pity of the gods can make him 'be well and get rid of this awful disease' (v. 25). For the philosopher, virtue may be its own reward, but for the love-sick poet, its only use is as a potential bargaining chip in the traditional reciprocal relationship with the gods – that is, *if* the gods really go in for reciprocity, something that may well remain the wishful thinking of the kind of person whom philosophers would not hesitate to call a fool.[69]

In the work of other classical poets, the role of philosophy has long been established. Horace, the self-proclaimed 'pig from the herd of Epicurus' (*Epist.* 1.4.16), in his *Odes* again and again enjoins his addressees to eat, drink and be merry, for tomorrow we die. Perhaps the most famous expression of this sentiment is *Odes* 1.11, whose final exhortation, *carpe diem*, has become – with some help from Robin Williams and the *Dead*

---

[69] Could Catullus be responding to Lucretius' diatribe against romantic love in *De rerum natura* 4, pointing out, as it were, that in the case of true love-sickness, Epicurean philosophy provides but cold comfort (generally on Catullus' rejection of philosophy, see Uden 2021)? The relationship of the two contemporary poets is vexed, and Lucretius has also been seen as reacting to Catullus (see Brown 1987: 139–42, with further references). It is probably safer to assume that both Epicureanism and erotic poetry were in the air in mid-first century Rome, and that the period's two surviving poets just happen to be where we see these ideologies clash.

*Poets Society* – one of the most popular Latin quotations of today. The poet here and in similar poems seems to have an actual philosophically informed message, viz. to keep in mind one's mortality, calmly meet the challenges of life whatever they might be[70] and, employing wisdom,[71] maximise one's pleasures by seizing the day.

Even so, *Odes* 1.11 serves up Epicurean hedonism with a twist: in telling his addressee Leuconoe about the necessity of enjoying the present moment, the poem's persona is not imparting impersonal philosophical teaching. Leuconoe, who has been trying to cast both her own and the poet's horoscope (vv. 1–3), is obviously a love interest, and her lover's insistence that they should 'stop talking' (*dum loquimur, fugerit inuida | aetas*, vv. 7–8) seems to be a none too subtle hint at what they ought to be doing instead. To his wider readership, Horace may be advertising the doctrine of the Garden, but within the poem, Epicureanism functions as a tongue-in-cheek means of seduction.

Philosophical reflections are even more prominent in Horace's *Satires* and *Epistles*, and it might be generally claimed that of all poetic genres practised at Rome, satire is the most openly philosophical. Quintilian famously maintains that *satura quidem tota nostra est* (*Inst.* 10.1.93), and in its intrinsic Romanness, the genre also presents an intrinsically Roman way of philosophising: irreverent, aggressive and often ostensibly non-elite as well as anti-Greek.[72] Drawing on the tradition of the Cynic diatribe, satire both proposes and deconstructs philosophical doctrines from all schools, presenting itself as both a vehicle for philosophy and its alternative – philosophy's evil twin, as it were. In addition, numerous Roman satires reflect on the social and institutional aspects of philosophy, bringing on stage philosophers as individuals or types, and not infrequently lambasting them for all sorts of failings, but especially for not living up to their own teachings.

We have already encountered the second-century satirist Lucilius, in both a mocking mode (the ridiculing of Albucius) and a more reflective one (the *uirtus* fragment). Numerous passages could be adduced from

---

[70] As Nisbet and Hubbard 1970 *ad loc.* point out, *quidquid erit pati* (v. 3) may be an Epicurean phrase and has a parallel in Cic. *Fam.* 9.17.4.
[71] Cf. *sapias* (v. 6).
[72] Generally on philosophy in Roman satire, see Mayer 2005. Among the many contributions on specific satirists, note Armstrong 2014 and Yona 2018 (on Horace), Bartsch 2012 (on Persius and Juvenal), Bartsch 2015a (on Persius), Uden 2015: 146–75 (on Juvenal).

Horace, Persius and Juvenal to demonstrate the (anti-)philosophical tendencies of satire, but I will here concentrate on a less obvious example, the *Menippean Satires* of the late-Republican polymath Varro.[73] Following in the footsteps of the Cynic Menippus of Gadara, Varro wrote a staggering 150 books of satires, of which we possess 591 fragments, most of which are cited by the fourth-century grammarian Nonius Marcellus, unfortunately without any context. It is thus extremely difficult to gauge the content or plot of any individual satire, though it is obvious that philosophy – and especially the Cynicism of the sub-genre's eponymous founder – played an important role in many. Let us take a quick look at *Eumenides*, at forty-nine fragments the best-preserved work in the corpus.

This satire features the first-person narrative of a protagonist who is widely considered mad, just like a latter-day Orestes harassed by the furies that give the work its title.[74] Madness, of course, is a stereotypical affliction of the philosophically unenlightened (according to the Stoics, for instance, everybody but the wise man is insane), and alarmed by his condition, the narrator embarks on the quest for a cure. In addition to temporarily joining the followers of Cybele and Serapis – which leads to various mishaps and gives Varro the opportunity of satirising foreign cults[75] – he tries out different schools of philosophy. However, this too leaves him only more confused:

> Postremo nemo aegrotus quicquam somniat
> tam infandum quod non aliquis dicat philosophus.   (fr. 122 Astbury)
>
> Finally, no sick man can dream of anything so unspeakable that some philosopher wouldn't say the same thing.

It turns out that everybody is mad – and philosophers may just be the craziest of them all.

Still, even if its all-too-human (and hence mad) acolytes fail to provide a cure for the soul, philosophy itself remains the answer. At the end of his ordeal, the protagonist encounters 'white-haired Truth, the foster child

---

[73] Written in prosimetrum, these admittedly only partly qualify as poetry – but their hybrid status in this respect fits well with their liminality in others (between Greek and Roman, serious philosophy and philosophical satire, etc.). There are two extensive commentaries on the *Menippeans*, Cèbe 1972–99 and Krenkel 2002, but few individual studies.
[74] Intriguingly, Varro also wrote a *Logistoricus* titled *Orestes de insania* (Gell. *NA* 13.4), whose content, however, is anyone's guess.
[75] On this motif, see Rolle 2017: 31–71 and 139–65.

of Attic philosophy'[76] and is able to recover his wits. To his great relief, his new-found sanity is officially acknowledged:

> Forenses decernunt ut Existimatio nomen meum in sanorum numerum referat. (fr. 147 Astbury)
>
> The judges decree that Reputation should enter my name in the roll of the sane.

While it has been suggested that the befuddled madman finds salvation in one school of philosophy specifically, namely Cynicism, this is not obvious from the fragments, and despite the Cynic pedigree of Menippean Satire, there is no need to assume that Varro's work preached a straightforward Cynic message.[77] It seems more likely that, just like the authors of the sister genre of hexameter satire, Varro felt free to come up with his own brand of satirical philosophising, which both reflected what was available in the philosophical marketplace and moved beyond it.

At the end of the first poem of his first book of *Satires*, Horace tells his readers that he does not want to be thought to 'have plundered the shelves of bleary-eyed Crispinus'.[78] Crispinus is a Stoic philosopher, and Horace has just given a lengthy disquisition on the folly of human beings, who are chronically dissatisfied with their lot, all because they are suffering from irrational greed. This all sounds philosophical enough – but Horace is at pains to distinguish himself from the 'real' philosopher, a man who suffers not just from an eye disease but also from logorrhea. Satire is all our own, and a specifically Roman way of doing philosophy.

## Cares of the Self

Our last glimpse of the dying republic was Cato's Stoic suicide, the most dramatic application of philosophy to politics on the part of a learned senator. With the arrival of a monarchic system, the political role of the Roman upper class changed drastically: while republican structures lived on, real power was concentrated in the hands of the emperor; ambitious men could still make a career in government, but they could not actually govern. Even so, philosophy continued to have the potential to inspire political action, most prominently in the case of the so-called 'Stoic

---

[76] Fr. 141 Astbury: *cana Veritas, | Attices philosophiae alumna.*
[77] In favour of a Cynic reading: Cèbe 1972–99: IV 543–747; sceptical: Relihan 1993: 65–71; cf. Scholz 2003.
[78] Hor. *Sat.* 1.120–1 *ne me Crispini scrinia lippi | compilasse putes.*

opposition' during the Neronian and Flavian periods. Stoic 'martyrs' like Thrasea Paetus and Helvidius Priscus paid with their lives for publicly dissenting from imperial policy, and more violent opponents, such as the members of the Pisonian conspiracy against Nero, may also in part have been inspired by philosophical principles.

These cases are fairly isolated, and as scholars have pointed out, there was nothing about philosophy in general and Stoicism in particular that dictated passive or active resistance to the imperial system or an individual emperor:[79] as in the case of the philosophically informed statesmen of the late Republic, men like Thrasea and Helvidius apparently simply decided for themselves that their chosen philosophy necessitated a certain course of political action, while other followers of the same creed interpreted their own duties differently.[80] After all, Seneca (Nero's tutor and longtime 'minister') and Marcus Aurelius (emperor himself) were likewise Stoics, as probably were many other people who never entered the limelight of history.

On the whole, the changed political landscape no doubt contributed to Roman philosophy's taking a more pronounced inward turn, focusing on what had always been a major concern of especially the Hellenistic schools but what now became the centre of philosophical attention: the self. Michel Foucault famously declared the first two centuries CE 'a kind of golden age' of what he called the 'cultivation' or 'care of the self' (*souci de soi*).[81] In teaching individuals how to achieve the goal of all philosophical endeavour, the good life, philosophers of all schools had developed certain cognitive-behavioural techniques that some scholars, adapting a Christian concept, have described as 'spiritual exercises' and which Foucault refers to as 'practices of the self'.[82] In what follows, I take a look at some applications of these techniques in the work of the period's foremost philosophical writer, the younger Seneca, with a small excursion into the writings of Marcus Aurelius. That both authors were Stoics – or at least strongly

---

[79] See Brunt 1975, Trapp 2007: 226–30; also Myles Lavan in this volume, pp. 823–4.
[80] See e.g. Mann 2016 on Helvidius Priscus' use of Stoic persona theory.
[81] Foucault 1986: 37–68, quotation on p. 45; see also Foucault 1988. I am not here concerned with the much-discussed question of whether Foucault's broad-strokes picture correctly represents the complexities of the period's philosophical theory and practice (for a helpful survey of, and response to, critiques of Foucault, see Ker 2009: 167–72); whatever the case may be, he uniquely succeeded in putting his finger on a central concern of the age.
[82] On ancient philosophical practices of the self, see Rabbow 1954, Foucault 1986: 37–68, Newman 1989, Hadot 1995. On the use of such techniques by Seneca, see Hadot 1969, Armisen-Marchetti 1986, Bartsch 2006: 183–281. Reydams-Schils 2005: 15–52 discusses the Roman Stoic self; Bartsch and Wray 2009 is a collection of essays on various aspects of the self in Seneca.

influenced by Stoicism[83] – is no coincidence: in the early Empire, Stoicism became a kind of default world-view of the Roman educated elite, ranging from well-informed orthodoxy to watered-down general ideas about cosmic order, self-sufficiency and virtue.

Whatever philosophical creed a person followed, he or she needed to know and assent to the school's doctrines. Given the intellectualism of ancient philosophy, such rational understanding ought in principle to have ensured the person's wisdom, virtue and happiness; however, in practice the progress toward the *uita beata* was often acknowledged to be a gradual one, during which the *proficiens* (to use the Stoic term) needed to exercise and develop his or her mental and emotional capacities. Such training could take place with the guidance of a philosophical mentor or otherwise take the form of a kind of self-help conducted by individuals on their own. In this, they had the choice of a number of self-shaping exercises: taking on the role of their own teachers, *proficientes* could engage in interior dialogues, interrogating and exhorting themselves; they could set aside special times during the day, especially in the morning and evening, for reflecting on their mental progress; they could inure themselves to the vicissitudes of fortune and condition themselves against anxiety by 'premeditating' evils that might befall them, including death; or they could even 'practise' feared conditions such as poverty to show themselves that such supposedly bad things were not in fact to be feared.

A famous example of the application of such a technique occurs toward the end of Seneca's *De ira*, in the context of the recommendation to review and critique one's own behaviour every day in order gradually to root out one's propensity to get angry:

> Vtor hac potestate et cotidie apud me causam dico. Cum sublatum e conspectu lumen est et conticuit uxor moris iam mei conscia, totum diem meum scrutor factaque ac dicta mea remetior; nihil mihi ipse abscondo, nihil transeo. (3.36.3)
>
> I make use of this opportunity and daily plead my own case before myself. When the light has been taken away and my wife, who already knows my habit, has grown silent, I examine my entire day and review what I have done and said. I hide nothing from myself, I leave nothing out.[84]

---

[83] While Seneca explicitly declares his allegiance to Stoicism, Marcus never does; however, the outlook of his *Meditations* is predominantly Stoic.
[84] Compare the whole of *De ira* 3.36–8, with Ker 2009. Seneca credits his technique to his teacher Sextius (3.36.1); on the school of the Sextii, see n. 92.

Seneca then provides an extensive example of such an interior dialogue, replete with analysis of his own behaviour and injunctions to himself to do better the next time.

We find similar techniques in the *Meditations* of Marcus Aurelius, a text apparently written for the private use of the emperor, which can be understood as a document of his philosophical self-formation.[85] One of Marcus' techniques is to exhort himself first thing in the morning, reminding himself not to get upset at all the annoying people he is likely to encounter in the course of his day (2.1). Even if he would prefer to remain in bed, it is his duty as a human being to get up:

> Ὄρθρου ὅταν δυσόκνως ἐξεγείρῃ, πρόχειρον ἔστω ὅτι ἐπὶ ἀνθρώπου ἔργον ἐγείρομαι· τί οὖν δυσκολαίνω, εἰ πορεύομαι ἐπὶ τὸ ποιεῖν ὧν ἕνεκεν γέγονα καὶ ὧν χάριν προῆγμαι εἰς τὸν κόσμον; (*Meditations* 5.1)

> Early in the morning, whenever you find it difficult to get up, have this thought ready at hand: 'I am getting up to do the work of a human being. Why then am I annoyed at doing that for which I was born and for whose sake I was brought into the cosmos?'

It is fascinating to observe the Roman emperor giving himself a pep talk to get out of bed and do his job of running the empire.

To return to Seneca, the most extensive use of the practices of the self occurs in the author's most popular work, the *Epistulae morales* written at the end of his life, while living in retirement from Nero's court. In the 124 extant letters to Lucilius, Seneca dramatises a process of philosophical progress, in which the author provides guidance to his younger friend while also reporting on his own state of mind and slow movement toward a more philosophically informed and happier life. Seneca imparts his own, increasingly more sophisticated teaching, which consists of both theoretical exposition and practical exhortation. In addition to such direct instruction, he advises Lucilius not just to study philosophical texts, but also to employ a number of cognitive and behavioural exercises, including *praemeditatio*, practice of poverty and self-interrogation.[86]

To take but one example, in Letter 26 Seneca discusses his own feelings at growing older. Since death is undoubtedly drawing closer, the author engages in an exercise whereby he imagines that his final day is already

---

[85] While the title *Meditationes* is modern, it is quite fitting, given the character of the work. On the text as a set of spiritual exercises, see Rutherford 1989: 15–21, Hadot 1998, Sellars 2012. Its private purpose explains Marcus' choice of writing in Greek: this was the language in which he had studied, and was used to 'doing', philosophy; if he had written for publication, he might have chosen Latin.
[86] See Edwards 1997, Schafer 2011, Bartsch 2015b.

here: 'as though the trial were at hand and the day had come that is going to pass judgement on all my years, I examine and address myself in the following way'.[87] Anticipating the 'trial' of his final hour, he both conditions himself not to be afraid of death and teaches himself to live his remaining life in a better way, keeping in mind those things that really count. Lucilius is still young, but according to Seneca, it is never too early to 'learn how to die' (*Ep.* 26.8): 'These sorts of things I say to myself, but imagine that I have said them to you too.'[88] By recounting his own methods of self-instruction, Seneca is instructing his addressee as well.

In the following letter, we see Lucilius for once bristling at this approach:

> 'Tu me' inquis 'mones? Iam enim te ipse monuisti, iam correxisti? Ideo aliorum emendationi uacas?' (*Ep.* 27.1)
>
> You say, 'Are you admonishing me? Have you already admonished and corrected yourself? Is that why you have time for improving others?'

Not at all, Seneca explains:

> Non sum tam improbus ut curationes aeger obeam, sed, tamquam in eodem ualetudinario iaceam, de communi tecum malo colloquor et remedia communico. (*Ep.* 27.1)
>
> I am not such a hypocrite as to offer a cure while I myself am sick. Instead, as if lying in the same hospital ward, I talk to you about the illness we have in common, and share remedies.

Seneca and Lucilius, teacher and student, are in the same situation: sick in soul and in need of the medicine that is philosophy. It is simply a matter of one patient sharing with another his experience of a regimen or course of medications that he himself has found particularly helpful.

Imagine, though, a person who enjoys being ill. Seneca also wrote tragedies, gruesome plays in which people act in pronouncedly un-Stoic way and nevertheless often prosper. It has been observed that such Senecan arch-villains as Atreus and Medea – though in their actions the very opposites of Stoic sages[89] – nevertheless exhibit some fairly philosophical attitudes (e.g. a disdain for fortune) and a mastery of the same practices of the self explored in Seneca's prose works.[90] Thus the Atreus of the *Thyestes*,

---

[87] Sen. *Ep.* 26.4 *Ego certe, uelut appropinquet experimentum et ille laturus sententiam de omnibus annis meis dies uenerit, ita me obseruo et alloquor.*
[88] Sen. *Ep.* 26.7 *haec mecum loquor, sed tecum quoque me locutum puta.*
[89] See Lefèvre 1997 on Atreus.
[90] See Littlewood 2004: 15–102, Bartsch 2006: 255–81, Star 2006 and, for a somewhat different take, Wiener 2014.

while in the grip of distinctly un-Stoic passion, remains in control throughout the play, using the very technique of self-command to rouse his own anger and effectively channel it into his plan for vengeance against his brother.[91] The fact that this perverted care of the self is highly successful makes a philosophical interpretation of the plays problematic: while they might be viewed as Stoic morality plays that warn against passion and vice, the triumph of the passionate and vicious raises serious questions about the wisdom and applicability of Stoicism. There is no obvious solution to this dilemma; Seneca's philosophical writing and his plays exist on an intellectual continuum, applying the same concepts (Stoic self-mastery, cosmic sympathy) to antithetical effect.

## How to Be a Philosopher

The care of the self as advocated by Seneca and others is largely concerned with a person's interiority: philosophy, the *ars uitae*, is the art of changing one's internal disposition in order to achieve the happy life. While this often necessitates modifying one's behaviour, it need not involve a noticeable change of lifestyle and appearance. In fact, Seneca warns against too drastic a refashioning of one's outward persona:

> Illud autem te admoneo, ne eorum more qui non proficere sed conspici cupiunt facias aliqua quae in habitu tuo aut genere uitae notabilia sint; asperum cultum et intonsum caput et neglegentiorem barbam et indictum argento odium et cubile humi positum et quicquid aliud ambitionem peruersa uia sequitur euita. Satis ipsum nomen philosophiae, etiam si modeste tractetur, inuidiosum est: quid si nos hominum consuetudini coeperimus excerpere? Intus omnia dissimilia sint, frons populo nostra conueniat. (*Ep.* 5.1–2)

> But I entreat you not to do anything that sticks out in your appearance or your lifestyle, in the manner of those who don't want to make progress but to be conspicuous: avoid shabby clothing, untrimmed hair, a matted beard, professed hatred of silverware, sleeping on the floor and every other perverse way of self-promotion. The very concept of philosophy, even if it is pursued in moderation, raises suspicion. What will happen if we remove ourselves from human convention? Let us be entirely different inside while our outside conforms to societal norms.

It is obvious why a Seneca would decry a kind of self-fashioning that is focused on the outside rather than the inside, but perhaps less clear to

---

[91] Note esp. *Thy.* 176–204, 241–3, 270–86, 491–507.

modern readers why a Lucilius might be tempted to walk around in rags and give up personal grooming. As it turns out, this kind of behaviour is associated with a particular social group: what the philosophical mentor tells his philosophical student to avoid is acting *like a philosopher*.

As mentioned above, philosophically interested upper-class Romans like Cicero and Seneca did not think of themselves as philosophers, a distinct group of intellectual professionals that was originally entirely Greek. In the course of the imperial period, however, this boundary became increasingly blurred, as a profession and way of life that had been a Greek 'other' gradually turned into something to which Romans themselves might aspire. Thus we find not only the occasional self-declared Roman philosopher[92] but also the option of embracing a philosophical lifestyle or at least nodding to what might be termed philosophical fashion. As Roman high society became ever more philhellenic, and the expansion of empire and citizenship led to administrative and cultural decentralisation, we encounter increasingly cosmopolitan manifestations of the philosopher. While the cultural and linguistic binary 'Roman/Latin vs. Greek' remained good to think, play and polemicise with, the intellectual and philosophical landscape of the High Empire was far more complex, confusing and contested.

No one better exemplifies this situation than the only major ancient Latin author who explicitly refers to himself as a *philosophus*:[93] Apuleius of Madaurus, who not only wrote the celebrated novel *Metamorphoses* and published excerpts of his display speeches (the so-called *Florida*), but also, among other titles, penned works on Plato's life and doctrine (*De Platone et eius dogmate*) and Platonist demonology (*De deo Socratis*).[94] Modern scholars have often been hesitant to consider this colourful figure a 'real' philosopher,[95] and some of Apuleius' contemporaries, too, appear to have questioned his intellectual identity. In a criminal case brought in the northern African city of Sabratha in 158/9 CE, Apuleius was accused by

---

[92] Possibly the first bona fide Roman 'philosophers', and founders of the only Roman philosophical school, were the Sextii (father and son), whose sect flourished in the early first century CE and who are mentioned approvingly by Seneca, their erstwhile follower. Often regarded as eclectics with a possible Pythagorean bent, they may instead have been Middle Platonists in the mould of Antiochus (Hadot 2007). Despite the fact that the school is described as a *Romani roboris secta* (Sen. *QNat.* 7.32.2), the Sextii apparently taught and wrote in Greek. However, their followers Celsus and Papirius Fabianus composed their works in Latin, with the latter reportedly writing more philosophical works than Cicero (Sen. *Ep.* 100.9). For testimonia and fragments of all four authors, see Garbarino 2003.

[93] See Hine 2016: 21–3, Trapp 2017a: 41–3.

[94] On Apuleius' Platonism, see Dillon 1996: 306–38, Fletcher 2014, Puccini 2017.

[95] Fletcher 2014: 19 n. 47 collects disparaging remarks.

## 13 Philosophy

relatives of the wife he had recently married of having won her affections by means of magic. In his flamboyant and successful defence speech, subsequently published under the Socratic title *Apologia*, Apuleius sets the record straight: he is by no means a magician, but a *philosophus Platonicus* through and through.[96]

Before addressing the major charge brought against him, Apuleius responds to a series of general accusations raised against his person and lifestyle. In doing so, he contends, he is defending philosophy itself against the attacks of the ignorant and the kinds of hackneyed complaints that are habitually levelled against philosophers.[97] What the prosecutors appear to have done was not to ignore the defendant's (apparently well-known) claim to the status of a *philosophus* but to challenge its justification, arguing that Apuleius' behaviour was by no means in keeping with his self-professed identity. The speaker's strategy, in turn, is to prove that all his doings are exactly what one would expect from a philosopher in general and a Platonist in particular. As Apuleius boldly maintains, 'no true charge can be brought against philosophers, and not even a false charge can be made up, against which, trusting in their innocence, they cannot defend themselves'.[98]

The activities called into suspicion by the prosecution but defended by Apuleius amount to a fascinating list. According to the speech, it is perfectly normal philosophical practice to write erotic verse; own a mirror; live in poverty; carry a staff and backpack; seek out and dissect various types of fish; attend to epileptics during their fits; own and conceal implements associated with mystery cults; and commission and purchase religious statues for private worship (*Apol.* 9–65). Even allowing for the tendentious and provocative nature of the argument, it is obvious that we have come quite a way from the amateur philosophising of a Cicero and Seneca, who would never have dreamed of engaging in most of the activities described and would probably have denied the specifically philosophical nature of a large number of them.

Most telling, however, is the prosecution's opening salvo against the defendant, which Apuleius quotes verbatim:

> Accusamus apud te philosophum formonsum et tam Graece quam Latine – pro nefas! – disertissimum. (*Apol.* 4)

---

[96] On the *Apologia*, see Harrison 2000: 39–88, Rives 2008, Fletcher 2014: 198–226; on Apuleius as a latter-day Socrates, see Schindel 2000, Riess 2008a; generally on Apuleius' self-representation as a *philosophus Platonicus*, see Puccini 2017: 33–82.
[97] Defence of philosophy: *Apol.* 1, 3, 103; typical anti-philosophical attacks: 3.
[98] *Apol.* 28 *nihil in philosophos non modo uere dici, sed ne falso quidem posse confingi, quod non ex innocentiae fiducia . . . habeant defendere.*

We bring charges before you against a 'philosopher' who is handsome and (shocking!) extremely eloquent in both Greek and Latin.

The defendant ironically deprecates these charges, taking special care to point to his matted hair, which is nothing like the luxuriant coiffure cited by the prosecution but instead – we are meant to understand – the neglected mane typical of the philosopher (compare Seneca's warning to Lucilius).[99] Nevertheless, Apuleius' alleged care for his appearance coupled with his indubitable rhetorical prowess appears to signal his membership in an intellectual subculture rather different from the philosophers: the sophists.

As scholars have often pointed out, Apuleius' work and career appear to have numerous points of contact with the phenomenon known as the Second Sophistic.[100] While the exact definition of 'sophist', and of the Second Sophistic itself, was and remains controversial,[101] the stereotypical imperial sophist might be described as a travelling intellectual superstar, who attracts vast followings with his virtuoso display speeches. In principle, then, sophists and philosophers were distinct in purpose, activity and even outer appearance:[102] sophists were well-groomed, well-dressed rhetorical performers who aimed to dazzle and entertain their audiences; philosophers were moral teachers who pointedly neglected their outer appearance to signal the sole importance of ethical values. In reality, however, the boundaries were fluid: sophists spoke on philosophical topics, and philosophers might put on sophistic displays or even the occasional clean garment. Apuleius seems to straddle both worlds, travelling the Mediterranean, giving epideictic speeches (the *Apology* itself has been termed 'a masterpiece of the Second Sophistic'),[103] writing philosophical treatises and even penning a bawdy novel whose interpretation still eludes critics.[104] Another boundary criss-crossed by this North African native is that of language.[105] As even his accusers avow, Apuleius is *tam Graece quam*

---

[99] On the significance of Apuleius' unkempt hair in the context of contemporary codes of self-fashioning, see Zanker 1995: 222–9.
[100] On Apuleius as a Latin sophist, see Sandy 1997, Harrison 2000; differently Swain 2001, 2006: 11–12.
[101] See Whitmarsh 2005: 3–22.
[102] On sophists vs. philosophers, see Bowersock 2002; on the authority and identity of imperial philosophers, see Hahn 1989, Trapp 2007: 1–27 and 226–57, 2017a and 2017b.
[103] See Helm 1955.
[104] There is no scholarly consensus about whether the *Metamorphoses* has a serious, possibly philosophical, message or subtext, with the story of Cupid and Psyche as well as the final, Isiac book particularly hotly debated.
[105] On the bilingualism and biculturalism of Roman intellectuals of the period (including Apuleius, Fronto, Gellius and Favorinus), see Swain 2006 and compare Simon Goldhill in this volume.

*Latine dissertissimus*, and we are told that in addition to his Latin output, he also wrote works in Greek.[106] While the Second Sophistic is typically considered a Greek phenomenon, intrinsically bound up with the question of Hellenic identity under Roman rule, the case of Apuleius shows that sophistry, just like philosophy, could be practised in Latin and by a person who, hailing from the periphery of the empire, was both a Roman citizen and an intellectual cosmopolitan.[107]

However idiosyncratic Apuleius' *Apologia* may appear, it is an enactment of some of the major concerns of the performative and combative intellectual culture of the High Empire. In Greek and Latin texts from the period, we find intellectuals (e.g. sophists, philosophers, religious figures, grammarians and doctors) publicly displaying their own expertise, competing with and attempting to get the better of others and continuously defining and redefining the boundaries of their own group.[108] What does it mean to be a sophist, a philosopher or (*pro nefas!*) a magician? Who has real authority and who is an impostor? Who is in and who is out? In his tour-de-force performance, Apuleius establishes himself as a *philosophus Platonicus* by the sheer power of his verbal skill. *Ratio* and *oratio* are intrinsically connected:[109] it is the arsenal of the sophist that provides the most effective defence of philosophy.

A similarly colourful cross-cultural, cross-linguistic second-century philosopher-sophist is immortalised in the *Attic Nights* of Aulus Gellius. The Roman miscellanist befriended and lionised Favorinus, a Latin-speaking Gaul from Arelate, who became an international celebrity as a Greek display speaker and philosopher in the Academic Sceptic tradition.[110] The fact that Favorinus was also a 'eunuch' (it may have been cryptorchism that created his famously soft, castrato-like voice without impinging on his sexual performance) and got into various spats with the emperor Hadrian further contributed to his notoriety.[111] In his *Life of*

---

[106] *Flor.* 9.29, *Apol.* 36, with Harrison 2000: 15.
[107] Considering the question 'Was there a Latin Second Sophistic?', Habinek 2017 largely answers in the negative, citing Apuleius as the 'exception that proves the rule' (p. 34); cf. Swain 2001, 2006: 11–12. It seems, however, that the binary Latin/Roman vs. Greek loses much of its significance in this period of proudly liminal figures. Compare the discussion immediately below of Aulus Gellius and Favorinus.
[108] On performance of identity and competition in the Second Sophistic, see Whitmarsh 2005: 23–40; on the construction and contestation of group identity and membership in imperial culture, see Eshleman 2012.
[109] For this pairing, see *Flor.* 13.3, 18.5; *De dog. Plat.* 1.3.
[110] On Favorinus in Gellius, see Beall 2001, Holford-Strevens 2003: 98–130, Howley 2018: 235–50.
[111] Philostratus reports that Favorinus liked to quip about the three 'paradoxes' of his life (*VS* 489): he was a Gaul who spoke Greek (ἑλληνίζειν), a eunuch who had been accused of adultery and a man who had quarrelled with the emperor and lived.

*the Sophists*, Philostratus includes him in a group of intellectuals who were in fact philosophers but also gained a reputation as sophists (*VS* 489–92).

Gellius, whose programmatically titled work purports to collect for a Roman readership the lucubrations of his study days in Athens, often presents his pieces of miscellaneous knowledge in the form of anecdotes that show intellectuals of various types and both languages displaying their own expertise and contesting that of others.[112] Philosophers and grammarians score points and humiliate their opponents, or otherwise find themselves cut down to size and shown up as impostors. A typical scene is found in *Attic Nights* 4.1, where Favorinus (as usual designated *philosophus*) is challenged by an importunate grammarian concerning the gender and declension of the Latin word *penus* ('store'). While the *grammaticus* is making a nuisance of himself (*nimis odiose blatiret*, 4.1.4), Favorinus responds in a genteel manner (*placide*, ibid.), dismissing the morphological discussion by asking the man to define what a *penus* actually is. The grammarian gets increasingly flustered when Favorinus tells him that 'wine and grain and oil and lentils and beans and the like' (4.1.7) does not qualify as a definition according to genus and difference, and he defensively objects that just because he has never studied philosophy, this doesn't mean that he doesn't know *litteras . . . alias* (4.1.13). As it turns out, however, the 'philosopher' Favorinus can just as easily talk grammar and proceeds with learned references to appearances of *penus* in both Virgil and juristic writing. At the end of his speech, he explains:

> 'Haec ego' inquit 'cum philosophiae me dedissem, non insuper tamen habui discere; quoniam ciuibus Romanis Latine loquentibus rem non suo uocabulo demonstrare non minus turpe est quam hominem non suo nomine appellare.' (4.1.18)

> 'Though I have dedicated myself to philosophy,' he said, 'I did not believe it superfluous to learn such things as well: for Roman citizens speaking Latin, it is no less shameful not to designate a thing by its correct word than to address a man by a wrong name.'

In demolishing the grammarian, Favorinus in his pleasant way has shown himself to be an intellectual for all seasons. Demonstrating his credentials as a philosopher, he has engaged in a Socratic interrogation on a topic dear

---

[112] See Keulen 2009 and Howley 2018, though note that Keulen believes that Gellius satirises the intellectuals whose interactions he describes, including himself (cf. also Keulen 2004 on Apuleius), while Howley treats such scenes as serious explorations of the acquisition and display of knowledge.

to Socrates' own heart, that of definition.[113] He has displayed his knowledge of Roman poetry and Roman law, presenting himself as a Roman citizen deeply concerned with proper Latin usage. And in good sophistic fashion, he has spontaneously risen to a rhetorical challenge and put on a winning performance for all bystanders, moving the discussion, as Gellius puts it, 'away from small and trivial matters toward those more worth hearing and learning'.[114] Fascinatingly, the interchange takes place among the crowd waiting for the emperor's morning *salutatio*, where Favorinus, the grammarian and, one assumes, the author himself are standing *in circulo doctorum hominum* (4.1.1). In Gellius' staging, the bilingual, gender-bending, philosopher–sophist has made it into the very heart of the empire.

From the very beginning, the history of Roman philosophy had been one of reacting to and negotiating with the philosophical theory and practice of the Greeks. Philosophers were Greek, and philosophy was written in Greek. While generations of Romans had proved that philosophy could also be practised by non-philosophers and written in Latin, and while the bilingual Roman upper classes moved easily between the languages, the dichotomy still largely held: a Roman could do philosophy but he could not be a philosopher. By the second century CE, however, cultural and political shifts had led to profound changes in the Roman empire's sociology of knowledge, as educated Romans not only continued to mingle with Greek intellectuals but increasingly began to play their interlocutors' own game. Cicero and Gellius were both deeply learned and competent in things Greek, but while the former translated one language and culture into the other, the latter was so steeped in what was increasingly becoming one and the same intellectual world that he chose his own 'Attic nights' as the peg from which to hang his Latin work.

Even so, an avid Roman student of philosophy and friend of philosophers such as Gellius was not yet ready to don the staff and backpack of the philosopher himself. This step was left to men from the western, Latinate parts of the empire, where alternative centres of culture were quickly developing. The African Apuleius and the Gaul Favorinus did not have the same need as a metropolitan Roman to agonise about the Greek–Roman divide. With their marginal and liminal identities, they could move between cultures as they moved around the Mediterranean, now wearing their Greek hats, now their Latin ones, and playing the

---

[113] The Socratic nature of Favorinus' *sermo* is made explicit by Gellius in his chapter heading, where he calls it *factus in Socraticum modum*.
[114] *NA* 4.1.18 *a rebus paruis et frigidis abducebat ad ea quae magis utile esset audire ac discere.*

philosopher as they played the sophist, the novelist, the grammarian, etc. What this cosmopolitanism meant, however, is that 'Roman' philosophy, even if written in Latin, lost its idiosyncratic Roman character as it no longer (as Lucretius, Cicero and Seneca had done) self-consciously pitted itself against the Greeks. However, a new dichotomy was about to open up, as Roman philosophy entered yet another chapter: with the arrival of a new religion, the question was no longer that of the Roman response to the Greeks, but of the Christian adaptation of pagan thought.

## Passing on the *pallium*

In the intellectual market place of the High Empire, Christians in many ways behaved just like their pagan counterparts: they aggressively policed the boundaries of their own group against impostors ('heretics') and engaged in rhetorical display and one-upmanship to convince their audience of the superiority of their own teachings *vis-à-vis* those of other contenders.[115] The first significant Christian writer in Latin, Tertullian, has even been called a 'Christian sophist':[116] he hailed from the same erudite North African milieu as Apuleius and was a similarly formidable and quirky orator. His status as a 'man between two worlds' is playfully brought to the fore in one of his most curious texts, *De pallio*, a speech of unclear date delivered to a Carthaginian audience, in which Tertullian defends his practice of wearing the Greek *pallium* rather than the Roman toga.[117] This sartorial choice is justified with a wide array of recherché arguments, ranging from cosmology to biology to mythology to history to the fact that togas are simply very uncomfortable. Crucially, though, the *pallium* (which in a whimsical *prosopopoeia* gets to make its own case) is the garment of the philosopher and the practitioners of all liberal arts.

Having thus established the overall superiority of the *pallium*, at the very end of the speech Tertullian adds a further twist. Addressing his own eloquent garment, the speaker concludes,

> At ego iam illi etiam diuinae sectae ac disciplinae commercium confero. Gaude pallium et exulta! Melior iam te philosophia dignata est ex quo Christianum uestire coepisti. (*De pallio* 6.4–5)

---

[115] On Christians as members of the same social world of intellectuals as philosophers and sophists, see Eshleman 2012.
[116] Barnes 1985: 211–32; differently Swain 2006: 12.
[117] On the speech, see Hunink 2005; the quotation is from p. 24.

But I will further grant to it [i.e. the *pallium*] communication with the divine sect and discipline. Rejoice and exult, *pallium*! Now a better philosophy has elected you, ever since you began to cloak a Christian.

As marked out by the *pallium*, Tertullian is a philosopher – but a philosopher of a new and infinitely better school, that of Christianity.

The redefined *pallium* provides Tertullian with a playful means of dramatising the strategic Christian redeployment of pagan learning. More often, however, we find Christian authors agonising over the role – if any – that classical thought and education ought to play in a Christian context.[118] In Jerome's famous dream, the writer finds himself before the judgement seat of Christ and, upon declaring himself a Christian, is told, 'You are lying. You are a Ciceronian, not a Christian!'[119] Beaten with lashes and racked by remorse, Jerome implores god's mercy and issues a solemn promise: 'Lord, if I ever possess or read secular books, I have denied you.'[120] As both contemporaries and later readers have been quick to point out, the saint failed to fulfil his vow: the siren call of *codices saeculares* proved too strong in the long run.

Jerome's contemporary Augustine proposes a more pragmatic attitude to pagan learning, including philosophy. Referring to Exodus 3:21–2 and 12:35–6, where the Israelites on their departure from Egypt despoil the Egyptians of their precious metal objects, he recommends that Christians take from the philosophers anything that might be useful for Christian purposes:

> Philosophi autem qui uocantur, si qua forte uera et fidei nostrae accommodata dixerunt, maxime Platonici, non solum formidanda non sunt, sed ab eis etiam tamquam ab iniustis possessoribus in usum nostrum uindicanda. (*De doctrina Christiana* 2.40.60)
>
> As for the so-called philosophers, if by chance they have said something true and compatible with our faith, especially Platonists, we not only should not fear such material but even claim it for our own use from them as from illegal possessors.

Any truth that pagan philosophers might have come up with is theirs only coincidentally: by right, it belongs to the Christians, who are encouraged in no uncertain terms to take it back.

---

[118] See Shanzer 2012: 161–4.
[119] *Ep.* 22.30 *mentiris, ait, Ciceronianus es, non Christianus*. On Jerome's relationship to the Latin classics, see Hagendahl 1958: 89–328; on his Ciceronianism, see MacCormack 2013: 266–70. For a psychoanalytical reading of the dream, which diagnoses Jerome with a 'neurotisierte Persönlichkeitsstruktur' (69), see Feichtinger 1991.
[120] *Ep.* 22.30 *domine, si unquam habuero codices saeculares, si legero, te negaui*.

Augustine's own extensive œuvre is, as it were, a treasure house of Egyptian spoils. The saint's very journey toward Christianity, as presented in his *Confessions*, proceeds via various encounters with pagan philosophy.[121] Thus it was reportedly Augustine's youthful reading of Cicero's protreptic *Hortensius* that first turned him toward god:

> Ille uero liber mutauit affectum meum, et ad te ipsum, domine, mutauit preces meas, et uota et desideria mea fecit alia. (*Conf.* 3.4.7)
>
> That book changed my feelings and turned my prayers to you, lord, and made my wishes and desires different.

Augustine knows that *philosophia* means 'love of wisdom', and since wisdom resides with god, to be inspired by philosophy is to feel drawn to god himself (3.4.8).

After numerous intellectual and emotional detours, Augustine finds himself in Milan under the influence of both Ambrose and 'certain books of the Platonists' (*quosdam Platonicorum libros*, 7.9.13), which prove eye-opening:

> Ibi legi, non quidem his uerbis sed hoc idem omnino multis et multiplicibus suaderi rationibus, quod in principio erat uerbum et uerbum erat apud deum et deus erat uerbum. (*Conf.* 7.9.13)
>
> There I read – not in the exact same words, but the very same thing was argued in many and multiform ways – that in the beginning was the word, and the word was with god, and the word was god.[122]

In a remarkable case of 'despoiling the Egyptians', Augustine recovers from these Platonic texts the very doctrine expressed in the opening of the Gospel of John. Explaining the episode in philosophical terms, we might say that Neoplatonism provided Augustine with an ontology on which to plot the biblical text: the transcendent realm of the intelligible (the 'word' or god) is fundamentally separated from that of the material, while at the same time constituting the origin and single source from which all physical reality flows.[123]

---

[121] On Augustine and classical literature, see the magisterial work of Hagendahl 1967, as well as O'Donnell 1980 and Shanzer 2012; on his reception esp. of Cicero, see MacCormack 2013: 273–82. For the passages from the *Confessions* which I discuss in the next paragraph, compare the commentary of O'Donnell 1992.

[122] *Conf.* 7.9.13. The exact identity of these Platonic works (Greek works translated into Latin by Marius Victorinus, *Conf.* 8.2.3) has been much debated (see O'Donnell 1992 ad loc.); they appear to have included texts by both Plotinus and Porphyry.

[123] See Mendelson 2018.

## 13 Philosophy

In the course of a long and eventful career, Augustine composed numerous works, tackling such central philosophical and theological topics as the nature of the soul, the problem of free will and political theory, among many others.[124] As scholars regularly point out, his opinions developed over time, to the extent that late in life he even published *Retractationes*, corrections of his earlier views. Notably, the saint became ever more pessimistic about the state of human beings in this world. While he remained a eudaimonist, convinced that all human beings naturally strive for happiness – he kept on quoting a favourite tag from his beloved *Hortensius*: 'we all want to be happy'[125] – Augustine ultimately came to the conclusion that the *uita beata* is unattainable in this life and granted only to a few by god's mercy in the next.

This radical departure from classical philosophical doctrine is explained in a sermon delivered to the Carthaginians in 413/14.[126] Taking his departure from Acts 17:17–34, where Paul during his sojourn in Athens debates with Epicurean and Stoic philosophers, Augustine explains why these philosophies are incompatible with Christianity. Yes, 'the desire for the happy life is something that philosophers and Christians have in common'.[127] However, the Epicureans and Stoics falsely believe that the *uita beata* is up to humans themselves and based either in the body (Epicurean pleasure) or in the mind (Stoic virtue). As so often, the Epicureans are quickly dispatched while the more serious Stoics are refuted at greater length:

> Stoicus in animo ponens summum hominis bonum in re quidem meliori hominis posuit; sed etiam ipse in se spem posuit. (*Serm.* 150.7.8)
>
> By placing man's greatest good in his mind, the Stoic did indeed place it in the better part of man – but he also placed his hope in himself.

Believing that man can achieve happiness by the strength of his own intellect and virtue involves a profound error:

> Non uirtus animi tui te facit beatum, sed qui tibi uirtutem dedit, qui tibi uelle inspirauit, et posse donauit. (*Serm.* 150.8.9)

---

[124] On Augustine's philosophy, with special attention to his relation to pagan thought, see Rist 1994 and Mendelson 2018, as well as, specifically on ethics, Kent 2001. See also Fuhrer 2017 on Augustine's pessimistic eudaimonism, discussed below.

[125] Cic. *Hort.* fr. 69/70 Straume-Zimmermann: *beati omnes esse uolumus*. Hagendahl 1967: 1 81–3 lists all occurrences of the quotation in Augustine's work.

[126] August. *Serm.* 150. The Carthaginians, having provided sophisticated audiences for Apuleius and Tertullian centuries earlier, are still complimented on their learning (150.2.3).

[127] *Serm.* 150.3.4 *appetitio igitur beatae uitae philosophis Christianisque communis est.*

> It is not the virtue of your mind that makes you happy, but he who gave you virtue, who inspired your wish and granted you the ability.

By definition, human beings are not capable of reaching *eudaimonia* without the grace of god. As Augustine triumphantly concludes his sermon, 'This is the Christian teaching, not just comparable but incomparably preferable to the teachings of the philosophers, the disgustingness of the Epicureans, the arrogance of the Stoics.'[128]

Augustine has been described as the first systematic philosopher writing in Latin,[129] and he is perhaps the earliest Latin philosopher studied and taken seriously by modern philosophers as a 'real' philosopher. At the same time, he marks the end of the era of Roman philosophy traced in this chapter. At the beginning of the first great philosophical work in Latin, Lucretius had celebrated the *Graius homo* Epicurus, who at a time when *religio* oppressed all human life, 'first dared to lift up his human eyes and first dared to resist'.[130] In triumph, Epicurus broke through the 'flaming ramparts of the world', 'traversed the universe in his mind' and brought back to humankind the truth about the nature of things (1.72–7). As Lucretius sums up:

> Quare religio pedibus subiecta uicissim
> opteritur, nos exaequat uictoria caelo. (1.78–9)
>
> Therefore religion in turn is ground down beneath our feet, while victory raises us to the sky.

The story of Roman philosophy is that of Romans taking over the various glad tidings brought by *Grai homines*, differing greatly in detail but agreeing on one thing: that humans beings qua human beings are capable of living the happy life or, to quote Lucretius again, *dignam dis degere uitam* (3.322). We all want to be happy, and philosophy is the *ars uitae* that will guide us to this end. Perhaps it involves a simple life in a villa far from town; perhaps it means committing suicide for a political cause. Perhaps it consists in dissecting fish and studying epilepsy, or perhaps in getting up early in the morning and running the Roman empire. There will be setbacks, and it is very difficult to become a sage; however, because we are endowed with reason we absolutely have the capability of being that person who is wise, virtuous and happy at the same time. Inheriting from

---

[128] *Serm.* 150.8.10 *haec est doctrina Christianorum, non plane conferenda, sed incomparabiliter praeferenda doctrinis philosophorum, immunditiae Epicureorum, superbiae Stoicorum.*
[129] Maurach 2006: 160.
[130] Lucr. 1.66–7 *primum Graius homo mortalis tollere contra | est oculos ausus primusque obsistere contra.*

Hellenistic philosophy the quest for happiness and its concomitant fundamental optimism, Roman thinkers show little interest in theoretically innovating on the doctrines they have learned. What they are interested in is applying Greek teaching to their own Roman situations, making it known – and making it work. If this picture conforms all too easily to the stereotype of the pragmatic Roman, so be it: what makes the history of Roman philosophy so fruitful is precisely that generations of learned amateurs with largely no professional aspirations got to play with a set of doctrines that came with the promise of actually working in real life. We all want to be happy – and we can do it. *Fac te ipse felicem*, as Seneca writes to Lucilius.[131] That, in a nutshell, is the moral imperative of Roman philosophy.

## References

Armisen-Marchetti, M. (1986) 'Imagination et méditation chez Sénèque: l'exemple de la praemeditatio', *REL* 64: 1985–95. English version in J. G. Fitch, ed., *Oxford Readings in Classical Studies: Seneca* (Oxford), 2008, 102–13.

Armstrong, D. (2011) 'Epicurean virtues, Epicurean friendship: Cicero vs the Herculaneum Papyri', in Fish and Sanders 2011, 105–28.

  (2014) 'Horace's Epicurean voice in the Satires', in Garani and Konstan 2014, 91–127.

Armstrong, D. et al., eds. (2004) *Vergil, Philodemus, and the Augustans*, Austin.

Baraz, Y. (2012) *A Written Republic: Cicero's Philosophical Politics*, Princeton.

Barnes, J. and M. Griffin, eds. (1997) *Philosophia togata* II: *Plato and Aristotle at Rome*, Oxford.

Barnes, T. D. (1985) *Tertullian: A Historical and Literary Study*, rev. edn, Oxford.

Bartsch, S. (2006) *The Mirror of the Self: Sexuality, Self-Knowledge, and the Gaze in the Early Roman Empire*, Chicago.

  (2012) 'Persius, Juvenal, and Stoicism', in S. Braund and J. Osgood, eds., *A Companion to Persius and Juvenal* (Chichester), 217–38.

  (2015a) *Persius: A Study in Food, Philosophy, and the Figural*, Chicago.

  (2015b) 'Senecan selves', in S. Bartsch and A. Schiesaro, eds., *The Cambridge Companion to Seneca* (Cambridge), 187–98.

Bartsch, S. and D. Wray, eds. (2009) *Seneca and the Self*, Cambridge.

Beall, S. M. (2001) '*Homo fandi dulcissimus*: the role of Favorinus in the *Attic Nights* of Aulus Gellius', *AJPh* 122: 87–106.

Benferhat, Y. (2005) *Ciues Epicurei: les épicuriens et l'idée de la monarchie à Rome et en Italie de Sylla à Octave*, Brussels.

Blyth, D. (2010–11) 'Cicero and philosophy as text', *CJ* 106: 71–98.

Boes, J. (1990) *La philosophie et l'action dans la correspondance de Cicéron*, Nancy.

---

[131] Sen *Ep.* 31.5: 'you yourself, make yourself happy'.

Booth, J. (1997) 'All in the mind: sickness in Catullus 76', in S. M. Braund and C. Gill, eds., *The Passions in Roman Thought and Literature* (Cambridge), 150–68.
Bowersock, G. W. (2002) 'Philosophy in the Second Sophistic', in G. Clark and T. Rajak, eds., *Philosophy and Power in the Graeco-Roman World: Essays in Honour of Miriam Griffin* (Oxford), 157–70.
Boyancé, P. (1936) 'Les méthodes de l'histoire littéraire: Cicéron et son œuvre philosophique', *REL* 14: 288–309.
Bringmann, K. (1971) *Untersuchungen zum späten Cicero*, Göttingen.
Brittain, C. (2016) 'Cicero's sceptical methods: the example of the *De finibus*', in J. Annas and G. Betegh, eds., *Cicero's De finibus: Philosophical Approaches* (Cambridge), 12–40.
Brown, R. D. (1987) *Lucretius on Love and Sex*, Leiden.
Brunt, P. A. (1975) 'Stoicism and the principate', *PBSR* 43: 7–35.
  (1986) 'Cicero's *officium* in the civil war', *JRS* 76: 12–32.
Burkert, W. (1961) 'Hellenistische Pseudopythagorica', *Philologus* 105: 16–43 and 226–46.
Campbell, G. L. (2003) *Lucretius on Creation and Evolution: A Commentary on De rerum natura Book Five, Lines 772–1104* (Oxford).
  (2011) 'Lucretius', *Oxford Bibliographies Online*.
Castner, C. J. (1988) *Prosopography of Roman Epicureans from the Second Century B.C. to the Second Century A.D.*, Frankfurt.
Catana, L. (2016) 'Intellectual history and the history of philosophy: their genesis and current relationship', in R. Whatmore and B. Young, eds., *A Companion to Intellectual History* (Chichester), 129–40.
Cèbe, J.-P. (1972–99) *Varron, Satires ménippées*, 13 vols., Rome.
Chase, M. (2013) 'Observations on Pierre Hadot's conception of philosophy as a way of life', in M. Chase, S. R. L. Clark and M. McGhee, eds., *Philosophy as a Way of Life: Ancients and Moderns* (Chichester), 262–86.
Clay, D. (2004) 'Vergil's farewell to education (Catalepton 5) and Epicurus' Letter to Pythocles', in Armstrong et al. 2004, 25–36.
Davis, G. and S. Yona, eds. (2022) *Epicurus in Rome: Philosophical Perspectives in the Ciceronian Age*, Cambridge.
Denecke, W. (2014) *Classical World Literatures: Sino-Japanese and Greco-Roman Comparisons*, Oxford.
Dillon, J. (1996) *The Middle Platonists*, rev. edn, Ithaca, NY.
Donohue, H. (1993) *The Song of the Swan: Lucretius and the Influence of Callimachus*, Lanham, MD.
Dutsch, D. (2014) 'The beginnings: philosophy in Roman literature before 155 B.C.', in Garani and Konstan 2014, 1–25.
Edwards, C. (1997) 'Self-scrutiny and self-transformation in Seneca's Letters', *G&R* 44: 23–38.
  (2007) *Death in Ancient Rome*, New Haven.
Erler, M. (1992) 'Cicero und "unorthodoxer" Epikureismus', *Anregung* 38: 307–22.

Eshleman, K. (2012) *The Social World of Intellectuals in the Roman Empire: Sophists, Philosophers, and Christians*, Cambridge.
Farrell, J. (2014) 'Philosophy in Vergil', in Garani and Konstan 2014, 61–90.
Feeney, D. (2016) *Beyond Greek: The Beginnings of Latin Literature*, Cambridge, MA.
Feichtinger, B. (1991) 'Der Traum des Hieronymus – Ein Psychogramm', *VChr* 45: 54–77.
Fish, J. (2011) 'Not all politicians are Sisyphus: what Roman Epicureans were taught about politics', in Fish and Sanders 2011, 72–104.
Fish, J. and K. R. Sanders, eds. (2011) *Epicurus and the Epicurean Tradition*, Cambridge.
Fletcher, R. (2014) *Apuleius' Platonism: The Impersonation of Philosophy*, Cambridge.
Fögen, T. (2000) *Patrii sermonis egestas: Einstellungen lateinischer Autoren zu ihrer Muttersprache*, Munich.
Foucault, M. (1986) *The History of Sexuality 3: The Care of the Self*, translated by R. Hurley, New York (French orig. 1984).
  (1988) 'Technologies of the self', in L. H. Martin, H. Gutman and P. H. Hutton, eds., *Technologies of the Self: A Seminar with Michel Foucault* (Amherst), 16–49.
Fuhrer, T. (2017) 'Erzählte Philosophie: Augustin und das Konzept der "Philosophie als Lebensform"', in C. Riedwed, ed., *Philosophia in der Konkurrenz von Schulen, Wissenschaften und Religionen: Zur Pluralisierung des Philosophiebegriffs in Kaiserzeit und Spätantike* (Berlin), 301–17.
Gale, M. R. (1994) *Myth and Poetry in Lucretius*, Cambridge.
  (2022) '*Otium* and *voluptas*: Catullus and Roman Epicureanism', in Davis and Yona 2022, 87–108.
Gale, M. R., ed. (2007) *Oxford Readings in Classical Studies: Lucretius*, Oxford.
Garani, M. and D. Konstan, eds. (2014) *The Philosophizing Muse: The Influence of Greek Philosophy on Roman Poetry*, Newcastle.
Garani, M., D. Konstan and G. Reydams-Schils, eds. (2023) *The Oxford Handbook of Roman Philosophy*, Oxford.
Garbarino, G. (1973) *Roma e la filosofia greca dalle origini alla fine del II secolo a. C.*, 2 vols., Turin.
  (2003) *Philosophorum Romanorum fragmenta usque ad L. Annaei Senecae aetatem*, Bologna.
Gawlik, G. and W. Görler (1994) 'Cicero', in H. Flashar, ed., *Die Philosophie der Antike, Band 4: Die Hellenistische Philosophie* (Basel), 991–1168.
Gee, E. (2013) *Aratus and the Astronomical Tradition*, New York.
Gilbert, N. (2015) 'Among friends: Cicero and the Epicureans', unpublished PhD dissertation, University of Toronto.
  (2022) 'Was Atticus an Epicurean?', in Davis and Yona 2022, 55–71.
Gildenhard, I. (2006) 'Reckoning with tyranny: Greek thoughts on Caesar in Cicero's *Letters to Atticus* in early 49', in S. Lewis, ed., *Ancient Tyranny* (Edinburgh), 197–209.

(2007) *Paideia Romana: Cicero's Tusculan Disputations*, Cambridge.
Gillespie, S. and P. Hardie, eds. (2007) *The Cambridge Companion to Lucretius*, Cambridge.
Görler, W. (1984) 'Zum *virtus*-Fragment des Lucilius (1326–1338 Marx) und zur Geschichte der stoischen Güterlehre', *Hermes* 112: 445–68.
Griffin, M. T. (1986) 'Philosophy, Cato, and Roman suicide', *G&R* 33: 64–77 and 192–202.
  (1995) 'Philosophical badinage in Cicero's letters to his friends', in J. G. F. Powell, ed., *Cicero the Philosopher: Twelve Papers* (Oxford), 325–46.
  (1997) 'From Aristotle to Atticus: Cicero and Matius on friendship', in Barnes and Griffin 1997, 86–109.
Habinek, T. (1994) 'Ideology for an empire in the prefaces to Cicero's dialogues', *Ramus* 23: 55–67.
  (2006) 'The wisdom of Ennius', *Arethusa* 39: 471–88.
  (2017) 'Was there a Latin Second Sophistic?' in D. S. Richter and W. A. Johnson, eds., *The Oxford Handbook of The Second Sophistic* (Oxford), 25–37.
Hadot, I. (1969) *Seneca und die griechisch-römische Tradition der Seelenleitung*, Berlin.
  (2007) 'Versuch einer doktrinalen Neueinordnung der Schule der Sextier', *RhM* 150: 179–210.
Hadot, P. (1995) *Philosophy as a Way of Life: Spiritual Exercises from Socrates to Foucault*, trans. M. Chase, Oxford (French orig. 1987, 2nd edn).
  (1998) *The Inner Citadel: The Meditations of Marcus Aurelius*, trans. M. Chase, Cambridge, MA (French orig. 1992).
  (2002) *What Is Ancient Philosophy?*, translated by M. Chase, Cambridge, MA (French orig. 1995).
Hagendahl, H. (1958) *Latin Fathers and the Classics: A Study of the Apologists, Jerome and Other Christian Writers*, Gothenburg.
  (1967) *Augustine and the Latin Classics*, 2 vols., Gothenburg.
Hahn, J. (1989) *Der Philosoph und die Gesellschaft: Selbstverständnis, öffentliches Auftreten und populäre Erwartungen in der hohen Kaiserzeit*, Stuttgart.
Hardie, P. R. (1986) *Virgil's Aeneid: Cosmos and Imperium*, Oxford.
  (1995) 'The speech of Pythagoras in Ovid *Metamorphoses* 15: Empedoclean epos', *CQ* 45: 204–14.
Harrison, S. J. (2000) *Apuleius: A Latin Sophist*, Oxford.
Helm, R. (1955) 'Apuleius' Apologie, ein Meisterwerk der zweiten Sophistik', *Altertum* 1: 86–108.
Hill, T. D. (2004) *Ambitiosa mors: Suicide and Self in Roman Thought and Literature*, New York.
Hine, H. (2016) 'Philosophy and *philosophi*: from Cicero to Apuleius', in Williams and Volk 2016, 13–29.
Holford-Strevens, L. (2003) *Aulus Gellius: An Antonine Scholar and His Achievement*, rev. edn, Oxford.
Holford-Strevens, L. and A. Vardi, eds. (2004) *The Worlds of Aulus Gellius*, Oxford.

Howley, J. A. (2018) *Aulus Gellius and Roman Reading Culture: Text, Presence, and Imperial Knowledge in the Noctes Atticae*, Cambridge.
Hunink, V. (2005) *Tertullian: De pallio*, Amsterdam.
Inwood, B. (2005) *Reading Seneca: Stoic Philosophy at Rome*, Oxford.
Keith, A. (2018). 'Epicurean philosophical perspectives in (and on) [Vergil] *Catalepton* 5', in S. Frangoulidis and S. Harrison, eds., *Life, Love and Death in Latin Poetry: Studies in Honor of Theodore D. Papanghelis* (Berlin), 189–203.
Kennedy, D. F. (2002) *Rethinking Reality: Lucretius and the Textualization of Nature*, Ann Arbor, MI.
Kenney, E. J. (1970) 'Doctus Lucretius', *Mnemosyne* 23: 366–92. Reprinted in Gale 2007, 300–27.
Kent, B. (2001) 'Augustine's ethics', in E. Stump and N. Kretzmann, eds., *The Cambridge Companion to Augustine* (Cambridge), 205–33.
Ker, J. (2009) 'Seneca on self-examination: rereading *On Anger* 3.36', in Bartsch and Wray 2009, 160–87.
Keulen, W. (2004) 'Gellius, Apuleius, and satire on the intellectual', in Holford-Strevens and Vardi 2004, 223–45.
    (2009) *Gellius the Satirist: Roman Cultural Authority in Attic Nights*, Leiden.
Krenkel, W. A. (2002) *Marcus Terentius Varro: Saturae Menippeae*, 4 vols., St. Katharinen.
Kruschwitz, P. and M. Schumacher (2005) *Das vorklassische Lehrgedicht der Römer*, Heidelberg.
Kurczyk, S. (2006) *Cicero und die Inszenierung der eigenen Vergangenheit: Autobiographisches Schreiben in der späten Republik*, Cologne.
Lapidge, M. (1979) 'Lucan's imagery of cosmic dissolution', *Hermes* 107: 344–70.
Lefèvre, E. (1997) 'Senecas Atreus – die Negation des stoischen Weisen?', in B. Zimmermann, ed., *Griechisch-römische Komödie und Tragödie* II (Stuttgart), 119–34.
Leonhardt, J. (1995) 'Theorie und Praxis der *deliberatio* bei Cicero: Der Briefwechsel mit Atticus aus dem Jahre 49', *ACD* 31: 153–71.
Lévy, C. (2017) 'Lucilius et la fondation de la culture philosophique romaine', in Vesperini 2017, 183–209.
Littlewood, C. A. J. (2004) *Self-Representation and Illusion in Senecan Tragedy*, Oxford.
Long, A. A. (1995) 'Cicero's politics in *De officiis*', in A. Laks and M. Schofield, eds., *Justice and Generosity: Studies in Hellenistic Social and Political Philosophy* (Cambridge), 213–40.
Loupiac, A. (1998) *La poétique des éléments dans La Pharsale de Lucain*, Brussels.
McConnell, S. (2014) *Philosophical Life in Cicero's Letters*, Cambridge.
MacCormack, S. (2013) 'Cicero in late antiquity', in C. Steel, ed., *The Cambridge Companion to Cicero* (Cambridge), 251–305.
McDonnell, M. (2006) *Roman Manliness: Virtus and the Roman Republic*, Cambridge.
MacKendrick, P. (1989) *The Philosophical Books of Cicero*, London.

Mann, W.-R. (2016) '"You're playing you now": Helvidius Priscus as a Stoic hero', in Williams and Volk 2016, 213–37.
Marenbon, J. (2018) 'Why we need a real history of philosophy', in M. van Ackeren, ed., *Philosophy and the Historical Perspective* (Oxford), 36–50.
Maso, S. (2012) *Filosofia a Roma: dalla riflessione sui principi all'arte della vita*, Rome.
Maurach, G. (2006) *Geschichte der römischen Philosophie*, 3rd edn, Darmstadt.
Mayer, R. (2005) 'Sleeping with the enemy: satire and philosophy', in K. Freudenburg, ed., *The Cambridge Companion to Roman Satire* (Cambridge), 146–59.
Mendelson, M. (2018) 'Saint Augustine', in E. N. Zalta, ed., *The Stanford Encyclopedia of Philosophy*, https://plato.stanford.edu/archives/win2016/entries/augustine/.
Michel, A. (1977) 'Cicéron, Pompée et la guerre civile: rhétorique et philosophie dans la "Correspondance"', *AAntHung* 25: 393–403.
Morford, M. (2002) *The Roman Philosophers: From the Time of Cato the Censor to the Death of Marcus Aurelius*, London.
Müller, G. M. (2015) 'Transfer und Überbietung im Gespräch: Zur Konstruktion einer römischen Philosophie in den Dialogen Ciceros', *Gymnasium* 122: 275–301.
Müller, G. M. and F. Mariani Zini, eds. (2018) *Philosophie in Rom – Römische Philosophie? Kultur-, literatur- und philosophiegeschichtliche Perspektiven*, Berlin.
Newman, R. J. (1989) '*Cotidie meditari*: theory and practice of the *meditatio* in imperial Stoicism', *ANRW* II.36.3: 1473–517.
Nisbet, R. G. M. and M. Hubbard (1970) *A Commentary on Horace: Odes Book 1*, Oxford.
O'Donnell, J. J. (1980) 'Augustine's classical readings', *RecAug* 15: 144–75.
  (1992) *Augustine: Confessions*, 3 vols., Oxford.
Powell, J. G. F. (1990) 'Two notes on Catullus', *CQ* 40: 199–206.
  (2013) 'The embassy of the three philosophers in 155 BC', in C. Kremmydas and K. Tempest, eds., *Hellenistic Oratory: Continuity and Change* (Oxford), 219–47.
Puccini, G. (2017) *Apulée: roman et philosophie*, Paris.
Rabbow, P. (1954) *Antike Seelenführung: Methodik der Exerzitien in der Antike*, Munich.
Rauh, S. H. (2018) 'Cato at Utica: the emergence of a Roman suicide tradition', *AJPh* 139: 59–91.
Rawson, E. (1985) *Intellectual Life in the Late Roman Republic*, London.
Reinhardt, T. (2016) 'To see and to be seen: on vision and perception in Lucretius and Cicero', in Williams and Volk 2016, 63–90.
Relihan, J. C. (1993) *Ancient Menippean Satire*, Baltimore.
Reydams-Schils, G. (2005) *The Roman Stoics: Self, Responsibility, and Affection*, Chicago.
  (2011) 'Philosophy, Roman', *Oxford Bibliographies Online*.

Riess, W. (2008a) 'Apuleius *Socrates Africanus*? Apuleius' defensive play', in Riess 2008b, 51–73.
Riess, W. ed. (2008b) *Paideia at Play: Learning and Wit in Apuleius*, Groningen.
Rist, J. M. (1994) *Augustine: Ancient Thought Baptized*, Cambridge.
Rives, J. B. (2008) 'Legal strategy and learned display in Apuleius' *Apology*', in Riess 2008b, 17–49.
Rolle, A. (2017) *Dall'Oriente a Roma: Cibele, Iside e Serapide nell'opera di Varrone*, Pisa.
Rorty, R., J. B. Schneewind and Q. Skinner (1984) 'Introduction', in R. Rorty, J. B. Schneewind and Q. Skinner, eds., *Philosophy in History: Essays on the Historiography of Philosophy* (Cambridge), 1–14.
Rosenmeyer, T. G. (1989) *Senecan Drama and Stoic Cosmology*, Berkeley.
Roskam, G. (2007) *Live Unnoticed (Λάθε βιώσας): On the Vicissitudes of an Epicurean Doctrine*, Leiden.
Rutherford, R. B. (1989) *The Meditations of Marcus Aurelius: A Study*, Oxford.
Sandy, G. (1997) *The Greek World of Apuleius: Apuleius and the Second Sophistic*, Leiden.
Schafer, J. (2011) 'Seneca's *Epistulae morales* as dramatized education', *CPh* 106: 35–52.
Schindel, U. (2000) 'Apuleius – Africanus Socrates? Beobachtungen zu den Verteidigungsreden des Apuleius und des platonischen Sokrates', *Hermes* 128: 443–56.
Schmidt, P. L. (1978–9) 'Cicero's place in Roman philosophy: a study of his prefaces', *CJ* 74: 115–27.
Schmitz, C. (1993) *Die kosmische Dimension in den Tragödien Senecas*, Berlin.
Schofield, M. (2008) 'Ciceronian dialogue', in S. Goldhill, ed., *The End of Dialogue in Antiquity* (Cambridge), 63–84.
Scholz, U. W. (2003) 'Varros Menippeische Satiren', in A. Haltenhoff, A. Heil and F. H. Mutschler, eds., *O tempora o mores! Römische Werte und römische Literatur in den letzten Jahrzehnten der Republik* (Munich), 165–85.
Schrijvers, P. H. (1978) 'Le regard sur l'invisible: étude sur l'emploi de l'analogie dans l'œuvre de Lucrèce', in O. Gigon, ed., *Lucrèce* (Vandœuvres), 77–114. English version in Gale 2007, 255–88.
Sedley, D. (1998) *Lucretius and the Transformation of Greek Wisdom*, Cambridge.
  (2009) 'Epicureanism in the Roman Republic', in J. Warren, ed., *The Cambridge Companion to Epicureanism* (Cambridge), 29–45.
  (2010) 'Philosophy', in A. Barchiesi and W. Scheidel, eds., *The Oxford Handbook of Roman Studies* (New York), 701–12.
Sellars, J. (2012) 'The *Meditations* and the ancient art of living', in M. van Ackeren, ed., *A Companion to Marcus Aurelius* (Chichester), 453–64.
  (2017) 'What is philosophy as a way of life?', *Parrhesia* 28: 40–56.
Shanzer, D. (2012) 'Augustine and the Latin classics', in M. Vessey, ed., *A Companion to Augustine* (Chichester), 161–74.
Smith, J. E. H. (2016) *The Philosopher: A History in Six Types*, Princeton.
Star, C. (2006) 'Commanding *constantia* in Senecan tragedy', *TAPhA* 136: 207–44.

Strasburger, H. (1990) *Ciceros politisches Spätwerk als Aufruf gegen die Herrschaft Caesars*, Hildesheim.
Swain, S. (2001) 'Apuleius Sophista' (review of Harrison 2000), *CR* 51: 269–70.
　(2006) 'Bilingualism and biculturalism in Antonine Rome: Apuleius, Fronto, and Gellius', in Holford-Strevens and Vardi 2006, 3–40.
Thorsrud, H. (2009) *Ancient Scepticism*, Berkeley.
Trapp, M. B. (2007) *Philosophy in the Roman Empire: Ethics, Politics and Society*, Aldershot.
　(2017a) 'Philosophical authority in the imperial period', in J. König and G. Woolf, eds., *Authority and Expertise in Ancient Scientific Culture* (Cambridge), 27–57.
　(2017b) 'Visibly different? Looking at *philosophi* in the Roman imperial period', in Vesperini 2017, 353–69.
Uden, J. (2015) *The Invisible Satirist: Juvenal and Second-Century Rome*, Oxford.
　(2021) 'Egnatius the Epicurean: the banalization of philosophy in Catullus', *Antichthon* 55: 94–115.
Vesperini, P. (2012) *La philosophia et ses pratiques d'Ennius à Cicéron*, Rome.
Vesperini, P., ed. (2017) *Philosophari: usages romains des savoirs grecs sous la République et sous l'Empire*, Paris.
Volk, K. (2002) *The Poetics of Latin Didactic: Lucretius, Vergil, Ovid, Manilius*, Oxford.
　(2009) *Manilius and His Intellectual Background*, Oxford.
　(2011) 'Manilian self-contradiction', in S. J. Green and K. Volk, eds., *Forgotten Stars: Rediscovering Manilius' Astronomica* (Oxford), 104–19.
　(2016) 'Roman Pythagoras', in Williams and Volk 2016, 33–49.
　(2021) *The Roman Republic of Letters: Scholarship, Philosophy, and Politics in the Age of Cicero and Caesar*, Princeton.
Volk, K. and G. D. Williams, eds. (2022) *Philosophy in Ovid, Ovid as Philosopher*, New York.
Wassmann, H. (1996) *Ciceros Widerstand gegen Caesars Tyrannis: Untersuchungen zur politischen Bedeutung der philosophischen Spätschriften*, Bonn.
Whitmarsh, T. (2005) *The Second Sophistic*, Oxford.
Wiener, C. (2014) '"Stoic tragedy": a contradiction in terms?', in Garani and Konstan 2014, 187–217.
Williams, G. D. and K. Volk, eds. (2016) *Roman Reflections: Studies in Latin Philosophy*, New York.
Woolf, R. (2015) *Cicero: The Philosophy of a Roman Sceptic*, London.
Yona, S. (2018) *Epicurean Ethics in Horace: The Psychology of Satire*, Oxford.
Zanker, P. (1995) *Die Maske des Sokrates: Das Bild des Intellektuellen in der antiken Kunst*, Munich.
Zetzel, J. E. G. (2016) 'Philosophy is in the streets', in Williams and Volk 2016, 50–62.

CHAPTER 14

# *Political Thought*

Michèle Lowrie

... the Romans, perhaps the most political people we have known ...
Arendt, *The Human Condition*[1]

From the *translatio imperii* of the Holy Roman Empire, to the new republics of the Renaissance and Enlightenment, to post-modern reflections on empire, Latin texts and Roman history have provided many and various models for political organisation and its conceptualisation in the West.[2] The legacy of ancient Rome includes the names of governmental forms (republic, empire), institutions (senate, tribunate), basic political concepts (liberty, civil war, domination, security), and the apparatus of law. Rome has been good for thinking about politics even though only three texts written in classical Latin comfortably fit political theory as a genre: Cicero's *De re publica* and *De legibus*, and Seneca's *De clementia*.[3] Nearly all Latin literature, however, addresses immediately pressing issues and, more generally, social organisation and institutions, law and justice, conflict and its management through rhetoric or violence, citizenship and its internal and external antonyms, slavery and enmity, internal and external relations. Roman political thought stands out in recognising the

---

[1] Arendt 1958: 7.
[2] Marx 1960: 115–16: the French Revolutions of 1789 and 1814 dressed first in republican then imperial garb. The idea of *translatio imperii* is ancient: Cresci and Gazzano 2018. On Rome as a model, Skinner 1978, Millar 2002, Murphy 2007, Hammer 2008, Smil 2010, Straumann 2016, Armitage 2017a, Dufallo 2018, Roche and Demetriou 2018, Fertik and Hanses 2019. Rome continues to serve as a political model, for good or ill, e.g.: Arendt 1963: 141–214, analysing the American and French Revolutions against a Roman backdrop; Agamben 2005 on sovereignty and the state of exception; McCormick 2011: 171–88, a thought experiment on incorporating a Roman-style tribunate into the American constitution; Houellebecq 2015: Augustus is the analogue to Mohammad Ben Abbes, the Muslim Brotherhood leader elected to the French presidency in a dystopian future.
[3] Unfortunately lost are: C. Sempronius Tuditanus' *Libri magistratuum* (books on magistracies, Macrobius, *Saturnalia* 1.13.21; Gellius, *Noctes Atticae* 13.15.4) on constitutional law; Marcus Junius Congus Gracchanus' *De potestatibus* (on magisterial powers, Ulpian, *Dig.* 1.13.1); Papirius Fabianus' *Libri qui inscribuntur ciuilium* (books entitled 'of civil matters', Sen. *Ep.* 100.1), translated 'On Politics' by Graver and Long 2015: *ad loc.* For Varro, Nelsestuen 2015.

753

centrality of emotion and imagination to politics.[4] Its ironic self-awareness, particularly of the contradictions in Roman, and indeed all politics, anticipates modern and indeed post-modern approaches.[5] As our post-Enlightenment age discovers increasingly that reason offers a poor guide for understanding decision-making,[6] Latin literature has become a compelling vehicle for thinking about politics beyond Rome's importance as the source of many institutional forms and political concepts.

I stake out a double claim: that a central purpose of writing Latin literature, among others, was to convey ideas about politics to a Roman audience; that the forms and processes of thinking about politics are as distinctive of Roman political thought as any substantive content. Therefore, Roman political thought as a modern discipline must grapple as much with Latin, the Romans' medium of expression, as with distinctively Roman concepts, institutions or constitutional forms.[7]

## Some Questions of Method

The lack of an 'easily defined canon' and Latin literature's generic fluidity make a diverse set of works required reading.[8] Conversely, totalising political interpretations risk diluting the specificity of politics and raise questions about the robustness of what we mean by 'thinking'.[9] The extent to which our interests produce Roman political thought as a subfield is an unresolved issue. 'Political theory' already takes considerable pressure off the high demands to qualify as 'political philosophy'. 'Thought' further erodes the generic restriction.

According to Crick's outdated definition, 'Political thought is the immediate and the concrete; political theories are concepts as to how social and political order adheres, develops and decays; political philosophy is the most abstract expression and the most general – political philosophy must, indeed, be philosophy.' Deconstruction has eroded similar distinctions between literature and philosophy, but the pressures tend to come from literary studies – analytic philosophers and hard-core political theorists still

---

[4] Kaster 2005; Hammer 2008: 7 and 2014: 3–4; Atkins 2013.
[5] Rimell 2015: 1–27; Connolly 2015: 19–20.
[6] In economics, e.g. Thaler 1991. Brown 1972: Augustine is closer to us than is 'classical' political theory.
[7] I focus on literary form as political content, while Lavan's complementary essay in this volume expands beyond political content to address literature's social function.
[8] Connolly 2010: 714–15.
[9] Greek scholarship faces similar challenges, e.g. Euben 1986; Goldhill 1986: 57–137, 222–43, 1999 and 2012: 38–55; Winkler and Zeitlin 1990; Loraux 1993, 1995 and 2002; Goff 1995; Wohl 2010 and 2015.

resist. Besides the sovereignty industry in Shakespeare studies, much literary scholarship analyses political thought without a strong theoretical apparatus. In Classics, Anderson's 'imagined communities' has become a go-to model; Castoriadis' 'social imaginary' and John Pocock's political languages are also sometimes invoked.[10] Crick includes within political thought 'the ordinary opinions that people hold, their immediate demands, assumptions and conditioned reflections about day to day public affairs – often called "public opinion"'.[11] On this broad view, literature, inscriptions, graffiti, images and monuments become valuable sources for Roman views on politics. Any artefact is game for cultural analysis through the lens of 'New Historicism';[12] the same for political thought. Historians in fact dominate the scholarship on Roman institutions and politics, and old and new historicists alike cast a wide evidentiary net. Scholars working in Roman political thought additionally desire to classify ancient works as political thought and look for signs of authorial self-awareness, such as abstraction or signs of contemplation, to legitimate the rubric as an ancient preoccupation, at least a mode, if not a full literary kind or genre.[13] I prefer a big tent that captures unexamined ideologies besides analysis and active deliberation, that highlights how forms of expression condition what is said, and that takes into account how explicitly political thinking unfolds.

The boundary is broad between Roman thinking about politics as a pervasive, even obsessive, cultural activity and the production of reified thought in the form of abstract principles or concepts.[14] Even without the category 'political thought', the Romans define or at least describe their institutions, customs and systems. Highly attuned to language's mediating properties and to how bodies make attachments and abstractions visible, they additionally ponder their own means of thinking.[15] Since their approach often tilts away from conceptual abstraction, toward embodied expression and the rhetorical manipulation of emotion, understanding what and how they thought their politics requires examining practices of

---

[10] Castoriadis 1975; Anderson 1983; Pocock 1981, 1987, 1989 and 2008.
[11] Crick 1967: 49. See also Griffin 1996; White 2002; Pocock 2008; Atkins 2013: 12 n. 26 summarises Nichols 1979: 129 as differentiating between 'the examination of philosophical principles, the analysis of particular societies, and prescriptions for immediate action as three different levels of political thought'.
[12] Payne 2005; critique in Goff 1995: 6–10.
[13] Fowler 1982 distinguishes between kinds, genres and modes.
[14] For specifically Roman approaches to philosophy, Müller and Zini 2018. Volk, in this volume, outlines the fall from prominence of Roman philosophy in the twentieth century, caused in part by its less argumentative mode, and points to its current revival, given the openness within some branches of philosophy to broader discursive modalities.
[15] Dressler 2016.

expression as well as substance. A cliché holds that 'explicit theorizing was not a Roman characteristic'.[16] This stands in the way of appreciating how much their political thought plays out indirectly through form and style. The medium both is and has a message.[17]

Despite Rome's influence on Western culture and thought, an unfortunate bifurcation between political theory and literary studies has arisen. For much of the twentieth century, Latin texts fell out of the political-theoretical canon, as well as many college curricula in the English-speaking world, in favour of Greek.[18] The Cambridge School's revival of republicanism as a theoretical field for analytic and normative political theory has reanimated the Roman tradition.[19] Beyond interest in a Roman constitutional form, their contextualist method accords well with the embeddedness of Roman thinking about politics. Furthermore, their methods of tracing actual influence share affinities with Latin philology.[20] Currently, a new appreciation for rhetoric and for the strong role of emotion in embodied and embedded practices has motivated broader nascent interest in Roman political thought.[21] Concomitantly, readings of Latin literature influenced by the so-called political turn in literary studies have proliferated.[22] But political theorists do not typically master Latin literature and Latinists typically lack formal training in political theory.

The disciplinary challenge is to enable communication between these fields. Both could benefit from connecting political questions about practices, norms and institutions to literary and historical analysis of the vast commentary in Latin on the actual and ideal organisation of human life and the obstacles to success. Such connections face hurdles of substance and method. Normative political theory has focused recently on republicanism, but does not usually look to Rome as a model for imperialism – despite the Roman Republic's demise and the Empire's longevity, despite the challenges to pluralism that the Empire shares with contemporary federalism and globalisation. Shared questions include: who deserves

---

[16] Wiedemann 2000: 517. For literature, not dogmatic statements, as a locus for thinking about religion, Feeney 1998 and 2004. On literature's indirect memory of history, Gowing 2013. The relationship between theory and history may also go the other way. Momigliano 1990: 129: modern political theory reproduces the Tacitean despot when direct analysis of contemporary situations was dangerous.

[17] Batstone 1991; Quint 1993; Henderson 1998; Damon 1999; Kraus 1999; Lowrie 2013; Batstone and Damon 2006: 33–84; Connolly 2015: 82–92.

[18] Hammer 2008: 13–37.

[19] Pocock 1975; Skinner 1978; Pettit 1997; Viroli 2002. Overview and critique: Ando 2011: 81–114; Connolly 2015: 9–18; Straumann 2016: 1–21.

[20] Method in Skinner 1969; Pocock 1981, 1987 and 1989; updated in Bevir 2011.

[21] Lucretius, Cicero and Seneca inform Nussbaum 2018.    [22] Habinek 1998; Oliensis 1998.

citizenship; how much tolerance the centre should show local customs of law, governance and religion; how to contain violence. The fall of nineteenth-century style imperialism has spawned an unexamined assumption – manifest in popular culture, with George Lucas' *Star Wars* as a prime example – that republics are unequivocally good and empires bad.[23] While theorists rightly look for models to bolster currently preferred political forms, a pressing question today might well be how to build a more humane empire.[24]

As Livy says (see p. 785), history teaches what to avoid as well as what to imitate. Much of Latin literature says less about success than about failure. Sallust attributes the republic's failure to the pressures of empire. Virgil grounds Rome's foundation in internal conflict. Cicero, Seneca and Pliny demonstrate how to manage potential tyrants through tactful speech. Literature reveals complexity – paradoxes, contradictions, conflict – beyond explicit theorising. Because it speaks concretely, through examples and metaphors, symbols and embodied figures, literature puts the conflict within systems on display.

Theorists, historians and literary scholars speak in different idioms. A range of styles maps fault lines in each field. Those committed to rigorous argumentation often fail to appreciate evocative analyses that better capture intangibles like tone.[25] Defining the task of research exclusively as the reconstruction of the genealogy of institutions or of abstract thought about them, or as the thorough explication of Latin texts, precludes alternative approaches. Particularly prone to misunderstanding are attempts to mine a wide variety of thinkers to construct new normative theories.[26] If politics concerns feeling as much as structures, then texts' aesthetic qualities must remain on the table. Scholarship focused on such qualities often communicates in non-traditional ways.

---

[23] Murphy 2007 unusually compares the United States of America to the Roman Empire instead of the Republic.
[24] Hardt and Negri 2000.
[25] Johnson 1976: Virgilian pathos is no mere mood, but comments on the potential for knowledge and action.
[26] Straumann's 2010 methodological investment in narratives of historical filiation makes Hammer's (2008) eclectic dialogue between ancients and moderns unintelligible to him. Taking the Romans' expressed regard for reason at their word, he undervalues the political power of attachment elucidated by Hammer. For more generous assessment and critique, Connolly 2015: 76–9. Similarly, Wiseman 2015 criticises Connolly 2015 on philological grounds, but her project does not aim for a complete account of Roman thinkers' views on, e.g., the capacity to resist as essential to non-domination (Chapter 1). She analyses representative passages toward a new republicanism that respects the power of aesthetic judgement beyond reason.

In a volume asking what Latin texts we read, how we read them and why, this essay surveys the intersection of political-theoretical and literary approaches. Because political theorists will need to expand their range to rhetoric and poetry and Latinists will better grasp the political weight of familiar texts, my analysis focuses largely on illustrative readings of canonical works from Ennius to Tacitus. The few gestures I make beyond – to Greek, to images, to inscriptions and traditions with classical Rome in view, especially Augustine and Machiavelli – point to rich opportunities for further exploration. I aim to outline a method for multidirectional viewing, for looking through literary and political-theoretical lenses at the same time. A focus on institutions or on tone would require different methods. Method in turn affects why we read what when and which aspects surface at different times. By grappling with the obstacles to appreciating Roman political thought, I hope to articulate a roadmap for reading Latin literature politically across a variety of forms and genres. Many works in Latin address political substance, for example the Romans' conception of liberty or constitutionalism, and I cite them, but the field's current burgeoning makes this a good moment to probe *how* the Romans thought about politics in their own language in addition to *what* their ideas were. The persistence of Roman analogies in the public sphere (comparisons between decadent emperors and political leaders) and the prevalence of Roman concepts and metaphors (civil war, security) make Rome still good to think with.

## Sources Standard and Less Usual

Beyond the properly political-theoretical works of Cicero and Seneca, scholarship on Roman political thought traditionally focuses on historians. Sallust and Tacitus are taken seriously as thinkers and Livy's reputation has recently been rising.[27] Speeches and letters by Cicero, Seneca, Pliny and Trajan attest to Roman attitudes and practices and also transmit and query active ideologies. Some of these texts are closely bound to their moment of composition, but others were heavily revised.[28] Cicero's letters fall to the more spontaneous and Pliny's *Panegyricus* the more edited end of

---

[27] Generally, Connolly 2009b; Feldherr 2009; Kapust 2011a. Sallust and Tacitus: Earl 1961; Gajda 2010; Kapust 2011b; Hammer 2014: 145–79, 321–57. Livy: Jaeger 1997; Feldherr 1998; Chaplin 2000; Lowrie 2010a, 2010b and 2013; Hammer 2014: 229–70; Vasaly 2015. Political thought has no chapter per se in Chaplin and Kraus 2009 or Mineo 2015, but comes under history's guise.

[28] Fronto's letters to Marcus Aurelius have little political interest. However, the emperor gives credit to his teachings on the vices of power (*Meditations* 1.11).

the spectrum. Highly polished works are not necessarily more perspicacious than impromptu communications, but curated production guarantees the author stands by the result.[29]

Roman political and cultural structures have themselves been influential as historical models. Much of our knowledge of Roman history depends on writings in Greek. Polybius supplies the basic framework for the mixed Republican constitution and Appian, Cassius Dio and others tell the standard narratives with greater or lesser deviation.[30] While these Greek authors were to differing degrees Roman,[31] this volume's focus on Latin precludes extensive treatment. I similarly exclude the historical or philosophical writings of Roman aristocrats in Greek, but merely note here signal instances at the beginning and end of the tradition. Fabius Pictor's history (late third century BCE), the first history written by a Roman, organises time annalistically and attests to the early assumption that Aeneas' arrival in Latium marked Rome's origin.[32] Marcus Aurelius' *Meditations* (121–180 CE) is a rare work of enduring influence by an active emperor.[33]

Inscriptions offer excellent para-literary sources for opinions about politics and basic conceptualisations.[34] Although many are formulaic and show little individual rumination, most weigh their words carefully. Those officially sanctioned by powerful authors or institutions can initiate change in standardised discourses. Mapping subtle shifts in political languages – from Republic to Empire, and from early to later Empire – requires attention to sometimes minute detail.[35] For this, training in literary techniques of close reading is an advantage. Although published only six years apart, stylistic differences between Augustus' *Res gestae* ('Accomplishments', 14 CE)[36] and the *Senatus consultum de Cn. Pisone patre* ('Decree of the senate on Gnaeus Piso, father', 20 CE)[37] correspond to evolving ideas about legitimacy. Augustus' celebration of his career conveys his position outside republican norms while respecting the very norms he oversteps. Even a *de facto* monarch whose actual power rested on extraordinary grants (as triumvir; tribunician power) found it expedient to

---

[29] Levene 2004; Gurd 2012.
[30] For Greek political thought as 'ideas in context', Cartledge 2009. For differences between Polybius' and Cicero's understandings of the mixed constitution, Atkins 2013: 85–119; 2018: 11–36. For Dio and Appian: Lange and Madsen 2016; Welch 2015.
[31] Goldhill in this volume.   [32] Rich 2017: 39–48.
[33] Reydams-Schils 2012; Hammer 2014: 358–81; Volk in this volume.
[34] Lavan in this volume calls for literary scholars to devote more attention to this corpus.
[35] Mebane 2017 is exemplary for method.   [36] Cooley 2009.
[37] Potter, Damon and Takács 1999.

hand – or to appear to hand – the administration of public affairs (*res publica*) back to the *senatus populusque Romanus* (*Res gestae* 34.1) after quelling civil war.[38] His claim to preside through personal authority rather than magisterial power respects the republican vocabulary of power while still wielding absolute control.[39] His insistence that his power over 'all things' came through the 'consensus of everyone' (*consensu uniuersorum potens rerum omnium*, 34.1) finds a correlate in the Piso inscription. Tiberius had requested an enquiry into Piso's treachery, alleged by Germanicus on his deathbed. The senate confirms Tiberius' response to and handling of the affair, in which Piso committed suicide, by praising the emperor and the various orders in terms of consensus in its etymological sense: the emperor, the equestrians and the plebs all *felt* the same way, within codes of decorum differing by status.[40] The senatorial inscription converts Augustus' bare formulation into a contemporary political idiom that emphasises the shared feeling always implied by *consensus*. The list of congruent reactions enacts the concept. That consensus concerns feeling and not just agreement accords with contemporary political language. Witness Velleius' insistence on the people's emotions when Augustus' succession was assured by his adoption of Tiberius (2.103) and at the actual moment of transition (2.124). The message may be the same, but the tone has become more emotive.

Besides providing evidence for social history, inscriptions commissioned by less powerful authors reveal ordinary presumptions about political order and how best to describe it. Much of the language used, however, appears flat without comparison to polished literary sources. Consider the inscription honouring Augustus, dedicated by a Spanish province in his Forum at Rome (2 BCE): *Imp. Caesari Augusto p. p. Hispania ulterior Baetica, quod beneficio eius et perpetua cura prouincia pacata est* ('Further Spain Baetica to the emperor Caesar Augustus, Father of the Fatherland, because by his benefit and unending care the province was made peaceful', *CIL* VI 31267 = *ILS* 103). Southern Spain, which submitted to Rome in 206 BCE and had subsequently undergone some Romanisation, largely escaped the first-century BCE civil war battles, although the northern part of the peninsula was a theatre of war. The Spanish provinces were reorganised under Augustus around 16–13 BCE. The inscription's encomiastic use of *cura* (care) accords with Augustan-age conceptions of the leader and his

---

[38] Lange 2019.
[39] Galinsky 2015 reviews the debate about Augustus' authority and his avowed restoration of the Republic.
[40] Potter 1999: 75.

delegates as caretakers (e.g. Virgil, *Georgics* 1.25–6; Horace, *Odes* 3.26).[41] Similarly, it expresses pacification not in the republican sense of terms imposed on the conquered, but in a new Augustan idiom. Hannah Cornwell shows that *pax* becomes generalised after the civil wars and comes to mean pervasive social stability.[42] The province gives thanks for the 'definitive delimitations of provincial boundaries' a decade before, but the language also suggests gratitude for 'the first extended period of peace and stability that Ulterior, and later Baetica, had enjoyed since the 50s B.C.'.[43] Conceptual history, better traced through literature, provides nuance to the inscription. It in turn provides evidence that the new conceptualisation of peace, which arose in the centre, spread abroad.

Some media convey political ideas even without Latin or indeed any language. Images can lend concepts visual form and convey their tone. The ranks of senators and priests on the Ara Pacis Augustae display the sociopolitical hierarchies upholding the Augustan peace. With its processions and foundational images, the altar, which was commissioned by the senate when Augustus returned from Gaul and Spain in 13 BCE, speaks in the same idiom as the *Aeneid*, particularly Anchises' parade of heroes in Book 6. The prosperity conveyed by the so-called Tellus relief (Figure 14.1) shares many elements with Horace, *Odes* 4.5 (peaceful cows and wheat-fields; seas pacified; babies born).[44] The registers of style and conventions used in such images, which are specific to their times,[45] participate non-verbally in contemporary political thought. Knowing that *pax* (peace) became a word for internal stability under Augustus supports the interpretation of the altar as addressing civil war's cessation – otherwise we might expect images of battles and subjected foreigners.[46] Similarly, the conceptual history of *securitas*, which comes to have a political meaning during this time, informs the tiny snake, intent on devouring chicks in their nest (Figure 14.2). Their abandonment and one's desperate, perhaps futile, attempt to escape in the acanthus frieze, is redolent of Virgilian pathos.[47] Latin *securitas* means a condition apart (*se-*) from worry (*cura*) and comes to apply to the Roman Empire (first at Velleius Paterculus 2.103.4–5). Just as worry lies encoded in the etymology of *securitas*, the small-scale threat cues

---

[41] For *cura*, Lowrie forthcoming.
[42] Cornwell 2017. Nicolet 1991: 43 sees Augustus' declarations of the pacification of Spain and Gaul among others as expressing at least 'indirect universal domination'.
[43] Haley 2003: 33–6. Laurence, Cleary and Sears 2011: 88 interpret *pacata* here as 'the peacefulness of their province' under Augustus' guidance.
[44] Zanker 1988: 172–6, 158–62; new identifications of mythic figures in Flower 2017: 323–5.
[45] Squire and Elsner in this volume.   [46] Cornwell 2017: 155–86.   [47] Johnson 1976.

Figure 14.1 'Tellus relief', Ara Pacis. With credit to Craig Jack Photographic/Alamy Stock Photo.

Figure 14.2 'Acanthus frieze', Ara Pacis: detail. Photo: Ralph Liebermann.

## 14 Political Thought

viewers to the logic of the *Pax Augusta*. The large-scale prosperity depicted on the Tellus relief dominates and reduces the snake's threat to a visual and conceptual footnote.[48] The reminder of anxiety overcome produces an icon of the Augustan Peace: not absolute tranquillity, but the cessation of internal discord. It would be impossible to appreciate the historical specificity of the altar's representation of peace without contemporary literature.

My examples mostly illustrate a single ideological node: the Augustan settlement. The hurdles to assembling evidence for any particular political idea in records of stone or bronze, however, are substantial. Access to the non-text-based building blocks of Roman history requires technical specialist expertise lacking among political theorists and literary scholars. Those of us who try to analyse material culture must rely on the scholarship of others.[49] The collaborative work needed to overcome non-specialist fears remains rare in the Anglo-American world; it is more typical in France and Germany, where funding structures encourage research groups.[50]

The formulaic language and visual codes of inscriptions and images, however, convey contemporary political thinking more economically than literature's cornucopia of stories, speeches and descriptions, which pose their own methodological challenges. They skirt argumentative forms of expression; verbal overabundance crowds out the clear articulation of distinct ideas; literature's interpretative openness is problematic for political theorists, as for historians.[51] Literature in verse has, of course, always been mined as a source for history and *mentalité*. For instance, Ennius' epigrammatic line, *moribus antiquis res stat Romana uirisque* ('the Roman state stands on ancient customs and men', *Annales* 156 Skutsch), is often cited for the centrality of *exempla* to Roman culture.[52] However, unlike the historians, the poets rarely receive attention as active contributors to political thought. The chapters on Latin authors in *The Cambridge History of Greek and Roman Political Thought* cover Cicero, Seneca and Pliny.[53] Additionally, Thomas Wiedemann addresses 'Reflections of Roman political thought in Latin historical writing'. He defines his task as 'isolating' political thought from history, narrative and rhetoric, and identifying what is properly Roman over against Greek.[54] The volume laudably extends its reach beyond political philosophy narrowly construed, even without treating any poets. Since then, the field has continued to broaden. Lucretius and

---

[48] Lowrie forthcoming.  [49] E.g. Thomas 2001: 73–4; Lowrie 2009: 279–326 on the Ara Pacis.
[50] The Centre national de la recherche scientifique and the Deutsche Forschungsgemeinschaft privilege collaboration, as does the European Research Council. See Fuhrer in this volume.
[51] Richlin 2017: 28–9: social historians of slavery do not know 'what to do with literature'.
[52] Wallace-Hadrill 2008: 229–30.  [53] Rowe and Schofield 2000.  [54] Wiedemann 2000: 517.

Virgil earn whole chapters in Dean Hammer's *Roman Political Thought*, organised around holistic treatment of authors. Jed Atkins' survey, based on topics, cites these and several other poets in his book of the same name. More unusually, Joy Connolly devotes a chapter to Horace's *Satires* in *The Life of Roman Republicanism*.[55] These exceptions bode well for a more expansive scope. The difference in Hammer's and Atkins' organising principles responds to productive tensions within conceptual history. Can reified ideas about topics be sifted out from the broader – and messier – contexts of individual authors' contributions and their thick articulation in aesthetic media?

Some literary studies explicitly embrace political thought,[56] but much scholarship on poetry does so implicitly. Latin literature is obsessed with generals, statesmen and emperors,[57] and perceptions of a realignment in power upon the republic's collapse. The Augustan poets' attitudes toward Augustus or where Lucan stands on empire, on Nero, therefore arise organically as topics.[58] Having opinions about particular political issues, however, somehow does not make a poet a political thinker. Political thought should be, well, more systematic. But if much thinking about politics in prose takes place through embedded story-telling, instead of explicit argumentation about principles and institutions, it becomes hard then to exclude poetry. It is not just the medium of expression, however, that excludes poets from seriousness. Modernity's expansion of political questions to include the disenfranchised makes much of ancient literature, written by elites, uninformative or, worse, obfuscatory. I limit my analysis here to political thought in the Latin textual record. Myles Lavan, in this volume, outlines ways literary scholars may shift perspectives to capture the interest of social historians.

It is one thing to treat Virgil, Horace, Lucan and Ovid seriously as political thinkers equal to Cicero and Tacitus when they address or describe statesmen,[59] outline the origins of or otherwise comment on institutions,[60] or show how Rome's foundation inscribes civil war into

---

[55] Hammer 2014: 93–144, 180–228; Connolly 2015: 115–54; Atkins 2018.
[56] Adler 2003; Vasaly 2015.　[57] Vout 2009.
[58] E.g. Ahl 1976; Lyne 1995; Thomas 2001: 25–54; Lowrie 2007c; Quint 2018.
[59] E.g. the *Aeneid*'s first simile comparing Neptune calming the waters to a statesman soothing a turbulent crowd, Feeney 2014: 209–21; Beck 2014; Horace's addresses to Augustus in the Roman Odes (*Odes* 3.1–6) or *Epist.* 2.1: Barchiesi 2001: 79–103; Feeney 2002; Lowrie 1997: 224–65; and 2009: 235–50; Ovid: Barchiesi 1997; Lowrie 2009: 259–75, 360–82; McGowan 2009.
[60] E.g. the aetiology of the *Ara maxima*, Virgil, *Aen.* 8.268–72; Ovid's comparison of the gods' ascent of Olympus to the senate ascending the Palatine hill, *Met.* 1.168–76.

its small-c constitution.⁶¹ It is quite another to approach poetry that proclaims an a- or anti-political orientation, as in Latin elegy at its most erotic. Reading what the elegists do *not* say requires reconstructing possible expectations under different circumstances. This is comparable to noticing the absence of conquered peoples on the Ara Pacis.⁶² No Augustan elegist taunts any political figure as Catullus does Cicero (poem 49) and Caesar (poems 57, 93), unless we read Ovid's *Tristia* 2, begging Augustus for recall from exile, as showcasing the emperor's arbitrary application of the rule of law.⁶³ Ovid no longer had anything to lose. Silences are readable as an index of a perceived danger to freedom of speech under the new Caesar. Elites, who felt disenfranchised, spoke coded language for those who chose to hear.⁶⁴ Poets used the *recusatio* to say something without saying it: Virgil, or Horace, or Ovid stages Apollo, Amor or some other god prohibiting him from singing of *reges et proelia* ('kings and battles', *Ecl.* 6.3) to signal generic allegiance.⁶⁵ They do not merely sidestep fraught issues, but flag their choice of small genres so as not to address Augustus' battles, many of which were fought against citizens. The metaphorical register of the *militia amoris* ('military service to love') similarly codes the life of love in terms defined by what it refuses, or what it intimates has been foreclosed to elites shut out of meaningful participation in running the state after the republic's demise.⁶⁶ A theoretical touchstone for reading the politics of lyric, and by extension other small genres devoted to love and quotidian affairs, is Adorno's essay, 'On lyric poetry and society' (1991): the more modern lyric dwells on privacy in bourgeois life, the more political a statement it makes *ex negativo*. By analogy, the emasculated stance of the Roman elegist loudly protests the loss of a political sphere.

Speaking by allegedly not speaking is nevertheless speech. However much elite voices lament lost power, all literature starts from the Roman presumption of speech's potency. To recover actual, as opposed to speaking, silences requires transgressing literature's bounds to social history. Although politics extends beyond representation, some minimal form of expression is necessary for political thought.

---

[61] Hardie 1993; James 1995.  [62] Goldhill in this volume makes much of telling silences.
[63] Lowrie 2009: 360–82.
[64] On analogous strategies in slave discourse, Richlin 2017: 311–50. Lavan in this volume stresses their actual hold on social and economic power.
[65] Also, e.g. *laudes egregii Caesaris* ('praise of outstanding Caesar', Horace, *Odes* 1.6.11), *arma ... uiolentaque bella* ('arms and violent battles', Ov. *Am.* 1.1.1). Freudenburg 2014 tracks parallels with the emperor's conventional refusal of proffered honours.
[66] Dufallo 2007: 76.

## Practices of Thinking

The Romans' famed pragmatism extends to thinking. The spiritual exercises of Hellenistic schools of philosophy, which thrived during the Empire, typically aimed to enable the blessed life, not to advance abstraction in itself.[67] Under the republic, Cicero defended abstract thought against Roman suspicions about philosophising on the grounds of its utility for public affairs. He gives logical and temporal priority in the *De re publica* to actual over theoretical states (1.2) and valorises statesmen (including himself) over philosophers as a source of knowledge about politics (1.10–13). His Scipio declares the superiority of historical Rome (1.70) and his intention to sketch out its real rather than Plato's ideal constitution (2.3).[68] Cicero's rhetorical salvo instantiates the practical Roman approach to thinking, particularly about politics.

Cicero's shift, from thought experiments toward the actual, is paradigmatic for Roman choices of topic. Moreover, Roman speech modes regardless of genre often embed their thinking about politics in contexts directed toward pragmatic ends. Oratory records assumptions about legitimacy and process by the way, while speakers argue particular cases or debate the proper course of action. Rhetoric systematises techniques of persuasion, always a pragmatic issue, whether in court or the senate house. History subordinates learning to public service: Cicero highlights history's exemplary function in calling it 'the schoolmistress of life' (*historia ... magistra uitae*, *De oratore* 2.36). Without his youthful passion for literature, Cicero claims, he never would have risked his own safety for the sake of public wellbeing – images of glory preserved in letters inspire him while administering affairs of state (*Pro Archia* 14). Telling the national myths in history, epic and other genres unifies an educated populace around an 'imagined community' (Anderson 1983). These address central questions of national character, shared values, institutions, constitutional forms and conflict resolution. The embedded nature of much Roman political thinking means that political theorists cannot simply pick up texts that distil concepts into rational arguments. They must wade through the stuff of living and of politics mediated through Latin.[69] Accessing Roman political

---

[67] Hadot 1995; Baraz 2012. On the Romans' love/hate for philosophy generally, see Volk in this volume.
[68] Atkins 2013: 5–6.
[69] Hammer 2014: 7: 'To the contemporary political theorist steeped in abstraction, Roman political thought seems mired in a hopelessly complex array of names, places, laws, and events. But in this complexity we can locate the conceptual core of Roman political thought.'

thought requires reading a plethora of texts whose primary subject matter and aims lie far from theoretical concerns.

The very messiness of embedded thinking makes it attractive as a model of engagement. Admittedly, elites – equestrian or aristocratic – wrote most of extant Latin literature. Even relatively impoverished writers received public support through festivals or private patronage. But the scribbling classes at Rome did not consist of intellectuals in an ivory tower. Many had experience in the military, statecraft and administration. Caesar, Cicero and Seneca held high positions; Tacitus and Pliny were prominent in the Senate; Sallust's career notoriously fell prone to the vices he excoriates. Some poets also brushed close to power, even if most shied away due to collapsing opportunity or personal inclination. Horace reveals he turned to poetry from a need to make money after serving as a military tribune on the losing side at Philippi (*Epist.* 2.2.51–2). His, Propertius' and Ovid's education prepared them for public careers. Their comments on the joy or regret each felt on declining or being excluded from public life indicate how much statecraft remained the default ambition.[70] Dean Hammer characterises Roman thinking about politics as 'practices of thinking' (2014: 5). He means that they performed a variety of modalities of thought, that their principles arose out of experience, but also that they practised 'applied thought'. Cicero's *De re publica* reads like the first inklings of political science – not theory – because of its orientation toward actuality.

Cicero's argument for granting Pompey an exceptional command against Mithridates in his speech *De imperio Cn. Pompei* shows how abstract principles bubble up inductively within deliberation on a particular problem. The tax collectors have been thwarted and Cicero recalls a prior instance of credit's collapse due to financial losses in Asia. He infers: 'For many in one state cannot lose property and fortunes without dragging more with them into the same calamity' (*non enim possunt una in ciuitate multi rem et fortunas amittere, ut non plures secum in eandem trahant calamitatem*, 19). We Romans, 'having learned from prior experience, should therefore hold it in memory' (*docti memoria retinere debemus*). Cicero does not argue abstractly for the economic interconnection of metropolis and empire, but uses a concrete, recent example, where Rome stands for metropolis and Asia for empire, to make a gnomic statement about finance. The link between metropolis and empire emerges from the consequences on the *plures* of what happens to the *multi*. He expands his statement of interconnection by piling up linked elements to argue for the

---

[70] Lowrie 2011.

war's importance, 'in which the glory of your name, the safety of the allies, the greatest revenues and the fortunes of many citizens are defended together with the republic' (*in quo gloria nominis uestri, salus sociorum, uectigalia maxima, fortunae plurimorum ciuium coniunctae cum re publica defendantur*). The criteria for going to war all join in a participle (*coniunctae*) expressing their link to the republic as common*wealth* – the *res* in *res publica* highlights financial concerns. The concept of linkage lurks in the participle instead of emerging clearly as an abstract noun. Experience produces the principle and the point of articulating it is to persuade the people of the necessity for action. Memory archives the gnomic statement for future retrieval. Pragmatism frames the argument throughout.

More overt political theorising likewise tends toward dynamic engagement with actual problems. The point is less to hand down principles than to guide readers toward producing them. Latin literature employs a variety of techniques that veil authorial and therefore authoritative interpretation in favour of establishing a puzzle. Cicero uses dialogue form in *De re publica* and *De legibus*, as well as many of his other rhetorical and philosophical works. In the preface to *De natura deorum*, he resists those curious to know what he thinks: people stop applying their own judgement (*iudicium*) and deem settled what an approved teacher has judged. We must work hard to reach our own judgement. Although Marcus often voices Cicero in his dialogues, he is not the only character representing the author's views and 'the dramatic action of the dialogue' provides a rich context from which his opinions emerge with greater complexity than they could from a single voice.[71] Discovering surrogates when the author does not participate in discussion is tempting, but fraught – witness the sense that Maternus speaks for Tacitus 'up to a point' in the *Dialogus de oratoribus*.[72]

The challenges shift when an adviser speaks directly to an addressee. The reader overhears an exchange conditioned by both roles, as when Seneca instructs Lucilius in Stoicism (*Epistulae morales*) or Nero in good governance (*De clementia*). Early in the letters, the teacher recommends several Epicurean precepts as first steps toward his own more demanding philosophy and expects his advancing tutee to outgrow them. A treatise would cut to the chase. The necessity of speaking tactfully to an emperor plants a hermeneutic thicket around Seneca's real assessment of Nero's character. The young ruler, pressed to sign convicted criminals' death warrants, expostulates he wished he had not learned to write (*Clem.* 2.2).

---

[71] Atkins 2013: 15 n. 7; 14–46.   [72] Mayer 2001: 47.

Seneca's lavish praise gives pause: if he trusted Nero's inclinations, why expatiate at length about clemency? Whether discussion is represented in dialogue or enacted through address, any discursive interaction situates the analysis of substance within a social exchange. Power and status are negotiated alongside the search for truth. The performance of niceties or of dispute between speakers and listeners models power relations in themselves beyond any precepts taught. Even in genres, like history, where the exchange between narrator and reader resides deep under the textual surface, authors rarely spell out the moral of the story. Readers must actively engage to disentangle contradictions and ambivalences. If Roman political thought amounts to any kind of system, it trains citizens in the processes of thinking within the social parameters available for exercising speech or action.

## Thinking about Talking

No politics exists without persuasion, no speech without style. The Romans compensate for their paucity of political theory by talking a lot about rhetoric. Republican freedom depended on deliberative oratory and they linked its decline to autocracy.[73] Effective speech is a means to achieving policy ends, but it performs other functions central to politics at Rome: it discloses the speaker as an agent and creates consensus, assent if not unanimity. Hannah Arendt speaks from a strong classical formation when she defines action less as getting things done than as the public revelation of self.[74] Speech is the medium of community: it forges a bond between leader and people through reasoned persuasion, but also through the speaker's embodiment of shared values and their symbolic display.[75] Republican restrictions on the right to speak made speaking a political act. Distortions of proper speech – lying and flattery – undermine freedom by putting relations of trust on a false basis.[76]

If speech reveals, it also masks. Romans of all philosophical stripes view speech as an authentic indication of the speaker's self: *talis oratio qualis uita* ('speech is such as the speaker's life').[77] The Elder Cato articulated this

---

[73] Kapust 2011a: 1–5: Cicero's identification of eloquence as the resource of a leader of a *bene moratae et bene constitutae ciuitatis* ('well-mannered and well-founded state', *Brutus* 7) contrasts with Maternus' downgrading of freedom of speech to rhetorical licence in Tacitus' *Dialogus* (40.2).
[74] Arendt 1958: 179.   [75] Connolly 2007.   [76] Kapust 2018a.
[77] The tag derives from Seneca's translation of a Greek maxim (*talis hominibus fuit oratio qualis uita*, 'people's speech matched their life', *Ep.* 114.1), but was already an important principle for Cicero: Möller 2004; Dugan 2005, with specific parallels at 2, 130 n. 196, 269.

assumption: *Orator est, Marce fili, uir bonus dicendi peritus. Rem tene, uerba sequentur* ('The orator is a good man, Marcus my son, one skilled in speaking. Keep to the topic, the words will follow', *De rhetorica* fr. 18–19 Cugusi). His definition and advice sum up Roman distrust of rhetoric's artifice and privilege morality over sheer skill.[78] Philosophers since Plato hate rhetoric for the same reason that Roman political thought fell out of the canon: style obscures argument; people make decisions based on emotion, not reason. Social historians also hate rhetoric because it privileges elite education: the cult of the genius speaker supports the great man theory of history. Verbal manipulation is a power play that naturalises, and thereby obscures, the power relations they would view clearly.[79] By insisting on the interconnection of subject (*res*) and a speaker's words (*uerba*) (*De oratore* 3.19), Cicero places the orator's irreducible individuality and therefore contingency at the centre of republican politics.[80]

The rhetorical turn in political theory resists the desire for rational argumentation bereft of style as a fiction imagined by Kant and Habermas and values persuasion's transformative power: rhetoric creates trust among the disappointed beyond mere inclusion in decision-making processes; by embodying shared values, the orator reaffirms the fabric of community.[81] His (at Rome always his) display of self-mastery – in judgement, virtue, bodily control – justifies his personal pre-eminence not for his sake, but everyone's. The terrain of political contestation between elite free men that characterised the republic depended on the impossibility of separating customs from the men who enacted them. Ennius' hendiadys – 'ancient customs and men' – well captures a messy truth, maddening to rationalists, that the medium of politics is the full person, with all his particularities. Statesmen competed in eloquence and accrued influence certainly from the strength of their arguments for the public good before the masses and their own peers, but also from the charisma of their personal style. At least such was the idea – military prowess in fact offered as or more effective a venue for amassing real sway.[82] The first simile of Virgil's *Aeneid*, where the simple sight of a man *pietate grauem ac meritis* ('respected for his reverence and accomplishments', 1.151) calms the turbulent crowd even before he speaks, illustrates authority's power prior to rational persuasion. This is sharply apparent in Augustus' self-avowed governance by *auctoritas* beyond the formal powers of office (*Res gestae* 34). This apparent good,

---

[78] Also, Cicero, *De or.* 3.125. For Cato as moralist, Edwards 1993: 17, 23.
[79] See Lavan in this volume.   [80] Fantham 2004: 237–47.   [81] Kapust 2011a: 13–21.
[82] E.g. Pompey was persuasive without stylistic brilliance, van der Blom 2011.

based on republican confidence in the public's ability to hold leaders to account and to choose whom to honour among competitors, runs aground when only one charismatic man hogs all the authority.

The contexts that authorise and enable political speech disclose the nature of agents' participation in larger cultural and political structures.[83] Differences in style and genre reveal available forms of political life. Seneca paints a portrait of Maecenas' style, commenting that taste for a corrupted style of speech (*corrupti generis oratio*, *Epist*. 114.1) indubitably accompanies a 'deviation' in *mores* 'from the straight path' (*a recto desciuisse*, 114.11). The close link between individual morals, political customs and aesthetic values makes the quality and freedom of speech an index of political conditions: the foreclosure of oratory altogether is the surest sign of crisis in the republic (e.g. Cic. *Brut*. 6; *Off*. 2.67, 3.2). Maternus in Tacitus' *Dialogus de oratoribus* attributes the current dearth of oratorical fireworks to the security of the age: under a 'single emperor most wise' (*sapientissimus et unus*, 41.4) no conflict remained and therefore no need for the admired oratory of the turbulent republic.[84] The extent of Tacitean irony here is contested, but the very shift from oratory to poetry as the new medium for expressing dissent, from deliberation to allegory as the privileged mode of speech, reveals the nature of the new political order. The worries of Maternus' friends, who gather after his recitation of his new drama *Thyestes* – a traditional theme for analysing tyranny – give the lie to his protestations that poetry offers a space for tranquil escape. Far from disappearing, political speech has migrated to a new genre. This shift is no mere one-off, but systematic: Maternus plans to write an even more inflammatory play about Cato, the exemplar of republican virtue. However much or little Maternus voices Tacitus' own opinions, the link he makes between political culture and the kinds of speech it affords builds on assumptions found in Cicero.[85] While the expression of such ideas through the example of the dialogue's characters remains republican, the contrast between Maternus' danger and his ostensible security speaks an allegorical code with an imperial flavour. Tacitus' own speech, grounded in literature's indirect modes of expression, operates according to the dialogue's analysis.

Romans talk about the public sphere when they talk about verbal expression. They thereby engage in and remake the sphere they talk

---

[83] Public speech belonged to free men. Lack of authority pushes slave speech into indirect expression, double meanings, joking and grumbling: Richlin 2017: 311–50.
[84] Sailor 2008: 130–2.   [85] Bartsch 2012b; Gallia 2009.

about.[86] Writing rhetoric was itself a form of virtuoso display; Cicero's interventions discuss and deploy power at the same time.[87] Cicero's assessment of Julius Caesar's famously elegant Latin as a domestic inheritance polished by diligence (*Brutus* 252) identifies two pillars of elite republicanism: his household signals aristocratic upbringing and hard study indicates personal virtue. Not all had such advantages.

Changes in elite education track shifts in the venues for public speaking from Republic to Empire: deliberative oratory falls off with the *contio*'s demise; forensic and epideictic become prevalent.[88] The *tirocinium fori* (apprenticeship in the Forum) yielded to schools for declamation without extending opportunity more broadly.[89] Education becomes a topic through which to address political and social change. The sheer volume of rhetorical treatises written during both Republic and Empire suggests Roman faith in the educability of the free elite: training could make them effective within the political venues available.[90] All this intellectual labour, however, hardly implies any free man could overcome deficiencies of class – *ars* overcomes deficiencies in *ingenium*. Only an exceptional individual managed to break into the senate as a 'new man' (*nouus homo*) under the republic. Like Cato, Quintilian emphasises the good man, but with a different valence: the empire requires less ostentation, more quiet competence.[91] The prime example is Tacitus' *Agricola*. Education under any regime has as much to do with acculturation as learning skills.[92] Declamation's artificial scenarios, preserved in the Elder Seneca and pseudo-Quintilian, entail coincidences involving pirates, tyrants and stepmothers, tortuous decisions about inheritance and rape. These were condemned as signs of decadence, encouraging specious reasoning and clever phrasing (entertainingly at Petronius, *Satyrica* 1), in contrast to the weighty matters of state that putatively marked republican oratorical exercises. Such

---

[86] Gurd 2012.
[87] Dugan 2005: 79–80: the *De oratore*'s mystifications burnish their author's genius instead of teaching others to follow in his footsteps.
[88] Morstein-Marx 2004.   [89] Corbeill 2002: 43–5.
[90] In addition to Cicero's early *De inventione* (late 90s BCE), the anonymous *Rhetorica ad Herennium* is generally dated to the time of Marius (late 80s BCE). After the *De oratore* (55 BCE), Cicero's own works devoted to rhetoric and the history of oratory cluster in 46 (*De optimo genere oratorum, Orator, Brutus*) or thereabouts (*De partitione oratoria*). Quintilian's *Institutio oratoria* and the declamations in pseudo-Quintilian attest to rhetorical training's continued centrality into the second century CE; the *triuium* enshrined rhetoric in education for pagan and Christian alike. For Roman education from the Republic to the early Empire, Corbeill 2002 and 2007.
[91] Dominik 1997: 50–68. Liebeschuetz 2013.
[92] Beard 1993. Play internalises ideologies, Habinek 2005: 111–16.

condemnation, ostensibly about education, comments indirectly on changes in political structure.

Triumviral and Augustan poets address contemporary reorderings of power by discussing and obsessively redefining their own media.[93] The recurrent theme of song's power or failure in Virgil's *Eclogues* responds to the discrete crisis of the land confiscations with larger questions about the function of speech when a few powerful men were ravaging the country in civil war.[94] The numerous *recusationes* of Augustan poetry situate their speaker just outside power – and tactfully protest the foreclosure of robust freedom of speech.[95] Horace expends much energy talking about his own and others' speech, from the fictive enactment of the orator's voice in *Epodes* 7 and 16, to his perennial redefinition of his lyric in terms of different Greek predecessors, each with varying degrees of power, to the voices and masks he stages according to the situation – ranging from slave (*Epistles* 1.1, 1.20) to high priest (*Odes* 3.1, 4.6; *Carmen saeculare*) to teacher of aristocratic sons, interested in writing tragedy when they have lost the chance to become orators like their fathers.[96] The frenzy of writing, attested of all classes at Horace, *Epist.* 2.1.108–10 and of the Younger Pliny's circle throughout his letters, remakes the intellectual sphere: the social realm moves into the space previously occupied by public affairs.[97] By shifting potent political speech in the *Dialogus* from oratory to poetry, Tacitus joins a debate about the closing of the public sphere with roots in both republican and Augustan-era literature. The ambivalence regularly expressed about what kind of speech to use, what capacities various forms actually have, analyses and engages in political discourse simultaneously.

## Directed Theorising

Roman authors often attempt to influence leaders by addressing them directly. These normative utterances reveal ideological assumptions, strategic thinking and historical pressures. Besides any message communicated, the medium itself lays bare tensions in language's ability to channel power. Advising leaders requires tact and risks flattery.[98] Whether the leader in question is presumed to live up to the values articulated therefore becomes ambiguous. Praise acknowledges the addressee's greater might. It

---

[93] Lowrie 2009.   [94] Habinek 2005; Breed 2006.   [95] Davis 1991; Freudenburg 2001 and 2014.
[96] Lowrie 1997 and 2014; Feeney 2009; Oliensis 1998; Geue 2014.
[97] Gurd 2012. For Pliny's social life and management of leisure, Gibson and Morello 2012. Generally on the letters, see Gibson and Whitton 2016.
[98] Ahl 1984; Kapust 2018a.

also thinly masks a speaker's real capacity to check the arbitrary exercise of power: setting norms in public makes their transgression perilous. Courtly discourse, declarations of mutuality, affection and even love soften implied threats while setting reciprocally binding parameters to speech and behaviour on speaker and honorand. Moderns, unfamiliar with these codes, can overlook the work they perform. Their political-theoretical interest resides less in their substance, often highly conventional, than in what they reveal about how language mediates affective ties.

Seneca's *De clementia*, a treatise addressed to Nero in his youth, and Pliny's *Panegyricus*, an oration praising Trajan before the senate, establish the rhetorical genre that mediaeval and later periods call the 'mirror of princes'.[99] Their portraits of the good leader have general applicability whether or not their addressees met their aspirations. The degree of explicitness with which they warn or even threaten the emperor if he falls short indicates how comfortable each felt speaking frankly. Historians analyse these authors' rhetoric for clues to contemporary evaluation of an emperor's reign and the period's climate. The theorist seeking abstract principles faces an inverse challenge: to translate into normative statements coded utterances made in a particular historical context.[100]

A representative leitmotif of the genre is that good governance averts assassination. Tracing evolving attitudes toward tyrannicide faces a methodological thicket. Authors tiptoe gingerly around voicing the ultimate threat and praise blunts the rhetorical blow. Higher praise can indicate a felt need to flatter an untrustworthy leader rather than rewarding excellence. The more a speaker avows sincerity, the worse the flattery – but how to tell?[101] Furthermore, responses to tyranny are continually reframed in texts spanning centuries, constitutions and genres. Justifications for regime change preoccupy political theorists; historians seek causes of assassination; literary historians often prioritise textual dependence. Since conventional elements may be absent in a text, knowledge of literary filiation may help tease out a fuller picture of cultural assumptions about tyrannicide's legitimacy at a particular time. Central recommendations are for the leader to subordinate himself to the gods, show respect for public interests and earn the people's love to minimise mutual fear.[102] Statements about revering the gods invoke shared norms without specifying what they are and emphasis on the emotive bond between people and ruler highlights the Roman understanding of politics' fundamentally affective nature. The

---

[99] Braund 1998; 2009: 17–23. Direct address of the sovereign may take place in any number of genres.
[100] Connolly 2009a.   [101] Bartsch 2012a; Roche 2011.   [102] Wallace-Hadrill 1982.

moral is banal: the good ruler need not fear assassination. If the message of the mirror of princes underwhelms, however, the genre becomes theoretically interesting for its political intervention. Such works performatively establish the bonds of mutuality they allege and thereby give leaders a positive incentive to meet the standards.

Cicero's *Pro Marcello* paves the way for the mirror of princes: warnings are encoded within his praise of Caesar. Thanking Julius Caesar for granting clemency to his friend Marcellus, whose opposition catalysed civil war, Cicero dwells repeatedly on Caesar's and the senate's mutual safety (*salus*, 21–34). Each has incentive to protect the other: the senate to avert a repeated outbreak of civil war, Caesar to earn the senate's protection. Their promise to put the *laterum nostrorum oppositus et corporum* ('the opposition of their flanks and bodies', 32) between him and harm, apparent assurance to Caesar, nevertheless threatens assassination through innuendo. Cicero never says so, but the implication is that the senate's protection is contingent: Caesar, apparently all-powerful, must exercise restraint; he has so far done so and his clemency is valued, but as dictator he must beware of turning tyrant. The intimated threat legitimates his eventual assassination on the grounds of aspiring to sole and unlimited rule against republican norms, but we must read between the lines.[103]

Seneca similarly withholds any overt threat in making clemency a defining difference between kings and tyrants: the one uses arms to foster peace, the other undermines his own security through mutual hatred and fear (*De clementia* 1.12.3–5). He cites Accius' 'execrable' verse, *oderint dum metuant* ('let them hate, provided they fear', *Atreus* fr. 5 Klotz), an exemplary tyrannical utterance, to excoriate the negative feedback loop where the tyrant, who 'is hated because he is feared, wants to be feared because he is hated'. The argument for granting clemency to foster love depends on the clear implication of danger through the assertion of its opposite: *unum est inexpugnabile munimentum amor ciuium* ('the one impregnable defence is citizens' love', 1.19). If structural similarities to *Pro Marcello* were insufficient, verbal citation cinches the link: *latera obiecti circumfusique defendunt, incurrentibus periculis se opponunt* ('they defend him, throwing their flanks in the way and circling around him, they put themselves before the onslaught of peril', 1.3.3).[104] The context, however, has shifted. Seneca

---

[103] For the history of debate over this speech's sincerity: Dyer 1990, Winterbottom 2002, Connolly 2011, Manuwald 2011, Dugan 2013. Warning, a conventional aspect of panegyric, does not necessarily undermine praise, Lowrie 1997: 258–65. On the politics of friendship: Kapust 2018a: 30–55.

[104] Lowrie 2016a: 79.

establishes rules for kings – acting like a king doomed Julius Caesar. The historical and textual background to Seneca's advice gains more or less importance depending on our interpretative aims. Seneca conveys a clear message to Nero: you may be loved and therefore safe, provided you exercise clemency. But a broader audience could infer a different message: Nero may be good so far, but our system is now kingship, so we must accept clemency in liberty's place. This message gains strength if we recognise the allusion to Cicero's speech. Deriving normative claims entails stripping off the message's particularity: clemency is good policy for winning trust.

Love cushions this rhetoric, but the threat of assassination becomes more explicit in proportion to the trust between speaker and addressee. Pliny displays liberty by voicing the usually unspoken threat: the affections of people and senate come with strings attached.[105] The good emperor must live up to his oath to govern in everyone's interest. This is the reciprocal correlate of the Roman people's oath to him: they pray for his safety on the condition of their security (*Panegyricus* 67.3–5). Their ultimate protection is inscribed in the emperor's oath, which consecrates 'his head and family to the wrath of the gods' (64.3) if he knowingly violates public interest. If Trajan does not meet these terms, Pliny openly, however politely, threatens assassination. Trajan possesses the peace of mind (*securus, securitatem*, 68.2, 4) based on a good conscience Pliny denies previous emperors, who deservedly felt 'worry and fear' (68.2) because they inspired hatred. He cannily projects onto Trajan an internalisation of the threat that keeps him honest: Trajan mulls over his vow, knowing he has armed the praetorian prefect against him if he does not work for the 'interests of all' (67.8). The people therefore respond in kind with entirely genuine and self-interested love (68.5). Unlike Cicero and Seneca, Pliny articulates the threat of assassination because he trusts Trajan will not abuse the people's trust. He therefore has no reason to suppose they will need to enact the threat. Knowledge of the literary filiation allows us to evaluate Pliny's threat differently. Contrary to first appearances, it indicates decreased political tension. Spelling out the logic of a now-conventional discourse binds the emperor to a commitment he has already made and highlights his good faith. Literary knowledge cues the historian to the speech's actual tenor. The theorist gains more explicit articulation of the logic underlying such expressions of reciprocity because the speaker may speak more freely.

[105] For unequal love here, Kapust 2018a: 55–63.

The degree of overlap between a general statement and targeted address may be opaque and each can inhibit appreciation of the other. Horace states broad principles without directly addressing Augustus. His implicit warning thereby falls short of a threat. To apply the principles to Augustus requires analogy, which the poems invite, but the reader at first assumes it follows only one track. The availability of another analogy flips the meaning. In the first Roman Ode, Horace outlines a hierarchy of power.

> Regum timendorum in proprios greges,
> reges in ipsos imperium est Iouis,
>   clari Giganteo triumpho,
>     cuncta supercilio mouentis.          (*Odes* 3.1.5–8)
>
> Fearsome kings rule their own flocks,
> kings themselves obey Jupiter's rule,
>   famous for triumph over the Giants,
>     moving all with his brow.

The obvious parallel between Jupiter and Augustus is backed up in *Odes* 3.4, where the Titanomachy, like Gigantomachy, stands as a conventional metaphor for civil war, checked by victorious Augustus. Divine and earthly rulers alike establish control over disorder.[106]

> Vis consili expers mole ruit sua:
> uim temperatam di quoque prouehunt
>   in maius, idem odere uiris
>     omne nefas animo mouentis.          (*Odes* 3.4.65–8)
>
> Force without a share in counsel goes to smash on its own weight: the gods also promote tempered force, the same hate strength moving all evil in its spirit.

At first, the force without counsel clearly belongs to the Titans, whom the gods defeat; Jupiter wins fame for defeating their analogue the Giants in *Odes* 3.1.7. If we put *Odes* 3.1 and 3.4 together, however, the fear kings should have of the gods in the first Roman Ode suggests Augustus should also show it in the fourth. Although he is like Jupiter over the forces of disorder, the analogy reveals he is also a ruler subject to Jupiter. The message transforms from praise for ending civil war to a warning he should make sure to follow the path of counsel. Otherwise, he risks falling into the other category: 'strength moving all evil in its spirit'. Horace intimates no threat, but the analogy between Augustus and the kings subject to divine

---

[106] Also *Odes* 3.6.5–6, Thomas 2001: 43; Lowrie 2018.

power conveys a subtle warning: he will be held accountable. The general statements, political-theoretical pablum, become more interesting once we understand that they enact a check on absolute power. The theoretical payoff lies not in their substance, but in the ability of apparently impotent voices to limit the powerful by publicly rearticulating shared norms.

To appreciate the political work accomplished by directed theorising in the later Roman tradition, which expands in scope, requires recognising the layering of political scenes. Machiavelli advises a solitary prince, Lorenzo de' Medici, in *The Prince*, but his *Discourses* innovate by addressing plural republican sympathisers.[107] Despite good inclinations, his dedicatees, Cosimo Rucellai and Zanobi Buondelmonti, expected an active role in governance on the basis of their nobility. They needed to hear arguments for republican as well as princely restraint. The bargain he proposes is that the *grandi* (big men) curb their appetite for dominating the people in return for glory. This they could win by being founders like Junius Brutus, who won eternal glory by betraying his class, and by imperial expansion through a well-armed and politically empowered citizenry. The imperial formula of the leader's safety in return for love overlays the Roman republican formula of glory for moderation. By making concessions to republican ambition, Machiavelli slips in a democratic point. He adapts the terms and the rhetorical context, derived from Roman models, to new political ends. Without intimate knowledge of this tradition, important aspects of his innovations pass under the radar.

## Institutions and Constitution

Foundation, the uncodified nature of the Roman constitution, the degree to which the Roman republic was democratic,[108] institutions,[109] their continuity and evolution, regime change, class conflict,[110] violence,[111] emergency measures,[112] the statesman,[113] citizenship and slavery,[114] civil religion,[115] the public sphere,[116] war,[117] law[118] and provincial governance[119]

---

[107] McCormick 2011: 36–61. His reading of Machiavelli as more democratic than usually understood currently organises discussion – pro and con – in the field.
[108] Cartledge 2016: 247–63 surveys the debate between Millar 1984 and 1998, championing the fundamentally democratic nature of the Roman Republic, and Hölkeskamp 2010, who stresses the structural predominance of elites; a host of features tilts against democracy.
[109] Lintott 1999a.   [110] Raaflaub 2005.   [111] Lintott 1999b; Riggsby 1999; Bryen 2018.
[112] Agamben 2005; Straumann 2016.   [113] Fantham 2004: Lowrie forthcoming.
[114] Richlin 2017: 21–40.   [115] Atkins 2018: 136–65.   [116] Gurd 2012; Russell 2016.
[117] Harris 1985: 9–53; Howarth 2013.   [118] Bryen 2014; du Plessis, Ando and Tuori 2016.
[119] Ando 2000; Richardson 2016.

are central preoccupations. I focus here on just one. Rome's famously uncodified constitution offers a good methodological test case for the role of letters in politics. Recovering Roman thinking on the topic entails piecing together latent or emergent features that later come to be identified with constitutions.[120] Fluidity in their thought about structures of governance matches the fluidity of their practices.

Since the Romans wrote no blueprint for either principles or process, but nevertheless managed a complex state for a good millennium, they relied on custom with an assumption that consensus was within reach, despite constant dispute and substantive formal change. The Roman genius was to project greater consensus and historical continuity than was warranted in fact. Everyone was assumed to know what virtue and ancestral custom were without much specification. Practices were therefore continually adapted for contingent circumstances. Norms and custom provided the *langue* for the creative *parole* of politics, which reshaped the adaptive organising structure.

Deliberative contexts disclose unspoken conventions short of rules. This makes it hard to determine when an exception is being made. When correct procedure was unclear, decisions depended on drumming up political backing. During the Catilinarian conspiracy, Cicero assumes without explanation that the senate's 'ultimate decree' overrides popular sovereignty, specifically the right to trial before the people's assembly, and argues before the senate for imposing the death penalty on Catiline, one of their own members, on the basis of this emergency measure (*Cat.* 1.3). Process was not self-evident but had to be learned and tested. Cicero's exile for authorising the conspirators' capital punishment, followed by swift recall, reveals real disagreement over process and sovereignty's ultimate location.[121] This is one instance among many controversial killings and exceptional measures challenged in the courts during the late republic. Each sparked procedural innovation in an attempt to legitimate extraordinary responses to crises.[122] These became exemplary for the next crisis. Under an emperor as decider-in-chief, sovereignty was clear, but custom lapsed. Pliny continually checks with Trajan on the rules and the legitimacy of bending them (*Epistles* 10): no, to exceptions on serving out full sentences (10.31, 32); yes, to an emergency passport for his wife (10.120.2). Without a meaningful *tirocinium fori* as in republican times, he comments

---

[120] Straumann 2016: 1–21; Atkins 2018: 11–36.   [121] Lowrie 2007b; Straumann 2016: 88–100.
[122] Fiori 1996.

on the obsolescence of practices by setting on display his consultation with an expert peer on process (*Ep.* 8.14).[123]

Constitutional thinking is scattered and ranges from terms embedded in the Latin language to proto-constitutional thinking. The name of the state, *Senatus populusque Romanus*, designates a shared national identity and identifies political players, if not full houses of governance.[124] *SPQR* enshrines basic aspects of the unwritten constitution and reveals unspoken principles and even contradictions. While the copula *-que* joins senate and people equally in an icon of governance, word order reveals assumptions about the priority of the senate's power: despite popular sovereignty, the senate is *primus inter pares* ('first among equals'). Senatorial intervention during crises indicates cracks in the people's hold on sovereignty. According to Carl Schmitt's controversial definition: 'sovereign is he who decides on the state of exception'.[125] If the senate decides, where does that leave the people? Once the emperor decides, how can the senate? The clash between articulation and practice – Cicero is a case in point – reveals that ultimate control remained unresolved. By the time of the principate, the dynamic struggle between senate and people revealed in *SPQR* no longer pertained, but the name of the state remained the same. Later shared power, between Augusti and Caesares, between Eastern and Western Empires, shifted structures yet again. My analysis, which reads state of exception theory out from the formal wordplay literary scholars delight in, is fruitful only before *SPQR* crystallises into a dead name.

Cicero's *De re publica* and the *De legibus* provide the most directly analytic statements about political organisation in Latin.[126] The latter is the republic's closest approximation to a constitution.[127] Cicero distinguishes between political bodies according to Latin's rich lexicon of power: 'since control lies in the people, authority in the senate . . .' (*cum potestas in populo, auctoritas in senatus sit, Leg.* 3.28).[128] His definition of the *res publica* as 'belonging to the people' directly articulates popular sovereignty and establishes the basis of governance as law and mutual interest.

> 'Est igitur,' inquit Africanus, 'res publica res populi, populus autem non omnis hominum coetus quoquo modo congregatus, sed coetus multitudinis

---

[123] Literary strategy in Whitton 2010, procedural substance in Ernst 2014.
[124] Roman identity surpasses citizenship, Syed 2005.
[125] Schmitt 1985: 2; Agamben 2005; Lowrie 2007b and 2010a. Straumann 2016 has greater confidence in the people's sovereignty.
[126] Zetzel 1995; Powell and North 2001; Dyck 2004.
[127] Asmis 2004 and 2005; Ando 2011: 84–5; Atkins 2013; Straumann 2016: 49–90.
[128] Heinze 1972; Galinsky 1996: 10–14.

iuris consensu et utilitatis communione sociatus. Eius autem prima causa coeundi est non tam imbecillitas quam naturalis quaedam hominum quasi congregatio.' (Cic. *Rep.* 1.39)

'Therefore,' Africanus said, 'the republic is the possession of the people. The people, however, is not every gathering of men aggregated in any old way, but the coming together of a multitude through agreement on rightful law and allied through the guardianship of mutual interest. And the first cause of its coming together is not so much weakness as a certain natural flocking together, so to speak, among humans.'

Scholars often quote the bare phrase, *res publica res populi*, out of context, creating a false sense of a properly theoretical statement, but Cicero's definition of the state morphs into a definition of a people. His statement exemplifies his evocative political thinking – metonymic, graced by linguistic concerns (the etymology *publica – populi*), with an excursus on the philosophical debate about weakness or innate sociability as society's cause.[129] Given the fragmentary state of both dialogues, it is uncertain how deeply he describes Roman structures of governance.

While Greek constitutional thought from Aristotle to Polybius focuses on form (kingship, oligarchy, democracy or mixed constitution), the Romans concentrated on power and norms.[130] This might explain why the modern division between republic and empire – shorthand for the formal mix before Augustus and the subsequent monarchical principate – does not correspond to Latin usage. The ostensibly unified republic extended real *imperium* overseas and the post-Augustan empire continued to call governance *res publica*.[131] 'Public affairs' or 'common wealth' specifies no particular constitutional shape and pertains as much to monarchy as to any other governmental permutations.

Constitutional order, determining who exercises the authority to do what under what circumstances, was enshrined not in formal statute but in custom (*mos*) and norms (*ius*).[132] Frequent appeal to the *mos maiorum* (custom of the ancestors) retrojected unity about process and values back into time immemorial despite formal change, high variability and contestation. The result was nominal conservatism blended with actual flexibility. But power tended to overwhelm constraints in the absence of strong rights.

---

[129] Zetzel 1995 ad loc.; Atkins 2013: 128–38.   [130] Wiedemann 2000.
[131] For a new periodisation of stages within the Republic, Flower 2009. For the conceptualisation of *imperium*, Richardson 2008.
[132] Straumann 2016 valorises *ius* over *mos* (pp. 27, 79); *ius* represents higher-order norms that legitimate exceptions to process in emergencies. A hierarchy of norms guides practice without need for judicial review or codification (p. 36).

The norm articulated by Cicero, *salus populi suprema lex esto* ('let the people's safety be the highest law', *De legibus* 3.8), to check the consuls, who otherwise held the highest authority, gave paltry guidance for actual emergencies, when exceptional circumstances challenge ordinary process.[133] Cicero, Rome's only serious constitutional thinker, imagines a thin roster of rights by modern standards: safety, appeal and private property.[134]

The most incisive expression of the Roman constitution is poetic. Ennius' *moribus antiquis res stat Romana uirisque* (quoted on p. 763) bases the state not on law or formal institutions, but on individuals sharing an inherited understanding of what is right. Powerful men who ran the *res Romana* could and did dispute the meaning of the tradition and therefore constitutional formalities. In Sallust's account, Caesar and Cato debate appropriate punishment for the Catilinarian conspirators. Their arguments, against and for the death penalty respectively, rest on not law, but the example of the latter's ancestor. Each reaches an antithetical conclusion (*Cat.* 51–2).[135] Cato the Elder, universally acknowledged as establishing standards, offers no unambiguous guide for action. The gorgeous balance of Ennius' line, where the verb denoting stability stands between words denoting the state, with the customs and men anchoring the whole at either end, tilts with *antiquis*, the apparent stabiliser.

If the ancestors' example is the source of moral and institutional guidance, the Roman informal constitution dwells beyond the legal order.

> The constitution of the Republic consisted of far more than statutes: it was based on traditional institutions defined by precedents and examples. These were above all embodied in stories, whether these related to more recent events and had good claims to historicity or were reconstructions of distant events with a strong element of myth.[136]

Customs lived because men re-enacted them. Only once civil war shut down republican performative politics did Livy amass the stories of Roman history into a continuous narrative. I suggest that Livy's history codifies the Roman republican constitution in literary form. His history is a storehouse for guiding action. For content, he projects constitutional debate backwards.[137] Formally, recording the stories that convey practices and values preserves them short of legal codification. This new vehicle for cultural memory filled the void in constitutional practices left by Augustus'

---

[133] Straumann 2016: 43, 183–4.   [134] Ibid. 118–45; Atkins 2018: 43–57.   [135] Levene 2000.
[136] Lintott 1999a: 26.
[137] Wiedemann 2000: Roman constitutional thinking via *exempla* contrasts with Greek abstract schematism.

accession to power.[138] Valerius Maximus systematised these and other stories in the next generation. As deliberative oratory fell off and epideictic and advocacy became eloquence's dominant modes, his handbook supplied a fossilised republican constitution as material for the new educational system. Collections of stories compiled after its collapse turn out to be the Roman republic's closest approximation to a written constitution.[139]

## Exemplarity

Telling stories to work through challenges is a central strategy of Roman political thinking.[140] The example may lead inductively to the generation of a principle or concept, but it may not. In Aristotle's analysis, the *paradeigma* is neither deductive nor even inductive, but leads from one particular to another.[141] In Latin, the rhetorical tradition classifies the *exemplum* as a figure of thought: it may be a discrete instance of something, but more often it offers a story that circulates as a cultural model in the aim of persuasion.[142] These models are rarely unproblematic. Historical figures who performed glorious deeds also violated norms (Romulus, Coriolanus, Camillus). They certainly stand for a kind of greatness, but their actions should not be emulated in entirety. Formally, the example may have or lack a supporting argument, clear hermeneutic signposts or an expressed moral. It has some narrative dimension, however minimal. Convention makes its meaning seem transparent, even if conflicted. It is a site for judgement, however ambivalent. Much political thinking takes place through *exempla* without generating any abstract take-away.

Exemplarity is the degree zero of Roman political thought. The particulars that map a conceptual field are offered not for the sake of pure contemplation, but to elicit engagement, to reproduce – or deflect – analogous actions pragmatically under new circumstances. Although the Roman propensity to particularistic thinking with *exempla* has received much attention in recent years, the extent of this method's challenge to political-theoretical assumptions about what constitutes thought remains insufficiently appreciated outside Classics.[143] *Exempla* embed

---

[138] For backward projection, Straumann 2016: 2.
[139] On stories' value for political theory, Honig 2009: 64; Connolly 2015: 7–8; for law, Brooks 2010; Bryen 2014; Lowrie 2016b.
[140] Chaplin 2000; Hölkeskamp 2004: 169–98; Roller 2004, 2009 and 2018; Kraus 2005; Lowrie 2007a; Wallace-Hadrill 2008: 225–339; Langlands 2008, 2011, 2015 and 2018; Lowrie and Lüdemann 2015.
[141] Lowrie and Lüdemann 2015: 2.   [142] *Rhet. Her.* 4.62, Quint. *Inst.* 5.11.6.
[143] Lowrie and Lüdemann 2015 attempt to correct this insufficiency.

unstated principles into instances of the application or violation of norms. To work, such a system requires shared assumptions to fill in what goes unsaid.

Cicero's citation of a substantial list of politically motivated deaths at the beginning of his first Catilinarian oration backs up his claim that Catiline should die (*Cat.* 1.4). The rhetorical function of the *exempla* is clear. Tiberius Gracchus, Spurius Maelius, Gaius Gracchus, Marcus Fulvius, Lucius Saturninus and Gaius Servilius all met their ends due to state violence; by analogy Catiline should too. The political-theoretical work done by the list, however, is powerful but unexpressed. Cicero joins four historical occasions of turbulence without specifying any similarity beyond posing a threat to the state. In the cases of Gaius Gracchus and Saturninus, the consuls had received, like Cicero, the *senatus consultum ultimum* (SCU) as authorisation for extraordinary measures. Their example therefore should be sufficient for his point. But Cicero includes Tiberius Graccus and Maelius as well, the former killed by Scipio Nasica in an extra-magisterial capacity while *pontifex maximus*, the latter by Servilius Ahala, master of the horse acting under the orders of the dictator Cincinnatus. These imprecise parallels muddy the waters and it would be easy to disdain Cicero's thinking here as mere rhetoric: the *a fortiori* argument about Tiberius Gracchus elevates his claim (if a private citizen killed Tiberius who was menacing the state only moderately, all the more should a consul backed by the SCU kill Catiline); the *praeteritio* about Maelius acknowledges his otiose status, but underscores the traditional nature of similar actions in the mythic past. In modernity, however, such acts are theorised under the broader rubric of the state of exception.[144] Cicero intuits that these events belong together even though he lacks an adequate classificatory category. This is political thinking in action that does not rise to the level of theory.

The Romans in fact reflect on how to think with *exempla* in programmatic statements across genres. They highlight the cognitive as well as pragmatic dynamism of the process. Ennius' phrase, *moribus antiquis ...,* assumes men know the customs they re-enact. Cicero's, *historia ... magistra uitae*, affirms the moral and political lessons available from history, among other functions, including illumination, memory and truth.[145] The orator, whose voice commends history to posterity, plays a strong role as

---

[144] Agamben 2005; Lowrie 2007b and 2010a; Straumann 2016: 88–100.　[145] Armitage 2012.

mediator between event and audience. Livy provides the most explicit articulation of history's teaching in his preface:[146]

> My intention is that each should devote his attention (*intendat animum*) for his own behalf to these things: what kind of life, what customs (*mores*) there were, through what sort of men and by what arts empire (*imperium*) was increased both in peace and in war. Then, let him follow in his mind (*animo*) how discipline gradually slipped and customs (*mores*) at first came into variance with one another, then slid more and more, and then began to go headlong (*praecipites*), until we have reached these times, when we cannot endure either our vices or their remedies. This is especially healthy and fruitful in thinking about things (*cognitione rerum*), for you to look at the records (*documenta*) of every *exemplum* that has been placed on an illustrious monument (*monumento*) and from there to take for yourself and your country (*rei publicae*) what you should imitate, from there to determine what you should avoid as foul in its beginning, foul in its end. But either the love of the endeavour I have undertaken has deceived me, or no other state (*res publica*) has ever been either greater or more reverent or richer in good *exempla*, nor have avarice and luxury come later from the outside into any other polity (*ciuitatem*) nor has there been such great honour given for so long to poverty and thrift. (*praef.* 9–11)

Although the third sentence is often excerpted as a concise explanation of how exemplarity works, removing it from the broader context obscures several characteristic ways the Romans theorise. Livy's general statement offers a guide to reading that assumes an active reader with an attentive mind. His lead-up emphasises cognitive processes. Reaching a decision to imitate or avoid a potential course of action entails a pragmatic response through thinking and judging.

Exemplary thinking is contestatory. As in the debate between Caesar and Cato in Sallust's *Catiline*, different meanings could be assigned to what an individual stood for. Furthermore, the same story could legitimate different interpretations. Livy's preface lends an illusory simplicity to making the judgements he calls for. Since, he alleges, the Romans have declined from a prior pinnacle of virtue, but their history still offers the richest storehouse of models for emulation, the materials he presents are mixed. The text does not prescribe any course of action, but demands active interpretation from readers. We learn to judge the actions depicted through observing how characters in his history make their own interpretations. Some *exempla* instruct, some persuade; characters succeed by

---

[146] This articulation is central to much scholarship on Livy: e.g. Jaeger 1997; Feldherr 1998; Chaplin 2000; Vasaly 2015.

learning history's lessons and fail by learning the wrong one; *exempla* structure debates between characters.¹⁴⁷ Even apart from deliberative contexts, however, the Roman system of thinking with particulars conveys norms holistically through their embodiment in leading figures.

The trials of the Scipios demonstrate how Livy's readership learns from the past indirectly. Various Cornelii are accused of breaches of justice (38.50–60). Although they may have committed minor infractions, these pale – the narrative intimates – in comparison to the family's service to the state. At issue is Rome's gratitude. Scipio Nasica defends his cousin Lucius Scipio, charged with diverting gold and silver from his defeat of Antiochus into his private purse. He invokes their family's distinction: Lucius' own, their fathers' and that of Lucius' brother Publius (Scipio Africanus). The speech does not sway the senate, but Roman values are represented through it.¹⁴⁸ This speech follows on the heels of Tiberius Sempronius Gracchus' similar defence of Scipio Africanus, again on the grounds of public service, against accusations based on challenging a man who had become too powerful. That a personal enemy of Africanus utters the defence strengthens the argument *a fortiori*: if even an enemy admires such virtue, how much more should we. The parallel between similar attacks and defences of two brothers shows how much exemplarity depends on analogy.¹⁴⁹ Repetition underscores the unexpressed point to be inferred.

Roman exemplarity is a system of thinking that was handed down despite radical re-evaluations – and even rejection – of traditional interpretations. In *De civitate Dei*, Augustine acknowledges classical Rome's model of virtue, one even Christians could admire: Romans put service to the state above all. Their aims were, however, misdirected because they served the city of men rather than of God (5.12). Their propensity for civil war – the prime, but not sole, example of the worst in human history (3.1) – overrides the admirable in Rome's model. Morally, he displaces Rome's exemplary virtue with Christian values, while formally, as he avers, he simply uses their authors' own words to reveal their misdirection (3.17). Although Augustine aims to supplant Rome with his vision of a new order as society's correct model, he nevertheless reproduces Roman methods of thinking by staging a debate between revered Roman authors.¹⁵⁰ He uses Livy's implicit point about ingratitude in the trials of the Scipios to argue

---

[147] Chaplin 2000.  [148] Chaplin 2000: 91–2.
[149] On Livy's citation and narrative strategies, Haimson Lushkov 2010.
[150] MacCormack 1998 and 1999; Hammer 2014: 416–30. Weithman's 2014: 248–9 emphasis on how his political thought corrects overestimation of the force of reason aligns him with a central characteristic of Roman political thought.

against Sallust, who claims this period was of the 'highest morals and in the greatest concord' (3.21). Roman exemplary history discredits classical Rome and its politics entirely.

Machiavelli looks to Livy both textually in his *Discourses on the First Decade of Livy* and in his aspiration to educate statesmen, but his thematic organisation advances in abstraction over the chronological format of the historian and thereby rises to the level of political theory.[151] His preface to the first book explains the value of exemplarity for politics. Unlike art, law and medicine, whose disciplines either derive from the classical tradition or aspire to offer ancient models for imitation, contemporary princes and republics have forgotten the ancient examples; if they do read, they see too great a gulf between ancient times and their own to imagine imitation. Machiavelli aspires to impart knowledge and assist readers in deriving 'utility' from it. His more analytic framework than Livy's or Augustine's does the work Livy hands off to his ideal reader. Machiavelli makes explicit comments about method, such as flagging his use of examples as evidence (e.g. Scipio, 1.11). Comparing instances sets up his articulation of general conclusions that remain implicit in his classical sources, particularly in history, where the primary job is to tell the story. Measuring the treatment of Scipio Africanus against the examples of Coriolanus and Camillus allows him to pronounce the first an exceptional error (1.29). With the latter, the people responded to injuries, but for Scipio, their defence of liberty against his excessive power may have been unnecessary. The stories sit within a larger argument that princes show more ingratitude than peoples and for worse reasons, which is undergirded by a secondary thesis, that there are two motives for ingratitude (1.29.1). The people's treatment of Scipio rested on the more laudable of the two: suspicion instead of avarice. He makes explicit what remained implicit in Livy and cites other Latin authors, here Tacitus, as well as historical instances to prove his argument. Unlike Roman authors, who often trust their audience to infer a story's implications, he controls the theoretical endgame by stating the point.

Literature continues to retell Roman history for political analysis.[152] Mention of Roman figures proliferates in the public sphere, particularly of emperors as tokens of decadence.[153] These look at first like a dry and elitist assumption of a shared frame of reference. But, as in Latin oratory, such parallels may imply an inflammatory argument without spelling it

---

[151] McCormick 2015 gives a foretaste of his forthcoming book on exemplarity in Machiavelli, *The People's Princes*.
[152] Camus' *Caligula* 1984 (orig. 1941); Nelson 2008; Houellebecq 2015.
[153] Connolly 2017; Freudenburg 2018a and 2018b; Kapust 2018b.

out. Exemplarity requires not just shared knowledge, but agreement about the rules of the game. A recent exchange demonstrates the pitfalls of delimiting analogies. Martha Nussbaum objects to an editorial by Paul Krugman, which compares President Donald Trump to Caligula.[154] She excoriates him for blaming the American Senate, which had to date refused 'to get rid of' Trump, on the grounds that he makes an implicit call for assassination; even without specialist knowledge, anyone may easily discover through Wikipedia that the praetorian guard assassinated Caligula and draw the parallel. Krugman's analogy, however, is rhetorically correct. He uses the *a maiore* argument standard in *exempla*. He explicitly contrasts the praetorians' conspiracy, the greater remedy, with the US Congress' lesser and constitutional remedy (impeachment or the fourteenth amendment), which would achieve removal from office without bloodshed. Under fraying democratic norms, it is not just political substance that has become fraught, but the rules of interpretation themselves.

## Conceptual History

> CICERO: An assistant of mine has compiled a list. (*He looks among his papers*.) Here it is. A list – of words. Words. That *I* have put into our language. Words that did not exist. Words I have – invented? So we could understand the great Greeks [...] 'Element. Quality, Vacuum. Moral. Individual. Definition. Induction. Property. Infinity. Comprehension. Appetite. Instance. Image. Difference. Notion. Science. Species ...' (*pause*) I read this over and I was amazed. I hadn't realized. I don't mean in a proud way. You don't realize all we *didn't* know. All we didn't have words for. How many more words will we need? How much more is there to know, to try and say? (R. Nelson, *Conversations in Tusculum* (scene 6), 2008: 77–8)

Roman history and Latin literature have established many fundamental concepts in Western political thought. Nelson highlights Greek philosophical terms mediated through Latin. However, many political concepts naturalised in modernity have Roman origins, sometimes forgotten, without Greek equivalents. The basic difference between a democracy and a republic, for instance, is fundamental to ancient history and political theory alike.[155] Concepts are the building blocks of abstract thought, but they do not arise in a vacuum. Parsing the exact valence of Latin words has

---

[154] Nussbaum 2018: 159; Krugman 2017.   [155] E.g. Cartledge 2016: 247–63.

helped historians shed light on Roman ideology, which is often defined by lists of virtues.[156] Concepts also help theorists access the contradictions underlying Roman politics and its interrogations.[157] Defining a concept in its cultural context requires examining its use by individuals who have their own agendas (*parole*) within broader semantic fields (*langue*). A further complication is that concepts contested within their times of origin also adapt to new circumstances. To trace the evolution of any concept across the *longue durée* entails serial recontextualisation that respects the multiplicity of use both synchronically and diachronically.[158]

There is a difference between 'essentially contested concepts'[159] and those offering sites for political contestation despite broad agreement about meaning. First, the latter. *Libertas*, universally acknowledged as grounding republicanism, provided a conceptual axis for political conflict in the late Republic.[160] The difference between the free man (*liber*) and the contrasting slave implicit in the word's etymology is fundamental. Particularly productive in modernity has been the distinction between positive and negative liberties, that is, the freedom to participate in politics versus freedom from domination, and furthermore, between non-domination proper and non-interference.[161] A good master, for instance, may happen not to interfere in a slave's activities, but nevertheless dominates because he has the legal right to do so. It is hard to avoid speaking in modern terms that lend clarity in retrospect and the contrast between slave and free leaves much room open. Still, the basics were not in dispute. Scholars agree that the Romans conceptualised *libertas* in strong terms as non-domination under the Republic – but not as positive freedom for all classes in society. The Romans fought bitterly about the institutional order needed to ensure *libertas* and who had a more legitimate claim on it. The *optimates* stressed the mixed constitution that distributed power in a system of checks without much balance, while *populares* strove for safeguards against domination with the tribunate and by giving greater power to the assembly.[162] Although class conflict might be the origins of politics,[163] the struggle that eventually destroyed the Republic was between elites, over whose freedom should prevail. All sides appealed to liberty in

---

[156] Such lists are fluid: Wallace-Hadrill 1981. [157] Connolly 2015: 111–13.
[158] Hampsher-Monk et al. 1998 compare German and Anglophone traditions of conceptual history. Armitage 2012 surveys old-school conceptual history, Big History, the Annales School, the Cambridge School, and *Begriffsgeschichte*. His method, 'history in ideas', effects rapprochement between intellectual history and the *longue durée*.
[159] Gallie 1956. I thank Michael Sevel for the reference. [160] Arena 2012: 8–10.
[161] Pettit 1997: 6, 21–2; Kapust 2011a: 11; Connolly 2015: 11–12. [162] Arena 2012; Kapust 2013.
[163] Connolly 2015: 23–64.

the civil wars. All sides lost it, to some degree, under monarchy. That the emperor was called *dominus* is a symptom of Roman acceptance of metaphorical enslavement. Tacitus frequently tars the senatorial order with this charge under the principate (e.g. *Agricola* 2.2, *Histories* 1.2).[164]

An example of an essentially contested concept is *populus*.[165] The collective of free citizens constituted into a political force, the *populus Romanus* is a whole defined always in opposition to some other. It contrasts first with non-Romans lacking citizen rights. But it is also defined against its component internal parts: senate versus *plebs*.[166] The *populus*, which as the collective citizenry includes senators, appears as a governing body with distinct powers over against the senate. In this sense, *populus* sometimes serves as a synonym of the *plebs*. But it may also be contrasted with the *plebs*, a distinct class within the greater whole. A *populus* in general distinguishes itself conceptually from a disorganised group, typically called a *multitudo*. While the dependence of a concept's different meanings on structural oppositions is semantically trivial, the ambiguities entailed in *populus* map onto politically fraught questions about who belongs, what groups have formal powers and how they are constituted. A whole ever internally divided, *populus* conceptually enacts the problem entailed when a group joins into a body politic, while displaying the exclusions constitutive of group identity.

Concepts outlive their original contexts.[167] Liberty remains a fundamental principle in modern nation-states that have outlawed slavery, so the essential contrast in Latin has become less determinative of freedom's meaning. Because concepts react dynamically to changing pressures, simply defining them even diachronically falls short. Concepts operate within larger semantic fields even without being mentioned.[168] Conversely, 'to think about words is not necessarily to define concepts'.[169] Besides balancing sometimes contradictory usages, untangling the work of concepts requires mapping constellations of conventional, often evolving metaphors that evoke a concept even when absent.

Even when broad agreement obtains about a concept's meaning, its semantic field can reveal underlying complexity. Latin *libertas*, to return to

---

[164] Sailor 2008: 10, 123, 127, 134–5.
[165] Amy Russell's research group, 'Who are "We the People"?' (Institute of Advanced Study, Durham University, Epiphany Term 2019) was helpful for reaching these formulations.
[166] Agamben 2000: 28–35.
[167] Farr 1989. Armitage 2017b: 182–4, with general bibliography at n. 11.
[168] Brunner, Conze and Koselleck 2004; Koselleck 2004.
[169] Connolly 2015: 3; the 'scene' is an alternative to conceptual representation (158).

the example above, circulates under the radar through widespread metaphors of mastery and slavery or by retaining implicit rankings. The Romans adopted the Greek political metaphor in which the rational part of the well-ordered soul (the *hegemonikon*) masters the body and the soul's irrational parts.[170] Freedom's metaphors reveal chinks in the hierarchies that define spheres of action: public *serv*ice depends on a metaphor of slave labour for the free dedication of effort to the public good. Magistrates and ministers all work in a system of greaterness and lesserness that subordinate those holding power to those with lesser responsibilities.[171] Much of a semantic sphere may be invisible. Dialogues between masters and slaves, in comedy or satire for instance, enact debate about *libertas* without necessarily mentioning the word.[172] The structure of *libertas* extends metaphorically beyond actual masters and slaves in Latin to define the relationships between political sectors and even of model forms of life.[173]

The formal properties of texts may also act out commentary on political conditions without naming the concepts at stake. Horace's choice to write small poems in multiple voices that fragment any unified statement or narrative responds to a perceived loss of freedoms, of speech, of political participation, in the early Augustan period.[174] Lucan's disjunctive style in itself protests the loss of republican freedom.[175] Literature's special gift to political thought is the enactment of politically fraught problems beyond explicit conceptualisations.[176]

## Metaphorology

Latin literature becomes legible as political thought once we recognise its consistent repertory of metaphors. Much of Latin studies continues to worry about textual allusion through close verbal repetition, and remains committed to discovering authorial intention despite protesting otherwise.[177] This method restricts analysis to authors and texts. The primary question is, 'What did $X$ (e.g. Tacitus) think about $y$, e.g. freedom?' Recent scholarship has broadened the scope beyond concepts to how texts function. For instance, Tacitus' ambivalence about freedom under the principate emerges symptomatically through conflict in his representation of Agricola, between Domitian to one side and the Stoic

---

[170] Gill 2006.   [171] Compare Ando's (2011: 64–80) discussion of *maiestas* and sovereignty.
[172] Richlin 2017; Horne 2018.   [173] Horne 2018.
[174] Johnson 1993; Lowrie 1997; McCarter 2015.   [175] Quint 1993; Bartsch 1997; Henderson 1998.
[176] Connolly 2015: 92.   [177] O'Rourke and Pelttari in this volume; also Sharrock in this volume.

suicides to the other.[178] Still, in such analyses, the author is presumed as the source or channel of the thought conveyed. To access Roman political thought as more than a collection of statements or even textual symptoms will require a concerted shift in focus from author to culture, intention to convention, reference to system.

Metaphorology, as invented by Hans Blumenberg, recognises clusters of words as cultural givens that transform diachronically without the texts transmitting shared figurations necessarily looking to each other, although they may. Lakoff and Johnson's seminal *Metaphors We Live By* locates many fundamental metaphors that structure human understanding of the world in universals derived from the body, such as the preference for 'up' over 'down'.[179] Blumenberg's 'absolute metaphor' bears a structural similarity to catachresis, which is a metaphor for an object, such as a table leg, that does not have a proper name; the absolute metaphor operates in the absence of a corresponding concept. Culturally specific, attested in texts, absolute metaphors provide a hinge between *parole* and *langue*. Their transmission shapes diachronic traditions, which are traceable through representative instances.[180] A high degree of metaphoricity, including absolute metaphors, characterises Roman political thought.[181] Not all conventional political metaphors in Latin are exclusive to the Romans – the ship of state already appears in Greek – but political languages in Pocock's sense evolve over time through minute changes in such metaphors whatever their origins.[182]

A good example of an absolute metaphor is the tendency for rape or its threat to attend moments of Roman foundation or refoundation in response to crisis. Ilia's (or Silvia's) conception of Romulus and Remus upon being raped by Mars establishes rape as a mytho-historical paradigm, repeated with the rapes of the Sabines, Lucretia, Verginia *et aliae*. Early Roman history functions as their equivalent of myth,[183] so these stories of violation reach deep into the culture regardless of the nuances of various authors' accounts.[184] The fragments of Ennius' version of Ilia's rape (*Annales* 1.29 Skutsch) give her pregnancy a foundational role in his narrative even without overt political language. Ovid, however, discloses the link through an obvious metaphor. He hammers home the parallel between Mars' literal seed and its purpose, 'that he might give great seed to this city'

---

[178] Sailor 2008: 51–118. [179] Lakoff and Johnson 1980; Short 2012.
[180] Blumenberg 1997, 2007 and 2010. [181] For Roman law and politics, Ando 2015.
[182] Mebane 2017: introduction, who examines the metaphor of the head of state. Classic works on Roman political languages include: Hellegouarc'h 1963; Jal 1963; Weinstock 1971.
[183] Beard 1993. [184] Kraus 1991; Matthes 2000; Joshel 2002; Lüdemann 2007.

(*ut huic urbi semina magna dares*, *Fasti* 3.10), commenting that 'now indeed within her entrails was the founder of the Roman city' (*iam scilicet intra | uiscera Romanae conditor urbis erat*, 3.23–4). Rape is no mere recurrent *topos* in these stories. An implicit relationship links the woman's body and the body politic, but no text fully spells this out. The metaphors of the *corpus rei publicae* ('body of the republic', e.g. Cicero, *De officiis* 1.85, *Philippics* 8.15) and the *corpus imperii* ('body of empire', e.g. Florus 2.14.5–6) exist in Latin, so the violation of a body at moments of crisis and its subsequent resolution in the foundation of Rome (Ilia), Roman society (the Sabines), of the republic (Lucretia) and the establishment of the law code (Verginia) is marked even when the body politic is not named.

Identifying exactly what concept undergirds these rapes is a challenge. Why sexuality? Why a woman's body? What difference does it make that Ilia is a Vestal Virgin, the Sabines marriageable daughters of a neighbouring people, Lucretia a matron and Verginia a nubile young Roman woman? Whether the rape results in a birth or the woman is killed? The point of an absolute metaphor is to do a kind of work that surpasses in complexity what a concept can do. As with exemplarity, the listener or reader cannot help but ask questions and engage in interpretation. Answers are not given, but produced. Mine – only one potential answer – runs as follows. Foundational rape starts from the assumption that politics begins with the bond between a man and a woman, recognised since Aristotle and prominent in Latin.[185] Furthermore, violation and violence are endemic to foundation.[186] These elements combined yield the violated woman's body as an absolute metaphor for a crisis, whose institutional solution results in rebirth in or of the body politic. A woman's violation captures the crisis' fundamentally socio-political nature without her body necessarily serving as an allegory for Rome.

Recognition of rape as a locus for thinking through political ruptures and transitions can elucidate passages that otherwise seem off target. Augustine's *De civitate Dei* opens with a shrug about the recent sack of Rome: not the cataclysmic fall of a great empire in preparation for the kingdom to come, but earthly history as usual. A long discussion ensues about how women raped by the enemy deserve compassion and should refrain from suicide. Augustine excoriates Lucretia, an exemplary model of classical Roman female virtue, for pride and exposes the logic that discredits her suicide: Lucretia was guilty of self-murder if her body only was unchaste, as she alleges in Livy, but if her suicide was honourable, that

---

[185] Aristotle, *Politics* 1252a25; Lucretius 5.962–5, 1012–23; Cicero, *De off.* 1.54.   [186] Lowrie 2005.

accuses her mind of unchastity. Augustine retropes the classical intersection of sexuality and politics for new ends. Rather than a digression sparked by an overwhelming obsession with sexual purity, his discussion of rape implicitly targets the pressing political question, whether earthly Rome's demise heralds the new foundation of a heavenly Jerusalem on earth. He could take for granted the unspoken assumption that rape marks political disruption prefatory to refoundation, that it indicates Rome's political condition. This conventional classical figuration intervenes in Christian debates about both sexuality and world order.[187]

Such a figural role for rape builds on the instrumental relationship between chastity and social virtue. Besides the utility of the legitimate production of heirs, the chastity of the women in these stories stands synecdochically for the virtue of society as a whole. Augustus certainly wanted to increase the birth rate through his marriage legislation. His restitution of the sanctity of marriage also stood symbolically for his restitution of the state after ending civil war.[188] For this reason, successful or failed marriage in Latin literature marks the wellness or dissolution of society respectively.[189]

Often, conventional figurations mix with absolute metaphors. *Bellum ciuile* (civil war), for instance, is a Roman concept that innovates on Greek *stasis* with two specifications: formal warfare, among citizens.[190] Actual treatments of civil war in Latin literature, however, use a figurative palette that extends its range to the collapse of the social bond more broadly.[191] Fratricide, suicide and sexual perversion figure civil war because they represent familial, psychic and societal degradation. A mix of fratricide, filicide, remarriage and maternal incest convey social collapse at Catullus 64.397–408. These tropes spread to civil war. Fratricide has been sufficiently naturalised as a metaphor for civil war that its figurative dimension escapes notice: it internalises the conflict between citizens into the microcosm of the family. The mix of friends, guests, relatives and personal enemies discovered on the battlefield in Sallust (*Cat.* 61.8) brings civil conflict chillingly into private life. Suicide internalises fratricide and twists the trope a conceptual notch further into the self. Romulus' murder of Remus, which becomes civil war's paradigmatic figuration,[192] combines with the city's suicide to produce a potent double metaphor (Hor. *Epod.* 7). Historical anecdotes about soldiers' committing suicide upon learning they

---

[187] Trout 1994.   [188] Treggiari 1991; Milnor 2005.   [189] Lowrie 2018; Lowrie and Vinken 2019.
[190] Armitage 2017a: 3–90 and 2017b; Lange 2017; Lange and Vervaet 2019. For a mix of literary and historical approaches, Breed, Damon and Rossi 2010.
[191] Lowrie and Vinken 2022.   [192] Wiseman 1995.

## 14 Political Thought

have killed a family foe in battle literalise the figure.[193] Civil war, figured by conventional metaphors, itself becomes a figure for pervasive collapse across dimensions – political, familial, cosmic – and in Lucan extends to a hyperbole surpassing language's analytic potential.[194]

### The Death of Turnus

The ending of Virgil's *Aeneid* is perhaps the weightiest conundrum for political thought in Latin literature.[195] At stake is nothing less than Rome's most canonical author's assessment of Rome's fundamental nature. The passage's density and apparent simplicity, the strong emotions it elicits in some, the intersection of and failure to resolve conflicting demands, the lack of authorial comment and abrupt ending – all unmoor interpretation.[196] The ending lacks closure to such an extent that subsequent authors – Ovid, the humanist Maphaeus Vegius – fill in the gaps, narrative and interpretative alike.[197] I stress the advantages of combining a wide set of interpretative strategies requiring different kinds of knowledge: Roman politics, values and types; political languages based on concepts and conventional metaphors; formal literary elements, such as internal consistency; techniques of verbal repetition and structural analogy. Each does a different kind of work. Some set up a dilemma, where choice is required at whatever price. Just as Aeneas must choose between divergent courses of action, the reader must judge the outcome. But others set up paradoxes incompatible with such antinomy. The absence of guideposts for interpretation demands the dynamic response that characterises Roman political thought. The layered and varied paradoxes informing the passage expose the contradictions of Roman politics, indeed of politics itself.

#### *Exemplarity*

Whether Aeneas is an *exemplar* instantiating Roman identity, an *exemplum* (an example in an argument) of what it means to be Roman, or Philip Hardie's 'synecdochic hero', part for Rome's

---

[193] Sisenna fr. 132 Cornell; Livy, *Epitome* 79; Val. Max. 5.5.4; Tac. *Hist.* 3.51.1–2. Bannon 1997: 150.
[194] Ahl 1976.
[195] Putnam 1965; Johnson 1976; Thomas 1998 and 2001: 278–96; Reed 2007: 55–72; Marincola 2010; Tarrant 2012: 16–30; Quint 1993: 65–96. For a general introduction to the *Aeneid*, see Perkell 1999.
[196] Thomas 2001: xix: the narrative voice 'does not instruct so much as demonstrate'. For ambiguity in ancient rhetoric, ibid. 7–14.
[197] Vegius' thirteenth book supplements the missing morality with a banal moral, Thomas 2001: 279–84.

whole,[198] he in some way embodies Rome. What he stands for, however, is hard to pin down. Augustus' direct analogue? A contrasting figure? A model for virtue? If so, for a heroic code that post-republican Rome needs to reinvent or to overcome? Or a failure of virtue tragically formative of Roman history? All the uncertainties of exemplarity attach to Aeneas and ask how far to press analogies to the current ruler and current politics. Judgement, therefore, is required. His act has invited judgement at the latest since Servius interpreted his hesitation before killing Turnus as an act of *pietas* no matter what.[199] The scene elicits judgement in a way that, say, Livy's brief version (1.1–3) where Turnus does not die, does not. Even Livy's Romulus, a founder whose acts – asylum, fratricide, rape – determine the character of the state for good or ill, does not bear so great a burden of signification. In Virgil, the morality of Aeneas' actions and the disposition of his character, part model, part warning, spur reflection about how a Roman citizen should act and be. When a new and sole ruler has suspended civil war and, they hoped, ended it for good, the pressing question is whether Rome can leave behind the internal conflict plaguing it since inception. Aeneas instantiates the contradictions and paradoxes of Roman history, the reprehensible and the laudatory together. He provokes hot judgement and cool analysis.

## *Repeated Words*

Like a textbook case in the New Criticism,[200] nearly every word in this brief scene has been set up throughout the epic (*furor, ira, cura, pater, immolare, cunctari*). Perhaps the most important is *condere*. Aeneas bears the task of founding Rome and therefore his final act is determinative even though Rome's actual foundation is deferred to a future on which the reader looks back. Romulus' foundation occurs in the gap and is first mentioned in an inset narrative, Jupiter's prophecy to Venus (1.275–7). There is no doubt Rome will be founded, only how. *Condere* marks foundation as Aeneas' task emphatically at the poem's beginning (*dum conderet urbem*, 'until he could found a city', 1.5; *Romanam condere gentem*, 'to found the Roman race', 1.33), so when Aeneas buries his sword in Turnus' breast (*condit*, 12.950), the framing repetition signals the act's metaphoric foundation.[201]

---

[198] Hardie 1993: 4–5.   [199] Servius on *Aen.* 12.940.   [200] Sharrock in this volume.
[201] James 1995.

## Contemporary Context

So much rides on the *Aeneid*'s conclusion because endings provide closure as sense-making or withhold it.[202] This is needed not just in a literary work, written to rival Homer in Latin, but because the poem speaks to contemporary politics, particularly the social and civil wars of the previous century.[203] The war between Trojans and the Latin looks retrospectively like an internal conflict. The clash between two 'peoples' who will join 'in eternal peace' (*aeterna gentes in pace futuras*, *Aen.* 12.504) is figured as a war between in-laws: Latinus and Aeneas evoke Pompey and Caesar.[204] Intersecting languages – some overt, some latent, each riven by contradiction – address whether the peace ending the civil wars will indeed turn out to be eternal. The tensions stressed by the New Criticism exceed the text itself and speak to problems in the poem's historical world. Virgil's procedure prevents facile conclusions and gives pause for reflection and analysis. Furthermore, a psychoanalytic approach would stress that it enables the emotional work needed for coming to terms with the horror of recent history and the prospect of civil war's return.[205]

## Unspoken Concepts

The evaluation of Aeneas' killing of Turnus depends on competing claims of vengeance and clemency, a fraught issue during the civil wars.[206] However, neither of these central political concepts appears here. To analyse his act in these terms requires translation into conceptual language. *Clementia* never appears in Virgil, perhaps because the word is too politically charged.[207] Neither *uenia* (pardon) nor *ulciscor* (avenge) or its nominal forms occurs at all in book 12;[208] and *parcere* (spare) is also absent here. Nevertheless, these concepts are still useful analytic tools. Virgil exercises

---

[202] Fowler 2000: 5–33, 239–307; Grewing et al. 2013.  [203] Toll 1997.
[204] Pompey and Caesar (6.830–1); Latinus and Aeneas (7.317).  [205] Oliensis 2009.
[206] Marincola 2010: 196: the scene replays Caesar and Cato's debate about punishing the Catilinarians, Sall. *Cat.* 51–2.
[207] *Inclementia*, however, pertains to death (*Georgics* 3.68) and the gods (*Aeneid* 2.602).
[208] *Venia* arguably goes wrong in every instance in the *Aeneid*, with the exception of Aeneas giving the *uenia* requested by the Latin orators who would bury their dead (11.101, 107), in Mezentius' poignant expression, the only *uenia* available to enemies (10.903). It is particularly fraught of Dido (1.519, 4.50, 4.435). Human vengeance in the *Aeneid* pertains to Rome's enemies (Sinon, 2.96; Dido, 4.625, 656, 659), civil war (Brutus, 6.818), is futile (Aeneas of his fatherland, 2.576; in the Helen episode, 2.587; Mezentius of Lausus, 10.864), archaic (Achaemenides of punishing the Cyclops, 3.638) or divine (Dirae, 4.473; Tisiphone, 6.570; Hercules over Cacus, 8.201; Opis of Camilla, 11.590, 847). But no paradigm validates vengeance among humans.

a particularly literary form of restraint: the scene illustrates rather than explains. Omitting inflammatory political language from the scene creates a more neutral analytic space, which invites reflection on the paradoxes, at the same time as ramping up the emotive tone.

The pressing and painful question of how to treat the losers in the civil wars poses challenges within and to Rome's moral, legal and constitutional order. Vengeance on citizens must appear to be not only just, but legitimate. Civil war's solution in sole rule changed the valence of clemency. Sparing and vengeance are mutually exclusive, but contemporary discourses distinguish between perpetrators of unlawful acts and citizens who made a pragmatically wrong decision to back the losing side. Augustus' vaunt of exacting vengeance (*ultus*) on the killers of his parent could justify Aeneas' revenge according to contemporary values, were it not for his boast in the following sentence about sparing those citizens who sought pardon (*ueniam petentibus ciuibus peperci*, Res gestae 2 and 3.1).[209] Augustus' establishment of the temple to Mars Ultor (*Res gestae* 21) legitimates vengeance as a means of justice,[210] but clemency was an inheritance from Caesar.[211] Ambivalence about clemency becomes explicit under monarchy because it is simultaneously desirable and reveals absolute power. Cicero is grateful for Caesar's clemency to Marcellus (*Pro Marcello* 1.1), Seneca urges it on Nero (*De clementia*), and Quintilian recommends extolling humanity over vengeance when arguing before an emperor (*Inst.* 5.13.6). Lucan casts his uncle Seneca's valorisation of clemency as a kingly virtue in the light of domination when Caesar pardons Domitius (2.510–25). As the Nazi legal theorist Carl Schmitt has shown, to suspend strict justice is a sovereign prerogative that puts the sovereign above the law.[212] Therefore, the failure to avenge signals superiority to the law. The benevolent gesture sets up a double bind. To kill or not to kill each have a principled moral and legal imperative as well as political drawbacks for Romans suspicious of kingship and the arbitrary application of justice. By staging a denied plea for pity, Virgil activates contemporary political anxieties: Romans craving clemency in civil war might recoil if its price is kingship.

---

[209] Thomas 1998: 274.
[210] Some, however, think postponing building – the temple was inaugurated in 2 BCE, Simpson 1977 – was meant to spare raw feelings; Harris 2001: 215, 244.
[211] One of the virtues on the *clipeus uirtutis* granted to Augustus in 28 BCE (*Res gestae* 34.2). Octavian took time to appreciate its advantages, Braund 2009: 290–1.
[212] Schmitt 1985, 2007; Agamben 1998, 2005.

## *Internal and External Consistency*

The comparanda cited in the previous paragraph come from outside the poem – this is a New Historicist gesture. They represent typical sources for Roman political thought: an inscription by Aeneas' contemporary analogue; a speech and directed theorising addressed to rulers of the same lineage before and after Augustus; rhetoric; and a poem on historical subject matter influenced by Virgil. Broader and shifting Roman attitudes toward vengeance and clemency validate the perception of ambivalence in the passage. Norms defined within the poem, available through formalist analysis, similarly spark a dilemma.

Anchises' declaration of Rome's excellence in the arts of imperial governance appears to establish a clear moral code.

> Tu regere imperio populos, Romane, memento
> (hae tibi erunt artes), pacique imponere morem,
> parcere subiectis et debellare superbos. (*Aeneid* 6.851–3)

> Roman, remember – these will be your arts – to govern peoples with rule and confer custom-based governance when peace treaties have been struck, to spare those you have made your subjects and war down the proud.

Virgil sets the question of sparing and the uses of and limits on total war within technical Roman political vocabulary: *pax, mos*. But the norm sets up another double bind. Turnus is both *subiectus* and *superbus* when Aeneas deliberates whether to spare him.[213] Turnus is notably *superbus* (*Aen.* 10.514, 12.326), markedly when he kills Pallas, the cause of Aeneas' anger, as are his people (8.613). But when he confesses that Aeneas has won (*uicisti*, 12.936), has he not been thrown down? Pride justifies driving home the sword, subjection clemency.

The poem also stresses clemency's urgency in civil war. Anchises addresses his descendant, Julius Caesar, with a plea that he spare first in his war against Pompey: *tuque prior, tu parce, genus qui ducis Olympo, | proice tela manu, sanguis meus!* ('you first, you spare, who draw your lineage from Olympus, throw your weapons from your hand, my blood!' *Aen.* 6.834–5). The subtle proximity of Anchises' two injunctions to spare invites both political-theoretical and historical questions: when do the subjected become citizens? Is a good Roman to war down the proud because they refuse to be folded into the empire on Roman terms and to spare the subjected so they may join the larger political order? As a breaker

---

[213] Scholarship often emphasises one or the other, e.g. Thomas 2001: 285.

of the proposed peace treaty, Turnus rejects inclusion with pride and therefore deserves war. But when he declares Aeneas has won, war is over. Turnus becomes an assimilable subject within the coming empire and therefore deserves mercy. The formal repetition of key words and structural analogies – Latinists' bread and butter – raises an institutional question: is Turnus in or outside the incipient political order? When can a subjected foe be legally assimilated?[214]

Turnus' death layers incompatible rationales over one another.[215] Submission could perhaps win him pardon for breaking the treaty, but Aeneas kills him not for legal reasons, but from anger. His anger against Turnus as Pallas' arrogant killer may be justified, but rage puts him on the wrong side of the cosmic order. The Romans understood politics not merely as a matter of constitutional or legal forms, but of regulating passion.[216] Attitudes about anger were conflicted in the philosophical tradition and the two categories characterising Aeneas' outburst provoke a dilemma: *furiis accensus et ira | terribilis* ('enflamed with rage and terrible in his anger', 12.946–7).[217] Aeneas does not reflect on Turnus' plea for mercy according to what he holds most normative and dear, that is, his care for his father, and then base his rational decision on righteous anger, justified because Turnus broke the treaty or because killing Pallas disqualifies his appeal. Rather, he flames up in fury. If anger (*ira*) can be rational, rage (*furia*) is illegitimate – it represents loss of control. We wonder: can anger redeem rage? Aeneas' hesitation encodes dilemma. Servius makes it a sign of Aeneas' essential goodness, but alternatively, it could make things worse: Aeneas' passion is not simply of the moment, but overwhelms listening and deliberation. Philosophical analysis is insufficient to the passage's power. A reader pondering moral questions will recall the simile comparing Aeneas to Aegaeon, a hundred-hander who fought against the Olympians – a conventional metaphor for civil war – when he flamed up in fury at Pallas' death (10.565). The literary figure elevates the moral and political dilemma to the cosmic sphere.

The morality of Aeneas' action is a political issue because of his exemplary function. Narratological analyses have used point of view to argue

---

[214] Turnus as the first imperial conquest, Marincola 2010: 199–204. Punitive citizenship as an instrument of domination, Ando 2011: 87–9.
[215] Thomas 2001: 291; Lowrie 2005.
[216] For social virtues, Kaster 2005. For the statesman's soul and his regulation of the souls of his people, Atkins 2013: 73–9; Lowrie forthcoming calls this metaphor 'the soul political'.
[217] Harris 2001; Thomas 2001: 290–1; Adler 2003; Gill 2006: 457–61.

for incompatible perspectives at the *Aeneid*'s end.[218] But the numerous dilemmas informing this scene surpass our judgement of Aeneas' particular character. His internal conflict when he kills Turnus matters not because it characterises an individual with a role in Rome's foundation, but because synecdochic transfer turns him into a general model for conflict within the Roman political order. Foundation is, well, foundational: what happened at Rome's beginning establishes a template for its subsequent history. His individual soul has political consequences. But it is not just a question of setting up an inevitable historical pattern. The exemplum encodes the conflict at the heart of Roman politics.

Roman exemplarity sets up an expectation that family members stay true to type. Any Appius Claudius is an extremist, reactionary senatorial hothead. The cognomen Poplicola inscribes the Valerii's role as champions of the plebs into their name. The Decii specialise in *deuotio*. Exemplarity, not just a textual phenomenon, actively forms politics, morality and culture. Brutus felt pressure to slay the tyrant Caesar on the model of his ancestor Lucius Junius Brutus, who drove out the tyrannical Tarquins. Sources attest to this pressure not in the hoary mythic times before the city's foundation, which Livy likens to 'poetic tales' (*poeticis ... fabulis, praef.* 6), but within the historical record.[219] In the *Aeneid*, Caesar, Augustus and Aeneas do not align. What does it mean then that Aeneas withholds clemency not only against his father's injunctions to spare – directed to his apostrophised descendant Caesar, known for clemency – but also against his further descendant Augustus' grant of pardon to citizens seeking it?[220] Differences between ancestor and descendant relieve the pressure to transfer judgement, positive or negative, from Aeneas onto Augustus or vice versa. Still, the conspicuous failure to conform to type puzzles. It certainly indicates a profound break – but of what sort? The *Aeneid* suggests answers to these questions not directly, but through a repertory of figurations.

### *Metaphors*

The double contexts of Anchises' call to pardon, civil war and empire, together inform Aeneas' failure to pardon and thereby link civil war and empire through figuration as decisively as Sallust's explicit derivation of

---

[218] For focalisation, Fowler 2000: 40–63; Thomas 2001: 296.   [219] Plutarch, *Brutus* 9.5–8.
[220] Much of the *Res gestae* was known before publication at Augustus' death (14 CE), probably because he recycled his autobiography: Lowrie 2009: 361 nn. 5 and 6; Lange 2019.

internal conflict from imperial expansion (*Cat.* 10–12). The tropes of foundation and of civil war are the same: fratricide, rape and suicide. They map the political order in its entirety: the new political entity established between refugees and the native population in this foundation instantiates empire; civil war inhabits Aeneas' killing of Turnus. The combination of implicit concepts with conventional and absolute metaphors says more than is spoken.

The density of civil war tropes is overwhelming and hard to process. Each – conveyed through literary techniques such as structural analogy and allusion to Homer – makes an implicit point beyond conveying learned aesthetic pleasure. Aeneas and Turnus become each other's figural twin.[221] Each, as is well known, is a new Iliadic Achilles, and the scholarship finds numerous other similarities.[222] Turnus defends his promised bride, Lavinia, snatched from him by a Trojan rapist (*Aen.* 7.362, 9.742), but plays Hector to Aeneas' Achilles in his death scene.[223] As twins, the one's killing the other evokes Romulus' fratricide, a metaphor by this time for civil war. If civil war inheres in Rome's foundation, it explains Rome's conflicted past and intimates the challenge facing Augustus as nothing less than breaking with the course of history, changing the imperative of his exemplary relation to his ancestor.

The parallels between Turnus and Aeneas make Aeneas' killing Turnus not just a metaphorical fratricide, however, but additionally a metaphorical suicide.[224] Like Achilles, who kills Hector wearing his own armour and thereby figuratively kills himself, Aeneas kills his own mirrored self and takes vengeance on himself for not preventing his beloved ward's death. The scene, however, rolls out yet another suicide. The actual armour shifts the figurative suicide to Pallas. The suicide is itself twinned. Turnus, like Hector, is wearing armour despoiled: a baldric ripped off Pallas, as dear to Aeneas as Patroclus was to Achilles. Turnus thereby stands in for Pallas, whose name rings out repeatedly when Aeneas declares he is Turnus' killer: *Pallas te hoc uulnere, Pallas | immolat et poenam scelerato ex sanguine sumit* ('With this wound Pallas sacrifices you and Pallas takes vengeance from this accursed blood', 12.948–9). Pallas as avenger – Italy's native-born son from the site of Rome – kills his own image, Pallas as Turnus, in a perverse human sacrifice, which overlays yet another trope for civil war onto the already dense image.[225]

[221] Thomas 1998; Quint 2018.   [222] Van Nortwick 1980.
[223] Lavinia's rape evokes Helen's (*Aen.* 7.359–64) among other, Homeric parallels, Anderson 1957: 21.
[224] Fratricide and suicide are tropes of civil war. For suicide's prominence in Lucan, Ahl 1976.
[225] For human sacrifice, Hardie 1993: 19–37.

If that were not enough imagistic overlay, foundational rape returns here. Internal analogues layer the blood of empire over the blood of civil war with metaphorical rapes, which engender monstrous and foundational political births. Penetration by the sword turns this into a scene first of a sterile homoerotic rape.[226] Io, on Turnus' shield, evokes rape and her descendants, the Danaids who are depicted on Pallas' baldric, pile on murder and gender reversal, in the women's wielding of the phallic sword. The scene does one worse, since no Hypermestra spares her Lynceus.[227] Furthermore, analogy with the rape of Dido – the baldric is also *infelix* – suggests a perversely fertile heterosexual register. The fruit of Dido's self-penetration with Aeneas' sword on the pyre (4.507, 664) – another rape/suicide – is Rome's most deadly imperial enemy, Hannibal, who will avenge her (*ultor*, 4.625). The fruit of Aeneas' rape of Turnus, who stands in for Pallas, is civil war. Dido's infertility (*infelix*), the baldric's infertility (*infelix*) are perversely fertile, not of children, but of war.

Virgil's metaphors bind external and internal enemy, empire and civil war inexorably together. The result, however, is not a clear and distinct analysis, as in Sallust's causal argument that empire engenders civil war, but a heap of bloodshed merged into a densely abject and conflicted figuration.[228] The interconnection between empire and civil war suggests that externalising internal violence onto empire, as Jupiter so cheerily predicts to Venus as the Augustan solution (1.286–90), may falter before Rome's foundational nature, which erases the distinction.[229] Civil war's inhering in Rome's foundation explains Rome's conflicted past and intimates the challenge facing Augustus as nothing less than changing the course of history. The current pause may be only temporary, like the golden ages that have come before. More than an explanatory function for history, however, the overlap of tropes for foundation and civil war unmasks the violence underlying the entire political order. Augustus would have to transcend history itself to change things. The golden age of the Augustan peace resides on a continual extension of empire through violence that continually re-inscribes the external as internal and thereby re-enacts civil war. To change the order of history would entail breaking the intrinsic link between empire, foundation and civil war.

---

[226] For the scene's displaced eroticism, Reed 2007: 44–55.
[227] Danaids: Spence 1991; Danaids and Io: Putnam 1994: 18–21, 188–209; homosexual rape: Mac Góráin 2016: 410–11 and 2018: 150; homo- and heterosexual rape and monstrous birth: Lowrie and Vinken 2023.
[228] For the *Aeneid*'s 'superabundance ... obsessively overwrought', Oliensis 2001: 61.
[229] For paradox in the *Aeneid*'s prophecies, O'Hara 1990.

Why so very many figural overlays? In case we miss one? To short-circuit our intellectual processing of the scene? Much figuration does its work latently. It touches on feelings not susceptible to reason, not even available to consciousness. Virgil's extraordinarily dense metaphorical register arouses conflicting, repressed emotions we may not even be aware of. Some of the figurations above – Pallas' suicide, Turnus' monstrous birth – have even (I think) escaped scholarly notice. And a long tradition of Augustanism has ignored even the ones recent scholarship emphasises.

I conclude with two methodological points about reading the ending of the *Aeneid* that I mean to be exemplary for the way Latin literature goes about political thought. The first is directed at political theorists. The conventional tropes identified here obey standard methods of formal literary analysis, where the figurative burden of repeated words, themes and motifs needs to be read out from the text. This kind of reading is analytic – intellectual and cool. The figurations speak to Roman anguish over contemporary politics. My reading dramatises the engagement required in Roman political thought to reach judgement – emotional and hot. Reading figuratively, that is, pulling out the unspoken concepts, the conventional and absolute metaphors, reveals the richly paradoxical dimension of how Romans thought their politics. If only Aeneas could resolve the merely logical contradiction of the poem's dilemmas, he would still face the paradoxes of the destructive political order. To literary readers, I would stress the structural parallel between the politics and the poem's figurative mode. Empire contains, but cannot erase, civil war in history, just as the poem's overt affirmation of empire contains, but does not erase, its metaphors.

## Conclusion

The Romans' contributions to the history of political thought include foundational institutions and concepts. These are well recognised and form the core of what the discipline recognises as their signature. Current approaches, however, have highlighted the affective, performative and embedded nature not only of the substance of their ideas, but also of their means of expression. Poetry is a rich source and should not be overlooked by theorists. The *Aeneid*'s fraught ending is an extreme instance of metaphorical density, but well exemplifies the need of figurative reading to access the creativity of political thinking in Latin. Conversely, literary scholars do well when they add inscriptions and material culture to their toolbox. The Romans' more methodological statements are located not in works conforming to political theory as a genre, but in history and rhetoric. Roman political thought revolves around conflict and power more than questions of constitutional form. It tends toward paradox and is eclectic. For this reason, the most fruitful approaches for its analysis share its broad palette.

## References

Adler, E. (2003) *Vergil's Empire: Political Thought in the Aeneid*, Lanham, MD.
Adorno, T. (1991) 'On lyric poetry and society', in *Notes to Literature*, Vol. 1 (trans. S. W. Nicholsen), New York (German orig. 1958).
Agamben, G. (1998) *Homo sacer: Sovereign Power and Bare Life* (trans. D. Heller-Roazen), Stanford (Italian orig. 1995).
   (2000) *Means without End: Notes on Politics* (trans. V. Binetti and C. Casarino), Minneapolis.
   (2005) *State of Exception*, Chicago.
Ahl, F. (1976) *Lucan: An Introduction*, Ithaca, NY.
   (1984) 'The art of safe criticism in Greece and Rome', *AJPh* 105: 174–208.
Anderson, B. (1983) *Imagined Communities: Reflections on the Origin and Spread of Nationalism*, London.
Anderson, W. S. (1957) 'Vergil's second *Iliad*', *TAPhA* 88: 17–30.
Ando, C. (2000) *Imperial Ideology and Provincial Loyalty in the Roman Empire*, Berkeley.
   (2011) *Law, Language, and Empire in the Roman Tradition*, Philadelphia.
   (2015) *Roman Social Imaginaries: Language and Thought in Context of Empire*, Toronto.
Arena, V. (2012) *Libertas and the Practice of Politics in the Late Roman Republic*, Cambridge.
Arendt, H. (1958) *The Human Condition*, Chicago.
   (1963) *On Revolution*, New York.
Armitage, D. (2012) 'What's the big idea? Intellectual history and the *longue durée*', *History of European Ideas* 38: 493–507.
   (2017a) *Civil Wars: A History in Ideas*, New York.
   (2017b) 'On the genealogy of quarrels', *Critical Analysis of Law* 4: 178–89.
Asmis, E. (2004) 'The state as partnership: Cicero's definition of *res publica* in his work *On the State*', *History of Political Thought* 25: 569–99.
   (2005) 'A new kind of model: Cicero's Roman constitution in *De republica*', *AJPh* 126: 377–427.
Atkins, J. W. (2013) *Cicero on Politics and the Limits of Reason*, Cambridge.
   (2018) *Roman Political Thought*, Cambridge.
Bannon, C. (1997) *The Brothers of Romulus: Fraternal pietas in Roman Law, Literature, and Society*, Princeton.
Baraz, Y. (2012) *A Written Republic: Cicero's Philosophical Politics*, Princeton.

Barchiesi, A. (1997) *The Poet and the Prince: Ovid and Augustan Discourse*, Berkeley.
  (2001) *Speaking Volumes: Narrative and Intertext in Ovid and Other Latin Poets*, London.
Bartsch, S. (1994) *Actors in the Audience*, Cambridge, MA.
  (1997) *Ideology in Cold Blood: A Reading of Lucan's Civil War*, Cambridge, MA.
  (2012a) 'The art of sincerity: Pliny's *Panegyricus*', in Rees 2012: 148–93 (reprint of Bartsch 1994: 148–87).
  (2012b) 'Praise and doublespeak: Tacitus' *Dialogus*', in Ash 2012: 119–54 (revised version of Bartsch 1994: 101–25).
Batstone, W. W. (1991) 'A narrative gestalt and the force of Caesar's plain style', *Mnemosyne* 44: 126–36.
Batstone, W. W. and C. Damon (2006) *Julius Caesar: The Civil War*, Oxford.
Beard, M. (1993) 'Looking (harder) for Roman myth: Dumézil, declamation and problems of definition', in F. Graf, ed., *Mythos in mythenloser Gesellschaft: Das Paradigma Roms* (Stuttgart and Leipzig), 44–64.
Beck, D. (2014) 'The first simile of the *Aeneid*', *Vergilius* 60: 67–83.
Bevir, M. (2011) 'The contextual approach', in G. Klosko, ed., *The Oxford Handbook of the History of Political Philosophy* (Oxford), 11–23.
Blumenberg, H. (1997) *Shipwreck with Spectator: Paradigm of a Metaphor for Existence* (trans. S. Rendall), Cambridge, MA.
  (2007) *Theorie der Unbegrifflichkeit* (ed. A. Haverkamp), Frankfurt.
  (2010) *Paradigms for a Metaphorology* (trans. R. Savage), Ithaca, NY.
Braund, S. (1998) 'Praise and protreptic in early imperial panegyric', in Whitby 1998, 53–76. Reprinted in Rees 2012, 85–108.
  (2009) *Seneca: De clementia*, Oxford.
Breed, B. (2006) *Pastoral Inscriptions: Reading and Writing Virgil's Eclogues*, London.
Breed, B., C. Damon and A. Rossi, eds. (2010) *Citizens of Discord: Rome and Its Civil Wars*, Oxford and New York.
Brooks, P. (2010) 'Literature as law's other', *Yale Journal of Law and Humanities* 22: 349–67.
Brown, P. R. L. (1972) 'Political society', in R. A. Markus, ed., *Augustine: A Collection of Critical Essays* (New York), 311–29.
Brunner, O., W. Conze and R. Koselleck (2004) *Geschichtliche Grundbegriffe: Historisches Lexikon zur politisch-sozialen Sprache in Deutschland*, Stuttgart.
Bryen, A. Z. (2014) 'Law in many pieces', *CPh* 109: 346–65.
  (2018) 'Labeo's *iniuria*: violence and politics in the age of Augustus', *Chiron* 48: 17–52.
Camus, A. (1984) *Caligula*, Paris.
Cartledge, P. (2009) *Ancient Greek Political Thought in Practice*, Cambridge.
  (2016) *Democracy: a Life*, Oxford.
Castoriadis, C. (1975) *L'Institution imaginaire de la société*, Paris. Trans. K. Blamey as *The Imaginary Institution of Society*, Cambridge, MA, 1987.
Chaplin, J. D. (2000) *Livy's Exemplary History*, Oxford.

Chaplin, J. D. and C. S. Kraus, eds. (2009) *Livy: Oxford Readings in Classical Studies*, Oxford.
Connolly, J. (2007) *The State of Speech: Rhetoric and Political Thought in Ancient Rome*, Princeton.
  (2009a) 'Fear and freedom: a new interpretation of Pliny's *Panegyricus*', in G. Urso, ed., *Ordine e sovversione nel mondo greco e romano* (Pisa), 259–78.
  (2009b) 'Virtue and violence: the historians on politics', in Feldherr 2009: 181–94.
  (2010) 'Political theory', in A. Barchiesi and W. Scheidel, eds., *The Oxford Handbook of Roman Studies* (Oxford), 713–27.
  (2011) 'Fantastical realism in Cicero's postwar panegyric', in G. Urso, ed., *Dicere laudes* (Pisa), 161–79.
  (2015) *The Life of Roman Republicanism*, Princeton.
  (2017) 'The Romans tried to save the republic from men like Trump. They failed', *Village Voice*, 17 January 2017.
Cooley, A. E., ed. (2009) *Res gestae Divi Augusti*, Cambridge.
Corbeill, A. (2002) 'Rhetorical education in Cicero's youth', in J. M. May, ed., *Brill's Companion to Cicero: Oratory and Rhetoric* (Leiden), 23–48.
  (2007) 'Rhetorical education and social reproduction in the Republic and early Empire', in W. Dominik and J. Hall, eds., *A Companion to Roman Rhetoric* (Malden, MA), 69–82.
Cornwell, H. (2017) *Pax and the Politics of Peace: Republic to Principate*, Oxford.
Cresci, L. R. and F. Gazzano, eds. (2018) *De imperiis: l'idea di impero universale e la successione degli imperi nell'antichità*, Rome.
Crick, B. (1967) 'Philosophy, theory and thought', *Political Studies* 15: 49–55.
Cugusi, P. and M. T. Sblendoria Cugusi, eds. (2001) *Marco Porcio Catone censore. Opere*, 2 vols., Turin.
Damon, C. (1999) 'The trial of Cn. Piso in Tacitus' *Annals* and the *Senatus consultum de C. Pisone patre*: new light on narrative technique', *AJPh* 120: 143–62.
Davis, G. (1991) *Polyhymnia: The Rhetoric of Horatian Lyric Discourse*, Berkeley.
Dominik, W. J. (1997) 'The style is the man: Seneca, Tacitus and Quintilian's canon', in W. J. Dominik, ed., *Roman Eloquence: Rhetoric in Society and Literature* (London), 50–68.
Dressler, A. (2016) *Personification and the Feminine in Roman Philosophy*, Cambridge.
Dufallo, B. (2007) *The Ghosts of the Past: Latin Literature, the Dead, and Rome's Transition to a Principate*, Columbus, OH.
Dufallo, B., ed. (2018) *Roman Error: Classical Reception and the Problem of Rome's Flaws*, Oxford.
Dugan, J. (2005) *Making a New Man: Ciceronian Self-Fashioning in the Rhetorical Works*, Oxford.
  (2013) 'Cicero and the politics of ambiguity: interpreting the *Pro Marcello*', in C. Steel and H. van der Blom, eds., *Community and Communication: Oratory and Politics in Republican Rome* (Oxford), 211–25.

du Plessis, P., C. Ando and K. Tuori, eds. (2016) *The Oxford Handbook of Roman Law and Society*, Oxford.
Dyck, A. (2004) *Cicero: De legibus*, Ann Arbor, MI.
Dyer, R. R. (1990) 'Rhetoric and invention in Cicero's *Pro Marcello*', *JRS* 80: 17–30.
Earl, D. C. (1961) *The Political Thought of Sallust*, Cambridge.
Edwards, C. (1993) *The Politics of Immorality in Ancient Rome*, Cambridge.
Ernst, W. (2014) 'Plinius, *Epistulae* 8.14: Abstimmungsprobleme im römischen Senat', *Fundamina* 20: 240–57.
Euben, J. P., ed. (1986) *Greek Tragedy and Political Theory*, Berkeley.
Fantham, E. (2004) *The Roman World of Cicero's De oratore*, Oxford.
Farr, J. (1989) 'Understanding conceptual change politically', in T. Ball, J. Farr and R. L. Hanson, eds., *Political Innovation and Conceptual Change* (Cambridge), 24–49.
Farrell, J. and D. Nelis, eds. (2013) *Augustan Poetry and the Roman Republic*, Oxford.
Feeney, D. C. (1998) *Literature and Religion at Rome: Cultures, Contexts and Beliefs*, Cambridge.
  (2002) '*Vna cum scriptore meo*: poetry, principate, and the traditions of literary history in the *Epistle to Augustus*', in A. J. Woodman and D. C. Feeney, eds., *Traditions and Contexts in the Poetry of Horace* (Cambridge), 172–87.
  (2004) 'Sacrificial ritual in Roman poetry', in A. Barchiesi, J. Rüpke and S. Stephens, eds., *Rituals in Ink* (Stuttgart), 1–22.
  (2009) 'Horace and the Greek lyric poets', in M. Lowrie, ed., *Horace's Odes and Epodes: Oxford Readings in Classical Studies* (Oxford), 202–31.
  (2014) 'First similes in epic', *TAPhA* 144: 189–28.
Feldherr, A. (1998) *Spectacle and Society in Livy's History*, Berkeley.
Feldherr, A., ed. (2009) *The Cambridge Companion to the Roman Historians*, Cambridge.
Ferenczi, A. and P. Hardie, eds. (2014) *New Approaches to Horace's Ars poetica* (= *MD* 72.1), Pisa.
Fertik, H. and M. Hanses, eds. (2019) *Above the Veil: Revisiting the Classicism of W. E. B. Du Bois* (= *IJCT* 26.1), Boston.
Fiori, R. (1996) *Homo sacer: dinamica politico-constituzionale di una sanzione giuridico-religiosa*, Naples.
Flower, H. I. (2009) *Roman Republics*, Princeton.
  (2017) *The Dancing Lares and the Serpent in the Garden: Religion at the Roman Street Corner*, Princeton.
Fowler, A. (1982) *Kinds of Literature: An Introduction to the Theory of Genres and Modes*, Cambridge, MA.
Fowler, D. (2000) *Roman Constructions: Readings in Postmodern Latin*, Oxford.
Freudenburg, K. (2001) *Satires of Rome: Threatening Poses from Lucilius to Juvenal*, Cambridge.
  (2014) '*Recusatio* as political theatre: Horace's letter to Augustus', *JRS* 104: 105–32.

(2018a) 'Donald Trump and Rome's mad emperors', *Common Dreams*, 29 April 2018.

(2018b) 'Donald Trump and the Tiberian lie', *Common Dreams*, 4 December 2018.

Gajda, A. (2010) 'Tacitus and political thought in early modern Europe, *c.* 1530–*c.* 1640', in A. J. Woodman, ed., *The Cambridge Companion to Tacitus* (Cambridge), 253–68.

Galinsky, K. (1996) *Augustan Culture: An Interpretation*, Princeton.

(2015) 'Augustus' *auctoritas* and *Res gestae* 34.3', *Hermes* 143: 244–9.

Gallia, A. (2009) '*Potentes* and *potentia* in Tacitus' *Dialogus de oratoribus*', *TAPhA* 139: 169–206.

Gallie, W. B. (1956) 'Essentially contested concepts', *PAS* 56: 167–98.

Geue, T. (2014) 'Editing the opposition: Horace's *Ars poetica*', in Ferenczi and Hardie 2014, 143–72.

Gibson, R. K. and R. Morello (2012) *Reading the Letters of Pliny the Younger: An Introduction*, Cambridge.

Gibson, R. K. and C. Whitton, eds. (2016) *The Epistles of Pliny*. Oxford Readings in Classical Studies, Oxford.

Gill, C. (2006) *The Structured Self in Hellenistic and Roman Thought*, Oxford.

Goff, B. (1995) 'Introduction', in B. Goff, ed., *History, Tragedy, Theory: Dialogues on Athenian Drama* (Austin), 1–37.

Goldhill, S. (1986) *Reading Greek Tragedy*, Cambridge.

(1999) 'Programme notes', in S. Goldhill and R. Osborne, eds., *Performance Culture and Athenian Democracy*, Cambridge.

(2012) *Sophocles and the Language of Tragedy*, Oxford.

Gowing, A. (2013) 'Afterword', in Farrell and Nelis 2013, 319–32.

Graver, M. and A. A. Long (2015) *Lucius Annaeus Seneca: Letters on Ethics*, Chicago.

Grewing, F., B. Acosta-Hughes and A. Kirichenko, eds. (2013) *The Door Ajar: False Closure in Classical Antiquity*, Heidelberg.

Griffin, M. T. (1996) 'When is thought political?', *Apeiron* 29: 269–82.

Gurd, S. A. (2012) *Work in Progress: Literary Revision as Social Performance in Ancient Rome*, Oxford.

Habinek, T. N. (1998) *The Politics of Latin Literature*, Princeton.

(2005) *The World of Roman Song*, Baltimore.

Hadot, P. (1995) *Philosophy as a Way of Life: Spiritual Exercises from Socrates to Foucault*, Oxford.

Haimson Lushkov, A. (2010) 'Intertextuality and source-criticism in the Scipionic trials', in W. Polleichtner, ed., *Livy and Intertextuality* (Trier), 93–133.

Haley, E. W. (2003) *Baetica felix: People and Prosperity in Southern Spain from Caesar to Septimius Severus*, Austin, TX.

Hammer, D. (2008) *Roman Political Thought and the Modern Theoretical Imagination*, Norman, OK.

(2014) *Roman Political Thought: From Cicero to Augustine*, Cambridge.

Hampsher-Monk, I., K. Tilmans and F. van Vree, eds. (1998) *History of Concepts: Comparative Perspectives*, Amsterdam.
Hardie, P. (1993) *The Epic Successors of Virgil: A Study in the Dynamics of a Tradition*, Cambridge.
Hardt, M. and A. Negri (2000) *Empire*, Cambridge, MA.
Harris, W. V. (1985) *War and Imperialism in Republican Rome, 327–70 BC*, Oxford.
  (2001) *Restraining Rage*, Cambridge, MA.
Heinze, R. (1972) '*Auctoritas*', in R. Heinze, *Vom Geist des Römertums* (Darmstadt), 43–58.
Hellegouarc'h, J. (1963) *Le vocabulaire latin des relations et des partis politiques sous la république*, Paris.
Henderson, J. (1998) *Fighting for Rome: Poets and Caesars, History and Civil War*, Cambridge.
Hölkeskamp, K.-J. (2004) *Senatus populusque Romanus*, Stuttgart.
  (2010) *Reconstructing the Roman Republic: An Ancient Political Culture and Modern Research*, Princeton.
Honig, B. (2009) *Emergency Politics: Paradox, Law, Democracy*, Princeton.
Horne, A. (2018) 'Making freedom in Cicero and Horace', unpublished PhD dissertation, University of Chicago.
Houellebecq, M. (2015) *Soumission*, Paris.
Howarth, R. S. (2013) 'War and warfare in ancient Rome', in B. Campbell and L. A. Tritle, eds., *The Oxford Handbook of Warfare in the Classical World* (Oxford), 29–45.
Jaeger, M. (1997) *Livy's Written Rome*, Ann Arbor, MI.
Jal, P. (1963) *La guerre civile à Rome. Étude littéraire et morale*, Paris.
James, S. (1995) 'Establishing Rome with the sword: *condere* in the *Aeneid*', *AJPh* 116: 623–37.
Johnson, W. R. (1976) *Darkness Visible: A Study of Vergil's Aeneid*, Berkeley.
  (1993) *Horace and the Dialectic of Freedom: Readings in 'Epistles' 1*, Ithaca, NY.
Joshel, S. R. (2002) 'The body female and the body politic: Livy's Lucretia and Verginia', in L. K. McClure, ed., *Sexuality and Gender in the Classical World* (Oxford), 163–87.
Kapust, D. J. (2011a) *Republicanism, Rhetoric, and Roman Political Thought: Sallust, Livy, and Tacitus*, Cambridge.
  (2011b) 'Tacitus and political thought', in V. A. Pagán, ed., *A Companion to Tacitus* (Malden, MA), 504–28.
  (2013) Review of Arena 2012, *BMCRev* 2013.08.51.
  (2018a) *Flattery and the History of Political Thought: That Glib and Oily Art*, Cambridge.
  (2018b) 'The founders hated excessive flattery. What would they think about the Trump administration?', *Washington Post*, 22 January 2018.
Kaster, R. A. (2005) *Emotion, Restraint and Community in Ancient Rome*, London.
Klotz, A. (1953) *Scaenicorum Romanorum fragmenta*, vol. 1, Munich.

Koschorke, A., S. Lüdemann, T. Frank and E. Matala de Mazza (2007) *Der fiktive Staat: Konstruktionen des politischen Körpers in der Geschichte Europas*, Frankfurt.
Koselleck, R. (2004) *Futures Past: On the Semantics of Historical Time* (trans. K. Tribe), New York.
Kraus, C. S. (1991) '*Initium turbandi omnia a femina ortum est*: Fabia Minor and the election of 367 BC', *Phoenix* 45: 314–25.
  (1999) 'Jugurthine disorder', in C. S. Kraus, ed., *The Limits of Historiography: Genre and Narrative in Historical Texts* (Leiden), 217–47.
  (2005) 'From *exempla* to *exemplar*? Writing history around the emperor in imperial Rome', in J. Edmondson, S. Mason and J. Rives, eds., *Flavius Josephus and Flavian Rome* (Oxford), 181–200.
Kraus, C. S., J. M. Marincola and C. B. R. Pelling, eds. (2010) *Ancient Historiography and Its Contexts: Studies in Honor of A. J. Woodman*, Oxford.
Krugman, P. (2017) 'Trump makes Caligula look pretty good', *New York Times*, 18 August 2017, page A25.
Lakoff, G. and M. Johnson (1980) *Metaphors We Live By*, Chicago.
Lange, C. H. (2017) '*Stasis* and *bellum civile*: a difference in scale?', *Critical Analysis of Law* 4: 129–40.
  (2019) 'Augustus, the *Res gestae*, and the end of civil war: unpleasant events?', in Lange and Vervaet 2019, 185–209.
Lange, C. H. and J. M. Madsen, eds. (2016) *Cassius Dio: Greek Intellectual and Roman Politician*, Leiden.
Lange, C. H. and F. Vervaet, eds. (2019) *The Historiography of Late Republican Civil War*, Leiden.
Langlands, R. (2008) '"Reading for the moral" in Valerius Maximus: the case of *severitas*', *The Cambridge Classical Journal* 54: 160–87.
  (2011) 'Roman *exempla* and situation ethics: Valerius Maximus and Cicero *De officiis*', *JRS* 101: 100–22.
  (2015) 'Roman exemplarity: mediating between general and particular', in Lowrie and Lüdemann 2015, 68–80.
  (2018) *Exemplary Ethics in Ancient Rome*, Cambridge.
Laurence, R., S. E. Cleary and G. Sears (2011) *The City in the Roman West c. 250 BC–c. AD 250*, Cambridge.
Levene, D. (2000) 'Sallust's *Catiline* and Cato the censor', *CQ* 50: 170–91.
  (2004) 'Reading Cicero's narratives', in J. Powell and J. Paterson, eds., *Cicero the Advocate* (Oxford), 117–46.
Liebeschuetz, W. (2013) 'The theme of liberty in the *Agricola* of Tacitus', in Ash 2012, 73–94.
Lintott, A. (1999a) *The Constitution of the Roman Republic*, Oxford.
  (1999b) *Violence in Republican Rome*, 2nd edn, Oxford.
Loraux, N. (1993) *The Children of Athena: Athenian Ideas about Citizenship and the Division between the Sexes* (trans. C. Levine), Princeton.
  (1995) *The Experiences of Tiresias* (trans. P. Wissing), Princeton.
  (2002) *The Divided City: On Memory and Forgetting in Ancient Athens* (trans. C. Pache), New York.

Lowrie, M. (1997) *Horace's Narrative Odes*, Oxford.
  (2005) 'Vergil and founding violence', *Cardozo Law Review* 27: 945–76.
  (2007a) 'Making an *exemplum* of yourself: Cicero and Augustus', in S. J. Heyworth, with P. G. Fowler and S. J. Harrison, eds., *Classical Constructions: Papers in Memory of Don Fowler, Classicist and Epicurean* (Oxford), 91–112.
  (2007b) 'Sovereignty before the law: Agamben and the Roman Republic', *Law and Humanities* 1: 31–55.
  (2007c) 'Horace and Augustus', in S. J. Harrison, ed., *Cambridge Companion to Horace* (Cambridge), 77–89.
  (2009) *Writing, Performance and Authority in Augustan Rome*, Oxford.
  (2010a) 'Spurius Maelius: dictatorship and the *homo sacer*', in Breed, Damon and Rossi 2010, 171–86.
  (2010b) 'Rom immer wieder gegründet', in T. Döring, B. Vinken and G. Zöller, eds., *Übertragene Anfänge: Imperiale Figurationen um 1800* (Munich), 23–49.
  (2011) 'Divided voices and imperial identity in Propertius 4.1 and Derrida, *Monolingualism of the Other and Politics of Friendship*', *Dictynna* 8, https://journals.openedition.org/dictynna/711.
  (2013) 'Foundation and closure', in Grewing et al. 2013, 83–102.
  (2014) 'Politics by other means: Horace's *Ars poetica*', in Ferenczi and Hardie 2014, 121–42.
  (2016a) 'Le corps du chef: transformations dans la sphère publique à l'époque d'Horace', in B. Delignon, N. Le Meur and O. Thevenaz, eds., *Le poète lyrique dans la cité antique: les Odes d'Horace au miroir de la lyrique grecque archaïque* (Paris), 71–86.
  (2016b) 'Roman law and Latin literature', in du Plessis, Ando and Tuori 2016, 70–82.
  (2018) 'Figures of discord and the Roman addressee in Horace, *Odes* 3.6', in S. J. Harrison, S. Frangoulidis and T. D. Papanghelis, eds., *Intratextuality and Latin Literature* (Berlin), 211–25.
  (forthcoming) *Security and Its Metaphors in Roman Political Thought*.
Lowrie, M. and S. Lüdemann (2015) *Exemplarity and Singularity: Thinking through Particulars in Philosophy, Literature, and Law*, London.
Lowrie, M. and B. Vinken (2019) 'Married to civil war: a Roman trope in Lucan's poetics of history', in Lange and Vervaet 2019, 263–91.
  (2022) *Civil War and the Collapse of the Social Bond: The Roman Tradition at the Heart of the Modern*, Cambridge.
Lüdemann, S. (2007) 'Weibliche Gründungsopfer', in Koschorke, Lüdemann, Frank and Matala de Mazza 2007, 36–46.
Lyne, R. O. A. M. (1995) *Horace: Behind the Public Poetry*, New Haven.
McCarter, S. (2015) *Horace between Freedom and Slavery*, Madison, WI.
MacCormack, S. (1998) *The Shadows of Poetry: Vergil in the Mind of Augustine*, Berkeley.
  (1999) 'Classical authors', in A. D. Fitzgerald, ed., *Augustine through the Ages: An Encyclopedia* (Grand Rapids), 202–6.
McCormick, J. (2011) *Machiavellian Democracy*, Cambridge.

(2015) 'Machiavelli's Agathocles: from criminal example to princely exemplum', in Lowrie and Lüdemann 2015, 123–39.
(forthcoming) *The People's Princes: Machiavelli, Leadership and Liberty.*
Mac Góráin, F. (2016) 'The poetics of vision in Virgil's *Aeneid*', *HSPh* 109: 383–427.
(2018) 'Vergil's Sophoclean Thebans', *Vergilius* 64: 131–56.
McGowan, M. (2009) *Ovid in Exile: Power and Poetic Redress in the Tristia and Epistulae ex Ponto*, Leiden.
Manuwald, G. (2011) 'Ciceronian praise as a step towards Pliny's *Panegyricus*', in Roche 2011, 85–103.
Marincola, J. (2010) '*Eros* and empire: Virgil and the historians on civil war', in Kraus, Marincola and Pelling 2010, 183–204.
Marx, K. (1960) 'Der achtzehnte Brumaire des Louis Bonaparte', in K. Marx and F. Engels, *Werke* 8 (Berlin), 111–207.
Matthes, M. (2000) *The Rape of Lucretia and the Founding of Republics*, University Park, PA.
Mayer, R. (2001) *Tacitus: Dialogus de oratoribus*, Cambridge.
Mebane, J. (2017) 'The body politic and Roman political languages', dissertation, University of Chicago; forthcoming as *The Body Politic in Roman Political Thought*, Cambridge.
Meconi, D. V. and E. Stump, eds. (2014) *The Cambridge Companion to Augustine*, 2nd edn, Cambridge.
Millar, F. (1984) 'The political character of the classical Roman Republic, 200–151 BC', *JRS* 76: 1–11.
(1998) *The Crowd in Rome in the Late Republic*, Ann Arbor, MI.
(2002) *The Roman Republic in Political Thought*, Hanover, NH and London.
Miller, J. F., C. Damon and K. S. Myers, eds. (2002) *Vertis in usum: Studies in Honor of Edward Courtney*, Leipzig.
Milnor, K. (2005) *Gender, Domesticity, and the Age of Augustus: Inventing Private Life*, Oxford.
Mineo, B., ed. (2015) *A Companion to Livy*, Malden, MA.
Möller, M. (2004) *Talis oratio – qualis vita: Zu Theorie und Praxis mimetischer Verfahrung in der griechisch-römischen Literaturkritik*, Heidelberg.
Momigliano, A. (1990) *The Classical Foundations of Modern Historiography*, Sather Classical Lectures 54, Berkeley.
Morstein-Marx, R. (2004) *Mass Oratory and Political Power in the Late Roman Republic*, Cambridge.
Müller, G. M. and F. M. Zini, eds. (2018) *Philosophie in Rom – Römische Philosophie?*, Berlin.
Murphy, C. (2007) *Are We Rome? The Fate of an Empire and the Fall of America*, Boston.
Nelsestuen, G. A. (2015) *Varro the Agronomist: Political Philosophy, Satire, and Agriculture in the Late Republic*, Columbus.
Nelson, R. (2008) *Conversations in Tusculum*, New York.

Nichols, J. H., Jr. (1979) 'On the proper use of ancient philosophy: a comment on Steven Taylor Holmes' "Aristippus in and out of Athens"', *American Political Science Review* 73.1: 129–33.
Nicolet, G. (1991) *Space, Geography and Politics in the Early Roman Empire*, Ann Arbor, MI.
Nussbaum, M. C. (2018) *The Monarchy of Fear: A Philosopher Looks at Our Political Crisis*, New York.
Oliensis, E. (1998) *Horace and the Rhetoric of Authority*, Cambridge.
　(2001) 'Freud's *Aeneid*', *Vergilius* 47: 39–63.
　(2009) *Freud's Rome: Psychoanalysis and Latin Poetry*, Cambridge.
Payne, M., ed. (2005) *The Greenblatt Reader*, Malden, MA.
Perkell, C., ed. (1999) *Reading Vergil's Aeneid: An Interpretive Guide*, Norman, OK.
Pettit, P. (1997) *Republicanism: A Theory of Freedom and Government*, Oxford.
Pocock, J. G. A. (1975) *The Machiavellian Moment: Florentine Political Thought and the Atlantic Political Tradition*, Princeton.
　(1981) 'The reconstruction of discourse: towards the historiography of political thought', *Modern Language Notes* 96: 959–80.
　(1987) 'The concept of a language and the *métier d'historien*: some considerations on practice', in A. Pagden, ed., *The Languages of Political Theory in Early-Modern Europe* (Cambridge), 21–5.
　(1989) *Politics, Language and Time: Essays on Political Thought and History*, Chicago.
　(2008) 'Theory in history: problems of context and narrative', in J. Dryzek, B. Honig and A. Phillips, eds., *The Oxford Handbook of Political Theory* (Oxford), 163–74.
Potter, D. S. (1999) 'Political theory in the *senatus consultum Pisonianum*', *AJPh* 120: 65–88.
Potter, D. S., C. Damon and S. A. Takács, eds. (1999) *The 'senatus consultum de Cn. Pisone patre'* (= *AJPh* 120.1), Baltimore.
Powell, J. G. F. and J. A. North, eds. (2001) *Cicero's Republic*, London.
Putnam, M. C. J. (1965) *The Poetry of the Aeneid*, Cambridge, MA.
　(1994) *Virgil's Epic Designs: Ekphrasis in the Aeneid*, New Haven.
O'Hara, J. (1990) *Death and the Optimistic Prophecy in Vergil's Aeneid*, Princeton.
Quint, D. (1993) *Epic and Empire: Politics and Generic Form from Virgil to Milton*, Princeton.
　(2018) *Virgil's Double Cross: Design and Meaning in the Aeneid*, Princeton.
Raaflaub, K., ed. (2005) *Social Struggles in Archaic Rome: New Perspectives on the Conflict of the Orders*, 2nd edn, Malden, MA.
Reed, J. D. (2007) *Virgil's Gaze: Nation and Poetry in the Aeneid*, Princeton.
Rees, R. (2012) *Oxford Readings in Classical Studies: Latin Panegyric*, Oxford.
Reydams-Schils, G. (2012) 'Social ethics and politics', in M. van Acheren, ed., *A Companion to Marcus Aurelius* (Malden, MA), 437–52.
Rich, J. (2017) 'Fabius Pictor, Ennius and the origins of Roman annalistic historiography', in K. Sandberg and C. Smith, eds., *Omnium annalium*

*monumenta: Historical Writing and Historical Evidence in Republican Rome* (Leiden), 17–65.
Richardson, J. (2008) *The Language of Empire: Rome and the Idea of Empire from the Third Century* BC *to the Second Century* AD, Cambridge.
  (2016) 'Provincial administration', in du Plessis, Ando and Tuori 2016, 111–23.
Richlin, A. (2017) *Slave Theater in the Roman Republic*, Cambridge.
Riggsby, A. M. (1999) *Crime and Community in Ciceronian Rome*, Austin.
Rimell, V. (2015) *The Closure of Space in Roman Poetics*, Cambridge.
Roche, H. and K. Demetriou, eds. (2018) *Brill's Companion to the Classics, Fascist Italy and Nazi Germany*, Leiden.
Roche, P., ed. (2011) *Pliny's Praise: The Panegyricus in the Roman World*, Cambridge.
Roller, M. B. (2004) 'Exemplarity in Roman culture: the cases of Horatius Cocles and Cloelia', *CPh* 99: 1–56.
  (2009) 'The exemplary past in Roman historiography and culture', in Feldherr 2009, 214–30.
  (2018) *Models from the Past in Roman Culture: A World of Exempla*, Baltimore.
Rowe, C. and M. Schofield, eds. (2000) *The Cambridge History of Greek and Roman Political Thought*, Cambridge.
Russell, A. (2016) *The Politics of Public Space in Republican Rome*, Cambridge.
Sailor, D. (2008) *Writing and Empire in Tacitus*, Cambridge.
Schmitt, C. (1985) *Political Theology: Four Chapters on the Concept of Sovereignty* (trans. G. Schwab), Cambridge, MA.
  (2007) *The Concept of the Political*, Chicago.
Short, W. M. (2012) 'A Roman folk model of the mind', *Arethusa* 45: 109–47.
Simpson, C. J. (1977) 'The date and dedication of the temple of Mars Ultor', *JRS* 67: 91–4.
Skinner, Q. (1969) 'Meaning and understanding in the history of ideas', *History and Theory* 8: 3–53.
  (1978) *The Foundations of Modern Political Thought*, 2 vols., Cambridge.
Skutsch, O. (1985) *The Annals of Quintus Ennius*, Oxford.
Smil, V. (2010) *Why America Is Not a New Rome*, Cambridge, MA.
Spence, S. (1991) 'Cinching the text: the Danaids and the end of the *Aeneid*', *Vergilius* 37: 11–19.
Straumann, B. (2010) Review of Hammer 2008, *Perspectives on Politics* 8: 660–2.
  (2016) *Crisis and Constitutionalism: Roman Political Thought from the Fall of the Republic to the Age of Revolution*, Oxford.
Syed, Y. (2005) *Vergil's Aeneid and the Roman Self: Subject and Nation in Literary Discourse*, Ann Arbor, MI.
Tarrant, R. J. (2012) *Virgil. Aeneid* XII. Cambridge.
Thaler, R. (1991) *Quasi Rational Economics*, New York.
Thomas, R. F. (1998) 'The isolation of Turnus', in H.-P. Stahl, ed., *Vergil's Aeneid, Augustan Epic and Political Context* (London), 271–302.
  (2001) *Virgil and the Augustan Reception*, Cambridge.
Toll, K. (1997) 'Making Roman-ness and the *Aeneid*', *ClAnt* 16: 34–56.

Treggiari, S. (1991) *Roman Marriage: Iusti Coniuges from the Time of Cicero to the Time of Ulpian*, Oxford.
Trout, D. (1994) 'Re-textualizing Lucretia: cultural subversion in the *City of God*', *JECS* 2: 53–70.
Van der Blom, H. (2011) 'Pompey in the *contio*', *CQ* 61: 553–73.
Van Nortwick, T. (1980) 'Aeneas, Turnus, and Achilles', *TAPhA* 110: 303–14.
Vasaly, A. (2015) *Livy's Political Philosophy*, Cambridge.
Viroli, M. (2002) *Republicanism*, New York.
Vout, C. (2009) 'Representing the emperor', in Feldherr 2009, 261–75.
Wallace-Hadrill, A. (1981) 'The emperor and his virtues', *Historia* 30: 298–323.
  (1982) '*Civilis princeps*: between citizen and king', *JRS* 72: 32–48.
  (2008) *Rome's Cultural Revolution*, Cambridge.
Weinstock, S. (1971) *Divus Julius*, Oxford.
Weithman, P. (2014) 'Augustine's political philosophy', in Meconi and Stump 2014, 231–50.
Welch, K. E., ed. (2015) *Appian's Roman History: Empire and Civil War*, Swansea.
Wiedemann, T. (2000) 'Reflections of Roman political thought in Latin historical writing', in Rowe and Schofield 2000, 517–31.
Winterbottom, M. (2002) 'Believing the *Pro Marcello*', in Miller, Damon and Myers 2002, 24–38.
Wiseman, T. P. (1995) *Remus: A Roman Myth*, Cambridge.
  (2015) Review of Connolly 2015, *AJPh* 136: 372–5.
Whitby, M., ed. (1998) *The Propaganda of Power: The Role of Panegyric in Late Antiquity*, Mnemosyne Supplement 183, Leiden.
White, S. K. ed. (2002) *What Is Political Theory?* (= *Political Theory* 30.4), London.
Whitton, C. L. (2010) 'Pliny, *Epistles* 8.14: senate, slavery and the *Agricola*', *JRS* 100: 118–39.
Winkler, J. J. and F. I. Zeitlin, eds. (1990) *Nothing to Do with Dionysus? Athenian Drama in Its Social Context*, Princeton.
Wohl, V. (2010) *Law's Cosmos: Juridical Discourse in Athenian Forensic Oratory*, Cambridge.
  (2015) *Euripides and the Politics of Form*, Princeton.
Zanker, P. (1988) *The Power of Images in the Age of Augustus* (trans. A. Shapiro), Ann Arbor, MI.
Zetzel, J. E. G. (1995) *Cicero: De re publica*, Cambridge.

CHAPTER 15

# Latin Literature and Roman History
### Myles Lavan

## Introduction

I put it to Latinists that too much work in the field is ignored by historians. There are certainly many scholars doing very productive work on the borderlands between Latin literature and Roman history (in the zone that one could style 'cultural history') that is read on both sides of the divide. But I am thinking of the main mass of the discipline. How many historians will read the next book on Ovid, Seneca, even Tacitus? A degree of mutual indifference is obviously to be expected between different specialisms, but I think Latinists ought to be worried by the degree of disinterest, which sometimes borders on alienation. Indeed it seems paradoxical that the intellectual divide has become wider at a time when once-dominant formalist modes of criticism that assumed the autonomy of literature have been marginalised by new historicist approaches that insist that texts must be studied not just as products of their time, but as embedded in, and indeed operating upon, the societies that produced them.[1] Is it not surprising, even deplorable, that so much work on literature and power is being ignored by scholars whose focus is the political structures and social and economic relations in which Latin literature was implicated?

If there is a problem, its roots surely lie as much in the openness of historians to different approaches as with critical practice in the field of Latin literature. But this is a volume aimed at Latinists, not historians. I will suggest three ways in which Latinists who conceive of their approach as historicist could seek to engage, even demand, the attention of historians.

---

[*] Thanks to the editors, the other participants in the stimulating workshop in Cambridge in 2018 and the many others with whom I have discussed these ideas. I am especially grateful to Tom Geue and Michèle Lowrie for their comments on a draft of the chapter.
[1] See Hinds 2010 on the current dominance of historicist approaches in both English and Anglophone Latin studies.

First, Latinists could take a much broader view of the structures of power in which Latin texts were embedded, rather than focusing on high politics and the phenomenon of autocracy – a narrow conception of the political that most historians long ago relinquished in order to pose wider question about economic, social and political structures. Second, they might profitably continue to extend their attention to non-literary texts, particularly to the highly heterogeneous corpus of texts we tend to subsume under the label 'inscriptions'. So long as Latinists continue to steer clear of inscriptions, their work is likely to remain of marginal interest to most historians. That is of course not a problem in itself. But it is a missed opportunity. There is no reason why Latinists' critical ambit should be restricted to texts transmitted through a manuscript tradition rather than on stone or other media. Finally, Latinists could work harder to speak to historians. I will take the long-running historiography debate as an example, not because I think that the critics of current work in the field have the right of it, but because the subfield illustrates a worrying degree of solipsism in Latin literary studies. There is too much preaching to the converted, too little effort to construct arguments that might engage and persuade potentially sympathetic readers among historians.

This essay is very much a personal reflection, grounded in my own experience of crossing a disciplinary boundary. My initial training was as a Latinist and my PhD began as a literary study of Tacitus, within the Ancient Literature caucus at Cambridge and under the supervision of a Latinist. As I began to reimagine my project as one of cultural history, I started to frequent the Ancient History caucus and eventually switched supervisor. Thereafter I was acutely conscious of trying to write for two distinct audiences, Latinists and ancient historians. I saw my first monograph as an attempt to find intellectual ground that would be common to both fields. I am not sure the experiment was successful. I was struck that almost all the reviewers were historians rather than Latinists (perhaps because the book appeared to be a work of ancient history), and yet at least one of them remarked that the book was 'strictly a work of Classical Philology rather than Ancient History'.[2] My subsequent work has taken me even further from my beginnings, to the comparative study of ancient empires, the history of Roman citizenship and the development of quantitative methods.

This trajectory may have accentuated my experience of the disciplinary divide. I have travelled a particularly long distance – from Latin literature as it is practised in Cambridge (a highly productive tradition, but one that is not necessarily representative of the field as a whole) to Roman history in the

[2] Lendon 2013.

modes of legal, social and demographic history. The divide may not seem so pronounced to those who keep closer to the borderlands between the disciplines. But I do think that the normal institutional requirement for scholars to identify as either Latinists or historians and the tendency for conferences and research networks to be either literary or historical in focus tends to pull even those on the borders into one orbit or another. I have certainly been conscious of a shift in the audience for whom I am writing: most of my dialogue is now with scholars who identify as historians, rather than with Latinists. This has brought with it subtle but significant changes in the way I write and even the questions I ask. When I do write about texts, I find myself producing fewer close readings of particular texts and more often trying to generalise about Latin language and discourse. Where I once contemplated a dissertation on 'religion in Tacitus', I now find the idea curiously blinkered.[3]

This is a reflection by a sympathetic bystander on how Latin studies looks from the other side of what I at least experience as a significant divide. My perspective is inevitably partial and limited. I find myself looking back at Latin literature much as I do at Ireland – as a community that is important to my identity and which shaped me into the scholar I am, but from which I am now somewhat estranged; I feel I still know it well, but my knowledge is certainly out of date. My view is also constrained by my own focus on the late republic and early empire, the period for which the divide between Latinists and historians is arguably most pronounced. And it is a perspective on a specifically Anglophone disciplinary landscape. (Therese Fuhrer in this volume discusses the idiosyncrasies of national traditions.) I therefore make no claim to exhaustiveness. Where I discuss the work of particular scholars, I am merely illustrating my arguments from my own, inevitably limited reading.

## 'Politics of' and 'Politics in'

'Power' has become the new critical master term, as Stephen Hinds put it two decades ago.[4] Contemporary Latinists tend to have a sophisticated understanding of the ways in which texts can be implicated in, and work to

---

[3] This is not meant to disparage Shannon-Henderson 2019, or for that matter Levene 1993 or Davies 2004. It is a distinguished tradition and the merit of such a focus once seemed obvious to me too. But I now wonder what it says about the field that author-focused projects are not just common, but the default approach to any topic. I share Emma Dench's reservations about what she calls the 'small worlds' approach of recent work on Tacitus: 'The world as it is figured remains narrow and centered on particular authors' (Dench 2009).
[4] Hinds 2001: 224.

support, power relations. Yet I would argue that they often have a relatively narrow view of the power relations in which Latin texts were in fact embedded. The ever-expanding corpus of political readings of Latin texts of the early empire, for example, largely focuses on the issue of autocracy, exploring how literature worked to legitimise the authority of the *princeps* or tried to subvert it. The focus on monarchy of course reproduces one of the main concerns of the texts themselves. Many authors writing in Latin in the early imperial period were indeed preoccupied with the nature of the principate and its relationship to the republican past. Much important work has been done on the relationship between Latin literature and the consolidation of a monarchical regime at Rome. 'The power of Augustus was a collective invention', as Duncan Kennedy put it in a seminal article, and language and literature made an important contribution.[5] Matthew Roller has helped to displace a constitutionalist model of the principate, which understood it as an amalgamation of legal powers, with a culturalist view that sees it as the product of intense and distributed debate among emperor and aristocrats about the emperor's authority.[6] In a very different vein Frederick Ahl's work on the rhetorical concept of 'figured speech' has primed a generation of critics to read imperial Latin literature for veiled criticism of oppressive regimes.[7] I certainly do not mean to deny the value of work in these traditions. Yet the almost total focus on relations between emperor and aristocrats reveals a surprisingly narrow conception of politics among those who profess to be interested in the politics of literature.

An adequate analysis of the politics *of* literature has to go beyond an account of politics *in* literature.[8] The scope of politics *in* literature is constrained by the limits of what a particular text or textual tradition recognises or admits as a matter of politics. But our understanding of the politics *of* literature ought to be determined by our own conception of the complex ways in which texts are implicated in the societies that produce and consume them. One would not easily guess from much recent work on Latin literature of the early empire that the senatorial and equestrian elite that produced the majority of surviving Latin literature were the primary beneficiaries of the new order, not its victims.[9] The senate appropriated a range of legislative, electoral and judicial powers that had previously been the preserve of the people. Its members enjoyed a range of new privileges,

---

[5] Kennedy 1992: 35.   [6] Roller 2001.   [7] Ahl 1984a and 1984b.
[8] The distinction has already been drawn by Martindale 2003: 109 and Leigh 2016: 424 and is implicit in Habinek 1998, with its programmatic title (*The Politics of Latin Literature*).
[9] On the social location of surviving Latin literature, see e.g. White 1993: 211–22 on the predominance of senators and equestrians among known writers of Latin verse.

both real and symbolic, and continued to monopolise the highest-ranking political offices. Senators and those equestrians who pursued careers in the emperor's service used the opportunities of office holding to increase their already massive wealth.[10] No adequate account of the politics of texts produced by (and largely for) this imperial elite can afford to ignore consideration of its situation and interests.

There are a few aspects of the social context of Latin literature that have been the subject of sustained investigation. Much has been written about literature's implication in the construction of gender norms in Roman society, explored in different ways by, for example, Alison Keith and Anthony Corbeill.[11] Slavery has also drawn especial attention, notably in three successive studies of Plautine drama by Katherine McCarthy, Roberta Stewart and Amy Richlin and also in William Fitzgerald's wider-ranging experiment in reading Latin literature as the product of a slave society.[12] Ellen O'Gorman, Nancy Shumate and others have adopted a post-colonial lens to read Roman representations of the provinces as expressions of what Edward Saïd would call a 'culture of imperialism'.[13] But readings in these traditions seem to have been marginalised to niche research interests by a predominant focus on high politics. Latinists who wish to explore the politics of literature would do well to attend to Thomas Habinek's programmatic *The Politics of Latin Literature*. Habinek called for more attention to the ways in which Latin literature intervened in society, rather than merely representing or responding to it.[14] Much Anglophone work in Latin studies might seem to be answering Habinek's call, by foregrounding the political in the reading of Latin texts. But not all critics have heeded his insistence on the need for a sociology rigorous enough to relate the ideology of the text to the material circumstances of ancient society.

Habinek's account of the politics of Latin literature was grounded in wide reading in the sociology of empire and of pre-modern societies. He recognised that Latin literature was a social institution that ultimately served the interests of 'the elite sector of a traditional aristocratic empire' – an allusion to John Kautsky's historical sociology of 'aristocratic empires'.[15] 'Many of the characteristics of Latin literature can be attributed to its production by and for an elite that sought to maintain and expand its dominance over other sectors of the population through reference to an

---

[10] See further Weisweiler 2016: 155–6, summarising the argument of a forthcoming book.
[11] Keith 2000, Corbeill 2015.   [12] McCarthy 2000, Stewart 2012, Richlin 2017; Fitzgerald 2000.
[13] O'Gorman 1993, Shumate 2006.   [14] Habinek 1998: 3.   [15] Ibid. 3, 45–6; Kautsky 1997.

authorising past.'[16] He also recognised that Latin literature continued to be produced by, and serve the interests of, an aristocracy after the transition to monarchy. To focus on the subordination of aristocrats, he argued, would be to collude in Latin literature's evasion of the exploitative political and economic practices that were the prerequisite for the leisured *otium* and to reduce politics to 'infighting among the elites'.[17] Avoiding these errors, he argued, required a 'contrapuntal' mode of reading (a term borrowed from Edward Said), 'an approach that observes the antitheses between text and context, or one text and another, and describes how they interact with one another'.[18]

Reading Ovid's exile poetry, for example, he refused to follow the texts in their focus on the relationship between poet and *princeps* (still less to internalise the conception of poet as 'victim' of autocratic outrage), but rather sought to elucidate the contribution that Ovid's representation of his life in Tomis made to the ideological structures that spurred the agents of Roman imperialism to accept the personal costs of mobility and dislocation that the maintenance of a colonial empire required.[19] Reading Seneca's *Letters*, he looked beyond their implication in the obvious subordination of aristocrats to the *princeps* to the less obvious – but arguably more important – question of how these texts served the interests of a social and political elite over and against other sectors of society.[20]

There have been surprisingly few attempts to take up Habinek's programme, but two recent exceptions illustrate what can be done.[21] Matthew Leigh returned to one of Habinek's models, Raymond Williams' cultural materialist critique of English pastoral, to develop an analysis of the politics *of* Virgil's *Eclogues*.[22] Rather than focusing on the political questions the poem raises relatively overtly, such as the dispossession of Italian landowners in the 40s BCE ('politics in the *Eclogues*'), he probes 'the more fundamental ideological work done by the collection as a whole'.[23] Like Habinek, his reading practice is 'contrapuntal' – juxtaposing the imaginary 'Sicily' and 'Arcadia' with what other texts and evidence reveals about contemporary conditions in those provinces. He reads with a particular focus on operations of mystification, evasion and occlusion. Arguing that Sicily is a 'constantly present absence' in the landscape of Virgil's pastoral, he highlights the evasion of conditions in contemporary Sicily: the brutal exploitation of slaves, depopulation, brigandage – in short, the negative

---

[16] Habinek 1998: 3; see also the definition of aristocrats at 45. [17] Ibid. 166–7 [18] Ibid. 167.
[19] Ibid. ch. 8, developed in Habinek 2002. [20] Ibid. ch. 7.
[21] The critical but sympathetic response in Hinds 2001 is a notable exception.
[22] Williams 1973, Leigh 2016. [23] Leigh 2016: 408.

effects of the integration of provincial landscapes into the Roman agrarian economy. For all their capacity to sympathise with 'those whom history has left behind', Leigh concludes, the *Eclogues* nevertheless participate in a broader ideology that works to mystify the sordid reality of the exploitation of provincial resources. In other words, there are limits to Virgil's sympathy – limits that are determined by his implication in an Italian elite that depended on the fruits of Rome's overseas conquests.

Inspired by both Habinek and Leigh, Tom Geue has penned a provocative reading of the *Georgics* as the product of a leisured elite dependent on coerced labour.[24] Geue deploys his own distinct critical practice, modelled on that of Pierre Macherey, that reads the text 'as a kind of social and psychoanalytic subject, the glitches and silences of which reveal its dark political unconscious' – these 'glitches and silences' doing the ideological work needed to convince a leisured elite that its privileges are natural and just. His method is to focus closely on the question of who works in the *Georgics*, and what sort of work they do. He argues that this reveals a development from a world in which all toil alike in Books 1 and 2, to a bifurcation between hard-working *pastores* and relatively leisured estate owners in Book 3, to relief from labour for a privileged few in Book 4. This amounts to an aetiology of *otium*, a narrative of a land-owning elite becoming able to displace labour onto others. 'The *Georgics* tells, performs, indeed trumpets the story of Virgil and posh reader/addressee moving from hard grind to slacking off.'[25] Geue's approach sidesteps the question of whether this structure should be understood as a 'glitch' or the product of design. (If the latter, it might seem to rehabilitate Virgil's capacity for sympathy with his social inferiors.) In any case, the paper stands out as an innovative attempt to grasp the deeper politics of a work of early Augustan literature by understanding it as the product of an Italian elite dependent on market-oriented agriculture, slave labour and the exploitation of provincial resources.

For inspiration in a different style, Latinists could turn to Brent Shaw's essay on Stoicism as ideology to see a historian's version of how to read texts as vehicles of ideology.[26] Shaw asks why Stoicism became and remained the dominant system of ideas in the Mediterranean for more than five centuries. His answer focuses on its intimate relationship with the new territorial states that gradually superseded city states as the principal form of political organisation throughout the Mediterranean, beginning with the Hellenistic kingdoms, large and small, and culminating in the

[24] Geue 2018.    [25] Ibid. 117.    [26] Shaw 1985.

Roman empire.[27] Highlighting the significance of Stoicism's reconceptualisation of social relations in the context of the cosmos rather than the polis, he suggests that this encouraged the subjects of these new states to identify with a social and political framework larger than the city-state – and even helped to foster the development of these new forms of political power. He also notes that Stoic ideas of a natural and beneficial order (the 'divine economy' of his title) tended to work to 'entrench' the current social order in a time of considerable social and political change. 'The enticement was that you actually knew what you were doing, and knew that it was right.'[28] Stoicism emerges as a system of ideas that served the interests of a propertied, slave-owning and educated elite whose material interests were aligned with those of the large 'kingdoms' or 'empires' to which they were subject. Stoic ideas worked to reassure them of the legitimacy of their privilege and to mobilise their energies in the service of the imperial projects their rulers were engaged in. Shaw's sweeping approach may seem characteristic of a historian; Latinists would probably be inclined to pursue similar questions through closer reading of particular texts. But they could still profitably reflect on Shaw's sense that the appropriate historical level at which to look for the operations of ideology is not the reigns of particular emperors or dynasties (the famous problem of the 'Stoic opposition' is demoted to mere detail), but rather *longue durée* patterns of state formation and social organisation.

Readings in this mode cannot – and should not – displace other, more formalist traditions of reading Latin literature. They can struggle to accommodate the ambiguity and playfulness that are particularly characteristic of literary texts and run the risk of reductiveness. Habinek, Leigh and Geue take great care to avoid this trap – indeed Habinek explicitly set out to combine 'a materialist interpretation of literature as ideological discourse and social institution with a playful or ludic approach to the process of reading' – but it remains a risk.[29] Their approach nevertheless seems the most promising way of interrogating the *politics* of literature.

The models I have cited might be subsumed under the umbrella of 'cultural materialism'. They are certainly all materialist in their approach, but so must be any serious attempt to investigate the politics *of* literature. They are far from dogmatic. They differ considerably in their operationalisation of concepts like ideology and their modes of reading. What they share is a broad and avowedly modern conception of politics as an analytical category and an understanding of the social and economic context in

---

[27] Shaw 1985: 25.   [28] Ibid. 54.   [29] Habinek 1998: 5.

which these texts were produced and consumed. They recognise that the text itself cannot be allowed to foreclose the critic's conception of its politics. Understanding what interests it might serve demands deep contextual knowledge and rigorous analysis. Being a good historicist requires being a good historian – and that is a non-trivial condition.

Latinists interested in the politics of imperial literature, for example, would do well to think about the producers and consumers of the texts they study not just as the subjects of a new monarchical order, but also as the members of a state elite that used the powers of the imperial state for its own enrichment, a metropolitan elite at the heart of an extensive and heterogeneous empire, a propertied urban class that dominated the empire through its control of the apparatus of government in the two or three thousand largely self-governing city states that constituted the empire and a class of slave-owners in a slave society of unprecedented scale. If we are to look for the ideological operations of literature, we might expect to find that its most important function was in naturalising these broader structures of power and privilege, rather than in legitimating or subverting monarchy.

## Beyond 'Literary' Texts

Although critical practice is increasingly willing to transgress what was once seen as a boundary between 'literary' and 'non-literary' texts, many Latinists still tend to steer clear of some of the texts that are most obviously implicated in the relations of power that they are interested in. For example, despite the universal interest in the development of the principate, the utterances of emperors – both private and public – have not attracted the attention one might expect. While most Latinists will have some familiarity with Trajan's replies to Pliny and Marcus Aurelius' *Meditations* (in Greek), I suspect that fewer have read the letters of Marcus, Lucius Verus and Antoninus Pius to Fronto, and even fewer will have read more than a handful of the letters, edicts and speeches that survive as inscriptions on bronze or stone. Indeed, it seems fair to say that many Latinists restrict their range to 'literary texts' in a sense peculiar to our field – texts transmitted through a manuscript tradition, as opposed to inscriptions, tablets or papyri. Merely because they happen to have been inscribed, many interesting texts are essentially left to specialists and thus deprived of the probing reading of those scholars who ought to be best placed to think about the imbrication of language, textuality and power.

Where the domain of the literary critic was once largely limited to verse, Anglophone critics now extend their hermeneutic efforts much more widely. The development is most obvious in English departments, where critical practice has freed itself from the structure of a canon, and even from the idea of 'literature'. The New Historicists in particular, with their provocative juxtapositions of 'literary' and 'non-literary' texts, have shown that even 'non-literary' texts can respond to the attentive, probing and imaginative strategies of close reading that the discipline of English promoted. A personal favourite is Stephen Greenblatt's virtuoso brief reading of a diary entry by an English merchant who participated in a raid on a village in Sierra Leone in 1586.[30] Latinists might also take note of a recent pamphlet by the influential Sanskritist Sheldon Pollock, who has called for philology to reimagine itself more ambitiously as 'the theory of textuality'.[31] However we identify ourselves – whether as 'philologists', 'critics' ('literary' or otherwise) or Latinists – the intellectual apparatus of the field has application well beyond the range of texts we might recognise as 'literary'.

Classicists have certainly been influenced by these new modes of reading. Critical attention has been extended not just to historiography (once largely left to historians, in the era of the 'historical commentary') and oratory, but also to technical writing. Yet it is worth observing that Latinists have largely steered clear of one technical discourse that is both voluminous in its remains and particularly apposite to consideration of power – namely legal writing. Wariness is entirely justified given the formidable complexities of the subject matter, the difficult textual tradition and – not least – the existence of an autonomous specialism devoted to the subject (at least on the continent, where the 'Romanist' tradition remains well established in university systems). But a number of recent attempts to reframe legal writing as 'literature' might encourage incursions in future.[32]

Even if Latinists are increasingly willing to transgress the boundaries of what used to be recognised as 'literature', however, their work still tends to be limited to what we often refer to, by an easy but misleading shorthand, as 'literary texts'. By common convention, texts transmitted through a manuscript tradition are referred to as 'literary texts' to distinguish them from inscriptions and texts on papyrus. The tripartite distinction

---

[30] Greenblatt 1980: 193–4.   [31] Pollock 2010.
[32] Mantovani 2018 offers a Romanist's perspective on law as literature; Harries 2018 re-situates juristic *Epistulae* in the context of contemporary literature. For a broader perspective on law and literature, see Lowrie 2016 and the results of Ioannis Ziogas' collaborative project on 'Roman Law and Latin Literature'.

has some disciplinary value, insofar as the media pose different challenges for the editors of a text. It is thus understandable that the work of editing manuscripts, inscriptions and papyri evolved into distinct specialisms. But it is not at all clear that the distinction is useful for those involved in the interpretation of texts. Yet many Latinists seem to have allowed not just their critical ambit but even their reading to be circumscribed by the limits of 'literary texts' in this banal sense. The most common exception proves the rule: Augustus' *Res gestae*, an inscribed text that is well known to Latinists not least because it has repeatedly been edited and published like 'literary' texts (including exceptional admission to the Loeb Classical Library). A chapter-length reading by Michèle Lowrie, in the context of a broader study of the relationship between performance and writing in Augustan culture, is a rare exception.[33]

The most obvious example of the neglect of texts that are not 'literary' in this sense is the very substantial corpus of inscribed Latin verse – amounting to a total of well over 4,000 texts.[34] Although they are familiar to Latinists working in the continental traditions, they have been largely marginalised in Anglophone Latin studies. Edward Courtney sought to stimulate interest in the corpus by publishing a selection of two hundred texts, with translation and commentary, in his *Musa lapidaria*.[35] But it has not had much obvious effect. The corpus certainly presents challenges: it can be hard to access (*CLE* is organised by metre and then type of inscription); there is considerable repetition (most examples being from epitaphs) and there are often considerable difficulties in establishing metre and text. Most importantly, they lack the comforting apparatus of editions, commentaries and translations that generally facilitate work on 'literary' texts. Yet one might have expected a critical community interested in re-embedding Latin texts in the society that produced them to give more attention to a corpus that takes us beyond the rarefied, metropolitan milieu that produced most surviving Latin texts of the late republic and high empire – out to the provinces and down to lower social strata.[36]

---

[33] Lowrie 2009: 279–308.
[34] See Schmidt 2015: 764 for an introduction. Bücheler and Lommatzsch 1930 (*Carmina Latina epigraphica* or *CLE*) compiled a corpus of *c.* 2,500 poems. New material from various provinces has been assembled in a series of papers by Paolo Cugusi and Maria Teresa Sblendorio Cugusi as preparation for the imminent Teubner *CLE*. In parallel, the *CIL* is publishing a new corpus arranged by province as *CIL* xviii.
[35] Courtney 1995.
[36] Peter Kruschwitz is preparing a new, thematic selection, focused on the themes of poverty, distress and social exclusion, that might make this material more accessible.

But the opportunities extend well beyond metrical texts. Mary Beard has shown how the unprepossessing genre of the elite *cursus* (career) inscription – minimalist and apparently conventional – can be approached as a form of life-writing.[37] Taking the funerary monument of the senatorial Plautii as a paradigmatic example, she illustrates that its epitaphs can be read as self-conscious texts that negotiate the challenges of narrating an individual's implication in the web of dynastic politics, making choices as to what to include or omit and where to deploy strategic vagueness. The essay also shows that even these short texts deserve critical attention to the manipulation of generic conventions and questions of readership.

Another category of texts that surely deserves wider attention is pronouncements of the state (both Roman and local), notably laws, *senatus consulta* and the letters, edicts, decrees, speeches and other constitutions of Roman emperors and provincial governors, and other agents of the Roman state.[38] These texts tend to be left to historians and epigraphers – sometimes cited for illustration or comparison, but not studied as texts in their own right. The 1999 *American Journal of Philology* volume dedicated to the recently published *Senatus consultum de Cn. Pisone patre*, co-edited by a Latinist (Cynthia Damon), was a partial exception.[39] Besides Damon's reading of the *senatus consultum* against Tacitus' parallel narrative, it also included some observations by the historians about ways in which the *senatus consultum* might respond to strategies of close reading.[40] But the imbalance between Latinists and historians still illustrates the typical division of labour.

It is an unfortunate accident of the epigraphic habit that we have more *senatus consulta*, imperial letters, edicts and speeches in Greek than we do in Latin. When the cities of the Greek east (where the Roman state normally spoke in Greek) chose to monumentalise an imperial pronouncement, they normally did so by inscribing it in stone. By contrast, the cities of the Latin-speaking west normally inscribed them on bronze, the by-word for permanence in Roman culture (hence Horace's *monumentum aere perennius*). Paradoxically, the value and fungibility of the medium (which was often melted down in late antiquity) meant that these texts tended to have

---

[37] Beard 1998. See also Henderson 1998.
[38] On the taxonomy of imperial pronouncements ('constitutions'), see the useful surveys in Oliver 1989: 1–24 and Millar 1977: 203–59. For a brief overview of where to find them, see Lavan 2013: 213–14.
[39] Potter, Damon and Takács 1999.
[40] Damon and Takács 1999. See Flower 1999: 101 on the theme of forgetting in the *senatus consultum* and Champlin 1999: 121 on its 'literary' character.

a lower survival rate than humbler monuments in stone. Nevertheless, there does remain a small but significant corpus of pronouncements in Latin that deserve to be better known to Latinists who work on this period – and which might respond to their reading strategies.[41] Michèle Lowrie's discussion of the *Senatus consultum de Cn. Pisone patre* in this volume (pp. 759–60) is an example of what can be done.

For models of how texts of this sort can respond to attention to genre and other forms of close reading, Latinists might look to the work of two Greek historians. In his programmatic study of the genres of Hellenistic political discourse, Jean-Marie Bertrand observed that there is no discourse in which form and expression are more closely intertwined than the discourse of the state.[42] He demonstrated the importance of genre in a political discourse dominated by civic decrees, inter-poliadic treaties and royal letters (all preserved in significant numbers as inscriptions). He showed, for example, that the genre of the civic decree was essential to the political culture of the polis. Indeed, he argues that it is primarily through decrees that 'the polis speaks'.[43] He highlighted the significance of the use of a homogeneous third-person narrative ('the people decreed', etc.) to obfuscate division and conflict within the city and evoke a unity of action. He also pointed to the tendency to signal the existence of an ongoing discourse of which a given decree is only one moment, implicitly asserting the continuity of the polis. Even when a polis obeys a king's instructions, he argued, it tends to do so by subordinating the king's words to its own pronouncements in 'a framework that pretends to control them'.[44]

Perhaps the most sophisticated development of Bertrand's approach can be found in John Ma's analysis of the idioms of civic decrees and royal letters in Seleukid Asia Minor.[45] Ma develops Bertrand's ideas about the role of the decree genre in constructing 'polis-centred narratives' of contemporary events. He also expands on the dialogue between the voice of the polis and the voice of the king, showing that the decree and letter forms take each other into account, sharing a generalising vocabulary of benefaction and gratitude in which what is praised is character as manifested in an ongoing relationship. Their idioms work to 'euphemise' domination, rewriting the king's power over the polis as a history of benefaction and care. Most recently Paola Ceccarelli has shown how the idioms of royal letters and civic decrees combine to construct a complex international

---

[41] See Lavan 2013: 211–16 for a survey of these texts and where they can be found.
[42] Bertrand 1990: 101.   [43] Ibid. 101.   [44] Ibid. 112, 106.   [45] Ma 2002.

community in an extraordinary dossier of texts from Magnesia on the Maeander (the responses of kings' leagues and cities to Magnesia's request for recognition of the contest for Artemis Leukophryene).[46] Latinists who read these works of history will recognise in them a kindred discipline of close reading, attentive to the significance of genre and language. They also illustrate the particular importance of close study of what Bertrand called 'la langue d'État'.

## Close Reading and Quotidian Texts

### A Wronged Trader

I illustrate the scope for productive incursions into 'non-literary' texts with two brief examples of quotidian texts that repay close reading, focusing in each case on a single but significant detail. The first is a fragmentary draft of a petition found at the fort at Vindolanda in Britain and dated to the early second century CE.[47] The beginning of the text has been lost and the central section of what remains is badly damaged (and restored merely *exempli gratia*), but two closing appeals are clearly preserved:

> Tuam maies[t]atem imploro ne patiaris me [i]nnocentem uirgis cas[t]-igatum esse et, domine, prou[t?] prae[fe]cto non potui queri quia ua[let]-udini detinebatur, ques[tu]s sum beneficiario [?frustra et? cen]turionibu[s ? ceteris?] numeri eius. [?Proinde? tu]am misericord[ia]m imploro ne patiaris me hominem trasmarinum et innocentem, de cuius f[ide] inquiras, uirgis cruent[at]u[m] esse, ac si aliquid sceler[i]s commississem. (*Tab. Vind.* II 344)

> I implore your majesty not to suffer me, an innocent man, to have been beaten with rods and, my lord, inasmuch as (?) I was unable to complain to the prefect because he was detained by ill-health, I have complained [in vain?] to the beneficiaries [and the rest of?] the centurions of his unit. [Accordingly?] I implore your mercifulness not to allow me, a man from overseas and an innocent one, about whose good faith you may inquire, to have been bloodied by rods as if I had committed some crime. (trans. Bowman and Thomas 1994)[48]

---

[46] Ceccarelli 2018.
[47] *Tab. Vind.* II 344. On the text and its context, see further Birley 1991: 17–18, Bowman and Thomas 1994: 329–34 (and on no. 180 for the text on the reverse), Peachin 1999: 227–31.
[48] I have omitted three badly damaged lines at the start of the surviving text and followed Peachin 1999: 228 in supplying the conjectures implied by the editors in their translation but not printed in their text in *Tab. Vind.* 344.

The text is written on the back of – and in the same hand as – a record of the disbursement of grain by a private trader. (Hence the inference that it is a draft.) The repeated *imploro* and highly deferential *tuam maiestatem* reveal this as a petition to a senior figure in the Roman administration, probably the governor, of a sort known from elsewhere in the empire.[49] A reference to wares (*merces*) in the fragmentary first lines and the handwriting suggest that the petitioner was the same trader whose accounts are preserved on the reverse, though his name and identity have been lost; they would have been specified at the outset of the petition. The trader's clients included soldiers and the tablet was found in a military context.[50] Although the petitioner's narrative account of the events that precipitated his petition has also been lost (again because it came earlier in the text), what survives makes it clear that he was complaining of having been wrongly beaten (*uirgis castigatum, cruentatum*) by a soldier or soldiers (implicit in the initial appeal to a prefect – presumably the equestrian *praefectus* commanding an auxiliary cohort or *ala* – and the reference to 'his unit').[51]

My focus is on the anonymous petitioner's rhetorical strategy as he sought to move his addressee to pity and outrage at the end of his petition. Besides showing due deference – implicit in the respectful *domine* and the use of abstract nouns as indirect address (*tuam maiestatem, tuam misericordiam*) – he twice asserts his innocence (*me innocentem, hominem ... innocentem*), hammering home – we can assume – the point of his narrative account of what had happened.[52] More interestingly, he yokes his claim of innocence to an assertion that he is a *homo transmarinus* (a man from across the sea).[53] The intrusion of *transmarinus* before *innocens* in *hominem tra(n)smarinum et innocentem* calls for some interrogation. What did the petitioner mean? And why did he think it appropriate here?

In metropolitan Latin, *transmarinus* normally has an Italocentric sense, denoting persons or things in the overseas provinces.[54] But it cannot mean that here. Instead it seems to be a local usage that gives us an unparalleled

---

[49] See the texts gathered in Hauken 1998 and (from Egypt) Kelly 2011. Note especially the petition of the *coloni* of the *saltus Burunitanus* who appeal to the emperor Commodus in similar terms (*[im]ploratum maiestatem tu[am]*, Hauken 1998 no. 1.1.1 col. II lines 19–20).
[50] See Bowman and Thomas 1994 on *Tab. Vind.* 180 for the text on the reverse and the depositional context.
[51] All this follows Bowman and Thomas 1994: 329–34.
[52] On *domine*, see Dickey 2002: 77–99 and Lavan 2018: 290–4; on abstract nouns as indirect address, see Hauken 1998: 18.
[53] On the spelling on the tablet, see Bowman and Thomas 1994: 333.
[54] See e.g. Varro, *Rust.* 2.5.9 and Plin. *HN.* 8.214.

glimpse into colonial dynamics in this peripheral province of the empire.[55] Insofar as scholars think of the Roman empire as a specifically colonial empire, they are usually thinking of the flow of magistrates, soldiers, traders and settlers from Italy to the provinces. Starting in the late third century BCE, Italians began to move into other regions of the Mediterranean as they came under Roman hegemony, parlaying their ethnic affiliation with the imperial power into positions of economic and political importance.[56] That first wave of individual settlement was reinforced in the last decades of the republic when Caesar, the triumvirs and Augustus settled hundreds of thousands of veterans in around a hundred new Roman *coloniae* in the provinces. But the situation in the imperial period was more complicated because of a shift in the direction of predatory population movements. The centrifugal flow of Italians to the provinces that characterised the republic was in the imperial period rivalled and eventually replaced by transverse movements between provinces, often from more to less urbanised regions.

Britain is a good example. In the first and second centuries, the men who ruled the province of Britain – the governor, his staff and the commanders of its garrisons – were mostly from Italy and the Mediterranean provinces.[57] Most of the soldiers stationed in Britain also seem to have been alien to the population they controlled, though drawn from a wider range of provinces.[58] There is also evidence to suggest that the economic opportunities opened up by the incorporation of the province into the imperial network – not least the opportunity to supply a population of 40,000 soldiers – were also disproportionately captured by foreigners, often from the neighbouring Gallic provinces, who were ideally placed to supply goods from the continent (addressing the army's taste for goods that could not be produced locally) and who might more easily secure the trust of imperial administrators and officers than native competitors.[59] The anonymous petitioner probably illustrates the phenomenon: a man from 'across the sea' (i.e. from an interior province, perhaps in Gaul), engaged in trade in Britain, who seems to have been closely integrated into the military community at Vindolanda.

In this case, of course, the shared colonial experience had not been enough to protect him from the depredations of some soldiers (whoever they were; the incident may not have happened at Vindolanda). But that

---

[55] See Goldhill in this volume on colonial dynamics between Italy and the Greek East.
[56] See especially Purcell 2006 and Eberle and LeQuéré 2017. [57] Birley 1979.
[58] Birley 1979: 82–96, Haynes 2013: 126. [59] Mattingly 2006: 108–9 and 297–8.

shared experience is precisely what he appeals to when he seeks to elicit solidarity from the governor (or whoever else the petition may have been addressed to), objecting not just to the injustice but also the indignity of the way he has been treated. Presumably he would have mentioned Roman citizenship if he had it. In its absence, he chose to focus on the fact that he was not a native Briton but a fellow *transmarinus* – from the (more civilised) world across the sea. Despite the social gulf between him and his addressee, the petitioner appeals for sympathy on the basis of a shared identity as members of a colonial elite in a subject land. As a perhaps unique example of a text that seeks to negotiate questions of identity and solidarity in a social situation with high stakes, this badly damaged draft is precious testimony to the complexities of the social landscape of Roman Britain. Such texts deserve to be much better known by those with an interest in identity and empire.

## *Humanitas and Slavery*

My second example is a letter written by the co-emperors Marcus Aurelius and Lucius Verus in response to a query from Voconius Saxa, a provincial governor (probably of Africa in 161–2 CE) – analogous to Trajan's replies to Pliny in Book 10 of his *Letters*.[60] This text is not an inscription but it comes from a similarly recondite corpus – the jurists. The letter was quoted by Ulpian in his early third-century work *On the Duties of the Proconsul* and later excerpted (with Ulpian's discussion) by Trebonian's jurists during the compilation of the *Digest* for Justinian.[61]

> Prudenter et egregia ratione humanitatis, Saxa carissime, Primitiuum seruum, qui homicidium in se confingere metu ad dominum reuertendi suspectus esset, perseuerantem falsa demonstratione damnasti quaesiturus de consciis, quos aeque habere se commentitus fuerat, ut ad certiorem ipsius de se confessionem peruenires. Nec frustra fuit tam prudens consilium tuum, cum in tormentis constiterit neque illos ei conscios fuisse et ipsum de se temere commentum. Potes itaque decreti gratiam facere et eum per officium distrahi iubere, condicione addita, ne umquam in potestatem domini reuertatur, quem pretio recepto certum habemus libenter tali seruo cariturum.

---

[60] For other examples of the genre, and for fuller discussion of the correspondence of emperors and governors and other officials, see Lavan 2018, on which this reading draws.

[61] *Dig.* 48.18.1.27 (Ulpian, *De off. procons.* 8). Imperial pronouncements quoted by the early jurists are most easily accessed through Gualandi 1963, a compilation of constitutions (the technical term for a ruling by the emperor) discussed by the jurists, which uses a different typeface to distinguish verbatim quotation from paraphrase and commentary by the jurists.

> You acted judiciously and with a fine regard for *humanitas*, dear Saxa, in condemning the slave Primitivus, who was suspected of having invented a charge of murder against himself out of fear of being returned to his master, when he persevered in his false testimony, with a view to interrogating him about the accomplices whom he had also falsely claimed to have, in order to get a more credible confession about himself. Your judicious plan was not in vain, since torture established both that he had no accomplices and that he had recklessly lied about himself. You may therefore annul your verdict and command him to be sold by your staff, with the proviso that he never be returned to the ownership of his master. We are certain that [the master] will be glad to be deprived of a slave of that sort, once he has been paid his value.

Saxa had tried a case in which a slave had confessed to being party to a murder but was suspected of having invented the story in order to escape from his master's power (testimony to the lengths to which cruelty could drive slaves). Saxa first condemned him based on his own confession and then had him tortured to test his claims about his accomplices. Having established that his story was false, Saxa then sought the emperor's approval to annul his initial finding. (Guilt, once established, could not be overturned by a mere governor.[62])

It is characteristic of the correspondence between emperors and the senatorial and equestrian elite that the emperors' familiar language contributes to the construction of a warm, personal relationship (*Saxa carissime*) and that their rhetoric of approval evokes a sense of partnership in the project of beneficial and just government (*prudenter et egregia ratione humanitatis ... damnauisti, tam prudens consilium*).[63] But I want to focus on a single word and its incongruity here – *humanitas*.

If any single word encapsulates the vision that the ruling class had of itself and its mission, it is *humanitas*. It is a word particularly associated with the activity of government and especially the creation and maintenance of a rational and beneficent legal order.[64] Yet its usage is deeply paradoxical. On the one hand, it suggests a sense of natural human solidarity (and hence is sometimes used to refer to sympathy and compassion towards others); on the other, it usually appears as a virtue specific to the powerful or to express the superiority of Graeco-Roman culture.[65] In

---

[62] Ulpian at *Dig.* 48.18.1.27.   [63] See further Lavan 2018.
[64] On legal discourse, see Bauman 1996 s.v. *humanitas* and Kreuzsaler and Urbanik 2008.
[65] Gildenhard 2011: 201–16 is an excellent survey of its semantic range in Cicero. On the superiority of Graeco-Roman culture, see e.g. Cic. *Div.* 2.80 (*humanitatis expertes barbaros*), Caes. *BGall.* 1.1.3 ([*Belgae*] ... *a cultu atque humanitate prouinciae longissime absunt*), Gell. 15.21.1 (*ferocissimos et immanes et alienos ab omni humanitate*).

other words, *humanitas* tends in practice to be invoked in order to elevate some human beings over others. A famous passage of Aulus Gellius attempts to foreclose (but merely highlights) this paradox, observing that most people think than *humanitas* means 'a sort of openness and benevolence towards all human beings' (*dexteritatem quandam beniuolentiamque erga omnis homines promiscam*), but insists that it really means *paideia* or mastery of the *bonae artes* – in other words a cultural competence exclusive to Graeco-Roman culture and specifically its educated, propertied elite.[66]

Although their rhetoric of *humanitas* has often been internalised by later writers inclined to idealise both the Roman empire in general and its legal order in particular, we ought to be alert to the ideological work it does. Perhaps nowhere more clearly than this passage can we see how the idea of *humanitas* serves to mystify a system characterised by extreme inequality and violence. What Saxa did was to torture an innocent slave. As he and the emperors would have seen it, of course, he was acting in pursuit of the truth and in the interests of the falsely accused conspirators (and indeed the slave himself, who would eventually be spared from capital punishment) and he had no choice but to use torture, since he could not otherwise admit evidence from a slave.[67] Hence the crucial force of *constat* in *in tormentis constiterit*: torture established the facts. Yet the fact remains that his intervention required torture to exonerate an innocent human being. Nor did it address the question of the slave's grievances or his master's faults. Besides the matter-of-fact ablative phrase (*metu ad dominum reuertendi*) that attributes Primitivus' false confession of murder to fear of being returned to his master, there is no acknowledgement of the extraordinary cruelty that it must have taken to drive a slave to such an extremity. On the contrary, the letter closes by insisting on the master's property rights (he must be compensated for the loss) and expressing masterly solidarity in imagining his likely exasperation with the slave – he will be delighted (*libenter*) to be rid of *a slave like that* (*tali seruo*).

In this context, the reference to *humanitas* is striking. As a typical virtue of judges and the legal order, it was of course conventional in a letter approving a legal decision. Yet it is revealing that no contradiction was felt between the ideals the word instantiated – founded in a recognition of the commonality of the human condition – and what this case revealed about the cruel reality of the slave system, a system which subjected one human being to the arbitrary cruelty of another and necessitated the torture of an innocent person. That *humanitas* could be invoked so casually and

[66] Gell. 13.17.   [67] Buckland 1908: 87.

unproblematically in this context demonstrates that the concept served to convince the ruling elite of the nobility of their own actions and the justice of the society they inhabited, much more than it did to encourage behaviour or foster the development of norms that we would recognise as enlightened.

## Historiography

The study of Latin historiography is a context in which the interests of Latinists and historians ought to overlap. Yet the subfield offers a striking example of the failure, or rather absence, of dialogue. The iconoclastic work of Peter Wiseman and Tony Woodman in the 1970s and '80s has inspired a substantial and growing literature on the genre of historiography, yet there has been little dialogue with historians. This is at least partly due to the marginalisation of ancient historiography in modern historical practice. Because historians increasingly focus on social and economic history, rather than traditional political history, the most important work in the field (at least for the imperial period) tends to be based on inscriptions, papyri and the juristic corpora, rather than the historiographical texts that once underpinned ancient history and are now much worked by Latinists.[68] But the lack of engagement from historians may also be due to a degree of alienation from work in this tradition.

A relatively rare example of overt engagement with recent developments in the study of historiography is Ted Lendon's essay in the recent *Cambridge Companion to the Roman Historians*, which opens by indicting the whole project: 'This essay weeps at the intellectual motion this volume exemplifies: the triumph of what now masquerades as "Roman historiography," the academic study of the ancient Roman historians as a discipline sundered from Roman history, the study of what happened in ancient Rome and why.'[69] The sparkling essay is a masterpiece of scholarly polemic. But it is unlikely to convince many Latinists that they need to fundamentally rethink their approach to historiography. First, his critique, which focuses on two (relatively early) works by Wiseman and Woodman, ignores the great diversity of approaches within the field.[70] There are in fact considerable and significant methodological differences not just between

---

[68] This will be evident from a glance at the *index locorum* of the most important recent studies of imperial political culture, such as Ando 2000, Rowe 2002 or Noreña 2011.
[69] Lendon 2009. [70] Lendon focuses on Wiseman 1979 and Woodman 1988.

Wiseman and Woodman (one writing as a historian, the other as a Latinist) but also between them and the many other scholars who have contributed to the proliferation of avowedly 'literary' approaches to Latin historiography over the past three decades. In reality, recent and current work on Latin historiography is widely dispersed along a spectrum from more historicising to more formalist approaches.[71] Second, it ignores the fact that verity remains a central preoccupation of much work on historiography. Scholarship on Tacitus, for example, tends to seize every opportunity to read him against parallel accounts in an attempt to elucidate the processes of selection, arrangement and framing that produced his narrative.[72] If anything, I would argue, scholarship remains *too* preoccupied with these questions, given the impossibility of establishing a 'true' account against which Tacitus can be measured. Third, the bulk of his paper is focused on rebutting two specific claims – Wiseman's thesis that most of the content of the history of early Rome was a later invention and Woodman's argument that history was regarded 'as a branch of rhetoric' – that are not in fact axiomatic for most current work on historiography. Even if one conceded these points to Lendon, the study of historiography could continue largely uninterrupted.[73] The corollary of this narrow focus is that Lendon's larger and more significant claims – that the ancient historian saw himself primarily as 'a teller of true tales about the past' and that the truth-orientation of the genre is an insuperable obstacle to the project of reading it as 'literature' – are left undeveloped.

Lendon is undoubtedly right that historians prized *veritas*, but the more important question is what they thought constituted *veritas*. Even granted the vulnerability of Woodman's extreme position that truth in historiography consisted purely in the avoidance of bias, it seems likely that Latin historians evaluated the truthfulness of historical narrative very differently from modern, academic historians, particularly when it came to the acceptability of supplying detail necessary to make sense of a narrative. It is generally accepted that the barbarian speeches that are a staple of Latin historiography are outright inventions, authorised by their antecedents in the genre rather than by any knowledge of what was actually said on the

---

[71] Note, for example, the distance separating two very different, but equally influential, readings of Tacitus: O'Gorman 2000 and Sailor 2008.

[72] See e.g. Damon 1999 (juxtaposing Tacitus' account of the trial of Piso against the *senatus consultum de Pisone patre*) and Damon 2003 and Ash 2007 (with considerable discussion of parallel narratives in Plutarch and Suetonius). More broadly, Tacitus' 'art of innuendo' (Ryberg 1942) continues to be documented and discussed.

[73] See Feldherr 2009a: 8.

occasion. Once some degree of invention is conceded, it is very hard to isolate its reach within any historical text. That should worry historians like Lendon more than it seems to.

Lendon also objects to the idea of reading a work of history 'as literature'. Lendon can be forgiven a degree of ambiguity here, since most of the writers he is responding to are similarly vague in their exhortations to read historiography 'as literature'. Insofar as he explains what he means by this, it consists in reading 'as if the historians they study were in fact authors of imaginative fiction, free to write absolutely as they pleased'. His notion of an 'unconstrained literary artist' ignores the fact that there are constraints and pressures in all genres: no artist is free of constraint. More importantly, his gloss seems to miss the essential core of most recent readings of historiography. It appears to me that the claim that historiography must be read 'as literature' is really a shorthand for a growing sensitivity to the ambition of the genre and the subtlety of its writing. It is becoming increasingly clear that history shares with epic the ambition of tackling profound questions about politics, society and culture. Moreover, again like epic, it requires interpretive work of its reader. Studied ambiguities, metaphorical language, significant juxtapositions and responsion within and between texts all demand interpretation. In this sense, the discourse of Latin history has many elements that we might identify as characteristic of 'literary' rather than expository writing.[74] In short, writers like Sallust or Tacitus are not merely describing and analysing a particular set of events (though they are doing that), but also using their narratives to offer complex and often elusive perspectives on the pressing issues of their own time. Of course, there is no programmatic passage that explains this so baldly – no more than there is in Virgil. That is not the nature of such writing. The test of such an approach can only lie in the felicity of the readings it produces. And the accumulated results of decades of work in this tradition is enough to convince me that authors like Sallust and Tacitus can and indeed must be read in this way.

A volume aimed at self-professed Latinists is not the place for a proper rebuttal of Lendon's arguments. In any case, the limits of Lendon's critique of current work on historiography do not mean that Latinists should be complacent. There is an additional dimension to his criticism that deserves separate consideration. Lendon closes his essay with a scathing survey of

---

[74] See Lowrie in this volume (pp. 783–8) on exemplarity and metaphor as characteristic modes of expression in embedded political thought in Latin and the challenges they pose for modern readers looking for explicit theorising. 'Answers are not given, but produced', in her pithy formulation.

what he regards as the excesses of recent critical work. It culminates in an extraordinary indictment:

> Finally, when history is cast out of the Latin historians, discarded also are the robust intellectual habits of the modern historian, to be replaced, if the restraint of stern philology fails, with the weak and whimsical instruments of the contemporary literary critic. A sense of argument, of proof, of scale, of proportion, even of logic and coherent language – all depart. Scholarship becomes indistinguishable from its parody, and the subject of inquiry shifts from the geysering fascination of antiquity to the dull, trend-obsessed, and self-obsessed mind of the critic.

This is unusual as an overt attack on the historical value and intellectual rigour of Latin studies as it is practised today (for that is what it amounts to). But I suspect that some other historians nodded in silent agreement. Lendon's exasperated tone has a notable parallel in Keith Bradley's review of William Fitzgerald's *Slavery and the Roman Literary Imagination* – a relatively rare example of a leading Roman historian reviewing a book at the cutting edge of Latin literature.[75] Fitzgerald's project was indicative of the growing interest among Latinists in the ways in which Latin literature is implicated in social relations. That was presumably what attracted the interest of Bradley, perhaps the single most influential historian of Roman slavery. But he was not impressed by what he found. He saw a profound difference in kind between Fitzgerald's project and his own: 'Literary scholars will welcome this particular book more, I imagine, than historians: indeed, it is written for them. To my mind, however, it confirms the pressing need not to confuse criticism that treats social themes with the history of society proper.' He goes so far as to question whether Fitzgerald's approach (and his comments could equally well apply to the field as a whole) can contribute anything of real value to our knowledge of the Roman world in a sentence that veers from a gesture of generosity to damning critique:

> Critics have every right to present their 'readings' of texts; but readings have to be recognised for what they are: personal and subjective reflections that may at times capture important truths but which devoid of historical and social context can make the texts studied 'mean' almost anything the critics wish them to mean. Ingenuity of argument, it seems, is all that is required.

Like Lendon, Bradley objects even to the mode of argument, singling out Fitzgerald's interpretation of the metaphor of the skill of the circus rider

---

[75] Bradley 2001, reviewing Fitzgerald 2000.

who jumps from horse to horse (*desultoria scientia*) that Apuleius applies to his writing in the prologue to the *Metamorphoses*. Starting from the relatively obvious connection between horses and the ass at the centre of the story, Fitzgerald reflects on the way in which the metaphor figures by inversion the knowledge of the narrator, which (as the reader will learn) is gained 'by lending his back to one owner after another – the reverse of the *desultor* who leaps from back to back'.[76] It is a relatively small detail in Fitzgerald's reading of slavery in the *Metamorphoses*, but Bradley will have none of it: 'The leaps made from the original image of the circus rider in the passages I have quoted are, well, desultory to say the least and to my mind stretch the limits of plausibility. They are far from unusual in the book as a whole.' Bradley's response is by no means representative of all ancient historians. One could contrast the much more sympathetic response by Brent Shaw, another leading social historian of the Roman empire: 'Provocative insights on the complexity of relationships between slave and free, and those between, abound on almost every page and cannot be adequately encompassed by this brief review.'[77] But Bradley's review shows that Lendon's concerns about intellectual rigour are shared more widely.

These two responses illustrate a growing intellectual divide between Latin literature and Roman history. It is a question not just of interest, or of intelligibility (all specialisms entail a degree of opacity even to related fields), but of recognition qua scholarship. The objections of Lendon and Bradley are not unlike the linguists' dismissal of literary readings as 'not even wrong', as discussed by James Clackson in this volume (p. 563). Whereas work in a more traditional vein – textual criticism, the dating of texts and even some New Criticism-style close readings of individual texts – has always been comprehensible (if not always of great interest) to Roman historians, newer currents of research that foreground the role of intertextuality (in the narrower sense that has become conventional in Classics) in determining the meaning of literary texts and/or deploy reading strategies drawn directly or indirectly from French post-structuralist criticism seem to alienate many historians. If there is a problem here, it is certainly not one-sided. It is at least partly an issue of historians' receptiveness to work in a different intellectual tradition, as can be seen in the contrast between Bradley's impatient and Shaw's more attentive review of *Slavery and the Roman Literary Imagination*. But Latinists could also do more to find common ground.

[76] Fitzgerald 2000: 96–7 on Apul. *Met.* 1.1.   [77] Shaw 2001: 187.

As it is, Latinists often seem to go out of their way to alienate historians, even in areas where the agendas of the two fields ought to converge, such as the study of historiography. It has become a commonplace of work on Latin historiography to open with a claim to have no interest in the question of the truth value of the narratives studied. What began as a radical call for rebellion, aimed at destabilising the conventional approach to these texts and precipitating new modes of reading, has become a mere motto. It functions as a shibboleth, signalling allegiance to a now well-established sub-discipline and alienating anyone who identifies as a historian. Rather than being a provocation to the establishment, it now serves mostly to foster a solipsistic culture in work on historiography. It gives Latinists an easy excuse for ducking complex questions about the relationship between historiography and history and forecloses on the possibility of productive dialogue with historians. This solipsism is all the more unfortunate since, for all the protestations of disinterest in 'what actually happened', much current work on historiography remains fundamentally historicist in approach. Besides the ubiquitous political readings of Latin texts, one could point to a recent swerve in the literature on intertextuality in historiography that foregrounds the complex entanglement of literary allusion and exemplary culture – what John Marincola called 'the intertextuality of real life'.[78] These are projects that ought to be conducted in dialogue with historians. Yet dialogue requires an effort to sympathise with and speak to the other. If nothing else, it might be a productive discipline for Latinists to imagine a 'Lendon' or 'Bradley' among their readers and to try to articulate their arguments in terms likely to persuade, not alienate them.

It is probably also fair to say that the echo-chamber of Latin studies and especially its subfield of Latin historiography is guilty of perpetuating a comforting stereotype of the reductiveness of historical practice.[79] It is common to contrast one's attention to the complexity of these 'texts' with historians' reductive use of them as 'sources'. But the figure of the reductive historian is a straw man that risks blinding its proponents to the diversity and sophistication of contemporary historical practice – particularly at the forefront of the discipline. The decades that have seen the consolidation of Latin historiography as a subfield of Latin literature have also brought fundamental changes to the way Roman history is written, tracking broader developments in the wider discipline of history. Social and economic history have displaced political history as the core of the discipline.

[78] Damon 2010, Marincola 2011 (quotation from p. 5), Chaplin 2013.   [79] So also Dench 2009.

The accumulation of quantitative evidence (a legacy of the *Annales* school in French history) and the construction of abstract models (reflecting the influence of the social sciences) have reduced historians' reliance on narrative or anecdotal evidence. At the same time, other historians have made ideology and culture the subject of historical analysis, reflecting another legacy of the *Annales* school (in its interest in *histoire des mentalités*) and the rise of a subfield of 'cultural history'. For example, Paul Kosmin's recent studies of space and time in the Seleukid empire stand at the forefront of current work in Hellenistic history.[80] In Roman history, Leslie Dossey's recent history of peasants in Roman Africa seamlessly integrates analysis of representations of the countryside with social and economic history, while Ari Bryen's study of violence in Roman Egypt places the act of narration at the centre of its analysis.[81] Indeed, there are now many self-professed 'historians' who could rival professional Latinists for the sensitivity and penetration of their readings of ancient texts. The late Keith Hopkins' reading of the *Life of Aesop* remains an outstanding model of how to read texts as the product of a slave society, while Mary Beard's innovative reading of the Ciceronian letter corpus opened up new ground for Latinists.[82] Many real historians offer much richer potential for dialogue than current stereotypes of the 'historian' suggest.

## Conclusion

The divide between Latinists and historians is probably no wider than that between Early Modernists (or scholars of any other period) in English and History departments. But it is surely more regrettable precisely because Latinists and Roman historians operate in such close proximity in Anglophone universities – one of the distinctive features of the idiosyncratic field of 'Classics'. Not only are they often located in the same departments, but they share departmental seminars and train in the same undergraduate and postgraduate programmes. Ancient historians are much more likely to be familiar with the discipline of close reading than historians in any other field. A porous boundary between literature and history ought surely to be one of the virtues of Classics as a field.

In the final analysis, the question of whether the prospect of a growing intellectual divide between the two fields is a concern for Latinists will depend on one's perspective. For formalists – those who approach

---

[80] Kosmin 2014 and 2018.   [81] Dossey 2010, Bryen 2013.
[82] Hopkins 1993, Beard 2002 (followed most recently by Martelli 2017).

literature as a relatively autonomous field of cultural production – a divide is only to be expected and hardly to be regretted. Nor will it seem a problem for those who reject any form of historicism, denying the possibility of recovering what a Latin text meant to its author or even to contemporary readers and insisting that we can only read them from our own historical and social location. But the alienation of historians ought to be a concern for the many who are committed to the admittedly fraught project of situating Latin texts in their original context and understanding how their authors were responding to, and seeking to act upon, their contemporary world. It seems particularly unfortunate that the divide is widening at a time when interest in such forms of historicism is growing in Latin literature. This essay is an attempt to persuade Latinists that this is a problem they should worry about, and to suggest some ways of addressing it.

## References

Ahl, F. (1984a) 'The art of safe criticism in Greece and Rome', *AJPh* 105: 174–208.
   (1984b) 'The rider and the horse: politics and power in Roman poetry from Horace to Statius', *ANRW* II.32.1: 40–124.
Ando, C. (2000) *Imperial Ideology and Provincial Loyalty in the Roman Empire*, Berkeley.
Ash, R. (2007) *Tacitus: Histories Book* II, Cambridge.
Bauman, R. A. (1996) *Crime and Punishment in Ancient Rome*, London.
Beard, M. (1998) 'Vita inscripta', in W. W. Ehlers, ed., *La biographie antique* (Geneva), 83–114.
   (2002) 'Ciceronian correspondences: making a book out of letters', in T. P. Wiseman, ed., *Classics in Progress* (Oxford), 103–44.
Bertrand, J.-M. (1990) 'Formes de discours politiques: décrets des cités grecques et correspondance des rois hellénistiques', in C. Nicolet, ed., *Du pouvoir dans l'antiquité: mots et réalités* (Paris and Geneva), 101–15.
Birley, A. (1979) *The People of Roman Britain*, London.
   (1991) 'Vindolanda: new writing tablets 1986–1989', in V. A. Maxfield and M. J. Dobson, eds., *Roman Frontier Studies 1989* (Exeter), 29–51.
Bowman, A. K. and J. D. Thomas (1994) *The Vindolanda Writing-Tablets (Tabulae Vindolandenses* II*)*, London.
Bradley, K. (2001). 'Imagining slavery: the limits of the plausible', *JRA* 14: 473–77.
Bryen, A. Z. (2013) *Violence in Roman Egypt: A Study in Legal Interpretation*, Philadelphia.
Bücheler, F. and E. Lommatzsch (1930) *Carmina Latina epigraphica*, 2nd edn, 2 vols., Leipzig.
Buckland, W. W. (1908) *The Roman Law of Slavery: The Condition of the Slave in Private Law from Augustus to Justinian*, Cambridge.

Ceccarelli, P. (2018) 'Letters and decrees: diplomatic protocols in the Hellenistic period', in P. Ceccarelli, L. Doering, T. Fögen and I. Gildenhard, eds., *Letters and Communities: Studies in the Socio-Political Dimensions of Ancient Epistolography* (Oxford), 148–83.
Champlin, E. (1999) 'The first (1996) edition of the *Senatus consultum*', *AJPh* 120: 117–22.
Chaplin, J. D. (2013) 'Alluding to reality: towards a typology of historiographical intertextuality', *Histos* working papers 2013.01.
Corbeill, A. (2015) *Sexing the World: Grammatical Gender and Biological Sex in Ancient Rome*, Princeton.
Courtney, E. (1995) *Musa Lapidaria: A Selection of Latin Verse Inscriptions*, Athens.
Damon, C. (1999) 'The trial of Cn. Piso in Tacitus' *Annales* and the *Senatus consultum de Cn. Pisone patre*', *AJPh* 120: 143–62.
  (2003) *Tacitus. Histories Book 1*, Cambridge.
  (2010) 'Déjà vu or déjà lu? History as intertext', *Papers of the Liverpool Latin Seminar* 14: 375–88.
Damon, C. and S. A. Takács (1999) 'The *senatus consultum de Cn. Pisone patre*: text, translation discussion', *AJPh* 120: 13–42.
Davies, J. P. (2004) *Rome's Religious History: Livy, Tacitus and Ammianus on Their Gods*, Cambridge.
Dench, E. (2009) 'The Roman historians and twentieth-century approaches to Roman history', in Feldherr 2009b, 394–406.
Dickey, E. (2002) *Latin Forms of Address: From Plautus to Apuleius*, Oxford.
Dossey, L. (2010) *Peasant and Empire in Christian North Africa*, Berkeley.
Eberle, L. P. and É. LeQuéré (2017) 'Landed traders, trading agriculturalists? Land in the economy of the Italian diaspora in the Greek East', *JRS* 107: 27–59.
Feldherr, A. (2009a) 'Introduction', in Feldherr 2009b, 1–8.
Feldherr, A., ed. (2009b) *The Cambridge Companion to the Roman Historians*, Cambridge.
Fitzgerald, W. (2000) *Slavery and the Roman Literary Imagination*, Cambridge.
Flower, H. I. (1999) 'Piso in Chicago: a commentary on the APA/AIA joint seminar on the *Senatus consultum de Cn. Pisone patre*', *AJPh* 120: 99–115.
Geue, T. (2018) 'Soft hands, hard power: sponging off the empire of leisure (Virgil, *Georgics* 4)', *JRS* 108: 115–40.
Gildenhard, I. (2011) *Creative Eloquence: The Construction of Reality in Cicero's Speeches*, Oxford.
Greenblatt, S. (1980) *Renaissance Self-Fashioning*, Chicago.
Gualandi, G. (1963) *Legislazione imperiale e giurisprudenza*, 2 vols., Milan.
Habinek, T. N. (1998) *The Politics of Latin Literature: Writing, Identity and Empire in Ancient Rome*, Princeton.
  (2002) 'Ovid and empire', in P. Hardie, ed., *The Cambridge Companion to Ovid* (Cambridge), 46–61.
Harries, J. (2018) 'Saturninus the helmsman, Pliny and friends: legal and literary letter collections', in König and Whitton 2018, 260–79.
Hauken, T. (1998) *Petition and Response: An Epigraphic Study of Petitions to Roman Emperors*, Bergen.

Haynes, I. (2013) *Blood of the Provinces: The Roman Auxilia and the Making of Provincial Society from Augustus to the Severans*, Oxford.
Henderson, J. (1998) *Roman Life: Rutilius Gallicus on Paper and in Stone*, Exeter.
Hinds, S. (2001) 'Cinna, Statius, and "immanent literary history" in the cultural economy', in E. A. Schmidt, ed., *L'histoire littéraire immanente dans la poésie latine* (Vandœuvres), 221–65.
  (2010) 'Between formalism and historicism', in A. Barchiesi and W. Scheidel, eds., *The Oxford Handbook of Roman Studies* (Oxford), 369–85.
Hopkins, K. (1993) 'Novel evidence for Roman slavery', *Past & Present* 138: 3–27.
Kautsky, J. H. (1997) *The Politics of Aristocratic Empires*, Chapel Hill, NC.
Keith, A. M. (2000) *Engendering Rome: Women in Latin Epic*, Cambridge.
Kelly, B. (2011) *Petitions, Litigation, and Social Control in Roman Egypt*, Oxford.
Kennedy, D. F. (1992) 'Augustan and anti-Augustan: reflections on terms of reference', in A. Powell, ed., *Roman Poetry and Propaganda in the Age of Augustus* (Bristol), 26–58.
König, A. and C. Whitton, eds. (2018) *Roman Literature under Nerva, Trajan and Hadrian: Literary Interactions, AD 96–138*, Cambridge.
Kosmin, P. J. (2014) *The Land of the Elephant Kings*, Cambridge, MA.
  (2018) *Time and Its Adversaries in the Seleucid Empire*, Cambridge, MA.
Kreuzsaler, C. and J. Urbanik (2008) 'Humanity and inhumanity of law: the case of Dionysia', *JJP* 38: 119–55.
Lavan, M. (2013) *Slaves to Rome: Paradigms of Empire in Roman Culture*, Cambridge.
  (2018) 'Pliny Epistles 10 and imperial correspondence: the Empire of letters', in König and Whitton 2018, 280–301.
Leigh, M. (2016) 'Vergil's second *Eclogue* and the class struggle', *CPh* 111: 406–33.
Lendon, J. E. (2009) 'Historians without history: against Roman historiography', in Feldherr 2009b, 41–61.
  (2013) Review of Lavan 2013, *Sehepunkte* 13.5.
Levene, D. S. (1993) *Religion in Livy*, Leiden.
Lowrie, M. (2009) *Writing, Performance, and Authority in Augustan Rome*, Oxford.
  (2016) 'Roman law and Latin literature', in P. J. du Plessis, C. Ando and K. Tuori, eds., *The Oxford Handbook of Roman Law and Society* (Oxford), 70–82.
Ma, J. (2002) *Antiochos III and the Cities of Western Asia Minor*, rev. edn, Oxford.
Mantovani, D. (2018) *Les juristes écrivains de la Rome antique: les oeuvres des juristes comme littérature*, Paris.
Marincola, J. (2011) 'Intertextuality and *exempla*', *Histos* working papers 2011.03.
Martelli, F. (2017) 'The triumph of letters: rewriting Cicero in *Ad fam.* 15', *JRS* 107: 90–115.
Martindale, C. (2003) 'Green politics', in C. Martindale, ed., *The Cambridge Companion to Virgil* (Cambridge), 107–24.
Mattingly, D. J. (2006) *An Imperial Possession: Britain in the Roman Empire, 54 BC–AD 409*, London.
McCarthy, K. (2000) *Slaves, Masters, and the Art of Authority in Plautine Comedy*, Princeton.

Millar, F. (1977) *The Emperor in the Roman World (31 BC–AD 337)*, London.
Noreña, C. F. (2011) *Imperial Ideals in the Roman West: Representation, Circulation, Power*, Cambridge.
O'Gorman, E. (1993) 'No place like Rome: identity and difference in the *Germania* of Tacitus', *Ramus* 22: 135–54.
 (2000) *Irony and Misreading in the Annals of Tacitus*, Cambridge.
Oliver, J. H. (1989) *Greek Constitutions of Early Roman Emperors from Inscriptions and Papyri*, Philadelphia.
Peachin, M. (1999) 'Five Vindolanda tablets, soldiers, and the law', *Tyche* 14: 223–35.
Pollock, S. (2010) 'Future philology? The fate of a soft science in a hard world', *Critical Inquiry* 35: 931–61.
Potter, D. S., C. Damon and S. A. Takács, eds. (1999) *The 'senatus consultum de Cn. Pisone patre'* (= *AJPh* 120.1), Baltimore.
Purcell, N. (2006) 'Romans in the Roman world', in K. Galinsky, ed., *The Cambridge Companion to the Age of Augustus* (Cambridge), 85–105.
Richlin, A. (2017) *Slave Theater in the Roman Republic: Plautus and Popular Comedy*, Cambridge.
Roller, M. B. (2001) *Constructing Autocracy: Aristocrats and Emperors in Julio-Claudian Rome*, Princeton.
Rowe, G. (2002) *Princes and Political Cultures: The New Tiberian Senatorial Decrees*, Ann Arbor, MI.
Ryberg, I. S. (1942) 'Tacitus' art of innuendo', *TAPhA* 73: 383–404.
Sailor, D. (2008) *Writing and Empire in Tacitus*, Cambridge.
Schmidt, M. G. (2015) 'Carmina Latina Epigraphica', in C. Bruun and J. Edmondson, eds., *The Oxford Handbook of Roman Epigraphy* (Oxford), 764–82.
Shannon-Henderson, K. E. (2019) *Religion and Memory in Tacitus' Annals*, Oxford.
Shaw, B. D. (1985) 'The divine economy: Stoicism as ideology', *Latomus* 44: 16–54.
 (2001) Review of Fitzgerald 2000, *Phoenix* 55: 185–7.
Shumate, N. (2006) *Nation, Empire, Decline: Studies in Rhetorical Continuity from the Romans to the Modern Era*, London.
Stewart, R. (2012) *Plautus and Roman Slavery*, Malden, MA.
Weisweiler, J. (2016) 'From empire to world-state: ecumenical language and cosmopolitan consciousness in the later Roman aristocracy', in M. Lavan, R. E. Payne and J. Weisweiler, eds., *Cosmopolitanism and Empire* (Oxford), 187–208.
White, P. (1993) *Promised Verse: Poets in the Society of Augustan Rome*, Cambridge, MA.
Williams, R. (1973) *The Country and the City*, London.
Wiseman, T. P. (1979) *Clio's Cosmetics: Three Studies in Greco-Roman Literature*, Leicester.
Woodman, A. J. (1988) *Rhetoric in Classical Historiography*, London.

CHAPTER 16

# Latin Literature and Greek

### Simon Goldhill

I

From the point of view of contemporary colonial theory, the literature from Rome, the mother of all empires, is a distinct anomaly. In recent decades, we have learned a great deal about the strategies of the colonised and the cultural dominance of the imperial power. The requirement of the colonised is to mimic, to pass, to write resistance from below. The ability of the subaltern to speak has been questioned, recalibrated and questioned again. The power of the colonisers, by contrast, is to objectify the other in its gaze, to represent empire as the necessary bringing of civilisation and value to an otherwise backwards culture, to exoticise, loot and then display the spectacle of heritage. The cultural oppressiveness of imperialism in its colonial form has become a commonplace of recent cultural history and literary criticism – with an ironically restricted set of geographical and temporal examples.[1]

Rome defeated and colonised Greece as it did much of the Mediterranean and beyond. It demonstrated its military power in all too well-known acts of military might, despoiling through taxation and the appropriation of material resources. Yet its relation to Greece, specifically in cultural terms, reverses the expected dynamics of power. As Horace famously wrote (*Epist.* 2.1.156–7), 'Captured Greece captured its savage conqueror and brought the arts to rustic Latium.' Horace's *bon mot* is a piece of knowing historical, national self-placement from the son of a freedman at the court of the newly flourishing Empire. It declares that a dominant, military imperial force found its own culture overtaken by the culture of its own enemy, as its own provinciality is exposed by one of its

---

[*] Thanks to the editors, John Henderson, Ingo Gildenhard and Emma Greensmith for comments on the draft of this chapter – as well as the other contributors for discussion.
[1] Acheraïou 2008 and 2011; Ashcroft, Griffiths and Tiffin 2002; Said 1994; Cronin 2008; Quayson 2000; Spivak 1988; Young 2000, and the seminal Bhabha 1990 and 1994; Young 1990 and 1995.

provinces. Horace himself was instrumental in adapting Greek lyric forms to the Latin language, and thus his comment on Greek culture is a gesture of self-representation too. Yet for all its ironies, this sentence does express an important recognition of Roman literary culture's extraordinary indebtedness to its colony. In contrast to the expectations of contemporary colonial theory, the politically and militarily dominant Rome found itself speaking the cultural language of the colonised.[2]

Denis Feeney, most recently, has provided a particularly provocative analysis of just how surprising Horace's celebrated claim is.[3] His history of early Latin literature emphasises that what might seem like a wry piece of cultural one-upmanship of self-recognition from an elite literary milieu actually conceals a long and fascinating history, which, above all, needs explanation. For, as Feeney argues, from the earliest days of contact in Magna Graecia in southern Italy, Roman literature, particularly Roman comedy and Roman epic, self-consciously models itself as adaptations, accommodations, imitations and translations of Greek comedy and epic. Roman literature starts as a translation of Greek. What is more, just as Lucretius translates Epicurus into Latin verse as a foundational act of Roman philosophy, so the *lingua franca* of education for the elite of empire society – rhetoric as much as philosophy – developed its models and terminology and practice from Greek authorities. And even the myths told to explain the world are peopled with a syncretic pantheon of stories and figures where Greek gods and Greek narratives are fully part of the repertoire of Roman mythology. When Quintilian, the great Roman rhetorical and literary theorist, looks back at the history of Roman literature, he concludes that only satire is a truly indigenous form. The rest is moulded by its engagement with Greek.[4] How, then, asks Feeney, are we to understand this unparalleled act of cultural transformation?

Feeney is concerned to trace the earliest history of the encounter, and there are, therefore, many speculative aspects to his analysis. In this chapter, I will be focusing on the later periods, from the late republic onwards, and, in particular, from the empire, where there are particularly rich evidence and particularly complex social contexts for Latin and Greek

---

[2] On Rome and post-colonial theory see Hose 1999; Quinn 2012; Webster and Cooper 1996. More generally, see Gruen 1992, Henrichs 1995, Huskinson 2000, Mattingly 2013 and 2014, Vanacker and Zuiderhoek 2017, Wallace-Hadrill 1998 and 2008; Woolf 2000.
[3] Feeney 2016; for a somewhat mechanical attempt to see how Romans wrote this history see Hutchinson 2013.
[4] Quint. *Inst.* 10.1.93. He also notes (10.1.100) that *sermo ipse Romanus*, 'the Latin language itself', prevents Romans reaching the grace of Greek comedy.

writing. I will also trace the encounter from both sides – to see the dynamics of interaction as a multi-sided process. The example of Rome's engagement with Greece is the most striking historical case where *translatio imperii* and *translatio scientiae* do not travel in the same direction, but fold back into a dynamic system where lines of power and knowledge are intricately intermeshed.

As Rome came into contact with other cultures through its imperial expansion, and included more and more communities in its polity, its increasingly pressing sense of self-definition – its privileged cultural and social values – is formed, as one might expect, in dynamic contrast with the others it faces. There has been fine critical analysis, for example, of the place of Germania in the imaginary of Rome, as a space where old values of austerity and integrity are on display.[5] The history of Rome itself, as told repeatedly by Romans, has its own ideological foundations and projections of a genealogy of aspirational virtue.[6] Alien communities within Rome – Jews and Christians have been most studied – acted as exemplary others, treated with fascination, repulsion, self-serving misrecognition and self-assertive violence.[7] Yet where literature and the arts are concerned, Greece occupies a unique definitional mirror for Roman self-expression. Roman elites expected each other to speak Greek and read Greek, not just for administrative purposes (as some British officials learned Hindi or Urdu for running the empire or missionary purposes), but even for some everyday exchanges between each other. Indeed, even at the sort of critical moment when the mother tongue might be expected, Greek could come to the lips: Julius Caesar, as he is killed, says to Brutus, *kai su teknon*, 'you too, child' (Suet. *Iul.* 82). Even if this is *ben trovato*, for Suetonius who reports it, the normality of speaking Greek – even and especially by the iconic Roman generalissimo to the noblest Roman of them all – is taken for granted. The education that Roman elites received across the empire included Homer, rhetorical theory, and philosophy in Greek: Cicero is typical in that he went to Athens for Further Education.[8] Again, the contrast with the British Empire is marked. The journey of Indian elites to Oxford and Cambridge was not matched by English men travelling to India for an education: indeed, Macaulay's famous minute presupposes

---

[5] Krebs 2011 goes further than O'Gorman 1993 and Lavan 2011.
[6] Langlands 2018 is the most recent study of this important topic.
[7] From a huge bibliography, see Benko 1984, Clark 2004, Lampe 2006, Lieu 2006, Carleton Paget and Lieu 2018, Lieu, North and Rajak 1992 and Rajak 2002, all with extensive further bibliography.
[8] Lee Too 2001 is an advance on Marrou 1956; Cribiore 2001 is standard for the later period.

the impossibility of yet getting an education in or from India at all.[9] Greek provided thus the furniture of the mind for Roman elites. If Germans, Gauls, Jews, Christians (for example) provided the opportunity for performative self-definition through projection of an other of the imaginary, Greece was internalised in Roman cultural experience. How this assimilation is negotiated, especially in and through Latin writing, is the subject of this chapter. Even when disavowed, Greece is a necessary alibi for Roman culture.

There is a marked asymmetry between this Roman experience and the production of Greek literature and culture during the empire. It is remarkable, as we will see in more detail later, that while Greek is fully absorbed as a language of Roman culture, it is still fiercely debated whether major Greek writers even read Latin; and the debate is necessary because many of these writers systematically fail to reveal any such knowledge, in a manner which is easily understood as an act of cultural self-assertion.[10] There are, as we will see, plenty of examples of Greek writers engaging directly with Rome: Lucian tells of his embarrassment when he uses the wrong term of greeting at the house of his *patronus*, and the annoyances of working as a hired academic; Aelius Aristides praises Rome in his most celebrated oration; Dio addresses the Roman Emperor, Trajan, in his kingship orations.[11] Yet much Greek prose bypasses Rome, either, as in the case of the genre of the novel, by constructing an imaginary contemporary or historical world without Rome, its institutions and authority; or by formulating a Greek cultural history which moves from the present back genealogically to the golden days of the classical city. Alciphron and Philostratus portray a world of farming, lovers, prostitutes, through their collections of fictional letters where the frame of reference is an Athens of the fourth century BCE, some six hundred years earlier. Philostratus' *Lives of the Sophists*, dedicated to a Roman consul, considers only Greek or Hellenised figures in his genealogy of rhetorical and intellectual expertise – Aelian, one of the few Romans to enter the roster, is praised precisely because he atticises (*attikizein*), that is, he speaks good Attic Greek – a cultural as much as a linguistic evaluation of what makes a good Greek. As a character in his *Life of Apollonius of Tyana* declares, 'to a wise man, everything is Greece', ἀνδρὶ σοφῷ πάντα "Ελλας (*VA* 1.35). If the history of

---

[9] See Vasunia 2013 and, on Macaulay, Hall 2012.
[10] Paradigmatic in its lack of conclusion is Gärtner 2005; the most recent discussion is Jolowicz 2021; see also Vian 1959 and 1963, James 2007, Keydell 1935, D'Ippolito 1994, Knox 1988, who argues against any influence of Latin on Greek epic.
[11] Aelius 14 and Dio 1–4: see Whitmarsh 2001.

Latin literature finds translation and hybridity at its very origin, Greek literature insists on finding its source in an authentic, pure, untrammelled Hellenism – and both Greek and Roman writers are aware of this difference, and negotiate their cultural self-expression within the matrix of such self-awareness. If Rome cannot find a literary and artistic identity without passing through Greece, Greek writers repeatedly strive to express themselves through a cultural heritage that starts before Rome and finds its authority without Rome.

While the Greek language and Greek literature were endemic in Roman education and the production of Latin literature, philosophy, rhetoric and art – and increasingly so from the early republic onwards – it also remained the case that the superiority of Rome to Greece could also always flare into violent self-assertion that took the shape of an aggressive opposition between Roman manly virtue and Greek effeminacy. It is no surprise to find a dominant masculine culture denigrating the other in gendered terms, but what is striking here is the combination of the recognition and practice of cultural deference on the one hand, and the hostile insistence of absolute cultural superiority on the other. Here, for example, is Livy (29.19) reporting without comment – he takes such strategies for granted – how a Roman commander was humiliated by his opponents (and victims):

> He was taunted with his style of dress (*cultus*) being un-Roman (*non Romanus*) and not even soldierly (*ne militaris quidem*). It was asserted that he walked about the gymnasium in a Greek mantle and Greek slippers, and spent his time in literature and athletics, and the whole of his staff were enjoying the attractions of self-indulgence and effeminacy (*molliter ... amoenitate frui*).

The Roman who in his public self-expression (*cultus*) does not look Roman enough puts at risk his privileged military and male status. This risk is embodied in wearing Greek clothes and Greek shoes in a Greek gymnasium (the Latin word for gymnasium is the transliterated Greek word: there is no real Latin term for such a place). This behaviour is upped in horror by the characteristic pairing of literature (*libellis*) and athletics (*palaestra* – another Greek word). Modern gender stereotypes would keep wrestling and poetry apart in the rhetoric of disparagement, but the Roman stereotype of Greek manhood easily associates poetry and naked wrestling as signs of an especially Greek effeminacy (*mollitia*) which cues the lures of unsuitable pleasure (*amoenitas*). Greek literature, in the Roman mind, could threaten to undermine the soldier's virtue. It was but a step from wearing slippers.

## 2

A particularly fascinating figure for this discussion is Marcus Porcius Cato (Cato the Elder). I say 'figure' because although Cato was a major character in the history of the early republic and a (brutal) force in the imperial conquest of Spain, and although his writings were prolific and widely read by many later intellectual stars including Cicero, I am interested here in how Cato was represented in discussions about cultural authority by later writers – how he became a figure of the imaginary through which the issue of Rome's relation to Greece was thought. Cato no doubt had his own political agenda to which any of his views on Greece were subordinate, and also was far more engaged with Greek knowledge than he performed,[12] but the figure of Cato for others often turns on how he represented his Romanness in contrast to Greek culture.[13]

Livy,[14] for example, depicts Cato speaking against the lures of Greece as a threat to the Romanness of the Romans, in terms that may seem to parallel Horace:

> The better and the happier the fortune of our commonwealth becomes day by day and the greater the empire grows – and already we have crossed into Greece and Asia, places filled with all the allurements of vice, and we are handling the treasures of kings – the more I fear that these things will capture [*ceperint*] us rather than we them. (34.4.3)

Like Horace, Cato recognises that imperialism's triumph is a challenge to the integrity of Roman self-definition, but sees this 'capture' not as the introduction of the arts but rather as the lure of vice and the threat of luxury. As with Horace, this is a mix of aesthetics and politics – but in Cato's case it is a fully religious horror of losing the old and therefore validated and authentic ways of worship: 'Altogether too many people do I hear praising the baubles of Corinth and Athens and laughing at the fictile antefixes of our Roman gods', he sneers (34.4.7). To Livy's Cato, it is a disgrace that the value of the divine art of Greeks is used to mock the

---

[12] Nep. *Cato* 3.2 is tellingly direct; see also Plut. *Cat. Mai., Min.* 2.4.
[13] The interest in Cato has been focused by Gruen 1992: 52–83, Feeney 2016: 177–8, Habinek 1998: 46–50, 60–4 and Sciarrino 2011. See also Astin 1978.
[14] In the scholarship on Livy, there are only scattered brief discussions specifically on Cato – see, with relevance to my discussion, Chaplin 2000: 97–101; Feldherr 1998: 42–6 – which do not compare Livy's depiction with others.

simple temple decorations of the Romans. With similar moral fervour, earlier in Livy's account, Cato successfully attacks the Greek rites of Dionysus, the Bacchanalia, and has them banned from Rome, precisely for their corrupting degeneracy. If Horace can sophisticatedly distance himself from a Roman lack of sophistication, Cato with his own rhetoric of authenticity insists on its necessity.

In Livy's representation, Cato goes on at length to contrast the earlier days of the republic with now. As Ennius paradigmatically states (and Michèle Lowrie in this volume puts this in its context of political thought), *moribus antiquis res stat Romana uirisque*, 'the Roman State stands on ancient customs and men' – and no one embodies this more stridently than Cato.[15] In those times, when true Roman values obtained, if offered extravagant bribes no Roman man or woman accepted them, and there was no need for the Oppian law against extravagance, because 'there was no extravagance to be restrained'. Relying on his own portrayal of early Roman history, Cato is portrayed thus as seeing Greece as the cause and sign of a collapse into the corruption marked by bribery and the degeneracy marked by extravagance. He makes this speech, however, against the background not just of a motion to repeal the Oppian law, but also that of a protest of Roman women who have blocked his way – and who actively wish to dress in finery, something Cato sees inevitably as leading to other crimes. He vitriolically upbraids the women for their protests, the men for not restraining the women, and the women and men for not resisting their desire for extravagance. Cato's Romanness is also fundamentally tied to the performance of his own manliness.

His opponent in the debate, however, Lucius Valerius, attacks Cato precisely for his dismissive and aggressive attitude towards the women, and, with brilliant rhetorical flair, theatrically unrolls Cato's own history, the *Origines*, and claims to read out from it examples of how often women have acted thus properly for the benefit of the republic. The *Origines* has the status of the first piece of Latin prose, the first history of Rome.[16] (In reality, it may not yet have been published by the date of the repeal of the Oppian law, but this is irrelevant to the power of Livy's representation of Cato.) The *Origines* told the story of the beginning of Rome (and the cities of Italy). Valerius sets Cato's own ideological foundational story of Roman beginnings against the history Cato himself mobilises in his rhetoric. Livy's history depicts his historical characters arguing through historical exemplars – and allows Cato's own written history to be quoted against the historian. It is a scene that demands therefore a certain self-reflexivity

---

[15] Cited, significantly, in August. *De ciu. D.* 2.21.  [16] Gotter 2009.

about a self-positioning in history. Cato sets himself up as a figure of old and now lost virtue – but is ambushed by his own history of Roman antiquity. Livy offers a carefully layered question to his Roman readers about their own use of the past in their projection of virtue – and about the place of Greece in their self-understanding.

Valerius sways the people, who engineer the overturning of the law: Cato was standing against history . . . But Livy's narrative continues with the story of Cato's inspired military leadership and brusque qualities as a general. For Livy, Cato's virtues are framed by a debate which uses Cato's own views of the past on both sides of the argument, and encourages both images of Roman virtue to resound – but it is a debate that Cato loses. Livy's eulogy of Cato captures the hard virtues Cato came to stand for:

> He was undoubtedly a man of a rough temper and a bitter and unbridled tongue, absolute master of his passions, of inflexible integrity, and indifferent alike to wealth and popularity. He lived a life of frugality capable of enduring toil and danger, with a mind and body tempered almost like steel, which not even old age that weakens everything could break. (39.40)

Cato's censoriousness is integrally linked to his dismissal of the threat that Greekness represented to his proclaimed and embodied Romanness. But Livy's complex narrative, for all its recognition of Cato's virtues, and for all that his own Preface states a theory of Rome's moral decline, does not allow his opposition to Greek culture to stand unchallenged. When Juvenal – a century later than Livy – has a character declare, 'Quirites, I can't bear a city that is Greek/a Greek Rome' (*'non possum ferre, Quirites,* | *Graecam urbem/Vrbem'*, *Sat.* 3.60–1), his satire is aimed as much at the speaker as it is at the cultural mix (and slipping hierarchies) marked by the juxtaposition of the archaic address *Quirites* and the adjective *Graecam*. In Juvenal's satire, the speaker is mocked for his pompous, old-fashioned posturing. Cato's commitment to the old ways is already problematic for Livy when it involves attacking the value of Greek culture for Roman self-definition, however much Cato embodies the virtues of old Rome.

Plutarch's account of Cato – written after Livy and before Juvenal – is framed by his intricate and fascinating engagement with Roman culture, both in his *Lives*, which regularly compare and contrast Greek and Roman political and military leaders, and in the *Moralia*, which construct an encyclopaedic view of what it means to be a knowing Greek under the Roman empire.[17] Plutarch's 'we' is Greek, but he is constantly negotiating

---

[17] For discussion, see Goldhill 2002 with bibliography, especially Duff 1999.

how his Greekness fits into the Roman world. In his *Life of Cato* Plutarch tells how Cato spent time in Athens and records the story that Cato made a public speech there in which 'he spoke to the people in Greek, stating that he admired the virtue of ancient Athenians and that he was happy to view so large and beautiful a city' (12.4). But Plutarch immediately corrects this story of bland diplomatic waffle. He spoke in Latin, Plutarch insists, and used a translator who had to use many phrases to expand Cato's taciturnity into anything like a speech. More to the point, Cato 'mocked people who admired Greekness'; 'in general he thought the words of Greeks came from the lips, the words of Romans from the heart' (12.5). Plutarch – writing in Greek and as a Greek, of course – concludes that Cato was desperate to keep his son from Greek influence and proclaimed that 'Rome would lose its empire if it became infected with Greek learning' (23.2–3). In Livy, Cato disparages Greek degeneracy and extravagance. For Plutarch, the issue is learning. Plutarch reframes Cato's objection as an objection not to vice but to what the Greeks praised themselves for, and were praised for amongst the Roman elite, their *paideia*. Cato in Greek looks different from Cato in Latin.

Plutarch immediately adds an authorial comment to the story. Cato spoke 'too rashly for his years', because 'history reveals the emptiness of his insult: as the city had risen to its greatest, so it has made Greek education and culture its own' (23.2). Cato's failure to assimilate Roman Hellenisation is defined now as precisely an inability to appreciate 'education and culture' – that core empire quality of *paideia*. The Greek writer, himself the epitome of the *pepaideumenos*, the cultured and educated citizen, corrects the self-proclaimed icon of Romanness for being too Roman, too rustic, too uncultured. Indeed, Plutarch goes on to tell that Cato refused to let his son see a Greek doctor on the grounds that Hippocrates asserted he would never serve a barbarian. Cato sees himself as a barbarian – the rejected other – in Greek eyes, and therefore dismisses Greek science in favour of his own herbal remedies (another sign of a commitment to the antique rusticity of early Rome). Pliny (*HN* 29.7) tells the same story and claims he is quoting the words of Cato himself: Cato calls the Greeks *nequissimum et indocile genus*, 'an evil and unteachable race' – 'unteachable' is a slur against the profession of *paideia* – and adds *quandoque ista gens suas litteras dabit, omnia corrumpet*, 'whenever that nation will give us its literature, it will corrupt everything' – where literary culture in general is held out as the source of corruption. But – and the contrast is pointed – when Plutarch tells the story, he adds drily that the result of Cato's intransigence was the death of his son and wife to a fatally mistreated disease (23.3–4). Cato's process of cultural self-assertion is troped as a fatal misrecognition of the value of Greece for Rome. Plutarch quietly delights in Cato's use of the word barbarian as a lethally misplaced certainty of his cultural integrity and superiority. Rather, Plutarch encourages his readers (Greek and Roman alike) to see themselves between two cultures, as between two mirrors, seeing oneself being seen and internalising the perspective of the other. These, suggests Plutarch, are the necessary transactions in the process of cultural contact between Rome and Greece. This all needs to be seen in the context of Plutarch's political treatises, too, which are designed to recognise how difficult it is for Greeks to negotiate the realities of Roman power in the Greek east.[18] For Plutarch, Cato becomes a complex and extreme case of the dangerous boundary between cultural resistance and acceptance.

Dionysius of Halicarnassus' *Rhōmaïkē archaiologia*, or *Roman Antiquities*, written roughly the same time as Horace and Livy, covers similar territory as Cato's *Origines* in telling the story of the early history of Rome and the cities around it.[19] But it does so in a way which would have dismayed Cato, or at least prompted his most intense scorn, even or especially when Cato is cited – and thus appropriated – as an authority. Dionysius is an extreme example of how Greek writers create their cultural authority through a genealogy back to a non-Roman, integrally Greek origin, by discovering a Greek origin for Rome itself. For Dionysius, the original inhabitants of the land, known as Aborigines, were Greeks from Arcadia (1.9): he cites Cato and Gaius Sempronius (with unnamed 'many others') to defend this claim. But it is Sophocles the tragedian and early Greek historians who provide him with the authorities he goes on to use: Greek sources for a Greek story. Dionysius returns to the Greek origin of Rome at the end of Book 1 with an explicit rehearsal of his claims at the beginning of the book. But now he turns to cult and explains a series of Roman cultic activity, including the Lupercalia's naked run through the city, through their Greek origins. This is further to prove 'the essential fact' that Rome is descended in its culture not from barbarians and vagabonds but from good Greek tribes. He is clear that the cults of the Romans follow Greek models; that these models pre-date the conquest of Greece; that each culture holds on to its cult practices with an innate conservatism. Through cult, then, Dionysius proves the Greekness of Roman culture. Cato may have pursued the origins of Rome to ground an authentic and integral Romanness, a Romanness which had to exclude any Greekness as

---

[18] See Goldhill 2002: 252–61; Stadter 2014; Liebert 2016.   [19] See Wiater 2011.

a corruption; but for Dionysius Rome was always 'a Greek city', not as the object of Juvenal's horror, but as an exclusion rather of the barbarian and vagabond. As in Livy's anecdote of Lucius Valerius, Cato's *Origines* is again cited against Cato's own agenda.

More surprisingly, Cato the Younger, Cato's great-grandson, also gets caught up in a similarly dismissive dynamic in the epigrammatist Martial's self-representation. Martial wrote his epigrams in part at least during the 'interesting times' of the rule of the emperors Domitian and Nerva in the first century; and an epigrammatist, by virtue of his funny, insulting, ludic poems, is necessarily always treading an awkward social line, especially in an imperial, court society where personal status, rumour and public persona interact in such a heady and potentially dangerous mix.[20] Martial is both a poet who aims to write Rome into a series of snapshots, a city defined by the epigrammatist's smart and jaundiced glance, and a poet who is obsessively self-reflexive in talking about what epigrams do and how to read them. If Plutarch writes as a Roman citizen from Greece to the east, Martial comes as an outsider from Spain in the west (not all Romans are 'from Rome').[21] Book 1 of his epigrams begins with a prose preface that turns at its close into verse. Typically – or, more precisely, with an aggressive self-posture that will become typical of his poetry – Martial is unapologetic about his ribaldry in poems for the festival of Flora, traditionally a time of licence. He promises *lasciuam uerborum ueritatem, id est epigrammaton linguam*, 'the dirty truth of words, that is, the tongue of epigrams'. This is not just the threat to call a spade a spade (and worse), but also suggests with the transliterated Greek word, *epigrammaton*, a certain tension between Greek lubricity and Latin smut (tongues can always be rude as well as linguistic ...). Indeed, Martial does imitate Greek epigrams, especially Lucillius, although he is usually at pains to disavow any such intellectual debt.[22] But he continues, *Si quis tamen tam ambitiose tristis est ut apud illum in nulla pagina latine loqui fas sit, potest epistula uel potius titulo contentus esse*, 'But if there is anyone so professionally miserable that Latin cannot be spoken on any page in his presence, he can be content with this letter, or better the title' (1.*pr*.15). The problem Martial anticipates is that any Roman committed to the public display of high morals will find his Latin too lascivious, and so

---

[20] The two best studies, with further bibliography, are Fitzgerald 2007 and Rimell 2008. See also Lorenz 2000.
[21] See Lavan 2020.   [22] Nisbet 2003.

he allows this self-promoting reader no more than the polite preface itself, or, more pointedly, the title of the book itself – the Greek word 'epigrams'. At which point, Martial turns to Cato: 'Cato should not enter to my theatre; or if he does enter, let him watch the show', a sentiment he then inscribes in verse:

> Nosses iocosae dulce cum sacrum Florae
> festosque lusus et licentiam uulgi,
> cur in theatrum, Cato seuere, uenisti?
> An ideo tantum ueneras ut exires? (Mart. 1.*pr*.15)

> You knew of giggling Flora's sweet ceremonies,
> The fun of the festival, and the freedom of the crowd;
> So why did you come to the theatre, stern Cato?
> Or had you come just so that you could walk out?[23]

Martial is positioning any negative criticism of his poetry as professional pomposity and self-regard, and does so by imagining a Roman reader dismissive of the vulgarity of Latin, a reader who should best stick with the one Greek word of the title (there is no Latin word for 'epigram'), a reader who is instantly troped as ... Cato. Cato the Younger, like his great-grandfather, the most professionally censorious of the old Romans, also emerges in Martial's eyes as a self-parading defender of traditional Roman ways – but who ironically enough cannot take good old Latin words and wit.

The figure of Cato the Elder becomes a node of contentious anxiety about the interaction of Greek and Roman culture, differently viewed from within Greek and Latin, and across different genres, and as different gestures of authorial self-positioning. In the face of evident and intricate cultural hybridity, where the colonisers and imperialist speak the cultural language of the colonised and defeated, Cato's extreme commitment to the politics of cultural purity, along with his active involvement in the military and political practice of imperial conquest and rule, make him particularly good to represent – to think with. For Roman and Greek writers and readers, the representation of Cato's extremism provokes a self-conscious awareness of the dynamics of historical self-placement and cultural self-understanding.

Three immediate conclusions can be drawn from this introduction. First, it is not possible to talk about Latin literature or Roman culture

---

[23] For the story in laudatory vein see Val. Max. 2.10.8.

especially of the later republic and empire, without passing through Greek territory. It would be hard to imagine a treatment of almost any work of literary Latin which did not need its recognition of how Greek informs it: Virgil writing the early history of Rome through Homer and Apollonius of Rhodes (among other Greek paradigms), Terence translating and adapting Menander – what is it to find one's comedy in another time and country? – Lucretius' deification of Epicurus, or Manilius recomposing Greek didactic texts on astronomy, or Cicero creating Roman thought through Greek philosophy;[24] the historians' recognition of Polybius, Thucydides, Herodotus (historiography's foundational role in the construction of the present's value) – all examples of how, as Katharina Volk discusses in this volume, Latin intellectualism strives with its bilingualism: inevitably, any such list could continue to expand, right through to Latin Christianity's uncomfortable relation to the Greek Gospels (and beyond). Even satire, a genre uniquely Roman according to Quintilian, stresses the Greekness of Rome and how Roman matrons cry out in Greek during sex. Latin's expressivity is mined at the centre with Greek.

Second, the zones of contact and cultural imbrication between Greek and Latin are also arenas of self-conscious debate in both Greek and Latin writing. What is more, both Roman and Greek writers are aware of such strategies of debate. When Pliny and Plutarch each tell the story of Cato's disdain for Greek physicians the story does not mean the same thing – and both echo against each other.[25] To cite Cato's *Origines* as a sign of Cato's extreme morality is a gesture differently and self-consciously mobilised. Such self-consciousness is also productive: the literary or cultural self-construction that is performed in and through the reading and writing of Latin is forged in this self-awareness of its own hybridity. Cato's longing for integrity – and other Roman writers' obsessive return to Cato's longing – takes shape as a fractured desire in and against this awareness of inevitable hybridity.

Third, however much the issue of what it is to be (truly) Greek or (authentically) Roman can flare into a localised argument – where extremes of prejudice, gestures of exclusion, wild or sophisticated arguments of self-assertion can come into play, and where Cato repeatedly becomes a key player of the imaginary – it should nonetheless be clear that the key terms of identification – Greek, Roman, Latin (Italian, Athenian, Lacedaemonian ...) – are synchronically and diachronically shifting and

---

[24] Gildenhard 2007 and more generally 2010 are particularly good on this. See in general Bishop 2019: 34 on how Cicero 'constructed himself as a classic' through Greek.
[25] See pp. 854–5.

repeatedly in a dynamic relation with each other and their own history. (Even to call the *Hellenes* (the usual Greek term for Greeks) *Graeci* (the Latin for Greeks) needs explanation, as at least Greek writers noted.)[26] I have tried not to use the term 'identity' in this chapter, although it would serve to link my arguments to a string of influential discussions in contemporary scholarship (and Alison Sharrock's chapter in this volume), because identity's implications of unity, singleness and continuity inevitably distort the intricate play of affiliation, identification, tacit knowledge, self-delusion and internal division which go into the make-up of a person, even when we allow identities to be multiple, as Amartya Sen insists.[27] To proclaim a fixed and pure cultural identity is always a mobile, interactive, divisive act of definition and placement. Modern scholarship, however, has often followed such ancient (and modern) proclamations of cultural purity or integrity in an insufficiently critical manner, a reflex perhaps of how such apparently flawed acts of self-awareness continue to have political purchase and consequence, often of a disastrously violent kind: 'The Second Sophistic has been – and remains in much current scholarship – a modern fantasy projected back on the ancient world, an *objet petit a*, an impossible idealization of a pure, untainted aristocratic tradition'[28] – as if, indeed, there is no blatant ideological projection when Philostratus imagines Herodes Atticus discovering a man in the middle of Attica who speaks pure Greek and lives in rustic simplicity.[29] (There is a certain and horrifying continuity that makes grim sense of the Nazi desire to possess the manuscript of Tacitus' *Germania*.)[30] Latin's relation to Greek – as we will further see – and Greek's relation to Latin have not only a long history but also a dynamic one, where fictiveness and contestation are constant factors in the performances of affiliation and assertion. We must be careful not to project an oversimplified notion of Greek or Roman identity onto the ancient world not only because it is historically insufficient, but also because such projections themselves have been so influential in a toxic modern politics of nationalism, religious supercessionism and racism.

3

There are four more precise areas of discussion that I wish to follow up from this general introduction. First, I will look at the vexed issue of how much Latin Greek writers can be assumed to know. This is not merely

---

[26] Aristotle, *Meteorologica* 1.14; Apollodorus 1.7.2; Pausanias 3.20.6.   [27] Sen 2006.
[28] Whitmarsh 2013: 3.   [29] Philostratus, *V S* 490; see Goldhill 2002: 76; Swain 1996: 80–4.
[30] Krebs 2011.

a question of the politics of knowledge or self-presentation in the empire, but is also related to the equally contentious issue of *where* the literature of resistance might be in empire culture. Second, reversing the perspective, I will look at how Roman culture adopted and adapted Greek myths: how did Roman authors negotiate the space where Greek longevity and cultural authority was so much in evidence? Third, I will look at the linguistics of translation and code-shifting between Latin and Greek: what are the pragmatics of moving between Greek and Latin and what are the social, ideological implications of such moves? Fourth, we will look at interactions of Greek and Latin in late antiquity, especially in a Christian framework. Jerome's linguistic versatility – and intellectual seriousness – opens a space where translation between Greek and Latin and Hebrew becomes a burning issue of theological contention – which in turn becomes a major flashpoint of Reformation violence. This leads to my final question: what are the questions which Greek literature allows but Latin literature eschews (and vice versa); and what does this tell us about our sense of 'classical antiquity'? That is, what are the boundaries we place – or are placed in antiquity – between Greek and Roman literature? What sorts of critical enterprise follow from this? Comprehensiveness would be an unrealistic aim, of course, for so rich a set of interactions, but these necessarily partial accounts will allow us at least to start to map a terrain that is of such importance for the unfolding of the west's history and sense of its own past in that history.

To ask how much Latin is known by Greek writers is not intended to provoke a statistical answer about bilingualism. On the one hand, notwithstanding the expectations of some public proclamations from the Mid-West of America, much of the world is happily bilingual or multilingual, and there have been fine studies both of localised cases in antiquity – how much Latin was required to serve in the army, for example – and of the general cultural and linguistic issues involved in the contact zones between Greeks and Romans.[31] It is inconceivable – indeed, demonstrably false – that no Greek writers could read Latin, and, on the basis of current evidence, it is also impossible to give anything but a very general horizon of expectation of how many of the elite who identified as ethnically Greek could comfortably read, write or speak Latin. On the other hand, the more vexed issue of whether specific literary texts written in Greek show knowledge of earlier Latin literature has been hampered by an insufficient

---

[31] Seminal is Adams 2003; Adams, Janse and Swain 2002; Elder and Mullen 2019.

attention to the underlying assumptions about intertextuality inherent in such debates. While Latin writers proclaim their intertextual relations to Greek works, as O'Rourke and Pelttari discuss in this volume, and criticism has been swift to follow such signposts in sophisticated (and less sophisticated) ways, Greek writers almost never indicate such indebtedness, and this has provoked a crisis of anxiety in critical thinking. When Greek appears to turn its back on Latin, can allusions to Latin texts nonetheless be heard – and should they?[32]

When Quintus of Smyrna, for example, in his *Posthomerica* tells the story of Aeneas fleeing Troy, scholars working from a traditional perspective have struggled to find convincing specific references or allusions to the *Aeneid*.[33] Quintus knows full well Aeneas' place in a history that Homer cannot tell. Any hints in Homer of Aeneas' future are turned by Quintus into a full-throated prophetic proclamation of the Roman empire to come, put into the mouth of the Greek seer, Calchas, who stops the Greeks from killing the future founder of Rome. Rome's future is thus God-given but proclaimed and authorised by a Greek voice, obeyed by Greek soldiers (13.333–52). Rome, Calchas asserts, will rule over 'far-flung nations' from west to east (339–41), but he does not mention their future rule over Greece (and thus revenge for the fall of Troy). With Aeneas, Rome is always troped in Quintus' language, even and especially when, with a certain irony, Quintus makes Aeneas instrumental in destroying Odysseus' military innovation of the *testudo*, the distinctively Roman instrument of war. Aeneas, then, without the *Aeneid*? Yet to a Roman reader brought up on the *Aeneid*, or to a Greek reader familiar with the *Aeneid* in any form or medium, and aware of its role in Roman literary culture, would not the refusal of recognition of the *Aeneid* itself signify – as a ghostly echo of distinctiveness if not as a strategy of cultural independence?

When Quintus narrates how Neoptolemus asked Philoctetes to return to Troy (9.354–528), Philoctetes, thanks to Athene's intervention, immediately gives up any anger and accepts. There is a long description of Philoctetes' agony in the cave leading up to this moment, and the very mention of Athene too may cue Sophocles in the minds of some readers. But the scene of anger melting away itself avoids any obvious reference to Sophocles. But it would be a surprisingly attenuated critical reading that did not recognise that the significance of the hero's change of heart makes

---

[32] See most recently with full bibliography Jolowicz 2021.
[33] See Gärtner 2005. On Quintus see Maciver 2012, Baumbach and Bär 2007, and now the outstanding Greensmith 2020.

sense against an unmentioned masterpiece of the literary tradition where Philoctetes, like Ajax before him, is unpersuadable. Such a contrast raises the question of what a hero's affective response should be, from the perspective of Quintus with his philosophical and aesthetic perspective. The silence speaks, if you can hear it. So, too, then, with the *Aeneid*?

For a Roman reader of this Greek text, that is, how can his (and it is paradigmatically his) Latin reading not be part of his horizon of comprehension, especially when the story matter overlaps? Why should a Greek writer, often from the elite or wishing to be in the elite, who is therefore in contact with Roman elites, not imagine that his Roman readers might have such a response, and work with it – especially a Greek writer called Quintus, a Roman name? For a Greek reader, there are multiple possible recognitions or misrecognitions of such a silence, depending on the multiple levels of knowledge of the *Aeneid* as a text or as a cultural symbol or as a plot-line or as no more than a name. Understanding the *Posthomerica* takes place in as many sites as it is read, and a discussion of its signification should take account of such dynamic differences, such horizons of possibility. It is, of course and of necessity, impossible, therefore, to insist on critical certainty about such allusivity. Uncertainty is usually part of the messy business of the social and aesthetic signification of literature. But my point here is not the familiar modernist celebration of uncertainty over a misleading requirement of scientific proof in traditional philology (as wittily defended but demonstrated by James Clackson in this volume). Rather, the uncertainty of how much Latin is heard in this Greek retelling of the story of Aeneas is an invitation to enter the cultural and aesthetic politics between Greece and Rome. Quintus' writing is also a canny and engaged response to the question of what an account of the founder of Rome could look like from a Greek epic perspective in the Roman empire – and, as such, prompts an engaged interaction from his readers, in the empire and beyond. For the *Posthomerica*, then, not so much Aeneas without the *Aeneid*, as Aeneas *after* the *Aeneid*.[34]

This sense of a cultural politics between Greek and Latin is also evident in the more explicit recognitions of knowing Latin in Greek authors. Plutarch provides one of the richest and most complex records of such an interface between Greek and Latin.[35] The *synkriseis* or 'comparisons' that conclude his pairs of *Lives* contrast Greek and Roman heroes in terms of their Greekness and Romanness as well as more abstract personal qualities;[36] his *Greek and Roman Questions* set cultural comparison into the intellectual environment

---

[34] For a fine study of Quintus' politics of affiliation see the last chapter of Greensmith 2020.
[35] Goldhill 2002.   [36] Duff 1999.

of sympotic curiosity;[37] his stories of cultural assimilation and difference are carefully layered and show a nuance that goes far beyond Dionysius of Halicarnassus (Plutarch's version of how Roman naked exercise developed makes a particularly vivid comparison with the analysis of Dionysius cited earlier).[38] His political theory emphasises the internal politics of empire and the difficult position of Greeks under the Romans. Plutarch's knowledge of Latin, therefore, is framed by – and must be understood within – his encyclopaedic self-positioning as an educated Greek in the Roman empire.

At one point, in passing, as it were, Plutarch mentions that 'everyone knows Latin', though in the context of the sympotic conversation it could mean little more than the educated chaps around the table share an understanding of the conversation's interest in etymology and its linguistic necessities.[39] But his best-known statement about knowing Latin is also an act of self-representation, which opens his account of the *Life of Demosthenes* (an orator who overcame his own problems with speech). 'I live in a small city,' he begins, 'and stay here lest it become smaller. In Rome and during my business in Italy, because of my political duties and the people who thronged to discuss philosophy, I had no leisure to work on [*gymnazesthai*] the Latin language. So I began to come across Latin works rather late and advanced in age' (*Dem.* 2). This statement has been taken at face value, and it has been proposed that since his necessary companions in Rome all spoke Greek, he had no need to learn any Latin; and that when he needed to do research, he used bilingual assistants. As Philip Stadter has shown, however, Plutarch clearly had read a good deal of Latin far earlier than this text may suggest, and for all the indications that he occasionally misread or misquoted an original, there is enough evidence of an active and informed encounter with Latin long before this passage appears to intimate.[40] Stadter suggests that Plutarch is comparing his Latin attainments with his exceptional knowledge of Greek literature and this explains his overstated modesty.

It is also important, however, that Plutarch begins, like Odysseus' *apologoi*, with a statement of where he lives. He announces himself as a small-town man, happy to be so, whose trips to the metropolis, where he was feted as a philosopher and had the duties of a politician, were both a contrast to and a temporary break in his life as a reclusive intellectual. It is a particular mix of boastfulness and restraint, replete with a familiar ideology of self-representation: a man who will fulfil his community's call to action brilliantly, but who wishes always to avoid the ambition

---

[37] Preston 2001.  [38] See Goldhill 2002: 261–5.  [39] Plut. *Quaest. Plat.* 1010d.  [40] Stadter 2014.

and corruption of the large stage of empire politics. Not knowing Latin superbly is also part of this image: not for him the cut and thrust of the law-court or imperial power plays. He had what Latin he had and really only needed it when he turned to research later on. Not knowing Latin is part of Plutarch's measured self-presentation as an outsider to Roman politics and very much the insider to the world of Greek *paideia*. Plutarch lives in Greek culture, and knowing Latin too well or for the wrong purposes might compromise the image of his sense of home. While there could be an empirical answer to the question of how well Plutarch read or spoke Latin, it is impossible to disentangle it from his self-representation as a master of Greek *paideia*.

Lucian offers a surprising parallel to such a self-presentation. His amusing short piece *On a Slip of the Tongue in Salutation* begins from his excruciated embarrassment at having said to his patron one morning 'be healthy' (*hygiainein*), rather than the normal form 'rejoice' (*chairein*). His letter of apology becomes a demonstration of linguistic éclat by way of defence. In a typical style of Greek *paideia*, epitomised by Athenaeus' *Deipnosophistae*, he catalogues different forms of greeting with examples from Greek literature, from Homer to Epicurus to king Ptolemy, to show that he was not as hopeless as might have been thought. He finally turns to Latin. He points out that the emperor in his book of instructions enjoins health as a primary aim, and ringingly declares that 'You yourselves, when you return a greeting, often reply with the word "health"' (*salue*). He glosses this observation with εἴ τι κἀγὼ τῆς Ῥωμαίων φωνῆς ἐπαΐω, 'if I too know any Latin' – or literally, 'if I too in some way hear the voice of Romans'. Lucian, a Syrian who made his way as a Greek-speaker in the Roman intellectual scene as an orator and satirist, does not admit to reading or writing Latin, just to being able to recognise a word he has heard spoken. Again, not knowing Latin is part of his self-presentation, part of a mock modesty framed by his elaborate demonstration of Greek *paideia* as he speaks to his Roman patron, or imagines for his Greek and Roman readers what he would say to his Roman patron under such circumstances. Lucian parades his Greekness in which his lack of Latin becomes a statement.

For all this pattern of pronounced and exclusive Greekness which grounds Greek self-representation, its ideological disavowal becomes strikingly evident when a writer such as Plutarch actually engages with Roman culture at a more detailed level. His treatise *Roman Questions* (which has *Greek Questions* as a mirror – *Barbarian Questions* has not survived) exposes a deeper, if sometimes performatively baffled awareness of Roman matters and the Latin language. He asks (*Quaest. Rom.* 45.275f) why the temple of the goddess Horta was always kept open in the old days. The goddess Horta is a deeply obscure, possibly Etruscan divinity, perhaps associated by Romans with the garden (*hortus*). The goddess barely matters, however: Plutarch asks the question only so that he can offer a set of potential etymological glosses to the name. First, he quotes Antistius Labeo, a Roman scholar, who derives the name from ***hortari***, 'to encourage', and suggests that the temple is always open to signify this incitement to action. Second, he wonders if the vowel should be long and the name derived from ***Hōra***, which he suggests is the current name: this goddess is *poly**hōrētikē*** (πολυωρητική), 'very caring' – an etymological suggestion which might justify the garden's continual openness as a sign of her continuing care for human affairs, where a Greek adjective justifies the understanding of the Roman word. Third, he suggests that actually the word is not Latin at all but Greek – 'as with many other cases' – and it indicates the goddess' supervision of human affairs (ἐφορῶσα, *ephorōsa*, 'over-seeing'). Finally, he comments that if Labeo is right and the word comes from *par**horman*** (παρορμᾶν) (he now gives a Greek translation of ***hor**tari* with the same sounding root ***hor***-), then this should be taken as the etymology of *orator* (he gives this Latin word in a Greek transliteration), indicating the role of the orator to incite the people, which he offers as a correction of the standard etymology from 'imprecating or praying' – and here he gives the Greek nouns *āra* and *euchē* – which must, however, refer to the unstated Latin word *orare*, 'to pray for', as an etymology for *orator*. This is an after-dinner piece of flamboyant linguistic virtuosity, part of Plutarch's display of learning. But it also depends on a complex network of interlingual puns between Greek and Latin terms, expressed and unexpressed. It presupposes an audience supremely comfortable between the two languages, and enjoying the interplay. When it suits him, Plutarch can show himself to be quite at home in Latin. The self-conscious demurrals of knowing Latin are evidently a strategy of self-representation, just as is this spectacle of competence.

Three conclusions follow. First, knowing Latin for a Greek writer is part of a politics of culture and a practice of self-representation. Not knowing Latin well is a strategic gesture within the work of proclaiming one's Greekness, with its displays of *paideia*. Second, this is not, however, a literature of resistance, at least in the strongest sense demanded by postcolonial theory and its political ideals. The writers who risked their lives by writing against the imperial court were figures such as Lucan, or, at least in safer retrospect, Tacitus, or perhaps even Ovid, who paid for a *carmen* with his exile, whatever the *error*. The Greek writers of the empire were constructing a genealogy of Greek culture against a claim of Roman authority, and it was undoubtedly a self-authorising cultural strategy. But it was also a gesture of aesthetic politics with which the Romans were complicit. There is nothing to suggest that Plutarch, Dionysius, Lucian and their pals ever suffered politically or socially for their literary output. Third, the silence about the place of Latin in the literary imaginary of Greek writers is a speaking silence: it becomes a place where readers find a mirror through which to express their own sense of cultural value. Lucian's Greekness was lauded as an ideal of the ludic integrity by Renaissance scholars such as Erasmus and Thomas More, and assaulted as the embodiment of hybridity and slyness by a German tradition from Luther through to the racist scholars of the nineteenth and twentieth centuries.[41] To read the Greek of the Roman empire without Latin, or to read it (over)hearing the silenced echoes of a Roman world, is not just a question of calibrating a Greek author's prior knowledge and commitment; it is to engage – for empire readers and readers since – in the politics of cultural integrity and resistance.

### 4

At some point around the middle of the nineteenth century, a shift in cultural commitments, rather than just a slide in aesthetic taste, changed the way that classical divinities were named in English and throughout Europe. During the eighteenth century, in literature, opera, and even in scholarly works, it was a commonplace to refer to Greek gods by Roman names. 'Jove' or 'Jupiter', 'Juno' and 'Minerva' stride across the stage in fully Greek settings, and enter the poetic arbours of Greek pastoral scenes with an ease of recognition. 'Myth' – the name given for the repertoire of stories which educated Europeans were expected to know and which provided a furniture of the mind as much as the furnishing of houses and galleries – was generally perceived as a product of a generic antiquity, authorised as such, and there was little thought to specify Greek rather than Roman narratives.[42] This (mis)use of Roman names was encouraged not just by the emphasis on the study of Latin and the value of Roman culture which dominated eighteenth-century artistic activity, but also by the timelessness of meaning with which myth was invested as a genre.[43] The huge influence and broad circulation of a text such as Ovid's *Metamorphoses*, where the

---

[41] See Goldhill 2002 and Baumbach 2002.  [42] Lincoln 1999, Winterer 2002, Greineder 2007.
[43] Williamson 2004.

repertoire of myth is enacted in Roman dress, certainly helped make such language easy.[44] When Ovid announces his poem's subject as *mutatas ... formas*, 'changed forms', do we hear the sound of the Greek title *Metamorphoses*, as well as recognise the shifting of Greek tales into Latin?

By the middle of the nineteenth century – and since then – it has become an oddity or, simply, an error to call Greek gods by Roman names (or, of course, Roman gods by Greek names). This change was a self-conscious and explicit decision, which can be seen, for example, when Wagner, in the mid-nineteenth century, rewrites the eighteenth-century operas of Gluck, and insists on a different nomenclature for the gods: Gluck's Diana appears as Artemis in Wagner's version.[45] From one perspective, this shift was a product of the increasingly prevalent Philhellenism across Europe which has been extensively studied in recent decades.[46] To find the origins of western values and thought in the glory that was Greece became a necessary strategy of the idealism and genealogical history that was a fundamental facet of the historical self-understanding of the era. The purity of this origin in Greece, as much as the privileging of Greece, demanded the Greekness of Greek names. From another perspective, such a change in naming is also the product of what could be called the archaeological imagination. In artistic representations, for example, it had been usual to depict biblical or classical scenes in the contemporary dress of the time of the artist, but by the mid-nineteenth century it had become a matter of principle to search for authenticity. Bible scenes now appeared as ancient Palestine, and the search to represent Greece as it was – material truth – was a lauded and debated paradigm for art, opera and eventually theatre too. Novels about Greece paraded archaeological knowledge in footnotes and appendices. Hence to give Greek gods in Greek stories Roman names appeared no less than a misidentification, a misuse of language, an inauthenticity when authenticity is a necessary ideal.

This motivated change in nomenclature indicates a fundamental issue for how Latin literature engages with Greek culture. From the beginnings of Latin literature, Roman writers encountered the full range of stories about gods and heroes in Greek writing and cult. They recognised that there were evident similarities between their pantheon and the Greek pantheon, as they also recognised that there were some gods – Priapus, for example – that had no equivalent in Greek ritual or representation.

---

[44] Barkan 1986, Martindale 1990, Miller and Newlands 2014.   [45] See Goldhill 2011a: 87–150.
[46] Marchand 2003; Valdez 2014; Roessel 2002; St. Clair 2002; Goldhill 2011a; Harloe 2013. Butler 1935 is seminal.

Roman culture seems to have had no difficulty in adapting the stories about Zeus and Hera to their own gods, and in adopting Greek heroes, such as Herakles, as their own.[47] If, as we have already seen, there is a real need to explain how and why Roman literature takes shape integrally in relation to the literature of another culture, namely Greece, there is also a pressing need to comprehend how a dominant imperial society could find it apparently so congenial to adopt the mythic repertoire of another culture, Greece.

We can make this question more precise. There are two basic strategies standard in contemporary analysis of Greek myth.[48] First, thanks to a strong integration of anthropological methodology, the telling of myth is seen as a key expression of how humans understand their position in the world, the categories of their world, their relation to the divine and the materiality of things. Myth appears as an ideologically charged articulation of how reality is experienced and categorised. The genealogies of myth express the structure of the world, and the cosmology of myth is deeply connected with the understanding of social order. Second, thanks to a combination of intellectual history and models of social evolution, there is an extended discussion of how myth itself, as a category, is a product of the fifth century BCE. Where *muthos* in Homer means no more than a privileged utterance,[49] in the fifth century it becomes a term placed in hierarchical opposition to a set of new categories: myth is opposed to *logos* (story to argument, irrationality to rationality); myth is opposed to history (fiction to reality); myth is opposed to truth or reality or science. Myth becomes a contested category, open to intellectual scrutiny and debate.[50] Nineteenth-century evolutionary arguments which claim that the change from mythic to logical thinking can first be found in ancient Greece – the Greek miracle – have been fundamentally challenged, of course, as an adequate historical account, but it is striking how often the thinkers of modernity (from Heidegger to Derrida) insist that to do philosophy is to speak Greek – that is, that the very categories of thought that we use have been significantly formed by a heritage from Greece, in which the invention of myth is an important move in our ideas of truth and language.

If myth, then, is how a society understands itself and represents itself to itself, and if myth as a notion is part of the intellectual history of engagement with the critique of such processes of self-representation, what can it mean

---

[47] See Beard 1993 for an interesting engagement with this issue.
[48] From a huge bibliography, see useful summaries in Edmunds 1990; Morford 1999; Powell 2011; Csapo 2005.
[49] Martin 1989.   [50] Detienne 1981.

that one culture adopts the myths of another so readily? If myth is a social charter of the self, how is the myth of the other to be integrated and retold?

The fluid movement between languages that Plutarch demonstrates when considering the etymology of the goddess Horta takes on a different light, then, when we turn to broader cultural appropriations, and view such processes from the perspective of the Roman writer, entangled in Greek stories, rather than from the perspective of the Greek intellectual, superior in his distance. To approach this complex issue we need to start with some ground-clearing background.

First, it cannot be emphasised too strongly that – once again – we cannot rely on a polarised opposition of Greece and Rome as discrete cultural entities. The south of Italy was known as Magna Graecia ('Greater Greece') and, although an Italian society, it was Hellenised from the fifth century BCE.[51] This is where Pythagoras came from. Romans as well as Greeks were fully aware of the integrated cultural history of this part of the Mediterranean. In the same way that this region has provided wonderful examples of so-called 'Greek art', we should expect that the shared or hybrid culture would produce shared or hybrid self-representations in and through mythic narratives. There was an organic development of Greek narratives in Italy from before the rise of Roman dominance.

Second, Greek and Roman narratives from the earliest evidence we have produce significant genealogical links between Greek culture and the rise of Rome, most pertinently through Aeneas. Such stories culminate in Virgil's *Aeneid*, which became a cultural artefact that was central to Roman education and Roman cultural projection. It became the mainstay of Latin as a written and taught language, and, of course, did so because it tells the story of the foundation of Rome by Aeneas.[52] The destruction of Troy by the Greeks is the condition of Aeneas' flight and thus the foundation of Rome. Homer already tells of Aeneas as surviving Troy (even if he does not mention Rome), giving an origin for Rome's story in the very earliest of Greek myth. To what degree Italy or even Rome were always already Greek is a subject debated by ancient writers – and most extensively by Dionysius of Halicarnassus – and in this discussion mythic narratives that link Greece and Rome are repeatedly retold and analysed.[53]

---

[51] For the archaeology see Cerchiai, Jannelli and Longo 2004; for the concept see Ceserani 2012.
[52] For introductions to the huge bibliography on the reception of Virgil see Tudeau-Clayton 1998; Thomas 2004; Kallendorf 2007; Farrell and Putnam 2010; Wilson-Okamura 2010; and, from a different angle, McGill 2005.
[53] Not only Dionysius. Varro, a Roman authority, also 'inserted the history of Rome into Greece' (Moatti 2015: 73).

## 16 Latin Literature and Greek

Indeed, a string of Latin and Greek writers list the Greek heroes who visited and lived in the Italian mainland. Ovid – to whom we will return – is paradigmatic. In the *Fasti*, he tells the story of April, the month dedicated to Venus, the mother of Aeneas, and in his account Ovid states that Italy was *Graecia Maior*, 'Greater Greece' (*Fasti* 4.64). He explains this name with a roll-call of Greek heroes of myth (4.65–76). The list begins *Venerat Evander plena cum classe suorum,* | *uenerat Alcides, Graius uterque genus*, 'There had come Evander, with a fleet full of his people, there had come Hercules, Greek by race, both of them.' The repetition of *uenerat* (and again at v. 73) is marked, not only establishing by repetition the repeated arrivals of the Greeks as a list, but also suggesting an etymological play with the name *Venus* (despite the different quantities in *uēnerat* and *Vĕnus*) in a passage whose subject is the origin of the name of the month. Both heroes, he emphasises, are of 'the Greek race'.[54] Ovid continues with Odysseus (v. 69), Homer's hero, the evidence for which, he adds (vv. 69–70), is the Laestrygonians and the shore still called Circe's. As is most articulately expressed in Strabo, scholars in antiquity doubted that the journeys of Odysseus could be mapped onto the real maritime map of the Mediterranean. At the same time, it was frequently suggested that Magna Graecia was the locale for these adventures, with the Cyclops located in Sicily. The promontory called Circeium is thus linked to Circe, and Ovid assumes that the Laestrygonians can be placed on the coast here too, as if there was no hesitation about finding cannibal giants in South Italy. The use of the word *testes*, 'witnesses', is an ironic recognition of how fast and loose the poet is being with a long-standing academic debate. After Odysseus, he mentions the walls built by Telegonus, the arrival (*uenerat*, v. 73) of Halaesus, and Antenor, who attempted to negotiate peace between Greeks and Trojans, and finally, late, Aeneas. Magna Graecia is thus written as a genealogy leading to Rome. In the mythic world, Greece and Rome are always already linked.

There is a further twist to this list as genealogy, however. With Aeneas, continues Ovid (vv. 79–83), came one Solymus, who founded Sulmo, Ovid's own home town. At this emotional juncture, Ovid addresses Germanicus, the dedicatee of the *Fasti* and the iconic hero of the imperial project, bringing the mythical history up to the moment: ... *patriae, Germanice, nostrae*, '... our, Germanicus, homeland'. Germanicus separates 'our' and 'homeland', as Ovid, the exile, cannot form a 'we' with his compatriots. As ever in exile, the mention of home prompts grief (vv. 82–3): *Me miserum, Scythio quam*

---

[54] Note that *Graius* is not a Greek word.

*procul illa solo est!* | *Ergo ego tam longe – sed supprime, Musa, querellas!*, . . . 'Ah, I am so miserable! How far Sulmo is from the Scythian land! Therefore I so far – but repress, Muse, these complaints!' The mythic history of Rome concludes with the poet in the here and now – but a poet banned from Rome. Mythic genealogy is designed to explain the present – or, as here, to reframe it. The Greek heroes could travel to Italy, but Ovid cannot. The painful aposiopesis, marked by the dash in the English punctuation, marks the gap between where he is and the 'so far' of his absence, his complaints, the distance that separates him, the history he tells from afar. The gap is the space of repression: *supprime*, he enjoins his Muse. The consequent aposiopesis leaves the words without a syntax, as fragments of a story, a buried desire, like a poem by Ezra Pound: 'therefore' . . . 'I' . . . 'so far'. What began as a story of how Greek heroes are part of the Roman past of Graecia Magna ends as a fractured story of how one Roman poet is separated from the very genealogy as well as the topography that grounded him. The myths of Greek heroes in Italy become a story of self-representation for the Roman poet.

A third element of necessary background concerns the word 'syncretism'. Syncretism is the term that scholars have repeatedly used to describe the process by which the Roman state incorporated the gods of defeated nations into their own system of ritual.[55] Cults from the east in particular were the object of historiographical fascination from the early republic onwards, and not just as the result of war. So Cybele, the Phrygian cultic divinity, known as Magna Mater or Mater Idaea in Rome, was taken into the ritual calendar of the city at the time of the second Punic war (218–201 BCE), and, from her origins in Phrygia, the goddess was sometimes associated specifically with the Trojan origin of the city of Rome.[56] One Sibylline oracle, we are told in Livy (29.10), was read to indicate that Rome would defeat an invading force if the Mater Idaea was brought from Pessinus to Rome ('Idaea' customarily indicates not just Phrygian but Trojan). A delegation to King Attalus resulted in the presentation of the sacred stone, that represented the goddess, to the Romans, and its ritual acceptance into the city. From this story of the arrival of the cult, however – and the winning of the war – the rituals of Cybele continued to be viewed with a stridently double aspect. The Magna Mater was for Romans and Greeks – and modern scholars – an obsessive object of prurience and even loathing. On the one hand, it is clear that many senior Roman noblemen and even emperors supported the introduction and practice of the cult, and that the

---

[55] Often with sophistication: Frankfurter 2018; more generally, Stewart and Shaw 1994.
[56] Roller 1999, followed here; also Latham 2012 with further bibliography.

Magna Mater was associated, as in the story told by Livy, with the role of protecting the city. On the other hand, the priests of Cybele, in the name of Attis, her youthful consort and devotee, were supposedly required to castrate themselves (thereby losing their citizenship), and the cult was associated also with Oriental barbarism and sexual perversion. A poem like Catullus 63 fully dramatises this fantasy and this ambivalence.[57]

Modern scholars have repeatedly and emphatically rehearsed and deprecated this doubleness.[58] It has even been asserted or assumed that either the Greeks (who also allowed the cult of Cybele into their ritual calendar, even in the classical city of Athens) or the Romans in Rome did not know what the cult involved when they accepted it, or that they rejected its sexual barbarism. 'The male attendant of the Great Goddess and his repulsive myth and ritual were obviously kept at bay', writes the historian of religion, H. S. Versnel (surprisingly, for one of the more imaginative and incisive writers on cult).[59] Garth Thomas is equally clear: 'It is beyond credibility that a Roman nobleman would have identified himself with the non-Roman aspect of the cult, or that such identification would have been acceptable within the social attitudes of the time.'[60] Roman practice, it is argued, could not involve the adoption of so grotesque a rite: syncretism has its limits.

Such demurrals could point to Dionysius of Halicarnassus (2.19) in support. Dionysius insists that the Romans, even though their manners are now corrupt, never allowed the full horror of eastern rites (frenzies, bacchic transports and the like) into the city, at least officially (δημοσίᾳ). When they *have* introduced a foreign cult, because of an oracle or other reasonable cause, then it is celebrated, asserts Dionysius, in a properly Roman style. So, he specifies, when it comes to the Idaean Mater, although the priest and priestess are Phrygian, the rites are completed according to Roman custom, and 'by law and decree of the senate no native Roman walks in procession through the city ..., so cautious are they about admitting any foreign rites'. Dionysius is defending the caution of the Romans, and he specifies that Romans have no stories of gods castrating their fathers and do not beat their breasts because of disappeared divinities, and when they take on a cult, they remove 'its mythic blather' (τερθρείαν μυθικήν). But Dionysius is constructing a polemical, apologetic argument here. The situation is evidently more complex. Both ancient writers and

---

[57] See Nauta 2004; Harrison 2004; Fantuzzi and Hunter 2004: 477–85; Janan 1994: 101–7; Wiseman 1984.
[58] Catalogued in Roller 1999.   [59] Versnel 1990: 107–8. But see Versnel 2011.
[60] Thomas 1984: 1504.

modern scholars seem not just to denigrate a goddess cult as such and an eastern cult as such (the history of patriarchal, western assumptions is long), but also, and perhaps more importantly, they seem to be disturbed by this combination of two apparently opposed aspects of the cult – although, of course, Bacchus/Dionysus is 'most gentle and most violent', as Euripides dramatises in the *Bacchae*, just as Artemis/Diana is both hunter and protective goddess of animals, virgin and goddess of childbirth. Dionysius wants to make Rome's cult more ordered, and less messy, bloody and painful than it clearly could be. He significantly praises 'caution' (εὐλαβῶς) at the beginning and the end of his paragraph of exposition about wild rites. Both ancient and modern scholars deny that the cult of Magna Mater could really fit into their image of the Romanness of the Romans.

There is, then, a deep ambivalence about the cults of Cybele, like the ecstatic rites of Dionysus/Bacchus, which were occasionally (and for now obscure reasons) temporarily banned from Rome. The ambivalence is present not just in modern scholars, struggling with the polymorphous contradictions of polytheism, but also in antiquity, where the eunuch priests were regarded with a certain prurient distaste, or entered the poetic imaginary as figures through which self-destructive desire could be figured – even while the cult continued in an honoured place in the city. The ambivalence, crucially, marks the site of contestation about how the foreign can or cannot become part of Rome, how the east and the female and the transgressive play a role in the self-understanding of Roman cultic practice. Syncretism becomes a term that veils rather than explains the complexities of these interactions.

Syncretism is rhetorically opposed to what? Perhaps most saliently to a fantasy of purity. That is, to the misplaced idea that any cultic system in the ancient world could develop without a dynamic interaction with its neighbours, and without significant change over time. Many religions, as we can call later systems, are committed to such a fantasy of their own authentic, original, simple purity (the early church, the companions in Medina, rabbi Akiva's school). 'Sprachreinheit' and the purity of the community go together, especially in the wake of Herder's influence.[61] Syncretism is also a term, therefore, which allows a certain dismissiveness towards Roman practices from a position of assumed superiority. In the study of the history of religion, it would be easy to find examples of scholars dismissing 'Roman religion' (a category I have

---

[61] Benes 2008.

avoided using so far) both because its practices are ritual without a concomitant requirement of internalised, committed belief – political religion; and because its myths, so often intertwined with Greek stories, lack the authenticity of cosmology or the authority of scripture.[62] Here, too, syncretism becomes a term which avoids discussing how Latin writings actually engage with Greek myth.

Let us return to Ovid, then. The *Fasti* is a six-book poem, dedicated to Germanicus, which narrates the ritual calendar of Rome (the six books tell the first six months only; it is usually assumed that the work is incomplete).[63] It runs through each month, and recounts the presiding god of the month, announces which festivals occur on which days, and what the stories are that explain the festivals, the myths, as it were, for the rituals. As we have seen, although the work was probably left unfinished when he went into exile, it also dramatises Ovid looking back to Rome from Tomi in Romania. The *Fasti* uses the structure of time, the calendar, to tell a mythic and topographical history of Rome, which imagines a life in the streets and temples of his longed-for and lost city, through the historical lens of myth and ritual. As Martial imagines Rome through the not quite ordered collection of witty, opportunistic *aperçus* of the epigrammatist, Ovid gives us Rome at its most structured, where any single moment of serendipity becomes the cause of repeated, lasting ritual action through the proleptic logic of aetiology. Where Martial is the amused, disgusted bystander, Ovid paints himself into the deep time of Rome as the educated, sophisticated man who knows, and narrates what he knows.[64] The Julian calendar, the emperor's regulation,[65] and glory[66] – his *nomina* and *tituli* (*Fasti* 2.15–16) – are now told as Ovid's poem, the poet's account of what counts for cultural memory.

The list of Greek heroes who had visited Magna Graecia that I have discussed on p. 871 was introduced to justify the fact that the very name of the month is Greek:

>    Sed Veneris mensem Graio sermone notatum
>       auguror: a spumis est dea dicta maris.      (*Fasti* 4.61–2)

---

[62] Nongbri 2015; Barton and Boyarin 2017.
[63] See Wallace-Hadrill 1987; Feeney 1992, who notes (p. 15) that the book breaks off just before July and August, the books most connected to the emperor; Boyd 2000; and the articles collected in Miller 1992b; Newlands 1995.
[64] Beard 1987; Newlands 1995; Feeney 1992; Wallace-Hadrill 1987.   [65] See Feeney 2007.
[66] Feeney 1992: 15, building on Wallace-Hadrill 1987.

> But the month of Venus is named from the Greek language,
> I divine: the goddess is called from the foam of the sea.

The Latin month 'April', dedicated to Venus, here is derived from ἀφρός, 'foam' in Greek, which is the etymology of Aphrodite, 'born of foam' [*aphros/aprilis*], and Aphrodite is the Greek name for the Latin Venus. Greece stands at the foundation of the Roman calendar. The month is named for Venus, as the narrator has explained by virtue of another genealogy, because Romulus always claimed his parents were Mars and Venus, and so he wanted the two months, March and its successor, to be named for his parents. Romulus is imagined doing genealogical research to get this conclusion. Iulus is said to have a 'fortunate name' (4.39), just as Venus did not hesitate to share the 'name of parent' with Anchises (4.36). Postumus, however, who was born in the woods (*siluis*), was called (*uocatus*) by the Latin people *Siluius*; but Epytus gave his son a 'revived name [*repetita uocabula*] from Troy, Capys'; Aventinus gave a name to the hill and the place (*uocatur*, 4.52). Before we get to April, named after Aphrodite, we get a series of names, changes of names, giving of names, and names from different cultures. The sheer variety and richness of cross-cultural naming is part and parcel of the interaction of Greek and Roman stories, the buried linguistic life of Roman history.

There is in the *Fasti*, then, a willing recognition of how Greek and Roman stories, even and especially when enshrined in single Greek and Roman words, interact. In Book 2, Ovid turns to explain why in the Lupercalia men run naked through the streets, hitting women with ritual objects – furry straps – exactly the sort of wild occasion that Dionysius denies for Roman practice, along with its absurd stories. Why, he asks, does Faunus avoid clothes? 'There is,' he begins, 'a story handed down full of ancient ribaldry', *traditur antiqui fabula plena ioci* (2.304). This will be, Ovid announces, a tale that has been often told – it is part of tradition, *traditur* – and it is ancient: it is, of course, therefore, a fully Hellenic narrative. This is the story of how Faunus saw Omphale walking with Hercules in the mountains and lusted after her, and plotted to have his way with her. Hercules and Omphale went into a cave for the night, where they swapped clothes as part of their partying. The image of Hercules in Omphale's clothes is a celebrated picture of the most manly man in a reverse gender role, a classic trope of assertive gender stereotypes. Faunus creeps into the dark cave, feels for the clothes in the pitch-black, finds a dress, begins to lift it, only to be confronted by an angry then laughing Hercules. Because Faunus was thus betrayed by clothes (*lusus*, 2.357) – this deception is a sign of play), the god now does not love clothes that deceive the eyes. The scene – opportunistic at all levels – is now the ground for what always happens, each year, in Rome.

But Ovid continues:

> Adde peregrinis causas, mea Musa, Latinas,
> inque suo noster puluere currat equus.           (*Fasti* 2.359–60)
>
> Add Latin reasons to the foreign ones, my Muse,
> And let our horse run in its own dust.

This story will be of a competiton between two bands of youths, one led by Romulus, the other by Remus, to recapture some stolen cattle. As they had been exercising naked, and there was no time to arm properly, in memory of this exploit, bands of naked men run through the streets of Rome. There is no apparent anxiety about naked exercising – of the type we have seen in Plutarch's articulating of Greek and Roman differences. The story takes the narrative back to the earliest days of the city itself, and has a *memorem famam* (2.380), a 'report that is remembered', 'a memorial through retelling'.

Ovid is explicit that he can give an ancient Greek source and a Roman one, homegrown and foreign, and offers both as evidence for why the Lupercal is as it is. Such narratives are incremental, not corrective.[67] They cross boundaries of time and culture. They are part of the polymorphously perverse narrative factory of myth in polytheistic Rome, where another story, with its pleasures, is always to be available (in a way that contrasts tellingly with the canonicity of scripture). The repertoire of stories is expanding across the empire; is an imperial resource; and is played with by Ovid. So, he will meet an old woman who tells him about why it is an old custom to walk barefoot at the festival of Vesta; he then adds in his own voice: 'The rest of the story I learnt ages ago in my childhood years, but I mustn't pass over it for that reason' (6.417–18) – a story of the Palladium, from the temple of Vesta, a story that takes him back to Troy to correct Homer's version, and forward to a past prophecy of Augustus' recent defeat of the Parthians (6.467–8) – to correct Parthian arrogance. An old woman's tale is made parallel to a story from childhood (two archetypally unreliable narrative voices) – that leads the narrative from a chance (*forte*) meeting near the Forum to the deepest mythic time of Homeric literature, through

---

[67] Miller 1992a.

some scholarly iffing and butting, to contemporary politics – a historical continuum from ancient to recent, Greece to Rome. With a similar bold openness to multiplicity, at the beginning of Book 5, he imagines even the Muses giving him contrasting stories to explain the naming of the month of May, and concludes that, as they have equal votes (like Orestes), he hopes he will never praise one more than the others. Multiple incompatible stories here are allowed equal divine authority, equal inspiration.

Ovid is, then, an exemplary, if a particularly literary and flamboyant, case of why 'syncretism' is not an adequate description of Roman engagement with Greek myth. From as early as we have evidence, Latin writing is intimately engaged with Greek stories, including a raft of tales about that very engagement between Greek heroes and Italy. By the imperial period – though this has roots at least as far back as Hellenistic Alexandria, and probably earlier – there is a self-conscious recognition of myth as a repertoire of stories that can be accessed and re-used in different ways. At its most mechanical, we have the collections of Greek myths in précis put together by Parthenius or Apollodorus, which in the case of Parthenius at least seem to have been partly for the express use of Latin writers.[68] In a more sophisticated form, the miscellanies of, say, Aelian, a Roman author writing in Greek, or Aulius Gellius weave anecdotes from history and the historians, scientific paradoxes and tales from the repertoire of myths, as a cultured collection of what an educated man can learn and re-use in his conversation – to appear as a *pepaideumenos*, a cultivated man about town. In *Leucippe and Cleitophon,* the Greek novel written by Achilles Tatius, the hero Cleitophon indeed uses some of the same stories that we also find in Aelian (though Aelian is, of course, later) to seduce the heroine, and we can see in action therefore how such mythic material is redeployed rhetorically to display one's character and persuade an audience.[69] At its most scholarly, a historian such as Dionysius of Halicarnassus polemically selects and retells mythical stories of the engagement of Greek and Roman pasts to argue his case for the historical origin of Rome in Greece and to privilege thus Greek cultural values over Rome. For Ovid – and in this he is typical of literary Latin – although he can happily draw attention to the difference between Greek and Latin aetiologies for Roman festival rites, it is not in order to oppose such stories in terms of authenticity or authority. All such stories – stories of the past, Greek or Roman, Greek and Roman – become grist to the mill of Ovid's self-representation as an educated writer – and

---

[68] Lightfoot 1999.
[69] Discussed in a broader context in Goldhill 2011b; in general, König and Woolf 2013.

thus call into being a similarly educated – or would-be educated – audience. There is an effortless slide from stories of Odysseus to stories of Aeneas to stories of Augustus to stories of Ovid himself. The past and the present have intricate and manipulable genealogical links, and Greek stories are fully part of this interlinked and intermeshed world.

These mythic stories still play a normative role in the construction of ideology: no one would doubt that Ovid's use of myth is informed by a set of gender values, for example, and expresses them forcefully, and expects our complicity. The *Metamorphoses* in particular has been analysed by recent critics as a text that expresses through its intricate, intertwined swirl of mythic narratives a political sensibility about change and stability as well as a set of challenging and amusing encounters with dominant Roman cultural values.[70] The self-conscious recognition of myth as a category and the literary and rhetorical deployment of these stories – equally self-conscious – does not stop myth being a profoundly expressive form in Latin writing. It does not, however, articulate meaning in the same way that myth is taken to do in standard anthropological theory (not least as evidenced by myth's role in the writing of the educated poet, who uses myth precisely as something distanced from but relevant to himself in his self-aware performance of self-representation). Nor does it function with the same topographical and ideological situatedness associated with traditional understandings of how myth expresses the established cosmology, physical and conceptual, of a group. Even and especially the myths of the foundation of Rome tell not of established fixity but of miscegenation at its origin(s), a constant reversion to the double perspective constructed between Greece and Rome. Paradigmatically, when Cicero terms Manius Curius' wit αὐτόχθων, 'born of the soil itself' (*Att.* 7.2.3, discussed on p. 888), his Greek vocabulary of pure, grounded origination sounds against Roman tales of multiple, fractured beginnings, and, in its very Greek, performs such doubling/fracturing of perspective. Latin writing and its use of Greek myth makes its own particular contribution to the theory and history of myth, and should be recognised as such. In Latin literature, the hybridity of myths and the myths of hybridity are an integral expression of Roman culture and its self-understanding – as a fissile, ongoing project.

[70] See Feldherr 2010; Brown 2005; Barchiesi 1993; Hardie 1990 and 1992, Curran 1972; the essays in Hardie, Barchiesi and Hinds 1999, esp. Rosati 1999; Horsfall 1979; Rosati 2002; Tarrant 2005; Keith 1992; Myers 1994.

5

What, then, does Greek know that Latin does not? How is thought changed when it is submerged in a new lexicon? As Virginia Woolf memorably expressed it, a thought thus plunged in the waters of a new language 'comes up dripping'.[71]

It is a mantra of modernist criticism that to do philosophy is to speak Greek. This comprehensive claim of the fundamental structuring role of the Greek philosophical tradition in western metaphysics finds a literal and local expression in the Roman labour of translation that set out to turn Greek knowledge into Latin words. Lucretius' *De rerum natura*, which is so important not just for the literary language of Rome but also for early modern classicism and the impact of past knowledge on the modern west through Latin, aims to turn Greek, Epicurean philosophy into Latin.[72] From the beginning, Lucretius is clear that the very resources of the Latin language are to be strained by his efforts:

> Nec me animi fallit Graiorum obscura reperta
> difficile illustrare Latinis uersibus esse,
> multa nouis uerbis praesertim cum sit agendum
> propter egestatem linguae et rerum nouitatem.   (1.136–9)

> Nor do I fail to understand that it is difficult
> to make clear the dark discoveries of the Greeks in Latin verses,
> especially since we have to express a good deal in new words,
> because of the poverty of our tongue and the novelty of things.

Greek is the source of discoveries – new knowledge – that are difficult to understand, but what makes his effort (*laborem*, 141) difficult is that the poet will need himself to invent 'new words'. A new lexicon is needed because of Latin's poverty of linguistic resource, and because of the novelty of the subject matter.[73] This last line performs what it is talking about. The prosaic 'because of the poverty of the language' is elided with the bumpiest of metrical compulsion – *linguae et* – into a further prosaic phrase where the very general *rerum*, 'things' also alludes to the title of the poem itself, *De rerum natura*, 'on the nature of things'. The line's compelling use of two

---

[71] '... as if thought plunged into a sea of words and came up dripping', Woolf 1925: 81.
[72] Hardie 2009; Warren 2009, esp. Sedley and Erler's chapters; Schrijvers 1970; Holmes and Shearin 2012; Gillespie and Hardie 2007; Gale 1994; Kennedy 2002; Shearin 2015; Greenblatt 2011.
[73] Symmetrical recognition in Greek exists but is far less common, and less charged: Cassius Dio 55.3.4–5 notes the impossibility of translating *auctoritas* into Greek: a recognition of the unique nature of Roman power?

long nouns, each more at home in prose than in verse, enacts the novelty of its own poetic language, as well as declaring the newness of its subject matter.

Lucretius returns to this theme repeatedly:

> Nunc et Anaxagorae scrutemur homoeomerian
> quam Grai memorant nec nostra dicere lingua
> concedit nobis patrii sermonis egestas,
> sed tamen ipsam rem facilest exponere uerbis. (1.832–5)

> Now let us investigate the *homoeomeria* of Anaxagoras,
> as the Greeks call it; it cannot be named in our language
> because of the poverty of the speech of our fatherland.
> But it is easy to expound the thing itself in words.

Here Lucretius demonstrates and explains the difficulty. The Greek word *homoeomeria* has no Latin equivalent. Again, he explains that this is because of the poverty (*egestas*) of Latin, but he adds two extra notes. First, he calls Latin the speech of the fatherland, *sermonis patrii*: there is connection asserted between the language and the political entity in which a citizen lives. This connection will be explored repeatedly in the coming centuries as the anxieties about cultural hybridity and linguistic purity go through cycles of salience – eventually bearing a sick and sad fruit in the 'mother-tongue nationalism' of the nineteenth and twentieth centuries.[74] In a lighter-hearted tone, but making the political connection between language and political belonging evident, Seneca (*Ep.* 120.4) wonders whether a Greek word – used in transliterated form – should therefore be given 'Roman citizenship'. Second, Lucretius is confident that he can express 'the thing itself' – *rem ipsam* – in words. Lucretius is a committed materialist. His subject is the nature of matter. Language – which has its own materialism in the swirl of letters and syllables that combine and explode like the atoms and particles of matter – is therefore a medium that offers a portal to the real, which exists outside language. This theory of language too has a long heritage. But not all languages construct equal portals. Here he is confident: Latin will get to 'the thing' – the materiality – that the Greek conceals. Later he confesses (3.260) that the 'poverty of the speech of the fatherland' (*patrii sermonis egestas* – the same phrase) compels him unwillingly to offer no more than a summary of what the Greeks can say. For Lucretius, to do philosophy in Latin is to fight against the limited resources

---

[74] Benes 2008; Bontempelli 2004; Hutton 1999.

of his own language — and to recognise when its expressivity trumps the abstractions of the Greek.

For the Romans themselves, as well as for later scholars, the key figure in the mediation of Greek philosophy into the Latin tongue is Cicero (who is himself never slow to promote his own importance in the culture of Latin as well as the politics of the state). Plutarch sums up Cicero's instrumental impact well, from the perspective of the Greek intellectual:

> The work and object which he set himself was to compose and translate philosophical dialogues and to render logical and physical terms into the Roman idiom. For he it was, as it is said, who first or principally gave Latin names to *phantasia, syncatathesis, epokhe, catalepsis, atomon, ameres, kenon* and other such technical terms, which, either by metaphors or other means of accommodation, he succeeded in making intelligible and expressible to the Romans. (Plut. *Cic.* 40)[75]

Romans could do philosophy — it became both comprehensible and expressible — because it found Latin words, thanks first to Cicero. But translations, in opening the potential of *noua uerba*, also have their treacheries. The Greek word λύπη (*lupē*) is commonly translated in English as 'grief' or 'pain'. It can be used both for physical pain and, more commonly, for mental anguish (and its physical symptoms). It becomes a term of art in philosophy as the force that is to be battled in the search for contentedness, and, at the extreme, *ataraxia*, 'imperturbability'.[76] When Cicero looks for a Latin word for *lupē*, he decides on *aegritudo*, which means not so much 'grief' as 'sickness' or even 'illness'. The consequence of this choice is that in Latin the response to *aegritudo* takes on a more emphatic sense of medical cure, and a shift in philosophical thinking from a care of the self to something closer to a medical treatment.[77]

The very heart of Roman moral values reflects this precarious translation from Greek to Latin. In Greek, *aretē* means the goodness of a thing or person: the *aretē* of an object, a spear, say, is the quality by which it does what it should and does it well. The *aretē* of a human is often translated therefore as 'virtue' or 'excellence'. *Andreia*, also a positive term, is derived from *anēr*, the word for a man — a male adult — and is often translated not so much as 'manliness', but as 'bravery'. But because of its root, it implies that which makes a man a proper man. Of course, Latin has words like *fortitudo* which implies the

---

[75] For another take on Cicero's lexical innovation see Michèle Lowrie in this volume (p. 788 on Richard Nelson).
[76] Nussbaum 2009.
[77] Erskine 2003, which this paragraph follows; see also Wolf 2015 and more generally, Griffin and Barnes 1999 and Williams and Volk 2016 on the Romanness of Latin philosophy.

sort of strength of spirit and body to stand firm in a battle line. But often the most general use of *andreia*, which usually praises a man for acting like a proper man, is to be translated by the Latin *uirtus*, also derived from the word for a man, *uir*. But so too *aretē* is rendered by *uirtus*. When Electra in Sophocles' *Electra* imagines that she and her sister will be praised for their *andreia*, because they have killed their mother, or when in Xenophon's *Oeconomicus* Ischomachus' wife, who will become a celebrated figure of scandal, is praised for her *andreia*, the ironic suggestion of unappreciated transgression is encoded through the gendered language of praise, inherent in the term *andreia*.[78] The *uirtus* of a woman, however, has, it seems, no such implication in Latin.[79] Greek distinguishes between two forms of excellence, which becomes overlaid in the single term in Latin. How a person's goodness can be discussed is inevitably informed by the affordances of the available language of praise. In the move between Greek and Latin, the differences in the framework of judgement are displayed in the differences in language.

This sense of how the translation between Greek and Latin produces a double lens through which to evaluate social qualities remains an active debate in Roman culture. Fronto was the tutor to the young Marcus Aurelius, who wrote his *Meditations* in Greek, and some of the letters of Fronto survive, in a somewhat battered state.[80] Their exchanges move between Greek and Latin in sexual, literary and cultural stylistics.[81] Here is Fronto writing a letter of recommendation to Lucius Verus, and he praises his friend with a list of Roman virtues – but finds that he has to turn to Greek to say what he means:

> Simplicitas, castitas, ueritas, fides Romana plane, φιλοστοργία uero nescio an Romana: quippe qui nihil minus in tota mea uita Romae repperi quam hominem sincere φιλόστοργον; ut putem, quia reapse nemo est Romae φιλόστοργος, ne nomen quidem huic uirtuti esse Romanum. (111.16–20 vdH²)

> Candour, modesty, truthfulness, loyalty – these are obviously Roman; but I doubt whether 'warmth of affection' is Roman; because I have come across nothing less in my whole life at Rome than a man who is genuinely 'warmly affectionate'; so that I think it is because in fact no one in Rome is 'warmly affectionate' that there is not even a Roman word for this quality.

---

[78] Soph. *El.* 983; Xen. *Oec.* 10.1 (with Goldhill 1995: 139–40).
[79] Tac. *Ann.* 12.51 has Rhadamistus admire his wife's *uirtus* as she flees pregnant on horseback to escape slavery; he kills her when she can no longer ride. But even here, where gender may be thought to be foregrounded, if *uirtus* has any echo of 'manhood', it is with the most flickering of irony.
[80] Richlin 2006; Freisenbruch 2007; Richlin 2011. Letters cited from van den Hout 1988 (= vdH²).
[81] On the language see Mullen 2015, further Elder and Mullen 2019.

I have translated the Greek words *philostorgia/philostorgos* into English for clarity's sake, but they are given in the manuscripts in Greek letters (Fronto also transliterates the term elsewhere in his letters). What is at stake for Fronto is not just the *egestas patrii sermonis* – 'there is no Roman word for this virtue' – but a comment – no doubt snide and knowing – about Roman society, and its general lack of emotional warmth – as he is recommending a friend be accepted warmly by another member of the elite. Fronto is engaging in the parade of values that a letter of recommendation requires, but in doing so he articulates a dynamic space between Greek and Roman qualities through a self-conscious use of the expectations of bilingualism. The self-consciousness of difference that the shift between languages entails is emphatically highlighted as a critique of Roman values.

As philosophy becomes part of the expectations of a Roman elite education, and as Stoic philosophy in particular becomes part of the *lingua franca* of the intellectual life of the empire, the moral evaluative language of Romans is increasingly shaped in dynamic interaction with its buried life as a translation from Greek. Even for the Christian polemicist Tertullian, over two hundred years after Cicero, philosophy's threat is still troped as Greek in his celebrated, outraged question, 'What has Athens to do with Jerusalem?' Tertullian can draw on a history of Roman performative displays of linguistic and thus normative distinctiveness and purity, for which, as we have already seen, the figure of Cato is iconic. Suetonius represents the emperor Tiberius, for example, enacting such gestures of emphatic Romanness:

> Sermone Graeco quamquam alioqui promptus et facilis, non tamen usque quaque usus est abstinuitque maxime in senatu; adeo quidem ut monopolium nominaturus ueniam prius postularet quod sibi uerbo peregrino utendum esset. Atque etiam cum in quodam decreto patrum ἔμβλημα recitaretur, commutandam censuit uocem et pro peregrina nostratem requirendam aut, si non reperiretur, uel pluribus et per ambitum uerborum rem enuntiandam. (*Tib.* 71)

> Though in general he [i.e. Tiberius] spoke Greek happily and fluently, he would not use it on all occasions, and especially avoided it in the senate; so much so that when he was about to use the word *monopolium*, he begged pardon for the necessity of employing a foreign term. Again, when the term *emblema* was read in a decree of the senate, he gave his judgement that it should be changed and a native word substituted for the foreign one; and, if one could not be found, that the idea should be expressed by several words, if necessary, and by periphrasis.

The power of language and the language of power go hand in hand. Or as Fronto puts it: *Imperium autem non potestatis tantummodo uocabulum sed etiam orationis est*, 'But *imperium* is a term not only of power but also of speech' (123.16–17 vdH²). The emperor in the senate apologises for using the word 'monopoly' – a wonderfully and ironically self-reflexive example for the insistence of monolingual purity – and Suetonius aptly gives the term not only in Roman letters but with a Latin ending, as if it were here a Roman word.[82] By drawing attention to his resistance to using foreign words (when his facility in Greek is, of course, to be acknowledged by us as by the senators) he is performing a power play. He makes his political circle complicit with his demand by insisting that they find a Roman equivalent or a suitable periphrasis for a technical term in Greek (given by Suetonius in untranslated Greek letters). What is required is a word that is 'ours': language becomes a sign and symptom of the political group, the projected fatherland of the imagination.

The resistance to Greek knowledge also took the form of spectacular political gestures. In 93/4 CE, the emperor Domitian expelled philosophers from Rome.[83] There had been specific individuals who were philosophers who had been forced out of the city in previous centuries, and occasional waves of political feeling against foreigners which may have resulted in expulsions. Tacitus had no doubt why Domitian took this drastic action, however: *expulsis insuper sapientiae professoribus atque omni bona arte in exilium acta, ne quid usquam honestum occurreret*, 'in addition, the teachers of philosophy were forced out and all honourable study sent into exile, to make sure nothing decent took place anywhere' (*Agr.* 2.2).[84] In Tacitus' heated rhetoric – he can at last tell the story of oppression and violence – the teachers of philosophy, the acme of Greek knowledge, are expelled because they are the guardians of civilised intellectual life (*bona ars*), which is the condition of possibility for decency (*honestum*). Domitian's corruption is such that his decision can only be explained as a desperate attempt to prevent decency breaking out. It is typical of Tacitus, however, that as he turns to praise Agricola, he immediately offers a different image of philosophy.[85] Agricola, Tacitus recalls, told him that in his early days – he had an excellent Greek teacher – he had been tempted to drink rather too keenly from the waters of philosophy (4.3), more keenly, that is, than should be allowed to a Roman and a senator (*ultra quam concessum Romano ac senatori*). Fortunately, the good sense (*prudentia*) of his mother restrained his overheated and burning spirit (*incensum ac flagrantem animum*). The result is that Agricola achieved the most difficult thing of all: as

---

[82] See Elder and Mullen 2019: 147.   [83] Whitton 2015: 15 for the date.
[84] For the translation of *sapientia*, see Gildenhard 2007.   [85] Noted by Whitmarsh 2006: 314–15.

age and reason tempered him, he maintained *ex sapientia modum*, a sense of proportion after studying philosophy. Although Tacitus sees the expulsion of the philosophers as the collapse of acceptable values in the Roman state, at the same time he emphasises that for a Roman and a Roman statesman, there is a real threat in philosophy – that it can lead to excess, to un-Roman values. A Roman needs real care in approaching philosphy's injunctions to care for the self lest he lose the very values that define the Roman self. Without a sense of proportion, Greek knowledge might unman a Roman. Tacitus' *Agricola* is a work riven with the tensions of decrying the old regime while negotiating the evident complicit silence (*tacere*, 2.3) that Tacitus himself needed to survive.[86] His double vision of philosophy as the very mark of decency and something that needs Roman proportion to control is part of the twisted rhetoric of post-Domitianic freedom as well as part of the tradition of Roman ambivalence about what Greek knows.

My discussion so far confirms the conclusion of Olivia Elder and Alex Mullen, in the most recent linguistic study of code-switching in Latin, that 'a defining characteristic of high-status Romans was full competence in both Latin and Greek linguistic and cultural spheres'.[87] This does not mean that all elite Romans were always fully comfortable with any form of Greek nor that elite Romans necessarily had long conversations in Greek on a regular basis with each other.[88] Rather, it suggests that bilingualism, cultural and linguistic, formed a horizon of expectation, which could flare into marked gestures of separation as well as functioning as linguistic passing with the circles of the elite. Greek, culturally and linguistically, remained a privileged *and* ambivalent source of value for Romans, part of Latin and yet other to it. Turville-Petre describes the early mediaeval culture of England as 'one culture in three voices' (Latin, English and French).[89] It is better to conceive of Rome and Greece as two interlocked circles like a Venn diagram, where there are regions of bounded and monocultural, monolingual Latinity and equivalent sites of bounded and monocultural, monolingual Hellenicity, both of which sometimes fiercely protect their boundaries. But literate, elite Rome, and large areas of zones of contact between this dominant world of the elites and the Greek-speaking communities of the empire, can be said to be one culture speaking in two voices – albeit with a regular self-awareness of the dynamics between this hybrid world and the real and imaginary monolingual space beyond it.

---

[86] See Rimell 2018, and in general, König and Whitton 2018. [87] Elder and Mullen 2019: 68.
[88] Swain 2002; *contra* Adams 2003. [89] Turville-Petre 1996: 181.

This shared or hybrid linguistic world is perhaps most vividly evident in the ways Latin writers, in more casual moments than we have so far been discussing, shift between Latin and Greek. In contrast, Greek writers almost never even transliterate Latin words – even Plutarch's use of the Latin word *orator* has Greek morphology – and they usually translate Roman technical terms into Greek equivalents.[90] Now, it must immediately be emphasised that the examples from letters that follow are still from published works of high-status educated Romans, who at best are offering a tailored image of themselves unbuttoned. It is striking that the Greek that is used is very rarely, if ever, *koinē* Greek, that is, the language closest to the Greek spoken on the street, and typified in its literary form by the Gospels; it comes instead from a higher register of literary Greek, often from Homer or the Classical period from many centuries earlier. The archaising Greek of Greek writers in the Roman empire, their so-called Atticism, has been extensively discussed by modern scholars – and was bickered over by the Greek writers themselves – and this is a necessary part of the interaction of Romans with Greek culture: the Greek culture displayed to them was always already layered with historicising gestures of self-representation.[91] Nonetheless, the letters of Cicero and others show in a way different from the grander literary texts how the strategic use of Greek is part and parcel of Latin self-expression.[92]

As they display their intimacy with each other and with the cultural value Greek embodies, Roman writers shift between Latin and Greek, between Greek of the street and Greek as a fetishised language of culture, in the process of exchanging letters between each other – with a constant eye on the third readers who overlook the exchange, that is, their contemporary extended audience and us, the readers of posterity. Greek – in Latin, but other to it – can be used to cover an awkwardness of social exchange. Cicero (*Fam.* 3.7.6) is quietly ticking off a colleague. 'If you are by nature,' he begins (*Si autem natura es*), and then puts the crucial term in Greek: φιλαίτιος. *Philaitios* means 'fond of complaining/finding fault'. It could no doubt be expressed in Latin. But the Greek term allows Cicero to distance himself slightly from the blow of the unpleasant adjective. Greek is not just a sign of elite bonding, but plays specific roles in its dynamic interactions. So, in his dismay at Pompey, Cicero again turns to Greek (*Att.* 8.16.1): *Ego hominem* ἀπολιτικώτατον *omnium iam ante cognoram, nunc uero etiam* ἀστρατηγιώτατον, 'I already before knew Pompey to be a most hopeless statesman; now I see he's really

---

[90] Mason 1974. See p. 882.
[91] Swain 1996; Whitmarsh 2004; Goldhill 2001; and the seminal Bowie 1970.
[92] For a fine study of Roman cultural policy here, see Spawforth 2012, which goes beyond Gruen 1996 or Ferrary 1988.

a most hopeless general too.' My translation cannot do justice to the effect of the code-shifting. The two Greek adjectives suggest, on the one hand, a background in political theory and historiography, setting Pompey against the *exempla* of the past and the value system that has constructed them as *exempla*; on the other hand, the shift allows Cicero to distance his critical judgement of a former associate from the bluntest of Roman abuse. Greek establishes a positionality. This can be the sharing of amusement. Cicero (who elsewhere talks of the difference between Roman and Greek humour, *Fam.* 9.15.2) praises his mate Curius for his natural Roman wit, but – in a joke I discussed on p. 879 – the word he uses for Curius' homegrown talent is αὐτόχθων – a Greek term, and indeed the word used by Athenians to assert their natural link to the soil of Attica, the home of Greek salty wit (*Att.* 7.2.3). The joke has its levels, but, above all, demands complicity. The use of Greek is also about fitting in and the boundaries of self-assertion. So, it is also inevitably possible to get the usage of Greek wrong and not to fit in: Cicero is sharply critical of a man who hears a Greek dirty joke (*binei* = βινεῖ 'he fucks') when he says in Latin *bini* 'two each' (*Fam.* 9.22.3). Humour always invokes regulation, and Cicero uses the man's misuse of Greek, as Cicero determines it, to put the fellow down. Greek, then, is not just good for Greeks to think with,[93] but also good to do business with – to lubricate the wheels of social and political discourse, to position and reposition speakers in the exchange of letters, to enact the micropolitics of exchange.[94]

Yet hybridity provokes contestation, even here. Horace – to return to where this chapter began – mocks a critic who praises Lucilius because he mixed Greek with Latin words (*quod uerbis Graeca Latinis miscuit*, *Sat.* 1.10.20–1). This, he declares, is to forget 'both the fatherland and your father' (*patriaeque patrisque*), and wrongly 'to prefer to intermix words found abroad with words from our fatherland, bilingual in the manner of a Canusian', *patriis intermiscere petita | uerba foris malis, Canusini more bilinguis* (*Sat.* 1.10.29–30). There are many layers of ironic self-representation here, for sure,[95] – Horace comes from Apulia, where Canusium is – but even Horace, the man who revels in his completely bilingual literary culture, can turn on the rhetoric of national linguistic purity when required. For Romans writing in Latin, Greek can never quite fully escape its cultural and linguistic ambivalence.

The introjection of Greek into Latin is fundamental, then, to the spread of philosophy and rhetoric as prime technical disciplines throughout the Latin

---

[93] Gildenhard 2007: 206; Bishop 2019.
[94] See Elder and Mullen 2019 for discussion of the letters I have cited and other examples from a linguistic perspective.
[95] Oliensis 1998: 40.

west and into Western Christianity. The process of translation (cultural as well as linguistic) required mediators – Lucretius, Cicero and others; but such mediation also provoked contestation to the degree that, as in the other areas we have looked at, Greek could be opposed to Latin, even as – and because – it was so prevalent and so important to Latin self-expression in these areas. The use of Greek by Roman elites can be seen too at the level of the word in code-switching performances where morality, humour, social nicety are articulated by gestures of complicity and distancing through momentary and strategic slipping into Greek. If philosophy as an art of self-understanding in Latin required a detour through Greek, so too self-expression among the elite found an alibi in Greek. Through the translation, transliteration and paraphrase of Greek, Latin literature as a language of elite expression has a constantly doubled perspective at its very heart, and this doubling – with its fissures and connections – becomes integral to the expressivity of the Latin as a social discourse.

## 6

The mixing of Greek and Latin in the exchange of elites continued to reach the heights of self-conscious sophistication. Ausonius, the fourth-century poet from Aquitaine, writes a bilingual letter to his friend Paulus which ends with three extraordinary lines:

> Ambo igitur nostrae παραθέλξομεν otia uitae,
>     dum res et aetas et sororum
>         νήματα πορφύρεα πλέκηται.
>
> We will both then charm the idleness of our life,
>     as long as there is money and time and the sisters
>         weave their dark thread.      (*Ep.* 6.43–5)

This does not just weave Greek and Latin together in the way that Horace dismissed, but actually both quotes Horace himself and translates Horace's verse into Greek! At line 44, the metre shifts from hexameters to alcaics, and, thus immediately marked out by its form, is a quotation from Horace's *Odes* 2.3 – as is line 45, but translated into Greek (as Horace himself boasted of turning Greek lyric into Latin . . .). Horace's sympotic poetry is re-purposed as an invitation to a friend; the literature of the past, by the poet's 'transitive reading',[96] becomes a cultural calling card; and by translating Horace into

---
[96] Pelttari 2014: 158.

Greek, Ausonius is not only performing his own cultural sophistication, but also inviting his reader – again both Paulus and all of us who eavesdrop on the exchange – to recognise a sophisticated game of cultural translation in which the literature of the past becomes part of the present, positioning the poet and his friends as the heirs to classical tradition; Latin becomes Greek, as here in the west now, bilingualism is enacted a sign of deep education; and the poet who famously laughed at mixing Greek and Latin is now transformed into Greek and Latin mixed – a game of literary critical wit. The invitation to 'charm the leisure of our life' is itself a charm: *parathelxomen* is a term which in Greek evokes not just the charm of a distracting spell, but also specifically, ever since the *Odyssey*, the charm of poetry.[97] The invitation demands leisure, leisure for the form of attention such sophisticated writing requires: a journey of slow reading Paulus is asked to share, as he makes his way to Ausonius.

The form of attention required by the later poet Optatian, however, is bizarre to the point of illegibility, or rather to the vanishing point of the doubleness of bilingualism (or so it seems at first sight). For Optatian sets letters in a grid which can be read sequentially across the grid, and also picks out letters in the grid to make shapes that relate to the poem's theme. In three of these figured poems, the highlighted Latin letters also add up to phrases that make semantic sense in Greek. In one of his most extraordinary works, poem 19, the grid's highlighted letters allow you to see a ship with rudder and a tiller and a sail with a chi-rho sign on it. Most remarkably of all, however, as Michael Squire writes, 'the Latin letters that make up the ship's mast, sail, tiller and rudder conceal a Greek elegiac couplet: hidden within the ground-text, the constituent letters of the image furnish a "paratextual" commentary on the picture seen'.[98] It is as if Optatian materialises the political discourse of Dionysius of Halicarnassus, who saw Greek history within Roman stories: here reading Latin is seeing Greek.

It might seem that Optatian offers no more than a hyper-aesthetic experience that only the post-modern critic will truly enjoy. His critical reputation would certainly encourage such a narrative (both in terms of his repeated dismissal and recent celebration).[99] But there is also a specifically Christian visionary agenda to his project. As the Christian viewer is asked not to see through a glass darkly, but to see God's Word written through the fabric of the world, a practice of visionary 'seeing through' is required by Optatian.[100] To see a chi-rho

---

[97] On *thelgein* see Goldhill 1991: 60–1, 64–6, with further bibliography.
[98] Squire 2016: 181; see Squire 2017 and Figure 12.8 in this volume.
[99] Squire and Wienand 2017.   [100] See Habinek 2017.

in the Latin letters is to perceive the Christian symbol, itself two Greek letters standing for a name and beyond a name a theology, emerging from within a perhaps trivial-seeming piece of Latin lettering.[101] It is the very sign that Constantine, to whom these poems were sent in order to bring Optatian back from exile, was said to have seen to foretell his own imperial victory – the turning point, in later historiography, of the Christianisation of empire.[102] Indeed, seeing Greek in Latin is a potent image for the history of translation between Greek and Latin in the Christian tradition. For if there is one area where the relation between Latin literature and Greek has proved continually consequential and repeatedly fraught it is in the Christian tradition. If the Word of God embodies truth, how can it be translated?

There is no figure more important to this story than Jerome. Jerome attracted controversy. Exiled from Rome for a host of reasons (sexual, intellectual, social), he established himself as a scholar in exile in Bethlehem, from where he continued his provocative and deeply ambitious work of scholarship, which set out 'to make the theological wisdom of the Greek east available to western readers in Latin translation'.[103] In particular, Jerome wished to bring the work of Origen's biblical commentaries to a wider, Latin-speaking audience.[104] Jerome consulted Origen's own autograph copy of the *Hexapla* in the library at Caesarea, which, thanks to Pamphilus, maintained Origen's own book collection. The *Hexapla* compared four different Greek translations of the Bible with the Hebrew text and a transliterated copy of the Hebrew; it proved to be a founding work of comparative linguistic scholarship on the scriptures. Jerome was one of few men who not only knew Greek, Latin and Hebrew, but also had the intellectual drive and ability to turn such knowledge into concentrated scholarship. He was prepared to emend passages of the transmitted texts of the Gospels based on his scholarly understanding of these multiple versions; and the Vulgate, the Latin translation of the Bible, was commissioned by Pope Damasus from Jerome. The Vulgate, even if it is not considered in its current form to be wholly the work of Jerome, became the dominant Bible of the Catholic Church, which was eventually declared authentic (or authenticated) by the Council of Trent. There is no work of Latin literature, translated from a Greek (and Hebrew) text, which has had

---

[101] See Lunn-Rockliffe 2017.
[102] On Optatian and Constantine, see Squire 2017: 32; on Constantine, Drake 2017: 49–74.
[103] Cain 2009: 48.   [104] Cain 2009; Chadwick 2001: 433–55 and especially Vessey 1993.

such importance, and where the business of translating Greek into Latin has such impact.

Jerome was attacked immediately for his translating work. He writes: 'I wanted to restore the corruption of the Latin manuscripts, which is evident from the variations present in them all, to their Greek original, from which my critics do not deny they were translated' (*Ep.* 27.1). His critics had accused him of tampering with the word of God, because his emendations set him 'against the authority of the ancients and the opinion of the entire world' (ibid.). The scholar known as Ambrosiaster, as Sophie Lunn-Rockliffe determines, is most probably one of the more articulate of these critics. Ambrosiaster pointed out that 'People want to pontificate to us from the Greek manuscripts as if these did not differ from one another' (*In Rom.* 5.14). He accused the textual critic of 'tampering with the words of Scripture to impose his own meaning on them'. What's more, he claimed, 'there are some Latin manuscripts which the innocence of the times has preserved and validates as incorrupt'. These, he concludes, were regarded as true by the great authorities, Tertullian, Victorinus and Cyprian.

Ambrosiaster did not know any Hebrew, and it is likely he could not read Greek either. His claim, dressed in the language of authority and tradition, was a cry against what he had inherited as knowledge. The argument between familiar knowledge and new scholarship would erupt repeatedly in the history of Christianity, most significantly, as we will see, in the Reformation. But Jerome's scholarship, both at the level of linguistics and at the level of hermeneutics – especially where the two approaches to scripture overlap, as they inevitably do – was instrumental in setting the agenda for a *scientia Scripturarum* which depended on the interface of Greek, Latin and Hebrew. This was not just a question of scholarly precision, nor even merely a sign and symptom of Jerome's continual struggle to establish his own authority within the church. Rather, it was a work to create a Christian reader, or to uncover how a Christian was made by reading. If Augustine – a great scholar who knew no Greek, it seems – constructed one dominant and brilliant model for understanding Christianity in and through its performance of reading,[105] Jerome offers a counter-case of the multilingual scholarly archaeology of the scriptures as the paradigm of engagement with the Word of God.

Fully to explore this matrix of the development of Christian intellectual life in late antiquity would be a major project in itself, but two examples

[105] Stock 1998, with the further discussion of Conybeare 2016.

here will have to suffice to indicate the fascination of Jerome's translation of the Greek scriptures into Latin. The first explores how his Latin is also layered by what he called *Hebraica ueritas*, his commitment to a hermeneutic method, one extremely challenging to Christians like Ambrosiaster, that 'privileges the Hebrew text as the holder of "truth" in all matters of Old Testament exegesis'.[106] The prophet Habakuk (3.18) wrote (in Hebrew): 'Yet I will rejoice in the Lord, I will joy in the God of my salvation' (the King James version). The Septuagint translates the final phrase accurately enough with ἐπὶ τῷ θεῷ τῷ σωτῆρί μου, 'in God my saviour'. Jerome translates the whole sentence into Latin as *Ego autem in Domino gaudebo et exsultabo in Deo Iesu meo*. *Sōtēri*, 'saviour', has been translated 'Jesus'. The Hebrew for 'my saviour' is *ye'shi*, and to Jerome's eyes this is close enough to the name *ye'shua*, 'Jesus', which is indeed formed from the root for 'salvation'. For Jerome, reading through the Greek to the Hebrew opens a new potential for seeing the truth of the text. Jerome's translation is a theologically creative rendering which not only sees in the name Jesus the root of (all) salvation, but also regards it as inevitable and right to imagine that a prophet who lived hundreds of years before the birth of Jesus could rejoice in Jesus, because in the temporality of Christianity, which through typology could see Jesus in Adam and Adam in Jesus, it was right and proper to uncover the timeless truth of Christianity in what was now an Old Testament. His Latin reads through Greek and through Hebrew to a deeper truth. Translation into Latin makes patent what the translation into Greek had buried.

My second example is so familiar that its extraordinariness is easy to forget. The Gospel of John begins ἐν τῇ ἀρχῇ ἦν ὁ λόγος. Jerome translates this with *In principio erat uerbum*, 'In the beginning was the Word'. *Logos* in Greek has a wide range of meanings, including 'reason', 'rationale', 'rational order', 'ratio', 'regulative law', 'explanation'. The term has a richly complex semantic nexus, including technical usages from the philosophical and rhetorical traditions, as well as being an everyday expression for a speech or an account. As a foundational expression, here in John, for example, it implies that there is a rational scheme of things that grounds all reality. It is not easy to translate. *Verbum* is translatable as 'word' (as the King James Bible duly has it). *Logos* is never used to mean a 'word' in any technical sense (the grammarians, for example, would use *epos* to mean a particular noun or verb). *Verbum* is used in grammatical treatises to mean a particular word, and it can be used to indicate a more general sense of

---

[106] Cain 2009: 54.

communication, as in the English expression, 'can we have a word?' In any normal usage, *uerbum* would be a very strange and difficult translation of *logos*. For Jerome, however, John is no ordinary usage, and the implications of Jerome's rendition are far-reaching indeed. For Jerome's philological *scientia Scripturarum*, every word is layered with the Word of God, every act of reading a work of discovering that truth. Jerome's *Verbum* is perhaps the limit case of how Latin's engagement with Greek reveals the creative, ideologically charged, culturally, intellectually, theologically explosive potential of translation.

The word 'word' was never less than contentious. Lactantius quotes Hermes Trismegistus, a figure whom, it appears, Christians around Constantine frequently mobilised to form a bridge between Christians and educated non-Christians (*Inst.* 4.7).[107] Hermes, says Lactantius, described the *logos* as *aporrhetos*, 'ineffable', because the name of the Son is inexpressible and unknown to humans and will not be known till the end of days. *Logos* is, in a manner which is both literal and theologically expressive, *unsayable*. Lactantius, who normally writes in Latin, here quotes in Greek, reminding us that understanding *logos* in John is always mediated for Latin speakers through an issue of translation. Lactantius is fully aware that *logos* has a range of meaning that includes both *sermo* and *ratio*, and is thus better than either insufficient Latin term (*Inst.* 4.9). Tertullian (*Adv. Prax.* 5) also debates whether *sermo*, *ratio* or *uerbum* is the best version of *logos*, depending on whether *logos* is taken to refer to God's reason itself or the instrumental power of God's reason embodied in the Word (as Augustine also argues).[108] So too Gregory of Elvira (*De fide* 6) links understanding the translation of *logos* to the central theological issue of the persons of the Father and Son, which dominated the conflict over the Arian heresy. The work to understand the relation between *logos* and *uerbum* is where Christian reading – and controversy – takes place.

This potential for divisiveness became violently evident when Erasmus, for whom Jerome was an intellectual and theological hero, re-translated the first line of John with *In principio erat sermo*.[109] *Sermo* can mean speech, discourse, conversation, and captures one side of the use of *logos* in Greek; but its challenge to the received – ingrained – knowledge that the regular use of Jerome's version had produced over the centuries was incendiary. Western and eastern Christianity had developed into radically separate

---

[107] Nicholson and Nicholson 1989: 198. See in particular Fowden 1986, especially pp. 205–11 on Lactantius. Thanks to my graduate student, Teresa Röger, for discussion here.
[108] *De diversis quaestionibus octaginta tribus* 63; *Tractatus in Iohannem* 108.3.
[109] Discussed in Goldhill 2002 with further bibliography.

traditions, to the degree that western Crusaders slaughtered eastern Christians in their thousands because they did not recognise them as Christians. Few western Christians knew any Greek: the Renaissance was fuelled by the re-discovery of Greek knowledge and knowledge of Greek. Erasmus was a key player in this return *ad fontes*, to the sources of learning in antiquity that knowing Greek made possible. Erasmus defended his shocking translation reasonably enough with the assertion that it better represented the Greek of the Gospels. In response, just as Ambrosiaster had attacked Jerome, so conservative clerics not only rebuked Erasmus but even went so far as to declare that 'Learning Greek is heresy'.[110] Indeed, Erasmus, against his own will, became an icon in the Reformation's religious wars, and the move first to understand the Gospels through the Greek rather than their Latin translation, and second to move from Latin into vernacular translations, became a battleground of change and conservatism across Europe.[111] It is against this background of theological, national and institutional conflict that Jerome's translation was declared authentic by the Council of Trent, asserting the authority of the Latin text independent of its Greek. As we have seen so often in this chapter, once again the desire to place a rigid boundary between Latin literature and Greek tradition is motivated by ideological pressures, and the normative longings for a purer self-definition.

The very question 'who owns Greek?' could flare into political contentiousness. The emperor Julian, echoing Dionysius of Halicarnassus, declared that 'the Greek colonies civilised the greater part of the world, thus preparing it to submit more easily to the Romans. For not only are the Romans Greek by origin, but so also are the sacred laws and pious beliefs in the gods.' For Julian Rome was Greek 'by origin and constitution'.[112] In line with his commitment to such Greekness, he banned Christians – or anyone who did not share a belief in Hellenic gods – from teaching traditional Greek texts. Gregory of Nazianzus was incensed (he was a Christian well versed in classical *paideia*). 'Whose property is the Greek language?', he exploded; 'O philhellene, O philologian, do you intend to debar us from speaking Greek?'[113] In the Roman empire, from the emperor down, for Christians and non-Christians, access to Greek learning remained essential for cultural capital, and thus became a battleground

---

[110] Erasmus, *Antibarbari*, Thompson 1978: I 32; Allen 1906–58: IV 400–11.
[111] McDonald 2016 (especially salient and good); Bentley 1983; Gelhaus 1989; Cummings 2002; McGrath 2004; Pelikan 1996.
[112] Jul. *Hel. R.* 152d–153a, superbly discussed in context by Elm 2012: 269–335.
[113] Greg. Naz. *Invective against Julian* 103, 105.

of belonging and affiliation. Translation in and out of Greek is always also framed by what is at stake in knowing Greek: not just the truth of scripture, not just one's own place in the tradition of learning and culture but also how Rome itself is to be conceived.

In the Christian tradition, translating from the Greek becomes an issue of theological and ideological passion: if translation is treacherous, is not the translation of the Word of God a treachery to God's truth? Or, can it, as Jerome would insist, make the truth visible, or, as Augustine would insist, open the unending work of interpreting the inexhaustible significance of scripture? The relation between Latin and Greek, when we turn to the Bible, sets at stake the authority of interpretation, the institutional stability of tradition, the role of received knowledge – or, simply, as Augustine and Jerome would agree, the soul of the Christian reader.

7

Rome offers, then, a fascinating and instructive example that contradicts the standard expectations of the relations between power and language that current critical thinking about empire demands. Latin writing is, from its beginnings, intertwined with the thinking, expression and narratives of its colony Greece – and, as we have seen, it *works through* such dynamic interactions with different ideological and pragmatic inflections, both nuanced and aggressive. For the colonised and coloniser, cultural privilege and cultural anxiety go hand in hand. For today, when naïve and toxic assertions of identity and strident claims of cultural purity, based on ideological fantasies of origin, are all too evident both in national agendas and in the academy, a more sophisticated and complex sense of the cultural politics of empire has never been more needed.

This imbrication of Latin with Greek has deeply affected the shape of classicism throughout the long history of the west's engagement with antiquity. When it comes to narratives of cultural purity, the lure of the origin, and the privileging of authenticity, it has been easy to turn to Greece, and this has been the fundamental imaginary of philhellenism. All too often, Latin has been treated as secondary to Greek (as the clichés have it, Greek gets the great literature, great myths and great bodies – that's the art – Rome gets roads, empire and the cruelty of gladiators; or, for the twentieth century, Greeks offer sexual freedom and democracy, Romans orgies and the military). Latin literature has had to struggle with its epigonal and hybrid condition in a way that Greek literature has not.

Especially while Latin remained the international language of scholarship and a basis of education, Latin literature was often normalised as the familiar schooltexts, while Greek had the exoticised glamour of the more ancient civilisation. Republican Rome could certainly be an inspiration of resistance to tyranny – the French revolution, Marx insisted, was enacted in Roman dress. Nor, of course, can there be any doubt about the influence of Ovid or Virgil, or the deep power of the Vulgate. Yet each of these masterpieces of Latin literature was always recognised to come trailing clouds of the glory that was Greek literature, there first.

For more recent critics, however, this secondariness has had its correlative benefits, as contemporary critical self-appraisal has insisted that modernity responds to antiquity as Latin does to Greek – appropriation, partiality, privilege, disdain, the structuring gestures of self-definition. Latin thus becomes a privileged mirror of contemporary self-scrutiny, as today's western society needs to understand well the anxiety of how an inherited tradition is to be managed in the process of cultural self-definition. In this, as Shelley could not say, we are all Latin.

How translation functions and distorts – between cultures as much as between languages; how self-identification deals with hybridity, multiple positionalities and self-assertion; how cultural value is ascribed in a multinational framework; how language forms a part of citizenship; how, in short, cultural difference is to be part of cultural identity – the grounding questions of this chapter – are indeed increasingly insistent problems in our contemporary era, and in public debate too often too shrilly treated, as if the answers to them were simple and single. In particular, as west and east (or the global north and global south) enter into more complex interactions and exchanges around politics, the shape of a good life, and comparative or competing values, understanding the questions which this chapter has aired will increasingly become a crucial task for humanities scholars, heirs to these older debates, which are formative of our own long traditions. What is lost and found in translation remains the problem and grounding opportunity of modern cosmopolitanism and its travails. It may well be that the example of Rome's relation to Greek, or, more precisely, Latin writing's relation to Greek language and culture, can yet provide a reflective model through which we can ourselves begin to think in a more sophisticated and historically informed manner. To understand the cultural hybridity at the very heart of Europe's self-understanding, along with the arguments weaponised against it in the name of the purity of national identity, remains a pressing task to which the study of classics and classicism is uniquely well placed to contribute.

## References

Acheraïou, A. (2008) *Rethinking Postcolonialism: Colonialist Discourse in Modern Literatures and the Legacy of Classical Writers*, Basingstoke.
  (2011) *Questioning Hybridity, Postcolonialism and Globalization*, London.
Adams, J. N. (2003) *Bilingualism and the Latin Language*, Cambridge.
Adams, J. N., M. Janse and S. Swain, eds. (2002) *Bilingualism in the Ancient World: Language Contact and the Written Text*, Oxford.
Allen, P. S. (1906–58) *Erasmi Epistoli*, 12 vols., Oxford.
Ashcroft, B., G. Griffiths and H. Tiffin (2002) *The Empire Writes Back: Theory and Practice in Post-Colonial Literatures*, 2nd edn, London.
Astin, A. (1978) *Cato the Censor*, Oxford.
Barchiesi, A. (1993) *Il poeta e il principe: Ovidio e il discorso Augusteo*, Rome. Translated as *The Poet and the Prince: Ovid and Augustan Discourse*, Berkeley, 1997.
Barkan, L. (1986) *The Gods Made Flesh: Metamorphosis and the Pursuit of Paganism*, New Haven.
Barton, C. and D. Boyarin (2017) *Imagine No Religion: How Modern Abstractions Hide Ancient Realities*, Fordham.
Baumbach, M. (2002) *Lukian in Deutschland: eine forschungs- und rezeptionsgeschichtliche Analyse vom Humanismus bis zur Gegenwart*, Munich.
Baumbach, M. and S. Bär, eds. (2007) *Quintus Smyrnaeus: Transforming Homer in Second Sophistic Epic*, Berlin.
Beard, M. (1987) 'A complex of times: no more sheep on Romulus' birthday', *PCPhS* 33: 1–15.
  (1993) 'Looking harder for Roman myth: Dumézil, declamation and the problems of definition', in Graf 1993, 44–64.
Benes, T. (2008) *In Babel's Shadow: Language, Philology, and Nation in Nineteenth-Century Germany*, Detroit.
Benko, S. (1984) *Pagan Rome and the Early Christians*, Bloomington, IN.
Bentley, J. (1983) *Humanist and Holy Writ: New Testament Scholarship in the Renaissance*, Princeton.
Bhabha, H. K. (1990) *Nation and Narration*, London and New York.
  (1994) *The Location of Culture*, London.
Bishop, C. (2019) *Cicero, Greek Learning and the Making of a Roman Classic*, Oxford.
Bontempelli, P. (2004) *Knowledge, Power and Discipline: German Studies and National Identity*, trans. G. Poole, Minneapolis.
Bowie, E. (1970) 'Greeks and their past in the Second Sophistic', *Past & Present* 46: 3–41.

Boyd, B. W. (2000) '*Celabitur auctor*: the crisis of authority and narrative patterning in Ovid's *Fasti 5*', *Phoenix* 54: 64–98.
Boyd, B. W., ed. (2002) *Brill's Companion to Ovid*, Leiden.
Brown, S. A. (2005) *Ovid: Myth and Metamorphosis*, Bristol.
Butler, E. (1935) *The Tyranny of Greece over the German Imagination*, Cambridge.
Cain, A. (2009) *The Letters of Jerome: Asceticism, Biblical Exegesis and the Construction of Christian Authority in Late Antiquity*, Oxford.
Carleton Paget, J. and J. Lieu, eds. (2018) *Christianity in the Second Century: Themes and Developments*, Cambridge.
Cerchiai, L., L. Jannelli and F. Longo (2004) *The Greek Cities of Magna Graecia and Sicily*, Los Angeles (trans. of *Città greche della Magna Grecia e della Sicilia*, Milan, 2002).
Ceserani, G. (2012) *Italy's Lost Greece: Magna Graecia and the Making of Modern Archaeology*, Oxford.
Chadwick, H. (2001) *The Church in Ancient Society: From Galilee to Gregory the Great*, Oxford.
Chaplin, J. (2000) *Livy's Exemplary History*, Oxford.
Clark, G. (2004) *Christianity and Roman Society*, Cambridge.
Conybeare, C. (2016) *The Routledge Guidebook to Augustine's Confessions*, London and New York.
Cribiore, R. (2001) *Gymnastics of the Mind: Greek Education in Hellenistic and Roman Egypt*, Princeton.
Cronin, S., ed. (2008) *Subalterns and Social Protest: History from below in the Middle East and North Africa*, New York.
Csapo, E. (2005) *Theories of Mythology*, Oxford.
Cummings, B. (2002) *Literary Culture of the Reformation: Grammar and Grace*, Oxford.
Curran, L. (1972) 'Transformation and anti-Augustanism in Ovid's *Metamorphoses*', *Arethusa* 5: 71–91.
Detienne, M. (1981) *L'invention de la mythologie*, Paris.
Drake, H. (2017) *A Century of Miracles: Christians, Pagans, Jews and the Supernatural, 312–410*, Oxford.
Duff, T. (1999) *Plutarch's Lives: Exploring Virtue and Vice*, Oxford.
Edmunds, L. (1990) *Approaches to Greek Myth*, Baltimore.
Elder, O. and A. Mullen (2019) *The Language of Roman Letters: Bilingual Epistolography from Cicero to Fronto*, Cambridge.
Elm, S. (2012) *Sons of Hellenism, Fathers of the Church: Emperor Julian, Gregory of Nazianzus and the Vision of Rome*, Berkeley.
Erskine, A. (2003) 'Cicero and the shaping of Hellenistic philosophy', *Hermathena* 175: 5–15.
Fantuzzi, M. and R. Hunter (2004) *Tradition and Innovation in Hellenistic Poetry*, Cambridge.
Farrell, J. and M. Putnam, eds. (2010) *A Companion to Vergil's Aeneid and Its Tradition*, Oxford.
  (2010) *Playing Gods: Ovid's Metamorphoses and the Politics of Fiction*, Princeton.

Feeney, D. (1992) '*Si licet et fas est*: Ovid's *Fasti* and the problem of free speech', in Powell 1992, 1–25.
  (2007) *Caesar's Calendar: Ancient Time and the Beginning of History*, Berkeley.
  (2016) *Beyond Greek: The Beginnings of Latin Literature*, Cambridge, MA.
Feldherr, A. (1998) *Spectacle and Society in Livy's History*, Berkeley.
Ferrary, J.-L. (1988) *Philhellénisme et impérialisme*, Rome.
Fitzgerald, W. (2007) *Martial: The World of the Epigram*, Chicago.
Fowden, G. (1986) *The Egyptian Hermes: A Historical Approach to the Late Pagan Mind*, Princeton.
Frankfurter, D. (2018) *Christianizing Egypt: Syncretism and Local Worlds in Late Antiquity*, Princeton.
Freisenbruch, A. (2007) 'Back to Fronto: doctor and patient in his correspondence with an emperor', in Morello and Morrison 2007, 235–56.
Gale, M. (1994) *Myth and Poetry in Lucretius*, Cambridge.
Gärtner, U. (2005) *Quintus of Smyrna und die 'Aeneis': Zur Nachwirkung Vergils in der griechischen Literatur der Kaiserzeit*, Munich.
Gelhaus, H. (1989) *Der Streit um Luthers Bibelverdeutschung im 16. und 17. Jahrhundert*, 2 vols., Tübingen.
Gildenhard, I. (2007) *Paideia Romana: Cicero's Tusculan Disputations*, Cambridge.
  (2010) *Creative Eloquence: the Construction of Reality in Cicero's Speeches*, Oxford.
Gillespie, S. and P. Hardie, eds. (2007) *The Cambridge Companion to Lucretius*, Cambridge.
Goldhill, S. (1991) *The Poet's Voice: Essays on Poetics and Greek Literature*, Cambridge.
  (1995) *Foucault's Virginity: Ancient Erotic Fiction and the History of Sexuality*, Cambridge.
  (2001) *Being Greek under Rome: Cultural Identity, the Second Sophistic and the Development of Empire*, Cambridge.
  (2002) *Who Needs Greek? Contests in the Cultural History of Hellenism*, Cambridge.
  (2011a) *Victorian Culture and Classical Antiquity: Art, Opera, Fiction and the Proclamation of Modernity*, Princeton.
  (2011b) 'The anecdote: exploring the boundaries between oral and literate performance in the Second Sophistic', in W. Johnson and H. Parker, eds., *Ancient Literacies: The Culture of Reading in Greece and Rome* (Oxford), 96–113.
Gotter, U. (2009) 'Cato's *Origines*: the historian and his enemies', in A. Feldherr, ed., *The Cambridge Companion to the Roman Historians* (Cambridge), 108–22.
Graf, F., ed. (1993) *Mythos in Mythenloser Gesellschaft: Das Paradigma Roms*, Berlin and New York.
Greenblatt, S. (2011) *The Swerve: How the World Became Modern*, New York.

Greensmith, E. (2020) *The Resurrection of Homer in Imperial Greek Epic: Quintus Smyrnaeus' Posthomerica and the Poetics of Impersonation*, Cambridge.
Greineder, D. (2007) *From the Past to the Future: The Role of Mythology from Winckelmann to the Early Schelling*, Bern.
Griffin, M. and J. Barnes, eds. (1999) *Philosophia Togata* I: *Essays on Philosophy and Roman Society*, Oxford.
Gruen, E. (1992) *Culture and National Identity in Republican Rome*, Ithaca, NY.
　(1996) *Studies in Greek Culture and Roman Policy*, Oakland, CA.
Habinek, T. (1998) *The Politics of Latin Literature: Writing, Identity and Empire in Ancient Rome*, Princeton.
　(2017) 'Optatian and his œuvre: explorations in ontology', in Squire and Wienand 2017, 391–426.
Hall, C. (2012) *Macaulay and Son: Architects of Imperial England*, New Haven, CT.
Hardie, P. (1990) 'Ovid's Theban History: the first anti-*Aeneid*?', *CQ* 40: 224–35.
　(1992) 'Augustan poets and the mutability of Rome', in Powell 1992, 59–82.
　(2009) *Lucretian Receptions: History, the Sublime, Knowledge*, Cambridge.
Hardie, P., A. Barchiesi and S. Hinds, eds. (1999) *Ovidian Transformations: Essays on Ovid's Metamorphoses and Its Reception*, Cambridge.
Harloe, K. (2013) *Winckelmann and the Invention of Antiquity: History and Aesthetics in the Age of Altertumswissenschaft*, Oxford.
Harrison, S. (2004) 'Altering Attis: ethnicity, gender and genre in Catullus 63', *Mnemosyne* 57: 520–33.
Henrichs, A. (1995) '*Graecia capta*: Roman views of Greek culture', *HSPh* 97: 243–61.
Holmes, B. and W. Shearin, eds. (2012) *Dynamic Reading: Studies in the Reception of Epicureanism*, New York.
Horsfall, N. (1979) 'Epic and burlesque in Ovid, *Met.* 8.260f.', *CJ* 74: 319–32.
Hose, M. (1999) 'Post-colonial theory and Greek literature in Rome', *GRBS* 40: 303–26.
Huskinson, J. (2000) 'Élite culture and the identity of empire', in J. Huskinson, ed., *Experiencing Rome: Culture, Identity and Power in the Roman Empire* (London), 95–124.
Hutchinson, G. (2013) *Greek to Latin: Frameworks and Contexts for Intertextuality*, Oxford.
Hutton, C. (1999) *Linguistics and the Third Reich: Mother-Tongue Fascism, Race and the Science of Language*, London.
D'Ippolito, G. (1994) *Studi nonniani. L'epillio nelle Dionisiache*, Palermo.
James, A. (2007) 'Quintus of Smyrna and Virgil: a matter of prejudice', in Baumbach and Bär 2007, 285–306.
Janan, M. (1994) *'When the Lamp Is Shattered': Desire and Narrative in Catullus*, Carbondale, IL.
Jolowicz, D. A. (2021) *Latin Poetry in the Ancient Greek Novels*, Oxford.
Kallendorf, C. (2007) *The Other Virgil: 'Pessimistic' Readings of the Aeneid in Early Modern Culture*, Oxford.

Keith, A. (1992) *The Play of Fictions: Studies in Ovid's Metamorphoses Book 2*, Ann Arbor, MI.
Kennedy, D. (2002) *Rethinking Reality: Lucretius and the Textualization of Nature*, Ann Arbor, MI.
Keydell, R. (1935) 'Quintus von Smyrna und Vergil', *Hermes* 82: 254–6.
Knox, P. E. (1988) 'Phaethon in Nonnus and Ovid', *CQ* 38: 536–51.
König, A. and C. Whitton, eds. (2018) *Roman Literature under Nerva, Trajan and Hadrian: Literary Interactions, AD 96–138*, Cambridge.
König, J. and G. Woolf, eds. (2013) *Encyclopedism from Antiquity to the Renaissance*, Cambridge.
Krebs, C. (2011) *A Most Dangerous Book: Tacitus' Germania from the Roman Empire to the Third Reich*, New York.
Lampe, P. (2006) *Christians at Rome in the First Two Centuries: from Paul to Valentinus*, London.
Langlands, R. (2018) *Exemplary Ethics in Ancient Rome*, Cambridge.
Latham, J. (2012) '"Fabulous clap-trap": Roman masculinity, the cult of Magna Mater, and literary constructions of the *Galli* at Rome from the late Republic to late antiquity', *Journal of Religion* 92: 84–122.
Lavan, M. (2011) 'Slavishness in Britain and Rome in Tacitus' *Agricola*', *CQ* 61: 294–305.
  (2020) 'Beyond Romans and others: identities in the long second century', in A. König, R. Langlands and J. Uden, eds., *Literature and Culture in the Roman Empire, 96–235: Cross-Cultural Interactions* (Cambridge), 37–57.
Lee Too, Y., ed. (2001) *Education in Greek and Roman Antiquity*, Leiden.
Liebert, H. (2016) *Plutarch's Politics: Between City and Empire*, Cambridge.
Lieu, J. (2006) *Christian Identity in the Jewish and Graeco-Roman World*, Oxford.
Lieu, J., J. North and T. Rajak, eds. (1992) *The Jews among Pagans and Christians in the Roman Empire*, London.
Lightfoot, J. (1999) *Parthenius of Nicaea: The Extant Works*, Oxford.
Lincoln, B. (1999) *Theorizing Myth: Narrative, Ideology and Scholarship*, Chicago.
Lorenz, S. (2000) *Erotik und Panegyrik: Martials epigrammatische Kaiser*, Tübingen.
Lunn-Rockliffe, S. (2017) 'The power of the jewelled style: Christian signs and names in Optatian's *versus intexti* and on gems', in Squire and Wienand 2017, 427–60.
McDonald, G. (2016) *Biblical Criticism in Early Modern Europe: Erasmus, the Johannine Comma and Trinitarian Debate*, Leiden.
McGill, S. (2005) *Virgil Recomposed: The Mythological and Secular Centos in Antiquity*, Oxford.
McGrath, A. (2004) *The Intellectual Origins of the European Reformation*, Oxford.
Maciver, C. (2012) *Quintus Smyrnaeus' Posthomerica: Engaging Homer in Late Antiquity*, Leiden.
Marchand, S. (2003) *Down from Olympus: Archaeology and Philhellenism in Germany, 1750–1970*, Princeton.
Marrou, H. (1956) *A History of Education in Antiquity* (trans. G. Lamb), London.

Martin, R. (1989) *The Language of Heroes: Speech and Performance in the Iliad*, Ithaca, NY.
Martindale, C. (1990) *Ovid Renewed: Ovidian Influences on Literature and Art from the Middle Ages to the Twentieth Century*, Cambridge.
Mason, H. (1974) *Greek Terms for Roman Institutions: A Lexicon and Analysis*, Toronto.
Mattingly, D. J. (2013) *Imperialism, Power, and Identity: Experiencing the Roman Empire*, Oxford.
  (2014) 'Identities in the Roman world: discrepancy, heterogeneity, hybridity, and plurality', in L. R. Brody and G. L. Hoffman, eds., *Roman in the Provinces: Art on the Periphery of Empire* (Chestnut Hill, MA), 35–59.
Miller, J. (1992a) 'The *Fasti* and Hellenistic didactic: Ovid's variant aetiologies', *Arethusa* 25: 11–32.
Miller, J., ed. (1992b) *Reconsidering Ovid's Fasti* (= *Arethusa* 25.1), Baltimore.
Miller, J. and C. Newlands, eds. (2014) *A Handbook to the Reception of Ovid*, Oxford.
Moatti, C. (2015) *The Birth of Critical Thinking in Republican Rome* (trans. J. Lloyd), Cambridge.
Morello, R. and A. Morrison, eds. (2007) *Ancient Letters: Classical and Late Antique Epistolography*, Oxford.
Morford, M. (1999) *Classical Mythology*, Oxford.
Mullen, A. (2015) '"In both our languages": Greek–Latin code-switching in Roman literature', *Language and Literature* 24: 213–32.
Myers, K. S. (1994) *Ovid's Causes: Cosmogony and Aetiology in the Metamorphoses*, Ann Arbor, MI.
Nauta, R. R. (2004) 'Catullus 63 in a Roman context', *Mnemosyne* 57: 596–628.
Newlands, C. (1995) *Playing with Time: Ovid and the Fasti*, Ithaca, NY.
Nicholson, C. and O. Nicholson (1989) 'Lactantius, Hermes Trismegistus and Constantinian obelisks', *JHS* 109: 198–200.
Nisbet, G. (2003) *Greek Epigram in the Roman Empire: Martial's Forgotten Rivals*, Oxford.
Nongbri, B. (2015) *Before Religion: A History of a Modern Concept*, New Haven.
Nussbaum, M. (2009) *The Therapy of Desire: Theory and Practice in Hellenistic Ethics*, 2nd edn, Princeton.
O'Gorman, E. (1993) 'No place like Rome: identity and difference in the *Germania* of Tacitus', *Ramus* 22: 135–54.
Oliensis, E. (1998) *Horace and the Rhetoric of Authority*, Cambridge.
Pelikan, J. (1996) *The Reformation of the Bible: The Bible of the Reformation*, New Haven.
Pelttari, A. (2014) *The Space that Remains: Reading Latin Poetry in Late Antiquity*, Ithaca, NY.
Powell, A., ed. (1992) *Roman Poetry and Propaganda in the Age of Augustus*, London.
Powell, B. (2011) *Classical Myth*, Harlow.

Preston, R. (2001) 'Roman questions, Greek answers: Plutarch and the construction of identity', in Goldhill 2001: 86–121.
Quayson, A. (2000) *Postcolonialism: Theory, Practice or Process?*, Malden, MA.
Quinn, J. C. (2012) 'Postcolonialism', in R. S. Bagnall, K. Brodersen, C. B. Champion, A. Erskine and S. R. Huebner, eds., *The Encyclopedia of Ancient History* (Oxford).
Rajak, T. (2002) *The Jewish Dialogue with Greece and Rome: Studies in Cultural and Social Interaction*, Leiden.
Richlin, A. (2006) *Marcus Aurelius in Love: Marcus Aurelius and Marcus Cornelius Fronto*, Chicago.
  (2011) 'Parallel lives: Domitia Lucilla and Cratia, Fronto and Marcus', *Eugesta* 1: 163–203.
Rimell, V. (2008) *Martial's Rome: Empire and the Ideology of Epigram*, Cambridge.
  (2018) 'I will survive (you): Martial and Tacitus on regime change', in König and Whitton 2018, 63–85.
Roessel D. (2002) *In Byron's Shadow: Modern Greece in the English and American Imagination*, Oxford.
Roller, L. (1999) *In Search of God the Mother: The Cult of Anatolian Cybele*, Berkeley.
Rosati, G. (1999) 'Form in motion: weaving the text in the *Metamorphoses*', in Hardie, Barchiesi and Hinds 1999, 241–53.
  (2002) 'Narrative techniques and narrative structures in the *Metamorphoses*', in Boyd 2002, 271–304.
Said, E. W. (1994) *Culture and Imperialism*, London.
Schrijvers, P. H. (1970) *Horror ac divina voluptas. Études sur la poétique et la poésie de Lucrèce*, Amsterdam.
Sciarrino, E. (2011) *Cato the Censor and the Beginnings of Latin Prose: From Poetic Translation to Elite Transcription*, Columbus, OH.
Sen, A. (2006) *Identity and Violence: The Illusion of Destiny*, London.
Shearin, W. (2015) *The Language of Atoms: Performativity and Politics in Lucretius' De rerum natura*, Oxford.
Spawforth, A. (2012) *Greece and the Augustan Cultural Revolution*, Cambridge.
Spivak, G. C. (1988) 'Can the subaltern speak?', in C. Nelson and L. Grossberg, eds., *Marxism and the Interpretation of Culture* (Chicago), 271–313.
Squire, M. (2016) '"How to read a Roman portrait?": Optatian Porfyry, Constantine and the *vultus Augusti*', *PBSR* 84: 179–240.
  (2017) 'POP art: the optical poetics of Publilius Optatianus Porfyrius', in J. Elsner and J. Hernández Lobato, eds., *The Poetics of Late Latin Literature* (Oxford), 25–99.
Squire, M. and J. Wienend, eds. (2017) *Morphogrammata/The Lettered Art of Optatian: Figuring Cultural Transformations in the Age of Constantine*, Paderborn.
St. Clair, W. (2002) *That Greece Might Still Be Free: The Philhellenes in the War of Independence*, Oxford.
Stadter, P. (2014) *Plutarch and His Roman Readers*, Oxford.

Stewart, C. and R. Shaw, eds. (1994) *Syncretism/Anti-Syncretism: The Politics of Religious Synthesis*, London.
Stock, B. (1998) *Augustine the Reader: Meditation, Self-Knowledge and Interpretation*, Cambridge, MA.
Swain, S. (1996) *Hellenism and Empire: Language, Classicism, and Power in the Greek World*, AD 50–250, Oxford.
  (2002) 'Bilingualism in Cicero? The evidence of code-switching', in Adams, Janse and Swain 2002, 128–67.
Tarrant, R. (2005) 'Paths not taken: untold stories in Ovid's *Metamorphoses*', *MD* 54: 65–89.
Thomas, G. (1984) 'Magna Mater and Attis', *ANRW* II.17.3: 1500–55.
Thomas, R. (2004) *Virgil and the Augustan Reception*, Cambridge.
Thompson, C. R., ed. (1978) *Collected Works of Erasmus. Vols. 23 and 24: Literary and Educational Writings*, 2 vols., Chicago.
Tudeau-Clayton, M. (1998) *Jonson, Shakespeare and Early Modern Virgil*, Cambridge.
Turville-Petre, T. (1996) *England the Nation: Language, Literature, and National Identity, 1290–1340*, Oxford.
Valdez, D. (2014) *German Philhellenism: The Pathos of the Historical Imagination from Winckelmann to Goethe*, New York.
Vanacker, W. and A. Zuiderhoek, eds. (2017) *Imperial Identities in the Roman World*, London.
van den Hout, M. (1988) *M. Cornelii Frontonis Epistulae*, Leipzig.
Vasunia, P. (2013) *The Classics and Colonial India*, Oxford.
Versnel, H. (1990) *Inconsistencies in Greek Religion*, Vol. 1, Leiden.
  (2011) *Coping with the Gods: Wayward Readings in Greek Theology*, Leiden.
Vessey, M. (1993) 'Jerome's Origen: the making of a Christian literary persona', *Studia Patristica* 28: 135–45.
Vian, F. (1959) *Recherches sur les 'Posthomerica' de Quintus de Smyrne*, Paris.
  (1963) *Quintus de Smyrne, 'La suite d'Homère'*, Vol. 1, Paris.
Wallace-Hadrill, A. (1987) 'Time for Augustus: Ovid, Augustus and the *Fasti*', in M. Whitby, P. Hardie and M. Whitby, eds., *Homo Viator: Classical Essays for John Bramble* (Bristol), 221–30.
  (1998) 'To be Roman, go Greek: thoughts on Hellenization at Rome', *BICS* 71: 79–91.
  (2008) *Rome's Cultural Revolution*, Cambridge.
Warren, J., ed. (2009) *The Cambridge Companion to Epicureanism*, Cambridge.
Webster, J. and N. Cooper, eds. (1996) *Roman Imperialism: Post-Colonial Perspectives*, Leicester.
Whitmarsh, T. (2001) *Greek Literature and the Roman Empire: The Politics of Imitation*, Oxford.
  (2004) *Greek Literature and the Roman Empire: The Politics of Imitation*, Oxford.

(2006) '"This in-between book": language, politics and genre in the *Agricola*', in B. McGing and J. Mossman, eds., *The Limits of Ancient Biography* (Swansea), 305–33.

(2013) *Beyond the Second Sophistic: Adventures in Greek Postclassicism*, Berkeley.

Whitton, C. (2015) 'Pliny's progress: on a troublesome Domitianic career', *Chiron* 45: 1–22.

Wiater, N. (2011) *The Ideology of Classicism: Language, History, and Identity in Dionysius of Halicarnassus*, Berlin.

Williams, G. and K. Volk, eds. (2016) *Roman Reflections: Studies in Latin Philosophy*, Oxford.

Williamson, G. (2004) *The Longing for Myth: Religion and Aesthetic Culture from Romanticism to Nietzsche*, Chicago.

Wilson-Okamura, D. (2010) *Virgil in the Renaissance*, Cambridge.

Winterer, C. (2002) *The Culture of Classicism: Ancient Greece and Rome in American Intellectual Life 1780–1910*, Baltimore.

Wiseman, T. P. (1984) 'Cybele, Virgil, and Augustus', in T. Woodman and D. West, eds., *Poetry and Politics in the Age of Augustus* (Cambridge), 117–28.

Wolf, R. (2015) *Cicero: The Philosophy of a Roman Sceptic*, London and New York.

Woolf, G. (2000) *Becoming Roman: The Origins of Provincial Civilization in Gaul*, Cambridge.

Woolf, V. (1925) *The Common Reader*, London.

Young, R. J. C. (1990) *White Mythologies*, London.

(1995) *Colonial Desire: Hybridity Theory, Culture and Race*, London.

(2000) *Postcolonialism: An Historical Introduction*, Oxford.

# *Envoi*

## Mary Beard

If you were studying Classics at the University of Cambridge in the late nineteenth century, your handy guide to the subject, and to what was expected of you, would have been Robert Burn's pamphlet *The Classical Tripos*. First published in 1863, it was originally just one section of the more compendious *Student's Guide to the University of Cambridge*, which told the student all the basics they needed to know about studying at the university, from the fees and the colleges, to how to succeed in their chosen field of study. But, for a couple of decades, students reading Classics bought the slim off-prints of the classical chapter, which was their closest equivalent to the modern course handbook.[1]

Burn, a Fellow of Trinity College, was a radical reformer of Classics at the time. A leading light in bringing the study of archaeology into the mainstream syllabus (he was one of the first to go field-walking in the countryside around Rome), he was firmly on the side of those at the time who were arguing that the study of Classics should be about more than just translating from Latin and Greek into English, and vice versa. But there is no hint of any such radicalism in his practical advice to students. The course he describes is mostly a diet of translation, with barely anything that we would think of as *literary* criticism. And his injunctions focus on what he unselfconsciously calls the 'best' or most 'important' authors (Cicero, Livy and Tacitus), and on a canon of Latin literature that never gets past the middle of the second century CE. It all seems to fit perfectly with the usual dreary stereotype of nineteenth-century Latin, at least as it was taught and studied in England. There is no sign of anything that relates to contemporary ideology, modern controversies or new ways of reading – or, to be honest, any 'ways of reading' at all.

---

[*] My thanks to the editors of this volume for the invitation to write these reflections, for their advice, and for their tolerance of my slowness. As often, Christopher Stray has shared his expertise and kept me on the right track.

[1] I have been referring to Burn 1874 (from the third edition of the complete *Student's Guide*).

It was worse than 'dreary'. Many observers have seen in the study of Latin and Greek at this period a way not just of rejecting modernity and its debates, but of underpinning a peculiarly conservative, self-serving and exploitative version of culture, which privileged a set of skills and knowledge that aimed to make modernity irrelevant. What more efficient way was there of simultaneously mystifying and policing the boundaries of elite status and existing social hierarchies than by making the terms of entry into that elite the mastery of a language which apparently had nothing to do with the here and now and certainly no claims whatsoever to be 'useful'?[2]

It did not need modern sociology to raise this question. That was the point made by classicist and poet Louis MacNeice when in the 1930s he wrote, ironically, in his autobiographical poem *Autumn Journal* of 'the *privilege* of learning a language / that is incontrovertibly dead' (my italics).[3] And, in a different idiom, a decade or so later it was one point of a clever cartoon which depicted Benjamin Hall Kennedy (1804–89), author of the famous Latin grammar book,[4] dressed up in the stereotypical kit of an imperial 'explorer' (or predator) and leading a strange animal out of the jungle. 'Kennedy discovers the gerund and leads it back into captivity', ran the caption. If this was in part a joke at the expense of the study-bound professor, who had never been near a jungle in his life, it was also a reminder that mastering Latin grammar was what guaranteed a boy (and I mean 'boy') a place in the hierarchy of empire.[5] The sting in the tail is that it has recently become clear that the bulk of 'Kennedy's' grammar book was actually written by his daughters Marion and Julia.[6] Whether that fact challenges the capacity of Latin to act as a gate keeper to elite status (showing that such intellectual 'defences' of the traditional hierarchy were always bound to fall to the intellectual talents of those they were constructed to exclude) or horribly confirms it (Marion and Julia are nowhere acknowledged in the book) is a moot point.

Different national traditions, as this *Guide* rightly insists, have always 'done Latin' differently.[7] And they have embedded the study of classical languages and literature into their social and political hierarchies in subtly and sometimes significantly different ways. England – and I am deliberately drawing a distinction with Scotland here – has often been at the extreme end of the spectrum. But there can be no doubt that a century or

---

[2] Some of the key studies of the 'Latin as exclusion' model are cited (and interrogated) by Uden in this volume.
[3] MacNeice 1939: 50.  [4] Kennedy 1866, still familiar as Kennedy 1931.
[5] Willans and Searle 1985: 158 (originally published 1954).  [6] Stray 1996.
[7] Fuhrer in this volume.

more ago Latin, and the cultural baggage that went with it, helped to underpin the position of elites across the West. That is, like it or not, the function of many, if not most, educational curricula. And, in some respects, Latin still does underpin claims to elite status in the UK, or at least some try to pretend that it does. The truth is that the Latin quotations – pretentiously, if not always accurately – dropped in British parliamentary debates by conservative politicians can now prompt as much ridicule as respect. But the role of Latin has always been more complicated than it might seem, as a harder look at some of the most ritualised, fetishised, some would say pointless, paedagogical exercises would suggest: notably the original composition of Latin verses or Latin prose essays as practised in Burn's Cambridge. Even in the depths of the nineteenth century there was more radicalism here than you would imagine, and more engagement with controversial issues of the here and now.[8]

One famous, slightly earlier example is the piece of work composed by the Cambridge undergraduate Thomas Clarkson in 1785 as an entry to a Latin essay competition set by the then Vice-Chancellor Peter Peckard (a one-time notorious wide boy who had mellowed into a university grandee, intellectual radical and committed anti-slavery campaigner). Peckard chose as the subject for the students to discuss in Latin, 'Anne liceat invitos in servitutem dare?' ('Is it right to make men slaves against their will?'). Clarkson won the prize with an essay – read aloud in the university's Senate House – about the evils of modern slavery, which became one of the most influential British contributions to the campaigns against the slave trade (especially after it had been published in an English translation).[9] It was as an explicit tribute to Peckard's subject and to Clarkson's essay that in 2020 the new Cambridge Centre for Animal Rights Law set 'Anne liceat invitos in servitutem dare?', as the theme of their first annual (English) essay competition – choosing to translate the Latin, in order to include animals, 'Is it lawful to enslave *the unconsenting?*'

But that topic of 1785 was not a one-off. Similar radical and contemporary themes, sometimes serious, sometimes satiric, can be found, for example, in the collection of so-called 'Tripos verses' – Latin poems written by students that, until 1894, were read or distributed as part of the rituals of Cambridge's Degree Day ('Commencement' as it was sometimes then called, as it still is in the USA). Of course, the role of these changed over

---

[8] Uden in this volume has further discussion of this; even though we start from very different places (he from the broader study of 'reception', myself from the history of my own institution), our conclusions on the cultural politics of Classics tend to converge.
[9] English translation: Clarkson 1786. Peckard's career: *ODNB* s.v. 'Peckard, Peter'.

their long history, starting in the late sixteenth century when Latin was still a 'live' medium of instruction and assessment in the university, as well as an intellectual *lingua franca*, and ending in the age when Latin verse composition was no more than an elite paedagogical exercise. One striking early example, written in 1679, more than a century before Clarkson's essay, also focused on the evils of slavery; its author boasted of adopting a 'free', or irregular metre ('pede libero') to allude to the 'freedom' of the slave (while glaringly punning on the *pede libero* of Horace, *Odes* 1.37.1). Later we find a celebration of the fall of the French July monarchy in 1848, a query about the merits of learning how to compose Latin verse, compared with the utility of studying hard science (1868), and praise of the intellectual achievements of women over the alleged bravery of male explorers, notably Henry Stanley (1890).[10]

I am not trying to claim that composing Latin poetry, particularly in the age of full 'paedagogical mystification' in the late nineteenth century, was a major medium of radical debate. Many 'Tripos verses', probably the majority, were on much safer themes. Robert Burn, for example, showing his intellectual colours while still a student, composed sixty-three lines of Latin hendecasyllables on the 'miseries' of the Cambridge examination system. And you might well argue, anyway, that turning important contemporary political issues into (sometimes ironic) Latin verses was a means of trivialising them, or of appropriating them for the bellettrist entertainment of the privileged elite. To write *in* Latin verse in order to question the merit *of* Latin verse might have been one way of laughing at the very idea of such a debate. Yet it would be wrong not to see a degree of cultural resistance in these compositions, and wrong to ignore attempts by students (and, in the case of Peckard, their teachers) to exploit the established forms of Latin paedagogy to subvert the very institutions that those forms were supposed to uphold.[11]

Modern students of Classics can be reluctant to recognise the interconnectedness of the reactionary and the radical in the teaching and scholarship of the past. It has often served our own interests better to paint the history of the discipline (particularly our immediate ancestors in the nineteenth and early twentieth centuries) as part of a dark age, its practitioners complicit in, or dupes of, a system of cultural, social, racial and gendered exclusion. That was, of course, partly true, and it remains so; the roster of contributors to this *Guide* reflects that. But the complexities, the

---

[10] Hall 2009.   [11] Compare Uden's nice phrase 'resistant allusion' (p. 412).

subversions and the modes of resistance within the subject are an important part of the story too.

How to incorporate that kind of complexity into our own understanding of the history of Latin studies is one important question that bubbles under the surface of this book. How can we be alert to the anxieties and ambivalences of our predecessors, not only to their orthodox, conservative and sometimes bombastic self-confidence? In part, we need to recognise our own stereotypes of the past for the oversimplifications that they are. Several of the contributions in this book effectively challenge some of those, notably the binary division between the 'secular' and the 'religious' in the history of Latin and Latin scholarship, and with it the comfortable notion that Classics has systematically been a champion of the secular against 'the culturally hegemonic reach of monotheistic religions'.[12] Some of the same work needs to be done in re-examining our assumptions about the cultural and social hegemony of Latin studies themselves.

Part of that re-examination would lie in telling a more nuanced, fragmented and ultimately subversive story. Of course, some young men at Oxford and Cambridge did find in Classics a route to (as they might have put it) 'ruling the world'. Many of them were certainly taught to see a justification, even an advertisement, for British imperialism in the 'ideals' of Roman conquest and empire, as mediated by some of the Latin texts which they had spent so many hours reading. The parallels between, for example, Agricola's campaigns in Scotland as detailed by Tacitus and the British campaigns in the Crimea could (be made to) seem obvious – even if the role of the British themselves, as the *victims* of Roman imperialism, was an awkward aspect to be negotiated. It is an awkwardness triumphantly brushed aside in the verses inscribed on the statue of the rebel queen Boudica, put up in 1902 on the Thames Embankment near the British Houses of Parliament: two lines from a poem by William Cowper, written a hundred years earlier: 'Regions Caesar never knew / Thy posterity shall sway'. Or, to put it simply, 'Don't worry Boudica, your descendants will "out-Roman" the Romans'.[13]

But again, that was only one side to it. It is easy to forget that most students who studied Classics even at Oxford or Cambridge, never mind at the less 'traditional' or elitist London colleges or the new metropolitan universities, did not go on to run the empire or play a leading role among

---

[12] Peirano Garrison in this volume.
[13] Cowper's poem *Boadicea: An Ode* was written in 1780 and published in 1782 (Milford 1905: 310–11). The history of the statue is discussed by Ward-Jackson 2011: 340–4.

the British governing elite. The majority went into far more 'ordinary' positions as teachers or Anglican parsons or the like. More strikingly, and more often forgotten, those who studied Classics were recruited to attack the empire (in print) almost as enthusiastically as they were recruited to defend it (on the ground). While the controversial Oxford classicist Benjamin Jowett was busy trying to persuade his students to serve the country and the empire, C. P. Scott – another Oxford classicist, who became the editor of the *Manchester Guardian*, the most powerful anti-imperial newspaper in the UK – was busy trying to persuade them to join *his* team. Scott's Tacitus was not the chronicler of Agricola's successful Roman campaigns, but the cynical analyst who scripted (to put into the mouth of Calgacus, another native British freedom fighter) one of the most powerful anti-imperial slogans ever: *ubi solitudinem faciunt, pacem appellant* ('they make a desert and call it peace').[14]

Jowett's partisan voice, insisting that a classical education (and an Oxford one at that) was the only one that properly trained a young man for governance, has been a powerful witness in the 'case for the prosecution'. And it makes very unappealing reading now. It is worth reflecting, though, that Jowett – who was far more complicated than the knee-jerk conservative he is sometimes painted[15] – might not have been stating the nineteenth-century obvious, but tendentiously responding to those who thought very differently. (There was always plenty of opposition, especially among some committed imperialists, to the idea that the empire was safe in the hands of the classically trained.) We run the risk, in other words, of treating Jowett's extreme, high-volume expression of one side of an *argument* as if it represented the standard view of the elite. It does nineteenth-century scholars an injustice to erase their differences and disagreements about the place of their subject within politics and culture, education and prestige, and to turn a blind eye to the questioning and uncertainty that lies behind the apparently confident (and conservative) image that their photographs and commemorative portraits project. We should perhaps reflect how we ourselves will appear in a hundred years' time, and what oversimplifications may be inflicted on our own approach to the subject.

Another major question that bubbles under the surface of the *Guide* is how Latin (as a disciplinary subject) should face its future, or even its

---

[14] Tac. *Agr.* 30.4. On the '*Manchester Guardian* Circle', see Symonds 1992: 80–98.
[15] The *ODNB* article (s.v. 'Jowett, Benjamin') is a brief introduction to some of the often overlooked complexities of Jowett's cultural, religious and political stance.

present. Some of the contributors rightly point to internal boundary disputes now being waged within Classics, or Ancient World Studies. How far, for example, does a Roman historian even need Latin? Is 'Classics' a useful disciplinary umbrella for subjects as apparently diverse as literary criticism, economic history and Roman archaeology, from sculpture to brick-stamps?[16] But we perhaps overestimate the novelty of these debates, or overinvest in simple solutions. Disciplinary boundaries have been contested for centuries, ever since there *were* disciplines (in a sense that is what underlies '*inter*-disciplinarity'). In the 1970s Moses Finley was keen to transfer Ancient History from the Faculty of Classics in Cambridge to the History Faculty, and G. E. L. Owen advocated a similar transfer for Ancient Philosophy, from Classics to Philosophy. A hundred years earlier, in Cambridge's disciplinary wars of the late nineteenth century, it was only by the skin of its teeth that Ancient History had not ended up with History anyway, in a combination with Law (both ancient and modern).[17] The truth is that there are pluses and minuses to wherever you decide to place, or move, these boundaries. Of course, you gain something if you study and teach the Roman empire alongside the comparative history of empires from China to Spain. There are also, different, gains in linking the study of the Roman empire with a close reading of Virgil or Tacitus. It is not a zero-sum game.

But beyond those internal disputes, Latinists cannot, or should not, avoid reflecting on how they might demonstrate the importance of their subject more widely, whether to colleagues in literature and the humanities, or to a more general public. It is not stupid or wilful for someone outside the discipline to want an answer to the question, 'why study a dead language and its literature?' I often sense that, despite our worries about underfunding and falling enrolments, we perhaps too easily turn our backs on big questions of that sort and take ourselves too much for granted, maybe even too seriously. Paradoxically, even the recent campaigns by some radical classicists to 'burn it all down' seem to assume that someone would notice if that happened.[18] The *Guide* does offer, implicitly at least, some powerful arguments here. It showcases some of the best in Latin scholarship and its contributions to literary and intellectual debates, which remain its strongest justification. And it reasserts the centrality of Latin as a language of creativity, argument and criticism that lasted for millennia,

---

[16] Gibson and Whitton, Lavan and others in this volume address precisely this question.
[17] Beard 1999; 2001.   [18] Zuckerberg 2019 is just one example.

not ending somewhere in the fourth century CE, or with the list of works in Robert Burn's canon.[19] But I wonder if we should push that further.

Should we not also be brave enough to insist that the history of 'western civilisation' is incomprehensible without Latin? That is emphatically *not* to say that western civilisation outranks other 'civilisations', that it is uniquely admirable, or that it is the only one in the world which deserves our attention. Nor is it to say that the classical tradition is the sole ancestor of western culture. Anyone who claims any of those things is (probably) politically toxic and (certainly) factually wrong. That said, it is a safe bet that there has never been a single day in history since 19 BCE on which someone somewhere has not been reading the *Aeneid*, reinterpreting it, and seeing their own world through its lens (and vice versa).[20] That gives Virgil a status in the hermeneutics of the West only rivalled, and marginally outranked, by the Bible. If we lost our understanding of the *Aeneid*, we would lose a lot more than 'just' a text, we would lose the glue of a major cultural tradition, with all its significance, and all its faults.

Let me sum up with one final example, a long way from the world of Robert Burn or B. H. Kennedy or the privileged paedagogy of Latin essays. It is a group of curious and now almost unknown Latin verses of around 1600, which bring together some of my themes: from the longevity of Latin culture to its potentially subversive properties. The verses were specially composed to accompany a series of prints which were one of the blockbuster bestsellers in European visual arts between the seventeenth and nineteenth centuries. The work of a notable Flemish engraver, Aegidius Sadeler, and dedicated to the Holy Roman Emperor, these reproduced (and extended, to form the canonical 'Twelve') Titian's paintings of the 'Eleven Caesars' – Julius Caesar to Titus – made for the Duke of Mantua in Italy in the early sixteenth century, and destroyed in a fire in Madrid in 1734. The Titians, with their expressive features and unique combination of antiquarian detail and striking modernity, were once *the* images of the early emperors in the European cultural imagination. Sadeler's prints gave them household familiarity across the continent.[21]

Few people now bother with the verses set underneath each emperor. Even learned catalogues rarely reprint the Latin, let alone translate it. The assumption, I think, is that the images were intended to add a bit of imperial lustre to the walls of the bourgeoisie, and so the individual

---

[19] See Stover and Haskell in this volume.
[20] I think John Henderson was the first to point this out to me. If not, I apologise.
[21] Beard 2021: 151–87.

poems were there to glorify the ruler concerned. But if you actually read them, a surprise is in store. The Latin is at best lumpy, though whoever composed it was familiar with Suetonius, whom he repeatedly half-quotes. His message, however, is almost universally satiric or unashamedly hostile. Julius Caesar was 'joined to the city in unspeakable ways' ('Iunctus et infandis cui fuit ille modis'). Nero 'made a pile of evil' ('Nequitiae cumulum fecit'). Vespasian is a rarity, 'at last a good emperor' ('Effigiem iam cerne boni nunc Principis'). And so on.[22]

How many of the thousands of people who proudly displayed these prints read the verses, could understand the Latin, or thought about the implications, we do not know. But the message *for us* is clear. This is another case of Latin being used not to uphold but to subvert the prestige of classical culture and to question its claims to power. And it is a reminder of how drastically we lose the point of many cultural debates over the last two millennia if we don't keep Latin centre stage.

## References

Beard, M. (1999) 'The invention (and re-invention) of "Group D": an archaeology of the Classical Tripos, 1879–1984', in C. Stray, ed., *Classics in 19th and 20th Century Cambridge* (Cambridge), 95–134.

(2001) 'Learning to pick the easy plums: the invention of Ancient History in nineteenth-century Classics', in J. Smith and C. Stray, eds., *Teaching and Learning in Nineteenth-Century Cambridge* (Woodbridge), 89–106.

(2021) *Twelve Caesars: Images of Power from the Ancient World to the Modern*, Princeton.

Burn, R. (1874) 'The Classical Tripos', in *The Student's Guide to the University of Cambridge* (3rd edn, Cambridge), 132–79 (multiple editions 1863–93); also published separately as an extract.

Clarkson, T. (1786) *An Essay on the Slavery and Commerce of the Human Species*, London.

Hall, J. J. (2009) *Cambridge Act and Tripos Verses, 1565–1894*, Cambridge.

Kennedy, B. H. (1866) *The Public School Latin Primer*, London.

(1931) *Kennedy's Revised Latin Primer* (ed. J. F. Mountford ), London.

MacNeice, L. (1939) *Autumn Journal*, London.

Milford, H. S., ed. (1905) *The Complete Poetical Works of William Cowper*, London.

Stray, C. (1996) 'Primers, publishing, and politics: the classical textbooks of Benjamin Hall Kennedy', *Papers of the Bibliographical Society of America* 90: 451–74.

---

[22] Ibid. 289–301.

Symonds, R. (1992) *Oxford and Empire: The Last Lost Cause*, Oxford.
Ward-Jackson, P. (2011) *Public Sculpture of Historic Westminster* vol. 1, Liverpool.
Willans, G. and R. Searle (1985) *The Compleet Molesworth*, London (orig. 1984). [misspelling deliberate]
Zuckerberg, D. (2019) 'Burn it all down? Editorial – April 2019', *Eidolon* (https://medium.com/eidolon/burn-it-all-down-182f5edb16e).

# *Index Locorum*

Abad, Diego, *Dissertatio ludicro-seria*: 350–1
Abbo of St Germain
  *Bella Parisiacae urbis*
    pr.: 306
    1.40–4: 307
    3.1–6: 307
Adam of St Victor *Pent.* 5.25–30: 312–13
Aldhelm
  *Carmen de virginitate* 1–7: 302–3
  *Prosa de virginitate* ch. 1, p. 229 Ehwald: 302
*Aldhelm* 12–17: 310
*Anthologia Latina* 87c.1–2: 228–9
Apuleius *Apol.* 4: 735–6
Archipoeta *carm.* 10.41–8: 313
Augustine
  *De ciu. D.* 11.3: 69
  *Conf.*
    3.4.7: 742
    7.9.13: 742
  *De doctrina Christiana*
    2.40.60: 741
    4.9: 72
  *Serm.*
    150.7.8: 743
    150.8.9: 743–4
Ausonius
  *Cento*: 246
  *Ep.* 6.43–5: 889

Baudri of Bourgeuil *carm.* 229.1–6: 311–12
Bede *Hist. Eccl. praef.*: 305–6
Besantinus *AP* 15.25: 628
Bidermann, Jacob, *Herodias*
    Book 1 §1: 365–6

Calpurnius Siculus
  *Ecl.*
    2.5: 232
    2.34–5: 232
    2.49–51: 232
    2.88–9: 232

Cato *De Rhetorica* fr. 18–19 Cugusi: 770
Catullus
  4.1–2: 577, 584
  7: 532
  10.2–3: 598
  10.25–6: 598–9
  13.12: 564
  36.3: 564
  64.64–5: 595
  76.5–6: 724
Chrodobertus of Tours *Ep. aev. Mer. coll.* 16: 304
Cicero
  *Ac.* 1.3: 61
  *Att.* 7.2.3: 879, 888
  *Brut.* 274: 238
  *Div.* 2.7: 719
  *Fin.* 1.6: 717
  *Imp. Cn. Pomp.* 19: 767–8
  *Leg.*
    3.8: 782
    3.28: 780
  *Marc.* 32: 775
  *Nat. Deor.* 1.7: 718, 720
  *Orat.* 2.36: 766
  *Re Pub.* 1.39: 780–1
[Cicero] *Rhetorica ad Herennium* 4.17: 582–3
*CIL*
  IV.1516: 601
  VI.1975: 631
  VI.11509: 679
St. Columba *Altus prosator*: 301

Dante *Ecl.* 2.4–10: 320–1
*Digest.* 48.18.1.27: 833–4
Dynamius of Marseille *Epistolae austrasiacae*
    12.1: 303

Egbert of Liège *Fecunda ratis* 1.3–4: 310–11
Einhard *Vita Karoli* 9: 294–5
Ennius *Ann.* 156 Sk. 763, 853
Erasmus *Ciceronianus* (*ASD* 1–2: 606): 344–5

Eucheria *ep.* 1–6, 31–2: 303–4
Eugenius of Toledo *Ep.* 1.3: 305
Euripides *HF* 952: 226
Eusebius 6.25.3: 69

Folengo, Teofilo, *Baldus* 2–3: 346–7
Fracastoro, Girolamo
  *Carm. lib.*
    3.30–47: 371–2
    3.88–95: 372–3
Fronto
  111.16–20 vdH: 883
  123.16–17 vdH: 885

Gellius
  1.10.2–4: 102–3
  4.1.1: 739
  4.1.18: 738
  15.24: 61–2
  18.9.5: 223
Giovanni de Virgilio *Ecl.* 1.1–7: 320
Gregorius Magnus *Hom.* 25.2: 299–300
Gregorius of Nazianzus *Invective against Julian* 103, 105: 895

Habakuk 3.18: 893
Heerkens, G.N. *De valetudine literatorum* (1790, 25–6): 349–50
Hermogenes *Prog.* 10.48: 654
*Hisperica famina* 1–6: 301–2
Homer
  *Il.*
    5.9–10: 283
    20.307–8: 218
Horace
  *Carm.*
    1.1.35: 63
    1.9.1–2: 626
    1.11.7–8: 726
    1.37.1: 910
    3.1.5–8: 777
    3.5.65–8: 777
    3.30.1: 626
  *Ep.*
    1.6.56–9: 487
    2.1.51: 62–3
    2.1.156–7: 847
  *Ars P.* 361: 627
  *Sat.*
    1.10.20–1: 888
    1.10.29–30: 888
*Hymni Homerici, Ven.* 196–7: 216

*Illa Iuventus* 1–7, 23–7: 314–15
Isidore
  *Etymologiae*
    1.1.1–2: 299
    10.44: 246–7

Jerome
  *Ep.*
    22.29: 71
    22.30: 70, 104, 142
    27.1: 892
    77.2: 71
  *In Esaiam* 3, 7.14: 248–9
  *In Rom.* 5.14: 892
  *Vulg. Ioh.* 1.1: 893
Jonas of Bobbio *Vita Columb.* 1.1: 300
Joyce, James, *Finnegan's Wake* (1939: 185): 317
Juvenal
  3.21–2: 220
  3.60–1: 854

*Laus Pisonis* 211–18: 66–7
Livy
  *praef.*
    6: 801
    9–11: 785
  29.19: 851
  34.4.3: 852
  34.4.7: 852
  39.40: 854
Llul, Raymond, *De ascensu* d.6: 314
Lovato, Lovati
  *carm.* 27.12–18, p. 21 Padrin: 319
  *Ep.* 4.83–90: 318–19
Lucan 7.794–5: 237
Lucian *Laps.* 18: 865
Lucilius fr. 84–5 W.: 239
Lucretius
  1.55–61: 716
  1.78–9: 744
  1.136–9: 880
  1.832–5: 881
  1.922–30: 712–13
  1.936–47: 713
  1.952–3: 255
  3.3–8: 715
  3.260: 881
  3.489: 597

Macrobius
  *Sat.*
    1.24.13: 75
    5.3.8: 212
    5.3.16–17: 252

# Index Locorum

Marcus Aurelius *Med.* 5.1: 731
Martial 1 *pr.* 15: 857–8
Martianus Capella *De nuptiis* 8.809–9: 297–8
Martius Valerius *Buc.* pr. 13–20: 289
Metellus of Tegernsee
   *Ecl.*
      1.1: 288
      2.35: 288
      3.70: 288

Optatian
   *carm.* 3: 639
   *carm.* 19: 634–5, 655
   *carm.* 26: 624–5
Ovid
   *Fast.*
      2.304: 876
      2.359–60: 877
      2.380: 877
      3.10: 793
      3.23–4: 793
      3.471–3: 230
      4.52: 876
      4.61–2: 875–6
      4.65–6: 871
      4.81–3: 871–2
      6.417–18: 877

Paleario, Aonio, *Actio in pontifices Romanos*: 342
Peter Damian *Serm.* 73, *PL* 144, 866b: 311
Petronius
   40.7: 254
   58.7: 681
Philostratus *Vit. Apollon.* 1.35: 850
Plautus
   *Men.*
      9–12: 224–5
      426–7: 229
      824: 226
Pliny the Elder
   *NH*
      praef. 1: 127–8
      29.7: 855
Pliny the Younger
   *Ep.*
      1.1: 173
      5.6.44: 654
Plutarch
   *Cato*
      12.4–5: 855
      23.2–3: 855
   *Cic.* 40: 882
   *Demosth.* 2: 864
   *Quaest. Rom.* 45.275f: 866

M. Porcius Iasucthan *Libya Antiqua* 1 (1995)
   79–123: 568–9
Proba
   *Cento*
      22–8: 245
      29–37: 241–4
Propertius
   2.34.31, 39: 490
   3.1.14: 231
   4.1.1: 234
   4.2.47: 233
   4.9.34, 53: 234
Prudentius *Apoth.* 393–6: 249–50

Quintilian
   *Inst.*
      1.4.3: 64–5
      6.2.29–30: 654
      10.1.45: 69
      10.1.54: 6
      10.1.57: 64
      10.1.93: 726
*Quondam fuit factus festus*: 315

Rahewin of Freising *Flosculus* 1, 9–10: 287–8
Rather of Verona *Sermo de Maria et Martha* 4: 309–10
*Res Gestae diui Augusti* 2: 798
*RIB* 2447.9: 674

Salutati, Coluccio, *Ep.* 9.9: 99–101
Seneca
   *Clem.*
      1.3.3: 775
      1.19: 775
   *De Ira* 3.36.3: 730
   *Ep.*
      5.1–2: 733
      27.1: 732
      114.1: 769, 771
Servius
   *Ad Aen.*
      *praef.*: 250
      3.97–8: 213
      6 *praef.*: 75
      12.940–1: 250–1
Servius Danielis 3.349: 75
Sidonius Apollinaris *Ep.* 2.9.4: 141
Statius *Theb.* 12.816–17: 231
Suetonius
   *Aug.* 40.5: 254
   *Jul.*
      52: 534–5
      82: 849
   *Tib.* 71: 884

*Tabulae Vindolandenses* ii.344: 830
Tacitus
  *Agr.*
    2.2: 885
    4.3: 885
    30.4: 912
    46.4: 235
  *Hist.* 2.70: 237
Terence
  *Adelph.* 8–14: 227–8
  *Eun.*
    7–8: 226
    23–4: 226
    40–3: 226
Tertullian
  *De Pallio* 6.4–5: 740–1
  *De praescr. haeret.* 7.1: 70–1
Theocritus *Id.* 4.2: 233
Theon *Prog.* 118.7: 653

Valerius Flaccus *Arg.* 3.596–7: 231
Varro
  *Men.*
    122: 727
    147: 728
    399: 62
Venantius Fortunatus *Carm.* 2.6.1–4: 132–3
Virgil
  *Ecl.*
    1.1: 288
    1.5: 231
    2.56: 288
    3.2, 5–6: 233
    3.60: 288–9
    6.3: 765
  *Geo.*
    3.8: 231
    3.89: 572
    4.13: 597
    4.411: 233

  *Aen.*
    1.5: 796
    1.33: 796
    1.151: 770
    1.261–2: 255
    1.450–85: 661–2
    1.459: 238
    1.462: 238
    2.27–30: 238
    2.711: 232
    3.100–2: 219
    3.393: 220, 250
    5.588: 230
    6.33: 233
    6.93–4: 230
    6.179: 232
    6.834–5: 799
    6.851–3: 799
    6.853: 426
    9.117–25: 649
    12.504: 797
    12.946–7: 800
    12.948–9: 802
[Virgil]
  *Cat.*
    5.8–13: 722
    5.8.23–4: 723
    15.3: 75
  *Culex* 351: 570
Virgilius Maro *Epit.* 15: 315–16
Vitruvius 7.5.2: 663
Volacius Sedigitus, *De Poetis*: 61–2

Walter of Châtillon *Past.*:
  289–90
Walther of Speyer *Vita Sancti Christophori*
  12–17: 308
Wilhelm of Grudencz
  *Probitate eminentem*: 322–4
  *Psalmodium exileratum* 1–8: 322

# General Index

Abad, Diego: 350–1
Abbo of St Germain: 306–7
Adam of St Victor: 312–13
Aldhelm: 302–3
ancient historians (Roman)
   and classical literature (study of): 28–30, 111, 817–43, 912–13
   and cultural materialism: 819–25
   and historiography (study of): 836–42
   ignore literary Latinists: 817–19
   and inscriptions: 818, 827–30
   and Latinists / Classicists: 28–30, 111, 817–43, 912–13
   and non-literary texts: 825–36
   and politics of literature: 819–25
*L'Année philologique*: 19, 462
*Anthologia Latina*: 58, 73–4
Apuleius: 12–14, 78, 81, 103, 118, 171–2, 467, 494, 702, 734–7
Arab conquests: 109
*Ara Pacis Augustae*: 761–3, 765
archaeology: *see* material culture
archaic Latin: *see* Classical Latin (and archaic Latin)
Augustine: 11, 14, 69–70, 71–2, 82, 98, 113, 131, 132, 141, 144–5, 147–8, 249, 321, 467, 478, 702, 741–4, 786–7, 793–4, 892, 896
Ausonius: 128, 142–3, 246, 479, 889–90
author, the (constructed): 179–84

Barbauld, Anna Letitia: 422–7
Barthes, R.: 67, 180, 185–7
Baudri of Bourgeuil: 311–12
Bede: 305–6
Black (identity) and Classics: 44 n. 4, 48–9, 168, 419–21, 430–1, 475, 480, 910–11
Boethius: 76–7, 98, 132, 285, 454
Budé editions (Latin): 117, 461–3, 483, 486, 501
Burke, E.: 411–15
'Byzantium' (invention of): 110

Caesar, Julius: 533–4, 551–2, 585, 775–6, 799, 849, 914–15
Callimachus: 64, 217, 231, 566, 713
Calpurnius Siculus: 84, 112, 139, 232, 285, 550–1
*Cambridge Greek and Latin Classics* (series): 19–20, 117, 494, 603–4
*Cambridge History of Classical Literature*: 2–3, 118, 292
canons: *see* Christians / Christian Latin, classical Latin, late antique Latin, mediaeval Latin, Neo-Latin, reception (canons of)
*Carmina Latina Epigraphica*: 613 n. 5, 827
Carter, Elizabeth: 417–18
Cassiodorus: 72, 98, 100, 126
Cato the Elder: 84, 769–70, 782, 852–9
Catullus: 83, 127–9, 146, 230, 309, 350–1, 361, 365, 532–3, 564–74, 577, 584, 590–1, 595–7, 598–601, 724–6
centos (Latin): 240–51, 285
Christian Latin (*see also* late antique Latin)
   canons in: 69–70
   continuity and change in: 22, 142–3
   and classical Latin: 13–14, 19, 21–2, 25, 32, 67–77, 98, 101, 107, 118, 140–3, 241–51, 602–3
   and close reading: 33
   genres (new) in: 142
   Gospels in: 640–8, 895
   and Greek language / texts: 640–8, 891–6
   and medieval Latin: 295–6
   and periodisations of Latin: 140–3
   and philosophy (Roman): 740–5
   rise of: 13, 23
Cicero: 61, 72, 76–7, 101, 103, 118–19, 126, 133–4, 135–6, 160, 175, 181, 190–1, 238–40, 254, 343–5, 462, 565, 676–7, 700, 705–6, 710, 717–22, 766–8, 775–6, 779, 780–1, 782, 784–5, 793, 882–3, 887–8
classical Latin: 104–6
   accent in: 578–82
   archaic Latin and: 103–4, 107–8, 122–3, 125, 126–7, 223, 580–1, 585–6, 603

921

classical Latin: (cont.)
  canon of: 14, 18–20, 21–2, 25, 30, 43–86, 194, 274–5
  and Christian Latin: *see* Christians / Christian Latin
  close reading of: 32–3, 34, 830–46
  and colonialism: 45–9, 431, 446–8, 450, 472, 476–8, 821, 847–52, 866–7, 908, 911–12
  corpus (size of): 14–17, 24–5, 112–13, 146–7
  decentering of: 24–5, 26
  decline of: 13, 31
  definitions of: 11–14, 97–9, 104–6, 410
  emperors and: 136–40, 764–5, 819–25
  and enslavement: 48–9
  eras within: 136–40
  and Eurocentrism: 45–7, 51, 421–33
  genres in: 66–7, 83
  grammars (modern) of: 594–8
  and Greek literature: 27, 59–67, 79, 80, 453, 702–45, 756, 847–96
  and Italic languages: 581, 591–2
  and late antique Latin: 13–14, 19, 32, 70–7, 112, 114–15, 118–19, 120–48, 241–51
  lexicon (associative) of: 589–94
  loss of: 17, 18–19
  and medieval Latin: 274–5, 292–6
  metre (verse) in: 126–33, 578–82
  'minor' Roman poetry and: 56–9
  and moral formation: 50–1
  orthography (modern) of: 124–5
  political thought central to: 754
  prose rhythm in: 133–6
  and Proto Indo-European: 590–3
  'representativeness' of surviving texts from: 18–19
  and Romance languages: 122, 583–4
  'silver' Latin and: *see* 'silver' Latin
  'spurious' texts in: 56–9
  and standard Latin: 582–5
  standardisation of: 13–14, 22, 112, 120–2, 123–5, 584–5
  stress and quantity in: 578–82
  texts researched from: 20
  texts taught from: 19–20, 47–8
  'triumviral' literature and: 139
  variation in: 584–5
  vowel lengths in: 598–601, 602–3
  and 'vulgar Latin': 583–4
Classics (as discipline): *see* Latinists (Classicists)
Claudian: 147, 258, 283, 363–4
close reading: 32–4, 150, 257, 259, 405, 759, 796, 826, 828, 829, 830–46, 913
codex, the (introduction of): 24, 143–8, 256–7, 632–52; *see also* textual transmission (manuscripts)

cognitive Classics: 9, 200, 260, 589–90
colonialism: 48–9, 847–52, 866–7
commentaries (Latin): 7, 19, 33, 57, 75–6, 82, 113, 142, 248, 250–1, 258, 273, 275, 284, 340–1, 377–8, 459, 462, 467, 482–3, 488–9, 498, 493–6, 537–40, 553–8, 565–7, 633, 826, 891
*Corpus Aristotelicum* (Latin): 313–14
*Corpus Christianorum* (series *Latina*): 467
*Corpus Inscriptionum Latinarum* (*CIL*): 455, 469, 614
*Corpus Scriptorum Ecclesiasticorum Latinorum* (*CSEL*): 456, 484

Dante: 102, 282, 320–1, 404
Dares Phrygius: 283
Darwin, Erasmus: 433–9
Derrida, J.: 173, 187–8, 403, 869
Dictys Cretensis: 81–2, 283
digital editions: 540–58
digital humanities: 6–7, 34, 53, 143, 211, 217, 257–62, 358, 379, 501–2, 517–18, 540–58, 601–3
Digital Latin Texts (Library of): 6–7, 502, 547–58
Dionysius of Halicarnassus: 68, 218–19, 856–7, 873–4
distant reading: 1, 33–4, 258–9
diversity (continental, national, racial) and inclusion / exclusion: 2, 6, 9, 168, 419–21, 428–31, 475, 480, 897–8, 910–11
Du Bois, W. E. B.: 420
Dynamius of Marseille: 303–4

*Eclogue of Theodulus*: 286–7
ecocriticism: 9
ecphrasis: 618, 652–72
education (Roman): 6, 18–20, 22, 72, 104–5, 125, 139–40, 584, 675–6, 711, 741, 772–3, 849–51, 855, 870, 884; *see also*: Quintilian
Eliot, T.S.: 45, 47, 185, 317, 500
Ennius: 18, 61–2, 126–7, 128–9, 234, 578–80, 707, 714–15, 763, 782, 792, 853
enslaved persons: 6, 48–9, 54, 81, 166–8, 168, 339, 412, 419–21, 426, 430–1, 678, 778, 789–91, 821, 822–5, 825, 833–6, 839–40, 909–10
Epictetus: 417
epigraphy: *see* inscriptions
Erasmus: 341–2, 344–5, 466–7, 536–7, 867, 894–5
Eusebius: 69, 256, 640

Foucault, M.: 173, 186–7, 729
Fracastoro, Girolamo: 371–3, 374–5

Fronto: 13, 65, 77, 82, 103, 825, 883–5

Gadamer, H.-G.: 45, 399–401, 406–7
Gellius: 13, 61–2, 65, 77, 102–5, 120–1, 145–6, 223–4, 519, 585, 737–9, 835, 878
gender: 2, 6, 9, 54, 166–9, 193–200, 374, 401, 410–15, 422–7, 433, 438, 448, 475, 497, 821, 851, 876–7, 910–11
Germanic scholarship (Latin): 77–9, 114, 453–8, 464–5, 483–93, 494–6, 497–501, 571
global classics: 9, 10, 21, 26, 45, 55, 395, 397, 398, 428–33, 439, 477–80
Gospels (Latin), the: 640–8, 859, 891, 895
Great Books programmes: 49–52, 396–7, 448, 483
*Greek Anthology*: 63, 81, 628
Greek literature
  and beginnings of Latin literature: 847–50
  canon of: 47
  corpus of (size of): 15–16
  decline of: 13
  ecphrasis in: 653–4
  Julian the Apostate and: 895
  knowledge of Latin in: 860–7
  and Latin language: 889–96
  mythology of (adopted by Romans): 867–80
  overshadows Latin: 453–4, 756, 867–8, 897
  and resistance to Rome: 850–1
  and Rome / Latin: 27, 59–67, 79, 80, 453, 702–45, 756, 847–96
Gregory the Great: 274, 283–4, 299–300

Habermas, J.: 400–1, 416, 770
*Handbuch der lateinischen Literatur der Antike*: 23–4, 117–18, 140–1
Heaney, Seamus: 208, 240, 261–2, 461
Hebrew: 52, 68, 132, 242, 249, 861, 891–3
Heerkens, G.N.: 349–50, 367–8
Herculaneum: 81, 711–12
Horace: 62–3, 164–5, 171, 176–7, 181–2, 485–8, 497–9, 626, 627, 725–7, 761, 773, 777–8, 847–8, 888, 889–90

inscriptions (Latin): 455, 469, 468–9, 601, 626–7, 628–32, 677–82, 759–63, 818, 827–30
intertextuality: 8, 33, 183, 208–62, 337, 359–60, 496–7, 501, 567–8, 569–70, 626, 675, 840–4, 862
Iser, W.: 402–3
Isidore: 246–7, 299

Jauss, H.R.: 398–9, 401–2, 406
Jerome: 22, 69–71, 98, 101, 104, 131, 142, 145, 248–9, 741, 861, 891–6

Jewish literature: 22, 76, 111, 242, 248; *see also* Hebrew
Jonas of Bobbio: 300–1
*Journal of Roman Studies*: 28–9, 460, 598
Joyce, James: 317
Juvenal: 19, 138, 161–5, 220, 495–6, 854

Kristeva, J: 209–10, 219–21

Lactantius: 98, 101, 709, 894
late antique Latin (*see also* Christians / Christian Latin): 20–6, 32
  and classical Latin: 70–7, 97–9, 101–2, 107, 114–15, 118–19, 123–5, 241–51, 602–3
  corpus (size of): 23–4, 113, 146–7
  definition of late antiquity and: 109–10
  eras within: 138
  'late Latin' and: 123–5
  manuscripts: 523–5
  as Platinum Latin: 119
  and philosophy (Roman): 740–5
  prose rhythm in: 134–6
  standardised Latin and: 13–14, 22, 112, 120–2, 123–5
late antiquity (definition of): 109–10
Latin (study of): *see also* classical Latin, late antique Latin, Latinists, linguistics (Latin), mediaeval Latin, Neo-Latin, philosophy (Roman)
  in Africa: 478–9
  and African Americans: 44 n. 4, 48–9, 168, 419–22, 430–1, 475, 480, 910–11
  and ancient historians: 817–43
  in Australia and New Zealand: 476
  in China: 479–80
  and class: 418–19, 907–9
  and colonialism: 45–9, 431, 446–8, 450, 472, 476–8, 821, 847–52, 866–7, 908, 911–12
  death of: 338–9, 351–2, 450–1
  democratisation of: 502–3
  dominance of English-language in: 448–9
  in Eastern Europe: 468–71
  and Eurocentrism: 447–8, 914
  as exclusion zone: 415–22
  future of: 502–3, 912–14
  history of: 449, 450–1, 907–12
  in France: 461–4
  German-American rivalry in: 472–3, 474
  German-Italian rivalry in: 464–5
  in German-speaking countries: 451–7, 469–70, 485–8, 571
  in Ireland: 460–1
  in Italy and the Mediterranean: 464–6
  in Japan: 479–80
  Jewish scholars and: 452, 459

Latin (study of): (cont.)
  and Latin grammars: 594–8
  and linguistics: 563–605
  national traditions in: 447–515
  in the Netherlands, Belgium and Scandinavia: 466–8
  by non-native speakers: 568–9
  in north America: 472–6, 499–501
  periodisations of: 97–157
  philhellenism overshadows: 52, 79, 453–4, 462, 756, 867–8, 896–7
  philosophy and: 700–45
  political thought and: 753–805, 909–10
  and radicalism: 909–10
  revival of: 352
  in Russia, 478
  in south America: 477
  and social hierarchies: 907–9
  as stifling: 415–16
  in Turkey: 477–8
  in the UK: 457–60, 485–8, 485–99
  and verse composition: 909–11
  and 'western' civilisation: 914
Latinists (Classicists):
  alienate historians: 841
  and ancient historians: 28–30, 111, 817–43, 912–13
  and ancient philosophy: 27, 700–2
  and archaeology / material culture: 28, 613–99, 827–36
  and close reading: 32–4, 150, 257, 259, 405, 759, 796, 826, 828, 829, 830–46, 913
  and Departments of Classics: 114–15, 842–3, 912–13
  and Eurocentrism: 396–7, 421–33, 447–8
  and historiography (study of): 836–42
  intellectual rigour (lacked by): 563–4, 836–42
  and interdisciplinarity: 29, 431–9, 912–13
  and intertextuality: 208–22
  ignored by ancient historians: 817–19, 836–42
  and linguistics: 26–7, 29, 563–605
  and non-literary texts: 825–36
  power (narrow view of in): 819–25
*Latinitas*: 582–5
law (Roman): 6, 31–2, 82–3, 140, 739, 826–7, 833–6
Lewis & Short (Latin dictionary of): 12, 117, 587
*Library of Digital Latin Texts*: 6–7, 502, 517, 547–58
Liddell, Scott and Jones (Greek dictionary of): 572–3
Lincoln, Abraham: 525–8
linguistics (Latin): 563–605
  diachronic and synchronic analysis in: 570–1
  in Germany: 454–5

  explanatory methods in: 564–74
  and linguistic universals: 570
  and literary explanations: 564–74
  and literary Latin: 574–8
  and Paelignian: 571–2
  and Latin grammars: 594–8
  and Proto-Indo-European: 27, 563–4, 577–8, 590–3
  and Sanskrit: 573
  and spoken language (as fundamental form): 574–6
  utility of (to literary Latinists): 585–601, 603–4
  and vowel lengths: 601–3
Livius Andronicus: 60, 67, 77, 126, 222–4, 253–4, 578
Livy: 62, 101, 134, 144, 494, 576, 626, 757, 782–3, 785–7, 796, 851–5, 907
*Loeb Classical Library*: 116–17, 356, 376, 474–6, 484, 488, 501, 827
Lovati Lovato: 272, 318–20
Lucan: 18, 32, 78, 82, 116, 128, 129, 138, 174, 230, 237, 245, 281, 343, 524, 764, 791, 798, 866
Lucian: 850, 865–7
Lucilius: 61, 238–40, 583, 709–10, 726, 888
Lucretius: 70, 83–4, 127–9, 174, 231–2, 233–4, 255–6, 335–6, 367, 340, 343, 360, 371–3, 432, 468, 492–3, 597, 600, 700, 702, 712–17, 744–5, 848, 880–1

'macaronic' writing: 133, 310, 314–17, 345–7, 470
Machiavelli: 778, 787
Macrobius: 74–6, 101, 212–14, 251–4, 284, 522
manuscripts: *see* textual traditions
Marcus Aurelius: 703–4, 729, 731, 759, 883–4
Martial: 19, 66, 254, 857–9
Martianus Capella: 73, 101, 284, 297–9
Marullus: 362, 370
material culture (study of): 613–99
  and archaeologists and art historians: 616–17
  ecphrasis and: 652–72
  and epigraphy: 625–32, 677–82, 759–63
  and the Gospels: 640–8
  and Latinists / Classicists: 614–17, 677–8
  and Latin literature: 617–82
  Roman (definitions of): 616–18
  and Virgil: 645–52, 658–72, 673–5
mediaeval Latin: 22, 272–333
  bucolic poetry in: 285–91
  and classical Latin: 101–2, 107–8, 133, 147–8, 274–5, 292–6
  canon (educational) of: 274
  canon (lack of) in: 275–7
  corpus (size of): 24, 112–13, 272–3, 274–5
  defies standardisation: 273

epic poetry in: 281–5
in France (study of): 463
genres (history of) in: 291–2
in Germany (study of): 456
grammar of: 273
and late antiquity: 109–10, 147–8
mannerism in: 296–318
national literatures and: 278–80
as period: 272
prose rhythm in: 134
recent discoveries in: 276–8
stylistic trends in: 292–318
unedited texts in: 277–9
Menander: 224, 226–8, 859
Metellus of Tegernsee: 288–9
metre (in Latin poetry): 126–33, 578–82, 827, 889

Neo-Latin: 25–6, 99–102, 119, 121, 126, 334–94, 482
and Anglophone scholarship: 355–6
beyond Europe: 339, 347–8, 356–7
canon of: 376–9
and classical Latin: 334–7, 354, 358, 604
and classical scholarship: 340–4
corpus (size of): 24, 359, 362–3
emotions in: 368–73
epic poetry in: 363–4, 365–6
and European literatures: 361–3
genres in: 363–8
intertextuality in: 359–61
Jesuits and: 336, 343, 366–7, 371–2, 462
and 'living' Latin: 357–8
and mediaeval Latin: 341–2
and national interests: 354, 471, 482
prose rhythm in: 135–6
regional variation in: 345–53
as research field: 353–63
stylistic variation in: 343–5
as teaching texts: 374–6
and women writers: 339–40
novel (pre-modern): 78, 81–2, 342–3, 702, 734, 850, 878

Optatian: 256, 617–40, 655, 681–2, 890–1
Ovid: 130, 160, 165, 166–70, 174, 177–8, 192, 199–200, 220–1, 230–1, 236, 367–8, 433–9, 521–2, 765, 792–3, 822, 866–7, 867–8, 871–2, 875–9
*Oxford Classical Texts*: 115–17, 459, 476, 483–4, 485–8, 488–93, 531–3, 614
*Oxford Latin Dictionary*: 3, 11–12, 16–17, 22, 117, 567, 571, 572, 586–9
*Oxford Latin Syntax*: 26–7, 576, 594–8

*Patrologia Latina*: 463, 502
*Peregrinatio Egeriae*: 122–4

Petrarch: 84, 101, 119, 128–9, 281, 341, 345
Petronius: 19, 81, 138–9, 146, 240, 254, 576, 583, 654–5, 663–4, 681, 772
philhellenism: 52, 79, 453–4, 462, 756, 867–8, 896–7
Philodemus: 81, 711–12
philosophy (Roman): 27, 700–45
Apuleius and: 734–7
care of the self and: 728–33
Cicero and: 717–22
distinctiveness of: 703–5
Epicureanism and: 710–17, 721, 724–7
Gellius and: 737–9
Greek foundations of: 705–10, 880–6
and history of philosophy: 700–2
Lucretius and: 712–17
poetry (Latin) and: 722–8
pragmatism of: 703–5
and (ancient) professional philosophers: 703–4
Seneca and: 729–33, 733–4
Stoicism and: 721–2, 728, 729–33, 733–4
Piccolomini, Aeneas Silvius: 322, 342–3
Plautus: 61–2, 82, 125–7, 183, 224–9, 454, 464, 493, 576, 600, 707–8
Pliny the Elder: 4, 127–8, 677, 706–7, 855
Pliny the Younger: 20, 173–8, 200, 236, 654–5, 773, 776
Plutarch: 47, 80, 277, 854–7, 863–5, 882–3
political thought (Roman): 30–1, 753–805
Augustine and: 786–7, 793–4
Cicero and: 766–8, 771, 775–6, 779, 780–1, 782, 784–5, 793
conceptual history and: 788–91, 797–8
constitution (Roman) and: 778–83
definitions of: 754–8
education and: 772–3
embeddedness of: 766–9
exemplarity in: 783–8, 795–6, 801
Horace and: 777–8
institutions (Roman) and: 778–83
Livy and: 782–3, 785–6, 787
metaphorology and: 791–5, 801–4
Pliny the Younger and: 776, 779
pragmatism of: 766
republican thought and: 756–7, 778, 780, 897
rhetoric and: 769–73
Seneca and: 768–9, 771, 774
sources for: 758–65
and *Star Wars*: 757
Virgil and: 795–805
and works addressed to leaders: 773–8
Polybius: 570, 759, 781
Pompeii: 520, 601, 628–9, 656, 664–8, 672
M. Porcius Iasucthan: 568–9, 579

posthumanism: 9
Proba (cento of): 241–6, 285
Propertius: 130, 146, 165, 231, 233, 234, 277, 488–92, 520, 533, 588–9, 600
prose rhythm: 133–6, 235–6
Prudentius: 73, 131, 142, 145, 147, 234, 249–50, 282, 342, 366
prosimetrum: 291–2
pseudepigraphy: 20, 53, 56–7, 180–1

queer theory: 9, 400, 423
Quintilian: 13, 18–20, 64–5, 69, 101, 123, 231, 239, 654, 675–6, 726, 772, 798, 848, 859
Quintus of Smyrna: 862–3

race: *see* diversity
Rahewin of Freising: 276–7, 287–9
Rather of Verona: 308–9
reception: 8, 21, 208–62, 395–440
 and anti-imperialism: 425–6
 canons in: 20–1, 397, 404–5
 definitions of: 406–10
 as dialogue: 409–10
 and diversity (national, racial): 419–22, 428–33
 and gender: 410–15, 422–7
 global focus of: 397, 398, 428–33
 as resistance to antiquity: 408, 410–15, 416
 as sub-discipline: 395–7
religion (Roman): 6, 140–3, 867–80
*Res Gestae diui Augusti*: 5, 81, 520, 759–60, 770, 798, 827
rhetoric (ancient): 6, 78, 83, 125, 136, 238, 259, 275, 285, 299–300, 305, 311, 399, 462, 582–3, 618, 626, 652–7, 675–7, 714, 722, 736, 740, 756, 766, 769–74, 778, 783–4, 831, 837, 848, 851, 893
Roman philosophy: *see* philosophy (Roman)

Saïd, E.: 821–2
Sallust: 14, 85, 105, 123, 134, 274, 283, 519, 757, 758, 767, 782, 785, 794, 801–2, 838
Salutati, Coluccio: 99–102, 105, 119, 121, 126
science (ancient): 6, 454, 480, 855
scrolls (papyrus): 144–8, 255, 631, 632, 636, 652
Second Sophistic: 47, 60, 736–7, 860, 887
*Senatus consultum de Cn. Pisone patre*: 759–60, 828–9
Seneca: 74, 78, 82, 101, 126, 138, 314, 343, 492–3, 495, 600, 655, 700–1, 704, 729–33, 733–4, 753, 758, 768–9, 771, 774, 775–6, 798, 822, 881
Septuagint: 70, 274, 893
Servius: 6, 23, 75–6, 213, 250–1, 290, 473, 537–40, 553–8, 572, 633, 796, 800
Sidonius Apollinaris: 98, 118, 128, 135, 141–2, 147

'silver' Latin: 83, 97–9, 108, 118–19, 141, 324
*Star Wars*: 757
Statius: 19, 78, 83, 85–6, 116, 128, 137, 191, 231, 240, 274, 287
Stoicism: 700–1, 703, 708–9, 721–2, 728–33, 743–4, 768, 823–4, 884
Strabo: 218–19, 871
Suetonius: 101, 254, 294, 519–20, 522, 528–31, 533–7, 544, 547–9, 849, 884–5, 915
Sulpicia: 194–8

*Tabula Iliaca Capitolina*: 668–70
Tacitus: 13–14, 21, 75, 101, 134, 136–7, 138, 144, 178, 235–8, 298, 340, 471, 758, 768, 771, 772, 787, 790, 791–2, 818, 828, 837–8, 860, 866–7, 885–6, 907, 911
Terence: 14, 32, 62, 81, 105, 125, 127, 224, 226–9, 274, 519, 600, 641–2, 708, 859
Tertullian: 10, 11, 22, 70–1, 78, 82, 98, 118, 272, 740–1, 884, 894
Teubner (*Bibliotheca Teubneriana Latina*): 117, 455, 470, 484, 485–8, 488–93, 532–3
textual criticism: 70, 182–3, 464–5, 483–93, 516–62
textual traditions (manuscripts): 518–40, 618–82; *see also* codex
 archetypes in: 525–30
 critical apparatus and: 530–7, 543–58
 digital editions and: 540–58
 as material culture: 613–99
 open and closed: 523–30, 537–40
theology (discipline of)
 and Classics / Latin: 12–13, 21, 27, 72–4, 114–16, 275, 431, 911
theory
 critical: 8–9, 158–201
 feminist: 193–200
 intentionalism and: 160–1, 173, 184–93, 214–15
 intertextuality and: 208–22
 and national traditions: 498–9
 persona: 158–60, 161–72
 political: 753–805
 post-colonial: 48–9, 847–52, 866–7
 queer: 9, 400, 423
 reception: 398–406
 text critical: 516–18
*Thesaurus Linguae Latinae*: 12, 15, 23, 117, 455, 469, 501–2, 572, 588
translation: 7, 22, 53, 60, 76, 78, 81, 132, 142, 211, 222–9, 240, 261–2, 275, 279, 283–4, 302, 313, 347, 374, 376, 378, 405, 433, 456, 461–3, 474–5, 477, 483, 501, 712, 714, 716, 827, 848, 851, 861, 880, 882, 883, 889, 891–7, 907, 909
trans-ness: 6

Varro: 62–3, 141, 727–8
Vindolanda tablets: 830–3
Virgil: 50–1, 74, 75, 85, 103, 104, 105, 114, 129–30, 144, 178–9, 181, 198–9, 213–20, 231, 232–3, 238, 241–6, 251–62, 285–6, 288–91, 365–6, 372, 423, 426, 427–8, 490–1, 499–501, 537–40, 641, 645–52, 658–72, 770–1, 795–805, 822, 823–4, 862–3, 870, 914
[Virgil]: 56–9, 75, 722–3

Vitruvius: 53, 98, 176, 615, 663

Walter of Châtillon: 128–9, 276, 289–91
Wheatley, Phillis: 420–2
Wilhelmi, Piotr: 321–4
Wolf, F. W.: 12, 44, 56, 79–80, 340–1, 453
Wollstonecraft, M.: 410–15, 422–3

XML (Extensible Markup Language): 546–58

Milton Keynes UK
Ingram Content Group UK Ltd.
UKHW051257200624
444506UK00002B/5